TWELFTH EDITION

Psychology Applied to Modern Life

ADJUSTMENT IN THE 21ST CENTURY

Wayne Weiten
University of Nevada, Las Vegas

Dana S. Dunn
Moravian College

Elizabeth Yost Hammer
Xavier University of Louisiana

CENGAGE
Learning

Australia • Brazil • Mexico • Singapore • United Kingdom • United States

*Psychology Applied to Modern Life
Adjustment in the 21st Century,*
Twelfth Edition
**Wayne Weiten, Dana S. Dunn,
Elizabeth Yost Hammer**

Product Director: Marta Lee-Perriard

Product Manager: Timothy Matray

Content Developer: Stefanie Chase

Product Assistant: Katie Chen

Marketing Manager: Andrew Ginsberg

Content Project Manager: Ruth Sakata Corley

Art Director: Vernon Boes

Manufacturing Planner: Karen Hunt

Production Service: Joan Keyes, Dovetail
    Publishing Services

Text Designer: Liz Harasymczuk

Cover Designer: Irene Morris

Cover Image: nmedia/Shutterstock.com;
    Rakic/Shutterstock.com

Compositor: Graphic World, Inc.

For product information and technology assistance, contact us at
Cengage Learning Customer & Sales Support, 1-800-354-9706.

For permission to use material from this text or product,
submit all requests online at **www.cengage.com/permissions.**
Further permissions questions can be e-mailed to
permissionrequest@cengage.com.

Library of Congress Control Number: 2016944085

Student Edition: ISBN: 978-1-305-96847-9
Loose-leaf Edition: ISBN: 978-1-337-11198-0

Cengage Learning
20 Channel Center Street
Boston, MA 02210
USA

Cengage Learning is a leading provider of customized learning solutions with employees residing in nearly 40 different countries and sales in more than 125 countries around the world. Find your local representative at **www.cengage.com.**

Cengage Learning products are represented in Canada by Nelson Education, Ltd.

To learn more about Cengage Learning Solutions, visit **www.cengage.com.** Purchase any of our products at your local college store or at our preferred online store **www.cengagebrain.com.**

Printed in the United States of America

Print Number: 04   Print Year: 2021

To two pillars of stability in this era
of turmoil—my parents
W.W.

To the memory of my mother,
Dah Kennedy Dunn, and brother,
James L. Dunn, Jr.
D.S.D.

To Elliott, of course
E.Y.H.

About the Authors

WAYNE WEITEN is a graduate of Bradley University and received his Ph.D. in social psychology from the University of Illinois, Chicago, in 1981. He has taught at the College of DuPage and Santa Clara University, and currently teaches at the University of Nevada, Las Vegas. He has received distinguished teaching awards from Division Two of the American Psychological Association (APA) and from the College of DuPage. He is a Fellow of Divisions 1, 2, and 8 of the American Psychological Association and a Fellow of the Midwestern Psychological Association. In 1991, he helped chair the APA National Conference on Enhancing the Quality of Undergraduate Education in Psychology. He is a former president of the Society for the Teaching of Psychology and the Rocky Mountain Psychological Association. In 2006, one of the six national teaching awards given annually by the Society for the Teaching of Psychology was named in his honor. Weiten has conducted research on a wide range of topics, including educational measurement, jury decision making, attribution theory, pressure as a form of stress, and the technology of textbooks. He is also the author of *Psychology: Themes & Variations* (Cengage, 2017, 10th edition). Weiten has created an educational CD-ROM titled *PsykTrek: A Multimedia Introduction to Psychology*, and he recently coauthored a chapter on the introductory psychology course for *The Oxford Handbook of Undergraduate Psychology Education* (Weiten & Houska, 2015).

DANA S. DUNN earned his B.A. in psychology from Carnegie Mellon and received his Ph.D. in social psychology from the University of Virginia. He is currently professor of psychology at Moravian College in Bethlehem, Pennsylvania. He chaired the psychology department at Moravian for six years. A Fellow of the Association for Psychological Science (APS) and the American Psychological Association (Divisions 1, 2, and 22), Dunn served as president of the Society for the Teaching of Psychology in 2010. A frequent speaker at national and regional disciplinary conferences, Dunn has written numerous articles, chapters, and book reviews concerning his areas of research interest: the teaching of psychology, social psychology, rehabilitation psychology, and educational assessment. He is the author or editor for thirty books, including *Pursuing Human Strengths: A Positive Psychology Guide* (2016), *The Social Psychology of Disability* (2015), and *The Oxford Handbook of Undergraduate Psychology Education* (2015). In 2013, Dunn received the Charles L. Brewer Award for Distinguished Teaching of Psychology from the American Psychological Foundation.

ELIZABETH YOST HAMMER earned her B.S. in psychology from Troy State University and received her Ph.D. in experimental social psychology from Tulane University. She is currently the Kellogg Professor in Teaching in the Psychology Department and Director of the Center for the Advancement of Teaching and Faculty Development (CAT+) at Xavier University of Louisiana in New Orleans. Her work in CAT+ includes organizing pedagogical workshops and faculty development initiatives. She is a Fellow of Division Two of the American Psychological Association and is a past president of Psi Chi, the International Honor Society in Psychology. She has served as the treasurer for the Society for the Teaching of Psychology. She is passionate about teaching and has published on collaborative learning, service learning, the application of social psychological theories to the classroom, and mentoring students.

To the Instructor

Many students enter adjustment courses with great expectations. They've ambled through their local bookstores, and in the "Psychology" section they've seen numerous self-help books that offer highly touted recipes for achieving happiness for a mere $15.95. After paying far more money to enroll in a college course that deals with the same issues as the self-help books, many students expect a revelatory experience. However, the majority of us with professional training in psychology or counseling take a rather dim view of self-help books and the pop psychology they represent. Psychologists tend to see this literature as oversimplified, intellectually dishonest, and opportunistic and often summarily dismiss the pop psychology that so many students have embraced. Instructors try to supplant pop psychology with more sophisticated academic psychology based on current scholarship, which is more complex and less accessible.

In this textbook, we have tried to come to grips with the problem of differing expectations between student and teacher. Our goal has been to produce a comprehensive, serious, research-oriented treatment of the topic of adjustment that also acknowledges the existence of popular psychology and looks critically at its contributions. Our approach involves the following:

- In Chapter 1 we confront the phenomenon of popular self-help books. We take students beneath the seductive surface of such books and analyze some of their typical flaws. Our goal is to make students more critical consumers of this type of literature by encouraging them to focus on substance, not on trendy claims.

- While encouraging a more critical attitude toward self-help books, we do not suggest that all should be dismissed. Instead, we acknowledge that some of them offer authentic insights. With this in mind, we highlight some of the better books in this genre in Recommended Reading boxes sprinkled throughout the text. These recommended books tie in with the adjacent topical coverage and show the student the interface between academic and popular psychology.

- We try to provide the student with a better appreciation of the merits of the empirical approach to understanding behavior. This effort to clarify the role of research, which is rare for an adjustment text, appears in the first chapter.

- Recognizing that adjustment students want to leave the course with concrete, personally useful information, we end each chapter with an Application section. The Applications are "how to" discussions that address everyday problems students encounter. While they focus on issues that are relevant to the content of the particular chapter, they contain more explicit advice than the text proper.

In summary, we have tried to make this book both challenging and applied. We hope that our approach will help students better appreciate the value and use of scientific psychology.

Philosophy

A certain philosophy is inherent in any systematic treatment of the topic of adjustment. Our philosophy can be summarized as follows:

- We believe that an adjustment text should be a resource book for students. We have tried to design this book so that it encourages and facilitates the pursuit of additional information on adjustment-related topics. It should serve as a point of departure for more learning.

- We believe in theoretical eclecticism. This book will not indoctrinate your students along the lines of any single theoretical orientation. The psychodynamic, behavioral, and humanistic schools of thought are all treated with respect, as are cognitive, biological, cultural, evolutionary, and other perspectives.

- We believe that effective adjustment requires taking charge of one's own life. Throughout the book we try to promote the notion that active coping efforts are generally superior to passivity and complacency.

Changes in the Twelfth Edition

One of the exciting things about psychology is that it is not a stagnant discipline. It continues to progress at what seems a faster and faster pace. A good textbook must evolve with the discipline. Although the professors and students who used the earlier editions of this book did not clamor for change, we have made countless content changes to keep up with new developments in psychology—adding and deleting some topics, condensing and reorganizing others, and updating everything (there are more than 1200 new references). A brief overview of some of these changes, listed chapter-by-chapter, can be found on pages viii–xii following this preface.

The most significant change in this edition is the addition of a feature we call *Spotlight on Research*. Each chapter has one Spotlight on Research, which provides a detailed but brief summary of a particular piece of research. Showing research methods in action should improve students' understanding of the research process.

In addition to this new feature, we have strived to enhance the pedagogical value of our photo program by pairing each photo with an explanatory caption and eliminating photos that were largely decorative. To increase the clarity of the book's organization, we now number all the major headings in the chapters. Moreover, we made a concerted effort to achieve more succinct writing. The manuscript length of each chapter (in words) has been reduced by 10% to 17%.

This reduction in length allowed us to move to a dramatically different book design, which for the first time is mostly a single-column design. This approach results in a much cleaner, open, student-friendly look. Instructors who know the book will notice that quite a few new figures have been added and that many familiar ones have been updated to resonate with the book's new look.

As already noted, we incorporated many new research citations into this edition in order to represent the expansion of the psychological literature since the previous edition went to print. At the same time, we were mindful about the problem posed to student readers when they are confronted with too many citations. Thus, at the same time that we added new references, we carefully culled many older ones to control the density of citations. So, even though we have added more than 1200 new references, the total number of citations in the chapters has declined by an average of 20%.

The online version of the text housed in MindTap features a variety of other changes. In MindTap, each chapter begins with an enticing engagement activity in which students attempt to answer questions about four common myths about behavior related to the chapter content. MindTap also incorporates twenty-six new Concept Clips, which are entertaining, animated, graphic overviews of important concepts, complete with audio narration. We are confident your students will greatly enjoy this new pedagogical aid. Furthermore, for each chapter, MindTap now provides three multiple-choice tests that can be assigned as Practice Tests or scored as low-stakes tests. Students' scores on these tests can automatically flow into instructors' electronic grade books. The MindTap version of the text also includes two other valuable features—the Appendix on Sustainability and the Reel Research boxes, which were formerly found in the print book.

Writing Style

This book has been written with the student in mind. We have tried to integrate the technical jargon of our discipline into a relatively informal and down-to-earth writing style. We use concrete examples extensively to clarify complex concepts and to help maintain student interest. Although we now have three authors, the original author of this book (Wayne Weiten) continues to do the final rewrite of all sixteen chapters to ensure stylistic consistency.

Features

This text contains a number of features intended to stimulate interest and enhance students' learning. These special features include the aforementioned Spotlights on Research, Applications, Recommended Reading boxes, Learn More Online boxes, Practice Tests, a didactic illustration program, cartoons, and the *Personal Explorations Workbook*.

Spotlights on Research

In each Spotlight on Research, an interesting study is presented in the conventional purpose-method-results-discussion format seen in journal articles, followed by critical thinking questions. The intent is to foster understanding of how empirical studies are conducted and to enhance students' ability to think critically about research while also giving them a painless introduction to the basic format of journal articles. The Spotlights on Research are fully incorporated into the flow of discourse in the text and are *not* presented as optional boxes. Some examples of the topics covered include:

- Stress-induced eating
- Hugs and social support
- Autism and vaccinations
- Internet therapy
- The effects of red clothing on attraction
- Oxytocin and fidelity

Applications

The end-of-chapter Applications should be of special interest to most students. They are tied to chapter content in a way that should show students how practical applications emerge out of theory and research. Although some of the material covered in these sections shows up frequently in adjustment texts, much of it is unique. Some of the Applications include the following:

- Understanding Intimate Violence
- Improving Academic Performance
- Understanding Eating Disorders
- Getting Ahead in the Job Game
- Building Self-Esteem
- Enhancing Sexual Relationships
- Boosting One's Own Happiness

Recommended Reading Boxes

Recognizing students' interest in self-help books, we have sifted through hundreds of them to identify some that may be especially useful. These books are featured in boxes that briefly review some of the higher-quality books, several of which were published recently. These Recommended Reading boxes are placed where they are germane to the material being covered in the text. Some of the recommended books are well known, whereas others are less so. Although we make it clear that we don't endorse every idea in every book, we think they all have something worthwhile to offer. This feature replaces the conventional suggested readings lists that usually appear at the ends of chapters, where they are almost universally ignored by students.

Learn More Online

The Internet is rapidly altering the landscape of modern life, and students clearly need help dealing with the information explosion in cyberspace. To assist them, we have come up with some recommendations regarding websites that appear to provide reasonably accurate, balanced, and empirically sound information. Short descriptions of these recommended Learn More Online websites are dispersed throughout the chapters, adjacent to related topical coverage. Because URLs change frequently, we have not included them in the book. Insofar as students are interested in visiting these sites, we recommend that they do so by using a search engine such as Google to locate and access the URLs.

Practice Tests

Each chapter ends with a ten-item multiple-choice Practice Test that should give students a fairly realistic assessment of their mastery of that chapter and valuable practice in taking the type of test that many of them will face in the classroom (if the instructor uses the Test Bank). This feature grew out of some research on students' use of textbook pedagogical devices (see Weiten, Guadagno, & Beck, 1996). This research indicated that students pay scant attention to some standard pedagogical devices. When students were grilled to gain a better understanding of this perplexing finding, it quickly became apparent that students are pragmatic about pedagogy. Essentially, their refrain was "We want study aids that will help us pass the next test." With this mandate in mind, we added the Practice Tests. They should be very realistic, given many of the items came from the Test Banks for previous editions (these items do not appear in the Test Bank for the current edition).

Didactic Illustration Program

The illustration program is once again in full color, and as already noted, many new figures have been added along with extensive redrawing of many graphics. Although the illustrations are intended to make the book attractive and to help maintain student interest, they are not merely decorative: They have been carefully selected and crafted for their didactic value to enhance the educational goals of the text.

Cartoons

A little comic relief usually helps keep a student interested, so we've sprinkled numerous cartoons throughout the book. Like the figures, these have been chosen to reinforce ideas in the text.

Personal Explorations Workbook

As mentioned earlier, the *Personal Explorations Workbook* can be found in the very back of the text. It contains experiential exercises for each text chapter, designed to help your students achieve personal insights. For each chapter, we have included one Self-Assessment exercise and one Self-Reflection exercise. The self-assessments are psychological tests or scales that students can take and score for themselves. The self-reflections consist of questions intended to help students think about themselves in relation to issues raised in the text. These exercises can be invaluable homework assignments. To facilitate assigning them as homework, we have printed the workbook section on perforated paper, so students can tear out the relevant pages and turn them in. In addition to providing easy-to-use homework assignments, many of these exercises can be used in class to stimulate lively discussion.

Learning Aids

A number of learning aids have been incorporated into the text to help the reader digest the wealth of material:

- The *outline* at the beginning of each chapter provides the student with a preview and overview of what will be covered.
- *Headings* are used extensively to keep material well organized.
- To help alert your students to key points, *learning objectives* are distributed throughout the chapters, after the main headings.
- *Key terms* are identified with **blue italicized boldface** type to indicate that these are important vocabulary items that are part of psychology's technical language.
- An *integrated running glossary* provides an on-the-spot definition of each key term as it is introduced in the text. These formal definitions are printed in **blue boldface** type.
- An *alphabetical glossary* is found in the back of the book, as key terms are usually defined in the integrated running glossary only when they are first introduced.
- *Italics* are used liberally throughout the text to emphasize important points.
- A *chapter review* is found at the end of each chapter. Each review includes a concise summary of the chapter's key ideas, a list of the key terms that were introduced in the chapter, and a list of important theorists and researchers who were discussed in the chapter.

Supplementary Materials

A complete teaching/learning package has been developed to supplement *Psychology Applied to Modern Life*. These supplementary materials have been carefully coordinated to provide effective support for the text. This package of supplementary materials includes the *Instructor's Manual*, *Cognero*®, online PowerPoints, and MindTap.

Instructor's Manual

The *Instructor's Manual* is available as a convenient aid for your educational endeavors. It provides a thorough overview of each chapter and includes a wealth of suggestions for lecture topics, class demonstrations, exercises, and discussion questions, organized around the content of each chapter in the text.

Cengage Learning Testing Powered by Cognero®

Cengage Learning Testing Powered by Cognero® is a flexible, online system that allows you to import, edit, and manipulate content from the text's Test Bank or elsewhere, including your own favorite test questions; create multiple test versions in an instant; and deliver tests from your Course Management System, your classroom, or wherever you want.

The content, revised by Jeremy Houska of Centenary College, is made up of an extensive collection of multiple-choice questions for objective tests, all closely tied to the learning objectives found in the text chapters. We're confident that you will find this to be a dependable and usable test bank.

Online PowerPoints

Vibrant Microsoft® PowerPoint® lecture slides for each chapter assist you with your lecture by providing concept coverage using images, figures, and tables directly from the textbook.

MindTap

MindTap® is the digital learning solution that helps instructors engage and transform today's students into critical thinkers. Through paths of dynamic assignments and applications that you can personalize, real-time course analytics, and an accessible reader, MindTap helps you turn cookie-cutter into cutting-edge, apathy into engagement, and memorizers into higher-level thinkers.

As an instructor using MindTap, you have at your fingertips the right content and a unique set of tools curated specifically for your course, all in an interface designed to improve workflow and save time when planning lessons and course structure. The control to build and personalize your course is all yours, focusing on the most relevant material while also lowering costs for your students. Stay connected and informed in your course through real-time student tracking that provides the opportunity to adjust the course as needed based on analytics of interactivity in the course.

Highlights of Content Changes in the Twelfth Edition

To help professors who have used this book over many editions, we are providing an overview of the content changes in the current edition. The following list is not exhaustive, but it should alert faculty to most of the major changes in the book.

CHAPTER 1: Adjusting to Modern Life

New discussion of how leisure time and sleep have declined in our fast-paced modern society

Updated information on the likelihood of choice overload

New discussion of possession overload and compulsive buying syndrome

New coverage of escalating financial stress and how materialism undermines well-being

New coverage of "affluenza" and its societal repercussions

New Spotlight on Research provides an example of naturalistic observation focusing on how larger plate sizes lead to increased eating at real-world buffets

New example of case study research evaluating anxiety and depressive disorders as risk factors for dementia

New example of survey research describes a Danish study on age trends in the experience of hangovers after binge drinking

New example of how correlational methods broaden the scope of phenomena that can be studied

New discussion of how subjective well-being is predictive of important life outcomes

New research on how spending on experiences rather than material goods, and on others rather than oneself, are associated with greater happiness

New data on gender and happiness

Revised coverage of the association between social relations and subjective well-being

New coverage of the link between leisure activity and subjective well-being

New data on how many students embrace flawed models of how they learn and remember

New discussion of how students overestimate their ability to multitask while studying

Revised discussion of the value of text highlighting in the coverage of study skills

New research on how surfing the Internet in class undermines academic performance and distracts fellow students

New research showing that taking notes on a laptop leads to shallower processing and reduced learning

New findings on test-enhanced learning

CHAPTER 2: Theories of Personality

New data on Big Five correlates of income, entrepreneurial activity, and longevity

New research relating reduced reliance on defense mechanisms to progress in therapy

New overview of empirical findings on the functions and health consequences of defensive behavior

New research on the effects of a repressive coping style

New discussion of how psychoanalytic theories depend too heavily on case studies

New summary of contradictory evidence related to Freudian theory

New research on the correlates of self-efficacy

New research supporting a key tenet of Maslow's hierarchy of needs

New meta-analytic findings on the heritability of personality

New findings on correlations between personality traits and reproductive fitness

New research relating narcissism to behavior on social media sites

New research relating narcissism to empathy, consumer preferences, and social class

New coverage of the distinction between grandiose narcissism and vulnerable narcissism

New findings on gender differences in narcissism

Revised assessment of the cross-cultural universality of the five-factor model

New data on the inaccuracy of perceptions of national character

New coverage of individualism versus collectivism in relation to self-enhancement

New featured study on individualism, collectivism, and the accuracy of self-perceptions

New, more favorable meta-analytic findings on the validity of Rorschach scoring

New discussion of the public exposure of the Rorschach inkblots on the Internet

CHAPTER 3: Stress and Its Effects

Revised to include a recent "Stress in America" survey from the American Psychological Association

New figure with recent national data on reported sources of stress

New data on physical health following Hurricane Katrina

New research on daily hassles and mortality in the elderly

New discussion of the stress mindset

New data on environmentally healthy neighborhoods and life satisfaction of residents

Expanded coverage of poverty as a source of stress

New research on antigay stigmas and health disparities

New coverage of the stress response and the ability to verbally characterize emotions

New data on positive emotional style and longevity

New discussion of stress and neurogenesis

New research on stress and memory improvement

New discussion of media exposure to trauma and PTSD symptoms

New discussion of the curvilinear relationship between lifetime adversity and mental health

New data on social support and inflammation

New discussion of superficial social interaction and well-being

New featured study on the role of hugs in social support

New cross-cultural data on optimism and health

CHAPTER 4: Coping Processes

Revised coverage of aggression and catharsis

New discussion of comfort foods and stress-induced eating

New Spotlight on Research on stress-induced eating

New discussion of stress-induced shopping

New description of the subtypes of Internet addiction

New cross-cultural research on the prevalence of Internet addiction

Expanded discussion of the correlates of Internet addiction

New discussion of research on the importance of timing when humor is used as a coping mechanism

New figure outlining the essential components of emotional intelligence

New discussion of research on mediation and compassion

New figure on the effect of meditation on helping behavior

New discussion of self-forgiveness as an emotion-based coping strategy

Two new websites profiled in the Learn More Online feature

CHAPTER 5: Psychology and Physical Health

New discussion of two causes of death that are not due to lifestyle factors—Alzheimer's and Parkinson's Diseases, respectively—that are linked instead to longer lifespan

New figure and discussion concerning leading causes of death linked to four ethnic groups in the United States

New discussion of other negative emotions beyond anger and hostility that are linked to heart disease

New, broader discussion of how lack of social support is a predictor of heart disease

New discussion of how working through anger constructively can prevent coronary incidents

New discussion of the very weak connections between psychosocial factors and cancer onset, and new focus on psychological interventions that improve cancer victims' quality of life

Updated figure illustrating the great variety of stress-linked health problems

New discussion of novel psychosocial factors, such as loneliness and social standing, which can compromise immune functioning

New research on college students' smoking habits, especially in relation to use of e-cigarettes and water pipes

New Spotlight on Research on whether smoking can be decreased via monetary incentives

New Recommended Reading profiling *The Longevity Project*

New information on the benefits of relatively modest amounts of exercise

New consideration of how walking is identified as a solid and beneficial form of exercise

New figure illustrates the declines in incidence, prevalence, and deaths from AIDS in the United States since the mid-1990s

New discussion of how to present medical instructions in order to increase adherence rates

New comparison of the term *narcotic*, which is seen as pejorative, with the term *opioid*, which is less recognized and understood by the public

New discussion of the context for legalization of marijuana for recreational and medicinal purposes in some locales, while highlighting benefits and liabilities of legalization

CHAPTER 6: The Self

New discussion of the fit between positive selves and situation contexts as a source of beneficial motivation

New Spotlight on Research on possible selves and late life depression

New review of social neuroscience work on social comparison theory, neural responses, and social status

New discussion of individualism and collectivism as being a part of social class differences within subcultures in the United States

Revised coverage of the correlates of self-esteem

New attention to the fact that a benefit of high self-esteem, such as task persistence following a negative evaluation, can come with interpersonal costs

New, extended discussion of the Dunning-Krueger effect and positive distortions in self-assessment

New examples of the better-than-average effect

New mention of how downward comparisons can be applied beneficially to oneself

New Recommended Reading profiling *The Marshmallow Test*

New studies revealing the benefits and risks of ingratiation as an impression management strategy

New figure illustrates the ways in which people use ingratiation and self-promotion in job interviews

New research indicating that self-promotion can be effective when an audience is cognitively busy during a presentation

New discussion of how people's high or low self-monitoring can be predicted reasonably well by their posts on Facebook

New suggestions on how to cultivate a new strength in the Application on building self-esteem

CHAPTER 7: Social Thinking and Social Influence

New discussion of an overlooked dimension of attributions: intentional versus unintentional behaviors

New discussion of research that reduces the incidence of the confirmation bias

New discussion indicating that older adults' health behaviors, which can be compromised by a crisis, are examples of health-related self-fulfilling prophecies

New and enhanced explanation of the costs of social categorization into groups

New explanation for the operation of the attractiveness stereotype

New fMRI study demonstrating that reliance on the fundamental attribution error is predictable based on activity in a particular part of the brain

New Spotlight on Research examining the influence of race and stereotypes on visual processing and behavior

New examples linking social dominance orientation to aggression in adolescence and efforts to maintain the status quo

New discussion of nationalism as a source of prejudice between groups

New Recommended Reading profiling *Blindspot: Hidden Biases of Good People*

New, broader discussion of social identity theory's influence on self-esteem as a source of aggression

New discussion of how imagined contact with stigmatized outgroup members can promote prejudice reduction

New figure listing most to least trustworthy occupational groups

New figure listing tactics for resisting persuasive appeals

New field study demonstrates a positive form of compliance in response to a prosocial request

CHAPTER 8: Interpersonal Communication

New Recommended Reading profiling *Clash! How to Thrive in a Multicultural World*

New Spotlight on Research on communicating social relationships by photo-messaging

New discussion of the lack of empirical evidence that online sources of social support lead to improved health or reduced negative outcomes

New material on why people sometimes fail to maintain privacy in online venues

New discussion of how the presence of rapid saccadic eye movements can nonverbally indicate when someone is lying

New discussion of research indicating closer personal distance can increase tipping by customers

New research on how the recognition of facial expressions is influenced by their frequency of occurrence

New material on display rules for emotion, which are discussed in terms of whether they occur in or outside of work, as well as whether they are influenced by the larger culture

New discussion of emoji, accompanied by a new graphic showing many emoji

New data on accuracy in detecting lies under high-stakes conditions

New coverage reviewing how higher assessed nonverbal sensitivity enables individuals to make more accurate judgments of others' personalities based on online profile information

New research concerning online self-disclosure as a predictor of honesty, intent, and whether status updates contain positive or negative content

New data linking laughter to self-disclosure

New discussion of how critical self-talk is associated with communication apprehension and anxiety regarding public speaking

New material on classroom layout as a means to enhance communication effectiveness as well as student comfort when presenting to others

New discussion of conversational rerouting and diversionary interrupting as forms of self-preoccupation associated with monopolizing conversations

New examples of aggressive, assertive, and submissive requests

CHAPTER 9: Friendship and Love

New research on the complexity of the link between familiarity and attraction

New coverage of the influence of red clothing on men's perceptions of women's attractiveness

New Spotlight on Research exploring limits to the link between the color red and attraction

New discussion of Montoya and Horton's two-dimensional model of attraction

New discussion of the relevance of reciprocal self-disclosure in establishing relationships

New introduction to the importance of relationship maintenance activities

New coverage of Hall's six friendship standards

New meta-analysis on gender differences in friendship expectations

New discussion of friendship maintenance strategies in response to conflict

New research on partner buffering to improve relational outcomes for individuals with insecure attachment

New discussion of the types of threats to relationships

New research on individual differences in adjustment after nonmarital breakups

New Recommended Reading profiling *Alone Together*

New discussion of advantages of online over face-to-face dating

New graphic on contemporary attitudes about online dating

New research finding a curvilinear relationship between the amount of communication in online dating and the quality of the initial face-to-face meeting

New coverage of the heritability of loneliness

New research on the link between loneliness and physical health

CHAPTER 10: Marriage and the Family

New discussion of the Supreme Court ruling that legalized same-sex marriage nationwide

Updated coverage of interracial couples

Updated data on voluntary childlessness, noting recent decline in rates

New discussion of postpartum depression as a "disease of modern civilization"

New research that challenges the view that nonparents are happier than parents

New Spotlight on Research comparing parents and nonparents in regard to positive emotions

New coverage of grandparents caregiving for children in later life

New research on division of labor among lesbian couples

New data on the financial practices of highly satisfied couples

New Recommended Reading profiling *The Seven Principles for Making Marriage Work*

New discussion of the "all-or-nothing" model of marriage

New section on same-sex marriages

New discussion of same-sex couples' stepfamilies

New data on the relationship between cohabitation motivation and relationship satisfaction

Updated data on the prevalence of date rape

CHAPTER 11: Gender and Behavior

New findings on the possible bases of gender disparities in spatial abilities

New discussion of gender differences in academic achievement in addition to cognitive abilities

Updated data from U.S. Department of Justice on female inmates (as an indicator of gender differences in aggression)

Introduced the concept of *neurosexism*

New discussion of the myth that hormones have a gender

New Spotlight on Research on the impact of gender-socialized play on career perceptions

New data on depictions of males and females in picture books

New discussion of how parents communicate gender messages while reading picture books

New discussion of the impact of the stereotype of the "underachieving male" in schools

Updated data from Neilsen Research Group on TV viewing habits of children

New research on how TV and video games promote gender stereotypes

New data on gender role distress and sexual risk taking in males

New coverage of transgendered identities

New coverage of gender fluidity

New Application on gender in the workplace

New discussion of benevolent sexism

Expanded coverage of the glass ceiling

New discussion of Queen Bees in the workplace

New coverage of who is likely to be a target of sexual harassment

New discussion of the mental and physical effects of sexism and sexual harassment

New information on ways a workplace can reduce sexism and sexual harassment

CHAPTER 12: Development and Expression of Sexuality

In discussion of sexual identity, added a definition for *asexuals*

New coverage of body image as a component of sexual identity

New recommended reading profiling *Sexual Intelligence*

New discussion of the effects of sexually explicit video games

New discussion of sexual fluidity in the coverage of sexual orientation

New discussion of how the belief that the vast majority of people are either straight or gay is a misleading oversimplification

New coverage of birth-order effects and sexual orientation

New data on attitudes toward homosexuality

New findings on the effects of others' reactions to one's coming out

New data on features of sexual fantasies

New data on the prevalence of hooking up among college students and outcomes of friends with benefits relationships

New discussion of sexting

New Spotlight on Research on the hormone oxytocin and its relationship to infidelity

Updated data on unintended and teen pregnancies

Updated data on HIV and HPV infections

CHAPTER 13: Careers and Work

Two new suggestions added to the discussion of the kinds of information one should pursue about specific occupations

New discussion of the value of job shadowing once potential professions are identified

New information on whether to pursue a job, a career, or a calling is discussed as an important consideration for planning one's future work

New data concerning women's participation in the labor force

New projections regarding the twenty occupations expected to grow the fastest between 2012 and 2022

New review of job quality dimensions where women lag behind men due to job segregation

New discussion of role overload as a source of workplace stress

New conclusion regarding how occupational stress can be reduced

New discussion of an experiment that reduced acceptance of myths regarding sexual harassment as well as the likelihood of engaging in harassment behaviors

New Spotlight on Research exploring how work-family conflict affects workers' quantity and quality of sleep

New discussion of how résumé-writing workshops can enhance students' skills at producing a good résumé

New information detailing questions an interviewee can ask during a job interview

New discussion of the importance of nonverbal cues in the job interview

CHAPTER 14: Psychological Disorders

Expanded discussion of how the stigma of mental illness is a source of stress and an impediment to treatment

New discussion of the exponential growth of the DSM system and its tendency to medicalize everyday problems

New Recommended Reading profiling *Saving Normal*

New discussion of how people with generalized anxiety disorder hope their worry will prepare them for the worst and its association with physical health problems

Agoraphobia covered as an independent disorder rather than a complication of panic disorder

Expanded description of agoraphobia, emphasizing the central role of fear that it will be difficult to escape threatening situations

Added discussion of whether people with OCD have insight into their irrationality and new information on the lack of gender differences in the prevalence of OCD

New research linking OCD to broad impairments in executive function

Added explanation of why multiple personality disorder was renamed dissociative identity disorder

Revised explanation of socio-cognitive views of dissociative identity disorder

New clarification that not all individuals with bipolar illness experience episodes of depression

Revised data on the prevalence and health consequences of depression

New data relating severity of depression and sense of hopelessness to suicidality

New research linking heightened reactivity in the amygdala to vulnerability to depression

New coverage of stormy social relations as a source of stress generation in the etiology of depression

New discussion of how stress becomes progressively less of a factor as people go through more recurrences of episodes of depression

New tabular overview of positive and negative symptoms in schizophrenia

New research linking low IQ to vulnerability to schizophrenia

New MRI data on schizophrenia linking it to reduced volume in the hippocampus, thalamus, and amygdala

Updated coverage of brain overgrowth as etiological factor in autism spectrum disorder

New Spotlight on Research on the myth that vaccines are a cause of autism

New section on personality disorders, including a table describing all ten DSM-5 personality disorder diagnoses

New coverage of antisocial personality disorder, narcissistic personality disorder, and borderline personality disorder

New discussion of the etiology of personality disorders

Streamlined coverage of eating disorders

New mention of peer influence and history of child abuse as etiological factors in eating disorders

Two new Learn More Online recommendations

CHAPTER 15: Psychotherapy

New findings on the importance of empathy and unconditional positive regard to therapeutic climate

New coverage of common factors as an explanation for the beneficial effects of therapy

New empirical effort to partition the variance in therapeutic outcomes to quantify the influence of common factors

Streamlined coverage of insight therapies

New data on prescription trends for antianxiety, antipsychotic, antidepressant, and mood-stabilizing drugs

New discussion of long-acting, injectable antipsychotic medications

Revised coverage of the side effects of SSRI antidepressants

New data on whether FDA warnings about antidepressants have impacted suicide rates

New data on antidepressant dosage levels in relation to suicide risk

New coverage of how the medicalization of psychological disorders has undermined the provision of insight therapy

New findings on relapse rates after ECT treatment

New research on ECT and autobiographical memory loss

New research on the effect of ethnic matching between therapist and client

New discussion of the need for culturally competent treatment of sexual minorities

New Spotlight on Research on whether Internet therapies are as effective as face-to-face therapies

CHAPTER 16: Positive Psychology

New figure allows readers to assess their current level of flourishing

New discussion of research pointing to clinical implications and interventions for increasing thought speed and positive mood

New research demonstrates that physical activity not only generates positive emotions but also builds psychosocial resource reserves, whereas sedentary behavior creates negative emotions and reduces psychosocial reserves

New discussion of flow's relationship to personality factors

New research linking mindfulness to the slowing of a progressively fatal disease

New figure enabling readers to assess the degree to which they savor their present moments

New Recommended Reading profiling *Love 2.0: How Our Supreme Emotion Affects Everything We Feel, Think, Do, and Become*

New Spotlight on Research on awe and prosocial behavior

New research on the noncognitive trait known as grit

New research concerning gratitude

New review of the intellectual divide between humanistic psychology and positive psychology

New material in the Application regarding gratitude journaling, a viable alternative to writing a gratitude letter

New suggestions for ways to spend money to promote happiness

Acknowledgments

This book has been an enormous undertaking, and we want to express our gratitude to the innumerable people who have influenced its evolution. To begin with, we must cite the contribution of our students who have taken the adjustment course. It is trite to say that they have been a continuing inspiration—but they have.

We also want to express our appreciation for the time and effort invested by the authors of various ancillary books and materials: Vinny Hevern (Le Moyne College), Bill Addison (Eastern Illinois University), Britain Scott (University of St. Thomas), Susan Koger (Willamette University), Jeffry Ricker (Scottsdale Community College), David Matsumoto (San Francisco State University), Lenore Frigo (Shasta College), Jeffrey Armstrong (Northampton Community College), and Jeremy Houska (Centenary College) have contributed excellent work either to this edition or to previous editions of the book. In spite of tight schedules, they all did commendable work.

The quality of a textbook depends greatly on the quality of the prepublication reviews by psychology professors around the country. The reviewers listed on pages xiv–xv have contributed to the development of this book by providing constructive reviews of various portions of the manuscript in this or earlier editions. We are grateful to all of them.

We would also like to thank Tim Matray, who has served as product manager for this edition. He has done a wonderful job following in the footsteps of Claire Verduin, Eileen Murphy, Edith Beard Brady, Michele Sordi, and Jon-David Hague, to whom we remain indebted. We are also grateful to Joan Keyes, who performed superbly as our production coordinator; Susan Gall, for an excellent job of copyediting; and Liz Harasymczuk, who created the new design. Others who have made significant contributions to this project include Stefanie Chase (content development), Michelle Clark and Ruth Sakata Corley (project management), Andrew Ginsberg (marketing), Adrienne McCrory (product assistant), and Vernon Boes (art director).

In addition, Wayne Weiten would like to thank his wife, Beth Traylor, who has been a steady source of emotional support despite the demands of her medical career, and his son, T. J., who adds a wealth of laughter to his dad's life. Dana S. Dunn thanks his children, Jacob and Hannah, for their usual support during the writing and production process. Dana continues to be grateful to Wayne and Elizabeth for their camaraderie as authors and friends. He also appreciates the excellent efforts of the Cengage team who supported his work during the preparation of this edition. Elizabeth Yost Hammer would like to thank CAT+ (Olivia Crum, Janice Florent, Bart Everson, Tiera Coston, Karen Nichols, and Jason Todd) for their patience and encouragement. She is especially grateful to Kimia Kaviani, Kyjeila Latimer, Chinyere Okafor, and Emma Ricks for their outstanding research assistance. Finally, she would like to thank Elliott Hammer—her partner in work and play—for far too much to list here.

Wayne Weiten
Dana S. Dunn
Elizabeth Yost Hammer

Reviewers

David Ackerman
Rhodes College

David W. Alfano
Community College of Rhode Island

Gregg Amore
DeSales University

Jeff Banks
Pepperdine University

David Baskind
Delta College

Marsha K. Beauchamp
Mt. San Antonio College

Robert Biswas-Diener
Portland State University (USA)/
Centre for Applied Positive Psychology

John R. Blakemore
Monterey Peninsula College

Barbara A. Boccaccio
Tunxis Community College

Paul Bowers
Grayson County College

Amara Brook
Santa Clara University

Tamara L. Brown
University of Kentucky

George Bryant
East Texas State University

James F. Calhoun
University of Georgia

Robert Cameron
Fairmont State College

David Campbell
Humboldt State University

Bernardo J. Carducci
Indiana University, Southeast

Richard Cavasina
California University of Pennsylvania

M. K. Clampit
Bentley College

Meg Clark
California State Polytechnic University–
Pomona

Stephen S. Coccia
Orange County Community
College

William C. Compton
Middle Tennessee State University

Dennis Coon
Santa Barbara City College

Katherine A. Couch
Eastern Oklahoma State College

Tori Crews
American River College

Salvatore Cullari
Lebenon Valley College

Kenneth S. Davidson
Wayne State University

Lugenia Dixon
Bainbridge College

Laura Duvall
Golden West College

Jean Egan
Asnuntuck Community College

Pamela Elizabeth
University of Rhode Island

Ron Evans
Washburn University

Belinda Evans-Ebio
Wayne County Community College

Richard Furhere
University of Wisconsin–Eau Claire

R. Kirkland Gable
California Lutheran University

Laura Gaudet
Chadron State College

Lee Gills
Georgia College

Chris Goode
Georgia State University

Lawrence Grebstein
University of Rhode Island

Bryan Gros
Louisiana State University

Kristi Hagen
Chippewa Valley Technical
College

David Hamilton
Canadore College

Kyle Max Hancock
Utah State University

Barbara Hansen Lemme
College of DuPage

Jerry Harazmus
Western Technical College

Christina Hawkey
Arizona Western College

Robert Helm
Oklahoma State University

Barbara Herman
Gainesville College

Jeanne L. Higbee
University of Minnesota

Robert Higgins
Central Missouri State University

Clara E. Hill
University of Maryland

Michael Hirt
Kent State University

Fred J. Hitti
Monroe Community College

William M. Hooper
Clayton College and State University

Joseph Horvat
Weber State University

Kathy Howard
Harding University

Teresa A. Hutchens
University of Tennessee–Knoxville

Howard Ingle
Salt Lake Community College

Brian Jensen
Columbia College

Jerry Jensen
Minneapolis Community & Technical
College

Walter Jones
College of DuPage

Wayne Joose
Calvin College

Bradley Karlin
Texas A&M University

Margaret Karolyi
University of Akron

Lambros Karris
Husson College

Liz Kiebel
Western Illinois University

Martha Kuehn
Central Lakes College

Susan Kupisch
Austin Peay State University

Robert Lawyer
Delgado Community College

Jimi Leopold
Tarleton State University

Harold List
Massachusetts Bay Community College

Corliss A. Littlefield
Morgan Community College

Louis A. Martone
Miami Dade Community College

Richard Maslow
San Joaquin Delta College

Sherri McCarthy
Northern Arizona Community College

William T. McReynolds
University of Tampa

Fred Medway
University of South Carolina–Columbia

Fredrick Meeker
*California State Polytechnic
University–Pomona*

Mitchell Metzger
*Pennsylvania State University–Shenago
Campus*

John Moritsugu
Pacific Lutheran University

Jeanne O'Kon
Tallahassee Community College

Gary Oliver
College of DuPage

William Penrod
Middle Tennessee State University

Joseph Philbrick
*California State Polytechnic University–
Pomona*

Barbara M. Powell
Eastern Illinois University

James Prochaska
University of Rhode Island

Megan Benoit Ratcliff
University of Georgia

Bob Riesenberg
Whatcom Community College

Craig Rogers
Campbellsville University

Katherine Elaine Royal
Middle Tennessee State University

Joan Royce
Riverside Community College

Joan Rykiel
Ocean County College

John Sample
Slippery Rock University

Thomas K. Savill
Metropolitan State College of Denver

Patricia Sawyer
Middlesex Community College

Carol Schachat
De Anza College

John Schell
Kent State University

Norman R. Schultz
Clemson University

Dale Simmons
Oregon State University

Gail Simpson
Wayne County Community College

Sangeeta Singg
Angelo State University

Valerie Smead
Western Illinois University

Krishna Stilianos
Oakland Community College

Dolores K. Sutter
Tarrant County College–Northeast

Karl Swain
*Community College of Southern
Nevada*

Diane Teske
Penn State Harrisburg

Kenneth L. Thompson
Central Missouri State University

Joanne Viney
University of Illinois Urbana/Champaign

Davis L. Watson
University of Hawaii

Deborah S. Weber
University of Akron

Monica Whitehead
University of Georgia

Clair Wiederholt
Madison Area Technical College

J. Oscar Williams
Diablo Valley College

Corinice Wilson
*Oklahoma State University Institute
of Technology*

David Wimer
*Pennsylvania State University,
University Park*

Raymond Wolf
Moraine Park Technical College

Raymond Wolfe
State University of New York at Geneseo

Michael Wolff
*Southwestern Oklahoma State
University*

Madeline E. Wright
Houston Community College

Norbet Yager
Henry Ford Community College

BRIEF CONTENTS

CONTENTS

Sergei Bachlakov/Shutterstock.com

Peter Cade/The Image Bank/Getty Images

CHAPTER 3   Stress and Its Effects   62

wavebreakmedia/Shutterstock.com

ZINQ Stock/Shutterstock.com

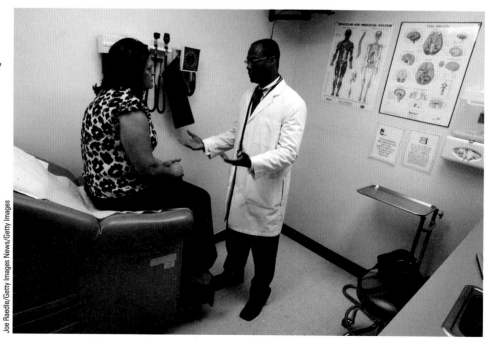

Joe Raadle/Getty Images News/Getty Images

Pressmaster/Shutterstock.com

Masterfile

Ting Hoo/Iconica/Getty Images

A and N photography/Shutterstock.com

Marmaduke St. John/Alamy Stock Photo

Monkey Business Image/Shutterstock.com

Thinkstock/Stockbyte/Getty Images

AP Images/Charles Sykes

Alexsokolov/Dreamstime.com

Patrizia Tilly/Shutterstock.com

To the Student

In most college courses, students spend more time with their textbooks than with their professors. Given this reality, it helps if you like your textbook. Making textbooks likable, however, is a tricky proposition. By its very nature, a textbook must introduce a great many new concepts, ideas, and theories. If it doesn't, it isn't much of a textbook, and instructors won't choose to use it—so you'll never see it anyway. Consequently, we have tried to make this book as likable as possible without compromising the academic content that your instructor demands. Thus, we have tried to make the book lively, informal, engaging, well organized, easy to read, practical, and occasionally humorous. Before you plunge into Chapter 1, let us explain some of the key features that can help you get the most out of the book.

Learning Aids

Mastering the content of this text involves digesting a great deal of information. To facilitate this learning process, we've incorporated a number of instructional aids into the book.

- *Outlines* at the beginning of each chapter provide you with both a preview and an overview of what will be covered. Think of the outlines as road maps, and bear in mind that it's easier to reach a destination if you know where you're going.
- *Headings* are used extensively to keep material well organized.
- To help alert you to key points, *learning objectives* are found throughout the chapters, immediately after the main headings.
- *Key terms* are identified with *blue italicized boldface* type to indicate that these are important vocabulary items that are part of psychology's technical language.
- An *integrated running glossary* provides an on-the-spot definition of each key term as it's introduced in the text. These formal definitions are printed in **blue boldface** type. It is often difficult for students to adapt to the jargon used by scientific disciplines. However, learning this terminology is an essential part of your educational experience. The integrated running glossary is meant to make this learning process as painless as possible.
- An *alphabetical glossary* is provided in the back of the book, as key terms are usually defined in the running glossary only when they are first introduced. If you run into a technical term that was introduced in an earlier chapter and you can't remember its meaning, you can look it up in the alphabetical glossary instead of backtracking to find the place where it first appeared.
- *Italics* are used liberally throughout the book to emphasize important points.
- A *chapter review* near the end of each chapter includes a thorough summary of the chapter and lists key terms and important theorists, with page references. Reading over these review materials can help ensure that you've digested the key points in the chapter.
- Each chapter ends with a ten-item *practice test* that should give you a realistic assessment of your mastery of that chapter and valuable practice taking multiple-choice tests that

will probably be representative of what you will see in class (if your instructor uses the test bank designed for this book).

Recommended Reading Boxes

This text should function as a resource book. To facilitate this goal, particularly interesting self-help books on various topics are highlighted in boxes within the chapters. Each box provides a brief description of the book. We do not agree with everything in these recommended books, but all of them are potentially useful or intriguing. The main purpose of this feature is to introduce you to some of the better self-help books that are available.

Learn More Online

To help make this book a rich resource guide, we have included Learn More Online boxes, which are recommended websites that can provide you with additional information on adjustment-related topics. As with the Recommended Reading boxes, we cannot say that we agree with everything posted on these websites, but we think they have some real value. The Learn More Online boxes are dispersed throughout the chapters, adjacent to related topical coverage. Because URLs change frequently, we have not included them for the Learn More Online boxes in the book. If you are interested in visiting these sites, we recommend that you use a search engine, such as Google, to locate the recommended websites.

Personal Explorations Workbook

The *Personal Explorations Workbook*, which can be found in the very back of the text, contains interesting, thought-provoking experiential exercises for each chapter. These exercises are designed to help you achieve personal insights. The Self-Assessment exercises are psychological tests or scales that you can take, so you can see how you score on various traits discussed in the text. The Self-Reflection exercises consist of questions intended to help you think about issues in your personal life in relation to concepts and ideas discussed in the text. Many students find these exercises to be quite interesting, even fun. Hence, we encourage you to use the *Personal Explorations Workbook*.

A Concluding Note

We sincerely hope that you find this book enjoyable. If you have any comments or advice that might help us improve the next edition, please write to us in care of the publisher, Cengage Learning, 500 Terry A. Francois Blvd., Second Floor, San Francisco, CA 94158. Finally, let us wish you good luck. We hope you enjoy your course and learn a great deal.

Wayne Weiten
Dana S. Dunn
Elizabeth Yost Hammer

CHAPTER 1 Adjusting to Modern Life

PIERRE VERDY/AFP/Getty Images

The immense Boeing 747 lumbers into position to accept its human cargo. The passengers make their way onboard. In a tower a few hundred yards away, air traffic controllers diligently monitor radar screens, radio transmissions, and digital readouts of weather information. At the reservation desk in the airport terminal, clerks punch up the appropriate ticket information on their computers and quickly process the steady stream of passengers. Mounted on the wall are video screens displaying up-to-the-minute information on flight arrivals, departures, and delays. Back in the cockpit of the plane, the flight crew calmly scans the complex array of dials, meters, and lights to assess the aircraft's readiness for flight. In a few minutes, the airplane will slice into the cloudy, snow-laden skies above Chicago. In a little more than four hours, its passengers will be transported from the piercing cold of a Chicago winter to the balmy beaches of the Bahamas. Another everyday triumph for technology will have taken place. ■

1.1 The Paradox of Progress

Learning Objectives

■ Describe three examples of the paradox of progress.

■ Explain what is meant by the paradox of progress and how theorists have explained it.

We are the children of technology. We take for granted such impressive feats as transporting 300 people over 1500 miles in a matter of hours. After all, we live in a time of unparalleled progress. Our modern Western society has made extraordinary strides in transportation, energy, communication, agriculture, and medicine. Yet despite our technological advances, social problems and personal difficulties seem more prevalent and more prominent than ever before. This paradox is evident in many aspects of contemporary life, as seen in the following examples.

Point. *Modern technology has provided us with countless time-saving devices.* Automobiles, vacuum cleaners, dishwashers, microwaves, personal computers, and communication via the Internet all save time. Today, smartphones allow people to fire off pictures or videos of what they are eating, doing, or seeing to friends who may be half a world away almost instantly. In a matter of seconds, a personal computer can perform calculations that would take months if done by hand.

Counterpoint. *Nonetheless, most of us complain about not having enough time.* Our schedules overflow with appointments, commitments, and plans. A recent survey of working parents revealed that a great many of them feel rushed, fatigued, and short on quality time with their family and friends (Pew Research Center, 2015). Part of the problem is that in our modern society, work follows people home or wherever they go, thanks to cell phones and email. Although work productivity has doubled since 1948, Mark Taylor (2014) points out that leisure time has declined steadily. Consistent with this observation, a recent *Time* magazine article reported that American workers are taking fewer and shorter vacations, leaving hard-earned paid vacation days on the table (Dickey, 2015). To deal with this time crunch, people have reduced their average sleep time from 8 hours a generation ago to just 6.5 hours a night (Crary, 2013). Sleep experts assert that American society suffers from an epidemic of sleep deprivation. Unfortunately, research indicates that chronic sleep loss can have significant negative effects on individuals' daytime functioning, as well as their mental and physical health (Banks & Dinges, 2011).

Point. *The range of life choices available to people in modern societies has increased exponentially in recent decades.* For example, Barry Schwartz (2004) describes how a simple visit to a local supermarket can require a consumer to choose from 285 varieties of cookies, 61 suntan lotions, 150 lipsticks, and 175 salad dressings. Although increased choice is most tangible in the realm of consumer goods and services, Schwartz argues that it also extends into more significant domains of life. Today, people tend to have unprecedented opportunities to make choices about how they will be educated (vastly more flexible college curricula are available, not to mention online delivery systems), how and where they will work (telecommuting presents employees with all sorts of new choices about how to accomplish their work), how their intimate relationships will unfold (people have increased freedom to delay

Barry Schwartz argues that people in modern societies suffer from choice overload. He maintains that the endless choices people are presented with lead them to waste countless hours weighing trivial decisions and ruminating about whether their decisions were optimal.

marriage, cohabit, not have children, and so forth), and even how they will look (advances in plastic surgery have made personal appearance a matter of choice).

Counterpoint. *Although increased choice sounds attractive, recent research suggests that an overabundance of choices has unexpected costs.* Studies suggest that when people have too many choices, they experience "choice overload" and struggle with decisions (White & Hoffrage, 2009). Having lots of choices does not *always* lead to choice overload, but it is a common phenomenon, especially when the choice set is complex, the decision task is difficult, and there is more uncertainty about one's preferences (Chernev, Böckenholt, & Goodman, 2015). Schwartz asserts that when choice overload occurs, it increases the potential for rumination, postdecision regret, and anticipated regret. Ultimately, he argues, the malaise associated with choice overload undermines individuals' happiness and contributes to depression. Interestingly, research data suggest that the incidence of depression has increased in recent decades (Twenge, 2014). Average anxiety levels have also gone up substantially (Twenge, 2011). It is hard to say whether choice overload is one of the chief culprits underlying these trends, but it is clear that increased freedom of choice has not resulted in enhanced tranquility or improved mental health.

Point. *Thanks in large part to technological advances, we live in an era of extraordinary affluence.* Undeniably, there are pockets of genuine poverty, but social critics argue convincingly that in North America and Europe the middle and upper classes are larger and wealthier than ever before (Easterbrook, 2003; Whybrow, 2005). Most of us take for granted things that were once considered luxuries, such as color television and air-conditioning. People spend vast amounts of money on expensive automobiles, computers, cell phones, and flat-screen TVs. Our homes bulge from "possession overload" even though the average size of new homes in the United States has doubled since the 1970s (de Graaf, Wann, & Naylor, 2014). The amount of money spent on luxury goods continues to increase at a rapid pace. Symptomatic of this trend, research suggests that many people in modern society are troubled by a *compulsive buying syndrome*, characterized by uncontrollable, impulsive, excessive shopping for things they don't need and often can't afford (Achtziger et al., 2015).

Counterpoint. *In spite of this economic abundance, research suggests that most people do not feel very good about their financial well-being.* For example, one recent survey found that almost three-quarters of Americans feel stressed about finances at least some of the time (APA, 2015). Another survey conducted by the Federal Reserve found that 47% of respondents could not cover an emergency expense of $400 without borrowing money. A huge part of the problem is that recent decades have seen a dramatic increase in income inequality (Piketty, 2014; Stiglitz, 2012). Moreover, the tone of public discourse about inequality has taken a cruel turn, as those with great wealth are often idolized, whereas those in poverty are frequently demonized and blamed for their fate (Wise, 2015). Ironically, however, those who embrace materialism are not necessarily all that satisfied with their lives. A recent analysis of 151 studies revealed that people who score high in materialism tend to report somewhat lower levels of subjective well-being than others (Dittmar et al., 2014). Why might materialism undermine well-being? One line of thinking is that advertising helps foster an insatiable thirst for consumption that is difficult to satisfy, resulting in frustration. Another proposed explanation is that the pursuit of material success can crowd out other experiences (leisure activities, time with family, exercise, and so forth) that satisfy important psychological needs and contribute to well-being. Unfortunately, research suggests that materialism has been on the rise in recent decades (Twenge & Kasser, 2013).

All these apparent contradictions reflect the same theme: *The technological advances of the past century, impressive though they may be, have not led to perceptible improvement in our collective health and happiness.* Indeed, many social critics argue that the quality of our lives and our sense of personal fulfillment have declined rather than increased. This is the paradox of progress.

What is the cause of this paradox? Many explanations have been offered. Robert Kegan (1994) maintains that the mental demands of modern life have become so complex, confusing, and contradictory that most of us are "in over our heads." Micki McGee (2005) suggests that modern changes in gender roles, diminished job stability, and other social trends have fostered an obsession with self-improvement that ultimately undermines many individuals' sense of security and satisfaction with their identity. Edward Hallowell (2006) argues that people in modern societies tend to be "crazy busy" and so overwhelmed by information overload that many feel like they suffer from attention deficit disorder. Sherry Turkle (2011) asserts that in our modern, digital, socially networked world, we spend more and more time with technology and less and less time with one another. Although people pile up huge numbers of "friends" on Facebook, Americans report that they have fewer friends than ever before. The resulting sense of loneliness and isolation just deepen people's dependence on superficial communication in the online world, leaving an increasing number of people suffering from an intimacy deficit. John De Graaf, David Wann, and Thomas Naylor (2014) argue that people in modern consumer societies suffer from "affluenza," a compulsive need to accumulate more stuff, better stuff, and newer stuff. They assert that this unbridled consumerism fuels a pernicious cycle of overconsumption, snowballing debt, escalating stress and anxiety, and fractured social relations, which undermine individuals' physical health, as well as their emotional well-being.

Whatever the explanation, many theorists, working from varied perspectives, agree that *the basic challenge of modern life has become the search for meaning, a sense of direction, and a personal philosophy* (Dolby, 2005; Emmons, 2003; Herbert & Brandsma, 2015). This search involves struggling with such problems as forming a solid sense of identity, arriving at a coherent set of values, and developing a clear vision of a future that realistically promises fulfillment. Centuries ago, problems of this kind were probably much simpler. As we'll see in the next section, today it appears that many of us are foundering in a sea of confusion.

1.2 The Search for Direction

Learning Objectives

- Provide some examples of people's search for direction.
- Describe some common problems with self-help books and what to look for in quality self-help books.
- Summarize the philosophy underlying this textbook.

We live in a time of unparalleled social and technological mutation. According to a number of social critics, the kaleidoscope of change that we see around us creates feelings of anxiety and uncertainty, which we try to alleviate by searching for a sense of direction. This search, which sometimes goes awry, manifests itself in many ways.

For example, we could discuss how hundreds of thousands of Americans have invested large sums of money to enroll in "self-realization" programs such as Scientology,

For the most part, the principal goal of most self-realization programs is to make money for their creators, as this protester suggests.

Silva Mind Control, John Gray's Mars and Venus relationship seminars, and Tony Robbins's Life Mastery seminars. These programs typically promise to provide profound enlightenment and quickly turn one's life around. Many participants claim that the programs have revolutionized their lives. However, most experts characterize such programs as intellectually bankrupt, and book and magazine exposés reveal them as simply lucrative money-making schemes (Behar, 1991; Pressman, 1993). In a particularly scathing analysis of these programs, Steve Salerno (2005) outlines the enormous financial benefits reaped by their inventors, such as Tony Robbins ($80 million in annual income), Dr. Phil ($20 million in annual income), and John Gray ($50,000 per speech). In his critique, Salerno also attacks the hypocrisy and inflated credentials of many leading self-help gurus. For example, he asserts that John Gray's doctorate came from a nonaccredited correspondence college; that Dr. Phil has a history of alleged marital infidelity and that some of his video segments are contrived to a degree that would make Jerry Springer proud; and that Dr. Laura is highly critical of premarital and extramarital sex, even though she has engaged in both. More than anything else, the enormous success of these self-help gurus and self-realization programs demonstrates just how desperate some people are for a sense of direction and purpose in their lives.

For the most part, self-realization programs are harmless scams that appear to give some participants an illusory sense of purpose or a temporary boost in self-confidence. But in some cases they lead people down ill-advised pathways that prove harmful. The ultimate example of the potential for harm unfolded in October 2009 in Sedona, Arizona, where three people died and eighteen others were hospitalized after participating in a "spiritual warrior" retreat that required them to spend hours in a makeshift sweat lodge (Harris & Wagner, 2009). The retreat was run by James Ray, a popular self-help guru who has written inspirational books and appeared on popular TV talk shows. The fifty to sixty people who participated in his ill-fated retreat paid more than $9000 apiece for the privilege. After spending 36 hours fasting in the desert on a "vision quest," they were led into a tarp-covered sweat lodge for an endurance challenge that was supposed to show them that they could gain confidence by conquering physical discomfort. Unfortunately, the sweat lodge turned out to be poorly ventilated and overheated, so that within an hour people began vomiting, gasping for air, and collapsing. Undaunted, Ray urged his followers to persevere. No one was physically forced to stay, but Ray was an intimidating presence who strongly exhorted everyone to remain. Tragically, he pushed their bodies too far; by the end of the ceremony many of the participants were seriously ill. Yet, according to one account, "At the conclusion, seemingly unaware of the bodies of the unconscious lying around him, Ray emerged triumphantly, witnesses said, pumping his fist because he had passed his own endurance test" (Whelan, 2009).

Some of the aftermath of this event has also proven revealing. Consistent with the assertion that it really is all about the money, Ray provided a *partial* refund to the family of Kirby Brown, a participant who *died* in the sweat lodge (Martinez, 2009). And the reactions of some of Ray's followers after the sweat lodge tragedy were illuminating. You might think that, after inadvertently but recklessly leading people "over a cliff," Ray might be discredited in the eyes of his followers. But think again. Reporters working on this horrific story had no trouble finding Ray advocates who continued to enthusiastically champion his vision for self-improvement (Kraft, 2009). This unwavering faith in Ray's teachings provides a remarkable testimonial to the persuasive power of the charismatic leaders who promote self-realization programs. Nonetheless, in 2011 an Arizona jury deliberated for less than 12 hours before convicting Ray on three counts of negligent homicide (Riccardi, 2011).

If you would like a more mundane, everyday example of people's search for direction, you need look no farther than your satellite radio, where you will find the long-running, highly popular show of "Dr. Laura" Schlessinger, who doles out advice to tens of thousands of listeners. An astonishing tens of thousands of people call each day to seek her unique brand of blunt, outspoken, judgmental advice. Dr. Laura, who is not a psychologist or psychiatrist (her doctorate is in physiology), analyzes callers' problems in more of a moral

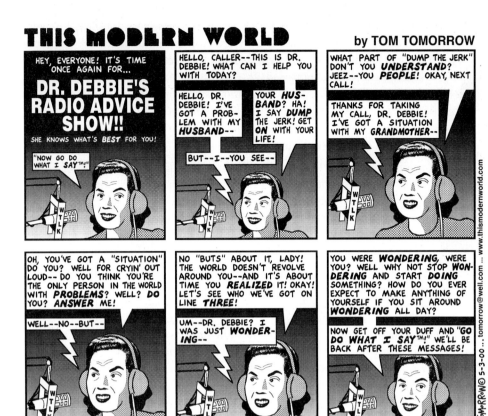

THIS MODERN WORLD   by TOM TOMORROW

than psychological framework. Unlike most therapists, she is confrontational, manifests little empathy for her callers, and preaches to her audience about how they ought to lead their lives (Arkowitz & Lilienfeld, 2010). In an editorial in *Psychology Today*, Robert Epstein (2001) concludes that "no legitimate mental health professional would ever give the kind of hateful, divisive advice that Schlessinger doles out daily" (p. 5). Yet, the remarkable popularity of her highly prescriptive advice demonstrates once again that many people are eager for guidance and direction.

Although there are countless examples of people's search for a sense of direction that we could discuss, we will reserve our in-depth analysis for a manifestation of this search that is even more germane to our focus on everyday adjustment: the spectacular success of bestselling "self-help" books.

Self-Help Books

Americans spend hundreds of millions of dollars annually on "self-help books" that offer do-it-yourself treatments for common personal problems. This fascination with self-improvement is nothing new. For decades American readers have displayed a voracious appetite for self-help books such as *I'm OK—You're OK* (Harris, 1967), *Ageless Body, Timeless Mind* (Chopra, 1993), *Don't Sweat the Small Stuff . . . and It's All Small Stuff* (Carlson, 1997), *The Secret* (Byrne, 2006), *Become a Better You: Seven Keys to Improving Your Life Every Day* (Osteen, 2009), *The Power of Habit: Why We Do What We Do in Life and Business* (Duhigg, 2012), *You're Stronger Than You Think* (Parrott, 2012), and *Rising Strong* (Brown, 2015).

With their simple recipes for achieving happiness, the authors of these books have generally not been timid about promising to change the quality of the reader's life. Unfortunately, merely reading a book is not likely to turn your life around. If only it were that easy! If only someone could hand you a book that would solve all your problems! If the consumption of these literary narcotics were even remotely as helpful as their

Self-help books have a long history, but their popularity began to spike back in the 1970s. Although they are especially big sellers in the United States, they are not a uniquely American phenomenon. Self-help books are widely read in many Western cultures.

publishers claim, we would be a nation of serene, happy, well-adjusted people. It is clear, however, that serenity is not the dominant national mood. Quite the contrary, as already noted, in recent decades the prevalence of anxiety and depression appear to have increased. The multitude of self-help books that crowd bookstore shelves represent just one more symptom of our collective distress and our search for the elusive secret of happiness.

The Value of Self-Help Books

It is somewhat unfair to lump all self-help books together for a critique because they vary widely in quality. Surveys exploring psychotherapists' opinions of self-help books suggest that there are some excellent books that offer authentic insights and sound advice (Bergsma, 2008). Many therapists encourage their patients to read carefully selected self-help books. Thus, it would be foolish to dismiss all these books as shallow drivel. In fact, some of the better self-help books are highlighted in the Recommended Reading boxes that appear throughout this text. Unfortunately, however, the gems are easily lost in the mountains of rubbish. A great many self-help books offer little of real value to the reader. Generally, they suffer from four fundamental shortcomings.

First, they are dominated by "psychobabble." The term *psychobabble*, coined by R. D. Rosen (1977), seems appropriate to describe the "hip" but hopelessly vague language used in many of these books. Statements such as "It's beautiful if you're unhappy," "You've got to get in touch with yourself," "You have to be up front," "You gotta be you 'cause you're you," and "You need a real high-energy experience" are typical examples of this language. At best, such terminology is ill-defined; at worst, it is meaningless. Clarity is sacrificed in favor of a jargon that prevents, rather than enhances, effective communication.

A second problem is that self-help books tend to place more emphasis on sales than on scientific soundness. The vast majority of these books are not based on solid, scientific research (Madsen, 2015). Even when books are based on well-researched therapeutic programs, interventions that are effective with professional supervision may not be effective when self-administered (Rosen et al., 2015). Moreover, even when responsible authors provide scientifically valid advice, sales-hungry publishers routinely slap outrageous, irresponsible promises on the books' covers, often to the dismay of the authors.

The third shortcoming is that self-help books don't usually provide explicit directions about how to change your behavior. These books tend to be smoothly written and "touchingly human" in tone. They often strike responsive chords in the reader by aptly describing a common problem that many of us experience. The reader says, "Yes, that's me!" Unfortunately, when the book focuses on how to deal with the problem, it usually provides only a vague distillation of simple common sense, which could be covered in 2 rather than 200 pages. These books often fall back on inspirational cheerleading in the absence of sound, explicit advice.

Fourth, many of these books encourage a remarkably self-centered, narcissistic approach to life (Justman, 2005). **Narcissism is a personality trait marked by an inflated sense of importance, a need for attention and admiration, a sense of entitlement, and a tendency to exploit others.** Although there are plenty of exceptions, the basic message in many self-help books is "Do whatever you feel like doing, and don't worry about the consequences for other people." According to McGee (2005), this mentality began to creep into books in the 1970s, as "bald proposals that one ought to 'look out for #1' or 'win through intimidation' marked a new ruthlessness in the self-help landscape" (p. 50). This "me first" philosophy emphasizes self-admiration, an entitlement to special treatment, and an exploitive approach to interpersonal relationships. Interestingly, research suggests that narcissism levels have increased among recent generations of college students (Twenge, Gentile, & Campbell, 2015; see Chapter 2). It is hard to say how much popular self-help books have fueled this rise, but they probably have contributed.

What to Look For in Self-Help Books

Because self-help books vary so widely in quality, it seems a good idea to provide you with some guidelines about what to look for in seeking genuinely helpful books. The following thoughts give you some criteria for judging books of this type (Norcross et al., 2013).

1. This may sound backward, but look for books that do not promise too much in the way of immediate change. The truly useful books tend to be appropriately cautious in their promises and realistic about the challenge of altering your behavior. As Arkowitz and Lilienfeld (2006) put it, "Be wary of books that make promises that they obviously cannot keep, such as curing a phobia in five minutes or fixing a failing marriage in a week" (p. 79).

2. Try to check out the credentials of the author or authors. Book jackets will often exaggerate the expertise of authors, but these days a quick Internet search can often yield more objective biographical information and perhaps some perceptive reviews of the book.

3. Try to select books that mention, at least briefly, the theoretical or research basis for the program they advocate. It is understandable that you may not be interested in a detailed summary of research that supports a particular piece of advice. However, you should be interested in whether the advice is based on published research, widely accepted theory, anecdotal evidence, clinical interactions with patients, or pure speculation by the author. Books that are based on more than personal anecdotes and speculation should have a list of references in the back (or at the end of each chapter).

4. Look for books that provide detailed, explicit directions about how to alter your behavior. Generally, these directions represent the crucial core of the book. If they are inadequate in detail, you have been shortchanged.

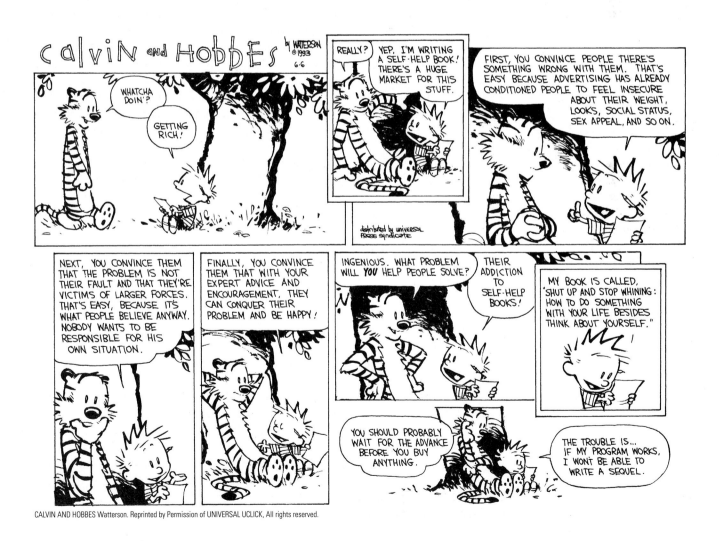

CALVIN AND HOBBES Watterson. Reprinted by Permission of UNIVERSAL UCLICK, All rights reserved.

5. More often than not, books that focus on a particular kind of problem, such as overeating, loneliness, or marital difficulties, deliver more than those that promise to cure all of life's problems with a few simple ideas. Books that cover everything and offer simple recipes for solving an endless list of problems tend to be the bestsellers (Bergsma, 2008), but they usually are superficial and disappointing. Books that devote a great deal of thought to a particular type of problem tend to be written by authors with genuine expertise on that topic. Such books are more likely to pay off for you.

The Approach of This Textbook

Clearly, living in our complex, modern society is a formidable challenge. This book is about that challenge. It is about you. It is about life. Specifically, it summarizes the scientific research on human behavior that appears relevant to the challenge of living effectively in contemporary society.

This text deals with the same kinds of problems addressed by self-help books, self-realization programs, and popular media "therapists." However, it makes no boldly seductive promises about turning your life around or helping you achieve tranquillity. Such promises simply aren't realistic. Psychologists have long recognized that changing a person's behavior is a difficult challenge, fraught with frustration and failure (Seligman, 1994).

That said, we would not be writing this text if we did not believe it could be beneficial to our readers. But it is important that you have realistic expectations. Reading this book will not be a revelatory experience. All this book can do is give you some useful information and point you in some potentially beneficial directions. The rest is up to you. In view of our criticisms of self-realization programs and self-help books, it seems essential that we explicitly lay out the philosophy that underlies the writing of this text. The following statements summarize the assumptions and goals of this book:

1. *This text is based on the premise that accurate knowledge about the principles of psychology can be of value to you in everyday life.* It has been said that knowledge is power. Greater awareness of why people behave as they do should help you in interacting with others as well as in trying to understand yourself.

2. *This text attempts to foster a critical attitude about psychological issues and to enhance your critical thinking skills.* Information is important, but people also need to develop effective strategies for evaluating information. Critical thinking involves subjecting ideas to systematic, skeptical scrutiny. Critical thinkers ask tough questions, such as: What exactly is being asserted? What assumptions underlie this assertion? What evidence or reasoning supports this assertion? Is there contradictory evidence? Are there alternative explanations? We have already attempted to illustrate the importance of a critical attitude in our evaluation of self-help books, and we'll continue to model critical thinking strategies throughout the text.

3. *This text should open doors.* The coverage in this book is broad; we tackle many topics. Therefore, in some places it may lack the depth or detail that you would like. However, you should think of it as a resource that can introduce you to other books or techniques or therapies, which you can then pursue on your own.

Learn More Online

Foundation for Critical Thinking

How can students best develop skills that go beyond merely acquiring information to actively weighing and judging information? The many resources of the Foundation for Critical Thinking at Sonoma State University are directed primarily toward teachers at every level to help them develop their students' critical thinking abilities.

Learning Objectives

- Describe the two key facets of psychology.
- Explain the concept of adjustment.

1.3 The Psychology of Adjustment

Now that we have spelled out our approach in writing this text, it is time to turn to the task of introducing you to some basic concepts. In this section, we'll discuss the nature of psychology and the concept of adjustment.

What Is Psychology?

Psychology **is the science that studies behavior and the physiological and mental processes that underlie it, and it is the profession that applies the accumulated knowledge of this science to practical problems.** Psychology leads a complex dual existence as both a *science* and a *profession.* Let's examine the science first. Psychology is an area of scientific study, much like biology or physics. Whereas biology focuses on life processes and physics focuses on matter and energy, psychology focuses on *behavior* and *related mental and physiological processes.*

Behavior **is any overt (observable) response or activity by an organism.** Psychology does *not* confine itself to the study of human behavior. Many psychologists believe that the principles of behavior are much the same for all animals, including humans. As a result, these psychologists often prefer to study animals—mainly because they can exert more control over the factors influencing the animals' behavior.

Psychology is also interested in the mental processes—the thoughts, feelings, and wishes—that accompany behavior. Mental processes are more difficult to study than behavior because they are private and not directly observable. However, they exert critical influence over human behavior, so psychologists have strived to improve their ability to "look inside the mind." Finally, psychology includes the study of the physiological processes that underlie behavior. Thus, some psychologists try to figure out how bodily processes such as neural impulses, hormonal secretions, and genetic coding regulate behavior.

The other facet of psychology is its applied side, represented by the many psychologists who provide a variety of professional services to the public. Although the profession of psychology is quite prominent today, this aspect of psychology was actually slow to develop. Until the 1950s psychologists were found almost exclusively in the halls of academia, teaching and doing research. However, the demands of World War II in the 1940s stimulated rapid growth in psychology's first professional specialty: clinical psychology. *Clinical psychology* **is the branch of psychology concerned with the diagnosis and treatment of psychological problems and disorders.** The emergence of clinical psychology gave the field of psychology a much more practical slant, which you will see reflected in this text.

What Is Adjustment?

We have used the term *adjustment* several times without clarifying its exact meaning. The concept of adjustment was originally borrowed from biology. It was modeled after the biological term *adaptation,* which refers to efforts by a species to adjust to changes in its environment. Just as a field mouse has to adapt to an unusually brutal winter, a person has to adjust to changes in circumstances such as a new job, a financial setback, or the loss of a loved one. Thus, *adjustment* **refers to the psychological processes through which people manage or cope with the demands and challenges of everyday life.**

The demands of daily life are diverse, so in studying the process of adjustment we will encounter a broad variety of topics. In our early chapters we discuss general issues, such as how personality affects people's patterns of adjustment and how individuals cope with stress. From there we move on to chapters that examine adjustment in an interpersonal context. We discuss topics such as prejudice, persuasion, friendship, love, gender roles, career development, and sexuality. Finally, toward the end of the book we discuss psychological disorders and their treatment, and delve into the newly developing domain of positive psychology. As you can see, the study of adjustment enters into nearly every corner of people's lives. Before we begin considering these topics in earnest, however, we need to take a closer look at psychology's approach to investigating behavior: the scientific method.

Learning Objectives

- Explain the nature of empiricism and the advantages of the scientific approach to behavior.
- Describe the experimental method, distinguishing between independent and dependent variables and between experimental and control groups.
- Distinguish between positive and negative correlation, and explain what the size of a correlation coefficient means.
- Describe three correlational research methods.
- Compare the advantages and disadvantages of experimental versus correlational research.

1.4 The Scientific Approach to Behavior

We all expend a great deal of effort in trying to understand our own behavior as well as the behavior of others. We wonder about any number of behavioral questions: Why am I so anxious when I interact with new people? Why is Sam always trying to be the center of attention at the office? Are extraverts happier than introverts? Given that psychologists' principal goal is to explain behavior, how are their efforts different from everyone else's? The key difference is that psychology is a *science*, committed to *empiricism*. **Empiricism is the premise that knowledge should be acquired through observation.** When we say that scientific psychology is empirical, we mean that its conclusions are based on systematic observation rather than on reasoning, speculation, traditional beliefs, or common sense. Scientists are not content with having ideas that sound plausible; they must conduct research to *test* their hypotheses. There are two main types of research methods in psychology: *experimental methods* and *correlational methods*. We discuss them separately because there is an important distinction between them.

Experimental Research: Looking for Causes

Does misery love company? This question intrigued social psychologist Stanley Schachter. When people feel anxious, do they want to be left alone, or do they prefer to have others around? Schachter hypothesized that increases in anxiety would cause increases in the desire to be with others, which psychologists call the *need for affiliation*. To test this hypothesis, Schachter (1959) designed a clever experiment. **The *experiment* is a research method in which the investigator manipulates one (independent) variable under carefully controlled conditions and observes whether any changes occur in a second (dependent) variable as a result.** Psychologists depend on this method more than any other.

Independent and Dependent Variables

An experiment is designed to find out whether changes in one variable (let's call it x) cause changes in another variable (let's call it y). To put it more concisely, we want to know how x affects y. In this formulation, we refer to x as the independent variable, and we call y the dependent variable. **An *independent variable* is a condition or event that an experimenter varies in order to see its impact on another variable.** The independent variable is the variable that the experimenter controls or manipulates. It is hypothesized to have some effect on the dependent variable. The experiment is conducted to verify this effect. **The *dependent variable* is the variable that is thought to be affected by the manipulations of the independent variable.** In psychology studies, the dependent variable is usually a measurement of some aspect of the subjects' behavior.

In Schachter's experiment, *the independent variable was the participants' anxiety level*, which he manipulated in the following way. Subjects assembled in his laboratory were told by a Dr. Zilstein that they would be participating in a study on the physiological effects of electric shock and that they would receive a series of shocks. Half of the participants were warned that the shocks would be very painful. They made up the *high-anxiety* group. The other half of the participants, assigned to the *low-anxiety* group, were told that the shocks would be mild and painless. These procedures were simply intended to evoke different levels of anxiety. In reality, no one was actually shocked at any time. Instead, the experimenter indicated that there would be a delay while he prepared the shock apparatus for use. The participants were asked whether they would prefer to wait alone or in the company of others. *This measure of the subjects' desire to affiliate with others was the dependent variable.*

Experimental and Control Groups

To conduct an experiment, an investigator typically assembles two groups of participants who are treated differently in regard to the independent variable. We call these groups the experimental and control groups. **The *experimental group* consists of the subjects who receive some special treatment in regard to the independent variable. The *control group* consists of similar subjects who do not receive the special treatment given to the experimental group.**

Let's return to the Schachter study to illustrate. In this experiment, the participants in the high-anxiety condition were the experimental group. They received a special treatment designed to create an unusually high level of anxiety. The participants in the low-anxiety condition were the control group.

It is crucial that the experimental and control groups be similar except for the different treatment they receive in regard to the independent variable. This stipulation brings us to the logic that underlies the experimental method. If the two groups are alike in all respects *except for the variation created by the manipulation of the independent variable*, then any differences between the two groups on the dependent variable *must be due to this manipulation of the independent variable*. In this way researchers isolate the effect of the independent variable on the dependent variable. In his experiment, Schachter isolated the impact of anxiety on need for affiliation. What did he find? As predicted, he found that increased anxiety led to increased affiliation. The percentage of people who wanted to wait with others was nearly twice as high in the high-anxiety group as in the low-anxiety group.

The logic of the experimental method rests heavily on the assumption that the experimental and control groups are alike in all important matters except for their different treatment with regard to the independent variable. Any other differences between the two groups cloud the situation and make it difficult to draw solid conclusions about the relationship between the independent variable and the dependent variable. To summarize our discussion of the experimental method, **Figure 1.1** provides an overview of the various elements in an experiment, using Schachter's study as an example.

Advantages and Disadvantages

The experiment is a powerful research method. Its principal advantage is that it allows scientists to draw conclusions about cause-and-effect relationships between variables. Researchers can draw these conclusions about causation because the precise control available in the experiment permits them to isolate the relationship between the independent variable and the dependent variable. No other research method can duplicate this advantage.

For all its power, however, the experimental method has its limitations. One disadvantage is that researchers are often interested in the effects of variables that cannot be manipulated (as independent variables) because of ethical concerns or practical realities. For example, you might want to know whether being brought up in an urban area as opposed to a rural area affects people's values. A true experiment would require you to assign similar families to live in urban and rural areas, which obviously is impossible to do. To explore this question, you would have to use correlational research methods, which we turn to next.

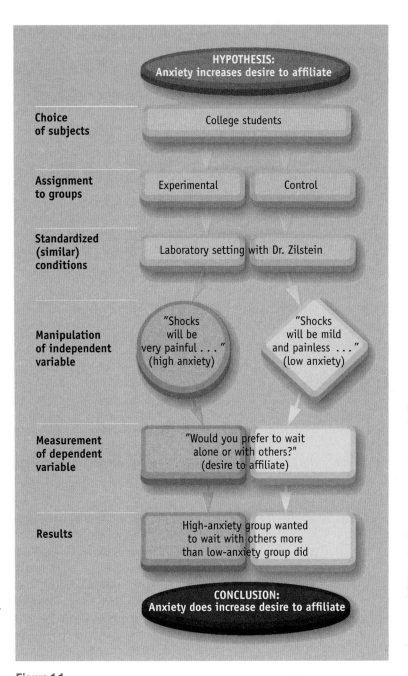

Figure 1.1

The basic elements of an experiment. This diagram provides an overview of the key features of the experimental method, as illustrated by Schachter's study of anxiety and affiliation. The logic of the experiment rests on treating the experimental and control groups alike except for the manipulation of the independent variable.

Correlational Research: Looking for Links

As we just noted, in some cases psychologists cannot exert experimental control over the variables they want to study. In such situations, all a researcher can do is make systematic observations to see whether a link or association exists between the variables of interest. Such an association is called a correlation. **A *correlation* exists when two variables are related to each other.** The definitive aspect of correlational studies is that the researchers cannot control the variables under study.

Measuring Correlation

The results of correlational research are often summarized with a statistic called the *correlation coefficient*. We'll be referring to this widely used statistic frequently as we discuss studies throughout the remainder of this text. **A *correlation coefficient* is a numerical index of the degree of relationship that exists between two variables.** A correlation coefficient indicates (1) how strongly related two variables are and (2) the direction (positive or negative) of the relationship.

Two kinds of relationships can be described by a correlation. A *positive* correlation indicates that two variables covary in the same direction. This means that high scores on variable *x* are associated with high scores on variable *y* and that low scores on variable *x* are associated with low scores on variable *y*. For example, there is a positive correlation between high school grade point average (GPA) and subsequent college GPA. That is, people who do well in high school tend to do well in college, and those who perform poorly in high school tend to perform poorly in college (see **Figure 1.2**).

In contrast, a *negative* correlation indicates that two variables covary in the opposite direction. This means that people who score high on variable *x* tend to score low on variable *y*, whereas those who score low on *x* tend to score high on *y*. For example, in most college courses, there is a negative correlation between how often a student is absent and how well the student performs on exams. Students who have a high number of absences tend to earn low exam scores, whereas students who have a low number of absences tend to get higher exam scores (see **Figure 1.2**).

While the positive or negative sign indicates whether an association is direct or inverse, the *size* of the coefficient indicates the *strength* of the association between two variables. A correlation coefficient can vary between 0 and +1.00 (if positive) or between 0 and −1.00 (if negative). A coefficient near 0 tells us there is no relationship between the variables. The closer the correlation to either −1.00 or +1.00, the stronger the relationship. Thus, a correlation of +.90 represents a stronger tendency for variables to be associated than a correlation of +.40 does (see **Figure 1.3**). Likewise, a correlation of −.75 represents a stronger relationship than a correlation of −.45. Keep in mind that the *strength* of a correlation depends only on the size of the coefficient. The positive or negative sign simply shows whether the correlation is direct or inverse. Therefore, a correlation of −.60 reflects a stronger relationship than a correlation of +.30.

Correlational research methods comprise a number of approaches, including naturalistic observation, case studies, and surveys. Let's examine each of these to see how researchers use them to detect associations between variables.

Figure 1.2

Positive and negative correlations. Variables are positively correlated if they tend to increase and decrease together and are negatively correlated if one variable tends to increase when the other decreases. Hence, the terms *positive correlation* and *negative correlation* refer to the *direction* of the relationship between two variables.

Naturalistic Observation

In *naturalistic observation* a researcher engages in careful observation of behavior without intervening directly with the subjects. This type of research is called *naturalistic* because behavior is allowed to unfold naturally (without interference) in its natural environment—that is, the setting in which it would normally occur. Of

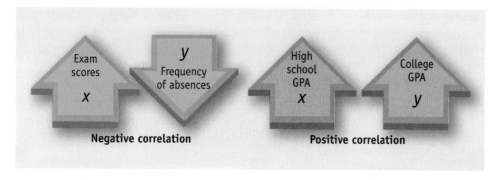

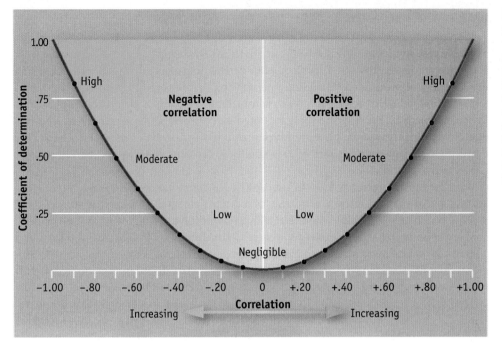

Figure 1.3

Interpreting correlation coefficients.
The magnitude of a correlation coefficient indicates the strength of the relationship between two variables. The closer a correlation is to either +1.00 or −1.00, the stronger the relationship between the variables. The square of a correlation, which is called the *coefficient of determination,* is an index of a correlation's strength and predictive power. This graph shows how the coefficient of determination and predictive power goes up as the magnitude of a correlation increases.

course, researchers have to make careful plans to ensure systematic, consistent observations (Heyman et al., 2014). The major strength of naturalistic observation is that it allows researchers to study behavior under conditions that are less artificial than in experiments, which brings us to our Spotlight on Research for this chapter.

Spotlight on **RESEARCH**

Does Plate Size Influence Food Consumption?

Source: Wansink, B., & van Ittersum, K. (2013). Portion size me: Plate-size induced consumption norms and win-win solutions for reducing food intake and waste. *Journal of Experimental Psychology: Applied, 19*(4), 320–332.

As we will discuss in Chapter 5, obesity is a major health problem that has been escalating in recent decades (Popkin, 2012). Although many factors contribute to the development of obesity, overeating obviously is a central consideration. Some theorists believe that overeating has increased because the size of grocery store packages, restaurant portions, and dinnerware has grown steadily (Wansink, 2012). Consistent with this notion, laboratory experiments have shown that people eat more when they are served with larger plates or bowls. Study two in a series of four studies reported by Wansink and van Ittersum was conducted to determine whether similar findings would be observed in real-world restaurants.

Method
The study was conducted at four Chinese restaurants with All-You-Can-Eat buffets. The eating behavior of 43 unsuspecting diners was monitored by carefully trained observers. On average, the diners made 2.7 trips to the buffet. The patrons could choose between two plate sizes; 18 chose the smaller plate and 25 chose the larger one. The observers unobtrusively estimated the diners' serving size, consumption, and waste.

Results
The diners who chose the larger plate served themselves 52% more food than those who used the smaller plate. Those using the larger plates ended up consuming 41% more food and wasted 135% more than those using the smaller plates. Thus, plate size had a significant impact on consumption and waste.

Discussion
The results of this field study were consistent with previous experiments, suggesting that the findings of the lab studies generalize to the real world. The data also provide further support for the hypothesis that larger dinnerware leads to increased eating, which may contribute to rising obesity.

Critical Thinking Questions
1. Why do you think that the size of plates and other dinnerware influences the amount that people eat?
2. The study found a correlation between plate size and amount consumed. Can you think of any factors besides plate size that might be responsible for this association?

Case Studies

A *case study* **is an in-depth investigation of an individual subject.** Psychologists typically assemble case studies in clinical settings where an effort is being made to diagnose and treat some psychological problem. To achieve an understanding of an individual, a clinician may use a variety of procedures, including interviewing the person, interviewing others who know the individual, direct observation, examination of records, and psychological testing. When clinicians assemble a case study for diagnostic purposes, they generally are *not* conducting empirical research. Case study *research* typically involves investigators analyzing a collection or consecutive series of case studies to look for patterns that permit general conclusions.

For example, a research team in the United Kingdom conducted a study of whether anxiety and depressive disorders are risk factors for dementia. *Dementia* is an abnormal condition marked by multiple cognitive deficits that revolve around memory impairment. Dementia can be caused by a variety of diseases, but Alzheimer's disease accounts for about 70% of the cases. Previous research had suggested that depression was a risk factor for dementia, but little was known about the possible role of anxiety disorders. Burton et al. (2013) took advantage of an existing, large database of medical case histories compiled from thirteen medical practices since 1998. They identified 400 new cases of dementia that were diagnosed during the 8-year period covered by the study. For each of these cases they identified three to four patients in the database who were similar in age and gender, but did not suffer from dementia. These 1353 cases served as controls for comparison purposes. All of the case records were then examined carefully to screen for preexisting anxiety disorders or depressive disorders. As expected, the prevalence of preexisting depressive disorders was elevated in the dementia cases. However, the prevalence of preexisting anxiety disorders was also elevated in the dementia cases, suggesting that anxiety disorders are a previously overlooked risk factor for dementia.

Researchers depend on surveys to investigate a wide range of issues. However, resentment of intrusive telemarketing and concerns about privacy have undermined individuals' willingness to participate in survey research. Today, many surveys are conducted online.

Surveys

Survey methods are widely used in psychological research (Krosnick, Lavrakas, & Kim, 2014). *Surveys* **are structured questionnaires or interviews designed to solicit information about specific aspects of participants' behavior, attitudes, and beliefs.** They are sometimes used to measure dependent variables in experiments, but they are mainly used in correlational research. Surveys are commonly used to gather data on people's attitudes and on aspects of behavior that are difficult to observe directly (marital interactions, for instance). As an example, consider a study that explored age trends in the experience of hangovers following episodes of binge drinking. Folk wisdom suggests that hangovers are thought to get worse with advancing age, but there were no data on age trends in hangovers until a recent survey study conducted by a research team in Denmark (Tolstrup, Stephens, & Gronbaek, 2014). Questions on drinking habits and the experience of hangovers were included in a broad survey of health habits. Binge drinking was defined as the consumption of more than five drinks on a single occasion. The incidence of hangovers was assessed with a 9-point scale based on symptoms reported after binge drinking. More than 76,000 participants responded to the survey. The study found clear age trends; the incidence of hangovers after binge drinking declined steadily with increasing age, as you can see in **Figure 1.4**. Contrary to folk wisdom, the incidence of *severe* hangovers also declined as subjects grew older.

Advantages and Disadvantages

Correlational research methods give psychologists a way to explore questions that they could not examine with experimental procedures. Consider, for instance, the study of hangovers after binge drinking. Obviously,

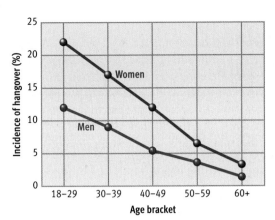

Figure 1.4

The incidence of hangovers in relation to age. The survey data collected by Tolstrup, Stephens, and Gronbaek (2014) show that older adults are less likely to experience a hangover after binge drinking than younger adults, even though older adults are thought to be more vulnerable to hangovers. The researchers speculate that older adults may tend to engage in less intense binge drinking or that they may become more skilled at avoiding hangovers.

investigators cannot conduct experiments in which they assign subjects to engage in serious binge drinking to determine the prevalence of hangovers in relation to age. But the use of correlational methods facilitated the collection of enlightening data on the link between age and the incidence and severity of hangovers. Thus, *correlational research broadens the scope of phenomena that psychologists can study.*

Unfortunately, correlational methods have one major disadvantage. *Correlational research cannot demonstrate conclusively that two variables are causally related.* The crux of the problem is that correlation is no assurance of causation. When we find that variables x and y are correlated, we can safely conclude only that x and y are related. We do not know *how* x and y are related. We do not know whether x causes y, whether y causes x, or whether both are caused by a third variable. For example, survey studies show a positive correlation between relationship satisfaction and sexual satisfaction (Schwartz & Young, 2009). Although it's clear that good sex and a healthy intimate relationship go hand in hand, it's hard to tell what's causing what. We don't know whether healthy relationships promote good sex or whether good sex promotes healthy relationships. Moreover, we can't rule out the possibility that both are caused by a third variable. Perhaps sexual satisfaction and relationship satisfaction are both caused by compatibility in values. The plausible causal relationships in this case are diagrammed for you in **Figure 1.5**, which illustrates the "third-variable problem" in interpreting correlations. This problem occurs often in correlational research. Indeed, it will surface in the next section, where we review the empirical research on the determinants of happiness.

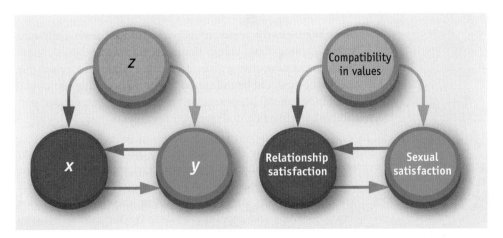

Figure 1.5

Possible causal relations between correlated variables. When two variables are correlated, there are several possible explanations. It could be that x causes y, that y causes x, or that a third variable, z, causes changes in both x and y. As the correlation between relationship satisfaction and sexual satisfaction illustrates, the correlation itself does not provide the answer. This conundrum is sometimes referred to as the "third-variable problem."

Learning Objectives

- Identify the various factors that are surprisingly unrelated to happiness.
- Describe the factors that are somewhat or very important to subjective well-being.
- Summarize conclusions about the determinants of happiness.

1.5 The Roots of Happiness: An Empirical Analysis

Commonsense hypotheses about the roots of happiness abound. For example, you have no doubt heard that money cannot buy happiness. But do you believe it? A television commercial says, "If you've got your health, you've got just about everything." Is health indeed the key? We often hear about the joys of parenthood, the joys of youth, and the joys of the simple, rural life. Are these the factors that promote happiness?

In recent years, social scientists have begun putting these and other hypotheses to empirical test. Quite a number of survey studies have been conducted to explore the determinants of *subjective well-being*—**individuals' personal assessments of their overall happiness or life satisfaction.** The findings of these studies are quite interesting. We review this research because it is central to the topic of adjustment and because it illustrates the value of collecting data and putting ideas to an empirical test. As you will see, many commonsense notions about happiness appear to be inaccurate.

The first of these ideas is the apparently widespread assumption that most people are relatively unhappy. Writers, social scientists, and the general public seem to believe that people around the world are predominantly dissatisfied, yet empirical surveys consistently find that the vast majority of respondents—even those who are poor or disabled—characterize themselves as fairly happy (Pavot & Diener, 2013). When people are asked to rate their happiness, only a small minority place themselves below the neutral point on the various scales used (see **Figure 1.6**). When the average subjective well-being of entire nations is computed, based on almost 1000 surveys, the means cluster toward the positive end of the scale, as shown in **Figure 1.7** (Tov & Diener, 2007). That's not to say that everyone is equally happy. Researchers have found substantial and thought-provoking disparities among people in subjective well-being, which we will analyze momentarily. But the overall picture seems rosier than anticipated. This is an encouraging finding, as subjective well-being tends to be relatively stable over the course of people's lives, and higher levels of happiness are predictive of better social relationships, greater career satisfaction, better physical health, and greater longevity (Lucas & Diener, 2015). Thus, one's subjective well-being can have important consequences.

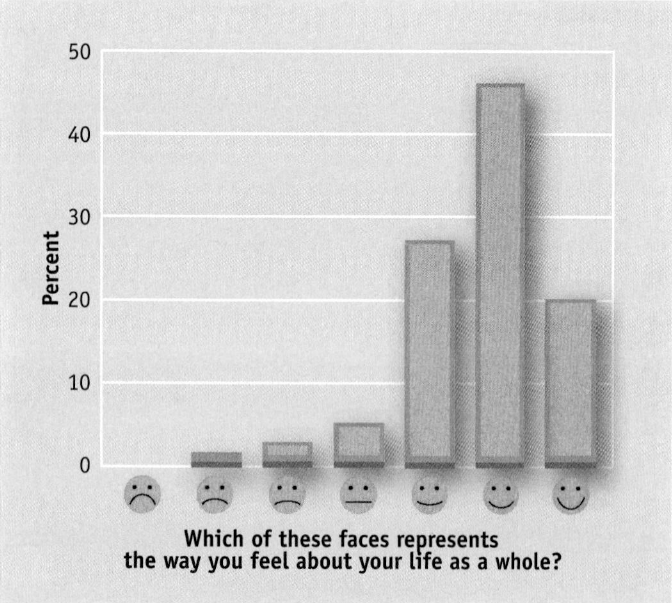

What Isn't Very Important?

Let us begin our discussion of individual differences in happiness by highlighting those things that turn out to be relatively weak predictors of subjective well-being. Quite a number of factors that one might expect to be influential appear to bear little or no relationship to general happiness, including money, age, gender, parenthood, intelligence, and attractiveness.

Money. Most people think that if they had more money, they would be happier. There *is* a positive correlation between income and feelings of happiness, but the association is surprisingly weak (Diener & Seligman, 2004). Within specific nations, the correlation between income and happiness tends to fall somewhere between .12 and .20. Obviously, being poor can contribute to unhappiness. Yet it seems once people ascend above a certain level of income, additional wealth does not foster greater happiness. One study in the United States estimated that once people exceed an income of around $75,000, little relation is seen between wealth and subjective well-being (Kahneman & Deaton, 2010). Why isn't money a

Figure 1.6

Measuring happiness with a nonverbal scale. Researchers have used a variety of methods to estimate the distribution of happiness. For example, in one study in the United States, respondents were asked to examine the seven facial expressions shown and to select the one that "comes closest to expressing how you feel about your life as a whole." As you can see, the vast majority of participants chose happy faces. (Data adapted from Myers, 1992)

better predictor of happiness? One reason is that a disconnect seems to exist between actual income and how people feel about their financial situation. Research suggests that the correlation between actual wealth and people's subjective perceptions of whether they have enough money is surprisingly modest (Johnson & Krueger, 2006).

Another problem with money is that in this era of voracious consumption, rising income contributes to escalating material desires. When these growing material desires outstrip what people can afford, dissatisfaction is likely. Thus, complaints about not having enough money are routine even among people who earn hefty six-figure incomes. Evidence also suggests that living in wealthy neighborhoods fuels increased materialism (Zhang, Howell, & Howell, 2014), providing yet another reason why wealth does not necessarily foster happiness.

Recent studies have provided some other interesting and unexpected insights about money and happiness. First, studies suggest that money spent purchasing *experiences*, such as concerts, travel, and outdoor activities, promotes more happiness than money spent purchasing *material goods*, such as clothes, jewelry, and appliances (Pchelin & Howell, 2014). Second, research indicates that across many cultures of varied wealth, people derive more happiness from money spent to help others than from money spent on themselves (Dunn, Aknin, & Norton, 2014).

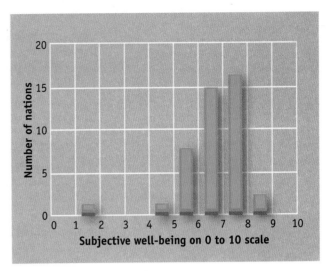

Figure 1.7

The subjective well-being of nations. Veenhoven (1993) combined the results of almost 1000 surveys to calculate the average subjective well-being reported by representative samples from forty-three nations. The mean happiness scores clearly pile up at the positive end of the distribution, with only two scores falling below the neutral point of 5. (Data adapted from Diener and Diener, 1996)

Age. Age and happiness are generally found to be unrelated. For example, a study of more than 7000 adults concluded that levels of happiness did not vary consistently with age (Cooper et al., 2011). The key factors influencing subjective well-being may shift some as people grow older, but people's average level of happiness tends to remain fairly stable over the lifespan.

Gender. Women are treated for depressive disorders about twice as often as men (Gananca, Kahn, & Oquendo, 2014), and women tend to make less money than men, so one might expect that women are less happy on the average. However, research suggests that gender has little impact on subjective well-being. For example, in a study of gender and happiness in seventy-three countries, statistically significant gender differences were found in only twelve mostly undeveloped countries and these differences were extremely small (Zweig, 2015).

Parenthood. Children can be a tremendous source of joy and fulfillment, but they can also be a tremendous source of headaches and hassles. Apparently, the good and bad aspects of parenthood balance each other out because the evidence indicates that people who have children are neither more nor less happy than people without children (Bhargava, Kassam, & Loewenstein, 2014).

Intelligence and attractiveness. Intelligence and physical attractiveness are highly valued traits in modern society. But researchers have *not* found an association between either characteristic and average happiness (Diener, Wolsic, & Fujita, 1995; Diener, Kesebir & Tov, 2009).

What Is Somewhat Important?

Research has identified five facets of life that appear to have a moderate impact on subjective well-being: health, social relations, religious belief, leisure activity, and culture.

Health. Good physical health would seem to be an essential requirement for happiness, but people adapt to health problems. Research reveals that

People who have lots of nice things tend to want even more and many fall into the trap of compulsive shopping. When they cannot afford what they want, frustration is likely. Thus, research shows that high materialism is correlated with lower subjective well-being.

individuals who develop serious, disabling health conditions aren't as unhappy as one might guess (Riis et al., 2005). Good health may not, by itself, produce happiness because people tend to take good health for granted. Such considerations may help explain why researchers find only a moderate positive correlation (average = .32) between health status and subjective well-being (Argyle, 1999). While health may promote happiness to a moderate degree, happiness may also foster better health, as research has found a positive correlation between happiness and longevity (Diener & Chan, 2011).

Social relations. Humans are social animals, and people's interpersonal relations *do* appear to contribute to their happiness. Assessments of the quantity and quality of one's friendships are predictive of greater happiness, and these relations hold across variations in age, ethnicity, and culture (Demir, Orthel, & Andelin, 2013). Similarly, researchers consistently find moderate positive correlations (typically in the .20s and .30s) between perceptions of social support from friends and family and measures of subjective well-being (Lakey, 2013).

Religious belief. The link between religiosity and subjective well-being is modest, but a number of surveys suggest that people with heartfelt religious convictions are more likely to be happy than people who characterize themselves as nonreligious (Myers, 2013). The association between religion and happiness appears to be stronger in societies where circumstances are difficult and stressful, and it is weaker in more affluent societies where circumstances are less threatening (Diener, Tay, & Myers, 2011). These findings suggest that religion may help people cope with adversity.

Leisure activity. Philosophers and poets have long extolled the importance of leisure for well-being. Empirical research has provided support for their insights. The amount of time allocated to leisure activities and the satisfaction one derives from these activities are both associated with subjective well-being (Newman, Tay, & Diener, 2014). That said, one study found that the sheer amount of leisure time is not as important as the degree to which leisure pursuits contribute to self-fulfillment and social interactions (Wang & Wong, 2014).

Culture. Surveys suggest that there are some moderate differences among nations in mean levels of subjective well-being. These differences correlate with economic development, as the nations with the happiest people tend to be affluent and those with the least happy people tend to be among the poorest (Diener, Kesebir, & Tov, 2009). Although wealth is a weak predictor of subjective well-being *within* cultures, comparisons *between* cultures tend to yield rather strong correlations between nations' wealth and their people's average happiness (Tov & Diener, 2007). How do theorists explain this paradox? They believe that national wealth is a relatively easy-to-measure marker associated with a matrix of cultural conditions that influence happiness. Specifically, they point out that nations' economic development correlates with greater recognition of human rights, greater income equality, greater gender equality, and more democratic governance (Tov & Diener, 2007). So, it may not be affluence per se that is the driving force behind cultural disparities in subjective well-being.

What Is Very Important?

The list of factors that turn out to be very important ingredients of happiness is surprisingly short. Only a few variables are strongly related to overall happiness: relationship satisfaction, work, and genetics and personality.

Relationship satisfaction. Romantic relationships can be stressful, but people consistently rate being in love as one of the most critical ingredients of happiness. Furthermore, although people complain a lot about their marriages, research shows that married people tend to be happier than people who are single or divorced (Saphire-Bernstein & Taylor, 2013). And among married people, their degree of marital satisfaction predicts their personal well-being (Carr et al., 2014). The research in this area generally has used marital status as a crude but easily measured marker of relationship satisfaction. In all likelihood, it is relationship satisfaction that fosters happiness. In other words, one does not have to be married to be happy. Relationship satisfaction probably has the same association with happiness in cohabiting heterosexual couples and gay couples. In support of this line of thinking, a study found that both married and cohabiting people were happier than those who remained single (Musick & Bumpass, 2012).

Work. Given the way people often complain about their jobs, we might not expect work to be a key source of happiness, but it is. Job satisfaction is strongly associated with general happiness (Judge & Klinger, 2008). Studies also show that unemployment has strong negative effects on subjective well-being, especially in men (van der Meer, 2014). It is difficult to sort out whether job satisfaction causes happiness or vice versa, but evidence suggests that causation flows both ways.

Genetics and personality. The best predictor of individuals' future happiness is their past happiness. Some people seem destined to be happy and others unhappy, regardless of their triumphs or setbacks. The limited influence of life events was highlighted in a classic study that found only modest differences in overall happiness between recent lottery winners and recent accident victims who became quadriplegics (Brickman, Coates, & Janoff-Bulman, 1978). Several lines of evidence suggest that happiness does not depend on external circumstances—buying a nice house, getting promoted—as much as on internal factors, such as one's outlook on life (Lyubomirsky, Sheldon, & Schkade, 2005).

With this finding in mind, researchers have investigated whether a hereditary basis might exist for variations in happiness. These studies suggest that people's genetic predispositions account for a substantial portion of the variance in happiness, perhaps as much as 50% (Lyubomirsky et al., 2005). How can one's genes influence one's happiness? Presumably, by shaping one's temperament and personality, which are known to be highly heritable. Indeed, personality traits show some of the strongest correlations with subjective well-being (Lucas & Diener, 2015). For example, *extraversion* is one of the better predictors of happiness. People who are outgoing, upbeat, and sociable tend to be happier than others (Gale et al., 2013). In contrast, those who score high in *neuroticism*—the tendency to be anxious, hostile, and insecure—tend to be less happy than others (Zhang & Howell, 2011).

Conclusions

We must be cautious in drawing inferences about the *causes* of happiness because most of the available data are correlational (see **Figure 1.8**). Nonetheless, the empirical findings suggest a number of worthwhile insights about the roots of happiness.

First, research on happiness demonstrates that the determinants of subjective well-being are precisely that: subjective. *Objective realities are not as important as subjective feelings.* In other words, your health, your wealth, your job, and your age are not as influential as how you *feel* about your health, wealth, job, and age.

Second, *when it comes to happiness, everything is relative.* In other words, you evaluate what you have relative to what the people around you have. People who are wealthy assess

Mark Davidson/Alamy Stock Photo

Happiness appears to depend on genetics, personality, and one's outlook on life more than the occurrence of positive or negative events in one's life.

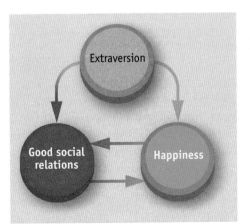

Figure 1.8

Possible causal relations among the correlates of happiness. Although we have considerable data on the correlates of happiness, it is difficult to untangle the possible causal relationships. For example, we know that a moderate positive correlation exists between good social relations and happiness, but we can't say for sure whether good social relations cause happiness or whether happiness causes people to experience better social relations. Moreover, in light of the finding that a third variable—extraversion—correlates with both variables, we have to consider the possibility that extraversion causes both better social relations and greater happiness.

by Daniel Gilbert (HarperCollins, 2006)

Do you think you know what will make you happy? Think again. If you read this book, you won't be nearly so confident about what will provide you with pleasure in the years to come. Daniel Gilbert is a Harvard psychologist who has pioneered research on *affective forecasting*—people's tendency to predict their emotional reactions to future events. This research shows that people tend to be reasonably accurate in anticipating whether events will generate positive or negative emotions, but they are often way off the mark in predicting the intensity and duration of their emotional reactions.

Why are people's predictions of their emotional reactions surprisingly inaccurate? A number of factors can contribute. One consideration is that people often assume they will spend a lot of time dwelling on a setback or relishing a triumph, but in reality a variety of other events and concerns will compete for their attention. Another consideration is that most people do not fully appreciate just how effective humans tend to be in rationalizing, discounting, and overlooking their failures and mistakes. People exhibit several cognitive biases that help them insulate themselves from the emotional fallout of life's difficulties, but they do not factor this peculiar "talent" into the picture when making predictions about their emotional reactions to setbacks.

In this wide-ranging book, Gilbert ventures far beyond the work on affective forecasting, profiling research on a host of related topics (especially peculiarities in decision making), but the central theme is that people's expectations about what will bring them happiness are surprisingly inaccurate. As you may have already gathered, this is not a self-help book per se, but it makes for fascinating reading that has some important implications for the never-ending pursuit of happiness. Although he describes a great deal of research, Gilbert's writing is so accessible, engaging, and humorous, it never feels like a review of research.

what they have by comparing themselves to their wealthy friends and neighbors, and their *relative ranking* is crucial (Boyce, Brown, & Moore, 2010). This is one reason for the surprisingly low correlation between wealth and happiness within specific societies. You might have a lovely home, but if it sits next to a neighbor's palatial mansion, this situation might be a source of more dissatisfaction than happiness.

Third, *research on happiness has shown that people are surprisingly bad at predicting what will make them happy*. We assume that we know what is best for us. But research on *affective forecasting*—**efforts to predict one's emotional reactions to future events**—suggests otherwise (Schwartz & Sommers, 2013). People routinely overestimate the pleasure that they will derive from buying an expensive automobile, taking an exotic vacation, earning an important promotion, or building their dream home (see the Recommended Reading Box and Chapter 6 for more on affective forecasting). Likewise, people tend to overestimate the misery and regret they will experience if they have a romantic breakup, don't get into the college they want, fail to get a promotion, or develop a serious illness. Thus, the roadmap to happiness is less clearly marked than widely assumed.

Fourth, *research on subjective well-being indicates that people often adapt to their circumstances. Hedonic adaptation* **occurs when the mental scale that people use to judge the pleasantness-unpleasantness of their experiences shifts so that their neutral point, or baseline for comparison, is changed** (*hedonic* means related to pleasure). Unfortunately, when people's experiences improve, hedonic adaptation may *sometimes* put them on a *hedonic treadmill*—their baseline moves upward, so that the improvements yield no real benefits (Kahneman, 1999). However, when people have to grapple with major setbacks, hedonic adaptation probably helps protect their mental and physical health. For example, people who are sent to prison and people who develop debilitating diseases are not as unhappy as one might assume because they adapt to their changed situations and evaluate events from a new perspective (Frederick & Loewenstein, 1999). That's not to say that hedonic adaptation in the face of life's difficulties is inevitable or complete, but people adapt to setbacks much better than widely assumed (Lucas, 2007).

We turn next to an example of how psychological research can be applied to everyday problems. In our first application section, we will review research evidence related to the challenge of being a successful student.

1.6 Improving Academic Performance

Learning Objectives

- List three steps for developing sound study habits.
- Discuss some strategies for improving reading comprehension and getting more out of lectures.
- Describe various study strategies that can aid memory.

Answer the following "true" or "false."

____ 1. If you have a professor who delivers chaotic, hard-to-follow lectures, there is little point in attending class.

____ 2. Cramming the night before an exam is an efficient way to study.

____ 3. In taking lecture notes, you should try to be a "human tape recorder" (that is, take down everything exactly as said by your professor).

As you will soon learn, all of these statements are false. If you answered them all correctly, you may already have acquired the kinds of skills and habits that lead to academic success. If so, however, you are not typical. Today, a huge number of students enter college with remarkably poor study skills and habits—and it's not entirely their fault. The U.S. educational system generally does not provide much in the way of formal instruction on good study techniques. Hence, it is not surprising that an influential review of research reported that a great many students embrace flawed models of how they learn and remember, waste precious time on activities that do not promote effective learning, and routinely misjudge their mastery of material (Bjork, Dunlosky, & Kornell, 2013). So, in this first Application, we'll start with the basics and try to remedy this deficiency to some extent by sharing some insights that psychology can provide on how to improve your academic performance.

Developing Sound Study Habits

People tend to assume that academic performance in college is largely determined by students' intelligence. This belief is supported by the fact that college admissions tests (the SAT and ACT), which basically assess general cognitive ability, predict college grades fairly well. What is far less well known, however, is that measures of study skills, habits, and attitudes also predict college grades pretty well. In a review of 344 independent samples consisting of more than 72,000 students, Crede and Kuncel (2008) reported that aggregate measures of study skills and habits predicted college grades almost as well as admissions tests did. The practical meaning of this finding is that most students

probably underestimate the importance of their study skills. And while most adults probably cannot increase their mental ability much, their study habits can usually be enhanced considerably.

In any event, the first step toward effective study habits is to face up to the reality that studying usually involves hard work. Once you accept the premise that studying doesn't come naturally, it should be apparent that you need to set up an organized program to promote adequate study. Such a program should include the following considerations.

Set up a schedule for studying. If you wait until the urge to study hits you, you may still be waiting when the exam rolls around. Thus, it is important to allocate definite times to study. Review your time obligations (work, housekeeping, and so on) and figure out in advance when you can study. In allotting certain times to studying, keep in mind that you need to be wide awake and alert. Allow time for study breaks; they can revive sagging concentration.

It's important to write down your study schedule (Tracy, 2006). Doing so serves as a reminder and increases your commitment to the schedule. As shown in **Figure 1.9**, you should begin by setting up a general schedule for the quarter or semester. Then, at the beginning of each week, plan the specific assignments that you intend to work on during each study session. This approach should help you avoid cramming for exams at the last minute. Cramming is an ineffective study strategy for most students (Wong, 2015). It will strain your memory, can tax your energy level, and may stoke the fires of test anxiety.

In planning your weekly schedule, try to avoid the tendency to put off working on major tasks such as term papers and reports. Time management experts point out that many of us tend to tackle simple, routine tasks first, saving larger tasks for later, when we supposedly will have more time. This common tendency leads many of us to delay working on major assignments until it's too late to do a good job. You can avoid this trap by

Learn More Online

Sites to Promote Academic Success

This site provides links to a number of other sites that provide advice on a diverse array of study-related topics, such as time management, effective note taking, memory-improvement strategies, and test-taking skills. Developed by Linda Walsh, a psychology professor at the University of Northern Iowa, it is an invaluable resource for students seeking to improve their chances of academic success.

	MON	TUES	WED	THURS	FRI	SAT	SUN
8 A.M.						Work	
9 A.M.	History	Study	History	Study	History	Work	
10 A.M.	Psych	French	Psych	French	Psych	Work	
11 A.M.	Study		Study		Study	Work	
Noon	Math	Study	Math	Study	Math	Work	Study
1 P.M.							Study
2 P.M.	Study	English	Study	English	Study		Study
3 P.M.	Study		Study		Study		Study
4 P.M.							
5 P.M.							
6 P.M.	Work	Study	Work				Study
7 P.M.	Work	Study	Work				Study
8 P.M.	Work	Study	Work				Study
9 P.M.	Work	Study	Work				Study
10 P.M.	Work		Work				

Figure 1.9

Example of an activity schedule. One student's general activity schedule for a semester is shown here. Each week the student fills in the specific assignments to work on during the upcoming study sessions.

breaking major assignments into smaller component tasks that you schedule individually.

Find a place to study where you can concentrate. Where you study is also important. The key is to find a place where distractions are likely to be minimal. Most people cannot study effectively while watching TV, listening to loud music, or overhearing conversations. Students routinely claim that they can multitask in these situations, but the research indicates that students tend to greatly overestimate their ability to multitask effectively (Chew, 2014).

Reward your studying. One of the reasons it is so difficult to motivate oneself to study regularly is that the payoffs for studying often lie in the distant future. The ultimate reward, a degree, may be years away. Even shorter-term rewards, such as an A in the course, may be weeks or months off. To combat this problem, it helps to give yourself immediate rewards for studying. It is easier to motivate yourself to study if you reward yourself with a tangible payoff, such as a snack, TV show, or phone call to a friend, when you finish. Thus, you should set realistic study goals and then reward yourself when you meet them.

Improving Your Reading

Much of your study time is spent reading and absorbing information. The keys to improving reading comprehension are to preview reading assignments section by section, work hard to actively process the meaning of the information, strive to identify the key ideas of each paragraph, and carefully review these key ideas after each section. Modern textbooks often contain a variety of learning aids that you can use to improve your reading. If a book provides a chapter outline, chapter summary, or learning objectives, don't ignore them. *Advance organizers* can encourage deeper processing and enhance your encoding of information (Marsh & Butler, 2013). A lot of effort and thought go into formulating these and other textbook learning aids. It is wise to take advantage of them.

Another important issue related to textbook reading is whether and how to mark up one's reading assignments. Many students deceive themselves into thinking that they are studying by running a marker through a few sentences here and there in their text. If they do so without thoughtful selectivity, they are simply turning a textbook into a coloring book. This situation probably explains why a recent review of the evidence on highlighting reported that it appears to have limited value (Dunlosky et al., 2013). That said, the review also noted that the value of highlighting probably depends on the skill with which it is executed. Consistent with this conclusion, other experts have asserted that highlighting textbook material *is* a useful strategy—*if* students are reasonably effective in focusing on the main ideas in the material and if they subsequently review what they have highlighted (Hayati & Shariatifar, 2009).

In theory, when executed effectively, highlighting can foster active reading, improve reading comprehension, and reduce the amount of material that one has to review later (Van Blerkom, 2012). The key to effective text marking is to identify (and highlight) only the main ideas, key supporting details, and technical terms. Most textbooks are carefully crafted such that every

Although many students underestimate the importance of study efforts, the reality is that effective study habits and skills are crucial to academic success.

paragraph has a purpose for being there. Try to find the sentence or two that best captures the purpose of each paragraph. Text marking is a delicate balancing act. If you highlight too little of the content, you are not identifying enough of the key ideas. But if you highlight too much of the content, you probably are not engaging in active reading and you are not going to succeed in making the important information stand out (Dunlosky et al., 2013). Overmarking appears to undermine the utility of highlighting more than undermarking.

Getting More out of Lectures

Although lectures are sometimes boring and tedious, it is a simple fact that poor class attendance is associated with poor grades. For example, Lindgren (1969) found that absences from class were much more common among "unsuccessful" students (grade average of C– or below) than among "successful" students (grade average of B or above), as shown in **Figure 1.10**. Even when you have an instructor who delivers hard-to-follow lectures from which you learn little, it is still important to go to class. If nothing else, you'll get a feel for how the instructor thinks. Doing so can help you anticipate the content of exams and respond in the manner your professor expects.

Fortunately, most lectures are reasonably coherent. Studies indicate that attentive note taking *is* associated with enhanced learning and performance in college classes (Marsh & Butler, 2013). However, research also shows that many students' lecture notes are surprisingly incomplete, with the average student often recording less than 40% of the crucial ideas in a lecture (Armbruster, 2000). Books on study skills (McWhorter, 2013; Wong, 2015) offer a number of suggestions on how to take good-quality lecture notes. These suggestions include:

- *Use active listening procedures.* With active listening, you focus full attention on the speaker. Try to anticipate what's coming and search for deeper meanings. Pay attention to nonverbal signals that may serve to further clarify the lecturer's intent or meaning.

- *Prepare for lectures by reading ahead on the scheduled subject in your text.* If you review the text, you have less information to digest that is brand new. This strategy is especially important when course material is complex and difficult.
- *Write down lecturers' thoughts in your own words.* Don't try to be a human tape recorder. Translating the lecture into your own words forces you to organize the ideas in a way that makes sense to you.
- *Look for subtle and not-so-subtle clues about what the instructor considers to be important.* These clues may range from simply repeating main points to saying things like "You'll run into this again."
- *Ask questions during lectures.* Doing so keeps you actively involved and allows you to clarify points you may have misunderstood. Many students are more bashful about asking questions than they should be. They don't realize that most professors welcome questions.

By the way, recent research has demonstrated that surfing the Internet while in class undermines learning and leads to lower performance on exams, regardless of one's academic ability (Ravizza, Hambrick, & Fenn, 2014). Another study found that students sitting nearby who could see a peer browsing the Internet in class also were distracted and earned lower grades (Sana, Weston, & Cepeda, 2013). Yet another study found that even when distractions are eliminated and students use their laptops exclusively for note taking, subsequent exam performance is impaired (Mueller & Oppenheimer, 2014). Why? Apparently, laptop note takers try to record lectures verbatim instead of putting the ideas into their own words, and this shallower processing results in reduced learning.

Applying Memory Principles

Scientific investigation of memory processes dates back to 1885, when Hermann Ebbinghaus published a series of insightful studies. Since then, psychologists have discovered a number of principles about memory that are relevant to helping you improve your study skills.

Engage in Adequate Practice

Studies show that memory improves with increased rehearsal. Evidence suggests that it even pays to overlearn material. *Overlearning* **is continued rehearsal of material after you have first appeared to master it.** In one classic study, after participants mastered a list of nouns (they recited the list without error), Krueger (1929) required them to continue rehearsing for 50% or 100% more trials (repetitions). Measuring retention at intervals of up to 28 days, Kreuger found that overlearning led to better recall of the list. Modern studies have also shown that overlearning can enhance performance on an exam that occurs within a week, although the evidence on its long-term benefits (months later) is inconsistent (Rohrer et al., 2005).

Although the benefits of practice are well known, people have a curious tendency to overestimate their knowledge of a topic and how well they will perform on a subsequent memory

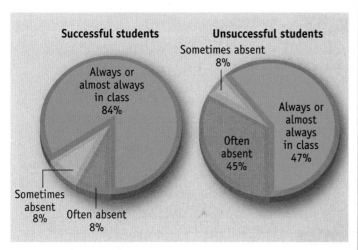

Figure 1.10

Successful and unsuccessful students' class attendance. Lindgren (1969) found that attendance was much better among successful students (grade of B or above) than among unsuccessful students (grade of C– or below).

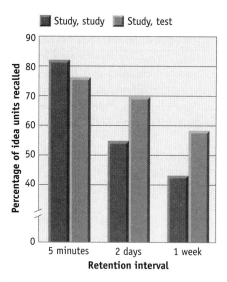

Figure 1.11

The testing effect. In one study by Roediger and Karpicke (2006), participants studied a brief prose passage for 7 minutes. Then, some of them studied it again for 7 minutes while others took a 7-minute test on the material. In the second phase of the study, subjects took another test on the material after either 5 minutes, 2 days, or 1 week. There wasn't much of a performance gap when subjects were tested over a 5-minute retention interval, but the testing group showed a significant advantage in recall when the retention interval was extended to 2 days or 1 week.

Source: Based on Roediger, III, H. L., & Karpicke, J. D. (2006). Test-enhanced learning: Taking memory tests improves long-term retention. *Psychological Science, 17*(3), 249–255.

test of this knowledge (Koriat & Bjork, 2005). After studying material, people also tend to underestimate the value of additional study and practice (Kornell et al., 2011). That's why it is a good idea to informally test yourself on information you think you have mastered before confronting a real test. In addition to checking your mastery, recent research suggests that testing actually enhances retention, a phenomenon dubbed the *testing effect* or *test-enhanced learning* (Pyc, Agarwal, & Roediger, 2014). Studies have shown that taking a test on material increases performance on a subsequent test even more than studying for an equal amount of time (see **Figure 1.11**). The testing effect has been seen across a wide range of different types of content, and the benefits grow as the retention interval gets longer. The favorable effects of testing are enhanced if participants are provided feedback on their test performance (Kornell & Metcalfe, 2014). Moreover, studies have demonstrated that the laboratory findings on the testing effect replicate in real-world educational settings (McDermott et al., 2014). Better yet, research suggests that testing improves not just the retention of information, but also the *application* of that information in new contexts (Carpenter, 2012). Unfortunately, given the recent nature of this discovery, relatively few students are aware of the value of testing.

Why is testing so beneficial? The key appears to be that testing forces students to engage in effortful retrieval of information, which promotes future retention (Roediger et al., 2010). In any event, self-testing appears to be an excellent memory tool, which suggests that it would be prudent to take the Practice Tests in this text.

Use Distributed Practice

Let's assume that you are going to study 9 hours for an exam. Is it better to "cram" all of your study into one 9-hour period (massed practice) or distribute it among, say, three 3-hour periods on successive days (distributed practice)? The evidence indicates that retention tends to be greater after distributed practice than massed practice (Carpenter, 2014). Moreover, a review of more than 300 experiments (Cepeda et al., 2006) showed that the longer the retention interval between studying and testing, the bigger the advantage for spaced practice, as shown in **Figure 1.12**. The same review concluded that the longer the retention interval, the longer the optimal "break" between practice trials. When an upcoming test is more than 2 days away, the optimal interval between practice periods appears to be around 24 hours. The superiority of distributed practice over massed practice provides another reason why cramming is an ill-advised approach to studying for exams.

Organize Information

Retention tends to be greater when information is well organized (Einstein & McDaniel, 2004). Hierarchical organization is particularly helpful when it is applicable. Thus, it may be a good idea to *outline* reading assignments for school. Consistent with this reasoning, there is some empirical evidence that

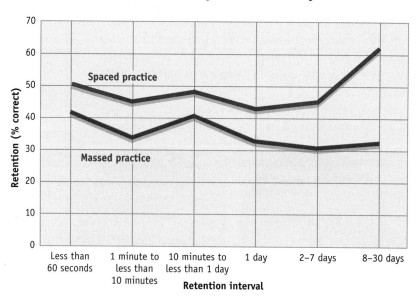

Figure 1.12

Effects of massed versus distributed practice on retention. In a review of more than 300 experiments on massed versus distributed practice, Cepeda et al. (2006) examined the importance of the retention interval. As you can see, spaced practice was superior to massed practice at all retention intervals, but the gap widened at longer intervals. These findings suggest that distributed practice is especially advantageous when you need or want to remember material over the long haul. (Based on data from Cepeda et al., 2006)

outlining material from textbooks can enhance retention of the material.

Emphasize Deep Processing

One line of research suggests that how *often* you go over material is less critical than the *depth* of processing that you engage in. Thus, if you expect to remember what you read, you have to wrestle fully with its meaning (Marsh & Butler, 2013). Many students could probably benefit if they spent less time on rote repetition and more on actually paying attention to and analyzing the meaning of their reading assignments. In particular, it is useful to make material *personally* meaningful. When you read your textbooks, try to relate information to your own life and experience.

Use Mnemonic Devices

Of course, it's not always easy to make something personally meaningful. When you study chemistry, you may have a hard time relating to polymers at a personal level. This problem has led to the development of many **mnemonic devices, or strategies for enhancing memory,** that are designed to make abstract material more meaningful.

Acrostics and acronyms. *Acrostics* are phrases (or poems) in which the first letter of each word (or line) functions as a cue to help you recall the abstract words that begin with the same letter. For instance, you may remember the order of musical notes with the saying "Every good boy does fine" (or "deserves favor"). A variation on acrostics is the *acronym*—a word formed out of the first letters of a series of words. Students memorizing the order of colors in the light spectrum often store the name "Roy G. Biv" to remember red, orange, yellow, green, blue, indigo, and violet. Acrostics and acronyms that individuals create for themselves can be effective memory tools (Hermann, Raybeck, & Gruneberg, 2002).

Link method. The *link method* involves forming a mental image of items to be remembered in a way that links them together. For instance, suppose you are going to stop at the drugstore on the way home and you want to remember to pick up a news magazine, shampoo, mouthwash, and pens. To remember these items, you might visualize a public figure likely to be on a magazine cover gurgling mouthwash with a pen in hand and shampoo on his or her head. Some researchers suggest that the more bizarre the images, the better they will be remembered (Iaccino, 1996).

Method of loci. The *method of loci* involves taking an imaginary walk along a familiar path where you have associated images of items you want to remember with certain locations. The first step is to commit to memory a series of loci, or places along a path. Usually, these loci are specific locations in your home or neighborhood. Then envision each thing you want to remember in one of these locations. Try to form distinctive, vivid images. When you need to remember the items, imagine yourself walking along the path. The various loci on your path should serve as retrieval cues for the images that you formed (see **Figure 1.13**). The method of loci assures that items are remembered in their correct order because the order is determined by the sequence of locations along the pathway. Empirical studies have supported the value of this method for memorizing lists (Gross et al., 2014).

Figure 1.13

The method of loci. In this example from Bower (1970), a person about to go shopping pairs items to be remembered with familiar places (loci) arranged in a natural sequence: (1) hot dogs/driveway; (2) cat food/garage; (3) tomatoes/front door; (4) bananas/coat closet; (5) whiskey/kitchen sink. As the last panel shows, the shopper recalls the items by mentally touring the loci associated with them.

Source: Adapted from Bower, G. H. (1970). Analysis of a mnemonic device. *American Scientist, 58,* 496–499. Copyright © 1970 by Scientific Research Society. Reprinted by permission.

CHAPTER 1 Review

Key Ideas

1.1 The Paradox of Progress

● Although our modern era has seen great technological progress, personal problems have not diminished. In spite of many time-saving devices, people tend to have less free time. The life choices available to people have increased greatly, but evidence suggests that choice overload undermines individuals' happiness.

● Although we live in an era of unprecedented affluence, the vast majority of people are stressed about financial matters, and the materialism cultivated by our consumer society appears to have undermined our subjective well-being. Thus, many theorists argue that technological progress has brought new, and possibly more difficult, adjustment problems.

1.2 The Search for Direction

● According to many theorists, the basic challenge of modern life has become the search for a sense of direction and meaning. This search has many manifestations, including the appeal of self-realization programs, self-help gurus, religious cults, and media "therapists."

● The enormous popularity of self-help books is an interesting manifestation of people's struggle to find a sense of direction. Some self-help books offer worthwhile advice, but most are dominated by psychobabble and are not based on scientific research. Many also lack explicit advice on how to change behavior and some encourage a self-centered, narcissistic approach to interpersonal interactions.

● Although this text deals with many of the same issues as self-realization programs, self-help books, and other types of pop psychology, its philosophy and approach are quite different. This text is based on the premise that accurate knowledge about the principles of psychology can be of value in everyday life.

1.3 The Psychology of Adjustment

● Psychology is both a science and a profession that focuses on behavior and related mental and physiological processes. Adjustment is a broad area of study in psychology concerned with how people adapt effectively or ineffectively to the demands and pressures of everyday life.

1.4 The Scientific Approach to Behavior

● The scientific approach to understanding behavior is empirical. Psychologists base their conclusions on formal, systematic, objective tests of their hypotheses, rather than reasoning, speculation, or common sense.

● Experimental research involves manipulating an independent variable to discover its effect on a dependent variable. The experimenter usually does so by comparing experimental and control groups, which must be alike except for the variation created by the manipulation of the independent variable. Experiments permit conclusions about cause-effect relationships between variables, but this method isn't usable for the study of many questions.

● Psychologists conduct correlational research when they are unable to exert control over the variables they want to study. The correlation coefficient is a numerical index of the degree of relationship between two variables. Correlational research methods include naturalistic observation, case studies, and surveys. Correlational research facilitates the investigation of many issues that are not open to experimental study, but it cannot demonstrate that two variables are causally related.

1.5 The Roots of Happiness: An Empirical Analysis

● A scientific analysis of happiness reveals that many commonsense notions about the roots of happiness appear to be incorrect, including the notion that most people are unhappy. Factors such as income, age, gender, parenthood, intelligence, and attractiveness are only weakly correlated with subjective well-being.

● Physical health, social relationships, religious faith, leisure activity, and culture appear to have a modest impact on feelings of happiness. The factors that are most strongly related to happiness are relationship satisfaction, work satisfaction, and personality, which probably reflects the influence of heredity.

● Happiness is a relative concept mediated by people's highly subjective assessments of their lives. Research on affective forecasting shows that people are surprisingly bad at predicting what will make them happy. Individuals adapt to both positive and negative events in their lives, which creates a hedonic treadmill effect.

1.6 Application: Improving Academic Performance

● Evidence suggests that study habits are almost as influential as ability in determining college success. To foster sound study habits, you should devise a written study schedule and reward yourself for following it. You should also try to find places for studying that are relatively free of distractions.

● You should use active reading techniques to select the most important ideas from the material you read. Highlighting textbook material can be a useful strategy—if you are reasonably effective in focusing on the main ideas in the material and if you subsequently review what you have highlighted. Good note taking can help you get more out of lectures. It's important to use active listening techniques and to record lecturers' ideas in your own words. Computer use in class appears to undermine learning.

● Rehearsal, even when it involves overlearning, facilitates retention. The process of being tested on material bolsters retention of that material. Distributed practice and deeper processing tend to improve memory. Evidence also suggests that organization facilitates retention, so outlining reading assignments can be valuable.

● Meaningfulness can be enhanced through the use of mnemonic devices such as acrostics and acronyms. The link method and the method of loci are mnemonic devices that depend on the value of visual imagery.

Key Terms

Adjustment p. 9
Affective forecasting p. 20
Behavior p. 9
Case study p. 14
Clinical psychology p. 9
Control group p. 11
Correlation p. 12
Correlation coefficient p. 12
Dependent variable p. 10
Empiricism p. 10
Experiment p. 10
Experimental group p. 11
Hedonic adaptation p. 20
Independent variable p. 10
Mnemonic devices p. 25
Narcissism p. 6
Naturalistic observation p. 12
Overlearning p. 23
Psychology p. 9
Subjective well-being p. 16
Surveys p. 14

CHAPTER 1 Practice Test

1. Technological advances have not led to perceptible improvement in our collective health and happiness. This statement defines
   a. escape from freedom.
   b. the point/counterpoint phenomenon.
   c. modern society.
   d. the paradox of progress.

2. Barry Schwartz (2004) argues that
   a. life choices have increased dramatically in modern society.
   b. an abundance of choices can lead to choice overload.
   c. choice overload often leads to rumination and postdecision regret.
   d. all of the above are true.

3. Which of the following is *not* offered in the text as a criticism of self-help books?
   a. They are infrequently based on solid research.
   b. Most don't provide explicit directions for changing behavior.
   c. The topics they cover are often quite narrow.
   d. Many are dominated by psychobabble.

4. The adaptation of animals when environments change is similar to _____ in humans.
   a. orientation
   b. assimilation
   c. evolution
   d. adjustment

5. An experiment is a research method in which the investigator manipulates the _____ variable and observes whether changes occur in a (an) _____ variable as a result.
   a. independent; dependent
   b. control; experimental
   c. experimental; control
   d. dependent; independent

6. A researcher wants to determine whether a certain diet causes children to learn better in school. In this study, the independent variable is
   a. the type of diet.
   b. a measure of learning performance.
   c. the age or grade level of the children.
   d. the intelligence level of the children.

7. A psychologist collected background information about a psychopathic killer, talked to him and people who knew him, and gave him psychological tests. Which research method was she using?
   a. Case study
   b. Naturalistic observation
   c. Survey
   d. Experiment

8. The principal advantage of experimental research is that
   a. it has a scientific basis and is therefore convincing to people.
   b. experiments replicate real-life situations.
   c. an experiment can be designed for any research problem.
   d. it allows the researcher to draw cause-and-effect conclusions.

9. Research has shown that which of the following is moderately correlated with happiness?
   a. Gender
   b. Intelligence
   c. Parenthood
   d. Good social relations

10. A good reason for taking notes in your own words, rather than verbatim, is that
    a. most lecturers are quite wordy.
    b. "translating" on the spot is good mental exercise.
    c. it reduces the likelihood that you'll later engage in plagiarism.
    d. it forces you to assimilate the information in a way that makes sense to you.

Answers
1. d Pages 1–3
2. d Pages 1–2
3. c Pages 6–7
4. d Page 9
5. a Page 10
6. a Page 10
7. a Page 14
8. d Page 11
9. d Pages 17–18
10. d Page 23

Personal Explorations Workbook

Go to the *Personal Explorations Workbook* in the back of your textbook for exercises that can enhance your self-understanding in relation to issues raised in this chapter.

Exercise 1.1 *Self-Assessment:* Narcissistic Personality Inventory

Exercise 1.2 *Self-Reflection:* What Are Your Study Habits Like?

Theories of Personality

wavebreakmedia/Shutterstock.com

magine that you are hurtling upward in an elevator with three other persons when suddenly a power blackout brings the elevator to a halt forty-five stories above the ground. Your companions might adjust to this predicament differently. One might crack jokes to relieve tension. Another might make ominous predictions that "we'll never get out of here." The third might calmly think about how to escape from the elevator. These varied ways of coping with the same stressful situation occur because each person has a different personality. Personality differences significantly influence people's patterns of adjustment. Thus, theories intended to explain personality can contribute to our effort to understand adjustment processes. In this chapter, we introduce you to various theories that attempt to explain the structure and development of personality. ∎

2.1 The Nature of Personality

Learning Objectives

- Clarify the meaning of personality and personality traits.
- Describe the five-factor model of personality and relations between the Big Five traits and life outcomes.

To discuss theories of personality effectively, we need to digress momentarily to come up with a definition of *personality* and to discuss the concept of personality traits.

What Is Personality?

What does it mean if you say that a friend has an optimistic personality? Your statement suggests that the person has a fairly *consistent tendency* to behave in a cheerful, hopeful, enthusiastic way, looking at the bright side of things, across a wide variety of situations. In a similar vein, if you note that a friend has an "outgoing" personality, you mean that she or he consistently behaves in a friendly, open, and extraverted manner in a variety of circumstances. Although no one is entirely consistent in his or her behavior, this quality of *consistency across situations* lies at the core of the concept of personality.

Distinctiveness is also central to the concept of personality. Everyone has traits seen in other people, but each individual has her or his own distinctive *set* of personality traits. Each person is unique. Thus, as illustrated by our elevator scenario, the concept of personality helps explain why people don't all act alike in the same situation. In summary, *personality* **refers to an individual's unique constellation of consistent behavioral traits.** Let's look more closely at the concept of traits.

What Are Personality Traits?

We all make remarks like "Melanie is very *shrewd*" or "Doug is too *timid* to succeed in that job" or "I wish I could be as *self-assured* as Antonio." When we attempt to describe an individual's personality, we usually do so in terms of specific aspects, called traits. **A** *personality trait* **is a durable disposition to behave in a particular way in a variety of situations.** Adjectives such as *honest, dependable, moody, impulsive, suspicious, anxious, excitable, domineering*, and *friendly* describe dispositions that represent personality traits.

Most trait theories of personality assume that some traits are more basic than others (Paunonen & Hong, 2015). According to this notion, a small number of fundamental traits determine other, more superficial traits. For example, a person's tendency to be impulsive, restless, irritable, boisterous, and impatient might all derive from a more basic tendency to be excitable. A number of theorists have taken on the challenge of identifying the basic traits that form the core of personality. In recent decades, the most influential theory has been the *five-factor model* developed by Robert McCrae and Paul Costa (2008).

The Five-Factor Model of Personality

The five-factor model of personality developed by McCrae and Costa (2003, 2008) asserts that the vast majority of personality traits derive from just five higher-order traits that have

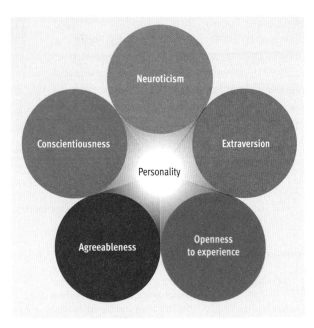

Figure 2.1

The five-factor model of personality. Trait models attempt to break down personality into its basic dimensions. McCrae and Costa (1987, 1997, 2003) maintain that personality can be described adequately with the five higher-order traits identified here, widely known as the Big Five traits.

come to be known as the "Big Five": extraversion, neuroticism, openness to experience, agreeableness, and conscientiousness (see **Figure 2.1**). Let's take a closer look at these traits:

1. *Extraversion.* People who score high in extraversion are characterized as outgoing, sociable, upbeat, friendly, assertive, and gregarious. They also have a more positive outlook on life and are motivated to pursue social contact, intimacy, and interdependence (Wilt & Revelle, 2009).

2. *Neuroticism.* People who score high in neuroticism tend to be anxious, hostile, self-conscious, insecure, and vulnerable. They also tend to exhibit more impulsiveness and emotional instability than others (Widiger, 2009).

3. *Openness to experience.* Openness is associated with curiosity, flexibility, vivid fantasy, imaginativeness, artistic sensitivity, and unconventional attitudes. People who are high in openness tend to be tolerant of ambiguity and have less need for closure on issues (McCrae & Sutin, 2009).

4. *Agreeableness.* Those who score high in agreeableness tend to be sympathetic, trusting, cooperative, modest, and straightforward. People who score at the opposite end of this personality dimension are characterized as suspicious, antagonistic, and aggressive. Agreeableness is associated with empathy and helping behavior (Graziano & Tobin, 2009).

5. *Conscientiousness.* Conscientious people tend to be diligent, disciplined, well organized, punctual, and dependable. Conscientiousness is associated with strong self-discipline and the ability to regulate oneself effectively (Roberts et al., 2009).

Correlations have been found between the Big Five traits and quite a variety of important life outcomes. For instance, higher college grades are associated with higher conscientiousness, probably because conscientious students work harder (McAbee & Oswald, 2013). Several of the Big Five traits are associated with occupational attainment (career success). Extraversion and conscientiousness are positive predictors of occupational attainment, whereas neuroticism is a negative predictor (Miller Burke & Attridge, 2011; Roberts, Caspi, & Moffitt, 2003). Agreeableness is negatively associated with income, especially among men (Judge, Livingston, & Hurst, 2012). Extraversion and openness to experience correlate with entrepreneurial activity (Leutner et al., 2014). The likelihood of divorce can also be predicted by personality traits because neuroticism elevates the probability of divorce, whereas agreeableness and conscientiousness reduce it (Roberts et al., 2007). Finally, and perhaps most important, several of the Big Five traits are related to health and mortality. Neuroticism is associated with an elevated prevalence of physical and mental disorders (Smith, Williams, & Segerstrom, 2015), whereas conscientiousness is correlated with the experience of less illness and with greater longevity (Friedman & Kern, 2014). Recent research suggests that openness to experience may also foster longevity (DeYoung, 2015).

Advocates of the five-factor model maintain that personality can be described adequately by measuring the five basic traits they've identified. Their bold claim has been supported in many studies, and the five-factor model has become the dominant conception of personality structure in contemporary psychology (McCrae, Gaines, & Wellington, 2013). However, some theorists have argued that only two or three traits are necessary to account for most of the variation seen in human personality, while others have suggested that more than five traits are needed to describe personality adequately (Saucier & Srivastava, 2015).

The debate about how many dimensions are necessary to describe personality is likely to continue for many years to come. As you'll see throughout the chapter, the study of personality is an area in psychology that has a long history of "dueling theories." We'll begin our tour of these theories by examining the influential work of Sigmund Freud and his followers.

2.2 Psychodynamic Perspectives

Learning Objectives

- Explain Freud's view of personality structure and the role of conflict and anxiety.
- Identify key defense mechanisms, and outline Freud's view of development.
- Summarize the psychodynamic theories proposed by Jung and Adler.
- Evaluate the strengths and weaknesses of the psychodynamic approach to personality.

Psychodynamic theories **include all the diverse theories descended from the work of Sigmund Freud that focus on unconscious mental forces.** Freud inspired many brilliant scholars who followed in his intellectual footsteps. Some of these followers simply refined and updated Freud's theory. Others veered off in new directions and established independent, albeit related, schools of thought. Today, the psychodynamic umbrella covers a large collection of related theories. In this section, we'll examine Freud's ideas in some detail and then take a brief look at the work of two of his most significant followers, Carl Jung and Alfred Adler.

Freud's Psychoanalytic Theory

Sigmund Freud was a physician specializing in neurology when he began his medical practice in Vienna near the end of the 19th century. Like other neurologists in his era, he often treated people troubled by nervous problems such as irrational fears, obsessions, and anxieties. Eventually, he devoted himself to the treatment of mental disorders using an innovative procedure he developed, called *psychoanalysis*, that required lengthy verbal interactions in which Freud probed deeply into patients' lives. Decades of experience with patients provided much of the inspiration for his theory of personality.

Although Freud's theory gradually gained prominence, most of his contemporaries were uncomfortable with it, for at least three reasons. First, he argued that unconscious forces govern human behavior. This idea was disturbing because it suggested that people are not masters of their own minds. Second, he claimed that childhood experiences strongly determine adult personality. This notion distressed many because it suggested that people are not masters of their own destinies. Third, he said that individuals' personalities are shaped by how they cope with their sexual urges. This assertion offended the conservative Victorian values of his time. Thus, Freud endured a great deal of criticism, condemnation, and outright ridicule, even after his work began to attract more favorable attention. What were these ideas that generated so much controversy?

Sigmund Freud is widely known for his invention of psychoanalysis, his interest in the unconscious, and his controversial emphasis on sexuality.

Structure of Personality

Freud (1901, 1920) divided personality structure into three components: the id, the ego, and the superego. He saw a person's behavior as the outcome of interactions among these three elements.

The *id* is the primitive, instinctive component of personality that operates according to the pleasure principle. Freud referred to the id as the reservoir of psychic energy. By this he meant that the id houses the raw biological urges (to eat, sleep, defecate, copulate, and so on) that energize human behavior. The id operates according to the *pleasure principle*, which demands immediate gratification of its urges. The id engages in *primary process thinking*, which is primitive, illogical, irrational, and fantasy oriented.

The *ego* is the decision-making component of personality that operates according to the reality principle. The ego mediates between the id, with its forceful desires for immediate satisfaction, and the external social world, with its expectations and norms regarding suitable behavior. The ego considers social realities—society's norms, etiquette, rules, and customs—in deciding how to behave. The ego is guided by the *reality principle*, which seeks to delay gratification of the id's urges until appropriate outlets and situations can be found. In short, to stay out of trouble, the ego often works to tame the unbridled desires of the id. As Freud put it, the ego is "like a man on horseback, who has to hold in check the superior strength of the horse" (Freud, 1923, p. 15).

In the long run, the ego wants to maximize gratification, just like the id. However, the ego engages in *secondary process thinking*, which is relatively rational, realistic, and oriented toward problem solving. Thus, the ego strives to avoid negative consequences from

Learn More Online

Sigmund Freud Museum, Vienna, Austria

This online museum, in both English and German versions, offers a detailed chronology of Freud's life and explanations of the most important concepts of psychoanalysis. The highlights, though, are the rich audiovisual resources, including online photos, amateur movie clips, and voice recordings of Freud.

society and its representatives (for example, punishment by parents or teachers) by behaving "properly." It also attempts to achieve long-range goals that sometimes require putting off gratification.

While the ego concerns itself with practical realities, **the *superego* is the moral component of personality that incorporates social standards about what represents right and wrong.** Throughout their lives, but especially during childhood, individuals receive training about what constitutes good and bad behavior. Eventually, they internalize many of these social norms, meaning that they truly *accept* certain moral principles, then *they* put pressure on *themselves* to live up to these standards. The superego emerges out of the ego at around 3 to 5 years of age. In some people, the superego can become irrationally demanding in its striving for moral perfection. Such people are plagued by excessive guilt.

According to Freud, the id, ego, and superego are distributed across three levels of awareness. He contrasted the unconscious with the conscious and preconscious (see **Figure 2.2**). **The *conscious* consists of whatever one is aware of at a particular point in time.** For example, at this moment your conscious may include the current train of thought in this text and a dim awareness in the back of your mind that your eyes are getting tired and you're beginning to get hungry. **The *preconscious* contains material just beneath the surface of awareness that can be easily retrieved.** Examples might include your middle name, what you had for supper last night, or an argument you had with a friend yesterday. **The *unconscious* contains thoughts, memories, and desires that are well below the surface of conscious awareness but that nonetheless exert great influence on one's behavior.** Material that might be found in your unconscious would include a forgotten trauma from childhood or hidden feelings of hostility toward a parent.

Conflict and Defense Mechanisms

Freud assumed that behavior is the outcome of an ongoing series of internal conflicts. Battles among the id, ego, and superego are routine. Why? Because the id wants to gratify its urges immediately, but the norms of civilized society frequently dictate otherwise. For example, your id might feel an urge to clobber a co-worker who constantly irritates you. However, society frowns on such behavior, so your ego would try to hold this urge in check, and you would find yourself in a conflict. Freud believed that internal conflicts are a routine part of people's lives. The following scenario provides a fanciful illustration of how the three components of personality interact to create constant conflicts.

Figure 2.2

Freud's model of personality structure. Freud theorized that people have three levels of awareness: the conscious, the preconscious, and the unconscious. To dramatize the size of the unconscious, it has often been compared to the portion of an iceberg that lies beneath the water's surface. Freud also divided personality structure into three components—id, ego, and superego—that operate according to different principles and exhibit different modes of thinking. In Freud's model, the id is entirely unconscious, but the ego and superego operate at all three levels of awareness.

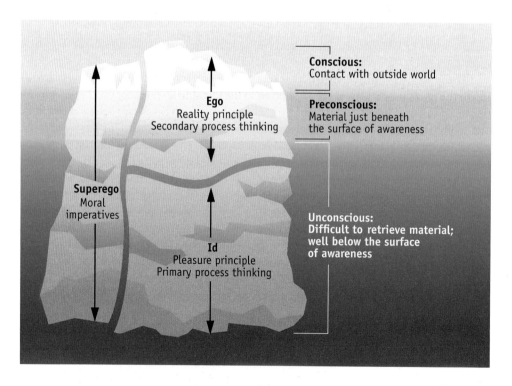

Ego
Reality principle
Secondary process thinking

Superego
Moral imperatives

Id
Pleasure principle
Primary process thinking

Conscious:
Contact with outside world

Preconscious:
Material just beneath the surface of awareness

Unconscious:
Difficult to retrieve material; well below the surface of awareness

Imagine your alarm clock ringing obnoxiously as you lurch across the bed to shut it off. It's 7 a.m. and time to get up for your history class. However, your id (operating according to the pleasure principle) urges you to return to the immediate gratification of additional sleep. Your ego (operating according to the reality principle) points out that you really must go to class since you haven't been able to decipher the textbook on your own. Your id (in its typical unrealistic fashion) smugly assures you that you will get the A that you need. It suggests lying back to dream about how impressed your roommate will be. Just as you're relaxing, your superego jumps into the fray. It tries to make you feel guilty about the tuition your parents paid for the class that you're about to skip. You haven't even gotten out of bed yet—and there is already a pitched battle in your psyche.

Freud believed that conflicts centering on sexual and aggressive impulses are especially likely to have far-reaching consequences. Why did he emphasize sex and aggression? Two reasons were prominent in his thinking. First, he thought that sex and aggression are subject to more complex and ambiguous social controls than other basic motives. Thus, people often get inconsistent messages about what's appropriate. Second, he noted that the aggressive and sexual drives are thwarted more regularly than other basic, biological urges. Think about it: If you get hungry or thirsty, you can simply head for a nearby vending machine or a drinking fountain. But when you see an attractive person who inspires lustful urges, you don't normally propose hooking up in a nearby broom closet. Freud ascribed great importance to these needs because social norms dictate that they're routinely frustrated.

Most psychic conflicts are trivial and are quickly resolved one way or the other. Occasionally, however, a conflict will linger for days, months, and even years, creating internal tension. Indeed, Freud believed that lingering conflicts rooted in childhood experiences cause most personality disturbances. More often than not, these prolonged and troublesome conflicts involve sexual and aggressive impulses that society wants to tame. These conflicts are often played out entirely in the unconscious. Although you may not be aware of these unconscious battles, they can produce *anxiety* that slips to the surface of conscious awareness. This anxiety is attributable to your ego worrying about the id getting out of control and doing something terrible.

The arousal of anxiety is a crucial event in Freud's theory of personality functioning (see **Figure 2.3**). Anxiety is distressing, so people try to rid themselves of this unpleasant emotion any way they can. This effort to ward off anxiety often involves the use of defense mechanisms. *Defense mechanisms* **are largely unconscious reactions that protect a person from painful emotions such as anxiety and guilt.** Typically, they are mental maneuvers that work through self-deception. A common example is *rationalization,* **which involves creating false but plausible excuses to justify unacceptable behavior.** You would be rationalizing if, after cheating someone in a business transaction, you tried to reduce your guilt by explaining that "everyone does it."

Freud's psychoanalytic theory was based on decades of clinical work. He treated a great many patients in the consulting room pictured here. The room contains numerous artifacts from other cultures—and the original psychoanalytic couch.

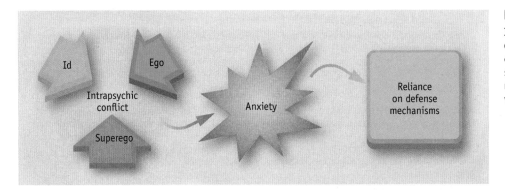

Figure 2.3

Freud's model of personality dynamics. According to Freud, unconscious conflicts among the id, ego, and superego sometimes lead to anxiety. This discomfort may lead to the use of defense mechanisms, which may temporarily relieve anxiety.

Characterized as "the flagship in the psychoanalytic fleet of defense mechanisms" (Paulhus, Fridhandler, & Hayes, 1997, p. 545), *repression* is the most basic and widely used defense mechanism. *Repression* **involves keeping distressing thoughts and feelings buried in the unconscious.** People tend to repress desires that make them feel guilty, conflicts that make them anxious, and memories that are painful. Repression is "motivated forgetting." If you forget a dental appointment or the name of someone you don't like, repression may be at work.

Self-deception can also be seen in the mechanisms of projection and displacement. *Projection* **involves attributing one's own thoughts, feelings, or motives to another.** For example, if your lust for a co-worker makes you feel guilty, you might attribute any latent sexual tension between the two of you to the *other person's* desire to seduce you. *Displacement* **involves diverting emotional feelings (usually anger) from their original source to a substitute target.** If your boss gives you a hard time at work and you come home and slam the door, yell at your dog, and lash out at your spouse, you are displacing your anger onto irrelevant targets. Unfortunately, social constraints often force people to hold back their anger until they end up expressing it toward the people they love the most.

Other prominent defense mechanisms include reaction formation, regression, and identification. *Reaction formation* **involves behaving in a way that is exactly the opposite of one's true feelings.** Guilt about sexual desires often leads to reaction formation. Freud theorized that many males who ridicule homosexuals are defending against their own latent homosexual impulses. The telltale sign of reaction formation is the exaggerated quality of the opposite behavior (such as trying to be ultra-nice in order to mask feelings of hostility).

Regression **involves a reversion to immature patterns of behavior.** When anxious about their self-worth, some adults respond with childish boasting and bragging (as opposed to subtle efforts to impress others). For example, a fired executive having difficulty finding a new job might start making ridiculous statements about his incomparable talents and achievements. Such bragging is regressive when it is marked by massive exaggerations that anyone can see through.

Identification **involves bolstering self-esteem by forming an imaginary or real alliance with some person or group.** For example, youngsters often shore up precarious feelings of self-worth by identifying with rock stars, movie stars, or famous athletes. Adults may join exclusive country clubs or civic organizations with which they identify.

Additional examples of the defense mechanisms we've described can be found in **Figure 2.4.** According to Freud, everyone uses defense mechanisms to some extent. They

Figure 2.4

Defense mechanisms. According to Freud, people use a variety of defense mechanisms to protect themselves from painful emotions. Definitions of seven commonly used defense mechanisms are shown on the left, along with examples of each on the right.

DEFENSE MECHANISMS, WITH EXAMPLES	
Definition	**Example**
Repression involves keeping distressing thoughts and feelings buried in the unconscious.	A traumatized soldier has no recollection of the details of a close brush with death.
Projection involves attributing one's own thoughts, feelings, or motives to another person.	A woman who dislikes her boss thinks she likes her boss but feels that the boss doesn't like her.
Displacement involves diverting emotional feelings (usually anger) from their original source to a substitute target.	After a parental scolding, a young girl takes her anger out on her little brother.
Reaction formation involves behaving in a way that is exactly the opposite of one's true feelings.	A parent who unconsciously resents a child spoils the child with outlandish gifts.
Regression involves a reversion to immature patterns of behavior.	An adult has a temper tantrum when he doesn't get his way.
Rationalization involves the creation of false but plausible excuses to justify unacceptable behavior.	A student watches TV instead of studying, saying that "additional study wouldn't do any good anyway."
Identification involves bolstering self-esteem by forming an imaginary or real alliance with some person or group.	An insecure young man joins a fraternity to boost his self-esteem.

become problematic only when a person depends on them excessively. The seeds for psychological disorders are sown when defenses lead to wholesale distortion of reality. Modern research provides some support for Freud's belief that mental health depends in part on the extent to which people rely on defense mechanisms. A study of patients undergoing long-term psychoanalytic therapy found that reductions in their reliance on defense mechanisms were associated with improvements in life functioning and decreases in psychiatric symptoms (Perry & Bond, 2012).

Recent decades have brought a revival of interest in research on defense mechanisms. Consistent with Freudian theory, empirical studies have found that (1) reliance on defense mechanisms increases when people experience stress or a threat to their sense of self, (2) defense mechanisms serve a protective function by shielding individuals from emotional distress, and (3) excessive dependence on defenses is associated with impairments in mental health (Cramer, 2015). One interesting line of research has investigated a *repressive coping style* and found that repressors have an impoverished memory for events that are likely to trigger unpleasant emotions (Alston et al., 2013). For example, one study found that repressors selectively forget more self-threatening information than control subjects (Saunders, Worth, & Fernandes, 2012). Another study found that repressors' recollections of negative events showed less specificity and detail than their recollections of positive events (Geraerts et al., 2012). In other words, their memory for negative experiences is degraded in quality.

Development: Psychosexual Stages

Freud made the startling assertion that the foundation of an individual's personality is laid down by the tender age of 5! To shed light on the crucial early years, he formulated a stage theory of development that emphasized how young children deal with their immature, but powerful, sexual urges (he used the term *sexual* in a general way to refer to many urges for physical pleasure, not just the urge to copulate). According to Freud, these sexual urges shift in focus as children progress from one stage to another. Indeed, the names for the stages (oral, anal, genital, and so on) are based on where children are focusing their erotic energy at the time. Thus, *psychosexual stages* **are developmental periods with a characteristic sexual focus that leave their mark on adult personality.**

Freud theorized that each psychosexual stage has its own unique developmental challenges or tasks, as outlined in **Figure 2.5**. The way these challenges are handled supposedly shapes personality. The notion of *fixation* plays an important role in this process. *Fixation* **is a failure to move forward from one stage to another as expected.** Essentially, the child's development stalls for a while. Fixation is caused by *excessive gratification* of needs at a particular stage or by *excessive frustration* of those needs. Either way, fixations left over from childhood affect adult personality. Generally, fixation leads to an overemphasis on the psychosexual needs that were prominent during the fixated stage. Freud described a series of five psychosexual stages. Let's examine some of the major features of each stage.

FREUD'S STAGES OF PSYCHOSEXUAL DEVELOPMENT			
Stage	Approximate ages	Erotic focus	Key tasks and experiences
Oral	0–1	Mouth (sucking, biting)	Weaning (from breast or bottle)
Anal	2–3	Anus (expelling or retaining feces)	Toilet training
Phallic	4–5	Genitals (masturbating)	Identifying with adult role models; coping with Oedipal crisis
Latency	6–12	None (sexually repressed)	Expanding social contacts
Genital	Puberty onward	Genitals (being sexually intimate)	Establishing intimate relationships; contributing to society through working

Figure 2.5

Freud's stages of psychosexual development. Freud theorized that people evolve through the series of psychosexual stages summarized here. The manner in which certain key tasks and experiences are handled during each stage is thought to leave a lasting imprint on one's adult personality.

According to Freudian theory, a child's feeding experiences are crucial to later development. Fixation at the oral stage could lead to an overemphasis on, for example, smoking or eating in adulthood.

Oral stage. During this stage, which usually encompasses the first year of life, the main source of erotic stimulation is the mouth (in biting, sucking, chewing, and so on). How caregivers handle the child's feeding experiences is supposed to be crucial to subsequent development. Freud attributed considerable importance to the manner in which the child is weaned from the breast or the bottle. According to Freud, fixation at the oral stage could form the basis for obsessive eating or smoking (among many other things) later in life.

Anal stage. In their second year, children supposedly get their erotic pleasure from their bowel movements, through either the expulsion or retention of feces. The crucial event at this time is toilet training, which represents society's first systematic effort to regulate the child's biological urges. Severely punitive toilet training is thought to lead to a variety of possible outcomes. For example, excessive punishment might produce a latent feeling of hostility toward the "trainer," who is usually the mother. This hostility might generalize to women in general. Another possibility is that heavy reliance on punitive measures might lead to an association between genital concerns and the anxiety that the punishment arouses. This genital anxiety from severe toilet training could evolve into anxiety about sexual activities later in life.

Phallic stage. Around age 4, the genitals become the focus for the child's erotic energy, largely through self-stimulation. During this pivotal stage, the *Oedipal complex* emerges. Little boys develop an erotically tinged preference for their mother. They also feel hostility toward their father, whom they view as a competitor for mom's affection. Little girls develop a special attachment to their father. At about the same time, they learn that their genitals are very different from those of little boys, and they supposedly develop *penis envy*. According to Freud, girls feel hostile toward their mother because they blame her for their anatomical "deficiency." To summarize, in **the *Oedipal complex* children manifest erotically tinged desires for their other-sex parent, accompanied by feelings of hostility toward their same-sex parent.** The name for this syndrome was taken from the Greek myth of Oedipus, who was separated from his parents at birth. Not knowing the identity of his real parents, he inadvertently killed his father and married his mother.

According to Freud, the way parents and children deal with the sexual and aggressive conflicts inherent in the Oedipal complex is of paramount importance. The child has to resolve the dilemma by giving up the sexual longings for the other-sex parent and the hostility toward the same-sex parent. Healthy psychosexual development is supposed to hinge on the resolution of the Oedipal conflict. Why? Because continued hostile relations with the same-sex parent may prevent the child from identifying adequately with that parent. Without such identification, Freudian theory predicts that many aspects of the child's development won't progress as they should.

Latency and genital stages. Freud believed that from age 6 through puberty, the child's sexuality is suppressed—it becomes "latent." Important events during this *latency stage* center on expanding social contacts beyond the family. With the advent of puberty, the child evolves into the *genital stage*. Sexual urges reappear and focus on the genitals once again. At this point the sexual energy is typically channeled toward peers of the other sex, rather than toward oneself, as in the phallic stage.

In arguing that the early years shape personality, Freud did not mean that personality development comes to an abrupt halt in middle childhood. However, he did believe that the foundation for one's adult personality is solidly entrenched by this time. He maintained that future developments are rooted in early, formative experiences and that significant conflicts in later years are replays of crises from childhood.

In fact, Freud believed that unconscious sexual conflicts rooted in childhood experiences cause most personality disturbances. His steadfast belief in the psychosexual origins of psychological disorders eventually led to bitter theoretical disputes with two of his most brilliant colleagues: Carl Jung and Alfred Adler. They both argued that Freud overemphasized sexuality. Freud summarily rejected their ideas, and the other two theorists felt compelled to go their own ways, developing their own psychodynamic theories of personality.

Jung's Analytical Psychology

Swiss psychiatrist Carl Jung called his new approach *analytical psychology* to differentiate it from Freud's psychoanalytic theory. Like Freud, Jung (1921, 1933) emphasized the unconscious determinants of personality. However, he proposed that the unconscious consists of two layers. The first layer, called the *personal unconscious*, is essentially the same as Freud's version of the unconscious. The personal unconscious houses material from one's life that is not within one's conscious awareness because it has been repressed or forgotten. In addition, Jung theorized the existence of a deeper layer he called the collective unconscious. **The *collective unconscious* is a storehouse of latent memory traces inherited from people's ancestral past that is shared with the entire human race.**

Jung called these ancestral memories *archetypes*. They are not memories of actual, personal experiences. Instead, *archetypes* **are emotionally charged images and thought forms that have universal meaning.** These archetypal images and ideas show up frequently in dreams and are often manifested in a culture's use of symbols in art, literature, and religion. Jung felt that an understanding of archetypal symbols helped him make sense of his patients' dreams.

Adler's Individual Psychology

Alfred Adler was a charter member of Freud's inner circle—the Vienna Psychoanalytic Society. However, he soon began to develop his own theory of personality, which he christened *individual psychology*. Adler (1917, 1927) argued that the foremost human drive is not sexuality, but a *striving for superiority*. He viewed such striving as a universal drive to adapt, improve oneself, and master life's challenges. He noted that young children understandably feel weak and helpless in comparison to more competent older children and adults. These early inferiority feelings supposedly motivate individuals to acquire new skills and develop new talents.

Adler asserted that everyone has to work to overcome some feelings of inferiority. *Compensation* **involves efforts to overcome imagined or real inferiorities by developing one's abilities.** Adler believed that compensation is entirely normal. However, in some people inferiority feelings can become excessive, resulting in what is widely known today as an *inferiority complex*—exaggerated feelings of weakness and inadequacy. Adler thought that either parental pampering or parental neglect (or actual physical handicaps) could cause an inferiority problem. Adler explained personality disturbances by noting that an inferiority complex can distort the normal process of striving for superiority (see **Figure 2.6**). He maintained that some people engage in *overcompensation* in order to conceal, even from themselves, their feelings of inferiority. Instead of working to master life's challenges, people with an inferiority complex work to achieve status, gain power over others, and acquire the trappings of success

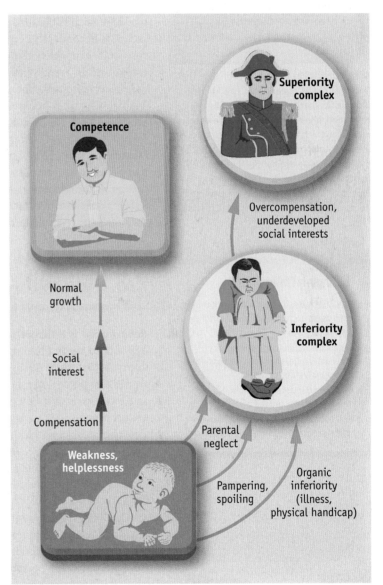

Figure 2.6

Adler's view of personality development. Like Freud, Adler believed that early childhood experiences exert momentous influence over adult personality. However, he focused on children's social interactions rather than on their grappling with their sexuality. According to Adler, the roots of personality disturbances typically lie in excessive parental neglect or pampering, which can lead to overcompensation.

POWOLNY, FRANK/ Album/Newscom

Adler's theory has been used to analyze the tragic life of the legendary actress Marilyn Monroe (Ansbacher, 1970). During her childhood, Monroe suffered from parental neglect that left her with acute feelings of inferiority. Her inferiority feelings led her to overcompensate by flaunting her beauty, marrying celebrities (Joe DiMaggio and Arthur Miller), keeping film crews waiting for hours, and seeking the adoration of her fans.

(fancy clothes, impressive cars, or whatever seems important to them) in an effort to cover up their underlying inferiority complex.

Evaluating Psychodynamic Perspectives

The psychodynamic approach has given us a number of far-reaching theories of personality. These theories yielded some bold new insights for their time. Psychodynamic theory and research have demonstrated that (1) unconscious forces can influence behavior, (2) internal conflict often plays a key role in generating psychological distress, (3) early childhood experiences can exert considerable influence over adult personality, and (4) people do rely on defense mechanisms to reduce their experience of unpleasant emotions (Bornstein, Denckla, & Chung, 2013; Westen, Gabbard, & Ortigo, 2008).

In a more negative vein, psychodynamic formulations have been criticized on several grounds, including the following (Crews, 2006; Kramer, 2006). First, some critics maintain that psychodynamic theories have often been too vague to permit a clear scientific test. Concepts such as the superego, the preconscious, and collective unconscious are difficult to measure. Second, critics note that psychodynamic theories depend too heavily on clinical case studies in which it's much too easy for clinicians to see what they expect to see. Reexaminations of Freud's own clinical work suggest that he frequently distorted his patients' case histories to make them mesh with his theory (Esterson, 2001) and that there were substantial disparities between Freud's writings and his actual therapeutic methods (Lynn & Vaillant, 1998). Third, although studies have supported some insights from psychodynamic theories, the weight of empirical evidence has contradicted many of the central hypotheses (Wolitzky, 2006). For example, we now know that development is a lifelong journey and that Freud overemphasized the importance of the first five years. The Oedipal complex is neither as universal nor as important as Freud believed, and struggles with sexuality are *not* the root cause of most disorders. Fourth, many critics have argued that psychodynamic theories have generally provided a rather male-centered, even sexist, view of personality.

Learning Objectives

- Describe Pavlov's classical conditioning and its contribution to understanding personality.
- Discuss how Skinner's principles of operant conditioning can be applied to personality development.
- Describe Bandura's social cognitive theory and his concept of self-efficacy.
- Evaluate the strengths and weaknesses of behavioral theories of personality.

2.3 Behavioral Perspectives

Behaviorism **is a theoretical orientation based on the premise that scientific psychology should study observable behavior.** Behaviorism has been a major school of thought in psychology since 1913, when John B. Watson published an influential article. In it, he argued that psychology should abandon its earlier focus on the mind and mental processes and focus exclusively on overt behavior. He contended that psychology could not study mental processes in a scientific manner because these processes are private and not accessible to outside observation.

In completely rejecting mental processes as a suitable subject for scientific study, Watson took an extreme position that is no longer dominant among modern behaviorists. Nonetheless, his influence was enormous, as psychology changed its primary focus from the study of the mind to the study of behavior.

The behaviorists have shown little interest in internal personality structures such as Freud's id, ego, and superego because such structures can't be observed. They prefer to think in terms of "response tendencies," which *can* be observed. Thus, most behaviorists view an individual's personality as a *collection of response tendencies that are tied to various stimulus situations*. A specific situation may be associated with a number of response tendencies that vary in strength, depending on an individual's past experience (see **Figure 2.7**).

Despite their lack of interest in personality structure, behaviorists have focused extensively on personality *development*. They explain development the same way they explain everything else—through learning. Specifically, they focus on how children's response tendencies are shaped through classical conditioning, operant conditioning, and observational learning. Let's look at these processes.

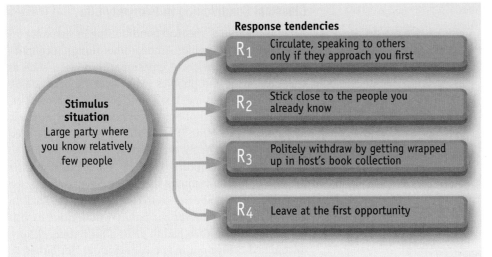

Response tendencies

Stimulus situation
Large party where you know relatively few people

R₁ Circulate, speaking to others only if they approach you first

R₂ Stick close to the people you already know

R₃ Politely withdraw by getting wrapped up in host's book collection

R₄ Leave at the first opportunity

Figure 2.7

A behavioral view of personality. Behaviorists devote little attention to the structure of personality because it is unobservable. But they implicitly view personality as an individual's collection of response tendencies. A possible hierarchy of response tendencies for a specific stimulus situation is shown here. In the behavioral view, personality is made up of countless response hierarchies for various situations.

Pavlov's Classical Conditioning

Do you go weak in the knees when you get a note at work that tells you to go see your boss? Do you get anxious when you're around important people? When you're driving, does your heart skip a beat at the sight of a police car—even when you're driving under the speed limit? If so, you probably acquired these common responses through classical conditioning. *Classical conditioning* **is a type of learning in which a neutral stimulus acquires the capacity to evoke a response that was originally evoked by another stimulus.** This process was first described back in 1903 by Ivan Pavlov, a prominent Russian physiologist who did Nobel Prize–winning research on digestion.

The Conditioned Reflex

Pavlov (1906) was studying digestive processes in dogs when he discovered that the dogs could be trained to salivate in response to the sound of a tone. What was so significant about a dog salivating when a tone was sounded? The key was that the tone started out as a *neutral* stimulus; that is, originally, it did not produce the response of salivation (after all, why should it?). However, Pavlov managed to change that by pairing the tone with a stimulus (meat powder) that did produce the salivation response. Through this process, the tone acquired the capacity to trigger the response. What Pavlov had demonstrated was *how learned reflexes are acquired*.

At this point we need to introduce the special vocabulary of classical conditioning. In Pavlov's experiment the bond between the meat powder and salivation was a natural association that was not created through conditioning. In unconditioned bonds, the *unconditioned stimulus (US)* **is a stimulus that evokes an unconditioned response without previous conditioning.** The *unconditioned response (UR)* **is an unlearned reaction to an unconditioned stimulus that occurs without previous conditioning.**

In contrast, the link between the tone and salivation was established through conditioning. In conditioned bonds, **the** *conditioned stimulus (CS)* **is a previously neutral stimulus that has acquired the capacity to evoke a conditioned response through conditioning.** The *conditioned response (CR)* **is a learned reaction to a conditioned stimulus that occurs because of previous conditioning.** Note that the unconditioned response and conditioned response often involve the same behavior (although there may be subtle differences). In Pavlov's initial demonstration, salivation was an unconditioned response when evoked by the US (meat powder) and a conditioned response when evoked by the CS (the tone). The procedures involved in classical conditioning are outlined in **Figure 2.8**.

Pavlov's discovery came to be called the *conditioned reflex*. Classically conditioned responses are viewed as reflexes because most of them are relatively involuntary. Responses that are a product of classical conditioning are said to be *elicited*. This word is meant to convey the idea that these responses are triggered automatically.

Ivan Pavlov was a Nobel-winning Russian physiologist who conducted pioneering work on what came to be known as classical conditioning.

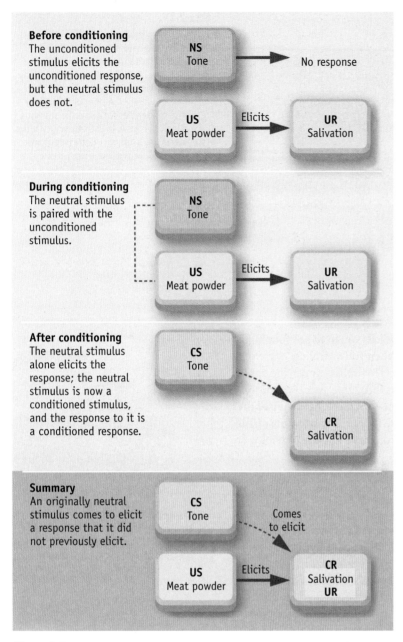

Before conditioning
The unconditioned stimulus elicits the unconditioned response, but the neutral stimulus does not.

NS Tone → No response

US Meat powder — Elicits → UR Salivation

During conditioning
The neutral stimulus is paired with the unconditioned stimulus.

NS Tone

US Meat powder — Elicits → UR Salivation

After conditioning
The neutral stimulus alone elicits the response; the neutral stimulus is now a conditioned stimulus, and the response to it is a conditioned response.

CS Tone

CR Salivation

Summary
An originally neutral stimulus comes to elicit a response that it did not previously elicit.

CS Tone — Comes to elicit

US Meat powder — Elicits → CR Salivation UR

Figure 2.8

The process of classical conditioning. The sequence of events in classical conditioning is outlined here. As we encounter new examples of classical conditioning throughout the book, you will see diagrams like that shown in the fourth panel, which summarizes the process.

Classical Conditioning in Everyday Life

What is the role of classical conditioning in shaping personality in everyday life? Among other things, it contributes to the acquisition of emotional responses, such as anxieties, fears, and phobias (Mineka & Zinbarg, 2006). This is a relatively small but important class of responses, as maladaptive emotional reactions underlie many adjustment problems. For example, one middle-aged woman reported being troubled by a bridge phobia so severe that she couldn't drive on interstate highways because of all the viaducts she would have to cross. She was able to pinpoint the source of her phobia. Back in her childhood, whenever her family would drive to visit her grandmother, they had to cross a little-used, rickety, dilapidated bridge out in the countryside. Her father, in a misguided attempt at humor, made a major production out of these crossings. He would stop short of the bridge and carry on about the enormous danger of the crossing. Obviously, he thought the bridge was safe or he wouldn't have driven across it. However, the naive young girl was terrified by her father's scare tactics, and the bridge became a conditioned stimulus eliciting great fear (see **Figure 2.9**). Unfortunately, the fear spilled over to all bridges, and 40 years later she was still carrying the burden of this phobia. Although a number of processes can cause phobias, it is clear that classical conditioning is responsible for many people's irrational fears.

Classical conditioning also appears to account for more realistic and moderate anxiety responses. For example, imagine a news reporter in a high-pressure job where he consistently gets negative feedback about his work from his bosses. The negative comments from his supervisors function as a US eliciting anxiety. These reprimands are paired with the noise and sight of the newsroom, so that the newsroom becomes a CS triggering anxiety, even when his supervisors are absent (see **Figure 2.10**).

Fortunately, not every frightening experience leaves a conditioned fear in its wake. A variety of factors influence whether a conditioned response is acquired in a particular situation. Furthermore, a newly formed stimulus-response bond does not necessarily last indefinitely. The right circumstances can lead to *extinction*—**the gradual weakening and disappearance of a conditioned response tendency.** What leads to extinction in classical conditioning? It is the consistent presentation of the CS *alone*, without the US. For example, when Pavlov consistently presented *only* the tone to a previously conditioned dog, the tone gradually stopped eliciting the response of salivation. How long it takes to extinguish a conditioned response depends on many factors. Foremost among them is the strength of the conditioned bond when extinction begins. Some conditioned responses extinguish quickly, while others are difficult to weaken.

Skinner's Operant Conditioning

Even Pavlov recognized that classical conditioning is not the only form of conditioning. Classical conditioning best explains reflexive responding controlled by stimuli that *precede* the response. However, both animals and humans make many responses that don't fit this description. Consider the response you are engaging in right now—studying. It is definitely not a reflex (life might be easier if it were). The stimuli that govern it (exams and grades) do not precede it. Instead, your studying response is mainly influenced by events that follow it—specifically, its *consequences*.

This kind of learning is called *operant conditioning*. **Operant conditioning is a form of learning in which voluntary responses come to be controlled by their consequences.** Operant conditioning probably governs a larger share of human behavior than classical conditioning because most human responses are voluntary rather than reflexive. Because they are voluntary, operant responses are said to be *emitted* rather than *elicited*.

The study of operant conditioning was led by B. F. Skinner (1953, 1974, 1990), a Harvard University psychologist who spent most of his career studying simple responses made by laboratory rats and pigeons. The fundamental principle of operant conditioning is uncommonly simple. Skinner demonstrated that *organisms tend to repeat those responses that are followed by favorable consequences, and they tend not to repeat those responses that are followed by neutral or unfavorable consequences.* In Skinner's scheme, favorable, neutral, and unfavorable consequences involve reinforcement, extinction, and punishment, respectively. We'll look at each of these concepts in turn.

The Power of Reinforcement

According to Skinner, reinforcement can occur in two ways, which he called *positive reinforcement* and *negative reinforcement*. **Positive reinforcement occurs when a response is strengthened (increases in frequency) because it is followed by the arrival of a pleasant stimulus.** Positive reinforcement is roughly synonymous with the concept of reward. Notice, however, that reinforcement is defined *after the fact*, in terms of its effect on behavior. Why? Because reinforcement is subjective. Something that serves as a reinforcer for one person may not function as a reinforcer for another. For example, peer approval is a potent reinforcer for most people, but not all.

Positive reinforcement motivates much of everyday behavior. You study hard because good grades are likely to follow as a result. You go to work because this behavior produces paychecks. Perhaps you work extra hard in the hope of winning a promotion or a pay raise. In each of these examples, certain responses occur because they have led to positive outcomes in the past.

Positive reinforcement influences personality development in a straightforward way. Responses followed by pleasant outcomes are strengthened and tend to become habitual patterns of behavior. For example, a youngster might clown around in class and gain appreciative comments and smiles from schoolmates. This social approval will probably reinforce clowning-around behavior (see **Figure 2.11**). If such behavior is reinforced with some regularity, it will gradually become an integral element of the youth's personality. Similarly, whether a youngster develops traits such as independence, assertiveness, or selfishness depends on whether the child is reinforced for such behaviors by parents and by other influential persons.

Negative reinforcement **occurs when a response is strengthened (increases in frequency) because it is followed by the removal of an unpleasant stimulus.** Don't let the word *negative* here confuse you. Negative reinforcement *is* reinforcement. Like positive reinforcement, it strengthens a response. However, this strengthening occurs because the response gets rid of an aversive stimulus. Consider a few examples: You rush home in the winter to get out of the cold. You clean your house to get rid of a mess. Parents give in to their child's begging to halt his whining.

Negative reinforcement plays a major role in the development of avoidance tendencies. As you may have noticed, many people tend to avoid facing up to awkward situations

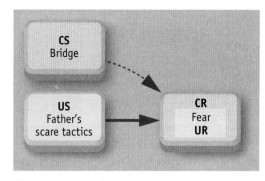

Figure 2.9

Classical conditioning of a phobia. Many emotional responses that would otherwise be puzzling can be explained as a result of classical conditioning. In the case of one woman's bridge phobia, the fear originally elicited by her father's scare tactics became a conditioned response to the stimulus of bridges.

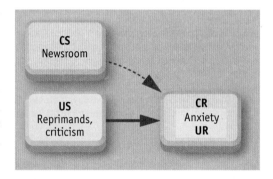

Figure 2.10

Classical conditioning of anxiety. A stimulus (in this case, a newsroom) that is frequently paired with anxiety-arousing events (reprimands and criticism) may come to elicit anxiety by itself, through classical conditioning.

B. F. Skinner was an American psychologist who highlighted the power of reinforcement in his work on operant conditioning.

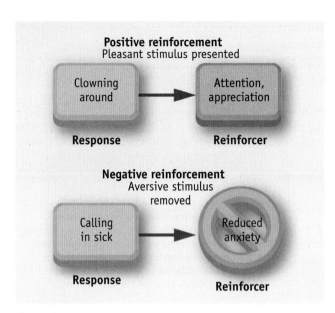

Positive reinforcement
Pleasant stimulus presented

Clowning around → Attention, appreciation

Response   Reinforcer

Negative reinforcement
Aversive stimulus removed

Calling in sick → Reduced anxiety

Response   Reinforcer

Figure 2.11

Positive and negative reinforcement in operant conditioning. Positive reinforcement occurs when a response is followed by a favorable outcome, so that the response is strengthened. In negative reinforcement, the removal (symbolized here by the "No" sign) of an aversive stimulus serves as a reinforcer. Negative reinforcement produces the same result as positive reinforcement: The person's tendency to emit the reinforced response is strengthened (the response becomes more frequent).

Albert Bandura's social cognitive theory emphasizes the importance of observational learning and individuals' perceptions of their self-efficacy.

and sticky personal problems. This personality trait typically develops because avoidance behavior gets rid of anxiety and is therefore negatively reinforced. Recall our imaginary newspaper reporter whose work environment (the newsroom) elicits anxiety (as a result of classical conditioning). He might notice that on days when he calls in sick, his anxiety evaporates, so this response is gradually strengthened—through negative reinforcement (shown in **Figure 2.11**). If his avoidance behavior continues to be successful in reducing his anxiety, it might carry over into other areas of his life and become a central aspect of his personality.

Extinction and Punishment

Like the effects of classical conditioning, the effects of operant conditioning may not last forever. In both types of conditioning, *extinction* refers to the gradual weakening and disappearance of a response. In operant conditioning, extinction begins when a previously reinforced response stops producing positive consequences. As extinction progresses, the response typically becomes less and less frequent and eventually disappears.

Thus, the response tendencies that make up one's personality are not necessarily permanent. For example, the youngster who found that his classmates reinforced clowning around in grade school might find that his attempts at comedy earn nothing but indifferent stares in middle school. This termination of reinforcement would probably lead to the gradual extinction of the clowning-around behavior.

Some responses may be weakened by punishment. In Skinner's scheme, *punishment* **occurs when a response is weakened (decreases in frequency) because it is followed by the arrival of an unpleasant stimulus.** The concept of punishment in operant conditioning confuses many students on two counts. First, it is often mixed up with negative reinforcement because both involve aversive (unpleasant) stimuli. Please note, however, that they are altogether different events with opposite outcomes! In negative reinforcement, a response leads to the *removal* of something aversive, and as a result this response is *strengthened*. In punishment, a response leads to the *arrival* of something aversive, and this response tends to be *weakened*.

The second source of confusion involves the tendency to view punishment only as a disciplinary procedure used by parents, teachers, and other authority figures. In the operant model, punishment occurs whenever a response leads to negative consequences. Defined in this way, the concept goes far beyond actions such as parents spanking children or teachers handing out detentions. For example, if you wear a new outfit and your friends make fun of it and hurt your feelings, your behavior has been punished, and your tendency to wear this clothing will decline. Similarly, if you go to a restaurant and have a horrible meal, in Skinner's terminology your response has led to punishment, and you are unlikely to return.

The impact of punishment on personality development is just the opposite of reinforcement. Generally speaking, those patterns of behavior that lead to punishing (that is, negative) consequences tend to be weakened. For instance, if your impulsive decisions always backfire, your tendency to be impulsive should decline.

Bandura's Social Cognitive Theory

Albert Bandura (1986, 2012b) is one of several theorists who have added a cognitive flavor to behaviorism since the 1960s. Bandura refers to his model as *social cognitive theory*. Bandura agrees with the basic thrust of behaviorism in that he believes that personality is largely shaped through learning. However, he contends that conditioning is not a mechanical process in which people are passive participants. Instead, he maintains that individuals actively seek out and process information about their environment in order to maximize their favorable outcomes.

Observational Learning

Bandura's foremost theoretical contribution has been his description of observational learning. *Observational learning* **occurs when an organism's responding is influenced by the observation of others, who are called models.** Bandura does not view observational learning as entirely separate from classical and operant conditioning. Instead, he asserts that both classical and operant conditioning can take place indirectly when one person observes another's conditioning.

To illustrate, suppose you observe a friend behaving assertively with a car salesman. Let's say that his assertiveness is reinforced by the exceptionally good buy he gets on the car. Your own tendency to behave assertively with salespeople might well be strengthened as a result. Notice that the favorable consequence is experienced by your friend, not you. Your friend's tendency to bargain assertively should be reinforced directly, but your tendency to bargain assertively may also be strengthened indirectly (see **Figure 2.12**).

The theories of Skinner and Pavlov make no allowance for this type of indirect learning. After all, observational learning requires that you pay *attention* to your friend's behavior, that you *understand* its consequences, and that you store this *information* in *memory*. Obviously, attention, understanding, information, and memory involve cognition, which behaviorists used to ignore.

As social cognitive theory has been refined, it has become apparent that some role models tend to be more influential than others (Bandura, 1986). Both children and adults tend to imitate people they like or respect more so than people they don't. People are also especially prone to imitate the behavior of those they consider attractive or powerful (such as celebrities). In addition, imitation is more likely when individuals see similarity between the model and themselves. Finally, as noted before, people are more likely to copy a model if they see the model's behavior leading to positive outcomes.

Self-Efficacy

Bandura (1997) believes that *self-efficacy* is a crucial element of personality. *Self-efficacy* **is one's belief about one's ability to perform behaviors that should lead to expected outcomes.** When a person's self-efficacy is high, he or she feels confident in executing the responses necessary to earn reinforcers. When self-efficacy is low, the individual worries that the necessary responses may be beyond her or his abilities. Perceptions of self-efficacy are subjective and specific to different kinds of tasks. For instance, you might feel extremely confident about your ability to handle difficult social situations but doubtful about your ability to handle academic challenges.

Perceptions of self-efficacy can influence which challenges people tackle and how well they perform. Studies have found that feelings of greater self-efficacy are associated with reduced procrastination (Wäschle et al., 2014), more effort to plan for the future (Azizli et al., 2015), greater success in giving up smoking (Perkins et al., 2012), greater adherence to exercise regimens (Ayotte, Margrett, & Hicks-Patrick, 2010), more-effective weight-loss efforts (Byrne, Barry, & Petry, 2012), greater physical activity among adolescents (Rutkowski & Connelly, 2012), reduced psychological distress among rheumatoid arthritis patients (Benka et al., 2014), better study habits (Prat-Sala & Redford, 2010), higher levels of academic engagement and performance (Ouweneel, Schaufeli, & Le Blanc, 2013), enhanced athletic

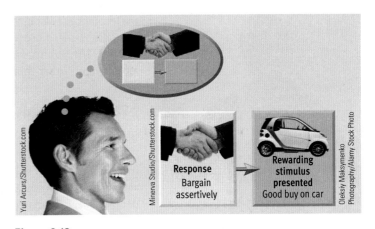

Figure 2.12

Observational learning. In observational learning, an observer attends to and stores a mental representation of a model's behavior (for example, assertive bargaining) and its consequences (such as a good deal on a purchase). According to social cognitive theory, many of our characteristic responses are acquired through observation of others' behavior.

Children acquire a diverse array of responses from their parents thanks to observational learning. Both classical and operant conditioning can occur vicariously through observational learning.

performance (Gilson, Chow, & Feltz, 2012), improved work performance (Tims, Bakker, & Derks, 2014), more proactive customer care by employees in the service industry (Raub & Liao, 2012), and reduced vulnerability to burnout among teachers (Brown, 2012), among many other things.

Evaluating Behavioral Perspectives

Behavioral theories are firmly rooted in empirical research rather than clinical intuition. Pavlov's model has shed light on how conditioning can account for people's sometimes troublesome emotional responses. Skinner's work has demonstrated how personality is shaped by the consequences of behavior. Bandura's social cognitive theory has shown how people's observations mold their characteristic behavior.

Behaviorists, in particular Walter Mischel (1973, 1990), have also provided the most thorough account of why people are only moderately consistent in their behavior. For example, a person who is shy in one context might be quite outgoing in another. Other models of personality largely ignore this inconsistency. The behaviorists have shown that it occurs because people behave in ways they think will lead to reinforcement in the situation at hand. In other words, situational factors are important determinants of behavior. Thus, a major contribution of the behavioral perspective has been its demonstration that personality factors and situational factors jointly and interactively shape behavior (Reis & Holmes, 2012).

Of course, each theoretical approach has its shortcomings, and the behavioral approach is no exception (Pervin & John, 2001). The behaviorists used to be criticized because they neglected cognitive processes. The rise of social cognitive theory blunted this criticism. However, social cognitive theory undermines the foundation on which behaviorism was built—the idea that psychologists should study only observable behavior. Thus, some critics complain that behavioral theories aren't very behavioral anymore. Other critics, especially humanistic theorists who we will discuss next, argue that behaviorists depend too much on animal research and that they are too cavalier in generalizing from the behavior of animals to the behavior of humans.

Daxiao Productions/Shutterstock.com

Perceptions of self-efficacy can influence which challenges people pursue and how well they perform. For example, research has linked self-efficacy to successful efforts to improve eating and exercise habits.

2.4 Humanistic Perspectives

Learning Objectives

- Describe the forces that gave rise to humanism and articulate Rogers's views on the self-concept.
- Describe Maslow's hierarchy of needs and summarize his findings on self-actualizing persons.
- Evaluate the strengths and weaknesses of humanistic theories of personality.

Learn More Online

Personality Theories

C. George Boeree, who teaches personality theory at Shippensburg University, has assembled an online textbook that discusses more than twenty important personality theorists in depth. All the major figures cited in this chapter (except for the behaviorists such as Skinner and Pavlov) receive attention at this valuable site.

Humanistic theory emerged in the 1950s as something of a backlash against the behavioral and psychodynamic theories. The principal charge hurled at these two models was that they were dehumanizing. Freudian theory was criticized for its belief that primitive, animalistic drives dominate behavior. Behaviorism was criticized for its preoccupation with animal research. Critics argued that both schools view people as helpless pawns controlled by their environment and their past, with little capacity for self-direction. Many of these critics blended into a loose alliance that came to be known as "humanism" because of its exclusive interest in human behavior. **Humanism is a theoretical orientation that emphasizes the unique qualities of humans, especially their free will and their potential for personal growth.** Humanistic psychologists do not believe that we can learn anything of significance about the human condition from animal research.

Humanistic theorists, such as Carl Rogers and Abraham Maslow, take an optimistic view of human nature. Humanistic theorists believe that (1) human nature includes an innate drive toward personal growth, (2) individuals have the freedom to chart their courses of action and are not pawns of their environment, and (3) humans are largely conscious and rational beings who are not dominated by unconscious, irrational needs and conflicts. Humanistic theorists also maintain that one's subjective view of the world is more important than objective reality. According to this notion, if you *think* you are homely or bright or sociable, that belief will influence your behavior more than the actual realities of how homely, bright, or sociable you are.

Rogers's Person-Centered Theory

Carl Rogers (1951, 1961) was one of the founders of the human potential movement, which emphasizes personal growth through sensitivity training, encounter groups, and other exercises intended to help people get in touch with their true selves. Like Freud, Rogers based his personality theory on his extensive therapeutic interactions with many clients. Because of his emphasis on a person's subjective point of view, Rogers called his approach a *person-centered theory*.

Carl Rogers was one of the chief architects of humanistic theory in psychology who emphasized the influential role of one's self-concept in guiding behavior.

The Self and Its Development

Rogers viewed personality structure in terms of just one construct. He called this construct the *self*, although it is more widely known today as the *self-concept*. **A *self-concept* is a collection of beliefs about one's own nature, unique qualities, and typical behavior.** Your self-concept is your mental picture of yourself. It is a collection of self-perceptions. For example, a self-concept might include such beliefs as "I am easygoing" or "I am pretty" or "I am hardworking."

Rogers stressed the subjective nature of the self-concept. Your self-concept may not be entirely consistent with your actual experiences. To put it more bluntly, your self-concept may be inaccurate. Most people are prone to distort their experiences to some extent to promote a relatively favorable self-concept. For example, you may believe that you are quite bright academically, but your grade transcript might suggest otherwise. Rogers used the term *incongruence* **to refer to the disparity between one's self-concept and one's actual experience.** In contrast, if a person's self-concept is reasonably accurate, it is said to be *congruent* with reality. Everyone experiences *some* incongruence; the crucial issue is how much (see **Figure 2.13**). Rogers maintained that a great deal of incongruence undermines a person's psychological well-being.

In terms of personality development, Rogers was concerned with how childhood experiences promote congruence or incongruence. According to Rogers, everyone has a strong need for affection, love, and acceptance from others. Early in life, parents provide most of this affection. Rogers maintained that some parents make their affection *conditional*. That is, they make it depend on the child's behaving well and living up to expectations. When parental love seems conditional, children often distort and block out of their memory those experiences that make them feel unworthy of love. At the other end of the spectrum, Rogers asserted that some parents make their affection *unconditional*. Their children have less need to block out unworthy experiences because they have been assured that they are worthy of affection no matter what they do.

Rogers believed that unconditional love from parents fosters congruence and that conditional love fosters incongruence. He further theorized that individuals who grow up believing that affection from others (besides their parents) is conditional go on to distort more and more of their experiences in order to feel worthy of acceptance from a wider and wider array of people, making the incongruence grow.

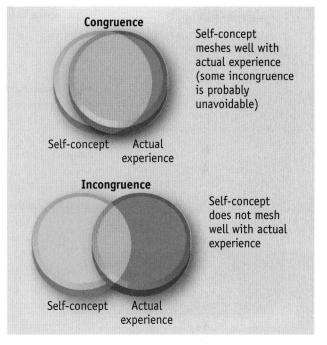

Figure 2.13

Rogers's view of personality structure. In Rogers's model, the self-concept is the only important structural construct. However, Rogers acknowledged that one's self-concept may not jell with the realities of one's actual experience—a condition called incongruence. Different people have varied amounts of incongruence between their self-concept and reality.

Anxiety and Defense

According to Rogers, experiences that threaten people's personal views of themselves are the principal cause of troublesome anxiety. Thus, people with highly incongruent self-concepts are especially likely to be plagued by recurrent anxiety (see **Figure 2.14**). To ward off this anxiety, individuals often behave defensively in an effort to reinterpret their experience so that it appears consistent with their self-concept. Thus, they ignore, deny, and twist reality to protect and perpetuate their self-concept. For example, a young lady

"Just remember, son, it doesn't matter whether you win or lose—unless you want Daddy's love."

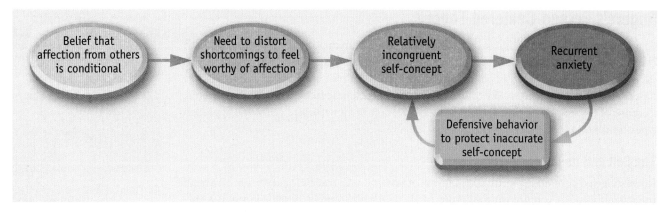

Figure 2.14

Rogers's view of personality development and dynamics. Rogers's theory of development posits that conditional love leads to a need to distort experiences, which fosters an incongruent self-concept. Incongruence makes one prone to recurrent anxiety, which triggers defensive behavior, which fuels more incongruence.

who is selfish but unable to face that reality might attribute friends' comments about her selfishness to their jealousy of her good looks.

Rogers's theory can explain defensive behavior and personality disturbances, but he also emphasized the importance of psychological health. Rogers held that psychological health is rooted in a congruent self-concept. In turn, congruence is rooted in a sense of personal worth, which stems from a childhood saturated with unconditional affection from parents and others. These themes are similar to those emphasized by the other major humanistic theorist, Abraham Maslow.

Maslow's Theory of Self-Actualization

Abraham Maslow (1970) was a prominent humanistic theorist who argued that psychology should take a greater interest in the nature of the healthy personality, instead of dwelling on the causes of disorders. "To oversimplify the matter somewhat," he said, "it is as if Freud supplied to us the sick half of psychology and we must now fill it out with the healthy half" (Maslow, 1968, p. 5). Maslow's key contributions were his analysis of how motives are organized hierarchically and his description of the healthy personality.

Hierarchy of Needs

Maslow proposed that human motives are organized into a *hierarchy of needs*—**a systematic arrangement of needs, according to priority, in which basic needs must be met before less basic needs are aroused.** This hierarchical arrangement is usually portrayed as a pyramid (see **Figure 2.15**). The needs toward the bottom of the pyramid, such as physiological or security needs, are the most basic. Higher levels in the pyramid consist of progressively less basic needs. When a person manages to satisfy a level of needs reasonably well (complete satisfaction is not necessary), *this satisfaction activates needs at the next level.*

Like Rogers, Maslow argued that humans have an innate drive toward personal growth—that is, evolution toward a higher state of being. Thus, he described the needs in the uppermost reaches of his hierarchy as *growth needs*. These include the needs for knowledge, understanding, order, and aesthetic beauty. Foremost among the growth needs is **the *need for self-actualization,* which is the need to fulfill one's potential; it is the highest need in Maslow's motivational hierarchy.** Maslow summarized this concept with a simple statement: "What a man *can* be, he *must* be." According to Maslow, people will be frustrated if they are unable to fully utilize their talents or pursue their true interests. For example,

Abraham Maslow is famous for his description of humans' hierarchy of needs, which is usually portrayed as a pyramid.

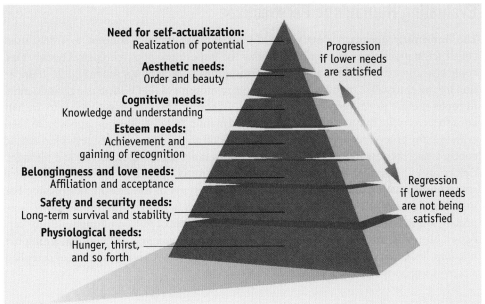

Figure 2.15

Maslow's hierarchy of needs. According to Maslow, human needs are arranged in a hierarchy, and individuals must satisfy their basic needs first, before progressing to higher needs. In the diagram, higher levels in the pyramid represent progressively less basic needs. People move upward in the hierarchy when lower needs are satisfied reasonably well, but they may regress back to lower levels if basic needs cease to be satisfied.

if you have great musical talent but must work as an accountant, or if you have scholarly interests but must work as a sales clerk, your need for self-actualization will be thwarted. Maslow's pyramid has penetrated popular culture to a remarkable degree. For example, Peterson and Park (2010) note that a Google search located more than 766,000 images of Maslow's pyramid on the Internet—a figure that topped the number of images for the *Mona Lisa* and *The Last Supper*!

Maslow's hierarchy of needs has proven to be a challenging subject for empirical study. However, a recent study that measured the satisfaction of various levels of needs in the hierarchy found that the satisfaction of needs at each level was predicted by satisfaction at the level just below it (Taormina & Gao, 2013). This finding provides some support for Maslow's thesis that satisfaction of needs at each level activates needs at the next level.

The Healthy Personality

Because of his interest in self-actualization, Maslow conducted research to analyze the nature of the healthy personality. He called people with exceptionally healthy personalities *self-actualizing persons* because of their commitment to continued personal growth. Maslow identified various traits characteristic of self-actualizing people; many of these traits are listed in **Figure 2.16**. In brief, Maslow found that self-actualizers are accurately tuned in to reality and that they're at peace with themselves. He found that they're open and spontaneous. They also retain a fresh appreciation of the world around them. Socially, they're sensitive to others' needs and enjoy rewarding interpersonal relations. However, they're not dependent on others for approval or uncomfortable with solitude. They thrive on their work, and they enjoy their sense of humor. Maslow also noted that they have "peak experiences" (profound emotional highs) more often than others. Finally, he found that they strike a nice balance between many polarities in personality. For instance, they can be both childlike and mature, both rational and intuitive, both conforming and rebellious.

CHARACTERISTICS OF SELF-ACTUALIZING PEOPLE
• Clear, efficient perception of reality and comfortable relations with it
• Spontaneity, simplicity, and naturalness
• Problem centering (having something outside themselves they "must" do as a mission)
• Detachment and need for privacy
• Autonomy, independence of culture and environment
• Continued freshness of appreciation
• Mystical and peak experiences
• Feelings of kinship and identification with the human race
• Strong friendships, but limited in number
• Democratic character structure
• Ethical discrimination between means and ends, between good and evil
• Philosophical, unhostile sense of humor
• Balance between polarities in personality

Figure 2.16

Characteristics of self-actualizing people. Humanistic theorists emphasize psychological health instead of maladjustment. Maslow's sketch of the self-actualizing person provides a provocative picture of the healthy personality.

Evaluating Humanistic Perspectives

The humanistic approach deserves credit for making the self-concept a widely used construct in psychology and for highlighting the importance of psychological health. One could also argue that the humanists' optimistic, growth-oriented approach laid the foundation for the emergence of the positive psychology movement that is increasingly influential in contemporary psychology (see Chapter 16). Of course, there is a negative side to the balance sheet as well (Burger, 2015). Like psychodynamic theorists, the humanists have been criticized for proposing hypotheses that are difficult to put to a scientific test. Humanistic concepts such as personal growth and self-actualization are difficult to define and measure. Critics also charge that the humanists have been overly optimistic in their assumptions about human nature and unrealistic in their descriptions of the healthy personality. For instance, Maslow's self-actualizing people sound *perfect*. In reality, Maslow had a hard time finding self-actualizing persons. Thus, humanistic portraits of psychological health are perhaps a bit unrealistic. Finally, humanistic theories are based primarily on discerning but uncontrolled observations in clinical settings. Humanistic psychologists have not compiled a convincing body of research to support their ideas.

Learning Objectives

- Outline Eysenck's view of personality and summarize behavioral genetics research on personality.
- Summarize evolutionary research on personality.
- Evaluate the strengths and weaknesses of biological theories of personality.

2.5 Biological Perspectives

Could personality be a matter of genetic inheritance? This possibility was largely ignored for many decades of personality research until Hans Eysenck made a case for genetic influence in the 1960s. In this section, we'll discuss Eysenck's theory and look at more recent behavioral genetics research on the heritability of personality. We'll also examine evolutionary perspectives on personality.

Eysenck's Theory

Hans Eysenck was born in Germany but fled to London during the era of Nazi rule. He went on to become one of Britain's most prominent psychologists. According to Eysenck (1967), personality is largely determined by one's genetic inheritance. How is heredity linked to personality in Eysenck's model? In part, through conditioning concepts borrowed from behavioral theory. Eysenck (1982) theorizes that some people can be conditioned more readily than others because of inherited differences in their physiological functioning (specifically, their level of arousal). These variations in "conditionability" are assumed to influence the personality traits that people acquire through conditioning.

Eysenck views personality structure as a hierarchy of traits. Numerous superficial traits are derived from a smaller number of more basic traits, which are derived from a handful of fundamental higher-order traits. Eysenck has shown a special interest in explaining variations in *extraversion-introversion*. He proposed that introverts are more easily aroused by events, which make them more easily conditioned than extraverts. According to Eysenck, such people acquire more conditioned inhibitions than others. These inhibitions make them more bashful, tentative, and uneasy in social situations, leading them to turn inward.

Recent Research in Behavioral Genetics

Recent twin studies have provided impressive support for Eysenck's hypothesis that personality is largely inherited (South et al., 2015). **In *twin studies* researchers assess hereditary influence by comparing the resemblance of identical twins and fraternal twins on a trait.** The logic underlying this comparison is as follows. *Identical twins* emerge from one egg that splits, so that their genetic makeup is exactly the same (100% overlap). *Fraternal twins* result when two eggs are fertilized simultaneously; their genetic overlap is only 50%. Both types of twins *usually* grow up in the same home, at the same time, exposed to the same relatives, neighbors, peers, teachers, events, and so forth. Thus, both kinds of twins normally develop under similar environmental conditions, but identical twins share more genetic kinship. Hence, if sets of identical twins exhibit more personality resemblance than sets of fraternal twins, this greater similarity is probably attributable to heredity rather than to environment. The results of twin studies can be used to estimate the *heritability* of personality traits and other characteristics. **A *heritability ratio* is an estimate of the proportion of trait variability in a population that is determined by variations in genetic inheritance.** Heritability can be estimated for any trait. For example, the heritability of height is estimated to be around 80% (Johnson, 2010), whereas the heritability of intelligence appears to be about 50%–70% (Petrill, 2005).

The accumulating evidence from twin studies suggests that heredity exerts considerable influence over personality. For instance, in research on the Big Five personality traits, identical twins have been found to be much more similar than fraternal twins on all five traits (Zuckerman, 2013). Especially telling is the finding that this is true even when the identical twins are reared in different homes. The latter finding argues against the possibility that environmental factors (rather than heredity) could be responsible for identical twins' greater personality resemblance. Overall, five decades of research on the determinants of the Big Five traits suggests that the heritability of each trait is in the vicinity of 40%–50% (South et al., 2013). Furthermore, a recent meta-analysis reported that there are no gender differences in the heritability of personality (Vukasović & Bratko, 2015). The same study also concluded that the Big Five traits are all pretty similar in terms of their degree of heritability.

Is personality determined in part by heredity? Twin studies have played a pivotal role in answering this question.

The Evolutionary Approach to Personality

Evolutionary psychologists assert that the patterns of behavior seen in a species are products of evolution in the same way that anatomical characteristics are. *Evolutionary psychology examines behavioral processes in terms of their adaptive value for members of a species over the course of many generations.* The basic premise of evolutionary psychology is that natural selection favors behaviors that enhance organisms' reproductive success—that is, passing on genes to the next generation. Evolutionary theorists assert that personality has a biological basis because natural selection has favored certain personality traits over the course of human history (Figueredo et al., 2009). Thus, evolutionary analyses of personality focus on how various traits—and the ability to recognize these traits in others—may have contributed to reproductive fitness in ancestral human populations.

For example, David Buss (1991, 1995) has argued that the Big Five personality traits stand out as important dimensions of personality across a variety of cultures because those traits have had significant adaptive implications. Buss points out that humans have historically depended heavily on groups, which afford protection from predators or enemies, opportunities for sharing food, and a diverse array of other benefits. In the context of these group interactions, people have had to make difficult but crucial judgments about the characteristics of others, asking such questions as: Who will make a good member of my coalition? Who can I depend on when in need? Who will share their resources? Thus, Buss argues that the Big Five emerge as fundamental dimensions of personality because humans have evolved special sensitivity to variations in the ability to bond with others (extraversion), the willingness to cooperate and collaborate (agreeableness), the tendency to be reliable and ethical (conscientiousness), the capacity to be an innovative problem solver (openness to experience), and the ability to handle stress (low neuroticism). In a nutshell, Buss argues that the Big Five reflect the most salient features of others' adaptive behavior over the course of evolutionary history.

Daniel Nettle (2006) takes this line of thinking one step further. He asserts that the traits themselves (as opposed to the ability to recognize them in others) are products of evolution that were adaptive in ancestral environments. For example, he discusses how extraversion could have promoted mating success, how agreeableness could have fostered the effective building of coalitions, and so forth. In line with this analysis, a handful of studies have found correlations between personality traits and variations in lifetime reproductive

Learn More Online

Great Ideas in Personality
At this site, personality psychologist G. Scott Acton demonstrates that scientific research programs in personality generate broad and compelling ideas about what it is to be a human being. He charts the contours of twelve research perspectives, including behaviorism, behavioral genetics, and sociobiology, and supports them with extensive links to published and online resources associated with each perspective.

success (Berg et al., 2014; Buss & Penke, 2015). The results vary somewhat from one study to the next, but the most consistent findings have been that high extraversion and low neuroticism are associated with higher fertility in modern societies (Jokela, 2012; Jokela et al., 2011).

Evaluating Biological Perspectives

Recent research in behavioral genetics has provided convincing evidence that hereditary factors help shape personality. Evolutionary theorists have developed thought-provoking hypotheses about how natural selection may have sculpted the basic architecture of personality. Nonetheless, we must take note of some weaknesses in biological approaches to personality. Some critics argue that efforts to carve personality into genetic and environmental components are ultimately artificial. The effects of heredity and environment are twisted together in complicated interactions that can't be separated cleanly (Asbury & Plomin, 2014; Rutter, 2012). Other critics note that *hindsight bias—***the common tendency to mold one's interpretation of the past to fit how events actually turned out***—presents thorny problems for evolutionary theorists (Cornell, 1997). Evolutionary theorists' assertion that the Big Five traits had major adaptive implications over the course of human history seems plausible, but what would have happened if other traits, such as dominance or shrewdness, had shown up in the Big Five? With the luxury of hindsight, evolutionary theorists surely could have constructed plausible explanations for how these traits promoted reproductive success in the distant past. Thus, some critics have argued that evolutionary explanations are post hoc, speculative accounts contaminated by hindsight bias.

Learning Objectives

■ Describe narcissism and its effects on behavior.

■ Explain the chief concepts and hypotheses of terror management theory.

2.6 Contemporary Empirical Approaches to Personality

So far, our coverage has been devoted to grand, panoramic theories of personality. In this section we'll examine some contemporary empirical approaches that are narrower in scope. In modern personality research programs, investigators typically attempt to describe and measure an important personality trait, shed light on its development, and ascertain its relationship to other traits and behaviors. To get a sense of this kind of research, we'll take a look at the burgeoning research on *narcissism*. We'll also look at an influential new approach called *terror management theory* that focuses on personality dynamics rather than personality traits.

Renewed Interest in Narcissism

As we noted in Chapter 1, *narcissism* **is a personality trait marked by an inflated sense of importance, a need for attention and admiration, and a sense of entitlement.** The concept of narcissism was originally popularized more than a century ago by pioneering sex researcher Havelock Ellis and by Sigmund Freud. Narcissism was not widely discussed outside of psychoanalytic circles until the 1980s, when some researchers developed scales intended to assess narcissism as a normal personality trait (as opposed to a pathological syndrome). Of these scales, the Narcissistic Personality Inventory (NPI) (Raskin & Hall, 1979, 1981) has become the most widely used measure of narcissism (Tamborski & Brown, 2011); the NPI has been used in hundreds of studies. You can see how you score on a variant of this scale in Exercise 1.1 in the *Personal Explorations Workbook* in the back of this text.

Studies have painted an interesting portrait of those who score high in narcissism. Narcissists have highly positive but easily threatened self-concepts. Above all else, their behavior is driven by a need to maintain their fragile self-esteem. They display a craving for approval and admiration. Hence, they tend to obsess about their looks, are prone to preening, and work overtime to impress people. As you might guess, in this era of social networking via the Internet, those who are high in narcissism tend to post relatively blatant self-promotional content on social media websites (Carpenter, 2012). On Facebook, they do not tend to post more updates than others (Deters, Mehl, & Eid, 2014), but they do post more updates about their personal accomplishments (Marshall, Lefringhausen, & Ferenczi, 2015). Males who are high in narcissism also post more "selfies" than less narcissistic males, although this disparity is not seen in females (Sorokowski et al., 2015).

Research also suggests that narcissists like to purchase products that make them stand out in a crowd; thus, they prefer products that are exclusive, distinctive, and personalized (Lee, Gregg, & Park, 2013). Because they are self-centered, they tend to show relatively little empathy for people in distress (Heppner, Hart, & Sedikides, 2014). In the sexual domain, one study found that narcissism is associated with an elevated likelihood of marital infidelity (McNulty & Widman, 2014). Narcissism is not distributed equally across socioeconomic classes; high narcissism is found more among the upper classes (Piff, 2014).

When they first meet people, narcissists are often perceived as charming, self-assured, and even charismatic. Thus, initially, they tend to be well liked. With repeated exposure, however, their constant need for attention, brazen boasting, and sense of entitlement tend to wear thin. Eventually, they tend to be viewed as arrogant, self-centered, and unlikable (Back, Schmukle, & Egloff, 2010).

Based on a variety of social trends, Jean Twenge and colleagues (2008) suspected that narcissism might be increasing in recent generations. To test this hypothesis they gathered data from eighty-five studies dating back to the 1980s in which American college students had been given the NPI. Their analysis revealed that NPI scores have been rising, going from a mean of about 15.5 in the 1980s to almost 17.5 in 2005–2006. This finding has been replicated and extended in several subsequent studies (Twenge, Gentile, & Campbell, 2015). In a discussion of the possible ramifications of this trend, Twenge and Campbell (2009) have argued that rising narcissism has fueled an obsessive concern in young people about being physically attractive, leading to unhealthy dieting, overuse of cosmetic surgery, and steroid-fueled body building. They also assert that narcissists' "me-first" attitude has led to increased materialism and overconsumption of the earth's resources, contributing to the current environmental crisis and economic meltdown.

In recent years, some theorists have argued that there are two types of narcissism: *grandiose narcissism* and *vulnerable narcissism* (Houlcroft, Bore, & Munro, 2012; Miller et al., 2013). Thus far, we have been discussing grandiose narcissism, which is characterized by arrogance, extraversion, immodesty, and aggressiveness. In contrast, vulnerable narcissism is characterized by hidden feelings of inferiority, introversion, neuroticism, and a need for recognition. To date, the vast majority of research has focused on grandiose narcissism, but recently there has been a surge of interest in the roots and ramifications of vulnerable narcissism (Lamkin et al., 2014). A recent study of gender differences found that males tend to score higher than females when grandiose narcissism is measured, but when the focus is on vulnerable narcissism, no gender disparities are found (Grijalva et al., 2015). Another study found that it is vulnerable narcissists who are most likely to exhibit "narcissistic rage," a syndrome marked by explosive anger and hostility in response to threats to one's sense of self (Krizan & Johar, 2015).

Terror Management Theory

Terror management theory emerged as an influential perspective in the 1990s. Although the theory borrows from Freudian and evolutionary formulations, it provides its own unique analysis of the human condition. Developed by Sheldon Solomon, Jeff Greenberg, and Tom Pyszczynski (1991, 2004), this fresh perspective is currently generating a huge volume of research.

One of the chief goals of terror management theory is to explain why people need self-esteem. Unlike other animals, humans have evolved complex cognitive abilities that permit self-awareness and contemplation of the future. These cognitive capacities make humans keenly aware that life can be snuffed out at any time. The collision between humans' self-preservation instinct and their awareness of the inevitability of death creates the potential for experiencing anxiety, alarm, and terror when people think about their mortality (see **Figure 2.17**).

How do humans deal with this potential for terror? According to terror management theory, "What saves us is culture. Cultures provide ways to view the world—worldviews—that 'solve' the existential crisis engendered by the awareness of death" (Pyszczynski, Solomon, & Greenberg, 2003, p. 16). Cultural worldviews diminish anxiety by providing answers to universal questions such as "Why am I here?" and "What is the meaning of life?" Cultures create stories, traditions, and institutions that give their members a sense of being part of an enduring legacy and thus soothe their fear of death.

Where does self-esteem fit into the picture? Self-esteem is viewed as a sense of personal worth that depends on one's confidence in the validity of one's cultural worldview and the belief that one is living up to the standards prescribed by that worldview. Hence, self-esteem helps protect people from the profound anxiety associated with the awareness that they are transient animals destined to die. In other words, self-esteem serves a *terror management* function (refer to **Figure 2.17**).

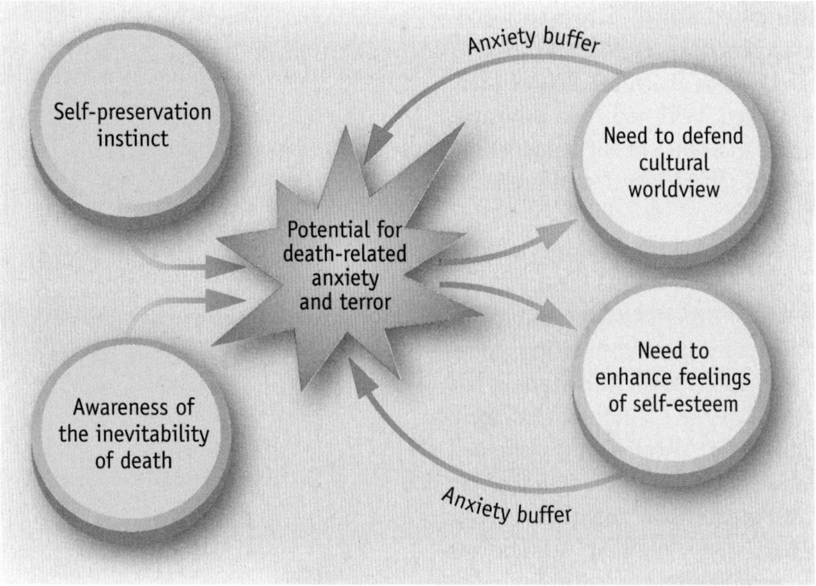

The notion that self-esteem functions as an *anxiety buffer* has been supported by numerous studies (Landau & Sullivan, 2015). In many of these experiments, researchers have manipulated what they call *mortality salience* (the degree to which subjects' mortality is prominent in their minds). Typically, mortality salience is temporarily increased by asking participants to briefly think about their own future death. Consistent with the anxiety buffer hypothesis, reminding people of their mortality leads subjects to engage in a variety of behaviors that are likely to bolster their self-esteem, thus reducing anxiety.

Increasing mortality salience also leads people to work harder at defending their cultural worldview (Landau & Sullivan, 2015). For instance, after

Figure 2.17

Overview of terror management theory. This graphic maps out the relations among the key concepts proposed by terror management theory. The theory asserts that humans' unique awareness of the inevitability of death fosters a need to defend one's cultural worldview and one's self-esteem, which serve to protect one from mortality-related anxiety.

briefly pondering their mortality, research participants (1) hand out harsher penalties to moral transgressors, (2) respond more negatively to people who criticize their country, and (3) show more respect for cultural icons, such as a flag. This need to defend one's cultural worldview may even fuel prejudice and aggression (Greenberg et al., 2009). Reminding subjects of their mortality leads to (1) more negative evaluations of people from different religious or ethnic backgrounds, (2) more stereotypic thinking about minority group members, and (3) more aggressive behavior toward people with opposing political views.

Terror management theory yields novel hypotheses regarding many phenomena (Pyszczynski, Sullivan, & Greenberg, 2015). For instance, Solomon, Greenberg, and Pyszczynski (2004a) explain excessive materialism in terms of the anxiety-buffering function of self-esteem. Specifically, they argue that "conspicuous possession and consumption are thinly veiled efforts to assert that one is special and therefore more than just an animal fated to die and decay" (p. 134). A number of studies have even applied terror management theory to the political process. This research suggests that mortality salience increases subjects' preference for "charismatic" candidates who articulate a grand vision that makes people feel like they are part of an important movement of lasting significance (Cohen & Solomon, 2011). Although terror management theory may seem a tad implausible at first glance, the predictions of the theory have been supported in hundreds of experiments (Burke, Martens, & Faucher, 2010).

Terror management theory has been applied to a remarkably wide range of phenomena. For example, it has even been used to explain conspicuous consumption.

2.7 Culture and Personality

Learning Objectives

- Discuss whether the five-factor model has any relevance in non-Western cultures.
- Explain how researchers have found both cross-cultural similarities and disparities in personality.
- Describe the Spotlight on Research regarding culture and the holier than thou phenomenon.

Are there connections between culture and personality? In recent decades psychology has become more interested in cultural factors, sparking a renaissance in culture-personality research (Church, 2010). This research has sought to determine whether Western personality constructs are relevant to other cultures and whether cultural differences can be seen in the strength of specific personality traits. These studies have found evidence of both continuity and variability across cultures.

For the most part, continuity has been apparent in cross-cultural comparisons of the *trait structure* of personality. When translated versions of the scales that tap the Big Five personality traits have been administered and subjected to analysis in other cultures, the usual five traits have typically surfaced (Chiu, Kim, & Wan, 2008). Admittedly, the results are not *always* consistent with the five-factor model (Kwan & Herrmann, 2015). The most common inconsistency has been that in some cultures a clear factor for the trait of openness to experience does not emerge (Saucier & Srivastava, 2015). Still, overall, the research tentatively suggests that the basic dimensions of personality trait structure may be nearly universal.

On the other hand, some cross-cultural variability is seen when researchers compare the average trait scores of samples from various cultural groups. For example, in a study comparing fifty-one cultures, McCrae et al. (2005) found that Brazilians scored relatively high in neuroticism, Australians in extraversion, Germans in openness to experience, Czechs in agreeableness, and Malaysians in conscientiousness, to give but a handful of examples. These findings should be viewed as very preliminary, as a variety of methodological problems make it difficult to ensure that samples and scores from different cultures are comparable (Church et al., 2011). Nonetheless, the findings suggest that genuine cultural differences may exist in some personality traits. That said, the observed cultural disparities in average trait scores were modest in size.

The availability of the data from the McCrae et al. (2005) study allowed Terracciano et al. (2005) to explore the concept of *national character*. Terracciano and his colleagues asked subjects from many cultures to describe the *typical* member of *their* culture on rating forms guided by the five-factor model. Generally, subjects displayed substantial agreement on these ratings of what was typical for their culture. The averaged ratings, which served as the measures of each culture's national character, were then correlated with the actual mean trait scores for various cultures compiled in the McCrae et al. (2005) study. The results were definitive: The vast majority of the correlations were extremely low and often even negative. In other words, there was little or no relationship between perceptions of national character and actual trait scores for various cultures (see **Figure 2.18**). People's beliefs about national character, which often fuel cultural prejudices, turned out to be profoundly inaccurate stereotypes (McCrae & Terracciano, 2006). Some doubts have been raised about this conclusion (Heine, Buchtel, & Norenzayan, 2008), but a recent replication found once again that perceptions of national character tend to be largely inaccurate (McCrae et al., 2013). Although the replication collected more fine-grained data on beliefs about national character (taking gender and age group into account) than the original study, these beliefs still showed little or no correlation with actual trait scores.

Personality has often been studied in relation to the cultural syndromes of *individualism versus collectivism*, which represent different value systems and worldviews. **Individualism involves putting personal goals ahead of group goals and defining one's identity in terms of personal attributes rather than group memberships.** In contrast, *collectivism* **involves putting group goals ahead of personal goals and defining one's identity in terms of the groups to which one belongs** (such as one's family, tribe, work group, social class, caste, and so on). Generally speaking, North American and Western European cultures tend to be individualistic, whereas Asian, African, and Latin American cultures tend to be collectivistic (Hofstede, 1983, 2001). These discrepant worldviews have a variety of implications for personality. For example, research has shown that individualism and collectivism foster cultural disparities in *self-enhancement*, which involves focusing on positive feedback from others, exaggerating one's strengths, and seeing oneself as above average. These tendencies tend to be pervasive in individualistic cultures, but far less common in collectivist cultures, where the norm is to reflect on one's shortcomings (Heine & Hamamura, 2007). This observation is the springboard for our Spotlight on Research for this chapter.

Figure 2.18

An example of inaccurate perceptions of national character. Terracciano et al. (2005) found that perceptions of national character (the prototype or typical personality for a particular culture) are largely inaccurate. The data shown here for one culture—Canadians—illustrates this inaccuracy. Mean scores on the Big Five traits for a sample of real individuals from Canada are graphed in red. Averaged perceptions of national character for Canadians are graphed in blue. The discrepancy between perception and reality is obvious. Terracciano et al. found similar disparities between views of national character and actual trait scores for a majority of the cultues they studied. (Adapted from McCrae & Terracciano, 2006)

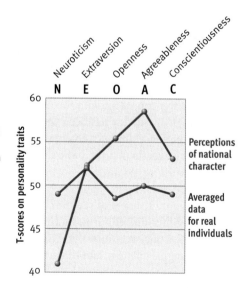

Individualism, Collectivism, and Self-Insight

Source: Balcetis, E., Dunning, D., & Miller, R. L. (2008). Do collectivists know themselves better than individualists? Cross-cultural studies of the holier than thou phenomenon. *Journal of Personality and Social Psychology, 95,* 1252–1267.

The evidence that individualism promotes self-enhancement led Balcetis and her colleagues to speculate that collectivists may tend to have more accurate views of themselves than individualists. Rather than asking subjects to rate themselves in comparison to others, which is highly *subjective*, they decided to ask participants to predict their own *objective* behavior. This focus on predicting actual behavior led them to investigate the "holier than thou phenomenon," which is the tendency for people to claim that they are more likely to engage in socially desirable behaviors than their peers are. For example, people tend to predict that they are more likely than their peers to give to a charity, read to the blind, vote, stop for pedestrians in a crosswalk, and so forth (Epley & Dunning, 2000). In the present research, Balcetis, Dunning, and Miller conducted four studies to explore the hypothesis that participants from collectivist backgrounds would make more accurate predictions about whether they would engage in socially admirable behaviors than those from individualistic backgrounds. We will focus on Study 2 in their series, and then briefly mention the companion studies.

Method

Participants. A total of forty-eight students from Cornell University participated in exchange for $5. The individualistic group consisted of twenty-four students who had two parents born in the United States. The collectivist group consisted of twenty-four Chinese students who had two parents born in China (most of the students were born in China themselves).

Design. Half of the subjects from each cultural group were randomly assigned to a *prediction condition* or an *actual behavior condition*. In the prediction condition, participants made predictions about how much of their $5 payment they might donate to three worthwhile charities if asked, and how much their peers would be likely to donate. In the actual behavior condition, participants were actually asked if they would like to donate a portion of their $5 payment to any of the three worthwhile charities. They were told that they could make their donation anonymously in a blank envelope to minimize the pressure to donate.

Procedure. Because all the subjects were currently living in an individualistic culture (the United States), they were put through a cultural immersion exercise to temporarily bolster the impact of their original cultural mindset. The exercise consisted of a 15–20 minute interview about their cultural background. Near the end of the experimental session, the experimenter handed the participants their $5 payment and either invited them to consider a donation to charity (in the actual behavior condition) or asked them to fill out a sheet asking for predictions about how much they and their peers might donate if asked (in the prediction condition).

Results

The crucial comparison looked at the predictions of donations in relation to the actual donations made by subjects from individualist and collectivist backgrounds. Individualists predicted that they would donate more than twice as much as was actually donated (the gap was $1.74). The collectivists predicted that they would donate *less* than was actually donated, but the gap ($0.69) between their predictions and actual behavior was much smaller than for the individualists.

Discussion

In other studies in the series, individualists overestimated their generosity in redistributing a reward and their willingness to avoid being rude to someone. In contrast, the collectivists were more accurate in making predictions of their actual behavior. Thus, the authors conclude that collectivism may promote greater self-insight than individualism, at least when people contemplate whether they will engage in socially desirable behaviors.

Critical Thinking Questions

1. Psychological research often relies on subjects rating their traits and characteristics. Why do you think the researchers did not want to depend on self-report in this study?
2. Can you think of a behavior for which you would probably fall prey to the holier than thou phenomenon, inaccurately claiming that you are superior to your friends regarding some admirable trait? Describe that behavior.
3. Can you think of some reasons why people from collectivist cultures appear to be less prone to a self-enhancement bias than those from individualistic cultures?

2.8 Assessing Your Personality

Learning Objectives

- Explain the concepts of standardization, test norms, reliability, and validity.
- Discuss the value and the limitations of self-report inventories and projective tests.

Answer the following "true" or "false."

____ **1.** Responses to personality tests are subject to unconscious distortion.

____ **2.** The results of personality tests are often misunderstood.

____ **3.** Personality test scores should be interpreted with caution.

____ **4.** Personality tests may be quite useful in helping people to learn more about themselves.

If you answered "true" to all four questions, you earned a perfect score. Yes, personality tests are subject to distortion. Admittedly, test results are often misunderstood, and they should be interpreted cautiously. In spite of these problems, however, psychological tests can be very useful.

We all engage in efforts to size up our own personality as well as that of others. When you think to yourself that "this salesman is untrustworthy," or when you remark to a friend that "Howard is too timid and submissive," you are making personality assessments. In a sense, then, personality assessment is part of daily life. However, psychological tests provide significantly more systematic assessments than casual observations do.

The value of psychological tests lies in their ability to help people form a realistic picture of their personal qualities. Thus, we have included a variety of personality tests in the *Personal Explorations Workbook* that can be found in the back of this text. We hope that you may gain some insights by responding to these scales. But it's important to understand the logic and limitations of such tests. To facilitate your use of these and other tests, this Application discusses some of the basics of psychological testing.

Key Concepts in Psychological Testing

A *psychological test* **is a standardized measure of a sample of a person's behavior.** Psychological tests are measurement instruments. They are used to measure abilities, aptitudes, and personality traits. Note that your responses to a psychological test represent a *sample* of your behavior. This fact should

alert you to one of the key limitations of psychological tests: It's always possible that a particular behavior sample is not representative of your characteristic behavior. We all have our bad days. A stomachache, a fight with a friend, a problem with your car—all might affect your responses to a particular test on a particular day. Because of the limitations of the sampling process, test scores should always be interpreted *cautiously*. Most psychological tests are sound measurement devices, but test results should not be viewed as the "final word" on one's personality and abilities because of the everpresent sampling problem.

Standardization and Norms

Psychological tests are *standardized* measures of behavior. *Standardization* **refers to the uniform procedures used to administer and score a test.** All subjects get the same instructions, the same questions, the same time limits, and so on, so that their scores can be compared meaningfully. The standardization of a test's scoring system includes the development of test norms. *Test norms* **provide information about where a score on a psychological test ranks in relation to other scores on that test.** Why do we need test norms? Because in psychological testing, everything is relative. Psychological tests tell you how you score *relative to other people*. They tell you, for instance, that you are average in impulsiveness, or slightly above average in assertiveness, or far below average in anxiety. These interpretations are derived from the test norms.

Reliability and Validity

Any kind of measuring device, whether it's a tire gauge, a stopwatch, or a psychological test, should be reasonably consistent (Geisinger, 2013). That is, repeated measurements should yield reasonably similar results. To appreciate the importance of consistency, think about how you would react if a tire pressure gauge gave you several very different readings for the same tire. You would probably conclude that the gauge was broken and toss it into the garbage because you know that consistency in measurement is essential to accuracy.

Reliability **refers to the measurement consistency of a test.** A reliable test is one that yields similar results upon repetition (see **Figure 2.19**). Like most other types of measuring devices, psychological tests are not perfectly reliable. They usually do not yield the exact same score when repeated. A certain amount of inconsistency is unavoidable because human behavior is variable. Personality tests tend to have lower reliability than mental

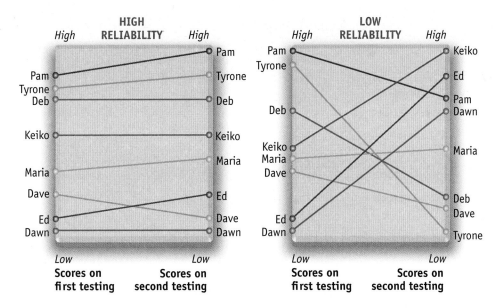

Figure 2.19

Test reliability. Subjects' scores on the first administration of an assertiveness test are represented on the left, and their scores on a second administration (a few weeks later) are represented on the right. If subjects obtain similar scores on both administrations, the test measures assertiveness consistently and is said to have high reliability. If subjects get very different scores when they take the assertiveness test a second time, the test is said to have low reliability.

ability tests because daily fluctuations in mood influence how people respond to such tests.

Even if a test is quite reliable, we still need to be concerned about its validity. *Validity* **refers to the ability of a test to measure what it was designed to measure.** If we develop a new test of assertiveness, we have to provide some evidence that it really measures assertiveness. Validity can be demonstrated in a variety of ways, depending on the nature of the test (Sireci & Sukin, 2013). Most of them involve correlating scores on a test with other measures of the same trait or with related traits.

Self-Report Inventories

The vast majority of personality tests are self-report inventories. *Self-report inventories* **are personality scales that ask individuals to answer a series of questions about their characteristic behavior.** When you respond to a self-report personality scale, you endorse statements as true or false as applied to you, you indicate how often you behave in a particular way, or you rate yourself with respect to certain qualities. For example, on the Minnesota Multiphasic Personality Inventory, people respond "true," "false," or "cannot say" to 567 statements such as the following:

I get a fair deal from most people.
I have the time of my life at parties.
I am glad that I am alive.
Several people are following me everywhere.

The logic underlying this approach is simple: Who knows you better than you do? Who has known you longer? Who has more access to your private feelings? Imperfect though they may be, self-ratings remain the gold standard for personality assessment (Paunonen & Hong, 2015).

The entire range of personality traits can be measured with self-report inventories. Some scales measure just one trait dimension, such as the Sensation Seeking Scale (SSS), which you can take in your *Personal Explorations Workbook* (found

in the back of this book). Others simultaneously assess a multitude of traits. The Sixteen Personality Factor Questionnaire (16PF), developed by Raymond Cattell and his colleagues (Cattell, Eber, & Tatsuoka, 1970), is an example of a multitrait inventory. The 16PF is a 187-item scale that measures 16 basic dimensions of personality, called source traits, which are shown in **Figure 2.20**.

As noted earlier, some theorists believe that only five trait dimensions are required to provide a full description of personality. The five-factor model led to the creation of the NEO Personality Inventory. Developed by Paul Costa and Robert McCrae (1992), the NEO Inventory is designed to measure the Big Five traits: neuroticism, extraversion, openness to experience, agreeableness, and conscientiousness. The NEO Inventory is widely used in research and clinical work, and updated revisions of the scale have been released (Costa & McCrae, 2008).

To appreciate the strengths of self-report inventories, consider how else you might assess your personality. For instance, how assertive are you? You probably have some vague idea, but can you accurately estimate how your assertiveness compares to other people's? To do that, you need a great deal of comparative information about others' usual behavior—information that all of us lack. In contrast, a self-report inventory inquires about your typical behavior in a wide variety of circumstances requiring assertiveness and generates

Learn More Online

Finding Information about Psychological Tests
Maintained by the American Psychological Association, this FAQ site answers all sorts of questions about the availability of various kinds of tests. It explains how to find specific tests, describes how to get information on tests, and outlines information on the proper use of tests.

Figure 2.20

The Sixteen Personality Factor Questionnaire (16PF). Cattell's 16PF is designed to assess sixteen basic dimensions of personality. The pairs of traits listed across from each other in the figure define the sixteen factors measured by this self-report inventory. The profile shown is the average profile seen among a group of airline pilots who took the test.

Source: Adapted from Cattell, R. B. (1973, July). Personality pinned down. *Psychology Today*, 40–46. Reprinted by permission of *Psychology Today* Magazine. Copyright © 1973 Sussex Publishers, Inc.

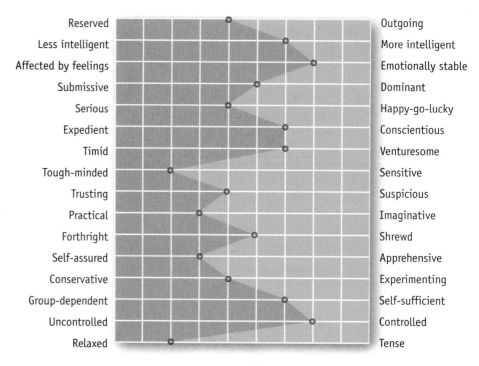

Reserved	Outgoing
Less intelligent	More intelligent
Affected by feelings	Emotionally stable
Submissive	Dominant
Serious	Happy-go-lucky
Expedient	Conscientious
Timid	Venturesome
Tough-minded	Sensitive
Trusting	Suspicious
Practical	Imaginative
Forthright	Shrewd
Self-assured	Apprehensive
Conservative	Experimenting
Group-dependent	Self-sufficient
Uncontrolled	Controlled
Relaxed	Tense

an exact comparison with the typical behavior reported by many other respondents for the same circumstances. Thus, self-report inventories are much more thorough and precise than casual observations.

However, these tests are only as accurate as the information that the test takers provide (Butcher, Bubany, & Mason, 2013). Deliberate deception can be a problem with these tests (Rees & Metcalfe, 2003), and some people are unconsciously influenced by the social desirability or acceptability of the statements (Paunonen & LeBel, 2012). Without realizing it, they tend to mostly endorse statements that make them look good. This problem provides another reason why personality test results should always be regarded as suggestive rather than definitive.

Projective Tests

Projective tests, which all take a rather indirect approach to the assessment of personality, are used extensively in clinical work. *Projective tests* **ask people to respond to vague, ambiguous stimuli in ways that may reveal the respondents' needs, feelings, and personality traits.** The Rorschach test, for example, consists of a series of ten inkblots. Respondents are asked to describe what they see in the blots. In the Thematic Apperception Test (TAT), a series of pictures of simple scenes is presented to subjects who are asked to tell stories about what is happening in them and what the characters are feeling. For instance, one TAT card shows a young boy contemplating a violin resting on a table in front of him.

The assumption underlying projective testing is that ambiguous materials can serve as a blank screen onto which people project their concerns, conflicts, and desires. Thus, a competitive

In taking the Thematic Apperception Test, a respondent is asked to tell stories about scenes such as this one. The themes apparent in each story can be scored to provide insight about the respondent's personality.

person who is shown the TAT card of the boy at the table with the violin might concoct a story about how the boy is contemplating an upcoming musical competition at which he hopes to excel. The same card shown to a person high in impulsiveness might elicit a story about how the boy is planning to sneak out the door to go dirt-bike riding with friends.

Proponents of projective tests assert that the tests have two unique strengths. First, they are not transparent to subjects. That is, the subject doesn't know how the test provides information to the tester. Hence, it may be difficult for people to engage in intentional deception (Weiner, 2013). Second, the indirect approach used in these tests may make them especially sensitive to unconscious, latent features of personality (Meyer & Viglione, 2008).

Unfortunately, the scientific evidence on projective measures is unimpressive (Wood et al., 2010). In a review of the relevant research, Lilienfeld, Wood, and Garb (2000) conclude that projective tests tend to be plagued by inconsistent scoring, low reliability, inadequate test norms, cultural bias, and poor validity estimates. They also assert that, contrary to advocates' claims, projective tests are susceptible to some types of intentional deception (primarily, faking poor mental health).

That said, advocates for one specific approach to scoring the Rorschach recently published a meta-analysis showing that there was good to excellent support for the validity of thirty of sixty-five variables assessed in their system and modest support for another ten of the variables (Mihura et al., 2013). Although these data are more favorable than previous findings, debate continues regarding the overall evidence base for the Rorschach (Mihura et al., 2015; Wood et al., 2015). Another problem related to the Rorschach is that all the inkblots have been posted on Wikipedia, along with common responses and their interpretation. Although psychologists have vigorously protested, copyright for the test has expired and the images are in the public domain. Clinicians are concerned that this exposure of the inkblots could compromise the utility of the test (Hartmann & Hartmann, 2014; Schultz & Brabender, 2013).

In spite of these problems, projective tests such as the Rorschach, continue to be used by many clinicians. Although the vigorously debated scientific status of these techniques is a very real issue, their continued popularity suggests that they yield subjective information that many clinicians find useful (Meyer et al., 2013).

CHAPTER 2 Review

Key Ideas

2.1 The Nature of Personality
- The concept of personality explains the consistency in individuals' behavior over time and situations while also explaining their distinctiveness. Personality traits are dispositions to behave in certain ways.
- Some theorists suggest that the complexity of personality can be reduced to just five basic traits: extraversion, neuroticism, openness to experience, agreeableness, and conscientiousness. The Big Five traits predict important life outcomes, such as grades, occupational attainment, divorce, health, and mortality.

2.2 Psychodynamic Perspectives
- Freud's psychoanalytic theory emphasizes the importance of the unconscious. Freud described personality structure in terms of three components (id, ego, and superego), operating at three levels of awareness, that are involved in conflicts, which generate anxiety.
- According to Freud, people often ward off anxiety and other unpleasant emotions with defense mechanisms, which work through self-deception. Freud believed that the first five years of life are extremely influential in shaping adult personality. He described five psychosexual stages of personality development.
- Jung's analytical psychology stresses the importance of the collective unconscious. Adler's individual psychology emphasizes how people strive for superiority to compensate for feelings of inferiority.

2.3 Behavioral Perspectives
- Behavioral theories view personality as a collection of response tendencies shaped through learning. Pavlov's classical conditioning can explain how people acquire emotional responses.
- Skinner's model of operant conditioning shows how consequences such as reinforcement, extinction, and punishment shape behavior. Bandura's social cognitive theory shows how people can be conditioned through observation. He views self-efficacy as an important trait.

2.4 Humanistic Perspectives
- Humanistic theories take an optimistic view of people's conscious, rational ability to chart their own courses of action. Rogers focused on the self-concept as the critical aspect of personality. He maintained that incongruence between one's self-concept and reality creates anxiety and leads to defensive behavior. Maslow theorized that needs are arranged hierarchically. He asserted that psychological health depends on fulfilling the need for self-actualization.

2.5 Biological Perspectives
- Eysenck argued that inherited individual differences in physiological functioning affect conditioning and thus influence personality. Recent twin studies have provided impressive evidence that genetic factors shape personality.
- Behavioral genetics research suggests that the heritability of each of the Big Five traits is around 50%. Evolutionary psychologists maintain that natural selection has favored the emergence of the Big Five traits as crucial dimensions of personality.

2.6 Contemporary Empirical Approaches to Personality
- Narcissism is a trait marked by an inflated sense of self, a need for attention, and a sense of entitlement. Research suggests that levels of narcissism have been increasing in recent generations. Some theorists distinguish beween grandiose narcisissm and vulnerable narcisissm.
- Terror management theory proposes that self-esteem and faith in a cultural worldview shield people from the profound anxiety associated with their mortality.

2.7 Culture and Personality
- Research suggests that the basic trait structure of personality may be much the same across cultures, as the Big Five traits usually emerge in cross-cultural studies. People's perceptions of national character appear to be remarkably inaccurate. People from collectivist cultures appear to be less prone to self-enhancement than those from individualistic cultures. Hence, collectivists have more accurate views of themselves than individualists.

2.8 Application: Assessing Your Personality
- Psychological tests are standardized measures of behavior. Psychological tests should produce consistent results upon retesting, a quality called reliability. Validity refers to the degree to which a test measures what it was designed to measure.
- Self-report inventories, such as the 16PF and NEO Personality Inventory, ask respondents to describe themselves. These tests can provide a better snapshot of personality than casual observations can.
- Projective tests, such as the Rorschach and TAT, assume that people's responses to ambiguous stimuli reveal something about their personality. Projective tests' reliability and validity appear to be relatively low.

Key Terms

Archetypes p. 37
Behaviorism p. 38
Classical conditioning p. 39
Collective unconscious p. 37
Collectivism p. 54
Compensation p. 37
Conditioned response (CR) p. 39
Conditioned stimulus (CS) p. 39
Conscious p. 32
Defense mechanisms p. 33
Displacement p. 34
Ego p. 31
Evolutionary psychology p. 49
Extinction p. 40
Fixation p. 35
Heritability ratio p. 49
Hierarchy of needs p. 46
Hindsight bias p. 50
Humanism p. 44
Id p. 31
Identification p. 34
Incongruence p. 45
Individualism p. 54
Narcissism p. 51
Need for self-actualization p. 46
Negative reinforcement p. 41
Observational learning p. 43
Oedipal complex p. 36

Operant conditioning p. 41
Personality p. 29
Personality trait p. 29
Positive reinforcement p. 41
Preconscious p. 32
Projection p. 34
Projective tests p. 58
Psychodynamic theories p. 31
Psychological test p. 56
Psychosexual stages p. 35
Punishment p. 42
Rationalization p. 33
Reaction formation p. 34
Regression p. 34
Reliability p. 56
Repression p. 34
Self-concept p. 45
Self-efficacy p. 43
Self-report inventories p. 57
Standardization p. 56
Superego p. 32
Test norms p. 56
Twin studies p. 48
Unconditioned response (UR) p. 39
Unconditioned stimulus (US) p. 39
Unconscious p. 32
Validity p. 57

Key People

Alfred Adler p. 37
Albert Bandura pp. 42–43
Hans Eysenck p. 48
Sigmund Freud pp. 31–36
Carl Jung p. 37

Abraham Maslow pp. 46–47
Ivan Pavlov pp. 39–40
Carl Rogers pp. 45–46
B. F. Skinner pp. 41–42

CHAPTER 2 Practice Test

1. Which of the following is *not* included in McCrae and Costa's five-factor model of personality?
   a. Neuroticism
   b. Extraversion
   c. Conscientiousness
   d. Authoritarianism

2. You're feeling guilty after your third bowl of ice cream. You tell yourself it's all right because yesterday you skipped lunch. Which defense mechanism is at work?
   a. Conceptualization
   b. Displacement
   c. Rationalization
   d. Identification

3. According to Adler, _____ is a universal drive to adapt, improve oneself, and master life's challenges.
   a. compensation
   b. striving for superiority
   c. avoiding inferiority
   d. social interest

4. The strengthening of a response tendency by virtue of the fact that the response leads to the removal of an unpleasant stimulus is
   a. positive reinforcement.
   b. negative reinforcement.
   c. primary reinforcement.
   d. punishment.

5. Self-efficacy is
   a. the ability to fulfill one's potential.
   b. one's belief about one's ability to perform behaviors that should lead to expected outcomes.
   c. a durable disposition to behave in a particular way in a variety of situations.
   d. a collection of beliefs about one's nature, unique qualities, and typical behavior.

6. According to Rogers, disparity between one's self-concept and actual experience is referred to as
   a. a delusional system.
   b. dissonance.
   c. conflict.
   d. incongruence.

7. According to Maslow, which of the following is *not* characteristic of self-actualizing persons?
   a. Accurate perception of reality
   b. Being open and spontaneous
   c. Being uncomfortable with solitude
   d. Sensitivity to others' needs

8. If identical twins exhibit more personality resemblance than fraternal twins, it's probably due mostly to
   a. similar treatment from parents.
   b. their greater genetic overlap.
   c. their strong identification with each other.
   d. others' expectations that they should be similar.

9. Research on terror management theory has shown that increased mortality salience leads to all of the following except
   a. increased striving for self-esteem.
   b. more stereotypic thinking about minorities.
   c. a preference for charismatic political candidates.
   d. reduced respect for cultural icons.

10. In psychological testing, consistency of results over repeated measurements refers to
    a. standardization.
    b. validity.
    c. statistical significance.
    d. reliability.

Answers
1. d Page 30
2. c Pages 33–34
3. b Page 37
4. b Pages 41–42
5. b Page 43
6. d Page 45
7. c Page 47
8. b Pages 48–49
9. d Pages 52–53
10. d Page 56

Personal Explorations Workbook

Go to the *Personal Explorations Workbook* in the back of your textbook for exercises that can enhance your self-understanding in relation to issues raised in this chapter.

Exercise 2.1 *Self-Assessment:* Sensation Seeking Scale

Exercise 2.2 *Self-Reflection:* Who Are You?

Stress and Its Effects

You're in your car headed home from school. Traffic is barely moving. You groan as the radio reports that the traffic jam is only going to get worse. Another motorist's car nearly hits you trying to cut into your lane. Your pulse quickens as you shout insults at the driver, who cannot even hear you. Your stomach knots up as you think about the term paper that you have to work on tonight. If you don't finish the paper soon, you won't be able to find any time to study for your math test, not to mention your biology quiz. Suddenly, you remember that you promised the person you're dating that the two of you would get together tonight. There's no way. Another fight looms on the horizon. You've been trying not to think about the tuition increase the college announced yesterday. You're already in debt. Your parents are bugging you about changing schools, but you don't want to leave your friends. Your heartbeat quickens as you contemplate the debate you'll have to wage with your parents. You feel wired with tension as you realize that the stress in your life never seems to let up.

As this example shows, many circumstances can create stress in people's lives. Stress comes in all sorts of packages: large and small, pretty and ugly, simple and complex. All too often, the package is a surprise. In this chapter, we analyze the nature of stress, outline the major sources of stress, and discuss how people respond to stressful events at several levels. We also discuss some factors that influence one's tolerance for stress. ■

3.1 The Nature of Stress

Over the years, the term *stress* has been used in different ways by different theorists. Some have viewed stress as a *stimulus* event that presents difficult demands (a divorce, for instance), while others have viewed stress as the *response* of physiological arousal elicited by a troublesome event. Many contemporary researchers view stress as neither a stimulus nor a response alone, but rather as a special stimulus-response transaction in which one feels threatened or experiences loss or harm. Hence, we will define *stress* as **any circumstances that threaten or are perceived to threaten one's well-being and thereby tax one's coping abilities.** The threat may be to one's immediate physical safety, long-range security, self-esteem, reputation, or peace of mind. Stress is a complex concept—so let's dig a little deeper.

Stress Is an Everyday Event

Stress is a part of everyday life. Indeed, a recent poll by the American Psychological Association (2015) shows that, for many of us, stress levels are higher than what is considered healthy. Women, younger Americans, and parents appear especially susceptible to symptoms of stress. It seems that being "stressed out" is a hallmark of modern life.

Undeniably, stress is associated with overwhelming, traumatic crises such as bombings, floods, earthquakes, and nuclear accidents. Studies conducted in the aftermath of

BABY BLUES

BABY BLUES © 2009 Baby Blues Partnership Dist. By King Features Syndicate

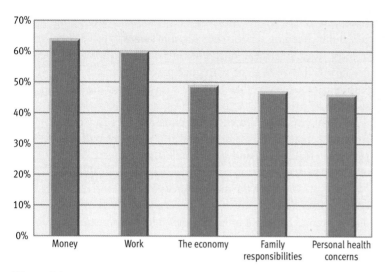

Figure 3.1

Reported causes of stress. In 2014, the American Psychological Association conducted a national survey on stress in America. This graph shows the percentage of respondents reporting various causes of stress. Note that economic issues dominate the top spots.

Source: Adapted from the American Psychological Association (2010). *Stress in America findings.* Washington, DC: APA.

such traumas typically find elevated rates of psychological problems and physical illness in the affected communities and individuals. For example, fifteen months after Hurricane Katrina devastated the New Orleans area, a survey of residents uncovered dramatic increases in physical and mental health problems (Kim et al., 2008). Even six years after Katrina, a study found that heart attack rates were three times higher than prior to the hurricane (Peters et al., 2014). However, these infrequent events represent the tip of the iceberg. Many everyday events, such as waiting in line, having car trouble, misplacing your keys, and staring at bills you can't pay, are also stressful. In fact, according to the national APA (2015) poll, daily problems concerning money, work, and the economy were the top three reported causes of stress (see **Figure 3.1**). Of course, major and minor stressors are not entirely independent. A major stressful event, such as going through a divorce, can trigger a cascade of minor stressors, such as looking for an attorney, taking on new household responsibilities, and so forth.

You might guess that minor stressors would produce minor effects, but that isn't necessarily true. Research shows that routine hassles may have significant negative effects on a person's mental and physical health (Pettit et al., 2010). One study looked at whether everyday hassles and major stressful events, both measured over a period of fifteen years, predicted mortality in an elderly sample of men (Aldwin et al., 2014). Elevated levels of both types of stress were associated with increased mortality, but the impact of hassles was actually somewhat greater than that of major stressors.

Why would minor hassles be related to mental health? Many theorists believe that stressful events can have a *cumulative* or *additive* impact. In other words, stress can add up. Routine stresses at home, school, and work might be fairly benign individually, but collectively they can create great strain. This is especially true for those who ruminate about or become preoccupied with hassles (Wrzus et al., 2015). Whatever the reason, it is evident that daily hassles make important contributions to psychological distress (Charles et al., 2013).

Not everyone becomes overwhelmed by stress from daily hassles. As we'll see in the next section, individual perceptions are important in how people experience stress.

Stress Lies in the Eye of the Beholder

The experience of feeling threatened depends on what events you notice and how you choose to interpret or *appraise* them. Appraisals account for many of the individual differences in reactions to potential stressors. Events that are stressful for one person may be routine for another. For example, many people find flying in an airplane somewhat stressful, but frequent fliers may not even raise an eyebrow. Thus, stress lies in the eye (actually, the mind) of the beholder.

In discussing appraisals of stress, Richard Lazarus and Susan Folkman (1984) distinguish between primary and secondary appraisal (see **Figure 3.2**). *Primary appraisal* is **an initial evaluation of whether an event is (1) irrelevant to you, (2) relevant but not threatening, or (3) stressful.** When you view an event as stressful, you are likely to make a *secondary appraisal,* **which is an evaluation of your coping resources and options for dealing with the stress.** For instance, your primary appraisal would determine whether you saw an upcoming job interview as stressful. Your secondary appraisal would determine how stressful the interview appeared, in light of your ability to deal with the event.

It should come as no surprise that people's appraisals of stressful events alter the impact of the events themselves. Research has demonstrated that negative interpretations of events are often associated with increased distress surrounding these events. In fact, when studying a sample of children after the September 11, 2001, terrorist

Richard Lazarus distinguished between primary and secondary appraisals as the mental processes that influence the impact of stress.

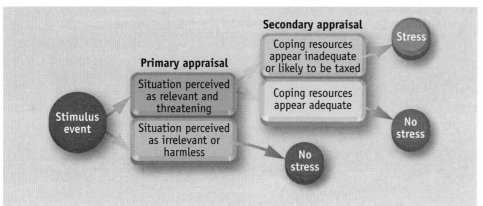

Figure 3.2

Primary and secondary appraisal of stress. *Primary appraisal* is an initial evaluation of whether an event is (1) irrelevant to you, (2) relevant but not threatening, or (3) stressful. When you view an event as stressful, you are likely to make a *secondary appraisal*, which is an evaluation of your coping resources and options for dealing with the stress. (Based on Lazarus & Folkman, 1984)

attacks, Lengua and her colleagues (2006) found that children's appraisals of the event predicted their stress symptoms as much as factors such as their coping styles or pre-attack stress loads.

In addition, appraisals can shift stress from being negative (a threat) to positive (a challenge) (Jamieson, Mendes, & Nock, 2013), and positive reappraisals of stress have both psychological and physiological benefits (Jamieson, Nock, & Mendes, 2012). Crum, Salovey, and Achor (2013) argue that most people assume that stress is generally harmful. They label this attitude a *stress-is-debilitating* mindset. However, they note that some people view stress as an invigorating challenge and opportunity for growth. They call this attitude a *stress-is-enhancing* mindset. They assert that a stress-is-enhancing mindset enhances our capacity to handle stress effectively. Their initial data provides some support for this line of thinking (Crum & Lyddy, 2014).

Stress May Be Embedded in the Environment

Although the perception of stress is a highly personal matter, many kinds of stress come from the environmental circumstances that individuals share with others. *Ambient stress* **consists of chronic environmental conditions that, although not urgent, are negatively valued and place adaptive demands on people.** Such features of urbanization as excessive noise, traffic, and pollution can threaten well-being and leave their mark on mental and physical health (White et al., 2013). In fact, individuals from neighborhoods that include greens spaces and clean air show higher life satisfaction than those from neighborhoods that do not include these characteristics (Diener, Oishi, & Lucas, 2015).

Crowding is an environmental condition that is a major source of stress. Even temporary experiences of crowding, such as being packed into a passenger train for a crowded commute, can be stressful (Evans & Wener, 2007). However, most of the research on crowding has focused on the effects of residential density. Generally, studies suggest an association between high density and increased physiological arousal, psychological distress, and social withdrawal (Evans & Stecker, 2004). Siddiqui and Pandey (2003) found crowding to be one of the most critical stressors for urban residents in northern India, indicating that this is an important issue that goes well beyond Western cities.

Another aspect of the environment that investigators have examined is poverty (Haushofer & Fehr, 2014). Poverty-related stress takes its toll on both mental and physical health (Evans & Kim, 2013). Children from lower-income homes tend to have higher levels of stress hormones than their higher-income peers (Blair et al., 2011). One study showed that younger children (birth to age 9) are especially susceptible to the detrimental effects of poverty (Evans & Cassells, 2014). These researchers argue that, unfortunately, many of the other ambient stress factors (e.g., crowding, noise, pollution) go hand in hand with poverty, thus making the problem worse.

Learn More Online

American Psychological Association: Stress

The American Psychological Association is the largest professional organization for psychologists. This website presents up-to-date coverage of stress research, including recent press releases and psychological research in the news. It also provides a peek into stress research currently being published.

Stress can be caused by environmental circumstances such as pollution, excessive noise, crowding, traffic jams, and urban decay.

Stress Is Influenced by Culture

Although certain types of events (such as the loss of a loved one) are probably viewed as stressful in virtually all human societies, cultures vary greatly in the predominant forms of stress their people experience. Obviously, the challenges of daily living encountered in modern Western cities such as Montreal or Philadelphia are quite different from the day-to-day difficulties experienced in indigenous societies in Africa or South America. Indeed, culture sets the context in which people experience and appraise stress. In some cases, a specific cultural group may be exposed to pervasive stress that is unique to that group. For example, the devastating and widespread destruction from the tsunami in Indonesia and regions of Southeast Asia in 2004 and the ongoing kidnapping and murder of Nigerian citizens by the Boko Haram are extraordinary forms of stress distinctive to these societies. Our discussion of stress largely focuses on the types of stressors confronted in contemporary Western society, but you should be aware that life in Western society is not necessarily representative of life around the world.

Moreover, even within the modern Western world, disparities can be found in the constellation of stressors experienced by specific cultural groups. Social scientists have explored the effects of ethnicity-related sources of stress experienced by African Americans, Hispanic Americans, Asian Americans, and other minority groups, and they have documented that racial discrimination negatively affects the mental health and well-being for targets of racism (Brondolo et al., 2011). Further, exposure to racism through social exclusion, stigmatization, and harassment affects appraisals of stressful events. For instance, researchers have linked mental and physical health disparities in lesbian, gay, and bisexual individuals to stress caused by antigay stigmas (Lick, Durso, & Johnson, 2013).

For immigrants, *acculturation*, **or changing to adapt to a new culture**, is a major source of stress related to reduced well-being. Indeed, acculturation stress is associated with depression and anxiety (Salas-Wright et al., 2015). Studies show that the discrepancy between what individuals *expect* before immigrating and what they actually *experience* once they do immigrate is related to the amount of acculturation stress they report (Negy, Schwartz, & Reig-Ferrer, 2009). The extra layers of stress experienced by minority group members clearly take their toll, but scientists are still exploring the degree to which ethnicity-related stress may have detrimental effects on individuals' mental and physical health.

3.2 Major Sources of Stress

Learning Objectives

- Distinguish between acute, chronic, and anticipatory stressors.
- Describe frustration and internal conflict in relation to stress.
- Summarize the research on life changes and pressure as sources of stress in modern life.

An enormous variety of events can be stressful for one person or another. To achieve a better understanding of stress, theorists have tried to analyze the nature of stressful events and divide them into subtypes. One sensible distinction involves differentiating between *acute stressors* and *chronic stressors*. *Acute stressors* **are threatening events that have a relatively short duration and a clear endpoint.** Examples would include having a difficult encounter with a belligerent drunk, waiting for the results of a medical test, or having your home threatened by severe flooding. *Chronic stressors* **are threatening events that have a relatively long duration and no readily apparent time limit.** Examples would include persistent financial strains produced by unemployment, ongoing pressures from a hostile boss at work, or the demands of caring for a sick family member over a period of years. Of course, this distinction is far from perfect. It is hard to decide where to draw the line between a short-lived versus lengthy stressor, and even brief stressors can have long-lasting effects.

Robert Sapolsky (2004), a leading authority on stress, points out another type of stressor. *Anticipatory stressors* **are upcoming or future events that are perceived to be threatening.** We may worry about breakups that never occur, bad grades we never receive, or hurricanes that never make landfall. The problem with anticipatory stress is that it can affect us psychologically and physically just as strongly as actual stressors do. However we classify them, stressors come from all aspects of our lives. Let's take a look at four major sources of stress. As you read about each of them, you'll surely recognize some familiar adversaries.

Frustration

As psychologists use the term, *frustration* **occurs in any situation in which the pursuit of some goal is thwarted.** In essence, you experience frustration when you want something and you can't have it. Everyone has to deal with frustration virtually every day. Long daily commutes, traffic jams, and annoying drivers, for instance, are routine sources of frustration that can produce negative moods and increase levels of stress. Such frustration often leads to aggression; even artificially induced frustration in a laboratory setting can lead to increased aggression from participants (Verona & Curtin, 2006). Some frustrations, such as *failures* and *losses*, can be sources of significant stress. Fortunately, most frustrations are brief and insignificant. You may be quite upset when you go to the auto shop to pick up your car and find that it hasn't been fixed as promised. However, a few days later you'll probably have your precious car back, and all will be forgotten.

More often than not, frustration appears to be the culprit at work when people feel troubled by ambient stress. Excessive noise, heat, pollution, and crowding are most likely stressful because they frustrate the desire for quiet, a comfortable body temperature, clean air, and adequate privacy. Frustration also plays a role in the aggressive behaviors associated with "road rage" (Carroll & Rothe, 2014). Further, frustration in the workplace often results in job insecurity and burnout (Elst et al., 2012), a specific effect of stress that we will discuss later in this chapter.

Internal Conflict

Like frustration, internal conflict is an unavoidable feature of everyday life. That perplexing question "Should I or shouldn't I?" comes up countless times on a daily basis. *Internal conflict* **occurs when two or more incompatible motivations or behavioral impulses compete for expression.** As we discussed in Chapter 2, Sigmund

Frustration, a common source of stress, occurs in any situation in which the pursuit of some goal is thwarted. Traffic jams, long lines, and technology problems are typical sources of frustration.

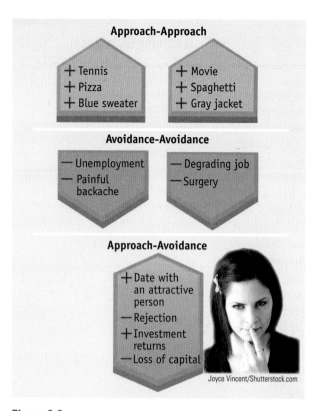

Approach-Approach

+ Tennis
+ Pizza
+ Blue sweater

+ Movie
+ Spaghetti
+ Gray jacket

Avoidance-Avoidance

– Unemployment
– Painful backache

– Degrading job
– Surgery

Approach-Avoidance

+ Date with an attractive person
– Rejection
+ Investment returns
– Loss of capital

Joyce Vincent/Shutterstock.com

Figure 3.3

Types of conflict. Psychologists have identified three basic types of conflict. In approach-approach and avoidance-avoidance conflicts, the person is torn between two goals. In an approach-avoidance conflict, only one goal is under consideration, but it has both positive and negative aspects.

Freud proposed more than a century ago that internal conflicts generate considerable psychological distress. This link between conflict and distress was measured with precision in studies by Laura King and Robert Emmons (1990, 1991). They used an elaborate questionnaire to assess the overall amount of internal conflict experienced by subjects. They found higher levels of conflict to be associated with higher levels of psychological distress.

Conflicts come in three types, which were originally described by Kurt Lewin (1935) and investigated extensively by Neal Miller (1944, 1959). These types are diagrammed in **Figure 3.3**.

In an *approach-approach conflict* **a choice must be made between two attractive goals.** The problem, of course, is that you can choose just one of the two goals. For example, you have a free afternoon; should you play tennis or go to the movies? Among the three kinds of conflict, the approach-approach type tends to be the least stressful. Nonetheless, if you are torn between two appealing college majors or two attractive job offers, you may find the decision-making process quite stressful.

In an *avoidance-avoidance conflict* **a choice must be made between two unattractive goals.** Forced to choose between two repelling alternatives, you are, as the expression goes, "caught between a rock and a hard place." For example, let's say you have painful backaches. Should you submit to surgery that you dread, or should you continue to live with the pain? Obviously, avoidance-avoidance conflicts are most unpleasant and highly stressful.

In an *approach-avoidance conflict* **a choice must be made about whether to pursue a single goal that has both attractive and unattractive aspects.** For instance, imagine that you're offered a job promotion that will mean a large increase in pay. The catch is that you will have to move to a city that you hate. Approach-avoidance conflicts are common, and they can be highly stressful. Any time you have to take a risk to pursue some desirable outcome, you are likely to find yourself in an approach-avoidance conflict. Fortunately, we are equipped to focus on the positive aspects of our decision once it has been made (Brehm, 1956).

Change

Life changes may represent a key type of stress. *Life changes* **are any noticeable alterations in one's living circumstances that require readjustment.** Research on life change began when Thomas Holmes, Richard Rahe, and their colleagues set out to explore the relation between stressful life events and physical illness (Holmes & Rahe, 1967; Rahe & Arthur, 1978). They interviewed thousands of tuberculosis patients to find out what kinds of events preceded the onset of their disease. Surprisingly, the frequently cited events were not uniformly negative. The list included plenty of aversive events, as expected, but patients also mentioned many seemingly positive events, such as getting married, having a baby, or getting promoted.

Why would positive events, such as moving to a nicer home, produce stress? According to Holmes and Rahe, it is because they produce *change*. Based on this analysis, Holmes and Rahe (1967) developed the Social Readjustment Rating Scale (SRRS) to measure life change as a form of stress (see **Figure 3.4**). The SRRS and similar scales have been used in thousands of studies by researchers all over the world. Overall, these studies have shown that people with higher scores on the SRRS tend to be more vulnerable to many kinds of physical illness—and many types of psychological problems as well (Scully, Tosi, & Banning, 2000). However, experts have criticized this research, arguing that the SRRS does not measure *change* exclusively (Anderson, Wethington, & Kamarck, 2011). The life changes listed on the SRRS potentially generate great frustration. Thus, it could be that frustration, rather than change, creates most of the stress assessed by the scale.

SOCIAL READJUSTMENT RATING SCALE

Life event	Mean value	Life event	Mean value
Death of a spouse	100	Son or daughter leaving home	29
Divorce	73	Trouble with in-laws	29
Marital separation	65	Outstanding personal achievement	28
Jail term	63	Spouse begins or stops work	26
Death of close family member	63	Begin or end school	26
Personal injury or illness	53	Change in living conditions	25
Marriage	50	Revision of personal habits	24
Fired at work	47	Trouble with boss	23
Marital reconciliation	45	Change in work hours or conditions	20
Retirement	45	Change in residence	20
Change in health of family member	44	Change in school	20
Pregnancy	40	Change in recreation	19
Sex difficulties	39	Change in church activities	19
Gain of a new family member	39	Change in social activities	18
Business readjustment	39	Loan for lesser purchase (car, TV, etc.)	17
Change in financial state	38	Change in sleeping habits	16
Death of a close friend	37	Change in number of family get-togethers	15
Change to a different line of work	36	Change in eating habits	15
Change in number of arguments with spouse	35	Vacation	13
Mortgage or loan for major purchase	31	Christmas	12
Foreclosure of mortgage or loan	30	Minor violations of the law	11
Change in responsibilities at work	29		

Figure 3.4

Social Readjustment Rating Scale (SRRS). Devised by Holmes and Rahe (1967), this scale is designed to measure the change-related stress in one's life. The numbers on the right are supposed to reflect the average amount of stress (readjustment) produced by each event. Respondents check off the events they experienced recently and add up the associated numbers to arrive at their stress scores.

Source: Adapted from Holmes, T. H., & Rahe, R. (1967). The Social Readjustment Rating Scale. *Journal of Psychosomatic Research, 11*, 213–218. Copyright © 1967 by Elsevier Science Publishing Co. Reprinted by permission.

Should we discard the notion that change is stressful? Not entirely. It is quite plausible that change constitutes a major type of stress in people's lives. However, we have little reason to believe that change is *inherently* or *inevitably stressful*. Some life changes may be quite challenging, whereas others may be quite benign.

Pressure

At one time or another, most of us have probably remarked that we were "under pressure." What does that expression mean? *Pressure* **involves expectations or demands that one behave in a certain way.** Pressure can be divided into two subtypes: the pressure to *perform* and the pressure to *conform*. You are under pressure to perform when you are expected to execute tasks and responsibilities quickly, efficiently, and successfully. For example, salespeople are usually under pressure to move lots of merchandise. Comedians are under pressure to get laughs. Pressures to conform to others' expectations are also common. Suburban homeowners are expected to keep their lawns manicured. College students are expected by their parents to get good grades.

We tend to think of pressure as something imposed from outside forces. However, pressure is often self-imposed. For example, one might sign up for extra classes to get through school quickly or actively seek additional leadership positions to impress one's

Pressure comes in two varieties: pressure to perform and pressure to conform. For example, workers on assembly lines are often expected to maintain high productivity with few mistakes (performance pressure), and suburban homeowners are typically expected to maintain well-groomed exteriors (conformity pressure).

family. People frequently put pressure on themselves to rapidly climb the corporate ladder or to be perfect parents. Even the pressure that modern people put on themselves to maintain a proper work-family balance can serve as a source of stress. Individuals who think that failure to meet exceedingly high standards is unacceptable (that is, negative perfectionists) are more prone to fatigue and depression (Dittner, Rimes, & Thorpe, 2011). In sum, because individuals might create stress by embracing unrealistic expectations for themselves, they might have more control over our stress than they realize.

Learning Objectives

- Summarize research on typical emotional responses (both positive and negative) to stress and discuss some effects of emotional arousal.

- Describe some physiological responses to stress, including the fight-or-flight response and the general adaptation syndrome.

- Describe the two major pathways along which the brain sends signals to the endocrine system.

- Discuss the concept of coping.

3.3 Responding to Stress

The human response to stress is complex and multidimensional. Stress affects people on several levels. Consider again the chapter's opening scenario, in which you're driving home in heavy traffic, thinking about overdue papers, relationship conflicts, tuition increases, and parental pressures. Let's look at some of the reactions we mentioned. When you groan in reaction to the traffic report, you're experiencing an *emotional response* to stress—in this case, annoyance and anger. When your pulse quickens and your stomach knots up, you're exhibiting *physiological responses* to stress. When you shout insults at another driver, your verbal aggression is a *behavioral response* to the stress at hand. Thus, we can analyze people's reactions to stress at three levels: (1) their emotional responses, (2) their physiological responses, and (3) their behavioral responses. **Figure 3.5** depicts these three levels.

Emotional Responses

Emotion is an elusive concept. Psychologists debate how to define emotion, and many conflicting theories purport to explain people's feelings. However, everybody has had extensive personal experience with emotions. Everyone has a good idea of what it means to be anxious, elated, gloomy, jealous, disgusted, excited, guilty, or nervous. So rather than pursue the technical debates about emotion, we'll rely on your familiarity with the concept and simply note that *emotions* **are powerful, largely uncontrollable feelings, accompanied by physiological changes.** When people are under stress, they often react emotionally.

Negative Emotions

More often than not, stress tends to elicit unpleasant emotions. In studying one of the most severe disasters of modern times, the Indian Ocean tsunami of 2004, researchers found

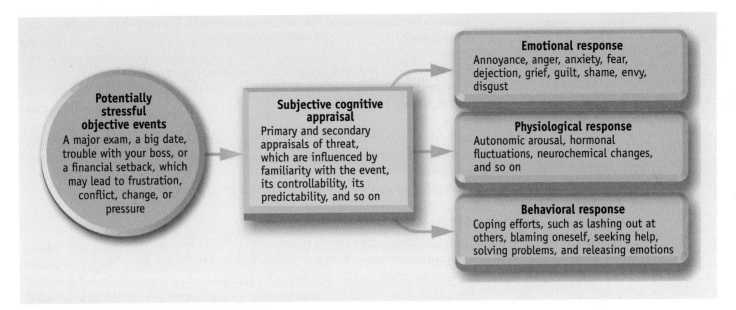

Figure 3.5

The multidimensional response to stress. A potentially stressful event, such as a major exam, will elicit a subjective, cognitive appraisal of how threatening the event is. If the event is viewed with alarm, the stress may trigger emotional, physiological, and behavioral reactions. The human response to stress is multidimensional.

that almost 84% of survivors showed signs of severe emotional distress, including depression and anxiety (Souza et al., 2007). Further, emotional responses to stress seem to transcend time and culture. For instance, a historical researcher, examining texts from 2100–2000 B.C., found evidence that core negative emotional reactions to trauma have not really changed over the millennia (Ben-Ezra, 2004).

There are no simple one-to-one connections between certain *types* of stressful events and particular emotions, but researchers *have* uncovered some strong links between specific *cognitive reactions to stress* and specific emotions. For example, self-blame tends to lead to guilt, helplessness to sadness, and so forth. Although stressful events can evoke many negative emotions, some are certainly more likely than others. According to Richard Lazarus (1993), common negative emotional responses to stress include the following:

The earthquake in Haiti in January 2010 produced overwhelming trauma for many people. Individuals experiencing severe stress have emotional, physiological, and behavioral reactions. Emotional responses to extreme stress (such as grief, anxiety, and fear) appear to transcend culture.

- *Annoyance, anger, and rage.* Stress often produces feelings of anger ranging in intensity from mild annoyance to uncontrollable rage. In fact, in a national survey, respondents reported irritability or anger as the most frequent symptom of their stress (American Psychological Association, 2010). As previously mentioned, frustration is particularly likely to generate anger.

- *Apprehension, anxiety, and fear.* Stress often evokes anxiety and fear. As we saw in Chapter 2, Freudian theory has long recognized the link between conflict and anxiety. However, anxiety can also be elicited by the pressure to perform, the threat of impending frustration, or the uncertainty associated with change.

- *Dejection, sadness, and grief.* Sometimes stress—especially frustration—simply brings one down. Routine setbacks, such as traffic tickets and poor grades, often produce feelings of dejection. More profound setbacks, such as deaths and divorces, typically leave one grief-stricken.

In addition to her work on cognitive appraisals, **Susan Folkman** has extensively investigated positive emotional reactions during periods of stress.

Research has demonstrated that the ability to verbally describe one's emotional experience (as opposed to struggling to put one's emotions into words) is associated with less severe reactions to stress (Kashdan, Barrett, & McKnight, 2015). In addition, people with the skills to recognize and communicate their emotions tend to engage less in maladaptive coping strategies (such as drinking or aggression). In short, negative emotions are to be expected in response to stressful events, and it might be one's ability to talk about them that makes the difference.

In the short term, emotional reactions to stressful events are to be expected. Experiencing such emotions does not mean that you are weak or that you are "losing it." For most people these reactions usually dissipate over time. However, if your reactions to a traumatic event are especially severe, persistent, and debilitating, it may be wise to seek professional help.

Positive Emotions

Investigators have tended to focus heavily on the connection between stress and negative emotions. However, research shows that positive emotions also occur during periods of stress (Folkman, 2008; Moskowitz et al., 2012). This finding may seem counterintuitive, but researchers have found that people experience a diverse array of pleasant emotions even while enduring the most dire of circumstances. Consider, for example, the results of a 5-year study of coping patterns in 253 caregiving partners of men with AIDS (Folkman et al., 1997). Surprisingly, over the course of the study the caregivers reported experiencing positive emotions about as often as they experienced negative ones—except during the time immediately surrounding the death of their partners.

Similar findings have been observed in some other studies of serious stress that made an effort to look for positive emotions. One study examined participants' emotional functioning early in 2001 and then again in the weeks following the 9/11 terrorist attacks in the United States (Fredrickson et al., 2003). Like most U.S. citizens, these individuals reported many negative emotions in the aftermath of 9/11, including anger, sadness, and fear. However, within this "dense cloud of anguish," positive emotions also emerged. For example, people felt gratitude for the safety of their loved ones, many took stock and counted their blessings, and quite a few reported renewed love for their friends and family. Fredrickson et al. (2003) also found that the frequency of pleasant emotions (such as happiness and contentment) correlated positively with a measure of subjects' resilience, whereas unpleasant emotions (such as sadness or irritation) correlated negatively with resilience. Based on their analyses, the researchers concluded that "positive emotions in the aftermath of crises buffer resilient people against depression and fuel thriving" (p. 365). This finding has been replicated in subsequent studies (Gloria & Steinhardt, 2014; Tugade, Devlin, & Fredrickson, 2014).

One particularly interesting finding is that a positive emotional style is associated with enhanced immune functioning and physical health (Moskowitz & Saslow, 2014). These effects probably contribute to the recently discovered association between positive emotions and longevity. Yes, people who report experiencing a high level of positive emotions appear to live longer than others! One recent study exploring this association looked at photos of major league baseball players taken from the Baseball Register for 1952. The intensity of the players' smiles was used as a crude index of their tendency to experience positive emotions, which was then related to how long they lived. As you can see in **Figure 3.6**, greater smile intensity predicted greater longevity (Abel & Kruger, 2010). A more recent study looked at the use of positive words in the autobiographies of eighty-eight well-known deceased psychologists (Pressman & Cohen, 2012). Once again, the results suggested that a positive mentality was associated with greater longevity.

Simply put, positive emotions can contribute to building social, intellectual, and physical resources that can be helpful in dealing with stress and allow one to experience flourishing mental health. In fact, the benefits of positive emotions are so strong that Fredrickson (2006) argues that people should "cultivate positive emotions in themselves and in those around them as means to achieving psychological growth and improved psychological and physical well-being over time" (p. 85). Chapter 16 discusses positive emotions in more detail.

Effects of Emotional Arousal

Emotional responses are a natural and normal part of life. Even unpleasant emotions serve important purposes. Like physical pain, painful emotions can serve as warnings that one needs to take action. However, strong emotional arousal can also hamper efforts to cope with stress.

The well-known problem of *test anxiety* illustrates how emotional arousal can hurt performance. Researchers have found a negative correlation between test-related anxiety and exam performance. That is, students who display high test anxiety tend to score low on exams. Test anxiety can interfere with test taking in several ways, but one critical consideration appears to be the disruption of attention to the test. Many test-anxious students waste too much time worrying about how they're doing and wondering whether others are having similar problems. In addition, there is evidence that test anxiety may deplete one's capacity for self-control, increasing the likelihood of poor performance. In other words, once distracted, test-anxious students might not have the self-control to get themselves back on course (Bertrams et al., 2013).

Although emotional arousal may hurt coping efforts, this isn't *necessarily* the case. The *inverted-U hypothesis* predicts that task performance should improve with increased emotional arousal—up to a point, after which further increases in arousal become disruptive and performance deteriorates. This idea is referred to as the inverted-U hypothesis because plotting performance as a function of arousal results in graphs that approximate an upside-down U (see **Figure 3.7**). In these graphs, the level of arousal at which performance peaks is characterized as the *optimal level of arousal* for a task.

This optimal level of arousal appears to depend in part on the complexity of the task at hand. The conventional wisdom is that *as tasks become more complex, the optimal level of arousal (for peak performance) tends to decrease*. This relationship is depicted in **Figure 3.7**. As you can see, a fairly high level of arousal should be optimal on simple tasks (such as driving 8 hours to help a friend in a crisis). However, performance should peak at a lower level of arousal on complex tasks (such as making a major decision in which you have to weigh many factors).

The research evidence on the inverted-U hypothesis is inconsistent and subject to varied interpretations. The original formulation of this hypothesis was more related to animal learning than to human performance in stressful situations. Hence, it may be risky to generalize this principle to the complexities of everyday coping efforts. However, scientists argue that the theory should be refined rather than discarded. In fact, recent research

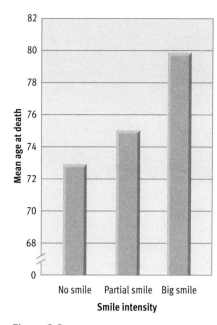

Figure 3.6

Positive emotions and longevity. To look at the relation between positive emotions and longevity, Abel and Kruger (2010) used the intensity of baseball players' smiles in photographs as a rough indicator of their characteristic emotional tone. All the photos in the *Baseball Register* for 1952 were reviewed and classified as showing no smile, a partial smile, or a big smile. Then the age of death was determined for the players (except the forty-six who were still alive in 2009). As you can see, greater smile intensity was associated with living longer.

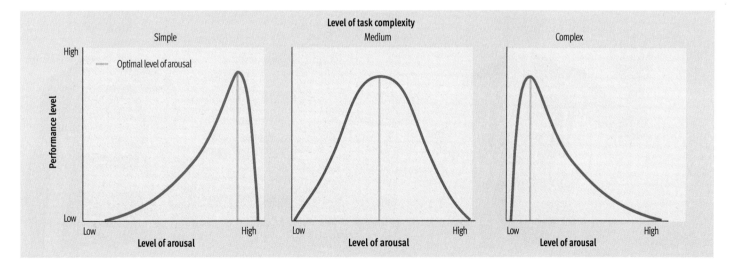

Figure 3.7

Arousal and performance. Graphs of the relationship between emotional arousal and task performance tend to resemble an inverted U, as increased arousal is associated with improved performance up to a point, after which higher arousal leads to poorer performance. The optimal level of arousal for a task depends on the complexity of the task. On complex tasks, a relatively low level of arousal tends to be optimal. On simple tasks, however, performance may peak at a much higher level of arousal.

indicates that this relationship might be due in part to physiological responses to stress (Human et al., 2013). Let's take a closer look at some of these responses.

Physiological Responses

As we have seen, stress frequently elicits strong emotional responses. These responses also bring about important physiological changes. Even in cases of moderate stress, you may notice that your heart has started beating faster, you have begun to breathe harder, and you are perspiring more than usual. How does all this (and much more) happen? Let's see.

The "Fight-or-Flight" Response

Even though he did not refer to it as stress, Walter Cannon (1929, 1932) was a pioneer in stress research with his work on the fight-or-flight response. **The** *fight-or-flight response* **is a physiological reaction to threat that mobilizes an organism for attacking (fight) or fleeing (flight) an enemy.** For instance, you see a threatening figure and your heart rate increases, blood pressure rises, respiration increases, digestion slows—all things that prepare you to act and that are evolutionarily advantageous. These responses occur in the body's autonomic nervous system. **The** *autonomic nervous system (ANS)* **is made up of the nerves that connect to the heart, blood vessels, smooth muscles, and glands.** As its name hints, the autonomic nervous system is somewhat *autonomous*. That is, it controls involuntary, visceral functions that people don't normally think about, such as heart rate, digestion, and perspiration.

The ANS can be broken into two divisions (see **Figure 3.8**). The *parasympathetic division* of the ANS generally conserves bodily resources. For instance, it slows heart rate and promotes digestion to help the body save and store energy. The fight-or-flight response is mediated by the *sympathetic division* of the ANS, which mobilizes bodily resources for emergencies. In one experiment, Cannon studied the fight-or-flight response in cats by confronting them with dogs. Among other things, he noticed an immediate acceleration in the cats' breathing and heart rate and a reduction in digestive processes.

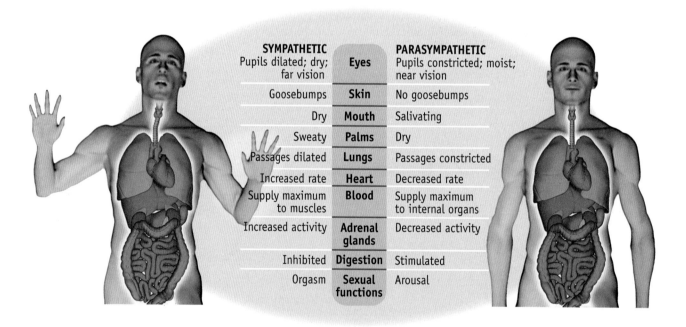

SYMPATHETIC		PARASYMPATHETIC
Pupils dilated; dry; far vision	**Eyes**	Pupils constricted; moist; near vision
Goosebumps	**Skin**	No goosebumps
Dry	**Mouth**	Salivating
Sweaty	**Palms**	Dry
Passages dilated	**Lungs**	Passages constricted
Increased rate	**Heart**	Decreased rate
Supply maximum to muscles	**Blood**	Supply maximum to internal organs
Increased activity	**Adrenal glands**	Decreased activity
Inhibited	**Digestion**	Stimulated
Orgasm	**Sexual functions**	Arousal

Figure 3.8

The autonomic nervous system (ANS). The ANS is composed of the nerves that connect to the heart, blood vessels, smooth muscles, and glands. The ANS is subdivided into the *sympathetic division*, which mobilizes bodily resources in times of need, and the *parasympathetic division*, which conserves bodily resources. Some of the key functions controlled by each division of the ANS are summarized in the center of the diagram.

Shelley Taylor and her colleagues (Taylor & Master, 2011) have questioned whether the fight-or-flight model applies equally well to both males and females. They note that in most species females have more responsibility for the care of young offspring than males do. Using an evolutionary perspective, they argue that this disparity may make fighting and fleeing less adaptive for females, as both responses may endanger offspring and thus reduce the likelihood of an animal passing on its genes. Taylor and colleagues maintain that evolutionary processes have fostered more of a "tend and befriend" response to stress in females. According to this analysis, in reacting to stress females allocate more effort to the care of offspring and to seeking help and support. Consistent with this theory, David and Lyons-Ruth (2005) found gender differences in how infants respond to threat. Specifically, when frightened, female infants showed more approach behaviors toward their mothers than male infants did. Taylor (2011a) speculates that the hormone oxytocin signals the need for affiliation in females in times of social distress, and recent evidence supports this theory (Cardoso et al., 2013). However, even though they hypothesize some gender differences in responses to stress, Taylor and her colleagues are quick to note that the "basic neuroendocrine core of stress responses" is largely the same for males and females.

Our physiological responses to stress are part of the fight-or-flight syndrome seen in many species. In a sense, this automatic reaction is a leftover from our evolutionary past. It is clearly an adaptive response for many animals, as the threat of predators often requires a swift response of fighting or fleeing (picture the gazelle escaping from the lion on the Discovery Channel). Likewise, the fight-or-flight response was probably adaptive among ancestral humans who routinely had to deal with acute stressors involving threats to their physical safety. But in our modern world, the fight-or-flight response may be less adaptive for human functioning than it was thousands of generations ago. Most modern stressors cannot be handled simply through fight or flight. Work pressures, marital problems, and financial difficulties require far more complex responses. Moreover, these chronic (and anticipatory) stressors often continue for lengthy periods of time, so that the fight-or-flight response leaves one in a state of enduring physiological arousal. Concern about the effects of prolonged physical arousal was first voiced by Hans Selye, a Canadian scientist who conducted extensive research on stress.

The General Adaptation Syndrome

The concept of stress was popularized in both scientific and lay circles by Hans Selye (1936, 1956, 1982). Although born in Vienna, Selye spent his entire professional career at McGill University in Montreal, Canada. Beginning in the 1930s, Selye exposed laboratory animals to a diverse array of unpleasant stimuli (heat, cold, pain, mild shock, restraint, and so on). The patterns of physiological arousal he observed in the animals were largely the same, regardless of which unpleasant stimulus elicited them. Thus, Selye concluded that stress reactions are *nonspecific*. In other words, they do not vary according to the specific type of circumstances encountered. Initially, Selye wasn't sure what to call this nonspecific response to a variety of noxious agents. In the 1940s, he decided to call it *stress*, and his influential writings gradually helped make the word part of our everyday vocabulary.

To capture the general pattern all species exhibit when responding to stress, Selye formulated a seminal theory called the general adaptation syndrome (see **Figure 3.9**).

Hans Selye popularized the concept of stress after noting that the patterns of physiological arousal he observed in the animals were largely the same, regardless of which unpleasant stimulus elicited them.

Learn More Online

The American Institute of Stress

The American Institute of Stress is a nonprofit organization established in 1978 at the request of stress pioneer Hans Selye. Its Board of Trustees reads like a who's who of stress research. The resources available online are a bit limited; one has to send for the information packets published by the institute. The site contains an interesting tribute to Selye.

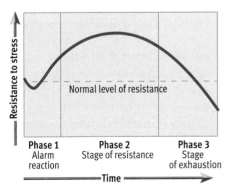

Figure 3.9

The general adaptation syndrome. According to Selye, the physiological response to stress can be broken into three phases. During the first phase, the body mobilizes its resources for resistance after a brief initial shock. In the second phase, resistance levels off and eventually begins to decline. If the third phase of the general adaptation syndrome is reached, resistance is depleted, leading to health problems and exhaustion.

The *general adaptation syndrome* **is a model of the body's stress response, consisting of three stages: alarm, resistance, and exhaustion.** In the first stage of the general adaptation syndrome, an *alarm reaction* occurs when an organism recognizes the existence of a threat (whether a lion, a big deadline, or a mugger). Physiological arousal increases as the body musters its resources to combat the challenge. Selye's alarm reaction is essentially the fight-or-flight response originally described by Cannon.

However, Selye took his investigation of stress a couple of steps further by exposing laboratory animals to *prolonged stress*, similar to the chronic stress often endured by humans. If stress continues, the organism may progress to the second phase of the general adaptation syndrome, called the *stage of resistance*. During this phase, physiological changes stabilize as coping efforts get under way. Typically, physiological arousal continues to be higher than normal, although it may level off somewhat as the organism becomes accustomed to the threat.

If the stress continues over a substantial period of time, the organism may enter the third stage, called the *stage of exhaustion*. According to Selye, the body's resources for fighting stress are limited. If the stress cannot be overcome, the body's resources may be depleted, and physiological arousal will decrease. Eventually, the individual may collapse from exhaustion. During this phase, the organism's resistance declines. This reduced resistance may lead to what Selye called "diseases of adaptation," such as cardiovascular disease or high blood pressure.

Selye's theory and research forged a link between stress and physical illness. He showed how prolonged physiological arousal that is meant to be adaptive could lead to diseases. His theory has been criticized because it ignores individual differences in the appraisal of stress, and his belief that stress reactions are nonspecific remains the subject of debate. However, his model provided guidance for generations of researchers who worked out the details of how stress reverberates throughout the body. Let's look at some of those details.

Brain-Body Pathways

When you experience stress, your brain sends signals to **the** *endocrine system,* **which consists of glands that secrete chemicals called hormones into the bloodstream.** These signals travel through the endocrine system along two major pathways (Dallman, Bhatnagar, & Viau, 2007). The *hypothalamus,* a small structure near the base of the brain, appears to initiate action along both pathways.

The first pathway (shown on the right in **Figure 3.10**) is routed through the autonomic nervous system. The hypothalamus activates the sympathetic division of the ANS. A key part of this activation involves stimulating the central part of the *adrenal glands* (the adrenal medulla) to release large amounts of *catecholamines* into the bloodstream. These hormones radiate throughout the body, producing many important physiological changes. The net result of catecholamine elevation is that the body is mobilized for action. Heart rate and blood flow increase, pumping more blood to the brain and muscles. Respiration and oxygen consumption speed up, facilitating alertness. Digestive processes are inhibited to conserve energy. The pupils of the eyes dilate, increasing visual sensitivity.

The second pathway (shown on the left in **Figure 3.10**) involves more direct communication between the brain and the endocrine system. The hypothalamus sends signals to the so-called master gland of the endocrine system, the *pituitary gland*. The pituitary secretes a hormone (ACTH) that stimulates the outer part of the adrenal glands (the adrenal cortex) to release another important set of hormones—*corticosteroids*. These hormones play an important role in the response to stress (Lucassen et al., 2014). They stimulate the release of chemicals that help increase your energy and help inhibit tissue

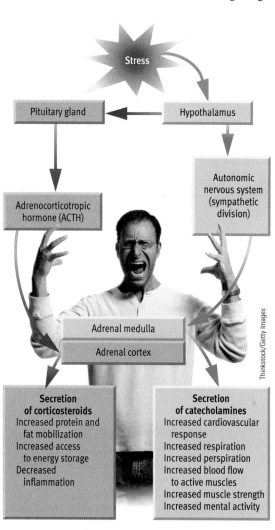

Figure 3.10

Brain-body pathways in stress. In times of stress, the brain sends signals along two pathways. The pathway through the autonomic nervous system (shown in blue on the right) controls the release of catecholamine hormones that help mobilize the body for action. The pathway through the pituitary gland and the endocrine system (shown in brown on the left) controls the release of corticosteroid hormones that increase energy and ward off tissue inflammation.

inflammation in case of injury. *Cortisol* is a type of corticosteroid that is often used as a physiological indicator of stress in humans. In fact, many of the studies discussed in this chapter used cortisol as a measure of subjects' response to stress.

Stress can also produce other physiological changes that we are just beginning to understand. The most critical changes occur in the immune system. Your immune system provides you with resistance to infections. However, evidence indicates that chronic stress can suppress certain aspects of the multifaceted immune response, reducing its overall effectiveness in repelling invasions by infectious agents. The exact mechanisms underlying immune suppression are complicated, but it appears likely that both sets of stress hormones (catecholamines and corticosteroids) contribute. Paradoxically, this state of high alert weakens the ability of the immune system to fend off illness over the long run. Contemporary research implicates stress-induced *chronic inflammation*, a risk factor for disease, as an indicator of an immune system that is chronically activated (Fagundes & Way, 2014). **Figure 3.11** shows common physical conditions associated with chronic inflammation.

In addition, researchers are finding that stress can interfere with *neurogenesis*—**the formation of new neurons,** in the brain (Maher et al., 2014). Specifically, scientists have recently discovered that the adult brain is capable of neurogenesis, primarily in key areas in the hippocampus (Cameron & Glover, 2015). Evidence suggests that suppressed neurogenesis may be a key cause of depression (Anacker, 2014). Thus, the capacity of stress to hinder neurogenesis may have important ramifications. This is currently the subject of intense research.

In sum, it is becoming clear that physiological responses to stress extend into every corner of the body. Moreover, some of these responses may persist long after a stressful event has ended. As you will see, these physiological reactions can have an impact on both mental and physical health.

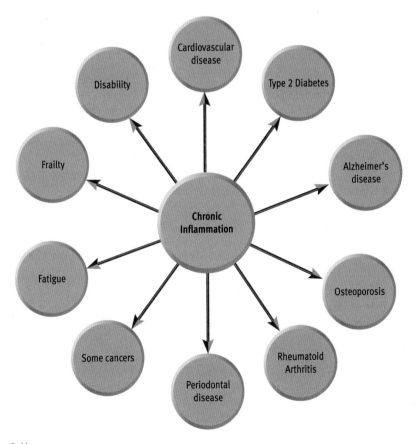

Figure 3.11

Physical conditions linked to chronic inflammation. Contemporary research suggests that chronic inflammation might be the key to the link between stress and physical illness. This figure shows common physical conditions associated with chronic inflammation.

Source: Fagundes, C. P., & Way, B. (2014). Early-life stress and adult inflammation. *Current Directions in Psychological Science, 23*(4), 277–283.

Why Zebras Don't Get Ulcers: The Acclaimed Guide to Stress, Stress-Related Diseases, and Coping

by Robert M. Sapolsky (W. H. Freeman, 2004)

This book provides a superb, wide-ranging discussion of the nature and effects of stress. The author is a neuroscientist at Stanford University whose research focuses on such issues as the relationship between stress and the cellular and molecular events underlying neural decay in the hippocampal area of the brain. That is not the type of résumé you would normally associate with lively, witty discourse, but the book is written with flair and humor. Sapolsky's basic thesis is that the physiological response to stress is a remnant of evolution that is no longer adaptive for the majority of stressful situations that humans face. He outlines in detail how neuroendocrine responses to stress can cause or worsen a host of physical and psychological afflictions, including cardiovascular disease, ulcers, colitis, diarrhea, infectious diseases, and depression.

Sapolsky does an excellent job of making complicated research understandable. Although opinionated, his overviews of research are scientifically sound and thoroughly documented in notes at the back of the book. This is not a coping manual, yet it is probably the most insightful and interesting dissection of the stress response available today and is highly worthwhile reading.

Behavioral Responses

Although people respond to stress at several levels, their behavior is a crucial dimension of these reactions. Emotional and physiological responses to stress—which are often undesirable—tend to be largely automatic. However, dealing effectively with stress at the behavioral level may shut down these potentially harmful emotional and physiological reactions.

Most behavioral responses to stress involve coping. *Coping* **refers to active efforts to master, reduce, or tolerate the demands created by stress.** Notice that this definition is neutral as to whether coping efforts are healthy or maladaptive. The popular use of the term often implies that coping is inherently healthy. In reality, coping responses may be either healthy or unhealthy. For example, if you were flunking a history course at midterm, you might cope with this stress by (1) increasing your study efforts, (2) seeking help from a tutor, (3) blaming your professor for your poor grade, or (4) giving up on the class. Clearly, the first two coping responses would more likely lead to a positive outcome than the second two would.

Because of the complexity and importance of coping processes, we devote all of the next chapter to ways of coping. At this point, it is sufficient to note that coping strategies help determine whether stress has any positive or negative effects on an individual. In the next section, you'll see what some of those effects can be as we discuss the possible outcomes of people's struggles with stress.

Learning Objectives

- Explain the influence of stress on task performance, cognitive functioning, and burnout.
- Assess the potential impact of stress on psychological and physical health.
- Articulate two ways in which stress might lead to beneficial effects.

3.4 The Potential Effects of Stress

People struggle with stressors every day, most of which come and go without leaving any enduring imprint. However, when stress is severe or when demands pile up, stress may have long-lasting effects, often called "adaptational outcomes." Although stress can have beneficial effects, research has focused mainly on negative outcomes, so you'll find our coverage slanted in that direction. Note that we will discuss *reducing* the effects of stress (that is, coping) in the next chapter.

Impaired Task Performance

Stress often takes its toll on the ability to perform effectively on a task. For instance, Roy Baumeister (1984) theorized that pressure to perform often makes people self-conscious and that this elevated self-consciousness disrupts their attention, thereby interfering with performance. He theorizes that attention may be distorted in two ways. First, elevated self-consciousness may divert attention from the demands of the task, creating a distraction. Second, on well-learned tasks that should be executed almost automatically, the self-conscious person may focus *too* much attention on the task. Thus, the person thinks too much about what he or she is doing.

Baumeister (1984) found support for his theory in a series of laboratory experiments in which he manipulated the pressure to perform on a simple perceptual-motor task. He found that many people tend to "choke" under pressure (Wallace, Baumeister, & Vohs, 2005). His theory also garnered some support in a pair of studies of the past performance of professional sports teams in championship contests (Baumeister, 1995; Baumeister & Steinhilber, 1984). These findings were particularly impressive in that gifted professional athletes are probably less likely to choke under pressure than virtually any other sample one might assemble.

Recent studies suggest that Baumeister was on the right track in looking to *attention* to explain how stress impairs task performance. According to Beilock (2010), choking under pressure tends to occur when worries about performance distract attention from the task at hand and use up one's limited cognitive resources. Let's consider the cognitive effects of stress more closely.

Disruption of Cognitive Functioning

The effects of stress on task performance often result from disruptions in thinking or in cognitive functioning. Ironically, simply being in a situation where you need cognitive resources the most (studying for a final exam, traveling in a foreign country) can produce this resource-sapping stress effect. In a study of stress and decision making, Keinan (1987) measured participants' attention under stressful and nonstressful conditions and found that stress disrupted two specific aspects of attention. First, it increased participants' tendency to jump to a conclusion too quickly without considering all their options. Second, it increased their tendency to do an unsystematic, poorly organized review of their available options.

In addition, studies suggest that stress can have detrimental effects on certain aspects of memory functioning. In order to affect memory, stressors do not have to be major; even minor day-to-day or anticipatory stressors can have a negative impact. Evidence suggests that stress can reduce the efficiency of the "working memory" system that allows people to juggle information on the spot (Markman, Maddox, & Worthy, 2006). Thus, in stressful situations, people may not be able to process, manipulate, or integrate new information as effectively as they normally would.

Researchers note, however, that stress has a complicated relationship with memory in that short-term, mild-to-moderate stressors can actually enhance memory, especially for emotional aspects of events (Sapolsky, 2004). Further, individuals who experienced early life stress (e.g., abuse) often show improved memory when it come to detecting dangers or threats, prompting researchers to ask if *adapted cognition* is a better term than *impaired cognition* when it comes to stress (Frankenhuis & de Weerth, 2013).

Burnout

Burnout is an overused buzzword that means different things to different people. Nonetheless, a few researchers have described burnout in a systematic way that has facilitated scientific study of the phenomenon (Leiter, Bakker, & Maslach, 2014). **Burnout is a syndrome involving physical and emotional exhaustion, cynicism, and a lowered sense of self-efficacy that is attributable to work-related stress.** Exhaustion, which is central to burnout, includes chronic fatigue, weakness, and low energy. Cynicism is manifested in highly negative attitudes toward oneself, one's work, and life in general. Reduced self-efficacy involves declining feelings of competence at work that give way to feelings of hopelessness and helplessness.

Figure 3.12

The antecedents, components, and consequences of burnout. Christina Maslach and Michael Leiter developed a systematic model of burnout that specifies its antecedents, components, and consequences. The antecedents on the left in the diagram are the stressful features of the work environment that cause burnout. The burnout syndrome itself consists of the three components shown in the center of the diagram. Some of the unfortunate results of burnout are listed on the right. (Based on Maslach & Leiter, 2007)

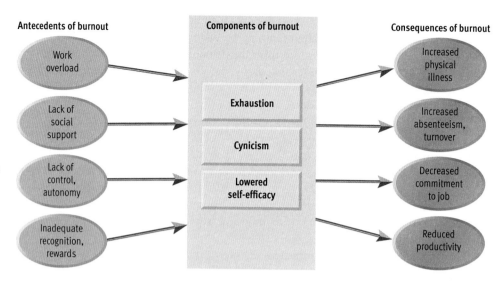

What causes burnout? According to Maslach and Leiter (2007), "Burnout is a cumulative stress reaction to ongoing occupational stressors" (p. 368). The conventional wisdom is that burnout occurs because of some flaw or weakness within the person, but Christina Maslach (2003) asserts that "the research case is much stronger for the contrasting argument that burnout is more a function of the situation than of the person" (p. 191). Factors in the workplace that appear to promote burnout include work overload, interpersonal conflicts at work, lack of control over responsibilities and outcomes, and inadequate recognition for one's work (see **Figure 3.12**). As you might expect, burnout is associated with increased absenteeism and reduced productivity, as well as increased vulnerability to a variety of health problems (Maslach & Leiter, 2007). Decades of research have shown that burnout is found all over the world in a wide variety of cultures (Maslach & Leiter, 2014).

Psychological Problems and Disorders

On the basis of clinical impressions, psychologists have long suspected that chronic stress might contribute to many types of psychological problems. Since the late 1960s, advances in the measurement of stress have allowed researchers to verify these suspicions in empirical studies. In the domain of common psychological problems, studies indicate that stress may contribute to poor academic performance (Hariharan, Swain, & Chivukula, 2014), insomnia and other sleep disturbances (Akerstedt, Kecklund, & Axelsson, 2007), lowered relationship satisfaction (Falconier et al., 2015), sexual difficulties (Slowinski, 2007), and substance abuse (Grunberg, Berger, & Hamilton, 2011). Beyond these everyday problems, research reveals that stress often contributes to the onset of full-fledged psychological disorders, including depression (Gutman & Nemeroff, 2011), schizophrenia (Diwadkar et al., 2014), anxiety disorders (Falsetti & Ballenger, 1998), and eating disorders (Loth et al., 2008).

Some individuals are exposed to extremely stressful, traumatic incidents that can leave a lasting imprint on their psychological functioning. *Posttraumatic stress disorder (PTSD)* **involves enduring psychological disturbance attributed to the experience of a major traumatic event.** Researchers began to appreciate the frequency and severity of posttraumatic stress disorder after the Vietnam War ended in 1975 and a great many psychologically scarred veterans returned home. These veterans displayed a diverse array of psychological problems and symptoms that in many cases lingered much longer than expected. Studies suggest that nearly a half million Vietnam veterans were still suffering from PTSD more than a decade after the end of the war (Schlenger et al., 1992). PTSD did not become an official psychological diagnosis until 1980, and since that time researchers have studied the disorder extensively to better understand the long-term impact of exposure to trauma. Currently, PTSD is being examined in military returnees from the Afghanistan and Iraq wars. Similar to Vietnam veterans, these U.S. troops show elevated rates of PTSD upon returning home, particularly if they experienced extreme combat exposure and involvement in harming civilians or prisoners (Dohrenwend et al., 2013).

Although PTSD is widely associated with the experiences of veterans, it is seen in response to other cases of traumatic stress as well. It is frequently seen after a rape or sexual assault, a serious automobile accident, a robbery or assault, or the witnessing of someone's death. PTSD is also common in the wake of major disasters, such as floods, hurricanes, earthquakes, fires, and so forth. Exposure to traumatic events such as the 9/11 terrorist attacks is also associated with PTSD, even several years later (Neria, DiGrande, & Adams, 2011).

Although PTSD is widely associated with the experiences of veterans, it also common in the wake of major disasters, such as floods, hurricanes, earthquakes, or fires.

Unfortunately, experiencing a traumatic event is not rare. Experts speculate that 50% of us will encounter a traumatic event at some point (Yehuda & Wong, 2007). In one study, 90% of older adults reported experiencing at least one traumatic event over the course of their lifetime (Ogle et al., 2013). Research suggests that approximately 9% of people have suffered from PTSD at some point in their lives, and it is twice as common in women as men (Feeny, Stines, & Foa, 2007). PTSD is seen in children as well as adults, and children's symptoms often show up in their play or drawings (La Greca, 2007). In some instances, PTSD does not surface until many months or years after a person's exposure to severe stress (Holen, 2007).

What are the symptoms of posttraumatic stress disorder? Common symptoms include reexperiencing the traumatic event in the form of nightmares and flashbacks, emotional numbing, alienation, problems in social relations, and elevated arousal, anxiety, and guilt. PTSD is also associated with an elevated risk for substance abuse, depression, and anxiety disorders, as well as a great variety of physical health problems. The frequency and severity of posttraumatic symptoms usually decline gradually over time, but in some cases the symptoms never completely disappear.

Recently, some psychologists have argued that traumatic events don't need to be experienced directly to lead to PTSD symptoms. Exposure can occur indirectly, such as by witnessing the event on television. Some evidence surrounding television exposure to 9/11 and the Iraq war supports this perspective (Silver et al., 2013). In addition, researchers have found that children who have preexisting anxiety before a traumatic event are especially vulnerable to PTSD after media exposure (Weems et al., 2012). Other researchers take exception to this notion of "virtual PTSD" arguing that, because viewing television is a voluntary act under one's control, it can't really lead to PTSD. In fact, in 2013, the American Psychiatric Association mandated that an individual must experience trauma directly and first hand in order to qualify for a diagnosis of PTSD.

Although PTSD is not unusual in the wake of traumatic events, the vast majority of people do *not* develop PTSD. Thus, a current focus of research is to determine what factors make certain people more (or less) susceptible than others to the ravages of severe stress. According to McKeever and Huff (2003), this vulnerability probably depends on complex interactions among a number of biological and environmental factors. One key predictor that emerged in a review of the relevant research is the *intensity of one's reaction at the time of the traumatic event* (Ozer et al., 2003). Individuals who have especially intense emotional reactions during or immediately after the traumatic event go on to show elevated vulnerability to PTSD. Vulnerability seems to be greatest among people whose reactions are so intense that they report *dissociative experiences* (such as a sense that things are not real, that time is stretching out, or that one is watching oneself in a movie).

Physical Illness

Stress can also have an impact on one's physical health (Erickson et al., 2014). The idea that stress can contribute to physical ailments is not new. Evidence that stress can cause physical illness began to accumulate back in the 1930s. By the 1950s, the concept of psychosomatic

David Baldwin's Trauma Information Pages
This site has long been recognized as the premier repository for web-based and other resources relating to emotional trauma, traumatic stress, and posttraumatic stress disorder. David Baldwin has assembled more than 1000 links to information about these issues.

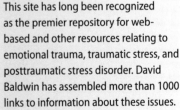

disease was widely accepted. *Psychosomatic diseases* **were defined as genuine physical ailments thought to be caused in part by stress and other psychological factors.** The classic psychosomatic illnesses were high blood pressure, peptic ulcers, asthma, skin disorders such as eczema and hives, and migraine and tension headaches. Please note, these diseases were not regarded as *imagined* physical ailments. The term *psychosomatic* has often been misused to refer to physical ailments that are "all in one's head," but that is an entirely different syndrome (see Chapter 14). Rather, psychosomatic diseases were viewed as authentic organic maladies that were heavily stress related.

Since the 1970s, the concept of psychosomatic disease has gradually fallen into disuse because research has shown that stress can contribute to the development of a diverse array of other diseases previously believed to be purely physiological in origin. Although there is room for debate on some specific diseases, stress may influence the onset and course of heart disease, stroke, gastrointestinal disorders, tuberculosis, multiple sclerosis, arthritis, diabetes, leukemia, cancer, various types of infectious disease, and probably many other types of illnesses. Thus, it has become apparent that there is nothing unique about the psychosomatic disease that requires a special category. Chapter 5 goes into greater detail, but suffice it to say that modern evidence continues to demonstrate that the classic psychosomatic diseases are influenced by stress, but so are numerous other diseases. In fact, scientists are now exploring how stress impacts the body at the DNA level to understand its link to physical illness (Lu, 2014).

Of course, some of the physical effects of stress might be exacerbated by the risky behaviors people are more likely to engage in when stressed. For example, stress appears to be related to increases in substance abuse, including problematic drinking and cigarette smoking. Obviously, these behaviors come with their own health hazards. Add stress to the mix and the person becomes even more vulnerable to disease and illness.

Positive Effects

The effects of stress are not entirely negative. Recent years have brought increased interest in positive aspects of the stress process, including favorable outcomes that follow in the wake of stress. To some extent, the new focus on the possible benefits of stress reflects a new emphasis on *positive psychology*. Some influential theorists have argued that the field of psychology has historically devoted too much attention to pathology, weakness, damage, and how to heal suffering (Seligman, 2003). The positive psychology movement seeks to shift the field's focus away from negative experiences. This movement is so relevant that we devote all of Chapter 16 to it. For now, know that advocates of positive psychology argue for increased research on well-being, contentment, hope, courage, perseverance, nurturance, tolerance, and other human strengths and virtues. One of these strengths is resilience in the face of stress. The beneficial effects of stress may prove more difficult to pinpoint than the harmful effects because they may be subtler. However, there appear to be at least two ways in which stress can have positive effects.

First, stress can promote positive psychological change, or what Tedeschi and Calhoun (1996) call *posttraumatic growth*. Experiences of posttraumatic growth are now well documented, and it appears that this phenomenon is evident in people facing a variety of stressful circumstances, including bereavement, cancer, sexual assault, and combat (Calhoun & Tedeschi, 2013; Tedeschi & Calhoun, 2004). Stressful events sometimes force people to develop new skills, reevaluate priorities, learn new insights, and acquire new strengths. In other words, the adaptation process initiated by stress may lead to personal changes for the better.

Second, today's stress can inoculate and psychologically prepare individuals so that they are less affected by tomorrow's stress. Some studies suggest that exposure to stress can increase stress tolerance—so long as the stress isn't overwhelming. Further, dealing with some adversity provides an opportunity to develop coping skills that can decrease distress when new stressors arise. That is, it can build "mental toughness" (Seery, 2011). One recent study that measured participants' exposure to thirty-seven major negative events found a curvilinear relationship between lifetime adversity and mental health (Seery, 2011). High levels of adversity predicted poor mental health, as expected, but people who had faced intermediate levels of adversity were healthier than those who experienced little adversity, suggesting that moderate amounts of stress can foster resilience. A follow-up study found a similar link between the amount of lifetime adversity and subjects' responses to laboratory stressors (Seery et al., 2013). Intermediate levels of adversity were predictive of the greatest resilience.

In light of the negative effects that stress can have, improved stress tolerance is a desirable goal. We'll look next at the factors that influence the ability to tolerate stress.

3.5 Factors Influencing Stress Tolerance

Learning Objectives

- Explain how social support, hardiness, and optimism moderate the impact of stress.
- Describe the Spotlight on Research regarding the stress buffering effects of hugging.

Some people seem to be able to withstand the ravages of stress better than others (Smith et al., 2013). Why? Because a number of *moderator variables* can soften the impact of stress on physical and mental health. To shed light on differences in how well people tolerate stress, we'll look at a number of key moderator variables, including social support, hardiness, and optimism. As you'll see, these factors influence people's emotional, physical, and behavioral responses to stress. These complexities are diagrammed in **Figure 3.13**, which builds on **Figure 3.5** to provide a more complete overview of the factors involved in individual reactions to stress.

Social Support

Friends may be good for your health! This encouraging conclusion emerges from studies on social support as a moderator of stress. *Social support* **refers to various types of aid and succor provided by members of one's social networks.** Over the last two decades, a vast body of literature has found evidence that social support is favorably related to physical health (Loving & Sbarra, 2015). Positive correlations between high social support and greater immune functioning have been observed in quite a number of studies with diverse samples (Kennedy, 2007; Stowell, Robles, & Kane, 2013). Social support has also been associated with lower levels of inflammation, which might help explain its relation to physical health (Fagundes et al., 2011). In contrast, the opposite of social support—loneliness and social isolation—is associated with immune dysregulation and increased inflammation (Jaremka et al., 2013).

The favorable effects of social support are even strong enough to have an impact on participants' life expectancy! A recent meta-analysis of the results of 148 studies reported that solid social support increased people's odds of survival by roughly 50% (Holt-Lunstad, Smith, & Layton, 2010). The strength of the impact of social support on life expectancy was surprising. To put this finding in perspective, the researchers compared the effect size of social support on life expectancy to other established risk factors. They note that the negative effect of inadequate social support is greater than the negative effects of being obese, not exercising, drinking excessively, and smoking (up to fifteen cigarettes per day). Meanwhile, studies have linked social isolation to poor health and increased mortality (Cacioppo & Cacioppo, 2014; Steptoe et al., 2013).

Social support seems to be good medicine for the mind as well as the body, as most studies also find an association between social

Over the last two decades, a vast body of research has found evidence that social support is favorably related to physical and mental health.

Ivonne Wierink/Shutterstock.com

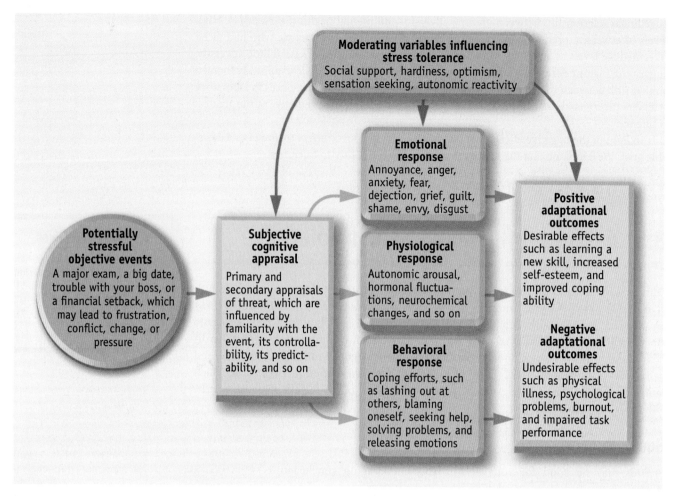

Figure 3.13

Overview of the stress process. This diagram builds on **Figure 3.5** (the multidimensional response to stress) to provide a more complete overview of the factors involved in stress. This diagram adds the potential effects of stress (seen on the far right) by listing some of the positive and negative adaptational outcomes that may result from stress. It also completes the picture by showing moderating variables (seen at the top) that can influence the effects of stress (including some variables not covered in the chapter).

support and mental health (Gleason & Masumi, 2014). It appears that social support serves as a protective buffer during times of high stress, reducing the negative impact of stressful events (American Psychological Association, 2015). In the workplace, social support has been shown to reduce the prevalence of burnout (Boren, 2014). With regard to more severe stress, social support appears to be a key factor in reducing the likelihood of PTSD among Vietnam veterans (King et al., 1998) and increasing the likelihood of posttraumatic growth (Prati & Pietrantoni, 2009).

Interestingly, a recent study suggests that even superficial social interactions with acquaintances and strangers, such as waiters, grocery store clerks, and people we see around our neighborhood, may be beneficial. Sandstrom and Dunn (2014) asked participants about their recent interactions involving people with whom they had either strong ties or weak ties. As expected, greater interactions with strong ties correlated with greater subjective well-being, but surprisingly, so did greater interactions with weak ties. Generally, researchers have assumed that our feelings of belongingness and social support derive from our interactions with close friends and family, but the Sandstrom and Dunn study raises the possibility that weak ties may also contribute.

The mechanisms underlying the connection between social support and mental health have been the subject of considerable debate. A variety of factors may be at work. Among other things, social support could promote wellness by making appraisals of stressful events more benign, dampening the intensity of physiological reactions to stress, reducing health-impairing behaviors such as smoking and drinking, encouraging preventive behaviors such as regular exercise and medical checkups, and fostering more constructive coping efforts (Taylor, 2007).

Researchers note that social support networks have their drawbacks (conflict role strain, additional responsibilities, dependency) (Rook, 2015). Further, support that is thought to be disingenuous or inappropriate can be counterproductive and decrease one's well-being (Rook, August, & Sorkin, 2011). Still, the benefits outweigh the costs, as we will see in the Spotlight on Research for this chapter.

Spotlight on RESEARCH

The Role of Hugs in Social Support

Source: Cohen, S., Janicki-Deverts, D., Turner, R. B., & Doyle, W. J. (2015). Does hugging provide stress-buffering social support? A study of susceptibility to upper respiratory infection and illness. *Psychological Science, 26*, 135–147.

As we have learned, friends can be good for you. There is a wealth of evidence that social support is important for both physical and mental health. However, little research has been conducted on how specific behaviors that convey social support (for instance, hugging) might relate to health. Therefore, the present researchers explored the role of one's perception of social support as well as the receiving of hugs in buffering one from the physical effects of stress. The researchers hypothesized that people who have a lot of social support and get frequent hugs will be less susceptible to infection and illness.

Method

Participants. The researchers put advertisements in newspapers seeking volunteers. Volunteers were excluded if a medical screening revealed health issues such as psychiatric illness, asthma, or pregnancy. The final sample included 404 healthy participants (46.3% female, 61.6% white, and 24.3% married).

Materials. Perceived level of *social support* was measured using a twelve-item questionnaire that asked participants to rate on a scale of 0 (definitely false) to 4 (definitely true) items such as: "If I decide one afternoon that I would like to go to a movie that evening, I could easily find someone to go with me." *Receiving hugs* was measured via telephone interviews on fourteen consecutive days by asking participants if they had been hugged that day (yes/no). *Infection* was measured by comparing virus-specific antibody levels taken before and after exposure to a virus. *Illness* was measured by the weight of daily nasal mucus production and the ability of the nasal passage to keep mucus from reaching the throat (also called clearance functioning). These indicators of illness were measured by daily weight of all tissues used to blow one's nose and the amount of time it took participants to taste a solution they sprayed into their nose, respectively.

Procedure. Participants first completed the twelve-item questionnaire and were phone-interviewed on fourteen consecutive evenings. Participants were then quarantined in single rooms at a local hotel. Blood was drawn to collect baseline measures of virus-specific antibodies. Baseline measures of mucus production and clearance functioning were also obtained. Participants were then exposed to a flu virus using nasal drops and remained in quarantine for up to 6 more days. Each day, nasal production and clearance functioning were measured. After 28 days, blood was collected to measure virus-specific antibodies.

Results

The researchers found support for their hypotheses. Participants who reported higher levels of social support showed fewer signs of infection after being exposed to the virus. These participants also showed fewer signs of illness (specifically as measured by more rapid clearance functioning). The same pattern emerged for receiving hugs. Those who reported more hugs showed fewer signs of infection and illness after being exposed to the virus. Interestingly, these results did not hold up for nasal production, perhaps because this indicator of illness is thought to be biochemical in nature.

Discussion

These results provide support for the stress-buffering effect of social support including receiving hugs. The authors note that hugs reduced the negative effects of stress whether they were received in times of tension or not. However, they note that they "cannot discount the possibility that those who are hugged more frequently also are more likely to use hugs to resolve conflicts" (p. 144), thus reducing stress. The authors note that the study has limitations in that they did not ask whom the participants were hugging or why. Nor can they draw causal conclusions from this nonexperimental data. Even so, their study highlights the importance of exploring touch and other behaviors that convey social support in reducing the effects of stress.

Critical Thinking Questions

1. The authors argue that hugging is a behavior that conveys social support. Can you identify other behaviors that might convey social support?
2. We have discussed emotional, physiological, and behavior responses to stress. How might receiving a hug relate to each of these response types?
3. Would you volunteer to be in a study that required you to be quarantined as well as exposed to a virus? Why or why not?

Hardiness

Another line of research indicates that an attribute called *hardiness* may moderate the impact of stressful events. Suzanne (Kobasa) Ouellette reasoned that if stress affects some people less than others, some people must be *hardier* than others. Kobasa (1979) used a modified version of the Holmes and Rahe (1967) stress scale (SRRS) to measure the amount of stress experienced by a group of executives. As in most other studies, she found a modest correlation between stress and the incidence of physical illness. However, she carried her investigation one step further than previous studies. She compared the high-stress executives who exhibited the expected high incidence of illness against the high-stress executives who stayed healthy. She administered a battery of psychological tests and found that the hardier executives "were more committed, felt more in control, and had bigger appetites for challenge" (Kobasa, 1984, p. 70). These traits have also shown up in many other studies of hardiness (Maddi, 2007; 2013).

Thus, *hardiness* **is a disposition marked by commitment, challenge, and control that is purportedly associated with strong stress resistance.** The benefits of hardiness showed up in a study of Vietnam veterans, finding that higher hardiness was related to a lower likelihood of developing posttraumatic stress disorders (King et al., 1998). Similar findings have been reported for veterans of the Iraq and Afghanistan wars (Escolas et al., 2013). In fact, research shows that hardiness is a good predictor of success in high-stress occupations such as the military (Bartone et al., 2008).

Hardiness may reduce the effects of stress by altering appraisals or fostering more active coping. Fortunately, it appears that hardiness can be learned, and it often comes from strong social support and encouragement from those around us (Maddi, 2007; 2013).

Optimism

Everyone knows someone whose glass is always half full, who sees the world through rose-colored glasses, who is an optimist. *Optimism* **is a general tendency to expect good outcomes.** Pioneering research in this area by Michael Scheier and Charles Carver (1985) found a correlation between optimism and relatively good physical health in a sample of college students. More recently, optimism has been associated with better cardiovascular health (Hernandez et al., 2015). In fact, more than 20 years of research has consistently shown that optimism is associated with better mental and physical health. Further, a recent study of representative samples from 142 countries yielded evidence that the link between optimism and health appears to be found around the world (Gallagher, Lopez, & Pressman, 2013).

Why does optimism promote a variety of desirable outcomes? Above all else, research suggests that optimists cope with stress in more adaptive ways than pessimists (Carver & Scheier, 2014). Optimists are more likely to engage in action-oriented, problem-focused, carefully planned coping and are more willing than pessimists to seek social support. By comparison, pessimists are more likely to deal with stress by avoiding it, giving up, or engaging in denial. Optimists also enjoy greater social support than pessimists, in part because they work harder on their relationships (Carver & Scheier, 2014).

Even with all these benefits, psychologists debate whether optimism is always beneficial. What about times when a rosy outlook is inaccurate and unrealistic? Unrealistic optimism can lead to false hope (Shepperd et al., 2015). Additionally, being optimistic can lead to risky behaviors if one holds an "it-can't-happen-to-me" attitude. Research shows that women with an optimistic bias toward their risk for breast cancer are less likely to go in for screening (Clarke at al., 2000). Gillham and Reivich (2007) argue that, when it comes to optimism, what is most adaptive is some sort of middle ground where one displays "optimism that is closely tied to the strength of wisdom" (p. 320).

3.6 Reducing Stress through Self-Control

Answer the following "yes" or "no."

___ **1.** Do you have a hard time passing up food, even when you're not hungry?

___ **2.** Do you wish you studied more often?

___ **3.** Would you like to cut down on your smoking or drinking?

___ **4.** Do you experience difficulty in getting yourself to exercise regularly?

It is clear that a sense of control is important to one's appraisal and experience of stress. If you answered "yes" to any of the above questions, you have struggled with the challenge of self-control. Self-control—or rather a lack of it—underlies many of the stressors that people struggle with in everyday life. Think back to the sources of stress. Many of them can be reduced through self-control. For instance, one can start exercising to reduce the *frustration* of poor fitness, or stop procrastinating to reduce *pressure* in a course. This Application discusses how you can use the techniques of behavior modification to improve your self-control.

Behavior modification **is a systematic approach to changing behavior through the application of the principles of conditioning.** Advocates of behavior modification assume that behavior is a product of learning, conditioning, and environmental control. They further assume that *what is learned can be unlearned.* Thus, they set out to "recondition" people to produce more desirable patterns of behavior. The technology of behavior modification has been applied with great success in schools, businesses, hospitals, factories, child-care facilities, prisons, and mental health centers (Goodall, 1972; Kazdin, 2001; Rachman, 1992). Behavior modification techniques have been used to treat a variety of issues, including attention disorders, autism spectrum disorders, and childhood obesity (Berry et al., 2004; Pelham, 2001; Roth, Gillis, & DiGennaro Reed, 2014).

Behavior modification techniques have proven particularly valuable in efforts to improve self-control. Our discussion will borrow liberally from an excellent book on self-modification by David Watson and Roland Tharp (2007, 2013). We will discuss five steps in the process of self-modification, which are outlined in **Figure 3.14.**

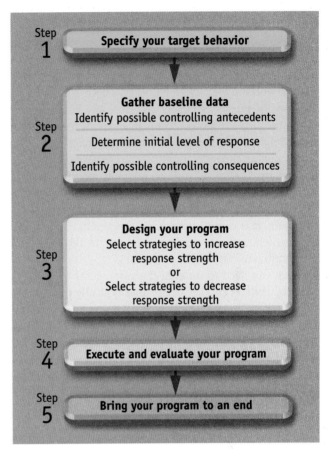

Figure 3.14

Steps in a self-modification program. This flowchart provides an overview of the steps necessary to execute a self-modification program.

Specifying Your Target Behavior

The first step in a self-modification program is to specify the target behavior(s) you want to change. Behavior modification can only be applied to a clearly defined response, yet many people have difficulty pinpointing the behavior they hope to alter. They tend to describe their problems in terms of unobservable personality *traits* rather than overt behaviors. For example, asked what behavior he would like to change, a man might say, "I'm too irritable." That may be true, but it is of little help in designing a self-modification program. To identify target responses, you need to think about past behavior or closely observe future behavior and list specific *examples* of responses that lead to the trait description. For instance, the man who regards himself as "too irritable" might identify two overly frequent responses, such as arguing with his wife and snapping at his children. These are specific behaviors for which he could design a self-modification program.

Gathering Baseline Data

The second step in behavior modification is to gather baseline data. You need to systematically observe your target behavior for a period of time (usually a week or two) before you work out the details of your program. In gathering your baseline data, you need to monitor three things.

First, you need to determine the initial response level of your target behavior. After all, you can't tell whether your program is working effectively unless you have a baseline for comparison. In most cases, you would simply keep track of how often the target response occurs in a certain time interval. Thus, you might count the daily frequency of snapping at your children, smoking cigarettes, or biting your fingernails. If studying is your target behavior, you will probably monitor hours of study. If you want to modify your eating, you will probably keep track of how many calories you consume. Whatever the unit of measurement, *it is crucial to gather accurate data*. You should keep permanent written records, preferably in the form of a chart or graph (see **Figure 3.15**).

Second, you need to monitor the antecedents of your target behavior. *Antecedents* **are events that typically precede the target response.** Often these events play a major role in evoking your target behavior. For example, if your target is overeating, you might discover that the bulk of your overeating occurs late in the evening while you watch TV. If you can pinpoint this kind of antecedent-response connection, you may be able to design your program to circumvent or break the link.

Third, you need to monitor the typical consequences of your target behavior. Try to identify the reinforcers that are maintaining an undesirable target behavior or the unfavorable outcomes that are suppressing a desirable target behavior. In trying to identify reinforcers, remember that avoidance behavior is usually maintained by negative reinforcement (see Chapter 2). That is, the payoff for avoidance is usually the removal of something aversive, such as anxiety or a threat to self-esteem. You should also take into account the fact that a response may not be reinforced every time because most behavior is maintained by intermittent reinforcement.

Designing Your Program

Once you have selected a target behavior and gathered adequate baseline data, it is time to plan your intervention program. Generally speaking, your program will be designed to either increase or decrease the frequency of a target response.

Increasing Response Strength

Efforts to increase the frequency of a target response depend largely on the use of positive reinforcement. In other words, you reward yourself for behaving properly. Although the basic strategy is quite simple, doing it skillfully involves a number of considerations.

Selecting a reinforcer. To use positive reinforcement, you need to find a reward that will be effective for you. Reinforcement is subjective—what is reinforcing for one person may not be reinforcing for another. **Figure 3.16** lists questions you can ask yourself to help you determine your personal reinforcers. Be sure to be realistic and choose a reinforcer that is really available to you.

You don't have to come up with spectacular new reinforcers that you've never experienced before. *You can use reinforcers that you are already getting.* However, you have to restructure the contingencies so that you get the reward only if you behave appropriately. For example, if you normally watch your favorite television show on Thursday nights, you might make this viewing contingent on studying a certain number of hours during the week. Making yourself earn rewards that you've taken for granted is often a useful strategy in a self-modification program.

Arranging the contingencies. Once you have chosen your reinforcer, you have to set up reinforcement contingencies. These contingencies will describe the exact behavioral goals that must be met and the reinforcement that may then be awarded. For example, in a program to increase exercise, you might make

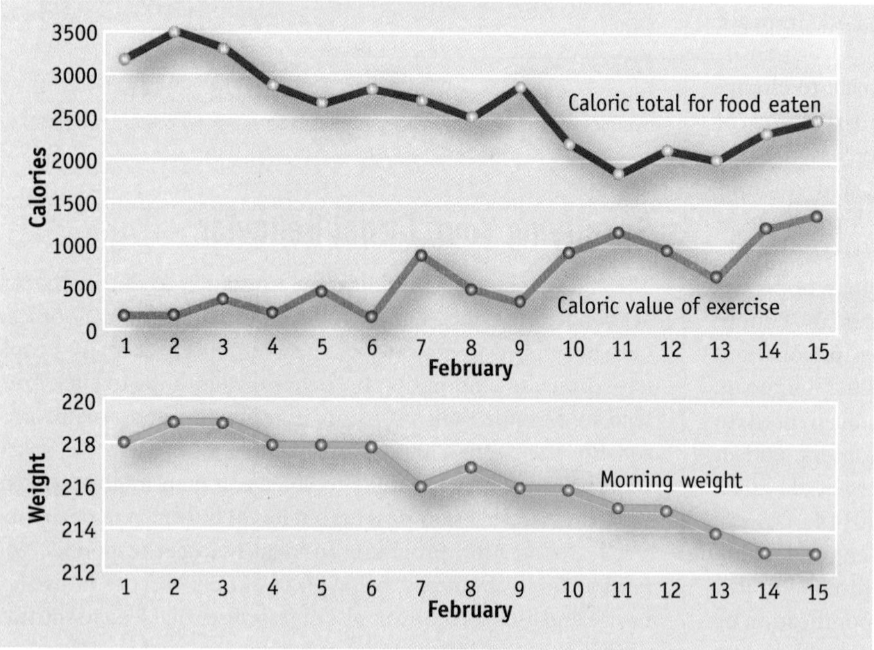

Figure 3.15

Example of recordkeeping in a self-modification program for losing weight. Graphic records are ideal for tracking progress in behavior modification efforts.

WHAT ARE YOUR REINFORCERS?	
1. What will be the rewards of achieving your goal?	12. What would be a nice present to receive?
2. What kind of praise do you like to receive, from yourself and others?	13. What kinds of things are important to you?
	14. What would you buy if you had an extra $20? $50? $100?
3. What kinds of things do you like to have?	15. On what do you spend your money each week?
4. What are your major interests?	16. What behaviors do you perform every day? (Don't overlook the obvious or commonplace.)
5. What are your hobbies?	
6. What people do you like to be with?	17. Are there any behaviors you usually perform instead of the target behavior?
7. What do you like to do with those people?	
8. What do you do for fun?	18. What would you hate to lose?
9. What do you do to relax?	19. Of the things you do every day, which would you hate to give up?
10. What do you do to get away from it all?	20. What are your favorite daydreams and fantasies?
11. What makes you feel good?	21. What are the most relaxing scenes you can imagine?

Figure 3.16

Selecting a reinforcer. The questions listed here may help you to identify your personal reinforcers.

Source: Adapted from Watson, D. L., & Tharp, R. G. (1997). *Self-directed behavior: Self-modification for personal adjustment.* Belmont, CA: Wadsworth. Reprinted by permission.

spending $40 on clothes (the reinforcer) contingent on having jogged 15 miles during the week (the target behavior).

Try to set behavioral goals that are both challenging and realistic. You want your goals to be challenging so that they lead to improvement in your behavior. However, setting unrealistically high goals—a common mistake in self-modification—often leads to unnecessary discouragement.

You also need to be concerned about handing out too much reinforcement. If reinforcement is too easy to get, you may become *satiated*, and the reinforcer may lose its motivational power. One way to avoid the satiation problem is to put yourself on a token economy. **A** *token economy* **is a system for doling out symbolic reinforcers that are exchanged later for a variety of genuine reinforcers.** Thus, you might develop a point system for exercise behavior, accumulating points that can be spent on clothes, movies, restaurant meals, and so forth. You can also use a token economy to reinforce a variety of related target behaviors, as opposed to a single specific response. The token economy in **Figure 3.17**, for instance, is set up to strengthen three different, though related, responses (jogging, tennis, and sit-ups).

Shaping. In some cases, you may want to reinforce a target response that you are not currently capable of making, such as speaking in front of a large group or jogging 10 miles a day. This situation calls for *shaping*, **which is accomplished by reinforcing closer and closer approximations of the desired response.** Thus, you might start jogging 2 miles a day and add a half-mile each week until you reach your goal. In shaping your behavior, you should set up a schedule spelling out how

RESPONSES EARNING TOKENS		
Response	**Amount**	**Number of tokens**
Jogging	1/2 mile	4
Jogging	1 mile	8
Jogging	2 miles	16
Tennis	1 hour	4
Tennis	2 hours	8
Sit-ups	25	1
Sit-ups	50	2

REDEMPTION VALUE OF TOKENS	
Reinforcer	**Tokens required**
Download an album of your choice	30
Go to movie	50
Go to nice restaurant	100
Take special weekend trip	500

Figure 3.17

Example of a token economy to reinforce exercise. This token economy was set up to strengthen three types of exercise behavior. The person can exchange tokens for four types of reinforcers.

and when your target behaviors and reinforcement contingencies should change. Generally, it is a good idea to move forward gradually.

Decreasing Response Strength

Let's turn now to the challenge of reducing the frequency of an undesirable response. You can go about this task in a number of ways. Your principal options are reinforcement, control of antecedents, and punishment.

Reinforcement. Reinforcers can be used in an indirect way to decrease the frequency of a response. This may sound paradoxical since you have learned that reinforcement strengthens a response. The trick lies in how you define the target behavior. For example, in the case of overeating you might define your target behavior as eating more than 1800 calories a day (a response that you want to decrease) or, alternatively, as eating less than 1800 calories a day (a response that you want to increase). If you choose the latter definition, you can reinforce yourself whenever you eat less than 1800 calories in a day, which ultimately decreases your overeating.

Control of antecedents. A worthwhile strategy for decreasing the occurrence of an undesirable response may be to identify its antecedents and avoid exposure to them. This strategy is especially useful when you are trying to decrease the frequency of a consummatory response, such as smoking or eating. In the case of overeating, for instance, the easiest way to resist temptation is to avoid having to face it. Thus, you might stay away from favorite restaurants, minimize time spent in your kitchen, shop for groceries just after eating (when willpower is higher), and avoid purchasing favorite foods.

Punishment. The strategy of decreasing unwanted behavior by punishing yourself for that behavior is an obvious option that people tend to overuse. The biggest problem with punishment in a self-modification effort is the difficulty in following through and punishing oneself. If you're going to use punishment, keep two guidelines in mind. First, do not use punishment alone. Use it in conjunction with positive reinforcement. If you set up a program in which you can earn only negative consequences, you probably won't stick to it. Second, use a relatively mild punishment so that you will actually be able to administer it to yourself. Nurnberger and Zimmerman (1970) developed a creative method of self-punishment. They had subjects write out a check to an organization they hated (for instance, the campaign of a political candidate they despised). The check was held by a third party who mailed it

if subjects failed to meet their behavioral goals. Such a punishment is relatively harmless, but it can serve as a strong source of motivation.

Executing and Evaluating Your Program

Once you have designed your program, the next step is to put it to work by enforcing the contingencies that you have carefully planned. During this period, you need to continue to accurately record the frequency of your target behavior so you can evaluate your progress. The success of your program depends on your not "cheating." The most common form of cheating is to reward yourself when you have not actually earned it.

You can do two things to increase the likelihood that you will comply with your program. One is to make up a *behavioral contract*—**a written agreement outlining a promise to adhere to the contingencies of a behavior modification program** (see **Figure 3.18**). The formality of signing such a contract in front of friends or family seems to make many people take their program more seriously. You can further reduce the likelihood of cheating by having someone other than yourself administer the reinforcers and punishments.

Behavior modification programs often require some fine-tuning, so don't be surprised if you need to make a few adjustments. Several flaws are especially common in designing self-modification programs. Among those you should look out for are (1) depending on a weak reinforcer, (2) permitting lengthy delays between appropriate behavior and delivery of reinforcers, and (3) trying to do too much too quickly by setting unrealistic goals. Often, a small revision or two can turn a failing program around and make it a success.

nemke/Shutterstock.com

Smoking and drinking are among the many self-control issues that can be conquered using the principles of self-modification.

Ending Your Program

Ending your program involves setting terminal goals such as reaching a certain weight, studying with a certain regularity, or going without cigarettes for a certain length of time. Often, it is a good idea to phase out your program by planning a gradual reduction in the frequency or potency of your reinforcement for appropriate behavior.

If your program is successful, it may fade away without a conscious decision on your part. Often, new, improved patterns of behavior such as eating right, exercising, or studying diligently become self-maintaining. Whether or not you end your program intentionally, you should always be prepared to reinstitute the program if you find yourself slipping back to your old patterns of behavior. Ironically, it can be the very stress we are trying to reduce that drives use back into old, unhealthy habits.

I, _____ , do hereby agree to initiate my self-change strategy as of (date) _____ and to continue it for a minimum period of _____ weeks—that is, until (date) _____ .

My specific self-change strategy is to _____
_____
_____ .

I will do my best to execute this strategy to my utmost ability and to evaluate its effectiveness only after it has been honestly tried for the specified period of time.

Optional Self-Reward Clause: For every _____ day(s) that I successfully comply with my self-change contract, I will reward myself with _____
_____

In addition, at the end of my minimum period of personal experimentation, I will reward myself for having persisted in my self-change efforts. My reward at that time will be _____
_____ .

I hereby request that the witnesses who have signed below support me in my self-change efforts and encourage my compliance with the specifics of this contract. Their cooperation and encouragement throughout the project will be appreciated.

Signed _____

Date _____

Witness:

Witness:

Figure 3.18

A behavioral contract. Behavior modification experts recommend the use of a formal, written contract similar to that shown here to increase commitment to one's self-modification program.

CHAPTER 3 Review

Key Ideas

3.1 The Nature of Stress

• Stress involves transactions with the environment that are perceived to be threatening and that tax one's coping abilities. Stress is a common, everyday event, and even routine hassles can be problematic. To a large degree, stress lies in the eye of the beholder. According to Lazarus and Folkman, primary appraisal determines whether events appear threatening, whereas secondary appraisal assesses whether one has the resources to cope with challenges. How one appraises an event can alter the impact of the event.

• Some of the stress that people experience comes from their environment. Examples of environmental stressors include crowding and poverty. Stress can vary with culture. Within Western culture, ethnicity and discrimination can be a source of stress in a variety of ways. Adapting to a new culture can also cause stress.

3.2 Major Sources of Stress

• Stress can be acute, chronic, or anticipatory. Major sources of stress include frustration, conflict, change, and pressure. Frustration occurs when an obstacle prevents one from attaining some goal. There are three principal types of internal conflict: approach-approach, avoidance-avoidance, and approach-avoidance.

• A large number of studies with the SRRS suggest that change is stressful. Although that may be true, it is now clear that the SRRS is a measure of general stress rather than just change-related stress. Pressure (to perform and to conform) also appears to be stressful. Often this pressure is self-imposed.

3.3 Responding to Stress

• Emotional reactions to stress typically involve anger, fear, or sadness. However, people also experience positive emotions while under stress, and these positive emotions promote well-being. Emotional arousal may interfere with task performance. As tasks get more complex, the optimal level of arousal declines.

• Physiological arousal in response to stress was originally called the fight-or-flight response by Cannon. Taylor has proposed an alternative response ("tend and befriend") that might be more applicable to females. Selye's general adaptation syndrome describes three stages in the physiological reaction to stress: alarm, resistance, and exhaustion. Diseases of adaptation may appear during the stage of exhaustion.

• In response to stress, the brain sends signals along two major pathways to the endocrine system. Actions along these paths release two sets of hormones into the bloodstream, catecholamines and corticosteroids. Stress can lead to suppression of the immune response and can interfere with the formation of new neurons.

• Behavioral responses to stress involve coping, which may be healthy or maladaptive. If people cope effectively with stress, they can short-circuit potentially harmful emotional and physical responses.

3.4 The Potential Effects of Stress

• Common negative effects of stress include impaired task performance, disruption of attention and other cognitive processes, and pervasive emotional exhaustion known as burnout. Other effects include a host of everyday psychological problems, full-fledged psychological disorders including posttraumatic stress disorder, and varied types of damage to physical health.

• However, stress can also have positive effects. Stress can lead to personal growth and self-improvement. Stress can also have an inoculation effect, preparing us for the next stressful event.

3.5 Factors Influencing Stress Tolerance

• People differ in how much stress they can tolerate without experiencing ill effects. A person's social support can be a key consideration in buffering the effects of stress. The personality factors associated with hardiness—commitment, challenge, and control—may increase stress tolerance. People high in optimism also have advantages in coping with stress, although unrealistic optimism can be problematic.

3.6 Application: Reducing Stress through Self-Control

• In behavior modification, the principles of learning are used to change behavior directly. Behavior modification techniques can be used to increase one's self-control. The first step in self-modification is to specify the overt target behavior to be increased or decreased.

• The second step is to gather baseline data about the initial rate of the target response and identify any typical antecedents and consequences associated with the behavior. The third step is to design a program. If you are trying to increase the strength of a response, you'll depend on positive reinforcement. A number of strategies can be used to decrease the strength of a response, including reinforcement (indirectly), control of antecedents, and punishment.

• The fourth step is to execute and evaluate the program. Self-modification programs often require some fine-tuning. The final step is to determine how and when you will phase out your program.

Key Terms

Acculturation p. 66	Fight-or-flight response p. 74
Acute stressors p. 67	Frustration p. 67
Ambient stress p. 65	General adaptation
Antecedents p. 88	syndrome p. 76
Anticipatory stressors p. 67	Hardiness p. 86
Approach-approach	Internal conflict p. 67
conflict p. 68	Life changes p. 68
Approach-avoidance	Neurogenesis p. 77
conflict p. 68	Optimism p. 86
Autonomic nervous system	Posttraumatic stress
(ANS) p. 74	disorder (PTSD) p. 80
Avoidance-avoidance	Pressure p. 69
conflict p. 68	Primary appraisal p. 64
Behavioral contract p. 90	Psychosomatic
Behavioral modification p. 87	diseases p. 82
Burnout p. 79	Secondary appraisal p. 64
Chronic stressors p. 67	Shaping p. 89
Coping p. 78	Social support p. 83
Emotions p. 70	Stress p. 63
Endocrine system p. 76	Token economy p. 89

Key People

Susan Folkman p. 72	Suzanne (Kobasa)
Thomas Holmes and	Ouellette p. 86
Richard Rahe pp. 68–69	Robert Sapolsky pp. 67, 78
Richard Lazarus pp. 64, 71	Hans Selye pp. 75–76
Neal Miller p. 68	Shelley Taylor p. 75

1. Secondary appraisal refers to
   a. second thoughts about what to do in a stressful situation.
   b. second thoughts about whether an event is genuinely threatening.
   c. initial evaluation of an event's relevance, threat, and stressfulness.
   d. evaluation of coping resources and options for dealing with a stressful event.

2. Don just completed writing a ten-page report. When he tried to save it, the computer crashed and he lost all his work. What type of stress is Don experiencing?
   a. Frustration
   b. Conflict
   c. Life change
   d. Pressure

3. Betty is having a hard time deciding whether she should buy a coat. On the one hand, it is a name brand coat on sale for a great price. On the other hand, it is an ugly mold-green color. Betty is experiencing what type of conflict?
   a. Approach-approach
   b. Avoidance-aviodance
   c. Approach-avoidance
   d. Life change

4. The optimal level of arousal for a task appears to depend in part on
   a. one's position on the optimism/pessimism scale.
   b. how much physiological change an event stimulates.
   c. the complexity of the task at hand.
   d. how imminent a stressful event is.

5. The fight-or-flight response is mediated by the
   a. sympathetic division of the autonomic nervous system.
   b. sympathetic division of the endocrine system.
   c. parasympathetic division of the autonomic nervous system.
   d. parasympathetic division of the endocrine system.

6. Selye exposed lab animals to various stressors and found that
   a. each type of stress caused a particular physiological response.
   b. each type of animal responded to stress differently.
   c. patterns of physiological arousal were similar, regardless of the type of stress.
   d. patterns of physiological arousal were different, even when stressors were similar.

7. Stress can _____ the functioning of the immune system.
   a. stimulate
   b. destroy
   c. suppress
   d. enhance

8. Salvador works as an art director at an advertising agency. His boss overloads him with responsibility but never gives him any credit for all his hard work. He feels worn down, disillusioned, and helpless at work. Salvador is probably experiencing
   a. an alarm reaction.
   b. burnout.
   c. posttraumatic stress disorder.
   d. a psychosomatic disorder.

9. Joan has a personal disposition marked by commitment, challenge, and control. She appears to be stress tolerant. This disposition is referred to as
   a. hardiness.
   b. optimism.
   c. courage.
   d. conscientiousness.

10. A system providing for symbolic reinforcers is called a (an)
    a. extinction system.
    b. token economy.
    c. endocrine system.
    d. symbolic reinforcement system.

Answers
1. d Page 64
2. a Page 67
3. c Page 68
4. c Page 73
5. a Page 74
6. c Page 75
7. c Page 77
8. b Pages 79–80
9. a Page 86
10. b Page 89

Personal Explorations Workbook

Go to the *Personal Explorations Workbook* in the back of your textbook for exercises that can enhance your self-understanding in relation to issues raised in this chapter.

Exercise 3.1 *Self-Assessment:* Pressure Inventory

Exercise 3.2 *Self-Reflection:* Stress—How Do You Control It?

Coping Processes

Dragon Images/Shutterstock.com

"I have begun to believe that I have intellectually and emotionally outgrown my partner. However, I'm not really sure what this means or what I should do. Maybe this feeling is normal and I should ignore it and continue my present relationship. This seems to be the safest route. Maybe I should seek a lover while continuing with my partner. Then again, maybe I should start anew and hope for a beautiful ending with or without a better mate."

Decisions about how to cope with life's difficulties can be incredibly complex. A person's mental and physical health depends, in part, on his or her ability to cope effectively with stress.

The woman quoted above is clearly experiencing substantial stress. What should she do? Is it psychologically healthy to remain in an emotionally hollow relationship? Is cheating a reasonable way to cope with this unfortunate situation? Should she just strike out on her own and let the chips fall where they may? These questions have no simple answers. As you'll soon see, decisions about how to cope with life's difficulties can be incredibly complex.

In the previous chapter we learned that stress can be a challenging, exciting stimulus to personal growth. However, we also saw that stress can prove damaging to people's psychological and physical health because it often triggers physiological responses that may be harmful. Controlling the effects of stress depends on the behavioral responses people make to stressful situations. Thus, a person's mental and physical health depends, in part, on his or her ability to *cope* effectively with stress.

In this chapter we will explore the concept of coping, including coping patterns that tend to have relatively little value and those that are healthier and more constructive. In the application, we discuss how to cope with one of the most common stressors: lack of time. We hope our discussion provides you with some new ideas about how to deal with the stressors of modern life. ■

4.1 The Concept of Coping

In Chapter 3, you learned that *coping* **refers to efforts to master, reduce, or tolerate the demands created by stress.** Let's take a closer look at this concept and discuss some general points about coping.

People cope with stress in many ways. A number of researchers have attempted to identify and classify the coping techniques that people use in dealing with stress. Their work reveals quite a variety of strategies; in fact, one review of the literature found more than 400 distinct coping techniques (Skinner et al., 2003). To simplify things, Carver suggests that we consider four important distinctions or groupings (Carver & Connor-Smith, 2010), which are listed in **Figure 4.1**. Although people can select their coping tactics from a large and varied menu of options, a national survey by the American Psychological Association (2015) found that 20% of Americans do *nothing* to manage their stress.

It is most adaptive to use a variety of coping strategies. Even with so many tactics to choose from, most people come to rely on some coping strategies more than others. However, Cheng (2001, 2003) has argued that the ability to use multiple strategies (called *coping flexibility*) is more desirable than consistently relying on the same strategy. Flexible copers can differentiate among stressful events in terms of controllability and impact, which is important information to know when choosing a coping strategy. In addition, the ability to select a particular coping tactic to deal with a specific adversity helps people avoid becoming hindered by a problematic strategy. Coping flexibility has been related to positive mental health outcomes (Liao, 2014) including increased resilience (Galatzer-Levy, Burton, & Bonanno, 2012) and reduced depression, anxiety, and distress (Kato, 2012).

Figure 4.1

Classifying coping strategies. There are literally hundreds of coping techniques. Carver and Connor-Smith (2010) point to four important distinctions or groupings of coping strategies that have proved to be meaningful. The groupings are listed here, along with a representative example from each category. As with other distinctions, there is significant overlap among the categories. As you can see, people use quite a variety of coping strategies.

Source: From Carver, C. S., & Connor-Smith, J. (2010). Personality and coping. *Annual Review of Psychology, 61*, 679–704.

TYPES OF COPING STRATEGIES	
Coping distinction/grouping	**Example**
Problem-focused vs. emotion-focused coping	Problem-focused: I save money in anticipation of layoffs. Emotion-focus: I engage in self-soothing relaxation exercises to handle the stress brought about by layoffs.
Engagement vs. disengagement coping	Engagement: I work on finding a new place to live after the looming divorce. Disengagement: I refuse to believe that the divorce is happening.
Meaning-focused coping	Losing my house and possessions in a fire reminded me of what is truly important in life—my family and friends.
Proactive coping	I know that this confrontation with my friend is going to be challenging, so I'm going to make sure I have my thoughts organized before I bring up our issues.

Coping strategies vary in their adaptive value. In everyday terms, when we say that someone "coped with her problems," we imply that she handled them effectively. In reality, however, not all strategies are created equal. For example, coping with a painful breakup by destroying your ex's car would clearly be a problematic way of coping (no matter what pop songs would lead us to believe). Hence, we distinguish between coping patterns that tend to be helpful and those that tend to be maladaptive. In general, the use of maladaptive strategies is associated with poorer psychological adjustment, whereas adaptive strategies are related to enhanced well-being. Bear in mind that our generalizations about the adaptive value of various coping strategies are based on trends or tendencies identified by researchers. No coping strategy can guarantee a successful outcome, and the adaptive value of a coping technique depends on the exact nature of the situation (Bonanno & Burton, 2013).

Learning Objectives

- Analyze the adaptive value of giving up and aggression as responses to stress.
- Evaluate the adaptive value of indulging yourself as a coping response and describe the Spotlight on Research regarding stress-induced eating.
- Discuss the adaptive value of self-blame as a response to stress.
- Evaluate the adaptive value of defense mechanisms, including recent work on healthy illusions.

4.2 Common Coping Patterns of Limited Value

Individuals don't always deal with it well when things take a turn for the worse. When one experiences academic setbacks, breakups, financial worries, or other stressors it is not uncommon to give up, lash out at others, turn to alcohol dull the pain, or to self-blame. In this section, we'll examine some relatively common coping patterns that tend to be less than optimal. Although some of these coping tactics may be helpful in certain circumstances, more often than not, they are counterproductive.

Giving Up

When confronted with stress, people sometimes simply give up and withdraw from the battle. Martin Seligman (1974, 1992) developed a model of this giving-up syndrome that sheds light on its causes. In Seligman's original research, animals were subjected to electric shocks they could not escape. The animals were then given an opportunity to learn a response that would allow them to escape the shock. However, many of the animals became so apathetic and listless that they didn't even try to learn the escape response. When researchers made similar manipulations with *human* subjects using inescapable noise (rather than shock) as the stressor, they observed parallel results (Hiroto & Seligman, 1975). This syndrome is referred to as learned helplessness. *Learned helplessness* **is passive behavior produced by exposure to unavoidable**

aversive events. Unfortunately, this tendency to give up may be transferred to situations in which one is not really helpless. Hence, some people routinely respond to stress with fatalism and resignation, passively accepting setbacks that they could have overcome.

Seligman originally viewed learned helplessness as a product of conditioning. However, research with human participants has led Seligman and his colleagues to revise their theory. Their current model proposes that people's *cognitive interpretation* of aversive events determines whether they develop learned helplessness. Specifically, helplessness seems to occur when individuals come to believe that events are beyond their control. This belief is particularly likely to emerge in people who exhibit a pessimistic explanatory style. Such people tend to attribute setbacks to personal inadequacies instead of situational factors.

Overall, giving up is not a highly regarded method of coping. Carver and his colleagues (1989, 1993) have studied this coping strategy, which they refer to as *behavioral disengagement*, and found that it is associated with increased rather than decreased distress. However, giving up could be adaptive in some instances, such as when goals are truly unattainable (Wrosch et al., 2012). For example, if you are thrown into a job that you are not equipped to handle, it might be better to quit rather than face constant pressure and diminishing self-esteem. Research suggests that people who are better able to disengage from unattainable goals report better health and exhibit lower levels of a key stress hormone (Wrosch, Scheier, & Miller, 2013). Thus, the researchers note that it might be better to engage in "goal adjustment" as opposed to giving up.

Acting Aggressively

A young man, age 17, cautiously edged his car into traffic on the Corona Expressway in Los Angeles. His slow speed apparently irritated the men in a pickup truck behind him. Unfortunately, he angered the wrong men—they shot him to death. During that same weekend there were six other roadside shootings in the Los Angeles area, all of them triggered by minor incidents or "fender benders."

Such tragic incidents of highway violence—so-called "road rage"—exemplify maladaptive ways in which drivers cope with the stress, anxiety, and hostility experienced while driving. They also vividly illustrate that people often respond to stressful events by acting aggressively. **Aggression is any behavior intended to hurt someone, either physically or verbally.** There are many forms of aggression, which can be either direct or indirect (Richardson, 2014). Snarls, curses, and insults are much more common than shootings or fistfights, but aggression of any kind can be problematic.

As you learned in Chapter 3, frustration is a major source of stress. Many years ago, a team of psychologists (Dollard et al., 1939) proposed the *frustration-aggression hypothesis*, which held that aggression is always due to frustration. Decades of research eventually showed that there isn't an inevitable link between frustration and aggression, but this research also supported the basic idea that frustration *does* frequently elicit aggression (Berkowitz, 1989).

People often lash out aggressively at others who had nothing to do with their frustration, especially when they can't vent their anger at the real source of their frustration. Thus, you'll probably suppress your anger rather than lash out verbally at a police officer who gives you a speeding ticket. Twenty minutes later, however, you might be downright brutal in rebuking a waiter who is slow in serving your lunch. As we discussed in Chapter 2, Sigmund Freud noticed this diversion of anger to a substitute target long ago; he called it *displacement*. Unfortunately, displaced aggression is not uncommon. In fact, displaced aggression is frequently a contributing factor to road rage (Sansone & Sansone, 2010).

The frustration of traffic delays can lead to aggressive driving or road rage. Unfortunately, lashing out at others is a common response to stress, which happens to be ineffective.

Freud theorized that behaving aggressively could get pent-up emotion out of one's system and thus be adaptive. He coined the term *catharsis* **to refer to the release of emotional tension.** The Freudian notion that it is a good idea to vent anger has become widely disseminated and accepted in modern society. Books, magazines, and self-appointed experts routinely advise that it is healthy to "blow off steam" and thereby release and reduce anger. However, experimental research generally has *not* supported the catharsis hypothesis. Indeed, most studies find just the opposite: *Behaving in an aggressive manner tends to fuel more anger and aggression* (Bushman & Huesmann, 2012).

For instance, conventional wisdom holds that viewing violent media or playing violent video games can be cathartic—that watching a fight on a TV or killing a fictional character in a game can release pent-up anger and hostility. However, the research evidence suggests that this is simply not true (Anderson et al., 2010). Craig Anderson and Brad Bushman (2001) conducted a groundbreaking review of the research on violent video games and found that playing these games was related to increased aggression, physiological arousal, and aggressive thoughts as well as to decreased prosocial behavior. In fact, they found that the relationship between media violence and aggressive behavior was almost as strong as the relationship between smoking and cancer (Bushman & Anderson, 2001; see **Figure 4.2**). Exposure to media violence not only desensitizes people to violent acts, but it also encourages aggressive self-views and automatic aggressive responses (Bartholow, Bushman, & Sestir, 2006), increases feelings of hostility (Arriaga et al., 2006), and decreases prosocial behaviors (Prot et al., 2014). Further, there is evidence that media violence can increase, as opposed to alleviate, stress (Hasan, Bègue, & Bushman, 2012; 2013). Interestingly, angry individuals who believe in catharsis are the very ones attracted to violent video games (Bushman & Whitaker, 2010).

Is there an upside to aggression? Some argue that there are cognitive, motivational, emotional, and social benefits to playing video games, even violent ones, and that these benefits need more research attention (Granic, Lobel, & Engels, 2014). However, as a coping strategy, acting aggressively has little value. Carol Tavris (1982, 1989) points out that aggressive behavior usually backfires because it elicits aggressive responses from others and generates more anger. She asserts, "Aggressive catharses are almost impossible to find in

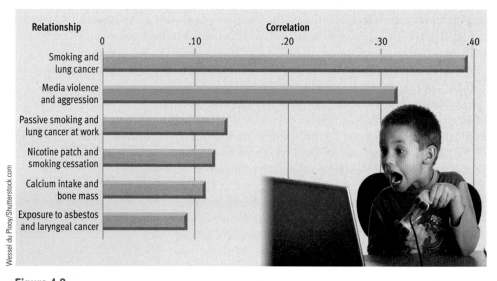

Figure 4.2

Comparison of the relationship between media violence and aggression to other correlations. Many studies have found a correlation between exposure to media violence and aggression. However, some critics have argued that the correlation is too weak to have any practical significance in the real world. In a rebuttal of this criticism, Bushman and Anderson (2001) note that the average correlation in studies of media violence and aggression is .31. They argue that this association is almost as strong as the correlation between smoking and the probability of developing lung cancer, which is viewed as relevant to real-world issues and notably stronger than a variety of other correlations shown here that are assumed to have practical importance.

Source: Adapted from Bushman, B. J., & Anderson, C. A. (2001). Media violence and the American public. *American Psychologist, 56*(6-7), 477–489. (Figure 2). Copyright © 2001 American Psychological Association. Reprinted by permission of the publisher and authors.

continuing relationships because parents, children, spouses, and bosses usually feel obliged to aggress back at you" (1982, p. 131). In fact, the interpersonal conflicts that often emerge from aggressive behavior actually induce additional stress.

Indulging Yourself

Stress sometimes leads to reduced impulse control, or *self-indulgence*. For instance, after an exceptionally stressful day, some people head for their kitchen, a grocery store, or a restaurant in pursuit of something sweet. Others cope with stress by making a beeline for the nearest shopping mall for a spending spree. Still others respond to stress by indulging in injudicious patterns of drinking, smoking, gambling, or drug use. It makes sense that when things are going poorly in one area of your life, you may try to compensate by pursuing substitute forms of satisfaction. Thus, it is not surprising that there is evidence of stress-induced eating (O'Connor & Conner, 2011), smoking (Slopen et al., 2013), gambling (Elman, Tschibelu, & Borsook, 2010), and alcohol and drug use (Grunberg, Berger, & Hamilton, 2011). In fact, psychologists speculate that the general relationship between stress and poor physical health might be attributable in part to these unhealthy behaviors (Carver, 2011).

Stress can also influence our food choices in unfortunate ways (Tryon, DeCant, & Laugero, 2013). When feeling stressed, it is not unusual for individuals to turn to their comfort foods in search of relief. In fact, these foods appear to be real sources of comfort. Researchers have found that comfort foods can remind us of meaningful relationships and reduce loneliness (Troisi & Gabriel, 2011). Of course, indulging in one's comfort foods can have negative effects such as an increase in consumption of unhealthy calories, ultimately increasing one's risk of obesity and other related health problems (Dallman, Pecoraro, & la Fleur, 2005; Roberts, Campbell, & Troop, 2014). Some of us are more prone to stress-induced eating than others, but there appears to be a bright side to this tendency, as we will see in the Spotlight on Research for this chapter.

Spotlight on RESEARCH

Stress-Induced Eating

Source: Sproesser, G., Schupp, H. T., & Renner, B. (2014). The bright side of stress-induced eating: Eating more when stressed but less when pleased. *Psychological Science, 25*(1), 58–65.

As we have learned, stress affects the mind and the body. One interesting and important area to explore is the effect that stress has on eating habits. Abundant research demonstrates how stress encourages unhealthy eating behaviors, but there is far less research on how positive experiences influence eating. The present researchers looked into preexisting eating tendencies and whether stressful situations increased unhealthy food consumption. In addition, they examined whether *not* being stressed (that is, being at ease) influenced eating patterns. They tested these ideas using very clever methods.

Method

Participants. The sample consisted of 251 participants from the University of Konstanz in Germany (29% men and 71% women). Using a questionnaire, participants were categorized as either stress hyperphagics (people who eat more in response to stress) or stress hypophagics (people who eat less in response to stress).

Materials and Procedure. Participants were told not to eat for 2 hours before arriving at the laboratory. Once there, they were told they would be exchanging video messages with another participant before meeting their "partner" face-to-face. The experimenter then showed all participants a prerecorded videotaped message of their partner, who was actually a research assistant, discussing his or her career plans. After watching the video, participants made one of their own to share with their partner. Participants were then given a questionnaire to evaluate their partner. At that point, the experimenter left the room, ostensibly to give the partner their video. Upon returning, experimenters manipulated a stressful, negative experience (social exclusion) or a nonstressful, positive experience (social inclusion). This was determined by random assignment. In the social exclusion condition, participants were told that their partner declined to meet them after viewing their videotape. In the social inclusion condition, participants were told that their partner gave them a positive evaluation and were looking forward to meeting them.

continued

Finally, after receiving the feedback, a bogus taste test of ice cream was administered, in which participants could eat as much as they liked. Afterward, the experimenter weighed the bowls of ice cream to determine exactly how much was eaten.

Results

The results showed that the experience of the positive or negative event interacted with participants' stress-eating status (hypo- or hyperphagic). As expected, hyperphagics ate more than hypophagics when socially excluded. However, when in a situation of ease (social inclusion), the opposite pattern emerged, and hyperphagics actually ate less!

Discussion

There is considerable evidence that stress influences eating habits, but this is the first evidence that stress-eaters adjust their eating habits in nonstressful times. This could explain research findings that show inconsistent weight gain among hyperphagics—perhaps they are increasing caloric intake during stressful times, but are making up for it by eating less when things are going smoothly. The authors argue that in order to get a complete picture of stress-induced eating, future researchers must consider both the person and the situation. The authors are quick to note that the participants self-reported their stress-eating status so these data could be inaccurate. Further, more research needs to be done before generalizing their laboratory results to a natural, real-world setting. Also, additional research is needed to see if other sources of stress besides social exclusion show similar patterns.

Critical Thinking Questions

1. The authors demonstrate that social inclusion/exclusion has an effect on stress-induced eating. What other sources of stress might influence one's eating habits?

2. Do you think you are hyperphagic or hyophagic? Why? When you have completed this chapter, describe some of the more constructive coping strategies, besides self-indulgence, that you might engage in when stressed.

Another example of self-indulgent coping is stress-induced shopping. One recent study examined the relations among stress, materialism, and compulsive shopping in two Israeli samples, one of which was under intense stress due to daily rocket attacks (Ruvio, Somer, & Rindfleisch, 2014). The findings indicated that stress increases compulsive consumption and that this coping strategy is particularly common among those who are highly materialistic. The authors essentially conclude that *when the going gets tough, the materialistic go shopping*.

Yet another manifestation of this coping strategy is the tendency to immerse oneself in the online world of the Internet. Kimberly Young (2009, 2015) has described a syndrome called *Internet addiction,* **which consists of spending an inordinate amount of time on the Internet and an inability to control online use.** People who exhibit this syndrome tend to feel anxious, depressed, or empty when they are not online. Their Internet use is so excessive that it begins to interfere with their functioning at work, at school, or at home, leading victims to start concealing the extent of their dependence on the Internet.

Internet addiction typically involves one of three subtypes: excessive gaming, preoccupation with sexual content, or obsessive socializing (via Facebook, texting, and so forth) (Weinsten et al., 2014). All three subtypes exhibit (1) excessive time online, (2) anger and depression when thwarted from being online, (3) an escalating need for better equipment and connections, and (4) adverse consequences, such as arguments and lying about Internet use, social isolation, and reductions in academic or work performance.

Estimates of the prevalence of Internet addiction vary considerably from one country to another, but a recent meta-analysis of findings from thirty-one nations estimates that the average prevalence is around 6% of the population (Cheng & Yee-lam Li, 2014). The exact percentage is not as important as the recognition that the syndrome is *not* rare and that it is a global problem. Studies suggest that Internet addiction *is* fostered by high stress (Chen et al., 2014; Tang et al., 2014). Among other things, Internet addiction is associated with increased levels of social anxiety (Weinstein et al., 2015), depression, and alcohol use (Ho et al., 2014). Although not all psychologists agree about whether excessive Internet use should be classified as an *addiction* (Hinic, 2011; Starcevic, 2013), it is clear that this coping strategy can be problematic (Muller et al., 2014).

Experts disagree about whether excessive Internet use should be characterized as an addiction, but the inability to control online use appears to be an increasingly common syndrome.

There is nothing inherently maladaptive about indulging oneself as a way of coping with life's stresses. If a hot fudge sundae, some new clothes, or chatting online can calm your nerves after a major setback, who can argue? However, if a person consistently responds to stress with excessive self-indulgence, obvious problems are likely to develop. For instance, excesses in drinking and drug use may endanger one's health and affect work or relationship quality. Additionally, these indulgences can cause emotional ambivalence, as immediate pleasure gives way to regret, guilt, or embarrassment (Ramanathan & Williams, 2007). Given the risks associated with self-indulgence, it has marginal adaptive value.

Blaming Yourself

In a postgame interview after a tough defeat, a prominent football coach was brutally critical of himself. He said that he had been outcoached, that he had made poor decisions, and that his game plan was faulty. He almost eagerly assumed all the blame for the loss himself. In reality, he had taken some reasonable risks that didn't go his way and had suffered the effects of poor execution by his players. Looking at it objectively, the loss was attributable to the collective failures of fifty or so players and coaches. However, the coach's unrealistically negative self-evaluation is not uncommon. When confronted by stress (especially frustration and pressure), people often become highly self-critical.

The tendency to engage in "negative self-talk" in response to stress has been noted by a number of influential theorists. As we will discuss in greater detail later in this chapter, Albert Ellis (1973, 1987) calls this phenomenon "catastrophic thinking" and focuses on how it is rooted in irrational assumptions. According to Ellis, catastrophic thinking perpetuates emotional reactions to stress that are often problematic. Supporting this assertion, researchers have found that self-blame is associated with increased distress and depression for individuals who have experienced traumas such as sexual assault, war, and natural disasters (DePrince, Chu, & Pineda, 2011; Kraaij & Garnefski, 2006). For victims of sexual assault specifically, self-blame is associated with heightened PTSD symptoms and greater feelings of shame (Ullman et al., 2007; Vidal & Petrak, 2007). Likewise, self-blame is related to difficulties in dealing with the loss of a loved one (Stroebe et al., 2014) and psychological distress (Nielsen & Knardahl, 2014).

Although being realistic and recognizing one's weaknesses has value, especially when one is engaging in problem solving, self-blame as a coping strategy can be enormously counterproductive. We cover Ellis's advice on more constructive thinking later in this chapter.

Using Defensive Coping

Defensive coping is a common response to stress. We noted in Chapter 2 that the concept of defense mechanisms was originally developed by Sigmund Freud. Though rooted in the psychoanalytic tradition, this concept has gained acceptance from psychologists of most persuasions. Building on Freud's initial insights, modern psychologists have broadened the scope of the concept and added to Freud's list of defense mechanisms.

The Nature of Defense Mechanisms

Defense mechanisms **are largely unconscious reactions that protect a person from unpleasant emotions such as anxiety and guilt.** A number of coping strategies fit this definition. In our discussion of Freud's theory in Chapter 2, we described several common defenses. **Figure 4.3** introduces another five defenses that people use with some regularity. Although widely discussed in the popular press, defense mechanisms

COMMON DEFENSE MECHANISMS	
Defense mechanism	**Example**
Denial. Refusal to acknowledge or face up to unpleasant realities in one's life.	A student allows her family to plan a trip to her graduation even though she is failing a class required for graduation.
Fantasy. Fulfilling conscious or unconscious wishes and impulses in one's imagination.	An unpopular man imagines that he has an extensive network of outgoing and popular friends.
Intellectualization. Dealing with difficulties by looking at them in a detached, abstract way, thus suppressing one's emotional reactions.	A man who has just been diagnosed with a terminal illness attempts to learn everything there is to know about the disease and the minute details of medical treatment.
Undoing. Attempting to counteract feelings of guilt through acts of atonement.	A daughter who feels guilty about insulting her mother compliments her mother's appearance after each insult.
Overcompensation. Making up for real or imagined deficiencies by focusing on, or exaggerating, desirable characteristics.	A transfer student who has not made any new friends focuses on excelling in her classes.

Figure 4.3

Additional defense mechanisms. Like the seven defense mechanisms described in the discussion of Freudian theory in Chapter 2 (see **Figure 2.4**), these five defenses are frequently used in people's efforts to cope with stress.

are often misunderstood. We will use a question-answer format to elaborate on the nature of defense mechanisms in the hopes of clearing up any misconceptions.

What do defense mechanisms defend against? Above all else, defense mechanisms shield the individual from the *emotional discomfort* elicited by stress. Their main purpose is to ward off unwelcome emotions or to reduce their intensity (Cramer, 2008; 2015). Foremost among the emotions guarded against is anxiety. People are especially defensive when the anxiety is the result of some threat to their self-esteem. Guilt is another emotion that people often try to evade through defensive maneuvers.

How do they work? Defense mechanisms work through *self-deception*. They accomplish their goals by distorting reality so it does not appear to be threatening. Let's say you're doing poorly in school and are in danger of flunking out. Initially, you might use *denial* to block awareness of the possibility that you could fail. If it becomes difficult to deny the obvious, you might resort to *fantasy*, daydreaming about how you get perfect scores on the upcoming final exams. Thus, defense mechanisms work their magic by bending reality in self-serving ways.

Are they conscious or unconscious? Mainstream Freudian theory originally assumed that defenses operate entirely at an unconscious level. However, the concept of defense mechanisms has been broadened to include maneuvers that people may have some awareness of. Thus, defense mechanisms operate at varying levels of awareness and can be conscious or unconscious.

Are they normal? Definitely. Most people use defense mechanisms on a fairly regular basis. The notion that only neurotic people use defense mechanisms is inaccurate.

Can Defense Mechanisms Ever Be Healthy?

This is a complicated question. Although some defenses appear more adaptive than others (Metzger, 2014), more often than not, the answer is no. In general, defense mechanisms are poor ways of coping, for a number of reasons. First, defensive coping is an avoidance strategy, and avoidance rarely provides a genuine solution to problems. In fact, Holahan and his colleagues (2005) found that avoidance coping is associated with increased life stressors as well as increased depressive symptoms. Second, defenses such as denial, fantasy, and projection represent "wishful thinking," which is likely to accomplish little. In a study of how students coped with the stress of taking the Medical College Admissions Test (MCAT), Bolger (1990) found that those who engaged in a lot of wishful thinking experienced greater increases in anxiety than other students as the exam approached. Third, a defensive coping style has been related to poor health, in part because it often leads people to delay facing up to their problems. For example, if you were to block out obvious warning signs of diabetes and failed to obtain needed medical care, your defensive behavior could be fatal. Although illusions may protect one from anxiety in the short term, they can create serious problems in the long term.

That said, there is some evidence suggesting that "positive illusions" may sometimes be adaptive for mental health (Taylor, 2011a; Taylor, 2011b). For example, Shelley Taylor and Jonathon Brown (1988, 1994) note that "normal" (that is, nondepressed) people tend to have overly favorable self-images. In contrast, depressed people exhibit less favorable— but more realistic—self-concepts. Also, "normal" participants overestimate the degree to which they control chance events. In comparison, depressed participants are less prone to this illusion of control. Finally, "normal" individuals are more likely than their depressed counterparts to display unrealistic optimism in making projections about the future.

As you might guess, critics have expressed considerable skepticism about the idea that illusions are adaptive. For example, Colvin and Block (1994) make an eloquent case for the traditional view that accuracy and realism are healthy. Moreover, they report data showing that overly favorable self-ratings are correlated with maladaptive personality traits (Colvin, Block, & Funder, 1995). One possible resolution to this debate is Roy Baumeister's (1989) theory that it's all a matter of degree and that there is an "optimal margin of illusion." According to Baumeister, extreme self-deception is maladaptive, but small illusions may often be beneficial.

Shelley Taylor notes that positive illusions may sometimes be adaptive for mental health.

4.3 The Nature of Constructive Coping

Our discussion thus far has focused on coping strategies that tend to be less than ideal. Of course, people also exhibit many healthy strategies for dealing with stress. We will use the term *constructive coping* to refer to **efforts to deal with stressful events that are judged to be relatively healthful.** Keep in mind that even the healthiest coping responses may turn out to be ineffective in some cases (Bonanno & Burton, 2013). The efficacy of a coping response depends to some extent on the person, the nature of the stressful challenge, and the context of events. Thus, the concept of constructive coping is simply meant to convey a healthy, positive connotation, without promising success.

What makes a coping strategy constructive? Frankly, in labeling certain coping responses constructive or healthy, psychologists are making value judgments. It's a gray area in which opinions will vary to some extent. Nonetheless, some consensus emerges from the research on coping and stress management. Key themes in this literature include the following (Kleinke, 2007):

1. Constructive coping involves confronting problems directly. It is task relevant and action oriented.

2. Constructive coping takes conscious effort. Using such strategies to reduce stress is an active process that involves planning.

3. Constructive coping is based on reasonably realistic appraisals of your stress and coping resources. A little self-deception may sometimes be adaptive, but excessive self-deception is not.

4. Constructive coping involves learning to recognize and manage potentially disruptive emotional reactions to stress.

5. Constructive coping involves learning to exert some control over potentially harmful or destructive habitual behaviors. It requires some behavioral self-control.

These points should give you a general idea of what we mean by constructive coping. They will guide our discourse in the remainder of this chapter as we discuss how to cope more effectively with stress. To organize our discussion, we will use a classification scheme proposed by Moos and Billings (1982) to divide constructive coping techniques into three broad categories: *appraisal-focused coping* (aimed at changing one's interpretation of stressful events), *problem-focused coping* (aimed at altering the stressful situation itself), and *emotion-focused coping* (aimed at managing potential emotional distress). **Figure 4.4** shows common coping strategies that fall under each category. It is important to note that many strategies could fall under more than one category. For instance, one could seek social

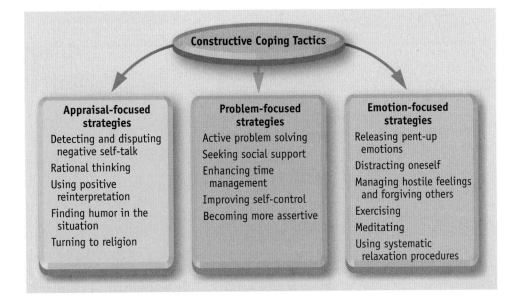

Figure 4.4

Overview of constructive coping tactics. Coping tactics can be organized in several ways, but we will use the classification scheme shown here, which consists of three categories: appraisal-focused strategies, problem-focused strategies, and emotion-focused strategies. The list of coping tactics in each category is not exhaustive. Most, but not all, of the listed strategies are discussed in our coverage of constructive coping.

support in order to talk through and come to a better understanding of a problem (appraisal focused), to get practical help (problem focused), or to gain emotional support (emotion focused). Further, these categories are not mutually exclusive. For example, tackling a problem head on can reduce unwanted negative emotions.

Learning Objectives

- Explain rational thinking as an appraisal-focused coping strategy by using Ellis's theory of catastrophic thinking.
- Discuss the merits of humor in coping with stress, including the research on different types of humor.
- Assess positive reinterpretation and benefit finding as appraisal-focused coping strategies.

4.4 Appraisal-Focused Constructive Coping

As we've seen, the experience of stress depends on how one interprets or appraises threatening events. People often fail to appreciate the highly subjective feelings that color the perception of threat to one's well-being. In fact, a useful way to cope with stress is to alter your appraisal of threatening events. In this section, we'll examine Albert Ellis's ideas about reappraisal and discuss the value of using humor and positive reinterpretation to cope with stress.

Ellis's Rational Thinking

Albert Ellis (1977, 1985, 1996, 2001b) was a prominent and influential theorist who died in 2007 at the age of 93. He believed that people could short-circuit their emotional reactions to stress by altering their appraisals of stressful events. Ellis's insights about stress appraisal are the foundation for his widely used system of therapy. His *rational-emotive behavior therapy* **is an approach to therapy that focuses on altering clients' patterns of irrational thinking to reduce maladaptive emotions and behavior.**

Ellis maintained that *you feel the way you think*. He argued that problematic emotional reactions are caused by negative self-talk, which, as we mentioned earlier, he called catastrophic thinking. *Catastrophic thinking* **involves unrealistic appraisals of stress that exaggerate the magnitude of one's problems.** Ellis used a simple A-B-C sequence to explain his ideas (see **Figure 4.5**):

A. *Activating event.* The A in Ellis's system stands for the activating event that produces the stress. The activating event may be any potentially stressful transaction. Examples might include a car accident, a delay while waiting in line at the bank, or a failure to get a promotion you were expecting.

Figure 4.5

Albert Ellis's A-B-C model of emotional reactions. Most people are likely to attribute their negative emotional reactions (C) directly to stressful events (A). However, Ellis argues that emotional reactions are really caused by the way individuals think about these events (B).

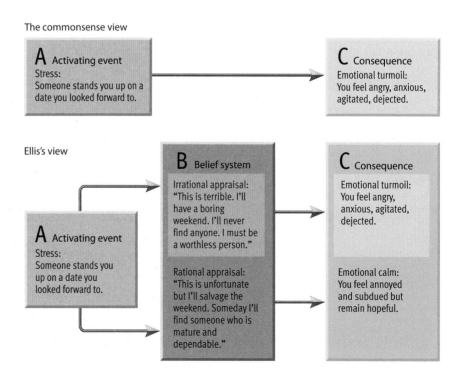

B. *Belief system.* B stands for your belief about the event, which represents your appraisal of the stress. According to Ellis, people often view minor setbacks as disasters, engaging in catastrophic thinking: "How awful this is. I can't stand it!" "I'll be in this line forever." "I'll never get promoted."

C. *Consequence.* C stands for the consequence of your negative thinking. When your appraisals of stressful events are highly negative, the consequence tends to be emotional distress. Thus, you feel angry, outraged, anxious, panic stricken, disgusted, or dejected.

Ellis asserts that most people do not understand the importance of phase B in this three-stage sequence. They unwittingly believe that the activating event (A) *causes* the consequent emotional turmoil (C). However, Ellis maintains that A does *not* cause C; it only appears to do so. Instead, Ellis asserts that B causes C. Emotional distress is actually caused by one's catastrophic thinking in appraising stressful events, which turns inconveniences into disasters and makes "mountains out of molehills."

Learn More Online

The Albert Ellis Institute
Albert Ellis developed rational-emotive behavior therapy in the mid-1950s as an effective alternative to psychoanalytically inspired treatment approaches. This site demonstrates the growth of Ellis's approach over the subsequent decades. The institute disseminates research and provides public self-help workshops.

The Roots of Catastrophic Thinking

Ellis theorized that unrealistic appraisals of stress are derived from the irrational assumptions people hold. He maintained that if you scrutinize your catastrophic thinking, you will find that your reasoning is based on an unreasonable premise, such as "I must have approval from everyone" or "I must perform well in all endeavors." These faulty assumptions, which most people hold unconsciously, generate catastrophic thinking. To facilitate emotional self-control, it is important to learn to spot irrational assumptions and the unhealthy patterns of thought they generate. Here are four particularly common irrational assumptions:

1. *I must have love and affection from certain people.* Everyone wants to be liked and loved. However, many people foolishly believe that everyone they come into contact with should like them. If you stop to think about it, that's clearly unrealistic. In addition, people tend to believe that if their current love relationship were to end, they would never again be able to achieve a comparable one. This is also an unrealistic view. Such views make the person anxious during a relationship and severely depressed if it comes to an end.

2. *I must perform well in all endeavors.* We live in a highly competitive society. We are taught that victory brings happiness. Consequently, we feel that we must always perform at our best level. However, by definition, our best level is not our typical level, and this sets us up for inevitable frustration.

3. *Other people should always behave competently and be considerate of me.* People are often angered by others' lack of competence and selfishness. For example, you may become outraged when a mechanic fails to fix your car properly or when a salesperson treats you rudely. It would be nice if others were always competent and considerate, but they are not. Yet many people go through life unrealistically expecting others' efficiency and kindness in every situation.

4. *Events should always go the way I like.* Some people simply won't tolerate any kind of setback. They assume that things should always go their way. For example, some commuters become tense and angry each time they get stuck in rush-hour traffic. They seem to believe that they are entitled to coast home easily every day. Such expectations are clearly unrealistic and doomed to be violated. Yet few people recognize the obvious irrationality of the assumption unless it is pointed out to them.

Albert Ellis maintained that you feel the way you think and that problematic emotional reactions are caused by negative self-talk.

Reducing Catastrophic Thinking

How can you reduce your unrealistic appraisals of stress? Ellis asserts that you must learn (1) how to detect catastrophic thinking and (2) how to dispute the irrational assumptions that cause it. Detection involves acquiring the ability to spot wild exaggeration in your thinking. Examine your self-talk closely. Force yourself to verbalize your concerns, covertly or out loud. Look for key words that often show up in catastrophic thinking, such as *should, ought, always, never,* and *must.*

People often turn to humor to help themselves cope during difficult times, as this photo taken in the aftermath of a natural disaster illustrates. Research suggests that humor can help reduce the negative impact of stressful events.

Disputing your irrational assumptions requires subjecting your entire reasoning process to scrutiny. Try to root out the source of your catastrophic thinking—the assumptions from which your conclusions are derived. Once these assumptions are unearthed, their irrationality may be quite obvious. Try to replace your catastrophic thinking with more low-key, rational analyses. Such strategies should help you to redefine stressful situations in ways that are less threatening.

Humor as a Stress Reducer

In the aftermath of Superstorm Sandy on the East Coast in late 2012, singer Aimee Mann performed a tongue-in-cheek song called "Sandy" (to the tune of Barry Manilow's "Mandy"). In a New Orleans suburb following Hurricane Katrina, a flooded, grimy Chevrolet pickup parked outside a shattered two-story house had a shiny new sign: "For Sale. Like New. Runs Great." Obviously, disasters don't destroy people's sense of humor. When the going gets tough, finding some humor in the situation is not uncommon and is usually beneficial.

Empirical evidence showing that humor moderates the impact of stress has been accumulating in recent decades (Lefcourt, 2005). For instance, in one influential study, Martin and Lefcourt (1983) found that a good sense of humor functioned as a buffer to lessen the negative impact of stress on mood. Their results showed that high-humor participants were less negatively affected by stress than their low-humor counterparts were. More recently humor has been linked to increases in self-efficacy, positive mood, and optimism, and with decreases in stress, depression, and anxiety (Crawford & Caltabiano, 2011).

It appears that some *types* of humor are more effective than others in reducing stress (Samson & Gross, 2012). Chen and Martin (2007) found that humor that is affiliative (used to engage or amuse others) or self-enhancing (maintaining a humorous perspective in the face of adversity) is related to better mental health. In contrast, coping through humor that is self-defeating (used at one's own expense) or aggressive (criticizing or ridiculing others) is related to poorer mental health. In addition, McGraw and colleagues have found that the *timing* of humor plays a role in how adaptive it is in reducing stress (McGraw, Williams, & Warren, 2014). To use humor, we need to have some psychological distance from the stressful event, especially if the event was severe. Otherwise, attempts at humor may be perceived as "too soon" (McGraw et al., 2012).

How does humor help reduce the effects of stress and promote wellness? Several explanations have been proposed (see **Figure 4.6**). One possibility is that humor affects *appraisals* of stressful events. Jokes can put a less-threatening spin on life's trials and tribulations. A second possibility is that humor increases the experience of *positive emotions*. A study comparing types of constructive coping found that strategies that increased positive emotions were most strongly associated with well-being (Shiota, 2006). A third hypothesis is that a good sense of humor buffers the effects of stress by facilitating positive social interactions, which promote social support. Studies have found positive associations between humor and liking, even in laboratory settings (Treger, Sprecher, & Erber, 2013). Finally, Lefcourt and colleagues (1995) argue that high-humor people may benefit from not taking themselves as seriously as low-humor people do. As they put it, "If persons do not regard themselves too seriously and do not have an inflated sense of self-importance, then defeats, embarrassments, and even tragedies should have less pervasive emotional consequences for them"

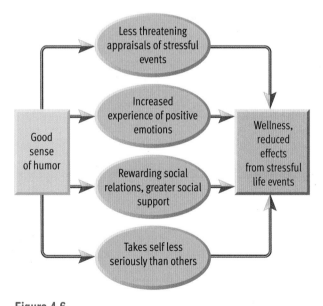

Figure 4.6

Possible explanations for the link between humor and wellness. Research suggests that a good sense of humor buffers the effects of stress and promotes wellness. Four hypothesized explanations for the link between humor and wellness are outlined in the middle column of this diagram. As you can see, humor may have a variety of beneficial effects.

(p. 375). Thus, humor is a rather versatile coping strategy that may have many benefits.

Positive Reinterpretation

When you are feeling overwhelmed by life's difficulties, you might try the commonsense strategy of recognizing that "things could be worse." No matter how terrible your problems seem, you probably know someone who has even bigger troubles. That is not to say that you should derive satisfaction from others' misfortune, but rather that comparing your own plight with others' even tougher struggles can help you put your problems in perspective. This strategy does not depend on knowing others who are clearly worse off. You can simply imagine yourself in a similar situation with an even worse outcome (two broken legs after a horseback-riding accident instead of just one). One healthy aspect of positive reinterpretation is that it can facilitate calming reappraisals of stress without the necessity of distorting reality. Over time this perspective can decrease the stress of the situation (Aldwin, 2007).

Another way to engage in positive reinterpretation is to search for something good in a bad experience. Distressing though they may be, many setbacks have positive elements. After experiencing divorces, illnesses, layoffs, and the like, many people remark, "I came out of the experience better than I went in" or "I grew as a person." Studies of victims of natural disasters, heart attacks, romantic break-ups, and bereavement have found an association between this type of *benefit finding* under duress and relatively sound psychological and physical health (Lechner, Tennen & Affleck, 2009; Nolen-Hoeksema & Davis, 2005; Samios, Henson, & Simpson, 2014; Stanko et al., 2015). Of course, the positive aspects of a traumatic experience or a personal setback may be easy to see after the stressful event is behind you. The challenge is to recognize these positive aspects while you are still struggling with the event so that it becomes less stressful.

off the mark .com — by Mark Parisi

I CAN DEAL WITH IT... I'VE BEEN EATEN BY A SNAKE, BUT I'LL JUST GO ON WITH MY LIFE... I'M OKAY!

LEWIS TESTS THE LIMITS OF POSITIVE THINKING.

Mark Parisi/Atlantic Features 1992 /offthemark.com

4.5 Problem-Focused Constructive Coping

Learning Objectives

- List and describe four steps in systematic problem solving.
- Discuss the adaptive value of seeking help as a coping strategy.
- Describe how people's time orientation might influence their time management.

Problem-focused coping includes efforts to remedy or conquer the stress-producing problem itself. This type of coping is associated with positive outcomes such as emotional growth in times of stress (Karlsen, Dybdahl, & Vitterso, 2006) and general well-being and adjustment (Mayordomo-Rodríguez et al., 2015; Riley & Park, 2014). In this section, we'll discuss using systematic problem solving, the importance of seeking help, and improving time management.

Using Systematic Problem Solving

In dealing with life's problems, the most obvious (and often most effective) course of action is to tackle them head on. In fact, problem solving has been linked to better psychological adjustment, lower levels of depression, reduced alcohol use, and fewer health complaints (Heppner & Lee, 2005). Obviously, people vary in their problem-solving skills. However, evidence suggests that these skills can be enhanced through training (Nezu & Nezu, 2014). With this thought in mind, we will sketch a general outline of how to engage in more systematic problem solving. The plan described here is a synthesis of observations by various experts, especially Mahoney (1979), Miller (1978), and Chang and Kelly (1993).

Clarify the Problem

You can't tackle a problem if you're not sure what it is. Therefore, the first step in any systematic problem-solving effort is to clarify the nature of the problem. Sometimes the problem will be all too obvious. At other times the source of trouble may be quite difficult to pin down. In any case, you need to arrive at a specific concrete definition of your problem.

Two common tendencies typically hinder people's efforts to get a clear picture of their problems. First, people often describe their problems in vague generalities ("My life isn't going anywhere" or "I never have enough time"). Second, they tend to focus too much on negative feelings, thereby confusing the consequences of problems ("I'm so depressed all the time" or "I'm so nervous I can't concentrate") with the problems themselves ("I don't have any friends at my new school" or "I have taken on more responsibilities that I can realistically handle").

Generate Alternative Courses of Action

The second step in systematic problem solving is to generate alternative courses of action. Notice that we did not call these alternative *solutions*. Many problems do not have a readily available solution that will completely resolve the situation. Instead, it is more realistic to search for alternatives that may produce some kind of improvement in your situation.

Besides avoiding the tendency to insist on solutions, you need to avoid the temptation to go with the first alternative that comes to mind. Many people thoughtlessly try to follow through on the first response that occurs to them when it is wiser to engage in brainstorming about a problem. *Brainstorming* **is generating as many ideas as possible while withholding criticism and evaluation.** This approach facilitates creative expression of ideas and can lead to more alternative courses of action to choose from.

Evaluate Your Alternatives and Select a Course of Action

Once you generate as many alternatives as you can, you need to start evaluating the possibilities. There are no simple criteria for judging the relative merits of your alternatives. However, you will probably want to address three general issues. First, ask yourself whether each alternative is realistic. In other words, what is the probability that you can successfully execute the intended course of action? Try to think of any obstacles you may have failed to anticipate. In making this assessment, it is important to try to avoid both foolish optimism and unnecessary pessimism.

Second, consider any costs or risks associated with each alternative. Sometimes the "solution" to a problem can be worse than the problem itself. Assuming you can successfully implement your intended course of action, what are the possible negative consequences? Third, compare the desirability of the probable outcomes of each alternative. In making your decision, you have to ask yourself, "What is important to me? Which outcomes do I value the most?" Through careful evaluation, you can select the best course of action.

Take Action while Maintaining Flexibility

You can plan your course of action as thoughtfully and intentionally as possible, but no plan works if you don't follow through with it. In so doing, try to maintain flexibility. You need to monitor results closely and be willing to revise your strategy.

In evaluating your course of action, try to avoid the simplistic success/failure dichotomy. You should look for improvement of any kind. If your plan doesn't work out too well, consider whether it was undermined by any circumstances that you could not have anticipated. Finally, remember that you can learn from your failures. Even if things did not work out, you may now have new information that will facilitate a new attack on the problem.

Seeking Help

In Chapter 3, we saw that social support is a powerful force that helps buffer the deleterious effects of stress and has positive effects of its own. In trying to tackle problems directly, it pays to keep in mind the value of seeking aid from trusted friends, family, and co-workers. So far, we have discussed social support as if it were a stable, external resource available to different people in varying degrees. In reality, social support fluctuates over time and evolves out of one's interactions with others. Some people have more support than others because they have personal characteristics that attract more support or because they make an effort to seek support.

Although the benefits of social support on mental and physical health are well documented, there are instances when the presence of friends or family is not experienced as supportive. Taylor (2011a) notes that friends can sometimes increase physiological reactivity to stress and increase evaluation apprehension. Further, there might be instances where social support networks are intrusive or give poor advice, or when the help offered doesn't match the need. Finally, merely having to ask for help might undermine one's sense of self, thus increasing one's stress.

Interestingly, cultural factors, often overlooked by researchers, seem to play an important role in what individuals see as problems and how they solve them (Chang, 2015). This is especially true with regard to who seeks social support (Taylor, 2011b). Taylor and colleagues (2004) found that Asians and Asian Americans are less likely to seek social support in times of stress than European Americans are. When examined closely, this difference appears to be rooted in cultural concerns about relationships. That is, individuals from cultures high in collectivism (discussed in Chapter 6) are cautious about straining relationships by calling on others for help in times of stress (Kim et al., 2006). Given that social support is such an important resource, researchers will no doubt continue to examine it within a cultural context.

Social support is quite helpful in dealing with stress, and the benefits of social support on mental and physical health are well documented.

Improving Time Management

Talk to the average person and you will discover that many of the stressors of modern life result from a lack of time. Individuals vary in their time perspectives. Some people are *future oriented*, able to see the consequences of immediate behavior for future goals, whereas others are *present oriented*, focused on immediate events and not worried about consequences. These orientations influence how people manage their time and meet their time-related commitments. Future-oriented individuals, for example, are less likely to procrastinate (Sirois, 2014) and are more reliable in meeting their commitments (Harber, Zimbardo, & Boyd, 2003). Regardless of orientation, most people could benefit from more effectively managing their time. Because it is such a crucial coping strategy, we devote the entire application at the end of this chapter to time management.

4.6 Emotion-Focused Constructive Coping

Let's be realistic: There are going to be occasions when appraisal-focused coping and problem-focused coping are not successful in warding off emotional turmoil. Some problems are too serious to be whittled down much by reappraisal, and others simply can't be "solved." Moreover, even well-executed coping strategies may take time to work before emotional tensions begin to subside. Therefore, we will discuss a variety of coping abilities and strategies that relate mainly to the regulation of emotions.

Enhancing Emotional Intelligence

According to some theorists, *emotional intelligence* is the key to being resilient in the face of stress. The concept of emotional intelligence was originally formulated by Peter

Learning Objectives

- Clarify the nature and value of emotional intelligence.
- Analyze the adaptive value of expressing emotions.
- Discuss the importance of managing hostility and forgiving others' transgressions.
- Understand how exercise can foster improved emotional functioning.
- Summarize the evidence on the adaptive value of meditation, relaxation, and spirituality.

Salovey and John Mayer (1990). *Emotional intelligence* **consists of the ability to perceive and express emotion, use emotions to facilitate thought, understand and reason with emotion, and regulate emotion.** As shown in **Figure 4.7**, emotional intelligence includes four essential components (Mayer, Salovey, & Caruso, 2008). First, people need to be able to accurately perceive emotions in themselves and in others and to have the ability to express their own emotions effectively. Second, people need to be aware of how their emotions shape their thinking, decision making, and coping with stress. Third, people need to be able to understand and analyze their emotions, which may often be complex and contradictory. Fourth, people need to be able to regulate their emotions so that they can dampen negative emotions and make effective use of positive ones.

Researchers have developed several tests to measure the concept of emotional intelligence. The test that has the strongest empirical foundation is the Mayer-Salovey-Caruso Emotional Intelligence Test (2002; 2012). The authors have strived to make this test a performance-based measure of the ability to deal effectively with emotions rather than a measure of personality or temperament. Results suggest that they have made considerable progress toward this goal, as evidenced by the scale's ability to predict intelligent management of emotions in real-world situations (Mayer et al., 2001). It has been found to reliably predict the quality of individuals' social interactions (Lopes et al., 2004), leadership effectiveness (Antoniou & Cooper, 2005), and mental and physical health (Martins, Ramalho, & Morin, 2010; Schutte et al., 2007). The scale has even been adapted for other cultures (Curci et al. 2013; Iliescu et al., 2013).

Emotional intelligence has been explored in relation to adaptive coping (Perera & DiGiacomo, 2015). Pashang and Singh (2008) found that those high in emotional intelligence were more likely to use problem-solving strategies to deal with anxiety, whereas those with lower levels used more distraction and denial. Low emotional intelligence has also been linked to increased worry and avoidance (Matthews et al., 2006). At work, low emotional intelligence is related to increased burnout (Xie, 2011). Because this construct appears to be important for general well-being, investigators are exploring ways to cultivate emotional intelligence in classrooms, workplaces, and counseling settings. One study found that positive emotional expression can lead to an increase in emotional intelligence (Wing, Schutte, & Byrne, 2006). That leads us to our next topic.

Expressing Emotions

Try as you might to redefine or resolve stressful situations, you no doubt will still go through times when you feel wired with stress-induced tension. When this happens, there's merit in the commonsense notion that you should express the emotions welling up inside. Why?

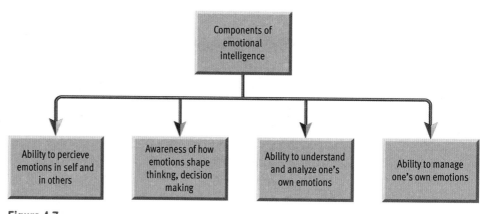

Figure 4.7

Essential components of emotional intelligence. According to Mayer, Salovey, and Caruso (2008), emotional intelligence includes four essential components. Individuals must possess each of these in order to effectively express their own emotions and cope with negative emotions.

Because the physiological arousal that accompanies emotions can become problematic. For example, research suggests that efforts to actively suppress emotions result in increased stress and autonomic arousal (Butler et al., 2003; Gross, 2001). Moreover, a meta-analysis that included more than 6500 participants found that coping by repressing negative feelings is related to an increase in cardiovascular diseases, especially hypertension (Mund & Mitte, 2012). Note that such findings do not mean you should act aggressively (a coping strategy of limited value discussed earlier in this chapter). Instead, our focus here is on appropriate, healthy expression of emotions.

James Pennebaker and his colleagues have shown that emotional expression through writing about traumatic events can have beneficial effects (Pennebaker & Ferrell, 2013). In one study of college students, half the subjects were asked to write three essays about their difficulties in adjusting to college. The other half wrote three essays about superficial topics. The participants who wrote about their personal problems and traumas enjoyed better health in the following months than the other subjects did (Pennebaker, Colder, & Sharp, 1990). Additionally, emotional disclosure, or "opening up," is associated with improved mood, more positive self-perceptions, fewer visits to physicians, and enhanced immune functioning (Niederhoffer & Pennebaker, 2005; Smyth & Pennebaker, 2001). Smyth and Pennebaker (1999) assert that "when people put their emotional upheavals into words, their physical and mental health seems to improve markedly." They conclude that "the act of disclosure itself is a powerful therapeutic agent" (p. 70). **Figure 4.8** summarizes some guidelines for writing about personal issues and trauma that should make this coping strategy more effective.

Managing Hostility and Forgiving Others

In 1944, when Eva Mozes was 10 years old, she and her twin sister were subjected to life-threatening experimentation at the Auschwitz concentration camp in Poland during World War II. She and her twin survived, although their parents and older sisters did not. In adulthood, she did something almost unimaginable: she forgave the Nazis, stating that forgiveness gave her "back the power" she lost as a victim (Pope, 2012). One might ask: Why did she choose this route? How did she manage to overcome the anger and hostility related to her early experiences? In fact, researchers have shown that Eva made a good choice, and we'll discuss why.

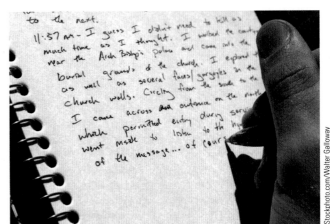

Research shows that emotional expression through writing about traumatic events can have beneficial effects.

INSTRUCTIONS FOR WRITING ABOUT PERSONAL EXPERIENCES

- Plan to spend 20 minutes or so writing each day.

- Try to write for three consecutive days or more.

- Write about your very deepest thoughts and feelings about any stressful or emotionally disturbing experiences going on in your life at the moment or traumatic events from the past.

- You may want to discuss how your topic is related to your relationships with others, such as parents, friends, or intimate others.

- You may want to analyze how your topic relates to who you are now or who you would like to be.

- Write spontaneously; you do not need to worry about spelling or grammar.

- Keep in mind that you are writing only for yourself; this is a private endeavor.

Figure 4.8

Using writing about emotional experiences as a coping strategy. Many studies have shown that writing about traumatic experiences and sensitive issues can have beneficial effects on mental and physical health. These guidelines can help you to use this coping strategy. (Based on Gortner, Rude, & Pennebaker, 2006)

In September 1994, Reg and Maggie Green were vacationing in Italy when their 7-year-old son, Nicholas, was shot and killed during a highway robbery. In an act of forgiveness that stunned Europe, the Greens chose to donate their son's organs, which went to seven Italians. The Greens, shown here 5 years after the incident, have weathered their horrific loss better than most, perhaps in part because of their willingness to forgive.

Scientists have compiled quite a bit of evidence that hostility is bad for you. It is related to increased risk for heart attacks and other types of illness (see Chapter 5). So how can individuals effectively regulate negative emotions that include anger and hostility? A variety of strategies can be used to decrease hostility, including positive reinterpretation of annoying events, distraction, and the kind of rational self-talk advocated by Albert Ellis. Efforts to increase empathy and tolerance can also contribute to hostility management, as can forgiveness, which has become the focus of a contemporary line of research in psychology.

People tend to experience hostility and other negative emotions when they feel "wronged"—that is, when they believe that the actions of another person were harmful, immoral, or unjust. In these cases, people's natural inclination is either to seek revenge or to avoid further contact with the offender (McCullough & Witvliet, 2005). Although there is debate among researchers about the exact definition, *forgiveness* **involves counteracting the natural tendencies to seek vengeance or avoid an offender, thereby releasing this person from further liability for his or her transgression.** Research suggests that forgiving is an effective emotion-focused coping strategy that is associated with better adjustment and well-being (Worthington, Soth-McNeff, & Moreno, 2007; Gull & Rana, 2013). For example, in one study of divorced or permanently separated women, the extent to which the women had forgiven their former husbands was positively related to several measures of well-being and was inversely related to measures of anxiety and depression (McCullough, 2001). Forgiveness not only decreases one's own psychological distress, it also increases one's empathy and positive regard for the offending person (Williamson & Gonzales, 2007; Riek & Mania, 2012). It has even been associated with better physical health (Silton, Flannelly, & Lutjen, 2013).

Recently, researchers have begun to examine self-forgiveness. Self-forgiveness is an emotion-focused coping strategy that involves reducing negative thoughts and emotions about oneself. Early studies indicate that it is associated with both better physical health and psychological well-being (Davis et al., 2015). Some psychologists caution that self-forgiveness has limits in that it might allow individuals to continue wrongful behaviors (Wohl & McLaughlin, 2014). The research in this area is still new and lags behind that on forgiving others, but it is an area that bears watching.

Exercising

There are numerous benefits to physical activity, both preventative and therapeutic. In Chapter 5 you will learn about the effects of exercise on health, so here we will limit our discussion to exercise as an emotion-focused coping strategy. Physical exercise is a healthy way to deal with overwhelming emotions related to stress (Weinstein, Lydick, & Biswabharati, 2014). In fact, one study found that people who participated in a 2-month program of regular exercise showed an increase in emotional control and a decrease in emotional distress (Oaten & Cheng, 2006). Exercise is an ideal coping strategy because it provides multiple coping-related benefits: an outlet for frustration, a distraction from the stressor, and benefits to physical and psychological health (Sapolsky, 2004). Although it appears that exercise decreases the impact of stress, it could be that those with lower stress are more likely to exercise (Stults-Kolehmainen & Sinha, 2014). Even with this caveat, however, exercise is an effective coping

Acey Harper/The LIFE Images Collection/Getty Images

strategy. In fact, psychologists are starting to question why mental health professionals don't recommend it more often (Walsh, 2011).

Sapolosky (2004) asserts that to get maximal benefits from physical exercise, you should engage in aerobic exercise (such as jogging, swimming, or bicycling) because most of the positive effects come from this type of exercise. You should also exercise on a regular basis. Of course, regular exercise requires discipline and self-control. If you are not currently as physically active as you would like, perhaps you could use the self-modification techniques covered in the Application section at the end of Chapter 3 to improve your exercise habits. Advice on devising an effective exercise program can also be found in Chapter 5.

"I'm learning how to relax, doctor —
but I want to relax *better* and *faster!*
I want to be on the cutting edge of relaxation!"

Using Meditation and Relaxation

Recent years have seen an increased interest in meditation as a method for regulating negative emotions caused by stress. *Meditation* **refers to a family of mental exercises in which a conscious attempt is made to focus attention in a nonanalytical way.** There are many approaches to meditation. In the United States, the most widely practiced approaches are those associated with yoga, Zen, transcendental meditation (TM), and mindfulness (Chapter 16 includes a discussion of mindfulness). Relaxation is one of the benefits of meditation, although meditation isn't the only way to achieve relaxation.

What are the *physical* effects of going into a meditative state? Most studies find decreases in participants' heart rate, respiration rate, oxygen consumption, and carbon dioxide elimination (Whitehouse, Orne, & Orne, 2007). Meditation has also been linked to improvements in blood pressure (Barnes, Treiber, & Davis, 2001) and other indicators of overall health (Schutte & Malouff, 2014). Taken together, these physical changes suggest that meditation can lead to a potentially beneficial physiological state characterized by relaxation and suppression of arousal.

What about the long-term *psychological* benefits that have been claimed for meditation? Research suggests that meditation may have some value in reducing the effects of stress (Walsh, 2011). In particular, regular meditation is associated with lower levels of some stress hormones (Infante et al., 2001). Research also suggests that meditative exercises can improve mental health by reducing anxiety and depression (Hofmann et al., 2010). Other studies report that meditation may have beneficial effects on self-control (Teper, Segal, & Inzlicht, 2013), mood (Johnson et al., 2015), happiness (Smith, Compton, & West, 1995), and overall well-being (Zwan et al. 2015).

Meditation might also have an influence on our behavioral choices. Condon and colleagues (2013) studied the effects of meditation on compassion. They examined whether participants who completed an 8-week meditation class were more likely to offer help to someone in pain than those in a control group. As seen in **Figure 4.9**, meditation made a difference—50% of the meditators offered help while only 16% of the control group did.

Researchers are just beginning to explore how meditation works to enhance well-being (see Chapter 16). It appears that the effects of meditation might be due in part to the increase in positive emotions brought on by meditative techniques (Garland et al., 2010). In fact, Garland and colleagues (2011) suggest that meditation and positive reappraisal of negative events mutually support each other, creating an "upward spiral" of mental health.

After studying various approaches to meditation, Herbert Benson, a Harvard Medical School cardiologist, concluded that what makes meditation beneficial is the relaxation

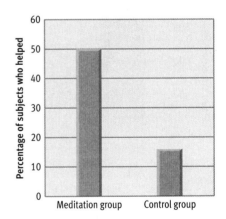

Figure 4.9

The effect of meditation on helping behavior. Research demonstrates that meditation may have beneficial effects on mood and behavior. For instance, Condon and colleagues (2013) found that an 8-week meditation class enhanced compassionate responding. Participants who completed the meditation class were more likely than control subjects to offer their seat to a hobbling person in pain who arrived in a crowded room with all seats occupied. (Based on Condon, Desbordes, Miller, & DeSteno, 2013)

it induces. Benson (1975) set out to devise a simple procedure that could provide similar benefits called the "relaxation response." To practice this response, you should sit comfortably with closed eyes and relaxed muscles. Breathe in through your nose, and as you breathe out say the word *one* to yourself. Continue for 10 to 20 minutes. For full benefit, the response should be practiced daily. According to Benson, four factors are critical to effective practice of the relaxation response:

1. *A quiet environment.* It is easiest to induce a relaxation response in a distraction-free environment. After you become skilled at the relaxation response, you may be able to accomplish it in a crowded subway. Initially, however, you should practice it in a quiet, calm place.

2. *A mental device.* To shift attention inward and keep it there, you need to focus it on a constant stimulus, such as a sound or word that you recite over and over. You may also choose to gaze fixedly at a bland object, such as a vase. Whatever the case, you need to focus your attention on something.

3. *A passive attitude.* It is important not to get upset when your attention strays to distracting thoughts. You must realize that such distractions are inevitable. Whenever your mind wanders from your focus, calmly redirect attention to your mental device.

4. *A comfortable position.* Reasonable body comfort is essential in order to avoid a major source of potential distraction. Simply sitting up straight works well for most people. Some people can practice the relaxation response lying down, but for most people such a position is too conducive to sleep.

Spirituality

Experts estimate that approximately 90% of people around the globe identify with a religion or spiritual practice (Koenig, 2004). People generally report that religious beliefs bring a sense of comfort in times of stress. Harold Koenig (2010, 2013), a medical doctor and leading researcher in the field, argues that spirituality is a means of coping with stress. Often linked with adaptive coping techniques such as social support, reappraisals, forgiveness, and mediation, spiritual practices are related to every aspect of the coping process. Like other strategies, spirituality can be viewed as appraisal, problem, or emotion focused, depending on the goal. Regardless of its goal, Koenig and his colleagues have found spiritual involvement to be linked to better physical and mental health.

Specifically, spirituality has been linked to lowered suicide rates, reduced substance abuse, lowered anxiety, and greater optimism. Physically, spirituality is associated with enhanced immune functioning, lower blood pressure, reduced heart disease, and better general health behaviors (Koenig, 2004). Evidence further suggests that religiosity is related to self-control, an important characteristic for both physical and mental health. In an innovative study, Rounding and colleagues (2012) found that psychology students who were primed to think about religion showed more self-control on a subsequent task than those who were not (see **Figure 4.10**).

Researchers note that the relationship between spirituality and well-being is more complex than it might appear (for a related discussion, see Chapter 16) in that it can be counterproductive as a stress reducer in some instances (Weber & Pargament, 2014). Religious involvement that focuses on punishment or guilt (as opposed to positive themes of love and forgiveness) tends to be detrimental to mental health (Walsh, 2011). Further, struggling with one's spiritual beliefs can induce stress (Pargament, 2011). Still, the evidence for the positive effects of spirituality are so strong that researchers recommend that psychologists and physicians alike take into account the "spiritual histories" of their patients when planning therapeutic treatment (Koenig, 2004).

Now that we have looked at numerous constructive coping tactics, in the following Application we turn to one of the most common sources of stress—poor time management—and examine ways to use time more effectively.

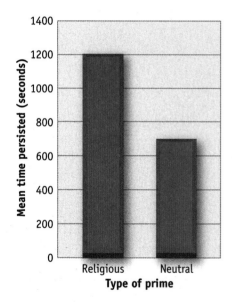

Figure 4.10

Self-control as a function of religious priming. Evidence suggests that spirituality is related to self-control, an important characteristic for coping with stress. Rounding and colleagues (2012) assessed self-control by measuring how long participants persisted in an impossible task, in this case solving impossible puzzles. The researchers found that psychology students who were primed to think about religion showed more self-control on the task than did those who received a neutral prime.

Source: Rounding, K., Lee, A., Jacobson, J. A., & Ji, L. (2012). Religion replenishes self-control. *Psychological Science, 23*(6), 635–642.

4.7 Using Time More Effectively

Learning Objectives

- Explain the common causes of wasted time.
- Identify the causes and consequences of procrastination.
- Summarize the advice on managing time effectively.

Answer the following "yes" or "no."

____ **1.** Do you constantly feel that you have too much to do and too little time in which to do it?

____ **2.** Do you feel overwhelmed by your responsibilities at work, at school, and at home?

____ **3.** Do you feel like you're always rushing around, trying to meet an impossible schedule?

____ **4.** Do you often procrastinate on school or work assignments?

____ **5.** Do you often jump around from one task to another?

If you answered "yes" to the majority of these questions, you're struggling with time pressure, a huge source of stress in modern life. You can estimate how well you manage time by responding to the brief questionnaire in **Figure 4.11**. If the results suggest that your time is out of your control, you may be able to make your life less stressful by learning sound time-management strategies.

R. Alec Mackenzie (1997), a prominent time-management researcher, points out that time is a nonrenewable resource. It can't be stockpiled like money, food, or other precious resources. You can't turn back the clock. Furthermore, everyone, whether rich or poor, gets an equal share of time—24 hours per day, 7 days a week. Although time is our most equitably distributed resource, some people spend it much more wisely than others. Let's look at some of the ways in which people let time slip through their fingers without accomplishing much.

The Causes of Wasted Time

When people complain about "wasted time," they're usually upset because they haven't accomplished what they really wanted to do with their time. Wasted time is time devoted to unnecessary, unimportant, or unenjoyable activities. There are many reasons people waste time on such activities.

Inability to set or stick to priorities. Time consultant Alan Lakein (1996) emphasizes that it's often tempting to deal with routine, trivial tasks ahead of larger and more difficult tasks. Thus, students (and professors for that matter) working on a major paper often check their texts, fold the laundry, or reorganize their desk instead of concentrating on the paper. Why?

Routine tasks are easy, and working on them allows people to rationalize their avoidance of more important tasks. Unfortunately, many of us spend too much time on trivial pursuits, leaving our more important tasks undone.

Inability to say "no." Other people are constantly making demands on our time. They want us to exchange gossip in the hallway, go out to dinner on Friday night, cover their hours at work, help with a project, listen to their sales pitch on the phone, join a committee, or coach Little League. Clearly, we can't do everything that everyone wants us to. However, some people just can't say "no" to others' requests for their time. Such people end up fulfilling others' priorities instead of their own. Thus, McDougle (1987) concludes, "Perhaps the most successful way to prevent yourself from wasting time is by saying *no*" (p. 112).

Inability to delegate responsibility. Some tasks should be delegated to others—assistants, subordinates, fellow committee members, partners, spouses, children, and so on. However, many people have difficulty delegating work. Barriers to delegation include unwillingness to give up any control, lack of confidence in subordinates, fear of being disliked, the need to feel needed, and the attitude that "I can do it better myself" (Mitchell, 1987). The problem, of course, is that people who can't delegate waste a lot of time on others' work.

Inability to throw things away. Some people are pack rats who can't throw anything into the wastebasket. Their desks are cluttered with piles of mail, newspapers, magazines, reports, and books. Their filing cabinets overflow with old class notes or ancient memos. At home, their kitchen drawers bulge with rarely used utensils and their closets bulge with old clothes that are never worn. Pack rats lose time looking for things that have disappeared among all the chaos and end up reshuffling the same paper, rereading the same mail, resorting the same files, and so on. According to Mackenzie (1997), they would be better off if they made more use of their wastebaskets and recycling bins.

Inability to avoid interruptions. Our lives are full of interruptions. Friends stop by when we are studying, co-workers want

HOW WELL DO YOU MANAGE YOUR TIME?

Listed below are ten statements that reflect generally accepted principles of good time management. Answer these items by circling the response most characteristic of how you perform your job. Please be honest. No one will know your answers except you.

1. Each day I set aside a small amount of time for planning and thinking about my job.
0. Almost never 1. Sometimes 2. Often 3. Almost always

2. I set specific, written goals and put deadlines on them.
0. Almost never 1. Sometimes 2. Often 3. Almost always

3. I make a daily "to do list," arrange items in order of importance, and try to get the important items done as soon as possible.
0. Almost never 1. Sometimes 2. Often 3. Almost always

4. I am aware of the 80/20 rule and use it in doing my job. (The 80/20 rule states that 80 percent of your effectiveness will generally come from achieving only 20 percent of your goals.)
0. Almost never 1. Sometimes 2. Often 3. Almost always

5. I keep a loose schedule to allow for crises and the unexpected.
0. Almost never 1. Sometimes 2. Often 3. Almost always

6. I delegate everything I can to others.
0. Almost never 1. Sometimes 2. Often 3. Almost always

7. I try to handle each piece of paper only once.
0. Almost never 1. Sometimes 2. Often 3. Almost always

8. I eat a light lunch so I don't get sleepy in the afternoon.
0. Almost never 1. Sometimes 2. Often 3. Almost always

9. I make an active effort to keep common interruptions (visitors, meetings, telephone calls) from continually disrupting my work day.
0. Almost never 1. Sometimes 2. Often 3. Almost always

10. I am able to say no to others' requests for my time that would prevent my completing important tasks.
0. Almost never 1. Sometimes 2. Often 3. Almost always

To get your score, give yourself

3 points for each "almost always"
2 points for each "often"
1 point for each "sometimes"
0 points for each "almost never"

Add up your points to get your total score.

If you scored

0–15	Better give some thought to managing your time.
15–20	You're doing okay, but there's room for improvement.
20–25	Very good.
25–30	You cheated!

Figure 4.11

Assessing your time management. The brief questionnaire shown here is designed to evaluate the quality of one's time management. Although it is geared more for working adults than college students, it should allow you to get a rough handle on how well you manage your time.

Source: From Le Boeuf, M. (1980, February). Managing time means managing yourself. *Business Horizons* magazine, p. 45. Copyright © by the Foundation for the School of Business at Indiana University. Used with permission.

Some people are pack rats who can't throw anything away. Pack rats can lose valuable time looking for things that have disappeared among all the chaos.

to chat while we are working under deadlines, and family emergencies arise whether we have time to deal with them or not. In addition, phone calls, texts, and emails can interrupt our workflow. As a result, people must protect blocks of uninterrupted time to accomplish their goals. Turning off your phone and shutting your door can go a long way toward protecting your time.

Inability to accept anything less than perfection. To maximize the use of one's time, one should avoid perfectionism (Pandey et al., 2011). High standards are admirable, but some people have difficulty finishing projects because they expect their work to be flawless. They are caught in what Emanuel (1987) calls the "paralysis of perfection." They end up spinning their wheels, redoing the same work over and over, instead of moving on to the next task. Perfectionism can be troublesome in many ways. For example, it is associated with increased fatigue (Dittner, Rimes, & Thorpe, 2011) and blood pressure (Albert, Rice, & Caffee, 2014). In a review of the literature on perfectionism, Leonard and Harvey (2008) report that it has been linked to depression, anxiety, job stress, substance abuse, eating disorders, interpersonal conflict, and procrastination, which we turn to next.

The Problem of Procrastination

Procrastination **is the tendency to delay tackling tasks until the last minute.** Almost everyone procrastinates on occasion. For example, 70%–90% of college students procrastinate before beginning academic assignments (Knaus, 2000). However, research suggests that about 20% of adults are chronic procrastinators (Ferrari, 2001). Not just a U.S. phenomenon, this trend appears to apply to a number of cultures (Ferrari et al., 2007). Procrastination is more likely when people have to work on aversive tasks or when they are worried about their performance being evaluated (Milgram, Marshevsky, & Sadeh, 1995; Senecal, Lavoie, & Koestner, 1997). Procrastination is associated with maladaptive coping and increased stress (Sirois & Kitner, 2015).

Why do people procrastinate? Procrastinators tend to focus less on the future (Sirois, 2014). In a review of the literature Steel (2007) found that procrastination was strongly related to low self-efficacy, low conscientiousness, lack of self-control, poor organization, low achievement motivation, and high distractibility. The type of irrational thinking described by Albert Ellis seems to foster procrastination (Bridges & Roig, 1997), as does a strong fear of failure (Chow, 2011; Krause & Freund, 2014) and excessive perfectionism (Flett, Hewitt, & Martin, 1995; Rice, Richardson, & Clark, 2012).

Other factors besides personality can affect procrastination. Schraw and colleagues (2007) identified six general principles related to academic procrastination, including these three:

1. *Desire to minimize time on a task.* As you know, the modern student is busy—studying, working, socializing, and maintaining a personal life. Time is at a premium. Sometimes delaying as much academic work as possible seems to be a way to safeguard some personal time. As one student reported, "The truth is, I just don't have time *not* to procrastinate. If I did everything the way it could be done, I wouldn't have a life" (Schraw et al., 2007, p. 21).

2. *Desire to optimize efficiency.* Procrastination can be viewed as allowing one to be optimally efficient, concentrating academic work into focused time frames. Students reported that being pressed for time means that there is less opportunity for busywork, boredom, or false starts.

3. *Close proximity to reward.* Students often procrastinate because they are rewarded for it. By putting off academic work until the last minute, students not only get more immediate feedback (the grade), but they also get a sudden release of stress. In this way, procrastination is similar to other thrill-seeking behaviors.

Although many people rationalize their delaying tactics by claiming that "I work best under pressure" (Ferrari, 1992; Lay, 1995), the empirical evidence suggests otherwise. Studies show that procrastination tends to have a negative impact on the quality of task performance (Ferrari, Johnson, & McCown, 1995) and is negatively associated with academic performance (Kim & Seo, 2015). In fact, Britton and Tesser (1991) found that time management was a better predictor of college GPA than SAT scores! Procrastinators may often underestimate how much time will be required to complete a task effectively, or they experience unforeseen delays and then run out of time because they didn't allow any "cushion." Another consideration is that waiting until the last minute may make a task more stressful—and while the release of this built-up stress might be exciting, performance often declines under conditions of high stress (as we saw in Chapter 3). Moreover, work quality may not be the only thing that suffers when people procrastinate. Studies indicate that as a deadline looms, procrastinators tend to experience elevated anxiety and increased health problems (Tice & Baumeister, 1997).

People who struggle with procrastination often impose deadlines and penalties on themselves. This practice can be helpful, but self-imposed deadlines are not as effective as externally imposed ones. Let's discuss some effective ways to manage your time.

Time-Management Techniques

What's the key to better time management? Most people assume that it's increased *efficiency*—that is, learning to perform tasks more quickly. Improved efficiency may help a little, but time-management experts maintain that efficiency is overrated. They emphasize that the key to better time management is increased *effectiveness*—that is, learning to allocate time to your most important tasks. This distinction is captured by a widely quoted slogan in the time-management literature: "Efficiency is doing the job right, while effectiveness is doing the right job." Here are some suggestions for using your time more effectively (based on Lakein, 1996; Mackenzie, 1997; Morgenstern, 2000).

1. *Monitor your use of time.* The first step toward better time management is to monitor your use of time to see where it all goes. Doing so requires keeping a written record of your activities, similar to that shown in **Figure 4.12**. At the end of each week, you should analyze how your time was allocated. Based on your personal roles and responsibilities, create categories of time use such as studying, child care, housework, commuting, working at the office, working at home, going online, spending time with friends, eating, and sleeping. For each day, add up the hours devoted to each category. Record this information on a summary sheet like that in **Figure 4.13**. Two weeks of recordkeeping should allow you to draw some conclusions about where your time goes. Your records will help you make informed decisions about reallocating your time. When you begin your time-management program, these records will also give you a baseline for comparison so you can see whether your program is working.

2. *Clarify your goals.* You can't wisely allocate your time unless you decide what you want to accomplish. Some people lack goals to guide their time, while others have so many goals it is impossible to meet them all. For short-term goals (such as finishing a term paper or completing a house project) set smaller priorities that will lead to the desired outcome, and then stick to them. Be sure they are realistic. For longer-term goals, Lakein (1996) suggests that you ask yourself, "What are my lifetime goals?" Write down all the goals you can think of, even relatively frivolous things like going deep-sea fishing or becoming a wine expert. Some of your goals will be in conflict. For instance, you can't become a vice president at your company in Wichita and still move to the West Coast. Thus, the tough part comes next. You have to wrestle with your goal conflicts. Figure out which goals are most important to you, and then order them in terms of priority. These priorities should guide you as you plan your activities on a daily, weekly, and monthly basis.

3. *Plan your activities using a schedule.* People resist planning because it takes time, but in the long run planning saves time. Thorough planning is essential to effective time management. At the beginning of each week, you should make a list of short-term goals. This list should be translated into daily "to do" lists of planned activities. To avoid the tendency to put off larger projects, break them into small, manageable components and set deadlines for completing the components. Your planned activities should be allocated to various time slots on a written schedule. Schedule your most important activities into the time periods when you tend to be most energetic and productive.

4. *Protect your prime time.* The best-laid plans can quickly go awry because of interruptions. There isn't any foolproof way to eliminate interruptions, but you may be able to shift most of them into certain time slots while protecting your most productive time. Reply to emails, texts, and phone messages at scheduled times, perhaps once in the morning and once in the later afternoon. The trick is to announce to your family, friends, and co-workers that you're blocking off certain periods of "quiet time" when visitors and phone calls will be turned away. Of course, you also have to block off periods of "available time" when you're ready to deal with everyone's problems.

5. *Increase your efficiency.* Although efficiency is not the key to better time management, it's not irrelevant. Time-management

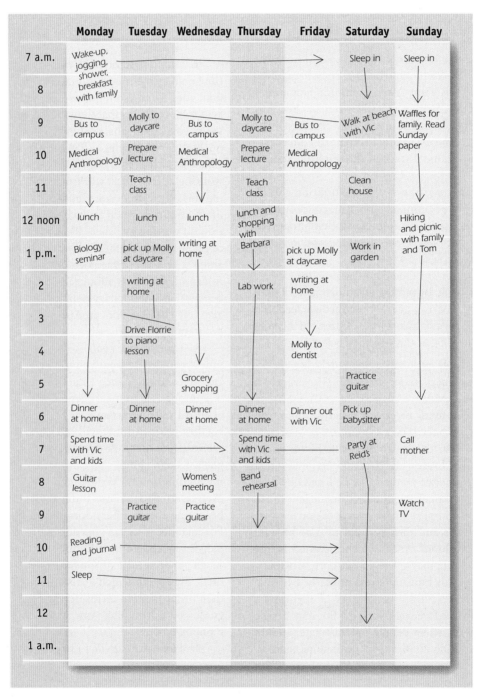

Figure 4.12

Example of a time log. Experts recommend keeping a detailed record of how you use your time if you are to improve your time management. This example shows the kind of recordkeeping that should be done.

experts do offer some suggestions for improving efficiency, including the following (Klassen, 1987; Schilit, 1987):

- *Handle paper once.* When emails, letters, reports, and such cross your desk, they should not be stashed away to be read again and again before you deal with them. Most paperwork can and should be dealt with immediately.

- *Tackle one task at a time.* Jumping from one problem to another is inefficient. As much as possible, stick with a task until it's done. In scheduling your activities, try to allow enough time to complete tasks.

- *Group similar tasks together.* It's a good idea to bunch up small tasks that are similar. This strategy is useful when you're paying bills, replying to emails, returning phone calls, and so forth.

- *Make use of your downtime.* Most of us endure a lot of "downtime," such as when we are waiting in doctors' offices, sitting in needless meetings, or riding on buses and trains. In many of these situations, you may be able to get some of your easier work done—if you think ahead and bring it along.

6. *Build in some time to relax.* Everyone needs time to recharge his or her batteries. Taking time to relax and engage in healthy, enjoyable activities can help individuals be more effective when work time rolls around.

It's not an easy skill to learn, but in today's fast-paced world, time management is crucial. By following the tips provided here and getting your tasks under control, you can avoid stress down the road.

TIME USE SUMMARY FORM									
Activity	**Mon.**	**Tues.**	**Wed.**	**Thurs.**	**Fri.**	**Sat.**	**Sun.**	**Total**	**%**
1. Sleeping	8	6	8	6	8	7	9	52	31
2. Eating	2	2	3	2	3	2	3	17	10
3. Commuting	2	2	2	2	2	0	0	10	6
4. Housework	0	1	0	3	0	0	2	6	4
5. In class	4	2	4	2	4	0	0	16	9
6. Part-time job	0	5	0	5	0	3	0	13	8
7. Studying	3	2	4	2	0	4	5	20	12
8. Relaxing	5	4	3	2	7	8	5	34	20
9.									
10.									

Figure 4.13

Time use summary. To analyze where your time goes, you need to review your time log and create a weekly time use summary like the one shown here. The exact categories to be listed on the left depend on your circumstances and responsibilities.

CHAPTER 4 Review

Key Ideas

4.1 The Concept of Coping
- Coping involves behavioral efforts to master, reduce, or tolerate the demands created by stress. People cope with stress in many ways, and flexibility is important when choosing a strategy. Coping strategies vary in their adaptive value.

4.2 Common Coping Patterns of Limited Value
- Giving up, possibly best understood in terms of learned helplessness, is a common coping pattern that tends to be of limited value. Another is engaging in aggressive behavior. Frequently caused by frustration, aggression tends to be counterproductive because it often creates new sources of stress. There is no evidence that acting aggressive can be cathartic.
- Indulging oneself is a common coping strategy that is not inherently unhealthy, but it is frequently taken to excess and thus becomes maladaptive. Stress-induced eating, compulsive shopping, and Internet addiction are common forms of self-indulgence. Blaming yourself with negative self-talk can also be quite counterproductive.
- Defensive coping is common and may involve any of a number of defense mechanisms. However, the adaptive value of defensive coping tends to be less than optimal. Although some illusions may be healthful, extreme forms of self-deception are maladaptive.

4.3 The Nature of Constructive Coping
- Constructive coping involves efforts to deal with stress that are judged as relatively healthful. Constructive coping is action oriented, effortful, and realistic. It involves managing emotions and self-control.

4.4 Appraisal-Focused Constructive Coping
- Appraisal-focused constructive coping depends on altering appraisals of threatening events. Ellis maintains that catastrophic thinking causes problematic emotional reactions. He asserts that catastrophic thinking can be reduced by digging out the irrational assumptions that cause it.
- Evidence indicates that the use of humor can reduce the negative effects of stress through a variety of mechanisms. Positive reinterpretation and benefit finding are also valuable strategies for dealing with some types of stress.

4.5 Problem-Focused Constructive Coping
- Systematic problem solving can be facilitated by following a four-step process: (1) clarify the problem, (2) generate alternative courses of action, (3) evaluate your alternatives and select a course of action, and (4) take action while maintaining flexibility.
- A problem-focused coping tactic with potential value is seeking help. There appear to be cultural differences regarding who seeks social support. Improving time management can also aid problem-focused coping.

4.6 Emotion-Focused Constructive Coping
- Emotional intelligence may help people to be more resilient in the face of stress. Inhibition of emotions appears to be associated with increased health problems. Thus, it appears that appropriate emotional expression is adaptive.
- Research suggests that it is wise for people to learn how to manage their feelings of hostility. New evidence also suggests that forgiving people for their offenses is healthier than nursing grudges.
- Exercise is a healthy way to deal with emotional distress. Physical activity provides an outlet for frustration, can distract one from the stress, and is related to improved physical and mental health.

- Meditation can be helpful in soothing emotional turmoil. Meditation is associated with lower levels of stress hormones, improved mental health, and other indicators of wellness. Relaxation procedures, such as listening to soothing music or Benson's relaxation response, can be effective in reducing troublesome emotional arousal.
- Spiritual practices are related to every part of the coping process. Spirituality is related to better physical and mental health outcomes. This relationship is complex in that religious involvement can increase stress under some circumstances.

4.7 Application: Using Time More Effectively
- There are many causes of wasted time, including the inability to stick with priorities, to say no, to delegate, to throw things away, to avoid interruption, and to accept anything less than perfection. Procrastination tends to have a negative impact on the quality of work, so it is helpful to avoid this common tendency.
- Effective time management doesn't depend on increased efficiency so much as on setting priorities and allocating time wisely. Engaging in sound time-management techniques can reduce time-related stress.

Key Terms

Aggression p. 97
Brainstorming p. 108
Catastrophic thinking p. 104
Catharsis p. 98
Constructive coping p. 103
Coping p. 95
Defense mechanisms p. 101
Emotional intelligence p. 110
Forgiveness p. 112
Internet addiction p. 100
Learned helplessness p. 96
Meditation p. 113
Procrastination p. 116
Rational-emotive behavior therapy p. 104

Key People

Herbert Benson pp. 113–114
Albert Ellis pp. 104–105
Sigmund Freud pp. 101–102
James Pennebaker p. 111
Martin Seligman pp. 96–97
Shelley Taylor p. 102

CHAPTER 4 Practice Test

1. Which of the following assertions about the cathartic effects of media violence is supported by research?
   a. Playing violent video games is related to increased aggression.
   b. Playing violent video games releases pent-up hostility.
   c. Playing violent video games is related to increased prosocial behavior.
   d. Playing violent video games decreases physiological arousal.

2. Richard feels sure that he failed his calculus exam and that he will have to retake the course. He is very upset. When he gets home, he orders a jumbo-size pizza and drinks two six-packs of beer. Richard's behavior illustrates which of the following coping strategies?
   a. Catastrophic thinking
   b. Defensive coping
   c. Self-indulgence
   d. Positive reinterpretation

3. Defense mechanisms involve the use of _____ to guard against negative _____.
   a. self-deception, behaviors
   b. self-deception, emotions
   c. self-denial, behaviors
   d. self-denial, emotions

4. When studying defensive illusions, Taylor and Brown found that "normal" people's self-images tend to be _____; depressed people's tend to be _____.
   a. accurate, inaccurate
   b. less favorable, more favorable
   c. overly favorable, more realistic
   d. more realistic, overly favorable

5. According to Albert Ellis, people's emotional reactions to life events result mainly from
   a. their arousal level at the time.
   b. their beliefs about events.
   c. congruence between events and expectations.
   d. the consequences following events.

6. Brainstorming is associated with which of the following appraisal-focused coping strategies?
   a. Systematic problem solving
   b. Catastrophic thinking
   c. Positive reinterpretation
   d. Self-enhancing humor

7. Wanda works at a software firm. Today, her boss unfairly blamed her for the fact that a new program is way behind schedule. The unjustified public criticism embarrassed Wanda. Later that evening, she went for a long run to get her anger under control. Wanda is engaging in which category of coping?
   a. Self-focused coping
   b. Appraisal-focused coping
   c. Problem-focused coping
   d. Emotion-focused coping

8. Research by James Pennebaker and his colleagues suggests that wellness is promoted by
   a. depending on more mature defense mechanisms.
   b. strong self-criticism.
   c. writing about one's traumatic experiences.
   d. inhibiting the expression of anger.

9. Which of the following is an emotion-focused coping strategy that provides an outlet for frustration, a distraction from the stressor, and benefits to physical and psychological health?
   a. Systematic problem solving
   b. Defensive coping
   c. Benefit finding
   d. Exercise

10. Research supports which of the following assertions about procrastination?
    a. Procrastination is associated with adaptive coping.
    b. Procrastinators tend to focus less on the future than nonprocrastinators.
    c. Procrastination is less likely for aversive tasks than pleasant ones.
    d. Procrastinators work best under pressure.

Answers

1. a Page 98
2. c Page 99
3. b Page 101
4. c Page 102
5. b Page 104
6. a Page 108
7. d Page 109
8. c Page 111
9. d Page 112
10. b Page 117

Personal Explorations Workbook

Go to the *Personal Explorations Workbook* in the back of your textbook for exercises that can enhance your self-understanding in relation to issues raised in this chapter.

Exercise 4.1 *Self-Assessment:* Barnes-Vulcano Rationality Test

Exercise 4.2 *Self-Reflection:* Analyzing Coping Strategies

CHAPTER 5 Psychology and Physical Health

Rocketclips, Inc./Shutterstock.com

Jamal is a fairly typical student. He carries a full course load, works a part-time job, and plans to pursue a challenging career in nursing. He hopes to work in a hospital for a few years before enrolling in graduate school. Right now, however, his life is regulated by work: homework, a part-time job, and more school-related work in the wards of the teaching hospital where he learns the science and practice of nursing. In a typical semester, Jamal feels under control for the first couple weeks, but then his work piles up: tests, papers, reading, appointments, labs, and so on. He feels anxious and stressed. Instead of getting 8 full hours of sleep, Jamal often gets by with much less. Fast food becomes a familiar and necessary comfort—he doesn't have time to prepare, let alone eat, healthy and well-balanced meals. His regular exercise routine at the gym often gives way to other time commitments. Sometimes he smokes to relieve his tension, a habit he gave up when he came to college. On the rare occasion he does take a break, it tends to involve watching television or texting with his girlfriend, who attends another school. By the end of the term, he is tense, tired, and run down. In fact, Jamal usually celebrates the end of the semester by getting sick rather than having relaxing times with his friends and family. And then this unfortunate cycle repeats itself the next semester.

Are you at all like Jamal? How often do you become ill in a typical semester? Do you begin strong and healthy but feel worn out and frayed by the end? If you are like many students, your lifestyle has a close connection to your health and well-being. Research now demonstrates quite clearly that health is affected by social and psychological factors as well as biological ones. In other words, health is affected not just by germs or viruses but also by the behavioral choices people make and the lives they lead.

Consider how the leading causes of mortality have changed from the start of the twentieth century to the early twenty-first century. In the United States in 1900, for example, cancer caused 3.7% of the recorded deaths, whereas in 2005 cancer led to 22.8% of recorded deaths (Kung et al., 2008). Over the same time period, heart disease rose from 6.2% to 26.6%. How do we explain the dramatic increases? Certainly, our life span has increased (in 1900, life expectancy was 47.3 years and for a child born in 2015 it is more than 78; U.S. Bureau of the Census, 2015), but that alone is not a sufficient explanation for the greater incidence of cancer and heart disease.

More than any other time in history, people's health is likely to be compromised by *chronic diseases*—conditions developing across many years—rather than by *contagious diseases*, those caused by specific infectious agents (such as measles, pneumonia, or tuberculosis). Moreover, lifestyle and stress play a much larger role in the development of chronic diseases than they do in contagious diseases. Today, the three leading chronic diseases (heart disease, cancer, and stroke) account for almost 60% of all deaths in the United States, and these mortality statistics reveal only the tip of the health iceberg. Psychological and social factors also contribute to many other, less serious maladies, such as headaches, insomnia, backaches, skin disorders, asthma, and ulcers.

Interestingly, there are also rising death rates linked to Alzheimer's disease and Parkinson's disease, yet these are not directly linked to behavioral or lifestyle causes (Kung et al., 2008). Instead, the increased lifespan of an expanding older population receiving quality health care, in part, accounts for the higher mortality rates linked to Alzheimer's and Parkinson's. How so? As people are enjoying significantly longer lifespans than in past generations, these and other diseases linked to aging are becoming more common.

In light of these trends, it is not surprising that the way we think about illness is changing. Traditionally, illness has been thought of as a purely biological phenomenon produced by an infectious agent or some internal physical breakdown in the body (Papas, Belar, & Rozensky, 2004). However, the shifting patterns of disease and new findings relating stress to physical illness have rocked the foundation of the traditional biological model. In its place a new model has gradually emerged (Leventhal, Musumeci, & Leventhal, 2006). **The biopsychosocial model holds that physical illness is caused by a complex interaction of biological, psychological, and sociocultural factors.** This model does not suggest that biological factors are unimportant. Rather, it simply asserts that biological factors operate in a psychosocial context that can also be highly influential. Medical and psychological professionals who adhere to the biopsychosocial model also focus on other factors, including cultural values and ethnicity, that can affect the ways individuals think about and deal with chronic illness, especially where interactions with healthcare providers and adherence to treatments are concerned (Ogedegbe, Schoenthaler, & Fernandez, 2007; Rakel et al., 2011). **Figure 5.1** illustrates how the three factors in the biopsychosocial model affect one another and, in turn, health.

The growing recognition that psychological factors influence physical health led to the development of a new specialty within psychology (Leventhal et al., 2008). *Health psychology* **is concerned with how psychosocial factors relate to the promotion and maintenance of health and with the causation, prevention, and treatment of illness.** This specialty is relatively young, having emerged in the late 1970s. In this chapter we focus on the rapidly growing domain of health psychology (Suls, Davidson, & Kaplan, 2010).

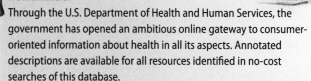

Learn More Online

healthfinder

Through the U.S. Department of Health and Human Services, the government has opened an ambitious online gateway to consumer-oriented information about health in all its aspects. Annotated descriptions are available for all resources identified in no-cost searches of this database.

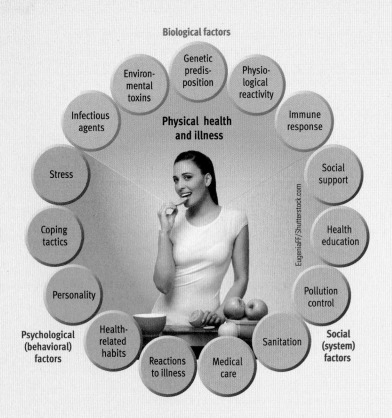

Biological factors

Genetic predisposition

Environmental toxins

Physiological reactivity

Infectious agents

Immune response

Physical health and illness

Stress

Social support

Coping tactics

Health education

Personality

Pollution control

Psychological (behavioral) factors

Health-related habits

Reactions to illness

Medical care

Sanitation

Social (system) factors

EugeniaFF/Shutterstock.com

Figure 5.1

The biopsychosocial model. Whether one's health is good or bad, the biopsychosocial model assumes that health is not just attributable to biological processes. According to this increasingly influential view, one's physical health depends on interactions among biolgical factors, psychological factors, and social system factors. Some key factors in each category are depicted here.

For example, health psychologists are interested in how being part of an ethnic group affects health. **Figure 5.2** identifies the ten leading causes of death among four ethnic groups in the United States. As you can see, no two of the groups have identical profiles regarding causes of death. Some causes do not even appear on the list for each group, a fact that emphasizes the influence that ethnicity—shared national or cultural traditions—may have on mortality. As we will see, there are many factors that determine people's health.

The chapter's first section analyzes the link between stress and illness. The second section examines common health-impairing habits, such as smoking and overeating. The third section discusses how people's reactions to illness can affect their health. The Application expands on one particular type of health-impairing habit: the use of recreational drugs. ◼

Figure 5.2

Ten leading causes of death for four ethnic groups in the United States. This figure shows the rankings of the ten leading causes of death for European Americans (Whites), Hispanic Americans, African Americans (Blacks), and Asian Americans. Note that a * indicates that this particular disease is not among ten leading causes of death for this ethnic group. As you can see, mortality varies with ethnicity.

Source: Adapted from Table 1.1, page 6, in Brannon, L., Feist, J., & Updegraff, J. A. (2014). *Health Psychology: An Introduction to Behavior and Health*. Belmont, CA: Wadsworth Cengage Learning. [Original source: Heron, M. (2011). Deaths: Leading causes for 2007. *National Vital Statistics Reports*, 59(8), Tables E and F.]

TEN LEADING CAUSES OF DEATH FOR FOUR ETHNIC GROUPS IN THE UNITED STATES, 2007

	European Americans	Hispanic Americans	African Americans	Asian Americans
Heart disease	1	1	1	2
Cancer	2	2	2	1
Chronic lower respiratory disease	3	7	8	7
Stroke	4	4	3	3
Unintentional injuries	5	3	4	4
Alzheimer's disease	6	*	*	10
Diabetes	7	5	5	5
Pneumonia & influenza	8	10	*	6
Kidney disease	9	*	7	9
Suicide	10	*	*	8
Septicemia	*	*	10	*
Chronic liver disease	*	6	*	*
Homicide	*	8	6	*
HIV	*	*	9	*
Conditions originating in perinatal period	*	9	*	*

5.1 Stress, Personality, and Illness

Learning Objectives

- Describe the Type A personality and its link to hostility and heart disease.
- Summarize evidence relating emotional reactions and depression to heart disease.
- Discuss the evidence linking stress to cancer, various diseases, and immune functioning.
- Evaluate the strength of the relationship between stress and illness.

What does it mean to say that personality can affect wellness? A guiding assumption is that a person's characteristic demeanor can influence his or her physical health (Friedman & Martin, 2011; Hill & Gick, 2011). As noted in Chapter 2, *personality* is made up of the unique grouping of behavioral traits that a person exhibits consistently across situations. Thus, an individual who is chronically grumpy, often hostile toward others, and routinely frustrated is more likely to develop an illness and perhaps even to die earlier than someone who is emotionally open, is routinely warm and friendly toward others, and leads a balanced life (Friedman, 2007). Of course, the link between personality and disease is somewhat more complex, but nonetheless real (Kern & Friedman, 2011a, b). We begin with a look at heart disease, far and away the leading cause of death in North America.

Personality, Emotions, and Heart Disease

As noted earlier, heart disease accounts for nearly 27% of the deaths in the United States every year. *Coronary heart disease* **results from a reduction in blood flow through the coronary arteries, which supply the heart with blood.** This type of heart disease causes about 90% of heart-related deaths. Atherosclerosis is the principal cause of coronary disease (American Heart Association, 2012). *Atherosclerosis* **is a gradual narrowing of the coronary arteries,** usually caused by a buildup of fatty deposits and other debris on the inner walls (see **Figure 5.3**). Atherosclerosis progresses slowly over many years. Narrowed coronary arteries may eventually lead to situations in which the heart is temporarily deprived of adequate blood flow, causing a condition known as *myocardial ischemia*. This ischemia may be accompanied by brief chest pain, called *angina*, as well as shortness of breath. If a coronary artery is blocked completely (by a blood clot, for instance), the abrupt interruption of blood flow can produce a full-fledged heart attack, or *myocardial infarction*.

Established risk factors for coronary disease include smoking, diabetes, high cholesterol levels, and high blood pressure (Fukushima et al., 2012). Smoking and diabetes are somewhat stronger risk factors for women than for men (Stoney, 2003). Contrary to public perception, cardiovascular diseases—those related to the heart and blood vessels—kill women just as much as men (Liewer et al., 2008), but these diseases tend to emerge in women about 10 years later than in men, presumably due to both physiology and lifestyle (Pilote et al., 2007).

Recently, attention has shifted to the possibility that inflammation may contribute to atherosclerosis and elevated coronary risk. Evidence is mounting that the swelling and reddening of arteries in the heart plays a key role in the initiation and progression of atherosclerosis, as well as the acute complications that trigger heart attacks (Abi-Saleh et al., 2008). The presence of stress, anxiety, and depression, too, can be related to inflammation (Shen et al., 2008; Whang et al., 2009).

Hostility and Coronary Risk

In the 1960s and 1970s a pair of cardiologists, Meyer Friedman and Ray Rosenman (1974), were investigating the causes of coronary disease. Originally, they were interested in the usual factors thought to produce a high risk of heart attack: smoking, obesity, physical inactivity, and so forth. Although they found these factors to be important, they eventually recognized that a piece of the puzzle was missing. Many people who smoked constantly, got little exercise, and were severely overweight still managed to avoid the ravages of heart disease. Meanwhile, others who seemed to be in much better shape with regard to these risk factors experienced the misfortune of a heart attack. What was their explanation

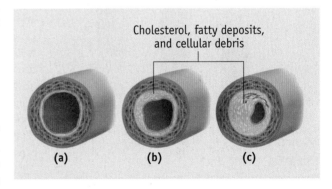

Figure 5.3

Atherosclerosis. Atherosclerosis, a narrowing of the coronary arteries, is the principal cause of coronary disease. **(a)** A normal artery. **(b)** Fatty deposits, cholesterol, and cellular debris on the walls of the artery have narrowed the path for blood flow. **(c)** Advanced atherosclerosis. In this situation, a blood clot might suddenly block the flow of blood through the artery.

for these perplexing findings? Stress! Specifically, they identified an apparent connection between coronary risk and a pattern of behavior they called the *Type A personality*, which involves self-imposed stress and intense reactions to stress (Allan, 2011).

Friedman and Rosenman divided people into two basic types (Friedman, 1996; Rosenman, 1993). **The *Type A personality* includes three elements: (1) a strong competitive orientation, (2) impatience and time urgency, and (3) anger and hostility.** In contrast, **the *Type B personality* is marked by relatively relaxed, patient, easygoing, amicable behavior.** Type A's are ambitious, hard-driving perfectionists who are exceedingly time conscious. They routinely try to do several things at once. They fidget frantically over the briefest delays, are concerned with numbers, and often focus on the acquisition of material objects. They tend to be highly competitive, achievement-oriented workaholics who drive themselves with many deadlines. They are easily aggravated and get angry quickly. In contrast, Type B's are less hurried, less competitive, and less easily angered than Type A's, and there is some evidence that Type B's engage in more preventive and less risky behaviors when facing stress (Korotkov et al., 2011).

Decades of research uncovered a tantalizingly modest correlation between Type A behavior and increased coronary risk. More often than not, studies found an association between Type A personality and an elevated incidence of heart disease, but the findings were not as strong or as consistent as expected (Smith & Gallo, 2001). However, in recent years, researchers have found a stronger link between personality and coronary risk by focusing on a specific component of the Type A personality: anger and hostility (Lampert, 2010). *Hostility* **refers to a persistent negative attitude marked by cynical, mistrusting thoughts, feelings of anger, and overtly aggressive actions.** In fact, an early researcher interested in hostility argued that individuals who use anger as a response for dealing with interpersonal problems were at an elevated risk for heart disease (Chida & Steptoe, 2009). For example, in one study of almost 13,000 men and women who had no prior history of heart disease, investigators found an elevated incidence of heart attacks among participants who exhibited an angry temperament (Williams et al., 2000). The participants, who were followed for a median period of 4.5 years, were classified as being low (37.1%), moderate (55.2%), or high (7.7%) in anger. Among those with normal blood pressure, the high-anger subjects experienced almost three times as many coronary events as the low-anger subjects (see **Figure 5.4**). Bear in mind that anger and hostility are not the only negative emotions that influence heart disease. Other negative emotions, such as fear or anxiety, are also linked to cardiac events (Betensky, Contrada, & Glass, 2012).

Why are anger and hostility associated with coronary risk? There are several reasons. First, let's be clear about some distinctions between these two responses. Anger is an unpleasant emotion that is accompanied by physiological arousal, whereas hostility involves a social component—a negative attitude and often reaction toward others (Suls & Bunde, 2005). People cannot avoid experiencing anger in their lives, however, which means it may be less of a risk factor in the development of heart disease. The manner in which individuals deal with their anger, though, may be quite consequential, creating a link to hostility toward others. Research has uncovered a number of possible explanations linking anger and hostility (see **Figure 5.5**). First, anger-prone individuals appear to exhibit greater physiological reactivity than those lower in hostility (Smith & Gallo, 1999). The frequent ups and downs in heart rate and blood pressure may create wear and tear in their cardiovascular systems.

Second, hostile people probably create additional stress for themselves (Smith, 2006). For example, their quick anger may provoke many arguments and conflicts with others, including friends and family members. Consistent with this line of thinking, Smith and colleagues (1988) found that subjects high in hostility reported more hassles, more negative life events, more marital conflict, and more work-related stress than subjects who were lower in hostility.

Third, thanks to their antagonistic ways of relating to others, hostile individuals tend to have less social support than others (Holt-Lunstad et al., 2008).

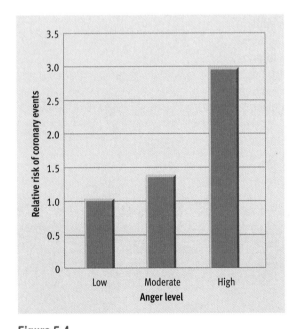

Figure 5.4

Anger and coronary risk. Working with a large sample of healthy men and women who were followed for a median of 4.5 years, Williams et al. (2000) found an association between trait anger and the likelihood of a coronary event. Among subjects who manifested normal blood pressure at the beginning of the study, a moderate anger level was associated with a 36% increase in coronary attacks, and a high level of anger nearly tripled participants' risk for coronary disease.

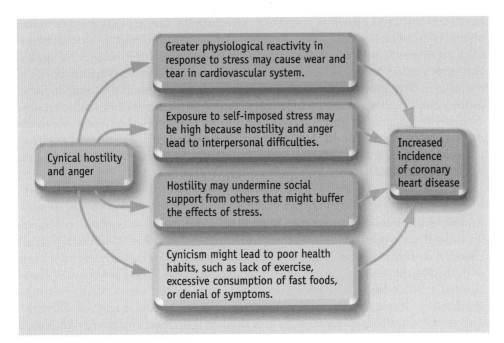

Figure 5.5

Mechanisms that may link hostility and anger to heart disease. Explanations for the apparent link between cynical hostility and heart disease are many and varied. Four widely discussed possibilities are summarized in the middle column of this diagram.

Why? One reason is that hostile behavior leads to reduced interaction with others: People avoid those who treat them poorly. In turn, the lack of social support available to angry or hostile individuals takes a toll. For example, women who perceive little or no social support at home or at work are at greater risk for mortality resulting from a heart attack than other women (Kawachi et al., 1994).

Fourth, perhaps because of their cynicism, people high in anger and hostility seem to exhibit a higher prevalence of poor health habits that may contribute to the development of cardiovascular disease. For example, people high in hostility are more likely to smoke, drink alcohol and coffee, and be overweight than others (Everson et al., 1997). One reason this matters is that physical fitness mediates cardiac reactivity: People who stay in good physical shape have lower reactivity than those in poor shape (Wright et al., 2007).

Finally, keep in mind that hostility does not always lead to the development of cardiovascular problems. One large-population project did not find any overall effect for hostility and the onset of heart disease (Surtees et al., 2005). This result does not mean that hostility is not a good predictor—ample evidence we already examined indicates that it can be. Instead, hostility may be a decided risk factor for some people but not others, just as it may exert its influence on promoting heart disease through some other pathway.

Emotional Reactions and Heart Disease

Although work on personality risk factors has dominated research on how psychological functioning contributes to heart disease, recent studies suggest that emotional reactions may also be critical. *One line of research has supported the hypothesis that transient mental stress and the resulting emotions can tax the heart.* Laboratory experiments with cardiology patients have shown that brief periods of mental stress can trigger acute symptoms of heart disease, such as myocardial ischemia and angina (Gottdiener et al., 1994).

Related research considers the impact of holding back or suppressing emotions, particularly anger. Ironically, perhaps, keeping

Research suggests that excessive anger and hostility are associated with an increased risk for various types of heart disease.

Psychology and Physical Health 127

negative emotions to oneself is potentially more harmful than expressing anger toward others (Jorgensen & Kolodziej, 2007). A related form of suppressed emotion is *rumination*—engaging in repetitive negative thinking about some event. Going over and over the incident heightens negative feelings as well as depression (Hogan & Linden, 2004). Over time, this relentless mental "stewing" can become a negative coping strategy that actually increases people's risk for cardiac problems. Learning to recognize one's impending emotional state, such as feeling angry, but then expressing the emotion as calmly and rationally as possible may be a healthier response. Individuals who work through their anger in ways that attempt to resolve disputes or cope with interpersonal problems tend to have better cardiovascular health (Davidson & Mostofsky, 2010). This finding is particularly true for men.

Depression and Heart Disease

Another line of research has recently implicated depression as a major risk factor for heart disease (Glassman, Maj, & Sartorius, 2011). *Depressive disorders*, which are characterized by persistent feelings of sadness and despair, are a fairly common form of psychological disorder (see Chapter 14). Over the years, many studies have found elevated rates of depression among patients suffering from heart disease, but most theorists have explained this correlation by asserting that being diagnosed with heart disease makes people depressed. Indeed, depression is the most common psychological reaction to having a heart attack (Artham, Lavie, & Milani, 2008). However, studies conducted in the last decade or so have suggested that the causal relation may also flow in the opposite direction—*that the emotional dysfunction of depression may cause heart disease* (Brown et al., 2011).

Overall, studies have found that depression roughly doubles one's chances of developing heart disease (Lett et al., 2004). Although the new emphasis is on how depression contributes to heart disease, experts caution that the relationship between the two conditions is surely bidirectional and that heart disease also increases vulnerability to depression.

Stress and Cancer

People generally view *cancer* as the most sinister, tragic, frightening, and unbearable of diseases. In reality, cancer is actually a *collection* of more than 200 related diseases that vary in their characteristics and amenability to treatment (Nezu et al., 2003). **Cancer refers to malignant cell growth, which may occur in many organ systems in the body.** The core problem in cancer is that cells begin to reproduce in a rapid, disorganized fashion. As this reproduction process lurches out of control, the teeming new cells clump together to form tumors. If this wild growth continues unabated, the spreading tumors cause tissue damage and begin to interfere with normal functioning in the affected organ systems.

Cancer is a psychological problem as much as it is a medical challenge (Green et al., 2015). It is widely believed by the general public that stress and personality play major roles in the development of cancer (McKenna et al., 1999), and researchers have considered the links between stressful circumstances and traits (Johansen, 2010). Some psychologists searched for evidence for the so-called Type C or "cancer-prone personality" but failed to find any link between personality traits and the development of the disease (Temoshok, 2004). In fact, the research linking psychological factors to the *onset* of cancer is extremely weak. For example, one prospective study of twins found that extraversion and neuroticism (two of the Big Five personality traits; see Chapter 2) were unrelated to increased risk of cancer (Hansen et al., 2005). Large-scale studies, too, have found only weak links between psychosocial factors and the incidence of cancer (Levin & Kissane, 2006; Stürmer, Hasselbach, & Amelang, 2006). In fact, the strongest links are between negative emotionality and an inclination to repress rather than express emotions.

Although efforts to link psychological factors to the onset of cancer have produced equivocal findings, more convincing evidence has shown that stress and personality influence the *course* of the disease. The onset of cancer frequently sets off a chain reaction of stressful events, and people display different responses as they try to adjust to the disease and its consequences (Helgeson, Snyder, & Seltman, 2004). Patients typically have to grapple with fear of the unknown; difficult and aversive treatment regimens; nausea, fatigue, and other treatment side effects; interruptions in intimate relationships; career disruptions; job discrimination; and financial worries.

At present, psychological interventions aimed at helping cancer patients cope can enhance their quality of life (Cameron et al., 2007). What about the quantity of life? Unfortunately, research does not suggest that such interventions prolong life or extend survival rates (Edwards et al., 2008).

Stress and Other Diseases

The development of questionnaires to measure life stress has allowed researchers to look for correlations between stress and a variety of diseases. On one end of the spectrum, consider headaches, a common problem or "everyday disease" but one that can sometimes point to more serious health conditions. So-called tension headaches, marked by muscle rigidity in the region of the head and neck, are what people most frequently experience. Stress is characterized as the one of the leading causes of headaches (Deniz et al., 2004). Among infectious diseases, stress has been clearly implicated in development of the common cold (Cohen, 2005). The typical research paradigm is to intentionally inoculate healthy volunteers with cold viruses, keep them under quarantine (in separate hotel rooms), and then observe who does or does not come down with a cold. The finding? People reporting higher levels of stress are more likely to become ill. Interestingly, people who are social and agreeable are at lower risk of getting a cold after exposure to a virus (Cohen, 2005; Cohen et al., 2003).

Figure 5.6 provides a longer list of health problems that have been linked to stress, including several chronic diseases. Many of these stress-illness connections are based on tentative or inconsistent findings, but the sheer length and diversity of the list is remarkable. Why should stress increase the risk for so many kinds of illness? A partial answer may lie in immune functioning.

Stress and Immune Functioning

The apparent link between stress and many types of illness probably reflects the fact that stress can undermine the body's immune functioning (Moynihan et al., 2014). **The immune response is the body's defensive reaction to invasion by bacteria, viral agents, or other foreign substances.** The human immune response works to protect the body from many forms of disease. Studies by Janice Kiecolt-Glaser and her colleagues have related stress to suppressed immune activity in humans (Kiecolt-Glaser, 2009). In one study, medical students provided researchers with blood samples so that their immune response could be assessed at various points (Kiecolt-Glaser et al., 1984). The students provided the baseline sample a month before final exams and contributed the "high-stress" sample on the first day of their finals. The subjects also responded to the Social Readjustment Rating Scale (SRRS; see Chapter 3) as a measure of recent stress. Reduced levels of immune activity were found during the extremely stressful finals week. Reduced immune activity was also correlated with higher scores on the SRRS.

Other research by Kiecolt-Glaser and colleagues indicates that immune function can be compromised by particular stressors, including loneliness (Jaremka et al., 2013a), depression (Fagundes et al., 2013), and marital problems (Jaremka et al., 2013b). There is

HEALTH PROBLEMS THAT MAY BE LINKED TO STRESS

Health problem	Representative evidence
Common cold	Mohren et al. (2005)
Ulcers	Kanno et al. (2013)
Asthma	Schmaling (2012)
Migraine headaches	Schramm et al. (2014)
Premenstrual distress	Nillni et al. (2013)
Herpes virus	Ashcraft & Bonneau (2008)
Skin disorders	Magnavita et al. (2011)
Rheumatoid arthritis	Davis et al. (2013)
Chronic back pain	Preuper et al. (2011)
Diabetes	Nezu et al. (2013)
Complications of pregnancy	Roy-Matton et al. (2011)
Hyperthyroidism	Vita et al. (2015)
Hemophilia	Perrin et al. (1996)
Stroke	Tsutsumi, Kayaba, & Ishikawa (2011)
Appendicitis	Schietroma et al. (2012)
Multiple sclerosis	Senders et al. (2014)
Periodontal disease	Parwani & Parwani (2014)
Hypertension	Emery, Anderson, & Goodwin (2012)
Cancer	Dalton & Johansen (2005)
Coronary heart disease	Bunker et al. (2003)
AIDS	Perez, Cruess, & Kalichman (2010)
Inflammatory bowel disease	Kuroki et al. (2011)
Epileptic seizures	Novakova et al. (2013)

Figure 5.6

Stress and health problems. The onset or progress of the health problems listed here *may* be affected by stress. Although the evidence is fragmentary in many instances, it's alarming to see the number and diversity of problems on this list.

Janice Kiecolt-Glaser has explored how stress can reduce beneficial immune system activity in humans, thereby putting affected people at risk for various illnesses.

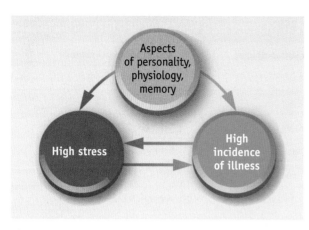

Figure 5.7

The stress/illness correlation. Based on the evidence as a whole, most health psychologists would probably accept the assertion that stress often contributes to the causation of illness. However, some critics argue that the stress-illness correlation could reflect other causal processes. One or more aspects of personality, physiology, or memory might contribute to the correlation between high stress and a high incidence of illness.

even evidence that where people perceive themselves on the "social ladder" can influence immune function (Derry et al., 2013). Those who see themselves as being lower in the social hierarchy experience frequent and high stress, which is predictive of poor health.

Conclusions

A wealth of evidence suggests that stress influences physical health. However, virtually all of the relevant research is correlational, so it cannot demonstrate conclusively that stress *causes* illness (Smith & Gallo, 2001). The association between stress and illness could be due to a third variable. Perhaps some aspect of personality or some type of physiological predisposition makes people overly prone to interpret events as stressful *and* overly prone to interpret unpleasant physical sensations as symptoms of illness (see **Figure 5.7**). Alternatively, stress may simply alter health-related behaviors, increasing the incidence of "bad habits"—smoking, eating poorly, drinking alcohol, using illegal drugs, sleeping less—all of which increase people's risk for diseases and disrupt their immunity (Segerstrom & Miller, 2004). In the next section we look at some of these factors as we examine health-impairing habits and lifestyles.

Learning Objectives

- Identify some reasons why people develop health-impairing habits.
- Discuss smoking's health effects, the rise in popularity of e-cigarettes, and the challenges of quitting smoking.
- Summarize data on patterns of alcohol use and the health risks and social costs of drinking.
- Discuss obesity's origins and health risks, as well as effective weight-loss and exercise programs.
- Describe AIDS, and summarize evidence on the transmission of the HIV virus.

5.2 Habits, Lifestyles, and Health

Some people seem determined to dig an early grave for themselves. They do precisely those things they have been warned are particularly bad for their health. For example, some people drink heavily even though they know they're corroding their liver. Others eat all the wrong foods even though they know they're increasing their risk for a heart attack. Unfortunately, health-impairing habits contribute to far more deaths than most people realize. In an analysis of the causes of death in the United States, Mokdad and colleagues (2004) estimate that unhealthy behaviors are responsible for about half of all deaths each year. The habits that account for the most premature mortality, by far, are smoking and poor diet/physical inactivity. Other leading behavioral causes of death include alcohol consumption, unsafe driving, sexually transmitted diseases, and illicit drug use.

It may seem puzzling that people behave in self-destructive ways. Why do they do it? Several factors are involved. First, many health-impairing habits creep up on people slowly. For instance, drug use may grow imperceptibly over years, or exercise habits may decline ever so gradually. Second, many health-impairing habits involve activities that are quite pleasant at the time. Actions such as eating favorite foods, smoking cigarettes, and getting "high" are potent reinforcing events that are often encouraged, even celebrated, by our culture. Third, the risks associated with most health-impairing habits are related to chronic diseases such as cancer that usually take 10, 20, or 30 years to develop. It is relatively easy to ignore risks that lie in the distant future.

Fourth, it appears that *people have a tendency to underestimate the risks associated with their own health-impairing habits* while viewing the risks associated with others' self-destructive behaviors much more accurately (Weinstein, 2003). In other words, most people are aware of the dangers associated with certain habits, but they often engage in *denial* when it is time to apply this information to themselves. Thus, some people exhibit *unrealistic optimism,* **in which they are aware that certain health-related behaviors are dangerous, but they erroneously view those dangers as risks for others rather than themselves.** In effect, they say to themselves "bad things may well happen to other people, but not to me" (Shepperd et al., 2013). Of course, we have already learned that, in general, optimism is a beneficial personality trait (see Chapter 3). However, in the context of taking health risks and engaging in unwise behavior, unrealistic optimism may prevent people from taking appropriate precautions to protect their physical and mental well-being (Waters et al., 2011).

In this section we discuss how health is affected by smoking, drinking, overeating and obesity, poor nutrition, and lack of exercise. We also look at behavioral factors that relate to AIDS.

Smoking

Here is a surprising and stark fact: Cigarettes lead to the death of more people each year than suicides, car accidents, homicides, alcohol, illegal drugs, fire-arm related incidents, and AIDS combined (American Cancer Society, 2008; CDC, 2014). And here is another: Smoking is actually the most preventable cause of mortality in the United States.

Why do people smoke? Tobacco smoking, a discovery in the "new world," became popular in the sixteenth century and has been with us ever since (Kluger, 1996). Social factors, such as peer pressure among adolescents (Stewart-Knox et al., 2005) and the influence of advertising (Pierce et al., 2005), are obvious candidates, but some people smoke in order to control their weight (Jenks & Higgs, 2007), and many smokers claim that cigarettes elevate their mood, suppress hunger pangs (which they believe helps them stay thin), and enhances alertness and attention.

Who smokes? Roughly one in five Americans smoke, which means there are currently about 42 million adult smokers. About 16 million of these smokers live with some chronic disease tied to their smoking habit. Fortunately, the percentage of people who smoke has declined noticeably since the mid-1960s (see **Figure 5.8**). Nonetheless, about 20.5% of adult men and 15.3% of adult women in the United States continue to smoke regularly (CDC, 2013).

Smoking among college-aged students has dropped from close to 30% to just under 20% (Harris, Schwartz, & Thompson, 2008). More college-aged men than women smoke, and one study argues that this gender gap is explained by males with low self-esteem who view smoking favorably (Hale et al., 2015). Some students are exploring a new way to smoke by using electronic cigarettes (also called e-cigarettes), which are battery-run devices that transport nicotine through a vapor that is then inhaled (Sutfin et al., 2013). One problem with e-cigarettes is that there is little research on either the short- or long-term health consequences of using them. Younger adults do not appear to use e-cigarettes as a way to quit smoking, a reason many older smokers seem to adopt them. Students may be drawn to e-cigarettes because they are perceived to be more acceptable for smoking in public than traditional cigarettes (Trumbo & Harper, 2013). E-cigarettes might also encourage some students to engage in more risky behaviors, such as smoking actual cigarettes, using

Learn More Online

Centers for Disease Control and Prevention (CDC)

The CDC is the federal agency charged with monitoring and responding to serious threats to the nation's health as well as taking steps to prevent illness. This site's "Health Information from A to Z" offers the public in-depth medical explanations of many health problems both common (flu, allergies) and unusual (fetal alcohol syndrome, meningitis).

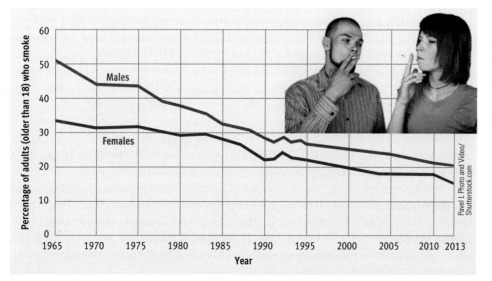

Figure 5.8

The prevalence of smoking in the United States. This graph shows how the percentage of U.S. adults who smoke has declined steadily since the mid-1960s. Although considerable progress has been made, smoking still accounts for about 435,000 premature deaths each year. (Data from Centers for Disease Control)

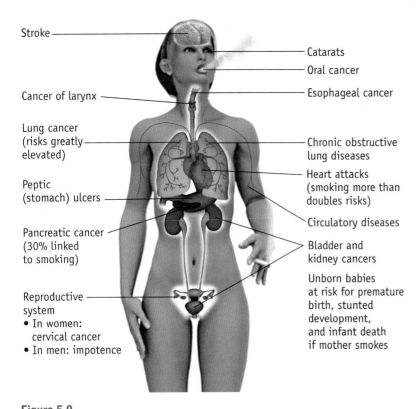

Stroke

Cataracts

Oral cancer

Esophageal cancer

Cancer of larynx

Lung cancer (risks greatly elevated)

Chronic obstructive lung diseases

Heart attacks (smoking more than doubles risks)

Peptic (stomach) ulcers

Circulatory diseases

Pancreatic cancer (30% linked to smoking)

Bladder and kidney cancers

Unborn babies at risk for premature birth, stunted development, and infant death if mother smokes

Reproductive system
• In women: cervical cancer
• In men: impotence

Figure 5.9

Health risks associated with smoking. This figure provides an overview of the various diseases that are more common among smokers than nonsmokers. As you can see, tobacco elevates one's vulnerability to a remarkably diverse array of diseases, including the three leading causes of death in the modern world—heart attack, cancer, and stroke.

Learn More Online

The QuitNet Community
The Boston University School of Public Health sponsors an online community of individuals who seek to quit smoking and tobacco use. A range of resources, including an online support "community" available 24 hours a day, can help make this behavioral health change a reality.

marijuana, and consuming alcohol (Saddleson et al., 2015). Still other students—approximately one in five—are smoking by using a hookah or waterpipe, often because they erroneously believe that waterpipe smoking has a less destructive effect on health than traditional cigarettes (Grekin & Ayna, 2015). Such attitudes may explain why college students are likely to try smoking hookah pipes initially (Sidani et al., 2014).

Health Effects

Accumulating evidence clearly shows that smokers face a much greater risk of premature death than nonsmokers. For example, the average smoker has an estimated life expectancy *13 to14 years shorter* than that of a similar nonsmoker (Schmitz & Delaune, 2005). The overall risk is positively correlated with the number of cigarettes smoked and their tar and nicotine content. Despite people's beliefs to the contrary, cigar smoking, which has increased dramatically in recent years, elevates health risks almost as much as cigarette smoking (Baker et al., 2000).

Why are mortality rates higher for smokers? In the first place, tobacco smoke contains about 7000 chemicals, and at least 70 of the latter are known cancer-causing agents, or carcinogens (U.S. Department of Health and Human Services, 2014). Smoking increases the likelihood of developing a surprisingly large range of diseases, as you can see in **Figure 5.9** (Schmitz & Delaune, 2005; Woloshin, Schwartz, & Welch, 2002). Lung cancer and heart disease kill the largest number of smokers; in fact, smokers are almost twice as likely to succumb to cardiovascular disease as nonsmokers are. Smokers also have an elevated risk of a wide variety of cancers throughout the body, including oral, bladder, and kidney cancer, as well as cancers of the larynx, esophagus, and pancreas; for atherosclerosis, hypertension, stroke, and other cardiovascular diseases; and for bronchitis, emphysema, and other pulmonary diseases (CDC, 2014).

Giving Up Smoking

Studies show that if people can give up smoking, their health risks decline reasonably quickly (Kenfield et al., 2008; Williams et al., 2002). Five years after people stop smoking, their health risk is already noticeably lower than that for people who continue to smoke. The health risks for people who give up tobacco continue to decline until they reach a normal level after about 15 years. About seven out of ten regular smokers would like to quit completely (CDC, 2011), but they are reluctant to give up a major source of pleasure and they worry about craving cigarettes, gaining weight, becoming anxious and irritable, and feeling less able to cope with stress (Grunberg, Faraday, & Rahman, 2001).

Research shows that long-term success rates for efforts to quit smoking are in the vicinity of only 25% (Cohen et al., 1989). Light smokers are somewhat more successful at quitting than heavy smokers, as are older smokers compared to younger ones (Ferguson et al., 2005). Discouragingly, people who enroll in formal smoking cessation programs are only slightly more successful than people who try to quit on their own (Swan, Hudman, & Khroyan, 2003). In fact, it is estimated that the vast majority of people who successfully give up smoking quit without professional help (Shiffman et al. 2008). And here is one myth that can be dispelled: Men do not have an easier time quitting smoking than women—there is virtually no difference between the sexes (O'Connor, 2012).

In recent years attention has focused on the potential value of *nicotine substitutes*, which can be delivered via gum, pills like Chantix, skin patches, nasal sprays, or inhalers. The rationale for nicotine substitutes is that insofar as nicotine is addictive, using a substitute might be helpful during the period when the person is trying to give up cigarettes. Do these substitutes work? They do help (Stead et al., 2008). Controlled studies have demonstrated that nicotine substitutes increase long-term rates of quitting in comparison to placebos (Stead et al., 2008). However, the increases are modest, and the success rates are still discouragingly low. Nicotine substitutes are not a magic bullet or a substitute for a firm determination to quit. The various methods of nicotine delivery seem to be roughly equal in effectiveness, but combining a couple of methods appears to increase the chances of quitting successfully (Schmitz & Delaune, 2005). Considering an alternative way to quit smoking is the focus of our Spotlight on Research in this chapter.

"There's no shooting—we just make you keep smoking."

Spotlight on RESEARCH

Quitting Smoking: Do Monetary Incentives Work?

Source: Halpern, S. D., French, B., Small, D. S., Saulsgiver, K., Harhay, M. O., Audrain-McGovern, J., Loewenstein, G., Brennan, T. A., Asch, D. A., & Volpp, K. G. (2015). Randomized trial of four financial-incentive programs for smoking cessation. *New England Journal of Medicine, 372* (22), 2108–2117. doi: 10.1056/NEJMoa1414293

Quitting smoking is difficult. Various programs designed to help people stop smoking have been tried. Few lead to success. Some research suggests that incentive programs—those that end up paying people money if they actually quit—can sometimes work. Here's an intriguing question: Would people be more likely to stop smoking if they got a big reward for succeeding or a smaller penalty for failing? Most incentive programs do not cost participants anything—if they succeed, they earn money. However, two groups in the present study were asked to provide a deposit of $150 to participate. If they successfully quit smoking for at least six months, they got their money and another $650 back. If they failed, they forfeited the $150. Other groups in the study were just offered the $800 reward for stopping. The investigators hypothesized that because losses loom larger than gains in people's experience, those who were at risk for losing $150 would be more likely to quit smoking than those who could only gain money if they succeeded.

Method

Researchers used a web portal to recruit CVS Caremark employees, friends, and family from around the United States. Participants had to be at least 18 years old, indicated they smoked more than five cigarettes per day, had access to the Internet, and expressed interest in learning about how to quit smoking. They were told they would be paid for filling out questionnaires, providing samples to confirm they abstained from smoking, and that

the study explored different approaches to providing financial incentives to encourage smoking cessation. The sample included 2538 men and women who were randomly assigned to one of four incentive programs or to a usual care (control) condition. Two incentive programs were aimed at individuals, and two were run in small groups of six participants each. Half the individual- and group-oriented programs were offered rewards of approximately $800 for quitting smoking. The remaining individuals and groups were asked to give refundable deposits of $150 and were told they would receive $650 if they quit smoking. The usual care group received informational resources and some free smoking-cessation aids (e.g., counseling, nicotine gum, nicotine patches, medication).

Results

The reward-based programs were more popular than the deposit programs, and 90% of those assigned to them agreed to participate. In contrast, only 13.7% of those placed in the deposit-based programs signed up. Six-month abstinence from smoking rates were higher in each of the four incentive programs (range of quitting was between 9.4% and 16% of the participants) as compared to the cessation rate in the usual care group (6% of the participants). The reward-based programs were not only more popular than the deposit-based program, they also led to higher rates of quitting. Being assigned to a group or an individual-oriented program had no effect on whether people quit smoking.

Discussion

Most of the people who took part in this study—more than 80%—were still smoking when it was over. Yet the overall

continued

success rate for those in the incentive groups was much higher than those who received the traditional (control) treatment. Thus, offering a "carrot" to people who want to quit smoking can be a good idea, but the intriguing result is that the "stick" associated with risking the $150 deposit doubled the chances of quitting for the relatively few in those conditions. Future research on smoking cessation should explore both the "carrot" and "stick" incentives to fight a disease that leads to the death of more than 480,000 Americans each year.

Critical Thinking Questions

1. Knowing what you know now, if you took part in this or a similar study, would you want to be assigned to the reward-based program or the deposit-based program? Why?

2. Were you surprised by the fact that more than 80% the study's participants were still smoking after six months? What does this fact suggest about nicotine addiction?

3. If you were to design the next study, would you focus on the incentive ("carrot") approach or the deposit ("stick") method? Why?

Drinking

Alcohol rivals tobacco as one of the leading causes of health problems in North America. *Alcohol* encompasses a variety of beverages containing ethyl alcohol, such as beers, wines, and distilled spirits. The concentration of alcohol in these drinks varies from about 4% in most beers up to 40% in 80-proof liquor (or more in higher-proof liquors). Survey data indicate that about half of adults in the United States drink (USDA & USDHHS, 2010). **Figure 5.10** shows the percentage of adults in the United States who are regular, infrequent, or former drinkers.

Drinking is particularly prevalent on college campuses. When researchers from the Harvard School of Public Health surveyed nearly 11,000 undergraduates at 119 schools, they found that 81% of the students drank (Wechsler et al., 2002). Moreover, 49% of the men and 41% of the women reported that they engage in binge drinking with the intention of getting drunk, and 40% of college students report drinking five or more alcoholic drinks at one sitting at least monthly (Johnston et al., 2009). For comparison, moderate drinking is defined as one drink per day for women and two drinks per day for men (USDA & USDHHS, 2010). College students who belong to fraternities and sororities consume more alcohol than those who do not belong to these organizations (Karam, Kypri, & Salamoun, 2007). Due to the hazards resulting from it (unintended injuries, homicide, suicide), binge drinking—five or more drinks at one time—is a particular problem for this age group (Panagiotidis

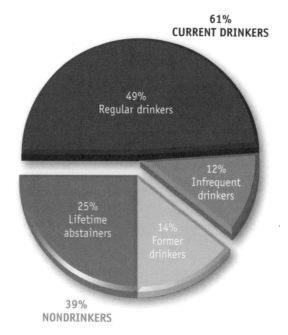

Figure 5.10

Types of Adult Drinkers in the United States. Just over 60% of adults in the United States categorize themselves as current drinkers. About one-quarter of all adults are lifelong abstainers.

Source: Adapted from *Healthy United States, 2007* (Table 68), 2007, by National Center for Health Statistics, Hyattsville, MD; U.S. Government Printing Office.

et al., 2008). Perhaps most telling, college students spend far more money on alcohol ($5.5 billion annually) than they do on their books.

Why Do People Drink?

The effects of alcohol are influenced by the user's experience, relative size and weight, gender, motivation, and mood, as well as by the presence of food in the stomach, the proof of the beverage, and the rate of drinking. Thus, we see great variability in how alcohol affects different people on different occasions. Nonetheless, the central effect is a "Who cares?" brand of euphoria that temporarily boosts self-esteem as one's problems and feelings of stress melt away (Ostafin & Brooks, 2011). Negative emotions such as tension, worry, anxiety, and depression are dulled, and inhibitions may be loosened (Johnson & Ait-Daoud, 2005). Thus, when first-year college students are asked why they drink, they say it's to relax, to

Alcohol is very popular on college campuses and many students engage in binge drinking.

feel less tense in social situations, to keep friends company, and to forget their problems. Of course, many other factors are also at work. Families and peer groups often encourage alcohol use. Drinking is a widely endorsed and encouraged social ritual in our culture, notably through media and advertising (Koordeman, Anschutz, & Engels, 2012). Its central role is readily apparent if you think about all the alcohol consumed at weddings, reunions, sports events, holiday parties, and so forth.

Short-Term Risks and Problems

Alcohol has a variety of side effects, including some that can be very problematic. To begin with, we have that infamous source of regret, the "hangover," which may include headaches, dizziness, nausea, and vomiting. In the constellation of alcohol's risks, however, hangovers are downright trivial. For instance, although it's possible to overdose with alcohol alone, a more common problem is overdosing on combinations of alcohol and sedative or narcotic drugs.

In substantial amounts, alcohol has a decidedly negative effect on intellectual functioning and perceptual-motor coordination. The resulting combination of tainted judgment, slowed reaction time, and reduced coordination can be deadly when people attempt to drive after drinking (Gmel & Rehm, 2003). Depending on one's body weight, it may take only a couple of drinks for driving to be impaired. It's estimated that alcohol contributes to 40% of all automobile fatalities in the United States (Yi et al., 2006). People with serious alcohol problems have more than twice the mortality risk compared to individuals who have no alcohol problems (Fichter, Quadflieg, & Fischer, 2011).

Long-Term Health Effects

Alcohol's long-term health risks are mostly (but not exclusively) associated with chronic, heavy consumption of alcohol. Estimates of the number of people at risk vary considerably. According to Schuckit (2000) approximately 5%–10% of American men and women engage in chronic alcohol abuse and another 10% of men and 3%–5% of women probably suffer from *alcohol dependence*, or *alcoholism*. **Alcohol dependence (alcoholism) is a chronic, progressive disorder marked by a growing compulsion to drink and impaired control over drinking that eventually interferes with health and social behavior.** Whether alcoholism is best viewed as a disease or as a self-control problem is the source of considerable debate, but experts have reached a reasonable consensus about the warning signs of a drinking problem and alcohol abuse. These signs include drinking in secret,

Learn More Online

National Institute on Alcohol Abuse and Alcoholism
Just two of the many scientific research sources from this NIH agency include the entire collection of the bulletin *Alcohol Alert*, issued since 1988 on specific topics related to alcoholism (such as "Alcohol and Sleep" and "Youth Drinking"), and the ETOH Database, a searchable repository of more than 100,000 records on alcoholism and alcohol abuse.

You may have a drinking problem if:

- You drink in secret.

- You feel worried about your drinking.

- You routinely consume more alcohol than you expected.

- You experience "blackouts" so that you forget what you did or said while drinking.

- You hear concern expressed by family and friends about your drinking.

- You cover up or lie about how often, and how much, you drink.

- You feel ashamed about your drinking.

- You get into arguments with those close to you about your drinking.

You may be abusing alcohol if:

- You frequently consume alcohol to deal with stress or worry.

- You know your drinking is harming your personal relationships, but you continue to drink anyway.

- Your drinking is causing you to neglect your responsibilities at home, at school, or at work.

- Your behavior is illegal and dangerous to others (e.g., you drink and drive).

- You want to stop drinking but you cannot seem to do it.

- You find yourself dropping other activities (e.g., exercise, hobbies, spending time with friends or family) because you need to have a drink.

Figure 5.11

Identifying an alcohol problem. Facing the reality that one has a problem with alcohol is always difficult. Here is a list of signs pointing to a possible drinking problem as well as a list indicating the likely presence of alcohol abuse, respectively.

Source: Based on http://www.helpguide.org/mental/alcohol_abuse_alcoholism _signs_effects_treatments.htm; http://www.med.unc.edu/alcohol/prevention/signs .html http://www.webmd.com/mental-health/alcoholabuse/alcohol-abuse-and -dependencesymptoms

experiencing "blackouts," drinking to cope with stress or worry, and neglecting responsibilities at home, school, or work, among the other indicators listed in **Figure 5.11**.

Alcoholism and problem drinking are associated with an elevated risk for a wide range of serious health problems, which are summarized in **Figure 5.12** (Mack, Franklin, & Frances, 2003). Although there is some thought-provoking evidence that moderate drinking may reduce one's risk for coronary disease (Klatsky, 2008) and Type 2 diabetes (Hendriks, 2007), it is clear that heavy drinking increases the risk for heart disease, hypertension, and stroke. Excessive drinking is also correlated with an elevated risk for various types of cancer, including oral, stomach, pancreatic, colon, and rectal cancer. Moreover, serious drinking problems can lead to cirrhosis of the liver, malnutrition, pregnancy complications, brain damage, and neurological disorders. Finally, alcoholism can produce severe psychotic states, characterized by delirium, disorientation, and hallucinations.

Overeating

Obesity is a common health problem (Sanger-Katz, 2015). About one-third (36 percent) of American adults are obese (Flegal et al., 2012). The percentage of obese citizens is projected to rise to 42% by 2030 (Trogdon et al., 2012). Obesity, then, is an immediate and growing problem: For instance, as recently as the 1980s, only 13% of adult Americans were considered to be obese (Ogden, Carroll, & Flegal, 2008).

Many experts prefer to assess obesity in terms of *body mass index (BMI)—weight (in kilograms) divided by height (in meters) squared (kg/m²).* This increasingly used index of weight controls for variations in height. A BMI of 25.0–29.9 is typically regarded as overweight, and a BMI over 30 is considered obese. If a BMI over 25 is used as the cutoff, almost two-thirds of American adults are struggling with weight problems (Sarwer, Foster, & Wadden, 2004). Moreover, they have plenty of company from their children, as weight problems among children and adolescents have increased 15%–22% in recent decades (West, Harvey-Berino, & Raczynski, 2004).

Obesity is similar to smoking in that it exerts a relatively subtle impact on health that is easy for many people to ignore. Nevertheless, the long-range effects can be quite dangerous; obesity is a significant health problem that elevates one's mortality risk (Wing & Phelan, 2012). In fact, obesity is probably responsible for the early deaths of well over a quarter of a million people in North America each year (DeAngelis, 2004). Overweight people are more vulnerable than others to heart disease, diabetes, hypertension, respiratory problems, gallbladder disease, stroke, arthritis, some cancers, muscle and joint pain, and back problems (USDA & USDHHS, 2010). For example, **Figure 5.13** shows how the prevalence of diabetes, hypertension, coronary disease, and musculoskeletal pain are elevated as BMI increases.

Determinants of Obesity

A few decades ago, obesity was thought to occur mostly in depressed, anxious, compulsive people who overeat to deal with their negative emotions or in individuals who are lazy and undisciplined. However, research eventually showed that there is no such thing as an "obese personality" (Rodin, Schank, & Striegel-Moore, 1989), although some traits are associated with weight fluctuation (Sutin et al., 2011). Instead, research indicated that a complex network of interacting factors—biological, social, and

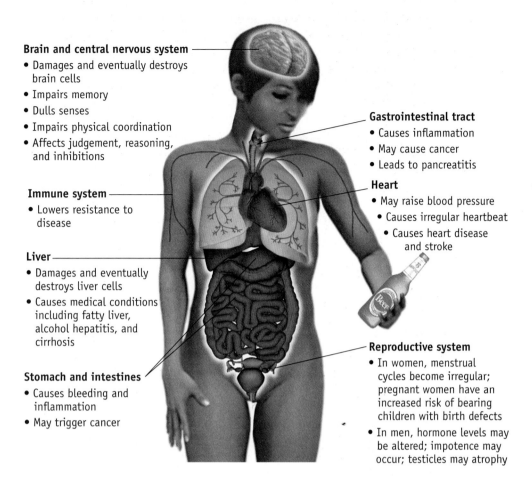

Brain and central nervous system
- Damages and eventually destroys brain cells
- Impairs memory
- Dulls senses
- Impairs physical coordination
- Affects judgement, reasoning, and inhibitions

Immune system
- Lowers resistance to disease

Liver
- Damages and eventually destroys liver cells
- Causes medical conditions including fatty liver, alcohol hepatitis, and cirrhosis

Stomach and intestines
- Causes bleeding and inflammation
- May trigger cancer

Gastrointestinal tract
- Causes inflammation
- May cause cancer
- Leads to pancreatitis

Heart
- May raise blood pressure
- Causes irregular heartbeat
- Causes heart disease and stroke

Reproductive system
- In women, menstrual cycles become irregular; pregnant women have an increased risk of bearing children with birth defects
- In men, hormone levels may be altered; impotence may occur; testicles may atrophy

Figure 5.12

Health risks associated with drinking. This figure provides an overview of the various diseases more common among drinkers than abstainers. As you can see, alcohol elevates one's vulnerability to a great variety of diseases.

---

psychological—determine whether people develop weight problems (Berthoud & Morrison, 2008).

Heredity. Chief among the factors contributing to obesity is *genetic predisposition* (Bouchard, 2002; Bradfield et al., 2012). In one influential study, adults raised by foster parents were compared with their biological parents in regard to body mass index (Stunkard et al., 1986). The investigators found that the adoptees resembled their biological parents much more than their adoptive parents. In a subsequent *twin study*, Stunkard and associates (1990) found that identical twins reared apart were far more similar in body mass index than fraternal twins reared together (see Chapter 2 for a discussion of the logic underlying twin studies). Based on a study of more than 4000 twins, Allison and colleagues (1994) estimate that genetic factors account for 61% of the variation in weight among men and 73% of the variation among women. These genetic factors probably explain why some people can eat constantly without gaining weight whereas other people grow chubby eating far less (Cope, Fernández, & Allison, 2004). However, keep in mind that hereditary explanations must still consider the interaction between genes and environmental constraints in order to understand the complexity inherent in weight control and obesity (Wells, 2011).

Excessive eating and inadequate exercise. The bottom line for overweight people is that their energy intake from food consumption chronically exceeds their energy expenditure from physical activities and resting metabolic processes.

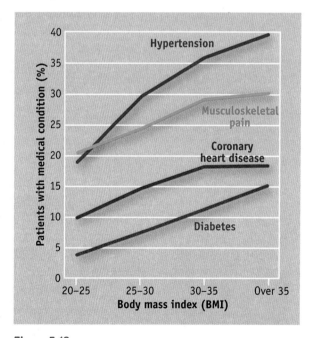

Figure 5.13

Weight and the prevalence of various diseases. This graph shows how obesity, as indexed by BMI, is related to the prevalence of four common types of illness. The prevalence of diabetes, heart disease, muscle pain, and hypertension increases as BMI goes up. Clearly, obesity is a significant health risk. (Data from Brownell & Wadden, 2000)

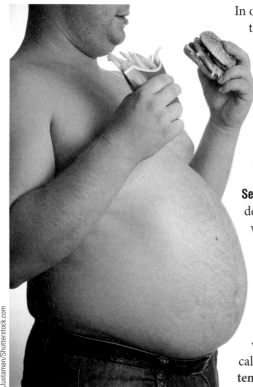

Justaman/Shutterstock.com

Obesity is a serious problem in the United States because many people eat high-caloric meals and get too little exercise.

In other words, they eat too much in relation to their level of exercise. In modern America, the tendency to eat too much and to exercise too little is easy to understand (Henderson & Brownell, 2004). Tasty, caloric, high-fat foods are readily available nearly everywhere, not just in restaurants and grocery stores but in shopping malls, airports, gas stations, schools, and workplaces. And when people eat out, they tend to eat larger meals and consume more high-fat food than they would at home (French, Harnack, & Jeffery, 2000). Portion sizes have grown (Young & Nestle, 2002), as has people's desire for sugar-sweetened soda (Tam et al., 2006) and sweet food more generally (Swithers et al., 2010). Unfortunately, the increased availability of these highly caloric foods in America has been paralleled by declining physical activity.

Set point. People who lose weight on a diet have a rather strong (and depressing) tendency to gain back all the weight they lose. The reverse is also true: People who have to work to put weight on often have trouble keeping it on (Leibel, Rosenbaum, & Hirsch, 1995). According to Richard Keesey (1995), these observations suggest that each body may have a *set point*, or a natural point of stability in body weight. *Set-point theory* **proposes that the body monitors fat-cell levels to keep them (and weight) fairly stable.** When fat stores slip below a crucial set point, the body supposedly begins to compensate for this change. This compensation apparently leads to increased hunger and decreased metabolism (Horvath, 2005). Studies have raised some doubts about various details of set-point theory, leading some researchers to propose an alternative called *settling-point theory* (Pinel et al., 2000). *Settling-point theory* **proposes that weight tends to drift around the level at which the constellation of factors that determine food consumption and energy expenditure achieve an equilibrium.** According to this view, weight tends to remain stable as long as there are no durable changes in any of the factors that influence it (e.g., diet, exercise or the lack thereof, stress, sleep). Settling-point theory casts a much wider net than set-point theory, which attributes weight stability to specific physiological processes. Another difference is that set-point theory asserts that an obese person's body will initiate processes that actively defend an excessive weight, whereas settling-point theory suggests that if an obese person makes long-term changes in eating or exercise, that person's settling point will drift downward without active resistance. Thus, settling-point theory is a little more encouraging to those who hope to lose weight.

Losing Weight

Whether out of concern about their health or just old-fashioned vanity, an ever-increasing number of people are trying to lose weight. One study found that at any given time, about 21% of men and 39% of women are dieting (Hill, 2002), and a subsequent survey yielded similar percentages by gender (Kruger et al., 2004). Research has provided some good news for those who need to lose weight. Studies have demonstrated that relatively modest weight reductions can significantly diminish many of the health risks associated with obesity. For example, a 10% weight loss is associated with reduced risks for diabetes, cancer, and heart disease (Jeffery et al., 2000). Thus, the traditional objective of obesity treatment—reducing to one's ideal weight—has been replaced by more modest and realistic goals (Sarwer et al., 2004).

Although many factors may contribute to obesity, there is only one way to lose weight: Individuals must change their ratio of energy intake (food consumption) to energy output (physical activities). To be quite specific, to lose 1 pound a person needs to burn up 3500 more calories than he or she consumes. Those wanting to shed pounds have three options in trying to change their ratio of energy input to energy output: (1) sharply reduce food consumption, (2) sharply increase exercise output, or (3) simultaneously decrease food intake and step up exercise output in more moderate ways. Dieting alone is unlikely to be sufficient to lose weight and maintain the loss (Jeffery et al.,

David Sipress/The New Yorker Collection/Cartoon Bank.com

2004), nor will an exclusive focus on exercise (Thorogood et al., 2011). Virtually all experts recommend the third option. Simply put, exercise is an essential ingredient of an effective weight-loss regimen (Manson et al., 2004). Exercise seems especially important for *maintaining* reduced weight because it is the single best predictor of long-term weight loss (Curioni & Lourenco, 2005).

Some people opt for surgery to reduce their weight, an increasingly popular choice for weight control (Vetter, Dumon, & Williams, 2011). This option is generally reserved for individuals who are seriously obese or who have other weight problems that warrant drastic action to cause weight loss quickly. One popular form of surgery essentially shrinks the size of the stomach by placing what is known as a gastric band around it. Another surgical option is a gastric bypass, in which food is rerouted around the bulk of the stomach and a portion of the intestines (Buchwald et al., 2004). Both procedures can lead to dramatic weight loss (Moldovan & David, 2011), but involve risks and are life altering; patients must usually take food supplements while carefully watching their food consumption for the rest of their lives (Tucker, Szomstein, & Rosenthal, 2007).

Poor Nutrition

Nutrition **is a collection of processes (mainly food consumption) through which an organism utilizes the materials (nutrients) required for survival and growth.** The term also refers to the *study* of these processes. Unfortunately, most of us don't study nutrition very much. Moreover, the cunning mass marketing of nutritionally worthless foods makes maintaining sound nutritional habits more and more difficult.

Nutrition and Health

We are what we eat. Evidence is accumulating that patterns of nutrition influence susceptibility to a variety of diseases and health problems. For example, in a study of more than 42,000 women, investigators found an association between a measure of overall diet quality and mortality. Women who reported poorer quality diets had elevated mortality rates (Kant et al., 2000). What are the specific links between diet and health? In addition to the problems associated with obesity, other possible connections between eating patterns and health include the following.

1. Heavy consumption of foods that elevate serum cholesterol level (eggs, cheeses, butter, shellfish, sausage) appears to increase the risk of cardiovascular disease (Stamler et al., 2000; see **Figure 5.14**). Regular diets high in saturated fats are also linked to cardiovascular problems (Levy & Brink, 2005; Iqbal et al., 2008). Eating habits are only one of

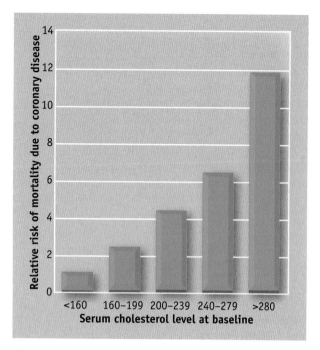

Figure 5.14

The link between cholesterol and coronary risk. In a review of several major studies, Stamler et al. (2000) summarize evidence on the association between cholesterol levels and the prevalence of cardiovascular disease. This graph is based on a sample of more than 11,000 men who were ages 18 to 39 at the beginning of the study when their serum cholesterol level was measured. The data shown here depict participants' relative risk for coronary heart disease during the ensuing 25 years. Although there is debate about whether cholesterol is a *causal* agent in heart disease, it is clear that there is a meaningful correlation between cholesterol and cardiovascular health.

several factors that influence serum cholesterol level, but they do make an important contribution.

2. Vulnerability to cardiovascular diseases may also be influenced by other dietary factors. For example, low-fiber diets may increase the likelihood of coronary disease (Timm & Slavin, 2008), and high intake of red and processed meats, sweets, potatoes, and refined grains is associated with increased cardiovascular risk (Hu & Willett, 2002). Research indicates that the omega-3 fatty acids found in fish and fish oils offer some protection against coronary disease (Din, Newby, & Flapan, 2004), as do foods that are high in fiber (Pereira et al., 2004).

3. High salt intake is thought to be a contributing factor in the development of hypertension (Havas, Dickinson, & Wilson, 2007), although there is still some debate about its exact role.

4. High caffeine consumption may elevate one's risk for hypertension (James, 2004) and for coronary disease (Happonen, Voutilainen, & Salonen, 2004), although the negative effects of caffeine appear relatively modest. In fact, there is other evidence suggesting that drinking coffee regularly in moderate amounts can protect against some types of cancer (Yu et al., 2011).

5. High-fat diets have been implicated as possible contributors to cardiovascular disease (Melanson, 2007) and to some forms of cancer, especially prostate cancer (Rose, 1997), colon and rectal cancer (Murtaugh, 2004), and breast cancer (Wynder et al., 1997). Some studies also suggest that high-fiber diets may reduce one's risk for breast cancer, colon cancer, and diabetes (Timm & Slavin, 2008).

Of course, nutritional habits interact with other factors—genetics, exercise, environment, and so on—to determine whether someone will develop a particular disease. Nonetheless, the examples just described indicate that eating habits can influence physical health.

Nutritional Goals

The most healthful approach to nutrition is to follow well-moderated patterns of food consumption that ensure nutritional adequacy while limiting the intake of certain substances that can be counterproductive. Here are some general guidelines for achieving these goals.

1. *Consume a balanced variety of foods.* Food is made up of a variety of components, six of which are essential to your physical well-being. These six *essential nutrients* are proteins, fats, carbohydrates, vitamins, minerals, and fiber. Proteins, fats, and carbohydrates supply the body with its energy. Vitamins and minerals help release that energy and serve other important functions as well. Fiber provides roughage that facilitates digestion. Educational efforts to promote adequate intake of all essential nutrients have generally suggested that people should be guided by the classic food pyramid published by the U.S. Department of Agriculture (see **Figure 5.15**). Although the food pyramid remains a useful benchmark, it has been subjected to considerable criticism and hotly debated revisions (Norton, 2004). The principal problem with the food pyramid is its failure to distinguish among different types of fat, different forms of carbohydrates, and different sources of protein (Willett & Stampfer, 2003). For example, the current thinking is that monounsaturated and polyunsaturated fats are healthy, whereas saturated fats should be consumed sparingly. A revised food diagram (**Figure 5.16**), which takes the form of a pie chart, takes distinctions such as these into consideration.

2. *Avoid excessive consumption of saturated fats, cholesterol, refined-grain carbohydrates, sugar, and salt.* Limit the intake of saturated fats by eating less beef, pork, ham, hot dogs, sausage, lunch meats, whole milk, and fried foods. Consumption of many of these foods should also be limited in order to reduce cholesterol intake, which influences vulnerability to heart disease. In particular, beef, pork, lamb, sausage, cheese, butter, and eggs are high in cholesterol. Refined-grain carbohydrates, such as white bread, pasta, and

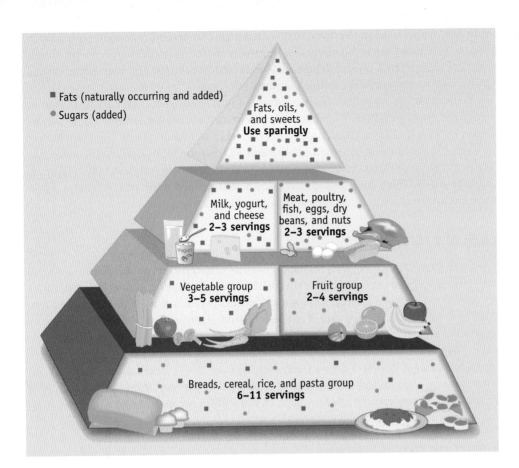

- Fats (naturally occurring and added)
- Sugars (added)

Fats, oils, and sweets
Use sparingly

Milk, yogurt, and cheese
2–3 servings

Meat, poultry, fish, eggs, dry beans, and nuts
2–3 servings

Vegetable group
3–5 servings

Fruit group
2–4 servings

Breads, cereal, rice, and pasta group
6–11 servings

Figure 5.15

The food guide pyramid. The food pyramid, endorsed in 1992 by the U.S. Department of Agriculture, is intended to provide a simple and easy guide to nutritionally balanced eating. It identifies key categories of food and makes recommendations about how many daily servings one should have in each category. As your text explains, it has been subjected to considerable criticism.

Figure 5.16

The healthy eating pie chart. This alternative food pyramid was developed by Walter Willett and colleagues at the Harvard Medical School. It corrects a variety of flaws that were apparent in the USDA food pyramid and incorporates recent scientific findings on healthy versus unhealthy fats and carbohydrates.

Source: Adapted from Willett, W. C. (2001). *Eat, drink, and be healthy: The Harvard Medical School guide to healthy eating.* New York: Free Press. Copyright © 2001 by the President and Fellows at Harvard College. Adapted with permission of Simon & Schuster Adult Publishing Group.

Elena Schweitzer/Shutterstock.com

white rice, are problematic because they increase glucose levels in the blood too quickly. Refined (processed) sugar is believed to be grossly overconsumed. Hence, people should limit their dependence on soft drinks, chocolate, candy, pastries, and high-sugar cereals. Finally, many people should cut down on their salt intake.

3. *Increase consumption of polyunsaturated fats, whole-grain carbohydrates, natural sugars, and foods with fiber.* To substitute polyunsaturated fats for saturated ones, people can eat more fish, chicken, turkey, and veal; trim skin and fat off meats more thoroughly; use skim (nonfat) milk; and switch to vegetable oils that are high in polyunsaturated fats. Healthy carbohydrates include whole-grain foods such as whole wheat bread, oatmeal, and brown rice, which are digested more slowly than refined-grain carbohydrates. Fruits and vegetables tend to provide natural sugars and ample fiber.

Lack of Exercise

A great deal of evidence suggests that there is a link between exercise and health. Research indicates that regular exercise is associated with increased longevity (Lee & Skerrett, 2001), yet only about 33% of Americans engage in it regularly (Pleis et al., 2009). Moreover, you don't have to be a dedicated athlete to benefit from exercise. Even a moderate level of reasonably regular physical activity is associated with lower mortality rates (Richardson et al., 2004; see **Figure 5.17**), even if the time involved is as low as 75 minutes per week (or 15 minutes per day for 5 days a week; Church et al., 2007). That's not a lot of time, yet our sedentary ways and love of technology often get in the way. Video games and other online pursuits may exercise the mind but, as you will see, we need rigorous, regular physical exercise to maintain health and well-being.

Benefits and Risks of Exercise

Exercise is correlated with greater longevity because it promotes a diverse array of specific benefits. First, an appropriate exercise program can enhance cardiovascular fitness

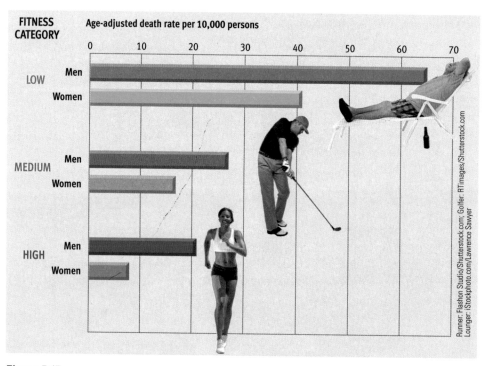

Figure 5.17

Physical fitness and mortality. Blair et al. (1989) studied death rates among men and women who exhibited low, medium, or high fitness. Even medium fitness was associated with lower mortality rates in both genders. The investigators note that one could achieve this level of fitness by taking a brisk half-hour walk each day.

and thereby reduce one's susceptibility to cardiovascular problems. Indeed, the reduced cardiovascular risk seems to benefit men and women equally and has a similar impact across different ethnicities (Bassuk & Manson, 2010; Warburton et al., 2010). Second, regular physical activity can contribute to the avoidance of obesity (Hill & Wyatt, 2005), reducing one's risk for a variety of obesity-related health problems, including diabetes, respiratory difficulties, arthritis, and back pain. Third, some studies suggest that physical fitness is also associated with a decreased risk for colon cancer and for breast and reproductive cancer in women (Monninkhof et al., 2007; Thune & Furberg, 2001).

Fourth, exercise may serve as a buffer that reduces the potentially damaging effects of stress and anxiety (Plante, Caputo, & Chizmar, 2000). This buffering effect may occur because people high in fitness show less physiological reactivity to stress than those who are less fit.

Physical fitness through regular exercise is important for all age groups.

Fifth, exercise may have a favorable impact on mental health, which in turn may have positive effects on physical health. Exercise increases people's happiness (Hyde et al., 2011). Studies have also found a consistent association between regular exercise over a period of at least 8 weeks and reduced depression (Phillips, Kiernan, & King, 2001), which is important given the evidence that depression is correlated with increased vulnerability to heart disease. Sixth, successful participation in an exercise program can produce desirable personality changes, such as enhanced self-esteem (Ryan, 2008), that may promote physical wellness. Research suggests that fitness training can lead to improvements in one's mood, self-esteem, and work efficiency, as well as reductions in tension and anxiety (Dunn, Trivedi, & O'Neal, 2001; Wipfli, Rethorst, & Landers, 2008).

Devising an Exercise Program

Putting together a good exercise program is difficult for many people. People who do not get enough exercise cite lack of time, lack of convenience, and lack of enjoyment as the reasons (Jakicic & Gallagher, 2002). To circumvent these problems, it is wise to heed the following advice (Greenberg, 2002; Jakicic & Gallagher, 2002).

1. *Look for an activity that you will find enjoyable.* You have a great many physical activities to choose from (see **Figure 5.18**). Shop around for one that you find intrinsically enjoyable. Doing so will make it much easier for you to follow through and exercise regularly. Walking is a good choice that meets health requirements (Lee & Buchner, 2008), and it does not require expensive equipment or a particular facility, such as a gym or health club. It can be done outdoors in pleasant weather or indoors (a shopping mall) when the weather is bad.

2. *Exercise regularly without overdoing it.* Sporadic exercise will not improve your fitness. At the other extreme, an overzealous approach can lead to frustration, not to mention injury. Moderation is key; more is not always better and may be counterproductive (Reynolds, 2012).

3. *Increase the amount of time you exercise gradually.* Don't rush it. Start slowly and build up because any amount of exercise is apt to be better than no exercise. For example, healthy people between the ages of 18 and 65 should do some moderate physical activity for half an hour, 5 days a week (or vigorous exercise three times a week for 20 minutes) (Haskell et al., 2007).

4. *Reinforce yourself for your participation.* To offset the inconvenience or pain that may be associated with exercise, it is a good idea to reinforce yourself for your participation. The behavior modification procedures discussed in Chapter 3 can be helpful in devising a viable exercise program.

5. *It's never too late to begin an exercise regimen.* Be forewarned: The number of people who engage in regular exercise declines with age. Yet even modest regular exercise has pronounced health benefits, as has been shown in studies with participants well into their 70s, 80s, and 90s (Everett, Kinser, & Ramsey, 2007).

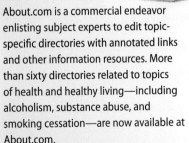

Learn More Online

About.Com: Health
About.com is a commercial endeavor enlisting subject experts to edit topic-specific directories with annotated links and other information resources. More than sixty directories related to topics of health and healthy living—including alcoholism, substance abuse, and smoking cessation—are now available at About.com.

Physical fitness	Jogging	Bicycling	Swimming	Skating (ice or roller)	Handball/ Squash	Skiing (Nordic)	Skiing (Alpine)	Basketball	Tennis	Calisthenics	Walking	Golf	Softball	Bowling
Cardiorespiratory endurance (stamina)	21	19	21	18	19	19	16	19	16	10	13	8	6	5
Muscular endurance	20	18	20	17	18	19	18	17	16	13	14	8	8	5
Muscular strength	17	16	14	15	15	15	15	15	14	16	11	9	7	5
Flexibility	9	9	15	13	16	14	14	13	14	19	7	9	9	7
Balance	17	18	12	20	17	16	21	16	16	15	8	8	7	6
General well-being														
Weight control	21	20	15	17	19	17	15	19	16	12	13	6	7	5
Muscle definition	14	15	14	14	11	12	14	13	13	18	11	6	5	5
Digestion	13	12	13	11	13	12	9	10	12	11	11	7	8	7
Sleep	16	15	16	15	12	15	12	12	11	12	14	6	7	6
Total	**148**	**142**	**140**	**140**	**140**	**139**	**134**	**134**	**128**	**126**	**102**	**67**	**64**	**51**

Figure 5.18

A scorecard on the benefits of fourteen sports and exercises. Here is a summary of how seven experts rated the value of fourteen sports activities (the highest rating possible on any one item was 21). The ratings were based on vigorous participation four times per week.

Source: Adapted from Conrad, C. C. (1976, May). How different sports rate in promoting physical fitness. *Medical Times*, p. 45.

Behavior and AIDS

At present, some of the most problematic links between behavior and health may be those related to AIDS, a pandemic, or worldwide epidemic (Antoni & Carrico, 2012). AIDS stands for *acquired immune deficiency syndrome (AIDS)*, **a disorder in which the immune system is gradually weakened and eventually disabled by the human immunodeficiency virus (HIV).** Being infected with the HIV virus is *not* equivalent to having AIDS. AIDS is the final stage of the HIV infection process, typically manifested about 7 to 10 years after the original infection (Carey & Vanable, 2003). With the onset of AIDS, one is left virtually defenseless against a number of opportunistic infectious agents. The symptoms of AIDS vary widely depending on the specific constellation of diseases that one develops (Cunningham & Selwyn, 2005). And, unfortunately, some people infected with HIV sincerely believe that there is no evidence the virus causes AIDS (Kalichman, Eaton, & Cherry, 2010).

Since the mid-1990s, U.S. death rates for people with AIDS have declined dramatically, but only recently have mortality rates started to level off around the world (UNAIDS, 2010). **Figure 5.19** illustrates the decline in AIDS cases reported each year (incidence) after 1992, as well as the decline in deaths after 1995. As shown in **Figure 5.19**, prevalence is a measure of all people affected by AIDS at a particular time. As you can see, due to accumulating cases and reduced mortality, this prevalence figure has been climbing steadily. Advances in the treatment of AIDS with drug regimens referred to as *highly active antiretroviral therapy* are responsible for the decline in AIDS-related mortality (Pichenot et al., 2012). Although considerable progress has been made, medical experts are concerned that the general public has gotten the impression that these treatments have transformed AIDS from a fatal disease to a manageable one, which is a premature conclusion. HIV strains are evolving, and many have developed resistance to the currently available antiretroviral drugs (Trachtenberg &

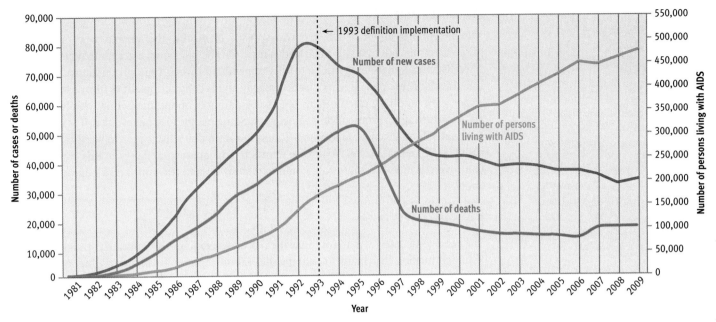

Figure 5.19

Incidence, prevalence, and deaths from AIDS cases by year, United States, 1981–2009.
In 1992, the Centers for Disease Control and Prevention revised its definition of HIV infection. Hence, incidence figures from 1992 and subsequent years are not directly comparable to earlier figures. This graph shows that the incidence of new cases and deaths due to AIDS have declined since the early 1990s. That said, the prevalence of individuals affected by AIDS has been increasing steadily.

Sources: Klevens, R. M. & Neal, J. J. (2002). Update, AIDS—United States: 2000. *Morbidity and Mortality Weekly Report, 51*(27), 593; *HIV/AIDS Surveillance Report, 2002,* by Centers for Disease Control and Prevention, 2004, vol. 14; *HIV/AIDS Surveillance Report, 2006,* by Centers for Disease Control and Prevention, 2008, vol. 18; *HIV/AIDS Surveillance Report, 2010,* by Centers for Disease Control and Prevention, 2012, vol. 22.

Sande, 2002). Moreover, many patients do not respond well to the new drugs, which often have adverse side effects (Beusterien et al., 2008).

Although the aforementioned drug regimens have played a crucial role, other factors have also contributed to recent progress in the battle against AIDS. Increases in longevity are due in part to early detection of the disease and behavioral changes that promote health and well-being. Thus, smoking, drinking alcohol, and enjoying illicit drugs are out, while regular exercise, healthy eating, and sufficient rest are helping people with HIV/AIDS live longer (Chou et al., 2004). Having a positive and optimistic attitude and seeking positive meaning is also linked with reduced AIDS mortality rates (Ikovics et al., 2006; Moskowitz, 2003).

Transmission

The HIV virus is transmitted through person-to-person contact involving the exchange of bodily fluids, primarily semen and blood. The two principal modes of transmission in the United States have been sexual contact and the sharing of needles by intravenous (IV) drug users. In the United States, sexual transmission has occurred primarily among gay and bisexual men, but heterosexual transmission has increased in recent years (Centers for Disease Control, 2006). In the world as a whole, infection through heterosexual relations has been more common from the beginning (UNAIDS, 2007). In heterosexual relations, male-to-female transmission is estimated to be about eight times more likely than female-to-male transmission (Ickovics, Thayaparan, & Ethier, 2001). Although the HIV virus can be found in the tears and saliva of infected individuals, the concentrations are low, and there is no evidence that the infection can be spread through casual contact. Even most forms of noncasual contact, including kissing, hugging, and sharing food with infected individuals, appear safe (Kalichman, 1995). Children of HIV-positive women can also acquire the disease during the pregnancy, the birthing process, or from breastfeeding (UNAIDS, 2007).

Misconceptions

Misconceptions about AIDS are widespread. Ironically, the people who hold these misconceptions fall into two polarized camps. On the one hand, a great many people have unrealistic fears that AIDS can be readily transmitted through casual contact with infected individuals. These people worry unnecessarily about contracting AIDS from a handshake, a sneeze, or an eating utensil. They tend to be paranoid about interacting with homosexuals, thus fueling discrimination against gays. Some people also believe that it is dangerous to donate blood when, in fact, blood donors are at no risk whatsoever. In sum, many myths about AIDS persist, despite extensive efforts to educate the public about this complex and controversial disease. **Figure 5.20** contains a short quiz to test your knowledge of the facts about AIDS.

Prevention

The behavioral changes that minimize the risk of developing AIDS are fairly straightforward, although making the changes is often easier said than done. In all groups, the more sexual

AIDS RISK KNOWLEDGE TEST
Answer the following "true" or "false."

T F	**1.**	The AIDS virus cannot be spread through kissing.
T F	**2.**	A person can get the AIDS virus by sharing kitchens and bathrooms with someone who has AIDS.
T F	**3.**	Men can give the AIDS virus to women.
T F	**4.**	The AIDS virus attacks the body's ability to fight off diseases.
T F	**5.**	You can get the AIDS virus by someone sneezing, like a cold or the flu.
T F	**6.**	You can get AIDS by touching a person with AIDS.
T F	**7.**	Women can give the AIDS virus to men.
T F	**8.**	A person who got the AIDS virus from shooting up drugs cannot give the virus to someone by having sex.
T F	**9.**	A pregnant woman can give the AIDS virus to her unborn baby.
T F	**10.**	Most types of birth control also protect against getting the AIDS virus.
T F	**11.**	Condoms make intercourse completely safe.
T F	**12.**	Oral sex is safe if partners "do not swallow."
T F	**13.**	A person must have many different sexual partners to be at risk for AIDS.
T F	**14.**	It is more important to take precautions against AIDS in large cities than in small cities.
T F	**15.**	A positive result on the AIDS virus antibody test often occurs for people who do not even have the virus.
T F	**16.**	Only receptive (passive) anal intercourse transmits the AIDS virus.
T F	**17.**	Donating blood carries no AIDS risk for the donor.
T F	**18.**	Most people who have the AIDS virus look quite ill.

Answers: 1.T 2.F 3.T 4.T 5.F 6.F 7.T 8.F 9.T 10.F 11.F 12.F 13.F 14.F 15.F 16.F 17.T 18.F

Figure 5.20

A quiz on knowledge of AIDS. Because misconceptions about AIDS abound, it may be wise to take this brief quiz to test your knowledge.

Source: Adapted from Kalichman, S. C. (1995). *Understanding AIDS: A guide for mental health professionals.* Washington, DC: American Psychological Association. Copyright © 1995 by the American Psychological Association. Adapted with permission of the author.

partners a person has, the higher the risk that he or she will be exposed to the HIV virus. Thus, people can reduce their risk by having sexual contacts with fewer partners and by using condoms to control the exchange of semen. It is also important to curtail certain sexual practices (in particular, anal sex) that increase the probability of semen/blood mixing. New cohorts of young people appear to be much less concerned about the risk of HIV infection than the generation that witnessed the original emergence of AIDS (Mantell, Stein, & Susser, 2008). This false sense of security among young adults may have dire consequences in the long run unless they adopt prevention practices and an attitude of vigilance.

5.3 Reactions to Illness

So far we have emphasized the psychosocial aspects of maintaining health and minimizing the risk of illness. Health is also affected by how individuals respond to physical symptoms and illnesses. Some people engage in denial and ignore early warning signs of developing diseases. Others engage in active coping efforts to conquer their diseases. In this section, we discuss the decision to seek medical treatment, the sick role, communication with health providers, and compliance with medical advice.

The Decision to Seek Treatment

Have you ever experienced nausea, diarrhea, stiffness, headaches, cramps, chest pains, or sinus problems? Of course you have; everyone experiences some of these problems periodically. However, whether you view these sensations as *symptoms* is a matter of individual interpretation, and the level of symptoms is what prompts people to seek medical advice (Ringström et al., 2007). When two persons experience the same unpleasant sensations, one may shrug them off as a nuisance, while the other may rush to a physician (Leventhal, Cameron, & Leventhal, 2005). Studies suggest that those who are relatively high in anxiety and neuroticism tend to report more symptoms of illness than others do (Charles et al., 2008). Those who are extremely attentive to bodily sensations and health concerns also report more symptoms than the average person (Barsky, 1988). When feeling ill, women report more symptoms and higher distress than men do (Koopmans & Lamers, 2007).

Variations in the perception of symptoms help explain why people vary so much in their readiness to seek medical treatment. Generally, people are more likely to seek medical care when their symptoms are unfamiliar, appear to be serious, last longer than expected, or disrupt their work or social activities (Martin et al., 2003). Social class matters, too. Higher socioeconomic groups report having fewer symptoms and better health, but when sickness occurs, member of these groups are more likely to seek medical care than lower-income people are (Matthews & Gallo, 2011; Stone, Krueger, et al., 2010).

Another key consideration is how friends and family react to the symptoms. Visibility of symptoms usually prompts people to seek medical care (Unger-Saldaña & Infante-Castañeda, 2011). Medical consultation is much more likely when friends and family view symptoms as serious and encourage the person to seek medical care, although nagging a person about seeking care can sometimes backfire (Martin et al., 2003). Gender also influences decisions to seek treatment because women are much more likely than men to utilize medical services (Galdas, Cheater, & Marshall, 2005). Finally, age matters: Young children (age 5 and under) and older adults (late middle age and beyond) are more likely to utilize health services. These facts should not be surprising, especially in the case of young children, who often experience illnesses and vaccinations and have parents or caregivers who take them for frequent checkups.

The process of seeking medical treatment can be divided into three stages of active, complex problem solving (Martin et al., 2003). First, people have to decide that their physical sensations *are* symptoms—that they are indicative of illness. Second, they have to decide that their apparent illness warrants medical attention. Third, they have to go to the trouble to make the actual arrangements for medical care, which can be complicated and time consuming.

The Sick Role

Although many people tend to delay medical consultations, some people are actually eager to seek medical care. Given this reality, it is not surprising that up to 60% of patients' visits to their primary care physicians appear to have little medical basis (Ellington & Wiebe, 1999). Many of the people who are quick to solicit medical assistance probably have learned that there are potential benefits in adopting the "sick role" (Hamilton, Deemer, & Janata, 2003). For instance, the sick role absolves people from responsibility for their incapacity and can be used to exempt them from many of their normal duties and obligations (Segall, 1997). Fewer demands are placed on sick people, who can often be selective in deciding which demands to ignore. Illness can provide a convenient, face-saving excuse for one's failures. Sick people may also find themselves receiving lots of attention (affection, concern, sympathy) from friends and relatives. This positive attention can be rewarding and can encourage the maintenance of symptoms (Walker, Claar, & Garber, 2002). Other individuals have medically unexplained symptoms which puts pressure on physicians to judge the legitimacy of their claims while also considering explanations linked to social problems or challenging personality traits (Mik-Meyer & Obling, 2012).

Communicating with Health Providers

When people seek help from physicians and other health-care providers, many factors can undermine effective communication. If a physician communicates poorly, patients will be less likely to follow whatever advice is offered (Zolnierek & DiMatteo, 2009). A large portion of medical patients leave their doctors' offices not understanding what they have been told and what they are supposed to do (Johnson & Carlson, 2004). Research indicates that

Communication between health-care providers and patients tends to be far from optimal for a variety of reasons.

female physicians tend to be more patient-centered, spend more time with patients, ask more questions, employ more emotionally focused language, and make more of an effort to form a behavioral partnership with their patients than their male counterparts (Hall, Blanch-Hartigan, & Roter, 2011).

There are many barriers to effective provider-patient communication (DiMatteo, 1997). Economic realities dictate that medical visits usually be quite brief, allowing little time for discussion. Illness and pain are subjective matters that may be difficult to describe. Many providers use too much medical jargon and overestimate their patients' understanding of technical terms. Doctors and nurses often believe their explanations are clear; however, patient misunderstanding can be a common phenomenon, one posing particular problems for individuals whose instructions regarding diagnosis, treatment, and medication are complex (Parker, 2000).

Adherence to Medical Advice

Many patients fail to adhere to the instructions they receive from physicians and other health-care professionals. Noncompliance with medical advice may occur 30% of the time when short-term treatments are prescribed for acute conditions and 50% of the time when long-term treatments are needed for chronic illness (Johnson & Carlson, 2004). Nonadherence takes many forms. Patients may fail to begin a treatment regimen, may stop the regimen early, may reduce or increase the levels of treatment that were prescribed, or may be inconsistent and unreliable in following treatment procedures (Clifford, Barber, & Horn, 2008). The high costs of medication and other out-of-pocket expenses can promote nonadherence among older adults who may be on fixed incomes (Zivin et al., 2010).

Nonadherence is a major problem that has been linked to increased sickness, treatment failures, and higher mortality (DiMatteo et al., 2002). What factors promote adherence to taking medications? A recent meta-analysis suggests that adherence rates increase with age; however, there is the related finding that it declines based on more frequent dosing (Assawasuwannakit et al., 2015; see also, Gellad et al., 2011). Advancing age reduces the likelihood of following dosing schedules. Here are some other considerations that influence the likelihood of adherence (Dunbar-Jacob & Schlenk, 2001; Johnson & Carlson, 2004).

1. *Frequently, noncompliance occurs because patients simply forget instructions or fail to understand the instructions as given.* Medical professionals often forget that what seems obvious and simple to them may be obscure and complicated to many of their patients.

2. *Instructions to patients are more effective when they are given verbally as well as in written form.* Instructions should be clear and delivered both ways in order to increase compliance with medical directives (Johnson et al., 2007).

3. *Another key factor is how aversive or difficult the treatments are.* If the prescribed regimen is unpleasant, compliance tends to decrease (Martin et al., 2010). For example, adherence is reduced when prescribed medications have many severe side effects and when instructions interfere with routine behavior.

4. *If a patient has a negative attitude toward a physician, the probability of noncompliance will increase.* When patients are unhappy with their doctors, they're more likely to ignore the medical advice provided. When a working alliance is formed between patient and physician, however, then compliance is likely to occur (Fuertes et al., 2007).

5. *Treatment adherence can be improved when physicians do follow-ups.* Patients are more likely to follow prescribed treatments if their doctors pay attention to them after the diagnosis has been made (Llorca, 2008).

5.4 Understanding the Effects of Drugs

Learning Objectives

■ Explain the concepts of drug tolerance, physical and psychological dependence, and overdose.

■ Summarize the main effects and risks of narcotics, sedatives, stimulant drugs, and hallucinogens.

■ Outline the main effects and risks of marijuana and ecstasy (MDMA).

Answer the following "true" or "false."

____ **1.** Smoking marijuana can make men impotent and sterile.

____ **2.** Overdoses caused by cocaine are relatively rare.

____ **3.** It is well documented that LSD causes chromosome damage.

____ **4.** Hallucinogens are addictive.

____ **5.** Ecstasy is a relatively harmless drug.

As you will learn in this Application, all of these statements are false. If you answered all of them accurately, you may already be well informed about drugs. If not, you *should* be. Intelligent decisions about drugs require an understanding of their effects and risks.

This Application focuses on the use of drugs for their pleasurable effects, commonly referred to as *drug abuse* or *recreational drug use*. Drug abuse reaches into every corner of our society and is a problematic health-impairing habit, one that accounts for about 2% of deaths in the United States each year (Kochanek et al., 2011). Although small declines appear to have occurred in the overall abuse of drugs in recent years, survey data show that illicit drug use has mostly been increasing since the 1960s (Musto & Wish, 2011). The onset of drug use is typically in adolescence (Swendsen et al., 2012).

Recreational drug use involves personal, moral, political, and legal, as well as occasionally religious, issues that are not matters for science to resolve. However, the more knowledgeable you are about drugs, the more informed your decisions and opinions about them will be. Accordingly, this Application is intended to provide you with nonjudgmental, realistic coverage of issues related to recreational drug

use. We begin by reviewing key drug-related concepts and then examine the effects and risks of six types of widely abused drugs: narcotics, sedatives, stimulants, hallucinogens, marijuana, and ecstasy (MDMA).

Drug-Related Concepts

The principal types of recreational drugs are described in **Figure 5.21**. This figure lists representative drugs in each of the five categories and indicates how the drugs are taken, their desired effects, and their common side effects.

Most drugs produce tolerance effects. *Tolerance* **is a progressive decrease in a person's responsiveness to a drug with continued use.** Tolerance effects usually lead people to consume larger and larger doses of a drug to attain the effects they desire. Tolerance builds more rapidly to some drugs than to others. The second column in **Figure 5.22** indicates whether various categories of drugs tend to produce rapid or gradual tolerance.

When evaluating potential problems associated with using specific drugs, a key consideration is the likelihood of either physical or psychological dependence. Although both forms of drug dependence have a physiological basis, important differences exist between the two syndromes. *Physical dependence* **exists when a person must continue to take a drug to avoid withdrawal illness (which occurs when drug use is terminated).** The symptoms of *withdrawal illness* (also called *abstinence syndrome*) vary depending on the drug. Withdrawal from heroin and barbiturates can produce fever, chills, tremors, convulsions, seizures, vomiting, cramps, diarrhea, and severe aches and pains. The agony of withdrawal from these drugs virtually compels addicts to continue using them. Withdrawal from stimulants leads to a different and somewhat milder syndrome dominated by fatigue, apathy, irritability, depression, and disorientation.

Psychological dependence **exists when a person must continue to take a drug to satisfy intense mental and emotional craving for it.** Psychological dependence is more subtle than physical dependence because it is not marked by a clear withdrawal reaction. However, psychological dependence can create a powerful, overwhelming need for a drug. The two types of dependence often coexist—that is, many people manifest both psychological and physical dependence on a specific drug. Both types of dependence are established gradually with repeated use of a drug. However, specific drugs vary greatly in their potential for creating dependence. The third and fourth columns in **Figure 5.22** provide estimates of the risk of each kind of dependence for the drugs covered in our discussion.

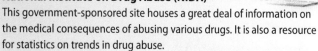

Learn More Online

National Institute on Drug Abuse (NIDA)

This government-sponsored site houses a great deal of information on the medical consequences of abusing various drugs. It is also a resource for statistics on trends in drug abuse.

COMPARISON OF MAJOR CATEGORIES OF ABUSED DRUGS

Drugs	Methods of administration	Desired effects	Short-term side effects
Narcotics (opiates) Morphine Heroin	Injected, smoked, oral	Euphoria, relaxation, anxiety reduction, pain relief	Lethargy, drowsiness, nausea, impaired coordination, impaired mental functioning, constipation
Sedatives Barbiturates (e.g., Seconal) Nonbarbiturates (e.g., Quaalude)	Oral, injected	Euphoria, relaxation, anxiety reduction, reduced inhibitions	Lethargy, drowsiness, severely impaired coordination, impaired mental functioning, emotional swings, dejection
Stimulants Amphetamines Cocaine	Oral, sniffed, injected, freebased, smoked	Elation, excitement, increased alertness, increased energy, reduced fatigue	Increased blood pressure and heart rate, increased talkativeness, restlessness, irritability, insomnia, reduced appetite, increased sweating and urination, anxiety, paranoia, increased aggressiveness, panic
Hallucinogens LSD Mescaline Psilocybin	Oral	Increased sensory awareness, euphoria, altered perceptions, hallucinations, insightful experiences	Dilated pupils, nausea, emotional swings, paranoia, jumbled thought processes, impaired judgment, anxiety, panic reaction
Cannabis Marijuana Hashish THC	Smoked, oral	Mild euphoria, relaxation, altered perceptions, enhanced awareness	Bloodshot eyes, dry mouth, reduced memory, sluggish motor coordination, sluggish mental functioning, anxiety

Figure 5.21

Major categories of abused drugs. This chart summarizes the methods of ingestion and principal effects of five major types of recreational drugs. Alcohol is covered in the main body of the chapter. (Based on Levinthal, 2014; Ruiz & Strain, 2011)

An overdose is an excessive dose of a drug that can seriously threaten one's life. Any drug can be fatal if a person takes enough of it, but some drugs carry more risk of overdose than others. In **Figure 5.22**, the fifth column estimates the risk of accidentally consuming a lethal overdose of various drugs. Drugs that are central nervous system (CNS) depressants—narcotics and sedatives—carry the greatest risk of overdose. It's important to understand that the effects of these drugs are additive. Many overdoses involve lethal *combinations* of CNS depressants. What happens when people overdose on these drugs? Their respiratory system usually grinds to a halt, producing coma, brain damage, and death within a brief period. In contrast, fatal overdoses with CNS stimulants (cocaine and amphetamines) usually involve a heart attack, stroke, or cortical seizure.

Now that our basic vocabulary is spelled out, we can begin to examine the typical effects and risks of major recreational drugs.

Narcotics

Narcotics are drugs derived from opium that are capable of relieving pain. Many people recognize the term *narcotic*

RISKS ASSOCIATED WITH MAJOR CATEGORIES OF ABUSED DRUGS

Drugs	Tolerance	Risk of physical dependence	Risk of psychological dependence	Fatal overdose potential
Narcotics	Rapid	High	High	High
Sedatives	Rapid	High	High	High
Stimulants	Rapid	Moderate	High	Moderate to high
Hallucinogens	Gradual	None	Very low	Very low
Cannabis	Gradual	None	Low to moderate	Very low

Figure 5.22

Specific risks for various categories of drugs. This chart shows the estimated risk potential for tolerance, dependence, and overdose for the five major categories of drugs discussed in this Application.

and can name an example, and they often view the word as having a negative connotation (Wallace et al., 2013). In contrast, the term *opioid* is less recognized by the general public, despite the fact that the overprescribing of opioid pain relievers is linked to a rise in opioid addiction (Kolodny et al., 2015). In government regulations, the term *narcotic* is used in a haphazard way to refer to a variety of drugs besides opiates. The most widely abused opiates are heroin, morphine, and a relatively new painkiller called Oxycontin (oxycodone). However, less potent opiates, such as codeine, Demerol, and Vicodin, are also subject to misuse.

Effects

The most significant narcotics problem in modern Western society is the use of heroin. Most users inject this drug intravenously with a hypodermic needle. The main effect is an overwhelming sense of euphoria. This "Who cares?" feeling makes the heroin high an attractive escape from reality. Common side effects include nausea, lethargy, drowsiness, constipation, and slowed respiration.

Risks

Narcotics carry a high risk for both *psychological and physical dependence* (Epstein, Phillips, & Preston, 2011; Lee, McNeely, & Gourevitch, 2011). Although heroin withdrawal usually isn't life threatening, it can be terribly unpleasant, so "junkies" feel a desperate need to continue their drug use. Once dependence is entrenched (Woodcock et al., 2015), users tend to develop a *drug-centered lifestyle* that revolves around the need to procure more heroin. This lifestyle occurs because the drug is expensive and available only through highly undependable black market channels. Obviously, it is difficult to lead a productive life if one's existence is dominated by a desperate need to "score" heroin. The inordinate cost of the drug forces many junkies to resort to criminal activities to support their habit. Heroin use in the United States has increased by more than 60% in recent years, and heroin is blamed for more than 8000 deaths annually, so *overdose* is a very real danger (Sifferlin, 2015). The effects of opiates are additive with those of other CNS depressants, and most narcotic overdoses occur in combination with the use of sedatives or alcohol. Junkies also risk *contracting infectious disease* because they often share hypodermic needles and tend to be sloppy about sterilizing them. The most common of these diseases used to be hepatitis, but in recent years AIDS has been transmitted at an alarming rate through the population of intravenous drug users (Goforth et al., 2011; Lee, McNeely, & Gourevitch, 2011). Finally, there is emerging evidence that heroin abuse damages white matter (neural tissue) in the brains of long-term users (Wollman et al., 2015).

Sedatives

Sedatives **are sleep-inducing drugs that tend to decrease central nervous system and behavioral activity.** In street jargon, they are often called "downers" because they induce a sense of relaxation and occasional intoxication, accompanied by lowered metabolic function (Julien et al., 2011). Over the years, the most widely abused sedatives have been the barbiturates, which are compounds derived from barbituric acid. However, barbiturates have gradually become medically obsolete and diminished in availability, so sedative abusers have had to turn to drugs in the benzodiazepine family, such as Valium (Ciraulo & Knapp, 2011).

Effects

People abusing sedatives generally consume larger doses than are prescribed for medical purposes. These overly large doses have a euphoric effect similar to that produced by drinking large amounts of alcohol (Ciraulo & Knapp, 2011). Feelings of tension, anxiety, and depression are temporarily replaced by a relaxed, pleasant state of intoxication in which inhibitions may be loosened. Sedatives carry a truckload of dangerous side effects: reduced motor coordination, slurred speech, and a staggering gait, among other problems. Intellectual functioning also becomes sluggish, and judgment is impaired. The user's emotional tone may become unstable, with feelings of dejection often intruding on the intended euphoric mood.

Risks

Sedatives have the potential to produce both *psychological and physical dependence*. They are also among the leading causes of *overdoses* in the United States because of their additive interactions with other CNS depressants (especially alcohol) and because of the degree to which they impair judgment. In their drug-induced haze, sedative abusers are likely to take doses they would ordinarily recognize as dangerous. Sedative users also elevate their risk for *accidental injuries* because these drugs can have significant effects on motor coordination.

Stimulants

Whereas sedatives slow people's metabolic rate (Julien et al., 2011), stimulants create a feeling of alertness and energetic awareness. *Stimulants* **are drugs that tend to increase central nervous system and behavioral activity.** They range from mild, widely available forms, such as caffeine and nicotine, to stronger, carefully regulated stimulants, such as cocaine and amphetamines ("speed"). All stimulants have some mood-altering effect. Here we focus on the latter two drugs.

Cocaine, an organic substance extracted from the coca shrub, is usually consumed as a crystalline powder that is snorted through the nasal cavities, although it can be consumed orally or intravenously. It is a dangerous drug (Huq, 2007). "Crack" is a processed variant of cocaine, consisting of little chips of cocaine that are usually smoked. Smoking crack tends to be more dangerous than snorting cocaine powder because smoking leads to a more rapid absorption of the drug into the bloodstream and more concentrated delivery of the drug to the brain. That said, all the forms of cocaine and all the routes of administration can deliver highly toxic amounts of the drug to the brain (Paczynski & Gold, 2011).

Effects

Amphetamines and cocaine have almost indistinguishable effects, except that cocaine produces a very brief high (20–30 minutes unless more is taken), while a speed high can last many hours. Stimulants create a euphoria very different from that created by narcotics or sedatives. They produce a buoyant, elated, enthusiastic, energetic, "I can conquer the world!" feeling accompanied by increased alertness. Common side effects include increased blood pressure, muscle tension, sweating, and restlessness. Some users experience unpleasant feelings of irritability, anxiety, and paranoia.

Risks

Stimulants can cause physical dependence, but the physical distress caused by withdrawal is mild compared to that caused by narcotic or sedative withdrawal. Psychological dependence on stimulants is a more common problem. Cocaine can create an exceptionally *powerful psychological dependence* that compels the user to pursue the drug with a fervor normally seen only when physical dependence exists (Paczynski & Gold, 2011).

Both cocaine and amphetamines can suppress appetite and disrupt sleep. Thus, heavy use of stimulants may lead to poor eating, poor sleeping, and ultimately, a *deterioration in physical health*. Furthermore, stimulant use increases one's risk for stroke, heart attack, and other forms of cardiovascular disease, and crack smoking is associated with a host of respiratory problems (Paczynski & Gold, 2011). Regular cocaine users show greater incidence of cardiovascular disease than nonusers, but even novice users place themselves at risk for cardiac symptoms (Darke, Kaye, & Duflou, 2006). Heavy stimulant use occasionally leads to the onset of a severe psychological disorder called *amphetamine* or *cocaine psychosis* (depending on the drug involved), which is dominated by intense paranoia (Hill & Weiss, 2011). All of the risks associated with stimulant use increase when more potent forms of the drugs (crack and ice) are used. Overdoses on stimulants used to be relatively infrequent. However, in recent years, *cocaine overdoses have increased sharply* as more people experiment with more dangerous modes of ingestion.

Hallucinogens

Hallucinogens **are a diverse group of drugs that have powerful effects on mental and emotional functioning, marked most prominently by distortions in sensory and perceptual experience.** The principal hallucinogens are LSD, mescaline, and psilocybin, which have similar effects, although they vary in potency. Mescaline comes from the peyote plant, psilocybin comes from a particular type of mushroom, and LSD is a synthetic drug. Common street names for hallucinogens include *acid, mushrooms, fry,* and *blotter.*

Effects

Hallucinogens intensify and distort perception in ways that are difficult to describe, and they temporarily impair intellectual functioning as thought processes become meteoric and jumbled. These drugs can produce awesome feelings of euphoria that sometimes include an almost mystical sense of "oneness" with the human race. This is why they have been used in religious ceremonies in various cultures. Unfortunately, at the other end of the emotional spectrum, they can also produce nightmarish feelings of anxiety, fear, and paranoia, commonly called a "bad trip."

Risks

There is no potential for physical dependence on hallucinogens, and no deaths attributable to overdose are known to have occurred. Psychological dependence has been reported but appears to be rare. Tolerance to LSD happens quickly but can dissipate within a week or two if use of the drug ends (Erikson, 2007).

Although the dangers of hallucinogens have probably been exaggerated in the popular press, there are some significant risks (Pechnick & Cunningham, 2011). Emotion is highly volatile with these drugs, so users can never be sure they won't experience *acute panic* from a terrifying bad trip. Generally, this disorientation subsides within a few hours, leaving no permanent emotional scars. However, in such a severe state of disorientation, *accidents and suicide* are possible. *Flashbacks* are vivid hallucinogenic experiences occurring long after the original drug ingestion. They do not appear to be a common problem, but repetitious flashbacks have proved troublesome for some individuals. In a small minority of users, hallucinogens may contribute to the emergence of a *variety of psychological disorders* (psychoses, depressive reactions, paranoid states) that may be partially attributable to the drug (Pechnick & Cunningham, 2011).

Marijuana

Cannabis **is the hemp plant from which marijuana, hashish, and THC are derived.** Marijuana (often called *pot, weed, reefer,* or *grass*) is a mixture of dried leaves, flowers, stems, and seeds taken from the plant, while hashish comes from the plant's resin. Although marijuana remains illegal in most states, it is now available for legal recreational use in Colorado, Oregon, Alaska, and Washington State, and for medical use in other states (Ghosh et al., 2015). Some researchers argue that the legalization of marijuana for medical purposes can provide appropriate regulation while establishing standards for the drug's potency, dosing, and method of delivery, thus minimizing problems (Loflin & Earleywine, 2015). Other researchers believe legalizing the drug for medicinal purposes will have long-term, negative consequences for young people (Wright, 2015).

Effects

When smoked, cannabis has an almost immediate impact that may last several hours. The effects of the drug vary greatly, depending on the user's expectations and experience with it, the drug's potency, and the amount smoked. The drug has subtle effects on emotion, perception, and cognition (Budney, Vandey, & Fearer, 2011). Emotionally, the drug tends to create a mild, relaxed state of euphoria. Perceptually, it enhances the impact of incoming stimulation, thus making music sound better, food taste better, and so on. Cannabis tends to produce a slight impairment in cognitive functioning (especially short-term memory) and perceptual-motor coordination while the user is high. However, there are huge variations among users.

Risks

Overdose and physical dependence are not problems with marijuana, but as with any other drug that produces pleasant feelings, it has the potential to produce *psychological dependence* (Budney, Vandey, & Fearer, 2011). Marijuana can also cause *transient problems with anxiety and depression* in some people. Of greater concern is recent research suggesting that marijuana use during adolescence *may help to precipitate schizophrenia* in young people who have a genetic vulnerability to the disorder (Compton, Goulding, & Walker, 2007; see Chapter 14). Studies also suggest that cannabis may have a more *negative effect on driving* than has been widely believed (Ramaekers, Robbe, & O'Hanlon, 2000). Indeed, people often make riskier decisions under the influence of marijuana

Marijuana is less dangerous than most abused drugs, but as the text notes, it is not without its risks.

(Lane et al., 2005), which may account for its link to increased risk for injuries (Kalant, 2004). Like tobacco smoke, marijuana smoke carries carcinogens and impurities into the lungs, thus increasing one's chances for *respiratory and pulmonary diseases, and probably lung cancer* (Kalant, 2004). Recent decriminalization of marijuana in some states has been found to be a risk factor for increased acceptance and use of the drug among young people (Miech et al., 2015). However, the evidence on other widely publicized risks remains controversial. Here is a brief overview of the evidence on some of these controversies.

- *Does marijuana reduce one's immune response?* Research with animals clearly demonstrates that cannabis can suppress various aspects of immune system responding (Cabral & Pettit, 1998). However, infectious diseases do not *appear* to be more common among marijuana smokers than among nonsmokers. Thus, it is unclear whether marijuana increases susceptibility to infectious diseases in humans (Bredt et al., 2002).
- *Does marijuana lead to impotence and sterility in men?* Research with humans has yielded weak, inconsistent, and reversible effects on testosterone and sperm levels (Brown & Dobs, 2002). At present, the evidence suggests that marijuana has little lasting impact on male smokers' fertility or sexual functioning (Budney, Vandey, & Fearer, 2011).
- *Does marijuana have long-term negative effects on cognitive functioning?* Some studies using elaborate and precise assessments of cognitive functioning have found an association between chronic, heavy marijuana use and measureable impairments in attention and memory that show up when users are not high (Solowij et al., 2002). However, the cognitive deficits that have been observed are modest and certainly not disabling, and one study found that the deficits vanished after a month of marijuana abstinence (Pope, Gruber, & Yurgelun-Todd, 2001).

Ecstasy (MDMA)

A relatively recent drug controversy in Western society centers on MDMA, better known as "ecstasy." Derived from methamphetamine, MDMA was originally formulated in 1912 but was not widely used in the United States until the 1990s, when it became popular in the context of "raves" and dance clubs. Popularity of the drug, which peaked around 2001 and then dropped (Johnston et al., 2008), is greater among high school students than young adults (Johnston et al., 2007; Wardle, Kirkpatrick, & de Wit, 2015). **MDMA is a compound related to both amphetamines and hallucinogens, especially mescaline; it produces a high that typically lasts a few hours or more.** Users report that they feel warm, friendly, euphoric, sensual, insightful, and empathetic, yet alert and energetic. Problematic side effects include increased blood pressure, muscle tension, sweating, blurred vision, insomnia, and transient anxiety.

MDMA does not appear to be especially addictive, but psychological dependence can clearly become a problem for some people. MDMA has been implicated in cases of stroke and heart attack, seizures, heat stroke, and liver damage, but its exact contribution is hard to gauge given all the other drugs that MDMA users typically consume (McCann, 2011). Chronic, heavy use of ecstasy appears to be associated with sleep disorders, depression, and elevated anxiety and hostility (Morgan, 2000). Recent research indicates that recreational MDMA users show increased levels of the stress hormone cortisol as well as significant memory impairments (Downey et al., 2015; Ruis et al., 2015). Other studies have found decreased performance on laboratory tasks requiring attention and learning (Gallagher et al., 2014). Thus, although more research is needed, there are many reasons to be concerned about the possible deleterious effects of ecstasy.

MDMA, better known as "ecstasy," surged in popularity in the 1990s in the context of "raves" and dance clubs. Although many people view MDMA as a relatively harmless drug, recent research suggests otherwise.

CHAPTER 5 Review

Key Ideas

5.1 Stress, Personality, and Illness

- The biopsychosocial model holds that physical health is influenced by a complex network of biological, psychological, and sociocultural factors. Stress is one of the psychological factors that can affect physical health. In particular, cynical hostility has been implicated as a contributing cause of coronary heart disease. A number of mechanisms may contribute to this connection.
- Emotional reactions may also influence susceptibility to heart disease. Recent research has suggested that transient mental stress and the negative emotions that result may tax the heart. Yet another line of research has identified the emotional dysfunction of depression as a risk factor for heart disease.
- The connection between psychological factors and the onset of cancer is not well documented, but stress and personality do appear to influence the course of the disease. Researchers have found associations between stress and the onset of a variety of other diseases. Stress may play a role in a variety of diseases because it can temporarily suppress immune functioning. Although there's little doubt that stress can contribute to the development of physical illness, the link between stress and illness is modest.

5.2 Habits, Lifestyles, and Health

- People commonly engage in health-impairing habits and lifestyles. These habits creep up slowly, and their risks are easy to ignore because the dangers often lie in the distant future.
- Smokers have much higher mortality rates than nonsmokers because they are more vulnerable to a variety of diseases. Giving up smoking can reduce one's health risks, but doing so is difficult and relapse rates are high. The Spotlight on Research suggested that monetary incentives may help people to give up smoking.
- Drinking rivals smoking as a source of health problems. In the short term, drinking can impair driving, cause various types of accidents, and increase the likelihood of aggressive interactions or reckless sexual behavior. In the long term, chronic, excessive alcohol consumption increases one's risk for numerous health problems, including cirrhosis of the liver, heart disease, hypertension, stroke, and cancer.
- Obesity elevates one's risk for many health problems. Body weight is influenced by genetic endowment, eating and exercise habits, and perhaps set point or settling point. Weight loss is best accomplished by decreasing caloric consumption while increasing exercise.
- Poor nutritional habits have been linked to many health problems, including cardiovascular diseases and some types of cancer, although some of the links are tentative. One's health can best be served by eating a balanced diet while limiting the intake of saturated fats, cholesterol, refined carbohydrates, sugar, and salt.
- Lack of exercise is associated with elevated mortality rates. Regular exercise can reduce one's risk for cardiovascular disease, cancer, and obesity-related diseases; buffer the effects of stress; and lead to desirable personality changes.
- Although misconceptions abound, HIV is transmitted almost exclusively by sexual contact and the sharing of needles by intravenous drug users. One's risk for HIV infection can be reduced by avoiding IV drug use, having fewer sexual partners, using condoms, and curtailing certain sexual practices.

5.3 Reactions to Illness

- Variations in seeking treatment are influenced by the severity, duration, and disruptiveness of one's symptoms and by the reactions of friends and family. The biggest problem is the tendency of many people to delay needed medical treatment. At the other extreme, a minority of people learn to like the sick role because it earns them attention and allows them to avoid stress.
- Good communication is crucial to effective health services, but many factors undermine communication between patients and health providers, such as short visits, overuse of medical jargon, and patients' reluctance to ask questions.
- Noncompliance with medical advice is a major problem, which appears to occur 30%–50% of the time. The likelihood of nonadherence is greater when instructions are difficult to understand, when recommendations are difficult to follow, and when patients are unhappy with their doctor.

5.4 Application: Understanding the Effects of Drugs

- Recreational drugs vary in their potential for tolerance effects, psychological dependence, physical dependence, and overdose. The risks associated with narcotics use include both types of dependence, overdose, and the acquisition of infectious diseases.
- Sedatives can also produce both types of dependence, are subject to overdoses, and elevate the user's risk for accidental injuries. Stimulant use can lead to psychological dependence, overdose, psychosis, and a deterioration in physical health. Cocaine overdoses have increased greatly in recent years.
- Hallucinogens can in some cases contribute to accidents, suicides, and psychological disorders, and they can cause flashbacks. The risks of marijuana use include psychological dependence, impaired driving, transient problems with anxiety and depression, and respiratory and pulmonary diseases. Recent studies suggest that marijuana use may have some long-term negative effects on cognitive processes.
- More research is needed, but it appears that the use of ecstasy (MDMA) may contribute to a variety of acute and chronic physical maladies. MDMA may also have subtle, negative effects on cognitive functioning.

Key Terms

Acquired immune deficiency syndrome (AIDS) p. 144
Alcohol dependence (alcoholism) p. 135
Atherosclerosis p. 125
Biopsychosocial model p. 123
Body mass index (BMI) p. 136
Cancer p. 128
Cannabis p. 153
Coronary heart disease p. 125
Hallucinogens p. 153
Health psychology p. 123
Hostility p. 126
Immune response p. 129

MDMA, p. 154
Narcotics p. 151
Nutrition p. 139
Overdose p. 151
Physical dependence p. 150
Psychological dependence p. 150
Sedatives p. 152
Set-point theory p. 138
Settling-point theory p. 138
Stimulants p. 152
Tolerance p. 150
Type A personality p. 126
Type B personality p. 126
Unrealistic optimism p. 130

Key People

Meyer Friedman and Ray Rosenman pp. 125–126

Janice Kiecolt-Glaser p. 129

CHAPTER 5   Practice Test

1. The greatest threats to health in our society today are
   a. environmental toxins.
   b. accidents.
   c. chronic diseases.
   d. contagious diseases caused by specific infectious agents.

2. Which of the following is *not* associated with elevated coronary risk?
   a. Cynical hostility
   b. Strong emotional reactions to transient mental stress
   c. Obsessive-compulsive disorder
   d. Depression

3. Why do people tend to act in self-destructive ways?
   a. Because many health-impairing habits creep up on them
   b. Because many health-impairing habits involve activities that are quite pleasant at the time
   c. Because the risks tend to lie in the distant future
   d. All of the above

4. Some short-term risks of alcohol consumption include all but which of the following?
   a. Hangovers and life-threatening overdoses in combination with other drugs
   b. Poor perceptual coordination and driving drunk
   c. Increased aggressiveness and argumentativeness
   d. Transient anxiety from endorphin-induced flashbacks

5. Twin studies and other behavioral genetics research suggest that
   a. genetic factors have little impact on people's weight.
   b. heredity has scant influence on BMI but does influence weight.
   c. heredity accounts for 60% or more of the variation in weight.
   d. heredity is responsible for severe, morbid obesity but has little influence over the weight of normal people.

6. Which of the following has *not* been found to be a mode of transmission for AIDS?
   a. Sexual contact among homosexual men
   b. The sharing of needles by intravenous drug users
   c. Sexual contact among heterosexuals
   d. Sharing food or a food utensil

7. Regarding the seeking of medical treatment, the biggest problem is
   a. the tendency of many people to delay seeking treatment.
   b. the tendency of many people to rush too quickly for medical care for minor problems.
   c. not having enough doctors to cover peoples' needs.
   d. the tendency of people in higher socioeconomic categories to exaggerate their symptoms.

8. In which of the following cases are people most likely to follow the instructions they receive from health-care professionals?
   a. When the instructions are complex and punctuated with impressive medical jargon
   b. When they do not fully understand the instructions but still feel the need to do something
   c. When they like and understand the health-care professional
   d. All of the above

9. Which of the following risks is *not* typically associated with narcotics use?
   a. Overdose
   b. Infectious disease
   c. Physical dependence
   d. Flashbacks

10. The use of sedatives may result in personal injury because they
    a. cause motor coordination to deteriorate.
    b. enhance motor coordination too much, making people overconfident about their abilities.
    c. suppress pain warnings of physical harm.
    d. trigger hallucinations such as flying.

Answers
1. c Page 123
2. c Pages 125–128
3. d Pages 130–131
4. d Page 135
5. c Page 137
6. d Page 146
7. a Page 147
8. c Page 149
9. d Pages 151–152
10. a Page 152

Personal Explorations Workbook

Go to the *Personal Explorations Workbook* in the back of your textbook for exercises that can enhance your self-understanding in relation to issues raised in this chapter.

   Exercise 5.1 *Self-Assessment:* Health Locus of Control Scale
   Exercise 5.2 *Self-Reflection:* How Do Your Health Habits Rate?

CHAPTER 6 The Self

NAS CRETIVES/Shutterstock.com

At last you are in college and on your own, away from home. You are a little nervous but excited about your new life and its challenges. Today is your first official day of college and psychology is your first class. You arrive early. You take a seat near the front of the lecture hall and immediately feel conspicuous. You don't know anyone in the class; in fact, you suddenly realize you don't know anyone at the university except your roommate, who is still a stranger. Many students seem to know one another. They are laughing, talking, and catching up while you just sit there, quiet and alone. They seem friendly, so why won't they talk to you? Should you speak to them first? Are you dressed okay—what about your hair? You begin to question yourself: Will you ever make any friends in this class or at the university? Oh, here comes the professor. She seems nice enough, but you wonder what she expects. Will this class be difficult? Well, you do plan to work hard and study a lot, but how will psychology help you in the future? Perhaps you should be taking a more practical class, maybe accounting, which will lead right to a career. Wait a minute: What if the professor calls on you in front of all these strangers who are already friends? Will you sound intelligent or look foolish? As the professor begins to take the class roll, your mind is racing. You feel tense and your stomach gets a little queasy as she gets closer in the alphabet to your name.

This scenario illustrates the process of self-perception and the effects it can have on emotion, motivation, and goal setting. People engage in this sort of self-reflection constantly, especially when they are trying to understand their own behavior or when they must decide how to act.

In this chapter, we highlight the self and its important role in adjustment. We begin by looking at two major components of the self: self-concept and self-esteem. Then we review some key principles of the self-perception process. Next, we turn to the important topic of self-regulation. Finally, we focus on how people present themselves to others. In this chapter's Application, we offer some suggestions for building self-esteem. ■

6.1 Self-Concept

Learning Objectives

- Identify some key aspects of the self-concept and describe the Spotlight on Research regarding possible selves.
- Cite two types of self-discrepancies and describe their effects and ways to cope with them.
- Discuss important factors that help form the self-concept.
- Explain how individualism and collectivism influence the self-concept.

If you were asked to describe yourself, what would you say? You'd probably start off with some physical attributes such as "I'm tall," "I have brown eyes," or "I'm blonde." Soon you'd move on to psychological characteristics: "I'm friendly," "I'm honest," "I have a good sense of humor," and so forth. People usually identify whatever makes them unique or distinct in a particular situation (McGuire & Padawer-Singer, 1978). These distinctive qualities fit into their self-definitions. As we will see, the self is both a cognitive and a social construct (Baumeister, Masicampo, & Twenge, 2013), one containing a subjective awareness (Klein, 2012) that emerges in early childhood and unfolds through adolescence (Harter, 2012). How did you develop beliefs about yourself? Have your self-views changed over time? Read on.

The Nature of the Self-Concept

Although the self-concept is usually talked about as a single entity, it is actually a multifaceted structure (Oyserman, Elmore, & Smith, 2012). As defined in chapter 2, **the self-concept is a collection of beliefs about one's own basic nature, unique qualities, and typical behavior.** The self-concept entails your beliefs about your personality (Markus & Cross, 1990), those things that come to mind when you think about yourself (Stets & Burke, 2003), what you believe to be true about yourself (Forgas & Williams, 2002), and your particular goals (Burkley et al., 2015). These beliefs, also called *self-schemas*, shape social perception (Showers & Zeigler-Hill, 2012), are developed from past experience, and are concerned with your personality traits, abilities, physical features, values, goals, and social and cultural roles (Brannon, Markus, & Taylor, 2015). For example, students' academic identities can frame their educational journeys in positive ways that promote engagement with the demands of college work (Landau et al., 2014). Thus, people have self-schemas on dimensions that are important to them, including both strengths and weaknesses. **Figure 6.1** depicts the self-concepts of two hypothetical individuals.

Hazel Markus, a social psychologist, identified the influence of possible selves in how people conceive of what they may become or be like in the future.

Each self-schema is characterized by relatively distinct thoughts and feelings. For instance, you might have considerable information about your social skills and feel quite self-assured about them but have limited information and less confidence about your physical skills. Your self-concept is apt to be "relational"—that is, your sense of self is based on your current and past relationships with significant others in your life, such as friends, family, and romantic partners (Chen, Boucher, & Tapias, 2006).

Beliefs about the self influence not only current behavior but also future behavior. *Possible selves* **are one's conceptions about the kind of person one might become in the future** (Destin & Oyserman, 2009; Erikson, 2007). If you have narrowed your career choices to personnel manager and psychologist, they would represent two possible selves in the career realm. According to Hazel Markus, possible selves are developed from past experiences, current behavior, and future expectations. They make people attentive to goal-related information and role models and mindful of the need to practice goal-related skills. As such, they help individuals not only to envision desired future goals but also to achieve them (McElwee & Haugh, 2010) while moderating reactions to both positive and negative feedback (Niedenthal, Setterlund, & Wherry, 1992). Interestingly, it has been found that, for individuals who have experienced traumatic events, psychological adjustment is best among those who are able to envision a variety of positive selves (Morgan & Janoff-Bulman, 1994). Sometimes, however, possible selves are negative and represent what you fear you might become—such as an alcoholic like Uncle George or a recluse lacking intimate relationships like your next-door neighbor. In these cases, possible selves function as images to be avoided (e.g., Lee & Oyserman, 2009).

What motivates people to approach or avoid particular possible selves? One answer appears to be motives that enhance one's identity. Vignoles and colleagues (2008) found that people desired possible selves that enhanced their self-esteem, self-perceived effectiveness, and sense of meaning or purpose, among other motives. At the same time, however, they feared developing identities in which such desired motives would be blocked. Other research finds that motivation linked to positive selves is contextually based (Oyserman, Destin, & Novin, 2015). When people are focused on success-likely contexts (an athlete competes in a familiar sport) rather than success-unlikely situations (competing in an unfamiliar sport), they are more motivated to perform if they are also thinking about a desired (winning) rather than an undesired possible future (losing). Thus, the fit between context and future self matters.

Individuals' beliefs about themselves are not set in concrete—but neither are they easily changed. People are strongly motivated to maintain a consistent view of the self across time and situations. Thus, once the self-concept is established, the individual has a tendency to preserve and defend it. In the context of this stability, however, self-beliefs do have a certain dynamic quality. For example, when coupled with educational strategies, "academic possible selves" led to positive changes in planning, test scores, grades, and attendance in a sample of low-income minority youth (Oyserman, Bybee, & Terry, 2006). Individuals with academic or career-oriented possible selves are also more persistent when it comes to scholastic achievement than those with different self-goals (Leondari & Gonida, 2008). Self-concepts seem to be most susceptible to change when people shift from an important and familiar social setting to an unfamiliar one, such as when they go off to college or to a new city for their first "real" job. Uncertainty can be motivating, leading to productive behavior if people believe they have the skills necessary to tackle desired goals (Smith et al., 2014).

How do possible selves influence our mental health in our later years? That question motivated this chapter's Spotlight on Research.

Jason's self-concept

Tall · Athlete · Friendly · Masculine · Aspiring sales manager · Son · Optimistic · Sense of humor · Helpful · Liberal · Student · Fraternity member · Attractive · Intelligent

Chris's self-concept

Son · Average-looking · Masculine · Energetic · Aspiring journalist · Helpful · Cynical · Intelligent · Student · Ambitious · Introverted · Conservative · Inquisitive · Determined

Figure 6.1

The self-concept and self-schemas. The self-concept is composed of various self-schemas, or beliefs about the self. Jason and Chris have different self-concepts in part because they have different self-schemas.

Possible Selves and Late Life Depression

Source: Bolkan, C., Hooker, K., & Coehlo, D. (2015). Possible selves and depressive symptoms in later life. *Research on Aging, 37*(1), 41–62. doi: 10.1177/0164027513520557

Psychologists know that having personal goals can promote general well-being, but not much is known about whether the goals of older adults can influence depression connected with age-related changes in health. Health-related goals in this study were assessed through possible selves, which can provide motivational incentives for the future by helping individuals develop, follow, avoid, or even abandon goals allowing them to achieve desirable outcomes or evade negative ones. For each person, health-related possible selves could include future images of the individual exercising, eating fruits and vegetables, and maintaining a healthy weight or losing excess pounds. The participants were older adults who lived in the same community. All the participants completed face-to-face, semi-structured interviews where they reacted to and thought about possible selves (future images of themselves) and completed measures of health and depressive symptoms. The investigators hypothesized that health-related possible selves would lead the participants to experience fewer depressive symptoms by encouraging them to strive for hoped-for possible selves while avoiding feared possible selves.

Method

Participants. The participants were eighty-five community-dwelling older adults (fifty-seven women, twenty-eight men) from two primary care clinics in a small city. They ranged in age from 60 to 92 (mean age was 74, standard deviation was 7.5). Most of the participants were white (99%), married (66%), retired (86%), and had at least a high school education (67%).

Materials and procedure. Trained researchers interviewed the participants. Each interview, which was conducted in the participants' homes or in a private office in the primary care clinic, lasted between 90 and 100 minutes. During the interview, the participants completed a fifteen-item geriatric depression scale, where a higher score indicates the presence of greater depression. The role of possible selves in future events was first explained (with an emphasis on hoped-for possible selves and feared possible selves), and then the participants were told to take a few minutes to think about their possible selves. They then generated up to three of their most hoped-for and three of their most feared possible selves. Their responses were then coded into one of several categories (e.g., lifestyle, independence/dependency,

death, bereavement). Finally, the participants rated their health on a 4-point scale, where higher numbers indicated better health.

Results

Across the sample, more hoped-for possible selves (203) were generated than were feared selves (133). As anticipated, the most frequently reported possible selves were related to health (seventy-one total; forty-five hoped-for selves and twenty-six feared selves). Most of the older adults reported good to excellent health (77%) and the average depression score was low (Mean = 2.3). Approximately 18% of the sample was at risk for depression. The results indicated that health-related possible selves (framed as a hope or a fear) were significantly related to fewer reported depressive symptoms. A subsequent analysis determined that the presence of feared selves was linked to significantly fewer reported depressive symptoms even when other variables such as age, gender, and self-reported health, were considered.

Discussion

It is likely that the demands of later life make some issues, such as health and well-being, very salient, which means that goal setting may be a way to effectively adapt. Most of the older adults who took part in this research were able to spontaneously generate health-related possible selves. These individuals reported significantly fewer depressive symptoms than those who did not possess health-related possible selves. Moreover, working to prevent the onset of disease (as represented by concern over feared health-related possible selves) by promoting or maintaining health was also linked to fewer reported depressive symptoms. Future research should consider exploring the precise mechanisms underlying motivational strategies linked to possible selves.

Critical Thinking Questions

1. Why do you think that feared possible selves had a stronger link with reduced depressive symptoms than did hoped-for possible selves?
2. There was no control condition in this study. Does that present any problems regarding the interpretation or use of the findings? Why or why not?
3. Could this study have also examined possible selves for mental rather than physical health? If yes, what changes would you introduce to the study's method to examine mental health?

Self-Discrepancies

Some people perceive themselves pretty much the way they'd like to see themselves. Others experience a gap between what they actually see and what they'd like to see. For example, Nathan describes his actual self as "shy" but his ideal self as "outgoing." According to E. Tory Higgins (1987), individuals have several organized self-perceptions: an *actual self* (qualities you believe you *actually* possess), an *ideal self* (characteristics you would *like* to have), and an *ought self* (traits you believe you *should* possess). The ideal and ought selves serve as personal standards or self-guides that direct behavior. *Self-discrepancy* consists of a mismatch between the self-perceptions that make up the actual self, ideal self, and ought self. These self-discrepancies are measureable and have consequences for how people think, feel, and act (Phillips & Silvia, 2010; Shah & Higgins, 2001).

Self-Discrepancies and Their Effects

The differences among one's actual, ideal, and ought selves influence how one feels about oneself and can create some particular emotional vulnerabilities (Higgins, 1999). When people live up to their personal standards (ideal or ought selves), they experience high self-esteem; when they don't meet their own expectations, their self-esteem suffers (Moretti & Higgins, 1990). In addition, certain types of self-discrepancies are associated with specific emotions (see **Figure 6.2**). One type of self-discrepancy occurs when the *actual* self is at odds with the *ideal* self. Such instances trigger *dejection-related* emotions (sadness, disappointment). As actual/ideal discrepancies outnumber actual/ideal congruencies, sadness increases and cheerfulness decreases (Silvia & Eddington, 2012). Consider Tiffany's situation: She knows that she's attractive, but she is also overweight and would like to be thinner. Self-discrepancy theory predicts that she would feel dissatisfied and dejected. Interestingly, research has shown an association between discrepant actual/ideal views of body shape and eating disorders (Sawdon, Cooper, & Seabrook, 2007).

A second type of discrepancy involves a mismatch between *actual* and *ought* selves. Let's say you don't stay in touch with your grandparents as often as you feel you should. According to Higgins, actual/ought self-discrepancies produce *agitation-related* emotions (irritability, anxiety, and guilt). As actual/ought discrepancies outnumber actual/ought congruencies, anxiety increases and calm emotions decrease (Higgins, Shah, & Friedman, 1997). Extreme discrepancies of this type can result in anxiety-related psychological disorders.

The self is a source of fascination for us. We think about ourselves all the time, wondering who we really are and what sort of person we will turn out to be.

Figure 6.2

Types of self-discrepancies, their effects on emotional states, and possible consequences. According to E. Tory Higgins (1989), discrepancies between actual and ideal selves produce disappointment and sadness, whereas discrepancies between actual and ought selves result in irritability and guilt. Such self-discrepancies can make individuals vulnerable to serious psychological problems, such as depression and anxiety-related disorders.

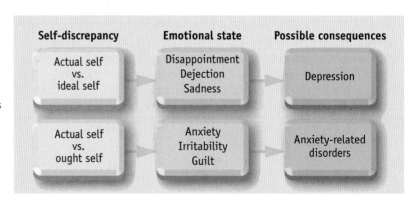

Self-discrepancy	Emotional state	Possible consequences
Actual self vs. ideal self	Disappointment Dejection Sadness	Depression
Actual self vs. ought self	Anxiety Irritability Guilt	Anxiety-related disorders

Everyone experiences self-discrepancies, yet most people manage to feel reasonably good about themselves. How is this possible? Three factors seem to be important: the amount of discrepancy experienced, the person's awareness of the discrepancy, and whether the discrepancy is actually important to the person (Higgins, 1999). Thus, a pre-med major who gets a C in calculus will probably feel a lot worse than an English major who gets a C in the course.

Coping with Self-Discrepancies

Can individuals do anything to blunt the negative emotions and blows to self-esteem associated with self-discrepancies? Yes! For one thing, people can *change their behavior* to bring it more in line with their ideal or ought selves. For instance, if your ideal self is a person who gets above-average grades and your actual self just got a D on a test, you can study more effectively for the next test to improve your grade. But what about the times you can't match your ideal standards? Perhaps you had your heart set on being on the varsity tennis team but didn't make the cut. One way to ease the discomfort associated with such discrepancies is to bring your ideal self a bit more in line with your actual abilities. You may not achieve your ideal self right away, if ever, but by behaving in ways that are consistent with that self, you will get closer to it and be more content (T. D. Wilson, 2011).

Caption: When people don't live up to their personal standards, self-esteem suffers, and some turn to alcohol to blunt their awareness of the discrepancy.

Heightened self-awareness intensifies people's internal sensations (Silvia & Duval, 2001), including through direct eye-contact with another person (Baltazar et al., 2014), but it doesn't always make people focus on self-discrepancies and negative aspects of the self. If that were true, most people would feel a lot worse about themselves than they actually do. As you recall, self-concepts are made up of numerous self-beliefs—many positive, some negative. Because individuals have a need to feel good about themselves, they tend to focus on their positive features rather than their "warts" (Tesser, Wood, & Stapel, 2005). In fact, when a person's self-concept is threatened (a job interview doesn't go well), the individual can recover by affirming competence in an unrelated domain (focusing on extraordinary talent as a salsa dancer) (Aronson, Cohen, & Nail, 1999).

Factors Shaping the Self-Concept

A variety of sources influence one's self-concept. Chief among them are one's own observations, feedback from others, and cultural values.

One's Own Observations

Individuals begin observing their own behavior and drawing conclusions about themselves early in life. Children will make statements about who is the tallest, who can run fastest, or who can swing the highest. Leon Festinger's (1954) **social comparison theory proposes that individuals compare themselves with others in order to assess their abilities and opinions.** People compare themselves to others to determine how attractive they are, how they did on the history exam, how their social skills stack up, and so forth (Dijkstra, Gibbons, & Buunk, 2010). Individuals cannot help themselves: They compare their own behavior with that of their peers (Suls & Wheeler, 2012).

Although Festinger's original theory claimed that people engage in social comparison for the purpose of accurately assessing their abilities, research suggests that they also engage in social comparison to improve their skills and to maintain their self-image (Wheeler & Suls, 2005). Sometimes social comparison is self-focused, such as when a successful professional woman compares her "current self" to the passive, withdrawn "past self" of high school (Ross & Wilson, 2002). Generally, however, people compare themselves against

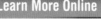

Learn More Online

Self-Concept at Simply Psychology
Self-concept, which falls under social psychology at the Simply Psychology website, appears with related constructs, including self-image, self-esteem and self worth, and the ideal self. Links to other related articles are provided.

others with particular qualities. **A *reference group* is a set of people who are used as a gauge in making social comparisons.** People choose their reference groups strategically. For example, if you want to know how you did on your first test in social psychology (ability appraisal), your reference group would likely be the entire class. In terms of acquiring accurate self-knowledge about your performance, this sort of comparison is a good one if you are confident your classmates are similar to you (Wheeler, Koestner, & Driver, 1982). Thus, people use others, even complete strangers, as social benchmarks for comparison (Mussweiler & Rütter, 2003).

What happens when people compare themselves to others who are better or worse off than themselves? For instance, if you want to improve your tennis game (skill development), your reference group should be limited to superior players, whose skills give you a goal to pursue. Such *upward social comparisons* can motivate you and direct your future efforts (Blanton et al., 1999). On the other hand, if your self-esteem needs bolstering, you will probably make a *downward social comparison*, looking to those you perceive to be worse off, thereby enabling you to feel better about yourself (Lockwood, 2002). Recent research in social neuroscience reveals that these two types of comparisons actually trigger pain- and pleasure-based neural responses in the brain, which in turn can predict whether individuals have aggressive or kind intentions toward others (Swencionis & Fiske, 2014). In status contexts, for example, comparing oneself to someone perceived to be more competent (upward comparison) can sometimes be a negative mental experience, while making downward comparisons to less fortunate individuals can trigger feelings of warmth due to one's relatively better standing. We'll have more to say about downward social comparison a little later in the chapter.

People's observations of their own behavior are not entirely objective. The general tendency is to distort reality in a positive direction (see **Figure 6.3**). In other words,

Figure 6.3

Distortions in self-images. How people see themselves may be different from how others see them. These pictures and text illustrate the subjective quality of self-concept and people's perception of others. Generally, self-images tend to be distorted in a positive direction.

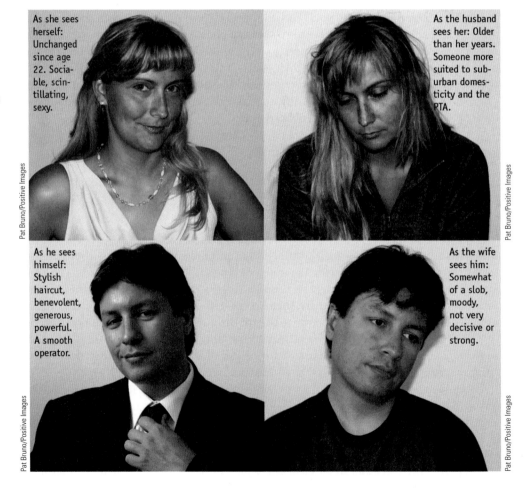

As she sees herself: Unchanged since age 22. Sociable, scintillating, sexy.

As the husband sees her: Older than her years. Someone more suited to suburban domesticity and the PTA.

As he sees himself: Stylish haircut, benevolent, generous, powerful. A smooth operator.

As the wife sees him: Somewhat of a slob, moody, not very decisive or strong.

Pat Bruno/Positive Images

most people tend to evaluate themselves in a more positive light than they really merit (Taylor & Brown, 1988), and they can extend this favorable distortion to include family and friends but not people in general (Pedregon et al., 2012). The strength of this tendency was highlighted in a large survey of high school seniors conducted as part of the SAT (Myers, 1980). By definition, 50% of students must be "above average" and 50% "below average" on specific questions. However, 100% of the respondents saw themselves as above average in "ability to get along with others." And 25% of the respondents thought that they belonged in the top 1%! This better-than-average effect seems to be a common phenomenon (Kuyper & Dijkstra, 2009), one driven by our motivational biases (Brown, 2012).

Whether positive or negative, feedback from others plays an important role in shaping a youngster's self-concept.

Feedback from Others

Individuals' self-concept is shaped significantly by the feedback they get from important people in their lives. Early on, parents and other family members play a dominant role. Parents give their children a great deal of direct feedback, saying such things as "We're so proud of you" or "If you just tried harder, you could do a lot better in math." Most people, especially when young, take this sort of feedback to heart. Thus, it comes as no surprise that studies find a link between parents' views of a child and the child's self-concept (Burhans & Dweck, 1995). There is even stronger evidence for a relationship between children's *perceptions* of their parents' attitudes toward them and their own self-views (Zhu et al., 2014).

Teachers, Little League coaches, Scout leaders, classmates, and friends also provide feedback during childhood. In later childhood and adolescence, parents and classmates are particularly important sources of feedback and support (Harter, 2003). Later in life, feedback from close friends and marriage partners assumes importance. In fact, there is evidence that a close partner's support and affirmation can bring the loved one's actual self-views and behavior more in line with his or her ideal self (Drigotas, 2002). For this situation to happen, the partner needs to hold views of the loved one that match the target person's ideal self and behave in ways to bring out the best in the person. If the target person's behavior can closely match the ideal self, then self-views can move nearer to the ideal self. Researchers have labeled this process the *Michelangelo phenomenon* to reflect the partner's role in "sculpting" into reality the ideal self of a loved one (Righetti, Rusbult, & Finkenauer, 2010).

Social Context

Receiving feedback from others reveals that the self-concept does not develop in isolation (Ledgerwood, 2014). Of course, it's not only people that matter; so do the social contexts where interactions occur. Think about it: You're much more boisterous (and less self-conscious) when you are out with friends at a dance or a diner than when you are sitting in class. Social context affects how people think and feel about others as well, including the impressions they may knowingly convey to others in different situations (Carlson & Furr, 2009). In office settings, for example, a superior will act and feel like a leader with subordinates but will quickly change demeanor and outlook in the presence of an equal (Moskowitz, 1994).

Cultural Values

Self-concept is also shaped by cultural values. Among other things, the society in which one is reared defines what is desirable and undesirable in personality and behavior. For

Learn More Online

Research Sources: Concepts of Person and Self

Over the past century psychologists, philosophers, and many others have wondered what is meant by terms like *person* and *self*. Professor Shaun Gallagher of the Department of Philosophy at the University of Memphis provides visitors with a variety of resources to explore these concepts.

example, American culture puts a high premium on individuality, competitive success, strength, and skill. When individuals meet cultural expectations, they feel good about themselves and experience increases in self-esteem (Cross & Gore, 2003). In the United States, for example, friends heap praise on one another with great regularity. Such self-congratulatory behavior puzzles Japanese visitors, who are apt to be more restrained when doling out praise. Kitayama (1996) found that Americans report praising a peer every day. When asked the same question, Japanese citizens, who are socialized to feel less pride in personal achievement, reported praising a peer once every 4 days or so.

Cross-cultural studies suggest that different cultures shape different conceptions of the self (Adams, 2012). One important way cultures differ is on the dimension of individualism versus collectivism (Triandis, 2001). *Individualism* **involves putting personal goals ahead of group goals and defining one's identity in terms of personal attributes rather than group memberships.** In contrast, *collectivism* **involves putting group goals ahead of personal goals and defining one's identity in terms of the groups to which one belongs** (such as one's family, tribe, work group, social class, caste, and so on). Narratives found in American and Japanese textbooks reflect this dichotomy, with the former emphasizing individual achievement and the latter focusing on group harmony (Imada, 2012). Although it's tempting to think of these perspectives in either/or terms, it is more appropriate to view them as qualities that vary in degree and that can be assessed (Fischer et al., 2009). Thus, it is more accurate to say that certain cultures are more or less individualistic (or collectivist) than others rather than see them as either one or the other.

Here is a clever but telling example illustrating the difference between individualistic and collectivist cultures where simple choice is concerned. American students and Indian students selected a pen from a group composed of one blue pen and four red ones. American students consistently picked the singular blue pen, while the Indian students always chose a red pen (Nicholson, 2006; see also Connor Snibe & Markus, 2005; Stephens, Markus, & Townsend, 2007). In Western culture, we need to remember that "agency," or how people express their sense of power or influence in the social world, is not always found in other cultures or cultural contexts (Markus & Kitayama, 2004). In a follow-up study, once the students made their choice, some were told "Actually, you can't have that pen. Here, take this one instead." All students were then told to try their new pen, either the one "chosen" for them or the one "given" to them, and to rate it. The Americans preferred the pens they originally chose, thus devaluing the pen they were "given." How did the Indian students react? They showed no preference for either the pen they freely chose or the one given to them. Individualistic cultures promote freedom and choice, and people who live in these cultures do not like to have either threatened.

Subcultures within a larger culture, too, can be revealing, as was shown in a conceptual replication of the pen studies examining choice differences linked to social class. In the United States, middle-class individuals tend to exhibit individualism, but their working-class counterparts act in ways that are more collectivist. Stevens, Markus, and Townsend (2007) found that middle-class American students routinely preferred a distinct pen (thereby emphasizing agency) while working-class students often chose a similar pen, thereby demonstrating a desire to connect with and be like others rather than to stand out.

Culture shapes thought, too (Varnum et al., 2010). Individuals reared in individualistic cultures usually have an *independent view of the self*, perceiving themselves as unique, self-contained, and distinct from others. In contrast, individuals reared in collectivist cultures typically have an *interdependent view of the self*. They see themselves as inextricably connected to others and believe that harmonious relationships with others are of utmost importance. Thus, in describing herself, a person living in an individualistic culture might say, "I am kind," whereas someone in a collectivist culture might respond, "My family thinks I am kind" (Triandis, 2001). **Figure 6.4** depicts the self-conceptions of representatives of these contrasting worldviews.

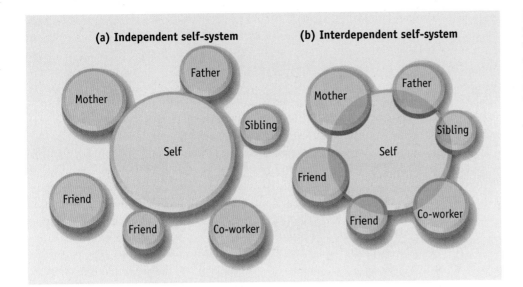

(a) Independent self-system

Mother
Father
Sibling
Self
Friend
Friend
Co-worker

(b) Interdependent self-system

Mother
Father
Sibling
Self
Friend
Friend
Co-worker

Figure 6.4

Independent and interdependent views of the self. (a) Individuals in cultures that support an independent view perceive the self as clearly separated from significant others. **(b)** Individuals in cultures that support an interdependent view perceive the self as inextricably connected to others.

Source: Adapted from Markus, H. R., & Kitayama, S. (1991). Culture and the self: Implications for cognition, emotion, and motivation. *Psychological Review, 98,* 224–253.

6.2 Self-Esteem

How do you evaluate yourself? Do you think of yourself in primarily positive or negative terms? One of the functions of the self-concept is to evaluate the self; the result of this self-evaluation is termed *self-esteem. Self-esteem* **refers to one's overall assessment of one's worth as a person.** Self-esteem is a global self-evaluation that blends many specific evaluations about one's adequacy as a student, an athlete, a worker, a spouse, a parent, or whatever is personally relevant. **Figure 6.5** shows how specific elements of the self-concept may contribute to self-esteem. If you feel basically good about yourself, you probably have high self-esteem.

People with high self-esteem are confident, taking credit for their successes in various ways (Blaine & Crocker 1993) while seeking venues for demonstrating their skills (Baumeister, 1998). High-self-esteem folks are not unduly discouraged by failure because they usually create personal strategies for downplaying or ignoring negative criticism (Heimpel et al., 2002). Compared to individuals with low self-esteem, they are also relatively sure of who they are (Campbell, 1990). In reality, the self-views of people with low self-esteem are not more negative; rather, they are more confused and tentative (Campbell & Lavallee, 1993), as such individuals often experience emotional highs and lows as well as mood swings (Campbell, Chew, & Scratchley, 1991). In other words, their self-concepts seem to be less clear, less complete, more self-contradictory, and more susceptible to short-term fluctuations than the self-views of high-self-esteem individuals. The problem is that such fluctuations among people with low self-esteem can lead to delinquency, aggression, and other forms of problem behavior (Donnellan et al., 2005). According to Roy Baumeister (1998), an eminent researcher on the self, this "self-concept confusion" means that individuals with low self-esteem simply don't know themselves well enough to strongly endorse many personal attributes on self-esteem tests, which results in lower self-esteem scores.

Although self-concept confusion may resolve itself over time if people learn who they truly are, there is compelling evidence that low self-esteem is a challenge at all phases of the adult lifespan. Recent longitudinal research reveals that self-esteem has a pronounced impact on real-life outcomes (Orth, Robins, & Widaman, 2012). For instance, it predicts depression as individuals make the transition to young adulthood (Rieger et al., 2015) and is found to be a consistent risk factor for depressive symptoms among people ages 18 to 88

Learning Objectives

- Clarify the implications of self-concept confusion and self-esteem instability.
- Explain how high and low self-esteem are related to adjustment.
- Distinguish between high self-esteem and narcissism, and discuss narcissism and aggression.
- Discuss some key influences in the development of self-esteem.

Roy Baumeister is a renowned expert in the positive and negative aspects of self-esteem.

Figure 6.5

The structure of self-esteem. Self-esteem is a global evaluation that combines assessments of various aspects of one's self-concept, each of which is built up from many specific behaviors and experiences. (Adapted from Shavelson, Hubner, & Stanton, 1976)

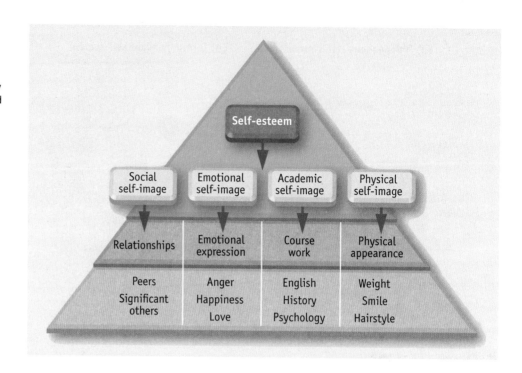

(Orth et al., 2009b). Further, low self-esteem's link to people's risk for depression is independent of other factors, such as stressful life events (Orth et al., 2009a).

Self-esteem can be construed in two primary ways: as a trait or as a state. *Trait self-esteem* refers to the ongoing sense of confidence people have regarding their abilities (athletic, assertive) and characteristics (friendliness, helpfulness). People's traits tend to stay with them and to remain constant; if one has high or low self-esteem in childhood, it will persist across young adulthood (Wagner, Lüdtke, & Trautwein, 2015), and chances are one will have a similar level of self-esteem as an adult and into old age (Trzesniewski, Donnellan, & Robins, 2003). **Figure 6.6** presents a basic self-report measure often used in research when self-esteem is studied as a trait. In contrast, *state self-esteem* is dynamic and changeable, referring to how individuals feel about themselves in the moment (Heatherton & Polivy, 1991). Feedback from others, self-observation, one's point in the lifespan, moods, a temporary financial setback, even the loss of one's alma mater's team (Hirt et al., 1992)—all can lower one's current sense of self-worth. Those whose self-esteem fluctuates in response to daily experiences are highly sensitive to interactions and events that have potential relevance to their self-worth, and they may even mistakenly view irrelevant events as having significance (Kernis & Goldman, 2003). They always feel their self-worth is on the line.

Investigating self-esteem is challenging for several reasons. For one thing, obtaining accurate measures of self-esteem is difficult. The problem is that researchers tend to rely on self-reports from subjects, which obviously may be biased. In fact, people with high self-esteem often believe they have higher intelligence or are more attractive than people with low self-esteem, but objective assessments indicate this is rarely true (Gabriel, Critelli, & Ee, 1994). These findings are not surprising; as you've seen, most individuals typically hold unrealistically positive views about themselves (Buss, 2012). Moreover, some people may choose not to disclose their actual self-esteem on a questionnaire. (What about you? Did you answer the questions in **Figure 6.6** truthfully and without any self-enhancing biases? How can you be sure?) Second, in probing self-esteem it is often quite difficult to separate cause from effect. Thousands of correlational studies report that high and low self-esteem are associated with various behavioral characteristics. For instance, it is true that students with high self-esteem tend to have slightly higher grades than those with low self-esteem (Baumeister et al., 2003). Yet high self-esteem is not the cause of these good grades, rather, the good grades are leading to the reported levels of high self-esteem. You

THE ROSENBERG (1965) SELF-ESTEEM SCALE			

Using the scale below, indicate your agreement with each of the following statements.

1	2	3	4
Strongly disagree	Disagree	Agree	Strongly agree

_____ 1. I feel that I am a person of worth, at least on an equal basis with others.

_____ 2. I feel that I have a number of good qualities.

_____ 3. All in all, I am inclined to feel that I am a failure.

_____ 4. I am able to do things as well as most other people.

_____ 5. I feel I do not have much to be proud of.

_____ 6. I take a positive attitude toward myself.

_____ 7. On the whole, I am satisfied with myself.

_____ 8. I wish I could have more respect for myself.

_____ 9. I certainly feel useless at times.

_____ 10. At times I think I am no good at all.

To calculate your score, first reverse the scoring for the five negatively worded items (3, 5, 8, 9, and 10) as follows: 1 = 4, 2 = 3, 3 = 2, 4 = 1. Then, sum your scores across the ten items. Your total score should fall between 10 and 40. A higher score indicates higher self-esteem.

Figure 6.6

A popular measure of self-esteem: The Rosenberg Self-Esteem Scale. The scale shown here is a widely used research instrument that taps respondents' feelings of general self-esteem. To calculate your score, first reverse the scoring for the five negatively worded items (3, 5, 8, 9, and 10) as follows: 1 = 4, 2 = 3, 3 = 2, 4 = 1. Then, sum your scores across the ten items. Your total should fall between 10 and 40. A higher score indicates higher self-esteem.

Source: Adapted from Rosenberg, M. (1965). *Society and the adolescent self-image.* Princeton, NJ: Princeton University Press.

should keep this problem in pinpointing causation in mind as we learn more about this fascinating topic.

The Importance of Self-Esteem

Popular wisdom holds that self-esteem is the key to practically all positive outcomes in life. In fact, its actual benefits are much fewer—but, we hasten to add, not unimportant (Krueger, Vohs, & Baumeister, 2009). Let's look at the findings that relate to self-esteem and adjustment.

Self-Esteem and Adjustment

The clearest advantages of self-esteem are in the *emotional sphere*. Namely, self-esteem is strongly and consistently related to happiness. Having high self-esteem feels good, and those who have it are happier than individuals with low self-esteem (Diener & Diener, 1995). In fact, Baumeister and his colleagues are persuaded that high self-esteem actually leads to greater happiness, although they acknowledge that research has not clearly established the direction of causation. On the other side, low self-esteem is more likely than high self-esteem to lead to depression.

In the area of *achievement*, high self-esteem has not been shown to be a reliable cause of good academic performance (Forsyth et al., 2007). In fact, it may actually be the (weak) result of doing well in school. Baumeister and his colleagues speculate that other factors may underlie both self-esteem and academic performance. Nonetheless, people with high self-esteem cope better with and respond constructively to receiving negative feedback on their performance (Sommer & Baumeister, 2002). They are less likely to quit trying to complete a task after a negative evaluation than are individuals with low self-esteem. Such persistence comes with a cost, however. For high-self-esteem people, negative feedback can make them more independent than their low-self-esteem counterparts, so much so that they can be perceived negatively, as arrogant, for example, by unfamilar peers after even a brief interaction (Vohs & Heatherton, 2001).

In the *interpersonal realm*, Baumeister and his colleagues report that people with high self-esteem claim to be more likable and attractive, to have better relationships, and to

Stephen Coburn/Shutterstock.com

Despite people's expectations, high self-esteem is not a solid predictor of academic success.

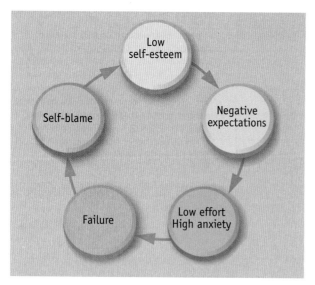

Figure 6.7

The vicious circle of low self-esteem and poor performance. Low self-esteem is associated with low or negative expectations about performance. These low expectations often result in inadequate preparation and high anxiety, heightening the likelihood of poor performance. Unsuccessful performance triggers self-blame, which feeds back to lower self-esteem.

Source: Adapted from Brehm, S. S., Kassin, S. M., & Fein, S. (2002). *Social psychology* (5th ed.). Boston: Houghton Mifflin.

"Can you believe this is happening to me? Her scores are very low in self-esteem."

make better impressions on others than people with low self-esteem do. Interestingly, as we already learned, these advantages seem to exist mainly in the minds of the beholders because objective data (ratings of peers) do not support these views. In fact, Mark Leary's *sociometer theory* suggests that self-esteem is actually a subjective measure of one's interpersonal popularity and success (Leary & Guadagno, 2011).

What about self-esteem and *coping*, a key aspect of adjustment? Individuals with low self-esteem *and* a self-blaming attributional style are definitely at a disadvantage here. For one thing, they become more demoralized after a failure than those with high self-esteem do. For them, failure contributes to depression and undermines their motivation to do better the next time. By contrast, individuals with high self-esteem persist longer in the face of failure. Second, as can be seen in **Figure 6.7**, individuals with low self-esteem often have negative expectations about their performance (in a social situation, at a job interview, on a test). Because self-esteem affects expectations, it operates in a self-perpetuating fashion. As a result, such people feel anxious and may not prepare for the challenge. Then, if they blame themselves when they do poorly, they feel depressed and deliver one more blow to their already battered self-esteem.

High Self-Esteem versus Narcissism

Although feeling good about oneself is desirable, problems arise when people's self-views are inflated and unrealistic. Indeed, high self-esteem may not be all it's cracked up to be. As we noted in Chapters 1 and 2, *narcissism* is the tendency to regard oneself as grandiosely self-important, to express excessive self-love, and to display a selfish orientation. Narcissistic individuals passionately want to think well of themselves, are highly sensitive to criticism (Twenge, 2006; Twenge & Campbell, 2009), and do not always make good partners or spouses (Campbell, 2005). Narcissists usually lack empathy, which means they are not concerned with others' problems and find it difficult to adopt others' perspectives (Konrath, O'Brien, & Hsing, 2011). They are preoccupied with fantasies of success, believe that they deserve special treatment, and react aggressively when they experience threats to their self-views (ego threats). Those with fragile (unstable) self-esteem also respond in this manner (Kernis, 2003a). Compared to narcissists, however, high-self-esteem individuals are able to moderate rather than exploit available self-enhancement opportunities (Horvath & Morf, 2010). Individuals whose positive self-appraisals are secure or realistic are not so susceptible to ego threats and are less likely to resort to hostility and aggression in the face of them. Note that narcissists' aggression must be provoked; without provocation, they are no more likely to aggress than non-narcissists (Twenge & Campbell, 2003).

Baumeister and his colleagues speculate that narcissists who experience ego threats have an elevated propensity to engage in aggressive acts such as partner abuse, rape, gang violence, individual and group hate crimes, and political terrorism (Bushman et al., 2003). Is there any evidence to support this idea? In a series of studies, researchers gave participants the opportunity to aggress against someone who had either insulted or praised an essay they had written (Bushman & Baumeister, 1998). The narcissistic participants reacted to their "insulters" with exceptionally high levels of aggression (see **Figure 6.8**).

These findings have important practical implications (Thomaes & Bushman, 2011). Most rehabilitation programs for spousal abusers, delinquents, and criminals are based on the faulty belief that

Edward Koren/www.cartoonbank.com

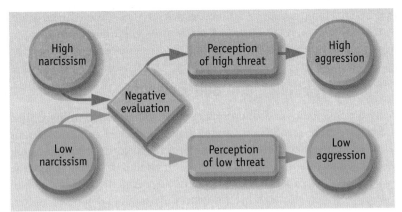

Figure 6.8

The path from narcissism to aggression. Individuals who score high on narcissism perceive negative evaluations by others to be extremely threatening. This experience of ego threat triggers strong hostile feelings and aggressive behavior toward the evaluator in retaliation for the perceived criticism. Low scorers are less likely to perceive negative evaluations as threatening and, therefore, behave much less aggressively toward evaluators. (Adapted from Bushman & Baumeister, 1998)

these individuals suffer from low self-esteem. So far, there is little empirical evidence that low self-esteem leads to either direct (e.g., hitting someone) or indirect (e.g., giving someone a negative evaluation) aggression (Bushman et al., 2009). Indeed, current research suggests that efforts to boost (already inflated) self-esteem are misguided. A better approach is to help such individuals develop more self-control and more realistic views of themselves. One researcher argues people should focus on developing self-compassion by treating ourselves with kindness while focusing less on comparions with others (Neff, 2011).

The Development of Self-Esteem

The foundations of self-esteem are laid early in life, and psychologists have focused much of their attention on the role of parenting in self-esteem development. Indeed, there is ample evidence that parental involvement, acceptance, support, and exposure to clearly defined limits have marked influence on children's self-esteem (Harter, 1998).

Two major dimensions underlie parenting behavior: acceptance and control. Diana Baumrind (2013) identified four distinct parenting styles as interactions between these two dimensions (see **Figure 6.9**). *Authoritative parenting* uses high emotional support and firm, but reasonable limits (high acceptance, high control). *Authoritarian parenting* entails low emotional support with rigid limits (low acceptance, high control). *Permissive parenting* uses high emotional support with few limits (high acceptance, low control), and *neglectful parenting* involves low emotional support and few limits (low acceptance, low control). Baumrind and others have found correlations between these parenting styles and children's traits and behaviors, including self-esteem (Furnham & Cheng, 2000) and children's social understanding of other people (O'Reilly & Peterson, 2014). Authoritative parenting is associated with the highest self-esteem scores, and this finding generally holds true across

Unfortunately, extreme or inflated views of the self can lead to narcissism.

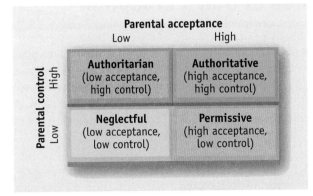

Figure 6.9

Baumrind's parenting styles. Four parenting styles result from the interactions of parental acceptance and parental control, as theorized by Diana Baumrind.

Source: Adapted from Baumrind, D. (1971). Current patterns of parental authority [Monograph]. *Developmental Psychology,* 4(1, Part 2), 1–103. American Psychological Association. Adapted by permission of the author.

Parents, teachers, coaches, and other adults play a key role in shaping self-esteem.

different ethnic groups (Wissink, Dekovic, & Meijer, 2006). In any case, these studies were correlational, so keep in mind they don't demonstrate that parenting style *causes* high or low self-esteem.

Ethnicity, Gender, and Self-Esteem

Because prejudice and discrimination are still pervasive in the United States, people commonly assume that members of minority groups have lower self-esteem than members of the majority group. Research both supports and contradicts this assumption. On the one hand, the self-esteem of Asians, Hispanics, and Native Americans is lower than that of whites, although the differences are small (Twenge & Crocker, 2002). On the other hand, the self-esteem of blacks is higher than that of whites (Twenge & Crocker, 2002). Adding gender to the mix complicates the picture even more. White males have higher self-esteem than white females, but minority males have lower self-esteem than minority females (Twenge & Crocker, 2002). Large-scale surveys reveal these patterns already exist in adolescence (Bachman et al., 2011).

Thus, ethnicity and gender interact in complex ways in self-esteem. The role of cultural differences in the self-concept may provide some insight here. Recall our earlier discussion of individualism and collectivism. Note that differences on this dimension are found not only between nations but also within a given country. And here's another fact: High individualism is associated with high self-esteem. What's interesting here is that the pattern of ethnic differences in individualism closely mirrors the pattern of ethnic differences in self-esteem (Twenge & Crocker, 2002). That is, blacks score higher than whites, whites do not differ significantly from Hispanics, and Hispanics score higher than Asian Americans. Thus, the ethnic differences in self-esteem are likely rooted in how the different groups view themselves based on cultural messages.

Although females are not a minority group, they resemble ethnic minorities in that they tend to have lower status and less power than males. The popular press abounds with reports of low self-esteem in adolescent girls and women (Orenstein, 1995). Is there any empirical basis for this assertion? One meta-analysis of 115 studies found that men had higher domain-specific self-esteem for physical appearance, athleticism, personal self (self-evaluation of personality independent of body or relationships to others), and self-satisfaction (happiness with self), while women did so in the domains of behavioral conduct (socially acceptable actions) and moral/ethical self-esteem (Gentile et al., 2009). Interestingly, the difference in self-esteem for physical appearance only appeared after 1980 and was largest among adult participants. The reason, Gentile and colleagues speculate, is increased media focus on how people look. However, men and women did not differ in their self-esteem levels for academic ability, social acceptance, family, or emotional well-being.

Learning Objectives

- Distinguish between automatic and controlled processing.
- Define self-attributions and identify the key dimensions of attributions.
- Explain how optimistic and pessimistic explanatory styles are related to adjustment.
- Identify three motives that guide self-understanding.
- Discuss four methods of self-enhancement.

6.3 Basic Principles of Self-Perception

Now that you're familiar with some of the major aspects of the self, let's consider how people construct and maintain a coherent and positive view of the self. First we look at the basic cognitive processes involved and then at the fascinating area of self-attributions. Then we move on to discuss explanatory style and the key motives guiding self-understanding, with a special emphasis on self-enhancement techniques.

Cognitive Processes

People are faced with an inordinate number of decisions on a daily basis. How do they keep from being overwhelmed? The key lies in how people process information. According to

Shelley Taylor (1981; Fiske & Taylor, 2013), people are "cognitive misers." Because cognitive resources (attention, memory, and so forth) are limited, the mind works to "hoard" them by taking cognitive shortcuts. For example, you probably have the same morning routine—shower, drink coffee, eat breakfast, check email, and so forth. Because you do these things without a lot of thought, you can conserve your attentional, decision-making, and memory capacities for important cognitive tasks. This example illustrates the default mode of handling information: *automatic processing*. On the other hand, when important decisions arise or when you're trying to understand why you didn't get that job you wanted, you spend those precious cognitive resources. This mode is termed *controlled processing*. Ellen Langer (1989) describes these two states as *mindlessness* and *mindfulness*, respectively. Mindfulness promotes cognitive flexibility, which in turn can lead to self-acceptance (Carson & Langer, 2006), stress reduction (Carmody & Baer, 2008), and well-being (Langer, 2009). In contrast, mindlessness leads to rigid thinking in which details and important distinctions are lost.

Another way that cognitive resources are protected is through *selective attention*, with high priority given to information pertaining to the self (Bargh, 1997). An example of this tendency is a phenomenon known as the "cocktail party effect"—the ability to pick out the mention of your name in a roomful of chattering people (Wood & Cowan, 1995). Sometimes our selective self-attention works against us, such as when we vastly overestimate how conspicuous we are in the minds of other people, a phenomenon known as the *spotlight effect* (Gilovich, Medvec, & Savitsky, 2000; Lawson, 2010). What would happen if you were to wear an embarrassing T-shirt—one emblazoned with none other than Barry Manilow on it—into a room of peers? Self-conscious participants guessed that half of the peers would notice their dorky fashion choice; in reality, less than 25% did.

Another principle of self-cognition is that people strive to understand themselves. One way they do so, as you saw in our discussion of social comparison theory, is to compare themselves with others (Wood & Wilson, 2003). Yet another is to engage in attributional thinking, our next topic.

Self-Attributions

Let's say that you win a critical match for your school's tennis team. To what do you attribute your success? Is your new practice schedule starting to pay off? Did you have the home court advantage? Was your opponent playing with a minor injury? This example from everyday life illustrates the nature of the self-attribution process. *Self-attributions* **are inferences that people draw about the causes of their own behavior.** People routinely make attributions to make sense out of their experiences (Malle, 2011a). These attributions involve inferences that ultimately represent guesswork on each person's part.

Fritz Heider (1958) was the first to assert that people tend to locate the cause of a behavior either within a person, attributing it to personal factors, or outside a person, attributing it to environmental factors. He thus established one of the crucial dimensions along which attributions are made: internal versus external. The other two dimensions are stable-unstable and controllable-uncontrollable. These three dimensions appear to be central in the attribution process. Let's discuss these various types of attributions in greater detail.

Internal or external. Elaborating on Heider's insight, various theorists have agreed that explanations of behavior and events can be categorized as internal or external attributions (Kelley, 1967; Weiner, 2006). *Internal attributions* **ascribe the causes of behavior to personal dispositions, traits, abilities, and feelings.** *External attributions* **ascribe the causes of behavior to situational demands and environmental constraints.** For example, if you credit your poor statistics grade to your failure to prepare adequately for the test or to getting overly anxious during the test, you are making internal attributions. An external attribution could be that the course is simply too hard, that the teacher is unfair, or that the book is incomprehensible.

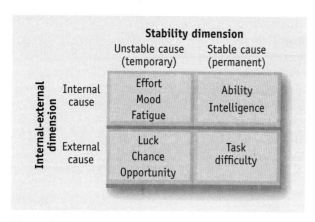

Figure 6.10

Key dimensions of attributional thinking. Weiner's model assumes that people's explanations for success and failure emphasize internal versus external causes and stable versus unstable causes. For example, if you attribute an outcome to great effort or to lack of effort, you are citing causes that lie within the person. Because effort can vary over time, the causal factors at work are unstable. Other examples of causal factors that fit into each of the four cells in Weiner's model are shown in the diagram.

Source: From Weiner, B., Frieze, I., Kukla, A., Reed, L.. & Rosenbaum, R. M. (1972). Perceiving the causes of success and failure. In E. E. Jones, D. E. Kanuouse, H. H. Kelly, R. E. Nisbett, S. Valins, & B. Weiner (Eds.), *Perceiving causes of behavior.* Morristown, NJ: General Learning Press. Reprinted by permission of the author.

Stable or unstable. A second dimension people use in making causal attributions is the stability of the causes underlying behavior (Weiner, 1994). A *stable* cause is one that is more or less permanent and unlikely to change over time. A sense of humor and intelligence are *stable internal* causes of behavior. *Stable external* causes of behavior include such things as laws and rules (speed limits, no-smoking areas). *Unstable* causes of behavior are variable or subject to change. *Unstable internal* causes of behavior include such things as mood (good or bad) and motivation (strong or weak). *Unstable external* causes could be the weather and the presence or absence of other people. According to Bernard Weiner (1994), the stable-unstable dimension in attribution cuts across the internal-external dimension, creating four types of attributions for success and failure, as shown in **Figure 6.10**.

Let's apply Weiner's model to a concrete event. Imagine that you are contemplating why you just landed the job you wanted. You might credit your situation to internal factors that are stable (excellent ability) or unstable (hard work on your attractive résumé). Or you might attribute the outcome to external factors that are stable (lack of top-flight competition) or unstable (luck). If you didn't get the job, your explanations would fall into the same four categories: internal-stable (lack of ability), internal-unstable (inadequate effort on your résumé), external-stable (too much competition in your field), and external-unstable (bad luck).

Controllable or uncontrollable. A third dimension in the attribution process acknowledges the fact that sometimes events are under one's control and sometimes they are not (Weiner, 1994). For example, the amount of effort you expend on a task is typically perceived as something under your control, whereas an aptitude for music is viewed as something you are born with (beyond your control). Controllability can vary with each of the other two factors.

Explanatory Style

Julio and Josh are freshmen who have just struck out trying to get their first college dates. After experiencing disappointment, they reflect on the possible reasons for it. Julio speculates that his approach was too subtle. Looking back, he realizes that he wasn't very direct because he was nervous about asking the woman out. When she didn't reply, he didn't follow up for fear that she didn't really want to go out with him. On further reflection, he reasons that she probably didn't respond because she wasn't sure of his intentions. He vows to be more direct the next time. Josh, on the other hand, responds to the situation by moping: "I'll never have a relationship. I'm a total loser." On the basis of these comments, who do you think is likely to get a date in the future? If you guessed Julio, you are probably correct. Let's see why.

According to Martin Seligman (1991), people tend to exhibit, to varying degrees, an *optimistic explanatory style* or a *pessimistic explanatory style* (see **Figure 6.11**). **Explanatory style refers to the tendency to use similar causal attributions for a wide variety of events in one's life.** The person with an optimistic explanatory style usually attributes setbacks to external, unstable, and specific factors (Peterson & Steen, 2009). A person who failed to get a desired job, for example, might attribute this misfortune to factors in the interview situation ("The room was really hot," "The questions were slanted") rather than to personal shortcomings. This style can be psychologically protective (Wise & Rosqvist, 2006), helping people to discount their setbacks and thus maintain a favorable self-image (Gordon, 2008). It also helps people bounce back from failure.

In contrast, people with a pessimistic explanatory style tend to attribute their setbacks to internal, stable, and global (or pervasive) factors. These attributions make them feel bad about themselves and doubtful about their ability to handle challenges in the future. As noted in Chapter 4, such a style can foster passive behavior and make people more

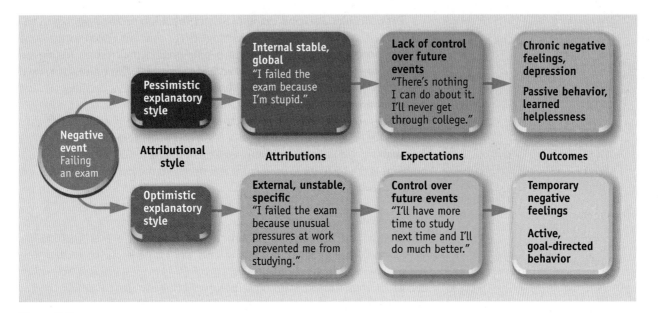

Figure 6.11

The effects of attributional style on expectations, emotions, and behavior. The pessimistic explanatory style is seen in the top row of boxes. This attributional style, which attributes setbacks to internal, stable, and global causes, tends to result in an expectation of lack of control over future events, depressed feelings, and passive behavior. A more adaptive, optimistic attributional style is shown in the bottom row of boxes.

vulnerable to *learned helplessness* and depression (Peterson, Maier, & Seligman, 1993), especially when they expect that things won't work out in their favor (Peterson & Vaidya, 2001). Of more concern is some suggestive evidence from a longitudinal sample of people that "catastrophizing"—attributing negative events to global causes—predicted accidental and violent deaths (Peterson et al., 1998). Luckily, explanatory style can be measured (Travers, Creed, & Morrissey, 2015), and cognitive-behavioral therapy appears to be effective at helping individuals at risk for depression (Seligman, Schulman, & Tryon, 2007) and at encouraging depressed individuals to change their pessimistic explanatory style (Seligman et al., 1999).

Motives Guiding Self-Understanding

Whether people evaluate themselves by social comparisons, attributional thinking, or other means, they are highly motivated to pursue self-understanding. In this pursuit, they are driven by two major motives: self-assessment and self-enhancement (Biernat & Billings, 2001).

Self-Assessment

The *self-assessment motive* is reflected in people's desire for truthful information about themselves. The problem is straightforward: Individuals don't know themselves all that well (Dunning, 2006)—in effect, we are ignorant of our own ignorance. The only good news about this flawed self-assessment is that people are typically unaware of this fact (Dunning, Heath, & Suls, 2004), presumably because evaluating one's own abilities is a formidable challenge (Carter & Dunning, 2008). Dubbed the *Dunning-Krueger effect*, this self-distorting bias occurs when we fail to recognize our own lack of skill in a given domain (baking), when we miss recognizing the genuine skill enacted by others (your roommate makes amazing cookies), and when we remain unaware of how inadequate we are when it comes to the ability in question (Dunning, 2011; Schlösser et al., 2013). Despite evidence to the contrary (everyone gobbles up your roommate's cookies but not yours), people often persist believing that they are more competent than everyone else.

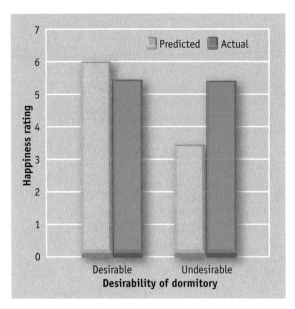

Figure 6.12

Bias in affective forecasting. Using a 7-point scale (where 1 = unhappy and 7 = happy), college students predicted how happy they would be a year later if they were randomly assigned to live in a desirable or an undesirable dormitory. Students anticipated that their dorm assignment would have a pronounced positive or negative impact on their overall happiness (yellow bars); however, a year later, those who ended up living in undesirable housing versus the desirable dorms showed nearly identical levels of happiness (green bars).

Source: Wilson & Gilbert (2005). Affective forecasting: Knowing what to want. *Current Directions in Psychological Science, 14*, 131–134, Fig. 1.

Let's consider a second example illustrating a limit to one's ability to engage in self-assessment. Social psychologists are now interested in the issue of emotional accuracy: How well do people predict their future feelings in response to good and bad events? As noted in Chapter 1, this process is known as *affective forecasting* (Wilson & Gilbert, 2003). Wilson and Gilbert (2005) have demonstrated repeatedly that people mispredict how much pleasure or displeasure they will feel once future events come to pass. The challenge people face is not the valence—or direction—of their feelings; individuals are reasonably good at judging what makes them happy or unhappy. Instead, the problem is the inability to predict the *intensity* and the *duration* of positive or negative feelings (Schwartz & Sommers, 2013).

One source of bias in affective forecasting is *impact bias*, which occurs when people misjudge the eventual intensity and duration of their emotional response to some future event. In this case, they overestimate rather than underestimate their feelings. Here's an example many readers can relate to: where they live on campus. Dunn, Wilson, & Gilbert (2003) asked college students to estimate how happy or unhappy they would be a year after being assigned to a desirable or an undesirable dormitory. As shown in **Figure 6.12**, the students expected that where they ended up living would have a fairly substantial impact on their overall levels of happiness. As you can see, however, a year after moving into the desired or less desired housing, self-reported happiness was virtually identical for the two groups (see **Figure 6.12**). In other words, people often overestimate the emotional impact of a single event because of what researchers call *focalism*, the tendency to overemphasize how much one will think about an event in the future while also underestimating how other events will compete for one's thoughts and feelings (Wilson et al., 2000).

Dorm life may not seem to be a very dramatic backdrop for adventures in affective forecasting, but other, more consequential life events have been studied. Research has found that people overestimate how unhappy they will be a couple months after a romance ends; women miscalculate their level of unhappiness on getting unwanted results from a pregnancy test; untenured college faculty misjudge how unhappy they will be 5 years after being turned down for tenure; and people fail to realize that acting in virtuous ways feels good, which means that their errors in emotional forecasting may keep them from doing good things (Sandstrom & Dunn, 2011). Thus, impact bias and focalism can distort expectations great and small, suggesting that the ability to accurately engage in self-assessment is limited.

Self-Enhancement

Finally, people are motivated by the *self-enhancement motive. Self-enhancement* **is the tendency to seek positive (and reject negative) information about oneself.** Psychologically, self-enhancement can appear in at least four ways: as an observed response or behavior, a process, a personality trait, or an underlying motive (Sedikides & Alicke, 2012). One example of self-enhancement is the tendency to hold flattering views of one's personal qualities, a tendency termed the *better-than-average effect* (Buckingham & Alicke, 2002). You've already seen an example of this effect in our earlier report that 100% of students who took the SAT rated themselves above average in the ability to get along with others—a mathematical impossibility. Students can take perverse pleasure in knowing that faculty also succumb to this bias: 94% of them regard their teaching as above average (Cross, 1977)! The effect is robust, as individuals routinely overrate their skills as public speakers (Keysar & Henley, 2002), selectively recall positive feedback while conveniently overlooking negative evaluations (Green, Sedikides, & Gregg, 2008), and are happy to credit themselves (but not others) for future outcomes, even when they are not yet realized (Williams, Gilovich, & Dunning, 2012).

Methods of Self-Enhancement

The powerful self-enhancement motive drives individuals to seek positive (and reject negative) information about themselves (Sanjuán, Magallares, & Gordillo, 2011). Let's examine four cognitive strategies people commonly use in this process.

Downward Comparisons

We've already mentioned that people routinely compare themselves to others as a means of learning more about themselves (social comparison). However, once a threat to self-esteem enters the picture, people often adjust their strategy and choose to compare themselves with those who are worse off than they are (Wood, 1989). *Downward social comparison* **is a defensive tendency to compare oneself with someone whose troubles are more serious than one's own.** Why do people change strategies under threat? Because they need to feel better, often doing so by connecting to the experience of others (Wayment & O'Mara, 2008). Research shows that downward social comparisons are associated with increases in both mood and self-esteem (Reis, Gerrard, & Gibbons, 1993).

If you have ever been in a serious traffic accident in which your car was "totaled," you probably reassured yourself by reflecting on the fact that at least no one was seriously injured. Similarly, people with chronic illnesses may compare themselves with those who have life-threatening diseases. The protective power of downward comparisons is apt to be quite robust. One recent study indicates that these strategic contrasts with the experience of others can save people from experiencing feelings of regret across their lives (Bauer & Wrosch, 2011). Another study indicates that we can make downward comparisons to our past selves instead of other people, thereby promoting self-enhancement by adopting the belief that "I'm better now than I used to be" (Zell & Alicke, 2009).

Self-Serving Bias

Suppose that you and three other individuals apply for a part-time job in the parks and recreation department and you are selected for the position. How do you explain your success? Chances are, you tell yourself that you were hired because you were the most qualified for the job. But how do the other three people interpret their negative outcome? Do they tell themselves that you got the job because you were the most able? Unlikely! Instead, they probably attribute their loss to "bad luck" or to not having had time to prepare for the interview. These different explanations for success and failure reflect **the** *self-serving bias,* **or the tendency to attribute one's successes to personal factors and one's failures to situational factors** (Shepperd, Malone, & Sweeny, 2008). One explanation for the self-serving bias is that unbiased self-judgments require a high degree of self-control, which is usually overridden by one's automatic drive toward self-enhancement (Krusemark, Campbell, & Clementz, 2008).

For example, in one experiment, two strangers jointly took a test. They then received bogus success or failure feedback about their test performance and were asked to assign responsibility for the test results. Successful participants claimed credit, but those who failed blamed their partners (Campbell et al., 2000). Still, people don't always rush to take credit. In another experiment in the just-cited study, participants were actual friends. In this case, participants shared responsibility for both successful and unsuccessful outcomes. Thus, friendship places limits on the self-serving bias.

Basking in Reflected Glory

When your favorite sports team won the national championship last year, did you make a point of wearing the team cap? And when your best friend won that special award, do you remember how often you told others the good news about her? If you played a role in someone's success, it's understandable that you would want to share in the recognition; however, people often want to share recognition even when they are on the sidelines of an outstanding achievement. *Basking in reflected glory* **is the tendency to enhance one's image by publicly announcing one's association with those who are successful.**

People frequently claim association with others who are successful (basking in reflected glory) to maintain positive feelings about themselves.

Robert Cialdini and his colleagues (1976) studied this phenomenon at colleges with nationally ranked football teams (see also Schaller, Kenrick, & Neuberg, 2012). The researchers predicted that, when asked how their team had fared in a recent football game, students would be more likely to say, "We won" (in other words, to bask in reflected glory, or to "BIRG"—pronounced with a soft "g") when the home team had been successful than to respond "We lost" when it had been defeated. Indeed, the researchers found that students were more likely to BIRG when their team won than when it lost. Also, subjects who believed that they had just failed a bogus test were more likely to use the words "We won" than those who believed they had performed well on the test.

A related self-enhancement strategy is "CORFing," or *cutting off reflected failure* (Ware & Kowalski, 2012). Because self-esteem is partly tied to an individual's associations with others, people often protect their self-esteem by distancing themselves from those who are unsuccessful (Miller, 2009). Thus, if your cousin is arrested for drunk driving, you may tell others that you don't really know him very well.

Self-Handicapping

When people fail at an important task, they need to save face. In such instances, individuals can usually come up with a face-saving excuse ("I had a terrible stomachache"). Curiously, some people actually behave in a way that sets them up to fail so that they have a readymade excuse for failure should it occur. *Self-handicapping* is the tendency to sabotage one's performance to provide an excuse for possible failure. For example, when a big test is looming, they put off studying until the last minute or go out drinking the night before the test. If, as is likely, they don't do well on the exam, they explain their poor performance by saying they hadn't prepared. (After all, wouldn't you rather have others believe that your poor performance is due to inadequate preparation rather than to lack of ability?) Such behavior is common in academic settings (Schwinger et al., 2014), where a lack of effort is often indicative of self-handicapping, as is a lack of self-control (Uysal & Knee, 2012); however, one study demonstrated that sometimes exerting too much effort—ironically, an active behavioral strategy—can reveal it, too. A group of men were led to believe that *too much* practice could hurt their future performance on a task. Within the group, those who scored high on a trait measure of self-handicapping were found to practice more compared to those low on this trait. Ironically, by overpreparing to ensure a poor performance, the high self-handicappers were able to save face—they could readily attribute their failure to

Recommended Reading

The Marshmallow Test: Mastering Self-Control

by Walter Mischel (Little, Brown and Company, 2014)

What are the roots of self-control? When does it appear? A classic study conducted by personality psychologist Walter Mischel found that being able to delay gratification in childhood predicted personal success later in life. Young children in a nursery school setting were presented with a simple but powerful challenge in the form of a marshmallow. They were told they could eat the one marshmallow right now or, if they waited a bit, they would receive and enjoy consuming two marshmallows. Some kids waited out the temptation in order to reap the larger reward, while others could not control themselves—they ate the solo sweet.

Are there long-term implications for such behavioral choices? Mischel says there are, and he demonstrates that self-control (or the lack thereof) in the form of delayed gratification is an essential part of later life success for the kids in the marshmallow study as well as the rest of us. Being able to wait for desired outcomes leads to better social connections with others, critical thinking, health, self-worth, and even higher college admissions test scores. The good news is that self-control can be learned and harnessed for positive ends in daily life, including weight loss, quitting cigarettes, dealing with romantic breakups, and saving for retirement, among other important life decisions.

their overpractice rather than a lack of skill, which is a more psychologically threatening explanation (Smith, Hardy, & Arkin, 2009). People use a variety of other tactics for handicapping their performance: alcohol, drugs, procrastination, a bad mood, a distracting stimulus, anxiety, depression, and being overcommitted (Baumeister, 1998).

6.4 Self-Regulation

Learning Objectives

■ Define *self-regulation* and explain the ego-depletion model of self-regulation.

■ Explain how self-efficacy develops and why it is important to psychological adjustment.

■ Describe the three categories of self-defeating behavior.

"Should I have that hot fudge sundae or not?" "I guess I'd better get started on that English paper." "Would I better off checking Facebook one more time or going to bed?" People are constantly trying to resist impulses and make themselves do things they don't really want to do. *Self-regulation* **is the process of directing and controlling one's behavior to achieve desired goals.** Clearly, the ability to manage and direct what you think, how you feel, and how you behave is tied to your success at work, your relationships, and your mental and physical health (Vohs & Baumeister, 2011), as well as the ability to avoid addiction (Baumeister & Vonasch, 2015). Being able to forgo immediate gratification (studying instead of partying) and focus your behavior on important, longer-range goals (graduating and getting a good job) is of paramount importance for success in life (Doerr & Baumeister, 2010).

It's possible that people have a limited amount of self-control resources. If you tax these resources resisting temptation in a given situation, you may have a hard time resisting the next temptation or persisting at a new task. As a result, self-control can have a cost (Baumeister & Alquist, 2009). At least that's the idea behind the *ego depletion model of self-regulation* (Baumeister et al., 1998). To investigate this hypothesis, researchers asked college students to participate in a study of taste perception (the study was actually on self-control) (Baumeister et al., 1998). Some participants were asked to eat two or three radishes in 5 minutes but not to touch the chocolate candy and chocolate chip cookies that were nearby. Others were asked to eat some candy or some cookies but were told not to eat any of the nearby radishes. A control group didn't participate in this part of the study. Then all subjects were asked to solve what were, unbeknownst-to-them, unsolvable puzzles while they supposedly waited for another part of the study. Researchers measured the subjects' self-control by the amount of time they persisted at the puzzles and the number of attempts they made. According to the ego depletion model, the radish eaters would use more self-control resources (resisting the chocolate) than the chocolate eaters (resisting the radishes) or the subjects in the no-food control group. Thus, this group should have the fewest self-control resources left to use for persisting at a difficult task. As you can see in **Figure 6.13**, the radish eaters gave up sooner and made fewer attempts on the puzzles than the chocolate eaters or the control group.

Self-regulation seems to develop early and remain relatively stable, and there is compelling evidence that self-regulation is transmitted from one generation (parents) to another (children) (Bridgett et al., 2015). One study reported that 4-year-olds who were better at delaying gratification did better in terms of both academic performance and social competence some 10 years later (Mischel, Shoda, & Peake, 1988; Shoda, Mischel, & Peake, 1990). Research also suggests that self-regulation is malleable and can be strengthened like a muscle, which means that with regular "exercise," people can become less vulnerable to ego depletion effects (Baumeister et al., 2006). Being in a good mood (Tice et al., 2007) and ingesting sugar, which fuels energy (Gailliot et al., 2007), can restore people's self-control, as can exposure to nature scenes (Chow & Lau, 2015). In the next section, we examine self-efficacy, a key aspect of self-regulation, and then discuss self-defeating behavior, a case of self-control failure.

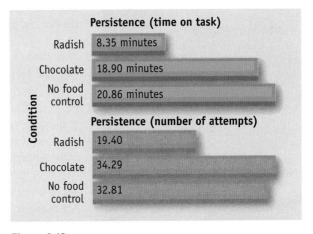

Figure 6.13

Persistence on unsolvable puzzles. Participants who were instructed to eat radishes and not to eat chocolate treats used more self-control resources than participants who were instructed to eat the chocolate and not touch the radishes or participants in the no-food control group. Because the radish eaters had relatively few self-control resources remaining to help them persist at a difficult task (unsolvable puzzles), they persisted for the shortest time and made the fewest attempts to solve the puzzles when compared to the other two groups. (Adapted from Baumeister et al., 1998)

Albert Bandura argues that self-efficacy represents a sense of confidence whereby a person believes he or she can achieve a desired goal.

Self-Efficacy

As explained in Chapter 2, *self-efficacy* **refers to one's belief about one's ability to perform behaviors that should lead to expected outcomes.** It represents people's conviction that they can achieve specific goals. According to Albert Bandura (2012, 2013), efficacy beliefs vary according to the person's skills. You may have high self-efficacy when it comes to making friends but low self-efficacy when it comes to speaking in front of a group. However, simply having a skill doesn't guarantee that you will be able to put it into practice. Like the Little Engine That Could, you must also *believe* that you are capable of doing so ("I *think* I can, I *think* I can . . ."). In other words, self-efficacy is concerned not with the skills you have, but with your *beliefs about what you can do* with these skills.

Correlates of Self-Efficacy

A number of studies have shown that self-efficacy affects individuals' commitments to goals, their performance on tasks, and their persistence toward goals in the face of obstacles (Maddux & Gosselin, 2003). Self-efficacy is related to health promotion (Bandura, 2004), academic performance (Prat-Sala & Redford, 2012), career choice (Betz & Klein, 1996), job satisfaction and performance (Alessandri et al., 2015; Peng & Mao, 2015), and coping with unemployment (Creed, Lehman, & Hood, 2009). Because of the importance of self-efficacy in psychological adjustment, it is worth keeping in mind that self-efficacy is learned and can be changed. Research shows that increasing self-efficacy is an effective way to improve health (losing weight, stopping smoking) (Maddux & Gosselin, 2003) and to treat a variety of psychological problems, including burnout (Ventura, Salanova, & Llorens, 2015), fear of computer use (Wilfong, 2006), phobias (Williams, 1995), eating disorders (Goodrick et al., 1999), and substance abuse (DiClemente, Fairhurst, & Piotrowski, 1995), including marijuana dependence (Lozano, Stephens, & Roffman, 2006).

Developing Self-Efficacy

Self-efficacy is obviously a valuable quality. How does one acquire it? Bandura (2000) identifies four sources of self-efficacy: mastery experiences, vicarious experiences, persuasion and encouragement, and interpretation of emotional arousal.

1. *Mastery experiences.* The most effective path to self-efficacy is through mastering new skills. Sometimes new skills come easily—learning how to use the copy machine in the library, for instance. Some things are harder to master, such as learning how to drive a stick-shift in a standard transmission car or how to play the piano. In acquiring more difficult skills, people usually make mistakes. If they persist through failure experiences to eventual success, they learn the lesson of self-efficacy: I *can* do it!

2. *Vicarious experiences.* Another way to improve self-efficacy is by watching others perform a skill you want to learn. It's important that you choose a model who is competent at the task, and it helps if the model is similar to you (in age, gender, and ethnicity). For example, if you're shy about speaking up for yourself, observing someone who is good at doing so can help you develop the confidence to do it yourself.

3. *Persuasion and encouragement.* Although it is less effective than the first two approaches, a third way to develop self-efficacy is through the encouragement of others. For example, if you're having a hard time asking someone for a date, a friend's encouragement might give you just the push you need.

4. *Interpretation of emotional arousal.* The physiological responses that accompany feelings and interpretations of these responses are another source of self-efficacy. Let's say you're sitting in class waiting for your professor to distribute an exam. You notice that your palms are moist, your stomach feels a little queasy, and your heart is pounding. If you attribute these behaviors to fear, you can temporarily dampen your self-efficacy, thus decreasing your chances of doing well. Alternatively, if you attribute your sweaty palms and racing heart to the arousal everyone needs in order to perform well, you may be able to boost your self-efficacy and increase your chances of doing well. Of course, self-regulation doesn't always succeed. That's the case in self-defeating behavior, our next topic.

Ironically, difficulties and failures can ultimately contribute to the development of a strong sense of self-efficacy. Self-efficacy tends to improve when youngsters learn to persist through difficulties and overcome failures.

Jgi/Blend Images/Corbis

Self-Defeating Behavior

People typically act in their own self-interest. But sometimes they knowingly do things that are bad for them—such as smoking, having unprotected sex, and completing important assignments at the last minute. *Self-defeating behaviors* **are seemingly intentional actions that thwart a person's self-interest.** Self-defeating behaviors generally provide short-term or immediate pleasures but lay the groundwork for long-term problems rather than gains (Baumeister & Bushman, 2011). According to Roy Baumeister (1997), there are three categories of intentional self-defeating behaviors: deliberate self-destruction, tradeoffs, and counterproductive strategies. The key difference among these three behaviors lies in how intentional they are. Attempts at deliberate self-destruction involve the most intent; counterproductive strategies are the least intentional, and tradeoffs fall in between.

In *deliberate self-destruction*, people want to harm themselves and choose courses of action that will forseeably lead to that result. This type of behavior typically occurs in individuals with psychological disorders; deliberate self-destruction appears to be infrequent in normal populations.

In *tradeoffs*, people foresee the possibility of harming themselves but accept it as a necessary accompaniment to achieving a desirable goal. Overeating, smoking, and drinking to excess are examples that come readily to mind. Other examples include procrastinating (putting off tasks feels good in the short run, but the struggle to meet looming deadlines results in poor performance and increased stress and illness), and self-handicapping (getting drunk before an exam explains poor performance but increases the chances of failure). People engage in tradeoffs because they bring immediate, positive, and reliable outcomes, not because they want to hurt themselves in the short or the long run.

In *counterproductive strategies*, a person pursues a desirable outcome but misguidedly uses an approach that is bound to fail. Of course, you can't always know in advance if a strategy will pay off. Thus, people must *habitually* use this strategy for it to qualify as self-defeating. For example, some people tend to persist in unproductive endeavors, such as pursuing an unreachable career goal or an unrequited love. People persist in these behaviors because they erroneously believe they'll be successful, not because they are intent on self-defeat.

To conclude, although most people engage in self-defeating behavior at some time, there is little evidence that they deliberately try to harm themselves or to fail at a task. Instead, self-defeating behavior appears to be the result of people's distorted judgments or strong desires to escape from immediate, painful feelings (Twenge, Catanese, & Baumeister, 2002).

Self-defeating behaviors come in many forms with many underlying motivations. Overeating is a matter of *tradeoffs*. People realize that excessive eating may be harmful in the long run, but it is enjoyable at the time.

6.5 Self-Presentation

Learning Objectives

■ Define *impression management* and cite some strategies people use to make positive impressions.

■ Understand how high self-monitors are different from low self-monitors.

Whereas your self-concept involves how you see yourself, your public self involves how you want others to see you. **A *public self* is an image presented to others in social interactions.** This presentation of a public self may sound deceitful, but it is perfectly normal, and everyone does it (Schlenker, 2003). Many self-presentations (ritual greetings, for example) take place automatically and without awareness. But when it really counts (job interviews, for example), people consciously strive to make the best possible impression so they are perceived favorably. Typically, individuals have a number of public selves that are tied to certain situations and certain people. For instance, you may have one public self for your parents and another for your peers. You may have still others for your teachers, your boss, your co-workers, and so forth. Also, people differ in the degree of overlap or congruence among their various public selves (see **Figure 6.14**). Does it matter whether you perceive yourself to be essentially the same person in different situations? It seems so. People who see themselves as being similar across different social roles (with friends, at work, at school, with parents, with romantic partners) are better adjusted than those who perceive less integration in their self-views across these roles (Lutz & Ross, 2003).

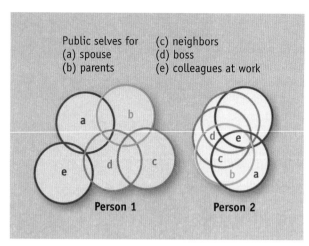

Figure 6.14

Public selves and adjustment. Person 1 has divergent public selves with relatively little overlap among them. Person 2, whose public selves are more congruent with each other, is likely to be better adjusted than Person 1.

Public selves for
(a) spouse
(b) parents
(c) neighbors
(d) boss
(e) colleagues at work

Person 1   Person 2

Impression Management

As noted earlier, the *spotlight effect* leads people to think others notice and evaluate them more than is the actual case (Gilovich, Kruger, & Medvec, 2002). In a related phenomenon, the *guilty by association effect*, people erroneously assume their social standing suffers as a result of embarrassing actions or blunders perpetrated by those they associate with ("My friend is making me look bad!") (Fortune & Newby-Clark, 2008). These two self-focused responses remind us that people normally strive to make a positive impression on others in order to be liked, respected, hired, and so forth (Baumeister & Twenge, 2003), just as they must be careful not to alienate others by bragging or drawing too much attention to themselves (Anderson et al., 2006). The sociologist Erving Goffman (1959) used the term *face* to describe the idealized image people try to create in the minds of others. **Impression management refers to usually conscious efforts by people to influence how others think of them.** As a skill, impression management is vital to social life (Koslowsky & Pindek, 2011). Consider how what you post on Facebook, for example, is a way for you to share your doings while still controlling what others know about you. Let's look at some common impression management strategies.

Impression Management Strategies

One reason people engage in impression management is to claim a particular identity (Baumeister, 1998). Thus, you select a type of dress, hairstyle, and manner of speech to present a certain image of yourself. Tattoos and body piercings also create a specific image. A second motive for impression management is to gain liking and approval from others—by editing what you say about yourself and by using various nonverbal cues such as smiles, gestures, and eye contact. Because self-presentation is practiced so often, people usually do it automatically. At other times, however, impression management may be used intentionally—to get a job, a date, a promotion, and so forth. Some common self-presentation strategies include ingratiation, self-promotion, and supplication (Jones, 1990). To this list, we add a rarely recognized strategy, negative acknowledgment:

1. *Ingratiation.* Of all the self-presentation strategies, ingratiation is the most fundamental and most frequently used. **Ingratiation is behaving in ways to make oneself likable to others.** For example, *giving compliments* is effective, so long as you are sincere (people dislike insincerity and can often detect it). One study found that waitresses could increase their tips simply by praising the food choices of customers as they ordered (Seiter, 2007). A recent study found that in a lab setting, ingratiation tactics displayed by a confederate worker led to higher likability ratings by observers than did the use of apologies, which caused negative evaluations (Bolino, Klotz, & Daniels, 2014). However, an accompanying field study using actual supervisors and their ratings found that apologies and justifications led to better evaluations. The effectiveness of ingratiation may well depend on good timing and how often (less may be more) it is used to manage the impressions of others. At the same time they are being "helpful," however, ingratiators run the risk of raising suspicion about their motives for doing so (Ham & Vonk, 2011). The top of **Figure 6.15** illustrates how ingratiation can be used during an employment interview.

2. *Self-promotion.* The motive behind self-promotion is earning respect. You do so by playing up your strong points so you will be perceived as competent. For instance, in a job interview, you might find ways to mention that you earned high honors at school and that you were president of the student body and a member of the soccer team. What about self-promotion in public venues? Some care is warranted or you will look boastful. However, when an audience is cognitively busy—their mental attention is split between two tasks or they are under some time pressure—they are more likely to give a self-promoter the benefit of the doubt, even when the social norms of modesty and politeness are violated (Fragale & Grant, 2015). The lower portion of **Figure 6.15** illustrates how self-promotion could be exercised when one is being interviewed for a job.

3. *Supplication.* This is usually the tactic of last resort. To get favors from others, individuals try to present themselves as weak and dependent—as in the song, "Ain't Too Proud to Beg" (Van Kleef, De Dreu, & Manstead, 2006). Students may plead or break into tears in an instructor's office in an attempt to get a grade changed. Because of the social norm to help those in need, supplication may work; however, unless the supplicator has something to offer the potential benefactor, it's not an effective strategy.

4. *Negative acknowledgment.* Can confessing you've made a relatively minor error motivate people to like you a bit more? Ward and Brenner (2006) found that making negative acknowledgments— candidly admitting to possessing some negative quality—triggered positive responses. In one study, when a hypothetical college student divulged that his high school record was by no means an outstanding one, his grades were judged more favorably than when he did not comment on his academic history. Perhaps negative acknowledgment leads people to see one as honest. Another possibility is that the presence of a negative acknowledgment makes it less likely that people will form counterarguments based on what they know or have heard (Pfeiffer et al., 2014). As long as the quality does not define the person, admitting that one is not perfect and that everyone makes small mistakes may sometimes be an advantage.

Individuals tailor their use of self-presentation strategies to match the situation. For instance, it's unlikely that you'd try intimidating your boss; you'd be more likely to ingratiate or promote yourself with him or her. All of these strategies carry risks. Thus, to make a good impression, you must use these strategies skillfully.

Self-Monitoring

According to Mark Snyder (1986; Fuglestad & Snyder, 2009), people vary in their awareness of how they are perceived by others. *Self-monitoring* **refers to the degree to which people attend to and control the impressions they make on others.** People who are high self-monitors seem to be very sensitive to their impact on others. Low self-monitors, on the other hand, are less concerned about impression management and behave more spontaneously.

Compared to low self-monitors, high self-monitors want to make a favorable impression and try to tailor their actions accordingly; they are skilled at deciphering what others want to see. In fact, high self-monitors manage their social relations well, earning status from others by offering them aid while avoiding asking for assistance themselves (Fuglestad & Snyder, 2010). Because they are able to control their emotions and deliberately regulate nonverbal signals, they are talented at self-presentation (Gangestad & Snyder, 2000). In contrast, low self-monitors are more likely to express their true beliefs or, possibly, to try to convey the impression that they are sincere and genuine individuals.

As you might infer, these two personality types view themselves differently (Gangestad & Snyder, 2000). Low self-monitors see themselves as having strong principles and behaving in line with them, whereas high self-monitors perceive themselves as flexible and pragmatic. Because high self-monitors don't perceive a necessary connection between their private beliefs and their public actions, they aren't troubled by discrepancies between beliefs and behavior, even when it involves mimicking group-based prejudice (Klein, Snyder, & Livingston, 2004).

Interestingly, people's posts on Facebook are reasonably good predictors of whether they are high or low self-monitors (He et al., 2014). What sorts of posts that you have seen

STRATEGIC SELF-PRESENTATION IN THE EMPLOYMENT INTERVIEW

In studies of the influence tactics that job applicants report using in employment interviews, the following uses of ingratiation and self-promotion were commonly reported.

Ingratiation
- I complimented the interviewer or organization.
- I discussed interests I shared in common with the recruiter.
- I indicated my interest in the position and the company.
- I indicated my enthusiasm for working for this organization.
- I smiled a lot or used other friendly nonverbal behaviors.

Self-Promotion
- I played up the value of positive events that I took credit for.
- I described my skills and abilities in an attractive way.
- I took charge during the interview to get my main points across.
- I took credit for positive events even if I was not solely responsible.
- I made positive events I was responsible for appear better than they actually were.

Figure 6.15

Using ingratiation and self-promotion for strategic self-presentation during an employment interview. Studies on influence tactics used by job applicants during interviews reveal the common, self-reported use of ingratiation and self-promotion.

Source: Kassin, Fein, & Markus (2014). *Social psychology* (9th ed.). Belmont, CA: Wadsworth Cengage Learning, Table 3.2, p. 93. (Based on data from Higgins & Judge, 2004; Stevens & Kristof, 1995)

on social media, including links and photographs, as well as text, do you think represent high or low self-monitors? Do you try to control the impression you convey of yourself when you post on Facebook or tweet on Twitter?

In the upcoming Application, we redirect our attention to the critical issue of self-esteem and outline eight steps for boosting it.

6.6 Building Self-Esteem

Learning Objectives

- List eight ways to build self-esteem.

Answer the following "yes" or "no."
____ **1.** I worry that others don't like me.
____ **2.** I have very little confidence in my abilities.
____ **3.** I often feel awkward in social situations and just don't know how to take charge.
____ **4.** I have difficulty accepting praise or flattery.
____ **5.** I have a hard time bouncing back from failure experiences.

If you answered "yes" to most of these questions, you may suffer from low self-esteem. As we noted earlier, people with low self-esteem are less happy and more prone to depression, become demoralized after failures, and are anxious in relationships. Moreover, even people with high global self-esteem may have pockets of low self-esteem. For example, you may feel great about your "social self" but not so good about your "academic self." Thus, this Application can be useful to many people, as research demonstrates clearly that people are willing to forgo other pleasures in order to boost their self-esteem (Bushman, Moeller, & Crocker, 2011).

As you saw in our discussion of self-efficacy, there is ample evidence that efforts at self-improvement can pay off by boosting self-esteem. Following are eight guidelines for building self-esteem. These suggestions are distilled from the advice of many experts, including Baumeister et al. (2003), McKay and Fanning (2000), and Zimbardo (1990).

Learn More Online

National Association for Self-Esteem (NASE)
This site is dedicated to fostering self-esteem. It explains the nature of self-esteem, permits browsers to estimate their self-esteem, discusses parenting and self-esteem, and provides links to other relevant websites.

Mike Twohy/The New Yorker Collection/Cartoon Bank.com

1. Recognize that You Control Your Self-Image

Recognize that *you* ultimately control how you see yourself. You *do* have the power to change your self-image. Your self-image resides in your mind and is a product of your thinking. Although others may influence your self-concept, you are the final authority.

2. Learn More about Yourself

People with low self-esteem don't seem to know themselves in as much detail as those with high self-esteem. Accordingly, to boost your self-esteem, you need to take stock of yourself. To do so, review what you know about your physical appearance, personality characteristics, relations with others, school and job performance, intellectual functioning, and sexuality. By thinking through each area, you may discover that you're fuzzy about certain aspects of yourself. To get a clearer picture, pay careful attention to your thoughts, feelings, and behavior and utilize feedback from others.

3. Don't Let Others Set Your Goals

A common trap that many people fall into is letting others set the standards by which they evaluate themselves. Others, including close friends, parents, and other family members, are constantly telling you that you should do this or ought to do that. Think about the source of and basis for your personal goals and standards. Do they really represent ideals that *you* value? Or are they beliefs that you have passively accepted from others without thinking?

4. Recognize Unrealistic Goals

Are your goals realistic? Many people demand too much of themselves. They want to always perform at their best, which is obviously impossible. Other delude themselves by selecting goals that are unlikely to be realized, often because they lack relevant skills. Some overly demanding people pervert the social comparison process by always comparing themselves to the *best* rather than to similar others. They assess their looks by comparing themselves with famous models, and they judge their finances by comparing themselves with the wealthiest people they know or hear about in the media. Such comparisons are unrealistic and almost inevitably undermine self-esteem. Set reasonable, realistic goals for yourself.

5. Modify Negative Self-Talk

How you think about your life influences how you see yourself (and vice versa). People who are low in self-esteem tend to engage in counterproductive modes of thinking. For example, when they succeed, they may attribute their success to good luck, and when they fail, they may blame themselves. Quite to the contrary, you should take credit for your successes and consider the possibility that your failures may not be your fault. Recognize the destructive potential of negative self-talk and bring it to a halt.

6. Emphasize Your Strengths

This advice may seem trite, but it has some merit. People with low self-esteem often derive little satisfaction from their accomplishments and virtues. They pay little heed to their good qualities while talking constantly about their defeats and frailties. The fact is that everyone has strengths and weaknesses. You should

If you like singing star Taylor Swift, that's fine, but she is not a sensible benchmark for evaluating your attractiveness or success. Some people distort the social comparison process.

accept those personal shortcomings that you are powerless to change and work on those that are changeable, without becoming obsessed about it. At the same time, you should embrace your strengths and learn to appreciate them.

7. Cultivate a New Strength

Besides recognizing the strengths you already have, you may want to cultivate some new ones. What particular personal strength would you like to improve? Try to select one that will help you develop meaningful connections to others. Perhaps you would like to be less shy or tongue-tied when speaking in front of groups of people. Consider taking a public speaking class so that you can gradually work up the wherewithal to give a public presentation. Select one new strength—not several—to work on and then find the right sort of setting or situation to gradually develop it. Adding a new strength to your list of strengths can provide a meaningful rise in self-esteem.

8. Approach Others with a Positive Outlook

Some people with low self-esteem try to cut others down to their (subjective) size through constant criticism. This fault finding and negative approach does not go over well. Instead, it leads to tension, antagonism, and rejection. This rejection lowers self-esteem still further (see **Figure 6.16**). You can boost your esteem-building efforts by recognizing and reversing this self-defeating tendency. Cultivate the habit of maintaining a positive, supportive outlook when you approach people. Doing so will promote rewarding interactions and help you earn others' acceptance. There is probably nothing that enhances self-esteem more than acceptance and genuine affection from others.

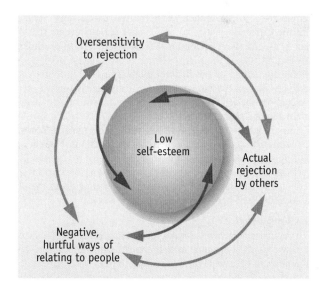

Figure 6.16

The vicious circle of low self-esteem and rejection. A negative self-image can make expectations of rejection a self-fulfilling prophecy because people with low self-esteem tend to approach others in negative, hurtful ways. Real or imagined rejections lower self-esteem still further, creating a vicious circle.

CHAPTER 6   Review

Key Ideas

6.1 Self-Concept
● The self-concept is composed of a number of beliefs about what one is like, and it is not easily changed. It governs both present and future behavior. Our possible selves can influence our future behavior and even our mental health. Discrepancies between one's ideal self and one's actual or ought self can produce negative emotions and lowered self-esteem. To cope with these negative states, individuals may bring their behavior in line with their ideal selves or blunt their awareness of self-discrepancies.
● The self-concept is shaped by several factors, including individuals' observations of their own behavior, which often involve social comparisons with others. Self-observations tend to be biased in a positive direction. In addition, feedback from others shapes the self-concept; this information is also filtered to some extent. Cultural guidelines also affect the way people see themselves. Members of individualistic cultures usually have an independent view of the self, whereas those in collectivist cultures often have an interdependent view of the self.

6.2 Self-Esteem
● Self-esteem is a person's global evaluation of his or her worth. Like the self-concept, it tends to be stable, but it can fluctuate in response to daily ups and downs.
● Compared to those with high self-esteem, individuals with low self-esteem are less happy, more likely to be depressed, more likely to give up after failure, and less trusting of others.
● Narcissistic individuals are prone to aggression when their self-esteem is threatened. Self-esteem develops through interactions with significant others. Self-esteem, ethnicity, and gender interact in complex ways.

6.3 Basic Principles of Self-Perception
● To avoid being overwhelmed with information, people tend to use automatic processing, but for important decisions, they shift to controlled processing. To explain the causes of their behavior, individuals make self-attributions. Generally, people attribute their behavior to internal or external factors and to stable or unstable factors. Controllability-uncontrollability is another key dimension of self-attributions.
● People tend to use either an optimistic explanatory style or a pessimistic explanatory style to understand various events that occur in their lives, and these attributional styles are related to psychological adjustment.
● People are guided by two distinct motives in seeking to understand themselves. The self-assessment motive directs people toward accurate feedback about the self. The self-enhancement motive enables people to maintain positive views of themselves.
● Common self-enhancement strategies include making downward comparisons to others whose problems are more serious than one's own, attributing successes to personal factors and failures to external factors (the self-serving bias), basking in the reflected glory of others who are successful, and sabotaging one's performance to provide an excuse for possible failure (self-handicapping).

6.4 Self-Regulation
● Self-regulation involves setting goals and directing behavior to meet those goals. Engaging in self-control can temporarily deplete what appears to be a limited underlying resource. A key aspect of self-regulation is self-efficacy—an individual's belief that he or she can achieve specific goals. Self-efficacy plays a key role in adjustment and can be learned through mastery experiences, vicarious experiences, persuasion, and positive interpretations of emotional arousal.
● Sometimes normal people knowingly do things that are bad for them. These self-defeating actions fall into three categories: deliberate self-destruction, tradeoffs, and counterproductive strategies.

6.5 Self-Presentation
● Public selves are the various images that individuals project to others. Generally, people try to manage the impressions they make by using a variety of strategies, including ingratiation, self-promotion, supplication, and negative acknowledgment. High self-monitors pay more attention to the impressions they make on others and tend to be more concerned about making favorable impressions than low self-monitors do.

6.6 Application: Building Self-Esteem
● The eight building blocks to higher self-esteem are (1) recognize that you control your self-image, (2) learn more about yourself, (3) don't let others set your goals, (4) recognize unrealistic goals, (5) modify negative self-talk, (6) emphasize your strengths, (7) cultivate new strengths, and (8) approach others with a positive outlook.

Key Terms

Basking in reflected glory p. 177	Self-attributions p. 173
Collectivism p. 166	Self-concept p. 159
Downward social	Self-defeating behaviors p. 181
comparison p. 177	Self-discrepancy p. 162
Explanatory style p. 174	Self-efficacy p. 180
External attributions p. 173	Self-enhancement p. 176
Impression management p. 182	Self-esteem p. 167
Individualism p. 166	Self-handicapping p. 178
Ingratiation p. 182	Self-monitoring p. 183
Internal attributions p. 173	Self-regulation p. 179
Possible selves p. 160	Self-serving bias p. 177
Public self p. 181	Social comparison
Reference group p. 164	theory p. 163

Key People

Albert Bandura p. 180	Hazel Markus p. 160
Roy Baumeister p. 167	

CHAPTER 6   Practice Test

1. Which of the following statements is *not* true about the self-concept?
   a. It is composed of one dominant belief about the self.
   b. It is composed of many self-beliefs.
   c. It is relatively stable over time.
   d. It influences present as well as future behavior.

2. Mismatches between one's actual and ought selves result in lower self-esteem and
   a. dejection-related feelings.
   b. agitation-related feelings.
   c. feelings of self-enhancement.
   d. no particular feelings.

3. A person reared in a collectivist culture is likely to have a(n) _____ self-view, whereas a person reared in an individualistic culture is likely to have a(n) _____ self-view.
   a. self-discrepant; self-consistent
   b. self-consistent; self-discrepant
   c. independent; interdependent
   d. interdependent; independent

4. Low self-esteem is associated with
   a. happiness.
   b. high trust of others.
   c. self-concept confusion.
   d. recovering after failure experiences.

5. Aggression in response to self-esteem threats is more likely to occur in people who are
   a. high in self-esteem.
   b. low in self-esteem.
   c. narcissistic.
   d. self-defeating.

6. Which of the following is *not* a basic principle of self-perception?
   a. People are "cognitive spenders."
   b. People's explanatory style is related to adjustment.
   c. People want to receive information that is consistent with their self-views.
   d. People want to maintain positive feelings about the self.

7. Keisha is upset when a textbook is stolen, but she feels better after she hears that a classmate's book bag, including her cell phone and wallet, was stolen. This is an example of
   a. the self-serving bias.
   b. basking in reflected glory.
   c. downward comparison.
   d. self-handicapping.

8. Which of the following statements about self-efficacy is true?
   a. It can be developed by persevering through failure until one achieves success.
   b. It is something that one is born with.
   c. It is essentially the same as self-esteem.
   d. It refers to conscious efforts to make a certain impression on others.

9. The self-presentation strategy of ingratiation involves trying to make others
   a. respect you.
   b. fear you.
   c. feel sorry for you.
   d. like you.

10. Which of the following will *not* help you build higher self-esteem?
    a. Minimizing negative self-talk
    b. Comparing yourself with those who are the best in a given area
    c. Working to improve yourself
    d. Approaching others with positive expectations

Answers

1. a Pages 159–160
2. b Page 162
3. d Pages 165–167
4. c Page 167
5. c Pages 170–171
6. a Pages 172–176
7. c Page 177
8. a Page 180
9. d Page 182
10. b Pages 184–185

Personal Explorations Workbook

Go to the *Personal Explorations Workbook* in the back of your textbook for exercises that can enhance your self-understanding in relation to issues raised in this chapter.

Exercise 6.1 *Self-Assessment:* Self-Control Schedule

Exercise 6.2 *Self-Reflection:* How Does Your Self-Concept Compare to Your Self-Ideal?

Digital Vision/Getty Images

You have a new boss at work. Your old boss was let go because of poor performance. The new boss looks very serious. Unlike your old boss, who was friendly and joked around a lot, this fellow is very reserved. He rarely even says hello to you when your paths cross in the halls or out in the parking lot. You wonder whether he doesn't like you or happens to treat everyone that way. Maybe he's just driven by his work. You resolve to ask around the office to see how he acts with your co-workers. You do know that he fired a woman who worked a few doors down the hall. You're not sure why; she seemed nice, always smiling and saying hello. She sure looked like a hard worker. Maybe he thought she was too friendly? The new boss is also not much older than you—in fact, he might be your age. What if he thinks you are not working hard enough? Could he be thinking about firing you?

This situation illustrates the process of person perception in everyday life. Everyone asks and answers "why" questions about the people around them. Individuals constantly form impressions to try to make sense of the people they encounter, not only to understand them but also to predict how they will behave. This chapter explores how people form impressions of others, as well as how and why such judgments can be incorrect. Our consideration of *social cognition* (how people think about others, as well as themselves) then broadens to examine the problems posed by prejudice. We then look at how others try to influence one's beliefs and behavior. To do so, we explore the power of persuasive messages and the social pressures to conform and obey. As you will learn, social thinking and social influence play important roles in personal adjustment. ■

7.1 Forming Impressions of Others

Learning Objectives

- Cite the five sources of information people use to form impressions of others.
- Explain the key differences between snap judgments and systematic judgments.
- Define *attributions* and describe two attribution-based expectations that can distort observers' perceptions.
- Recognize four important cognitive distortions and how they operate.
- Identify some ways in which perceptions of others are efficient, selective, and consistent.

Do you recall the first time you met your roommate? She seemed friendly but a little shy, and perhaps a bit on the neat side—so much so that you wondered whether you would get along. You like things less structured; not messy, but decidedly lived-in or comfortable. You worried that you'd have to change your ways, straightening up your space all the time. Happily, once you got to know her better, she warmed up to you and your clutter, and now you are close friends. As people interact with others, they constantly engage in *person perception,* **the process of forming impressions of others.** Because impression formation is usually such an automatic process, people are unaware that it is occurring. Nonetheless, the process is a complex one, involving perceivers, their social networks, and those who are perceived (Moskowitz & Gill, 2013). Let's review some of its essential aspects.

Key Sources of Information

We are dependent on *observations* of people to determine what they are like (Uleman & Saribay, 2012). When forming impressions, people rely on five key sources of observational information: appearance, verbal behavior, actions, nonverbal messages, and situational cues.

1. *Appearance.* Despite the admonition "You can't judge a book by its cover," people frequently do exactly that. Physical features such as height, weight, skin color, clothing style, and hair color are some of the cues used to "read" other people. Regardless of their accuracy, beliefs about physical features are used to form impressions of others (Olivola & Todorov, 2010), including people's personalities (Naumann et al., 2009).

2. *Verbal behavior.* Another obvious source of information about others is what they say. People form impressions based on what and how much others self-disclose (Derlega, Winstead, & Greene, 2008), how often they give advice and ask questions, and how judgmental they are. If Tanisha speaks negatively about most of the people she knows, you will probably conclude that she is a critical person.

3. *Actions.* Because people don't always tell the truth, you have to rely on their behavior to provide insights about them. For instance, when you learn that Wade volunteers 5 hours a week at the local homeless shelter, you are likely to infer that he is a caring person.

4. *Nonverbal messages.* As discussed in Chapter 8, a key source of information about others is nonverbal communication: facial expressions, eye contact, body

Jupiterimages/Stockbyte/Getty Images

In forming impressions of others, people rely on cues, such as appearance, actions, and verbal and nonverbal messages, as well as the nature of the situation.

language, and gestures. These nonverbal cues provide information about people's emotional states and dispositions. For example, in our culture, we make judgments about others based on their faces (Ito, 2011); thus, a bright smile and steady eye contact signal friendliness and openness, just as a handshake can indicate extraversion (Bernieri & Petty, 2011). Also, because people know that verbal behavior is easily manipulated, they often rely on nonverbal cues to determine the truth of what others say (Jacks & Lancaster, 2015). And we should not forget about nonverbal cues that appear in written form (*how* we say what we say), as the content of email messages or Facebook posts can suggest personality traits or emotional states of the sender (Fleuriet, Cole, & Guerrero, 2014).

5. *Situational cues.* The setting where behavior occurs provides crucial information about how to interpret a person's behavior. For instance, without situational cues (such as being at a wedding versus a funeral), it would be hard to know whether a person crying is happy or sad.

When it comes to drawing inferences about people, one bad piece of information can outweigh or undo a collection of positive characteristics. Social psychological research repeatedly demonstrates that the presence of a trait perceived to be negative ("untrustworthy") can have more influence on forming impressions than several positive qualities ("warm," "open," "friendly," "clever") (Vonk, 1993). When an immoral act is performed, other good or virtuous behaviors cannot undo the damage to people's perceptions of the offender's character (Riskey & Birnbaum, 1974). In fact, a single bad deed can eliminate a good reputation, but one good deed cannot redeem an otherwise bad standing in the eyes of others (Skowronski & Carlston, 1992). Thus, in the realm of perception *bad impressions tend to be stronger than good ones* (Sparks & Baumeister, 2008).

Snap Judgments versus Systematic Judgments

In daily life, we are bombarded with more information than we can possibly handle. To avoid being overwhelmed, we rely on alternative ways to process information (Kahneman, 2011). *Snap judgments* about others are those made quickly and based on only a few bits of information and preconceived notions. Thus, they may not be particularly accurate. Indeed, there is evidence that when a stranger looks very similar to someone we know well, such as a romantic partner, we automatically, effortlessly, and more or less nonconsciously like the person (Günaydin et al., 2012). Nevertheless, people can get by with superficial assessments of others quite often. As Susan Fiske (2004) puts it, "Good-enough accuracy in forming impressions allows us to navigate our social seas and not collide or run aground too often" (p. 132). Often, interactions with others are so fleeting or inconsequential that it makes little difference that such judgments are imprecise.

On the other hand, when it comes to selecting a friend, a partner, or an employee, it's essential that impressions be as accurate as possible. Thus, it's not surprising that people are motivated to take more care in such assessments. In forming impressions of those who can affect their welfare and happiness, people make *systematic judgments* rather than snap decisions (see **Figure 7.1**). That is, they take the time to observe the person in a variety of situations and to compare that person's behavior with that of others in similar situations. To determine the cause of others' behavior, people engage in the process of causal attribution.

Susan Fiske argues that people generally use off the cuff or snap judgments when forming impressions of others. More systematic or careful judgments are reserved for important decisions.

Attributions

As noted in earlier chapters, *attributions* **are inferences that people draw about the causes of their own behavior, others' behavior, and events.** In Chapter 6, we focused on self-attributions. Here, we'll apply attribution theory to the behavior of *other people* (Malle, 2011a).

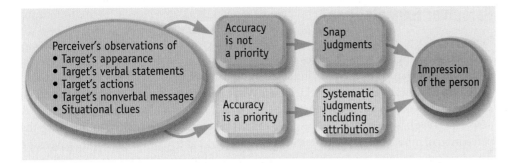

Figure 7.1

The process of person perception. In forming impressions of others, perceivers rely on various sources of observational information. When it's important to form accurate impressions of others, people are motivated to make systematic judgments, including attributions. When accuracy isn't a priority, people make snap judgments about others. (Adapted from Kassin, Fein, & Markus, 2011)

For example, suppose that your boss bawls you out for doing a sloppy job on an insignificant project. To what do you attribute this tongue lashing? Was your work really that bad? Is your boss under too much pressure?

In Chapter 6, we noted that attributions have three key dimensions: internal versus external, stable versus unstable, and controllable versus uncontrollable (Jones & Davis, 1965; Weiner, 1974). For this discussion, we focus primarily on the internal/external dimension (Heider, 1958). When people ascribe the causes of someone's behavior to personal dispositions, traits, abilities, or feelings, they are making *internal* attributions. When they impute the causes of a person's behavior to situational demands and environmental constraints, they are making *external* attributions. For example, if a friend's business fails, you might attribute the failure to your friend's lack of business skills (an internal factor) or to negative trends in the economy (an external factor).

There is also a fourth dimension of attributions that is receiving renewed attention. Malle (2011b) notes that Heider also discussed intentional versus unintentional acts as a source of attributional processing. Intentional acts are those we choose to perform, so that observers assume our behavior has a reason behind it—and that reason is the cause of our behavior. In contrast, unintentional acts are often triggered by causes outside the person (something in the situation, another person). If an unintentional act happens because of something inside an individual, it may be due to something the affected individual doesn't know about (such as an unrecognized illness or the side effect of a medication).

The types of attributions people make about others can have a tremendous impact on everyday social interactions (Tetlock & Fincher, 2015). Consider the judgments people make about the nature of others' emotional experiences or reactions, for example. People often assume that women are the more emotional gender when, in fact, they are no more emotional than men except where outward displays of emotion are concerned (DeAngelis, 2001; see Chapter 11). This bias can color the conclusions observers make about the emotional experiences of men and women in similar circumstances.

Obviously, people don't make attributions about every person they meet. Research suggests that people are relatively selective in this process (Malle, 2004). It seems they are most likely to make attributions (1) when others behave in unexpected or negative ways, (2) when events are personally relevant, and (3) when they are suspicious about another person's motives. For example, if Serena laughs loudly at the local student hangout, no one bats an eye. But if she does so in the middle of a serious lecture, it raises eyebrows and generates speculation about why she behaved this way.

Some aspects of the attribution process are logical (Weiner, 2012). Nonetheless, research also shows that the process of person perception is sometimes illogical and unsystematic, as in the case of snap judgments. Perceivers may agree on the nature of people's behavior but because of their own implicit biases get the cause of the behavior wrong (Robins et al., 2004). Other sources of error also creep into the process, a topic we take up next.

Learn More Online

Social Psychology Network

Wesleyan University social psychologist Scott Plous offers a broad collection of more than 5,000 Learn More Onlines related to all aspects of social and general psychology, including how people understand and influence one another interpersonally.

Perceiver Expectations

Remember Evan, that bully from the fourth grade? He made your life miserable—constantly looking for opportunities to poke fun at you and beat you up. Now when you meet someone named Evan, your initial reaction is negative, and it takes awhile to warm up to him (Andersen & Przybylinski, 2014). Why? Your negative past experiences with an Evan have led you to expect the worst, whether or not it's warranted (Andersen, Reznik, & Manzella, 1996). This is just one example of how *perceiver expectations* can influence the perception of others (de Calvo & Reich, 2009). Let's look at two of the principles governing perceiver expectations: confirmation bias and self-fulfilling prophecy.

Confirmation Bias

Shortly after you begin interacting with someone, you start forming hypotheses about what the person is like. In turn, these hypotheses can influence your behavior toward that person in such a way as to confirm your expectations. Thus, if on your first encounter with Xavier he has a camera around his neck, you will probably hypothesize that he has an interest in photography and question him selectively about his shutterbug activities. You might also neglect to ask more wide-ranging questions that would give you a more accurate picture of him. *Confirmation bias* **is the tendency to seek information that supports one's beliefs while not pursuing disconfirming information.**

Confirmation bias is a well-documented phenomenon (Nickerson, 1998). It occurs in casual social interactions and in gender relations (Traut-Mattausch et al., 2011), as well as in job interviews and in courtrooms, where the interviewer or attorney may ask leading questions. Law enforcement officers, for example, should be careful to evaluate evidence without any preconceived notion of a suspect's guilt or innocence (Lilienfeld & Landfield, 2008). When it comes to forming first impressions of others, the principle is not so much "seeing is believing" as "believing is seeing" (see **Figure 7.2**), and some people may be more susceptible to displaying confirmation biases than others (Rassin, 2008).

Confirmation bias also occurs because individuals selectively recall facts to fit their views of others. In one experiment, participants watched a videotape of a woman engaging in a variety of activities, including listening to classical music, drinking beer, and watching TV (Cohen, 1981). Half of them were told that the woman was a waitress and the other half were told that she was a librarian. When asked to recall the woman's actions on the videotape, participants tended to remember activities consistent with their stereotypes of waitresses and librarians. Thus, those who thought that the woman was a waitress recalled her drinking beer; those who thought she was a librarian recalled her listening to classical music.

Can anything be done to reduce conformation bias? There is some evidence that intentionally presenting people with information that is inconsistent with their perceptions and preferences can encourage them to engage in more divergent thinking (Schwind et al.,

Figure 7.2

Confirmation bias. Confirmation bias is a two-pronged process in which people seek and remember information that supports their beliefs while discounting and forgetting information that is inconsistent with their beliefs. This common cognitive slant often distorts the process of person perception, leading to inaccurate impressions of people.

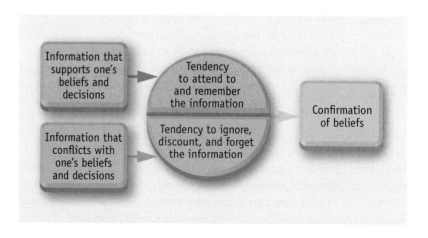

2012), but this is unlikely to happen very often in daily life. Other research suggests that when information is difficult for perceivers to process—they experience "disfluency"—it can reduce the confirmation bias (Hernandez & Preston, 2013). When confronted with disfluent information, perceivers have to switch to more careful and analytical processing, which turns out to reduce the incidence of the confirmation bias.

Self-Fulfilling Prophecies

Sometimes a perceiver's expectations can actually change another person's behavior (Madon et al., 2011). **A *self-fulfilling prophecy* occurs when expectations about a person cause him or her to behave in ways that confirm the expectations.** This term was originally coined by sociologist Robert Merton (1948) to explain phenomena such as "runs" on banks that occurred during the Depression. That is, when unfounded rumors would circulate that a bank couldn't cover its deposits, people would rush to the bank and withdraw their funds, thereby draining the deposits from the bank and making real what was initially untrue.

Figure 7.3 depicts the three steps in a self-fulfilling prophecy. First, the perceiver has an initial impression of someone. (A teacher believes that Jennifer is highly intelligent.) Then the perceiver behaves toward the target person according to his or her expectations. (He asks her interesting questions and praises her answers.) The third step occurs when the target person adjusts his or her behavior to the perceiver's actions, confirming the perceiver's hypothesis about the target person. (Jennifer performs well in class.) Note that both individuals are unaware that this process is operating. Also note that because perceivers are unaware of their expectations and of the effect they can have on others, they mistakenly attribute the target person's behavior to an internal cause (Jennifer is smart), rather than an external one (their own expectations).

The best-known experiments on self-fulfilling prophecy have been conducted in classroom settings, looking at the effect of teachers' expectations on students' academic performance (Rosenthal, 2006; Rubie-Davies et al., 2015). A review of 400 studies of this phenomenon over a period of 30 years reported that teacher expectations significantly influenced student performance in 36% of the experiments. In a related vein, perhaps the "storm and stress" of early adolescence, particularly teen rebellion and risk taking and the predictable parental reactions, are sometimes expectation based (Buchanan & Hughes, 2009). When both teens and parents anticipate tension and alienation, for example, they may look for, instigate, or see other behaviors as fitting their respective perceptions. Still, there is research suggesting that in some venues, such as aging, people's expectations—their self-perceptions of aging following a health crisis—can impair later positive health behaviors and beliefs (Wurm et al., 2013). Instead of engaging in self-regulation strategies that promote a healthy lifestyle, they may assume that physical loss and compromised health are inevitable, thereby becoming a self-fulfilling prophecy.

Cognitive Distortions

Another source of error in person perception comes from distortions in the minds of perceivers. These errors in judgment are most likely to occur when a perceiver is in a hurry, is distracted, or is not motivated to pay careful attention to another person.

Social Categorization

One of the ways people efficiently process information is to classify objects (and people) according to their distinctive features (North & Fiske, 2014). Thus, people quite often categorize others on the basis of nationality, race, ethnicity, gender, age, religion, sexual orientation, and so forth (Crisp & Hewstone, 2006). Indeed, age, race, and gender lead to especially

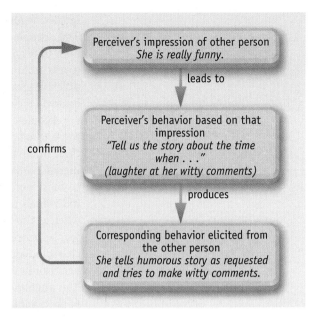

Figure 7.3

The three steps of the self-fulfilling prophecy. Through a three-step process, your expectations about a person can cause that person to behave in ways that confirm those expectations. First, you form an impression of someone. Second, you behave toward that person in a way that is consistent with your impression. Third, the person exhibits the behavior that you encourage, which confirms your initial impression.

Source: Adapted from Smith, E. R., & Mackie, D. M. (1995). *Social psychology.* New York: Worth, p. 103. Copyright © 1995 Worth Publishing. Reprinted with permission.

quick categorization because they dominate our perception (Yzerbyt & Demoulin, 2010). Thus, people frequently take the easy path of categorizing others into groups, thereby saving both time and effort. The cost of doing so is that such reduced cognitive effort often leads to less accurate impressions. A particular problem associated with categorizing people into different groups is that we tend to overestimate the differences between groups and underestimate the differences within groups (Krueger & DiDonato, 2008).

People classify those who are similar to them as members of their *ingroup* ("us") and those who are dissimilar to them as being in the *outgroup* ("them"). Such categorizing has three important results. First, people usually have less favorable attitudes toward outgroup members than ingroup members (Brewer & Brown, 1998), such that empathic reactions to those perceived to be in their ingroup are often exaggerated (Brewer, 2007). Second, individuals usually see outgroup members as being much more alike than they really are, whereas they see members of their ingroup as unique individuals (Oakes, 2001). In other words, people frequently explain the behavior of outgroup members on the basis of the characteristic that sets them apart ("Those *Nerdians* are *all* drunks") but attribute the same behavior by an ingroup member to individual personality traits ("*Brett* is a heavy drinker"). This phenomenon, in which others are seen as "all alike" and one's own group is perceived to be "diverse," is termed the *outgroup homogeneity effect* (Ostrom & Sedikides, 1992).

The third result of categorizing is that it heightens the visibility of outgroup members when there are only a few of them within a larger group. In other words, minority group status in a group makes more salient the quality that distinguishes the person—ethnicity, gender, whatever. When people are perceived as being unique or distinctive, they are also seen as gaining more attention in a group, and their good and bad qualities are given extra weight (Crocker & McGraw, 1984). Significantly, distinctiveness—some quality that makes one person stand out from others—can also trigger stereotyping. People tend to define others by those traits or actions that are rare, uncommon, or otherwise distinctive.

Finally, based on their proclivity to categorize, people are even likely to see outgroup members as looking more like one another than they actually do. Various studies clearly show that eyewitnesses are better at identifying people of their own race than those who belong to a different racial group (Meissner & Brigham, 2001). In fact, to observers, outgroup members even look alike, which means that people are not very accurate when it comes to distinguishing among and recognizing faces of racial outgroup members as compared to ingroup members (Young et al., 2012). An exception to this rule occurs when outgroup members are angry (Ackerman, et al., 2006). That is, angry outgroup members are much easier to identify than angry ingroup members, suggesting that the human mind carefully tracks strangers who may pose a threat.

Stereotypes

Stereotypes **are widely held beliefs that people have certain characteristics because of their membership in a particular group.** For example, many people assume that Italians are loud and passionate, that African Americans have special athletic and musical abilities, and that Muslims are religious fanatics. Although a kernel of truth may underlie some stereotypes, it should be readily apparent that not all Italians, African Americans, Muslims, and so forth behave alike. If you take the time to think about it, you will recognize that there is enormous diversity in behavior within any group. So, despite the fact that stereotypes can employ reality-based information, they are also often based on biased expectations (Spears & Strobe, 2015). The very real problem, of course, is that stereotypes are linked with prejudice and discrimination (Bodenhausen & Richeson, 2010).

Stereotypes may also be based on physical appearance. In particular, there is plenty of evidence that physically attractive people are believed to have desirable personality traits. This widespread perception is termed the *"what-is-beautiful-is-good"* stereotype (Dion, Berscheid, & Walster, 1972). Specifically, beautiful people are usually viewed as happier, more socially competent, more assertive, better adjusted, and more intellectually competent than those who are less attractive (Jackson, Hunter, & Hodge, 1995). In fact, people believe they remember more positive qualities associated with attractive people and more

Learn More Online

Social Cognition Paper Archive and Information Center

Eliot R. Smith at Indiana University maintains a popular site that includes information about papers (abstracts, mostly) and people in the field of social cognition. The site also provides extensive links to the wider social psychological research community.

negative characteristics with unattractive individuals (Rohner & Rasmussen, 2012). Interestingly, some researchers believe that attributing desirable characteristics to physically attractive people is a way to project our interpersonal goals onto others (LeMay, Clark, & Greenberg, 2010). In essence, we want to bond with beautiful people, whether as friends or romantic partners. Yet most such perceptions have little basis in fact.

Attractive people *do* have an advantage in the social arena. Attractive children, for example, tend to be perceived as more popular than less attractive ones; sad to say, their teachers like them better, too (Dion, 1973). Is there a long-term consequence? Well, good-looking adults have better social skills, are more popular, are less socially anxious (especially about interactions with the other gender), are less lonely, and are more sexually experienced (Feingold, 1992b). However, they are not any different from others in intelligence, happiness, mental health, or self-esteem (Langlois et al., 2000). Thus, attractive people are perceived in a more favorable light than is actually justified. Unfortunately, the positive biases toward attractive people also operate in reverse. Hence, unattractive people are unjustifiably seen as less well adjusted and less intellectually competent than others.

How does the attractiveness stereotype affect most people? First, the bad news: Highly attractive people end up with one another (all else being equal, a perfect "10" might marry a "9," for example, but is unlikely to pair off with a "4" or a "5"). If there is any solace in this news, it's this: Most people pair up with others who match their own level of attractiveness. Thus, individuals are likely to date those who match their own level of attractiveness (Berscheid et al., 1971).

Stereotypes can be spontaneously triggered when people—even in those who are not prejudiced—encounter members of commonly stereotyped groups (Dunning & Sherman, 1997). Worse still, racially based stereotypes can cause regrettable—and potentially dangerous—split-second decisions in which people see a weapon that isn't actually there (Payne, 2006). Stereotypes can exist outside a person's awareness (Nosek et al., 2007). Because stereotyping is automatic, some psychologists are pessimistic about being able to control it (Bargh, 1999); others take a more optimistic view (Uleman et al., 1996). For example, one study found less automatic race bias when men and women of different races (except blacks) were surreptitiously induced to smile while looking at photographs of blacks (Ito et al., 2006). If people put forth effort to respond in a friendly and open manner to individuals who are different from them on some important dimension (race, sexual orientation), perhaps the positive behaviors will lead to a reduction in automatic biases when reacting to others.

There is also some intriguing new evidence that imagining an encounter between oneself and an outgroup member can reduce hostile feelings linked to stereotyping (Crisp & Turner, 2013). Brambilla, Ravenna, and Hewstone (2012) had participants imagine interacting with someone from an outgroup usually rated as either high or low on warmth and competence. The imagined encounters promoted feelings of warmth and competence toward the members of groups usually dehumanized (e.g., poor people), envied (e.g., wealthy people), or otherwise targeted for condescending behavior (e.g., elderly people). A key component of imagined intergroup contact theory is that the imagined contact must be positive and high quality, otherwise, negative attitudes toward particular outgroups (e.g., homeless persons, people with schizophrenia) can remain (Falvo et al., 2015; West, Holmes, & Hewstone, 2011).

The Fundamental Attribution Error

When explaining the causes of others' behavior, people invoke personal attributions and discount the importance of situational factors. Although this tendency is not universal (Miyamoto & Kitayama, 2002), it is strong enough that Lee Ross (1977) called it the "*fundamental* attribution error." The *fundamental attribution error* **refers to the tendency to explain other people's behavior as the result of personal, rather than situational, factors.**

This tendency differs from stereotyping in that inferences are based on actual behavior. Nonetheless, those inferences may still be inaccurate. If Jeremy leaves class early, you may be correct in inferring that he is inconsiderate, but he might also have had a previously scheduled job interview. Thus, a person's behavior at a given time may or may not reflect his or her personality or character—but observers tend to assume that it does. The situations people encounter can have profound effects on their behavior, often overpowering the influence of their dispositions—they just don't realize it.

What's behind this tendency to discount situational influences on people's behavior? Once again, the culprit is people's tendency to be cognitive misers. It seems that making attributions is a two-step process (Gilbert & Malone, 1995). As you can see in **Figure 7.4**, in the first step, which occurs automatically, observers make an internal attribution because they are focusing on the person rather than the situation. (At your bank, if you observe the man ahead of you yell at the teller, you might infer that he is a hostile person.) In the second step, observers weigh the impact of the situation on the target person's behavior and adjust their inference. (If you overhear the customer claim this is the third time in three weeks that the bank has made the same error in his account, you're likely to temper your initial judgment about his hostile tendencies.)

The first step in the attribution process occurs spontaneously, but the second step requires cognitive effort and attention. Thus, it is easy to stop after step one—especially if one is in a hurry or distracted. Failure to take the effortful second step can result in the fundamental attribution error. However, when people are motivated to form accurate impressions of others (Webster, 1993) or when they are suspicious about another's motives (Fein, 1996), they do expend the effort to complete the second step. In these cases, they are more likely to make accurate attributions. Some evidence suggests that these two steps may be related to different types of brain activity (Lieberman et al., 2004). One recent study using fMRI (functional magnetic resonance imaging) technology, which measures brain activity, found that observers spontaneously process others' mental states, such as their momentary feelings or their presumed personality traits. Participants read a series of stories that described ambiguous behaviors performed by a target person in a social setting, and then judged whether the behaviors were attributable to an internal disposition or external situational factors. The fMRI revealed that areas of the brain associated with mental state inferences (based on previous research) predicted use of dispositional rather than situational attributions.

Defensive Attribution

Observers are especially likely to make internal attributions in trying to explain the calamities and tragedies that befall other people. When a woman is abused by a boyfriend

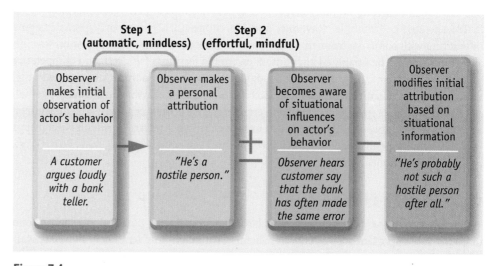

Figure 7.4

Explaining the fundamental attribution error. People automatically take the first step in the attribution process (making a personal attribution). However, they often fail to take the second step (considering the possible influence of situational factors on a person's behavior) because that requires extra effort. The failure to consider situational factors causes observers to exaggerate the role of personal factors in behavior—that is, they make the fundamental attribution error. (Adapted from Kassin, Fein, & Markus, 2011)

or husband, for example, people frequently blame the victim by remarking on how stupid she is to stay with the man, rather than condemning the aggressor for his behavior (Summers & Feldman, 1984). Similarly, rape victims are often judged to have "asked for it" (Abrams et al., 2003).

Defensive attribution **is a tendency to blame victims for their misfortune, so that one feels less likely to be victimized in a similar way.** Blaming victims for their calamities also helps people maintain their belief that they live in a "just world" where people get what they deserve and deserve what they get (Haynes & Olson, 2006). Bystanders to a crime, too, can be subject to blame based on defensive attributions ("He should have done something to help even if it was risky to do so—he's almost as bad as the perpetrator") (Levy & Ben-David, 2015). Acknowledging that the world is not just—that unfortunate events can happen as a result of chance factors—would mean having to admit the frightening possibility that the catastrophes that happen to others could also happen to oneself (Lambert, Burroughs, & Nguyen, 1999), especially when the victim is perceived to be like oneself (Correia, Vala, & Aguiar, 2007). Defensive attributions are a self-protective, but irrational, strategy that allows people to avoid such unnerving thoughts and helps them feel in control of their lives (Hafer, 2000).

A common example of defensive attribution is the tendency to blame the homeless for their plight.

Key Themes in Person Perception

The process of person perception—how people mentally construe one another's behavior—is a complex one (Trope & Gaunt, 2003). Nonetheless, we can detect three recurrent themes in this process: efficiency, selectivity, and consistency.

Efficiency

In forming impressions of others, people prefer to exert no more cognitive effort or time than is necessary. Thus, much social information is processed automatically and effortlessly. According to Susan Fiske (1993), people are like government bureaucrats, who "only bother to gather information on a 'need to know' basis" (p. 175). Efficiency has two important advantages: People can make judgments quickly, and it keeps things simple, for example, by searching for similarities between the target person and comparison criteria already held by the perceiver (Corcoran, 2013). The big disadvantage is that snap judgments are error-prone. Still, on balance, efficiency works pretty well as an operating principle.

Selectivity

The old saying that "people see what they expect to see" has been confirmed repeatedly by social scientists. In a classic study, Harold Kelley (1950) showed how a person is preceded by his or her reputation. Students in a class at the Massachusetts Institute of Technology were told that a new lecturer would be speaking to them that day. Before the instructor arrived, the students were given a short description of him, with one important variation. Half the students were led to expect a "warm" person, while the other half were led to expect a "cold" one. All the participants were exposed to exactly the same 20 minutes of lecture and interaction with the new instructor. However, those who were led to expect a warm person rated the instructor as significantly more considerate, sociable, humorous, good natured, informal, and humane than those who expected a cold person.

Consistency

How many times did your parents remind you to be on your best behavior when you were meeting someone for the first time? As it turns out, they were onto something! Considerable research supports the idea that first impressions are powerful (Belmore, 1987). **A** *primacy effect* **occurs when initial information carries more weight than subsequent information.** Primacy effects are likely to occur when perceivers—the people who meet us for the first time—are in good rather than bad moods (Forgas, 2011). We risk being labeled a hypocrite, for example, if we say one thing and then do another (such as claiming to have an open mind and then make a cutting, judgmental remark about someone) rather than the reverse (Barden, Rucker, & Petty, 2005). Initial negative impressions may be especially hard to change (Mellers, Richards, & Birnbaum, 1992) because, as we learned earlier, bad can indeed be stronger than good. Only if people are motivated to form an accurate impression and are not tired will they be less likely to lock in their initial impressions (Webster, Richter, & Kruglanski, 1996). Interestingly, such primacy effects may be culturally based, as one recent investigation finds first impressions to hold greater weight in judgments made by American than by Japanese observers (Noguchi, Kamada, & Shrira, 2014). Why are primacy effects so potent? Because people find comfort in cognitive *consistency*; cognitions that contradict each other create tension and discomfort.

To conclude, although the process of person perception is highly subjective, people are relatively accurate perceivers of others. Even when misperceptions occur, they are often harmless. However, there clearly are occasions when such inaccuracies are problematic, which is certainly true in the case of prejudice.

7.2 The Problem of Prejudice

Learning Objectives

- Explain how old-fashioned and modern discrimination differ and describe the Spotlight on Research regarding stereotypes.
- Understand how authoritarianism and cognitive distortions can contribute to prejudice.
- Clarify how intergroup competition and threats to social identity can foster prejudice.
- Describe the operation of some strategies for reducing prejudice.

Let's begin our discussion by clarifying a couple of terms. *Prejudice* **is a negative attitude toward members of a group;** *discrimination* **involves behaving differently, usually unfairly, toward members of a group.** Prejudice and discrimination do tend to go together, but that is not always the case (see **Figure 7.5**). One classic social psychology study found almost no discriminatory behavior aimed at a Chinese couple traveling around the country with a white professor in the 1930s. Before making the trips, the professor anticipated that they would encounter some prejudice about where they could stay or dine, but the three were declined service only a few times. Months later, when the professor wrote to all the establishments they had visited to ask whether Chinese guests were welcome, however, the majority of the responses were, in fact, prejudiced and rather uninviting, showing that attitudes don't always predict behavior (LaPiere, 1934). Why can people respond in discriminatory ways sometimes, but not always? It is possible that a restaurant owner would be prejudiced against Chicanos and yet treat them like anyone else because he needed their business. This is an example of prejudice without discrimination. Although it is probably less common, discrimination without prejudice may also occur. For example, an executive who has favorable attitudes toward blacks may not hire them because he thinks his boss would be upset.

Sometimes, too, prejudices and stereotypes can be triggered without conscious awareness (Greenwald et al., 2009) and can have consequences for behavior. For example, in one study, college students were given a sentence completion task in which half of them received a word list containing words stereotypically associated with elderly people (wrinkle, gray, Florida). Once the idea of old age was surreptitiously "primed" in their thoughts, these same college students were later found to take 13% longer to walk to an elevator than a control group that received a neutral word list (Bargh, Chen, & Burrows, 1996). Our Spotlight on Research deals with the ways race and stereotypes can guide visual perception and have decided consequences for behavior.

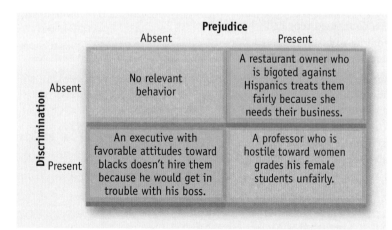

Figure 7.5

Prejudice and discrimination. Prejudice and discrimination are highly correlated, but they don't necessarily go hand in hand. As the examples in the blue cells show, prejudice can exist without discrimination and discrimination without prejudice.

When Seeing Is Stereotypically Believing—and Reacting

Source: Correll, J., Wittenbrink, B., Crawford, M. T., & Sadler, M. S. (2015). Stereotypic vision: How stereotypes disambiguate visual stimuli. *Journal of Personality and Social Psychology, 108*(2), 219–233. doi:10.1037/pspa0000015

Stereotypes are powerful guides for our perceptions, allowing us to process social information in consistent ways, direct our attention to particular aspects of a stimulus or a target person, and adding information that is not necessarily present. This experiment examined how race and racial stereotypes influence visual perception in what is known as a first-person-shooter task, or FPST. Participants saw a series of men (who were either black or white), each of whom was holding either a weapon (e.g., gun) or some innocuous object (e.g., wallet). The participants' goal was to shoot any armed targets but to avoid shooting any unarmed targets. The research goal was to demonstrate that racial stereotypes actually shape what people see—literally their visual perception—so that participants (shooters) actually "see" different objects based on the target's race. Thus, black male targets are associated stereotypically with feelings of danger, whereas white male targets (all else being equal) are not. This study hypothesized that participants would rely on more ambiguous information (assessed by eye-tracking equipment that followed the angle of each participant's gaze and visual search of target figures) when responding to stereotypic targets (i.e., black target holding gun, white target not holding a gun). Doing so indicates a reliance on stereotypes to guide decisions. When responding to counter-stereotypic targets (i.e., white target holding a gun, black target not holding a gun) they were expected to achieve greater clarity before responding by shooting or not shooting a target.

Method

Participants and design. Participants were forty-two nonblack undergraduates who participated for course credit. The experiment manipulated the race (black versus white) of the stimulus person and the type of object the person held (gun versus nongun). Each participant in FPST made a decision to shoot or not shoot targets over a series of 120 trials.

Apparatus. An eye-tracking device that recorded where and what participants viewed during each trial recorded participants' eye movements.

Procedure. Each participant was run individually. After being seated in front of a computer screen, the experimenter explained the FPST task and then gave the participant a gun-gaming mouse that had two buttons. One button would "shoot" the target, the other represented "don't shoot" the target (this nonshoot button was described as the gun's

safety switch). Because the gun mouse was designed for right-handed players, all participants were right handed. After completing the trials, the participants were debriefed, thanked, and dismissed.

Results

Participants made fewer decision errors when confronted with armed rather than unarmed targets; however, this finding was qualified by the fact that participants were more likely to shoot an unarmed target if he was black rather than white. When targets were armed, the pattern was reversed: Participants were less likely to choose "don't shoot" if the armed target was white rather than black. Where visual search was concerned, responses (shooting or not) were made for black targets when participants had poorer visual resolution regarding relevant information (what was the object in the target's hand?). When targets where white, participants waited to achieve greater visual acuity before responding. Participants who displayed more racial bias ended their visual searches sooner and relied on less clear visual information when responding to the stereotypic targets. These results suggest that racial stereotypes are used together with visual processing, so that stereotypic decisions are made more quickly and require less clarity.

Discussion

Eye-tracking results found that when confronted with stereotypic target information, participants were more likely to end their visual search before full clarity regarding what they saw was realized. They were also less likely to actually focus on the object held by the target before they made a "shoot" or "don't shoot" decision, presumably because the target's race guided their interpretation and often their choice. The research implications are that when information is ambiguous, people may react by relying on stereotypes to guide their decisions and behavior. Sadly, stereotypes may affect response tendencies—especially when time is limited—so that the presence of black targets leads to more hostile decisions than white targets.

Critical Thinking Questions

1. Do you think there are methods to counteract the influence of racial stereotypes, so that participants in a variation of this study could somehow be trained to avoid relying on biased beliefs? How might that be achieved?

2. Does this research have any implications for other types of decisions that people make in daily life?

3. How do you think law enforcement officers might view this research?

Old-Fashioned versus Modern Discrimination

Prejudice and discrimination against minority groups have diminished in the United States. Racial segregation is no longer legal, and discrimination based on race, ethnicity, gender, and religion is much common it was in the 1950s and 1960s. Thus, the good news is that overt, or *old-fashioned, discrimination* against minority groups has declined. The bad news is that a more subtle form of prejudice and discrimination has emerged (Gawronski et al., 2012). People may privately harbor racist or sexist attitudes but express them only when they feel such views are justified or when it's safe to do so. This new phenomenon is termed *modern discrimination* (also called *modern racism*). Modern discrimination also operates when people endorse equality as an abstract principle but oppose programs intended to promote equality on the grounds that discrimination against minority groups no longer exists (Wright & Taylor, 2003).

Although modern racists do not wish to return to the days of segregation, they also feel that minority groups should not push too fast for advancement or treatment by the government. Individuals who endorse statements that favor modern discrimination are much more likely to vote against a black political candidate, to oppose affirmative action, and to favor tax laws that benefit whites at the expense of blacks compared to those who do not endorse such views (Murrell et al., 1994).

One important trend in the study of prejudice is the recognition that most white people consider the possibility that they might hold racist views to be very upsetting; indeed, they are conflicted about it. As a result, they avoid acting in ways that might be construed as racist by others or even by themselves. The upshot is that well-intentioned whites can engage in *aversive racism*, an indirect, subtle, ambiguous form of racism that occurs when their conscious endorsement of egalitarian ideals conflicts with unconscious, negative reactions to minority group members (Hodson, Dovidio, & Gaertner, 2010). One study found that black patients had less positive interactions with white physicians who harbored feelings consistent with aversive racism (Penner et al., 2010). An aversive racist might act in a racist manner when a nonracist excuse is available ("I interviewed several qualified blacks for the job but I had to hire the best candidate, who happened to be white"). Aversive racism may have its roots in childhood, as intergroup biases based on race appear among elementary school aged children (de França & Monteiro, 2013). Fortunately, researchers are seeking ways to combat such unintended but real bias toward others (Gaertner & Dovidio, 2005). When people cannot reconcile the conflict between their expressed attitudes and how they act, for example, their prejudice decreases (Son Hing, Li, & Zanna, 2002).

Causes of Prejudice

Prejudice is a complex issue with multiple causes. Although we can't thoroughly examine all causes of prejudice, we'll examine some of the major psychological and social factors that contribute to this vexing problem.

Authoritarianism

In early research on prejudice, Theodor Adorno and his colleagues (1950) identified the *authoritarian personality*, a personality type characterized by prejudice toward *any* group perceived to be different from oneself. Subsequent research found serious methodological weaknesses in the study, calling into question the validity of the personality type.

Over the intervening years, both the definition and measurement of authoritarianism have evolved (Dion, 2003). The construct is now termed *right-wing authoritarianism (RWA)* (Altemeyer, 1988a), and it is characterized by authoritarian submission (exaggerated deference to those in power), authoritarian aggression (hostility toward targets sanctioned by authorities), and conventionalism (strong adherence to values endorsed by authorities). Because authoritarians tend to support established authority, RWA is more commonly found among political conservatives than among political liberals (who are more likely to challenge the status quo). RWA has even been linked to the Big Five personality traits (recall

Chapter 2) in that authoritarian individuals tend to score low on openness to experience and conscientiousness (Sibley & Duckitt, 2008). A recent study, for example, found that lower levels of openness and high RWA predicted antigay prejudice (Cramer et al., 2013).

What causes RWAs to be prejudiced? According to Altemeyer (1998), there are two key factors. First, they organize their social world into ingroups and outgroups, and they view outgroups as threatening their cherished traditional values. Second, they tend to be self-righteous: They believe that they are more moral than others, feeling justified in derogating groups that authority figures define as immoral. RWAs have typically been reared in highly religious and socially homogeneous groups, with little exposure to minority groups and unconventional behavior (Rowatt et al., 2013). They feel unduly threatened by social change—a fear picked up from their parents who believe that "the world is a dangerous and hostile place" (Altemeyer, 1988b, p. 38). Altemeyer also notes that fearful attitudes are reinforced by the mass media's emphasis on crime and violence. However, exposure to cultural empathy and open-mindedness (Nesdale, De Vries Robbé, & Van Oudenhoven, 2012), as well as to diverse people and perspectives can reduce RWA (Dhont & Van Hiel, 2012).

Authoritarian behavior is linked with other types of personalities. Recently, a related personality type, *social dominance orientation (SDO)*, has received much research attention (Ho et al., 2012). People high in SDO prefer inequality among social groups, believing in a hierarchy where some are destined to dominate others, such as men over women, majorities over minorities, or heterosexuals over homosexuals (Kteily, Ho, & Sidanius, 2012). Those low in SDO are less likely to think in terms of a social pecking order where society's "haves" should control what happens to the "have nots." Such behavior is found among adolescents, where SDO is linked with both popularity and relational aggression, where social standing is damaged by gossip, disrupted relationships, and covert bullying (Mayeux, 2014). Individuals who score high in SDO are likely to endorse the use of cognitive ability tests for college admissions (Kim & Berry, 2015), which is a way to endorse and maintain the status quo on many campuses.

Cognitive Distortions and Expectations

Much of prejudice is rooted in automatic cognitive processes that operate without conscious intent (Wright & Taylor, 2003). As you recall, *social categorization* predisposes people to divide the social world into ingroups and outgroups. This distinction can trigger negativity toward outgroup members.

Perhaps no factor plays a larger role in prejudice than *stereotyping* (Carlston & Schneid, 2015; Stangor & Crandall, 2013). Many people subscribe to derogatory stereotypes of various ethnic groups. Although racial stereotypes have declined, they're not entirely a thing of the past (Dovidio et al., 2003). Racial profiling, where law enforcement officers stop motorists, pedestrians, or airline passengers solely on the basis of skin color, is a case in point.

People are more likely to make the *fundamental attribution error* when evaluating targets of prejudice (Levy, Stroessner, & Dweck, 1998). Pettigrew (2001) suggests that perceiving negative characteristics as being dispositional (personality based) and due to group membership is the *ultimate attribution error*. Thus, when people take note of ethnic neighborhoods dominated by crime and poverty, they blame these problems on the residents ("they're lazy and ignorant") and downplay or ignore situationally based explanations (job discrimination, poor police service, and so on). The old saying, "They should pull themselves up by their own bootstraps" is a blanket dismissal of how situational factors may make it especially difficult for minorities to achieve upward mobility.

Which man looks guilty? If you picked the man on the right, you're wrong. Wrong for judging people based on the color of their skin. Because if you look closely, you'll see they're the same man. Unfortunately, racial stereotyping like this happens every day. On America's highways, police stop drivers based on their skin color rather than for the way they are driving. For example, in Florida 80% of those stopped and searched were black and Hispanic, while they constituted only 5% of all drivers. These humiliating and illegal searches are violations of the Constitution and must be fought. Help us defend your rights. Support the ACLU. www.aclu.org **american civil liberties union**

This clever poster, sponsored by the American Civil Liberties Union, focuses a spotlight on the sensitive issue of racial profiling. Racial profiling, which is a manifestation of modern racism, reflects the influence of stereotyping. The phenomenon of racial profiling shows how simple, often automatic, cognitive distortions can have unfortunate consequences in everyday life.

Defensive attributions, in which people unfairly blame victims of adversity to reassure themselves that the same thing won't happen to them, can also contribute to prejudice. For example, individuals who claim that people who contract AIDS deserve it may be trying to reassure themselves that they won't suffer a similar fate (Kouabenan et al., 2001).

Competition between Groups

In 1954, Muzafer Sherif conducted a now-classic study at Robbers' Cave State Park in Oklahoma to look at competition and prejudice (Sherif et al., 1961; Platow & Hunter, 2014; Reicher & Haslam, 2014). In this study, 11-year-old boys were invited to attend a 3-week summer camp. What the boys didn't know was that they were participants in an experiment. The boys were randomly assigned to one of two groups; at camp, they went directly to their assigned campsites and had no knowledge of the other group's presence. During the first week, the boys got to know members of their own group through typical camp activities (hiking, swimming, camping out); each group also chose a name (the Rattlers and the Eagles).

In the second week, the Rattlers and Eagles were introduced to each other through intergroup competitions. Events included a football game, a treasure hunt, and a tug of war, with medals, trophies, and other desirable prizes for the winning team. Almost immediately after competitive games were introduced, hostile feelings erupted between the two groups, quickly escalating to highly aggressive behavior: Food fights broke out in the mess hall, cabins were ransacked, and group flags were burned. This classic study and more recent research (Dreu, Aaldering, & Saygi, 2015; Puurtinen, Heap, & Mappes, 2015) suggest that groups often respond more negatively to competition than individuals do.

This experimental demonstration of the effects of competition on prejudice is often mirrored in the real world (Jackson, 2011). For example, disputes over territory often provoke antagonism, as is the case in the Israeli-Palestinian conflict. A strong sense of nationalism, the belief that your country is better than all others, can also lead to prejudicial feelings and even conflict (Falomir-Pichastor & Frederic, 2013). Nationalism can be an especially potent source of prejudice that becomes aimed at immigrants, who are perceived as social, cultural, and economic threats (Kosic, Phalet, & Mannetti, 2012). A lack of empathy for members of another group is clearly a powerful force (Castano, 2012), but a scarcity of jobs or other important resources can also create competition among social groups. Still, competition does not always breed prejudice. In fact, the *perception* of threats to one's ingroup (loss of status, for example) is much more likely to cause hostility among groups than actual threats to the ingroup are (Greenaway et al., 2014).

Threats to Social Identity

Although group membership provides identity and pride, it can also foster prejudice and discrimination, as we just noted. Members' individual psychologies become merged with group and even societal processes (Spears, 2011), which can lead to feelings that one's group is superior to others. To explore a different facet of this idea, we turn to *social identity theory*, developed by Tajfel (1982) and Turner (1987). According to this theory, self-esteem is partly determined by one's *social identity*, or collective self, which is tied to one's group memberships (nationality, religion, gender, major, occupation, political party affiliation, fraternity, sorority, self-help clubs, and so forth) (Ellemers & Haslam, 2012). At times, perception of group membership is subtle, as we are also drawn to those who look like us or sound like us (sharing an accent or regional speech), so much so that we like them virtually automatically (Gluszek & Dovidio, 2010).

How do rises in personal self-esteem differ from this more collective form of self-esteem? Whereas your personal self-esteem is elevated by individual accomplishments (you got an A on a history exam), your collective self-esteem is boosted when an ingroup is successful (your team wins the football game). Likewise, your self-esteem can be threatened on both the personal level (you didn't get that job interview) and the collective level (your football team loses the championship).

Threats to both personal and social identity motivate individuals to restore self-esteem, but threats to social identity are more likely to provoke responses that foster prejudice and discrimination (Crocker & Luhtanen, 1990). When collective self-esteem is threatened, individuals react in two key ways to bolster it. The most common response is to show *ingroup favoritism*—for example, tapping an ingroup member for a job opening or rating the performance of an ingroup member higher than that of an outgroup member (Stroebe, Lodewijkx, & Spears, 2005; Ellemers & Haslam, 2012). The second way to deal with threats to social identity is to engage in *outgroup derogation*—in other words, to "trash" outgroups perceived to be threatening. This latter tactic is especially likely to be used by individuals who identify strongly with an ingroup (Perreault & Bourhis, 1999). Young people who affiliate with gangs often do so to obtain feelings of pride, worth, security, and social identity, so that as the distinction between self and group ebbs they become willing to fight and even sacrifice themselves for the group (Gomez et al., 2011). **Figure 7.6** depicts the various elements of social identity theory.

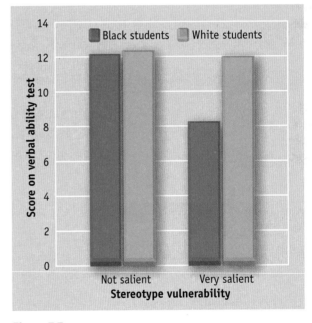

Figure 7.6

Social identity theory. According to Tajfel (1982) and Turner (1987), individuals have both a personal identity (based on a unique sense of self) and a social identity (based on group memberships). When social identity is threatened, people are motivated to restore self-esteem by either showing favoritism to ingroup members or derogating outgroup members. These tactics contribute to prejudice and discrimination. (Adapted from Kassin, Fein, & Markus, 2011)

Stereotype Threat

Our discussion in this chapter has focused on stereotypes that are directed at others—that is, how each person relies on simplified beliefs associating groups of people with particular traits. What happens when individuals are the targets of a stereotype used by others to characterize the group they belong to? Is the stereotype ignored, or does the person internalize its impact?

Consider African Americans. One pernicious stereotype is that African American students perform poorly on standardized tests compared to, say, white students. Claude Steele (1997) suggests that although socioeconomic disadvantages can serve as an explanatory factor for the underperformance of blacks relative to whites on such tests, there may be other legitimate reasons. How so? Steele suggests that the availability and awareness of derogatory stereotypes connected to various stigmatized groups, including blacks, leads to *stereotype vulnerability*, otherwise known as *stereotype threat*. Feelings of stereotype vulnerability can undermine group members' performance on standardized tests, as well as other measures of academic achievement. Thus, stereotype threat poses a variety of challenges for intergroup relations (Schmader, Hall, & Croft, 2015).

In a study by Steele and Aronson (1995), for example, black and white college students who scored well above average in academic ability were recruited (their comparable academic backgrounds ruled out cultural disadvantage as a factor in the research). All participants completed a challenging 30-minute test of verbal ability composed of items drawn from the Graduate Record Exam (GRE). In one condition, stereotype vulnerability was made salient: The test was described as being an excellent index of a person's general verbal ability. In the other condition, the test was described as a means for researchers to analyze people's problem-solving strategies (thus, not as a measure of intellectual ability). What did Steele and Aronson find? When the African American students' stereotype vulnerability was not emphasized, the performances of black and white students did not differ (see the bars on the left side of **Figure 7.7**). Yet when the same test was presented in a way that increased stereotype threat, the black students scored significantly lower than the white test takers (see the two bars on the right side of **Figure 7.7**).

Steele and his colleagues have demonstrated that the stereotype threat can influence the performance of a variety of groups, not just minorities, suggesting its applicability to a variety of behavioral phenomena (Steele, 2011). Thus, for example, women have been shown to be vulnerable to

Figure 7.7

Stereotype vulnerability and test performance. Steele and Aronson (1995) compared the performances of African American and white students of equal ability on a thirty-item verbal ability test constructed from difficult GRE questions. When the black students' stereotype vulnerability was not obvious, their performance did not differ from that of the white students; when the threat of stereotype vulnerability was raised, however, the black students performed significantly worse than the white students.

Source: Adapted from Steele, C. M., & Aronson, J. (1995). Stereotype threat and the intellectual test performance of African Americans. *Journal of Personality and Social Psychology, 69,* 797–811. Copyright © 1995 by the American Psychological Association. Reprinted by permission of the author.

stereotype threat concerning the belief that men perform better on math-related tasks (Stone & McWhinnie, 2008). In turn, white men have been found to be "threatened" by the stereotype that men of Asian descent are superior when it comes to doing well at mathematics (Aronson et al., 1999). Among older people, stereotype threat—worrying that one's advanced age will impact functioning—is found to be one explanation for underperformance on various physical and cognitive tasks, as opposed to actual changes linked to age (Krendl, Ambady, & Kensinger, 2015; Lamont, Swift, & Abrams, 2015).

Reducing Prejudice

For decades, psychologists have searched for ways to reduce prejudice (Zárate et al., 2014). Such a complicated problem requires solutions on a number of levels. Let's look at a few interventions that can help.

Cognitive Strategies

Although it's true that stereotypes kick in automatically, unintentionally, and unconsciously, individuals *can* override them—with some cognitive effort (Fiske, 2002). Thus, if you meet someone who speaks with an accent, your initial, automatic reaction might be negative. However, if you believe that prejudice is wrong and if you are aware that you are stereotyping, you can intentionally inhibit such thoughts and work to avoid speaking or behaving in a biased manner. According to Devine's (1989) model of prejudice reduction, this process requires an intentional shift from *automatic processing* to *controlled processing*—or from *mindlessness* to *mindfulness*, in Langer's terms (see Chapters 6 and 16). Thus, you can reduce prejudice if you are motivated to pay careful attention to what and how you think. There is even some suggestive evidence that using imagery to envision a negative followed by a positive encounter with an outgroup member can reduce prejudicial feelings (Birtel & Crisp, 2012). This imagined exposure therapy led to reduced anxiety in perceivers as well as enhanced intentions to interact positively with members of stigmatized groups, such as gay men, adults with schizophrenia, and British Muslims (see also, Crisp & Birtel, 2014; McDonald et al., 2014).

Intergroup Contact

Let's return to the Robbers' Cave study. When we left them, the Rattlers and Eagles were engaged in food fights and flag burning. Understandably, the experimenters were eager to

 **Recommended Reading**

Blindspot: Hidden Biases of Good People

by Mahzarin R. Banaji and Anthony G. Greenwald (Delacorte, 2013)

As considerable research in social psychology attests, stereotypes are alive and well, and very influential where our social perception and thinking are concerned. Research on attitudes reveals that hidden biases, implicit pieces of knowledge based on social categories (e.g., race, gender, religion, ethnicity, social class, sexual orientation, disability) can subtly direct how we behave toward other people. The chief problem is that we are largely unaware of how these biases influence our behavior in everyday settings.

Social psychologists Banaji and Greenwald developed what is known as the Implicit Association Test (IAT), which assesses the presence and magnitude of hidden prejudices. They demonstrate convincingly that even the most open-minded person can harbor prejudicial "mindbugs" that lead him to behave in ways that do not match his personal, often espoused, beliefs. Their analysis means that the tolerant, open-minded person is possibly a secret chauvinist because his perceptions of various social groups are outside of his awareness or conscious control.

The book contains several paper-and-pencil IATs so that readers can learn about their own social blindspots concerning race and gender. There are also two thoughtful appendices supporting the book's main narrative—one explores whether American citizens carry racist beliefs, the other examines race, discrimination, and social disadvantage. The authors are brutally honest in this book, one everyone should read and heed.

restore peace. First, they tried speaking with each group, talking up the other group's good points and minimizing their differences. They also made the groups sit together at meals and "fun" events like movies. Unfortunately, these tactics fell flat. Mere contact between groups is not sufficient to reduce prejudicial feelings (Al Ramiah & Hewstone, 2013).

Next, the experimenters designed intergroup activities based on the principle of *superordinate goals*—goals requiring two or more groups to work together to achieve mutual ends. For example, each boy had to contribute in some way to a cookout (building a fire, preparing food) so that all could eat. After the boys participated in a variety of such activities, the hostility between the groups was much reduced. By the end of the 3-week camping period, the Eagles and the Rattlers voted to ride the same bus home. Cooperating to reach common goals, then, can reduce conflict (Bay-Hinitz, Peterson, & Quilitch, 1994).

Researchers have identified four necessary ingredients in the recipe for reducing intergroup hostility (Brewer & Brown, 1998). First, groups must *work together for a common goal*—merely bringing hostile groups into contact is not effective in reducing intergroup antagonism and may worsen it. Second, cooperative efforts must have *successful outcomes*—if groups fail at a cooperative task, they are likely to blame one another for the failure. Third, group members must have opportunities to establish *meaningful connections* with one another, not merely going through the motions of interacting. The fourth factor, *equal status contact*, requires bringing together members of different groups in ways that ensure that everyone has equal status. A large meta-analysis demonstrated clear support for intergroup contact that meets these conditions as a means of reducing prejudice (Tropp & Page-Gould, 2015).

7.3 The Power of Persuasion

Every day you are bombarded by attempts to alter your attitudes through persuasion. You may not even be out of bed before you hear radio advertisements meant to persuade you to buy specific tooth-whiteners, smartphones, athletic shoes, and fast food. On your way to school, you see billboards showing attractive models draped over cars in the hopes that they can induce positive feelings that will transfer to the vehicles. "Does it ever end?" you wonder.

When it comes to persuasion, the answer is "no." As Pratkanis and Aronson (2000) note, Americans live in the "age of propaganda." In light of this situation, let's examine some factors that determine whether persuasion works.

Persuasion involves **the communication of arguments and information intended to change another person's attitudes.** What are attitudes? For the purposes of our discussion, we'll define *attitudes* **as beliefs and feelings about people, objects, and ideas.** Let's look more closely at two of the terms in this definition. We use the term *beliefs* to mean thoughts and judgments about people, objects, and ideas. For example, you may *believe* that equal pay for equal work is a fair policy or that capital punishment is not an effective crime deterrent. The "feeling" component of attitudes refers to the positivity and negativity of one's feelings about an issue as well as how strongly one feels about it. For example, you may *strongly favor* equal pay for equal work but only *mildly disagree* with the idea that capital punishment reduces crime. Psychologists assume that attitudes predict behavior (Ajzen, 2012)—if you are favorably disposed toward some new product, you are likely to buy it; if not, you won't (Eagly & Chaiken, 1998). Of course, there is more to the persuasion side of the attitude-behavior relation: Read on.

Elements of the Persuasion Process

The process of persuasion or attitude change (Crano & Prislin, 2008) includes four basic elements (see **Figure 7.8**). The *source* **is the person who sends a communication, and the** *receiver* **is the person to whom the message is sent.** Thus, if you watched a presidential

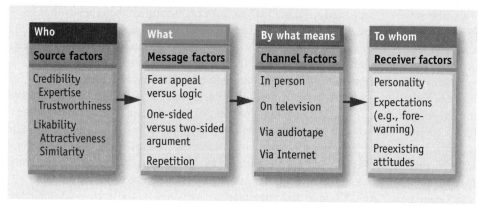

Figure 7.8

Overview of the persuasion process. The process of persuasion essentially boils down to *who* (the source) communicates *what* (the message) *by what means* (the channel) *to whom* (the receiver). Thus, four sets of variables influence the process of persuasion: source, message, channel, and receiver factors. The diagram lists some of the more important factors in each category (including some that are not discussed in the text because of space limitations).

address on TV, the president would be the source, and you and millions of other viewers would be the receivers in this persuasive effort. **The *message* is the information transmitted by the source; the *channel* is the medium through which the message is sent.** In examining communication channels, investigators often compare face-to-face interaction with appeals sent via mass media (television, radio). Although the research on communication channels is interesting, we'll confine our discussion to source, message, and receiver variables.

Source Factors

Persuasion tends to be more successful when the source has high *credibility* (Pornpitakpan, 2004) or when perceivers believe the communicator will actually deliver on a promise (Clark, Evans, & Wegener, 2011). Two subfactors make a communicator credible: expertise and trustworthiness (Hovland & Weiss, 1951). People try to convey their *expertise* by mentioning their degrees, training, and experience or by showing an impressive grasp of the issues (Clark et al., 2012). As to *trustworthiness*, whom would you believe if you were told that your state needs to reduce corporate taxes to stimulate its economy—the president of a huge corporation in your state or an economics professor from out of state? Probably the latter. Trustworthiness is undermined when a source, such as the corporation president, appears to have something to gain. In contrast, trustworthiness is enhanced when people appear to argue against their own interests (Petty et al., 2001), which explains why salespeople often make remarks like "Frankly, my snowblower isn't the best—they have a better brand down across town if you're willing to spend more . . ."

Advertisers frequently employ well-liked celebrities such as Gwyneth Paltrow to pitch their products, hoping that the positive feelings of the audience toward the source will transfer to the product.

Likability, a second major source factor, includes a number of subfactors (Petty et al., 1997). A key consideration is a person's *physical attractiveness* (Petty et al., 1997). For example, one researcher found that attractive students were more successful than less attractive ones in obtaining signatures for a petition (Chaiken, 1979). People also respond better to sources who are *similar* to them in ways that are relevant to the pertitnent issue (Mackie, Worth, & Asuncion, 1990). Thus, politicians stress the values they and voters hold in common.

Source variables are used to great effect in advertising. Many companies spend a fortune to obtain spokespersons, such as Ellen DeGeneres or Rachael Ray, who combine trustworthiness, likability, and a knack for connecting with the average person. Companies quickly abandon spokespersons whose likability declines. For example, in 2015 the NBC Network dropped Donald Trump's television show "The Apprentice" following controversial remarks he made concerning immigrants.

Who do we trust in everyday life? The Gallup Organization polled a sample of Americans and asked them to rate the honesty and ethical standards of individuals who worked in eleven occupations. **Figure 7.9** indicates that nurses, doctors, and pharmacists topped the list—they were seen as most credible. Sadly, car salespeople and members of Congress were viewed as least credible, ending up at the list's bottom.

Message Factors

Imagine that you advocate selecting a high-profile entertainer as the speaker at your commencement ceremony. In preparing your argument, you ponder the most effective way to structure your message. On the one hand, you're convinced that hosting a well-known entertainer would be popular with students and would boost the university's image in the community and among alumni. Still, you realize the performer would cost a lot and that some people believe that entertainers are not appropriate commencement speakers. Should you present a *one-sided argument* that ignores the problems? Or should you present a *two-sided argument* that acknowledges the problems but then downplays them?

In general, two-sided arguments are more effective (Crowley & Hoyer, 1994). In fact, just mentioning that there are two sides to an issue can increase your credibility with an audience (Jones & Brehm, 1970). One-sided messages work only when your audience is uneducated about the issue or when they already favor your point of view.

Persuaders also use emotional appeals to shift attitudes, as message factors are more likely to be attended to as a problem's seriousness increases (Feng, & MacGeorge, 2010). Insurance companies show scenes of homes on fire to arouse fear. Antismoking campaigns emphasize the threat of cancer. Deodorant ads prey on the fear of embarrassment. Does *fear arousal* work? Yes. Studies involving various issues (nuclear policy, auto safety, and dental hygiene, among others) show that arousing fear often increases persuasion (Perloff, 1993). And fear appeals are influential if people feel susceptible to the threat (De Hoog, Stroebe, & De Wit, 2007). If you induce strong fear in your audience without providing a workable solution to the problem (such as a surefire stop-smoking program), however, you may make your audience defensive, causing them to tune you out (Petty & Wegener, 1998).

Generating *positive feelings* is also an effective way to persuade people. Providing people with comfort—food, drinks, a cozy setting, an easy chair—can reduce people's defenses and open them up to persuasion (Schwartz, Bless, & Bohner, 1991). Other familiar examples of such tactics include the use of music and physically attractive actors in TV commercials, the use of laugh tracks in TV programs, and the practice of wining and dining prospective customers. People attend better to humorous messages than to sober ones (Duncan & Nelson, 1985); later, however, they may recall that something was funny but forget what it was about (Cantor & Venus, 1980).

Receiver Factors

What about the receiver of the persuasive message? Are some people easier to persuade than others? Yes, but the answer is complicated. For instance, receptivity to a message can sometimes depend on people's *moods*: Optimistic people process uplifting messages better than pessimists, who are drawn to counter-attitudinal communications, or those opposing their current views (Wegener & Petty, 1994). Other people want to think deeply about issues, possessing a so-called **need for cognition, the tendency to seek out and enjoy**

U.S. CITIZENS' VIEWS ON HONESTY AND ETHICAL STANDARDS IN PROFESSIONS	
Profession	**Honesty and Ethical Standards**
Nurses	80%
Medical doctors	65%
Pharmacists	65%
Police officers	48%
Clergy	46%
Bankers	23%
Lawyers	21%
Business executives	17%
Advertising practitioners	10%
Car salespeople	8%
Members of Congress	7%

Figure 7.9

Trustworthiness of various professions. A 2014 Gallup Poll asked people to rate the level of honesty and ethical standards attributed to people who work in eleven occupations. Listed in the figure are the percentages of respondents who rated the members of each occupational group as "high" or "very high" in honesty.

Source: Adapted from www.gallup.com/poll/180260/americans-rate-nurses-highest-honesty-ethical-standards.aspx

"You're right. It does send a powerful message."

Peter Steiner/www.cartoonbank.com

TACTICS FOR RESISTING PERSUASIVE APPEALS

Tactic	Example
Attitude bolstering	"I remind myself of the facts that support the validity of how I feel."
Counter-arguing	"I talk to myself and play the Devil's advocate."
Social validation	"I know others who share my same opinions are there to support me."
Negative affect	"I get angry whenever someone tries to get me to change my mind about what I believe and feel."
Assertions of confidence	"I don't believe anyone can change my mind; it's set."
Selective exposure	"I usually just ignore those opinions and perspectives I neither share nor agree with."
Source derogation	"I search for faults in the individual who is challenging my beliefs."

Figure 7.10

Tactics for resisting persuasive appeals. Jacks and Cameron (2003) asked research participants to describe the tactics they used to combat persuasive appeals dealing with controversial social issues, such as abortion or the death penalty. Seven tactics were revealed and are shown in the figure. They are ranked from the most to the least commonly used. (Based on data from Jacks & Cameron, 2003)

Source: Adapted from Table 6.4 (p. 235) of Kassin, S., Fein, S., & Markus, H. R. (2014), *Social Psychology* (9th ed.), Belmont, CA: Cengage Learning.

effortful thought, problem-solving activities, and in-depth analysis. People who truly relish intellectual give-and-take as well as debate are more likely to be convinced by high-quality arguments than those who prefer more superficial analyses (Nettelhorst & Brannon, 2012).

Transient factors also matter in receptivity to persuasive messages. *Forewarning* the receiver about a persuasive effort and a receiver's initial position on an issue, for instance, seem to be more influential than a receiver's personality. When you shop for a new TV or a car, you expect salespeople to work at persuading you. To some extent, this forewarning reduces their arguments' impact (Petty & Wegener, 1998). When receivers are forewarned about a persuasion attempt on a personally important topic, it is harder to persuade them than when they are not forewarned (Wood & Quinn, 2003). Thus, the old saying "To be forewarned is to be forearmed" is often true. Understandably, receivers are harder to persuade when they encounter a position that is incompatible with their existing beliefs. In general, people display a *disconfirmation bias* in evaluating such arguments (Edwards & Smith, 1996).

Jacks and Cameron (2003) invited research participants to share and then rate the tactics they use to resist persuasive appeals aimed at undermining their beliefs regarding controversial social issues (e.g., abortion, the death penalty). Seven tactics for resisting persuasive communications were found (see **Figure 7.10**). The tactics are listed from the most to the least commonly used.

The Whys of Persuasion

Why do people change their attitudes in response to persuasive messages? Thanks to the work of Richard Petty and John Cacioppo (1986), psychologists have a good understanding of the cognitive processes that underlie attitude change.

According to the *elaboration likelihood model,* **an individual's thoughts about a persuasive message (rather than the actual message itself) determine whether attitude change will occur** (O'Keefe, 2013; Petty & Briñol, 2014). As we know, sometimes people make quick, sloppy decisions (automatic processing, mindlessness, snap judgments), whereas at other times they process information carefully (controlled processing, mindfulness, systematic judgments). Sometimes people choose to think; others times they choose not to. These processes also operate in persuasion, with messages sometimes persuading receivers through a *peripheral* route and sometimes through a *central* route.

When people are distracted, tired, or uninterested in a persuasive message, they fail to key in on the true merits of the product or issue. They do process information, but not mindfully. Being in a happy mood can produce the same effect (Sinclair, Mark, & Clore, 1994). Surprisingly, even when people do not carefully evaluate a message, attitude change can occur (Petty & Cacioppo, 1990). What happens is that the receiver is persuaded by cues that are peripheral to the message—thus the term *peripheral route* (see **Figure 7.11**). Just because you're not mindfully analyzing a TV commercial for a new fruit drink doesn't mean that you're totally tuned out. You may not be paying attention to the substance of the commercial, but you are aware of an ad's superficial aspects—you like the music, your favorite basketball player is pitching the product, and boy, that beach scene is appealing.

Although persuasion usually occurs via the peripheral route, senders can also use another route to attitude change—the *central route* (see **Figure 7.11**). In this case, receivers process persuasive messages mindfully, by thinking about the logic and merits of the pertinent (or central) arguments. In other words, the receiver cognitively *elaborates* on the persuasive message—hence, the model's name—and messages that receive greater and deeper processing are more resistant to persuasion (Blankenship & Wegener, 2008). If people have a favorable reaction to their thoughtful evaluation of a message, positive attitude change occurs; an unfavorable reaction results in negative attitude change.

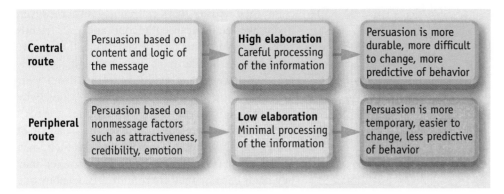

Central route	Persuasion based on content and logic of the message	**High elaboration** Careful processing of the information	Persuasion is more durable, more difficult to change, more predictive of behavior
Peripheral route	Persuasion based on nonmessage factors such as attractiveness, credibility, emotion	**Low elaboration** Minimal processing of the information	Persuasion is more temporary, easier to change, less predictive of behavior

Figure 7.11

The peripheral and central routes to persuasion. Persuasion can occur via two different routes. The central route, which results in high elaboration, tends to produce longer-lasting attitude change and stronger attitudes than the peripheral route.

For the central route to override the peripheral route, two requirements must be met. First, receivers must be *motivated* to process the persuasive message carefully. Motivation is triggered when people are interested in the issue, find it personally relevant, have a high need for cognition, and have time and energy to think about it carefully. For example, if your university is considering changing its grading system, you will probably think carefully about the various options and their implications. Second, receivers must have the *ability* to grasp the message—that is, the message must be comprehensible, and individuals must be capable of understanding it. If people are distracted, tired, or find the message uninteresting or irrelevant, they will not pay careful attention, and superficial cues will become salient.

Ultimately, the two routes to persuasion are not equally effective. Attitudes formed via the central route are longer lasting and more resistant to challenge than those formed via the peripheral route (Petty & Wegener, 1998). They are also better predictors of a person's behavior (Petty, Priester, & Wegener, 1994).

Although we can't stem the tide of persuasive messages bombarding you daily, we hope you will be a vigilant recipient of persuasion attempts. Of course, persuasion is not the *only* method through which people try to influence you, as you'll learn in the next section.

Blend Images-Hill Street Studios/Getty Images

Political candidates use music, flags, and slogans to persuade via the peripheral route; when they present their views on an issue, they are going for the central route.

7.4 The Power of Social Pressure

Learning Objectives

- Summarize what Asch discovered about conformity.
- Distinguish between normative and informational influences on conformity.
- Describe Milgram's research on obedience and explain how to resist demands from an authority.

In the previous section, we showed you how others attempt to change your *attitudes*. Now you'll see how people attempt to change your *behavior*—by trying to get you to agree to their requests and demands.

Conformity and Compliance Pressures

If you extol the talent of the popular group Imagine Dragons or keep a well-manicured lawn, are you exhibiting conformity? According to social psychologists, it depends on whether your behavior is freely chosen or due to group pressure. *Conformity* **occurs when people yield to real or imagined social pressure.** Such social influence is powerful in groups (Levine & Tindale, 2015). For example, if you like Imagine Dragons because you truly

Conformity is far more common than most people appreciate. We all conform to social expectations in an endless variety of ways. There is nothing inherently good or bad about conforming to social pressures; it all depends on the situation. However, it is prudent to be aware of how social expectations can sometimes have a profound influence on our behavior.

enjoy their music, that's not conformity. However, if you like them because it's "cool" and your friends would question your taste if you didn't, then you're conforming. Similarly, if you maintain a well-groomed lawn just to avoid complaints from your neighbors, you're yielding to social pressure (why not have a wildflower meadow instead of a yard?). In short, people are apt to explain the behavior of others as conforming but not think of their own actions this way (Pronin, 2008). Your friends may buy iPads because they are conformists; you buy one for what seem to be justifiable personal reasons (failing to realize that all those "conformists" believe this to be their motivation, too). As you read this section, remember that individuals often believe they are "alone in a crowd of sheep" because everyone else is conforming (Pronin et al., 2007).

The Dynamics of Conformity

To introduce this topic, we'll re-create a classic experiment devised by Solomon Asch (1955). The participants are male undergraduates recruited for a study of visual perception. Seven participants are shown a large card with a vertical line on it and asked to indicate which of three lines on a second card matches the original "standard line" in length (see **Figure 7.12**). All seven participants are given a turn at the task, and each announces his choice to the group. The participant in the sixth chair doesn't know it, but everyone else in the group is an accomplice of the experimenter.

The accomplices give accurate responses on the first two trials. On the third trial, line 2 is clearly the correct response, but the first five participants all say that line 3 matches the standard line. The genuine participant can't believe his ears. Over the course of the experiment, the accomplices all give the same incorrect response on twelve out of eighteen trials. Asch wanted to see how people would respond in these situations. The line judgments are easy and unambiguous. Without group pressure, matching errors occur less than 1% of the time. So, if the participant consistently agrees with the accomplices, he isn't making honest mistakes—he is conforming. Will the participant stick to his guns, or will he go along with the group? Asch found that the men conformed (made mistakes) on 37% of the twelve trials. The subjects varied considerably in their tendency to conform, however. Of the fifty participants, thirteen never caved in to the group, while fourteen conformed on more than half the trials. One could argue that the results show that people confronting a unanimous majority generally tend to *resist* the pressure to conform. But given how clear and easy the line judgments were, most social scientists viewed the findings as a dramatic demonstration of humans' propensity to conform.

In subsequent studies, Asch (1956) determined that group size and group unanimity are key determinants of conformity. To examine group size, Asch repeated his procedure with groups that included one to fifteen accomplices. Little conformity was seen when a subject was pitted against just one accomplice. Conformity increased rapidly as group size went from two to four, peaked at a group size of seven, and then leveled off (see **Figure 7.13**). Asch concluded that as group size increases, conformity increases—up to a point. Significantly, Asch found that group size made little difference if just one accomplice "broke" with the others, wrecking their unanimous agreement. The presence of another dissenter lowered conformity to about one-quarter of its peak, even when the dissenter made inaccurate judgments that happened to conflict with the majority view. Apparently, the participants just needed to hear a second person question the accuracy of the group's perplexing responses. Asch's classic study has been replicated without the use of confederates and similar

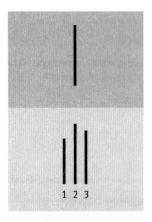

Figure 7.12

Stimuli used in Asch's conformity studies. Subjects were asked to match a standard line (top) with one of three other lines displayed on another card (bottom). The task was easy—until experimental accomplices started responding with obviously incorrect answers, creating a situation in which Asch evaluated subjects' conformity.

Source: Adapted from illustration on p. 35 by Sarah Love in Asch, S. (1955, November). Opinions and social pressure. *Scientific American, 193*(5), 31–35. Copyright © 1955 by Scientific American, Inc.

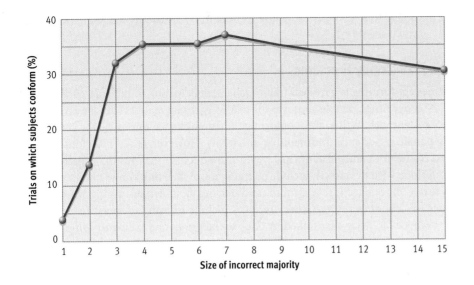

Figure 7.13

Conformity and group size. This graph shows the percentage of trials on which participants conformed as a function of the number of individuals with an opposing view. Asch found that conformity became more frequent as group size increased, up to about seven persons, and then leveled off.

Source: Adapted from illustration on p. 32 by Sarah Love in Asch, S. (1955, November). Opinions and social pressure. *Scientific American,* 193(5), 31–35. Copyright © 1955 by Scientific American, Inc.

results were observed (Mori & Arai, 2010), including a study where 6-year-old children were the participants (Hanayama & Mori, 2011).

Conformity versus Compliance

Did the conforming participants in Asch's study really change their beliefs in response to social pressure, or did they just pretend to change them? Subsequent studies asked participants to make their responses privately, instead of publicly (Insko et al., 1985). Conformity declined dramatically when participants wrote down their responses. Thus, it is likely that Asch's participants did not really change their beliefs. Based on this evidence, theorists concluded that Asch's experiments evoked a particular type of conformity, called compliance. *Compliance* **occurs when people yield to social pressure in their public behavior, even though their private beliefs have not changed.** For example, many people comply with modest group pressure daily—they "dress up" for work by wearing suits, ties, dresses, and so on—when they would prefer to wear more casual clothing. A recent field study in France found that people were more likely to agree to organ donation requests when the solicitor wore a religious symbol (here, a Christian cross on a chain) than no symbol in a control condition (Guéguen, Bougeard-Delfosse, & Jacob, 2015). Men and women complied at similar levels. Perhaps the presence of the symbol primed thoughts of compassion, which in turn led to greater compliance as respondents came to view the request positively.

The Whys of Conformity

People often conform or comply because they are afraid of being criticized or rejected. *Normative influence* **operates when people conform to social norms for fear of negative social consequences.** Compliance often results from subtle, implied pressure. For example, for fear of making a negative impression, you may remove your eyebrow ring or cover your tattoo for a job interview. However, compliance also occurs in response to explicit rules, requests, and commands. Thus, you'll probably follow your boss's instructions even when you think they're lousy ideas.

People often conform when they are uncertain how to behave (Cialdini, 2001). Thus, if you're at a nice restaurant and don't know which fork to use, you may watch others to see what they're doing. *Informational influence* **operates when people look to others for how to behave in ambiguous situations.** In such cases, using others as a source of information about appropriate behavior is a good thing. Yet,

"He's one of our own, so let's give him a big welcome."

Charles Barsotti/The New Yorker Collection/www.cartoonbank.com

relying on others to know how to behave in unfamiliar situations can sometimes be problematic, as you'll see shortly.

Resisting Conformity Pressures

Sometimes conforming is harmless fun—such as participating in Internet-generated "flash mobs." At other times, people conform for relatively trivial matters (dressing up for dinner at a nice restaurant). In this case, conformity and compliance minimize the confusion and anxiety people experience in unfamiliar situations. However, when individuals feel pressured to conform to antisocial norms, tragic consequences may result. Negative examples of "going along with the crowd" include drinking more than one knows one should because others say "C'mon, have just one more" and driving at someone's urging when under the influence of alcohol or drugs. Other instances include refusing to socialize with someone simply because the person isn't liked by one's social group and failing to come to another's defense when it might make one unpopular.

These examples all concern normative influence, but pressure can come from informational influence as well. A useful example concerns a paradox called the *bystander effect*—**the tendency for individuals to be less likely to provide help when others are present than when they are alone.** Numerous studies have confirmed that people are less helpful in emergency situations when others are around (Fischer et al., 2011). Even young children are not immune from the effect (Plötner et al., 2015). Thankfully, the bystander effect is less likely to occur when the need for help is very clear (Fischer, Greitemeyer, & Pollozek, 2006), when people experience heightened self-awareness (van Bommel et al., 2012) such as when a security camera is present to record their actions (van Bommel et al., 2014), or when the needed help requires the aid of many people, not just one (Greitemeyer & Mügge, 2015).

What accounts for the bystander effect? Several factors are at work, and conformity is one of them. The bystander effect is most likely to occur in *ambiguous situations* because people look around to see whether others are acting as if there's an emergency (Harrison & Wells, 1991). If everyone hesitates, this inaction (informational influence) suggests that help isn't needed. So the next time you witness what you think might be an emergency, don't automatically give in to the informational influence of inaction.

To resist conformity pressures, we offer these suggestions: First, pay more attention to the social forces operating on you. Second, if you are in a situation where others are pressuring you, identify someone in the group whose views match yours. Recall that just one dissenter in Asch's groups significantly reduced conformity pressures. Finally, if you know in advance that you're heading into this kind of situation, invite a friend with similar views to go along.

Pressure from Authority Figures

Obedience **is a form of compliance that occurs when people follow direct commands, usually from someone in a position of authority.** In itself, obedience isn't good or bad; it depends on what one is being told to do (Ent & Baumeister, 2014). For example, if the fire alarm goes off in your classroom building and your instructor "orders" you to leave, obedience is a good idea. On the other hand, if your boss asks you to engage in an unethical or illegal act, *disobedience* is probably in order. A key issue is that obedience entails an element of social power and whether individuals can resist such influence (Forsyth, 2013).

The Dynamics of Obedience

Following World War II, social psychologist Stanley Milgram was troubled by how readily German citizens followed the orders of dictator Adolf Hitler, even when the orders required morally repugnant actions, such as the slaughter of millions of Jews, Russians,

Stanley Milgram explored the dynamics of obedience to authority in his classic social psychological research.

Nazi Germany and its symbols represent a collective example of obedience to authority, which was the inspiration for Milgram's research on obedience.

Poles, Gypsies, and homosexuals (Russell, 2011). This observation was Milgram's motivation to study the dynamics of obedience. Milgram's (1963) participants were a diverse collection of forty men from the local community who volunteered for a study on the effects of punishment on learning. Once at the lab, they drew slips of paper from a hat to get their assignments. The drawing was rigged so that the participant always became the "teacher" and an experimental accomplice (a likable 47-year-old accountant) became the "learner."

The teacher watched while the learner was strapped into a chair and electrodes were attached to his arms (for delivering shocks whenever he made a mistake on the task). The participant was then taken to an adjoining room that housed the shock generator that he would control in his role as the teacher. Although the apparatus looked and sounded realistic, it was a fake, and the learner was never shocked. The experimenter played the role of the authority figure who told the teacher what to do and who answered any questions that arose.

The experiment was designed so that the learner would make many mistakes, and the teacher was instructed to increase the shock level after each wrong answer. At 300 volts, the learner began to pound on the wall between the two rooms in protest and soon stopped responding to the teacher's questions. From this point forward, participants frequently turned to the experimenter for guidance. Whenever they did so, the experimenter (authority figure) firmly stated that the teacher should continue to give stronger and stronger shocks to the now-silent learner. Milgram wanted to know the maximum shock the teacher was willing to administer before refusing to cooperate.

As **Figure 7.14** shows, 65% of the subjects administered all thirty levels of shock. Although they mostly obeyed the experimenter, many participants voiced and displayed considerable distress about harming the learner. They protested, groaned, bit their lips, trembled, and broke into a sweat—but they continued administering shocks. Based on these findings, Milgram concluded that obedience to authority was even more common than he or others had anticipated. A replication by Burger (2009) suggests Milgram's conclusion still stands: Although participants were stopped at the 150-volt level for ethical

Learn More Online

Stanley Milgram
This site provides a wealth of accurate information about the work of Stanley Milgram, arguably one of the most controversial and creative social psychologists in the field's history. The site is maintained by Thomas Blass, a psychology professor at the University of Maryland (Baltimore County), who has published many articles and books on the life and work of Milgram.

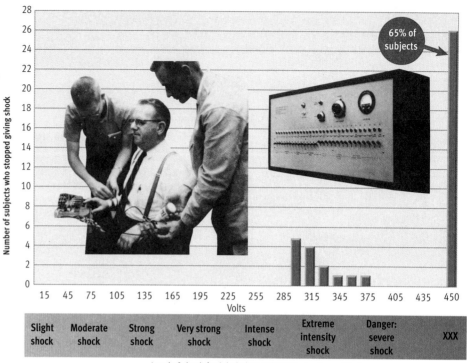

Figure 7.14

Milgram's (1963) experiment on obedience. The photos show the fake shock generator and the "learner" being connected to the shock generator during an experimental session. The results of the study are summarized in the bar graph. The vast majority of subjects (65%) delivered the entire series of shocks to the learner.

Source: Photos from the film *Obedience*, copyright ©1968 by Stanley Milgram; copyright renewed 1993 by Alexandra Milgram and distributed by Alexander Street Press. Reprinted by permission of Alexandra Milgram.

reasons, 70% continued to shock the learner despite hearing anguished cries (80% of Milgram's participants continued to shock after 150 volts).

The Causes of Obedience

What caused the obedient behavior observed by Milgram? First, the demands on the participants (to shock the learner) escalated gradually, so that very strong shocks were required only after the participant was well into the experiment. Second, participants were told that the authority figure, not the teacher, was responsible if anything happened to the learner. Third, subjects evaluated their actions based on meeting the authority figure's expectations, not by their harmful effects on the victim. Fourth, participants had little time to think about their decisions (Burger, 2014). Taken together, these findings suggest that human behavior is determined not so much by the *kind of person* one is as by the *kind of situation* one is in (Lewin, 1935). Applying this insight to Nazi war crimes and other atrocities, Milgram made a chilling assertion: Inhuman and evil visions may originate in the disturbed mind of an authority figure like Hitler, but only through the obedient actions of normal people do such ideas become a frightening reality.

Milgram's study has been consistently replicated, in diverse settings, with a variety of participants and procedural variations (Blass, 2012). Overall, the evidence supports Milgram's results. Of course, critics have questioned the ethics of Milgram's procedure (Nicholson, 2011). Today, at most universities it would be difficult to obtain permission to replicate Milgram's study—an ironic epitaph for what may be psychology's best-known experiment.

In the Application, we'll alert you to some social influence strategies that people use to get you and others to agree to their requests.

7.5 Seeing through Compliance Tactics

Which of the following statements is true?

____ **1.** It's a good idea to ask for a small favor before soliciting the larger favor that you really want.

____ **2.** It's a good idea to ask for a large favor before soliciting the smaller favor that you really want.

Would you believe that *both* of these conflicting statements are true? Although the two approaches work for different reasons, both can be effective ways to get people to comply. It pays to understand these and other social influence strategies because advertisers, salespeople, and fundraisers (not to mention friends and neighbors) use them frequently to influence people's behavior. To consider the strategies' relevance to your own life, we've grouped them by the principles that make them work. Much of our discussion is based on the work of Robert Cialdini (2007), a social psychologist who spent years observing social influence tactics used by compliance professionals.

The Consistency Principle

Once people agree to something, they tend to stick with their initial commitment (Guadagno & Cialdini, 2010). This tendency to prefer behavioral consistency is used to gain compliance in two ways. Both involve a person getting another individual to commit to an initial request and then changing the terms of the

Robert Cialdini has spent his career examining how compliance tactics can influence people in a variety of formal and informal settings.

agreement to the requestor's advantage. Because people often prefer their initial commitments, the target will likely agree to the revised proposal, even though it may not be to his or her benefit.

The Foot-in-the-Door Technique

Door-to-door salespeople have long recognized the importance of gaining a *little* cooperation from sales targets (getting a "foot in the door") before presenting their real sales pitch. **The *foot-in-the-door (FITD)* technique involves getting people to agree to a small request to increase the chances that they will agree to a larger request later** (see Figure 7.15). This technique is widely used. For example, groups seeking donations often ask people to simply sign a petition first. Salespeople routinely ask individuals to try a product with "no obligations" before they launch their hard sell.

The FITD technique was first investigated by Freedman and his colleagues. In one study (Freedman & Fraser, 1966), the large request involved telephoning homemakers, asking whether six consumer researchers could come into their home to classify all their household products. Imagine six strangers trampling through your home, pulling everything out of your closets and cupboards, and you can understand why only 22% of the control group members agreed to this outlandish request. Participants in the experimental group were contacted 3 days *before* the unreasonable request was made and asked to answer a few questions about the soaps used in their home. When the large request was made 3 days later, 53% of the experimental group complied with that request.

Why does this strategy work? The best explanation is rooted in Bem's *self-perception theory*, or the idea that people sometimes infer their attitudes by observing their own behavior (Burger & Guadagno, 2003). When Joe agrees to sign a petition, he infers that he is a helpful person. When confronted with a second, larger request to collect petition signatures, "helpful person" comes to mind, and Joe complies with the request. Confirming a theory offered by Cialdini and Sagarin (2005), a recent study found that when people answer a series of "yes or no" questions with several "yes" answers, they are more likely to comply with a later request (Guéguen et al., 2013).

The Lowball Technique

A second commitment-based strategy is **the *lowball technique*, which involves getting someone to commit to an attractive proposition before its hidden costs are revealed.** The technique's name derives from a common practice in automobile sales, where a customer is offered a terrific bargain on a car. The bargain price gets the customer to commit to buying, but soon

Figure 7.15

The foot-in-the-door and door-in-the-face techniques. These two influence techniques are essentially the reverse of each other, but both can work. (a) In the foot-in-the-door technique, you begin with a small request and work up to a larger one. (b) In the door-in-the-face technique, you begin with a large request and work down to a smaller one.

after, the dealer starts revealing some hidden costs. Typically, the customer discovers that options expected to be included in the original price will cost extra. Once the customer has committed to buying a car, most customers are unlikely to cancel the deal. Car dealers aren't the only ones who use this technique. For instance, a friend might invite you to spend a week with him at his charming lakeside cabin. After you accept this seemingly generous offer, he may add, "Of course, there's a little work to do. We need to paint the doors, repair the pier, and . . ." You might think

Used car dealers are notorious for using compliance tactics like the lowball technique.

that people would become angry and back out of a deal once its hidden costs are revealed. Sometimes they do, but lowballing is a surprisingly effective strategy (Burger & Cornelius, 2003), even when the follow-up requests are challenging or deviant (Guéguen & Pascual, 2014).

The Reciprocity Principle

Most people are socialized to believe in the *reciprocity principle—* **the rule that one should pay back in kind what one receives from others.** Charities frequently make use of this principle. Groups seeking donations for the disabled, the homeless, and so forth routinely send "free" address labels, key rings, and other small gifts with their pleas for donations. The belief that people should reciprocate others' kindness is a powerful norm; thus, people often feel obliged to reciprocate by making a donation in return for the gift. According to Cialdini (2007), the reciprocity norm is so powerful that it often works even when (1) the gift is uninvited, (2) the gift comes from someone you dislike, or (3) the gift results in an uneven exchange. Let's review some reciprocity-based influence tactics that take advantage of our belief in reciprocity.

The door-in-the-face technique reverses the request sequence used with the foot-in-the-door technique. **The *door-in-the-face (DITF)* technique involves making a large request that is likely to be turned down in order to increase the chances that people will agree to a smaller request later** (see Figure 7.15).

The strategy's name is derived from the expectation that an initial request will be quickly rejected. For example, a wife who wants to coax her frugal husband into buying a $30,000 sports car might begin by proposing purchasing a $40,000 sports car. After talking his wife out of the more expensive car, the $30,000 price tag may look quite reasonable to him. For the DITF to work, there must be no delay between the two requests (O'Keefe & Hale, 2001). Guéguen, Jacob, and Meineri (2011) found that restaurant customers who declined to order dessert were more likely to order coffee or tea when the waitress proposed a beverage immediately rather than a few minutes later. Another study, which dealt with motivating employees to stop smoking in the workplace, found that the DIFT was superior to an informational campaign (Pansu, Lima, & Fointiat, 2014).

Salespeople who distribute free samples to prospective customers are also using the reciprocity principle. Cialdini (2007) describes the procedures used by the Amway Corporation, which sells such household products as detergent, floor wax, and insect spray. Amway's door-to-door salespeople give homemakers their products for a "free trial." When they return a few days later, most homemakers feel obligated to buy some of the products.

The Scarcity Principle

It's no secret that telling people they can't have something only makes them want it more. According to Cialdini (2007), this principle derives from two sources. First, people have learned that items that are hard to get are of better quality than items that are easy to obtain. From there, they often assume, erroneously, that anything that is scarce must be good. Second, when people's choices (of products, services, romantic partners, job candidates) are constrained in some way, they often want what they can't have even more (Williams et al., 1993). The psychological term for this is *reactance* (Quick, Shen & Dillard, 2013).

Companies and advertisers frequently use the scarcity principle to drive up the demand for their products. Thus, you constantly see ads that scream "limited supply available," "for a limited time only," "while they last," and "time is running out." Although both messages work, limited-quantity messages are more effective (Aggarwal, Jun, & Huh, 2011). Perhaps the scarcity principle accounts for the reason so many antique and "vintage" items on eBay generate so much interest and auction dollars.

In summary, people use various methods to coax compliance from one another. Although many of these influence techniques are more or less dishonest, they're still widely used. There is no way to completely avoid being hoodwinked by influence strategies, and sometimes individuals are more susceptible to such influence such as when someone feels ostracized and wants to get back into a group's good graces (Carter-Sowell, Chen, & Williams, 2008). However, being alert to these techniques can reduce the likelihood that you'll be a victim of influence artists. As noted in our discussion of persuasion, "to be forewarned is to be forearmed."

Advertisers often try to artificially create scarcity to make their products seem more desirable.

CHAPTER 7 Review

Key Ideas

7.1 Forming Impressions of Others
- In forming impressions of other people, individuals rely on appearance, verbal behavior, actions, nonverbal messages, and situational cues. Individuals usually make snap judgments about others unless accurate impressions are important. To explain the causes of other people's behavior, individuals make attributions (either internal or external).
- People often try to confirm their expectations about what others are like, which can result in biased impressions. Self-fulfilling prophecies can actually change a target person's behavior in the direction of a perceiver's expectations.
- Categorization of people into ingroups and outgroups can slant social perceptions. Stereotypes, which are widely held beliefs about the typical characteristics of various groups, can distort one's perceptions of others. When people make the fundamental attribution error, they discount situational factors and explain others' behavior in terms of internal attributions. Defensive attribution often leads people to blame victims for their misfortunes. The process of person perception is characterized by the themes of efficiency, selectivity, and consistency.

7.2 The Problem of Prejudice
- Prejudice is a particularly unfortunate outcome of the tendency to view others inaccurately. Blatant (old-fashioned) discrimination occurs relatively infrequently today, but subtle expressions of prejudice and discrimination (modern discrimination, aversive racism) have become more common. Stereotypes can have subtle, but important effects on our perceptions of others.
- Common causes of prejudice include right-wing authoritarianism, a strong social dominance orientation, cognitive distortions due to stereotyping and attributional errors, actual competition between groups, and threats to one's social identity. Stereotype threat represents a case of internalized prejudice that can be countered. Strategies for reducing prejudice are rooted in social thinking and collaborative intergroup contact.

7.3 The Power of Persuasion
- The success of persuasive efforts depends on several factors. A source of persuasion who is expert, trustworthy, likable, physically attractive, and similar to the receiver tends to be relatively effective. Although there are some limitations, two-sided arguments, arousal of fear, and generation of positive feelings are effective elements in persuasive messages. Persuasion is undermined when receivers are forewarned or have beliefs that are incompatible with the position being advocated.
- Persuasion takes place via two processes. The central route to persuasion requires a receiver to be motivated to process persuasive messages carefully (elaboration). A favorable reaction to such an evaluation will result in positive attitude change. When a receiver is unmotivated or unable to process persuasive messages carefully, persuasion may take place via the peripheral route (on the basis of simple cues such as a catchy tune). Persuasion undertaken via the central route tends to have more enduring effects on attitudes.

7.4 The Power of Social Pressure
- Asch found that subjects often conform to the group, even when the group reports inaccurate judgments. Asch's experiments may have produced public compliance while subjects' private beliefs remained unchanged. Both normative and informational influence can produce conformity. Being mindful of social pressures and getting support from others with similar views are ways to resist conformity pressures.

- In Milgram's landmark study of obedience to authority, subjects showed a remarkable tendency to follow orders to shock an innocent stranger. Milgram's findings highlight the influence of situational pressures on behavior. Although people often obey authority figures, sometimes they are disobedient, usually because they have social support.

7.5 Application: Seeing through Compliance Tactics
- Although they work for different reasons, all compliance tactics have the same goal: getting people to agree to requests. The foot-in-the-door and the lowball technique are based on the fact that people prefer consistency in their behavior.
- The door-in-the-face technique and the tactic of offering "giveaway" items are manipulations of the principle of reciprocity, the rule that one should pay back in kind what one receives from others. When advertisers suggest that products are in short supply, they are taking advantage of the scarcity principle. Understanding these strategies can make you less vulnerable to manipulation.

Key Terms

Attitudes p. 205
Attributions p. 190
Bystander effect p. 212
Channel p. 206
Compliance p. 211
Confirmation bias p. 192
Conformity p. 209
Defensive attribution p. 197
Discrimination p. 198
Door-in-the-face technique p. 216
Elaboration likelihood model p. 208
Foot-in-the-door technique p. 215
Fundamental attribution error p. 195
Informational influence p. 211
Lowball technique p. 215
Message p. 206
Need for cognition p. 207
Normative influence p. 211
Obedience p. 212
Person perception p. 189
Persuasion p. 205
Prejudice p. 198
Primacy effect p. 197
Receiver p. 205
Reciprocity principle p. 216
Self-fulfilling prophecy p. 193
Source p. 205
Stereotypes p. 194

Key People

Solomon Asch pp. 210–211
Robert Cialdini p. 214
Susan Fiske p. 190
Stanley Milgram pp. 212–214
Richard Petty and John Cacioppo p. 208
Muzafer Sherif p. 202
Claude Steele pp. 203–204

CHAPTER 7   Practice Test

1. Inferences that people draw about the causes of events, their own behavior, and others' behavior are called
   a. snap judgments.
   b. self-fulfilling prophecies.
   c. attributions.
   d. attitudes.

2. Which of the following is *not* a potential source of cognitive distortion in perception?
   a. Categorizing
   b. The bystander effect
   c. Stereotypes
   d. Defensive attribution

3. Which of the following is *not* a theme in person perception?
   a. Efficiency
   b. Selectivity
   c. Consistency
   d. Mindfulness

4. Old-fashioned discrimination is _____; modern discrimination is _____.
   a. blatant; subtle
   b. legal; illegal
   c. common; rare
   d. race based; gender based

5. Which of the following is a cause of prejudice?
   a. Mindfulness
   b. Right-wing authoritarianism
   c. The fundamental attribution error
   d. Activities based on superordinate goals

6. Receivers who are forewarned that someone will try to persuade them will most likely
   a. be very open to persuasion.
   b. listen intently but openly argue with the speaker.
   c. be more resistant to persuasion.
   d. heckle the persuader.

7. Compared to attitudes formed via the peripheral route, those formed via the central route
   a. operate subliminally.
   b. are more enduring and harder to change.
   c. last only a short time.
   d. are poor predictors of behavior.

8. When people change their outward behavior but not their private beliefs, _____ is operating.
   a. conformity
   b. persuasion
   c. obedience
   d. compliance

9. The results of Milgram's (1963) study imply that
   a. situational factors can exert tremendous influence over behavior.
   b. in the real world, most people resist pressures to act in harmful ways.
   c. most people are willing to give obviously wrong answers on rigged perceptual tasks.
   d. disobedience is far more common than obedience.

10. When charities send prospective donors free address labels and the like, which of the following social influence principles are they manipulating?
    a. The consistency principle
    b. The scarcity principle
    c. The reciprocity principle
    d. The foot-in-the-door principle

Answers
1. c Pages 190–191
2. b Pages 193–197
3. d Pages 197–198
4. a Page 200
5. b Pages 200–204
6. c Page 208
7. b Pages 208–209
8. d Page 211
9. a Page 214
10. c Page 216

Personal Explorations Workbook

Go to the *Personal Explorations Workbook* in the back of your textbook for exercises that can enhance your self-understanding in relation to issues raised in this chapter.

Exercise 7.1 *Self-Assessment:* Argumentativeness Scale

Exercise 7.2 *Self-Reflection:* Can You Identify Your Prejudicial Stereotypes?

CHAPTER 8 Interpersonal Communication

Peter Bernik/Shutterstock.com

eronica is getting ready for the prom. Her date, Javier, is waiting downstairs. As she fixes her hair, checks her makeup, and smoothes the front of her new and costly dress, her 13-year-old sister, Amy, wanders into the room. As Veronica looks at her own reflection in a full-length mirror, she hears Amy snort, "*Nice* dress. Really *nice*." Amy's voice brims with the sort of sarcasm that is refined in middle-school hallways, but it is enough to shake Veronica's confidence. "What do you mean? What's wrong with this dress? It's beautiful—isn't it?" she says quickly, worry creeping into her voice. "*Oh, that* dress," grins Amy. "Why there's *not* a thing wrong with it, I am *so* sure Javier will just *love* it." While making that last statement, Amy rolls her eyes. A shouting match ensues. Veronica's mother intervenes, telling Veronica she "must have misunderstood—Amy would never make fun of such a nice dress."

Minutes later, her confidence still a bit rattled, Veronica descends the stairs, wondering if it is too late to put on something else—maybe the dress she wore to the junior-senior dance last year? Would anyone remember she wore it before?

Would Javier? A moment later, she hears Javier say, "Wow—that is a *really* nice dress. You look terrific, even amazing." Thoughts of changing dresses flee her mind as quickly as they arrived. She smiles at Javier and says, "Thanks, I think it's a nice dress, too." A memorable night begins.

Sometimes it's not so much what people say that matters but how they say it. The same word—like the word *nice*—can drip with sarcasm (as Amy demonstrated) or sincerity (as Javier showed us). Learning to manage interpersonal communication in daily life is an important way to deal with people and to interpret their intentions accurately.

Communication skills are highly relevant to adjustment because they can be critical to happiness and life success. In this chapter, we begin with an overview of the communication process and then turn to the important topic of nonverbal communication. Next, we discuss ways to communicate more effectively and examine common communication problems. Finally, we look at interpersonal conflict, including constructive ways to deal with it. In the Application, we consider ways to develop an assertive communication style. ■

8.1 The Process of Interpersonal Communication

Communication can be defined as the system and process of sending, receiving, and interpreting messages that have meaning (Wood, 2015). Your personal thoughts have meaning, of course, but when you "talk to yourself," you are engaging in *intra*personal communication. In this chapter, we will focus on *inter*personal communication—the transmission of meaning between two or more people (Smith & Wilson, 2010). For the most part, we'll concentrate on two-person interactions.

We define *interpersonal communication* as **an interactional process in which one person sends a message to another.** Note several points here. First, for communication to qualify as *interpersonal*, at least two people must be involved. Second, interpersonal communication is a *process* (Hargie, 2011). By this, we simply mean that it usually involves a series of actions: Kelli talks/Jason listens, Jason responds/Kelli listens, and so on. Third, this process is *interactional*. Effective communication is not a one-way street: Both participants send as well as receive information when they're interacting. Communicators also interpret and create messages by reflecting on their own experiences. People with similar backgrounds are apt to understand each other better (at least initially) than individuals with different frames of reference (Schramm, 1955). A key implication of these facts is that you need to pay attention to both *speaking* and *listening* if you want to be an effective communicator, just as you should learn to ask focused questions to clarify the meaning or intent of the communications you receive.

Components and Features of the Communication Process

Let's take a look at the essential components of the interpersonal communication process. The key elements (most of which were introduced in Chapter 7) are (1) the sender, (2) the receiver, (3) the message, (4) the channel through which the message is sent, (5) noise or interference, and (6) the context in which the message is communicated. As we describe these components, refer to **Figure 8.1** to see how they work together.

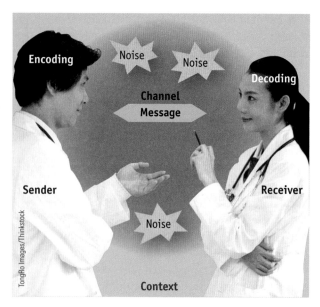

Figure 8.1

A model of interpersonal communication. Interpersonal communication involves six elements: the sender, the receiver, the message, the channel through which the message is transmitted, distorting noise, and the context in which the message is sent. In conversations, both participants function as sender and receiver.

The *sender* is the person who initiates the message. In a typical two-way conversation, both people serve as senders (as well as receivers). Keep in mind that each person brings a unique set of expectations and understandings to each communication situation. The *receiver* is the person to whom the message is sent.

The *message* refers to the information transmitted by the source. The message is the *content* of the communication—that is, the ideas and feelings conveyed. Two important cognitive processes underlie the transmission of messages: Speakers *encode* or transform their ideas and feelings into symbols and organize them into a message; receivers *decode* or translate a speaker's message into their own ideas and feelings (see **Figure 8.1**). Generally, fluent speakers of a language are unaware of these processes. If you've ever learned a new language, however, you have consciously experienced encoding (groping for the right word to express an idea) and decoding (trying to discover a word's meaning by how it is used).

The *channel* refers to the medium through which the message is sent. Typically, people receive information from multiple channels simultaneously. They not only hear what the other person says, they also see the person's facial expressions, observe his or her gestures, experience eye contact, and sometimes feel the person's touch. Note that the messages in the various channels may be consistent or inconsistent with each other, making their interpretation more or less difficult. Sometimes sound is the only channel available for receiving information—when you talk on the telephone, for instance. Through sound, people hear both the literal content of messages and vocal inflections. In digital communication (texts, tweets, email), only the visual channel is in play, as individuals communicate in writing (although some people add emoticons or emojis—digital icons representing facial expressions like happiness or upset to their messages).

Whenever two people interact, miscommunication can occur. *Noise* refers to any stimulus that interferes with accurately expressing or understanding a message. Noise sources include environmental factors (traffic, loud music, computer spam or pop-ups, crowds), physical factors (hearing limitations, poor vision), physiological factors (hunger, headaches), and psychological factors (worry, preoccupation) (Wood, 2010). Noise can also have semantic origins (Verderber, Verderber, & Berryman-Fink, 2008). For instance,

---

Recommended Reading

Clash! How to Thrive in a Multicultural World

by Hazel Rose Markus and Alana Connor (Plume, 2015)

As discussed in Chapter 6, we know that some cultures create selves that are independent (Western culture, including the United States), where focus is on the individual, while others nurture selves that are primarily interdependent or relational in nature (Eastern culture, including Japan). Markus and Connor explore how these two perspectives govern people's thoughts, feelings, and behaviors where gender, race, social class, regional cultures in the United States (i.e., Northern and Southern folkways), religion and faith, and the workplace are concerned.

This book offers readers insights and guidance for making their way in our increasingly small, global community. Cultural clashes and misunderstandings are commonplace as people travel from familiar settings to exotic places for work or vacation.

The authors offer suggestions for navigating these brave new worlds in order to understand and communicate effectively and sensitively with people from different cultures.

Who will benefit from reading this thoughtful and engaging book? Students, especially those who plan to study abroad, will learn a great deal of useful information from this book. Teachers who work with foreign exchange students can become equipped with knowledge that can prevent embarassing moments in the classroom or office. Businesspeople who travel frequently will certainly learn a great deal of helpful insights regarding cultural meaning and difference. Really, anyone who wants to sucessfully engage with our multicultural world will find much to think about in this well-written work.

profanity, ethnic slurs, or sexist language can cause a listener to disregard the larger message being sent. Similarly, effective communications can be disrupted by unavoidable events that can inadvertently send the wrong message (arriving late to an important meeting due to heavy traffic could convey unintended disinterest or disrespect) (Tazelaar, Van Lange, & Ouwerkerk, 2004). In addition, psychological factors such as defensiveness and anxiety can contribute to noise, as we'll see later in the chapter.

John Klossner / The New Yorker Collection / www.cartoonbank.com

All social communication occurs in and is influenced by a *context,* **the environment in which communication takes place.** Context includes the *physical environment*—such as location, time of day, and noise level—and how a conversation takes place: face-to-face, in a telephone call, or via the Internet. Other important aspects of context include the nature of the participants' *relationship* (work associates, friends, family), their *history* (previous interactions), their current *mood* (happy, stressed), and their *cultural backgrounds* (Verderber et al., 2008). In other words, *context* refers to how people are influenced by their situations. Culture is especially important in the United States because of the varieties of subcultures, many with different rules of communication. The Recommended Reading *Clash!* is an excellent guide to the cultural variety in communication practices around the world.

Most person-to-person communications are characterized by common features. For example, you are probably not interested in engaging in intimate or private exchanges with everyone you meet. Instead, you are *selective* in initiating or responding to communications. Communications between people are not isolated events; rather, they have a *systemic* quality because of time, situation, social class, education, culture, personal histories, and other influences that are beyond individuals' control but that nonetheless affect how they interact with each other. Communications within a given relationship (between you and a close friend) are also *unique,* possessing special patterns, vocabulary, even rhythms (Nicholson, 2006). When you become close to someone, you may establish particular roles and rules for how you interact with each other that are distinct from the roles or rules used in other relationships (Duck, 2006). For example, close friends often share private or "inside" jokes with each other that a bystander simply would not understand.

Technology and Interpersonal Communication

The explosion in electronic and wireless communication technology has revolutionized our notions of interpersonal communication. Today, communication via email, Skype, text or instant messaging, "tweets," Facebook, blogs and vlogs, chat rooms, and videoconferencing must be considered along with face-to-face interactions. *Electronically mediated communication* **is interpersonal communication that takes place via technology** (cell or smartphones, computers, and tablet or other handheld devices). Even a new slang ("netlingo") has developed to facilitate quick and easy communication for use in text messaging, email messages, and chat rooms (Ellis, 2006). **Figure 8.2** provides some popular examples of the slang that is often used when texting.

Smartphones have both advantages and disadvantages. On the positive side, they are convenient, provide a sense of security, and can summon aid in an emergency. Camera and video features on smartphones allow your friends and family to share your experiences even when they are hundreds or thousands of miles away. On the down side, however, they erode the barrier between private and public life. Some phone features automatically update your friends about your current location ("Karen Persa is at Taco Junction") as you go about your daily life. Cell phones also tie people to their jobs, can disrupt classrooms and public events, and bring private conversations into public places. Who hasn't been forced to listen to someone yelling his or her personal business into a cell phone in a public place? By now, most people are

EXAMPLES OF NETLINGO	
Acronymn	**Meaning**
B4N or BFN	Bye For Now
FUD	Fear, Uncertainty, and Disinformation
GTG	Got To Go
IDK	I Don't Know
LOL	Laughing Out Loud
LYLAS	Love You Like a Sister
PAL	Parents Are Listening
RUOK	Are You OK?
OT	Off Topic
WEG	Wicked Evil Grin
DGT	Don't Go There
SITD	Still in the Dark
LDR	Long Distance Relationship
SAPFU	Surpassing All Previous Foul Ups
XOXO	Hugs and Kisses

Figure 8.2

A sample of popular texting terms. A new type of slang has developed that allows quick and easy communication in text messages. Here you can see some frequently used text messaging acronyms and their meanings. Theses acronyms are variously termed *netlingo, techspeak,* or *e-talk.* Although netlingo is obviously useful for cybercommunication, its use in more formal settings (school, work) is problematic. (Information from NetLingo.com)

Cell phone etiquette in public places calls for turning off your phone or putting it on vibrate mode, keeping your voice low, and making your calls short.

familiar with the basic rules of etiquette for cell phone use in public: (1) turn off your phone (or put it on "vibrate" mode) when any ringing will disturb others, (2) keep calls short, and (3) make and receive calls unobtrusively, preferably out of earshot from others. Of course, many people now send texts instead of making calls, but the activity of typing away at your phone in a classroom setting or when spending time with a friend, for example, can still be rude and disruptive.

This chapter's Spotlight on Research deals with a now ubiquitous aspect of digital communication—sending photos to family and friends. An intriguing issue is whether these electronic images play a large role in creating and maintaining our social relationships with others.

Spotlight on RESEARCH

Communicating Social Relationships by Photo-Messaging

Source: Hunt, D. S., Lin, C. A., & Atkin, D. J. (2014). Communicating social relationships via the use of photo-messaging. *Journal of Broadcasting and Electronic Media, 58*(2), 234–252. doi:10.1080/08838151.2014.906430

Many people routinely send photos of themselves ("selfies"), images of what they are eating, whom they are with, or their location to others. Smartphones and tablet devices have made sharing photos with others easy to do on sites like Facebook, Flickr, and Instagram, among others. Most smartphone owners report taking and sending photos, just as more than half of all Internet users have posted photos to the Web. The ubiquity of this practice has encouraged researchers to wonder what the psychosocial purpose of such photo sharing and swapping might be. The article's authors believed that photo-messaging friends serves social and psychological purposes beyond simply keeping contacts apprised of one's activities. Instead, they hypothesized that photo-messaging is a means to

form personal relationships with others and to maintain established relationships within one's network. Specifically, the investigators explored two hypotheses. First, they expected that the level of photo-message activity to and from people's social networks would positively predict relationship formation motives. Second, they anticipated that the level of photo-messaging activity to and from people's social networks would predict relationship maintenance motives.

Method
Participant sample and procedure. Participants were undergraduate students from a university in the northeastern United States. An online survey yielded 682 valid responses. Participants were asked questions concerning photo-messaging activity present in their personal social networks; what

technologies (e.g., smartphone, tablet, laptop) they owned; and their relational motives, behavioral intentions, and the frequency of photo-messaging. Demographic data were also collected.

Measures. Social network activity was measured by asking respondents if their personal networks engage in photo-messaging, as measured using five items that were gauged on a 7-point scale (ranging from strongly disagree to strongly agree) such as "Most of my friends send photo-messages" and "None of my friends or family send photo-messages." Relationship formation motives were assessed by items such as "I send photo-messages to develop new relationships" and "I send photo-messages as a way of bonding with new friends." Relationship maintenance motives were discerned by five items such as "I send photo-messages to keep up with my friends or family" and "I send photo-messages as a way of communicating with my friends or family."

Results

To analyze the results, the researchers used advanced data analysis techniques, including factor analysis and structural equation modeling. We will focus on the general descriptive findings here. Social network activity based on photo-messaging was found to significantly predict relationship formation motives. People who received photo-messages from others were motivated to form relationships with them. Social network activity performed by respondents who engaged in photo-messaging was also found to significantly predict relationship maintenance motives; people sent images to friends and relatives as a means to maintain existing social ties.

Discussion

Relational maintenance motives were strong predictors of behavioral intentions to engage in photo-messaging. Although relationship formation motives did not influence the intention to send and share photo-messages, they did influence maintenance motives. These findings suggest that although people use socially mediated communication such as Facebook and Instagram to form and develop new relationships, maintaining relationships remains a prominent motive for the use of these sites, as well. The results imply an important role for relationship maintenance as a key motivation for photo-messaging and online photo-sharing. In effect, people adopt new technologies and develop skills using them in order to stay connected with people in their social networks. It's not just about fun or letting people know what we are up to—it's about establishing or keeping close connections with others.

Critical Thinking Questions

1. How often do you send or share photos with your friends and family? Did you ever attribute a motive, such as the desire to form or to maintain a relationship, to this practice?
2. Do you think the type of photo-messages people share can affect relationship formation or maintenance? How so? Think of some examples.
3. How do you react to the photo-messages you receive? Have you ever presumed that the senders had another purpose besides keeping you updated on their lives?

As we have noted, face-to-face communication relies on the spoken word, while Internet communication largely depends on the written word. You can see other important differences in **Figure 8.3**. The absence of nonverbal cues in computer-mediated communication also means that you need to take special care that the other person understands your intended meaning. Thus, you should choose your words carefully, provide clarifying details, and describe your feelings, if necessary. It's also a good idea to review what you have written before you send it!

Social Networking Sites: Privacy and Security Issues

Do you participate in any social networking site (SNS), such as Facebook, Twitter, LinkedIn, or Instagram? If you are a typical college student or a young adult, there is a good chance you have posted a profile of yourself on one of these popular Internet destinations. The primary benefit of any SNS is presenting yourself virtually to other people who may already know you, remember you from a shared past (high school, for example), or want to connect with you ("friend you," in Internet parlance) because of some common interest. Most online profiles contain all kinds of personal or private information—everything from your favorite books, movies, or food to your political, social, and even religious beliefs. In effect, an SNS allows you to express yourself and your personality. Another reason that social networking sites are popular is because they are believed to provide a form of social support to some individuals who may need it due to life experiences or personal challenges. Such sites often provide emotional or informational support. Yet there is still relatively little evidence that such sites actually lead to decreased use of health services or to any reduction in negative outcomes (Mehta & Atreja, 2015).

Is there any drawback to taking part in an SNS? There can be if you do not take appropriate steps to maintain your online privacy. Why should privacy be a concern? Simply put,

ASSERTIVE RESPONSES TO SOME COMMON PUTDOWNS		
Dimension	**Face-to-face**	**Internet**
Physical distance	People need to be in the same place at the same time to meet.	People can meet and develop a relationship with someone thousands of miles away.
Anonymity	One can't be anonymous in real-life interactions.	People take greater risks in disclosing personal information than they otherwise do. Thus, feelings of intimacy can develop more quickly.
Richness of communication	People have access to nonverbal cues such as facial expressions and tone of voice to detect nuances in meaning or deception.	In cyberspace, these cues are absent, making social and status cues, such as gender, age, social class, race, and ethnicity less discernible.
Visual cues	Physical appearance and visual cues play a big role in attraction in face-to-face relationships.	These cues are generally absent on the Internet (although people can exchange photographs online).
Time	Two people have to connect at the same time.	Although instant messaging and chat room conversations take place in real time, there is no need for an immediate response, so time becomes relatively unimportant. On the Internet, you can take as long as you like to craft a response so you can more completely explain yourself.

Figure 8.3

Differences between face-to-face and electronically mediated communication. Electronically mediated communication applications (cell phone text messaging, email, chat rooms, news groups, and so forth) have dramatically changed the ways people interact and develop relationships. These two types of communication differ from each other in five important ways. (Adapted from Bargh & McKenna, 2004; Boase & Wellman, 2006; Verderber & Verderber, 2004)

you never know who is reading your profile or what they are doing with the information you have shared (Lewis, Kaufman, & Christakis, 2008). Surely, you are already aware that you should be careful what financial information (such as PIN numbers) you share online and that interfacing with a website is never a good idea unless you know it is secure (LaRose & Rifon, 2007). But what about the information you post on your SNS? Should you worry about that?

Possibly yes. Consider that Facebook has more than 1.6 billion active users, yet users assume others, not they themselves, are at risk when it comes to posting private information (Debatin et al., 2009). To presume all those users are well intentioned seems somewhat foolhardy. There is also ample evidence that the content of student postings has been used to raid student parties (Hass, 2006) and to keep individuals from getting jobs (Finder, 2006). In short, private information is not always so private. Think for a moment: Is your SNS profile set so that it cannot be read, accessed, or searched by nonfriends (strangers)? Or can anyone see your personal pages?

One reason people fail to use available privacy protections is because they assume their own online privacy is fine but that of others is likely to be at risk (Baek, Kim, & Bae, 2014). When individual users compare themselves to younger persons, for example, they tend to display this comparative optimistic bias ("I'm not at risk where my privacy is concerned, but you probably are"). Privacy concerns can also be disrupted when people believe their online anonymity is more assured than it may actually be or when they feel that social rewards (e.g., new online friendships) are available (Jiang, Heng, & Choi, 2013).

Communication and Adjustment

Before we plunge further into the topic of interpersonal communication, let's take a moment to emphasize its significance. Communication with others—friends, lovers, parents, spouses, children, employers, workers—is such an essential and commonplace aspect of everyday life that it's hard to overstate its role in adjustment. Many of life's gratifications (and frustrations and heartaches) hinge on one's ability to communicate effectively with others. Numerous studies have shown that good communication can enhance satisfaction in relationships (Vangelisti, 2015) and that poor communication ranks high as a cause of breakups among both straight and gay couples (Angulo, Brooks, & Swann, 2011). Our language—the words we use to convey what we say—also matters in our interpersonal relationships (Duck & Usera, 2014). What about the messages we convey without words?

8.2 Nonverbal Communication

Learning Objectives

- List five general principles of nonverbal communication.
- Discuss the dynamics of personal space and what can be discerned from facial cues and eye contact.
- Summarize the research findings on body movement, posture, gestures, touch, and paralanguage in communication.
- Understand the difficulty in detecting deception and clarify the nonverbal cues linked to deception.

You're standing at the bar in your favorite hangout, gazing across a dimly lit room filled with people drinking, dancing, and talking. You signal to the bartender that you'd like another drink. Your companion comments on the loud music, and you nod your head in agreement. You spot an attractive stranger across the bar; your eyes meet briefly and you smile. In a matter of seconds, you sent three messages without uttering a syllable. To put it another way, you just sent three *nonverbal* messages. **Nonverbal communication is the transmission of meaning from one person to another through means or symbols other than words.** Communication at the nonverbal level occurs through various behaviors: interpersonal distance, facial expression, eye contact, body posture and movement, gestures, physical touch, and tone of voice (e.g., Knapp, Hall, & Horgan, 2014).

Clearly, considerable information is exchanged through nonverbal channels—more than most people realize. You can significantly enhance your communication skills by learning more about this important aspect of communication.

General Principles

Let's begin by examining some general principles of nonverbal communication.

1. *Nonverbal communication conveys emotions.* People can communicate their feelings without saying a word—for example, "a look that kills." Nonverbal demonstrations of positive feelings include sitting or standing close to those you care for, touching them often, and looking at them frequently (Buck & Miller, 2015). Negative emotions, such as fear, can be conveyed through facial expressions (Kostić & Chadee, 2015). Still, nonverbal signals alone are not the precise indicators of emotional states that they were once believed to be (App et al., 2011), so you should be cautious in making inferences.

2. *Nonverbal communication is multichanneled.* Nonverbal communication typically involves simultaneous messages sent through several channels. For instance, information may be transmitted through gestures, facial expressions, eye contact, and vocal tone at the same time. In contrast, verbal communication is limited to one channel: speech. If you have ever tried to follow two people speaking at once, you understand how difficult it is to process multiple inputs of information. Thus, many nonverbal transmissions can sail by the receiver unnoticed.

3. *Nonverbal communication is ambiguous.* A shrug or a raised eyebrow can mean different things to different people. Moreover, receivers may have difficulty determining whether nonverbal messages are being sent intentionally. Although some popular books on body language imply otherwise, few nonverbal signals carry universally accepted meanings, even within the same culture. Thus, nonverbal cues are informative, but they are most reliable when accompanied by verbal messages and embedded in a familiar cultural and social context (Samovar, Porter, & McDaniel, 2007).

4. *Nonverbal communication may contradict verbal messages.* How often have you seen people proclaim "I'm not angry" even though their bodies shout that they are positively furious? When confronted with such an inconsistency, which message should you believe? Because of their greater spontaneity, you're probably better off heeding the nonverbal signs. Research shows that when someone is instructed to tell a lie, deception is most readily detected through nonverbal signals (Vrij, 2015). Some recent research finds that saccadic eye movements—those extremely rapid movements we all make when we fixate on something in our visual field—can indicate when someone is lying (Virj et al., 2015). The trick is to observe their saccadic eye movements when they are *not*

In Tibet, friends greet their friends by sticking out their tongue.

looking at any particular thing, as this behavior indicates retrieval of information from memory. Deception is associated with more rather than less memory searching, so the presence of fewer saccadic eye movements suggests someone is telling the truth.

5. *Nonverbal communication is culture-bound.* Like language, nonverbal signals are different in different cultures (Weisbuch & Amady, 2008). Culture influences how people notice, retain, and decode nonverbal behaviors (Mandal & Awasthi, 2015; Matsumoto & Hwang, 2013a, 2013b). Sometimes cultural differences can be quite dramatic. For example, in Tibet people greet their friends by sticking out their tongues (Ekman, 1975).

Elements of Nonverbal Communication

Nonverbal signals can provide a great deal of information in interpersonal interactions. As we discuss specific nonverbal behaviors, we will focus on what they communicate about interpersonal attraction and social status.

Personal Space

Proxemics **is the study of people's use of interpersonal space.** *Personal space* **is a zone of space surrounding a person that is felt to "belong" to that person.** Personal space is an invisible bubble or barrier you carry around with you in your social interactions (Andersen, Gannon, & Kalchik, 2013). The size of this mobile zone is related to your cultural background, social status, personality, age, and gender.

Distance in relationships is psychological as well as physical. The amount of interpersonal distance people prefer depends on the nature of the relationship and the situation (E. T. Hall, 2008). The appropriate distance between people is also regulated by social norms and varies by culture (Hall & Whyte, 2008). Culture influences people's spatial behavior (Høgh-Olesen, 2008). For instance, people of northern European heritage tend to engage in less physical contact and keep a greater distance between themselves than people of Latin or Middle Eastern heritage. The United States is usually characterized as a medium-contact culture, but there is a lot of variability among ethnic groups. Situations matter, too: Consider how much distance from others people desire when they are using an ATM. Those waiting behind you in line know that you want your privacy in order to preserve the personal information you enter into the machine during a transaction (Li & Li, 2007). They, in turn, expect the same courtesy. Similarly, when strangers expect to interact with one another directly in a group setting, they are likely to move their seats closer to one another (Novelli, Drury, & Reicher, 2010). When no expectation of direct interaction exists, people automatically retain greater personal space between one another.

Anthropologist Edward T. Hall (1966) described four interpersonal distance zones that are appropriate for middle-class encounters in American culture, as shown in **Figure 8.4**. The general rule is that the more you like someone, the more comfortable you feel being physically close to that person. Women have smaller personal-space zones than men do (Holland et al., 2004). When talking, women sit or stand closer together than men do. Of course, there are obvious exceptions, such as in crowded subways and elevators, but these situations are often experienced as stressful. For example, one study examined train commuters' experiences during rush hour (Evans & Wener, 2007). Interestingly, density (crowding) within the train car had little impact on commuters' stress, but stress associated with seating density (the proximity of other passengers) was quite high, as indicated by self-reports, physiological measures, and behavioral measures of feeling "closed in."

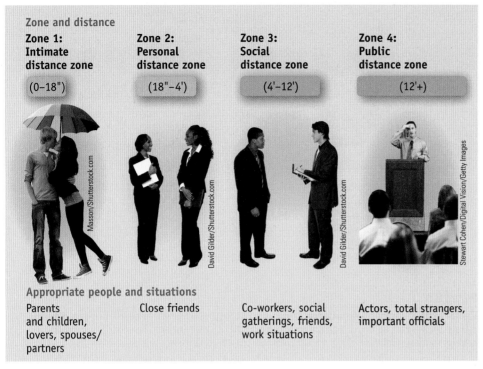

Zone and distance

Zone 1: Intimate distance zone	Zone 2: Personal distance zone	Zone 3: Social distance zone	Zone 4: Public distance zone
(0–18")	(18"–4')	(4'–12')	(12'+)

Appropriate people and situations

| Parents and children, lovers, spouses/ partners | Close friends | Co-workers, social gatherings, friends, work situations | Actors, total strangers, important officials |

Figure 8.4

Interpersonal distance zones. According to Edward Hall (1966), people like to keep a certain amount of distance between themselves and others. The distance that makes one feel comfortable depends on whom one is interacting with and the nature of the situation.

Imagine the long-term impact of such personal space distress on people who commute twice a day for 5 or more days per week.

On the other hand, the context where contact occurs may matter a great deal. Another study found that closer—not farther—interpersonal distance between waitresses and customers had an impact on the latter's tipping behavior (Jacob & Guéguen, 2012). Standing closer to restaurant patrons increased both the frequency and amount of tips waitresses received.

Personal distance can also convey status information. People generally stand farther away from high-status communication partners versus partners of lower power (Holland et al., 2004). Moreover, it is the prerogative of the more powerful person in an interaction to set the "proper" distance (Henley, 1986).

Facial Expression

More than anything else, *facial expressions* convey emotions (Awasthi & Mandal, 2015). Paul Ekman and Wallace Friesen identified six distinctive facial expressions that correspond with six basic emotions: anger, disgust, fear, happiness, sadness, and surprise (Ekman, 1994). Early research involving participants from many countries supported the idea that these six emotions are universally recognized (Ekman, 1972). In such studies, researchers showed photographs depicting different emotions to participants from a variety of Western and non-Western cultures, asking them to match the photographs with an emotion (Ekman & Matsumoto, 2011). Some representative results from this research are depicted in **Figure 8.5**.

One meta-analysis of ninety-seven studies (based on studies in more than forty countries) looked at whether these six emotions are universally recognized or are culturally specific (Elfenbein & Ambady, 2002). Interestingly, there was evidence for both perspectives. In support of the universal view, individuals do accurately recognize emotions in photographs of people from other cultures. Favoring cultural specificity, there was evidence of an "ingroup advantage." Thus, observers are better at recognizing the emotions in photographs from their own cultural groups than those from other cultural groups. A few basic

Emotion displayed

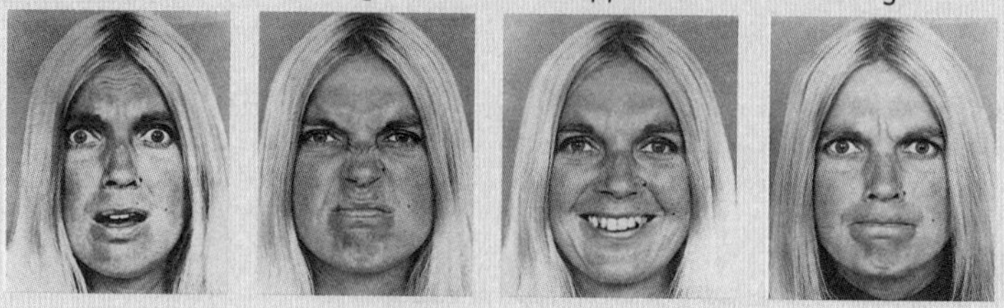

Country	Fear	Disgust	Happiness	Anger
	Agreement in judging photos (%)			
United States	85	92	97	67
Brazil	67	97	95	90
Chile	68	92	95	94
Argentina	54	92	98	90
Japan	66	90	100	90
New Guinea	54	44	82	50

Paul Ekman, Ph.D./ Paul Ekman Group, LLC

Figure 8.5

Facial expressions and emotions. Ekman and Friesen (1984) found that people in highly disparate cultures showed fair agreement on the emotions portrayed in these photos. This consensus across cultures suggests that the facial expressions associated with certain emotions may have a biological basis.

Source: Photos from *Unmasking the Face,* Copyright © 1975 by Paul Ekman, photographs courtesy of Paul Ekman.

facial expressions are universally recognizable, but other emotional expressions vary from culture to culture—as we noted in the earlier example of Tibetans sticking out their tongues to greet friends.

Recent research suggests that the recognition of facial expressions of emotion is based on the frequency with which they occur in daily life (Calvo et al., 2014). Thus, happy and surprised faces were observed the most frequently, and disgusted and fearful faces the least. An implication of this research is that people are more efficient at processing facial emotion based on the relative familiarity of the expression. Perhaps that is one reason that we can readily tell when someone is happy but have to ask questions when confronted with a fearful expression ("Is everything OK?").

Interestingly, other research suggests that there may also be a seventh distinct facial expression for anxiety that occurs in ambiguous situations where perceived threats (e.g., feelings of being watched or followed) are unclear. Anxiety is marked by darting of the eyes and head swivels. As an emotion, anxiety is often confused with fear, a reaction that occurs when perceived threats are more apparent (e.g., confronting a snarling dog) (Perkins et al., 2012).

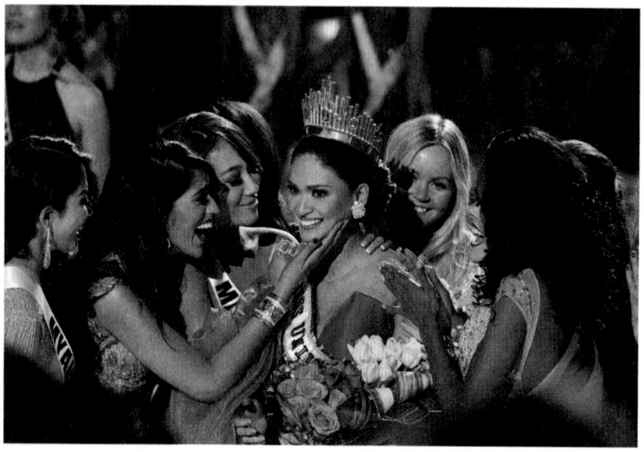

VALERIE MACON/AFP/Getty Images

Display rules require unsuccessful contestants in beauty pageants to suppress the display of resentful, envious, or angry feelings.

Each society has rules that govern whether and when it is appropriate to express feelings (Koopmann-Holm & Matsumoto, 2011). ***Display rules*** **are norms that govern the appropriate display of emotions in a culture.** In the United States, for instance, it is considered bad form to gloat over one's victories or to show envy or anger in defeat. Generally speaking, people also show less emotion in the workplace than when they are outside of work, but this observation is also qualified by culture (Moran, Diefendorff, & Greguras, 2013). In Singapore, for example, display rules dictate less public expression of anger, sadness, and fear as compared with the United States, where sharing those emotions outside the workplace would be deemed acceptable.

Eye Contact

Eye contact (or mutual gaze) is another major channel of nonverbal communication. The duration of eye contact is its most meaningful aspect. The ability to use eye contact as a means to gauge the mental and emotional states of others appears in humans older than 6 years of age (Vida & Maurer, 2012). Among European Americans, people who engage in high levels of eye contact are usually judged to have effective social skills and credibility. Similarly, speakers, interviewers, and experimenters receive higher ratings of competence when they maintain high rather than low eye contact with their audience. As a rule, people engage in more eye contact when they're listening than when they're talking (Bavelas, Coates, & Johnson, 2002). People display an interesting self-serving bias regarding eye contact: They assume attractive people are more likely to make eye contact with them than persons deemed less attractive (Kloth, Altmann, & Schweinberger, 2011). Liars are found to make greater eye contact with those they are trying to dupe, presumably because they believe deliberately engaging in mutual gaze conveys the message that they are telling the truth (Mann et al., 2013).

Gaze also communicates the *intensity* (but not the positivity or negativity) of feelings. For example, couples who say they are in love spend more time gazing at each other than other couples do (Patterson, 1988). Also, maintaining moderate (versus constant or no) eye contact with others typically generates positive feelings in them. When women make eye contact with men, a longer gaze can generate the latter's interest, sustaining it when smiling is part of the interaction (Guéguen et al., 2008).

In a negative interpersonal context, a steady gaze becomes a stare that causes most people to feel uncomfortable (Kleinke, 1986). Moreover, like threat displays among nonhuman primates such as baboons and rhesus monkeys, a stare can convey aggressive intent (Henley, 1986). So, if you want to avoid road rage incidents, avoid making eye contact with hostile motorists. People also communicate by *reducing* eye contact with others. Unpleasant interactions, embarrassing situations, or invasions of personal space usually trigger this behavior (Kleinke, 1986). Indeed, in the absence of verbal or contextual information, such looking away can communicate fear; in effect, people sometimes "point" to danger with their eyes (Hadjikhani et al., 2008).

Culture strongly affects patterns of eye contact (Samovar et al., 2007). For example, Americans should be sensitive to the fact that direct eye contact is perceived as an insult in Mexico, Latin America, Japan, and Africa, and in some Native American tribes. By contrast, people from Arab countries look directly into the eyes of their conversational partners for longer periods than Americans are used to.

In the United States, gender and racial differences have been found in eye contact. For instance, women tend to gaze at others more than men do (Briton & Hall, 1995). However, the patterning of eye contact also reflects status, and gender and status are often confounded. Higher-status individuals look at the other person more when speaking than when listening, while lower-status people behave just the opposite. Women usually show the lower-status visual pattern because they are typically accorded lower status than men. As shown in **Figure 8.6**, when women are in high-power positions, they show the high-status visual pattern to the same extent that men do (Dovidio et al., 1988). African Americans use more continuous eye contact than European Americans when speaking, but less when listening (Samovar & Porter, 2004). Misunderstandings can arise if gaze behaviors that are intended to convey interest and respect are interpreted as being disrespectful or dishonest.

Body Language

Body movements—those of the head, trunk, hands, legs, and feet—also provide nonverbal avenues of communication (Sinke, Kret, & de Gelder, 2012). *Kinesics* **is the study of communication through body movements.** By noting a person's body movements, observers may be able to tell an individual's level of tension or relaxation, or whether a

Coupled with facial expression, our body language can convey a variety of messages, including dissatisfaction, as shown here.

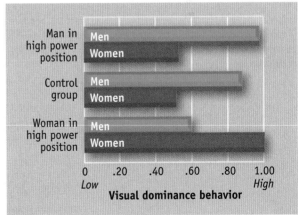

Figure 8.6

Visual dominance, status, and gender. Women typically show low visual dominance (see control condition) because they are usually accorded lower status than men (Dovidio et al. 1988). However, when researchers placed women in a high-power position and measured their visual behavior, women showed the high visual dominance pattern and men showed the low visual dominance pattern. When men were placed in the high-power position, the visual dominance patterns reversed. Thus, visual dominance seems to be more a function of status than of gender.

"O.K., big cheer here, but nothing that might be construed as pressure. Quiet now, but a supportive quiet. Watch your body language"

The potential force of body language can be seen in these photos showing Lyndon Baines Johnson, who was the U.S. Senate majority leader at the time (1957), working over a fellow senator (Theodore Green). The status difference between Johnson and his colleague is obvious, and they way Johnson leans into Green is a clear attempt at intimidation.

person's expressed remorse is sincere and genuine or merely fabricated "crocodile tears" (ten Brinke et al., 2012). For instance, frequent touching or scratching suggests nervousness (Harrigan et al., 1991).

Posture, too, conveys information. Leaning back with arms or legs arranged in an asymmetrical or "open" position conveys a feeling of relaxation. Posture can also indicate someone's attitude toward you (McKay, Davis, & Fanning, 1995); indeed, we interpret both action and emotion from people's posture (Kana & Travers, 2012). A body leaning toward you typically indicates interest and a positive attitude. Conversely, a body angled away from you or a position with crossed arms may indicate a negative attitude or defensiveness. People can even judge the emotion shared by a crowd of people based on their body language and posture, even when the perceiver's exposure to the crowd's behavior is brief (McHugh et al., 2010).

Posture can also convey status differences. Generally, a higher-status person will look more relaxed. By contrast, a lower-status person will tend to exhibit a more rigid body posture, often sitting up straight with feet together, flat on the floor, and arms close to the body (a "closed" position) (Vrugt & Luyerink, 2000). Again, status and gender differences are frequently parallel. That is, men are more likely to exhibit the high-status "open" posture and women the lower-status "closed" posture (Cashdan, 1998).

Our hands also help us think and communicate (Goldin-Meadow, 2003). People use *hand gestures* to describe and emphasize the words they speak, as well as to persuade (Maricchiolo et al., 2009). You might point to give directions or slam your fist on a desk to emphasize an assertion. To convey "no," you can extend the index finger of your dominant hand and wave it back and forth from left to right. Children know that when adults slide their right index finger up and down their left index finger, it means "shame on you." As travelers frequently discover, the meaning of gestures is not universal (Samovar et al., 2007). For instance, a circle made with the thumb and forefinger means that everything is "OK" to an American, but it is considered an obscene gesture in some countries.

Touch

Touch takes many forms and can express various meanings (Hertenstein, 2011), including support, consolation, and sexual intimacy. Touch can also convey messages of status and power (Hall, 2006a), just as it sometimes can be helpful and therapeutic (Field, 2014) or used to help us recall information or recognize objects (Klatzky & Lederman, 2013). In the United States, people typically "touch downward"—i.e., higher-status individuals are freer to touch subordinates than vice versa (Henley & Freeman, 1995). Higher-status people who touch others while making requests ("I'm conducting a survey—will you answer some questions for me?") actually increase compliance rates (Guéguen, 2002). How people interpret the possible messages communicated by touch depends on the age and gender of the individuals involved, the setting where the touching takes place, and the relationship between the toucher and recipient, among other things (Major, Schmidlin, & Williams, 1990).

For example, consider the impact of being touched while you are out shopping. Consumers who are accidentally touched by a stranger (a confederate of the researcher) while shopping end up rating products more negatively, and then spend less time in stores compared to their untouched counterparts (Martin, 2012). There are also gender differences related to status and touch: Adult women use touch to convey closeness or intimacy, whereas men use touch as a means to control or indicate their power in social situations (Hall, 2006a). Finally, there are strong norms about *where* on the body people are allowed to touch their friends.

These norms are quite different for same-gender as opposed to cross-gender interactions, as can be seen in **Figure 8.7**.

Paralanguage

The term *paralanguage* refers to *how* something is said rather than to *what* is said. Thus, *paralanguage* **includes all vocal cues other than the content of the verbal message itself.** Cues to paralanguage include grunts, sighs, murmurs, gasps, and other vocal sounds. Paralanguage also entails how loudly or softly people speak, how fast they talk, and the pitch, rhythm, and quality (such as accent, pronunciation, sentence complexity) of their speech. Each vocal characteristic can affect the message being transmitted.

Variations in vocal emphasis can give the same set of words very different meanings. Consider the sentence "I really enjoyed myself." By varying the word that is accented, you can speak this sentence in three ways, each suggesting a different meaning:

- *I* really enjoyed myself! (Even though others may not have had a good time, I did.)
- I *really* enjoyed myself! (My enjoyment was exceptional.)
- I really *enjoyed* myself! (Much to my surprise, I had a great time.)

As shown in these examples, you can actually reverse the meaning of a verbal message by how you say it (using sarcasm). The vignette opening this chapter also illustrates how paralanguage can change the meaning of words.

In cyberspace communication, emailers use various substitutes for the paralanguage cues found in spoken communication. For instance, capital letters are used for emphasis ("I had a GREAT vacation"); however, using capital letters throughout a message is viewed as shouting and considered rude behavior. Using *emoticons* (punctuation marks arranged to indicate the writer's emotions) has also become a common practice; thus, :-) indicates a smile and :-(indicates a frown. Emoticons are rapidly being replaced by *emojis*, which are small digital images or icons used to express an idea or an emotion in an electronic communication. The word *emoji* means "picture letter" in Japanese. No doubt you have received a message from someone punctuated with a smiley face icon or perhaps a wink or frown icon—these are all emojis. If you have any type of smartphone, chances are good that you also have a large selection of emojis to use in your text messages. Examples of emojis are shown in **Figure 8.8**.

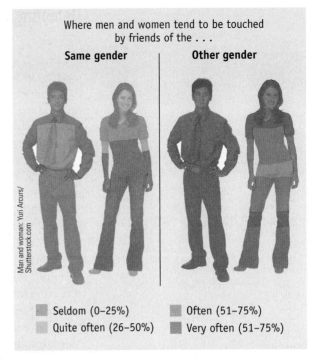

Where men and women tend to be touched by friends of the . . .

Same gender | Other gender

- Seldom (0–25%)
- Quite often (26–50%)
- Often (51–75%)
- Very often (51–75%)

Figure 8.7

Where friends touch each other. Social norms govern where friends tend to touch each other. As these figures show, the patterns of touching are different in same-gender as opposed to cross-gender interactions.

Source: Adapted from Marsh, P. (Ed.). (1988). *Eye to eye: How people interact.* Topsfield, MA: Salem House. Copyright © 1988 by Andromeda Oxford Ltd. Reprinted by permission of HarperCollins, Publishers, Inc. and Andromeda Oxford Ltd.

Figure 8.8

Conveying emotion in cyberspace by using emojis. People sometimes complain that online communication, chiefly email or text messaging, does not allow recipients to read senders' emotional states. Emojis are small digital images or icons used to express an idea or an emotion in an electronic communication. The word *emoji* means "picture letter" in Japanese. People often punctuate their messages with emojis in order to express how they are feeling.

Source: Wikipedia entry "Emoji" with "OS X mini character palette showing Emoji emoticons" by Source (WP:NFCC#4). Licensed under Fair use via Wikipedia, https://en.wikipedia.org/wiki/File:OS_X_mini_character_palette_showing_Emoji_emoticons.png#/media/File:OS_X_mini_character_palette_showing_Emoji_emoticons.png on September 1, 2015.

Detecting Deception

Like it or not, lying is a part of everyday life (DePaulo, 2004). People typically tell one to two lies a day (DePaulo et al., 1997). Most everyday lies are inconsequential "white lies," such as claiming to be better than one actually is or lying to avoid hurting someone's feelings ("Say, I like your new haircut—really, I do"). Of course, people tell more serious lies, too. When they do, such lies are used to gain some advantage—that is, to get what they want or to obtain something they feel entitled to, such as gaining credit for an idea (DePaulo et al., 2004). People tell serious lies, too, when they want to avoid conflict or to protect or even harm other people.

Is it possible to catch people in a lie? Yes, but it's difficult—even for experts (Granhag, Vrij, & Verschuere, 2015). As shown in **Figure 8.9**, some studies have found that professionals whose work involves detecting lies (police officers, FBI agents, psychiatrists) are slightly more accurate judges of liars than nonexperts are (Ekman, O'Sullivan, & Frank, 1999). Still, even these individuals have accuracy rates around 57%—not much better than chance (50%), which means their "edge" is only slight. However, motivation may matter. One recent study that used real-life, high-stakes lies and stimulus materials found that a sample of police officers achieved 72% accuracy as compared to 68% accuracy for nonpolice observers (Whelan, Wagstaff, & Wheatcroft, 2015.) Even married people cannot necessarily tell when their spouse is lying unless the marital bond has been disrupted and suspicion is running high (McCormack & Levine, 1990). Moreover, meta-analyses find no significant differences in the accuracy rates of experts and nonexperts (Ekman, 2009), yet people routinely overestimate their ability to detect liars (DePaulo et al., 1997).

The popular stereotypes about how liars give themselves away don't necessarily correspond to the actual clues related to dishonesty. For example, observers tend to focus on the face (the least-revealing channel), ignoring more useful information (Burgoon, 1994). In **Figure 8.10**, you can review the research findings on the nonverbal behaviors actually associated with deception (based on DePaulo, Stone, & Lassiter, 1985). By comparing the second and third columns in the figure, you can see which cues are actually associated with deception and which are erroneously linked with it. Contrary to popular belief, lying is *not* associated with slow talking, long pauses before speaking, excessive shifting of posture, reduced smiling, or lack of eye contact. A meta-analysis of more than 300 studies generally supported these findings, concluding that liars say less, tell less-compelling stories, make a more negative impression, are more tense, and include less unusual content in their stories than truth tellers do (DePaulo et al., 2003).

So, how *do* liars give themselves away? As you may have noted in **Figure 8.10**, many clues "leak" from nonverbal channels because speakers have a harder time controlling these channels (DePaulo & Friedman, 1998). For example, liars may blink less than usual while telling a lie because of cognitive demand (Leal & Vrij, 2008). Eye blinks then accelerate once the lie is told. Vocal cues include speaking with a higher pitch, giving relatively short answers, and excessive hesitations. Visual cues include dilation of the pupils and the aforementioned rapid saccadic eye movements. It's also helpful to look for inconsistencies between facial expressions and lower body movements. For example, a friendly smile accompanied by a nervous shuffling of feet could signal deception. People can also deplete their self-presentational resources over time—they tire of creating and conveying the same impression over and over—thereby rousing observers' suspicions that they are being deceptive (Vohs, Baumeister, & Ciarocco, 2005).

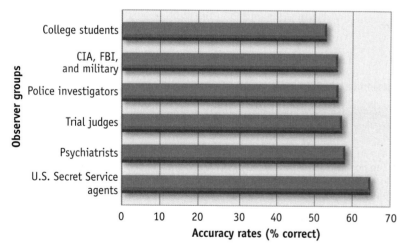

Figure 8.9

How well do experts distinguish truth and deception? Lie-detection experts with experience making judgments of truth and deception were shown brief videotapes of ten women telling the truth or lying about their feelings (Ekman & O'Sullivan, 1991). Considering that there was a 50-50 chance of guessing correctly, the accuracy rates were remarkably low. Only a sample of U.S. Secret Service agents posted better-than-chance performance. (Adapted from Kassin, Fein, & Markus, 2011)

NONVERBAL CUES AND DECEPTIONS

Kind of cue	Are cues associated with actual deception?	Are cues believed to be a sign of deception?
Vocal cues		
Speech hesitations	YES: Liars hesitate more	YES
Voice pitch	YES: Liars speak with higher pitch	YES
Speech errors (stutters, stammers)	YES: Liars make more errors	YES
Speech latency (pause before starting to speak or answer)	NO	YES: People think liars pause more
Speech rate	NO	YES: People think liars talk slower
Response length	YES: Liars give shorter answers	NO
Visual cues		
Pupil dilation	YES: Liars show more dilation	(No research data)
Adapters (self-directed gestures)	YES: Liars touch themselves more	NO
Blinking	YES: Liars blink less	(No research data)
Postural shifts	NO	YES: People think liars shift more
Smile	NO	YES: People think liars smile less
Gaze (eye contact)	NO	YES: People think liars engage in less eye contact

Figure 8.10

Detecting deception from nonverbal behaviors. This chart summarizes evidence on which nonverbal cues are *actually* associated with deception and which are *believed* to be a sign of deception, based on a research review by DePaulo, Stone, and Lassiter (1985).

Bella DePaulo (1994), a noted researcher in this area, isn't too optimistic about the prospects of teaching people to spot lies because the cues are usually subtle. If she's correct, perhaps *machines* can do better. **The *polygraph* is a device that records fluctuations in physiological arousal as a person answers questions.** Although called a "lie detector," it's really an emotion detector (Meijer & Verschuere, 2015). The polygraph monitors key indicators of autonomic arousal such as heart rate, blood pressure, respiration rate, and perspiration, or galvanic skin response (GSR). The assumption is that when people lie, they experience emotion that produces noticeable changes in these physiological indicators.

Polygraph experts claim that lie detector tests are 85%–90% accurate and that there is empirical support for the validity of polygraph testing (Honts, Raskin, & Kircher, 2002). These claims are clearly not supported by the evidence. Methodologically sound research is surprisingly sparse (largely because the research is difficult to do), and the limited evidence available is not very impressive (Iacono, 2009). One problem is that when people respond to incriminating questions, they may experience emotional arousal even when they are telling the truth. Thus, polygraph tests often lead to accusations against the innocent. Another problem is that some people can lie without experiencing physiological arousal. Thus, because of high error rates, polygraph results are not admitted as evidence in most courtrooms (Iacono, 2008).

One promising method is the use of brain-imaging procedures for detecting lies (Bell & Grubin, 2010; Choi, 2015), which may represent a new and promising direction for detecting deception in law enforcement settings (Gamer, 2014). Such tools enable researchers to create computer images of brain structures and to assess changes, such as blood flow, during thought tasks. Some preliminary evidence is that, under highly controlled conditions, brain-imaging technology can separate liars from those who are telling the truth with a higher degree of success than conventional polygraphs (Simpson, 2008). Drawbacks include the practicality of implementing such technology, the costs involved, and ethical issues surrounding the ability to peer inside people's heads. A less-expensive and more practical method may involve the use of a reaction time (RT) paradigm for detecting concealed information in noncriminal contexts (Verschuere, Suchotzki, & Debey, 2015). Slower response times to controlled questions, for example, might point to deception, and preliminary evidence indicates the approach is as valid as the polygraph.

To summarize, deception is potentially detectable, but the nonverbal behaviors that accompany lying are subtle and difficult to spot.

The Significance of Nonverbal Communication

Good nonverbal communication skills are associated with good social adjustment and with relationship satisfaction (Schachner, Shaver, & Mikulincer, 2005). Experts give particular attention to *nonverbal sensitivity*—**the ability to accurately encode (express) and decode (understand) nonverbal cues.** Nonverbal sensitivity is related to social, emotional, and academic competence (Bänziger et al., 2011), even in children (Izard et al., 2001), and some standardized tests exist for assessing it (Ivan, 2013). In fact, people who score highly on measures of nonverbal sensitivity are capable of making reasonably accurate personality judgments of strangers after reviewing their Facebook profiles (Lueders et al, 2014). This nonverbal decoding resulted in accurate assessments of personality for the Big Five traits (i.e., openness, conscientiousness, extraversion, agreeableness, and neuroticism; recall Chapter 2).

What about sensitivity for decoding and responding to facial expressions of emotion? Generally, women are better encoders and decoders of nondeceptive messages than men (Hall, 2006b). It is not that women are innately better at these skills or that they have lower status than men, but rather that women are more motivated than men to exert effort acquiring these skills (Hall, Coats, & Smith-LeBeau, 2005). The good news is that men (and women) who are willing to exert effort can improve their nonverbal communication skills—and enjoy happier and more satisfying relationships.

Learning Objectives

■ Identify five steps involved in making small talk.

■ Explain why self-disclosure is important to adjustment, citing ways to reduce risks associated with it.

■ Discuss the role of self-disclosure in relationship development.

■ Analyze gender differences in self-disclosure.

■ Cite four points good listeners need to keep in mind.

8.3 Toward More Effective Communication

If you are like most people, you probably overestimate how effectively you communicate with others (Keysar & Henly, 2002). In this section, we turn to practical issues that will help you become a more effective communicator with your family, friends, romantic partner, and co-workers. We'll review conversational skills, self-disclosure, and effective listening.

Conversational Skills

When meeting strangers, some people launch right into a conversation, while others break into a cold sweat as their minds go completely blank. If you fall into the second category, don't despair! The art of conversation is actually based on conversational *skills*, which can be learned. To get you started, we'll offer a few general principles, gleaned primarily from *Messages: The Communication Skills Book* by McKay, Davis, and Fanning (2009).

First, follow the Golden Rule: Give to others what you would like to receive from them. In other words, give others your attention and respect, and let them know that you like them. Second, focus on the other person, not yourself. Concentrate on what the person is saying, rather than on how you look, what you're going to say next, or how you are going to win the argument. Third, as we have noted, use nonverbal cues to communicate your interest in the other person. Like you, others also find it easier to interact with a person who signals friendliness. A welcoming smile can make a big difference in initial contacts.

Now, how do you actually get the conversational ball rolling? Psychologist Bernardo Carducci (1999) suggests five steps for making successful small talk. We'll use his template and fill it in with additional suggestions:

1. *Indicate that you are open to conversation by commenting on your surroundings.* ("This line sure is slow.") You can begin with other topics, too, but you should be careful about your opening line. Because cute lines often backfire ("Hi, I'm easy—are you?"), your best bet is probably the conventional approach.

2. *Introduce yourself.* You don't have to be an extravert to behave like one in unfamiliar situations. If no one is saying anything, why not make the first move by extending your hand, looking the person in the eye, introducing yourself, and sharing some information to find common ground? A simple introduction will work ("I'm Adam Weaver. I'm a psychology major").

3. *Select a topic others can relate to.* Look for similarities and differences between you and your conversational partner. Consider things you have in common—a class, a hometown, campus happenings—building conversation around that ("I heard a great band last night"). Alternatively, explore your differences ("How did you get interested in science fiction? I'm a mystery fan myself").

4. *Keep the conversational ball rolling.* Keep things going by elaborating on your initial topic ("After the concert, we walked to the coffeehouse and tried their dessert special"). Alternatively, you can introduce a related topic or start a new one.

5. *Make a smooth exit.* Politely end the conversation ("Well, I've got to run. I enjoyed our talk"). When you see the person again, give a friendly smile and a wave. You need not become friends in order to be friendly.

After you've learned a little about another person, you could move the relationship to a deeper level. This is where self-disclosure comes into play.

Self-Disclosure

Self-disclosure **is the act of sharing personal information about yourself with another person.** Self-disclosure involves opening up about yourself to others. The information you share need not be a secret, but it may be. Conversations with strangers and acquaintances typically begin with superficial self-disclosure—your opinion of a new film or speculation about who will win the Super Bowl. Typically, once people come to like and trust each other, then they begin to share private information—such as self-consciousness about their weight, health worries (Park, Bharadwog, & Blank, 2011), or sibling jealousy (Greene, Derlega, & Mathews, 2006). **Figure 8.11** illustrates how self-disclosure varies according to type of relationship.

In discussing self-disclosure, we focus on verbal communication—how disclosers and recipients decide to share information with each other (Ignatius & Kokkonen, 2007). But keep in mind that nonverbal communication plays an equally important role in self-disclosure (Laurenceau & Kleinman, 2006). For example, you have already seen how nonverbal cues can support or completely change the meaning of the words they accompany. Also, nonverbal behaviors can determine whether interactions have positive, neutral, or negative outcomes. Thus, if you tell a friend about a distressing experience and she signals her concern via sympathetic nonverbal cues (eye contact, leaning forward), your feelings about the interaction will be positive. But if she conveys a lack of interest (minimal eye contact, a bored facial expression), you will walk away with negative feelings.

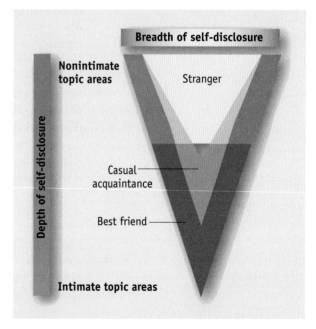

Figure 8.11

Breadth and depth of self-disclosure. *Breadth of self-disclosure* refers to how many topics one opens up about; *depth* refers to how far one goes in revealing private information. Both the breadth and depth of one's disclosures are greater with best friends as opposed to casual acquaintances or strangers. (Adapted from Altman & Taylor, 1973)

Self-disclosure is critically important to adjustment for several reasons. First, sharing fears, problems, or good news with others who are trustworthy and supportive plays a key role in mental health (Greene et al., 2006). Recall from Chapter 4 that sharing your feelings can reduce stress. Following mutual self-disclosures, people experience a boost in positive feelings (Vittengl & Holt, 2000). Second, self-disclosure can build relationships with friends and co-workers (Tardy & Dindia, 2006). Third, emotional (but not factual) self-disclosures lead to feelings of closeness, as long as disclosers feel that listeners are understanding and accepting (Laurenceau & Kleinman 2006). Fourth, self-disclosure in romantic relationships correlates positively with relationship satisfaction (Greene et al., 2006).

Still, self-disclosure may not be beneficial for specific people in particular contexts. Consider individuals with low self-esteem who hoped that Facebook, a social networking site where self-disclosure is rife (Special & Li-Barber, 2012), would help them form social connections with others. On the one hand, entertaining status updates that are high in self-disclosure can create feelings of connection (Utz, 2015). On the other hand, one study found that although people found Facebook to be a low-threat way to engage in self-disclosure, the content of their online disclosures, which were either too low in positivity or too high in negativity, led to undesired reactions from their online "friends" (Forest & Wood, 2012). Individuals with higher self-esteem, for example, tend to engage in more positive self-disclosure online as a way to maintain relationships, doing so by being honest, intentional, and generally positive concerning what they share (Hollenbaugh & Ferris, 2015). In contrast, those individuals who rely on Facebook as a virtual community or for companionship are likely to share more dishonest, negative, and unintentional information online. Other research confirms that recogntion of others' low self-esteem hinders positive self-disclosure because the respondent fears the exchange will go poorly, but not because they are worried about hurting others' feelings (MacGregor & Holmes, 2011).

Self-Disclosure and Relationship Development

Earlier, we noted that self-disclosure leads to feelings of intimacy. Actually, the process is a little more complicated than that. Research suggests that only certain types of disclosures lead to feelings of closeness (Laurenceau, Barrett, & Rovine, 2005). For instance, emotional-evaluative self-disclosures (e.g., your feeling about your sister) do, but factual-descriptive self-disclosures (e.g., that you have three siblings) do not. Moreover, for intimacy to develop, a discloser must feel understood and cared for (Lin & Huang, 2006). In other words, self-disclosure alone doesn't promote intimacy—how listeners respond matters, too (Maisel, Gable, & Strachman, 2008). Interestingly, the presence of laughter in a situation can lead to greater intimacy and self-disclosure, presumably because the act of laughing leads to positive emotion which, in turn, creates connections between people (Gray, Parkinson, & Dunbar, 2015).

Self-disclosure varies over the course of relationships. At the beginning of a relationship, high levels of mutual disclosure prevail (Taylor & Altman, 1987). Once a relationship is well established, the level of disclosure tapers off, although responsiveness remains high (Reis & Patrick, 1996). Also, in established relationships people are less likely to reciprocate disclosures in the same conversation. Thus, when a lover or a good friend reveals private information, you frequently respond with words of sympathy and understanding rather than a similar disclosure. This movement away from equal exchanges of self-disclosure appears to be based on twin needs that emerge as intimate relationships develop: (1) the need for connection (via openness) and (2) the need for autonomy (via privacy) (Planalp, Fitness, & Fehr, 2006).

Gender and Self-Disclosure

What about gender? In the United States, females tend to be more openly self-disclosing than males, although the disparity seems smaller than once believed (Fehr, 2004). This gender difference is strongest in *same-gender* friendships, with female friends sharing more personal information than male friends (Wright, 2006). In *other-gender* relationships, self-disclosure is more equal, although men with traditional gender-role attitudes are less likely to self-disclose because they view sharing personal information as a sign of weakness. Women also share more personal information and feelings, whereas men share more nonpersonal information, both in conversations and email messages (Kilmartin, 2007).

What about the disclosure styles of men and women in more intimate relationships? One theory argues that such intimate interactions are best fostered by a combination of self-disclosure and empathic responding—that is, being a compassionate listener and supportive partner (Reis & Shaver, 1988). Men and women appear to differ in the emphasis placed on these two behaviors. One study found that men's degree of disclosure and empathic responding predicted their own feelings of closeness and confidence in the relationship. Women's feelings of intimacy, however, were more likely to be based on their male partner's degree of disclosure and empathic responding (Mitchell et al., 2008). And, in the early stages of other-gender relationships, men often disclose more than women (Derlega et al., 1985). This finding is consistent with the traditional expectations that males should initiate relationships and females should encourage males to talk. Thus, it is an oversimplification to say that women are always more open than men.

Effective Listening

Listening and hearing are distinct processes that are often confused. *Hearing* is a physiological process that occurs when sound waves come into contact with our eardrums. In contrast, *listening* **is a mindful activity and complex process requiring one to select and organize information, interpret and respond to communications, and recall what was heard.** Thus, listening well is an active skill.

Effective listening is a vastly underappreciated skill. There's truth in the old saying "We have two ears and only one mouth, so we should listen more than we speak." Because listeners process speech much more rapidly than people speak (between 500 and 1000 words per minute versus 125–175 words per minute), it's easy for them to become bored, distracted, and inattentive (Hanna, Suggett, & Radtke, 2008). Fatigue and self-preoccupation are other factors that interfere with effective listening.

To be a good listener, you need to keep four points in mind. First, *signal your interest in the speaker via nonverbal cues.* Face the speaker squarely and lean toward him or her (rather than slouching or leaning back in a chair). This posture shows that you are interested in what the other person has to say. Communicate your feelings about what the speaker is saying by nodding your head or raising your eyebrows.

Second, *hear the other person out before responding.* Listeners often tune out or interrupt a conversational partner when (1) they know someone well (they assume they already know what the speaker will say), (2) a speaker has mannerisms listeners find frustrating (speaking in a monotone), and (3) a speaker discusses ideas (abortion, politics) that generate strong feelings or uses terms (*welfare cheat, redneck*) that push "hot buttons." Although it is challenging not to tune out a speaker or lob an insult in these situations, you'll be better able to formulate an appropriate response if you allow the speaker to complete his or her thought.

Third, *engage in active listening* (Verderber et al., 2008). Pay attention to what the speaker says, mindfully processing the information. Active listening also involves the skills of clarifying and paraphrasing. Inevitably, a speaker will skip over an essential point or say something that is confusing. When this happens, ask for clarification. "Was Bill her boyfriend or her brother?" Clarifying ensures that you have an accurate picture of the message and also tells the speaker that you are interested. Paraphrasing goes beyond clarifying. To paraphrase means to state concisely what you believe the speaker said. You might say, "Let me see if I've got this right . . ." or "Do you mean . . . ?" It's silly to paraphrase everything a speaker says; you need to paraphrase only when a speaker says something important. Paraphrasing has several benefits: It reassures the speaker that you are "with" him or her, it derails misinterpretations, and it keeps you focused on the conversation.

Listening attentively to a speaker is an important part of the communication process.

Finally, *pay attention to the other person's nonverbal signals*. Listeners use a speaker's words to get a message's "objective" meaning, but they rely on nonverbal cues for the emotional and interpersonal meanings of a message. Your knowledge of body language, voice tone, and other nonverbal cues can provide deeper understanding of communications (Akhtar, 2007). Remember that these cues are available not only when another person is speaking but also when you are talking. If your listener is drifting away, you might be going overboard on irrelevant details or even hogging the conversation. The antidote is active listening.

8.4 Communication Problems

In this section, we focus on two problems that can interfere with effective communication: communication apprehension and barriers to effective communicatioin.

Communication Apprehension

You have just learned that a 30-minute oral presentation is a course requirement for your child psychology class. Do you welcome this requirement as an opportunity to polish your public speaking skills or, panic-stricken, do you race to drop the class? If you opted for the latter, you may suffer from *communication apprehension*, **or anxiety caused by having to talk with others.** Some people experience communication apprehension in all speaking situations (including one-on-one encounters), but most people who have the problem notice it only when speaking before groups.

Communication apprehension is a concern for students as well as teachers because it can adversely affect general academic success as well as performance related to classroom public speaking requirements (Blume, Baldwin, & Ryan, 2013). One study found that individuals with higher levels of communication apprehension were found to have lower critical thinking skills as well as less-developed oral communication skills (Blume, Dreher, & Baldwin, 2010). Other research suggests that communication apprehension can disrupt skills needed for effective career planning (Meyer-Griffith, Reardon, & Hartley, 2009). A recent study revealed that students with higher communication apprehension engaged in more frequent and critical self-talk ("I'll never be able to introduce the speaker effectively, I talk too softly") and had higher levels of public speaking anxiety (Shi Brinthaupt & McCree, 2015). Individuals who engaged in reinforcing self-talk ("I only have to give a brief introduction about the speaker and I can do that because I have cue cards"), however, were found to have lower levels of anxiety and less communication apprehension.

Researchers have identified four responses to communication apprehension (Richmond & McCroskey, 1995). The most common is *avoidance*, or choosing not to participate when confronted with voluntary communication opportunities. If people believe that speaking will make them uncomfortable, they will typically avoid the experience. *Withdrawal* occurs when people unexpectedly find themselves trapped in a communication situation they can't escape. Here they may clam up entirely or say as little as possible. *Disruption* refers to the inability to make fluent oral presentations or to engage in appropriate verbal or nonverbal behavior. Naturally, inadequate communication skills can produce this same behavioral effect, so it isn't always possible for the average person to identify the problem's actual cause. *Overcommunication* is a relatively unusual response to high communication apprehension, but it does occur, as when someone who attempts to dominate social situations talks nonstop.

Image Source/Getty Images

Many people suffer from communication apprehension when they have to speak in front of a group. Doing so can lead to feelings of stress and anxiety.

Although such individuals are seen as poor communicators, they are not usually perceived as having communication apprehension.

Happily, there are effective ways to reduce speech anxiety. With the technique of visualization, for example, you picture yourself successfully going through all of the steps involved in preparing for and making a presentation. Research shows that people who practice visualization have less anxiety and fewer negative thoughts when they actually speak compared to previsualitization levels (Ayres, Hopf, & Ayres, 1994). Where student presentations are concerned, the layout of the classroom can be used to reduce communication apprehension and to promote effective discourse (Rae & Sands, 2013). Having students give an initial, informal presentation from their seats before doing a more formal or prepared talk from behind the instructor's desk, a podium, or in front of the classroom is probably a good idea. Arranging classroom chairs in a circle, too, can promote a sense of equality while allowing everyone to feel comfortable looking at and exchanging remarks with one another.

Other research demonstrates that repeatedly practicing a presentation while being digitially vidoed can help some people with communication apprehension (Leeds & Maurer, 2009). In particularly acute cases of communication apprehension, substituting a recorded talk may be preferable to a live presentation (Leeds & Maurer, 2009).

Learn More Online

Effective Presentations
Students often tell teachers that they are terrified of making a presentation in front of a class. Professor Jeff Radel (University of Kansas Medical Center) has crafted an excellent set of guides to show the best ways of communicating by means of oral presentations, visual materials, and posters.

Barriers to Effective Communication

Earlier in the chapter, we discussed noise and its disruptive effects on interpersonal communication. Now we want to check out some psychological factors contributing to noise. These barriers to effective communication can reside in the sender, the receiver, or sometimes both. Common obstacles include defensiveness, ambushing, and self-preoccupation.

Defensiveness

Perhaps the most basic barrier to effective communication is *defensiveness*—**an excessive concern with protecting oneself from being hurt.** People usually react defensively when they feel threatened, such as when they believe that others are evaluating them or trying to control or manipulate them (Trevithick & Wengraf, 2011). Defensiveness is also triggered when others act in a superior manner. Thus, those who flaunt their status, wealth, brilliance, or power often put receivers on the defensive. Dogmatic people who project "I'm always right" also breed defensiveness. Strive to cultivate a communication style that minimizes defensiveness in others.

Ambushing

Some listeners are really just looking for opportunities to attack a presenter. Although the person who is about to attack—a verbal "bushwhacker"—is really listening carefully and intently to what is being said, his or her purpose in doing so is simply to assail or harass the speaker (Wood, 2015). Understanding, discussing, or having an otherwise thoughtful exchange of ideas and opinions is not the point. People who engage in ambushing almost always arouse defensiveness from others, especially in those whom they attack. Sadly, ambushing can be an effective barrier to communication because few people relish being hassled or bullied in front of others.

Self-Preoccupation

Who hasn't experienced the frustration of trying to communicate with someone who is so self-focused that two-way conversation is impossible? Self-preoccupied people often engage in *pseudolistening*, or pretending to listen while their minds are occupied with other topics (O'Keefe, 2002). Pseudolistening occurs when a student feigns interest in class discusson while actually daydreaming or surreptitiously using his smartphone. Other annoying, self-centered individuals seem to talk to hear themselves speak, and then end up monopolizing the conversation. If you try to slip in a word about *your* problems, they may cut you off by engaging in *conversational rerouting* (Wood, 2015) by proclaiming, "That's nothing. Listen to what happened to me!" Other preoccupied listerners use what is known as *diversionary interrupting*, which can entail conversational rerouting but usually just steers the discussion off to a new and possibly unrelated topic that is of interest to the self-preoccupied monopolizer (Wood, 2015). Further, self-preoccupied people are poor listeners. When someone else is talking, they're mentally rehearsing their next comments. Because they are self-focused, these individuals are usually oblivious to their negative impact on others.

8.5 Interpersonal Conflict

Learning Objectives
- Assess the pros and cons of avoiding versus facing conflict.
- Describe five personal styles for dealing with conflict.
- Articulate some tips for coping effectively with interpersonal conflict.

People do not have to be enemies to be in conflict, and being in conflict does not make people enemies. *Interpersonal conflict* **exists whenever two or more people disagree.** By this definition, conflict occurs between friends and lovers as well as between competitors and enemies, even between perfect strangers. Interpersonal conflict is present anytime people have disparate views, opposing perspectives, incompatible goals, emotional reactions, and a desire to try to address and resolve their differences (Ruz & Tudela, 2011). Discord may be caused by a simple misunderstanding, or it may be due to incompatible goals, values, attitudes, or beliefs. Because conflict is unavoidable and can be constructive as well as disruptive, knowing how to deal constructively with it is essential (Jehn, 2014). Many studies report associations between effective conflict management and relationship satisfaction (Kline et al., 2006).

Beliefs about Conflict

How do you respond when a conflict arises between yourself and another person? Why do you react that way? Your approach to or avoidance of conflict may be rooted in how conflict was dealt with in your family (Mikulincer & Shaver, 2011).

Conflict is neither inherently bad nor inherently good. It is a natural phenomenon that may lead to either good or bad outcomes, depending on how people deal with it. When people see conflict as negative, they tend to avoid dealing with it. Of course, sometimes avoiding conflict is good. If a relationship or an issue is of little importance to you, or if the costs of confrontation are too high (your boss might fire you), avoidance might be the best way to handle a conflict. Also, cultures differ in how conflict should be handled. Collectivist cultures (such as China and Japan) often avoid conflict, whereas individualistic cultures tend to encourage direct confrontations (Samovar et al., 2007). In individualistic cultures, the consequences of avoiding conflict depend on the nature of the relationship. When relationships and issues are important, avoiding conflict is generally counterproductive. For one thing, it can lead to a self-perpetuating cycle (see **Figure 8.12**).

Styles of Managing Conflict

How do you react to conflict? Some approaches are more constructive than others (Deutsch, 2011), such as knowing who has a stake or a voice in a conflict situation (Shapiro & Burris, 2014). Most people have a habitual way or personal style of dealing with dissension. Studies have consistently revealed five distinct patterns of dealing with conflict: avoiding/withdrawing, accommodating, competing/forcing, compromising, and collaborating (Lulofs & Cahn, 2000). Two dimensions underlie these different styles: interest in satisfying one's own concerns and interest in satisfying others' concerns (Rahim & Magner,

Radius Images/Alamy Stock Photo

Disagreements are a fact of everyday life, so effective communicators need to learn how to deal with them constructively.

1995). You can see the location of these five styles on the two dimensions in **Figure 8.13**. Where do you fit?

- *Avoiding/withdrawing* (low concern for self and others). Some people find conflict extremely distasteful. When a conflict emerges, the avoider will change the subject, deflect discussion with humor, make a hasty exit, or pretend to be preoccupied with something else. Usually, people who prefer this style hope that ignoring a problem will make it go away. Yet some researchers argue this style is actually very goal directed and not a passive response to conflict (Wang, Fink, & Cai, 2012). For minor problems, this tactic is often a good one—there's no need to react to every little annoyance. For bigger conflicts, avoiding/withdrawing is not a good strategy; it usually delays an inevitable clash.

- *Accommodating* (low concern for self, high concern for others). Like the avoider, the accommodator feels uncomfortable with conflict. However, instead of ignoring the disagreement, this person brings the conflict to a quick end by giving in easily. People who are overly concerned about acceptance and approval from others commonly use this strategy of surrender. Habitual accommodating is a poor way of dealing with conflict because it does not generate creative thinking and effective solutions. Moreover, feelings of resentment (on both sides) may develop because the accommodator often plays the role of a martyr. Of course, when you don't have strong preferences (where to eat out), occasional accommodating is perfectly appropriate.

- *Competing/forcing* (high concern for self, low concern for others). The competitor turns every conflict into a black-and-white, win-or-lose situation. Competitors will do virtually anything to emerge victorious from confrontations; thus, they can be deceitful and aggressive—including using verbal attacks and physical threats. They rigidly adhere to one position and will use threats and coercion to force the other party to submit. This style is undesirable because, like accommodation, it fails to generate creative solutions to problems. Moreover, this approach is especially likely to lead to postconflict tension, resentment, and hostility.

- *Compromising* (moderate concern for self and others). Compromising is a pragmatic approach to conflict that acknowledges the divergent needs of both parties. Compromisers are willing to negotiate and to meet the other person halfway. With this approach, each person gives up something so both can have partial satisfaction. Because both parties gain some satisfaction, compromising is a fairly constructive approach to conflict, especially when the issue is moderately important.

- *Collaborating* (high concern for self and others). Whereas compromising simply entails "splitting the difference" between positions, collaborating involves a sincere effort to find a solution that will optimally satisfy both parties. Here, conflict is viewed as a mutual problem to be solved as effectively as possible. Collaborating encourages openness and honesty, stressing the importance of criticizing the other person's *ideas* in a disagreement rather than the other *person*. To collaborate, you have to work on clarifying differences and similarities in positions so that you can build on the similarities. Generally, this is the most mature and productive approach for dealing with conflict. Instead of resulting in a postconflict residue of tension and resentment, collaborating tends to produce a climate of trust.

Dealing Constructively with Conflict

Collaborating is the most effective approach to conflict management. We offer some specific suggestions to help you implement this approach. But, before we get down to specifics, there are a few principles to keep in mind (Verderber et al., 2007). First, in a conflict situation, try to give the other person the benefit of the doubt; don't automatically assume that those who

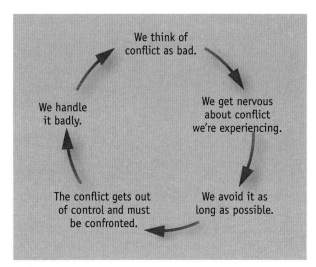

Figure 8.12

The conflict avoidance cycle. Avoiding conflict can lead to a self-perpetuating cycle: (1) People think of conflict as bad, (2) they get nervous about a conflict they are experiencing, (3) they avoid the conflict as long as possible, (4) the conflict gets out of control and must be confronted, and (5) they handle the confrontation badly. In turn, this negative experience sets the stage for avoiding conflict the next time—usually with the same negative outcome. (Adapted from Lulofs, 1994)

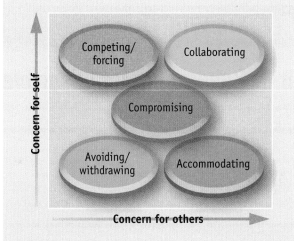

Figure 8.13

Five styles of handling interpersonal conflict. In dealing with discord, individuals typically prefer one of five styles. The two dimensions of *concern for self* and *concern for others* underlie each of the five styles.

Learn More Online

The Conflict Resolution Information Source

This excellent resource on conflict management is provided by the University of Colorado's Conflict Information Consortium. The site is actually a gateway to a huge variety of resources on conflict management and is easy to navigate.

disagree with you are ignorant or mean-spirited. Show respect for their position and do your best to empathize with, and fully understand, their frame of reference. Second, approach the other person as an equal. If you have a higher status or more power (parent, supervisor, club officer), try to set this difference aside. Third, define the conflict as a mutual problem to be solved cooperatively, rather than as a win-lose proposition. Fourth, choose a mutually acceptable time to sit down and work on resolving the conflict. It is not always wise to tackle the conflict when and where it first arises. Finally, communicate your flexibility and willingness to modify your position.

Here are some explicit guidelines for dealing effectively with interpersonal conflict (Verderber et al., 2007):

- *Make communication honest and open.* Don't withhold information or misrepresent your position. Avoid deceit and manipulation. Try being agreeable (Barry & Friedman, 1998).
- *Exhibit trust.* Being trustworthy and dependable can lead to smooth and successful negotiations (De Dreu et al., 2006).
- *Use specific behaviors to describe another person's annoying habits rather than general statements about their personality.* You'll probably get further with your roommate if you say something like "Please throw your clothes in the hamper" rather than "You're an inconsiderate slob." Remarks about specific actions are less threatening and are less likely to be taken personally. They also clarify what you hope will change.
- *Avoid "loaded" words.* Certain words tend to trigger negative emotional reactions in listeners. For example, you can discuss politics without using terms such as *right-winger, knee-jerk liberal,* or *lunatic fringe.*
- *Use a positive approach and help the other person save face.* Saying "I love it when we cook dinner together" will go over better than "I resent it that you never help with dinner."
- *Limit complaints to recent behavior and to the current situation.* Dredging up past grievances only rekindles old resentments and distracts you from the current problem. And avoid saying things like "You *always* say you're too busy" or "You *never* do your fair share of the housework." Such categorical statements are bound to put the other person on the defensive.
- *Assume responsibility for your own feelings and preferences.* Rather than "*You* make me mad," say "*I* am angry." Or try "I'd appreciate it if you'd water the garden" instead of "Do you think the garden needs to be watered?"
- *Use an assertive (not submissive or aggressive) communication style.* This approach will make it easier to head off and deal constructively with conflict situations. In the upcoming Application, we elaborate on *assertive communication* and its usefulness in a wide variety of interpersonal communication situations.

APPLICATION

8.6 Developing an Assertive Communication Style

Learning Objectives

- Distinguish among assertive, submissive, and aggressive communications.
- List five steps that lead to more assertive communication.

Answer the following questions "yes" or "no."

____ **1.** When someone asks you for an unreasonable favor, is it difficult to say no?

____ **2.** Do you feel timid about returning flawed merchandise?

____ **3.** Do you have a hard time requesting even small favors from others?

____ **4.** When a group is hotly debating an issue, are you shy about speaking up?

____ **5.** When a salesperson pressures you to buy something you don't want, is it hard for you to resist?

If you answered "yes" to several of these questions, you may need to increase your assertiveness, that is, your confidence and self-assuredness. Many people have difficulty being assertive; however, this problem is more common among females because they are socialized to be more submissive and obliging than males—to "be nice." Consequently, assertiveness training is especially popular among women. Men, too, find assertiveness training helpful, both because some have been socialized to be passive and because others want to become less aggressive and more assertive. In this Application we elaborate on the differences among assertive, submissive, and aggressive behavior and discuss some procedures for increasing assertiveness (Hays, 2014), which can build self-esteem.

The Nature of Assertiveness

Assertiveness **involves acting in one's own best interests by expressing one's thoughts and feelings directly and honestly.** Essentially, assertiveness involves standing up for your rights when someone else is about to infringe on them. To be assertive is to speak out rather than pull your punches.

The nature of assertive communication can best be clarified by contrasting it with other types of communication. *Submissive communication* is deferential, as it involves giving in to others on points of possible contention. Submissive people often let others take advantage of them. Typically, their biggest problem is that they cannot say "no" to unreasonable requests. A common example is the college student who can't tell her roommate not to borrow her clothes. In traditional trait terminology, submissive people are timid or reticent.

Although the roots of submissiveness have not been investigated fully, they appear to lie in excessive concern about gaining the social approval of others. However, the strategy of "not making waves" is more likely to garner others' contempt than their approval. Moreover, individuals who use this style often feel bad about themselves (for being "pushovers") and resentful of those they allow to take advantage of them. These feelings often lead submissive individuals to try to punish others by withdrawing, sulking, or crying (Bower & Bower 2004). Such manipulative attempts to get one's own way are sometimes referred to as "passive aggression" or "indirect aggression" (Hopwood & Wright, 2012).

At the other end of the spectrum, *aggressive communication* focuses on saying and getting what one wants at the expense of others' feelings and rights. With assertive behavior, however, one strives to respect others' rights while defending one's own. The problem in real life is that assertive and aggressive behaviors *may* overlap. When someone is about to infringe on their rights, people often lash out at the other party (aggression) while defending their rights (assertion). The challenge, then, is to be firm and assertive without becoming aggressive and demanding.

Learn More Online

Assertiveness
In an online brochure, this site clarifies the nature of assertiveness in a diverse world and describes specific techniques for becoming more assertive. The site is maintained by the Counseling Center at the University of Illinois at Urbana–Champaign.

Advocates of assertive communication argue that it is much more adaptive than either submission or aggression (Bower & Bower, 2004). They maintain that submissive behavior leads to poor self-esteem, self-denial, emotional suppression, and strained interpersonal relationships. Conversely, aggressive communication tends to promote guilt, alienation, and disharmony. In contrast, assertive behavior is said to foster high self-esteem, satisfactory interpersonal relationships, and effective conflict management. Here are three different ways to express the same desire:

Aggressive: I want to watch football all day today, so that is the only thing that will be on the TV. End of story.
Assertive: I feel like watching football on the TV today—do you?
Submissive: It's okay with me if we don't watch football; whatever you feel like watching is fine with me.

The essential point with assertiveness is that you are able to state what you want clearly, directly, and honestly. Being able to do so makes you feel good about yourself and will usually make others feel good about you, too. And, although being assertive doesn't guarantee your chances for getting what you want, it certainly enhances them.

Steps in Assertiveness Training

Here we summarize the key steps in assertiveness training.

1. Understand What Assertive Communication Is

To produce assertive behavior, you need to understand what it looks and sounds like. Assertiveness trainers often ask clients to imagine situations calling for assertiveness and compare hypothetical submissive, aggressive, and assertive responses. Let's consider an example: A woman in assertiveness training asks her roommate to cooperate in cleaning their apartment weekly. The roommate, who is uninterested in the problem, is listening to music when the conversation begins. In this example, the roommate is playing the role of the antagonist, called a "downer," in the following scripts (adapted from Bower & Bower, 2004, pp. 8, 9, 11).

Being assertive can be done in a friendly rather than threatening manner, ensuring that both parties benefit from the outcome.

The Submissive Scene

She: Uh, I was wondering if you would be willing to take time to decide about the housecleaning.

Downer: (listening to music) Not now, I'm busy.

She: Oh, okay.

The Aggressive Scene

She: Listen, I've had it with you not even talking about cleaning this damn apartment. Are you going to help me?

Downer: (listening to music) Not now, I'm busy.

She: Why can't you look at me when you turn me down? You don't give a damn about the housework or me! You only care about yourself!

RULES FOR ASSERTIVE SCRIPTS	
Do	**Don't**
Describe	
Describe the other person's behavior objectively.	Describe your emotional reaction to it.
Use concrete terms.	Use abstract, vague terms.
Describe a specified time, place, and frequency of the action.	Generalize for "all time."
Describe the action, not the "motive."	Guess at your Downer's motives or goals.
Express	
Express your feelings.	Deny your feelings.
Express them calmly.	Unleash emotional outbursts.
State feelings in a positive manner, as relating to a goal to be achieved.	State feelings negatively, making Downer attack.
Direct yourself to the specific offending behavior, not to the whole person.	Attack the entire character of the person.
Specify	
Ask explicitly for change in your Downer's behavior.	Merely imply that you'd like a change.
Request a small change.	Ask for too large a change.
Request only one or two changes at one time.	Ask for too many changes.
Specify the concrete actions you want stopped and those you want performed.	Ask for changes in nebulous traits or qualities.
Take account of whether your Downer can meet your request without suffering large losses.	Ignore your Downer's needs or ask only for your satisfaction.
Specify (if appropriate) what behavior you are willing to change to make the agreement.	Consider that only your Downer has to change.
Consequences	
Make the consequences explicit.	Be ashamed to talk about rewards and penalties.
Give a positive reward for change in the desired direction.	Give only punishments for lack of change.
Select something that is desirable and reinforcing to your Downer.	Select something that only you might find rewarding.
Select a reward that is big enough to maintain the behavior change.	Offer a reward you can't or won't deliver.
Select a punishment of a magnitude that "fits the crime" of refusing to change behavior.	Make exaggerated threats.
Select a punishment that you are actually willing to carry out.	Use unrealistic threats or self-defeating punishment.

Figure 8.14

Guidelines for assertive behavior. Gordon and Sharon Bower (1991, 2004) outline a four-step program intended to help readers create successful assertive scripts for themselves. The four steps are (1) *describe* the unwanted behavior from another person (called your "Downer") that is troubling you, (2) *express* your feelings about the behavior to the other person, (3) *specify* the changes needed, and (4) try to provide rewarding *consequences* for the change. Using this framework, the table shown here provides some useful dos and don'ts for achieving effective assertive behavior.

Source: Adapted from Bower, S. A., & Bower, G. H. (1991). *Asserting yourself: A practical guide for positive change* (2nd ed.). Reading, MA: Addison-Wesley. Copyright © 1991 by Sharon Anthony Bower and Gordon H. Bower. Reprinted by permission of Perseus Books Publishers, a member of Perseus Books, L.L.C.

Downer: That's not true.

She: You never pay any attention to the apartment or to me. I have to do everything around here!

Downer: Oh, shut up! You're just neurotic about cleaning all the time. Who are you, my mother? Can't I relax with my music for a few minutes without you pestering me? This was my apartment first, you know!

The Assertive Scene

She: I know housework isn't the most fascinating subject, but it needs to be done. Let's plan when we'll do it.

Downer: (listening to music) Oh, c'mon—not now! I'm busy.

She: This won't take long. I feel that if we have a schedule, it will be easier to keep up with the chores.

Downer: I'm not sure I'll have time for all of them.

She: I've already drawn up a couple of rotating schedules for housework, so that each week we have an equal division of tasks. Will you look at them? I'd like to hear your decisions about them, say, tonight after supper?

Downer: [indignantly] I have to look at these now?

She: Is there some other time that's better for you?

Downer: Oh, I don't know.

She: Well, then let's discuss plans after supper for 15 minutes. Is that agreed?

Downer: I guess so.

She: Good! It won't take long, and I'll feel relieved when we have a schedule in place. I'm sure you will, too.

A helpful way to distinguish among the three communication types is in terms of how people deal with their own rights and the rights of others. Submissive people sacrifice their own rights. Aggressive people tend to ignore others' rights. Assertive people consider both their own rights *and* the rights of others. You'll find some additional guidelines for behaving assertively in **Figure 8.14**.

2. Monitor Your Assertive Communication

Most people's assertiveness varies from situation to situation. They may be assertive in some social contexts (when complaining about service in a restaurant) but timid in others (dealing with a bullying boss or co-worker). Consequently, once you understand assertive communications, you should monitor yourself and identify when you are nonassertive. In particular, figure out *who* intimidates you, on *what topics*, and in *which situations*.

3. Observe a Model's Assertive Communication

Once you have identified the situations in which you are nonassertive, think of someone who communicates assertively in those situations and observe that person's behavior closely. In other words, find someone to model yourself after. This is an

easy way to learn how to behave assertively in situations crucial to you. Your observations should also allow you to see how rewarding assertive communication can be, which should strengthen your assertive tendencies.

4. Practice Assertive Communication

To achieve assertive communication, practice it and work toward gradual improvement. Practice can take several forms. In *covert rehearsal*, imagine a situation requiring assertion and the dialogue you would engage in. In *role playing*, ask a friend or therapist to play the role of an antagonist, then practice communicating assertively in this artificial situation. Eventually, you will transfer your assertiveness skills to real-life situations.

5. Adopt an Assertive Attitude

Most assertiveness training programs have a behavioral orientation, focusing on specific responses for specific situations (see **Figure 8.15**). However, real-life situations rarely match those portrayed in books. Thus, some experts maintain that acquiring a repertoire of verbal responses for certain situations is not as important as developing a new attitude that you're not going to let people push you around (or allow yourself to push others around if you're aggressive) (Alberti & Emmons, 2001). Although most programs don't talk explicitly about attitudes, they do appear to instill a new attitude indirectly. Attitude change is probably crucial to achieving flexible, assertive behavior.

ASSERTIVE RESPONSES TO SOME COMMON PUTDOWNS		
Nature of remark	**Put-down sentence**	**Suggested assertive reply**
Nagging about details	"Haven't you done this yet?"	"No, when did you want it done?" (Answer without hedging, and follow up with a question.)
Prying	"I know I maybe shouldn't ask, but ..."	"If I don't want to answer, I'll let you know." (Indicate that you won't make yourself uncomfortable just to please this person.)
Putting you on the spot socially	"Are you busy Tuesday?"	"What do you have in mind?" (Answer the question with a question.)
Pigeonholing you	"That's a woman for you!"	"That's one woman, not *all* women." (Disagree—assert your individuality.)
Using insulting labels for your behavior	"That's a dumb way to ..."	"I'll decide what to call my behavior." (Refuse to accept the label.)
Basing predictions on an amateur personality analysis	"You'll have a hard time. You're too shy."	"In what ways do you think I'm too shy?" (Ask for clarification of the analysis.)

Figure 8.15

Assertive responses to common put-downs. Having some assertive replies at the ready can increase your confidence in difficult social interactions.

Source: Adapted from Bower, S. A., & Bower, G. H. (1991). *Asserting yourself: A practical guide for positive change* (2nd ed.). Reading, MA: Addison-Wesley. Copyright © 1991 by Sharon Anthony Bower and Gordon H. Bower. Reprinted by permission of Perseus Books Publishers, a member of Perseus Books, L.L.C.

CHAPTER 8 Review

Key Ideas

8.1 The Process of Interpersonal Communication
- Interpersonal communication is the interactional process that occurs when one person sends a message to another. Communication takes place when a sender transmits a message to a receiver either verbally or nonverbally. The widespread use of electronic communication devices has raised new issues in interpersonal communication. Although people often take it for granted, effective communication contributes to their adjustment in school, in relationships, and at work.

8.2 Nonverbal Communication
- Nonverbal communication conveys emotions, above all. It tends to be more spontaneous than verbal communication, and it is more ambiguous. Sometimes it contradicts what is communicated verbally. It is often multichanneled and, like language, is culturally bound.
- The amount of personal space that people prefer depends on culture, gender, social status, and situational factors. Facial expressions can convey a great deal of information about people's emotions. Variations in eye contact can influence nonverbal communication in a host of ways.
- Body postures can hint at interest in communication, and they often reflect status differences. Touch can communicate support, consolation, intimacy, status, and power. Paralanguage refers to *how* something is said rather than *what* is said.
- Certain nonverbal cues are associated with deception, but many of these cues do not correspond to popular beliefs about how liars give themselves away. Discrepancies between facial expressions and other nonverbal signals may suggest dishonesty. The vocal and visual cues associated with lying are so subtle, however, that the detection of deception is difficult. Machines used to detect deception (polygraphs) are not particularly accurate.
- Nonverbal communication, particularly nonverbal sensitivity, plays an important role in adjustment, especially in the quality of interpersonal relationships. Women are typically more nonverbally sensitive than men because they exert more effort at it.

8.3 Toward More Effective Communication
- To be an effective communicator, it's important to develop good conversational skills, including knowing how to make small talk with strangers.
- Self-disclosure—opening up to others—is associated with good mental health, happiness, and satisfying relationships. The emotional content of an experience may determine whether individuals will share it with others or keep it to themselves.
- Self-disclosure can foster emotional intimacy in relationships. Emotional-evaluative self-disclosures lead to feelings of closeness, but factual-descriptive disclosures do not. The level of self-disclosure varies over the course of relationships. American women tend to disclose more than men, but this disparity is not as large as it once was. Effective listening is an essential aspect of interpersonal communication.

8.4 Communication Problems
- A number of problems can arise that interfere with effective communication. Individuals who become overly anxious when they talk with others suffer from communication apprehension. This difficulty can cause problems in relationships and in work and educational settings. Sometimes communication can produce negative interpersonal outcomes. Barriers to effective communication include defensiveness, ambushing, and self-preoccupation.

8.5 Interpersonal Conflict
- Dealing constructively with interpersonal conflict is an important aspect of effective communication. Individualistic cultures tend to encourage direct confrontations, whereas collectivist cultures often avoid them. Nonetheless, many Americans have negative attitudes about conflict.
- In dealing with conflict, most people have a preferred style: avoiding/withdrawing, accommodating, competing, compromising, or collaborating. This last style is the most effective in managing conflict.

8.6 Application: Developing an Assertive Communication Style
- Assertiveness enables individuals to stand up for themselves while respecting the rights of others. To become more assertive, individuals need to understand what assertive communication is, monitor their assertive communication, observe a model's assertive communication, practice being assertive, and adopt an assertive attitude.

Key Terms

Assertiveness p. 245
Channel p.222
Communication apprehension p. 240
Context p. 223
Defensiveness p. 241
Display rules p. 230
Electronically mediated communication p. 223
Interpersonal communication p. 221
Interpersonal conflict p. 242
Kinesics p. 231

Listening p. 239
Message p. 222
Noise p. 222
Nonverbal communication p. 227
Nonverbal sensitivity p. 236
Paralanguage p. 233
Personal space p. 228
Polygraph p. 235
Proxemics p. 228
Receiver p. 222
Self-disclosure p. 237
Sender p. 222

Key People

Bella DePaulo pp. 234–235
Paul Ekman and Wallace Friesen pp. 229–230

Edward T. Hall pp. 228–229

CHAPTER 8 Practice Test

1. Which of the following is *not* a component of the interpersonal communication process?
   a. The sender
   b. The receiver
   c. The channel
   d. The monitor

2. Research shows that individuals from a variety of cultures
   a. agree on the facial expressions that correspond with all emotions.
   b. agree on the facial expressions that correspond with fifteen basic emotions.
   c. agree on the facial expressions that correspond with six basic emotions.
   d. do not agree on the facial expressions that correspond with any emotions.

3. Which of the following is *not* an aspect of nonverbal communication?
   a. Facial expressions
   b. Homogamy
   c. Posture
   d. Gestures

4. According to research, which of the following cues is associated with dishonesty?
   a. Speaking with a higher than normal pitch
   b. Speaking slowly
   c. Giving relatively long answers to questions
   d. Lack of eye contact

5. With regard to self-disclosure, it is best to
   a. share a lot about yourself when you first meet someone.
   b. share very little about yourself for a long time.
   c. gradually share information about yourself.
   d. give no personal information on a first encounter, but share a lot the next time.

6. Paraphrasing is an important aspect of
   a. nonverbal communication.
   b. active listening.
   c. communication apprehension.
   d. assertiveness.

7. When people engage in pseudolistening, it is usually due to
   a. ambushing.
   b. self-preoccupation.
   c. motivational distortion.
   d. defensiveness.

8. The conflict style that reflects low concern for self and low concern for others is
   a. competing/forcing.
   b. compromising.
   c. accomodating.
   d. avoiding/withdrawing.

9. Generally, the most productive style for managing conflict is
   a. collaboration.
   b. compromise.
   c. accommodation.
   d. avoidance.

10. Expressing your thoughts directly and honestly without trampling on other people is a description of which communication style?
    a. Aggressive
    b. Empathic
    c. Submissive
    d. Assertive

Answers

1. d Pages 221–223
2. c Pages 229–230
3. b Pages 227–236
4. a Pages 234–236
5. c Pages 237–238
6. b Page 239
7. b Page 241
8. d Page 243
9. a Page 243
10. d Pages 244–247

Personal Explorations Workbook

Go to the *Personal Explorations Workbook* in the back of your textbook for exercises that can enhance your self-understanding in relation to issues raised in this chapter.

Exercise 8.1 *Self-Assessment:* Opener Scale

Exercise 8.2 *Self-Reflection:* How Do You Feel about Self-Disclosure?

CHAPTER 9   Friendship and Love

iStockphoto.com/AndreyPopov

Antonio was so keyed up, he tossed and turned all night. When morning finally arrived, he was elated. In less than two hours, he would be meeting Sonia! In his first class, thoughts and images of Sonia constantly distracted him from the lecture. When class was finally over, he had to force himself not to walk too fast to the Student Union, where they had agreed to meet. Chances are that you recognize Antonio's behavior as that of someone falling in love.

Friendship and love play major roles in psychological adjustment. Recall from Chapter 1 that one of the strongest predictors of happiness is social connectedness. Conversely, social isolation is associated with poor physical and mental health. We begin this chapter by defining close relationships. Next, we consider why people are attracted to each other, and why they stay in or leave relationships. Then we probe more deeply into friendship and romantic love and discuss how the Internet influences relationships. Finally, we focus on the painful problem of loneliness and how to overcome it. ■

9.1 Relationship Development

Close relationships **are those that are important, interdependent, and long lasting.** In other words, people in close relationships spend a lot of time and energy maintaining the relationship, and what one person says and does affects the other. Close relationships come in many forms, from family relationships, friendships, and work relationships to romantic relationships and marriage. As you are aware, close relationships can arouse intense feelings—both positive (passion, concern, caring) and negative (rage, jealousy, despair). As a result, close relationships are related to some of the best aspects of life (well-being, happiness, health), but they do have a dark side (abuse, deception, rejection). This phenomenon is termed the *paradox of close relationships* (Perlman, 2007). This paradox makes friendship and love perennial interests for poets, philosophers, and psychologists alike.

As we discuss how relationships develop, we divide our coverage into three segments. First, we review the factors that operate in initial encounters. Then we consider elements that come into play as people become acquainted and relationships deepen. Finally, we review what's involved in maintaining relationships.

Our review of research in this section pertains to both friendships and romantic relationships. In some cases, a particular factor (such as physical attractiveness) may play a more influential role in love than in friendship. However, all the factors discussed in this section enter into both types of relationships. These factors also operate in the same way in both straight and gay friendships and romantic relationships (Peplau & Fingerhut, 2007).

Initial Encounters

Attraction is the initial desire to form a close relationship. Sometimes initial encounters begin dramatically with two strangers' eyes locking across a room. More often, two people become aware of their mutual attraction, usually triggered by each other's looks and early conversations. What draws two strangers together as either friends or lovers? Three factors stand out: proximity, familiarity, and physical attractiveness.

Proximity

Attraction usually depends on proximity (Sprecher et al., 2015). *Proximity* **refers to geographic, residential, and other forms of spatial closeness.** Of course, proximity is not an issue in cyberspace interactions, but in everyday life people become attracted to, and acquainted with, someone who lives, works, shops, or plays nearby. Proximity effects may seem self-evident, but it is sobering to realize that your friendships and love interests are often shaped by seating charts, apartment availability, shift assignments, and office locations.

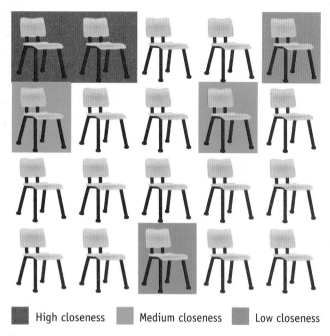

High closeness   Medium closeness   Low closeness

Figure 9.1

Friendship intensity as a function of initial seat assignment.
To show that friendships are sometimes the result of mere chance, Back, Schmukle, and Egloff (2008) found that college students' initial seat assignments predicted how close the students would be a year later. Sitting in neighboring seats yielded the closest friendships, followed by sitting in the same row, and finally sitting in no obvious proximity.

Source: Adapted from Back, M. D., Schmukle, S. C., & Egloff, B. (2008). Becoming friends by chance. *Psychological Science, 19*(5), 439–440.

The importance of proximity was apparent in a study that examined friendship development in a real-life context (Back, Schmukle, & Egloff, 2008). College students in a psychology course were randomly assigned to sit in neighboring seats, in the same row but not in neighboring seats, or without any physical relation to one another (control). One year later, the researchers measured the friendship development among classmates. As proximity would suggest, those who sat in neighboring seats were more likely to be friends than those in the same row, while those in the same row were more likely to be friends than those in the control condition (see **Figure 9.1**).

How does proximity increase attraction? Goodfriend (2009) asserts that first, people who are near each other are more likely to get acquainted and find out their similarities. Second, individuals who live or work close by may be seen as more convenient and less costly (in terms of time and energy) than those farther away. Finally, people might develop attraction just because someone in close proximity becomes familiar to them.

Familiarity

You probably walk the same route to your classes several times a week. As the term progresses, you begin to recognize some familiar faces along the way. Have you found yourself nodding or smiling at these people? If so, you've experienced **the *mere exposure effect*, or an increase in positive feelings toward a novel stimulus (such as a person) based on frequent exposure to it** (Zajonc, 1968). Note that the positive feelings arise just on the basis of seeing someone frequently—not because of any interaction.

The implications of the mere exposure effect on initial attraction should be obvious. Generally, the more familiar someone is, the more you will like him or her. And greater liking increases the probability that you will strike up a conversation and, possibly, develop a relationship with the person. However, contemporary researchers argue that the familiarity-attraction link is not that simple; one must consider the nature and stage of the relationship. For instance, familiarity can lead to *decreased* attraction if the target person becomes progressively less appealing or more competitive (Finkel et al., 2015). In addition, after a certain point in a relationship, familiarity fails to add anything new to the attraction and can even lead to boredom. In one study, men who were exposed to female faces twice rated them as less attractive on the second rating, indicating they liked novelty over familiarity (Little, DeBruine, & Jones, 2014). Future research will no doubt continue to explore this complex interaction.

Physical Attractiveness

Physical attractiveness plays a major role in initial face-to-face encounters (Finkel & Eastwick, 2015). As you might expect, the importance of physical appearance is different for a future spouse or life partner than it is for casual relationships. Physical attractiveness is highly important in a dating partner—for both sexes, but especially for men (Buss et al., 2001). For a sexual partner, both men and women ranked "attractive appearance" as the most important characteristic (Regan & Berscheid, 1997). Good looks play a role in friendships as well. People, especially males, prefer attractiveness in their same- and other-gender friends (Fehr, 2000).

Do gays and straights differ in the importance they place on the physical attractiveness of prospective dating partners? It seems not. In fact, researchers often find gender rather than sexual orientation to be the more important factor in partner preferences. Men, whether gay or straight, place more emphasis on physical attractiveness than women do (Franzoi & Kern, 2009).

The emphasis on beauty may not be quite as great as the evidence reviewed thus far suggests. In an online survey of more than 200,000 participants, intelligence, humor, honesty, and kindness were ranked as the most important traits in a partner, with good looks coming in fifth. However, when results were separated by gender, attractiveness was ranked higher by men than by women (Lippa, 2007). Keep in mind that verbal reports don't always reflect people's actual priorities and behavior, and some people might not be aware of what truly attracts them. Finally, judgments about physical attractiveness can and do change as one learns about the personality of the individual in question.

What makes someone attractive? Although people can hold different views about what makes a person attractive, they tend to agree on the key elements of good looks. Researchers who study attractiveness focus primarily on facial features and physique. Both aspects are important in perceived attractiveness, but an unattractive body is seen as a greater liability than an unattractive face. In one study, when evaluating potential short-term partners, if men were allowed to see only a portion of the woman, they were more likely to choose to look at her body than her face (Confer, Perilloux, & Buss, 2010).

Michael Cunningham (2009a) identified four categories of qualities that cause someone to be seen as more or less attractive: neonate (baby-face) qualities, mature features, expressiveness, and grooming. Even across different ethnic groups and countries, there seems to be strong agreement on attractive facial features (Langlois et al., 2000). Women who have *neonate qualities* such as large eyes, prominent cheekbones, a small nose, and full lips tend to get high ratings.

In particular, the combination of these youthful features with *mature features* (prominent cheekbones, wide smile) seems to be the winning ticket (Cunningham, Druen, & Barbee, 1997)—think of Angelina Jolie. Men who have mature features, such as a strong jaw and a broad forehead, get high ratings on attractiveness (Cunningham, Barbee, & Pike, 1990)—George Clooney and Denzel Washington come to mind. Women also rate men with wide faces as more attractive than those with slim features (Valentine et al., 2014).

Currently in the United States, thinness receives heightened emphasis, especially for girls and women, although African American men and women prefer a larger body type than European American men and women do (Franko & Roehrig, 2011). Many studies show that repeated exposure to media portrayals of the thin ideal are associated with body dissatisfaction. Thus, it is not surprising that high school girls underestimate the body size that boys find attractive (Paxton et al., 2005). Also, many college women perceive themselves to be heavier than they actually are, and they often wish to be thinner (Vartanian, Giant, & Passino, 2001). Further, women who associate positive attributes with being underweight have a higher incidence of eating disorders (Ahern, Bennett, & Hetherington, 2008). We explore the important issue of eating disorders in the Chapter 14 Application.

Men, both gay and straight, also desire to be thinner and more muscular, and this dissatisfaction increases with age (Tiggemann, Martins, & Kirkbride, 2007). As American media increasingly objectify male bodies and men feel greater pressure to meet the ideals of the male body shape, there is a need for more research on underdiagnosed and undertreated eating disorders in men.

In addition to the physical characteristics we are born with, we also have *grooming qualities*, such as cosmetics, hairstyle, clothing, and accessories, that we use to enhance our physical attractiveness, (Cunningham, 2009a). Individuals will go to great lengths to improve their physical attractiveness, as demonstrated by the increased rate of cosmetic surgery. In 2014, more than 10 million cosmetic procedures were performed in the United States, costing more than $12 billion (see **Figure 9.2**). Liposuction, breast augmentation, and eyelid surgery were the three most common procedures. Additionally, procedures for men have increased 43% in the past five years (American Society for Aesthetic Plastic Surgery, 2015).

A specific grooming quality, our clothing choices, has garnered recent research attention. Interestingly, there is increasing evidence that wearing the color red increases a woman's perceived sexual attractiveness (Elliot & Niesta, 2008). Researchers speculate that

The color red is associated with increased perceptions of women's sexual attractiveness, perhaps because the color red signals peak fertility.

Studio 1One/Shutterstock.com

Figure 9.2

Top five surgical cosmetic procedures in 2014. The number of cosmetic surgeries annually is on the rise. In 2014, more than 10 million cosmetic procedures were performed.

Source: Retrieved from the American Society for Aesthetic Plastic Surgery (2015), www.surgery.org /media/statistics.

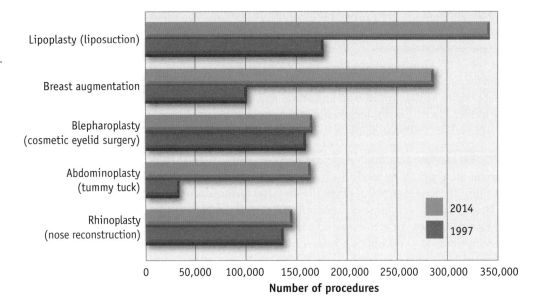

this is an evolutionary artifact related to displays of sexual receptivity (such as reddening of the chest or genitalia in nonhuman primates) (Kayser, Elliot, & Feltman, 2010). In support of this theory, studies have found that women are more likely to wear red around the time of their peak fertility (Beall & Tracy, 2013; Eisenbruch, Simmons, & Roney, 2015). Additionally, the influence of the color red on attractiveness appears to hold only for men's attraction to women, not the other way around. (Elliot et al, 2010). Let's take a deeper look at this phenomenon in the following Spotlight on Research.

Spotlight on RESEARCH

Is the Woman in Red Always Attractive?

Source: Young, S. G. (2015). The effect of red on male perceptions of female attractiveness: Moderation by baseline attractiveness of female faces. *European Journal of Social Psychology, 45*(2), 146–151.

As we have learned, the color red is associated with increased perceptions of women's sexual attractiveness, perhaps because the color red signals peak fertility. From an evolutionary perspective, this should both make women more attractive to potential mates and make women more likely to wear red when their fertility is high. Both of these assertions are supported by research. However, the red-attraction link appears to have boundaries. For instance, it holds only for young women, not those who are menopausal and thus incapable of childbearing. Additionally, little is known about the role of baseline attractiveness in the red-attraction link. If red is an indicator of sexual receptivity, could unattractive women in red be rated as *less* attractive by men as a way of avoiding sexual interest? The present research explored this question by manipulating the physical attractiveness of women's faces.

Method

Participants. Forty-six heterosexual men participated in the study (eleven black, fourteen Latino, five Asian, sixteen white). The average age was 21.1 years.

Materials. Attractive and unattractive photos of female faces were identified through pretesting. They were displayed on red, gray, and blue color panels matched in size and lightness.

Procedure. Participants were told the study was about "forming impressions of other people." At individual computer stations, they viewed forty female faces (twenty attractive, twenty unattractive) on a red, gray, and blue background. Each face was shown three times, once on each color background, for a total of 120 trials. Immediately after viewing each trial, participants rated the attractiveness of the face on a scale of 1 (extremely unattractive) to 7 (extremely attractive).

Results

The researchers found that facial attractiveness impacted the red-attraction link. The red background increased men's ratings of women's attractiveness, but only for the attractive faces. There was no influence of background color on unattractive faces.

Discussion

These results replicate findings that red enhances ratings of attractiveness. However, this study illustrates the importance of examining factors such as baseline attractiveness that might play a role in the red-attraction link. The researcher points out that there was no evidence that red *reduced* the attractiveness of unattractive faces, going against the idea that men might want to distance themselves from those potential mates. He also notes that some of the differences in the ratings, though statistically significant, were small. Even so, this study highlights the notion that the influence of color on perceptions of physical attractiveness is "nuanced and sensitive to social cues" (p. 150) and warrants further research.

Critical Thinking Questions

1. This study examined how facial attractiveness influenced the red-attraction link. What other of Cummingham's qualities of physical attractiveness do you think might influence this link? Explain why.
2. What other factors related to attraction discussed in this chapter, besides physical attractiveness, might influence the red-attraction link? Explain how.

Matching up on looks. Thankfully, people can enjoy rewarding social lives without being spectacularly good looking. In the process of dating and mating, people apparently take into consideration their own level of attractiveness. **The *matching hypothesis* proposes that people of similar levels of physical attractiveness gravitate toward each other.** This hypothesis is supported by findings showing that both dating and married heterosexual couples tend to be similar in physical attractiveness (Feingold, 1988; Hatfield & Sprecher, 2009). When measuring weight and body mass indexes, one study found that women's physiques were positively correlated to those of their fiancés (Prichard et al., 2015)

Although people often lust after others who are extremely attractive, the matching hypothesis kicks in when one is thinking about actually initiating a relationship. Montoya and Horton (2014) argue that the matching effects (as well as other considerations in attraction) result from one's assessment of two fundamental factors. One is the willingness of the target person to form a relationship with you (how much they like you). The other is their capacity to do so (how good a fit you think the person is). As such, someone "out of your league" might be judged as a poor fit, and therefore low in capacity. In this two-dimensional model, attraction occurs when someone is high on both factors.

According to the matching hypothesis, people tend to wind up with someone similar to themselves in attractiveness. However, other factors, such as personality, intelligence, and social status, also influence attraction.

Attractiveness and resource exchange. Physical attractiveness can be viewed as a resource that partners can exchange in relationships. A number of studies have shown that, in heterosexual dating, men value physical attractiveness in a mate more than do women, while women value social and occupational status more than do men (Li et al., 2013). Evolutionary social psychologists such as David Buss (1988, 2009) believe that these findings on status and physical attractiveness reflect gender differences in inherited reproductive strategies that have been sculpted over thousands of generations by natural selection. Their thinking has been guided by *parental investment theory*, **which maintains that a species' mating patterns depend on what each sex has to invest—in the way of time, energy, and survival risk—to produce and nurture offspring.** According to this model, members of the gender that makes the smaller investment will compete with each other for mating opportunities with the gender that makes the larger investment, and the gender with the larger investment will tend to be more discriminating in selecting its partners (Kenrick, Neuberg, & White, 2013).

David Buss uses an evolutionary perspective to explain gender differences in mate selection.

How does this analysis apply to humans? Like many mammalian species, human males are required to invest little in the production of offspring beyond the act of copulation, so mating with as many females as possible maximizes their reproductive potential. Also, males should prefer young and attractive females because these qualities are assumed to signal fertility, which should increase the chances of conception and passing genes on to the next generation. The situation for females is quite different. Females have to invest 9 months in pregnancy, and our female ancestors typically had to devote at least several additional years to nourishing offspring through breastfeeding. These realities limit the number of offspring women can produce, regardless of how many males they mate with. Hence, females have little or no incentive for mating with many males. Instead, females can optimize their reproductive potential by selectively mating with reliable partners who have greater material resources. These preferences should increase the likelihood that a male partner will be committed to a long-term relationship and will be

Evolutionary theory can explain why attractive women often become romantically involved with much older men who happen to be wealthy.

able to support the woman and their children, thus ensuring that her genes will be passed on (see **Figure 9.3**).

Are there alternatives to the evolutionary explanation for patterns of mate selection and resource exchange in heterosexual relationships? Yes, sociocultural models can also provide plausible explanations that center on traditional gender-role socialization and men's greater economic power. Some theorists argue that women have learned to value men's economic clout because their own economic potential has been severely limited in virtually all cultures by a long history of discrimination. Consistent with this hypothesis, women in countries with limited educational and career opportunities for females show the strongest preferences for men with high incomes (Eagly & Wood, 1999). Moreover, societies with more gender equality show less of the traditional gender differences in mate preferences (Zenter & Mitura, 2012).

Getting Acquainted

After several initial encounters, people typically begin the dance of getting to know each other. Is it possible to predict which budding relationships will flower and which will die on the vine? We'll examine two factors that can keep the ball rolling: reciprocal liking and similarity.

Reciprocal Liking

An old adage advises, "If you want to *have* a friend, *be* a friend." This suggestion captures the idea of the reciprocity principle in relationships. *Reciprocal liking* **refers to liking those who show that they like you.** Many studies show that if you believe another person likes you, you will like him or her, especially if you find that other person attractive (Montoya & Horton, 2012). Think about it. You respond positively when others sincerely flatter you, do favors for you, and use nonverbal behavior to signal their interest in you (eye contact, leaning forward). These interactions are enjoyable, validating, and positively reinforcing. As such, you usually reciprocate such behavior.

A specific type of reciprocity, *reciprocal self-disclosure*, is especially important in getting acquainted. As noted in Chapter 8, *self-disclosure* **is the voluntary act of sharing personal information about yourself with another person.** Self-disclosure typically starts slowly and gradually builds in terms of intimacy. It is associated with increases in positive relationship outcomes such as liking and closeness (Sprecher, Treger, & Wondra, 2013). When getting to know someone, taking turns sharing information is crucial (Sprecher et al., 2013; Sprecher & Treger, 2015). Researchers speculate that it is through this reciprocal exchange that potential partners obtain information about their degree of similarity.

Similarity

Do "birds of a feather flock together," or do "opposites attract"? Research offers far more support for the first saying than the second. In a longitudinal study of best friends, researchers found that similarity among friends in 1983 actually predicted their closeness in 2002—19 years later (Ledbetter, Griffin, & Sparks, 2007). We've already explored similarity in physical attractiveness (the matching hypothesis). Now, let's consider other similarities that contribute to attraction.

Heterosexual married and dating couples tend to be similar in *demographic characteristics* (age, race, religion, socioeconomic status, and education), *physical attractiveness, intelligence,* and *attitudes* (Watson et al., 2004). Support for similarity in *personality* as a factor in attraction is weaker and

BIZARRO

ONE SECOND BEFORE THE BLIND DATE

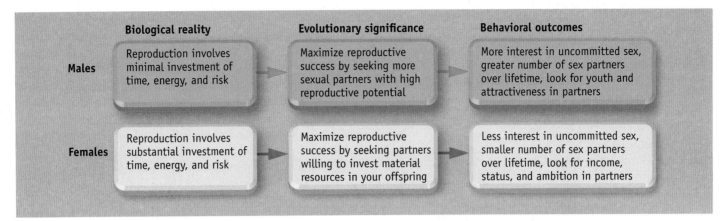

Figure 9.3

Parental investment theory and mating preferences. Parental investment theory suggests that basic differences between males and females in parental investment have great adaptive significance and lead to gender differences in mating propensities and preferences, as outlined here.

mixed. Results indicate that perceived similarity in personality might be more important than actual similarity, at least in the early phases of getting aquainted (Selfhout et al., 2009). For instance, a recent study revealed that perceived, but not actual, similarity significantly predicted romantic interest in a speed-dating context (Tidwell, Eastwick, & Finkel, 2013). Once people are in committed relationships, however, actual similarity in personality is associated with relationship satisfaction (Gonzaga, Campos, & Bradbury, 2007).

What is the appeal of similarity? For one thing, you might assume that a similar person will probably like you. Second, when others share your beliefs, you feel validated and accepted. Finally, people who are similar are more likely to react to situations in the same way, thus reducing the chances for conflicts and stress. However, it could be that liking actually leads to increased similarity as people become acquainted, rather than the other way around (Sprecher, 2014).

Established Relationships

Over time, some acquaintanceships evolve into established relationships. Individuals mutually determine the desired level of intimacy they want in a relationship, whether friendship or romantic. Although not all relationships need to be highly intimate to be satisfying, for some, intimacy is an essential ingredient of satisfaction. In either case, if they are to continue, close relationships must be maintained.

Maintenance of Ongoing Relationships

Although relationships are rewarding, they provide plenty of opportunities for conflict. Friends can have differing priorities, offend each other, and romantic partners can be tempted by others (Karremans, Pronk, & van der Wal, 2015). In sum, close relationships take work to maintain. *Relationship maintenance* **involves the actions and activities used to sustain the desired quality of a relationship.** These actions can be used to promote interdependence and stability or can protect a relationship from threat (Agnew & VanderDrift, 2015). In **Figure 9.4**, you can see a list of commonly occurring relationship maintenance behaviors. Often, these behaviors come about spontaneously (calling to check in, eating meals together); at other times, behaviors are more intentional and require more planning (traveling to visit family and friends). Obviously, strategies vary depending on the nature of a

RELATIONSHIP MAINTENANCE STRATEGIES	
Strategy	**Behavioral example**
Positivity	Try to act nice and cheerful
Openness	Encourage him/her to disclose thoughts and feelings to me
Assurances	Stress my commitment to him/her
Social networking	Show that I am willing to do things with his/her friends and family
Task sharing	Help equally with tasks that need to be done
Joint activities	Spend time hanging out
Mediated communication	Use email to keep in touch
Avoidance	Respect each other's privacy and need to be alone
Antisocial behaviors	Act rude to him/her
Humor	Call him/her by a funny nickname
No flirting	Do not encourage overly familiar behavior (relevant in cross-gender friendships)

Figure 9.4

Relationship maintenance strategies. College students were asked to describe how they maintained three different personal relationships over a college term. Their responses were grouped into eleven categories. You can see that, ironically, some people behave negatively in an attempt to enhance relationships. Openness was the most commonly nominated strategy. (Adapted from Canary & Stafford, 1994)

relationship (familial, friendship, romantic) and its stage of development (new, developing, mature). For example, married couples engage in more assurances than dating partners do (Stafford & Canary, 1991).

In long-distance relationships, communication is especially crucial for effective relationship maintenance. When coding the content of emails for long-distance romantic partners, Johnson and colleagues (2008) found that the most common categories used were assurances, openness, and positivity, in that order. More recent research shows that partners also use communicative maintenance behaviors through social network sites (Billedo, Kerkhof, & Finkenauer, 2015).

Relationship Satisfaction and Commitment

How do you gauge your satisfaction in a relationship? What determines whether you will stay in or get out of a relationship? *Interdependence* or *social exchange theory* **postulates that interpersonal relationships are governed by perceptions of the rewards and costs exchanged in interactions.** Basically, this model predicts that interactions among acquaintances, friends, and lovers will continue as long as the participants feel that the benefits they derive from the relationship are reasonable in comparison to the costs of being in the relationship. Harold Kelley and John Thibaut's interdependence theory (1978) is based on B. F. Skinner's principle of reinforcement, which assumes that people try to maximize their rewards in life and minimize their costs (see Chapter 2).

Rewards include such things as emotional support, status, and sexual gratification (in romantic relationships); examples of costs are the time and energy that a relationship requires, emotional conflicts, and the inability to engage in other rewarding activities because of relationship obligations. According to interdependence theory, people assess a relationship by its *outcome*—their subjective perception of the rewards of the relationship minus its costs (see **Figure 9.5**).

Individuals assess their *satisfaction* with a relationship by comparing the relationship outcomes (rewards minus costs) to their subjective expectations. **A *comparison level* is a personal standard of what constitutes an acceptable balance of rewards and costs in a relationship.** It is based on the outcomes you have experienced in previous relationships and the outcomes you have seen others experience in their relationships. Your comparison level may also be influenced by your exposure to fictional relationships, such as those you have read about or seen on television. Consistent with the predictions of exchange theory, research shows that relationship satisfaction is higher when rewards are perceived to be high and costs are viewed as relatively low.

To understand the role of *commitment* in relationships, we need to consider two additional factors. The first is **the *comparison level for alternatives*, or one's estimation of the available outcomes from alternative relationships.** In using this standard,

Figure 9.5

The key elements of social exchange theory and their effects on a relationship. According to social exchange theory, relationship *outcome* is determined by the rewards minus the costs of a relationship. Relationship *satisfaction* is based on the outcome matched against comparison level (expectations). *Commitment* to a relationship is determined by one's satisfaction minus one's comparison level for alternatives plus one's investments in the relationship.

Source: Adapted from Brehm, S. S., & Kassin, S, M. (1993). *Social psychology*. Boston: Houghton Mifflin. Copyright © 1993 by Houghton Mifflin Company. Adapted with permission.

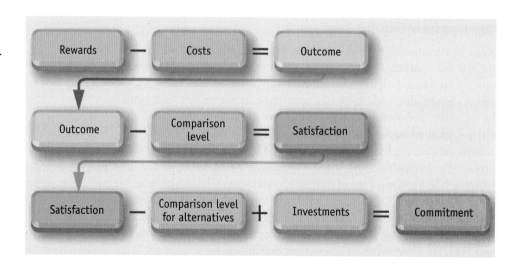

individuals assess their current relationship outcomes in comparison to the potential outcomes of other, similar relationships that may be available to them. This principle helps explain why many unsatisfying relationships are not terminated until another love interest actually appears. It also explains why someone might leave a seemingly happy relationship, if that person's expectations and standards were not being met. The second factor that figures in relationship commitment is *investments,* **or things that people contribute to a relationship that they can't get back if the relationship ends.** Investments include past costs (time, money) that they can never recover if the relationship fails. Understandably, putting investments into a relationship strengthens one's commitment to it.

Figure 9.5 demonstrates how interdependence theory works. If both members of a couple feel that they are getting a lot out of the relationship (lots of support, high status) compared to its costs (a few arguments, occasionally giving up preferred activities), they will probably perceive the relationship as satisfactory and will keep it going. However, if either partner begins to feel that the ratio of rewards to costs is falling below his or her comparison level, dissatisfaction is likely to occur. The dissatisfied person may attempt to alter the balance of costs and rewards or try to ease out of the relationship. The likelihood of ending the relationship depends on the number of important investments a person has in the relationship and whether the person believes that an alternative relationship that could yield greater satisfaction is available.

Research generally supports interdependence theory and its extensions (Van Lange & Balliet, 2015). However, many people resist the idea that close relationships operate according to an economic model. Much of this resistance probably comes from discomfort with the idea that self-interest plays such an important role in the maintenance of relationships. Resistance may also stem from doubts about how well social exchange principles apply to close relationships. In fact, there is some empirical support for this position. Margaret Clark and Judson Mills (1993) distinguish between *exchange relationships* (with strangers, acquaintances, co-workers) and *communal relationships* (with close friends, lovers, family members). Research suggests that in exchange relationships, the usual principles of social exchange dominate, but in communal relationships these principles don't apply (Morrow, 2009). For example, in communal relationships, you help people who are close to you without calculating whether and when they will reward you in kind.

9.2 Friendship

Learning Objectives

- Summarize the research on what makes a good friend.
- Describe some key gender and sexual orientation differences in friendships.
- Explain the friendship repair ritual as a way of dealing with conflict in friendships.

It's hard to overestimate the importance of friends. They give help in times of need, advice in times of confusion, consolation in times of failure, and praise in times of achievement. Friends clearly are important to individuals' adjustment. In fact, friendship quality is predictive of overall happiness, in part because friends satisfy basic psychological needs (Demir & Özdemir, 2010).

What Makes a Good Friend?

Exactly what makes someone a good friend? One approach to this question comes from a cross-cultural study of students in England, Italy, Japan, and Hong Kong (Argyle & Henderson, 1984). Notably, in this diverse sample, there was enough agreement on how friends should conduct themselves to identify several informal rules governing friendships, including sharing good news, providing emotional support, helping in times of need, making each other happy when together, trusting and confiding in each other, and standing up for each other. Notice that the common thread running through these rules seems to be providing emotional and social support.

Men's friendships, more so than women's, are based on shared interests and activities.

These informal rules seem to stand the test of time. More recently, Hall (2012) identified six friendship standards or expectations. First, *symmetrical reciprocity* relates to mutual loyalty and trust, characteristics that are often seen as central to relationships. Second, *agency* refers to the rewards or benefits friends provide us (such as popularity or money). Third, *enjoyment* reflects the importance of having fun with friends. Fourth, *instrumental aide* reflects direct support friends provide (for example, advice, a shoulder to cry on). Fifth, *similarity* in terms of attitudes, dispositions, and preferred activities is important. Finally, *communion* involves intimacy and self-disclosure. How well a friend meets these expectations is related to friendship satisfaction (Hall, Larson, & Watts, 2011).

Gender and Sexual Orientation

While men's and women's same-gender friendships have a lot in common, there are some interesting differences likely rooted in traditional gender roles and socialization. Consider the friendship expectations described previously. In a meta-analysis of thirty-seven studies, Hall (2011) found that women's friendships were higher than men's in symmetrical reciprocity, communion, enjoyment, and similarity; while men's friendships were higher in agency. There were no gender differences in instrumental aide. The current belief is that men's friendships are typically based on shared interests and doing things together, whereas women's friendships more often focus on talking—usually about personal matters (Fehr, 1996, 2004). So whose friendships are more intimate, men's or women's? Currently, there is controversy over this question. The most widely accepted view is that women's friendships are closer and more satisfying because they involve more intimacy and self-disclosure (Fehr, 2004).

The boundaries between the friendship and romantic or sexual relationships of gay men and lesbians appear to be more complex than those of heterosexuals. Many intimate relationships among lesbians begin as friendships and progress to romance and then to a sexual relationship (Diamond, 2007). Obviously, discerning and negotiating these shifts can be difficult. Also, both lesbians and gay men are more likely than heterosexuals to maintain social contacts with former sexual partners (Solomon, Rothblum, & Balsam, 2004). One possible explanation for this phenomenon is the small size of some gay and lesbian social networks (Peplau & Fingerhut, 2007). Also, compared to heterosexual couples, gay and lesbian couples have less support from families and societal institutions (Kurdek, 2005). So, maintaining close connections with friends and creating "safe spaces" through these connections is especially important (Goode-Cross & Good, 2008).

Conflict in Friendships

Friends, especially long-term ones, are bound to experience conflicts. As with other types of relationships, conflicts can result from incompatible goals, mismatched expectations, or changes in individuals' interests over time. When conflict arises, individuals might engage in strategies to preserve the friendship, such as attempting to make the friendship more enjoyable, providing extra emotional support, engaging in deeper conversations, or spending more time together (Oswald, Clark, & Kelly, 2004).

When conflicts occur, friends can work to overcome them. Cahn (2009) describes three steps in friendship repair rituals. First, there is a *reproach*, in which the offended party acknowledges the problem and asks the offender for an explanation. Second, the offender offers a *remedy* by taking responsibility and offering a justification, a concession, an apology, or a combination of these three. Finally, in the *acknowledgment* stage, the offended party acknowledges the remedy and the friendships progresses. Of course, at any point, either party can call off the ritual and dissolve the friendship.

9.3 Romantic Love

Although there are cultural differences in romantic attitudes and behaviors, romantic love is experienced in all cultures. Love is difficult to define, difficult to measure, and frequently difficult to understand. Nonetheless, psychologists have conducted thousands of studies and developed a number of interesting theories on love and romantic relationships.

Learning Objectives

- Identify some gender differences regarding love.
- Clarify the research findings on the experience of love in gay and straight couples.
- Compare Sternberg's triangular theory of love with the theory of adult attachment styles.
- Discuss the course of romantic love over time, including what couples go through as they dissolve a relationship.
- Explain why relationships fail and what couples can do to help relationships last.

Gender and Sexual Orientation

Stereotypes hold that women are more romantic than men. Nonetheless, research suggests just the opposite—that men are the more romantic gender (Fehr, 2015). For example, men hold more romantic beliefs ("Love lasts forever" or "There is one perfect love in the world for everyone") (Peplau, Hill, & Rubin, 1993). In addition, men fall in love more readily than women, whereas women fall out of love more easily than men (Hill, Rubin, & Peplau, 1976; Rubin, Peplau, & Hill, 1981). In an international survey, 48% of men reported experiencing "love at first sight" compared to 28% of women (Northrup, Schwartz, & Witte, 2012). Research also finds that while participants (both male and female) *believe* that women are more likely to confess love first, in *reality*, men are more likely to say "I love you" first, and they report more happiness when receiving confessions of love (Ackerman, Griskevicius, & Li, 2011) (see **Figure 9.6**). We should note, however, that there is more similarity than disparity in men's and women's conceptions of love.

Sexual orientation **refers to a person's preference for emotional and sexual relationships with individuals of the same gender, the other gender, or either gender.** *Heterosexuals* seek emotional-sexual relationships with members of the other gender. *Homosexuals* seek emotional-sexual relationships with members of the same gender. *Bisexuals* seek emotional-sexual relationships with members of both genders. In recent years, the terms *gay* and *straight* have become widely used to refer to homosexuals and heterosexuals, respectively. *Gay* can refer to homosexuals of either gender, but most homosexual women prefer to call themselves *lesbians*. Chapter 12 goes into more details regarding sexual orientation.

Many studies of romantic love and relationships suffer from **heterosexism, or the assumption that all individuals and relationships are heterosexual.** For instance, many questionnaires on romantic love and romantic relationships fail to ask participants about their sexual orientation. Thus, when data are analyzed, there is no way to know whether subjects are referring to same- or other-gender romantic partners. Assuming that their subjects are all heterosexuals, some researchers proceed to describe their findings without any mention of homosexuals. Because most people identify themselves as heterosexual, heterosexism in research isn't likely to distort conclusions about heterosexuals; however, it renders homosexual relationships invisible.

We discuss gay and lesbian committed relationships more in Chapter 10, so we will just touch on the basics here. Homosexuals face three unique dating challenges (Peplau & Spalding, 2003): They have a smaller pool of potential partners; they are often under pressure to conceal their sexual orientation; and they have limited ways to meet prospective partners. Also, fears of hostility or rejection may cause them to guard their self-disclosures to acquaintances and friends.

Even with these challenges, homosexual romances and relationships are essentially the same as those of heterosexuals. Both groups experience romantic and passionate love and make commitments to relationships (Fingerhut & Peplau, 2013). Both heterosexual and homosexual couples hold similar values about relationships, report similar levels of relationship satisfaction, perceive their relationships to be loving and satisfying, and say they want their partners to have characteristics similar to theirs (Peplau & Fingerhut, 2007). Further, both groups desire positive qualities, such as caring and friendliness, in a partner (Felmlee, Hilton, & Orzechowicz, 2012). When relationship differences are found, they are much more likely to be rooted in gender than in sexual orientation, as we'll see next.

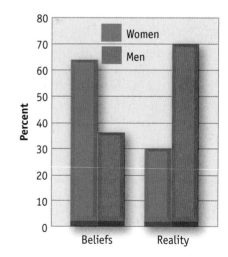

Figure 9.6

Who is the more romantic gender?
Ackerman and colleagues (2011) found that although both males and females believe that women are more likely to confess love first, in reality men are more likely to say "I love you" first.

Source: Adapted from Ackerman, J. M., Griskevicius, V., & Li, N. P. (2011). Let's get serious: Communicating commitment in romantic relationships. *Journal of Personality and Social Psychology 100*(6), 1079–1094.

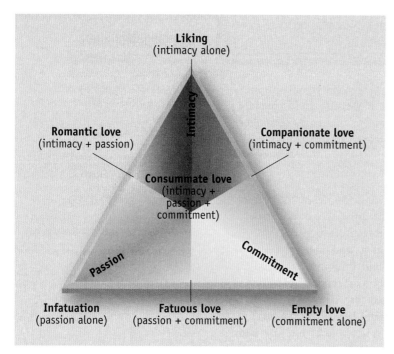

Figure 9.7

Sternberg's triangular theory of love. According to Robert Sternberg (1986), love includes three components: intimacy, passion, and commitment. These components are portrayed here as points on a triangle. The possible combinations of these three components yield the seven types of relationships mapped out here. The absence of all three components is called nonlove, which is not shown in the diagram.

Source: From Sternberg, R. J. (1986). A triangular theory of love. *Psychological Review, 93*, 119–135. Copyright © 1986 by the American Psychological Association. Reprinted by permission of the author.

Robert Sternberg's triangular theory of love includes three components: intimacy, passion, and commitment.

Theories of Love

Can the experience of love be broken down into certain key components? How are romantic love relationships similar to other types of close relationships? These are the kinds of questions that two current theories of love address.

Triangular Theory of Love

Robert Sternberg's (1986, 2012, 2013) *triangular theory of love* posits that all love experiences are made up of three components: intimacy, passion, and commitment. Each of the components is represented as a point of a triangle, from which the theory derives its name (see **Figure 9.7**).

Intimacy **refers to warmth, closeness, and sharing in a relationship.** Signs of intimacy include giving and receiving emotional support, valuing the loved one, wanting to promote the welfare of the loved one, and sharing oneself and one's possessions with another. Self-disclosure is necessary in order to achieve and maintain feelings of intimacy in a relationship, whether platonic or romantic.

Passion **refers to the intense feelings (both positive and negative) experienced in love relationships, including sexual desire.** Passion is related to drives that lead to romance, physical attraction, and sexual consummation. Although sexual needs may be dominant in many close relationships, other needs also figure in the experience of passion, including the needs for nurturance, self-esteem, dominance, submission, and self-actualization. For example, self-esteem is threatened when someone experiences jealousy. Passion obviously figures most prominently in romantic relationships.

Commitment **involves the decision and intent to maintain a relationship in spite of the difficulties and costs that may arise.** According to Sternberg, commitment has both short-term and long-term aspects. The short-term aspect concerns the conscious decision to love someone. The long-term aspect reflects the determination to help a relationship endure. Although the decision to love someone usually comes before commitment, that is not always the case (in arranged marriages, for instance).

Sternberg described eight types of relationships that can result from the presence or absence of each of the three components of love, as depicted in **Figure 9.7**. One of these relationship types, nonlove, is not pictured in the diagram because it is defined as the absence of any of the three components. Most casual interactions are of this type. When all three components are present, *consummate love* is said to exist.

Sternberg's model has generated considerable interest and research. In support of his theory, researchers report that Sternberg's three components characterize not only how people think about love in general but also how they personally experience love. All three components are positively related to satisfaction in dating relationships (Madey & Rodgers, 2009). In addition, they are applicable to same-sex romantic relationships as well (Bauermeister et al., 2011). Critics argue that the triangular theory alone doesn't fully capture the complexity of love. It seems that how people bond with others plays a role. To see why that might be the case, let's turn our attention to attachment theory.

Romantic Love as Attachment

In a groundbreaking theory of love, Cindy Hazan and Phillip Shaver (1987) asserted that romantic love can be conceptualized as an attachment process, with similarities to the bond between infants and their caregivers. According to these theorists, adult romantic love and infant attachment share a number of features: intense fascination with the other person, distress at separation, and efforts to stay close and spend time together. Of course, there are also differences: Infant-caregiver relationships are one-sided, whereas caregiving in romantic relationships works both ways. A second difference is that romantic relationships usually have a sexual component, whereas infant-caregiver relationships do not.

Today, adult attachment theory is one of the most influential approaches to the study of close relationships. Researchers who study attachment are keenly interested in the nature and development of *attachment styles,* **or typical ways of interacting in close relationships.** Their interest is fueled by the belief that attachment styles develop during the first year of life and strongly influence individuals' interpersonal interactions from then on.

Some researchers view romantic love as an attachment process, with similarities to the bond between infants and their caregivers.

Infant attachment. Hazan and Shaver's ideas build on earlier work in attachment theory by John Bowlby (1980) and Mary Ainsworth (Ainsworth et al., 1978). Based on actual observations of infants and their primary caregivers, they identified three attachment styles. More than half of infants develop a *secure attachment style.* However, other infants develop insecure attachments. Some infants are very anxious when separated from their caregiver and show resistance at reunion, a response characterized as an *anxious/ambivalent attachment style.* A third group of infants never connect very well with their caregiver and are classified in the *avoidant attachment style.* How do attachments in infancy develop? As you can see in **Figure 9.8**, three parenting styles have been identified as likely determinants of attachment quality. A *warm/responsive* approach seems to promote secure attachments, whereas a *cold/rejecting* style is associated with avoidant attachments. An *ambivalent/inconsistent* style seems to result in anxious/ambivalent attachments.

Adult attachment. What do these attachment styles look like in adulthood? To answer this question, we'll summarize the findings of a number of studies (Mickelson, Kessler, & Shaver, 1997; Shaver & Hazan, 1993). You can also see capsule summaries of adult attachment styles in **Figure 9.8**.

- *Secure adults* (about 55% of participants). These people trust others, find it easy to get close to them, and are comfortable with mutual dependence. They rarely worry about being abandoned by their partner. Secure adults have the longest-lasting relationships and the fewest divorces. They describe their parents as behaving warmly toward them and toward each other.
- *Avoidant adults* (about 25% of participants). These individuals both fear and feel uncomfortable about getting close to others. They are reluctant to trust others and prefer to maintain emotional distance from others. They have the lowest incidence of positive relationship experiences of the three groups. Avoidant adults describe their parents as less warm than secure adults do and see their mothers as cold and rejecting.
- *Anxious/ambivalent adults* (about 20% of participants). These adults are obsessive and preoccupied with their relationships. They want more relationship closeness than their partners do and suffer extreme feelings of jealousy, based on fears of abandonment. Their relationships have the shortest duration of the three groups. Ambivalent adults describe their relationship with their parents as less warm than secure adults do and feel that their parents had unhappy marriages.

The current thinking assumes that attachment style is determined by where people fall on two continuous dimensions (Brennan, Clark, & Shaver, 1998). *Attachment anxiety* reflects how much a person worries that a partner will not be available when needed. This fear of abandonment stems, in part, from a person's doubts about his or her lovability. *Attachment avoidance* reflects the degree to which a person distrusts a partner's goodwill and has tendencies to maintain emotional and behavioral distance from a partner. People's scores on these two dimensions as measured by self-report data yield four attachment

Figure 9.8

Infant attachment and romantic relationships. According to Hazan and Shaver (1987), romantic relationships in adulthood are similar in form to attachment patterns in infancy, which are determined in part by parental caregiving styles. The theorized relations between parental styles, attachment patterns, and intimate relations are outlined here. Hazan and Shaver's (1987) study sparked a flurry of follow-up research, which has largely supported the basic premises of their groundbreaking theory, although the links between infant experiences and close relationships in adulthood appear to be somewhat more complex than those portrayed here. (Based on Hazan & Shaver, 1986, 1987; Shaffer, 1989)

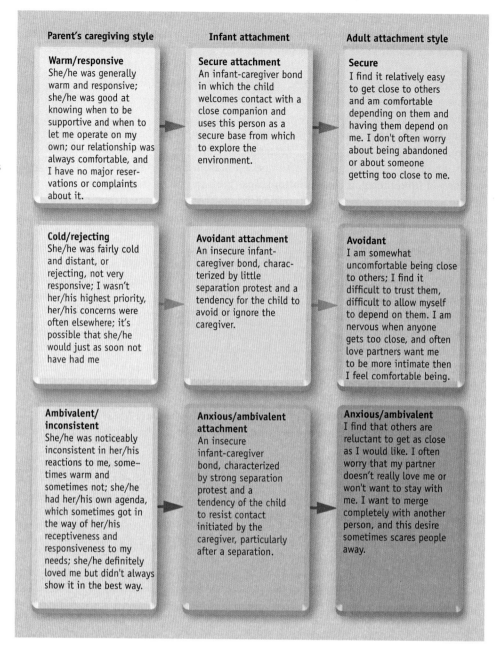

Parent's caregiving style

Warm/responsive
She/he was generally warm and responsive; she/he was good at knowing when to be supportive and when to let me operate on my own; our relationship was always comfortable, and I have no major reservations or complaints about it.

Cold/rejecting
She/he was fairly cold and distant, or rejecting, not very responsive; I wasn't her/his highest priority, her/his concerns were often elsewhere; it's possible that she/he would just as soon not have had me

Ambivalent/ inconsistent
She/he was noticeably inconsistent in her/his reactions to me, sometimes warm and sometimes not; she/he had her/his own agenda, which sometimes got in the way of her/his receptiveness and responsiveness to my needs; she/he definitely loved me but didn't always show it in the best way.

Infant attachment

Secure attachment
An infant-caregiver bond in which the child welcomes contact with a close companion and uses this person as a secure base from which to explore the environment.

Avoidant attachment
An insecure infant-caregiver bond, characterized by little separation protest and a tendency for the child to avoid or ignore the caregiver.

Anxious/ambivalent attachment
An insecure infant-caregiver bond, characterized by strong separation protest and a tendency of the child to resist contact initiated by the caregiver, particularly after a separation.

Adult attachment style

Secure
I find it relatively easy to get close to others and am comfortable depending on them and having them depend on me. I don't often worry about being abandoned or about someone getting too close to me.

Avoidant
I am somewhat uncomfortable being close to others; I find it difficult to trust them, difficult to allow myself to depend on them. I am nervous when anyone gets too close, and often love partners want me to be more intimate then I feel comfortable being.

Anxious/ambivalent
I find that others are reluctant to get as close as I would like. I often worry that my partner doesn't really love me or won't want to stay with me. I want to merge completely with another person, and this desire sometimes scares people away.

styles: secure, preoccupied (anxious/ambivalent), avoidant/dismissing, and avoidant/ fearful. You are already familiar with the secure style, and "preoccupied" is just a different label for the anxious/ambivalent style. The dismissing and fearful styles are two variations of the avoidant style.

As you can see in **Figure 9.9**, securely attached individuals (low on both anxiety and avoidance) enjoy close relationships and are not worried that others will leave them. Those in the *preoccupied* category (high on anxiety, low on avoidance) desire closeness with others but fear rejection. Those with an *avoidant/dismissing* style (high on avoidance, low on anxiety) prefer to maintain their distance from others and are not concerned about rejection, while those with an *avoidant/fearful* style (high on both avoidance and anxiety) are uncomfortable being close to others but still worry about rejection.

Although it might appear from **Figure 9.9** that the four attachment styles are distinctly different categories or typologies, that is not the case. Recall that the two underlying dimensions of anxiety and avoidance are distributed along a continuum (as indicated by the arrows in the figure) from low to high. This means that people are *more* *or less* anxious (or avoidant) versus totally consumed by anxiety or totally without anxiety. So, as you read about the four attachment styles, keep in mind that they are "convenient labels for sets of anxiety and avoidance scores rather than distinctly different categories that have nothing in common" (Miller, Perlman, & Brehm, 2007).

Correlates of attachment styles. The idea of adult attachment styles has stimulated a huge body of research. When researchers study the connection between attachment style and relationship quality, the findings generally support attachment theory predictions. Securely attached individuals have more committed, satisfying, interdependent, and well-adjusted relationships while insecurely attached individuals experience poorer relationship quality (Meyer et al., 2015; Pietromonaco & Beck, 2015). In a meta-analysis of more than 21,000 participants, high anxiety and avoidance were associated with problems in all aspects of relationships—cognitive, emotional, and behavioral (Li & Chan, 2012). Attachment styles have also been related to sexual satisfaction in heterosexual relationships: Anxious attachment in men is predictive of their female partners' sexual dissatisfaction, whereas avoidant attachment in women is related to male partners' sexual dissatisfaction (Brassard et al., 2012). Insecure attachment has also been linked to poor physical health (for example, impaired immune functioning) (Stanton & Campbell, 2014).

Given these findings, you might ask yourself, how do insecurely attached individuals maintain relationships? The answer might lie with their partner. Simpson and Overall (2014) argue that a person's partner can protect or buffer against the negative outcomes associated with an insecure attachment by providing reassurances of commitment, thus helping them feel more secure in the relationship. The idea of "partner buffering" illustrates the importance of examining the attachment styles of the couple, not just the individual (Tran & Simpson, 2012). This is an emerging research area that bears watching.

Stability of attachment styles. It appears that early bonding experiences do influence relationship styles later in life (Pietromonaco & Beck, 2015). A meta-analysis of longitudinal studies concluded that attachment styles are moderately stable over the first 19 years of life (Fraley, 2002). However, despite the relative stability of attachment styles, they are not set in stone. In childhood, changes from secure to insecure attachment are typically related to negative life events (divorce or death of parents, parental substance abuse, maltreatment) (Waters et al., 2000). Experiences later in life, such as consistent support (or lack thereof) from one's partner, can either increase or decrease one's attachment anxiety (Shaver & Mikulincer, 2008). One study reported that a significant number of individuals (ages 26–64) in short-term psychotherapy shifted from an insecure to a secure attachment style (Travis et al., 2001). Thus, therapy may be a helpful option for those with attachment difficulties. Contemporary researchers argue that social scientists should continue to explore how social experiences "accumulate" over time to influence adult romantic relationships (Simpson, Collins, & Salvatore, 2011).

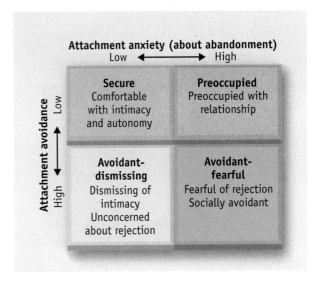

Figure 9.9

Attachment styles and their underlying dimensions. Attachment styles are determined by where people fall along two continuous dimensions that range from low to high: attachment avoidance and attachment anxiety (about abandonment). This system yields four attachment styles, which are described here. (Adapted from Brennan, Clark, & Shaver, 1998; Fraley & Shaver, 2000)

One's partner can buffer against the negative outcomes associated with an insecure attachment by providing assurances of commitment and security.

The Course of Romantic Love

Most people find being in love exhilarating and wish the experience could last forever. Must passion fade? Regrettably, the answer to this question seems to be "yes." Consistent with this view, Sternberg's (1986) triangular theory holds that passion peaks early in a relationship and then declines in intensity. In contrast, both intimacy and commitment increase as

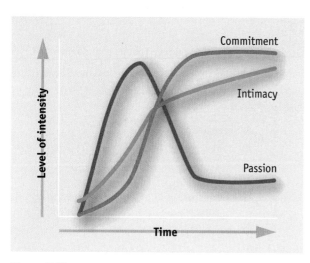

Figure 9.10

The course of love over time. According to Sternberg (1986), the three components of love typically progress differently over time. He theorizes that passion peaks early in a relationship and then declines. In contrast, intimacy and commitment are thought to build gradually.

time progresses, although they develop at different rates (see **Figure 9.10**). Research supports the idea that the intense attraction and arousal one feels for a lover do tend to subside over time—for both gay and straight couples (Fingerhut & Peplau, 2013).

Why does passion fade? It seems that three factors kick into high gear early, then begin to dissipate: fantasy, novelty, and arousal (Miller et al., 2007). At first, love is "blind," so individuals usually develop a fantasy picture of their lover (often a projection of their own needs). However, as time passes, the intrusion of reality undermines this idealized view. Also, the novelty of a new partner fades with increased interactions and knowledge. Finally, people can't exist in a state of heightened physical arousal forever.

Does the decline of passion mean the demise of a relationship? Not necessarily. Some relationships do dissolve when early passion fades, but many others evolve into different, yet deeply satisfying, mixtures of passionate/companionate love.

Why Relationships End

The question of why some relationships last while others end is a popular issue in relationship research. Nonetheless, the matter is complex, so easy answers have not been forthcoming. Furthermore, when it comes to breakups, there are often differences in what people *report publicly* as the cause, what they actually *think* is the cause, and what the cause actually *is* (Powell & Fine, 2009).

Threats to a relationship can be internal to the individual (insecure attachment, low self-esteem), internal to the relationship (unwillingness to sacrifice, waning commitment) or external (attractive alternatives, familial disapproval) (Agnew & VanderDrift, 2015). In a meta-analysis of 137 studies, Le and colleagues (2010) found that relationship-level factors such as commitment were better predictors of breakups than individual factors such as attachment style.

Let's take a look at a classic study, the Boston Couples Study (Hill et al., 1976). Here, 200 heterosexual couples (predominantly college students in Boston) were followed over 2 years. To participate, couples had to be "going steady" and believe that they were in love. If couples split, researchers asked them to give their reasons. The results of this and other studies (Buss, 1989; Powell & Fine, 2009; Sprecher, 1994) suggest that five prominent factors contribute to romantic breakups:

1. *Premature commitment.* Sometimes couples make romantic commitments without taking the time to get to know each other. These individuals may find out later that they don't really like each other or that they have little in common. For these reasons, "whirlwind courtships" are risky. Intimacy needs to be combined with commitment if relationships are to survive.

2. *Ineffective communication and conflict management skills.* Poor conflict management skills are a key factor in relationship distress and can lead to a breakup. Distressed couples tend to have more negativity in their communication, which can decrease problem solving and increase withdrawal (Cordova & Harp, 2009). In one study of more than 5000 participants in ninety-six countries, "lack of communication" was the most commonly reported reason for breakup (Morris, Reiber, & Roman, 2015). As we saw in Chapter 8, the solution to this problem is not to stifle all disagreements because conflict can be helpful to relationships. The key is to manage conflict constructively through effective communication.

3. *Becoming bored with the relationship.* As we have noted, once couples have been together for a period of time, the novelty of the relationship usually fades, passion decreases, and boredom can set in. Although predictability in close relationships is also important (Sprecher, 1994), becoming bored with one's partner can make others look even more attractive.

4. *Availability of a more attractive relationship.* Whether a deteriorating relationship actually ends depends, in great part, on the availability and awareness of a more attractive alternative (Lydon & Quinn, 2013). We all know of individuals who remained in unsatisfying relationships only until they met a more appealing prospect.

5. *Low levels of satisfaction.* The four factors above all contribute to low levels of relationship satisfaction. Obviously, many other factors play a role in relationship satisfaction, including one's expectations of a partner, attachment style, and stress level. Ultimately, becoming dissatisfied in a relationship erodes one's commitment and increases the chances of relationship dissolution.

How Relationships End

Sometimes relationships deteriorate to the point where one or both partners decide the relationship should end. Breakups are not single events; they are instead a process. Steve Duck and colleagues proposed a model describing six stages that partners go through in relationship dissolution (Duck, 1982; Rollie & Duck, 2006). First, the relationship experiences *breakdown processes*, in which one or both partners become dissatisfied. If this breakdown becomes extreme, either partner might engage in *intrapsychic processes*—ruminating about his or her dissatisfaction, the cost of the relationship, and attractive alternatives. If commitment wavers, the couple will engage in *dyadic processes* by discussing and negotiating the conflict. At this point the relationship can be repaired. However, if partners reach the decision to end their relationship, *social processes* occur as friends and family are alerted to the problem. As the couple moves toward breaking up, *grave-dressing processes* occur in which each partner develops a separate account of the breakup for his or her social network. Finally, each partner engages in *resurrection processes* to prepare for his or her new life. Interestingly, this model appears to apply to the dissolution of both romantic relationships and friendships (Norwood & Duck, 2009).

As one might expect, there are individual differences in adjusting to breakups. For instance, securely attached individuals tend to have more amicable breakups, blame their partner less, and are ready to date sooner than those who are insecurely attached (Madey & Jilek, 2012). In addition, being the initiator of the breakup and having a new partner are associated with better adjustment (Barutçu Yıldırım, & Demir, 2015), as is finding benefits in the breakup (Samios, Henson, & Simpson, 2014). Researchers are finding that the pain of breaking up might activate the same brain regions as actual physical pain (Eisenberger, 2012). That is, love (or the loss of it) can actually hurt.

Helping Relationships Last

Close relationships are important to our health and happiness (Loving & Sbarra, 2015; Loving & Slatcher, 2013), so how can we increase the likelihood that they will last? Research supports the following suggestions:

1. *Take plenty of time to get to know the other person before you make a long-term commitment.* Research based on Sternberg's theory shows that intimacy built through meaningful self-disclosure is a good predictor of whether dating couples' relationships will continue. Other advice comes from long-married couples who were asked why they thought their relationship had lasted (Lauer & Lauer, 1985). The most frequently cited responses of 351 couples who had been married for 15 years or more were (1) friendship ("I like my spouse as a person"); (2) commitment to the relationship ("I want the relationship to succeed"); (3) similarity in values and relationship issues ("We agree on how and how often to show affection"); and (4) positive feelings about each other ("My spouse has grown more interesting"). Thus, early attention to the intimacy foundations of a relationship and ongoing mutual efforts to build a commitment can foster more enduring love.

2. *Emphasize the positive qualities in your partner and relationship.* It is essential to communicate more positive than negative feelings to your partner. Early in a relationship, this is easy to do, but it gets harder as relationships continue. Unfortunately, when one

Figure 9.11

Most frequently cited causes of boredom in dating and married relationships. In a 2010 study of dating and married individuals, Harasymchuk and Fehr (2010) obtained participants' perceived causes of relational boredom. Many of these factors—including "doing the same things," which was the most frequently cited for both groups—overlap, but some are unique to one of the groups. As you can see, central to relational boredom is the lack of novelty.

Rank	Dating	Married
	CAUSES OF BOREDOM IN RELATIONSHIPS	
1	Doing same things	Doing same things
2	Fighting/arguments	Not going out, staying in
3	Watching movies together all the time	Not seeing partner
4	Spend too much time together	No communication
5	Routine	Work spillover
6	Not going out, staying in	Partner does things without spouse
7	Talk about the same things	Routine
8	Doing something partner likes, but you do not	Not socializing with others
9	Nothing to talk about	Watching movies together all the time
10	No communication	Talk about the same things

Research shows that couples who engage in exciting, novel activities together have higher relationship satisfaction.

partner makes more negative than positive statements, the other often responds in kind, which can set in motion a pattern of reciprocal negativity that makes things worse. Partners who see the best in each other, even in conflict, are more likely to stay together and experience greater satisfaction.

3. *Develop effective conflict management skills.* Conflicts arise in all relationships, so it's essential to handle them well. For one thing, it's helpful to distinguish between minor annoyances and significant problems. You need to learn to see minor irritations in perspective and recognize how little they matter. With big problems, however, it's usually best to avoid the temptation to sweep them under the rug in the hope that they'll disappear. Important issues rarely vanish on their own, and if you postpone the inevitable discussion, the "sweepings" will have accumulated, making it harder to sort out the various issues. For more specific suggestions on handling conflict, refer to our discussion in Chapter 8.

4. *Find ways to bring novelty to long-term relationships.* As romantic partners learn more about each other and develop feelings of intimacy, they also become more predictable to each other. But, too much predictability can translate into loss of interest. As you can see in **Figure 9.11**, central to relationship boredom is the lack of novelty. One way to keep things interesting is to engage in new activities together. In fact, one study reported that couples who participated in exciting activities together (versus just spending time together) showed increases in relationship satisfaction over a 10-week period (Reissman, Aron, & Bergen, 1993).

Learning Objectives

- Clarify how differences between Internet and face-to-face interactions affect relationship development.
- Describe the pros and cons of building intimacy online.
- Discuss the role of the Internet in face-to-face interactions.

9.4 The Internet and Close Relationships

The Internet has dramatically expanded opportunities for people to meet and to develop relationships through social networking services (Facebook, Twitter, Instagram), online dating services (eHarmony, Match.com), interactive virtual worlds, online multiple player games, chat rooms, and blogs. Critics of these social networking trends fear the demise of face-to-face interactions, widespread loneliness and alienation, and millions being lured into dangerous liaisons by unscrupulous people. But research to date generally paints a positive picture of the Internet's impact on people's connections with one another. For example,

Alone Together: Why We Expect More from Technology and Less from Each Other

by Sherry Turkle (Basic Books, 2012)

With advances in technology and the rise of the Internet, we have the opportunity to connect with others digitally as well as face-to face. In this book, Turkle (a clinical psychology professor at MIT) explores the "illusion of companionship" that these mediums provide. Drawing on hundreds of interviews, Turkle argues that technology is changing communication among individuals and can lead to emotionally empty relationships. She covers the gamut of technologies from robotic pets to social network sites to virtual realities, detailing their impact as we substitute these for human interaction. Part One describes the "robotic movement," including those involved in child care and elder care. Part Two explores how the Internet works as a social network, albeit a shallow and distancing one. She concludes by discussing how computers shape our behavior, arguing that computers are keeping us busy rather than the other way around. If we can see the problems inherent in expecting more and more from technology and less and less from one another, we can take steps to resist this trend and improve our relationships.

This is a well-written, well-referenced book that would be relevant to anyone interested in technology or interpersonal relationships. *Alone Together* is the third in a series including *The Second Self: Computers and the Human Spirit* (2005) and *Life on the Screen: Identity in the Age of the Internet* (1997).

the web offers a wealth of interaction opportunities for those normally separated because of geography or physical infirmity. However, experts caution that the distinction between online and face-to-face relationships is not as clear as many people assume, given that face-to-face relationships today usually have an online element (Whitty, 2013).

Developing Close Relationships Online

In a short period of time, the Internet has become an indispensable vehicle for making acquaintances and developing relationships. As seen in **Figure 9.12**, the majority of single Americans see online dating as socially acceptable (Statista, 2015). Finkel and colleagues (2012) argue that the Internet provides three unique advantages over face-to-face dating: (1) access to a wide array of potential partners, (2) easy and convenient communication between partners, and (3) the ability to match individuals with compatible potential partners. Madden and Lenhart (2006) asked Internet users who said they were single and looking for a romantic partner to identify how they used the Internet for dating. You can see their responses in **Figure 9.13**.

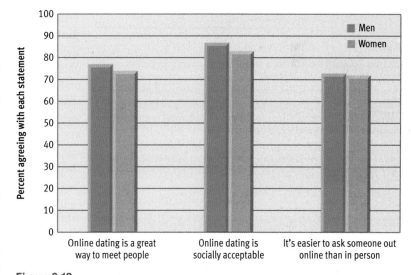

Figure 9.12

Attitudes toward online dating by gender. The Internet has dramatically expanded opportunities for people to meet and develop relationships. Among singles, online dating is now seen as socially acceptable by the majority of both men and women.

Source: Retrieved from Statista: The Statistics Portal (2015), www.statista.com/statistics/316481/us-beliefs-online-dating/.

The differences between online and face-to-face communication require psychologists to reexamine the established theories and principles of relationship development that we discuss in this chapter. For example, good looks and close physical proximity are powerful factors in initial attraction in the real world. On the Internet, where people often form relationships sight unseen, these factors are less relevant. In the absence of physical appearance, similarity of interests and values kicks in earlier and assumes more power than it does in face-to-face relationships (McKenna, 2009). Research indicates that the more similar an online friend, the stronger the bond (Mesch & Talmud, 2007). Even in long-term friendships, enhanced self-disclosure through emails or text messaging increases feelings of closeness (McKenna, 2009).

DATING-RELATED ACTIVITIES ONLINE	
Online activities	Single and looking Internet users (%)
Flirt with someone	40
Go to an online dating website	37
Ask someone out on a date	28
Find a place offline, like a nightclub or singles event, where you might meet someone to date	27
Been introduced to a potential date by a third party using email or instant messaging	21
Participate in an online group where you hope to meet people to date	19
Search for information about someone you dated in the past	18
Maintain a long-distance relationship	18
Search for information about someone you are currently dating or are about to meet for a first date	17
Break up with someone you are dating	9

Figure 9.13

Dating-related activities online. Researchers asked Internet users who were single and looking for a romantic partner how they used the Internet (including email and instant messaging) for dating (Madden & Lenhart, 2006). Flirting and going to an online dating website were most frequently mentioned. Most respondents engaged in three or fewer of these activities.

Source: Adapted from Madden & Lenhart (2006). Online dating. Retrieved April 29, 2007 from http://www.pewinternet.org/pdfs/PIP_Online_Dating.pdf. (Dating-Related Activities Online table, p. 5) Reprinted by permission of PEW Internet & American Life Project. Washington, D.C.

"Your online profile stated that you were tall, dark and handsome. Have you ever considered a career in fiction writing?"

Jerry King Cartoons, Inc.

Building Online Intimacy

Although critics are concerned that Internet relationships are superficial, research suggests that virtual relationships can be just as intimate as face-to-face ones and are sometimes even closer. In fact, a recent survey of more than 5000 users of eHarmony.com found that "interpersonal communication" was the main goal of usage (Menkin et al., 2015). Because the Internet provides the cloak of anonymity, people can take greater risks in online self-disclosure. Thus, feelings of intimacy can develop more quickly (Sprecher et al., 2105). Sometimes this experience can set up a false sense of intimacy, which can create uncomfortable feelings if a face-to-face meeting ensues— that is, meeting with a stranger who knows "too much" about you (Hamilton, 1999). Of course, such face-to-face meetings can also go smoothly. Experts caution, however, that whenever you share private information online, you are sharing it in a public space (DeAndrea, Tong, & Walther, 2011).

In addition to facilitating self disclosure, anonymity also allows people to construct a virtual identity. Obviously, this can be a problem if one person adopts a fictional persona and another assumes that it is authentic and begins to take the relationship seriously. A related concern is truthfulness. In one survey a whopping 86% of participants in an online dating site felt that others misrepresented their physical appearance (Gibbs, Ellison, & Heino, 2006). The most common factors that online daters misrepresent are age, appearance, and marital status (Byrm & Lenton, 2001). In fact, one study found that the lower the online daters' attractiveness, the more likely they were to lie about their physical descriptors such as height, weight, and age (Toma & Hancock, 2010). Another study of online daters age 53 to 74 found that both men and women attempted to represent themselves as more youthful than they really were (McWilliams & Barrett, 2014).

Some people rationalize lying online because it has practical advantages: Men on dating sites who claim to earn high salaries receive more replies than those who say they earn less money (Epstein, 2007). In addition, there are semantic misunderstandings: One person's "average" may be another person's "plump." Finally, creating an accurate online representation of oneself is a complex process: Individuals need to put their best self forward to attract potential dates, but they also need to present themselves authentically—especially if they expect to meet a person face-to-face.

Moving beyond Online Relationships

Many virtual interactions migrate to face-to-face relationships. Researchers find that romantic relationships that begin on the Internet seem to be just as stable over 2 years as traditional relationships (McKenna, Green, & Gleason, 2002). Additionally, there seems to be a curvilinear relationship between amount of communication online and the quality of the initial face-to-face meeting (Ramirez et al., 2015). That is, there appears to be a "tipping point" where continued interacting online becomes associated only with detriments in intimacy and information seeking in the initial meeting.

The Internet has definitely changed the relationship landscape, and not just in the initial stages of relationships (Finkel et al., 2012). Individuals can use the Internet to sustain contacts, reconnect, and even break up with others. Research shows that while social network sites allow for relationship maintenance behaviors in long-distance relationships, they also provide opportunities for partner surveillance and increased jealousy (Billedo, Kerkhof, & Finkenauer, 2015). In addition, research indicates that individuals who feel that their romantic partners use social network sites a lot also feel less intimacy with their partner (Hand et al., 2013). More research in this fascinating area will not only provide valuable information about virtual relationships but also reveal interesting new perspectives on face-to-face relationships.

APPLICATION

9.5 Overcoming Loneliness

Learning Objectives

- Describe loneliness and discuss its prevalence.
- Explain how early experiences and current social trends contribute to loneliness.
- Understand how shyness, poor social skills, and self-defeating attributions contribute to loneliness.
- Summarize the suggestions for conquering loneliness.

Answer the following "true" or "false."
____ 1. Adolescents and young adults are the loneliest age group.
____ 2. Many people who are lonely are also shy.
____ 3. The seeds of loneliness are often sown early in life.
____ 4. Effective social skills can be learned relatively easily.

All of the above are true, as you'll learn shortly. But let's start with a couple of general points. First, being alone doesn't necessarily produce feelings of loneliness. In these fast-paced times, solitude can provide needed down time to recharge your batteries. People also need time alone to deepen self-understanding, wrestle with decisions, and contemplate important life issues. Second, people can feel lonely even when surrounded by others (at a party or concert, for instance). It's possible to have a large social network but not feel close to anyone in particular.

The Nature and Prevalence of Loneliness

Loneliness **occurs when a person has fewer interpersonal relationships than desired or when these relationships are not as satisfying as desired.** Of course, people vary in their needs for social connections. Thus, if you're not distressed by the quantity or quality of your social and emotional ties, you wouldn't be considered lonely.

We can think about loneliness in various ways. One approach is to look at the type of relationship deficit involved (Weiss, 1973). *Emotional loneliness* stems from the absence of an intimate attachment figure. For a child, this figure is typically a parent; for an adult, it is usually a spouse, partner, or best friend. *Social loneliness* results from the lack of a friendship network (typically provided in school, work, or church settings and in community groups). For example, a married couple who moves to a new city might experience social loneliness until they make

A couple who moves to a new city might experience social loneliness until they make new friends. However, because they have each other, they should not experience emotional loneliness.

new social connections; however, because they have each other, they should not experience emotional loneliness. On the other hand, a recently divorced person will likely feel emotional loneliness but should not experience social loneliness if work and friendship networks remain intact.

Emotional loneliness seems to be tied to the absence of a romantic partner in both college students and senior adults (Green et al., 2001). Social loneliness, however, seems to spring from different roots, depending on age. In college students, it's the *quantity* of friendship contacts that counts; among the older group, it's the *quality* of contacts. It's also worth noting that social support can't compensate for emotional loneliness—for example, the presence of friends and family cannot substitute for a loved one who has died. Of course, this is not to say that social support is unimportant. The point is that different types of loneliness require different responses; therefore, you need to pinpoint the exact nature of your social deficits to cope effectively with loneliness.

A second way to look at loneliness is in terms of its duration (Young, 1982). *Transient loneliness* involves brief and sporadic feelings of loneliness, which many people may experience even when their social lives are reasonably satisfying. *Transitional loneliness* occurs when people who have had adequate social relationships in the past become lonely after experiencing a disruption in their social network (the death of a loved one, say, or a divorce or a move). *Chronic loneliness* is a condition that affects people who have been unable to develop a satisfactory interpersonal network over a period of years. Here we focus on chronic loneliness.

How many people are plagued by loneliness? Although we don't have a precise answer to this question, anecdotal evidence suggests that the number is substantial. The prevalence of loneliness in specific age groups actually contradicts stereotypes. For example, many assume that the loneliest age group is the elderly, but this "distinction" actually belongs to adolescents and young adults (Snell & March, 2008). Gay and lesbian adolescents are particularly likely to be lonely (Westefeld et al., 2001). Loneliness is also common among college students (Knox, Vail-Smith, & Zusman, 2007). Another surprising finding is that loneliness decreases with age, at least until the much later years of adulthood when one's friends begin to die or one becomes widowed (DePaulo, 2011).

Women are found to be lonelier than men, but only on measures that use words such as *lonely* or *loneliness* (Borys & Perlman, 1985). Thus, it is likely that this apparent gender difference is really men's reluctance to admit to feeling lonely. In fact, when surveying men and women in the Netherlands, researchers found that divorced men are more likely to suffer from emotional loneliness than divorced women are (Dykstra & Fokkema, 2007).

The Roots of Loneliness

Any event that ruptures the social fabric of a person's life may lead to loneliness, so no one is immune. We'll consider the roles of early experiences and social trends.

Early Experiences

A key problem in chronic loneliness seems to be early negative social behavior that leads to rejection by peers (Pedersen et al., 2007). Children who are aggressive or withdrawn are likely to suffer peer rejection even in preschool (Ray et al., 1997). What prompts inappropriate social behavior in young children? One factor is an insecure attachment style. Because of difficult early parent-infant interactions, children often develop social behaviors (aggression, aloofness, competitiveness, overdependence) that "invite" rejection by adults and peers (Bartholomew, 1990). You can see how a vicious cycle gets set up. A child's inappropriate behavior prompts rejection, which in turn triggers negative expectations about social interactions in the child, which can lead to more negative behavior, and so on. To help break this self-defeating cycle (and head off the loneliness that can result), it is crucial to help children learn appropriate social skills early in life. Without intervention, this cycle can continue and result in chronic loneliness. Indeed, one study found that attachment style at the age of only 24 months was predictive of later childhood loneliness (Raikes & Thompson, 2008).

Interestingly, researchers are starting to explore the genetics of loneliness. Studies suggest that the heritability of loneliness may be in the vicinity of 50% (Goossens et al., 2015). Of course, environmental factors are likely to interact with genetic predispositions. For example, social factors (such as rejection or low social support) might have a greater effect on those genetically predisposed to loneliness (Goossens et al., 2015).

Social Trends

Some social commentators and social scientists are concerned that recent trends are undermining social connections in our culture, making us "lonely in a social world" (Cacioppo & Patrick, 2008). A number of factors come into play. Parents (especially if they are single) may be so pressed for time that they have little time to cultivate adult relationships (Olds & Schwartz, 2009). Because of busy schedules, face-to-face interactions at home are reduced as family members eat on the run, on their own, or in front of the TV without meaningful family conversation. Further, superficial social interactions become prevalent as people order their meals and do their banking at drive-up windows, purchase their groceries via automated checkout stations, and so forth.

Even with the ubiquitous presence of social network sites, loneliness appears to be on the rise (Cacioppo et al. 2015b). While technology makes life easier in some respects and does provide opportunities for developing relationships, it has its downsides. As previously mentioned, online relationships can be devoid of true connection and intimacy, which can leave us feeling lonely.

Correlates of Loneliness

For people who are chronically lonely, painful feelings are a fact of life. Three factors that figure prominently in chronic loneliness are shyness, poor social skills, and a self-defeating attributional

Thanks to automation and online technology, people today are able to take care of many of life's necessities without interacting with other human beings. These reduced opportunities for social interaction help fuel increased loneliness.

style. Of course, the link between these factors and loneliness could be bidirectional. Feeling lonely might cause a person to make negative attributions about others, but making negative attributions can also lead to loneliness.

Shyness

Shyness is in associated with increased loneliness. *Shyness refers to discomfort, inhibition, and excessive caution in interpersonal relations.* Specifically, shy people tend to (1) be timid about expressing themselves, (2) be overly self-conscious about how others react to them, (3) embarrass easily, and (4) experience physiological symptoms of their anxiety, such as a racing pulse, blushing, or an upset stomach. In pioneering research on shyness, Philip Zimbardo (1977, 1990) and his associates report that 60% of shy people indicated that their shyness was *situationally specific.* That is, their shyness was triggered only in certain social contexts, such as asking someone for help or interacting with a large group of people. Shyness might be one reason some lonely people engage in unhealthy Internet usage (Huan et al., 2014). Supporting the importance of the situation, one study found that self-reported shyness was related to decreased self-disclosures in an online conversation, but only when a webcam was present. Shyness was not related to self-disclosure when there was no webcam (Brunet & Schmidt, 2007).

Learn More Online

The Shyness Homepage
The Shyness Institute (Portola Valley, CA) offers a "gathering of network resources for people seeking information and services for shyness." The site contains many online resources and provides access to research on shyness.

Poor Social Skills

A variety of problematic social skills are associated with loneliness. A common finding is that lonely people show lower responsiveness to their conversational partners and are more self-focused (Rook, 1998). Similarly, researchers report that lonely people are relatively inhibited and unassertive, speaking less than nonlonely people. They also seem to disclose less about themselves than those who are not lonely or who are less socially anxious (Cuming & Rapee, 2009). This (often unconscious) tendency has the effect of keeping people at an emotional distance and limits interactions to a relatively superficial level. These interactional problems are based, in part, on heightened fears of rejection (Jackson et al., 2002). It seems that people with "rejection anxiety" believe that their signaled interest is obvious to others when it is not (Vorauer et al., 2003). Thus, unaware that their signal was invisible, those with rejection anxiety may perceive rejection where none exists. The fact that social skills deficits and peer acceptance are predictive of loneliness isn't simply a Western phenomenon; it has been demonstrated among Japanese and Chinese students as well (Aikawa, Fujita, & Tanaka, 2007; Liu & Wang, 2009).

Self-Defeating Attributional Style

It's easy to see how repeated rejections can foster negative expectations about social interactions. Thus, lonely people are prone to irrational thinking about their social skills, the probability of their achieving intimacy, the likelihood of their being rejected, and so forth. Unfortunately, once people develop these negative ideas, they often behave in ways that confirm their expectations, again setting up a cycle of counterproductive behavior.

Jeffrey Young (1982) points out that lonely people engage in *negative self-talk* that prevents them from pursuing intimacy in an active and positive manner. He has identified some clusters of ideas that foster loneliness. **Figure 9.14** gives examples of typical thoughts from six of these clusters of cognitions and the overt behaviors that result. As you can see, several of the cognitions in **Figure 9.14** are stable, internal self-attributions. This tendency to attribute loneliness to stable, internal causes constitutes a self-defeating attributional style. That is, lonely people tell themselves that they're lonely because they're basically unlovable individuals. Not only is this a devastating belief, it is self-defeating because it offers no way to change the situation. Happily, it *is* possible to reduce loneliness, as you'll see.

Conquering Loneliness

The emotional consequences associated with chronic loneliness can be painful and sometimes overwhelming: low self-esteem, hostility, depression, alcoholism, possibly even suicide (McWhirter, 1990). Chronic loneliness also is associated with reduced physical health (Cacioppo et al., 2015a). A meta-analysis of seventy studies found that loneliness and social isolation are associated with early mortality to the same degree as risk factors such as obesity and lack of physical activity (Holt-Lunstad et al., 2015). Research indicates that the loneliness–physical

CLUSTERS OF COGNITIONS TYPICAL OF LONELY PEOPLE		
Clusters	**Cognitions**	**Behaviors**
A	1. I'm undesirable. 2. I'm dull and boring.	Avoidance of friendship
B	1. I can't communicate with other people. 2. My thoughts and feelings are bottled up inside.	Low self-disclosure
C	1. I'm not a good lover in bed. 2. I can't relax, be spontaneous, and enjoy sex.	Avoidance of sexual relationships
D	1. I can't seem to get what I want from this relationship. 2. I can't say how I feel, or he/she might leave me.	Lack of assertiveness in relationships
E	1. I won't risk being hurt again. 2. I'd screw up any relationship.	Avoidance of potentially intimate relationships
F	1. I don't know how to act in this situation. 2. I'll make a fool of myself.	Avoidance of other people

Figure 9.14

Patterns of thinking underlying loneliness. According to Young (1982), negative self-talk contributes to loneliness. Six clusters of irrational thoughts are illustrated here. Each cluster of cognitions leads to certain patterns of behavior (right) that promote loneliness.

Source: From a paper presented at the annual convention of the American Psychological Association, September 2, 1979. An expanded version of this paper appears in Emery, G., Hollan, S. D., & Bedrosian, R. C. (Eds.) (1981). *New directions in cognitive therapy.* NY: Guilford Press, and in Peplau, L. A., & Perlman, D. (Eds.) (1982). *Loneliness: A sourcebook of current theory, research and therapy.* NYk: Wiley. Copyright © 1982 by John Wiley & Sons, Inc. and Jeffrey Young.

health link might exist because lonely people are more susceptible to inflammation in response to stress (Jaremka et al., 2013). Although there are no simple solutions to loneliness, there are some effective ones. Let's look at four useful strategies.

One option is to use the Internet to overcome loneliness, although this approach has its hazards as well. On the plus side, the Internet is an obvious boon to busy people, those with stigmatized social identities, and those who find physical mobility difficult (for example, people with serious medical conditions). Among lonely people, Internet use is associated with benefits such as the formation of online friendships, improved social support, and ultimately reduced loneliness (Morahan-Martin & Schumacher, 2003; Shaw, & Gant, 2002). Moreover, socially anxious people can interact without the pressure involved in face-to-face communication (Bonetti, Campbell, & Gilmore, 2010). On the other hand, if lonely people spend a lot of time online, they might devote less time to face-to-face relationships and might not develop the self-confidence to pursue relationships offline. One study found that over time, excessive Internet use increased loneliness (Yao & Zhong, 2014).

A second suggestion is to resist the temptation to withdraw from social situations. A study that asked people what they did when they felt lonely found the top responses to be "read" and "listen to music" (Rubenstein & Shaver, 1982). These days, playing computer games and using the Internet are also options. If done occasionally, these activities can be constructive ways of dealing with loneliness. However, as long-term strategies, they do nothing to help a lonely person acquire new "real-world" friends. The importance of staying active socially cannot be overemphasized. Recall that proximity is a powerful factor in the development of close relationships. To make friends, you have to be around people.

A third strategy to thwart loneliness is to cultivate one's social skills. You'll find a wealth of information on this important topic in Chapter 8 (Interpersonal Communication). Lonely people, especially, should focus on attending to others' nonverbal signals, deepening the level of their self-disclosure, engaging in active listening, improving their conversational skills, and developing an assertive communication style.

A final strategy is to break out of the habit of the self-defeating attributional style we just discussed ("I'm lonely because I'm unlovable"). There are other attributions a lonely person could make, and these alternative explanations point to solutions (see **Figure 9.15**). If someone says, "My conversational skills are weak" (unstable, internal cause), the solution would be: "I'll try to find out how to improve them." Or, if someone thinks, "It always takes time to meet people when you move to a new location" (unstable, external cause), this attribution suggests the solution of trying harder to establish new relationships and giving them time to develop. The attribution "I've really searched, but I just can't find enough compatible people at my workplace" (stable, external cause) may lead to the decision, "It's time to look for a new job." As you can see, the last three attributions lead to active modes of coping rather than the passivity fostered by a self-defeating attributional style. Research finds this strategy to be the most effective in combating loneliness (Cacioppo et al. 2015b).

Anyone who feels overwhelmed at the prospect of tackling loneliness on his or her own should consider seeing a counselor

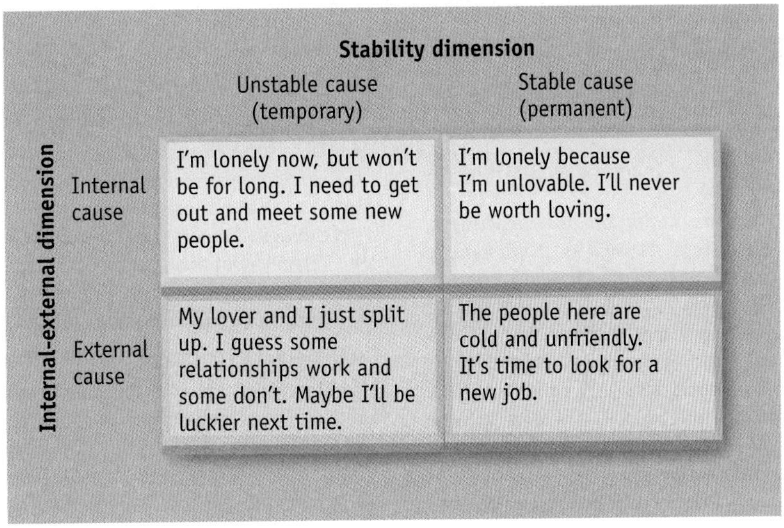

	Unstable cause (temporary)	Stable cause (permanent)
Internal cause	I'm lonely now, but won't be for long. I need to get out and meet some new people.	I'm lonely because I'm unlovable. I'll never be worth loving.
External cause	My lover and I just split up. I guess some relationships work and some don't. Maybe I'll be luckier next time.	The people here are cold and unfriendly. It's time to look for a new job.

Internal-external dimension

Figure 9.15

Attributions and loneliness. Lonely people often have a self-defeating attributional style, in which they attribute their loneliness to stable, internal causes (see upper right quadrant). Learning to make alternative attributions (see other quadrants) can bring to light ways to deal with loneliness and facilitate active coping.

Source: Based on Shaver, P., & Rubenstein, C. (1980). Childhood attachment experience and adult loneliness. In L. Wheeler (Ed.), *Review of personality and social psychology* (Vol.1, pp. 42–73). Thousand Oaks, CA: Sage Publications.

or therapist. Dealing with loneliness and shyness usually involves work on two fronts. First, counselors help people improve social skills through *social skills training*. In this program, individuals learn and practice the skills involved in initiating and maintaining relationships. Second, counselors use *cognitive therapy* (see Chapter 15) to help lonely and shy individuals break the habit of automatic negative thoughts and self-defeating attributions. Over a series of sessions, individuals learn to change their negative views of themselves ("I'm boring") and other people ("They're cold and unfriendly"). Both of these approaches have high success rates, and they can pave the way to more positive social interactions that are critical to adjustment.

CHAPTER 9 Review

Key Ideas

9.1 Relationship Development
- Close relationships are those that are important, interdependent, and long lasting. They include friendships as well as work, family, and romantic relationships. They can elicit both positive and negative emotions.
- People are initially drawn to others who are nearby, who are seen often, and who are physically attractive. Although physical attractiveness plays a key role in initial attraction, people also seek other desirable characteristics, such as kindness and intelligence. There is general agreement about what makes a person attractive. Red clothing may enhance attractiveness in women. People often match up on looks, but sometimes men trade status for physical attractiveness in women, and vice versa.
- As people get acquainted, they prefer others who like them and who are similar to them in various ways. Couples tend to be similar in age, race, religion, education, and attitudes.
- Once relationships are established, people engage in various maintenance behaviors and actions to sustain them. Interdependence (or social exchange) theory uses principles of reinforcement to predict relationship satisfaction and commitment. How individuals apply social exchange principles depends on whether they are in exchange or communal relationships.

9.2 Friendship
- A key component of friendship is emotional support. Women's same-gender friendships are usually characterized by self-disclosure and intimacy, whereas men's same-gender friendships typically involve doing things together. Some friendship issues are more complex for homosexuals than heterosexuals. Friends must engage in friendship repair if they are dealing with conflict.

9.3 Romantic Love
- Contrary to stereotypes, men may be more romantic in some ways than women. Many studies of romantic love and relationships suffer from heterosexism. Research indicates that the experience of romantic love is similar for heterosexual and homosexual individuals.
- Sternberg's triangular theory of love proposes that passion, intimacy, and commitment combine into eight types of love. Hazan and Shaver theorize that love relationships follow the form of attachments in infancy. Researchers subsequently expanded the number of attachment styles from three to four: secure, preoccupied, avoidant-dismissing, and avoidant-fearful. Each style has a characteristic profile. Although attachment styles show stability over time, it is possible for them to change.
- Initially, romantic love is usually characterized by passion, but strong passion appears to fade over time for a number of reasons. In relationships that continue, passionate love evolves into a less intense, more mature form of love.
- The chief causes of relationship failure are the tendency to make premature commitments, ineffective conflict management skills, boredom with the relationship, and the availability of a more attractive relationship. Breakups are a process, and there are individual differences in adjusting to breakups. To help relationships last, couples should take the time to know each other very well, emphasize the positive qualities in their partner and relationship, develop effective conflict management skills, and engage in novel activities together.

9.4 The Internet and Close Relationships
- The Internet offers many new vehicles for meeting others and developing relationships. The differences between Internet and face-to-face communication have important implications for established psychological theories and principles of relationship development.
- Virtual relationships can be just as intimate as face-to-face ones. However, people often misrepresent themselves online. Many online relationships go on to become face-to-face ones.

9.5 Application: Overcoming Loneliness
- Loneliness involves discontent with the extent and quality of one's interpersonal network. A surprisingly large number of people in our society are troubled by loneliness. The age groups most affected by loneliness contradict stereotypes.
- The origins of chronic loneliness can often be traced to early negative behavior that triggers rejection by peers and teachers. Social trends may also promote loneliness. Loneliness is associated with shyness, poor social skills, and self-defeating attributions.
- The keys to overcoming loneliness include resisting the temptation to withdraw from social situations, avoiding self-defeating attributions, and working on one's social skills.

Key Terms

Attachment styles p. 263
Close relationships p. 251
Commitment p. 262
Comparison level p. 258
Comparison level for
   alternatives p. 258
Heterosexism p. 261
Interdependence theory p. 258
Intimacy p. 262
Investments p. 259
Loneliness p. 271
Matching hypothesis p. 255
Mere exposure effect p. 252
Parental investment theory p. 255
Passion p. 262
Proximity p. 251
Reciprocal liking p. 256
Relationship maintenance p. 257
Self-disclosure p. 256
Sexual orientation p. 261
Shyness p. 273
Social exchange theory p. 258

Key People

David Buss p. 255
Michael Cunningham p. 253
Cindy Hazan and Phillip Shaver
   pp. 262–264
Harold Kelley and John
   Thibaut p. 258
Robert Sternberg p. 262
Philip Zimbardo p. 273

CHAPTER 9   Practice Test

1. The *mere exposure effect* refers to an increase in positive feelings due to
   a. seeing someone often.
   b. interacting with someone.
   c. communicating via email often.
   d. seeing someone once.

2. Jack and Liz have been dating for two years. They are a good example of the matching hypothesis. This means that they are matched on the basis of
   a. religion.
   b. personality.
   c. socioeconomic status.
   d. looks.

3. Tracey's personal standard of what constitutes an acceptable balance of rewards and costs in a relationship is termed
   a. *social exchange.*
   b. *comparison level.*
   c. *proximity level.*
   d. *relationship satisfaction.*

4. A sociocultural explanation for the finding that women emphasize economic potential more than men in choosing partners is that women
   a. have better vision than men.
   b. have historically had less economic power than men.
   c. are less superficial than men.
   d. have to compensate for being more romantic than men.

5. Women's same-gender friendships are typically based on _____; men's are typically based on _____.
   a. shopping together; hunting together
   b. attending sports events; watching sports events on televison
   c. shared activities; intimacy and self-disclosure
   d. intimacy and self-disclosure; shared activities

6. If a researcher fails to determine the sexual orientation of her research participants and reports her findings without any mention of homosexuals, her study suffers from
   a. homosexism.
   b. sexual dysfunction.
   c. heterosexism.
   d. homophobia.

7. Jenna tends to keep her distance from others and is unconcerned about social rejection. She would be classified in which of the following attachment styles?
   a. Secure
   b. Preoccupied
   c. Avoidant-dismissing
   d. Avoidant-fearful

8. Ross is going through a painful breakup. He is ruminating about his dissatisfaction, the costs of his relationship, and his alternatives. Steve Duck would say Ross is going through which of the following?
   a. Breakdown processes
   b. Intrapsychic processes
   c. Dyadic processes
   d. Social processes

9. Which of the following statements regarding self-disclosure in online communication is accurate?
   a. Because online communication is anonymous, people take fewer risks in online self-disclosure.
   b. Because online communication is anonymous, people take greater risks in online self-disclosure.
   c. Because there is a potential record of one's online communication, people take fewer risks in online self-disclosure.
   d. There is no difference in self-disclosure in online versus face-to-face communication.

10. A self-defeating attributional style associated with loneliness involves attributing loneliness to
    a. internal, stable factors.
    b. internal, unstable factors.
    c. external, stable factors.
    d. external, unstable factors.

Answers
1. a Page 252
2. d Page 255
3. b Page 258
4. b Page 256
5. d Page 260
6. c Page 261
7. c Pages 264–265
8. b Page 267
9. b Page 270
10. a Page 273

Personal Explorations Workbook

Go to the *Personal Explorations Workbook* in the back of your textbook for exercises that can enhance your self-understanding in relation to issues raised in this chapter.

Exercise 9.1 *Self-Assessment:* Social Avoidance and Distress Scale

Exercise 9.2 *Self-Reflection:* How Do You Relate to Friends?

CHAPTER 10 Marriage and the Family

Maksim Mazur/Shutterstock.com

"My hands are shaky. I want to call her again but I know it is no good. She'll only yell and scream. It makes me feel lousy. I have work to do but I can't do it. I can't concentrate. I want to call people up, go see them, but I'm afraid they'll see that I'm shaky. I just want to talk. I can't think about anything besides this trouble with Nina. I think I want to cry." —A recently separated man quoted in Marital Separation *(Weiss, 1975, p. 48)*

This man is describing his feelings a few days after he and his wife separated. He is still hoping for reconciliation. In the meantime, he feels overwhelmed by anxiety, remorse, and depression. His emotional distress is so great that he can't think straight or work effectively. Although this anecdote is from more than 40 years ago, his experience remains familiar. Breakups and divorce are devastating for most people—a reality that illustrates the enormous importance of intimate relationships in people's lives.

In the previous chapter, we explored the important role of close relationships in personal adjustment. In this chapter we focus on marriage and the family. We discuss why people marry and how they progress toward the selection of a mate. To shed light on marital adjustment, we describe the life cycle of the family, highlighting key vulnerable spots in marital relations and issues related to divorce. We will also address same-sex marriages and alternatives to marriage, including cohabitation and singlehood. Finally, in the Application we examine the tragic problem of violence in intimate relationships. Let's begin by discussing recent challenges to the traditional concept of marriage. ■

10.1 Challenges to the Traditional Model of Marriage

Learning Objectives
- Define *marriage* and discuss the current status of same-sex marriage.
- Discuss six social trends that are affecting the institution of marriage.

Marriage **is the legally and socially sanctioned union of sexually intimate adults.** In June 2015, the Supreme Court issued a landmark ruling that same-sex marriage was legal nationwide (Liptak, 2015), thus expanding the definition of *marriage* to include all adults regardless of gender and sexual orientation. Obviously, this changing landscape will stimulate research in years to come. It is important to note that for now, research in the area of marriage relies almost exclusively on heterosexual relationships and, when comparisons are made, they are typically with same-sex committed relationships as opposed to marriages. Unless otherwise noted, the research in this chapter involves heterosexual married couples. It will be interesting to watch how research progresses and how same-sex marriages will impact social trends.

Traditionally, the marital relationship has included economic interdependence, common residence, sexual fidelity, and shared responsibility for children. Although the institution of marriage remains popular, it sometimes seems to be under assault from shifting social trends (Teachman, Tedrow, & Kim, 2013). The percentage of married adults has been decreasing gradually since the 1960s. Take the past decade for instance: In 2014 the percentage of young adults (age 18 to 29) who have never been married was 64%, up from 52% in 2004 (Saad, 2015). This trend has prompted many experts to ask whether marriage is in serious trouble. Although it appears that the institution of marriage will weather the storm, we should note some of the social trends that are shaking up the traditional model (Helms, 2013).

1. *Increased acceptance of singlehood.* As previously mentioned, remaining single is a trend that has been on the rise for several decades. In part, this trend reflects longer postponement of marriage than before. **Figure 10.1** shows that the median age at which people marry has been increasing gradually since the mid-1960s. In 2015, the median age of first marriages was 27.1 years for women and 29.2 years for men (U.S. Census Bureau, 2015). Thus, remaining single is becoming a more acceptable lifestyle. As a result, the negative stereotype of people who remain single—lonely, frustrated, and unchosen—is gradually evaporating.

2. *Increased acceptance of cohabitation.* **Cohabitation is living together in a sexually intimate relationship without the legal bonds of marriage.** The prevalence of cohabitation has grown dramatically in recent decades, as has its social acceptance (Rose-Greenland

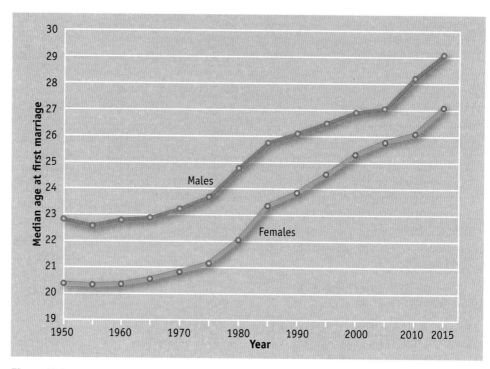

Figure 10.1

Median age at first marriage. The median age at which people in the United States marry for the first time has been creeping up for both males and females since the mid-1960s. This trend indicates that more people are postponing marriage. (Data from U.S. Bureau of the Census)

& Smock, 2013). Moreover, cohabiting relationships increasingly include children (Pew Research Center, 2015c).

3. *Reduced premium on permanence.* Most people still view marriage as a permanent commitment, but an increasing number of people regard divorce as justifiable if their marriage fails to foster their interests. Accordingly, the social stigma associated with divorce has lessened, and divorce rates in the United States are high, hovering around 40% (Kreider & Ellis, 2011).

4. *Transitions in gender roles.* Gender-role expectations are different for people entering marriage today than they were a generation or two ago. The traditional breadwinner and homemaker roles for the husband and wife are being discarded by many couples as more and more married women enter the workforce (Halpern, 2005; see **Figure 10.2**). In 2011, the number of families with a mother as the sole or primary breadwinner reached an all-time high of 40% (Wang, Parker, & Taylor, 2013). Role expectations for husbands and wives are becoming more varied, more flexible, and more ambiguous. Many people regard this trend as a move in a positive direction. However, changing gender roles create new potential for conflict between marital partners.

5. *Increased voluntary childlessness.* In the past decades, the percentage of women without children has climbed in all age groups as an increasing number of married couples have chosen not to have children or to delay having children (Shaw, 2011). Indeed, when compared to other countries worldwide, the United States has one of the highest childlessness rates (Livingston, 2014a). Researchers speculate that this trend is a result of new career opportunities for women, the tendency to marry at a later age, and changing attitudes (such as a desire for independence or concerns about overpopulation) (Hatch, 2009).

6. *Decline of the traditional nuclear family.* In the eyes of many Americans the ideal family should consist of a husband and wife married

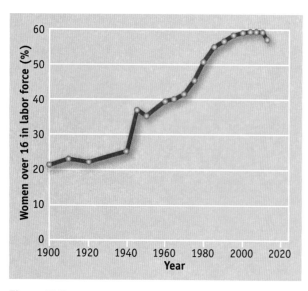

Figure 10.2

Women in the workforce. The percentage of women in the United States (older than age 16) who work outside the home has been rising steadily, although it has leveled off in recent years. (Data from U.S. Bureau of Labor Statistics)

for the first time, rearing two or more children, with the man serving as the primary breadwinner. In reality, this image was never all that accurate, and it still isn't. According to the Pew Research Center, fewer than half (46%) of American children live at home with both heterosexual parents (Livingston, 2014c). The diversity of modern family structures—including same-sex marriages, single-parent households, stepfamilies, and childless marriages—make the traditional nuclear family a bit of a mirage (Peterson & Bush, 2013). Interestingly, television shows today are beginning to depict these diverse family structures (for instance, *Modern Family*).

In summary, traditional marriage is no longer the only acceptable lifestyle that defines a family. The norms that mold marital and intimate relationships have been restructured in fundamental ways in recent decades. Thus, the institution of marriage is in a period of transition, creating new adjustment challenges for modern couples. Support for the concept of monogamy remains strong, but changes in society are altering the traditional model of marriage. The impact of these changes can be seen throughout this chapter as we discuss various facets of married life.

10.2 Deciding to Marry

Although alternatives to marriage are more viable than ever, experts project that more than 90% of Americans will marry at least once (Cordova & Harp, 2009). Some will do it several times! Further, most young people still view marriage as central to their future (Willoughby, Hall, & Goff, 2015). Why? As shown in **Figure 10.3**, American women overwhelmingly cite *love* as the reason they decided to marry. But how does culture influence marriage? How do individuals choose their partners? And what are some predictors of successful marriages? We'll address these questions as we discuss the factors that influence the decision to marry.

Cultural Influences on Marriage

Although it appears that romantic love is experienced in all cultures, there are cultural differences in romantic behaviors (Eastwick, 2013). For instance, cultures vary in their emphasis on romantic love as a prerequisite for marriage. Modern Western cultures are somewhat unusual in permitting free choice of one's marital partner. According to Elaine Hatfield and Richard Rapson (1993), "Marriage-for-love represents an ultimate expression of individualism" (p. 2). By contrast, marriages arranged by families and other go-betweens remain common in cultures high in collectivism (Merali, 2012). In fact, experts estimate

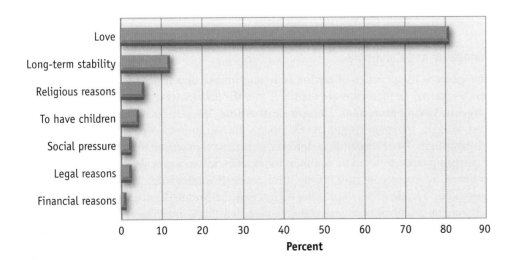

Figure 10.3

Why do women decide to marry? Campbell, Wright, and Flores (2012) conducted an online survey of 197 women who had been married less than 2 years and asked them the primary reasons they got married. As the figure shows, "love" was by far the most common response. (Adapted from Campbell, Wright, & Flores, 2012).

Marriages based on romantic love are the norm in Western cultures, whereas arranged marriages prevail in collectivist cultures.

that up to 80% of world cultures have arranged marriages (Pasupathi, 2009). This practice is declining in some societies, especially in urban settings, as a result of Westernization (Moore & Wei, 2012). Still, when people in collectivist societies contemplate marriage, they strongly weigh the impact the relationship will have on their family, rather than relying solely on what their heart says (Triandis, 1994).

People from Western societies often hold a simplistic view of collectivist cultures' deemphasis on romantic love and their penchant for arranged marriages, assuming that the modern conception of romantic love as the basis for marriage must result in better marital relationships than collectivist cultures' "antiquated" beliefs and practices (Grearson & Smith, 2009). However, there is little empirical support for this ethnocentric view. Take, for example, a study of couples in India, which found that love grew over the years in arranged marriages, whereas it declined among couples who married for romantic love (Gupta & Singh, 1982). Another study found that Indian couples in arranged marriages living in the United States reported higher marital satisfaction than U.S. couples who married by choice (Madathil & Benshoff, 2008). Further, it's estimated that the divorce rate for arranged marriages worldwide is only about 6% (Statistic Brain Research Institute, 2015). Granted, individuals in arranged marriages might be less likley to view divorce as an option, but perhaps assumptions about the superiority of Western ways are misguided, given our high divorce rates.

Selecting a Mate

Mate selection in American culture has typically been a gradual process that begins with dating and moves on to sometimes lengthy periods of courtship before marriage. Let's look at some of the factors that influence this important process.

Monogamy and Polygamy

Monogamy **is the practice of having only one spouse at a time.** In our society, monogamous marital relationships are the norm and the law. However, many cultures practice *polygamy,* **having more than one spouse at a time.** Westerners typically associate polygamy with the Mormon religion, even though the Mormon Church officially denounced polygamy in the late 19th century. However, polygamy is practiced worldwide. The practice of polygamy tends to be most common in societies where women have little or no independence, access to education, or political power (Cunningham, 2009b). In a review of cross-cultural studies from Australia, Africa, and the Middle East, Shepard (2013) found that women in polygamous marriages (also called plural marriages) had decreased life satisfaction, lower self-esteem, and higher rates of depression and anxiety compared to those in monogamous marriages. Women report that unhappiness, loneliness, a sense of competition, and jealousy are disadvantages of polygamy. Commonly reported ways of dealing with these disadvantages include believing that this way of life is God's will, allocating household resources equally, and maintaining an attitude of respect for the other wives (Slonim-Nevo & Al-Krenawi, 2006).

Endogamy and Homogamy

Endogamy **is the tendency for people to marry within their own social group.** Research demonstrates that people tend to marry others of the same race, religion, ethnic background, and social class (Surra & Boelter, 2013). This behavior is promoted by cultural norms and by the way similarity fosters interpersonal attraction. Although endogamy appears to be declining, this decrease has been gradual. For example, in 2010, 10% of all households reported an interracial marriage, up from 7% in 2000 (U.S. Bureau of the Census, 2012). This

People tend to marry others who are similar in race, religion, and social class—a phenomenon called endogamy.

is up from just 1% in 1970 (Gaines, 2009). Although some people speculate that interracial relationships carry an extra burden, research suggests that there are no differences between interracial couples and same-race couples in terms of relationship quality, conflict patterns, and attachment. In fact, interracial couples tend to report higher relationship satisfaction than others (Troy, Lewis-Smith, & Laurenceau, 2006), especially when partners feel positive about their own race while being accepting of others (Leslie & Letiecq, 2004). Interracial married couples report that race doesn't play a role in their everyday relationship experiences (Killian, 2012). However, it appears that biases still exist. When individuals were asked directly if they would be in favor of a family member having an interracial marriage, 54% of black participants said yes compare to only 26% of whites (Djamba & Kimuna, 2014).

Homogamy **is the tendency for people to marry others who have similar personal characteristics.** Among other things, marital partners tend to be similar in age and education, physical attractiveness, attitudes and values, marital history, and even vulnerability to psychological disorders. Interestingly, homogamy is associated with longer-lasting and more satisfying marital relations (Gonzaga, 2009). Even in dating relationships, similarity on a variety of characteristics is related to stability and satisfaction (Peretti & Abplanalp, 2004).

Gender and Mate Selection Preferences

Research reveals that males and females exhibit both similarities and differences in what they look for in a marital partner. Many characteristics, such as physical attractiveness, intelligence, humor, honesty, and kindness, are rated highly by both sexes (Lippa, 2007). Both male and female college students gave high ratings to the traits of honesty and trustworthiness for marriage partners (Regan & Berscheid, 1997). However, a few reliable differences between men's and women's priorities have been found, and these differences appear to be nearly universal across cultures.

As we saw in Chapter 9, women tend to place a higher value than men on potential partners' socioeconomic status, intelligence, ambition, and financial prospects. In contrast, men consistently show more interest than women in potential partners' youthfulness and physical attractiveness (Buss & Kenrick, 1998). Fletcher (2002) asserts that mate selection criteria can be grouped into three major categories: warmth/loyalty, vitality/attractiveness, and status/resources. Compared to men, women tend to place a greater emphasis on warmth/loyalty and status/resources and less of an emphasis on vitality/attractiveness. This gender difference is greater for long-term as opposed to short-term mate selection (Fletcher et al., 2004). Most theorists explain these gender disparities in terms of evolutionary concepts (Griskevicius, Haselton, & Ackerman, 2015).

Predictors of Marital Success

Are there any factors that reliably predict marital success? A great deal of research has been devoted to this question. This effort has been plagued by one obvious problem: How do you measure "marital success"? Some researchers have simply compared divorced and intact couples in regard to premarital characteristics. The problem with this strategy is that it assesses only commitment and not satisfaction. Many intact couples obviously do not have happy or successful marriages. Other researchers have used elaborate questionnaires to measure couples' marital satisfaction. Unfortunately, these scales appear to measure complacency and lack of conflict more than satisfaction (Fowers et al., 1994). Although research shows some thought-provoking correlations between couples' premarital characteristics and marital adjustment, most of the correlations are relatively small. Thus, there are no foolproof predictors of marital success. Nevertheless, here are some of the factors that researchers have investigated.

Family background. The marital adjustment of partners is correlated with the marital satisfaction of their parents. People whose parents were divorced are more likely than others to experience divorce themselves (Frame, Mattson, & Johnson, 2009). Researchers speculate that this intergenerational "divorce cycle" may be due in part to how individuals learn to resolve conflicts. For better or worse, they often learn this behavior from their parents. Rhoades and colleagues (2012) found that spouses whose parents were divorced reported more negative communication than those with parents who were still married. Further, Whitton and colleagues (2008) found that hostility levels of parents in family interactions predicted the marital hostility levels of their offspring 17 years later. This hostility level, in turn, predicted marital adjustment, especially for men. The researchers note, however, that other factors, such as the development of insecure attachment styles, might be at play here.

Age. The age at which one marries is also related to the likelihood of marriage success. Couples who marry young have higher divorce rates (Bramlett & Mosher, 2002), as **Figure 10.4** shows. Perhaps people who marry later have more carefully selected their mate or are less likely to undergo dramatic personal change that would render them incompatible with their partners.

Length of courtship. Longer periods of courtship are associated with a greater probability of marital success (Cate & Lloyd, 1988). Longer courtships may allow couples to evaluate their compatibility more accurately. Alternatively, the correlation between courtship length and marital success may exist because people who are cautious about marriage have attitudes and values that promote marital stability.

Personality. Generally, studies have found that partners' specific personality traits are not strong predictors of marital success. That said, there are some traits that show modest correlations with marital adjustment. For example, two predictors of marital dissolution are perfectionism (Haring, Hewitt, & Flett, 2003) and insecurity (Crowell, Treboux, & Waters, 2002). Recently, researchers have had more success exploring the link between people's underlying emotional dispositions and marital adjustment. They found that the intensity of smiling in college yearbooks (an indicator of positive emotional expression) was predictive of a lower likelihood of divorce in later life (Hertenstein et al., 2009). These researchers found similar results when they rated childhood photos of older adults; smiling in photos predicted marital success later in life. Although Hertenstein acknowledges that there are other explanations for the link (such as that smiling people might attract more friends and have more social support), he asserts that these results demonstrate the important role of positive emotional dispositions in life.

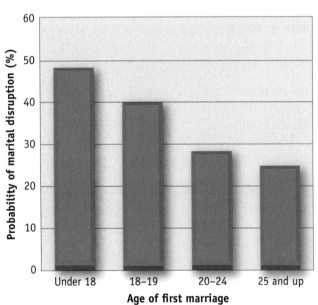

Figure 10.4

Age at marriage and probability of marital disruption after 10 years. Researchers have estimated the likelihood of marital disruption (either divorce or separation) after 10 years for various age groups. The data summarized here show that the probability of marital disruption is substantially higher among those who marry young. (Data from the Centers for Disease Control)

Premarital communication. As you might expect, how well couples get along during their courtship is predictive of their marital adjustment. The quality of premarital communication appears to be especially crucial. For example, the more that prospective mates are negative, sarcastic, insulting, and unsupportive during courtship, the greater the likelihood of marital distress and divorce (Clements, Stanley, & Markman, 2004). Close relationships that include self-disclosure and acceptance of what is learned through disclosure are likely to be the most satisfying over long periods of time (Harvey & Omarzu, 1999). Although most research in the area of communication has focused on discussions of conflict, one study found that being understood and validated in conversation is strongly related to satisfaction, even when the conversation is about a positive event (Gable, Gonzaga, & Strachman, 2006).

Stressful events. So far we have talked about issues that individual partners bring to a marriage, but these relationships don't exist in a vacuum. Stressful situations surrounding a marriage (unemployment, chronic illness, caregiving for an aging parent) can cause conflict, increase distress, and harm marital stability (Lavee, 2013). Partners who report higher levels of external stress also report more stress and tension in their close relationships (Ledermann et al., 2010). That is, when stress is high, partners have more negative interactions, thus eroding satisfaction (Buck & Neff, 2012). Neff (2012) suggests that stress harms marriages over time by limiting one's ability to engage in relationship-promoting behaviors. One exception to the stress-distress link is the stress related to becoming new parents, a topic we will talk about in more detail shortly.

10.3 Marital Adjustment across the Family Life Cycle

Learning Objectives

- Describe the family life cycle.
- Identify factors couples weigh in deciding whether to have children and analyze the dynamics of the transition to parenthood.
- Identify common problems that surface as a family's children reach adolescence and discuss the transitions that occur in the later stages of the family life cycle.

There are predictable patterns of development for families, just as there are for individuals. These patterns make up **the** *family life cycle,* **an orderly sequence of developmental stages that families tend to progress through.** The institutions of marriage and family are inevitably intertwined. With the advent of marriage, two persons create an entirely new family. Typically, this new family forms the core of one's life as an adult.

Sociologists have proposed a number of models to describe family development. Our discussion is organized around a six-stage model outlined by Carter and McGoldrick (1988, 1999). **Figure 10.5** provides an overview of their model. It spells out the developmental tasks during each stage of the life cycle for families that eventually have children and remain intact. Stress on the couple is typically highest as they transition from one stage to another, adjusting to new roles and redefining their relationship (McGoldrick & Shibusawa, 2012).

Admittedly, not all families progress through the family life cycle in an orderly fashion, and some researchers find that marital problems are similar whether a couple are newly married, have young children, or have been married for many years. Nevertheless, the model does appear to be a useful predictive tool for the marriage experience. Although Carter and McGoldrick have described variations on this basic pattern that are associated with remaining childless or going through a divorce (McGoldrick & Carter, 2003), we will focus primarily on the typical, basic pattern in this section. Note that the focus is on heterosexual couples in this section. It will be interesting to see how this model applies to gay and lesbian families in future research.

Between Families: The Unattached Young Adult

As young adults become independent of their parents, they go through a transitional period during which they are "between families" until they form a new family through marriage.

THE FAMILY LIFE CYCLE		
Family life cycle stage	**Key developmental task**	**Additional changes in family status required to proceed developmentally**
1. Between families: The unattached young adult	Accepting parent/offspring separation	a. Differentiation of self in relation to family of origin b. Development of intimate peer relationships c. Establishment of self in work
2. The joining of families through marriage: The newly married couple	Commitment to new system	a. Formation of marital system b. Realignment of relationships with extended families and friends to include spouse
3. The family with young children	Accepting new members into the system	a. Adjusting marital system to make space for child(ren) b. Taking on parenting roles c. Realignment of relationships with extended family to include parenting and grandparenting roles
4. The family with adolescents	Increasing flexibility of family boundaries to include children's independence	a. Shifting of parent-child relationships to permit adolescent to move in and out of system b. Refocus on midlife marital and career issues c. Beginning shift toward concerns for older generation
5. Launching children and moving on	Accepting a multitude of exits from and entries into the family system	a. Renegotiation of marital system as a dyad b. Development of adult-to-adult relationships between grown children and their parents c. Realignment of relationships to include in-laws and grandchildren d. Dealing with disabilities and death of parents (grandparents)
6. The family in later life	Accepting the shifting of generational roles	a. Maintaining own or couple functioning and interests in face of physiological decline; exploration of new familial and social role options b. Support for a more central role for middle generation c. Making room in the system for the wisdom and experience of the elderly; supporting the older generation without over-functioning for them d. Dealing with loss of spouse, siblings, and other peers and preparation for own death; life review and integrations

Figure 10.5

Stages of the family life cycle. The family life cycle can be divided into six stages, as shown here (based on Carter & McGoldrick, 1988). The family's key developmental task during each stage is identified in the second column. The third column lists additional developmental tasks at each stage.

What is interesting about this stage is that more and more people are prolonging it. As we saw in **Figure 10.1**, the median age for marriage has been gradually increasing for several decades. The extension of this stage is probably the result of a number of factors, including the availability of new career options for women, increased educational requirements in the world of work, an increased emphasis on personal autonomy, and more positive attitudes about remaining single.

Joining Together: The Newly Married Couple

The next phase begins when the unattached adult becomes attached. If the couple marries, the new spouses gradually settle into their new roles. For some couples, this phase can be quite troublesome, as the early years of marriage are often marred by numerous problems and disagreements. When reporting on marital satisfaction, 8%–14% of newlyweds score in the distressed range; the most commonly reported problems are balancing work and marriage and financial concerns (Schramm et al., 2005). In general, however, this stage tends to be characterized by great happiness—the proverbial "honeymoon stage" and "marital bliss." Spouses' satisfaction with their relationship tends to be relatively high early in marriage, before the arrival of the first child.

The prechildren phase used to be rather short for most newly married couples, as they quickly went about the business of adding to their family. Traditionally, couples have simply *assumed* that they would proceed to have children. In fact, remaining childless by choice used to be virtually unthinkable for women, as having a child was viewed as the ultimate fulfillment of womanhood (Ulrich & Weatherall, 2000). In recent decades, however, ambivalence about having children has clearly increased, and the Pew Research Center reports that about 15% of women will not have children by age 44, up from 10% in the 1970s (Livingston, 2015). It is worth noting that these data suggest that the childlessness trend might be on the decline, given that the rates peaked at 20% in 2005.

Couples who choose to remain childless cite the great costs incurred in raising children. Women especially cite career issues as playing a role in their decisions (Park, 2005), and voluntarily childless women tend to have higher incomes and more work experience than do other women (Abma & Martinez, 2006). Most voluntarily childless women do not regret their decision; however, those who wish to have children but cannot (due to infertility, for instance) express distress over their childlessness (McQuillan et al., 2012).

Although more couples are choosing not to have children, they are still in the minority. Most couples decide to have children, citing the responsibility to procreate, the joy of watching youngsters mature, the sense of purpose that children create, and the satisfaction associated with emotional nurturance and the challenges of childrearing (Cowan & Cowan, 2000). Further, the vast majority of parents report no regret about their choice (Demo, 1992).

The Family with Young Children

Although most parents are happy with their decision to have children, the arrival of the first child represents a major transition, and the disruption of routines can be emotionally draining, lessening parents' well-being. The transition to parenthood tends to have a greater impact on mothers than fathers (Nomaguchi & Milkie, 2003). The new mother, already physically exhausted by the birth process, is particularly prone to postpartum distress. According to the Centers for Disease Control and Prevention (2015b) approximately 8% to 19% of women report postpartum depressive symptoms. Risk factors for developing postpartum depression include past depression, high stress levels, and marital dissatisfaction (O'Hara, 2009). Issues such as infants' sleeps patterns and crying are also associated with mothers' depressive symptoms (Meijer & van den Wittenboer, 2007).

Recently researchers have been asking whether postpartum depression might be a "disease of modern civilization" (Hahn-Holbrook & Haselton, 2014). They argue that there have been cultural shifts—such as early weaning, poor diets, lack of physical activity, and isolation from extended family—that coincide with increasing postpartum depression. More research in this area will be helpful in testing these interesting theories.

The transition to parenthood is more difficult when a mother's expectations regarding how much the father will be involved in child care are not met (Fox, Bruce, & Combs-Orme, 2000). A review of decades of research on parenthood and marital satisfaction found that (1) parents exhibit lower marital satisfaction than comparable nonparents, (2) mothers of infants report the steepest decline in marital satisfaction, and (3) the more children couples have, the lower their marital satisfaction tends to be (Twenge, Campbell, & Foster, 2003).

Crisis during the transition to first parenthood is not a forgone conclusion, however. Nelson, Kushlev, and Lyubomirsky (2014) propose that the real question isn't whether parents are happier than nonparents, but under what circumstances parents experience the most well-being. Their review found that parents who focused on a greater meaning in life and had more positive emotions in parenthood showed increased well-being, whereas well-being decreased with increases in financial problems, sleep disturbance, and marital distress. The following Spotlight on Research further examines the circumstances in which parents are happier than nonparents.

Learn More Online

American Psychological Association: Parenting
The American Psychological Association is the largest professional organization for psychologists. This website presents up-to-date coverage of parenting research, including recent press releases and psychological research in the news. It also provides a peek into parenting research currently being published.

The arrival of the first child represents a major transition, and the disruption of routines can be emotionally draining, especially for mothers.

michaeljung/Shutterstock.com

Finding the Bundles of Joy in Parenting

Source: Nelson, S. K., Kushlev, K., English, T., Dunn, E. W., & Lyubomirsky, S. (2013). In defense of parenthood: Children are associated with more joy than misery. *Psychological Science, 24*(1), 3–10.

As we discussed, the transition to parenthood can be difficult. The birth of a new baby has been linked to increases in depression and reductions in marital satisfaction, life satisfaction, and overall well-being. These findings seem to fly in the face of the evolutionary perspective that holds reproduction and parenting most central to one's life. In fact, some studies do not find such negative outcomes for parents and indeed find positive outcomes (increased gratification, meaning) associated with parenting. The researchers speculate that these conflicting findings might be due to the use of different methodologies in the studies. Most studies are retrospective in that they ask parents to reflect back on and recall their feelings; this technique is susceptible to bias because parents might report what they want to believe they felt (or wanted to feel) as opposed to what they actually felt. Therefore, the researchers conducted a study to examine moment-to-moment experiences of parents and nonparents to see if there was a difference in their emotions.

Method

Three hundred and twenty-nine adults (53% women, 47% men) participated in the study. Each participant received an electronic pager, and over the course of 1 week was randomly paged five times a day. Each time participants were paged, they completed a brief response sheet rating their emotional experiences at the moment. At the end of the week, they mailed all response sheets to the researchers.

Results

Results showed that parents reported more moment-to-moment positive emotions overall than nonparents, but these findings rest predominantly on the experiences of fathers. Whereas fathers reported significantly higher happiness, positive emotion, and meaning in life, as well as lower levels of depression, than did childless men, mothers experienced greater positivity than childless women only in lower levels of depression.

Discussion

These results demonstrate that parenting doesn't necessary mean a decline in one's life satisfaction, and in fact can be a source of well-being. Obviously, the transition to parenthood is complex, and many factors can come into play (marital status of parents, age, financial stability, social support, to name a few). Furthermore, the researchers note that there could be selection effects in their data, in that perhaps happier people were more likely to choose parenthood. Although more research is needed, this study challenges the current belief that having children reduces a couple's happiness.

Critical Thinking Questions

1. Why might a moment-to-moment study yield more positive parenting experiences than a retrospective study?
2. What factors from your life might make you more or less likely to experience positive effects from being a parent?

Learn More Online

American Academy of Child and Adolescent Psychiatry (AACAP): Facts for Families
Many new parents may need help coping with emerging problems in their children. The brochures here (in a variety of languages, including English, Spanish, and Chinese) cover a wide range of psychological issues and psychiatric conditions.

The key to making the transition to parenthood less stressful may be to have *realistic expectations* about parental responsibilities (Belsky, 2009). Studies find that stress tends to be greatest in new parents who have overestimated the benefits and underestimated the costs of their new role. Reactions to parenthood may also depend on how well a couple's marriage is going (Lawrence et al., 2008). Couples with high levels of affection and commitment prior to the first child's birth are likely to maintain a stable level of satisfaction after the child's birth (Shapiro, Gottman, & Carrère, 2000). Although children clearly bring their share of challenges to a marriage, divorce rates are higher for those who remain childless (Shapiro et al., 2000).

The Family with Adolescent Children

Parents typically rate adolescence as the most difficult stage of parenting. However, problematic parent-teen relationships appear to be the exception rather than the rule (Smetana, 2009). As adolescent children seek to establish their own identities, parents must teach them the skills necessary to become competent, well-adjusted adults (Gavazzi, 2013). During this transition to independence, parents deal with the challenges of maintaining open communication and providing support while also maintaining some control (Longmore, Manning, & Giordano, 2013). Unsurprisingly, adolescents tend to exhibit better adjustment in families in which they are encouraged to participate in decision making but parents ultimately maintain control (Smetana, 2009).

When children hit adolescence, parental influence tends to decline while the influence of peer groups tends to increase. Parents tend to retain more influence than peers over important matters such as educational goals and career plans, but peers gradually gain more influence over less critical matters such as style of dress and recreational plans (Gecas & Seff, 1990). Thus, conflicts between adolescent children and their parents tend to involve everyday matters such as chores and dress more than substantive issues such as sex and drugs (Barber, 1994). Parents seem to learn from their experience in dealing with an adolescent child, as they report less conflict with their second adolescent child than their first (Whiteman, McHale, & Crouter, 2003).

In addition to worrying about their children, middle-aged couples are often at the stage where they must also focus on the care of their aging parents. Adults caught between these conflicting responsibilities have been called the *sandwich generation* (Boyczuk & Fletcher, 2015). According to the Pew Research Center (Parker & Patten, 2013), approximately 15% of middle-aged adults are caring for both an aging parent and a child, and they face increased financial strains as a result. These caregivers, especially those dealing with parents with dementia, experience increased stress, anxiety, and sadness (Solberg, Solberg, & Peterson, 2014). On the positive side, many caregivers describe the experience as gratifying in that it allowed them to repair or enhance damaged relationships (Fruhauf, 2009).

Launching Children into the Adult World

When children begin to reach their twenties, the family has to adapt to a multitude of exits and entries, as children leave and return, sometimes with their own families. This period, during which children normally become independent, brings a variety of transitions. In many instances, conflict subsides and parent-child relations become closer and more supportive.

One might argue that launching children into the adult world tends to be a lengthier and more difficult process today than it once was. As shown in **Figure 10.6**, the number of adults living with their parents is increasing. In 2014, the number of young adult women living at home reached a high (36%) that hasn't been seen since the 1940s (Fry, 2015). The rapidly rising cost of a college education and the shrinking job market have probably led many young adults to linger in their parents' homes. Moreover, crises such as separation, divorce, job loss, and single-parent pregnancy force many children who have ventured out on their own to return to their parents.

When parents do manage to get all their children launched into the adult world, they find themselves faced with an "empty nest." This period was formerly thought to be a difficult transition for many parents, especially mothers who were familiar only with the

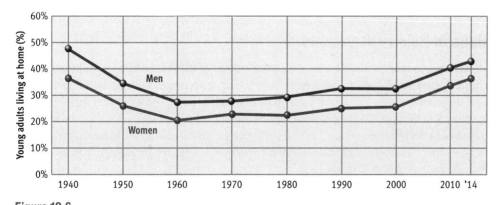

Figure 10.6

The percentage of adults living at home. According to the Pew Research Center, the percentage of adults ages 18 to 34 living at home with parents or relatives has increased since the 1960s. The recent upturn might be a result of the economic recession. (Data from the Pew Research Center)

maternal role. In recent decades, however, more women have experience with other roles outside the home and look forward to their "liberation" from childrearing responsibilities. Most parents adjust effectively to the empty nest situation, and this stage is generally a positive one for the family (Bouchard, 2014). In fact, parents are more likely to have problems if their children *return* to the once-empty nest, especially if these returns are frequent (Bookwala, 2009).

The Family in Later Life

Marital satisfaction tends to climb in the postparental period as couples find they have more time to devote attention to each other. This trend appears to be the result of partners' time together being more relaxed and enjoyable (Gorchoff, John, & Helson, 2008). Older couples rate children or grandchildren, good memories, and traveling together as the top three sources of pleasure (Levenson, Carstersen, & Gottman, 1993). However, spouses do have to adapt to spending more time with each other and often need to renegotiate role expectations. Of course, age-related considerations that are independent of the relationship, such as the increased likelihood of physical illness, can make the later years stressful. The three most commonly reported problems in late-life marriages are disagreements or disappointments about leisure activities, intimacy, and finances (Henry, Miller, & Giarrusso, 2005).

Being done parenting is not a forgone conclusion for this age group, however. In 2011, one in ten children were living with a grandparent, a trend more common for low-income families (Livingston, 2013). This increase is attributed to the increase in mothers' employment (Geurts et al., 2015). Taking on these parenting responsibilities adds to the stress of a family in later life. However, experts argue that caregiving also can provide older adults benefits such as cognitive stimulation (Arpino & Bordone, 2014).

Learning Objectives

■ Discuss how role expectations, work, and financial issues may affect marital adjustment.

■ Summarize evidence on the relationship between communication quality and marital adjustment.

10.4 Vulnerable Areas in Marital Adjustment

During courtship, couples tend to focus on pleasurable activities. But once couples are married, they deal with a variety of problems, such as arriving at acceptable role compromises, paying bills, and raising a family. All couples encounter problems, but successful marriages depend on couples' ability to handle their problems. Most of the sources of conflict faced by heterosexual couples are the same for same-sex couples; however, these couples have the burden of dealing with additional challenges within the context of stigmatization and prejudice (Patterson, 2013). In this section we analyze the major kinds of difficulties that couples are likely to face. Although there are no simple solutions for these problems, it helps to know where you're likely to encounter them.

Gaps in Role Expectations

When couples marry, they assume new roles—those of husband and wife, in heterosexual couples—and these tend to be gender based. Each role comes with certain expectations that the partners hold about how each spouse should behave. These expectations may vary greatly from one person to another. Gaps between partners in their role expectations can have a negative effect on couples' marital satisfaction. Unfortunately, substantial differences in role expectations seem particularly likely in this era of transition in gender roles, a topic we discuss in depth in Chapter 11.

Once upon a time, the role expectations for husbands and wives were fairly clear, but gender roles have changed as the structures of modern families have become more varied (Murry, Mayberry, & Berkel, 2013). A husband traditionally was supposed to act as the principal breadwinner, make the important decisions, and take care of certain household chores, such as car or yard maintenance. A wife was supposed to raise the children, cook,

SALLY FORTH

clean, and follow the leadership of her husband. As such, spouses had different spheres of influence (Coltrane & Shih, 2010). The working world was the domain of the husband, the home the domain of the wife. In recent decades, however, forces of social change have led to new expectations about marital roles. Thus, modern couples need to negotiate and renegotiate role responsibilities throughout the family life cycle.

Men's contribution to housework has increased noticeably since the 1960s, but wives are still doing the bulk of the household chores in America, even when they work outside the home (Blair, 2013). For example, research indicates that wives take responsibility for about 65% of total housework (not including child care), with husbands doing the remaining 35%. Moreover, wives still account for 78% of the essential "core housework" such as cooking, cleaning, and laundry, while men continue to handle more discretionary, traditional "male chores," such as yard or auto maintenance (Bianchi et al., 2000).

Although married women perform the majority of all housework, only about one-third of wives characterize their division of labor as unfair because most women don't expect a 50–50 split (Coltrane, 2001). Nevertheless, this one-third of wives constitutes a sizable population of women for whom housework is a source of discontent. As you might expect, wives who perceive their housework burden to be unfair tend to report lower levels of marital satisfaction (Coltrane & Shih, 2010). Interestingly, men who have lived independently for a longer period of time (that is, not with their parents, partners, or in dorms) are more egalitarian in their views about housework than are those who have had less of an independent "bachelorhood" (Pitt & Borland, 2008).

What about same-sex partners, where gender roles should be more similar? Moore (2008) found that for lesbian stepfamilies, the biological mother took more responsibility for child care and household chores than the stepmother. Interestingly, this gave these mothers more power in the home, both over childrearing and finances. Continued research in this area will provide more information about the influence of roles when gender differences are not an issue in the relationship (Murry, Mayberry, & Berkel, 2013).

Couples in which the husband holds egalitarian gender-role attitudes have higher levels of marital happiness than those where the husband holds more traditional attitudes (Frieze & Ciccocioppo, 2009). Given this finding, it is imperative that couples discuss role expectations in depth before marriage. If they discover that their views are divergent, they need to take the potential for problems seriously. Many people casually dismiss gender-role disagreements, thinking they can "straighten out" their partner later on. But assumptions about marital roles, whether traditional or not, may be deeply held and not easily changed.

Work and Career Issues

The possible interactions between one's occupation and one's marriage are numerous and complex. Although the data on the effect of income and employment on marital stability are inconsistent, individuals' job satisfaction and involvement can affect their own marital satisfaction, their partner's marital satisfaction, and their children's development. Conversely, being a parent seems to have an impact on one's career, especially for women. According to the Pew Research Center (2013), more than 51% of women say having children makes it more difficult to advance in their career, compared to only 16% of men.

Work and Marital Adjustment

Many studies have compared the marital adjustment of male-breadwinner versus dual-career couples. The interest in this comparison arises from traditional views that regard men's *lack* of employment and women's *employment* as departures from the norm. Typically, these studies simply categorize women as working or nonworking and evaluate couples' marital satisfaction. Most of these studies find little in the way of consistent differences in the marital adjustment of these two types of couples, and they often find some benefits for dual-career couples, such as increased social contacts, self-esteem, and egalitarian attitudes (Haas, 1999; Steil, 2009). Although dual-career couples do face special problems in negotiating career priorities, child-care arrangements, and other practical matters, their marriages need not be negatively affected.

However, the frustration and stress of an unsatisfying job might spill over to contaminate one's marriage. When pressures at work increase, husbands and wives report more role conflicts and often feel overwhelmed by their multiple commitments (Crouter et al., 1999). Furthermore, studies find that spouses' stress at work can have a substantial negative effect on their marital and family interactions (Perry-Jenkins, Repetti, & Crouter, 2001). For example, after highly stressful days at work, spouses tend to withdraw from family interactions (Repetti & Wang, 2009).

Although the difficulties involved in juggling work and family roles can be challenging, some theorists have argued that in the long run multiple roles are beneficial to both men and women. Barnett and Hyde (2001) assert that negative effects of stress in one role can be buffered by success and satisfaction in another role. They also note that multiple roles can increase sources of social support and opportunities to experience success. Moreover, when both spouses work outside the home, income tends to be greater, and spouses often find they have more in common. Interestingly, one study of gay fathers found that most men didn't report stress related to their roles and were generally satisfied with their work-family balance (Richardson, Moyer, & Goldberg, 2012).

Parents' Work and Children's Development

Another issue of societal concern has been the potential impact of parents' employment on their children. Virtually all of the research in this area has focused on the effects of mothers' employment outside the home. In 2010, approximately 21 million mothers were employed (U.S. Bureau of the Census, 2011). What does the research on maternal employment show? Although many Americans believe that maternal employment is detrimental to children's development, the vast majority of empirical studies have found little evidence that a mother's working is harmful to her children (Gottfried & Gottfried, 2008). A meta-analysis of sixty-nine studies found no link between maternal employment and children's achievement or behavioral problems (Lucas-Thompson, Goldberg, & Prause, 2010). In a longitudinal study spanning two decades, early maternal employment showed no apparent "sleeper effects"; that is, there were no negative outcomes that showed up later in life. These results have led researchers to conclude that the adverse outcomes of maternal employment are a "public myth" (Gottfried & Gottfried, 2008, p. 30).

In fact, maternal employment has been shown to have positive effects on children's development in some cases (Bush & Peterson,

Although many Americans seem to believe that maternal employment is detrimental to children's development, the vast majority of empirical studies have found little evidence that a mother's working is harmful to her children.

2013). Data from the Canadian National Longitudinal Survey of Children and Youth indicate that maternal employment is related to decreased hyperactivity, lower levels of anxiety, and increased prosocial behavior at age 4 (Nomaguchi, 2006). However, experts are careful to note that any benefits of maternal employment might also come at the cost of fewer positive interactions between the mother and child (Nomaguchi, 2006).

Financial Difficulties

Neither financial stability nor wealth can ensure marital satisfaction. However, financial difficulties can cause stress in a marriage, and finances are one of the top concerns for newlyweds (Schramm et al., 2005). According to a recent poll by the American Psychological Association (2015), 72% of Americans reported financial stress in the past month. Without money, families live in constant dread of financial drains such as illness, layoffs, or broken appliances. Thus, it is not surprising that serious financial worries among couples are associated with increased hostility in husbands, increased depression in wives, and lower marital happiness in both husbands and wives (White & Rogers, 2001). Further, children brought up in poverty exhibit poorer physical health, reduced mental health, lower academic performance, and increased delinquency in comparison to other children (Seccombe, 2001).

Even when financial resources are plentiful, money can be a source of marital strain. Studies have found that perceptions of financial problems (regardless of a family's actual income) are associated with decreased marital satisfaction (Dean, Carroll, & Yang, 2007). Further, differences in spending habits (tightwad, spendthrift) can also lead to marital conflict (Rick, Small, & Finkel, 2011).

So how do happily married couples deal with finances? Researchers asked couples who thought they had "great marriages" about their financial practices and found three common themes (Skogrand et al., 2011). First, one partner tended to handle the day-to-day money matters. Second, these couples had little debt or were actively paying off the debt they had. Third, these couples lived within their means and avoided buying what they couldn't afford. Ultimately, these highly satisfied couples emphasized the importance of constructive *communication* in financial matters.

Inadequate Communication

Effective communication is crucial to the success of any relationship, including marriage, and is consistently associated with greater marital satisfaction (Vangelisti, 2015). When examining couples in the process of a divorce, researchers found that communication difficulties were the most frequently cited problem among both husbands and wives (Bodenmann et al., 2007). In addition, communication is a highly ranked source of conflict for long-term married couples (Levenson et al., 1993). Research supports the notion that marital adjustment depends not on whether there is conflict (because conflict is virtually inevitable) but rather on how conflict is handled when it occurs (Gottman et al., 2014).

The importance of marital communication was underscored in a widely cited study by John Gottman and his colleagues that attempted to predict the likelihood of divorce in a sample of fifty-two married couples (Buehlman, Gottman, & Katz, 1992). Each couple provided an oral history of their relationship and a 15-minute sample of their interaction style, during which they discussed two problem areas in their marriage. The investigators rated the spouses on a variety of factors that most reflected the participants' ways of communicating with each other. Based on these ratings, they were able to predict which couples would divorce within 3 years with 94% accuracy!

Gottman, who is probably the world's foremost authority on marital communication, asserts that conflict and anger are normal in marital interactions and are not, in and of themselves, predictive of marital dissolution. Instead, Gottman (1994, 2011) identifies four other communication patterns, which he calls the "Four Horsemen of the Apocalypse," that are risk factors for divorce: contempt, criticism, defensiveness, and stonewalling. *Contempt* involves communicating insulting feelings that one's spouse is inferior. *Criticism*

John Gottman supports the notion that marital adjustment depends not on whether there is conflict, but rather on how conflict is handled when it occurs.

Recommended Reading

The Seven Principles for Making Marriage Work

by John M. Gottman (with Nan Silver) (Harmony Books, 2015)

Gottman, a leading expert in communication in intimate relationships, has studied this topic intensively for more than 30 years. A psychology professor at the University of Washington, Gottman is well known for his landmark research on the prediction of divorce. He has demonstrated that he can predict which couples will divorce with remarkable accuracy, based on careful examination of the couples' communication patterns. According to Gottman, the marriages that last are not those that appear to be free of conflict but those in which couples are able to resolve the conflicts that inevitably arise in intimate relationships. Gottman summarizes his work by introducing seven principles that, if followed, can save, protect, or enhance your marriage.

The Seven Principles for Making Marriage Work was originally published in 1999 and has sold millions of copies. It has been updated to account for the last 15 years of research. It is an outstanding book loaded with exercises, quizzes, and tips that should help readers improve their marital interactions. It is practical and readable, with plenty of case histories to make ideas come alive. Gottman has written other highly practical books on marriage that are also worth consulting: *The Relationship Cure* (2001), *10 Lessons to Transform Your Marriage* (2006), and *Baby Makes Three: The Six-Step Plan for Preserving Marital Intimacy and Rekindling Romance after Baby Arrives* (2008).

---

involves constantly expressing negative evaluations of one's partner. It typically begins with the word *you* and involves sweeping negative statements. *Defensiveness* refers to responding to contempt and criticism by invalidating, refuting, or denying the partner's statements. This obstructive communication style escalates marital conflict. *Stonewalling* is refusing to listen to one's partner, especially to the partner's complaints. Gottman eventually added a fifth troublesome communication pattern, *belligerence*, which involves provocative, combative challenges to the partner's power and authority (Gottman, Gottman, & DeClaire, 2006). Given the importance of good communication, many approaches to marital therapy emphasize the development of better communication skills in partners (Gottman & Gottman, 2008).

Learning Objectives

- Describe the evidence on changing divorce rates and the factors that go into deciding to divorce.
- Analyze how spouses and children tend to adjust to divorce.
- Summarize data on remarriage and the impact of stepfamilies on children.

10.5 Divorce and Its Aftermath

Divorce **is the legal dissolution of a marriage.** It tends to be a painful and stressful event for most people. Any of the problems discussed in the previous section might lead a couple to consider divorce. However, people appear to vary in their threshold for divorce, just as they do in their threshold for marriage. Some couples will tolerate a great deal of disappointment and bickering without seriously considering divorce. Other couples are ready to call their attorney as soon as it becomes apparent that their expectations for marital bliss were somewhat unrealistic. Typically, however, divorce is the culmination of a gradual disintegration of the relationship brought about by an accumulation of interrelated problems, which often date back to the beginning of a couple's relationship (Huston, Niehuis, & Smith, 2001).

Recently, researchers have noted that as a society our expectations for marriage have grown increasingly more demanding. We often expect help in everything from the basics of meeting everyday needs to the more substantive facilitation of one's growth in esteem and self-actualization. It seems that our expectations have become so high that many marriages can't live up to them. On the positive side, those marriages that can meet those high standards are highly fulfilling. Researchers have referred to this trend as the "all-or-nothing" model of marriage, in that we want it all or we don't want marriage (Finkel et al., 2015).

Divorce Rates

It is clear that divorce rates in the United States increased dramatically between the 1950s and 1980s, but they appear to have stabilized and even declined slightly since then. When divorce rates were at their peak, the most widely cited estimates of future divorce risk were around 50%. However, the modest reductions in divorce rates in recent years appear to have lowered the risk of divorce to about 40% (Kreider & Ellis, 2011). Nevertheless, because some marriages end in permanent separation instead of legal divorce, Amato (2010) suggests that the common belief that about half of marriages end is reasonable. Although most people realize that divorce rates are high, they have a curious tendency to underestimate the likelihood that they will personally experience a divorce. When asked directly, newlywed women pegged their probability of divorce at about 13%. Further, a full 97% of these women said they expected to remain married to their current spouse for life (Campbell, Wright, & Flores, 2012). Obviously, these estimations are far beyond the actual probability for the population as a whole.

Divorce rates are higher among blacks than whites or Hispanics, among lower-income couples, among couples with less education, among couples who cohabitated, among people who marry at a relatively young age, and among those whose parents divorced (Amato, 2010). As **Figure 10.7** shows, the vast majority of divorces occur during the first decade of a marriage (Copen et al., 2012). What types of marital problems are predictive of divorce? Frequently cited problems include communication difficulties (not talking; being moody, critical, and easy to anger), infidelity, jealousy, growing apart, careless spending behavior, and substance abuse problems (Amato & Previti, 2003).

A wide variety of social trends have probably contributed to increasing divorce rates. The stigma attached to divorce has gradually eroded. Many religious denominations are becoming more tolerant of divorce, and marriage has thus lost some of its "sacredness." The shrinking size of families probably makes divorce a more viable option for many couples. Also, the entry of more women into the workforce has made many wives less financially dependent on the continuation of their marriage. New attitudes emphasizing individual fulfillment seem to counter older attitudes that encouraged dissatisfied spouses to suffer in silence. Finally, the legal barriers to divorce have also diminished (Braver & Lamb, 2013).

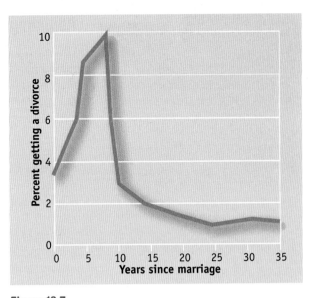

Figure 10.7

Divorce rate as a function of years married. This graph shows the distribution of divorces in relation to how long couples have been married. As you can see, the vast majority of divorces occur in the early years, with divorce rates peaking between the fifth and tenth years of marriage. (Data from National Center for Health Statistics)

Deciding on a Divorce

Divorces are often postponed repeatedly, and they are rarely executed without a great deal of agonizing forethought. The decision to divorce is usually the outcome of a long series of smaller decisions or relationship stages that may take years to unfold, so divorce should be viewed as a process rather than as a discrete event. Wives' judgments about the likelihood of their marriages ending in divorce tend to be more accurate than husbands' judgments (South, Bose, & Trent, 2004). This finding may be related to the fact that wives initiate the majority of divorce actions (Hetherington, 2003).

It is difficult to generalize about the relative merits of divorce as opposed to remaining in an unsatisfactory marriage. Extensive research shows that people who are currently divorced suffer a higher incidence of both physical and psychological maladies and are less happy than those who are currently married (Sbarra & Beck, 2013). In a meta-analysis involving thirty-two studies across eleven countries, Sbarra and colleagues (2011) found that divorce was associated with early death risk, especially for men. Nevertheless, as painful as marital dissolution may be, remaining in an unhappy marriage is also potentially detrimental. Research has shown that in comparison to divorced individuals, unhappily married people tend to show poorer physical health and lower levels of happiness, life satisfaction, and self-esteem (Hawkins & Booth, 2005; Wickrama et al., 1997). In addition, divorce is often related to higher rates of autonomy, self-awareness, and job success, especially when individuals have a stable financial situation and a strong social support network (Trotter, 2009). So the picture is not entirely negative.

Adjusting to Divorce

Divorce is a major disruption that has negative impacts on the entire family, but some of those impacts vary by gender (Sbarra & Beck, 2013). Although divorce seems to have a more negative impact on men's health and mortality (Amato, 2010), it appears to be more difficult and disruptive for women in terms of finances (Trotter, 2009). Women are more likely to assume the responsibility of raising the children, whereas men tend to reduce their contact with their children, some losing contact with them altogether. Another key consideration is that divorced women are less likely than their ex-husbands to have an adequate income or a satisfying job (Smock, Manning, & Gupta, 1999). Although the economic consequences of divorce can be more severe for women than for men, in this era of two-income families, many men also experience a noticeable decline in their standard of living after going through a divorce (McManus & DiPrete, 2001).

The process of getting divorced is stressful for both spouses. Researchers do *not* find consistent gender differences in psychological adjustment to divorce (Amato, 2001). In the aggregate, the magnitude of the negative effects of divorce on individuals' psychological well-being seems to be pretty similar for husbands and wives. Factors associated with favorable postdivorce adjustment include having higher income, getting remarried, and having more positive attitudes about divorce (Wang & Amato, 2000). In addition, it helps to be the partner who initiated the divorce (Frisby et al., 2012). After a divorce, having social relationships, including both one-to-one friendships and a circle of friends, is important to adjustment (Krumrei et al., 2007). Forgiveness of the ex-spouse is also associated with increased well-being and lowered depression (Rye et al., 2004). Similarly, evidence suggests that self-compassion (showing kindness to and forgiving oneself about the divorce) is associated with less postdivorce distress (Sbarra, Smith, & Mehl, 2012).

Effects of Divorce on Children

As divorce rates increase, so do the number of children from divorced families. When couples have children, decisions about divorce must take into account the potential impact on their offspring. Widely publicized research by Judith Wallerstein and her colleagues has painted a rather bleak picture of how divorce affects youngsters (Wallerstein & Blakeslee, 1989; Wallerstein, Lewis, & Blakeslee, 2000). This research followed a sample of 60 divorced couples and their 131 children for 25 years, beginning in 1971. At the 10-year follow-up, almost half of the participants were characterized as "worried, underachieving, self-deprecating, and sometimes angry young men and women" (Wallerstein & Blakeslee, 1989, p. 299). Even *25 years* after their parents' divorce, a majority of subjects were viewed as troubled adults who found it difficult to maintain stable and satisfying intimate relationships (Wallerstein, 2005; Wallerstein & Lewis, 2004).

Critics, however, point to a variety of potential flaws in Wallerstein's research (Amato, 2003; Cherlin, 1999). For example, it was based on a small sample of children from a wealthy area in California that was not representative of the population at large. Also there was no comparison group, and conclusions were based on impressions from clinical interviews, in which it is easy for interviewers to see what they expect to see. Further, critics caution against drawing causal conclusions from such correlational data (Gordon, 2005).

Are Wallerstein's findings consistent with other research? Yes and no. The results of another long-running study by E. Mavis Hetherington (1993, 1999, 2003), which used a larger and more representative sample, a control group, and conventional statistical comparisons, suggest that Wallerstein's conclusions are unduly pessimistic. According to Hetherington, divorce can be traumatic for children, but a substantial majority adjust reasonably well after 2 to 3 years, and only about 25% show serious psychological or emotional problems in adulthood (versus 10% in the control group). That is, most children of divorce do not show long-term adjustment problems (Lansford, 2009). Other research has highlighted some positive outcomes of parental divorce for children: enhancing personal growth, teaching life management skills, encouraging realistic relationship expectations, and enhancing empathy (Demo & Fine, 2009).

Although Wallerstein's conclusions appear overly discouraging, they differ from the results of other research only in *degree* (Amato, 2003). In a recent study using two national data sets, researchers found that for both younger children and adolescents, divorce was associated with some declines in achievement and poorer adjustment (Amato & Anthony, 2014). Experiencing divorce during childhood is a risk factor for many subsequent problems in one's adult years, including maladjustment, marital instability, and reduced occupational attainments (Amato, 1999). Factors that moderate the impact of divorce on children's adjustment include their age, coping resources, and adjustment prior to the divorce (Lansford, 2009; Shelton & Harold, 2007).

Stepfamilies, or blended families, are an established part of modern life. However, adaptation to remarriage can be difficult for children.

Remarriage and Stepfamilies

Although many marriages end in divorce, this is not the end of the marital line for many people. Statistics indicate that the majority of divorced people eventually remarry. In fact, in 2013, 40% of new marriages included at least one spouse who had been married before, and for half of those, it was at least the second marriage for both spouses (Livingston, 2014b). The mean length of time between divorce and remarriage is 3 to 4 years (Kreider, 2005).

How successful are second marriages? The answer depends on your standard of comparison. Divorce rates *are* higher for second than for first marriages, though the average duration for second marriages is about the same as for first, about 8 to 9 years (Kreider, 2005). However, this statistic may simply indicate that people who have been divorced are those who see divorce as a reasonable alternative to an unsatisfactory marriage. Nonetheless, studies of marital adjustment suggest that second marriages are slightly less successful than first marriages, especially for women who bring children into the second marriage (Teachman, 2008). Further, research suggests that individuals in second marriages tend to have lower marital satisfaction than those in first marriages (Mirecki et al., 2013).

Another major issue related to remarriage is its effect on children. *Stepfamilies* or *blended families* (where both spouses bring in children from a previous relationship) are an established part of modern life, and adaptation to remarriage can be difficult for children (Bray, 2009). **Figure 10.8** summarizes the developmental stages through which most stepfamilies progress. Wallerstein and Lewis (2007) argue that in stepfamilies there is an inherent instability in parenting, as parents are caught between their desires to create a new intimate relationship and to maintain their parenting role. These differing loyalties can cause conflict for the couple (Martin-Uzzi & Duval-Tsioles, 2013) and can create a negative experience for children who feel powerless or who undergo dramatic changes in living spaces, rules, and expectations (Stoll et al., 2005). The evidence suggests that children in stepfamilies are a bit less well adjusted than children in first marriages and are roughly similar in adjustment to children in single-parent homes (van Eeden-Moorefield & Pasley, 2013). However, the differences between stepfamilies and other types of families in the adjustment of their children tend to be modest.

In sum, much research remains to be conducted in the area of divorce and its impact on the family. Given the complexity of the modern family structure, the dissolution and reconstitution of families is similarly complex. As a result, it is hazardous to generalize research on the effects of divorce across all individuals and situations.

PATTERNS OF DEVELOPMENT IN STEPFAMILIES

Stage	Description	Example
Stage One: Fantasy	Family has unrealistic, ideal expectations.	I love my new wife, so I'll certainly love her children.
Stage Two: Immersion	Real life challenges expectations.	It seems like my husband is closer to his daughter than he is to me.
Stage Three: Awareness	Family members attempt to make sense out of the new arrangements.	I understand that my stepchildren are resistant to the new family structure, not because they are bad kids but because it is hard for them.
Stage Four: Mobilization	Family members attempt to negotiate difficulties.	Eating together as a family is important enough to me that I am willing to speak with my husband about it.
Stage Five: Action	Family creates strategies to resolve differences.	We will have weekly family meetings to air frustrations.
Stage Six: Contact	Positive emotional bonds begin to form.	My stepson and I can resolve this issue by having a heart-to-heart.
Stage Seven: Resolution	Norms are established and new family rituals emerge.	My teenage stepdaughter appreciates my perspective on her new boyfriend.

Figure 10.8

Patterns of development in stepfamilies. Papernow (1993) developed a model of seven stages through which most stepfamilies pass as they move from fantasy toward resolution.

Source: Adapted from Papernow, P. L. (1993). *Becoming a stepfamily: Patterns of development in remarried families.* San Francisco: Jossey-Bass. Reprinted by permission of the author.

- Discuss one challenge unique to same-sex couples.
- Compare homosexual and heterosexual couples in regard to their relationship stability and adjustment.
- Describe the dynamics of same-sex families and the adjustment of children with same-sex parents.

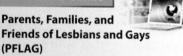

Learn More Online

Parents, Families, and Friends of Lesbians and Gays (PFLAG)

PFLAG is a national nonprofit organization dedicated to supporting the well-being of gay, lesbian, bisexual and transgender persons, as well as their families, friends, and allies. This comprehensive site includes educational as well as advocacy information.

10.6 Same-Sex Marriage

As previously noted, much of the research included in this chapter was conducted exclusively on heterosexual married couples. Indeed, given the recency of legalized same-sex unions, researchers have not had sufficient time to study marriage in same-sex couples. Devoting a separate section to same-sex couples may seem to imply that the dynamics of their close relationships are different from those seen in heterosexual couples, but research does not justify that assumption. However, same-sex couples do face the unique challenge of sexual stigmatization (Diamond, 2015). As Garnets and Kimmel (1991) point out, gay and lesbian relationships "develop within a social context of societal disapproval with an absence of social legitimization and support; families and other social institutions often stigmatize such relationships and there are no prescribed roles and behaviors to structure such relationships" (p. 170). It is reasonable to predict that legalized same-sex marriage will lessen this stigma. Although same-sex relationships evolve in a different social context, research has documented that close relationships, gay or heterosexual, generally function in similar ways (Herek, 2006).

Relationship Stability and Adjustment

Contrary to some stereotypes, most gay men and lesbians desire a stable, long-term relationship, and at any one time roughly 40%–60% of gay males and 45%–80% of lesbians are involved in committed relationships (Kurdek, 2004). In fact, in 2013, more than half of gay men (56%) and lesbians (58%) reported that they would like to get married (Motel & Dost, 2015). The top reported reasons for marriage included love, companionship, and making a lifetime commitment.

Given the lack of societal support for same-sex relationships, are gay unions less stable than heterosexual unions? Researchers have not yet been able to collect adequate data on this question, but the limited data available suggest that gay couples' relationships *are* somewhat briefer and more prone to breakups than heterosexual marriages; however, they are similar to that of heterosexual, cohabiting couples (Diamond, 2013).

Research shows that same-sex couples basically "meet, fall in love, and maintain their relationship" through processes very similar to heterosexual couples (Diamond, 2015, p. 534). Both heterosexual and homosexual couples hold similar values about relationships, report similar levels of relationship satisfaction, perceive their relationships to be loving and satisfying, and say they want their partners to have characteristics similar to theirs (Peplau & Fingerhut, 2007). Furthermore, homosexual and heterosexual couples are similar in terms of the factors that predict relationship satisfaction, the sources of conflict in their relationships, and their patterns of conflict resolution (Kurdek, 2004; Peplau & Ghavami, 2009).

Same-Sex Families

According to the 2010 U.S. Census, out of the 594,000 same-sex households, 115,000 (19%) are rearing children, 84% of whom are their own biological children. Many of these parental responsibilities are left over from previous marriages, as about 20%–30% of homosexuals have been heterosexually married (Kurdek, 2004). Researchers are beginning to examine stepfamilies in this population. So far research indicates that experiences of gay and lesbian stepfamilies are similar to their heterosexual counterparts (van Eeden-Moorefield & Pasley, 2013). Still, the stigma associated with homosexuality introduces

Marmaduke St. John/Alamy Stock Photo

Although same-sex relationships evolve in a different social context, research has documented that they generally function in similar ways to heterosexual couples.

added stressors that can impact family functioning (Berger, 1998). In addition, children in same-sex stepfamilies report stigmatization from having a gay or lesbian parent or stepparent (Robitaille & Saint-Jacques, 2009).

What do we know about gay men and lesbians as parents? The evidence suggests that gays are similar to their heterosexual counterparts in their approaches to parenting and that their children are similar to the children of heterosexual parents in terms of personal development and peer relations (Patterson, 2001, 2006, 2009, 2013). The overall adjustment of children with same-sex parents appears similar in quality to that of children of heterosexual parents (van Gelderen et al., 2012). Moreover, the vast majority of children in same-sex families grow up to identify themselves as heterosexual (Patterson, 2013). In sum, decades of research indicates that the quality of child-parent interactions is much more important to a child's development than parental sexual orientation (Crowl, Ahn, & Baker, 2008; Patterson, 2006, 2009, 2013).

67photo/Alamy Stock Photo

Children reared by gay or lesbian parents do not seem more poorly adjusted than other children. Research indicates that the quality of child-parent interactions is much more important to a child's development than parental sexual orientation.

10.7 Alternatives to Marriage

Learning Objectives

■ Discuss the prevalence of cohabitation and its relationship to marital success.

■ Describe stereotypes of single life and summarize evidence on the adjustment of single people.

So far we have been discussing the traditional model of marriage, which, as we noted at the beginning of the chapter, has been challenged by a variety of social trends. More and more people are experiencing alternative relationship lifestyles, including cohabitation and remaining single.

Cohabitation

As we noted earlier in the chapter, *cohabitation* refers to living together in a sexually intimate relationship outside of marriage. Recent decades have witnessed a tremendous increase in the percentage of couples who are cohabiting (see **Figure 10.9**). Recent estimates suggest that 66% of couples live together prior to their marriage (Manning, Brown, & Payne, 2014). Thus, cohabitation has become the norm, rather than the exception. Increasing rates of cohabitation are not unique to the United States and are even higher in many European countries (Kiernan, 2004).

Although many people see cohabitation as a threat to the institution of marriage, many theorists see it as a new stage in the courtship process—a sort of trial marriage or premarriage (Surra & Boelter, 2013). However, research shows that individuals also cohabitate for practical reasons (such as financial necessity or convenience) (Sassler & Miller, 2011). The couple's motivation to cohabit appears to be a factor in the continued success of the relationship. One study examined reported reasons for living together and found that cohabitating to "spend time together" (as opposed to "test the relationship" or "for convenience") was associated with greater relationship commitment and satisfaction (Tang, Curran, & Arroyo, 2014).

As a prelude to marriage, cohabitation should allow people to experiment with marriage-like responsibilities and reduce the likelihood of entering marriage with unrealistic expectations; thus, couples who cohabit before they marry should go on to more successful marriages than those who do not. Although this analysis sounds plausible, researchers have *not* found that premarital cohabitation increases the likelihood of subsequent marital success. In fact, many studies have found an association between premarital cohabitation and higher divorce rates (Pew Research Center, 2015b). This association is referred to as the *cohabitation effect* (Cohan, 2013),

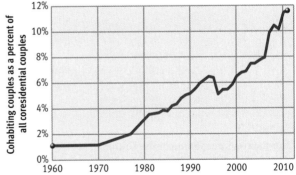

Figure 10.9

Cohabitation in the United States. The percentage of coresidential couples cohabiting (rather than being married) has been increasing rapidly since the 1960s, rising from 1.1% to nearly 12% in 2011. This increase shows no signs of leveling off. Please note, this graph shows the percentage of couples who are unmarried in any specific year; the percentage of couples who have cohabited at one time or another is much higher. As your text notes, that figure has increased to 66% (Manning, Brown, & Payne, 2014). (Data from U.S. Bureau of the Census)

and it holds true even for second marriages (Stanley et al., 2010). However, recent research suggests that the cohabitation effect might be weakening or disappearing for recent cohorts of married couples, as cohabitation has become a common, normative part of the relationship cycle (Manning & Cohen, 2012).

Remaining Single

The pressure to marry is substantial in our society. People are socialized to believe that they are not complete until they have found their "other half" and have entered into a partnership for life. And reference is often made to people's "failure" to marry. In spite of this pressure, an increasing proportion of young adults are remaining single (DePaulo, 2014). In 2010, more than a quarter of all households in the United States were one-person households (Lofquist et al., 2012) (see **Figure 10.10**).

Does the greater number of single adults mean that people are turning away from the institution of marriage? Perhaps a little, but not completely. Indeed, fewer Americans are getting married, and that trend appears to be holding steady (Fry, 2012). However, a variety of factors have contributed to the growth of the single population. Much of this growth is a result of the higher median age at which people marry and the increased rate of divorce. In addition, the vast majority of single, never-married people *do* hope to eventually marry. In a national survey of never-married adults, only 12% reported that they did not want to get married at some point (Cohn et al., 2011).

Singles continue to be stigmatized and plagued by two rather contradictory stereotypes. On the one hand, single people are sometimes presumed to be carefree swingers who are too busy enjoying the fruits of promiscuity to shoulder marital responsibilities. On the other hand, they are seen as losers who have not succeeded in snaring a mate; they may be perceived as socially inept, maladjusted, frustrated, lonely, and bitter. These stereotypes do a great injustice to the diversity that exists among those who are single. In fact, the negative stereotypes of singles have led some researchers to coin the term *singlism* to refer to prejudice and discrimination against unmarried adults (DePaulo, 2011, 2014).

Moving beyond stereotypes, what do scientists know about singlehood? It is true that being married, especially if there is high marital satisfaction, is associated with better mental and physical health (Robles, 2014). Further, singles rate themselves as less happy than their married counterparts (Waite, 2000). However, we must use caution in interpreting these results; in many studies, "singles" include those who are divorced or widowed, which inflates this finding (DePaulo, 2011; Morris & DePaulo, 2009). Not surprisingly, adults who *choose* singlehood associate it with positive outcomes in their lives such as self-fulfillment and independence; conversely, those who are unmarried due to external constraints report feelings of regret and loneliness (Timonen & Doyle, 2014). Furthermore, the differences are modest, and the happiness gap has shrunk, especially among women.

In sum, as traditional married households become less common in modern life, psychological researchers must answer the call to explore these alternatives to marriage and their impact on families.

Figure 10.10

One-person households in the United States. This graph depicts the increase in the number of U.S. households with only one person living in them. It shows that the percentage has more than doubled in the last 50 years. (Data from U.S. Bureau of the Census)

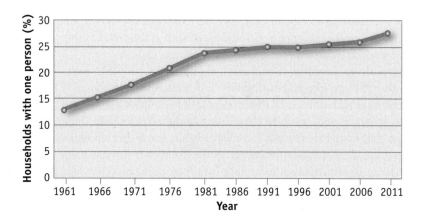

10.8 Understanding Intimate Partner Violence

Learning Objectives

- Discuss the incidence of partner abuse and the characteristics of batterers, and explain why some partners stay in abusive relationships.
- Discuss the incidence and consequences of date rape, as well as the factors that contribute to it.
- Understand ways to reduce the likelihood of date rape.

Answer the following statements "true" or "false."

____ **1.** Most rapes are committed by strangers.

____ **2.** Women are almost never perpetrators of intimate violence.

____ **3.** Most women in abusive relationships are attracted to violent men.

____ **4.** Most men who have witnessed domestic violence as children will batter their intimate partners.

All of the above statements are false, as you will see in this Application, which examines the darker side of intimate relationships. Most people assume they will be safe with those they love and trust. Unfortunately, some people are betrayed by individuals to whom they feel closest. *Intimate partner violence* **is aggression toward those who are in close relationship to the aggressor.** Intimate partner violence takes three forms: psychological, physical, and sexual abuse. Tragically, this violence sometimes ends in homicide. In this Application, we'll focus on two serious social problems: partner abuse and date rape. Much of our discussion is based on the work of the Rape, Abuse, and Incest National Network (RAINN).

Partner Abuse

Celebrity cases such as those involving former Baltimore Ravens star Ray Rice and his wife, Janay, have dramatically heightened public awareness of partner violence, particularly wife battering. *Battering* **encompasses physical abuse, emotional abuse, and sexual abuse of an intimate partner.** *Physical abuse* can include kicking, biting, punching, choking, pushing, slapping,

Celebrity cases such as Ray Rice's abuse of his wife, Janay, have dramatically heightened public awareness of intimate partner violence.

hitting with an object, and threatening with or using a weapon. Examples of *emotional abuse* include humiliation, name-calling, controlling what the partner does and with whom the partner socializes, refusing to communicate, unreasonably withholding money, and questioning the partner's sanity. *Sexual abuse* is characterized as using sexual behavior to control, manipulate, or demean the other person. Let's explore the research on physical abuse of intimate partners.

Incidence and Consequences

As with other taboo topics, obtaining accurate estimates of physical abuse is difficult. According to the Centers for Disease Control and Prevention (2011a), twenty-four people per minute are victims of rape, physical violence, or stalking by an intimate partner in the United States. As shown in **Figure 10.11**, most first-time victims of intimate partner violence are young adults. Both men and women are victims of and commit intimate partner violence (Finkel & Eckhardt, 2013). That said, women are more likely to be victims of abuse. In 2010, females accounted for 91.9% of reported rape and sexual assault incidents (Bureau of Justice Statistics, 2011). Further, a woman is the victim in 85% of nonfatal violent crimes committed by intimate partners and in 75% of murders by spouses (Rennison & Welchans, 2000).

The effects of battering reverberate beyond the obvious physical injuries. Victims of partner abuse are at a high risk for depression, feelings of helplessness and humiliation, stress-induced physical illness, alcohol and drug abuse, posttraumatic stress disorder, and suicide (Eckhardt, Sprunger, & Hamel, 2014). Children who witness marital violence also experience ill effects, such as anxiety, depression, reduced self-esteem, and increased delinquency (Johnson & Ferraro, 2001; Lloyd, 2013).

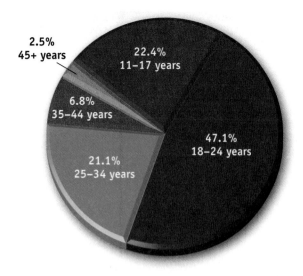

Figure 10.11

Age and intimate partner violence. This graph show the ages of women when they first experienced intimate partner violence. As you can see, most were young adults. A similar pattern holds for men. (Data from the Centers for Disease Control)

Characteristics of Batterers

Sexual assault perpetrators are a diverse group, so a single profile has not emerged. Some factors associated with an elevated risk for domestic violence include unemployment, drinking and drug problems, a tendency to anger easily, attitudes that condone aggression, and high stress (Stith et al., 2004). Studies indicate that men who were beaten as children or who witnessed their mothers being beaten are more likely to abuse their wives, although most men who grow up in these difficult circumstances do *not* become batterers themselves (Wareham, Boots, & Chavez, 2009). Batterers tend to be jealous in relationships, have unrealistic expectations of their partners, blame others for their own problems, and have their feelings hurt easily (Lundberg-Love & Wilkerson, 2006). Other relationship factors associated with domestic violence include having frequent disagreements, exhibiting a heated style of dealing with disagreements, and pairing a man holding traditional gender-role attitudes with a woman who has nontraditional views of gender roles (DeMaris et al., 2003).

Why Do People Stay in Abusive Relationships?

Individuals leave abusive partners more often than popular stereotypes suggest, but people are still perplexed by the fact that many partners remain in abusive relationships that seem horrible and degrading. However, research shows that this phenomenon is not really that perplexing. A number of seemingly compelling reasons explain why some individuals feel that leaving is not a realistic option, and many of the reasons revolve around fear. Some individuals lack financial independence and fear that they won't be able to survive financially without their partner (Kim & Gray, 2008). Others simply have no place to go and fear becoming homeless (Browne, 1993a). Still others feel

guilty and ashamed about their failing relationship and don't want to face disapproval from family and friends, who are likely to fall into the trap of blaming the victim (Barnett & LaViolette, 1993). Above all else, many fear that if they try to leave, they may incur more brutal violence and even murder (Grothues & Marmion, 2006). Unfortunately, this fear is not altogether unrealistic, as many abusers have shown remarkable persistence in tracking down, stalking, threatening, beating, and killing their ex-partners.

Although it is important to understand why people stay, it is also important to explore why individuals batter and what interventions can prevent partners from being brutalized or killed when they do leave. To really understand and prevent intimate partner violence, researchers argue for additional study of cultural factors that lead to a tolerance of it (Bartholomew, Cobb, & Dutton, 2015).

Date Rape

Intimate violence is not limited to marital relations. *Date rape* **refers to forced and unwanted intercourse in the context of dating.** It can occur on a first date, with someone you've dated for a while, or with someone to whom you're engaged. The key factor in distinguishing this type of abuse is a partner's *consent.* There are two important considerations to keep in mind regarding consent. First, relationship status (either current or previous) and past acts of intimacy are *not* indicators of consent. Second, to ensure that activity is consensual, partners should seek consent with each sexual activity as the level of sexual intimacy increases (for instance when kissing, moving from kissing to petting, and from petting to oral sex or intercourse).

Incidence and Consequences

Most people naively assume that the vast majority of rapes are committed by strangers who leap from bushes or dark alleys to surprise their victims. In reality, research indicates that most victims are raped by someone they know (Frazier, 2009). It's difficult to estimate how often date rape occurs because the majority of instances go unreported, but it is clearly a major problem on college campuses and beyond. One recent study found that by the start of the second year of college, 26% of women had been raped while incapacitated (by alcohol or drugs) and 22% had experienced forcible rape (which includes threats or actual use of physical force) (Carey et al., 2015a).

In the aftermath of date rape, victims typically experience a variety of emotional reactions, including fear, anger, anxiety, self-blame, and guilt (Kahn & Andreoli Mathie, 1999). Many rape victims suffer from depression, symptoms of posttraumatic stress disorder, and increased risk for suicide. Research also shows that rape affects a woman's self-esteem, desire to have sex, and self-perception of her value as a mate (Perilloux, Duntley, & Buss, 2012). In addition to the trauma of the rape, women also have to cope with the possibility of pregnancy. Further, if the rape survivor presses charges against the attacker, he or she may have to deal with lengthy and difficult legal proceedings, negative publicity, and social stigma.

Contributing Factors

To understand the phenomenon of date rape, it's essential to know something about the factors that contribute to this behavior. It probably comes as no surprise to learn that alcohol plays a major role in sexually aggressive incidents (Carey et al., 2015b). Alcohol impairs judgment and reduces inhibitions, making people more willing to assert their power. Drinking also undermines one's ability to interpret ambiguous social cues, making one more likely to overestimate a date's interest in sex. The more intoxicated perpetrators are, the more aggressive they tend to be (Abbey, 2009). Alcohol also increases one's vulnerability to sexual coercion. Drinking can cloud people's assessments of their risk and their ability to mount firm resistance or find a way to escape the situation.

So-called "date rape drugs" are also a cause for concern. Rohypnol ("roofies") and gamma hydroxybutyrate (GHB) are two drugs used to subdue dates. Although these drugs are colorless, odorless, and tasteless, their effects are anything but benign, and they can even be fatal. Victims typically pass out and have no recall of what happened while they were under the influence of the drug. To make it easier to spike a drink, predators typically look for individuals who are already intoxicated.

Gender differences in sexual standards also contribute to date rape. Society still encourages a double standard for males and females. Men are encouraged to have sexual feelings, to act on them, and to "score," whereas women are socialized to be coy about their sexual desires. These social norms can encourage game playing, so dating partners may not always say what they mean or mean what they say.

Alcohol plays a role in sexually aggressive incidents, especially on college campuses. Alcohol impairs judgment and reduces inhibitions. The more intoxicated perpetrators are, the more aggressive they tend to be.

Protecting Oneself from Date Rape

To protect oneself, RAINN suggests that is useful to understand the three stages of date rape. First, *intrusion* is when an offender violates the victim's personal space or level of comfort with unwelcomed touches, stares, or sharing of information. *Desensitization*, the second stage, occurs when the victim gets used to the intrusive actions and sees them as less threatening. In this stage the victim might still feel uncomfortable but might convince herself that the feeling is unfounded. Finally, *isolation* occurs when the offender isolates the victim from others. Understanding these three stages can help one identify warning signs of sexual aggression.

It is imperative to recognize date rape for what it is: an act of sexual aggression, and victims are never to blame for others' acts of aggression. There are steps one can take, however, to reduce one's likelihood of victimization: (1) Beware of excessive alcohol and drug use, which may undermine self-control and self-determination in sexual interactions. (2) Don't leave your drink unattended or accept drinks from people you don't know or trust. (3) When dating someone new, agree to go only to public places, and always carry enough money for transportation back home. (4) Watch out for your friends and have them watch out for you. (5) Finally, clearly and accurately communicate your feelings and expectations about sexual activity by engaging in appropriate self-disclosure.

CHAPTER 10 Review

Key Ideas

10.1 Challenges to the Traditional Model of Marriage

- The traditional model of marriage is being challenged by the increasing acceptability of singlehood, the increasing popularity of cohabitation, the reduced premium on permanence, changes in gender roles, the increasing prevalence of voluntary childlessness, and the decline of the traditional nuclear family. Nonetheless, marriage remains quite popular.

10.2 Deciding to Marry

- A multitude of factors influence an individual's decision to marry, including one's culture. The norm for our society is to select a mate and engage in a monogamous marriage. Mate selection is influenced by endogamy, homogamy, and gender. Women place more emphasis on potential partners' ambition and financial prospects, whereas men are more interested in a partner's youthfulness and physical attractiveness.
- There are some premarital predictors of marital success, such as family background, age, length of courtship, and personality, but the relations are weak. The nature of a couple's premarital communication is a better predictor of marital adjustment. Stressful events surrounding the marriage influence marital stability.

10.3 Marital Adjustment across the Family Life Cycle

- The family life cycle is an orderly sequence of developmental stages through which families tend to progress. Newly married couples tend to be very happy before the arrival of children. Today, more couples are struggling with the decision about whether to have children. The arrival of children is a major transition that is handled best by parents who have realistic expectations about the difficulties inherent in raising a family.
- As children reach adolescence, parents should expect more conflict as their influence declines. They must learn to relate to their children as adults and help launch them into the adult world. Most parents no longer struggle with the empty nest syndrome. Adult children returning home may be more of a problem.

10.4 Vulnerable Areas in Marital Adjustment

- Gaps in expectations about marital roles may create marital stress. Disparities in expectations about gender roles and the distribution of housework may be especially common and problematic. Work concerns can clearly spill over to influence marital functioning, but there is little evidence that maternal employment is detrimental to children's development.
- Wealth does not ensure marital happiness, but financial difficulties can put strain on a marriage. Inadequate communication is a commonly reported marital problem, which is predictive of divorce.

10.5 Divorce and Its Aftermath

- Divorce rates have increased dramatically in recent decades, but they appear to be stabilizing. Deciding on a divorce tends to be a gradual process rather than a single event. Most couples underestimate their likelihood of divorce.
- Wallerstein's research suggests that divorce tends to have negative effects on children. Hetherington's research suggests that most children recover from divorce after a few years. The effects of divorce on children vary, but negative effects can be long lasting.
- A substantial majority of divorced people remarry. These second marriages have a somewhat lower probability of success than first marriages. The adjustment of children in stepfamilies appears to be somewhat lower than for other families, but differences are modest.

10.6 Same-Sex Marriage

- Given the stigma associated with homosexuality, same-sex relationships develop in a different social context than heterosexual relationships. Most homosexuals desire long-term intimate relationships, and studies have found that heterosexual and homosexual couples are similar in many ways. Children raised by gay parents do not show poorer adjustment than other children

10.7 Alternatives to Marriage

- The prevalence of cohabitation has increased dramatically. Logically, one might expect cohabitation to facilitate marital success, but research has consistently found an association between cohabitation and marital instability.
- An increasing proportion of the young population are remaining single, yet some stereotypes about singles persist. Although singles generally have the same adjustment problems as married couples, evidence suggests that singles tend to be somewhat less happy and less healthy.

10.8 Application: Understanding Intimate Partner Violence

- Both men and women are victims of intimate partner violence. Women are the principal victims of serious, dangerous abuse. Perpetrators of intimate partner violence are diverse, but they tend to anger easily, be jealous, and have unrealistic expectations of their partner. Partners stay in abusive relationships for a variety of compelling, practical reasons, including economic realities.
- The majority of rapes are committed by someone the victim knows. Rape is a traumatic experience that has many serious consequences. Alcohol abuse, drug use, and gender-based sexual standards all contribute to date rape. Miscommunication revolving around token resistance is particularly problematic. There are steps one can take to protect oneself from date rape.

Key Terms

Battering p. 301
Cohabitation p. 279
Date rape p. 302
Divorce p. 294
Endogamy p. 283
Family life cycle p. 285
Homogamy p. 283
Intimate partner violence p. 301
Marriage p. 279
Monogamy p. 282
Polygamy p. 282

Key People

John Gottman pp. 293–294
E. Mavis Hetherington p. 296
Judith Wallerstein p. 296

CHAPTER 10 Practice Test

1. Which of the following is a social trend that is undermining the traditional model of marriage?
   a. Decreased acceptance of singlehood
   b. Less voluntary childlessness
   c. Reduced acceptance of cohabitation
   d. Reduced premium on permanence in marriage

2. *Endogamy* refers to
   a. the tendency to marry within one's social group.
   b. the tendency to marry someone with similar attitudes.
   c. the final marriage in serial monogamy.
   d. norms that promote marriage outside of one's social unit.

3. Based on trends in the data, which of the following couples has the greatest likelihood of marital success?
   a. Stephanie and David, whose parents are divorced
   b. Jane and Brian, who are both perfectionists
   c. Ruth and Randy, who had a long courtship
   d. Chris and Abby, who married at a very young age

4. The transition to parenthood tends to be easier when
   a. the parents hold traditional gender roles.
   b. the parents have realistic expectations.
   c. the new parents are relatively young.
   d. the father is not heavily involved in child care.

5. Which of the following characteristics in young children is related to maternal employment?
   a. Increased hyperactivity
   b. Higher anxiety
   c. Increased positive interactions with the mothers
   d. Increased prosocial behavior

6. Truc and Hiroshi have plenty of financial resources. In their marriage, arguments about money
   a. may be common.
   b. don't occur.
   c. are a big problem only if the wife earns more than her husband.
   d. are unrelated to marital satisfaction.

7. The evidence suggests that the negative effects of divorce on former spouses' physical health and mortality are
   a. exaggerated for both sexes.
   b. greater for men than women.
   c. greater for women than men.
   d. about the same for men and women.

8. Which of the following has been supported by research on intimate relationships among gay men and lesbians?
   a. The majority of same-sex couples have open relationships.
   b. Same-sex couples avoid becoming involved in long-term relationships.
   c. Same-sex couples have impoverished family relations.
   d. Most gay men and lesbians desire a stable, long-term relationship.

9. Which of the following reasons for cohabitation is associated with greater relationship commitment and satisfaction?
   a. Convenience
   b. Spending time together
   c. Testing the relationship
   d. Trial marriage

10. Which of the following can an individual do to reduce the likelihood of being victimized by date rape?
    a. Offer token resistance to sexual advances
    b. Avoid communicating about sex altogether
    c. Beware of excessive alcohol and drug use
    d. View intrusive actions as nonthreatening

Answers
1. d Page 280
2. a Page 283
3. c Page 284
4. b Page 288
5. d Pages 292-293
6. a Page 293
7. b Page 296
8. d Page 298
9. b Page 299
10. c Page 303

Personal Explorations Workbook

Go to the *Personal Explorations Workbook* in the back of your textbook for exercises that can enhance your self-understanding in relation to issues raised in this chapter.

Exercise 10.1 *Self-Assessment:* Self-Report Jealousy Scale

Exercise 10.2 *Self-Reflection:* Thinking through Your Attitudes about Marriage and Cohabitation

CHAPTER 11 Gender and Behavior

Olesya Feketa/Shutterstock.com

On January 14, 2005, the then-president of Harvard University Lawrence H. Summers spoke publicly about Harvard's policies regarding diversity. Dr. Summers focused his remarks on the issue of women's underrepresentation in tenured positions in science and engineering at top universities. He offered three broad hypotheses about this gender disparity. The one that attracted the most media attention was what he called a "different availability of aptitude at the high end." While he acknowledged that there are differences in socialization and patterns of discrimination between men and women, he cited innate gender differences in mathematical and scientific ability as having greater "importance" in explaining the gender disparity (Harvard Crimson, 2005).

Summers's remarks on this issue sparked a contentious debate among academics, scientists, and the public. The war of words lingered for months and eventually led to Summers's resignation as president of Harvard. This scenario demonstrates in a highly compelling way that gender research is relevant, important, and frequently controversial. Obviously, psychologists have a lot to offer in this area. In this chapter, we explore some intriguing and controversial questions: Are there genuine behavioral and cognitive differences between males and females? If so, what are their origins? Are traditional gender-role expectations healthy or unhealthy? Why are gender roles in our society changing, and what does the future hold? After addressing those questions, in the Application we explore gender in the workplace. ■

11.1 Gender Stereotypes

Learning Objectives

■ Explain the nature of gender stereotypes and their connection to instrumentality and expressiveness.

■ Discuss three important points about gender stereotypes.

Surprisingly, there is little consensus about when to use the term *sex* and when to use the term *gender* (Eagly, 2013). Some scholars prefer to use the term *gender* to refer to male-female differences that are learned and *sex* to designate biologically based differences between males and females. Others argue that making this sharp distinction fails to recognize that biology and culture interact. Still others use the terms interchangeably. For the sake of simplicity, we'll broadly use **gender to mean the state of being male or female. Figure 11.1** sorts out a number of gender-related terms that we will use in our discussions. As we will discuss later, some contemporary researchers are challenging the binary perspective on gender. Nevertheless, the coverage in this chapter will generally focus on male and female as distinct gender categories.

Obviously, males and females differ biologically—in their genitals and other aspects of anatomy, and in their physiological functioning. These readily apparent physical differences between males and females lead people to expect other differences as well, especially with regard to social roles. Recall from Chapter 7 that *stereotypes* are widely held beliefs that people possess certain characteristics simply because of their membership in a particular group. Thus, *gender stereotypes* **are widely shared beliefs about males' and females' abilities, personality traits, and social behavior.** These stereotypes can bias your perceptions and expectations of and interactions with others.

Research indicates that beliefs about the attributes characteristic of men and women are widely shared. For example, a survey of gender stereotypes in twenty-five countries revealed considerable similarity of views (Williams, Satterwhite, & Best, 1999). Because of the widespread gains in educational and occupational attainment by American women since the 1970s, you might expect to find changes in contemporary gender stereotypes for both genders. However, although gender stereotypes in this country have become more complex, they remain largely stable.

Gender stereotypes are too numerous to summarize here. Instead, you can examine **Figure 11.2**, which lists a number of characteristics people commonly link with femininity and masculinity. Note that

GENDER-RELATED CONCEPTS	
Term	**Definition**
Gender	The state of being male or female
Gender identity	An individual's perception of himself or herself as male or female
Gender stereotypes	Widely held and often inaccurate beliefs about males' and females' abilities, personality traits, and social behavior
Gender differences	Actual disparities in behavior between males and females, based on research observations
Gender roles	Culturally defined expectations about appropriate behavior for males and females
Gender-role identity	A person's identification with the traits regarded as masculine or feminine (one's sense of being masculine or feminine)
Gender schemas	Cognitive structures that guide the processing of gender-relevant information

Figure 11.1

Terminology related to gender. The topic of gender involves many closely related ideas that are easily confused. The gender-related concepts introduced in this chapter are summarized here for easy comparison.

GENDER STEREOTYPES	
Masculine	**Feminine**
Active	Artistic
Analytical	Aware of others' feelings
Athletic	Creative
Competitive	Devotes self to others
Financial provider	Emotional
Good at numbers	Gentle
Good at problem solving	Graceful
Independent	Kind
Physically strong	Soft voice
Self-confident	Takes care of children
Stands up to pressure	Tends the house
Takes a stand	Understanding

Figure 11.2

Traditional gender stereotypes. Gender stereotypes are widely known and relate to many diverse aspects of psychological functioning. This is a partial list of the characteristics that college students associate with a typical man and a typical woman. Gender stereotypes have remained remarkably stable in spite of all the recent changes relating to gender issues in modern societies.

Source: Adapted from Kite, M. E. (2001). Gender stereotypes in J. Worell (Ed.). *Encyclopedia of women and gender: Sex similarities and differences and the impact of society on gender* (Vol. 1), (pp. 561–570). San Diego, CA: Academic Press.

the stereotyped attributes for males generally reflect the quality of *instrumentality,* **an orientation toward action and accomplishment,** whereas the stereotypes for females reflect the quality of *expressiveness,* **an orientation toward emotion and relationships**.

When it comes to stereotypes, there are some important points to keep in mind. First, despite the general agreement on a number of gender stereotypes, variability also occurs. The characteristics in **Figure 11.2** represent stereotypes for white, middle-class, heterosexual, and Christian males and females. But it is obvious that not everyone fits this set of characteristics. For example, the stereotypes for African American males and females are more similar on the dimensions of competence and expressiveness than those for white American males and females (Kane, 2000).

A second point about gender stereotypes is that since the 1980s, the boundaries between male and female stereotypes have become less rigid. In the past, male and female stereotypes were seen as separate and distinct categories (for example, men are strong and women are weak). However, there is more support for viewing gender attributes as a continuum rather than a dichotomy (Carothers & Reis, 2013; Reis & Carothers, 2014).

A third consideration is that the traditional male stereotype is more complimentary than the conventional female stereotype. There is considerable evidence that, in the United States, masculinity is associated with higher overall status and competence (Ridgeway & Bourg, 2004). For instance, in the workplace a man might be described as "good with details," whereas a woman is viewed as "picky." Likewise, a man might be viewed as "exercising authority," whereas a woman would be described as "controlling" for the same behaviors. This discrepancy is related to *androcentrism,* **or the belief that the male is the norm.** Ironically, this bias is evident even in psychological studies of gender (Hegarty et al., 2013). Hegarty and Buechel (2006), for example, examined 388 articles on gender differences from journals published by the American Psychological Association and found evidence of androcentric reporting. Specifically, gender differences were reported in terms of *women* (as opposed to men) being different. The implication, then, is that men are the norm from which women deviate.

Let's shift from gender stereotypes to what males and females are actually like. Keep in mind that our discussion focuses on modern Western societies; the story may be different in other cultures (Cuddy et al., 2015).

11.2 Gender Similarities and Differences

Learning Objectives

- Explain how meta-analyses have helped researchers who study gender.
- Articulate the gender similarities hypothesis.
- Summarize the findings on gender similarities and differences in verbal, mathematical, and spatial abilities.
- Summarize the findings on gender similarities and differences in personality, social behavior, and psychological disorders.
- Give two explanations for why gender differences appear larger than they actually are.

Are men more aggressive than women? Do more women than men suffer from depression? For decades researchers have attempted to answer these and related questions about gender and behavior. Moreover, new evidence is constantly pouring in, and many researchers report conflicting findings. It is an almost overwhelming task to keep up with the research in this area. Thankfully, a statistical technique called meta-analysis helps clarify this body of research. *Meta-analysis* **combines the statistical results of many studies of the same question, yielding an estimate of the size and consistency of a variable's effects.** This approach allows a researcher to assess the overall trends across all the previous studies of how gender is related to, say, math abilities or conformity. Meta-analysis has been a great boon to researchers, and hundreds of meta-analyses on gender differences have now been conducted.

Based on the results of more than forty-six meta-analyses, Janet Shibley Hyde, a noted authority in the field, proposed the *gender similarities hypothesis*. Hyde (2005, 2014) notes that men and women are similar on most psychological variables and that most of the time when researchers report a difference, it is quite small. She further asserts that overinflated claims of gender differences have costs associated with them for the workplace and relationships. Subsequent studies have supported her hypothesis (Zell, Krizan, & Teeter, 2015).

Researchers also debate whether gender differences that do exist are attributable to environmental factors or to biological ones, and there is evidence on both sides. Before we examine the possible causes of these differences, let's thread our way through the available research in the following areas: cognitive abilities, personality traits and social behavior, and psychological disorders.

Cognitive Abilities

We should first point out that gender differences have *not* been found in *overall* intelligence (Priess & Hyde, 2010). Of course, this fact shouldn't be surprising because intelligence tests are intentionally designed to minimize differences between the scores of males and females. But what about gender differences in *specific* cognitive skills?

Verbal Abilities

Verbal abilities include a number of distinct skills, such as vocabulary, reading, writing, spelling, and grammar abilities. Girls and women generally have the edge in the verbal area, although the gender differences are small (Hyde, 2007, 2014). Among the findings worth noting are that girls usually start speaking a little earlier, have larger vocabularies and better reading scores in grade school, and are more verbally fluent (on tests of writing, for instance). Boys seem to fare better on verbal analogies (Priess & Hyde, 2010). However, they are three to four times more likely to be stutterers (Skinner & Shelton, 1985) and five to ten times more likely than girls to be dyslexic (Vandenberg, 1987). With regard to writing, females seem to have a slight advantage over males that tends to increase over time in school (Scheiber et al., 2015). It is important to remember that while gender differences in verbal abilities generally favor females, the overlap between males and females in verbal abilities is much greater than the gap between them.

Mathematical Abilities

Researchers have looked extensively at gender differences in *mathematical abilities*, including performing computations and solving word problems. Although it is conventional wisdom that males have greater mathematical abilities than females, a recent meta-analysis representing the data of more than 1 million participants over the past 20 years indicates otherwise (Lindberg et al., 2010). This research led Lindberg and colleagues to conclude that that there are no longer gender differences in general mathematical performance. Another meta-analysis including almost 500,000 students from more than sixty-nine countries

Janet Shibley Hyde proposed that men and women are similar on most psychological variables. She called this the gender similarity hypothesis.

Learn More Online

Women in Science, Technology, Engineering, and Mathematics ON THE AIR!
At this website, sponsored by the National Science Foundation, you can listen to stories about women working in science, technology, engineering, and mathematics (STEM) fields. You can also subscribe to the podcast.

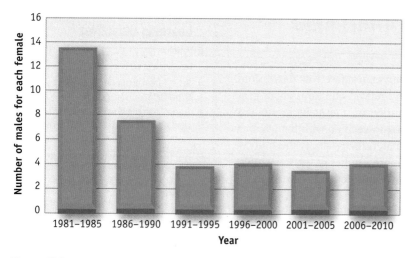

Figure 11.3

Male-to-female ratio for math SAT scores of 700 and above. Research shows that males outperform females at the high end of the mathematical ability distribution. As you can see in this graph, this gap has been shrinking since the 1980s. Between 1981 and 1985, boys who scored a 700 and above outnumbered girls 13 to 1; by 2010, this ratio was only 4 to 1.

Source: Adapted from Wai, J., Cacchio, M., Putallaz, M., & Makel, M. C. (2010). Sex differences in the right tail of cognitive abilities: A 30 year examination. *Intelligence, 38,* 412–423.

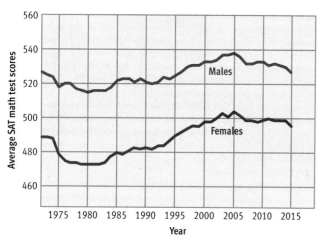

Figure 11.4

Gender differences in math performance on the SAT. Females historically score lower than males on the math portion of the SAT. Researchers continue to question whether this is an innate cognitive difference or a difference in socialization. (Adapted from College Board, 2015)

Can the set of blocks on the left be rotated to match the set at the right?

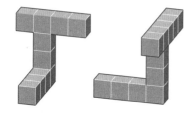

Figure 11.5

Mental rotation test. Spatial reasoning tasks can be divided into a variety of subtypes. Studies indicate that males perform slightly better than females on most, but not all, spatial tasks. The tasks on which males are superior often involve mentally rotating objects, such as in the problem shown here, for which the answer is "no."

Source: From Kalat, J. W. (2013). *Biological psychology* (11th ed.). Belmont, CA: Wadsworth. Reproduced with permission. www.cengage.com/permissions

found that "on average, males and females differ very little in math achievement," even though males have a more positive attitude toward math (Else-Quest, Hyde, & Linn, 2010, p. 125).

Thus, the current view is that gender differences in mathematical abilities in the general population are essentially nil. However, this conclusion has a few exceptions. Males, for example, outperform females at the high end of the mathematical ability distribution (Dweck, 2007). This gap, however, has shrunk since the 1980s (Ceci, Williams, & Barnett, 2009) (see **Figure 11.3**). Also, in mathematical *complex problem solving*, boys start to slightly outperform girls when they reach high school (Lindberg et al., 2010). Given that this pattern does not emerge until later in life, researchers do not see it as an innate cognitive difference, but instead as a difference in socialization, an issue that we will discuss in more depth shortly. However, boys historically outperform girls on the math portion of the SAT (see **Figure 11.4**). Because math skills and problem-solving ability are essential for success in scientific courses and careers (arenas currently underpopulated by women), this finding is a concern.

Spatial Abilities

In the cognitive area, the most compelling evidence for gender differences is in *spatial abilities*, which include perceiving and mentally manipulating shapes and figures. Males typically outperform females in most spatial abilities, and gender differences favoring males are consistently found in the ability to perform mental rotations of a figure in three dimensions—a skill important in occupations such as engineering, chemistry, and the building trades (Hyde, 2014) (see **Figure 11.5**). This gender gap in the ability to handle mental rotations is relatively large and has been found repeatedly (Halpern, 2000, 2004). Using creative methods, researchers have demonstrated this difference in infants as young as 5 months old (Moore & Johnson, 2008). Experience and training can improve mental rotation in both girls and boys (Newcombe, 2007). In fact, playing action video games has been shown to improve mental rotation skills for both genders (Spence, Feng, & Marshman, 2009). One study found benefits for women in rotation skills after only 1 hour of training on an action video game (Cherney, Bersted, & Smetter, 2014). This leads researchers to speculate that activities associated with masculine gender roles (such as playing action video games) might actually contribute to the development of these skills (Reilly & Neumann, 2013).

In sum, there appear to be few strong gender differences in cognitive *abilities*. However, when it comes to academic *achievement* (typically measured by grades in school) females tend to have the edge (Voyer & Voyer, 2014). A study of more than 1 million adolescents from seventy-four countries found that girls outperformed boys in all subjects most of the time (Stoet & Geary, 2015). Interestingly, even with this achievement advantage, females report more anxiety about, and lower confidence in, abilities associated with boys (such as math) than do males (Goetz et al., 2013). This could, in turn, lead females away from careers in science and engineering.

Personality Traits and Social Behavior

Turning to personality and social behavior, let's examine those factors for which gender differences are reasonably well documented.

Self-Esteem

Females typically score lower than males on tests of global self-esteem, but the difference in scores is small (Stake & Eisele, 2010). Hyde (2014) argues that this difference has been exaggerated in the popular press. For example, a meta-analysis of several hundred studies that included respondents from 7 to 60 years of age found only a small difference in self-esteem that favored males (Kling et al., 1999). The authors found no support for claims that girls' self-esteem drops dramatically during adolescence. A second meta-analysis also reported only a small overall gender difference favoring males (Major et al., 1999). Other research reports self-esteem differences between white men and women, but no such differences are found for black men and women (Sprecher, Brooks, & Avogo, 2013). Obviously, the findings on self-esteem are complex.

Females are more likely than males to use relational aggression, such as talking behind another's back or spreading rumors. However, the gender difference is small.

Aggression

Aggression **involves behavior that is intended to hurt someone, either physically or verbally** (see Chapter 4). Common stereotypes hold that males are more aggressive than females, but the picture is more complex (Frieze & Li, 2010). Gender differences in aggression vary depending on the form aggression takes. Cross-cultural meta-analyses conclude that males consistently engage in more *physical aggression* than do females (Archer, 2005). This difference is evident even in young children (Baillargeon et al., 2007). On the other hand, although the differences are small, females are more likely than males to commit *relational aggression*, such as giving someone the "silent treatment" to get one's way, talking behind another's back, or spreading rumors (Archer, 2005; Richardson, 2014).

When you consider extreme forms of aggression such as violent crimes, however, there is no getting around the fact that men commit a grossly disproportionate share. According to the U.S. Department of Justice, in 2014 only about 7% of all state and federal inmates were women (Bureau of Justice Statistics (2015). In addition, 54% of the males in state facilities were violent offenders compared to only 37% of women (Carson, 2015). **Figure 11.6** shows the stark gender differences in such crimes as assault, robbery, rape, and homicide.

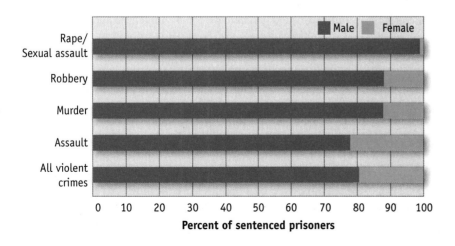

Percent of sentenced prisoners

Figure 11.6

Gender differences in violent crime arrests in suburban areas. Males are much more likely to be arrested and sentenced for violent crimes than women are. These data support the findings of laboratory studies showing that males are more physically aggressive than females. (Data from the Federal Bureau of Investigation, 2011)

Sexual Attitudes and Behavior

We cover the relation between gender and sexuality in more depth in Chapter 12, so we will address only the basics here. In the sexual domain, a meta-analysis by Petersen and Hyde (2010b, 2011) found that men are slightly more likely to engage in sexual activity and tend to have more sexual partners. Men are slightly more permissive in their attitudes toward sex in general, whereas women are more likely than men to feel negative emotions (such as shame or guilt) in response to sexual activity. The researchers found larger differences for some other aspects of sexuality. Specifically, males are more likely than females to engage in casual sex, use pornography, and masturbate (Petersen & Hyde, 2010).

Emotional Expression

Conventional wisdom holds that women are more "emotional" than men. Does research support this belief? If by being "emotional" we mean outwardly displaying one's emotions, the answer is "yes"; a number of studies have found that women express more emotion than men (Fisher & Evers, 2013). Gender differences "favoring" women have been found on such emotions as sadness, disgust, fear, surprise, and happiness.

Do women actually *experience* more emotion? To answer this question, Ann Kring and Albert Gordon (1998) had college students view films selected to evoke sadness, happiness, and fear. The researchers videotaped the participants' facial expressions and asked them to describe their emotional experiences. As expected, the researchers found gender differences in the facial expression of emotion. However, they failed to find any gender differences in *experienced* emotions. Thus, gender differences in emotional functioning may be limited to the outward expression of feelings and likely stem from societal norms about how males and females should display emotions.

Communication

Gender differences in communication are quite complex and, as with other characteristics, are typically small (Carli, 2013). Popular stereotypes suggest that females are much more talkative than males. In fact, the opposite seems to be true: men talk more than women (Cameron, 2007). In addition, men tend to interrupt women more than women interrupt men (Eckert & McConnell-Ginet, 2003). However, when women have more power in work or personal relationships, women interrupt more (Aries, 1998). Perhaps some gender differences in communication are better seen as representing a status difference.

Many studies indicate that women are more skilled than men in nonverbal communication. For example, they are better at reading and sending nonverbal messages (Hall & Matsumoto, 2004) and are more facially expressive (Brody & Hall, 2010). In addition, studies have found that women speak more tentatively ("I may be wrong, but . . .") than men, especially when discussing masculine topics in mixed-gender groups (McHugh & Hambaugh, 2010; Palomares, 2009). In a meta-analysis of more than twenty-nine studies, Leaper and Robnett (2011) found support for this phenomenon, although the difference was small. In general, gender differences in communication are a matter of degree, not kind. In other words, it's not a matter of men being from Mars and women from Venus, but more like men are from North Dakota and women are from South Dakota (Dindia, 2006).

Popular stereotypes suggest that females are much more talkative than males. In fact, men talk more than women and tend to interrupt women more, especially when there is a power differential.

Psychological Disorders

In terms of the *overall* incidence of mental disorders, only minimal gender differences have been found. When researchers assess the prevalence of *specific* disorders, however, they do find some rather consistent gender differences. Alcohol abuse and other drug-related disorders are far more prevalent among men than among

women (Nolen-Hoeksema, 2013). On the other hand, women are more likely than men to suffer from depression and anxiety disorders (Hatzenbuehler et al., 2010; Nolen-Hoeksema, 2012). Even when comparing opposite-sex fraternal twins, females have a higher rate of mood disorders than males (Kendler, Myers, & Prescott, 2005).

Females also show higher rates of eating disorders (see the Chapter 14 Application), which have been linked to distorted body images (Devlin & Steinglass, 2014). *Body image consists of one's attitudes, beliefs, and feelings about one's body.* Typically, women have a greater drive for thinness and are more concerned with dieting than are men (Herman & Polivy, 2010). For many years, this concern with thinness has existed among white and Asian Americans, but has been a lesser concern among Hispanics and black Americans (Polivy & Herman, 2002). Some evidence suggests that the very-thin female ideal may be spreading to these two groups as well (Barnett, Keel, & Conoscenti, 2001). While ultra-thinness for women has been a longtime media message, muscular body types for men are becoming more heavily promoted (Murnen & Don, 2012). Thus, the pressure to live up to an ideal body shape is a significant adjustment challenge facing both males and females today.

Putting Gender Differences in Perspective

It pays to be cautious when interpreting gender differences. Although research has uncovered some genuine differences in various domains, remember that these are *group* differences. That is, they tell us nothing about individuals. Essentially, we are comparing the "average man" with the "average woman." **Figure 11.7** shows how scores on a trait might be distributed for men and women. Although the group averages are detectably different, you can see that there is great variability within each group (gender) and huge overlap between the two group distributions. Furthermore, as we have repeatedly noted, the differences between these groups are usually relatively small. *Ultimately, the similarities between women and men greatly outweigh the differences.*

A second essential point is that gender accounts for only a minute proportion of the differences between individuals. Using complicated statistical procedures, it is possible to gauge the influence of gender (or other factors) on behavior. These tests often show that factors other than gender (for example, the social context in which behavior occurs) are far more important determinants of differences between individuals (Yoder & Kahn, 2003).

Another point to keep in mind is that when gender differences are found, they do not mean that one gender is better than the other. As Diane Halpern (1997) humorously notes, "It is about as meaningful to ask 'Which is the smarter sex?' . . . as it is to ask 'Which has the better genitals?'" (p. 1092). The problem is not with gender differences, but with how these differences are evaluated by the larger society.

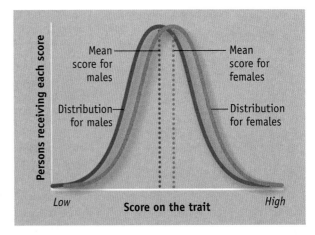

Figure 11.7

The nature of group differences. Gender differences are group differences that tell us little about individuals because of the great overlap between the groups. For a given trait, one gender may score higher on the average, but there is far more variation within each gender than between the genders.

Although gender differences in abilities, personality, and behavior are relatively few in number and small in size, sometimes it seems otherwise. How come? One explanation focuses on gender-based differences in social roles. Alice Eagly's (1987) *social role theory* **asserts that minor gender differences are exaggerated by the different social roles that males and females occupy.** For example, because women are assigned the role of caregiver, they learn to behave in nurturing ways. Over time, people come to associate such role-related behaviors with individuals of a given gender, not with the roles they play (Eagly & Wood, 2012). In other words, people come to see nurturing as a female trait rather than as a characteristic that anyone in a nurturing role would demonstrate. This is one way that gender stereotypes develop and persist.

Another explanation for discrepancies between beliefs and reality is that the differences actually reside in the eye of the beholder, not the beholdee. *Social constructionism* **asserts that individuals construct their own reality based on societal expectations, conditioning, and self-socialization** (Hyde, 1996). According to social constructionists, people's specific beliefs about gender (as well as their tendency to look for gender differences) are rooted in the "gendered" messages and conditioning that permeate socialization experiences. To better understand these issues, we next explore the role of biological and environmental factors as likely sources of gender differences.

Learning Objectives

- Summarize evolutionary explanations for gender differences.
- Review the evidence linking gender differences in cognitive abilities to brain organization.
- Describe the evidence relating hormones to gender differences.

11.3 Biological Origins of Gender Differences

Are the gender differences that *do* exist biologically built in, or are they acquired through socialization? This is the age-old question of nature versus nurture. The "nature" theorists concentrate on how biological disparities between the genders contribute to differences in behavior. "Nurture" theorists, on the other hand, emphasize the role of learning and environmental influences. Although we will discuss biological and environmental influences separately, keep in mind that most contemporary researchers and theorists in this area recognize that biological and environmental factors interact. Further, biological factors can influence gender differences without specifically determining them (Eagly & Wood, 2013). Let's first look at three biologically based lines of inquiry on this topic: evolutionary explanations, brain organization, and hormonal influences.

Evolutionary Explanations

Evolutionary psychologists suggest that gender differences in behavior reflect different natural selection pressures operating on the genders over the course of human history (Byrd-Craven & Geary, 2013). That is, natural selection favors behaviors that maximize the chances of passing on genes to the next generation (reproductive success).

To support their assertions, evolutionary psychologists look for gender differences that are consistent across cultures. Is there consistency across cultures for the better-documented gender differences? Despite some fascinating exceptions, gender differences in personality, cognitive abilities, aggression, and sexual behavior *are* found in many cultures (Lippa, 2010). According to evolutionary psychologists, these consistent differences have emerged because males and females have been confronted with different adaptive demands. For example, males are thought to be more *sexually active and permissive* because they invest less than females in the process of procreation and can maximize their reproductive success by seeking many sexual partners (Webster, 2009).

The gender gap in *aggression* is also explained in terms of reproductive fitness. Because females are more selective about mating than males are, males have to engage in more competition for sexual partners than females do. Greater aggressiveness is thought to be adaptive for males in this competition for sexual access because it should foster social dominance over other males. Evolutionary theorists assert that gender differences in *spatial abilities* reflect the division of labor in ancestral hunting-and-gathering societies in which males typically handled the hunting and females the gathering. Males' superiority on most spatial tasks has been attributed to the adaptive demands of hunting (Newcombe, 2010).

Evolutionary analyses of gender differences are interesting, but controversial. Although it is certainly plausible that evolutionary forces could have led to some divergence between males and females in typical behavior, evolutionary hypotheses are highly speculative and difficult to test empirically. In addition, evolutionary theory can be used to claim that the status quo in society is the inevitable outcome of evolutionary forces. Thus, if males have dominant status over females, natural selection must have favored this arrangement. The crux of the problem is that evolutionary analyses can be used to explain almost anything. For instance, if the situation regarding mental rotation were reversed—if females scored higher than males—evolutionary theorists might attribute females' superiority to the adaptive demands of gathering food, weaving baskets, and making clothes—and it would be difficult to prove otherwise.

Brain Organization

Some theorists propose that male and female brains are organized differently, which might account for gender differences in some gender-specific abilities. As you may know, the human brain is divided into two halves. The *cerebral hemispheres* **are the right and left halves of the cerebrum, which is the convoluted outer layer of the brain.** The cerebrum, the largest and most complicated part of the human brain, is responsible for most complex mental activities. Some evidence suggests that the right and left cerebral hemispheres are specialized to handle different cognitive tasks (Sperry, 1982; Springer & Deutsch, 1998). For example, it appears that the *left hemisphere* is more actively involved in *verbal and mathematical processing*, while the *right hemisphere* is specialized to handle *visual-spatial and other nonverbal processing*. Still, it is important to note that the brain functions as a unified structure, in that these two hemispheres do not act completely independently.

After these findings on hemispheric specialization surfaced, some researchers began looking for disparities between male and female brain organization as a way to explain the observed gender differences in verbal and spatial skills. Some thought-provoking findings have been reported. For instance, males exhibit more cerebral specialization than females (Hines, 1990). In other words, males tend to depend more heavily than females on the left hemisphere in verbal processing and on the right hemisphere in spatial processing. Additionally, some studies suggest that females tend to have a larger *corpus callosum,* **the band of fibers connecting the two hemispheres of the brain.** This greater size might allow for better transfer of information across hemispheres, which in turn might underlie the more bilateral (less hemispherically specialized) organization of female brains (Lippa, 2005). Thus, some theorists have argued that these differences in brain organization are responsible for gender differences in verbal and spatial ability (Clements et al. 2006).

Although this idea is intriguing, there are some important limitations in this line of reasoning. First, studies have not consistently found that males have more specialized brain organization than females (Kaiser et al., 2009), and the finding of a larger corpus callosum in females does not always emerge (Fine, 2010). Second, because a significant amount of brain development occurs over the first 5 to 10 years after birth, during which time males and females are socialized differently, it is possible that different life experiences may accumulate to produce slight differences in brain organization (Hood et al., 1987). In other words, because the brain responds to the environment, the biological factors that

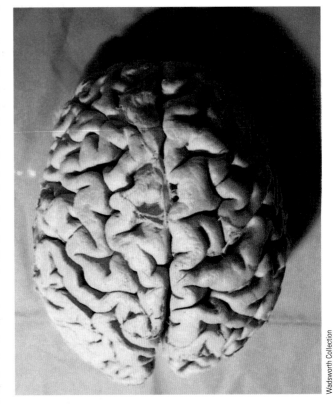

Studies have shown that the brain's cerebral hemispheres, shown here, are somewhat specialized in the kinds of cognitive tasks they handle and that such specialization is more pronounced in males than in females. Whether this difference bears any relation to gender differences in behavior is yet to be determined.

supposedly cause gender differences in cognitive functioning may actually reflect the influence of environmental factors. Third, gender accounts for only a small amount of the variance in lateralization; it's more dependent on the type of task (Boles, 2005). Finally, it's important to remember that male and female brains are much more similar than they are different. Taken together, Fine (2013) argues that we must be wary of engaging in *neurosexism*, or using these biological findings to support our preexisting gender stereotypes.

Hormonal Influences

As we discussed in Chapter 3, *hormones* **are chemical substances released into the bloodstream by the endocrine glands.** Biological gender is determined by sex chromosomes: An XX pairing produces a female, and an XY pairing produces a male. However, both male and female embryos are essentially the same until about 7 to 12 weeks after conception. Around this time, male and female gonads (sex glands) begin to produce different hormonal secretions. The high level of *androgens* (hormones such as testosterone) in males and the low level of androgens in females lead to the differentiation of male and female genital organs. It is important to note that androgens are found in and are important for both males and females. Even though testosterone is often referred to as a "male" hormone while estrogen is referred to as a "female" hormone, the idea that hormones have a gender is a myth (Crocetti, 2013).

The influence of prenatal hormones on genitalia is clear, but their impact on behavior is harder to establish. However, researchers have found that hormones play an important role in the development of sex-typical childhood behavior, including toy preferences (Hines, 2010, 2011). Much of what researchers know about this topic comes from studying endocrine disorders—that is, those caused by interference with normal prenatal hormonal secretions (Bussey, 2013). Scientists have studied children born to mothers given an androgen-like drug to prevent miscarriage. Two trends have been noted in this research (Collaer & Hines, 1995). First, girls exposed prenatally to abnormally high levels of androgens exhibit more male-typical behavior (for instance, choosing "boy" toys) than other girls do. Second, boys exposed prenatally to abnormally low levels of androgens exhibit more female-typical behavior (such as choosing "girl" toys) than other boys.

These findings suggest that prenatal hormones shape gender differences in humans. But there are a number of problems with this evidence (Bussey, 2013). First, behavior is always subject to social factors after birth. Second, it's always dangerous to draw conclusions about the general population based on small samples of people who have rare conditions. Third, most of the endocrine disorders studied have multiple effects (besides altering hormone level) that make it difficult to isolate actual causes. Finally, most of the research is necessarily correlational, and it is always risky to draw causal conclusions from correlational data.

Postnatally, the hormone testosterone plays an important role in *sexual desire* for both men and women (Petersen & Hyde, 2010a). That is, when testosterone is reduced or eliminated, both men and women show decreases in sexual drive. Additionally, high levels of testosterone in men and women correlate with higher rates of *sexual activity* (Petersen & Hyde, 2011), although research suggests that there might be social factors at play in this link (van Anders, 2012). Testosterone has also been linked with higher levels of *aggression* (impulsive and antisocial behavior) in humans (Platje et al., 2015), but the picture is complicated because aggressive behavior can produce increases in testosterone. In fact, one study demonstrated that simply interacting with a gun increased testosterone levels in males (Klinesmith, Kasser, & McAndrew, 2006).

The overall evidence suggests that, aside from obvious physical differences, biological factors such as evolution, brain structure, and hormones play a relatively minor role in gender differences. In contrast, efforts to link gender differences to disparities in the way males and females are socialized have proved more fruitful. We consider this perspective next.

11.4 Environmental Origins of Gender Differences

Learning Objectives

- Define *socialization* and *gender roles*.
- Explain how reinforcement and punishment, observational learning, and self-socialization operate in gender-role socialization.
- Describe how parents, peers, schools, and the media serve as sources of gender-role socialization.

Socialization **is the acquisition of the norms and roles expected of people in a particular society.** This process includes all the efforts made by a society to ensure that its members learn to behave in a manner that's considered appropriate. Teaching children about gender roles is an important aspect of the socialization process. *Gender roles* **are cultural expectations about what is appropriate behavior for each gender.** For example, in our culture women have traditionally been expected to rear children, cook meals, clean house, and do laundry. On the other hand, men have been expected to be the family breadwinner, do yardwork, and tinker with cars.

Keep in mind that gender roles and gender stereotypes are intertwined, each fueling the other. As we noted earlier, Eagly's social role theory suggests that gender differences often occur (and seem bigger than they actually are) because males and females are guided by different role expectations. In the next section, we'll discuss how society teaches individuals about gender roles.

Processes in Gender-Role Socialization

How do people acquire gender roles? Several key learning processes come into play, including reinforcement and punishment, observational learning, and self-socialization.

Reinforcement and Punishment

In part, gender roles are shaped by the power of rewards and punishment—the key processes in operant conditioning (see Chapter 2). Parents, teachers, peers, and others often reinforce (usually with tacit approval) "gender-appropriate" behavior. For example, a young boy who has hurt himself may be told that "big boys don't cry." If he succeeds in inhibiting his crying, he may get a pat on the back or a warm smile—both powerful reinforcers. Over time, a consistent pattern of such reinforcement will strengthen the boy's tendency to "act like a man" and suppress emotional displays.

Most parents take gender-appropriate behavior for granted and don't go out of their way to reward it. However, many are much less tolerant of gender-inappropriate behavior, especially for males. For instance, a 10-year-old boy who enjoys playing with dollhouses will probably elicit strong disapproval. Reactions usually involve ridicule or verbal reprimands rather than physical punishment.

Children learn behaviors appropriate to their gender roles very early in life. According to social learning theory, girls tend to do the sorts of things their mothers do, whereas boys tend to follow in their fathers' footsteps.

Observational Learning

Younger children commonly imitate the behavior of a parent or an older sibling. This imitation, or *observational learning*, occurs when a child's behavior is influenced by observing others. These others are called *models*. Parents serve as models for children, as do siblings, teachers, relatives, and others who are important in children's lives. Models are not limited to real people; television, movie, and cartoon characters can also serve as models.

According to *social cognitive theory* (see Chapter 2), young children are more likely to imitate people who are nurturant, powerful, and similar to them (Bussey & Bandura, 1984, 2004). Children imitate both genders, but most children are prone to imitate same-gender models. Interestingly, same-gender peers may be even more influential models than parents are (Maccoby, 2002).

Self-Socialization

Children are not merely passive recipients of gender-role socialization. Rather, they play an active role in this process, beginning early in life. Because society labels people, characteristics, behavior, and activities by gender, children learn that gender is an important social category. Around 2 to 3 years of age, children begin to identify themselves as male or female (Martin, Ruble, & Szkrybalo, 2002). Once children have these labels, they begin to organize the various pieces of gender-relevant information into gender schemas. **Gender schemas are cognitive structures that guide the processing of gender-relevant information.** Basically, gender schemas work like lenses that cause people to view and organize the world in terms of gender (Bem, 1993).

Self-socialization begins when children link the gender schema for their own gender to their self-concept. Once this connection is made, children are motivated to selectively attend to activities and information that are consistent with the schema for their own gender. For example, Terrance knows that he is a boy and also has a "boy" schema that he attaches to himself. Now his self-esteem is dependent on how well he lives up to his boy schema. In this way, children get involved in their own socialization. They are "gender detectives," working diligently to discover the rules that are supposed to govern their behavior (Halim & Ruble, 2010).

Sources of Gender-Role Socialization

Four major sources of gender-role messages are parents, peers, schools, and the media (Leaper & Farkus, 2015). Keep in mind that gender-role socialization varies depending on one's culture. For example, black families typically make fewer distinctions between girls and boys than do white families (Hill, 2002); as a result, gender roles are more flexible for black women (Littlefield, 2003). By contrast, gender roles are relatively rigidly defined in Asian and Hispanic families (Chia et al., 1994; Comas-Diaz, 1987). Also, gender roles are changing, so the generalizations that follow may say more about how *you* were socialized than about how your children will be.

Parents

Parents are arguably the most important agents of socialization (Grusec & Davidov, 2015). Although a meta-analysis of 172 studies of parental socialization practices suggests that parents don't treat girls and boys as differently as one might expect (Lytton & Romney, 1991), there are some important disparities. For one thing, there is a strong tendency for both mothers and fathers to emphasize and encourage *play activities* that are "gender appropriate." For example, studies show that parents encourage boys and girls to play with different types of toys (Wood, Desmarais, & Gugula, 2002). Generally, boys have less leeway to play with "feminine" toys than girls do with "masculine" toys. It is clear that children are socialized to play with "girl" toys or "boy" toys, but could this play also be a *source* of gender-role socialization? The following Spotlight on Research explores this possibility.

Boys are under more pressure than girls to behave in gender-appropriate ways. Little boys who show an interest in dolls are likely to be chastised by both parents and peers.

Jennie Hart/Alamy Stock Photo

Can Barbie Be a Firefighter?

Source: Sherman, A. M., & Zurbriggen, E. L. (2014). "Boys can be anything": Effect of Barbie play on girls' career cognitions. *Sex Roles, 70*(5–6), 195–208.

As we have discussed, men are more likely to be employed in math-based occupations such as engineering or computer science, but psychologists speculate that this gap is not due to gender differences in cognitive abilities. Instead, gender-role socialization plays an important role in one's academic interests and career choices. Childhood play is central to socialization in that children learn appropriate behaviors for their gender. The researchers examined the impact of gender-socialized play (that is, girls playing with Barbie dolls) on perceptions about careers. If Barbie dolls carry gendered messages about how girls should look, then perhaps these dolls affect the perception about what jobs girls can do as well.

Method

Participants. Thirty-seven girls, ages 4 to 7, participated in the study. All parents gave consent for their daughters to participate.

Materials and Procedures. Girls were randomly assigned to play with either a Barbie doll or a Mrs. Potato Head doll. After 5 minutes of "free play," the experimenter removed the dolls and told the participants that they were going to play a picture game. The girls viewed eleven pictures showing various occupations (one neutral, five stereotypically female, and five stereotypically male). Each photo had a caption and no humans were shown. For example, there was a picture of a fire station captioned, "This is a fire station. A firefighter works here." Pictures were presented in random order and for each one the girls were asked "Could you do this job when you grow up? And "could a boy do this job when he grows up?" "Yes" or "no" responses were recorded.

Results

Regardless of which doll they played with, the girls reported that boys had more job options overall than they did. However, the difference in the number of jobs the girls thought were possible for themselves versus the number possible for boys was significantly greater after the girls played with a Barbie doll. That is, girls who played with Barbie reported fewer job possibilities for themselves than the girls who played with Mrs. Potato Head.

Discussion

These results demonstrate that childhood play can affect children's expectations about their future career possibilities at an early and impressionable age. As children are building their gender schemas, even their toys provide them with information. The researchers noted some limitations. Specifically, the girls were asked to report on themselves and a hypothetical boy. Perhaps the results would be different if the girls were asked to report on a hypothetical girl, as opposed to themselves. Future researchers are encouraged to include other outcomes such as self-concept or well-being in addition to career possibilities. Although more research is needed, this study presents evidence that gender gaps in career domains might be due in part to early childhood socialization.

Critical Thinking Questions

1. Did you play with gender-stereotypical toys? How might this play have influenced your academic choices so far (such as your choice of major)?
2. The researchers suggest that future studies consider other outcomes besides career possibilities (for example, self-concept)? Can you think of other outcomes than might be affected by gender-socialized childhood play?

In addition to toys, the *picture books* parents buy for their children typically depict characters engaging in gender-stereotypic activities (Gooden & Gooden, 2001). One study of more than 5,600 books from 1900 to 2000 found that males are twice as likely as females to be in the book's title and 1.6 times more likely to be the main character (McCabe et al., 2011). Further, a content analysis of 20 years of award-winning children's books revealed that females were more often depicted using household items (spoons, sewing machines), whereas male characters were more often depicted using production items outside the home (such as cars and tools), a pattern that has not changed over time (Crabb & Marciano, 2011). Even books that parents and teachers rate as "nonsexist" portray female characters with stereotypic personalities, chores, and leisure activities (Diekman & Murnen, 2004).

Further, the way parents communicate with their children about picture books provides clues for gender schemas. One study found that even with gender-neutral books, parents reinforce gender stereotypes by providing gender labels (Endendijk et al., 2014). For instance, while reading picture books with gender-neutral characters to their preschoolers, parents were more likely to label angry characters as male while labeling sad or happy characters as female (van der Pol et al., 2015).

Rob Van Petten/Photodisc/Getty Images

The way parents read to their children can provide clues for gender schemas. Even with gender-neutral books, parents can reinforce gender stereotypes by labeling angry characters as male while labeling sad or happy characters as female.

Of course, parents communicate gender roles in more direct ways. For instance, one study found that fathers were more attentive to their daughters' submissive emotions such as sadness, whereas they were more attentive to their sons' disharmonious emotions such as anger (Chaplin, Cole, & Zahn-Waxler, 2005). Through these conversational patterns, parents subtly (or not so subtly) reinforce what emotions and behaviors are appropriate for girls and boys to display.

Peers

Peers form an important network for learning about gender-appropriate and gender-inappropriate behavior, especially as children get older (Bussey, 2013). Between the ages of 4 and 6, children tend to separate into same-gender groups, and these preferences appear to be child- rather than adult-driven (Fabes, Hanish, & Martin, 2003). From age 6 to about 12, boys and girls spend much more time with same-gender than other-gender peers. Moreover, according to Eleanor Maccoby (1998, 2002), over time boys' and girls' groups develop different "subcultures" (shared understandings and interests) that strongly shape youngsters' gender-role socialization. One study that examined friendship stability from seventh through twelfth grade found that mixed-gender friendships were more likely than same-gender ones to dissolve (Hartl, Laursen, & Cillessen, 2015).

Because both boys and girls are critical of peers who violate traditional gender norms, they perpetuate stereotypical behavior. Among children ages 3 to 11, boys are devalued more than girls for dressing like the other gender, whereas girls are evaluated more negatively than boys for playing like the other gender—for instance, loudly and roughly versus quietly and gently (Blakemore, 2003). Further, "gender-atypical boys" report more often being victims of bullying, more loneliness, and greater distress than their "typical" peers (Young & Sweeting, 2004). Associations between negative adjustment and gender-atypical behavior, however, appear to be reduced with positive parenting styles (Alanko et al., 2008).

Schools

The school environment figures importantly in socializing gender roles (Wentzel & Looney, 2007). One way that gender bias shows up in schools is in *teachers' treatment of boys and girls*. Preschool and grade school teachers often reward gender-appropriate behavior in their pupils. Teachers also tend to pay greater attention to boys—helping them, praising them, and scolding them more than girls (Beaman, Wheldall, & Kemp, 2006). By contrast, girls tend to be less visible in the classroom and to receive less encouragement for academic achievement from teachers. Overall, these teacher-student interactions reinforce the gender stereotype of male competence and dominance (Meece & Scantlebury, 2006). In contrast, given that females tend to have higher academic achievement than boys, teachers' stereotypes about the "underachieving male" can also bias their perceptions. For instance, one study found that teachers rated males (especially those who behaved in a gender-typical manner) as less academically engaged than females (Heyder & Kessles, 2015). This finding indicates that gender stereotypes can cut both ways.

Gender bias also shows up in *academic and career counseling*. Despite the fact that females obtain higher grades than males (on the average) in all subjects from elementary school through college (Stoet & Geary, 2015), many counselors continue to encourage male students to pursue high-status careers in medicine or engineering while guiding female students toward less-prestigious careers. Stereotypic beliefs that lead to differential treatment by counselors and teachers can facilitate barriers to women's career choices, especially in the areas of science and math.

The Media

Television, videos, and other forms of media are sources of gender-role socialization (Scharrer, 2013). According to a Nielsen Research Group (2014) report, the average American child (ages 2–11) spends 24 hours, 16 minutes a week watching traditional TV (the time is even greater if you include recorded shows). And that doesn't include DVDs, videos, or streaming content. Given this high level of consumption, researchers are quite interested in gender messages in the media.

In traditional children's adventure *cartoons* (as opposed to educational cartoons), male characters appear more often and engage in more physical aggression, whereas female characters are much more likely to show fear, act romantic, be polite, and act supportive (Leaper et al., 2002). An analysis of male and female characters on *prime-time television programs* showed that the number and variety of roles of female TV characters have increased but that these shifts lag behind the actual changes in women's lives (Glascock, 2001). Compared to males, females appear less often, are less likely to be employed in prestigious positions, are more likely to be younger, and are more likely to appear in secondary and comedy roles. As compared to female characters, males are still more likely to demonstrate acompetence-related behaviors such as reaching a goal, showing ingenuity, and answering questions (Aubrey & Harrison, 2004). In shows geared toward tweens (those considered too old to be a child but not yet a teenager), females are more likely to be attractive and receive comments or display concern about their looks (Gerding & Signorielli, 2013). Even in the news, use of the pronoun "he" is nine times more likely than "she" and is associated with more positive contexts (Sendén, Sikström, & Lindholm, 2014).

Television commercials are even more gender stereotyped than TV programs (Lippa 2005). When analyzing more than 450 after-school commercials from the popular children's network *Nickelodeon*, researchers found that gender-role stereotypes were pervasive (Kahlenberg & Hein, 2010). Commercials were gender orientated, and even gender-neutral toys were often marketed toward one gender (see **Figure 11.8**). Further, boys tended to be depicted outdoors more than girls, and they were shown engaged in a wider variety of activities. In a content analysis comparing the major U.S. networks to an African American niche station (Black Entertainment Television—BET), researchers found that

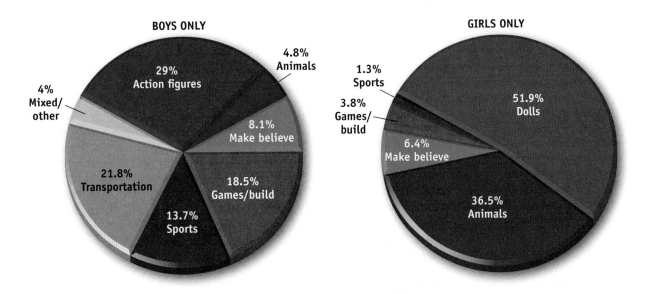

Figure 11.8

Toys presented in commercials with boys or girls in them. A content analysis of commercials airing on Nickelodeon demonstrated that commercials with only boys promoted very different toys than those with only girls. These differences highlight the role of gender-role stereotypes in the media. (Adapted from Kahlenberg & Hein, 2010)

the majority of the characters in primetime commercials are male and white, even on BET (Messineo, 2008).

TV is not the only medium that perpetuates gender stereotypes; gender-role socialization is a multimedia phenomenon. Most *video games* push a hypermasculine stereotype featuring search-and-destroy missions, fighter pilot battles, and male sports (Lippa, 2005). Females, if depicted at all, tend to be hypersexualized. One study found that including a hypersexualized, but noncentral, female character on the box for the game was associated with increased sales (Near, 2013). Of the few video games directed at girls, the great majority are highly stereotypic (shopping and Barbie games).

Do the media actually influence children's views about gender? Evidence suggests that the answer is "yes." A meta-analysis reported a link between children's exposure to gender stereotyping in the media and the acquisition of gender-stereotyped beliefs (Oppliger, 2007). Even among adults, viewing sexualized portrayals of women appears to influence viewers' gender-role and sexual attitudes (Kistler & Lee, 2010). One study found that men who watched a sexually objectifying TV clip were subsequently more likely to endorse stricter gender roles and engage in coercive and harassing behavior than were those who viewed a non-objectifying clip (Gladi, Maass, & Cadinu, 2014). Admittedly, gender-role socialization is complex, and other factors such as parental values come into play as well. Nonetheless, Greenwood and Lippman (2010) argue that our perceptions of gender differences might be an "artifact of the gender-stereotyped landscape of the mass media" (p. 662).

Learning Objectives

- List the key elements of the traditional male role and identify common problems associated with the traditional male role.
- List the major expectations of the female role and identify common problems associated with the female role.

11.5 Gender-Role Expectations

Traditional gender roles are based on several unspoken assumptions: that all members of the same gender have basically the same traits, that the traits of one gender are very different from the traits of the other gender, and that masculine traits are more highly valued. In this section, we review the research and theory in this area and note changes in gender roles in the recent past. We begin with the male role.

Role Expectations for Males

A number of psychologists have sought to pinpoint the essence of the traditional male role (Levant, 2011; Pleck, 1995). Many consider *anti-femininity* to be the central theme that runs through the male gender role. That is, "real men" shouldn't act in any way that might be perceived as feminine. Five key attributes constitute the traditional male role (Brannon, 1976; Jansz, 2000).

1. *Achievement.* To prove their masculinity, men need to beat out other men at work and at sports. Having a high-status job, driving an expensive car, and making lots of money are aspects of this element.
2. *Aggression.* Men should be tough and fight for what they believe is right. They should aggressively defend themselves and those they love against threats.
3. *Autonomy.* Men should be self-reliant and not admit to being dependent on others.
4. *Sexuality.* Real men are heterosexual and are highly motivated to pursue sexual activities and conquests.
5. *Stoicism.* Men should not share their pain or express their "soft" feelings. They should be cool and calm under pressure.

There is evidence that manhood, as opposed to womanhood, is more precarious (Bosson, Vandello, & Caswell, 2013). That is, it is more susceptible to threat and requires social proof and validation. Unfortunately, harmful demonstrations of masculinity such as displays of physical aggression are typical ways of defending one's manhood when this status is threatened. This behavior is often at odds with modern gender-role expectations. According to Joseph Pleck (1995), who has written extensively on this issue, in the *traditional male role*, masculinity is validated by individual physical strength, aggressiveness, and emotional inexpressiveness. In the *modern male role*, however, masculinity is validated by economic achievement, organizational power, emotional control (even over anger), and emotional sensitivity and self-expression, but only with women.

This flux in expectations means that males are experiencing role inconsistencies and pressures to behave in ways that conflict with traditional masculinity; that is, they have gender-role strain (Levant & Richmond, 2016). Brooks (2010) argues that distress over ever-changing gender roles fuels three major problems—violence, substance abuse, and sexual misconduct—as men channel their distress into these destructive behaviors. Ironically, endorsement of gender roles becomes a barrier to seeking help for such problems (Yousaf, Popat, & Hunter, 2015).

Problems with the Male Role

It is often assumed that only females suffer from the constricting binds of traditional gender roles. Not so. As we just discussed, the costs of the male role are an increasing cause for concern.

Pressure to Succeed

Most men are socialized to be highly competitive and are taught that a man's masculinity is measured by the size of his paycheck and job status. The majority of men who have internalized the success ethic are unable to fully realize their dreams. This is a particular problem for African American and Hispanic men, who experience more barriers (due to discrimination) to financial success than European American men do. How does this "failure" affect men? Although many are able to adjust to it, some are not. The men in this latter group are likely to suffer from shame and low self-esteem (Kilmartin, 2000). Regardless of ethnicity, losing his job can threaten a man's sense of manhood, increasing his risk for depression and anxiety (Bosson et al., 2013).

Gender differences in pressure to succeed might be more perceived than real. When asked about *perceptions*, college students rated the typical man as worrying about achievement more that the typical woman. However, when asked about their *own* worry, women reported more worry about achievement than men did (Wood et al., 2005). Perhaps this finding reflects men's not wanting to admit that they are worrying about anything.

The Emotional Realm

Most young boys are trained to believe that men should be strong, tough, cool, and detached. Thus, they learn early to hide vulnerable emotions such as love, joy, and sadness because they believe that such feelings are feminine and imply weakness (Fischer & Evers, 2013). As a result, over time, some men lose touch with their own emotional lives. With the exception of anger, men with traditional views of masculinity are more likely to suppress outward emotion, supposedly because having feelings may lead to a loss of composure (Jakupcak et al., 2003).

Males' difficulty with "tender" emotions has serious consequences. First, as we saw in Chapter 3, suppressed emotions can contribute to stress-related disorders. And, men are less likely than women to seek social support or help from health professionals. Second, men's emotional inexpressiveness can cause problems in their relationships with partners and children. For example, compared to husbands who

Because most men are taught that their masculinity is measured by their job status, losing a job can threaten a man's sense of manhood, increasing his risk for depression and anxiety.

endorse traditional masculine roles, those who endorse egalitarian gender roles report greater marital happiness, as do their wives (Frieze & Ciccocioppo, 2009). Further, children whose fathers are warm, loving, and accepting toward them have higher self-esteem and lower rates of aggression and behavior problems than those with colder, more distant fathers (Rohner & Veneziano, 2001).

Sexual Problems

Traditional gender-role socialization gives men a "macho" sexual image to live up to. As a result, a great fear for many men is the inability to achieve an erection. Unfortunately, this very fear often *causes* the dysfunction that men dread (see Chapter 12). The upshot is that men's obsession with sexual performance can produce anxiety that may interfere with their sexual responsiveness. Alternatively, distress about being perceived as "masculine enough" can lead to overcompensation in the sexual arena. One study found that men who felt distress about living up to gender roles were more likely to engage in risky sexual behaviors and were more likely to be diagnosed with a sexually transmitted infection as a result (Reidy et al., 2015).

Another problem is that many men learn to confuse feelings of intimacy and sex. In other words, if a man experiences strong feelings of connectedness, he is likely to interpret them as sexual feelings. This confusion has a number of consequences. For one thing, sex may be the only way some men can allow themselves to feel intimately connected to someone else. In addition, the confusion of intimacy and sex may underlie the tendency for men (but not women) to perceive eye contact, a compliment, an innocent smile, a friendly remark, or a brush against the arm as a sexual invitation (Kowalski, 1993). Finally, the sexualization of intimate feelings causes inappropriate anxiety when men feel affection for another man, thus promoting *homophobia* or sexual prejudice, *the intense intolerance of homosexuality*. Indeed, endorsement of traditional gender roles and hypermasculinity are related to negative attitudes toward homosexuality (Parrott et al., 2008). This tendency can put a strain on developing male friendships.

Role Expectations for Females

Male roles aren't the only ones in flux; the role expectations for American women have undergone dramatic changes, especially with regard to work. Prior to the 1970s, a woman was expected to be a housewife and a stay-at-home mother. Today, there are three major expectations for women:

1. *The marriage mandate.* Remaining single is a choice that has been growing in popularity for several decades; however, there is still a stigma attached to singlehood in a society where marriage is the norm (DePaulo, 2014). Most women are socialized to feel incomplete until they find a mate.

2. *The motherhood mandate.* A major imperative of the female role is to have children. This expectation has been termed the *motherhood mandate* (Rice & Else-Quest, 2006). The prevailing ideology of today's motherhood mandate is that women should desire to have children, mothering should be wholly child-centered, and mothers should be self-sacrificing rather than persons who have their own needs and interests.

3. *Work outside the home.* Most of today's young women, especially those who are college educated, expect to work outside the home, and they also want a satisfying family life. The percentage of women in the labor force has been steadily rising over the last 30 years. Yet even when they work outside the home, women still perform the bulk of the household chores (Blair, 2013).

Problems with the Female Role

Writers in the feminist movement generated some compelling analyses of the problems associated with the pre-1970s traditional role of wife and mother (Friedan, 1964; Millett, 1970). Many criticized the assumption that women, unlike men, did not need an independent identity; it should be sufficient to be a wife and a mother. Since that time, girls and women have increasingly been encouraged to develop and use their talents, and work opportunities for women have greatly expanded. Still, there are problems with the female role.

Learn More Online

Voice of the Shuttle: Gender Studies

The VOS maintains one of the broadest databases of web resources across many topics. The multiple links cited here cover the spectrum of gender-related issues from women's and men's studies to gay and lesbian identity resources.

Diminished Career Aspirations

As we have discussed, gender roles can dictate a woman's academic interests and career choices (Eccles, 2014). Despite recent efforts to increase women's opportunities for achievement, young women are more likely to underestimate their achievement than boys (who overestimate theirs), especially when estimating performance on "masculine" tasks such as science and math (Eccles, 2001, 2007). As a result, girls might shy away from taking math-intensive courses at school. This is a problem because science and math are the foundations for many high-paying, high-status careers, and the lack of a math background (as opposed to ability) often contributes to the inferior performance of some women. Further, researchers speculate that it is gender differences in attitudes about math-centered careers (again, as opposed to actual ability) that lead fewer women to pursue those jobs (Ceci et al., 2014).

The discrepancy between women's abilities and their level of achievement has been termed the *ability-achievement gap* (Hyde, 1996). The roots of this gap seem to lie in the conflict between achievement and femininity that is built into the traditional female role. The marriage and motherhood mandates fuel women's focus on *heterosexual success*— learning how to attract and interest males as prospective mates. The resulting emphasis on dating and marriage can lead some women away from *occupational success*—they worry that they will be seen as unfeminine if they boldly strive for a challenging career. Of course, this is not a concern for all women. And, because younger men are more supportive of their wives' working than older men are, this conflict should ease for younger women.

Juggling Multiple Roles

Another problem with the female role is that societal institutions have not kept pace with the reality of women's lives, especially if women choose motherhood. In 2014, approximately 70% of mothers with children younger than 18 years of age were employed or looking for work (Bureau of Labor Statistics, 2014a). Yet some workplaces (and many husbands and fathers) still operate as if all women were stay-at-home moms and as if there were no single-parent families. This gap between outdated policies and modern reality means that women who "want it all" experience burdens and conflicts that most men do not. This is because most men typically have *major* day-to-day responsibilities in only *one* role: worker. But most women have major day-to-day responsibilities in *three* roles: spouse, parent, and worker.

Of course multiple roles, in themselves, are not inherently problematic. In fact, there is some evidence that multiple roles can be beneficial to mental health, as you'll see in Chapter 13. Rather, the problem stems from the tensions among these roles and the unequal sharing of role responsibilities. Greater participation in household tasks and child care by husbands or others, as well as family-friendly workplaces and subsidized quality child-care programs, help alleviate women's stress in this area. However, this issue is not clear cut. Goldberg and Perry-Jenkins (2004) note that women with traditional gender roles and whose husbands did *more* child care after the birth of their first child experienced substantial distress. This finding may be due to the conflict of performing *less* child care than they expected and, thus, not living up to their own gender-role expectations.

Although multiple roles are not inherently problematic, most women have major day-to-day responsibilities in three roles: spouse, parent, and worker.

Ambivalence about Sexuality

Like men, women may have sexual problems that stem, in part, from their gender-role socialization (Katz-Wise

& Hyde, 2014). For many women, the problem is difficulty in enjoying sex. Why? Research shows that adherence to traditional gender roles is associated with a decrease in women's sexual satisfaction (Sanchez, Fetterrolf, & Rudman, 2012). For instance, many girls are still taught to suppress or deny their sexual feelings. Further, they are told that a woman's role in sex is a passive one. In addition, girls are encouraged to focus on romance rather than on gaining sexual experience. As a result, many women feel uncomfortable (guilty, ashamed) with their sexual urges. Thus, when it comes to sexuality, women are likely to have ambivalent feelings instead of the largely positive feelings that men have. Unfortunately, this ambivalence is often viewed as sexual "dysfunction" for women, as opposed to an attitude resulting from narrow gender roles.

11.6 Gender in the Past and in the Future

In Western society, gender roles are in a state of transition. As we have noted, sweeping changes have already occurred in the female role. It's hard to imagine today, but less than 100 years ago, women were not allowed to vote or to manage their own finances. It wasn't that long ago when it was virtually unheard of for a woman to initiate a date, manage a corporation, or run for public office. In this section, we discuss why gender roles are changing and what the future might bring.

Why Are Gender Roles Changing?

A number of theories attempt to explain why gender roles are in transition. Basically, these theories look at the past to explain the present and the future. A key consideration is that gender roles have always constituted a division of labor. In earlier societies, such as hunting-and-gathering and herding societies, the gender-based division of labor was a natural outgrowth of some simple realities. For instance, men tend to be stronger than women, so they were better equipped to handle such jobs as hunting and farming. Thus, traditional gender roles are a carryover from the past. Once traditions are established, they have a way of perpetuating themselves. Over the last century or so in Western society, these divisions of labor have become increasingly antiquated. For example, the widespread use of machines to do work has rendered differences in physical strength relatively unimportant. Therein lies the prime reason for changes in gender roles. *Traditional gender roles no longer make economic sense.*

The future is likely to bring even more dramatic shifts in gender roles. We can see the beginnings of these changes now. For example, although women still bear children, nursing responsibilities are now optional. Moreover, as women become more economically independent, they have less need to get married solely for economic reasons. Further, with the recent legalization of same-sex marriage, a gender-based division of labor for these families is irrelevant. In light of these and other changes in modern society, it is safe to say that gender roles are likely to remain in flux for some time to come.

Per Magnus Persson/Getty Images

Traditional gender roles are in flux. The recent legalization of same-sex marriage and other changes in modern society make a gender-based division of labor irrelevant.

Alternatives to Traditional Gender Roles

Gender-role identity **is a person's identification with the qualities regarded as masculine or feminine.** Initially, gender-role identity was conceptualized as either "masculine" or "feminine." All males were expected to develop masculine role identities and females, feminine gender-role identities. Individuals who did not identify with the role expectations for their gender or who identified with the characteristics for the other gender were judged to be few in number and to have psychological problems.

In the 1970s, social scientists began to rethink their ideas about gender-role identity. One assumption that was called into question is that males should be "masculine" and females should be "feminine." For one thing, it appears that the number of people who don't conform to traditional gender-role norms is higher than widely assumed, as is the amount of strain that some people experience trying to conform to conventional roles (Pleck, 1981, 1995). In addition, the evidence suggests that "masculine" males and "feminine" females may be less well adjusted, on the average, than those who are less traditional. As people have become aware of the possible costs of conventional gender roles, there has been much debate about moving beyond them. A big question has been: What should we move toward? Let's examine some options.

Androgyny

Like masculinity and femininity, androgyny is a type of gender-role identity. *Androgyny* **refers to the coexistence of both masculine and feminine personality traits in a single person.** In other words, an androgynous person is one who scores above average on measures of *both* masculinity and femininity.

To help you fully appreciate the nature of androgyny, we need to briefly review other kinds of gender identity (see **Figure 11.9**). Males who score high on masculinity and low on femininity, and females who score high on femininity and low on masculinity, are said to be *gender-typed*. Males who score high on femininity but low on masculinity, and females who score high on masculinity but low on femininity, are said to be *cross-gender-typed*. Finally, males and females who score low on both masculinity and femininity are characterized as *gender-role undifferentiated*.

In groundbreaking research more than four decades ago, Sandra Bem (1975) challenged the then-prevailing view that males who scored high in masculinity and females who scored high in femininity are better adjusted than "masculine" women and "feminine" men. She argued that traditionally masculine men and feminine women feel compelled to adhere to rigid and narrow gender roles that unnecessarily restrict their behavior. In contrast, androgynous individuals ought to be able to function more flexibly.

How have Bem's ideas played out over time? Androgynous people do seem more flexible than others. That is, they can be nurturing (feminine) or independent (masculine), depending on the situation (Bem, 1975). In contrast, gender-typed males tend to have difficulty behaving in a nurturing manner, while gender-typed females often have trouble with independence. Also, individuals whose partners are either androgynous or feminine (but not masculine or undifferentiated) report higher relationship satisfaction and fewer depressive symptoms (Bradbury, Campbell, & Fincham, 1995). This finding holds for both cohabiting heterosexuals and lesbian and gay couples (Kurdek & Schmitt, 1986). Thus, in these areas androgyny seems to be advantageous.

However, researchers speculate that, due to changing gender roles, the traits Bem used to categorize gender identities are now outdated. Case in point—in a sample of college students, Auster and Ohm (2000) found that although eighteen of the twenty feminine traits still qualified as feminine, only eight of the twenty masculine traits were still perceived as strictly masculine. These problems with the concept of androgyny and its measurement have led Bem and other psychologists to take a different view of gender roles, as you'll see next.

Gender-Role Transcendence

As psychologists thought more about androgyny, they realized that the concept had some additional problems. For one thing, the idea that people should have both masculine and feminine traits reinforces the assumption that gender is an integral part of human behavior. That is, if people use gender-based labels ("masculine" and "feminine") to describe certain

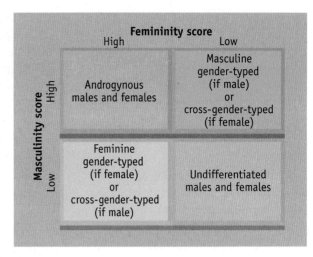

Figure 11.9

Possible gender-role identities. This diagram summarizes the relations between participants' scores on measures of masculinity and femininity and four possible gender identities.

Sandra Bem challenged the view that males who scored high in masculinity and females who scored high in femininity are better adjusted than "masculine" women and "feminine" men.

Researchers recognize that gender can be fluid, varying over time. As a result, gender-fluid individuals move between identities. Jaden Smith (son of Will and Jada Pinkett Smith) has been public in his gender nonconformity, bringing greater attention to gender fluidity.

human characteristics and behavior, they are likely to associate these traits with one gender or the other, creating a self-fulfilling prophecy of sorts (Batalha & Reynolds, 2013). Another criticism of androgyny is that it implies that the solution to gender bias is to change the individual rather than to address the gender inequities in society and its institutions (Matlin, 2004).

Many gender theorists maintain that masculinity and femininity are really only arbitrary labels that we have learned to impose on certain traits through societal conditioning. This assertion is the foundation for the *gender-role transcendence* perspective (Bem, 1983, 1993; Spence, 1983). **The *gender-role transcendence perspective* proposes that to be fully human, people need to move beyond gender roles as a way of organizing their perceptions of themselves and others.** This goal requires that instead of dividing human characteristics into masculine and feminine categories (and then combining them, as the androgyny perspective suggests), we should dispense with the artificially constructed gender categories and labels altogether. How would this work? Instead of the labels *masculine* and *feminine*, we would use gender-neutral terms such as *instrumental* and *expressive*, respectively, to describe personality traits and behaviors. This "decoupling" of traits and gender could reduce the self-fulfilling prophecy problem. Given that individuals today have had years of exposure to gender messages, moving toward gender-role transcendence would likely be a gradual process.

Gender Variance

Contemporary researchers agree that gender labels are arbitrary and socially constructed. Instead of defining new labels, they are more interested in *gender variance*, or gender nonconformity. Due to outspoken celebrities such as Caitlyn Jenner and Laverne Cox, the concept of *transgender* has received mainstream media attention and entered public discourse. *Transgendered* individuals are those whose sense of gender identity differs from the biological sex they were labeled with at birth (typically based on genitals) (Bockting, 2014). As such, transgendered individuals typically don't adhere to traditional gender roles in terms of physical appearance or behaviors, and often reject traditional gender labels. Given that gender expression is diverse and culturally bound, researchers argue that gender variations, such as transgender, are not pathological and most adjustment problems that do occur typically result from stressors outside the individual (from sexism or sexual prejudice) (Hidalgo et al., 2013).

More recently, researchers have begun to explore the idea of *gender fluidity* (Baker & Richards, 2015). These researchers recognize that the construct of gender can vary over time. As a result, gender-fluid individuals move between identities—identifying as a woman at times, a man at other times, or rejecting a gender label altogether. Looking at gender as an unstable continuum is complex and challenges deep-rooted ideas about gender. This research is still in its infancy, and it will be interesting to see where it leads. However, it has researchers and practitioners alike questioning the notion of an either/or approach to gender.

11.7 Gender in the Workplace

Learning Objectives

- Describe sexism and explain benevolent sexism.
- Discuss two forms of economic discrimination. Describe the glass ceiling and explain what might account for it.
- Define *sexual harassment*, describe two forms of it, and explain some characteristics of targets.
- Discuss the effects of sexism and harassment as well as ways to reduce each.

Answer the following questions "true" or "false."

____ 1. Sexism can stem from positive feelings toward a person.

____ 2. Women in high-status positions can contribute to the stereotyping of other women in the workplace.

____ 3. Women who behave in ways that go against traditional gender-role expectations are more likely to be harassed.

____ 4. Clear, transparent policies for hiring and promotion decisions reduce the chances of sexism in the workplace.

If you answered "true" to all of these statements, you were correct. As we have discussed, gender stereotypes bias our perceptions and expectations of others. They go beyond merely *describing* our beliefs about males and females to *prescribing* behaviors that are deemed appropriate (Barreto & Ellmers, 2013). These gender-based prescriptions can present particular difficulties in the workplace. Although the issues are relevant for men (especially gay men in low-status positions), they are more commonly a problem for women. As a result, you will find our coverage tilted in that direction.

Sexism

Sexism **is discrimination against people on the basis of their gender.** Sexism usually refers to discrimination by men against women. However, sometimes *women* discriminate against other women and sometimes *men* are the victims of gender-based discrimination. Sexism is not limited to American culture; it is a cross-cultural phenomenon (Brandt, 2011). Further, sexism does not have to come from an individual, but rather can be a result of institutional policies that value one gender over another (Barreto & Ellemers, 2013).

Sexism can be hostile, if one is expressing clearly negative attitudes toward one gender. However, sometimes people behave in sexist ways without having negative attitudes toward the target. Instead, they have positive feelings toward the target, but still treat the target in restricting ways. For example, men might behave in ways toward women (for instance, treating them in

a child-like fashion, placing them on a pedestal) ostensibly to protect them, implying that they cannot protect themselves. Researchers call this *benevolent sexism*. Although benevolent sexism might seem less problematic than hostile discrimination, it still has a negative impact. It conveys the belief that women are inferior and need protection and help from men, thus perpetuating the gender stereotype that males are more competent and have more agency than women. This type of sexism is subtle and largely legitimized in society, making it difficult for women to identify and combat it (Jetten et al., 2013). Let's look at the impact of sexism in the workplace.

Economic Discrimination

Women are victimized by two forms of economic discrimination: differential access to jobs and differential treatment once on the job. Concerning *job access*, the problem is that women still lack the same employment opportunities as men. A meta-analysis showed that there was a gender bias in that men were preferred over women for stereotypically male jobs, but no such preference emerged for female jobs (Kock, D'Mello, & Sackett, 2015). For example, in 2011 women were more than twice as likely as men to have occupations with wages below the poverty level (Institute for Women's Policy Research, 2012). Ethnic minority women are even less likely than white women to work in high-status, male-dominated occupations. Across all economic sectors, men are more likely than women to hold positions with decision-making authority (Eagly & Sczesny, 2009). In contrast, women are overrepresented in "pink-collar ghetto" occupations, such as secretary and preschool and kindergarten teacher. Additionally, motherhood can be a liability on the job market. One study found that there is a bias against mothers (but not fathers) applying for a job, in terms of anticipated competence (Heilman & Okimoto, 2007).

The second aspect of economic discrimination is *differential treatment* on the job. For example, women typically earn lower salaries than men in the same jobs (see **Figure 11.10**). And occupations that are male dominated typically pay more than those that are female dominated (Pratto & Walker, 2004). Further, when women demonstrate leadership qualities such as confidence, ambitiousness, and assertiveness, they are evaluated less favorably than men, perhaps because this behavior contradicts the female gender stereotype (Lyness & Heilman, 2006). Thus, they are often penalized for their success.

The Glass Ceiling

There appears to be a *glass ceiling* that prevents most women and ethnic minorities from being advanced to top-level professional positions (Reid, Miller, & Kerr, 2004). It is called a "glass"

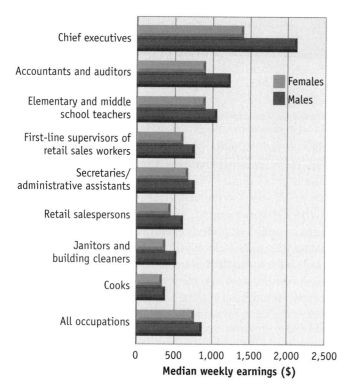

Figure 11.10

The gender gap in weekly wages. Women continue to earn less than men in almost all occupational categories, as these 2011 data for selected occupations make clear. Many factors can contribute to this gender gap in earned income, but economic discrimination is probably a major consideration. (Data from the Institute for Women's Policy Research, 2012)

ceiling because it is largely unseen, but still a barrier. For example, in 2012 there were only eighteen female CEOs of Fortune 500 companies—still an all-time record high (Huffington Post, 2012). One of the reasons for the glass ceiling is the perception by bosses that female subordinates have greater family-work conflict than their male counterparts (Hoobler, Lenmon, & Wayne, 2011). Ironically, men employed in traditionally female fields are promoted more quickly than their female counterparts, a phenomenon dubbed the *glass escalator* (Hultin, 2003).

What might account for the glass ceiling? Recall that the traditional male stereotype is more complimentary than the conventional female stereotype. These stereotypes can lead to different interpretations of men and women's behaviors. For instance, in the workplace a man demonstrating leadership might be described as "strong," whereas a woman is viewed as "bossy" for the same behaviors. Any time a woman behaves counter to gender stereotypes, she risks negative evaluation. That is, she could be judged as not feminine enough. Yet, masculine behaviors are often the very ones valued in hiring and promotion decisions for high-status jobs (Phelan, Moss-Racusin, & Rudman, 2008).

Of course, women can climb the ladder in their male-dominated professions in the face of direct discrimination. Research shows that many of these women (referred to as *Queen Bees*) do so by distancing themselves from their gender

identity and acting "masculine" (Derks et al., 2011). In doing so, they are contributing to the stereotyping of other women in the workplace by perpetuating the idea that only masculinity will get you to the top. However, Derks and colleagues (2016) argue that the Queen Bee phenomenon isn't just another source of gender inequality in the workplace, but instead is a result of gender bias. Reminding Queen Bees of gender biases in the workplace can motivate them to actually improve the conditions for other women (Derks et al., 2011).

Sexual Harassment

Sexual harassment **is unwelcome conduct on the basis of gender.** The key components of sexual harassment are that it is unwelcome, unreciprocated, and socially inappropriate (Maass, Cadinu, & Galdi, 2013). It can include sexual advances, requests for sexual favors, and other verbal or physical harassment of a sexual nature. Sexual harassment has become recognized as a widespread problem that occurs not only on the job but also at home (obscene telephone calls), while walking outside (cat-calls and whistles), and in medical and psychotherapy settings. It also takes place in schools and colleges. Sexual harassment is more about dominance and power than desire. Women in male-dominated organizations are more likely to be harassed than those in female-dominated ones, and women who break traditional gender roles (such as being assertive and showing leadership abilities) in male-dominated organizations are the most likely to be targets (Berdahl, 2007).

Betz (2006) distinguishes between two categories of sexual harassment in the workplace. In *quid pro quo harassment*, employees are expected to give in to sexual demands in exchange for employment, raises, promotions, and so forth. In *hostile environment harassment*, employees are exposed to sexist or sexually oriented comments, cartoons, posters, and so forth. The experience of sexual harassment is related to poorer job outcomes (Settles et al., 2006), as well as increased psychological

Sexual harassment is a problem in the workplace, and women in male-dominated organizations are more likely to be harassed than those in female-dominated ones. The key components of sexual harassment are that it is unwelcome, unreciprocated, and socially inappropriate.

distress (Nielsen & Einarsen, 2012). Given that harassment continues to be a major problem in the workplace, future researchers will no doubt continue to explore this issue.

Targets of Harassment

As we will discuss further in Chapter 13, anyone can be the target of harassment, though researchers have uncovered some trends. In general, women who are seen as vulnerable are often targets (perhaps because they are perceived as easily dominated), whereas women who are seen as strong are also targets (perhaps because they challenge the idea of male dominance). In particular, women who work in a male-dominated workplace, who have already experienced interpersonal violence, or who go against gender-role expectations, are more likely to be harassed (Maass et al., 2013). Research shows that minority women experience a form of "double jeopardy" when it comes to workplace harassment. When Berdahl and Moore (2006) surveyed employees from five ethnically diverse companies, they found that women experience more harassment than men, that minorities experience more harassment than whites, and that minority women experience more harassment than any other group.

Men are less likely to be targets of harassment, with some exceptions. Specifically, gay men and straight men who do not conform to gender-role expectations are often targets of harassment by other men, especially if they are in low-status positions.

Effects of Sexism and Sexual Harassment

Experiencing discrimination in the form of sexism and sexual harassment has detrimental effects on one's mental and physical well-being. A meta-analysis of almost 200 studies found that *perceived discrimination* is associated with increases in depression and distress, as well as a heightened stress response (Pascoe & Richman, 2009). The negative effects of sexism decrease when women themselves endorse traditional gender stereotypes or if they view the perceived discrimination as a challenge rather than a threat (Barreto & Ellemers, 2013). Sexism is a stressor, and as with other stressors, women's appraisals of discrimination (as challenge or threat) play a role in its impact (Matheson & Foster, 2013).

Experiencing sexual harassment at work increases stress. It is related to lower job satisfaction, reduced commitment to work, and poorer physical and mental health.

There are negative effects of *sexual harassment* for individuals as well as organizations. In a meta-analysis of more than 70,000 participants, harassment was related to lower job satisfaction, reduced commitment to the organization, becoming less engaged at work, and poorer physical and mental health (Willness, Steel, & Lee, 2007). In severe cases, it is associated with symptoms of posttraumatic stress disorder (see Chapter 3). Given these negative effects, researchers continue to explore experiences of sexism and harassment.

Reducing Sexism and Sexual Harassment

Reducing sexism and sexual harassment requires a shift in social norms. Traditional gender stereotypes labeling women as weak and passive and men as strong and agentic perpetuate gender inequalities and support male-dominance as the status quo. To combat sexism, organizations need to recognize that sexism and discrimination exist, provide opportunities for success for disadvantaged group members, and have clear, transparent policies for hiring and promotion (Stroebe, Barreto, & Ellemers, 2010).

To combat workplace harassment, organizations must develop a culture that discourages it. Researchers recommend that organizations adopt a clearly communicated zero-tolerance policy, safe and visible ways to report violations, and diversity training (Maass et al., 2013). In addition, these policies must be embraced from the top. Shifting societal and organizational norms takes time and effort, but they yield benefits to all employees and the workplace as a whole.

CHAPTER 11 Review

Key Ideas

11.1 Gender Stereotypes

• Many stereotypes have developed around behavioral differences between the genders, although the distinctions between the male and female stereotypes are less rigid than they used to be. Gender stereotypes may vary depending on ethnicity, and they typically favor males.

11.2 Gender Similarities and Differences

• Some contemporary researchers have adopted the gender similarity hypothesis, emphasizing the fact that males and females are more similar than different on most psychological variables.

• There are no gender differences in general intelligence. When it comes to verbal abilities, gender differences are small, and they generally favor females. Gender differences in mathematical abilities are typically small as well, and they favor males. Males perform much better than females on the spatial ability of mental rotation; however, this skill can be improved through practice.

• Research shows that males typically are somewhat higher in self-esteem, although the findings are complex. Males tend to be more physically aggressive than females, whereas females are higher in relational aggression. Males have more permissive attitudes about casual sex and are more sexually active than females. Males and females are similar in the experience of emotions, but females are more likely to outwardly display emotions. Gender differences in communication are complex. Men tend to talk more and interrupt more than women. Women tend to be more skilled in nonverbal communication. Males and females are similar in overall mental health, but they differ in prevalence rates for specific psychological disorders.

• The gender differences that do exist are quite small. Moreover, they are group differences that tell us little about individuals. Nonetheless, some people still adhere to the belief that psychological differences between the genders are substantial. Social role theory and social constructionism provide two explanations for this phenomenon.

11.3 Biological Origins of Gender Differences

• Biological explanations of gender differences include those based on evolution, brain organization, and hormones. Evolutionary psychologists explain gender differences on the basis of their purported adaptive value in ancestral environments. These analyses are speculative and difficult to test empirically.

• Regarding brain organization, some studies suggest that males exhibit more cerebral specialization than females. However, linking this finding to gender differences in cognitive abilities is questionable for a number of reasons.

• Efforts to tie hormone levels to gender differences have also been troubled by interpretive problems. Nonetheless, there probably is some hormonal basis for gender differences in aggression and in some aspects of sexual behavior.

11.4 Environmental Origins of Gender Differences

• The socialization of gender roles appears to take place through the processes of reinforcement and punishment, observational learning, and self-socialization. These processes operate through many social institutions, but parents, peers, schools, and the media are the primary sources of gender-role socialization.

11.5 Gender-Role Expectations

• Five key attributes of the traditional male role include achievement, aggression, autonomy, sexuality, and stoicism. The theme of anti-femininity cuts across these dimensions. Problems associated with the traditional male role include excessive pressure to succeed, difficulty in dealing with emotions, and sexual problems. Homophobia is a particular problem for men.

• Role expectations for females include the marriage mandate, the motherhood mandate, and working outside the home. Among the principal costs of the female role are diminished aspirations, juggling of multiple roles, and ambivalence about sexuality.

11.6 Gender in the Past and in the Future

• Gender roles have always represented a division of labor. They are changing today, and they seem likely to continue changing because they no longer mesh with economic reality. Consequently, an important question is how to move beyond traditional gender roles. The perspectives of androgyny and gender-role transcendence provide two possible answers to this question.

• Many contemporary researchers view binary gender labels as arbitrary and are more interested in gender variance or gender nonconformity. Transgender and gender fluidity are two types of gender variance.

11.7 Application: Gender in the Workplace

• Sexism is discrimination against people on the basis of their gender. It can be hostile or benevolent. Sexism can lead to differential access to jobs and differential treatment once on the job. The glass ceiling, a result of traditional gender stereotypes, prevents many women from advancing to top positions in their careers.

• Sexual harassment is unwelcome, unreciprocated, and socially inappropriate. Women who work in a male-dominated workplace are more likely to be harassed. Though less likely in men, gay men and straight men who do not conform to gender-role expectations are often targets of same-gender harassment.

• Sexism and sexual harassment have detrimental effects on mental and physical well-being. Reducing sexism and sexual harassment requires a shift in social and organizational norms.

Key Terms

Aggression p. 311
Androcentrism p. 308
Androgyny p. 327
Body image p. 313
Cerebral hemispheres p. 315
Corpus callosum p. 315
Expressiveness p. 308
Gender p. 307
Gender-role identity p. 326
Gender-role transcendence
  perspective p. 328
Gender roles p. 317
Gender schemas p. 318
Gender stereotypes p. 307
Hormones p. 316
Instrumentality p. 308
Meta-analysis p. 309
Sexism p. 329
Sexual harassment p. 330
Social constructionism p. 314
Social role theory p. 314
Socialization p. 317

Key People

Sandra Bem p. 327
Alice Eagly p. 314
Janet Shibley Hyde p. 309
Joseph Pleck p. 323

CHAPTER 11 Practice Test

1. Taken as a whole, gender differences in verbal abilities are
   a. small and favor females.
   b. large and favor females.
   c. nonexistent.
   d. small and favor males.

2. Among the following traits, the largest gender differences are found in
   a. verbal abilities.
   b. mathematical abilities.
   c. spatial abilities.
   d. general intelligence.

3. The finding that males exhibit more cerebral specialization than females supports which of the following biologically based explanations for gender differences?
   a. Evolutionary theory
   b. Brain organization
   c. Hormones
   d. Social constructionism

4. Four-year-old Rachel seems to pay particular attention to what her mother and her older sister do, and she often imitates them. What is taking place?
   a. Punishment
   b. Observational learning
   c. Reinforcement
   d. Self-socialization

5. Parents tend to respond negatively to _____ behavior, especially in _____.
   a. gender appropriate; boys
   b. gender appropriate; girls
   c. gender inappropriate; boys
   d. gender inappropriate; girls

6. Which of the following is *not* a problem associated with the male role?
   a. Pressure to succeed
   b. Emotional inexpressiveness
   c. Sexual problems
   d. The marriage mandate

7. Aaron exhibits both masculine and feminine personality traits. According to gender identity theory, he would be classified as
   a. androgynous.
   b. androcentric.
   c. undifferentiated.
   d. cross-gender-typed.

8. Which of the following perspectives proposes that to be fully human, people need to move beyond gender roles as a way of organizing their perceptions of themselves and others?
   a. Social constructivism
   b. Evolutionary theory
   c. Gender-role identity
   d. Gender-role transcendence

9. The idea that individuals can move between gender identities is referred to as
   a. gender nonconformity.
   b. gender fluidity.
   c. transgender.
   d. androgyny.

10. Sara's supervisor implied that she would get a promotion if she would go out on a date with him. This is an example of
    a. quid pro quo harassment.
    b. hostile environment harassment.
    c. benevolent sexism.
    d. the Queen Bee phenomenon.

Answers

1. a Page 309
2. c Page 310
3. b Page 315
4. b Page 318
5. c Page 318
6. d Pages 323–324
7. a Page 327
8. d Page 328
9. b Page 328
10. a Page 330

Personal Explorations Workbook

Go to the *Personal Explorations Workbook* in the back of your textbook for exercises that can enhance your self-understanding in relation to issues raised in this chapter.

Exercise 11.1 *Self-Assessment:* Personal Attributes Questionnaire (PAQ)

Exercise 11.2 *Self-Reflection:* How Do You Feel about Gender Roles?

CHAPTER 12 Development and Expression of Sexuality

ImageDJ/Alamy Stock Photo

Rachel and Marissa, both college students and new roommates, headed out to a local club on a Friday night. After a while, they were joined by Luis and Jim, whom they knew a little from one of their classes. After a couple of hours, Rachel took Marissa aside and asked if she would drive the car back to their apartment so Rachel could leave with Luis. Marissa agreed and went home. When she woke up the next morning, Marissa realized that Rachel hadn't come home yet. Questions raced through Marissa's mind. How could Rachel have spent the night with a guy she barely even knew? Was it being prudish to think that? Did Rachel or Luis have a condom? Marissa knew she would have been afraid of getting pregnant, or maybe getting a disease of some kind. As this scenario illustrates, sexuality raises a lot of issues in people's lives. In this chapter we consider key aspects sexuality and adjustment. ■

12.1 Becoming a Sexual Person

People vary greatly in how they express their sexuality. While some eagerly reveal the intimate details of their sex lives, others can't even utter sexual words without embarrassment. To understand this diversity, we need to examine developmental influences on human sexual behavior.

Before beginning, we should note that sex research has some unique problems. Given the difficulties in conducting direct observation, sex researchers depend mostly on survey methods such as interviews and questionnaires (Schick, Calabrese, & Herbenick, 2014). As a result, sex studies are especially susceptible to participant bias. People who are willing to volunteer information tend to be more sexually experienced and have more positive attitudes about sex than does the general population (Chivers et al., 2014). In addition, respondents may shade the truth about their sex lives because of shame, embarrassment, boasting, wishful thinking, or simply wanting to be viewed favorably. Thus, you need to evaluate the results of sex research with more than the usual caution.

Key Aspects of Sexual Identity

Identity refers to a clear and stable sense of who one is in the larger society. We'll use the term *sexual identity* to refer to the complex set of personal qualities, self-perceptions, attitudes, values, and preferences that guide one's sexual behavior. In other words, your sexual identity is your sense of yourself as a sexual person. It includes four key features: sexual orientation, body image, sexual values and ethics, and erotic preferences.

1. *Sexual orientation.* Sexual orientation is an individual's preference for emotional and sexual relationships with individuals of one gender or the other. *Heterosexuals* seek emotional-sexual relationships with members of the other gender. *Homosexuals* seek emotional-sexual relationships with members of the same gender. *Bisexuals* seek emotional-sexual relationships with members of both genders. *Asexuals* feel little need for emotional-sexual relationships with either gender. However, as we will see later in this chapter, sexual orientation is more complicated and multidimensional than this simple categorization implies.

2. *Body image.* Your body image is how you see yourself physically. Your view of your physical self affects how you feel about yourself in the sexual domain. A positive body image is correlated with greater sexual activity, higher sexual satisfaction, and fewer sexual problems (Nobre & Pinto-Gouveia, 2008; Weaver & Byers, 2006). The popularity of face-lifts and breast enhancements testifies to the importance of body image to many people.

3. *Sexual values and ethics.* In forming their values, people are taught that certain expressions of sexuality are "right," while others are "wrong." The nature of these sexual messages is culture-specific and varies depending on gender, race, ethnicity, and socioeconomic status. For example, a lingering sexual double standard encourages sexual activity

in males, but not females. Individuals are faced with the daunting task of sorting through these often-conflicting messages to develop their own sexual values and ethics.

4. *Erotic preferences.* Within the limits imposed by sexual orientation and values, people still differ in what they find enjoyable. People's erotic preferences encompass their attitudes about self-stimulation, oral sex, intercourse, and other sexual activities. For instance, researchers found that although men and women were equally interested in erotic photos, they differed in terms of their preferences for the sexual activities depicted (Rupp & Wallen, 2009). Such preferences develop through a complex interplay of physiological and psychosocial influences—issues we take up next.

Physiological Influences

Among the various physiological factors involved in sexual behavior, hormones have been of particular interest to researchers. As you will see, hormones have important effects on sexual development. Their influence on sexual *anatomy*, however, is much greater than their influence on sexual *activity* (Brotto & Smith, 2014).

Hormones and Sexual Differentiation

During the prenatal period, a number of biological developments result in a fetus that is male or female. Hormones play an important role in this process, which is termed *sexual differentiation*. Around the third month of prenatal development, different hormonal secretions begin to be produced by male and female *gonads*—**the sex glands.** In males, the testes produce *androgens*, **the principal class of male sex hormones.** Testosterone is the most important of the androgens. In females, the ovaries produce *estrogens*, **the principal class of female sex hormones.** Actually, both classes of hormones are present in both genders, but in different proportions. During prenatal development, the differentiation of the genitals depends primarily on the level of testosterone produced—high in males, low in females.

There are instances, though rare, in which sexual differentiation is incomplete and individuals are born with ambiguous genitals, sex organs, or sex chromosomes. These persons, called *intersex individuals* (formerly called *hermaphrodites*), are born with a combination of male and female hormonal or anatomical features (Agocha, Asencio, & Deccenta, 2014). Though their sex is usually difficult to determine at birth, some intersex individuals might not be identified until puberty, and it is often difficult for them to determine their "true" sexual identity.

After Caster Semenya, a South African athlete who is intersex, won the 800-meter world championship, questions were raised about her eligibility to compete as a woman. This controversy brought gender issues to the forefront of athletics.

Sexual Maturation and Puberty

At puberty, hormones reassert their influence on sexual development. Adolescents attain reproductive capacity as hormonal changes trigger the maturation of the *primary sex characteristics*, the structures necessary for reproduction (sex organs). Hormonal shifts also regulate the development of *secondary sex characteristics* (physical features that distinguish the genders but are not directly involved in reproduction). For instance, in females, more estrogen leads to breast development, widened hips, and rounded body contours. In males, more androgen results in developing facial hair, a deeper voice, and angular body contours.

In females, a pivotal point in pubertal development is *menarche*—**the first occurrence of menstruation.** American girls typically reach menarche between ages 12 and 13, with further sexual maturation continuing for 2 to 3 more years (Peper & Dahl, 2013). In males, there is no clear-cut marker of the onset of sexual maturity, although the capacity to ejaculate is used as an index of puberty. *Spermarche*, **or the first ejaculation,** is often experienced through nocturnal ejaculations (O'Sullivan & Thompson, 2014). Experts note that ejaculation may not be a valid index of actual maturity, as early ejaculations may contain seminal fluid but not active sperm.

Psychosocial Influences

The principal psychosocial influences on sexual identity are essentially the same as the main sources of gender-role socialization discussed in Chapter 11. Sexual identity is shaped by one's family, peers, schools, and religion, as well as the media.

Families

Parents and the home environment are significant influences on sexual identity in the early years. Before they reach school age, children usually engage in some sex play and exploration, such as "playing doctor." They also display curiosity about sexual matters, asking questions such as "Where do babies come from?" This curiosity increases with age. One study of more than 1000 preadolescents found that 70% of 12-year-olds were eager to learn about sex (Miller et al., 2012). Parents who punish innocent, exploratory sex play and who stutter and squirm when kids ask sexual questions convey the idea that sex is "dirty." As a result, children may begin to feel guilty about their sexual urges and curiosity.

Direct communication between parents and children about issues related to sex is important. However, only 79% of girls and 70% of boys report talking to their parents about sex (Martinez, Abma, & Casey, 2010). As you can see in **Figure 12.1**, almost 50% of teens report getting information about birth control from someone other than their parents. And even when communication does occur, many young people feel dissatisfied with the sexual information they receive from their parents, in terms of both quantity and quality. Although most parents recognize that it is important to communicate with their children about issues related to sexuality, many don't because they simply don't know how. Further, even when parents do provide information, it is not uncommon for their knowledge about sexually related topics to be incorrect, incomplete, or outdated, prompting experts to encourage sex education for the parents of teens (Brookes et al., 2010).

Peers

Friends provide a lot of information regarding sex, and positive peer influence is associated with less risky sexual behavior and reduced risk of sexually transmitted infections (Dunn, Gilbert, & Wilson, 2011; Vivancos et al., 2013). Indeed, the sexual behaviors of one's friends is a strong predictor of one's own sexual behavior (Lyons et al., 2011).

Figure 12.1

Sources of information about birth control among teens. Many young people do not get their information about contraception from either their parents or their schools. (Adapted from Alan Guttmacher Institute, 2012b)

But it's not just actual *behaviors* that individuals use for information; adolescents' sexual attitudes and behavior are also positively associated with their *perceptions* of their friends' sexual attitudes and behavior (Sprecher, Christopher, & Cate, 2006). Unfortunately, peers can be a source of highly misleading information and often champion sexual behavior at odds with parents' views.

Schools

Surveys show that the vast majority of parents and other adults support sex education programs in the schools, despite the media attention given to isolated, vocal protests (Tortolero et al., 2011). As of 2015, twenty-two states and the District of Columbia mandated sex education (Alan Guttmacher Institute, 2015). The type of sexual education schools offer varies. "Abstinence only" programs offer no information about contraceptive methods but encourage students to abstain from sex, while "abstinence plus" programs include additional information about sexually transmitted diseases and contraception. "Comprehensive programs" offer information on a wide variety topics such as contraception, abortion, sexually transmitted diseases, relationships, sexual orientation, and responsible decision making (Kendall, 2014).

What is the effectiveness of these various programs? *Abstinence only* programs do not deter adolescents from engaging in sex, nor do they delay first intercourse or reduce the number of sexual partners (U.S. Department of Health and Human Services, 2007). In fact, they have been associated with a decrease in reliable contraceptive use (Isley, 2010). In contrast, *comprehensive programs* result in a wide range of positive outcomes: increased use of contraception, fewer pregnancies, and reduced high-risk sexual behavior (Chin et al., 2012). In addition, comprehensive programs do not promote (and may even delay) having early sex and do not increase (and may decrease) the number of sexual partners (Katz-Wise & Hyde, 2014). Even with these statistics, most schools do not offer students comprehensive sexual education (Kendall, 2014).

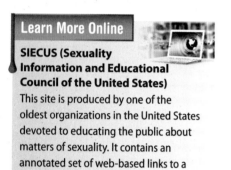

Religion

One's religious background (or lack thereof) can play a major role in the development of sexual identity (Hernandez, Mahoney, & Pragament, 2014). Religious teachings and traditions can dictate what is seen as sexually natural or unnatural. For example, religious institutions historically have had a lot to say about issues such as guilt, monogamy, and homosexuality (Francoeur, 2007). Using data from three national surveys, Regnerus (2007) found that the predominant message that teens receive about sex from their religious institutions is "Don't do it until you're married." This message is conveyed through church-based initiatives such as abstinence pledges, chastity vows, and purity rings. This message is largely ineffective, however. Teens who take these pledges tend to be just as sexually active (but less likely to use condoms or other forms of birth control) as their equally religious nonpledging peers. They do, however, tend to feel guiltier about it (Rosenbaum, 2009). These findings suggest that although religious teachings might affect sexual attitudes, they do not always influence behavior. However, there is evidence that teens and young adults who view religion as very important and who frequently attend church are less likely to have had sex and, if they have, to have had fewer sex partners than their nonreligious peers (Haglund & Fehring, 2010). Additionally, Hernandez and her colleagues (2014) found that married couples who view sex as a sacred bond (that is, having a spiritual component) report higher marital and sexual satisfaction.

The Media

Americans see thousands of sexual encounters a year on television, movie, and computer screens. And the portrayal of sexual content, both in terms of sex talk and behavior, appears to be on the rise. In movies,

Teens who take abstinence pledges or wear purity rings tend to be just as sexually active as their peers who don't.

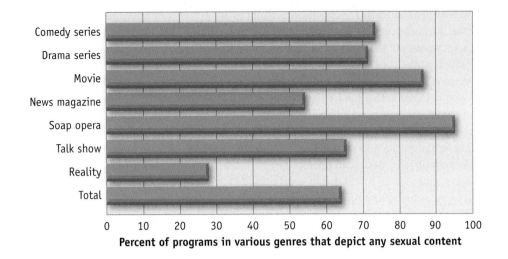

Figure 12.2

Sexual content in television programs by genre. Kunkel and colleagues (2007) examined more than 100 hours of television per week for the 2001–2002 television season. They measured both sexual talk (conversations about sex, comments about sexual actions) and sexual behavior (intimate touching, implied sexual intercourse). As you can see, sexual content is common in a variety of television genres.

Figure axis: Percent of programs in various genres that depict any sexual content

Genres: Comedy series, Drama series, Movie, News magazine, Soap opera, Talk show, Reality, Total

sexual content has increased over the years, especially for female characters (Bleakley, Hennessy, & Fishbein, 2012). O'Hara and colleagues (2012) analyzed movies over a 6-year period and found that 84% of them contained sexual content (including 68% of G-rated films). The percentage of television shows containing sexual content has been increasing as well. When analyzing more than 2000 television programs, Kunkel and his colleagues (2007) found that depictions of sexual intercourse doubled over a 5-year period. They also found that topics related to sexual risks and responsibilities, though increasing, were still incredibly rare, with such references appearing in only 6% of all sexual scenes. **Figure 12.2** shows how sexual content is distributed over common television genres.

Movies and televisions shows aimed at young people also contain sexual content. One study found that 16% of characters involved in sexual intercourse on television are teenagers or young adults (Eyal & Finnerty, 2009). Media portrayals of sexual behavior can influence an individual's beliefs about typical sexual practices. For adolescents, exposure to sexual content is associated with earlier sexual activity as well as increased sexual risk taking (O'Hara et al., 2012).

Music lyrics and music videos are additional vehicles of sexual socialization, and the sexualization of music has also increased over time (Hall, West, & Hill, 2012). Listening to music with sexually explicit and degrading lyrics is associated with higher levels of sexual behaviors in teenagers (Primack et al., 2009). In one study, male college students who viewed sexually explicit music videos were more sexually permissive, were more likely to objectify women, expressed more stereotypic gender attitudes, and showed a greater acceptance of rape (Kistler & Lee, 2010). Rap music videos tend to sexualize female characters more than male ones, and for African American adolescents, exposure to these stereotypes is associated with increases in sexual partners, negative body image, and acceptance of rape myths (Burgess & Burpo, 2012; Conrad, Dixon, & Zhang, 2009; Peterson et al., 2007).

Video games also contain sexually explicit content, often depicting women in highly sexualized ways and combining sex with violence. Research shows that exposure to these games is associated with increased sexist attitudes (Stermer & Burkley, 2012) and sexually harassing behaviors (Yao, Mahood, & Linz, 2010). Playing these video games is also related to increased sexual risk taking (Fischer et al., 2011).

Turning to cyberspace, experts estimate that there were about 7.26 billion (42.4% of the total world population) Internet users worldwide in 2015 (Internet World Stats, 2015). The Internet has become a common way to both explore and express one's sexuality. Online pornography is extremely popular, especially among males. And exposure to sexually explicit material online is related to problematic sexual

Video games can contain sexually explicit content, often depicting women in highly sexualized ways. Research shows that exposure to these games is associated with increased sexist attitudes, sexually harassing behaviors, and sexual risk taking.

attitudes such as unrealistic expectations (Buhi et al. 2014; Owens et al., 2012). On the up side, the Internet provides easy, private access to useful information on a variety of sexual topics, including contraceptive methods and resources for the LGBT communities.

Note that the causal link between sexual behavior and sexual media viewing can be bidirectional. While those exposed to sex in the media are more sexually active, those who are more sexually active tend to seek out more sexual content. In addition, the link between media exposure and sexual behaviors may actually be due to outside factors, such as permissive parenting or having sexually active peers—factors that could influence both viewing sexual media and sexual behaviors simultaneously.

Admittedly, the media can promote responsible sexual behavior and an understanding of issues such as sexual orientation (Ward et al., 2014). However, whatever advantages there might be to sexual content in the media, experts agree that media depictions of sexuality would have to change dramatically for consumption of sexual media to be considered a healthy part of sexual development.

Gender Differences in Sexual Socialization

Americans have many deeply held beliefs about how men and women express themselves sexually. From an early age, we are taught that men simply like sex more than women do—they are more interested in it, want more of it, and are more open in their attitudes than women are. As we saw in Chapter 11, such gender differences can become exaggerated, leading to harmful gender stereotypes. So how do these commonly held beliefs hold up under scientific scrutiny? To explore this question, Jennifer Petersen and Janet Shibley Hyde (recall that she is the proponent of the *gender similarity hypothesis*) conducted a large-scale meta-analysis that included more than 800 published articles and seven large national data sets. Petersen and Hyde (2010b, 2011) conclude that while gender differences exist in both sexual behaviors and sexual attitudes, most of these differences are quite small—the sexes have a lot more in common than was previously thought. Here is a summary of some of the smaller differences they uncovered:

- Men have sex somewhat more frequently and have more sex partners.
- Men are more permissive in their attitudes toward sex in general (again, the magnitude of this difference has decreased over time).
- Women are more likely than men to feel negative emotions (e.g., shame, guilt, fear) in response to sex.

There were a few areas in which men and women differ to a greater degree. Here is a summary of some of the larger differences they uncovered:

- Men are more likely to engage in casual sex (sex with a stranger or acquaintance).
- Men are more likely to engage in masturbation.
- Men are more likely to use pornography.

Although biological and evolutionary factors can explain some of these differences, societal values and gender roles obviously come into play here (Katz-Wise & Hyde, 2014). American males are encouraged to experiment sexually, to initiate sexual activities, and to enjoy sex without emotional involvement. They also get the message to be conquest oriented and to desire multiple partners. Females are typically taught to view sex in the context of a loving relationship with one partner. They learn about romance and the importance of physical attractiveness and catching a mate. Unlike males, they are not encouraged to experiment with sex or to have numerous sexual partners. In fact, sexually active women may be chastised for their behavior.

With differing views of sexuality and relationships, males and females can be out of sync with each other—particularly in adolescence and early adulthood. These gender differences can lead to confusion and mean that communication is essential for mutually satisfying sexual relationships. Because both members of homosexual couples have been socialized similarly, they are less likely than heterosexual couples to have problems with incompatible expectations. Let's consider sexual orientation next.

12.2 Sexual Orientation

Learning Objectives

- Compare Kinsey's continuum of sexuality with Diamond's theory of sexual fluidity.
- Summarize the current thinking on the origins of sexual orientation.
- Describe contemporary attitudes toward homosexuality.
- Explain the process of disclosing one's sexual orientation, and the adjustment of lesbians and gay males.

In this section, we'll explore the intriguing and complex topic of sexual orientation. The terms *gay* and *straight* are widely used to refer to homosexuals and heterosexuals, respectively. Male homosexuals are called *gay*, whereas female homosexuals are referred to as *lesbians*. Frequently, the term *LGB* is used to refer, collectively, to lesbians, gay men, and bisexuals. *Transgendered* individuals are those whose sense of gender identity differs from the sex they were labeled with at birth (Bockting, 2014). As such, transgendered individuals typically don't adhere to traditional gender roles in terms of physical appearance or behaviors. Because the lesbian, gay, bisexual, and transgendered communities often have intersecting interests, the term *LGBT* is used to refer to these groups. However, it is important to note that transgender is related to gender identity and *not* to sexual orientation.

Models of Sexual Orientation

Most people view heterosexuality and homosexuality as two distinct categories: you're either one or the other. However, many individuals who define themselves as heterosexuals have had homosexual experiences, and vice versa. Thus, it is more accurate to view heterosexuality and homosexuality as endpoints on a continuum. Indeed, Alfred Kinsey and colleagues (1948) devised a 7-point scale, shown in **Figure 12.3**, to characterize sexual orientation.

Some researchers argue that even Kinsey's model is too simplistic, inaccurately depicting sexual orientation as fixed and stable. For instance, how would you categorize a man who was married for 10 years, has children, is divorced, and is now involved in a committed homosexual relationship? What about a woman who dates only men but who has homosexual fantasies? Instead, contemporary research supports a complex and malleable view of sexual orientation. Lisa Diamond (2014) uses the term *sexual fluidity* to reflect this complexity. She rejects the idea that sexual orientation is a stable trait and argues that our attractions can change depending on interpersonal and situational factors (Diamond, 2013a). That is, our sexuality is "fluid," a phenomenon that appears to apply more strongly for women. This explains how someone could have same-sex attraction and behaviors without identifying with a homosexual orientation (Kleinplatz & Diamond, 2014).

Diamond (2014) also notes that it has been widely assumed that most of those who report same-sex attractions are exclusively homosexual, with bisexuals presumed to be infrequent exceptions, who were often viewed skeptically as gays in denial about their homosexuality. In reality, recent, more fine-grained data from a variety of surveys suggest that among those who are not exclusively heterosexual, only a minority are exclusively homosexual, especially among women. These data suggest that bisexuality is much more common than previously appreciated, but Diamond (2014) points out that the term *bisexuality* suggests an equal attraction to both sexes, whereas many of the people in this category are predominantly, but not exclusively, attracted to one sex or the other. She argues that it is probably more accurate to characterize these individuals as *nonexclusive* in their sexuality, as opposed to bisexual. As you can see, models of sexual orientation are complicated and evolving.

Origins of Sexual Orientation

There is no consensus among researchers as to what determines one's sexual orientation. A number of *environmental explanations* have been proposed as causes of sexual orientation. Freud believed that homosexuality originates from an unresolved Oedipus complex (see Chapter 2). That is, instead of coming to identify with the parent of the same gender, the child continues to identify with the parent of the other gender. Learning theorists asserted that homosexuality results from early negative heterosexual encounters or early positive

Chaz Bono (born Chastity Bono to parents Sonny and Cher) is a transgender man. Born female, he identifies as male and underwent a female-to-male gender transition as an adult. He is now an LBGT advocate.

Alfred Kinsey is a pioneer in sexuality research and founder of the Kinsey Institute at the University of Indiana.

Figure 12.3

Heterosexuality and homosexuality as endpoints on a continuum. Kinsey and other sex researchers view heterosexuality and homosexuality as ends of a continuum rather than as all-or-none distinctions. Kinsey created this 7-point scale (from 0 to 6) for describing sexual orientation.

0	1	2	3	4	5	6
Exclusively heterosexual	Predominantly heterosexual only incidentally homosexual	Predominantly heterosexual more than incidentally homosexual	Equally heterosexual and homosexual	Predominantly homosexual more than incidentally heterosexual	Predominantly homosexual only incidentally heterosexual	Exclusively homosexual

Sexual fluidity reflects the idea that sexual orientation is not a fixed, stable trait. Instead, our attractions can change depending on interpersonal and situational factors. Actress Cynthia Nixon referred to this concept when addressing the media about why she left a long-term relationship with a man to be with a woman.

homosexual experiences. Sociologists proposed that homosexuality develops because of poor relationships with same-gender peers or because being labeled a homosexual sets up a self-fulfilling prophecy. However, a comprehensive review of the causes of sexual orientation found no compelling support for *any* of these explanations (Bell, Weinberg, & Hammersmith, 1981).

Some theorists speculate that *biological factors* are involved in the development of sexual orientation. Several lines of research suggest that hormonal secretions during prenatal development may shape sexual development, organize the brain in a lasting manner, and influence subsequent sexual orientation. Because of advances in technology that allow researchers to actually map the activity in the brain, we can begin to explore brain differences in sexual orientation. However, it is important to keep in mind that it is difficult to determine whether any brain differences are the cause or the consequence of sexual orientation.

There are interesting trends in birth-order effects and sexual orientation, with gay men more likely to be born after their heterosexual siblings (Mustanski, Kuper, & Greene, 2014). This trend holds especially for older brothers, in that having older brothers tends to increase the likelihood of the younger brother being gay (Bogaert & Skorska, 2011). Researchers speculate this is due to changes in the maternal prenatal immune response for each male she carries.

Genetic factors are also of interest. In an important study, investigators identified gay and bisexual men who had a twin brother or an adopted brother (Bailey & Pillard, 1991). They found that 52% of the participants' identical twins were gay, 22% of their fraternal twins were gay, and only 11% of their adoptive brothers were gay. A companion study of lesbian women with twin or adopted sisters reported a similar pattern of results (Bailey et al., 1993; see **Figure 12.4**).

The bottom line is that there probably isn't a single determining factor for an individual's sexual orientation. Contemporary researchers endorse a more interactive, biopsychosocial

Figure 12.4

Genetics and sexual orientation. A concordance rate indicates the percentage of twin pairs or other pairs of relatives that exhibit the same characteristic. If relatives who share more genetic relatedness show higher concordance rates than relatives who share less genetic overlap, this evidence suggests a genetic predisposition to the characteristic. Studies of both gay men and lesbian women have found higher concordance rates among identical twins than fraternal twins, who in turn exhibit more concordance than adoptive siblings. These findings are consistent with the hypothesis that genetic factors influence sexual orientation. If *only* genetic factors were responsible for sexual orientation, the identical twin concordance rates would push 100%; because they are much lower, environmental factors must also play a role. (Data from Bailey & Pillard, 1991; Bailey et. al., 1993)

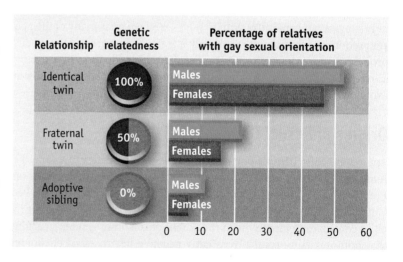

model of sexual orientation to capture the influence of biological, psychological, and social factors. This issue is exceedingly complex and needs additional research.

Attitudes toward Homosexuality

Gay and lesbian rights have gained attention in the political arena, as evidenced by the historic Supreme Court ruling on June 26, 2015, making same-sex marriage legal across the United States. Although the public discussion of gay marriage can be divisive, it has allowed the gay community to educate straight citizens about the realities and diversity of same-sex couples and their family relationships. Second, it has helped raise the nation's awareness about the facets of prejudice and discrimination against the LGBT community.

Homophobia **is the fear and intolerance of homosexuals.** Because few people with negative attitudes toward homosexuals have the psychopathology that "phobia" implies, some psychologists believe that *sexual prejudice* is a more appropriate term. The lowest levels of sexual prejudice are associated with individuals who personally know someone who is gay (Fingerhut, 2011). Viewing homosexuality as biological or genetic in origin (as opposed to attributing it to choice) is also associated with more favorable attitudes (Savin-Williams et al., 2010). Higher levels of sexual prejudice are associated with being older, male, less educated, and living in the South or Midwest and in rural areas (Herek & Capitanio, 1996). Sexual prejudice is also correlated with such psychological factors as authoritarianism, traditional gender-role attitudes (see Chapter 11), and conservative religious and political beliefs.

Tragically, negative attitudes sometimes translate into violence. In 2013, 20.8% of reported hate crimes were based on the offender's bias against the victim's sexual orientation (Federal Bureau of Investigation, 2013). In a national survey, 23% of the LGB participants had been threatened with violence, and 49% reported verbal harassment. These percentages were even higher when just considering gay males (35% for violence and 63% for harassment; Herek, 2009). These forms of discrimination are by no means exclusively an American problem, as violence related to sexual prejudice is reported around the world (Turner-Frey, 2014).

Although many Americans still exhibit sexual prejudice, general attitudes appear to be moving in a positive direction. As shown in **Figure 12.5**, a 2015 national poll found that more than half (57%) of Americans would not be upset if their child was gay, up from just 9% in 1985 (Gao, 2015). Greater acceptance is due, in part, to the increasing visibility of lesbians and gays in society. For instance, homosexual content on television has increased dramatically over the past two decades, including having more openly gay and transgendered characters (*Modern Family, Orange Is the New Black*) and celebrities (Ellen DeGeneres).

Disclosing One's Sexual Orientation

Coming to terms with one's sexual identity is difficult when it must take place in a climate of sexual prejudice. For gays, lesbians, and bisexuals, *coming out* involves recognizing and accepting one's sexual orientation, then disclosing it to others. Coming out can be a difficult process for many people. Gay and lesbian teenagers report losing more friends and worrying more about friendship loss than their heterosexual counterparts (Diamond & Lucas, 2004). Negative reactions from those to whom one is disclosing is associated with decreased well-being (Ryan, Legate, & Weinstein, 2015). Typical negative reactions include denying the disclosure, asking inappropriate questions, or shaming the person (Manning, 2015).

In deciding to disclose one's sexual orientation to others, individuals must balance the psychological and social benefits (being honest, having social support) against the costs (losing

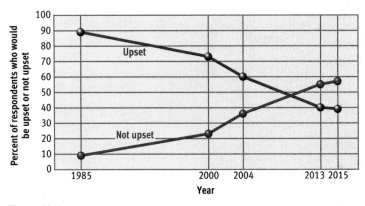

Figure 12.5

Reactions to having a gay or lesbian child. Although many Americans still exhibit sexual prejudice, general attitudes appear to moving in a positive direction. As shown in this graph, a national poll found that more than half of Americans would not be upset if their child was gay. Greater acceptance may be due, in part, to the increasing visibility of lesbians and gays in society.

Source: From Gao, G. (2015). Most Americans now say learning their child is gay wouldn't upset them. Retrieved October 18, 2015, from www.pewresearch.org/fact-tank/2015/06/29/most-americans-now-say-learning-their-child-is-gay-wouldnt-upset-them/.

friends, being fired, falling victim to hate crimes, losing custody of children). When the costs are too high or fear is too great, some individuals choose not to make known their sexual identity and are said to be *in the closet*.

Adjustment

The mental health community initially classified homosexuality as a psychological disorder, but researchers demonstrated that view to be a myth. That is, homosexuals and heterosexuals are indistinguishable in their general levels of psychopathology (Cochran & Mays, 2013). As a result of this research, changes in public attitudes, and political lobbying, homosexuality was deleted from the official list of psychological disorders in 1973 (Newmahr, 2011).

Although there is no reliable evidence that one's homosexual orientation *per se* impairs psychological functioning, exposure to sexual prejudice and discrimination can cause acute distress and lead to mental and physical health problems (Lick, Durso, & Johnson, 2013). For instance, gay men experience an increase in depression shortly after coming out (Pachankis, Cochran, & Mays, 2015). Other studies suggest that gay males and lesbians are at greater risk than their straight peers for anxiety, depression, self-injurious behavior, substance dependence, suicidal ideation, and suicide attempts (Balsam et al., 2005; Cochran & Mays, 2013). Fortunately, like their heterosexual counterparts, most LGBT individuals are able to cope with this stress and thrive despite the adversity.

Learning Objectives

■ Describe the four phases of the human sexual response cycle.

■ Discuss gender differences in patterns of orgasm and give some reasons for them.

12.3 The Human Sexual Response

When people engage in sexual activity, exactly how does the body respond? Surprisingly, until William Masters and Virginia Johnson conducted their groundbreaking research in the 1960s, little was known about the physiology of the human sexual response. Masters and Johnson used physiological recording devices to monitor the bodily changes of volunteers engaging in sex. Their observations and interviews with these subjects yielded a detailed description of the human sexual response.

The Sexual Response Cycle

Masters and Johnson's (1966, 1970) description of the sexual response cycle is a general one, outlining typical rather than inevitable patterns—people vary considerably. **Figure 12.6** shows how the intensity of sexual arousal changes as women and men progress through the four phases of the sexual response cycle.

Excitement Phase

During the initial phase of excitement, the level of arousal usually escalates rapidly. In both sexes, muscle tension, respiration rate, heart rate, and blood pressure increase quickly. In males *vasocongestion—engorgement of blood vessels*—produces penile erection, swollen testes, and the movement of the scrotum (the sac containing the testes) closer to the body. In females, vasocongestion leads to a swelling of the clitoris and vaginal lips, vaginal lubrication, and enlargement of the uterus. Most women also experience nipple erection and a swelling of the breasts.

Plateau Phase

The name given to the "plateau" stage is misleading because physiological arousal does not level off. Instead, it continues to build, but at a much slower pace. In women, further vasocongestion produces a tightening of the lower third of the vagina and a "ballooning" of the upper two-thirds, which lifts the uterus and cervix away from the end of the vagina.

William Masters and **Virginia Johnson** conducted groundbreaking research in the 1960s on the physiology of the human sexual response.

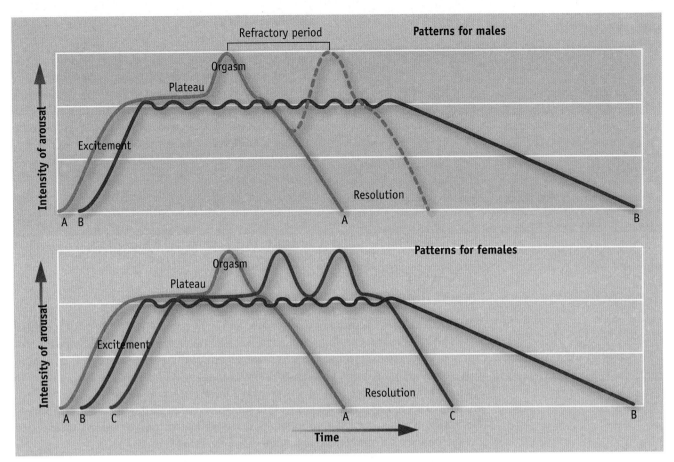

Figure 12.6

The human sexual response cycle. There are similarities and differences between men and women in patterns of sexual arousal. Pattern A, which culminates in orgasm and resolution, is the most typical sequence for both sexes. Pattern B, which involves sexual arousal without orgasm followed by a slow resolution, is also seen in both genders, but it is more common among women. Pattern C, which involves multiple orgasms, is seen almost exclusively in women, as men go through a refractory period before they are capable of another orgasm. (Based on Masters & Johnson, 1966)

In men, the head of the penis may swell, and the testicles typically enlarge and move closer to the body. Many men secrete a bit of pre-ejaculatory fluid from the tip of the penis that may contain sperm.

Distractions during the plateau phase can delay or stop movement to the next stage. These include ill-timed interruptions like a phone ringing or a child's knocking on the bedroom door. Equally distracting can be internal factors such as physical discomfort, pain, guilt, frightening thoughts, feelings of insecurity or anger toward one's partner, and anxiety about sexual performance.

Orgasm Phase

Orgasm **occurs when sexual arousal reaches its peak intensity and is discharged in a series of muscular contractions that pulsate through the pelvic area.** Heart rate, respiration rate, and blood pressure increase sharply during this exceedingly pleasant spasmodic response. The male orgasm is usually accompanied by ejaculation of seminal fluid. Some women report that they ejaculate some kind of fluid at orgasm, but the prevalence of female ejaculation and the source and nature of the fluid are matters still under debate. The subjective experience of orgasm appears to be essentially the same for men and women, although the relationship between subjective experience and physical response seems to be greater for men (Suschinsky, Lalumiere, & Chivers, 2009). That is, there is a higher degree of agreement between a man's physical response (erection) and his self-report of arousal than there is for a woman.

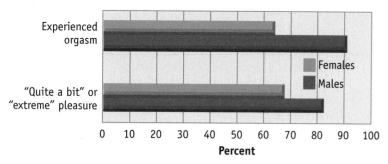

Figure 12.7

Gender differences in sexual experiences within the past year. A national survey regarding Americans' most recent sexual experiences revealed that men were more likely than women to report having experienced orgasm and to report experiencing high levels of pleasure during sex. (Adapted from Herbenick et al., 2010a)

Resolution Phase

During the resolution phase, the physiological changes produced by sexual arousal subside. If one has not had an orgasm, the reduction in sexual tension may be relatively slow and sometimes unpleasant. After orgasm, men generally experience a *refractory period*, **a time following orgasm during which males are largely unresponsive to further stimulation.** The refractory period varies from a few minutes to a few hours and increases with age.

Critics note that the Masters and Johnson model focuses entirely on genital changes during sex and ignores cognitive factors. Because people's thoughts and views about sex underlie many sexual problems, it is helpful to keep in mind that the sexual response involves more than just physical factors.

Gender Differences in Patterns of Orgasm

As a whole, the sexual responses of women and men parallel each other fairly closely. Nonetheless, there are some interesting differences between the genders in their patterns of experiencing orgasm. During *intercourse*, women are less likely than men to reach orgasm (that is, they are more likely to follow pattern B in **Figure 12.6**). Women are more likely to orgasm when they engage in a variety of sexual behaviors such as oral sex, whereas men are more likely to orgasm when sex includes intercourse. According to a national survey (Herbenick et al., 2010b), 91% of men report having had an orgasm during their sexual activities in the past year compared to 64% of women (see **Figure 12.7**).

How do we account for these disparities? First, although most women report that they enjoy intercourse, it is not the optimal mode of stimulation for them. This is because intercourse provides rather indirect stimulation to the clitoris, the most sexually sensitive genital area in most women. Thus, more lengthy *foreplay*, including manual or oral stimulation of the clitoris, is usually the key to enhancing women's sexual pleasure. Many men mistakenly assume that women experience the same degree of pleasurable sensations as they do during sexual intercourse. But this is not the case, as the upper two-thirds of the vagina has relatively few nerve endings—a good thing given that the vagina serves as the birth canal! Manual or oral stimulation of the clitoris is typically more effective in producing female orgasm than sexual intercourse alone. Unfortunately, many couples are locked into the idea that orgasms should be achieved only through intercourse (as often depicted in movies). Even the word *foreplay* suggests that any other form of sexual stimulation is merely preparation for the "main event."

Because women reach orgasm through intercourse less consistently than men, they are more likely than men to fake an orgasm. Some 67% of women and 28% of men report that they have faked an orgasm (Muehlenhard & Shippee, 2010). People typically do so to make their partner feel better or to bring sexual activity to an end when they're tired. Frequent faking is not a good idea because it can become a cycle that undermines communication about sex.

Learning Objectives

- Describe six different forms of sexual expression.
- Discuss the preferred sexual activities of gay males and lesbians.
- Describe common barriers in communicating about sex.

12.4 Sexual Expression

People experience and express sexuality in myriad ways. Most individuals engage in a variety of sexual practices (see **Figure 12.8**), and the menu of sexual activities is quite similar for heterosexual and same-sex couples. *Erogenous zones* **are areas of the body that are sexually sensitive or responsive.** The genitals and breasts usually come to mind when people think of erogenous zones because these areas are particularly sensitive for most

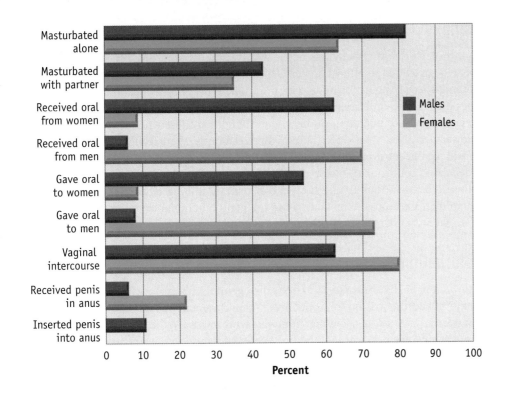

Figure 12.8

Percentages of sexual activities for American men and women, ages 20 to 24. Data from a national survey show the distribution of reported sexual activities for men and women, ages 20 to 24, in the past year. It is clear that young adults engage in a variety of sexual activities. (Adapted from Herbenick, et al., 2010b)

people. But it's worth noting that virtually any area of the body can function as an erogenous zone. Indeed, the ultimate erogenous zone may be the mind. An individual's mental state is extremely important to sexual arousal. Skillful genital stimulation by a partner may have absolutely no impact if a person is not in the mood. Yet fantasy in the absence of any other stimulation can produce great arousal. Ultimately, communication between partners is crucial for a satisfying sexual experience. In this section, we'll consider the most common forms of sexual expression.

Fantasy

Have you ever fantasized about having sex with someone other than your partner? If so, you've had one of the most commonly reported fantasies. In fact, a study of university students and employees reported that 98% of men and 80% of women had sexual fantasies involving someone other than their current partner (Hicks & Leitenberg, 2001). As you might expect, women's fantasies tend to be more romantic, while men's tend to contain more explicit imagery (Impett & Peplau, 2006). However, the presence of romantic emotions is the most commonly reported element of sexual fantasies for both men and women (Joyal, Cossette, & Lapierre, 2015). Most sex therapists view sexual fantasies as a harmless, and even healthy, way to enhance sexual excitement and achieve orgasm either during masturbation or with a partner. **Figure 12.9** shows some commonly reported features of sexual fantasies (Joyal, Cossette, & Lapierre, 2015).

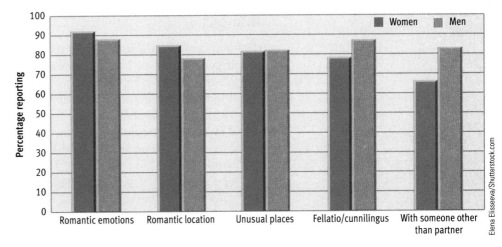

Figure 12.9

Commonly reported features of sexual fantasy. Sexual fantasy is a normal component of sexuality. Both men and women report that their sexual fantasies increase their excitement. This graph shows some of the most commonly reported features of sexual fantasy. (Adapted from Joyal, Cossette, & Lapierre, 2015).

Kissing

Most two-person sexual activities begin with kissing. Kissing usually starts at the lips but may be extended to almost any area of the partner's body. In fact, there seems to be something special about kissing as a form of nonverbal communication. Floyd and colleagues (2009) randomly assigned heterosexual partners to either increase their romantic kissing frequency or not. After 6 weeks, they found that those who had increased kissing had lower perceived stress levels and higher relationship satisfaction. These differences were still significant even after the researchers controlled for increased verbal affections and decreased conflict, two factors that might be expected with increased romantic kissing. Research shows that kissing is especially relevant in long-term relationships—not as a way to increase arousal, but as a way to maintain emotional closeness and attachment (Wlodarski & Dunbar, 2013, 2014).

Masturbation

Masturbation, **or the stimulation of one's own genitals,** has historically been condemned as immoral because it is nonreproductive. Disapproval and suppression of masturbation (often referred to as *self-abuse* at the time) were truly intense in the 19th and early 20th centuries, when people believed that the practice was harmful to physical and mental health. Yet Kinsey discovered more than six decades ago that most people masturbate with no ill effects, and sexologists now recognize it as normal and healthy. In fact, sex therapists often prescribe masturbation to treat both male and female sexual problems. Nonetheless, many of those who engage in the practice feel guilty about it.

Masturbation, also referred to as *self-stimulation* or *autoeroticism,* is quite common in our society. In a national survey, 85% of women and 94% of men reported having engaged in self-stimulation at some point in their lives (Herbenick et al., 2010b). Among married couples, up to 71% of men and 51% of women report engaging in self-stimulation (Herbenick et al., 2010c; Reece et al., 2010). In fact, masturbation in marriage is often associated with a greater degree of marital and sexual satisfaction (Leitenberg, Detzer, & Srebnik, 1993).

Sometimes people, more often women, use vibrators or other sex toys for self-stimulation. One study found that 46% of women reported having used a vibrator during masturbation (Herbenick et al., 2010d). Recent evidence suggests that vibrator use for women is associated with more positive sexual functioning and better sexual health practices (Herbenick et al., 2009). The findings are similar for men who incorporate vibrators into foreplay with their partners (Reece et al., 2009).

Oral Sex

Oral sex refers to oral stimulation of the genitals. *Cunnilingus* **is oral stimulation of the female genitals;** *fellatio* **is oral stimulation of the penis.** Oral sex is a common practice in adolescent sexual experiences and most couples' (both homosexual and heterosexual) sexual relationships. According a national survey, about two-thirds of males and females ages 15 to 24 have had oral sex (Copen, Chandra, & Martinez, 2012). Oral sex may be one of several activities in a sexual encounter, or it may be the main event. It is a major source of orgasms for many heterosexual couples, and it plays a central role in homosexual relationships.

A positive aspect of oral sex for some people is that it does not result in pregnancy. This fact partly accounts for the finding that younger teens are more likely to engage in oral sex than in intercourse. However, some sexually transmitted diseases (HIV, for example) can be contracted through oral-genital stimulation, especially if there are small cracks in the mouth or if the mouth is exposed to semen. In addition, a person with a cold sore can pass along the herpes virus during oral sex or kissing. Unfortunately, data suggest that up to 40% of sexually active teens either don't know that one can become infected with HIV through unprotected oral sex or are unsure about it (Centers for Disease Control and Prevention, 2009).

Anal Sex

Anal intercourse **involves insertion of the penis into a partner's anus and rectum.** Legally, it is termed *sodomy* (and it is still illegal in some states). In a national survey, up to 27% of men and 22% of women reported having practiced anal sex in the past year (Herbenick et al., 2010b). Anal intercourse is more popular among homosexual male couples than among heterosexual couples. However, even among gay men it ranks behind oral sex and mutual masturbation in prevalence.

Although we will discuss sexually transmitted infections later in the chapter, it is worth noting here that anal sex is risky. Gay men who engage in it without a condom (referred to as *bareback sex*) run a high risk for HIV infection in that rectal tissues are easily torn, facilitating HIV transmission. Anal sex is associated with increased risk for infections in women as well (Benson, Martins, & Whitaker, 2015).

Intercourse

Penile-vaginal intercourse, known more technically as *coitus*, **involves the insertion of the penis into the vagina and (typically) pelvic thrusting.** It is the most widely endorsed and practiced sexual act in our society. In a national survey, 80% of male and 86% of female respondents said that they had practiced coitus in their most recent sexual encounter (Herbenick et al., 2010a). Frequent intercourse is associated with greater sexual and relationship satisfaction, higher life satisfaction, and better mental health (Brody & Costa, 2009).

Inserting the penis generally requires adequate vaginal lubrication or intercourse may be painful for the woman. In a national survey, about 30% of women reported mild pain during intercourse (Herbenick et al., 2015). This is a good reason for couples to spend plenty of time on foreplay, as sexual excitement induces vaginal lubrication. In the absence of adequate lubrication, partners may choose to use artificial lubricants.

What kinds of sexual activities do homosexuals prefer in the absence of coitus (which is, by definition, a heterosexual act)? As is true with heterosexual couples, the preliminary activities of gay and lesbian couples include kissing, hugging, and caressing. Gay men also engage in fellatio, mutual masturbation, and anal intercourse. Lesbians engage in cunnilingus, mutual masturbation, and *tribadism* (also known as humping or scissoring), in which partners rub their genitals together so that both receive genital stimulation at the same time.

Communicating about Sex

Regardless of the activity, it is clear that communication is the key ingredient to a satisfying sexual relationship (Byers & Rehman, 2014). Because individuals differ in sexual motives, attitudes, and appetites, disagreements about sex are to be expected. Couples have to negotiate whether, how often, and when they will have sex. They also have to decide what kinds of erotic activities will take place and what sexual behavior means to their relationship. Unresolved disparities can be an ongoing source of frustration in a relationship. Still, many people find it difficult to talk with their partner about sex. Couples can encounter four common barriers to sexual communication.

1. *Fear of appearing ignorant.* Many Americans are ignorant and misinformed about sex, often because media sources present incorrect information or perpetuate sexual myths. (You can test your own knowledge about some aspects of sex by responding to the questions in **Figure 12.10**.) Because most people feel that they should be experts about sex and know that they are not, they feel ashamed. To hide their lack of knowledge, they avoid talking about sex.

HOW KNOWLEDGEABLE ABOUT SEX ARE YOU?

1. Massage oil, petroleum jelly, and body lotions are good lubricants to use with a condom or diaphragm.
   _____ True _____ False _____ Don't know

2. A homosexual orientation is related to impaired psychological adjustment.
   _____ True _____ False _____ Don't know

3. A teenage girl or woman can get pregnant during her menstrual period.
   _____ True _____ False _____ Don't know

4. Most cases of sexually transmitted diseases occur in people ages 26–50.
   _____ True _____ False _____ Don't know

5. In the United States, heterosexually-transmitted HIV infections rarely occur.
   _____ True _____ False _____ Don't know

Scoring: 1. False. (Oil-based creams, lotions, and jellies can produce microscopic holes in rubber products within 60 seconds of their application.) 2. False. (Research does not support this view.) 3. True. (While the chance of a woman's becoming pregnant during her menstrual period is lower than at other times, pregnancy can occur if she has unprotected sex during her period. Sperm can live for several days in a woman's reproductive tract, and if the menstrual cycle is irregular, as it is likely to be in adolescence, sperm may still be present in the reproductive tract a week later to fertilize a new egg.) 4. False. (Most cases of sexually transmitted diseases occur in the younger-than-25 age group.) 5. False. (There is currently an upsurge in heterosexually transmitted HIV infections in the United States)

Figure 12.10

How knowledgeable about sex are you? Check your basic sexual knowledge by answering these five questions. Information about each of the questions is discussed in this chapter.

2. *Concern about partner's response.* Both men and women say they want their partners to tell them what they want sexually. Ironically, both can feel uncomfortable doing so. People usually hold back because they're afraid of hurting each other's feelings. Or they fear that their partner won't respect and love them if they are truthful. However, extensive disclosure of sexual likes and dislikes positively predicts sexual and relationship satisfaction in committed relationships (Byers, 2011).

3. *Conflicting attitudes about sex.* Many people, particularly women, are burdened with the negative sexual messages they learned as children. Also, many individuals have contradictory beliefs about sex ("Sex is 'beautiful'" and "Sex is 'dirty'"), and this dissonance produces internal psychological conflicts that can make communication difficult.

4. *Negative early sexual experiences.* Some people have had negative sexual experiences that inhibit their enjoyment of sex. If these experiences are due to ignorant or inconsiderate sexual partners, subsequent positive sexual interactions will usually resolve the problem over time. If earlier sexual experiences have been traumatic, as in the case of rape or incest, counseling may be required to help a person view sex positively and enjoy it.

Even with these barriers, communicating one's sexual likes and dislikes to one's partner is related to higher sexual satisfaction and functioning for both men and women (Rehman, Rellini, & Fallis, 2011). To communicate more easily and effectively about sex, you may want to review Chapter 8. Most of the advice on how to improve verbal and nonverbal communication can be applied to sexual relationships. Assertive communication and constructive conflict resolution strategies can keep sexual negotiations healthy. A basic rule is to accentuate the positive ("I like it when you . . .") rather than the negative ("I don't like it when you . . .").

12.5 Patterns of Sexual Behavior

The context of a sexual interaction influences the interaction itself. In this section we examine how the type of relationship one is in relates to sexual behavior.

Sex outside of Committed Relationships

"Hooking up" involves two uncommitted people having a sexual encounter with no expectation of a romantic relationship, and experts estimate that 60%–80% of college students have participated in a hookup (Garcia et al., 2012). Hookups don't always involve intercourse (manual stimulation and oral sex are common). When looking at hookups that did include sexual intercourse, Eshbaugh and Gute (2008) found that 36% of sexually active women reported having sex with someone only once, and 29% reported having sex with someone they had known less than 24 hours. Further, hookups that included sex were linked to regret for women. Hookups are often related to drinking alcohol (Johnson & Chen, 2015), and typically end when one or both partners reach orgasm or one person leaves or passes out (Paul, Wenzel, & Harvey, 2008).

Friends with benefits (FWB) refers to friends who engage in sex but who don't label their relationship as romantic. This situation is different from hooking up because participants in a FWB relationship anticipate maintaining their friendship. In one study, 54% of young adult men and 43% of women reported maintaining this kind of relationship (Owen & Fincham, 2011). People who engage in a FWB arrangement are more likely to be casual daters, to be nonromantics, and to hold more hedonistic (anything goes) sexual values (Puentes, Knox, & Zusman, 2008). Obviously, negotiating such relationships can be tricky. Friendships are jeopardized if unreciprocated desires for romantic commitment develop or if one person wants to end the sexual relationship. However, one study of FWBs found that 50% reported feeling as close or closer when the sexual relationship ended, especially if the relationship was more friendship than sexually based (Owen, Fincham, & Manthos, 2013).

Monkey Business Image/Shutterstock.com

Hooking up involves two uncommitted people having a sexual encounter with no expectation of a romantic relationship. Experts estimate that 60%–80% of college students have participated in a hookup. Hookups are often related to drinking alcohol.

Sex in Committed Relationships

Sex is a key aspect of most romantic relationships. In this section, we examine patterns of sexual activity in the context of committed relationships.

Sex between Dating Partners

With the average age of first marriage rising, most couples confront the issue of premarital sex. Some worry that sex might adversely affect the relationship; others fear that not having sex will cause trouble. Is there evidence to support either view? As it turns out, sexual intimacy is a positive predictor of relationship stability (Sprecher & Cate, 2004). However, gender plays a role in this relationship. For men, sexual (but not relationship) satisfaction is significantly correlated with relationship stability; for women, relationship (but not sexual) satisfaction is significantly associated with relationship stability (Sprecher, 2002). For both men and women, though, there is evidence that delaying sexual intercourse (even for a few weeks into the relationship) is associated with higher relationship satisfaction and stability (Willoughby, Carroll, & Busby, 2014).

"Sexting," or sharing sexual images or messages via a text or social media site, is getting increased notice from researchers. This area of research is still new, but initial studies indicate that sexting is not uncommon. One study found that 38% of participants had sent or received a sext, and of those, the vast majority were within the context of a romantic relationship (Perkins et al., 2014). In addition, sexting is more common among adults than adolescents and men report higher levels of sexting than woman (Dir & Cyders, 2015; Klettke, Hallford, & Mellor, 2014). Generally, information shared in a sext is intended to be private, but there is a risk that it can be shared to hurt or humiliate the sender. As a result, some view sexting as a new opportunity for cyberbullying or intimate partner violence (Bauman, 2015; Drouin, Ross, &, Tobin, 2015).

Marital Sex

Couples' sexual satisfaction is strongly related to their overall marital satisfaction (Sprecher et al., 2006). Of course, it is difficult to know whether good sex promotes good marriages or good marriages promote good sex; in all probability, it's a two-way street. Married couples vary greatly in how often they have sex (see **Figure 12.11**). The majority of couples report engaging in sex in a range of two to three times per week to a few times per month, with the frequency of sex decreasing as the years pass (Herbenick et al., 2010c; Reece et al., 2010). Biological changes play some role in this trend, but social factors are also compelling. Many couples attribute this decline to increasing fatigue from work and childrearing and to a growing familiarity with their sexual routine.

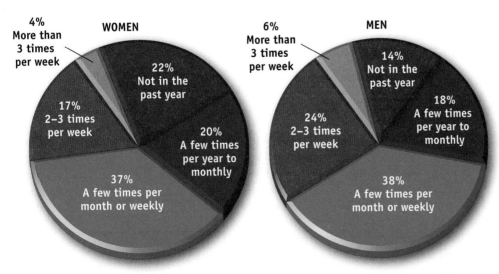

Figure 12.11

Frequency of sex among married men and women. In a large-scale national survey, married individuals were asked how often they had vaginal intercourse. Their responses were wide ranging. The majority of couples report engaging in sex between two to three times per week and a few times per month. (Adapted from Herbenick et al., 2010c, and Reece et al., 2010)

As men and women age, sexual arousal tends to build more slowly and orgasms tend to diminish in frequency and intensity. Males' refractory periods lengthen, and females' vaginal lubrication and elasticity decrease. Nevertheless, older people, especially those in good health, remain capable of and interested in rewarding sexual encounters. In a national survey, 43% of men and 22% of women older than the age of 70 reported having had sex in the previous year (Herbenick, 2010b). Marrying for love, still being in love, and being financially stable are associated with sexual activity in later adulthood (Papaharitou et al., 2008).

Sex in Homosexual Relationships

Because the ability for same-sex partners to legally marry is so new, researchers have yet to tease apart dating relationships versus marriages. However, Peplau and her colleagues (2004) explored the frequency of sex among lesbian, gay, and heterosexual committed couples and found three patterns. First, there is a general decline in the frequency of sexual behavior over time. Second, in the early stages of a relationship, gay males engage in sex more frequently than the other types of couples. Third, lesbian couples have sex less often than other couples. Comparative studies find comparable levels of sexual satisfaction in gay, lesbian, and heterosexual couples. And for all groups, sexual satisfaction is correlated with overall relationship satisfaction (Fingerhut & Peplau, 2013).

Infidelity in Committed Relationships

Sexual infidelity occurs when a person who is in a committed relationship engages in erotic activity with someone other than his or her partner. Among married couples, this behavior is also called "adultery" or "extramarital sex." Infidelity among couples in committed but unmarried relationships is termed *extradyadic sex*. The vast majority of people (91%) in our society believe that extramarital sex is "always" or "almost always wrong" (Saad, 2007). Nonetheless, Americans engage in infidelity, as evidenced by the success of *Ashley Madison*, the online dating site marketed specifically to those who are married or in a committed relationship.

Although it's not common, some couples condone extramarital sex. Two examples include "swinging" and "open marriage." Swingers are married couples who agree to exchange partners for sex. In open marriage, now typically called *polyamory*, both partners agree that it is okay for each to have sex with others.

Prevalence

Because of the associated stigma and secrecy, accurate estimates of infidelity are difficult to come by. Yet experts estimate that approximately 21% of men and 11% of women have engaged in sexual infidelity (Baucom, Snyder, & Abbott, 2014). In one study of more than 1300 undergraduates, approximately 20% had engaged in extradyadic oral sex or intercourse without telling their partner (Knox, Vail-Smith, & Zusman, 2008).

Sexual openness is more common in committed gay male relationships, and the rates of extradyadic sex for this group are higher than for all other groups (Fingerhut & Peplau, 2013). Committed lesbian relationships are more exclusive, in principle and in practice, than gay male relationships (Peplau & Fingerhut, 2007). Rates of lesbian extradyadic sex are also lower than those for married women.

Motivations

Why do people pursue sexual encounters outside of their committed relationships? Common reasons include dissatisfaction with a relationship, anger toward a partner, and boredom. Sometimes people need to confirm that they are still desirable, or they want to trigger the end of an unsatisfying relationship. Then again, extramarital sexual activity can occur simply because two people are attracted to each other. Erotic reactions to people other than one's partner do not cease when one makes a permanent commitment, though most people suppress these sexual desires because they disapprove of adultery.

The gender differences in motivations for infidelity parallel the gender differences in sexual socialization. Men tend to engage in extradyadic affairs to obtain sexual variety or more frequent sex, whereas women usually seek an emotional connection (Buunk & Dijkstra, 2006). Men are also more motivated by sexual excitement, whereas women are more motivated by relationship unhappiness (Mark, Janssen, & Milhousen, 2011). Low levels of positive communication are associated with infidelity for both genders (Allen et al., 2008). Further, for both men and women, holding power positions is related to increased instances of infidelity (Lammers et al., 2011). Interestingly, recent evidence suggests that our hormones might play a role in maintaining fidelity, as the following Spotlight on Research shows.

Spotlight on **RESEARCH**

Oxytocin Promotes Fidelity

Source: Scheele, D., Striepens, N., Güntürkün, O., Deutschländer, S., Maier, W., Kendrick, K. M., & Hurlemann, R. (2012). Oxytocin modulates social distance between males and females. *The Journal of Neuroscience, 32*(46), 16,074–16,079.

As we learned in Chapter 3, oxytocin is associated with affiliation and bonding in women. It has also been related to attraction and attachment for men. Thus far, oxytocin has been explored in initial encounters, but it has not been examined in relation to the maintenance of committed relationships. Therefore, the present researchers explored the role of oxytocin in fidelity-promoting behaviors in men, specifically keeping one's social distance in a first encounter. The researchers wondered whether oxytocin would play a role in the willingness of men to approach an attractive, unfamiliar woman.

Method
Participants. Participants included fifty-seven healthy heterosexual men, twenty-seven of whom were single and thirty of whom were in a monogamous relationship.

Materials and procedures. Prior to beginning the experiment, participants were randomly assigned to receive a nasal spray containing either oxytocin or a placebo. The study employed a double-blind design, where neither the experimenters nor the participants knew which nasal spray participants received. After 45 minutes, the men were introduced to an attractive female experimenter and using a "stop-distance paradigm" were asked to determine the boundary of personal space. In this paradigm, participants stood at the end of the room with their toes on a line, and the female experimenter moved toward and away from them. While she did this, participants indicated the "ideal distance" for interacting with the experimenter and the distance that felt "slightly uncomfortable" for interaction. Then the roles were reversed, and the participants moved toward and away from the experimenter. The final chin-to-chin distance was measured as an indicator of social distance.

Results
The results demonstrated that men in committed relationships who received the hormone oxytocin chose to keep a greater distance between themselves and the unfamiliar, attractive female experimenter than men in committed relationships who received the placebo. In addition, oxytocin led the men in committed relationships, but not those who were single, to keep a greater distance between themselves and the experimenter. In addition, oxytocin seemed to influence only behaviors, but not attitudes, in that both those who received the oxytocin and those who received the placebo rated the experimenter as being equally attractive. In a separate study, the researchers found that oxytocin had no effect on the distance men kept between themselves and a male experimenter.

Discussion
These results support the idea that oxytocin promotes fidelity behaviors in committed relationships. Approach behaviors (such as seeking a close social distance) are important signals of romantic interest in initial encounters with someone. By preferring a greater distance in the oxytocin condition, monogamous men avoided signaling romantic interest and thus fidelity was enhanced. The authors note that both the presence of oxytocin and the relationship status acted together in leading to this result. Obviously, this study looked at only one attraction behavior (i.e., social distance), and oxytocin was artificially introduced to the participants. However, the researchers note that this is the "first direct evidence for a behavior-modifying role of [oxytocin] in helping maintain monogamous pair-bonds in humans" (p. 16,078). Future research is needed to understand exactly how this hormone exerts its influence on relationship behaviors.

Critical Thinking Questions
1. The premise of this study is based on the assumption that a closer social distance is a signal of romantic interest. What other behaviors can you think of that signal interest in initial encounters with someone?
2. Would you volunteer to be in a study that required you to take a nasal spray with hormones? Why or why not?
3. How does using a double-blind design make this study stronger?

Impact

Infidelity can lead to breaking up or divorce. Still, it's hard to know in these cases whether extradyadic sex is a symptom of a disintegrating relationship or its cause. When a partner cheats, men tend to react with anger and violence, whereas women tend to show sadness and seek out support from friends (Miller & Maner, 2008). Additionally, women are more distressed by emotional infidelity, while men are more distressed by sexual infidelity (Treger & Sprecher, 2011). Participants in extramarital affairs, whether or not they are discovered, may experience loss of self-respect, guilt, stress, and complications of sexually transmitted diseases. Occasionally, extramarital affairs can have a positive effect on a marriage if they motivate a couple to resolve relationship problems through marital counseling (Baucom et al., 2014).

Learn More Online

Planned Parenthood

Planned Parenthood maintains an accurate, up-to-date website with information on STDs, contraception, emergency contraception, and abortion. This site is a useful resource when considering one's contraceptive options.

12.6 Practical Issues in Sexual Activity

Regardless of the context of sexual activity, two practical issues are often matters of concern: contraception and sexually transmitted diseases. These topics are more properly in the domain of medicine than of psychology, but birth control and sex-related infections certainly do have their behavioral aspects.

Contraception

Most people want control over whether and when they will conceive a child, so they need reliable contraception and need to know how to use it effectively. Despite the availability of effective contraceptive methods, however, many people fail to exercise much control. In 2008, 51% of pregnancies were either mistimed or unwanted (Finer & Zolna, 2014), with the unintended pregnancy rate being five times higher for lower income women (Sonfiled, Hasstedt, & Gold, 2014). Teenage birth rates are also a concern, although these rates have been declining in recent years. In 2013, there were 26.5 births for every 1000 adolescent females (Hamilton et al., 2015).

Constraints on Effective Contraception

Effective contraception requires that intimate couples negotiate their way through a complex sequence of steps. First, both people must define themselves as sexually active. Second, both must have accurate knowledge about fertility and conception. Third, their chosen method of contraception must be readily accessible. Finally, both must have the motivation and skill to use the method correctly and consistently. Failure to meet even one of these conditions can result in an unintended pregnancy.

Why do some individuals and couples engage in risky sexual behavior? Reasons can range from not having the contraception on hand, to fearing a partner's reaction, to religious restrictions, to having inaccurate information about contraception (Ayoola, Nettleman, & Brewer, 2007). Once again, conflicting norms about gender and sexual behavior play a role. Men are socialized to be the initiators of sexual activity, but when it comes to birth control, they often rely on women to take charge. It is hard for a woman to maintain an image of sexual naiveté and also be responsible for contraception. The mixed messages sent by some sexual education programs ("Use a condom but we can't supply you with one") add to the confusion. In addition, many individuals have inaccurate knowledge about contraception effectiveness (Frost, Lindberg, & Finer, 2012).

Selecting a Contraceptive Method

How should one go about selecting a contraceptive technique? A rational choice requires accurate knowledge of the effectiveness, benefits, costs, and risks of the various methods.

Figure 12.12 summarizes information on most of the methods currently available. The *ideal failure rate* estimates the probability of conception when the technique is used correctly and consistently. The *typical failure rate* is what occurs in the real world, when users' negligence is factored in.

Contraception is a joint responsibility. Hence, it's essential for partners to discuss their preferences, to decide what method(s) they are going to use, and to *act* on their decision. Let's look in more detail at two of the most widely used birth control methods in the Western world: hormone-based contraceptives and condoms.

Hormone-based contraceptives contain synthetic forms of estrogen and progesterone (or progesterone only, in the minipill), which inhibit ovulation in women. Types of hormone-based contraceptives include "the pill," hormonal injectables (Depo-Provera), the transdermal patch (worn on the skin), the vaginal ring (inserted once a month), and contraceptive implants. Many couples prefer these birth control options because contraceptive use is not tied to the sex act. However, these contraceptives do not protect against sexually transmitted diseases. Women considering these options should speak with their healthcare providers about risks and side effects.

The male *condom*, a barrier method of contraception, is a sheath worn over the penis during intercourse to collect ejaculated semen. The condom is the only widely available contraceptive device for use by males. Eighty percent of adolescent males (and 69% of females) reported using a condom the most recent time they had intercourse (Fortenberry et al., 2010). Other barrier methods include female condoms (which are inserted into the vagina), diaphragms, and spermicides.

Condoms can be purchased in any drugstore without a prescription. If used correctly, the condom is highly effective in preventing pregnancy (see **Figure 12.12**). It must be placed over the penis after erection but before any contact with the vagina, and space must be left

Most excuses provided by women for having unprotected sex fall into three categories: individual (such as forgetting or having unexpected sex), interpersonal (for example, fear of partner's reaction), or societal (for instance, limited access or incorrect information).

Reggie Casagrande/Photographer's Choice RF/Getty Images

CONTRACEPTIVE METHODS

Methods	Ideal failure rate (%)	Typical failure rate (%)	Advantages	Disadvantages
Hormonal methods				
Birth control pills combination	0.3	9	Highly reliable; coitus-independent; has some health benefits	Side effects; daily use; continual cost; health risks for some women; no protection against STDs
Minipill (progestin only)	0.5	3	Thought to have low risk of side effects; coitus-independent; has some health benefits	Breakthrough bleeding; daily use; continual cost; health risks for some women; no protection against STDs
Hormonal injectables (Depo-Provera)	0.2	6	Highly reliable; coitus-independent; no memory or motivation required for use; reduces risk of endometrial and ovarian cancer	Side effects; use may increase risk of certain cancers; continual cost; injection every 3 months; no protection against STDs
Hormonal ring (NuvaRing)	0.3	9	Highly reliable; coitus-independent; no memory or motivation required for use; may offer protection against endometrial and ovarian cancer	Side effects; no data on extended use; no protection against STDs
Subdermal implants (Implanon)	0.05	0.05	Highly reliable; coitus-independent; no memory or motivation required for use	Side effects; painful removal; possible scarring at site; no protection from STDs
Transdermal patch	.03	9	No memory or motivation required to use; coitus-independent; very reliable; has some health benefits	Continual cost; skin irritation for some women; no protection against STDs

(continued on next page)

Figure 12.12

A comparison of widely used contraceptive techniques. Couples can choose from a variety of contraceptive methods. This chart summarizes the advantages and disadvantages of each method. Note that the typical failure rate is much higher than the ideal failure rate for all methods because couples do not use contraceptive techniques consistently and correctly. (Based on Alan Guttmacher Institute, 2012a)

CONTRACEPTIVE METHODS				
Methods	Ideal failure rate (%)	Typical failure rate (%)	Advantages	Disadvantages
Barrier methods				
IUD	0.2–0.6	0.2–0.8	No memory or motivation required for use; very reliable; some health benefits	Cramping, bleeding, expulsion; risk of pelvic inflammatory disease; no protection against STDs
Diaphragm with spermicidal cream or jelly	6	12	No major health risks; inexpensive	Aesthetic objections; initial cost
Condom (male)	2	18	Protects against STDs; simple to use; male responsibility; no health risks; no prescriptions required	Unaesthetic to some; requires interruption of sexual activity; continual cost
Condom (female)	5	21	Protects against STDs; reduces post-coital drip; can be used without partner knowledge	Difficult to insert; uncomfortable; can be noisy during intercourse
Sponge	9–20	12–24	24-hour protection; simple to use; no taste or odor; inexpensive; effective with several acts of intercourse	Aesthetic objections; continual cost; no protection against STDs
Cervical cap with spermicidal cream or jelly	9–20	20–40	48-hour protection; no major health risks	May be difficult to insert; may irritate cervix; initial cost
Spermicides	18	28	No major health risks; no prescription required	Unaesthetic to some; must be properly inserted; continual cost; no protection against STDs
Fertility awareness (rhythm)	1–9	24	No cost; acceptable to Catholic Church	Requires high motivation and periods of abstinence; unreliable; no protection against STDs
Surgical methods				
Female sterilization (tubal ligation)	0.5	0.5	Effective; permanent; doesn't interfere with sexual activity; reduces risk of ovarian cancer	Side effects associated with surgery; doesn't protect against STDs; expensive; irreversible
Male sterilization (vasectomy)	0.1	0.15	Effective; permanent; doesn't interfere with sexual activity	Side effects associated with surgery; doesn't protect against STDs; expensive; irreversible
Other methods				
Withdrawal	4	22	No cost or health risks	Reduces sexual pleasure; unreliable; requires high motivation; no protection against STDs
No contraception	85	85	No immediate monetary cost	High risk of pregnancy and STDs

Figure 12.12 *(continued)*
A comparison of widely used contraceptive techniques.

at the tip to collect the ejaculate. The man should withdraw before completely losing his erection and firmly hold the rim of the condom during withdrawal to prevent any semen from spilling into the vagina.

Condoms are made of polyurethane, latex rubber, or animal membranes ("skin"). Skin condoms do *not* offer protection against sexually transmitted diseases. Polyurethane condoms are thinner than latex condoms; however, they are more likely to break and to slip off than latex condoms. Using latex condoms definitely reduces the chances of contracting or passing on various sexually transmitted diseases. However, oil-based creams and lotions (petroleum jelly, massage oil, baby oil, and hand and body lotions, for example) should never be used with latex condoms. Within 60 seconds, these products can make microscopic holes in the rubber membrane that are large enough to allow passage of HIV and organisms produced by other sexually transmitted infections. Instead, water-based lubricants such as Astroglide or K-Y Warming Liquid should be used.

Emergency Contraceptive

There are a variety of reasons that individuals have unprotected sex, and in some cases they might turn to emergency contraception after the fact. Women may seek emergency contraception in cases of sexual assault, contraceptive failure, or unplanned sex. Progestin pills (also called Plan B or "morning after" pills) are available from pharmacies without a prescription. Plan B pills are 89% effective when started within 72 hours after unprotected sex. The drug works like birth control pills, by preventing ovulation or fertilization and implantation of the fertilized egg into the uterine wall (Planned Parenthood Federation of America, 2014a). By contrast, mifepristone (also called the "abortion pill") is a drug that can induce a miscarriage in pregnancies of less than 9 weeks. Prescribed by a physician, mifepristone is typically administered in the form of two pills taken several days apart (Planned Parenthood Federation of America, 2014b). Although no substitute for regular birth control, these drugs can be used after unprotected sex. They do not, however, provide any protection against sexually transmitted diseases.

Sexually Transmitted Diseases

A *sexually transmitted disease (STD)* **is a disease or infection transmitted primarily through sexual contact.** When people think of STDs (also referred to as sexually transmitted infections or STIs), they typically think of chlamydia and gonorrhea, but these diseases are only the tip of the iceberg. There are actually around twenty-five sexually transmitted diseases. Some of them—for instance, pubic lice—are minor nuisances that can be readily treated. Others, however, are severe afflictions that are difficult to treat. For instance, if it isn't detected early, syphilis can cause heart failure, blindness, and brain damage, and AIDS is eventually fatal. The principal types of sexually transmitted diseases are listed in **Figure 12.13**, along with their symptoms and modes of transmission. Most of these infections are spread from one person to another through intercourse, oral-genital contact, or anal-genital contact.

Prevalence

No one is immune to sexually transmitted diseases. Health authorities estimate that about 19 million new cases occur in the United States each year, with nearly half occurring in the under-25 age group (Centers for Disease Control and Prevention, 2012b).

The Centers for Disease Control and Prevention (2012a) estimate that 1.2 million people are living with HIV/AIDS. Since the mid-1990s, new diagnoses of HIV have remained relatively stable at about 50,000 infections per year (Hall et al., 2008). HIV disproportionately affects sexual minorities and people of color (Pellowski et al., 2013).

In 2010, women made up 20% of the new HIV infections in the United States, with 84% of these infections stemming from heterosexual contact (Centers for Disease Control and Prevention, 2015a). An increasing concern is that a woman's partner may be secretly having sex with other men. This phenomenon, known as being on the "down low," is more common among black and Latinos than white men, possibly because of cultural differences in attitudes toward homosexuality and bisexuality. In one study, 22% of men on the down low had recently had both unprotected anal and vaginal sex (Siegel et al., 2008). These men report that they didn't use protection because they didn't always have condoms available, they enjoyed sex more without a condom, and they perceived their females partners as "safe" (Dodge, Jeffries, & Sandfort, 2008). Obviously, this

SEXUALLY TRANSMITTED DISEASES (STDS)

STD	Transmission	Symptoms
Acquired immune deficiency syndrome (AIDS)	The AIDS virus is spread by coitus or anal intercourse. There is a chance the virus may also be spread by oral-genital sex, particularly if semen is swallowed. (AIDS can also be spread by nonsexual means: contaminated blood, contaminated hypodermic needles, and transmission from an infected woman to her baby during pregnancy or childbirth.)	Most people infected with the virus show no immediate symptoms; antibodies usually develop in the blood 2 to 8 weeks after infection. People with the virus may remain symptom-free for 5 years or more. No cure for the disease has yet been found. Common symptoms include fevers, night sweats, weight loss, chronic fatigue, swollen lymph nodes, diarrhea and/or bloody stools, atypical bruising or bleeding, skin rashes, headache, chronic cough, and a whitish coating on the tongue or throat.
Chlamydia infection	The *Chlamydia trichomatis* bacterium is transmitted primarily through sexual contact. It may also be spread by fingers from one body site to another.	In men, chlamydial infection of the urethra may cause a discharge and burning during urination. Chlamydia-caused epidydimitis may produce a sense of heaviness in the affected testicle(s), inflammation of the scrotal skin, and painful swelling at the bottom of the testicle. In women, pelvic inflammatory disease caused by chlamydia may disrupt menstrual periods, temperature, and cause abdominal pain, nausea, vomiting, headache, infertility, and ectopic pregnancy.
Human papillomavirus (HPV)	Virus is often on genital skin areas not covered by a condom (vulva, scrotum, etc.); virus is spread primarily through penile-vaginal, oral-genital, oral-anal, or genital-anal contact; transmission most often occurs by asymptomatic individuals.	Often asymptomatic; 10% of infections lead to contagious genital warts, which may appear 3 to 8 months after contact with infected person; HPV is associated with various cancers.
Gonorrhea ("clap")	The *Neisseria gonorrhoeae* bacterium (gonococcus) is spread through penile-vaginal, oral-genital, or genital-anal contact.	Most common symptoms in men are a cloudy discharge from the penis and burning sensations during urination. If the disease is untreated, complications may include inflammation of the scrotal skin and swelling at the base of the testicle. In women, some green or yellowish discharge is produced, but the disease commonly remains undetected. At a later stage, pelvic inflammatory disease may develop.
Herpes	The genital herpes virus (HSV-2) appears to be transmitted primarily by penile-vaginal, oral-genital, or genital-anal contact. The oral herpes virus (HSV-1) is transmitted primarily by kissing, or oral-genital contact.	Small red, painful bumps (papules) appear in the region of the genitals (genital herpes) or mouth (oral herpes). The papules become painful blisters that eventually rupture to form wet, open sores.
Pubic lice ("crabs")	*Phthirus pubis,* the pubic louse, is spread easily through body contact or through shared clothing or bedding.	Persistent itching. Lice are visible and may often be located in pubic hair or other body hair.
Syphilis	The *Treponema pallidum* bacterium (spirochete) is transmitted from open lesions during penile-vaginal, oral-genital, oral-anal, or genital-anal contact.	*Primary stage:* A painless chancre (sore) appears at the site where the spirochetes entered the body. *Secondary stage:* The chancre disappears and a generalized skin rash develops. *Latent stage:* There may be no observable symptoms. *Tertiary stage:* Heart failure, blindness, mental disturbance, and many other symptoms may occur. Death may result.
Trichomoniasis	The protozoan parasite *Trichomonas vaginalis* is passed through genital sexual contact or less frequently by towels, toilet seats, or bathtubs used by an infected person.	In women, white or yellow vaginal discharge with an unpleasant odor; vulva is sore and irritated. Men are usually asymptomatic.
Viral hepatitis	The hepatitis B virus may be transmitted by blood, semen, vaginal secretions, and saliva. Manual, oral, or penile stimulation of the anus is strongly associated with the spread of this virus. Hepatitis A seems to be spread primarily via the fecal-oral route. Oral-anal sexual contact is also a common mode of sexual transmission for hepatitis A.	Vary from nonexistent to mild flulike symptoms to an incapacitating illness characterized by high fever, vomiting, and severe abdominal pain.

Figure 12.13

Overview of common sexually transmitted diseases (STDs). This chart summarizes the symptoms and modes of transmission of nine STDs. Note that intercourse is not required to transmit all STDs—many can be contracted through oral-genital contact or other forms of physical intimacy. (Adapted from Carroll, 2007; Crooks & Baur, 2008; Hatcher et al., 2004)

lifestyle has serious implications for unknowing female partners in terms of increasing their risk for HIV infection or any STD.

Human papillomavirus (HPV), the infection that causes genital warts, is the most common STD. In fact, it's estimated that nearly all sexually active men and women acquire HPV at some point in their lives (Centers for Disease Control, 2014). HPV tends to be more problematic for women than men because certain types of HPV can lead to cervical cancer. In 2006, the U.S. Food and Drug Administration approved a vaccine (Gardisil) that prevents infection with the types of HPV that lead to cervical cancer. The vaccination is recommended for both girls and boys, starting at age 11 (Alan Guttmacher Institute, 2012b).

Prevention

Abstinence is obviously the best way to avoid acquiring STDs. Of course, for many people this is not an appealing or realistic option. Short of abstinence, the best strategy is to engage in sexual activity only in the context of a long-term relationship, where partners have an opportunity to know each other reasonably well. You need to talk openly about safer sexual practices with your partner. But if you don't carry the process one step further and practice what you preach, you remain at risk.

We offer the following suggestions for safer sex:

- If you are not involved in a sexually exclusive relationship with someone free of disease, always use latex condoms with spermicides; they have a good track record of preventing STDs and offer effective protection against the AIDS virus. (And never use oil-based lubricants with latex condoms; use water-based lubricants instead.)
- If there is any possibility that you or your partner has an STD, abstain from sex, always use condoms, or use other types of sexual expression such as hand-genital stimulation. People can be carriers of sexually transmitted diseases without knowing it. For instance, in its early stages gonorrhea may cause no readily apparent symptoms in women, who may unknowingly transmit the infection to their partners.
- Don't have sex with lots of people. This increases your risk of contracting STDs.
- Don't have sex with someone who has had lots of previous partners. People won't always be honest about their sexual history, so it's important to know whether you can trust a prospective partner's word.
- You should consider *any* activity that exposes you to blood (including menstrual blood), semen, vaginal secretions, urine, feces, or saliva as high-risk behavior *unless* you and your partner are in a mutual, sexually exclusive relationship and neither of you is infected.
- Because HIV is easily transmitted through anal intercourse, it's a good idea to avoid this type of sex. Rectal tissues are delicate and easily torn, thus letting the virus pass through the membrane. Always use a condom during anal sex.
- Oral-genital sex may also transmit some STDs. Use a condom or a Sheer Gylde dam to make this safer.
- Watch for sores, rashes, or discharge around the vulva or penis, or elsewhere on your body, especially the mouth. If you have cold sores, avoid kissing or oral sex.

If you have any reason to suspect that you have an STD, find a good health clinic and get tested *as soon as possible*. It's normal to be embarrassed or afraid of getting bad news, but don't delay. Health professionals are in the business of helping people, not judging them. To be really sure, get tested twice. If you have several sexual partners in a year, you should have regular STD checkups. You will have to ask for them because most doctors and health clinics won't perform them otherwise.

If your test results are positive, it's essential to get the proper treatment *right away*. Notify your sexual partners so they can be tested immediately, too. And avoid sexual intercourse and oral sex until you and your partner are fully treated and a physician or clinic says you are no longer infectious.

Human papillomavirus (HPV) is the most common STD. In 2006, the U.S. Food and Drug Administration approved a vaccine that prevents infection with the types of HPV that lead to cervical cancer. The vaccination is recommended for both girls and boys, starting at age 11.

12.7 Enhancing Sexual Relationships

Learning Objectives

■ List five general suggestions for enhancing sexual relationships.

■ Discuss the nature, prevalence, causes of common sexual dysfunctions, as well as some strategies to cope with them.

Answer the following statements "true" or "false."

____ **1.** Sexual problems are unusual.

____ **2.** Sexual problems belong to couples rather than individuals.

____ **3.** Sexual problems are highly resistant to treatment.

____ **4.** Sex therapists sometimes recommend masturbation as a treatment for certain types of problems.

The answers are (1) false, (2) true, (3) false, and (4) true. If you missed several of these questions, you are by no means unusual. Misconceptions about sexuality are the norm rather than the exception. Fortunately, there is plenty of useful information on how to improve sexual relationships.

For the sake of simplicity, our advice is directed to heterosexual couples, but much of what we have to say is also relevant to same-gender couples. For advice aimed specifically at same-gender couples, we recommend *Permanent Partners: Building Gay and Lesbian Relationships that Last* by Betty Berzon (2004).

General Suggestions

Let's begin with some general ideas about how to enhance sexual relationships. Even if you are satisfied with your sex life, these suggestions may be useful as "preventive medicine."

1. *Become knowledgeable about sex.* The first step in promoting sexual satisfaction is to acquire accurate information about sex. The shelves of most bookstores are bulging with popular books on sex, but many of them are loaded with inaccuracies. A good bet is to pick up a college textbook on human sexuality. Enrolling in a course on human sexuality is also a good idea. Most colleges offer such courses today.

2. *Review your sexual values system.* Many sexual problems stem from a negative sexual values system that associates sex with immorality. The guilt feelings caused by such a perspective can interfere with sexual functioning. Thus, sex therapists often encourage adults to examine the sources and implications of their sexual values.

3. *Learn to communicate about sex.* Sexual communication is linked to both sexual and relationship satisfaction. It is essential in a sexual relationship. Many common problems—such as choosing an inconvenient time or too little erotic activity before intercourse—are traceable largely to poor communication. Your partner is not a mind reader! You have to share your thoughts and feelings.

4. *Avoid focusing on sexual performance.* Sexual encounters are not tests or races. People can get overly concerned with issues like both partners reaching orgasm simultaneously. This mindset can lead to disruptive habits like judging one's performance. Sexual experiences are usually best when you adopt the philosophy that getting there is at least half the fun.

5. *Enjoy your sexual fantasies.* As we noted earlier, the mind is the ultimate erogenous zone. Men and women both report that their sexual fantasies increase their excitement. Don't be afraid to use fantasy to enhance your sexual arousal.

Understanding Sexual Dysfunction

Many people struggle with *sexual dysfunctions*—**impairments in sexual functioning that cause subjective distress.** Figure 12.14 shows the prevalence of some of the most common sexual problems. Physical, psychological, and interpersonal factors can contribute to sexual problems. *Physical factors* include chronic illness, disabilities, some medications, alcohol, and drugs. *Individual psychological factors* include performance anxiety, negative attitudes about sexuality learned during childhood, fears of pregnancy and STDs, life stresses such as unemployment, and prior sexual abuse. *Interpersonal factors* include ineffective communication about sexual matters and unresolved relationship issues that fuel anger and resentment.

People commonly assume that a sexual problem resides in just one partner (physical or individual psychological factors). While this is sometimes the case, most sexual problems emerge from partners' unique ways of relating to each other (interpersonal factors). In other words, sexual problems belong to couples rather than to individuals.

Learn More Online

American Psychological Association: Sex

APA's website offers information and resources on many important contemporary psychological issues. Under the topic of "sex," the site provides answers to common questions and information about common problems as well as links to books and additional web resources.

Unresolved sexual problems can be a source of tension and frustration in relationships. Physical, psychological, and interpersonal factors can contribute to sexual difficulties.

Lucky Business/Shutterstock.com

Let's examine the symptoms and causes of four common sexual dysfunctions: erectile difficulties, premature ejaculation, orgasmic difficulties, and hypoactive sexual desire.

Erectile difficulties **are the male sexual dysfunction characterized by the persistent inability to achieve or maintain an erection adequate for intercourse.** The traditional name for this problem is *impotence*, but sex therapists have discarded the term because of its demeaning connotation. A man who has never had an erection sufficient for intercourse is said to have *lifelong erectile difficulties*. A man who has had intercourse in the past but who is currently having problems achieving erections is said to have *acquired erectile difficulties*. The latter problem is more common and easier to overcome.

Erectile difficulty is the most commonly reported sexual problem for men (Stassberg, Perelman, & Walter, 2014). In a study of twenty-seven countries, nearly half the men surveyed reported having erectile difficulties if a broad criterion (the inability to get an erection adequate for satisfactory sexual performance) is used (Mulhall et al., 2008). In a national survey of American adults over the age of 50, 44% of men reported some erectile difficulty (Schick et al., 2010).

Physical factors besides aging can play a role in erectile difficulties. For example, many cases may be the result of side effects from medication. A host of common diseases (such as obesity, diabetes, heart disease, and high blood pressure) can produce erectile problems as a symptom. Many temporary conditions, such as fatigue, worry about work, an argument with one's partner, a depressed mood, or too much alcohol can cause such incidents. The most common psychological cause of erectile difficulties is anxiety about sexual performance. This anxiety can be amplified if one's partner turns an incident into a major catastrophe.

Premature ejaculation **is characterized as impaired sexual relations because a man consistently reaches orgasm too quickly.** What is "too quickly"? To address this question, researchers asked a random sample of sex therapists from the United States and Canada for their expert opinions (Corty & Guardiani, 2008). They found that sustaining intercourse for 3 to 13 minutes

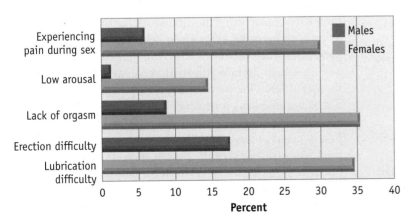

Figure 12.14

Gender differences in reported sexual difficulties within the past year. This graph shows the results of a national survey of sexual behavior in Americans ages 18 to 59. The most commonly reported problem among men is erectile difficulties; in women common problems include orgasmic and lubrication difficulties. (Adapted from Herbenick et al., 2010a)

is not worthy of concern. Obviously, time estimates, even from "experts," are arbitrary. The critical consideration is the subjective feelings of the partners. If either partner feels that the ejaculation is persistently too fast for sexual gratification, the couple has a problem. Although estimates of the pervasiveness of premature ejaculation vary, as many as one in three men might deal with this issue at some point in their lives (Mayo Clinic, 2011).

What causes this dysfunction? Some men who have a life-long history of quick ejaculation may have a neurophysiological predisposition to the condition. Biological causes include hormones, thyroid problems, or inflammation of the prostate. Psychological causes can include stress, depression, or anger at one's partner. Some therapists believe that early sexual experiences in which a rapid climax was advantageous (or necessary to avoid being discovered) can establish a habit of rapid ejaculation (Mayo Clinic, 2009).

Orgasmic difficulties **occur when people experience sexual arousal but have persistent problems in achieving orgasm.** When this problem occurs in men, it is often called *male orgasmic disorder*. The traditional name for this problem in women, *frigidity*, is no longer used because of its derogatory implications. Because this problem is much more common among women, we'll limit our discussion to them. A woman who has never experienced an orgasm through any kind of stimulation is said to have *generalized lifelong orgasmic difficulties*. Women who experience orgasms in some situations or only rarely are said to have *situational orgasmic difficulties*. Although lifelong orgasmic difficulties would seem to be the more severe problem, they are actually more responsive to treatment than situational orgasmic difficulties.

Physical causes of orgasmic difficulties are rare (medications can be a problem). One of the leading psychological causes is a negative attitude toward sex. Women who have been taught that sex is dirty or sinful are likely to approach it with shame and guilt. These feelings can undermine arousal, inhibit sexual expression, and impair orgasmic responsiveness. Arousal may also be inhibited by fear of pregnancy or excessive concern about achieving orgasm.

Hypoactive sexual desire **is the lack of interest in sexual activity.** Individuals with this problem rarely initiate sex or tend to avoid sexual activities with their partner. It occurs in both men and women, but it is more common among women and tends to increase with age (Bradford & Schwartz, 2014). In women, low sexual desire is most often associated with relationship difficulties. Other factors related to hypoactive desire include sexual abuse in childhood, stress, distraction, anxiety, depression, and body image dissatisfaction (Brotto et al., 2010). In men, low sexual desire is often related to embarrassment about erectile dysfunction (Carvalho & Nobre, 2011).

Coping with Specific Problems

With modern sex therapy techniques, sexual problems no longer have to be chronic sources of frustration and shame. *Sex therapy* **involves the professional treatment of sexual dysfunctions.**

Learn More Online

The American Association of Sexuality Educators, Counselors and Therapists (AASECT)

This professional organization is for sexual educators, counselors, and therapists. The website includes books and articles by members. It also has a link to locate sex therapists or educators on a state-by-state basis.

Masters and Johnson reported high success rates for their treatments of specific problems, and there is a consensus that sexual dysfunctions can be overcome with regularity. However, the advent of medications (such as Viagra) to treat sexual problems has resulted in an increased emphasis on medical and individual treatments over relationship interventions (Perelman, 2014). Nonetheless, couple-based treatment approaches definitely have their place and are often recommended. If you're looking for a sex therapist, be sure to find someone who is qualified to work in this specialized field. One professional credential to look for is that provided by the American Association of Sex Educators, Counselors, and Therapists (AASECT).

Erectile Difficulties

According to Pfizer, the company that makes Viagra, the much-touted pill for treating erectile disorders is effective for up to four out of five men. Still, it is not without its drawbacks—some of them life threatening. Cialis and Levitra are two similar pills that enhance erections over a longer period (24 to 36 hours) than Viagra. These drugs affect the muscles in the penis, allowing them to relax, which in turn increases the blood flow and results in an erection. To work effectively, these pills must be incorporated into the couple's lovemaking style. There is evidence that exercising and staying physically active help maintain healthy erectile functioning (Janiszewski, Janssen, & Ross, 2009).

The expectation that a pill alone will solve sexual problems that stem from relationship or psychological issues can set a couple up for disappointment. To overcome psychologically based erectile difficulties, the key is to decrease the man's performance anxiety. It is a good idea for a couple to discuss the problem openly. Obviously, it is crucial for partners to be emotionally supportive rather than hostile and demanding.

Masters and Johnson introduced an effective procedure for the treatment of erectile difficulties and other dysfunctions. *Sensate focus* **is an exercise in which partners take turns pleasuring each other while giving guided verbal feedback and in which certain kinds of stimulation are temporarily forbidden.** One partner stimulates the other, who simply lies back and enjoys it while giving instructions and feedback about what feels good. Initially, the partners are not allowed to touch each other's genitals or to attempt intercourse. This prohibition should free the man from feelings of pressure to perform. Over a number of sessions, the couple gradually include genital stimulation in their sensate focus, but intercourse is still banned. With the pressure to perform removed, many men spontaneously get erections. Repeated arousals should begin to restore the man's confidence in his sexual response. As his confidence returns, the couple can move on gradually to attempts at intercourse.

Premature Ejaculation

Men troubled by premature ejaculation range from those who climax almost instantly to those who cannot last the time that their partner prefers. In the latter case, simply slowing down the tempo of intercourse may help. Sometimes the problem can be solved indirectly by discarding the traditional assumption that orgasms should come through intercourse. If the female partner enjoys oral or manual stimulation, these techniques can be used to provide her with an orgasm either before or after intercourse. This strategy can reduce the performance pressure for the male partner, and couples may find that intercourse starts to last longer.

For the problem of instant ejaculation, two treatments are very effective: the *stop-start method* (Semans, 1956) and the *squeeze technique* (Masters & Johnson, 1970). With both, the woman brings the man to the verge of orgasm through manual stimulation. Then, she either stops stimulating him (stop-start technique) or squeezes the base or the end of his penis firmly for 3 to 5 seconds (squeeze technique) until he calms down. She repeats this procedure three or four times before bringing him to orgasm. These exercises can help a man recognize preorgasmic sensations and teach him that he can delay ejaculation. Medications such as certain antidepressants and topical anesthetic creams may also help (Mayo Clinic, 2009).

Orgasmic Difficulties

In some cases, couples can deal with women's orgasmic difficulties by exploring sexual activities such as manual or oral stimulation of the clitoris that are more effective in producing female orgasm than sexual intercourse alone. However, if negative attitudes and embarrassment about sex are at the root of the problem, therapy might be needed. Therapeutic discussions are usually geared toward helping nonorgasmic women reduce their ambivalence about sexual expression, become clearer about their sexual needs, and become more assertive about them. Sex therapists often suggest that women who have never had an orgasm try to have one by first using a vibrator and then shifting to masturbation because the latter more closely approximates stimulation by a partner. Sensate focus is also an effective technique for treating orgasmic difficulties (Donahey, 2010).

Hypoactive Sexual Desire

Therapists consider reduced sexual desire the most challenging sexual problem to treat (Aubin & Heiman, 2004). This is because the problem usually has multiple causes that can be difficult to identify. If the problem is a result of fatigue from overwork, couples may be encouraged to allot more time to personal and relationship needs. Sometimes hypoactive sexual desire reflects relationship problems. Treatment for reduced sexual desire is usually more intensive than that for more specific sexual disorders, and it is usually multifaceted to deal with the multiple aspects of the problem.

Medications can be used for low sexual desire if the problem is chemical in nature. Hormonal therapies are used for both men and women. The medical and financial success of Viagra has opened the door to the recent introduction of a drug to increase women's sexual desires. However, drugs will not solve relationship problems. For these, sex therapy is recommended (Kennedy, Martinez, & Garo, 2010). And as we have seen for most problematic issues in this chapter, communication between partners is crucial (Herbenick et al., 2014).

CHAPTER 12   Review

Key Ideas

12.1 Becoming a Sexual Person

- One's sexual identity is made up of sexual orientation, body image, sexual values and ethics, and erotic preferences. Physiological factors such as hormones influence sexual differentiation and anatomy more than they do sexual activity. Psychosocial factors appear to have more impact on sexual behavior.
- Sexual identity is shaped by families, peers, schools, religion, and the media. Because of differences in sexual socialization, sexuality can have different meanings for males and females.

12.2 Sexual Orientation

- Experts believe that sexual orientation should be viewed on a continuum and that it is more complex and fluid than widely appreciated. The determinants of sexual orientation are not yet known but appear to be a complex interaction of biological, psychological, and environmental factors.
- Negative attitudes toward homosexuals can lead to discrimination. Attitudes appear to be changing in a positive direction. Coming to terms with and disclosing sexual orientation is a complicated process. Evidence suggests that homosexuals are at greater risk for depression and suicide attempts than are heterosexuals, a phenomenon linked to their membership in a stigmatized group.

12.3 The Human Sexual Response

- The physiology of the human sexual response was described by Masters and Johnson. They analyzed the sexual response cycle into four phases: excitement, plateau, orgasm, and resolution. For a more complete view of this process, individuals' cognitive experiences during sexual encounters also need to be factored in.
- Women reach orgasm in intercourse less consistently than men, usually because foreplay is too brief and intercourse is not the optimal mode of stimulation. Gender differences in sexual socialization might also play a role.

12.4 Sexual Expression

- Sexual fantasies are normal and are an important aspect of sexual expression. Kissing is an important erotic activity linked to attachment in long-term relationships. Despite historically negative attitudes about masturbation, this practice is quite common, even among married people. Oral-genital sex is a common element in most couples' sexual repertoires. Anal sex is less common.
- Coitus is the most widely practiced sexual act in our society. Sexual activities between gay males include mutual masturbation, fellatio, and, less often, anal intercourse. Lesbians engage in mutual masturbation, cunnilingus, and tribadism.
- Disparities between partners in sexual interest and erotic preferences lead to disagreements that require negotiation. Common barriers to sexual communication include fear of appearing ignorant, concern about partner's response, conflicting attitudes, and negative early experiences. Effective communication plays an important role in sexual and relationship satisfaction.

12.5 Patterns of Sexual Behavior

- Hooking up is a common practice for young adults. The casual sex associated with hookups is risky. Many young adults engage in friends-with-benefits arrangements. These relationships can be tricky to negotiate.
- Sexual intimacy is a predictor of relationship stability. Younger married couples report having sex about two or three times a week. This frequency declines with age in both heterosexual and same-sex couples, though sexual activity in late adulthood is still common. Sexting in the context of sexual relationships is not uncommon.
- Most Americans disapprove of extramarital sex, though some couples condone it. Infidelity is less common among married couples and lesbians and more common among gay male couples. People become involved in extradyadic relationships for a variety of reasons, and it can lead to the dissolution of the relationship. The findings of our Spotlight on Research suggest that oxytocin may inhibit infidelity.

12.6 Practical Issues in Sexual Activity

- Contraception and sexually transmitted diseases are two practical issues that concern many sexually active individuals. Many people who do not want to conceive a child fail to use contraceptive procedures effectively, if at all. Contraceptive methods differ in effectiveness and have various advantages and disadvantages.
- STDs are prevalent, especially among those younger than 25. Since the mid-1990s, the rate of newly diagnosed HIV cases is holding steady. HIV disproportionally affects sexual minorities and people of color. HPV is very common and is more problematic for women. There is now an HPV vaccine.
- The danger of contracting STDs is higher among those who have had more sexual partners. Using condoms decreases the risk of contracting STDs. Early detection and treatment of STDs are important.

12.7 Application: Enhancing Sexual Relationships

- To enhance their sexual relationships, individuals need to have adequate sex education and positive values about sex. They also need to be able to communicate with their partners about sex and avoid focusing on sexual performance. Enjoying sexual fantasies is also important.
- Common sexual dysfunctions include erectile difficulties, premature ejaculation, orgasmic difficulties, and hypoactive sexual desire. Treatments for low sexual desire are less effective than those for more specific sexual problems. Sex therapy can be useful.

Key Terms

Anal intercourse p. 349	Masturbation p. 348
Androgens p. 336	Menarche p. 337
Asexuals p. 335	Orgasm p. 345
Bisexuals p. 335	Orgasmic difficulties p. 362
Coitus p. 349	Premature
Cunnilingus p. 348	ejaculation p. 361
Erectile difficulties p. 361	Refractory period p. 346
Erogenous zones p. 346	Sensate focus p. 362
Estrogens p. 336	Sex therapy p. 362
Fellatio p. 348	Sexual dysfunctions p. 360
Gonads p. 336	Sexual identity p. 335
Heterosexuals p. 335	Sexually transmitted
Homophobia p. 343	disease (STD) p. 357
Homosexuals p. 335	Spermarche p. 337
Hypoactive sexual desire p. 362	Vasocongestion p. 344

Key People

Lisa Diamond p. 341	William Masters and Virginia
Alfred Kinsey p. 341	Johnson pp. 344–345

CHAPTER 12 Practice Test

1. Which of the following is a problem unique to research on sexuality?
   a. Sex studies typically do not produce generalizable results.
   b. Sex studies do not meet ethical guidelines.
   c. Sex studies must rely on direct observation.
   d. Sex studies are especially susceptible to participant bias.

2. Which of the following statements about sexual orientation is true?
   a. Heterosexuality and homosexuality are best viewed as two distinct categories.
   b. Sexual orientation is complex and malleable.
   c. Biological factors alone probably determine sexual orientation.
   d. Environmental factors alone probably determine sexual orientation.

3. Stacy is in the initial phase of sexual arousal. Her muscles are tense and her heart rate and blood pressure are elevated. She is in which phase of Masters and Johnson's sexual response cycle?
   a. Foreplay
   b. Orgasm
   c. Excitement
   d. Resolution

4. Sexual fantasies
   a. are signs of abnormality.
   b. are quite normal.
   c. rarely include having sex with someone other than one's partner.
   d. are an excellent indication of what people want to experience in reality.

5. Regarding overall marital satisfaction and sexual satisfaction, research indicates there is
   a. a strong relationship.
   b. a weak relationship.
   c. no relationship.
   d. a strong relationship, but only in the first year of marriage.

6. Which of the following statements is true regarding infidelity?
   a. Women are more distressed by emotional infidelity, while men are more distressed by sexual infidelity.
   b. Women are more motivated by sexual excitement, whereas men are more motivated by relationship unhappiness.
   c. People between the ages of 18 and 30 are less likely to engage in sex outside a committed relationship than people older than 50.
   d. The majority of people in American society today approve of extramarital sex.

7. A man is orally stimulating his female partner. In which of the following is he engaging?
   a. Fellatio
   b. Cunnilingus
   c. Coitus
   d. Sodomy

8. Which of the following statements about condoms is true?
   a. It's okay to use oil-based lubricants with latex condoms.
   b. Polyurethane condoms are thicker than latex condoms.
   c. Skin condoms provide protection against STDs.
   d. It's okay to use water-based lubricants with latex condoms.

9. Sexually transmitted diseases
   a. are all very serious.
   b. have immediate symptoms.
   c. are most common among people younger than age 25.
   d. are most common among people between the ages of 26 and 40.

10. Which of the following is one of the text's suggestions for enhancing your sexual relationships?
    a. Set clear goals for each sexual encounter.
    b. Adhere to negative sexual values.
    c. Avoid giving your partner feedback.
    d. Pursue adequate sex education.

Answers

1. d Page 335
2. b Page 341
3. c Page 344
4. b Page 347
5. a Page 351
6. a Page 354
7. b Page 348
8. d Page 357
9. c Page 357
10. d Page 360

Personal Explorations Workbook

Go to the *Personal Explorations Workbook* in the back of your textbook for exercises that can enhance your self-understanding in relation to issues raised in this chapter.

Exercise 12.1 *Self-Assessment:* Sexuality Scale

Exercise 12.2 *Self-Reflection:* How Did You Acquire Your Attitudes about Sex?

CHAPTER 13 Careers and Work

Pressmaster/Shutterstock.com

"Love and work . . . work and love, that's all there is." This quote is attributed to Sigmund Freud, whose opinions on love and sex are well known, if sometimes misunderstood. Less well known, however, is the fact that Freud viewed work as an important element in understanding the human condition. Work is a defining characteristic in the lives of many people; it may be *the* defining characteristic for Americans. Consider this: Do most people you know identify themselves by what they do in their careers? When you meet someone new, isn't one of the first things you ask, "So, what do you do for a living?" How people reply to this question reveals information not only about their occupation but also about their social status, educational background, lifestyle, personality, interests, aspirations, and aptitudes. In other words, work plays a pivotal role in adult life. According to a Gallup poll, 73% of Americans rate work as either "extremely" or "very important" in their life (Moore, 2003). In **Figure 13.1**, you can see that how people view their jobs is strongly correlated with their income. In a real sense, people *are* what they do at work. Therefore, it should come as no surprise that being unemployed can have devastating consequences for people's sense of self, well-being, and even happiness.

Because work is a significant aspect of life, psychologists take great interest in it. *Industrial/organizational (I/O) psychology is* **the study of human behavior in the workplace.** Industrial/organizational psychologists strive to increase the dignity and performance of workers and the organizations for which they labor (Schmitt, Highhouse, & Weiner, 2013). Among other issues, I/O psychologists study worker motivation and satisfaction, job performance and training, ethics in the workplace, leadership, occupational hazards, personnel selection, and diversity in organizations. A recent concern is how individuals balance work and family life. An imbalance between these two spheres can lead to what I/O psychologists call work-family conflict (e.g., Allen, 2013).

We begin this chapter by reviewing some important considerations in choosing a career. Then we explore two models of career development and discuss women's career issues. Next, we examine how the workplace and workforce are changing and look at some occupational hazards such as job stress, sexual harassment, and unemployment. Finally, we address the important issues involved in balancing work, relationships, and leisure. In the Application, we offer some concrete suggestions for enhancing your chances of landing a desirable job. ■

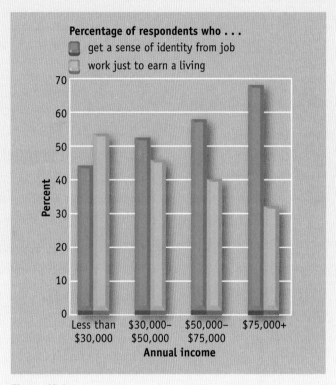

Figure 13.1

How workers view their jobs. The way workers view their jobs is strongly related to their income. Those who earn higher salaries are more likely to obtain a sense of identity from their work, whereas those who earn lower salaries typically see their jobs merely as a way to make a living. (Data from Moore, 2001)

13.1 Choosing a Career

Learning Objectives

■ Describe personal and family influences on job choice.

■ List helpful sources of career information and important aspects of potential occupations.

■ Clarify the role of occupational interest inventories in career decisions.

■ Outline important considerations in choosing an occupation.

One of life's biggest decisions is choosing a career. Consider this: The average person works at least 8 hours a day, 5 days a week, 50 weeks a year, for 40 to 45 years. Some people work much more and, admittedly, some work considerably less. Still, such a time commitment—really, a lifetime commitment—implies that you should both enjoy and be proficient at what you do for a living. Imagine the dissatisfaction, if not drudgery, that people who neither like their careers nor are adept at them feel all the time. Aside from sleeping, most people spend more time working than performing any other activity. Just consider a typical weekday:

Sleep	6–8 hours
Commute to and from work	1–2 hours
Work	8 hours
Prepare and eat meals	2 hours
TV and Internet time	1–3 hours
Other activities	1–2 hours

As you can see, the importance of your career decision is enormous. It may determine whether you are employed or unemployed, financially secure or insecure, happy or unhappy. Rapidly advancing technology and the increased training and education required to break into most fields make it more important than ever to choose carefully. In theory, what's involved in making a successful career choice is pretty straightforward. First, you need a clear grasp of your personal characteristics. Second, you need realistic information about potential careers. From there, it's just a matter of selecting an occupation that is a good match with your personal characteristics. In reality, however, the process is a lot more complicated than simply finding a match between these two elements. Let's take a closer look.

Examining Personal Characteristics and Family Influences

People with limited job skills and qualifications (education, training, experience) have limited job options; they often take whatever job is available rather than one that is well suited for them. In a real sense, these individuals do not choose their jobs—the jobs choose them. In fact, *choosing* a career is a luxury usually afforded to the middle and upper classes. For those who *are* able to select a career, personal qualities and family influences come into play.

Personal Qualities

Making career decisions can be scary. Individuals who exhibit *secure attachment* (see Chapter 9) and who have a sense of *self-efficacy* about career-relevant abilities (see Chapter 6) find it easier to make career choices (Braunstein-Bercovitz et al., 2012). What other personal characteristics affect career choice? Although *intelligence* does not necessarily predict occupational success (Griffeth, Hom, & Gaertner, 2000), it does predict the likelihood of entering particular occupations. That's because intelligence is related to academic success—the ticket required to enter certain fields. Professions such as law, medicine, and engineering are open only to those who can meet increasingly selective criteria as they advance from high school to college to graduate education and professional training. The relationship between intelligence and occupational level generally holds well for men, but an ability-achievement gap exists for women, as we noted in Chapter 11.

Some psychologists have also wondered about the link between intelligence and job satisfaction. One study indicates that smart people tend to have lower job satisfaction than less-intelligent workers when the work in question is not complex or challenging (Ganzach, 1998). Thus, pursuing a career that matches one's intellectual abilities may be a wise decision (Ganzach & Fried, 2012).

Still, in many occupations, special talents are more important than general intelligence. *Specific aptitudes* that might make a person well suited for certain occupations include creativity, artistic or musical talent, mechanical ability, clerical skills, mathematical ability, and persuasive talents. A particularly crucial characteristic is *social skills* because teams and networking are increasingly important in organizations (Kozlowski & Bell, 2003). Workers must be able to get along well with peers and to also counsel or supervise them. Certainly, social-emotional or interpersonal intelligence—the ability to behave wisely in human relations and to accurately interpret emotions and intentions—is an important part of such social skills (Meisler, 2014).

As people travel through life, they acquire *interests*. Are you intrigued by the business world? the academic world? international affairs? the outdoors? physical sciences? music? athletics? art and culture? human services? hospitality and recreation? The list of potential interests is virtually infinite. Because interests underlie your motivation for work and your job satisfaction, they should definitely be considered in your career planning. Whether you perceive your work as *meaningful* has an impact, as well, because it can influence how self-directed you are in the workplace (Hall, Feldman, & Kim, 2013).

Finally, it is important to choose an occupation that is compatible with your *personality* (Swanson & D'Achiardi, 2005). We'll examine the relationship between personality types and career choice in a later section.

Lloyd Bridges' sons decided to emulate their father by pursuing acting careers.

Family Influences

Individuals' career choices are strongly influenced by their family backgrounds (Duck et al., 2013) and social class (Blustein et al., 2011, 2015). That is, the jobs that appeal to people tend to be like those of their parents. Thus, people who grow up in middle-class homes are likely to aspire to high-paying professions in law, medicine, or business. In contrast, individuals from low-income families often lean toward blue-collar jobs in construction work, office work, and food services.

Family background influences career choice for several reasons. First, a key predictor of occupational status is the number of years of education an individual has completed (Arbona, 2005). And because parents and children often attain similar levels of education, they are likely to have similar jobs. Second, career attainment is related to socioeconomic status. The factors that mediate this relationship are educational aspirations and attainment during the school years (Schoon & Parsons, 2002). This means that parents and teachers can help boost children's career aspirations and opportunities by encouraging them to do well in school.

Finally, parenting practices come into play. Most children from middle-class homes are encouraged to be curious and independent, qualities that are essential to success in many high-status occupations. In contrast, children from lower-status families are often taught to conform and obey (Hochschild, 2003), thus they may have less opportunity to develop the qualities demanded in high-status jobs. As we noted in Chapter 11, parents' gender-role expectations also influence their children's aspirations and sometimes interact with socioeconomic status and ethnicity.

Researching Job Characteristics

The second step in selecting an occupation is seeking out information about jobs. Because the sheer number of jobs is overwhelming, you must narrow your search before you start gathering information.

Sources of Career Information

Once you select some jobs that might interest you, the next question is, Where do you get information about them? A helpful place to start is the *Occupational Outlook Handbook*, available in most libraries and on the Internet. This government document, published every 2 years by the U.S. Bureau of Labor Statistics, is a comprehensive guide to occupations. It includes job descriptions, education and training requirements, salaries, and employment outlooks for more than 800 occupations.

If you're interested in a career in psychology, you can obtain materials from the American Psychological Association (APA) or consult a book dedicated to careers in psychology (Hettich & Landrum, 2014; Landrum & Davis, 2013). Also, the APA website provides links to other sites describing more than fifty subfields in psychology, many of which provide useful career information. Related professions (social work, school psychology, and so on) also have webpages. You can find the addresses of these pages on Marky Lloyd's Careers in Psychology website.

Learn More Online

Occupational Outlook Handbook (OOH) Online

Every 2 years the Bureau of Labor Statistics publishes the OOH, now available via the Internet. This guide to every occupation in the United States includes descriptions of the nature of each job and its working conditions, educational requirements, future employment, and earnings prospects. You can also find information about job and workforce trends here.

Learn More Online

Marky Lloyd's Careers in Psychology Page

For those who think they might want a job or career in psychology or allied fields, Professor Marky Lloyd has put together a fine set of resources to help in both planning and making the choice. Many of the resources are helpful to any student seeking career guidance and employment tips.

Essential Information about Occupations

When you examine the occupational literature and interview professionals, what kinds of information should you seek? To some extent, the answer depends on your interests, values, and needs. However, some things are of concern to virtually anyone. Workers typically give high ratings to good health insurance, retirement plans, limited job stress, and recognition for performing well (Saad, 1999), as well as whether the organization is a great place to work (Wentland, 2015). Some key issues include:

- *The nature of the work.* What would your daily duties and responsibilities be?
- *Working conditions.* Is the work environment pleasant or unpleasant, low key or high pressure?
- *Job entry requirements.* What education and training are required for an occupation?
- *Ongoing training or education.* Will you need to continue learning in order to remain proficient?
- *Chance to collaborate.* Will you have the opportunity to work with others on a team?
- *Potential earnings.* What are entry-level and average salaries, and how much can you hope to earn if you're exceptionally successful? Are there fringe benefits?
- *Potential status.* What is the social status associated with this occupation?
- *Opportunities for advancement.* How do you move up in this field? Are there adequate opportunities for promotion and advancement?
- *Trust and respect.* Are all the employees in this workplace treated well and fairly?
- *Intrinsic job satisfaction.* Apart from money and benefits, what can you derive in the way of personal satisfaction from this job? Will it allow you to help people, have fun, be creative, or shoulder responsibility?
- *Future outlook.* What is the projected supply and demand for this occupation?
- *Security.* Is the work stable, or can the job disappear if there is an economic downturn?

By the way, if you're wondering whether your college education is worth the expense, the answer is "yes." As we'll discuss shortly, the jobs that you can obtain with a college degree typically yield higher pay than those requiring less education, so, despite the costs involved, a college education is worth the money (Leonhardt, 2014). Indeed, by current estimates, across a lifetime a typical bachelor's degree leads to in excess of $1 million of earnings more than a high school diploma (Reuters, 2012). But educational attainment alone does not predict who performs well in a given job setting (Hunter & Hunter, 1984). In other words, having a degree is not as important as the grades you earn during college. Why? Higher grade point averages (GPAs) point to the ability to be trained, which in turn influences subsequent job performance (Roth et al., 1996) and salary level (Roth & Clarke, 1998). Still, experts agree that the future belongs to those who are better educated, and a main reason is the appeal education has for employers. Ng and Feldman (2009) found that employees with more education performed better at work, were good organizational citizens, were absent less frequently, and were much less likely to engage in on-the-job substance abuse than workers with less education.

Using Psychological Tests for Career Decisions

If you are undecided about an occupation, you might consider taking some tests at your school's counseling center. *Occupational interest inventories* **measure one's interests as they relate to various jobs or careers.** These inventories help users identify vocational areas for choosing potential careers (Burns, 2015). Two widely used tests are the Strong Interest Inventory (SII) (Kantamneni, 2014) and the Self-Directed Search (SDS) (Behrens & Nauta, 2014). Another popular interest inventory is the Kuder Career Search with Person Match (Ihle-Helledy, Zytowski, & Fouad, 2004; Zytowski, 2001).

Occupational interest inventories do not predict whether you would be successful in various occupations based on your interests, skills, motivations, values, and other personal factors (Harrington & Long, 2013). Rather, they focus more on potential job *satisfaction* than job *success* (Nye et al., 2011). After taking an inventory, you receive many scores indicating how

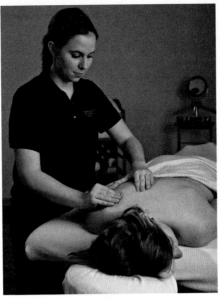

People vary in their preferences for work environments. Some like high pressure work; others prefer more low-key jobs.

similar your interests are to those of people in various occupations. For example, a high score on the accountant scale of a test means that your interests are similar to those of the average accountant. This correspondence in interests does not guarantee that you would enjoy a career in accounting, but it is a moderately good predictor of job satisfaction (Hansen, 2005).

Although interest inventories can be helpful in working through career decisions, several cautions are worth noting. First, you may score high on some occupations that you're sure you would hate or that simply do not interest you. Given the sheer number of occupational scales on these tests, this can easily happen by chance. However, avoid dismissing the remainder of the test results just because you're sure that a few specific scores are "wrong."

Second, don't let a test make career decisions for you. Some students naively believe that they should pursue whatever occupation yields their highest score. That is not how the tests are designed to be used. They merely provide information for you and to give you some directions or possibilities to consider. Ultimately, you have to think things out for yourself and do a bit of research on the suggested options. A very good idea is to learn about potential careers indicated by these tests by talking to professionals who hold such jobs. Once you think a particular career seems to be appealing to you, ask to "job shadow" a professional who currently works in field of interest for a day or two (sometimes campus career services can set up such opportunities for you). Observing firsthand what a lawyer or a physical therapist or a landscape architect does all day can be very informative.

Third, be aware that most occupational interest inventories have a lingering gender bias (Einarsdóttir & Rounds, 2009). Many of these scales were originally developed decades ago when outright discrimination or more subtle discouragement prevented women from entering many traditionally "male" occupations. Critics assert that interest inventories have helped channel women into gender-typed careers, such as nursing and teaching, while guiding them away from more prestigious "male" occupations, such as medicine and engineering. Undoubtedly, this was true in the past. Recently, progress has reduced but not completely eliminated gender bias in occupational tests. Research suggests that ethnic bias on interest tests is less of a concern than gender bias (Hansen, 2005; but see Einarsdóttir & Rounds, 2009).

Taking Important Considerations into Account

As you contemplate career options, here are some important points to keep in mind.

1. *You have the potential for success in a variety of occupations* (Spokane & Cruza-Guet, 2005). Considering the huge variety of job opportunities, it's foolish to believe that only one career would be right for you. If you expect to find one perfect job, you may spend your entire lifetime searching for it.

2. *Career success is apt to be linked to mobility.* Career paths are now more turbulent and subject to sudden unexpected changes than before. Career success can hinge on your flexibility and willingness to move from one job to another; viewing such change as a positive event rather than a negative event is associated with career evolution (Chudzikowski, 2011).

3. *Be cautious about choosing a career solely on the basis of salary.* Because of the tremendous emphasis on material success in America, people are often tempted to choose careers solely on income or status. However, research suggests that meaning and purpose, not money, lead to happiness and well-being (e.g., Berg, Dutton, & Wrzesniewski, 2013; Wrzesniewski, 2012). Experts advise against following a strategy aimed at choosing a career based solely on projected earnings (Pollack, 2007). When people ignore personal characteristics in choosing a career, they risk being mismatched. Such job mismatching can result in boredom, frustration, and unhappiness with one's work, and these negative feelings can spill over into other spheres of life.

4. *There are limits on your career options.* Entry into a particular occupation is not simply a matter of choosing what you want to do. Although you get to make choices, you also have to persuade schools and employers to choose you. Your career options will be limited by factors beyond your control, including economic fluctuations and the job market.

5. *Career choice is an ongoing developmental process.* Occupational choice involves not one but a series of decisions. Once believed to extend only from prepuberty to the early 20s, authorities now recognize that this process continues throughout life. Some experts predict that the average person will have eleven or more jobs over the course of his or her working life (U.S. Bureau of Labor Statistics, 2015c). Thus, making occupational choices is not limited to youth.

6. *Some career decisions are not easily undone.* Although it's never too late to try new career directions, it is clear that many decisions are not readily reversed. Learning to exercise control over your career and the environment where you work is important (Converse et al., 2012). Few middle-aged lawyers suddenly decide to attend medical school or become elementary school teachers, for example, but it does happen. Once you invest time, money, and effort following one career path, it may not be easy to change paths.

7. *Do you want a job, a career, or a calling?* Some I/O psychologists draw distinctions among these three work options (Wrzesniewski, 2012; Wrzesniewski et al., 1997). A *job* allows people to earn money in order to survive, while work is something to be done in exchange for pay, not identity. A *career* enables people to achieve, to compete with others in the workplace, and to raise their status or their prestige. A *calling* exists when individuals see work as means to becoming personally fulfilled, to serve a greater social purpose by serving the self and others. Research on these approaches to work suggests that about one-third of workers fall into each of the three categories (Wrzesniewski et al., 1997). Which one describes your orientation toward work?

In the next section, we explore in greater detail how personal characteristics are related to career choice and career development.

Learning Objectives

- Summarize Holland's model of career choice and Super's stage model of career development.
- Identify some differences between women's and men's career development.

13.2 Models of Career Choice and Development

How do people choose a career? Before interest inventories existed, career counselors asked people to share likes and dislikes, to identify individuals they admired, and to catalog their hobbies (Reardon et al., 2009). Self-reports and interest tests have their place, but psychologists are interested in more theoretically based approaches for understanding how individuals make career choices and how their careers evolve. Here we examine two influential models that are often used to provide college students with career counseling (Hartung & Niles, 2000).

Holland's Person-Environment Fit Model

The most influential trait model of career choice was developed by John Holland (1997; see also Wilkins & Tracey, 2014). According to Holland, career choice is related to an individual's personality characteristics (e.g., values, interests, needs, skills, learning styles, attitudes), which are assumed to be relatively stable over time. In Holland's system, people are classified into one of six personality types, called *personal orientations*. Similarly, occupations are classified into six ideal *work environments*.

According to Holland, people search for environments that allow them to exercise their abilities and skills, share their attitudes or values, and adopt agreeable problems and roles. They flourish when their personality type is matched with a work environment that is congruent with their abilities, interests, and self-beliefs. The term *work environment* should be viewed broadly, as it can be a job or an occupation, a field of study, an educational program, a college or a university, a leisure time activity, or a particular organization's culture. In fact, in Holland's view, a work environment can even be construed as a social relationship with another person or persons (Reardon et al., 2009). A good match between one's personality and a work environment typically results in career satisfaction, achievement, and stability (Wilkins & Tracey, 2014). Workers who fit well in their professional environments, for example, are less likely to report job conflicts or to display aggression in the workplace (Pseekos, Bullock-Yowell, & Dahlen, 2011). Holland's six personal orientations and their optimal work environments are shown in **Figure 13.2**.

Those with a social personal orientation in Holland's theory are understanding and want to help others. Teachers typically score high on social orientation.

HOLLAND'S PERSONAL ORIENTATIONS AND RELATED WORK ENVIRONMENTS

Themes	Personal orientations	Work environments
Realistic	Values concrete and physical tasks. Perceives self as having mechanical skills and lacking social skills.	*Settings:* concrete, physical tasks requiring mechanical skills, persistence, and physical movement *Careers:* machine operator, pilot, draftsperson, engineer
Investigative	Wants to solve intellectual, scientific, and mathematical problems. Sees self as analytical, critical, curious, introspective, and methodical.	*Settings:* research laboratory, diagnostic medical case conference, work group of scientists *Careers:* marine biologist, computer programmer, clinical psychologist, architect, dentist
Artistic	Prefers unsystematic tasks or artistic projects: painting, writing, or drama. Perceives self as imaginative, expressive, and independent.	*Settings:* theater, concert hall, library, radio or TV studio *Careers:* sculptor, actor, designer, musician, author, editor
Social	Prefers educational, helping, and religious careers. Enjoys social involvement, church, music, reading, and dramatics. Is cooperative, friendly, helpful, insightful, persuasive, and responsible.	*Settings:* school and college classrooms, psychiatrist's office, religious meetings, mental institutions, recreational centers *Careers:* counselor, nurse, teacher, social worker, judge, minister, sociologist
Enterprising	Values political and economic achievements, supervision, and leadership. Enjoys leadership control, verbal expression, recognition, and power. Perceives self as extraverted, sociable, happy, assertive, popular, and self-confident.	*Settings:* courtroom, political rally, car sales room, real estate firm, advertising company *Careers:* realtor, politician, attorney, salesperson, manager
Conventional	Prefers orderly, systematic, concrete tasks with verbal and mathematical data. Sees self as conformist and having clerical and numerical skills.	*Settings:* bank, post office, file room, business office, Internal Revenue office *Careers:* banker, accountant, timekeeper, financial counselor, typist, receptionist

Figure 13.2

Overview of Holland's theory of occupational choice. According to John Holland (1985), people can be divided into six personality types (personal orientations) that prefer different work environments, as outlined here.

Source: Adapted from Holland, J. L. (1985). *Making occupational choices: A theory of occupational personalities and work environments* (2nd ed.). Englewood Cliffs, NJ: Prentice-Hall. Adapted by permission of Prentice-Hall, Inc.

The six personal orientations are ideal types, and no one person will fit perfectly into any one type. Indeed, most people are a combination of two or three types (Holland, 1996). Try categorizing your own personal orientation by studying **Figure 13.2**. Look at the matching work environments to get some ideas for possible career options. In contrast to trait models such as Holland's that view occupational choice as a specific event, stage theories view occupational choice as a developmental process. We consider that approach next.

Super's Developmental Model

Donald Super (1988, 1990) outlined a highly influential developmental model of career choice. Super views occupational development as a process that begins in childhood, unfolds and matures gradually across most of the lifespan, and ends with retirement. Super asserts that the person's *self-concept* is the critical factor in this process, so that decisions about work and career commitments reflect people's attempts to express their changing views of themselves. To map these changes, Super breaks the occupational life cycle into five major stages and various substages (see **Figure 13.3**).

Growth Stage

The growth stage occurs during childhood, when youngsters fantasize about exotic jobs they would enjoy. Generally, they imagine themselves as detectives, airplane pilots, and brain surgeons rather than plumbers, salespersons, and bookkeepers. Until the end of this period, children are largely oblivious to realistic considerations such as the abilities or education required for specific jobs. Naturally, children's aspirations and expectations may vary widely because of home and educational environments (Cook et al., 1996).

Figure 13.3

Overview of Super's theory of occupational development. According to Donald Super, people go through five major stages (and a variety of substages) of occupational development over the lifespan.

Source: Adapted from Zaccaria, J. (1970). *Theories of occupational choice and vocational development.* Boston: Houghton Mifflin. Copyright © 1970 by Time Share Corporation, New Hampshire.

STAGES OF OCCUPATIONAL DEVELOPMENT		
Stage	**Approximate ages**	**Key events and transitions**
Growth stage	**0–14**	**A period of general physical and mental growth**
Prevocational substage	0–3	No interest or concern with vocations
Fantasy substage	4–10	Fantasy is basis for vocational thinking
Interest substage	11–12	Vocational thought is based on individual's likes and dislikes
Capacity substage	13–14	Ability becomes the basis for vocational thought
Exploration stage	**15–24**	**General exploration of work**
Tentative substage	15–17	Needs, interests, capacities, values, and opportunities become bases for tentative occupational decisions
Transition substage	18–21	Reality increasingly becomes basis for vocational thought and action
Trial substage	22–24	First trial job is entered after the individual has made an initial vocational commitment
Establishment stage	**25–44**	**Individual seeks to enter a permanent occupation**
Trial substage	25–30	Period of some occupational change due to unsatisfactory choices
Stabilization substage	31–44	Period of stable work in a given occupational field
Maintenance stage	**45–65**	**Continuation in one's chosen occupation**
Decline stage	**65+**	**Adaptation to leaving workforce**
Deceleration substage	65–70	Period of declining vocational activity
Retirement substage	71+	A cessation of vocational activity

Exploration Stage

Pressures from parents, teachers, and peers to develop a general career direction begin to intensify during high school. By the end of high school, individuals are expected to turn a general career direction into a specific one. Young people try to get a sense of their intended occupation through reading about it or taking on part-time work. In effect, it's better to explore a particular career and discover it does not meet one's expectations sooner rather than later. Helwig (2008) found that while parent and teacher support are important, not enough career preparation occurs during the high school years, which means that the subsequent stage in Super's model becomes a very important one.

Establishment Stage

Vacillation in career commitment is common early in the establishment stage. Once people make gratifying occupational choices, their career commitment is strengthened. With few exceptions, future job moves will take place *within* the preferred occupational area. Having made a commitment, the person now needs to demonstrate the ability to function effectively in the area. To succeed, individuals must use known skills, learn new ones, and display flexibility in adapting to organizational and technological changes.

Maintenance Stage

Across time, opportunities for further career advancement and occupational mobility decline. However, both formal and informal forms of lifelong learning are often necessary so that workers can keep pace with the ever-changing aspects of their current and future jobs (Pang, Chua, & Chu, 2008). Around their mid-40s, many people cross into the maintenance stage, during which they worry more about *retaining* their achieved status than *improving* it. Although middle-aged employees may need to update their skills to compete with younger workers, their primary goal is to protect the security, power, advantages, and perks that they have attained. With decreased emphasis on career advancement, many people shift energy and attention away from work toward family or leisure activities.

Decline Stage

Deceleration involves a decline in work activity in the years prior to retirement. People redirect their energy and attention toward planning for this major transition. Super's original formulation, which was based on research in the 1950s, projected that deceleration ought to begin around age 65. Since the 1970s, however, the large Baby Boom cohort has created an oversupply of skilled labor and professional talent. This social change spawned pressures that promote early retirement, so deceleration often begins earlier than Super initially indicated. However, the recent economic recession and accompanying financial worries experienced by people in the United States and around the world may change things yet again. Individuals who lost their job or retirement savings may be planning a longer time horizon, so that career deceleration may not begin until closer to age 70.

Retirement brings work activity to a halt. People approach this transition with varied attitudes. Many individuals look forward to it eagerly. Others are apprehensive, unsure about how they will occupy themselves and worried about their financial viability. Still others approach retirement with both hopeful enthusiasm and anxious concern. Although retirement may mean less income, it can also mean more time to spend with friends and on hobbies, travel, and volunteer or charity work. For some, retirement from a primary career may prompt the launching of a new career.

In support of Super's model, research shows career maturity is correlated with self-esteem and self-efficacy (Creed, Prideaux, & Patton, 2005). A serious problem with Super's theory, however, is that it assumes that people will remain in the same careers all of their working lives. Today's American workers will have many career changes, a reality that is incompatible with the assumptions of long-term models like Super's. The current thinking about career stages or cycles is that they are shorter and recur periodically over the course of a person's career (Greenhaus, 2003). To be useful, stage models must reflect today's workplace realities while also providing career counseling that can help people to see meaning in their work and careers despite the reality of change (Sterner, 2012).

Women's Career Development

Currently, estimates are that 57.2% of adult women (versus 69.7% of men) are in the labor force (Bureau of Labor Statistics, 2013a). In terms of ethnicity, 99.5 million women of working age were white, 16.6 million were black or African American, 7.1 million were Asian, and 18.7 million were Hispanic or Latino (U.S. Bureau of Labor Statistics, 2013a,b). Will women's presence in the workforce rise? Between 2012 and 2022, the number of women present in the civilian labor force will increase by 5.4% (compared to an estimated 5.6% increase for men; U.S. Bureau of Labor Statistics, 2013c). However, women are estimated to represent only 46.8 % of the labor force by 2022 (U.S. Bureau of Labor Statistics, 2013c).

Gender also affects career paths. Men's career paths are usually *continuous*, whereas women's tend to be *discontinuous* (Betz, 1993). Thus, once men start working full-time, they usually continue to work. Women often interrupt their careers to concentrate on childrearing or family crises (Hynes & Clarkberg, 2005). Because women are having fewer children and are returning to work sooner, the amount of time they are out of the labor force is decreasing. Although labor force discontinuity is a factor in women's lower salaries and status, there is other evidence that women are simply paid less than men (Dey & Hill, 2007). Women who do not have children usually remain in the labor force, following a pattern of career advancement similar to men's (Blair-Loy & DeHart, 2003).

13.3 The Changing World of Work

Before entering the working world, it's important to get your bearings. In this section we look at several important background issues: contemporary workplace trends, the relationship between education and earnings, and workforce diversity.

Contemporary Workplace Trends

Work is an activity that produces something of value for others. For some people, work is just a way to earn a living; for others, work is a way of life (recall our discussion of jobs, careers, and callings). For virtually all workers, the nature of work is undergoing dramatic changes that are affecting people's identities (Crafford et al., 2015). Because such changes can affect your future job prospects, you need to be aware of seven important trends.

1. *Technology is changing the nature of work.* Computers and electronic equipment have dramatically transformed the workplace. For workers, these changes have both down sides and up sides. On the negative side, computers automate many tasks that people perform, eliminating jobs. The digital workplace also demands that employees have more education and skills than ever before. Workers must upgrade their technology skills, which can be stressful. On the positive side, technological advances allow employees to work at home and to communicate with others while traveling. Working at home when electronically connected to the office is called *telecommuting* (Lautsch, Kossek, & Ernst, 2011), and approximately 45% of organizations use some form of it (SHRM, 2011). Telecommuting provides psychological and practical benefits for workers, including lower levels of work-family life conflict, lower employee turnover, and higher job satisfaction (Gajendran & Harrison, 2007).

The growth of technology is significantly changing the nature of work, with both positive and negative effects.

Monty Rakusen/Cultura/Getty Images

2. *New work attitudes are required.* Yesterday's workers could usually count on job security, but today's workers have job security only as long as they can add value to a company; organizational change is a frequent event (Burke, 2011). Thus, workers must take a more active role in shaping their careers, developing a variety of valuable skills, being productive workers, and skillfully marketing themselves to prospective employers. In the new work environment, the keys to job success are self-direction, self-management, up-to-date knowledge and skills, flexibility, and mobility (Smith, 2000).

3. *Lifelong learning is a necessity.* Experts predict that today's jobs are changing so rapidly that in many cases, work skills will become obsolete over a 10- to 15-year period (Lock, 2005a). Thus, lifelong learning and training will become essential for employees (Boyer et al., 2014). Continuing education, retraining, and even self-directed learning can occur on the job, in community colleges, or in technical institutes. Online or distance learning courses also provide skill development and maintenance opportunities. Workers who know "how to learn" will be able to keep pace with change and will be highly valued. Those who cannot, may be left behind.

4. *Independent workers are increasing.* Corporations are downsizing and restructuring to cope with the changing economy and to be competitive globally. In doing so, they are slashing thousands of permanent jobs and doling out the work to temporary employees or to workers in other countries, a practice termed *outsourcing*. By reducing their workforce, companies can chop their expenditures on payroll, health insurance, and pension plans, as temporary employees don't typically receive such benefits. A leaner workforce also enables organizations to respond quickly to fast-changing markets. Many professionals now thrive on contract work, which, while often short-term, can provide freedom, flexibility, and high incomes. But for those who are short on skills and entrepreneurial spirit, this work can be stressful and risky. About one-third of independent employees would prefer to work for someone else than to work for themselves (Bond et al., 2003).

5. *The boundaries between work and home are disappearing.* As already noted, technological advances allow people to work at home and stay in touch with the office via the Internet or smartphones. Working at home is convenient—workers save time (no commuting) and money (on gas, parking, clothes). Still, family members and friends may interrupt home-workers, necessitating setting rules to protect work time. With expanding wireless networks, smartphones, and tablet computers, employees can be contacted anywhere and any time, making some workers feel they are on an "electronic leash." Looking at

Thinkstock/Stockbyte/Getty Images

People who telecommute have the flexibility to work at home.

TWENTY FASTEST GROWING OCCUPATIONS: 2012–2022	
Industrial-organizational psychologists	53%
Personal care aides	49%
Home health aides	48%
Insulation workers, mechanical	47%
Interpreters and translators	46%
Diagnostic medical sonographers	46%
Helpers—brickmasons, blockmasons, stonemasons, and tile and marble setters	43%
Occupational therapy assistants	43%
Genetic counselors	41%
Physical therapist assistants	41%
Physical therapist aides	40%
Skincare specialists	40%
Physician assistants	38%
Segmental pavers	38%
Helpers—electricians	37%
Information security analysts	37%
Occupational therapy aides	36%
Health specialties teachers, postsecondary	36%
Medical secretaries	36%
Physical therapists	36%

Figure 13.4

The twenty fastest-growing occupations. According to the U.S. Bureau of Labor Statistics, the occupations listed are expected to show a large increase in job openings between 2012 and 2022. The percentages represent the rate of expanded growth in the number of people holding these occupations by 2022.

Source: Adapted from the Occupational Outlook Handbook (2014). Bureau of Labor Statistics: Fastest growing occupations, 2012–2022. Retrieved from www.bls.gov/ooh/fastest-growing.htm.

the flip side, the availability of onsite day care in some large companies means that a traditional home function has moved to the office (Payne, Cook, & Diaz, 2012). This development is largely a response to increases in the number of single-parent families and *dual-earner households,* **in which both partners are employed.** Consider this fact: More than 70% of today's workers have children younger than the age of 18 (U.S. Bureau of the Census, 2012b). Thus, quality onsite day care is a big draw to workers because it allows parents to interact with their children during the day.

6. *The highest job growth will occur in the professional and service occupations.* The United States, like many industrialized nations, continues to shift from a manufacturing, or "goods-producing," economy to a service-producing one (U.S. Bureau of Labor Statistics, 2006). Whereas the bulk of yesterday's jobs were in manufacturing, construction, agriculture, and mining, the jobs of the next decade will be in the professional (and related technical) occupations and service occupations. **Figure 13.4** depicts twenty occupations expected to grow the fastest between 2012 and 2022 (Occupational Outlook Handbook, 2014).

7. *Job sharing is becoming more common.* Not everyone wants to work a 40-hour week or can do so. Having the opportunity to job share—that is, sharing one job between two people—may be beneficial to workers' well-being (Westman, 2010). Approximately 13% of organizations currently provide this option (Society for Human Resource Management, 2011). Job sharing often occurs when both spouses work in similar professions. For example, high school teaching is a good fit; the husband, a history instructor, can teach his classes in the morning, while his wife, a math teacher, can schedule her courses in the afternoons. When sharing a job, each person usually works 20 hours per week at separate times. A few hours per week may be conjoined so that each partner can update the other, as well as meet with their supervisor and other workforce members. Job sharing is ideal for couples who have small children or other family obligations (caring for elderly parents), are enrolled in degree programs, want to work part-time, or are considering gradually winding down their careers. Employers like job sharing because it promotes commitment to the organization while also attracting well-qualified individuals who could not otherwise accept a full-time position.

Education and Earnings

Although many jobs exist for individuals without a college degree, these jobs usually offer the lowest pay and benefits. In fact, all but one of the fifty highest-paying occupations require a college degree or higher (U.S. Bureau of Labor Statistics, 2004). (The high-paying job that doesn't require a college degree is air traffic controller.) Many construction management jobs, too, do not require a bachelor's degree (U.S. Bureau of Labor Statistics, 2012a). In **Figure 13.5**, you can see that the more you learn, the more you earn. Having a college degree is also associated with more career options, greater opportunities for professional advancement, and lower unemployment (Dohm & Wyatt, 2002). The link between learning and earning holds for both males and females, although, as you can see, men are paid approximately $7000 to $30,000 more than women with the same educational credentials. Despite legislation aimed at reducing discrepancies related to gender, research indicates that women continue to receive lower wages than men for holding the same or similar jobs (Lips, 2013). One estimate indicates that women are now earning about 79% of what men earn (AAUW, 2015).

On the other hand, a college degree is no guarantee of a great job. In fact, many college graduates are underemployed. *Underemployment* **is settling for a job that does**

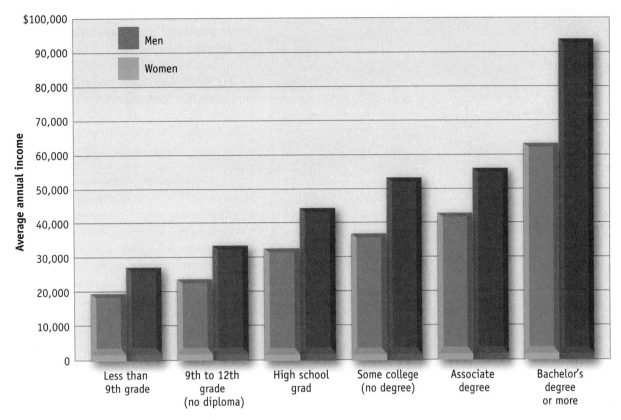

Figure 13.5

Education and income. This graph shows the average incomes of year-round, full-time workers age 18 and older, by gender and educational attainment. As you can see, the more education people have, the higher their income tends to be. However, at all levels women earn less than men with comparable education. (Data from U.S. Bureau of the Census, 2012a)

Source: U.S. Bureau of the Census. (2012). *Statistical abstract of the United States: 2012*. Washington, DC: U.S. Government Printing Office.

not fully utilize one's skills, abilities, and training. Besides having implications for worker satisfaction, underemployment poses social, psychological, and physical health challenges (Anderson & Winefield, 2011). About 48% of college graduates take jobs that don't usually require a college degree, and experts predict that this situation is unlikely to change in the near future (Adams, 2013). And while it's true that the jobs one can obtain with a college degree pay more than those requiring less education, the higher-paying jobs go to college graduates with *college-level* reading, writing, and quantitative skills. College graduates without these skills more often end up in high-school-level jobs (Pryor & Schaffer, 1997).

Workforce Diversity

The *labor force* consists of all those who are employed, as well as those who are currently unemployed but are looking for work. In this section, we look at some of the demographic changes affecting the labor force and consider how women and other minorities fare in the workplace.

Demographic Changes

The workforce is becoming increasingly diverse with regard to both gender and ethnicity. In 2005, 61% of married women worked, compared to 41% in 1970 (U.S. Bureau of the Census, 2012a). This percentage increase holds even for women with very young children. For instance, in 1975 only 33% of women with children younger than the age of 3 worked outside the home; by 2005, this number had grown to 57% (U.S. Bureau of the Census, 2012b).

Learn More Online

U.S. Department of Labor
With primary responsibility for many job- and work-related matters in the U.S. government, the Labor Department offers a site that can serve as a base to explore a variety of topics, including wages and compensation, worker productivity, and the legal rights of workers (such as protection from sexual harassment).

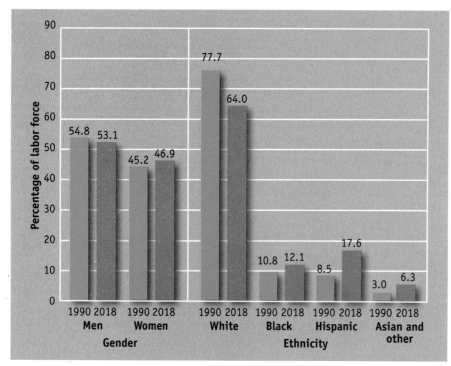

Figure 13.6

Increasing diversity in the workforce. Women and minority group members are entering the workforce in greater numbers than before. This graph projects changes in the share of the labor force by gender and by ethnicity between 1990 and 2018, according to the U.S. Bureau of Labor Statistics. (Data from Toossi, 2009)

The workforce is also becoming more ethnically diversified (see **Figure 13.6**) (U.S. Bureau of Labor Statistics, 2006). High school graduation rates for Asian Americans match those for European Americans, but college graduation rates for Asian Americans exceed those of European Americans. Both high school and college graduation rates of Hispanics and African Americans lag behind those of European Americans, although they have been improving in recent decades (Worthington, Flores, & Navarro, 2005). Consequently, both groups are at a disadvantage when it comes to competing for the better jobs.

Although gay, lesbian, and bisexual workers have been longstanding participants in the workplace, they are often "closeted" for fear of discrimination. The recent and rapid cultural changes in the United States, notably the 2015 Supreme Court Decision declaring the legality of same-sex marriage, will likely change things. Yet, most gay and lesbian workers do not have the same legal protections against employment discrimination as their heterosexual counterparts (Barron & Hebl, 2011); thus, wage gaps can exist because of sexual orientation. One study suggests that gay men tend to earn somewhat less than heterosexual men, while lesbians may earn somewhat more than heterosexual women (Antecol, Jong, & Steinberger, 2008), findings that were confirmed in a separate study concerning the sexual orientation wage gap for racial minorities (Douglas & Steinberger, 2015). Regrettably, wage penalties may be associated with disclosing one's sexual orientation (Cushing-Daniels & Tsz-Ying, 2009). Factors associated with the decision to disclose one's sexual orientation at work include employer policies and perceived gay supportiveness of the employer (Griffith & Hebl, 2002).

John Browne, the long-time chief executive of British Petroleum and close associate of former British Prime Minister Tony Blair, had little choice but to resign after a judge cleared the way for a newspaper to publish allegations made by a former boyfriend. The exposé of Browne's private life ended his 41-year career at British Petroleum. The stunning demise of Browne's career demonstrates why many gay individuals choose to remain "closeted" in the workplace out of concern about recrimination.

Today's Workplace for Women and Minorities

Recent years have seen a dramatic upsurge in the number of females and ethnic minorities in the workplace. Is today's workplace essentially the same for these groups as it is for white males? The answer appears to be "no" (Denmark, German, & Brodsky, 2011). Although job discrimination based on race and gender has been illegal for more than 40 years, women and minority group members continue to face obstacles to occupational success. Foremost among these obstacles is *job segregation*. Jobs are simultaneously typed by gender and by race. For example, skycaps are typically African American males, and most hotel maids are minority females. Most white women and minority workers tend to be concentrated in jobs where there is little opportunity for advancement or increase in salary (Equal Employment Opportunity Commission, 2007). As a result, they lag behind men where key dimensions of job quality are concerned, such as opportunities to achieve autonomy over time, job security, and good physical and emotional work settings (Stier & Yaish, 2014). However, there is reason for hope. As the relative share of occupational positions held by women increases, the existing gender gaps in job quality dimensions should decrease.

More women and ethnic minorities are entering higher-status occupations, but they still face discrimination because they are frequently *passed over for promotion* in favor of white men (Whitley & Kite, 2006). This seems to be a problem especially at higher levels of management. For example, in 2013, about 14.6% of corporate officer positions in Fortune 500 companies were held by women (Catalyst, 2014), a percentage that has not changed much over the past 5 years. An earlier estimate found that only about 1.5% were held by women of color (Catalyst, 2007), who also hold only 3.2% of all the board seats of Fortune 500 companies (Warner, 2014). Furthermore, discrimination toward women and ethnic and other minorities (gays, lesbians) is now more covert, subtle, and indirect (Nadal & Haynes, 2012). Employers and fellow employees are less likely to display overt discriminatory behaviors. Instead, however, they may hold onto prejudices that leak out unconsciously in exchanges with members of diverse groups (Nadal, 2008).

There appears to be a *glass ceiling,* **or invisible barrier that prevents most women and ethnic minorities from advancing to the highest levels of occupations.** That very few black women are in managerial positions has caused some to term the glass ceiling a *concrete wall* for women of color. Women are underrepresented at the upper levels of corporate life (Barreto, Ryan, & Schmitt, 2009). Largely because of these reduced opportunities for career advancement, some female corporate managers are quitting their jobs and starting their own firms. In 2007, women owned 28.7% of nonfarm U.S. businesses (National Association of Women Business Owners, 2010). At the other end of the job spectrum, there seems to be a *sticky floor* that causes women and minorities to get stuck in low-paying occupations (Brannon, 2005).

When only one woman or minority person is employed in an office, that person becomes a *token*—**or a symbol of all the members of that group.** Tokens are more distinctive or visible than members of the dominant majority (Richard & Wright, 2010). And, as we discussed in Chapter 7, distinctiveness makes a person's actions subject to intense scrutiny, stereotyping, and judgments. Thus, if a white male makes a mistake, it is explained as an *individual* problem. When a token woman or minority person errs, it is seen as evidence that *all* members of that group are incompetent. Hence, tokens experience a great deal of *performance pressure,* an added source of job stress (King et al., 2010). There is even evidence that women who believe they are tokens in a work setting perceive they receive less support from same-gender rather than opposite-gender supervisors (Ryan et al., 2012). Interestingly, if tokens are perceived as being "too successful," they may be labeled "workaholics" or may be accused of trying to "show up" members of the dominant majority.

The Challenges of Change

The increasingly diverse workforce presents challenges for organizations and workers (Podsiadlowski et al., 2013). These challenges can occur within the workplace, as well as within the community where the workplace and workers reside. Important cultural differences exist in managing time and people, in identifying with work, and in making decisions (Konyu-Fogel, 2015). These differences can contribute to conflict. Not surprisingly, perhaps, members of majority groups (generally white males) do not perceive discrimination as often as the members of minority groups do (Danaher & Branscombe, 2010). Another challenge is that some individuals feel that they are personally paying the price of prejudice in the workplace, and this perception causes resentment. Recognizing the problem, some corporations offer diversity training programs for employees (Green, 2013; Roberson, Kulik, & Tan, 2013).

Many who advocate abandoning affirmative action programs that are intended to promote access to jobs for women and minorities argue that these programs promote "reverse discrimination" through the use of unfair hiring and promotion practices (Thompson & Morris, 2013). For some, this perception reflects a sense of *privilege,* an unquestioned assumption that white males should be guaranteed a place in society and that others should compete for the remaining jobs (Nkomo & Ariss, 2014). Not surprisingly, women and ethnic minority group members hold more positive views of affirmative action than do males and nonminority group members (Harrison et al., 2006). Some also argue that affirmative action undercuts the role of merit in employment decisions and sets up (supposedly) underprepared workers for failure. Many laboratory studies show that individuals have negative feelings about employees who may have been hired under affirmative action (Brandts, Groenert, & Rott, 2015). However, studies conducted with actual workers have not found this situation (Taylor, 1995). Regardless, this potential negative effect can be counteracted when workers know that decisions are based on merit as well as on group membership.

13.4 Coping with Occupational Hazards

Work can bring people deep satisfaction; indeed, it can promote psychological health and well-being (Duffy, Autin, & Bott, 2015). Yet work can also be a source of frustration and conflict. In this section, we explore three challenges to today's workers: job stress, sexual harassment, and unemployment.

Job Stress

You saw in Chapter 3 that stress can emerge from any corner of your life. However, many theorists suspect that the workplace is the primary source of stress in modern society. To begin, let's consider this sobering statistic: More than 80% of the workers in the United States claim that something about their jobs is stressful (Smith, 2014). To put this statistic into context, let's compare the typical stressors experienced by younger adults (ages 17–21) and those of older (25+), working adults. As you can see in the left column of **Figure 13.7**, younger people are troubled more by personal stressors, whereas older adults are troubled primarily by work-related stressors (right column). Let's examine the pervasive problem of job stress and see what employers and workers can do about it.

COMMON STRESSORS FOUND IN YOUNGER AND OLDER ADULTS	
Young adults (age 17–21)	**Older adults (age 25 and beyond)**
Graduating from high school	Organizational change
Beginning college	Job insecurity (downsizing)
Leaving home	Balancing work and family demands
Nagging parents	Paying bills
Peer pressure	Increasing job demands
Taking exams	Dull or unchallenging work
Fear of the future	Work overload (time pressure)
Graduating from college	Lack of supervisor or co-worker support
Job search	Unpleasant or dangerous work settings
Starting a new job	Pay inequity
Interviewing for jobs	Attending school while working full time
Financial concerns (school loans)	Job relocation
Other financial concerns	Planning for retirement

Figure 13.7

Common stressors found in younger and older adults. Compare and contrast the typical sources of stress reported by younger and older adults. Do any of these stressors reflect your own experiences? As you can see, as people get older, their stress increasingly comes from work-related issues.

Adapted from Aamodt, M. (2010). *Industrial/organizational psychology: An applied approach*. Belmont, CA: Wadsworth/Cengage. © 2010 Wadsworth, a part of Cengage Learning, Inc.

Sources of Stress on the Job

In addition to long hours, common job stressors include lack of privacy, high noise levels, unusual hours (such as rotating shifts), the pressure of deadlines, lack of control over one's work, inadequate resources to do a job, and perceived inequities at work (Fairbrother & Warn, 2003). Environmental conditions, such as workplace temperature (e.g., extreme heat in a steel mill, excessive cold in a meat-packing plant), can affect physical, cognitive, and perceptual tasks (Evans et al., 2012). Fears of being downsized, concerns about health-care benefits (losing them or paying increasingly higher premiums), and worries about losing pension plans also dog workers in today's economy (Clay, 2011). Office politics and conflict with supervisors, subordinates, and co-workers also make the list of job stressors (Chang, Rosen, & Levy, 2009).

Women may experience certain workplace stressors, such as sex discrimination and sexual harassment, at higher rates than men (Betz, 2008). African Americans and ethnic minorities must cope with racism and other types of discrimination on the job (Betz, 2006), which means members of minority groups may experience higher levels of stress than nonminorities do (Sulsky & Smith, 2005). Discrimination is also a problem for gay and lesbian employees (Badgett, 2003). Workers from lower socioeconomic groups typically work in more dangerous jobs than workers from higher socioeconomic status do.

Why are American workers so stressed out? Many factors are probably at work, including the following.

1. *More workers are employed in service industries.* Workers in these jobs must interact with a variety of individuals on a daily basis. While most customers are civil and easy to deal with, some are decidedly difficult. Nonetheless, even obnoxious and troublesome customers are "always right," so workers have to swallow their frustration and anger, and doing so is stressful. Such situations may contribute to residual stress, where strain and tension from work are carried over because workers have a hard time "letting go." Imagine the frustration some workers must feel if their jobs do not allow them to be "right" or to speak candidly to customers.

2. *The economy is unpredictable.* In the age of takeovers and bankruptcies, even excellent workers aren't assured of keeping their jobs. Change in response to economic pressures often comes in the form of downsizing, restructuring, and job insecurity (De Witte, Vander Elst, & De Cuyper, 2015). Thus, the fear of job loss may lurk in the back of workers' minds.

3. *Rapid changes in computer technology tax workers' abilities to keep up.* Computers have taken over some jobs, forcing workers to develop new skills and to do so quickly. In other jobs, the stress comes from rapid and ongoing advances in technology (software as well as hardware) that force workers to keep pace with change.

4. *The workplace is becoming more diverse.* Individuals from all groups must learn to interact more with people who are unfamiliar to them. Developing these skills takes time and may be stressful.

5. *Role overload.* Amid all this organizational change and disruption, some workers feel that they lack the skills or resources to complete their work tasks, often coupled with the fact that the tasks are simply not doable in the available time (or the workers perceive it that way). Such role overload is not only stressful (Bolino & Turnley, 2005), but it can compromise workers' health (Shultz, Wang, & Olson, 2010).

Taking a broader view, Robert Karasek contends that the two key factors in occupational stress are the *psychological demands* made on a worker and a worker's amount of *decision control* (Dollard & Karasek, 2010). Psychological demands are measured by asking employees questions such as "Is there excessive work?" and "Must you work fast (or hard)?" To measure decision control, employees are asked such questions as "Do you have a lot of say in your job?" and "Do you have freedom to make decisions?" In Karasek's demand-control model, *stress is greatest in jobs characterized by high psychological demands and low decision control.* Based on survey data, he has tentatively mapped out where various jobs fall on these two key dimensions of job stress, as shown in **Figure 13.8**. The jobs thought to be most stressful are those with heavy psychological demands and little control over decisions (see the lower right area of the figure). Considerable research has been conducted on the demand-control model, most of which has been supportive (Sonnentag & Frese, 2003).

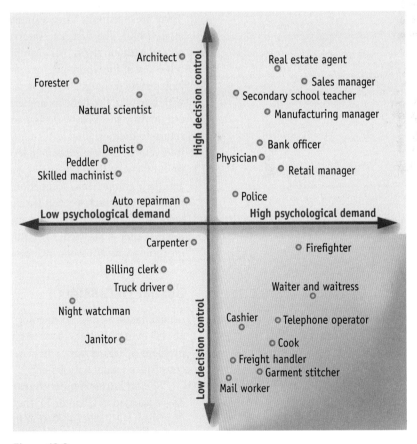

Figure 13.8

Karasek's model of occupational stress as related to specific jobs. Robert Karasek (1979) theorizes that occupational stress is greatest in jobs characterized by high psychological demands and low decision control. Based on survey data, this chart shows where various familiar jobs fall on these two dimensions. According to Karasek's model, the most stressful jobs are those shown in the shaded area on the lower right.

COMMON SIGNS OF BURNOUT AMONG WORKERS	
Low energy	Negativity and complaining attitude
Lessened productivity	Increased forgetfulness
Apathy	Dread of going to work
Routinely late for work	Sense of being overwhelmed
Limited concentration	Frustration and tension
Feelings of low impact on organization or peers	

Figure 13.9

Common signs of job burnout among workers. Here are some of the commonly observed symptoms of stress-induced burnout, a physical and psychological condition that is marked by fatigue, pessimism, and a lowered quality of work or job performance. Burnout is most likely to occur when the stress and strain of work are continuous rather than occasional or sporadic.

(Adapted from Aamodt, M. (2010). *Industrial/organizational psychology: An applied approach.* Belmont, CA: Wadsworth/Cengage. © 2010 Wadsworth, a part of Cengage Learning, Inc.)

Effects of Job Stress

As with other forms of stress, occupational stress is associated with numerous negative effects (Hurrell & Sauter, 2012). Job stress has been linked to an increased number of industrial accidents, heightened absenteeism, poor job performance, and higher turnover rates (Colligan & Higgins, 2005). Experts estimate that stress-related reductions in workers' productivity may cost American industry hundreds of billions of dollars per year. Just under 3% of the workforce is absent on any given workday in the United States (Bureau of Labor Statistics, 2014), and 13% of all employee absences can be chalked up to the impact of stress (Commerce Clearing House, 2007).

When job stress is temporary (a looming deadline), workers usually suffer only minor, brief effects of stress, such as sleeplessness or anxiety. Prolonged high levels of stress are more problematic, as those who work in people-oriented jobs such as human services, education, and health care can attest (Maslach, 2005). A chief reason for the prevalence of burnout in these professions is the ongoing amount of "people work," that is, performing the emotional labor required by clients, customers, students, and patients (Brotherridge & Grandey, 2002). As we noted in Chapter 3, prolonged stress can lead to *burnout*, characterized by exhaustion, cynicism, and poor job performance (Leiter, Bakker, & Maslach, 2014; Maslach, & Leiter, 2014). People's personalities and the nature of the work and careers they choose, too, can influence burnout (Lohmer, 2012). **Figure 13.9** lists some of the most common signs of burnout among workers.

Dealing with Job Stress

There are essentially three avenues of attack for dealing with occupational stress (Ivancevich et al., 1990). The first is to intervene at the *individual* level by modifying workers' ways of coping with job stress. For example, workers often try to deal with job stress by taking themselves out of the workplace for a short time, such as taking a vacation. Although vacations can help people recharge their professional batteries by reducing stress and the feelings associated with burnout, the benefits are temporary. Research indicates symptoms of stress and burnout do drop just before, during, and immediately following vacations; however, they tend to return to their original levels a few weeks later (de Bloom et al., 2010, 2011). The second is to intervene at the *organizational* level by redesigning the work environment itself. The third is to intervene at the *individual-organizational interface* by improving the fit between workers and their companies. Occupational stress and burnout can be treated, ideally by ensuring a proactive approach where a strong fit between work demands and worker strengths is made, work-family balance is sought, and resources for coping are present in the workplace and the home (Leiter & Maslach, 2014; Rupert, Miller, & Dorociak, 2015). Other concrete suggestions for coping with stressors, including those found in the workplace, are discussed in Chapter 4.

Sexual Harassment

Sexual harassment is an ongoing problem in the workplace (Gibbons, Cleveland & Marsh, 2014; Levin & Rotter, 2014). Although most workers recognize that they need to take the problem of sexual harassment seriously, many people remain relatively naive about what constitutes sexual harassment.

Sexual harassment **is characterized by unwelcome conduct on the basis of gender.** As we learned in Chapter 11, there are two types of sexual harassment. The first is *quid pro quo* (from the Latin expression that translates as "something given or received in exchange for something else"). In the context of sexual harassment, quid pro quo involves making submission to unwanted sexual advances a condition of hiring, advancement (raise, promotion), or not being fired. In other words, the worker's survival on the job depends on agreeing to engage in unwanted sex. The second type of harassment is *hostile environment*, or any type of unwelcome sexual behavior that creates hostile work situations that can inflict psychological harm and interfere with job performance.

Sexual harassment can take a variety of forms: unsolicited and unwelcome flirting, sexual advances, or propositions; insulting comments about an employee's appearance, dress, or anatomy; unappreciated dirty jokes and sexual gestures; intrusive or sexual questions about an employee's personal life; explicit descriptions of the harasser's own sexual experiences; abuse of familiarities such as "honey" and "dear"; unnecessary and unwanted physical contact such as touching, hugging, pinching, or kissing; catcalls; exposure of genitals; physical or sexual assault; and rape. Sexual harassment is an abuse of power by a person in authority (Elias, Gibson, & Barney, 2013). To determine what legally constitutes sexual harassment, the courts take into account "whether the behavior is motivated by the gender of the victim, whether it is unwelcome, whether it is repetitive, and whether it could lead to negative psychological or organizational outcomes" (Goldberg & Zhang, 2004, p. 823). Same-sex sexual harassment also occurs and is prosecuted according to the same standards applied in opposite-sex sexual harassment, although little research has been done on the topic (but see Rabelo & Cortina, 2014).

Prevalence and Consequences

Sexual harassment in the workplace is more widespread than most people realize, but the topic is now better understood because of increased research attention (O'Leary-Kelly et al., 2009). By one estimate, nearly one-quarter of all women in the United States have experienced some form of sexual harassment in the workplace (Ilies et al., 2003). A reasonable estimate for male workers is 16.3% (Catalyst, 2012). The typical female victim is young, divorced or separated, in a nonsenior position, and in a masculine-stereotyped field (Davidson & Fielden, 1999). A review of studies on women in the military reported rates of sexual harassment ranging from 55% to 79% (Goldzweig et al., 2006). Women in blue-collar jobs are also at high risk, but sexual harassment also occurs in the professions. Sadly, sexual harassment is often associated with other forms of workplace discrimination for blacks and other ethnic or minority groups (Rospenda, Richman, & Shannon, 2009).

Unfortunately, sexual harassment is all too common in the workplace. Both men and women can be the targets of this unwanted form of workplace discrimination.

Experiencing sexual harassment can have negative effects on psychological and physical health (Pina & Gannon, 2012). Problematic reactions include anger, reduced self-esteem, depression, and anxiety. Victims may also have difficulties in their personal relationships and in sexual adjustment (loss of desire, for example). Increased alcohol consumption, smoking, and dependence on drugs are also reported (Rospenda et al., 2008). In addition, sexual harassment can produce fallout on the job: Women who are harassed may be less productive, less satisfied with their jobs, and less committed to their work and employer (Woodzicka & LaFrance, 2005). Women who are sexually harassed also report lower job satisfaction and may withdraw from work as the result of physical and mental health problems. Some of these women are even found to display symptoms of posttraumatic stress disorder (Willness, Steel, & Lee, 2007). Finally, sexual harassment can heighten the incidence of job withdrawal while decreasing job satisfaction and undermining an individual's organizational commitment (Kath et al., 2009).

Stopping Sexual Harassment

Responses to sexual harassment may be personal and organizational. Researchers have developed a typology of possible responses to this problem (see **Figure 13.10**) and have studied their relative effectiveness (Bowes-Sperry & Tata, 1999). Unfortunately, the most frequently used strategy—avoidance/denial—is also the least effective one. Confrontation/negotiation and advocacy seeking are two effective strategies but are infrequently used.

One recent experiment with college students found that learning about how victims of sexual harassment suffered led to a reduction in both the acceptance of myths about sexual harassment (e.g., "Jokes about sex never hurt anybody—they are being too sensitive") and men's likelihood to sexually harass (Diehl, Glaser, & Bohner, 2014). When seeing things from the victims' perspectives, participants also expressed higher levels of empathy. Although this research was conducted in a controlled lab situation, the investigators hope that insights

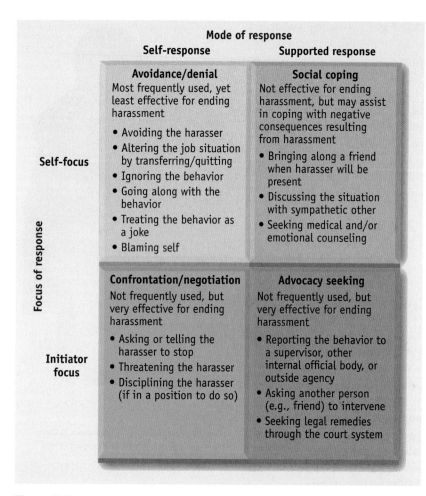

Mode of response

Self-response	Supported response
Avoidance/denial Most frequently used, yet least effective for ending harassment • Avoiding the harasser • Altering the job situation by transferring/quitting • Ignoring the behavior • Going along with the behavior • Treating the behavior as a joke • Blaming self	**Social coping** Not effective for ending harassment, but may assist in coping with negative consequences resulting from harassment • Bringing along a friend when harasser will be present • Discussing the situation with sympathetic other • Seeking medical and/or emotional counseling
Confrontation/negotiation Not frequently used, but very effective for ending harassment • Asking or telling the harasser to stop • Threatening the harasser • Disciplining the harasser (if in a position to do so)	**Advocacy seeking** Not frequently used, but very effective for ending harassment • Reporting the behavior to a supervisor, other internal official body, or outside agency • Asking another person (e.g., friend) to intervene • Seeking legal remedies through the court system

Self-focus (top row), Initiator focus (bottom row). Focus of response (vertical axis label).

Figure 13.10

Effectiveness of responses to sexual harassment. Responses to sexual harassment can be classified into four categories based on the focus of the response (directed toward self or toward the harasser) and the mode of the response (involving the self or others). Unfortunately, the most frequent reactions turn out to be the least helpful. Effective strategies are available, but they are infrequently used.

Source: From Bowes-Sperry, L., & Tata, J. (1999). A multiperspective framework of sexual harassment. In G. N. Powell (Ed.), *Handbook of gender and work* (pp. 263–280). Thousand Oaks, CA: Sage Publications.

from it can be used to design workplace interventions to reduce the incidence of sexual harassment.

Unemployment

A major consequence of recent economic upheavals is *displaced workers*—individuals who are unemployed because their jobs have disappeared. Losing one's job is difficult at best and devastating at worst, ranking among the most stressful events a person can experience. As of June 2015, the unemployment rate was 5.3% (U.S. Bureau of Labor Statistics, 2015a), a drop from previous highs (in late 2012, for example, it was around 8.1%; U.S. Bureau of Labor Statistics, 2012b). Still, many Americans have found themselves out of work and continue to worry about their futures. Not only can unemployment cause economic distress, but it can cause health problems and such psychological difficulties as loss of self-esteem, depression, and anxiety (Wanberg, 2012). A meta-analysis found that the rate of psychological problems was more than doubled among unemployed persons compared to those who were working (Paul & Moser, 2009). Also, the rate of attempted and completed suicides is higher among those who are unemployed (Yang, Tsai, & Huang, 2011). Longer unemployment is also a risk factor linked with higher rates of suicide (Classen & Dunn, 2012). Gender, however, does not affect the amount of distress experienced as the result of job loss (Kulik, 2000). Even "survivors," those who retain their jobs following a round of layoffs during downsizing, are not immune from psychological distress (Paulsen et al., 2005).

Although losing a job at any age is highly stressful, those who are laid off in middle age seem to find the experience most difficult (Breslin & Mustard, 2003). For one thing, they typically have more financial responsibilities than those in other age groups (e.g., children still at home). Second, if other family members aren't able to provide health insurance, the entire family's health and welfare is jeopardized. Third, older workers typically remain out of work longer than younger workers. Thus, economic hardship can be a real possibility and can threaten quality of life for the worker's family. Finally, middle-aged workers have been on the job for a number of years, which means they identify with and are involved in their work.

Coping with Unemployment

Mental health experts view job loss as a devastating life experience—similar to death, divorce, and serious illness or disability. Foremost, people are hit with the frightening prospect of loss of income and must deal with the stressful practicalities of how to live on less. Job loss also deals a psychological blow because it strikes at a key component of adult identity—having a job, which provides purpose as well as an income. And victims of downsizing must deal with the anger and resentment that stem from the unfairness of the situation.

Understandably, job loss negatively affects mental health (Shupe & Buchholz, 2013; Ziersch et al., 2014) and is associated with decreases in self-confidence, feelings of failure and rejection, and increases in anxiety and depression (Bobek & Robbins, 2005). Some experts suggest that individuals' reactions to job loss are similar to what they experience when they confront their own death (Bobek & Robbins, 2005).

For some practical suggestions for coping with job loss, we draw on the advice of career experts Laskoff (2004) and Lock (2005b).

1. *Apply for unemployment benefits as soon as possible.* The average length of unemployment in June 2015 was 28.1 weeks (U.S. Bureau of Labor Statistics, 2015b). Thus, you need to look into unemployment benefits, which you may be able to collect for 26 weeks (or longer in some cases). Contact the nearest office of your state's Employment Security Commission or Department of Labor.

2. *Determine your income and expenses.* Determine precisely your sources of income (unemployment benefits, spouse or partner's income, savings) and how much you can count on per month. Itemize your monthly expenses. Set up a realistic budget and stick to it. Talk with your creditors if you need to.

3. *Lower your expenses and think of ways to bring in extra income.* Cut out unnecessary expenses for now. Minimize your credit card purchases and pay off the credit card bills every month to avoid building up huge debt. For extra income, consider selling a car, having a garage sale, or putting items up for sale on Craigslist or for auction on eBay. Use your skills as a temporary or seasonal worker.

4. *Stay healthy.* To save money on medical expenses, eat well-balanced meals, maintain an exercise regimen, and get adequate sleep. Keep yourself in a positive frame of mind by recalling past successes and imagining future ones.

5. *Reach out for support.* Although it is difficult to do, explain your job situation to your family and friends. You need their support, and they need to know how your unemployment will affect them. If you are having relationship problems, consult a counselor. Let your friends know that you are looking for work; they may have job leads.

6. *Get organized and get going.* Start by setting aside time and space to work on your job search. Is your résumé up to date? Can you find a similar job, or do you need to think about other options? Do you need to relocate? Do you need more education or retraining? Some people decide to go into business for themselves, so don't overlook this option. Check out some of the excellent career planning books (see this chapter's recommended reading, *What Color Is Your Parachute?*, for example) and visit relevant websites. Expect to spend 15 to 25 hours a week on job-searching activities.

13.5 Balancing Work and Other Spheres of Life

Learning Objectives

- Articulate current perspectives on workaholism.
- Explain work-family conflict and discuss the benefits of multiple roles.
- Define *leisure* and list several leisure activities.

A major challenge for individuals today is balancing work, family, and leisure activities in ways that are personally satisfying (Major & Morganson, 2011). We noted earlier that dual-earner families are becoming increasingly common and that the traditional boundaries between family and paid work life are breaking down. These two developments are related. Historically, traditional gender roles assigned women's work to the home and men's work outside the home. This division of labor created boundaries between family and work life. With more women entering the workforce, these boundaries have become blurred. The technology-based changes in the workplace are also eroding these distinctions between family and work life. Here we examine three issues related to balancing various life roles: workaholism, work and family roles, and leisure and recreation.

Workaholism

Workaholics devote nearly all their time and energy to their jobs; for them, work is addictive (Andreassen, 2015). They put in lots of overtime, take few vacations, regularly bring work home, sacrifice other roles in their lives, and think about work constantly, yet they may not necessarily enjoy the job (Ng, Sorenson, & Feldman, 2007). They are energetic, intense, and ambitious, which are generally positive traits; however, two unfavorable traits, perfectionism and negative emotionality, also predict workaholism (Bovornusvakool et al., 2012).

"If only I'd thought to take my damn phone with me, I could be getting some work done."

Besides personal factors, situational forces can promote workaholism (Aziz & Burke, 2015). Thus, it is more common where organizational climates support imbalances between work and personal life (Burke, 2001). Research finds a link between workaholism and aggression (interpersonal conflict) in the workplace (Balducci et al., 2012). Workaholism has even been labeled a 21st-century addiction (Griffths, 2011).

Psychologists are divided on the issue of whether workaholism is problematic. Should workaholics be praised for their dedication and encouraged in their single-minded pursuit of fulfillment through work (Baruch, 2011)? Or is workaholism a form of addiction (Shifron & Reysen, 2011), a sign that an individual is driven by uncontrollable compulsions? In support of the former view is evidence that some workaholics tend to be highly satisfied with their jobs and with their lives (Bonebright, Clay, & Ankenmann, 2000). They work hard simply because work is the most meaningful activity they know. Yet other evidence suggests that workaholics may have poorer emotional and physical well-being than nonworkaholics (Bonebright et al., 2000). How can these conflicting findings be reconciled?

There may be two types of workaholics (Aziz & Zickar, 2006). One type, the *enthusiastic workaholic*, works for the pure joy of it. Such people derive immense satisfaction from work and generally perform well in highly demanding jobs. They also qualify as being high in *work engagement*, an emerging positive and fulfilling construct linked to absorption in work (Shimazu et al., 2015). The other type, the *nonenthusiastic workaholic*, feels driven to work but reports low job enjoyment. Moreover, these people report lower life satisfaction and less purpose in life than enthusiastic workaholics. Thus, it is not surprising that the nonenthusiastic group is more likely to develop *burnout* (Maslach, 2005).

Both types of workaholics experience an imbalance between work and personal time. Not surprisingly, this situation translates into a high degree of work-family conflict for both groups (Shimazu, Kubota, & Bakker, 2015). Moreover, the families of both groups suffer (Robinson, Flowers, & Ng, 2006).

Work and Family Roles

One of the biggest changes in the labor force has been the emergence of dual-earner households, now the dominant family form in the United States (U.S. Bureau of the Census, 2006). Dual-earner couples struggle to balance family life and work demands. These changes in work and family life draw the interest of researchers in many disciplines, including psychology.

Being pulled between the needs of the workplace and the needs of the family is a cause of conflict for many of today's workers.

An important fact of life for dual-earner couples is juggling *multiple roles*: spouse/partner and employee. TICKS (two-income couples with kids) add a third role: parent. Thus, today's working parents experience **work-family conflict, or the feeling of being pulled in multiple directions by competing demands from job and family.** In heterosexual dual-earner families, men are taking on more household chores and childcare, but most wives still have greater responsibilities in these areas (Drago, 2007) and neither spouse may accurately recognize the work-family conflict experienced by the other (Nomaguchi & Milkie, 2015). In gay and lesbian dual-earner households, responsibilities are more evenly divided (Kurdek, 2005). Single parents are especially likely to have work-family conflicts.

How does work-family conflict affect workers' quality of sleep, an important factor in both physical and mental health? The lack of consistent sleep is a factor that can have consequences for performance in the workplace and at home. This issue is the focus of this chapter's Spotlight on Research.

Work-Family Conflict's Connections to a Good Night's Sleep (Or the Lack Thereof)

Source: Crain, T. L., Hammer, L. B., Bodner, T., Kossek, E. E., Moen, P., Lilienthal, R. & Buxton, O. M. (2014). Work-family conflict, family-supportive supervisor behaviors (FSSB) and sleep outcomes. *Journal of Occupational Health Psychology, 19*(2), 155–167.

Stressors at work are thought to affect the quality of family life, just as family challenges, in turn, should influence well-being at work. Such work-family conflict is the subject of considerable research in psychology but little is known about how such conflict relates to other domains of daily life, including leisure time, community involvement, and sleep.

Sleep is crucial to physical health. Yet little or no research examines the role of sleep outcomes for workers who experience work-family conflict. Too little sleep (less than 7 hours per night) and too much sleep (more than 8 hours per night) are linked with chronic health problems, such as cardiovascular disease, obesity, diabetes, and hypertension. This study hypothesized that work-family conflict can impact both the quantity and quality of workers' sleep cycles. Specifically, the investigators predicted that work role demands are incompatible with family role demands, which means that work to family conflict (WTFC) or family to work conflict (FTWC) could both adversely affect sleep quality (initiating and maintaining sleep without insomnia) and quantity of sleep (duration of nightly rest).

Method

Sample and procedure. Participants were 637 employees at a large Fortune 500 company. The employees, who received $20 for their participation, were interviewed for 1 hour by trained interviewers. The participants wore a sleep-monitoring device at night for the duration of the study.

Measures. Employee WTFC and FTWC were assessed using two five-item subscales that were rated on a 5-point scale from 1 (strongly disagree) to 5 (strongly agree). A sample WTFC item read, "The demands of your work interfere with your family or personal time" and a sample for FTWC stated, "The demands of your family

or personal relationships interfere with work-related activities." Participants also completed a sleep quality index, self-reporting items dealing with sleep insufficiency, sleep duration, and insomnia symptoms.

Results

Employees who reported higher levels of WTFC experienced less sufficient sleep and displayed more insomnia symptoms. However, FTWC was not associated with either sleep insufficiency or insomnia symptoms. WTFC was also negatively associated with self-reported sleep duration as well as device-monitored total sleep time. Thus, employees who reported higher levels of WTFC had to live with less sleep than those with lower levels of WTFC. FTWC was not associated with sleep duration.

Discussion

Discovering which aspects of work-family conflict influence sleep is an important concern for workers as well as I/O psychologists. Measures of WTFC were found to predict the quality and duration of sleep in this study. The fact that FTWC did not predict outcomes is interesting but, given the cross-sectional nature of this research, it is difficult to determine why the work to family conflict direction was predictive while the family to work side was not. Future research should further explore whether bidirectional relationships exist between work-family conflict and patterns of sleep.

Critical Thinking Questions

1. Can you think of reasons why WTFC would influence measures of sleep duration and quality while FTWC did not?
2. What can organizations and workplaces do to foster improved sleep quality and quantity in their workers?
3. Do these results have anything to say about the experience of college students and sleep? In other words, is college life like work life, indicating that stress related to course work and the classroom has similar affects as WTFC?

Although employers are reducing their contributions to employee benefits such as pension and retirement plans, health-care benefits, and the like, they do not seem to be cutting back on flexible work schedules, family leave, and child and elder care support (SHRM, 2011). A key reason employers are retaining these programs is that they help recruit and retain employees. Still, the fact is that most employees do not have access to such programs. Some believe that this situation is partly to blame for the downward drift in the percentage of mothers with infant children who are in the labor force (Stone & Lovejoy, 2004). In 1998, the participation rate for this group had reached a high of 59%; by 2005, it had fallen to 56%. According to Ellen Galinsky, president of the Families and Work Institute, "They're not fleeing work—they're fleeing the demanding way of work" (Armour, 2004). Indeed, the more hours women work, the more their marital satisfaction tends to suffer (but keep in mind that this is a correlational relationship and not a causal one). However, it makes sense that longer work hours can spill over into time once reserved for family

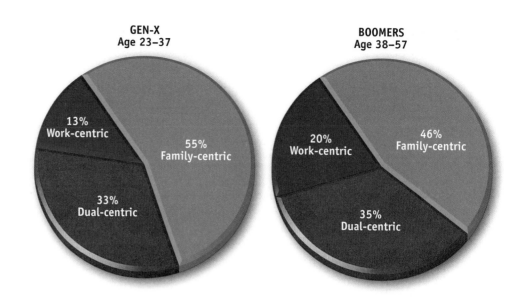

Figure 13.11

Generational differences in work and family priorities. Gen-X parents were significantly more likely than Boomer parents to be family-centric (place more emphasis on family than work), whereas Boomer parents were significantly more likely than Gen-Xers to be work-centric (place greater emphasis on work than family). The fact that both groups had children younger than 18 living at home suggests that this was a generational, rather than a life cycle, difference.

Source: From Families and Work Institute (2004, October). *Generation and gender in the workplace.* New York: Families and Work Institute.

commitments, thereby introducing strain in family life (Hughes & Parkes, 2007). To gain more control over their lives, some women are temporarily opting out of the workforce; others are going into business for themselves.

Some decline in women's labor force participation rates is probably due to generational shifts in the views of the optimal balance of work and family roles. As you can see in **Figure 13.11**, more Gen-X employees with children endorsed a family-centric view over a work-centric view compared to a comparable group of Boomers. Some suggest that these generational differences are due, in part, to many Gen-Xers seeing their hardworking parents lose their jobs because of downsizing (Families and Work Institute, 2004).

Leisure and Recreation

Given the pace of contemporary American life, it's no surprise that almost 60% of Americans say that having leisure time is either "extremely important" or "very important" in their lives, according to a Gallup poll (Moore, 2003). Yet many Americans are taking less vacation time than they did in the past (Dickey, 2015; Schor, 2011). U.S. workers take an average of 14 days of paid annual vacation *after* 5 years of service (U.S. Bureau of Labor Statistics, 2009). The paid vacation time of American workers lags far behind that of many European workers. Moreover, workers in many European Union countries get 4 weeks of vacation time mandated by law (Roughton, 2001). A generous number of public holidays pushes the average vacation time in the European Union to about 7 weeks!

We define *leisure* as **unpaid activities people choose to engage in because the activities are personally meaningful.** How might we distinguish activities that are meaningful from those that aren't? Although people may lounge in front of the TV or surf the Internet for hours at a time, most would also acknowledge that an important difference exists between this use of time and, say, hiking around a beautiful lake. While one activity merely provides respite from a boring or exhausting day (which you sometimes need), the other can be genuinely revitalizing. Being a couch potato will probably contribute nothing to your state of mind and may even contribute to feelings of apathy and depression. Participating in activities that are meaningful and fulfilling, however, can contribute to one's well-being and quality of life (Brajša-Žganec, Merkaš, & Šverko, 2011).

Leisure time should be relaxing and personally meaningful; cultivating a garden can be both of those things. Some research suggests that being satisfied with one's job and one's leisure activities is predictive of psychological health.

Types of Leisure Activities

The leisure activities that people enjoy are quite diverse. Popular leisure pursuits include:

- *Hobbies.* Among the most popular hobbies are photography; acting; music (playing and listening); dancing; gardening; knitting; drawing; collecting stamps, autographs, and so forth; hiking; camping; fishing; and birdwatching.

- *Reading.* Although fewer individuals read now than in the past, plenty of people still love to curl up with a good book. Books allow readers to escape from daily cares, solve mysteries, travel to real or imaginary places, learn useful information, and find inspiration.

- *Surfing the Internet.* A relatively new entry into the world of leisure, the Internet offers an amazing array of activities: emailing friends and relatives, social networking on Facebook or Instagram, posting on message boards or Twitter, and playing multiuser games are just a few options.

- *Travel.* Many choose their destinations spontaneously, but others are more systematic in their travel plans. For example, some individuals want to travel to all the U.S. national parks or to every state. Others travel abroad—to get a taste of real French cooking or a firsthand look at what remains of ancient Egypt.

- *Games and puzzles.* Some individuals enjoy playing bridge for relaxation; others like to play board games such as Scrabble or chess. Computerized and video games are highly popular. For some, the day isn't complete without the daily crossword or Sudoku puzzle.

- *Sports.* Many people play team sports such as bowling or softball, enjoying both physical exercise and social interaction. Others enjoy individual sports such as jogging, swimming, surfing, ice skating, or skiing.

- *Volunteer activities.* People can use their skills to help others in diverse settings: homeless shelters, hospitals, schools, battered women's shelters, boys' and girls' clubs, and sports teams, for example.

Being aware of the broad range of leisure activities heightens your chances of selecting those that are most meaningful to you.

In the upcoming Application, we describe how to conduct a productive job search and offer a few tips for more effective job interviews.

APPLICATION

13.6 Getting Ahead in the Job Game

Learning Objectives

- Summarize some guidelines for putting together an effective résumé.
- Discuss strategies for targeting companies you would like to work for.
- Outline several strategies for landing an interview and discuss how to behave when interviewing for a job.

Answer the following statements "true" or "false."

____ **1.** The most common and effective job-search method is answering classified ads.

____ **2.** Your technical qualifications are the main factor in determining the success of your job search.

____ **3.** Employment agencies are a good source of leads to high-level professional jobs.

____ **4.** Your résumé should be very thorough and include everything you have ever done.

____ **5.** It's a good idea to inject some humor into your job interviews to help you and your interviewer relax.

Most career counselors would agree that all these statements are generally false. Although there is no one method for obtaining a desirable job, recommended guidelines can increase your chances of success. These insights appear in this Application. To ensure that you get the best job you can, you'll need to know more details than we can provide here. A good place to start is to read *What Color Is Your Parachute?*, one of the best job-search manuals available.

Above all else, conduct a job search that is well organized, thorough, and systematic. Sending out a hastily written résumé to a few randomly selected companies is a waste of effort. An effective job search requires time and careful planning. Thus, it is crucial to begin your search well in advance of the time when you will need a job.

Of course, no amount of planning and effort can guarantee favorable results in a job search. Most hiring decisions are based on subjective impressions gleaned from résumés, telephone conversations, and face-to-face interviews. These impressions are based on perceptions of personality, appearance, social skills, and body language. Knowing these truths, you can practice certain strategies that may increase the odds in your favor.

No matter what job you're looking for, successful searches contain certain steps. First, you must prepare a résumé. Next, you must target specific companies you would like to work for. Then, you must inform these companies of your interest in such a way as to get them interested in you.

Putting Together a Résumé

The purpose of a strong résumé is not to get you a job, but to get you an interview. To be effective, your résumé must show that you have at least the minimum technical qualifications for the position, know standard conventions of the work world, and are someone who is on the fast track to success. Furthermore, it must achieve these goals without being flashy or gimmicky, yet it must tell your story and make you stand out from other applicants (Akpan & Notar, 2012). No spelling or grammatical errors can be present.

Here are a few basic guidelines for a résumé projecting a positive, yet conservative image.

1. Use high-quality white, ivory, or beige paper for hard copies.

2. Make sure the résumé contains no typographical errors.

3. Keep it short. One side of an 8.5" × 11" sheet of paper will suffice for most students; do not go over two pages.

4. Don't write in full sentences, and avoid using the word *I*. Instead, begin each statement with an "action" word describing a specific achievement, such as "Supervised a staff of fifteen" or "Handled all customer complaints."

5. Avoid including personal information that is unrelated to the job. Such information is distracting, giving a reader cause to dislike you and to reject your application.

Effective résumés generally contain the following elements (**Figure 13.12** shows an attractively prepared, easily read résumé):

Heading. At the page's top, list your name, address, phone number, and email address. This is the only unlabeled section of the résumé. (You do not need to label the document "Résumé.")

Objective. State precisely and concisely the position you are seeking, remembering to use action words. An example might be "Challenging, creative position in the communication field requiring extensive background in newspaper, radio, and television."

Education. List any degrees you've earned, giving major field, date, and granting institution for each. List the highest degree you received first. If you have a college degree, you don't need to mention your high school diploma. If you received *academic* honors or awards, mention them here.

Experience. This section should be organized chronologically, beginning with your most recent job and working backward. For each position, provide dates of employment and describe

TERESA M. MORGAN

Campus Address
1252 River St., Apt. 808
East Lansing, MI 48823
(517)332-6086
tmorgan@michstate.edu

Permanent Address
1111 W. Franklin
Jackson, MI 49203
(517)782-0819
tmmor@gmail.com

OBJECTIVE	To pursue a career in interior design, or a related field, in which I can utilize my design training. Willing to relocate after June 2018.
EDUCATION Sept. 2016– June 2018	**Michigan State University,** East Lansing, MI 48825. Bachelor of Arts–Interior Design, with emphasis in Design Communication and Human Shelter. Courses include Lighting, Computers, Public Relations and History of Art. (F.I.D.E.R. accredited) 3.0 GPA (4.0 = A).
July 2016– Aug. 2016	**Michigan State University overseas study,** England and France, Decorative Arts and Architecture. 4.0 GPA (4.0 = A).
Sept. 2013– June 2015	**Jackson Community College,** Jackson, MI 49201. Associate's Degree. 3.5 GPA (4.0 = A).
EMPLOYMENT Dec. 2017– June 2018	**Food Service and Maintenance,** Owen Graduate Center, Michigan State University. • Prepared and served food. • Managed upkeep of adjacent Van Hoosen Residence Hall.
Sept. 2016– June 2017	**Food Service and Maintenance,** McDonel Residence Hall, Michigan State University. • Served food and cleaned facility. • Handled general building maintenance.
June 2012– Dec. 2012	**Waitress,** Charlie Wong's Restaurant, Jackson, MI. • Served food, dealt with a variety of people on a personal level. • Additional responsibilities: cashier, hostess, bartender, and employee trainer.
HONORS AND ACTIVITIES	• Community College Transfer scholarship from MSU. • American Society of Interior Design Publicity Chairman; Executive Board, MSU Chapter. • Sigma Chi Little Sisters. • Independent European travel, summer 2012. • Stage manager and performer in plays and musicals.

REFERENCES and PORTFOLIO available upon request.

Figure 13.12

Example of an attractively formatted résumé. The physical appearance of a résumé is very important. This example shows what a well-prepared résumé should look like. (Adapted from Lock, 2005b)

Learn More Online

CollegeGrad
This site bills itself as "The #1 entry-level job site." Key sections include "Job Preparation" (explore careers, résumés, and cover letters), "Job Searching" (advice and posting résumés), and "Offers" (salary, negotiating, and new job advice). You can also search for internships here.

isn't feasible, do some volunteer work and list it under an "Honors and Activities" section on your résumé.

Technology is changing aspects of the job-search process, including the preparation and screening of résumés. Increasingly, companies are electronically scanning résumés for key words that match job specifications (Lock, 2005a). Thus, it's helpful to create an electronic résumé in addition to the traditional paper version. You can get this information at your campus career services office. In fact, find out if your career services office sponsors any résumé-writing workshops. Attending one is likely to improve your résumé quite a bit, as demonstrated by a study exploring the impact of a résumé-writing workshop on students' résumé-writing skills (Tillotson & Osborn, 2012). Also, many organizations post formatting instructions on their websites for people who want to submit electronic résumés.

Finding Companies You Want to Work For

Initially, you need to determine what general type of organization will best suit your needs.

your responsibilities and accomplishments. Be specific, making sure your most recent position highlights the greatest achievements. Don't list trivial attainments: Readers find such material annoying.

Also, beware of padding your résumé with misrepresentations or outright untruths. One résumé-writing business reported that 43% of 1000 résumés they received over a 6-month period contained one or more "significant inaccuracies" (Cullen, 2007). If you are wondering whether to include a questionable entry on your résumé, use the "sniff test." Could you talk easily with an interviewer about what you claim on your résumé without feeling nervous? If not, delete the information.

If you are currently a student or are a recent graduate, your schooling will provide the basis for both your experience and your qualifications. You can get a jump on the competition by gaining experience in the field in which you want to work—through internships or part-time or summer jobs. If this option

"Oops! The padding just fell out of your résumé."

Leo Cullum/The New Yorker Collection/ www.cartoonbank.com.

Do you want to work in a school? A hospital? A small business? A large corporation? A government agency? A human services agency? To select an appropriate work environment, you need an accurate picture of your personal qualities and knowledge of various occupations and their characteristics. Job-search manuals like *Parachute* can provide you with helpful exercises in self-exploration. To learn about the characteristics of various occupations, check out relevant websites such as the *Occupational Outlook Handbook* or visit your career services office.

Landing an Interview

No one is going to hire you without first "checking out the goods." This inspection process typically involves one or more formal interviews. How do you get invited for an interview? If you are applying for an advertised vacancy, the traditional approach is to send a résumé with a cover letter to the hiring organization. If your letter and résumé stand out from the crowd, you may be invited for an interview. A good way to increase your chances is to persuade the prospective employer that you are interested enough in the company to have done some research on the organization.

If you are approaching an organization in the absence of a known opening, your strategy may be somewhat different. You may still opt to send a résumé, along with a more detailed cover letter explaining why you have selected this particular company. Another option, suggested by Bolles (2007), is to introduce yourself (by phone or in person) directly to the person in charge of hiring and request an interview. You can increase your chances of success by using your network of personal contacts to identify some acquaintance that you and the person in charge have in common. Then you can use this person's name to facilitate your approach.

Polishing Your Interview Technique

The final, and most crucial, step in the process of securing a job is the face-to-face interview. If you've gotten this far, the employer already knows that you have the necessary training and experience to do the job. Your challenge is to convince the employer that you're the kind of person who would fit well in the organization. Your interviewer will attempt to verify that you have the intangible qualities that will make you a good hire. More importantly, he or she will try to identify any "red-flag" behaviors, attitudes, or traits that mark you as an unacceptable risk.

racorn/Shutterstock.com

To be successful on a job interview, candidates need to dress appropriately and convey confidence, enthusiasm, and interest in the job.

To create the right impression, you must appear confident, enthusiastic, and ambitious. By the way, a firm (not wishy-washy or bone-crushing) handshake helps create a positive first impression, especially for women (Stewart et al., 2008). Your demeanor should be somewhat formal and reserved; avoid any attempts at humor—you never know what might offend your interviewer. Above all, never give more information than the interviewer requests, especially negative information. If asked directly what your weaknesses are—a common ploy—respond with a "flaw" that is really a positive, as in "I tend to work too hard at times." Finally, don't ever blame or criticize anyone, especially previous employers, even if you feel that the criticism is justified (Lock, 2005b).

Developing an effective interview technique requires practice. Many experts suggest that you never turn down an interview because you can always benefit from the practice even if you don't want the job. Preparation is crucial: Never go into an interview cold. Find out all you can about the company before you go. Try to anticipate the questions that will be asked and have some answers ready. You can review commonly asked interview questions on websites and in career books (Yate, 2006). Know, however, that many untrained interviewers treat interviews as informal and unplanned, which means they rely on unstructured questions. In contrast, trained interviewers usually rely on a set of standardized questions for prospective employees. Sample questions associated with both interviewer styles are shown in **Figure 13.13**. In general, you will not be asked simply to reiterate information from your résumé. Remember, it is your personal qualities that are being assessed at this point.

Interviews are not a one-way street: Your interviewer will expect that you will have some questions to ask about the position. In fact, the sorts of questions you ask will be another source of information for determining your fit in that workplace. **Figure 13.14** lists some sample questions that you might ask. And remember, it is very bad form to tell an interviewer that "I don't have any questions about the position at this point" because it conveys a lack of interest in the job and that you are not taking the interview very seriously.

Unstructured interview questions

1. What are your weaknesses?
2. Why should we hire you?
3. What are your goals?
4. Why do you want to work here?
5. What are three positive things a former boss would say about you?
6. What salary are you seeking?
7. If you were an animal, what animal would you want to be? Why?

Structured interview questions

1. Tell me in specific detail about a time when you had to deal with a difficult person.
2. Give me an example of a time when you had to make a decision without having a supervisor present to help you.
3. Give me a specific example of when you demonstrated initiative in your last job.
4. Tell me about a time when you had to work with a team of other people.
5. Describe a situation where you had to be creative when it came to solving some problem.

Figure 13.13

Some typical unstructured and structured interview questions. Untrained interviewers treat interviews as informal and unplanned; they tend to ask unstructured questions. In contrast, trained interviewers usually rely on a set of standardized questions for prospective employees. Sample questions associated with unstructured or structured interviews, respectively, are shown here. (Adapted from Baumeister & Bushman, 2011)

One more thing: As we learned in Chapter 8, nonverbal behavior matters, so your smiles, eye contact, posture, rate of speaking, amount of time you speak, and paralanguage all matter, as they will create an impression in the mind of your interviewer (Frauendorfer & Mast, 2015). Your nonverbal behavior should convey interest, enthusiasm, and honesty. No doubt, too, you will be trying to "read" the nonverbal cues the interviewer displays, which is understandable; however, you should focus more on the nonverbal as well as verbal messages you are sending.

Some questions a job candidate might ask during an interview

1. What particular skills are appropriate for this position?
2. Please explain to me the responsibilities and duties associated with this position.
3. What is the ideal candidate for this position like?
4. Is this a new position in the company?
5. Who would I work with in this position?
6. If I join the company in this position, how will I be evaluated? Who will perform my evaluation?
7. What are the strengths of this company?
8. What direction will the company be taking in the next 5 years?

Figure 13.14

Some questions job candidates might ask during an interview. Job seekers need to ask as well as answer questions. Having good questions at the ready during an interview can demonstrate to the employers that you are serious and interested in working for them. Review the questions here before you go on an interview and adjust them as needed to fit the job and the needs of your possible future employer.

A final word of advice: If possible, avoid discussing salary in an initial interview. The appropriate time for salary negotiation is *after* a firm offer of employment has been extended. You can scope out salary information for many jobs through judicious searching of the Internet. After you have an interview, you should follow up with a thank-you note and a résumé that will jog the prospective employer's memory about your training and talents.

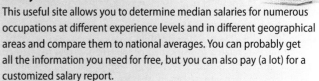

Learn More Online

Salary.com
This useful site allows you to determine median salaries for numerous occupations at different experience levels and in different geographical areas and compare them to national averages. You can probably get all the information you need for free, but you can also pay (a lot) for a customized salary report.

CHAPTER 13 Review

Key Ideas

13.1 Choosing a Career
• Ideally, people look for jobs that are compatible with their personal characteristics. Thus, individuals need to have a sense of their own abilities, interests, and personality. Family background also influences career choices.
• There are abundant resources for those who want to learn about possible career options. In researching prospective careers, it is important to find out about the nature of the work, working conditions, entry requirements, potential earnings, potential status, opportunities for advancement, intrinsic satisfactions, and the future outlook for jobs.
• Individuals who have trouble making career decisions may find it helpful to take an occupational interest inventory. People have the potential for success in a variety of occupations, and they need to keep this and other considerations in mind as they make career decisions.

13.2 Models of Career Choice and Development
• John Holland's person-environment fit model of career development asserts that people select careers based on their own personality characteristics. Holland's well-supported theory includes six personal orientations and matching work environments.
• Super's stage theory holds that self-concept development is the basis for career choice. According to this model, there are five stages in the occupational life cycle: growth, exploration, establishment, maintenance, and decline. However, the assumption that people will remain in the same career all of their working lives is out of sync with current workplace realities.
• Models of career development in women are still being developed. Women's career paths are often less orderly and predictable than men's because of the need to juggle multiple roles and because many women interrupt their careers to devote time to childrearing.

13.3 The Changing World of Work
• Work is an activity that produces something of value for others. A number of contemporary trends are changing the world of work. Generally, the more education individuals obtain, the higher their salaries will be.
• In the future, more women and minorities will join the labor force. Although women and minorities participate in the workforce at all occupational levels, they tend to be concentrated in lower-paying and lower-status positions. Furthermore, women and minorities face discrimination in a number of areas. Increasing diversity in the workforce presents challenges to both organizations and workers.

13.4 Coping with Occupational Hazards
• Major hazards related to work include job stress, sexual harassment, and unemployment. Stress affects both employers and employees. Interventions to manage stress in the workplace can be made at the individual level, the organizational level, and the individual-organizational interface.
• Victims of sexual harassment often develop physical and psychological symptoms of stress that can lead to decreased work motivation and productivity. Many organizations are educating their workers about this problem. Individuals can also take steps to reduce sexual harassment, although the most popular strategies tend to be the least effective.
• Because of dramatic changes in the economy, unemployment is a problem for both skilled and unskilled workers. Job loss is highly stressful. Middle-aged workers are most distressed by the experience. Unemployed workers who believe that they have been treated unfairly and arbitrarily often feel angry. In coping with unemployment, social support is critical.

13.5 Balancing Work and Other Spheres of Life
• A major challenge for workers today is balancing work, family, and leisure activities in ways that are personally satisfying. Workaholism may be based on positive or negative motives, but it still creates work-family conflict for workaholics and their families.
• As dual-earner families have become the norm, juggling multiple roles has emerged as a challenge, especially for women. Nonetheless, multiple roles are generally beneficial to mental, physical, and relationship health. Leisure plays an important role in promoting well-being and quality of life.

13.6 Application: Getting Ahead in the Job Game
• The essential elements of a successful job search include (1) determining the type of organization that will best suit one's needs, (2) constructing an effective résumé, (3) obtaining a job interview, and (4) developing an effective interview technique.
• Résumés should be brief and project a positive, yet conservative image. To locate prospective employers, it is good to use a variety of strategies.
• Nonverbal communication skills can be crucial in job interviews. You should try to appear confident and enthusiastic. Try to avoid salary discussions in your initial interview.

Key Terms

Displaced workers p. 386
Dual-earner households p. 378
Glass ceiling p. 381
Industrial/organizational (I/O) psychology p. 367
Labor force p. 379
Leisure p. 390
Occupational interest inventories p. 370
Sexual harassment p. 384
Token p. 381
Underemployment p. 378
Work p. 376
Work-family conflict p. 388

Key People

John Holland pp. 373–374
Robert Karasek p. 383
Donald Super pp. 374–375

CHAPTER 13   Practice Test

1. Individuals' career choices are often
   a. much higher in status than those of their parents.
   b. similar to those of their parents.
   c. much lower in status than those of their parents.
   d. unrelated to their family background.

2. Findings on education and earnings show that
   a. at all levels of education, men earn more than women.
   b. at all levels of education, women earn more than men.
   c. there are no gender differences in education and earnings.
   d. there is no relationship between education and earnings.

3. Occupational interest inventories are designed to predict
   a. how successful an individual is likely to be in a job.
   b. how long a person will stay in a career.
   c. how satisfied a person is likely to be in a job.
   d. all of the above.

4. Holland's theory of occupational choice emphasizes
   a. the role of self-esteem in job choice.
   b. the unfolding of career interests over time.
   c. parental influences and job choice.
   d. matching personality traits and job environments.

5. Which of the following is *not* a work-related trend?
   a. Technology is changing the nature of work.
   b. New work attitudes are required.
   c. Most new jobs will be in the manufacturing sector.
   d. Lifelong learning is a necessity.

6. When there is only one woman or minority person in a workplace setting, that person becomes a symbol of his or her group and is referred to as a
   a. token.
   b. scapegoat.
   c. sex object.
   d. protected species.

7. Job stress has been found to lead to all but which of the following negative effects?
   a. Burnout
   b. Bipolar disorder
   c. High blood pressure
   d. Anxiety

8. According to law, the two types of sexual harassment are
   a. quid pro quo and hostile environment.
   b. legal and illegal.
   c. caveat emptor and confrontational.
   d. industrial and organizational.

9. Compared to European workers, American workers receive
   a. much less paid vacation time.
   b. about the same amount of paid vacation time.
   c. much more paid vacation time, but less sick leave.
   d. much more paid vacation and more sick leave.

10. Which of the following is a good tip for preparing an effective résumé?
    a. Make your résumé as long as possible.
    b. Use complete sentences.
    c. Keep it short.
    d. Provide a lot of personal information.

Answers

1. b Page 369
2. a Pages 378–379
3. c Pages 370–371
4. d Pages 373–374
5. c Pages 376–378
6. a Page 381
7. b Pages 382–384
8. a Page 384
9. a Page 390
10. c Pages 392–393

Personal Explorations Workbook

Go to the *Personal Explorations Workbook* in the back of your textbook for exercises that can enhance your self-understanding in relation to issues raised in this chapter.

Exercise 13.1 *Self-Assessment:* Assertive Job-Hunting Survey

Exercise 13.2 *Self-Reflection:* What Do You Know about the Career that Interests You?

Dotshock/Shutterstock.com

ctress Jessica Alba used to unplug every single appliance in her house because she worried it would catch fire. She would also check and recheck her doors to ensure that they were locked. Soccer star David Beckham acknowledges more elaborate concerns that involve symmetry and matching. He is not comfortable unless everything is arranged in straight lines or in pairs. For instance, if he has five cans of Pepsi in a refrigerator, he has to get rid of one to restore even pairs. When he enters a hotel room he immediately has to put away all the leaflets and books to restore order to the room.

For Alba and Beckham, these aren't just little eccentricities of being a celebrity. They're manifestations of obsessive-compulsive disorder (OCD). Comedian and talk show host Howie Mandel explains it in his 2009 autobiography, *Here's the Deal: Don't Touch Me*. Mandel doesn't shake hands, due to his fear of germs, but "it's not just that I'm scared of germs," he says. There's nothing wrong with shaking hands with someone and then washing your hands. But "there *is* something wrong with being totally consumed that you didn't get everything off your hand, that there's things crawling, so you wash it again, and you're so consumed that you wash it again, and you wash it again and you wash it again and you wash it again," Mandel says. "When you can't get past that, that's obsessive-compulsive disorder. It's not that you're afraid of germs, it's that you obsess about that thought and have to do things like handwashing to relieve the worry. I always have intrusive thoughts and rituals."

What causes such abnormal behavior? Does Mandel have a mental illness, or does he just behave strangely? What is the basis for judging behavior as normal versus abnormal? How common are such disorders? Can they be cured? These are just a few of the questions that we address in this chapter as we discuss psychological disorders and their complex causes. ■

Howie Mandel has written an insightful and amusing account of his struggles with obsessive-compulsive disorder.

AP Images/Charles Sykes

14.1 General Concepts

Learning Objectives

- Describe and evaluate the medical model of abnormal behavior.
- Identify the key criteria of abnormality and discuss the development of DSM-5.

Misconceptions about abnormal behavior are common. We therefore need to clear up some preliminary issues before we describe the various types of psychological disorders. In this section, we discuss the medical model of abnormal behavior, the criteria of abnormal behavior, and the classification of psychological disorders.

The Medical Model Applied to Abnormal Behavior

There's no question that Howie Mandel's extreme fear of germs is abnormal. But does it make sense to view his unusual and irrational behavior as an *illness*? This is a controversial question. **The *medical model* proposes that it is useful to think of abnormal behavior as a disease.** This point of view is the basis for many of the terms used to refer to abnormal behavior, including mental *illness*, psychological *disorder*, and psycho*pathology* (*pathology* refers to manifestations of disease). The medical model gradually became the conventional way of thinking about abnormal behavior during the 19th and 20th centuries, and its influence remains dominant today.

The medical model clearly represented progress over earlier models of abnormal behavior. Prior to the 18th century, most conceptions of abnormal behavior were based on superstition. People who behaved strangely were thought to be possessed by demons, to be witches in league with the devil, or to be victims of God's punishment. Their disorders were "treated" with chants, rituals, exorcisms, and such.

The rise of the medical model brought improvements in the treatment of those who exhibited abnormal behavior. As victims of an illness, they were viewed with more sympathy and less hatred and fear. Although living conditions in early asylums were often deplorable, gradual progress was made toward more humane care of the mentally ill.

However, in recent decades, some critics have suggested that the medical model may have outlived its usefulness (Boyle, 2007; Deacon, 2013). A particularly vocal critic has been the late Thomas Szasz (1993). He asserted that "strictly speaking, disease or illness can affect only the body; hence there can be no mental illness. . . . Minds can be 'sick' only in the sense that jokes are 'sick' or economies are 'sick' " (1974, p. 267). He further argued that abnormal behavior usually involves a deviation from social norms rather than an illness. He contended that such deviations are "problems in living" rather than medical problems. According to Szasz, the medical model's disease analogy converts moral and social questions about what is acceptable behavior into medical questions.

Some critics are also concerned because medical diagnoses of abnormal behavior pin potentially derogatory labels on people (Overton & Medina, 2008). Being labeled as psychotic, schizophrenic, or mentally ill carries a social stigma that can be difficult to shake. Those characterized as mentally ill are viewed as erratic, dangerous, incompetent, and inferior. These stereotypes fuel prejudice, which is a significant source of stress for people who suffer from mental illness (Rüsch et al., 2014). Perhaps even more important, the stigma associated with psychological disorders prevents many people from seeking the mental health care that they need and could benefit from (Corrigan, Druss, & Perlick, 2014). Unfortunately, this stigma appears to be deep rooted and not easily reduced (Schnittker, 2008).

Although critics' analyses of the medical model have some merit, we'll take the position that the disease analogy continues to be useful, although you should keep in mind that it is *only* an analogy. Medical concepts such as *diagnosis, etiology*, and *prognosis* have proven valuable in the treatment and study of abnormality. *Diagnosis* **involves distinguishing one illness from another.** *Etiology* **refers to the apparent causation and developmental history of an illness. A** *prognosis* **is a forecast about the probable course of an illness.** These medically based concepts have widely shared meanings that permit clinicians, researchers, and the public to communicate more effectively in their discussions of abnormal behavior.

Criteria of Abnormal Behavior

If your next-door neighbor scrubs his front porch twice every day and spends virtually all his time cleaning and recleaning his house, is he normal? If your sister-in-law goes to one physician after another seeking treatment for ailments that appear imaginary, is she psychologically healthy? How are we to judge what's normal and what's abnormal? Formal diagnoses of psychological disorders are made by mental health professionals. In making these diagnoses, clinicians rely on a variety of criteria, the foremost of which are the following.

1. *Deviance.* As Szasz pointed out, people are often said to have a disorder because their behavior deviates from what their society considers acceptable. What constitutes normality varies somewhat from one culture to another, but all cultures have such norms. When people ignore these standards and expectations, they may be labeled mentally ill.

2. *Maladaptive behavior.* In many cases, people are judged to have a psychological disorder because their everyday adaptive behavior is impaired. This is the key criterion in the diagnosis of substance use (drug) disorders. In and of itself, alcohol and drug use are not terribly unusual or deviant. However, when the use of cocaine, for instance, begins to interfere with a person's social or occupational functioning, a substance use disorder exists. In such cases, it is the maladaptive quality of the behavior that makes it disordered.

3. *Personal distress.* Frequently, the diagnosis of a psychological disorder is based on an individual's report of great personal distress. This is usually the criterion met by people who are troubled by

Hoarding behavior clearly represents a certain type of deviance, but should it be regarded as a mental disorder? The criteria of mental illness are subjective and complicated. Hoarding *is* viewed as a disorder, but as with any disorder, it is all a matter of degree. In many cases, it can be very difficult to draw a line between normality and abnormality.

depression or anxiety disorders. Depressed people, for instance, may or may not exhibit deviant or maladaptive behavior. Such people are usually labeled as having a disorder when they describe their subjective pain and suffering to friends, relatives, and mental health professionals.

Although two or three criteria may apply in a particular case, people are often viewed as disordered when only one criterion is met. As you may have already noticed, diagnoses of psychological disorders involve *value judgments* about what represents normal or abnormal behavior. The criteria of mental illness are not nearly as value-free as the criteria of physical illness. Judgments about mental illness reflect prevailing cultural values, social trends, and political forces, as well as scientific knowledge (Frances & Widiger, 2012; Kirk, Gomory, & Cohen, 2013).

Antonyms such as *normal* versus *abnormal* and *mental health* versus *mental illness* imply that people can be divided neatly into two distinct groups: those who are normal and those who are not. In reality, it is often difficult to draw a line that clearly separates normality from abnormality. On occasion, everyone experiences personal distress. Everybody acts in deviant ways once in a while. And everyone displays some maladaptive behavior. People are judged to have psychological disorders only when their behavior becomes *extremely* deviant, maladaptive, or distressing. Thus, normality and abnormality exist on a continuum. It's a matter of degree, not an either-or proposition (see **Figure 14.1**).

Psychodiagnosis: The Classification of Disorders

Lumping all psychological disorders together would make it extremely difficult to understand them better. A sound taxonomy of mental disorders can facilitate empirical research and enhance communication among scientists and clinicians (Widiger & Crego, 2013). Thus, a great deal of effort has been invested in devising an elaborate system for classifying psychological disorders. This classification system, published by the American Psychiatric Association, is outlined in a book titled the *Diagnostic and Statistical Manual of Mental Disorders*. The fourth edition, titled DSM-IV, was used from 1994 until 2013, when the current fifth edition was released. The fifth edition is titled DSM-5 (instead of DSM-V) to facilitate incremental updates (such as DSM 5.1). It is the product of more than a decade of research (Kupfer, Kuhl, & Regier, 2013). Clinical researchers collected extensive data, held numerous conferences, and engaged in heated debates about whether various syndromes should be added, eliminated, redefined, or renamed (Sachdev, 2013).

One area of concern related to the DSM has been its nearly exponential growth. The number of specific diagnoses in the DSM has increased from 128 in the first edition to 541 in the current edition (Blashfield et al., 2014; see **Figure 14.2**). Some of this growth has

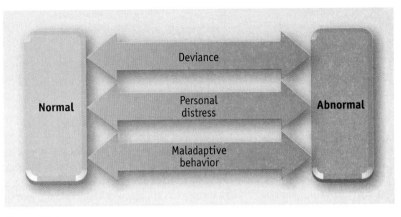

Figure 14.1

Normality and abnormality as a continuum. No sharp boundary divides normal and abnormal behavior. Behavior is normal or abnormal in degree, depending on the extent to which it is deviant, personally distressing, or maladaptive.

Learn More Online

NAMI: The National Alliance for the Mentally Ill
Professional and lay evaluators have consistently found NAMI among the most helpful and informative organizations dealing with the entire spectrum of mental disorders, including schizophrenia and depression. The NAMI site offers a rich array of information on specific mental disorders and on how patients and their families can find support.

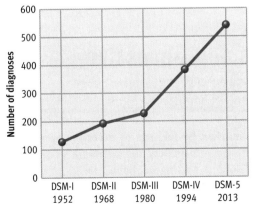

Figure 14.2

Growth of the DSM diagnostic system. Published by the American Psychiatric Association, the *Diagnostic and Statistical Manual of Mental Disorders* has grown dramatically with each new edition. The number of specific diagnoses has more than quadrupled since the first edition was released. (Based on Blashfield et al., 2014)

by Allen Frances (William Morrow, 2013)

In *Saving Normal*, psychiatrist Allen Frances takes a very critical look at contemporary trends in psychiatric diagnosis. The subtitle of the book provides a snapshot of its themes: *An Insider's Revolt against Out-of-Control Psychiatric Diagnosis, DSM-5, Big Pharma, and the Medicalization of Ordinary Life*. Frances brings an interesting perspective to the table in analyzing various controversies, as he chaired the task force that created the previous edition of the diagnostic system (DSM-IV). Frances's principal concern is what he calls *diagnostic inflation*, the trend toward taking the routine, everyday problems of the worried well and turning them into formal psychiatric disorders, thus leading countless people to seek unnecessary treatment, often with powerful medications that can prove harmful.

Frances begins by discussing the fuzzy boundaries between normality and abnormality, and describes the development of earlier editions of the DSM. He readily acknowledges that some of the decisions made under his guidance for DSM-IV

unexpectedly contributed to diagnostic inflation, much to his chagrin and regret. He then outlines how a variety of decisions made for DSM-5 appear likely to lead to diagnostic hyperinflation. Along the way, Frances explains how a variety of forces in modern society and modern medicine are fueling diagnostic inflation, such as diagnostic fads, insurance reimbursement pressures for formal diagnoses, epidemiology methods that greatly overestimate the prevalence of disorders, and so forth. First and foremost among these forces, he indicts the pharmaceutical industry for overselling the benefits of psychiatric drugs through brilliant marketing and its copious funding of highly biased research on new medications. Frances wraps up his compelling analyses in the final chapters by offering a variety of suggestions for bringing diagnostic inflation under control, followed by a highly practical chapter on how to be a smart and savvy consumer of clinical services. *Saving Normal* is a very insightful, readable, and thought-provoking examination of contemporary issues in psychodiagnosis.

been due to splitting existing disorders into narrower subtypes, but much of it has been due to adding entirely new disorders. Some of the new disorders encompass behavioral patterns that used to be regarded as mundane, everyday adjustment problems, rather than mental disorders. For example, DSM-5 includes diagnoses for caffeine intoxication (getting really buzzed from coffee), tobacco use disorder (inability to control smoking), disruptive mood dysregulation disorder (problems with recurrent temper tantrums in youngsters), binge-eating disorder (gluttonous overeating more than once a week for at least 3 months), and gambling disorder (inability to control gambling). Some of these syndromes can be serious problems for which people might want to seek treatment, but should they merit a formal designation as a mental illness? Some critics of the DSM argue that this approach "medicalizes" everyday problems and casts the stigma of pathology on normal self-control issues (Frances, 2013). Critics also worry that making everyday problems into mental disorders may trivialize the concept of mental illness.

We are now ready to start examining the specific types of psychological disorders. Obviously, we cannot cover all of the diverse disorders listed in DSM-5. However, we will introduce most of the major categories of disorders to give you an overview of the many forms abnormal behavior takes. In discussing each set of disorders, we begin with brief descriptions of the specific syndromes or subtypes that fall in the category. Then we focus on the *etiology* of the disorders in that category.

Learning Objectives

- Describe four types of anxiety disorders and obsessive-compulsive disorder.
- Discuss how biological factors and conditioning contribute to the etiology of anxiety-related disorders.
- Explain how cognitive processes and stress play a role in anxiety-related disorders.

14.2 Anxiety Disorders and Obsessive-Compulsive Disorder

Anxiety disorders **are a class of disorders marked by feelings of excessive apprehension and anxiety.** In DSM-5 the principal types of anxiety disorders are generalized anxiety disorder, specific phobia, panic disorder, and agoraphobia. DSM-5 removed obsessive-compulsive disorder (OCD) from the anxiety disorders category and put it in its own special category with other compulsive problems, such as hoarding disorder. The wisdom of this decision has been questioned as the new category consists of a hodgepodge of disorders whose resemblance may be superficial (Abramowitz & Jacoby, 2015). In any event, due to space limitations, we will cover OCD with the anxiety disorders.

Generalized Anxiety Disorder

Generalized anxiety disorder **is marked by a chronic high level of anxiety that is not tied to any specific threat.** People with this disorder worry constantly about minor matters related to family, finances, work, and personal illness. Their anxiety is frequently accompanied by physical symptoms, such as muscle tension, diarrhea, dizziness, faintness, sweating, and heart palpitations. They hope that their worrying will prepare them for the worst that could possibly happen, but the net result is they just generate negative emotions and prolonged physiological arousal (Newman & Llera, 2011). People with generalized anxiety disorder sound like the "worried well," but the disorder can be very disabling and is associated with an increased risk for a variety of physical health problems (Newman et al., 2013). Generalized anxiety disorder tends to have a gradual onset, has a lifetime prevalence of about 5%–6%, and is seen more frequently in females than males (Schneier et al., 2014).

Specific Phobia

In a phobic disorder, an individual's troublesome anxiety has a precise focus. **A *specific phobia* is marked by a persistent and irrational fear of an object or situation that presents no realistic danger.** Although mild phobias are extremely common, people are said to have a phobic disorder only when their fears seriously interfere with their everyday behavior. The following case provides an example of a specific phobia:

Hilda is 32 years of age and has a rather unusual fear. She is terrified of snow. She cannot go outside in the snow. She cannot even stand to see snow or hear about it on the weather report. Her phobia severely constricts her day-to-day behavior. Probing in therapy revealed that her phobia was caused by a traumatic experience at age 11. Playing at a ski lodge, she was buried briefly by a small avalanche of snow. She had no recollection of this experience until it was recovered in therapy. (Adapted from Laughlin, 1967, p. 227)

As Hilda's unusual snow phobia illustrates, people can develop phobic responses to virtually anything. Nonetheless, certain types of phobias are relatively common, as the data in **Figure 14.3** show. Particularly common are acrophobia (fear of heights), claustrophobia (fear of small, enclosed places), brontophobia (fear of storms), hydrophobia (fear of water), and various animal and insect phobias (McCabe & Antony, 2008). People troubled by phobias typically realize that their fears are irrational, but they still are unable to calm themselves when they encounter a phobic object.

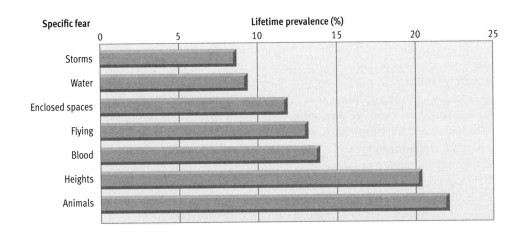

Figure 14.3

Common phobic fears. This graph shows the lifetime prevalence of the most common types of phobic fears reported by participants in a study by Curtis et al. (1998). As you can see, a substantial number of people struggle with a variety of specific phobias. Bear in mind that only a portion of these people qualify for a diagnosis of phobic disorder, which is merited only if individuals' phobias seriously impair their everyday functioning.

Panic Disorder

A *panic disorder* is characterized by recurrent attacks of overwhelming anxiety that usually occur suddenly and unexpectedly. These paralyzing attacks are accompanied by physical symptoms of anxiety and are sometimes misinterpreted as heart attacks. After a number of anxiety attacks, victims often become apprehensive, wondering when their next attack will occur. About two-thirds of people who are diagnosed with panic disorder are female, and the onset of the disorder typically occurs during late adolescence or early adulthood (Schneier et al., 2014).

Agoraphobia

People with panic disorder often become increasingly concerned about exhibiting panic in public to the point where they are afraid to leave home. This fear creates a condition called *agoraphobia,* **which is a fear of going out to public places** (its literal meaning is "fear of the marketplace"). In particular, agoraphobics tend to experience great discomfort in shopping malls, theaters, restaurants, and when using buses, trains, and subways. The crux of the problem is that in these situations they fear that it may be difficult to escape or get help if they panic. Some agoraphobics manage to venture out, but they endure crowds with intense dread. As its name suggests, agoraphobia was originally viewed as a phobic disorder. However, in DSM-III and DSM-IV it was characterized as a common complication of panic disorder. In DSM-5 it is listed as a separate anxiety disorder that may or may not coexist with panic disorder because it turns out that it can coexist with a variety of disorders (Asmundson, Taylor, & Smits, 2014).

Obsessive-Compulsive Disorder

Obsessions are *thoughts* that repeatedly intrude on one's consciousness in a distressing way. Compulsions are *actions* that one feels forced to carry out. Thus, **an *obsessive-compulsive disorder (OCD)* is marked by persistent, uncontrollable intrusions of unwanted thoughts (obsessions) and urges to engage in senseless rituals (compulsions).** To illustrate, let's examine the bizarre behavior of a man once reputed to be the wealthiest person in the world:

The famous industrialist Howard Hughes was obsessed with the possibility of being contaminated by germs. This led him to devise extraordinary rituals to minimize the possibility of such contamination. He would spend hours methodically cleaning a single telephone. He once wrote a three-page memo instructing assistants on exactly how to open cans of fruit for him. The following is just a small portion of the instructions that Hughes provided for a driver who delivered films to his bungalow. "Get out of the car on the traffic side. . . . Carry only one can of film at a time. Step over the gutter opposite the place where the sidewalk dead-ends into the curb from a point as far out into the center of the road as possible. Do not ever walk on the grass at all, also do not step into the gutter at all." (Adapted from Barlett & Steele, 1979, pp. 227–237)

Obsessions often center on fear of contamination, inflicting harm on others, personal failures, suicide, or sexual acts. Compulsions usually involve rituals that temporarily relieve the anxiety produced by one's obsessions. Common examples include constant handwashing; repetitive cleaning of things that are already clean; endless rechecking of locks, faucets, and such; and excessive arranging, counting, and hoarding of things. Specific types of obsessions tend to be associated with specific types of compulsions. For example, obsessions about contamination tend to be paired with cleaning compulsions, and obsessions about symmetry tend to be paired with ordering and arranging compulsions. People with OCD vary considerably in regard to how much insight they have into their disorder. Some are keenly aware that their obsessions and compulsions are irrational, whereas others are convinced that their behavior is rational (Abramowitz & Jacoby, 2015).

Handwashing is one of the most common compulsions among OCD patients, second only to checking and rechecking. Some theorists believe these compulsions are driven by a need to reduce irrational feelings of guilt.

Many of us can be compulsive at times. Indeed, in samples of people without a mental disorder many individuals report significant obsessions or compulsions (Clark et al., 2014). However, full-fledged obsessive-compulsive *disorders* occur in roughly 2%–3% of the population (Zohar, Fostick, & Juven-Wetzler, 2009). Although OCD is often trivialized in the media (Pavelko & Myrick, 2015), OCD can be a very serious disorder, as it is often associated with severe social and occupational impairments (Dougherty, Wilhelm, & Jenike, 2014), as well as elevations in suicidal behavior (Angelakis et al., 2015). OCD is unusual among anxiety-related problems in that it is seen in males and females in roughly equal numbers (Gallo et al., 2013).

Etiology of Anxiety-Related Disturbances

Like most psychological disorders, anxiety disorders and OCD develop out of complicated interactions among a variety of factors. Conditioning and learning appear especially important, but biological factors may also contribute.

Biological Factors

Recent studies suggest that there may be a weak to moderate genetic predisposition to anxiety-related disorders, depending on the specific type of disorder (Fyer, 2009). These findings are consistent with the idea that inherited differences in temperament might make some people more vulnerable than others to anxiety problems. Kagan and his colleagues (1992) found that about 15%–20% of infants display an *inhibited temperament*, characterized by shyness, timidity, and wariness, which appears to have a strong genetic basis. Research suggests that this temperament is a risk factor for the development of anxiety disorders (Coles, Schofield, & Pietrefesa, 2006).

Recent evidence suggests that a link may exist between anxiety-dominated disturbances and neurochemical activity in the brain. *Neurotransmitters* **are chemicals that carry signals from one neuron to another.** Therapeutic drugs (such as Valium or Xanax) that reduce excessive anxiety appear to alter activity at synapses for a neurotransmitter called GABA. This finding and other lines of evidence suggest that disturbances in the neural circuits using GABA may play a role in some types of anxiety disorders (Rowa & Antony, 2008). Abnormalities in other neural circuits using the transmitter serotonin have been implicated in obsessive-compulsive disorders (Sadock, Sadock, & Ruiz, 2015). Thus, scientists are beginning to unravel the neurochemical bases for these kinds of disorders.

Conditioning and Learning

Many anxiety responses may be *acquired through classical conditioning* and *maintained through operant conditioning* (see Chapter 2). According to Mowrer (1947), an originally neutral stimulus (the snow in Hilda's case, for instance) may be paired with a frightening event (the avalanche) so that it becomes a conditioned stimulus eliciting anxiety (see **Figure 14.4**). Once a fear is acquired through classical conditioning, the person may start

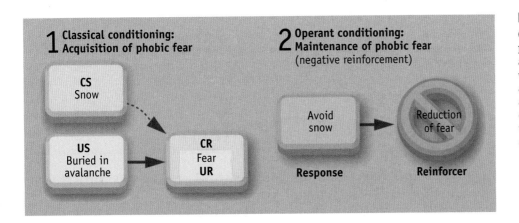

Figure 14.4

Conditioning as an explanation for phobias. (1) Many phobias appear to be acquired through classical conditioning when a neutral stimulus is paired with an anxiety-arousing stimulus. (2) Once acquired, a phobia may be maintained through operant conditioning because avoidance of the phobic stimulus leads to a reduction in anxiety, resulting in negative reinforcement.

People tend to develop phobias to snakes very easily but to hot stoves rarely, even though the latter can be just as painful. Preparedness theory can explain this paradox.

avoiding the anxiety-producing stimulus. The avoidance response is *negatively reinforced* because it is followed by a reduction in anxiety. This process involves operant conditioning (also shown in **Figure 14.4**). Thus, separate conditioning processes may create and then sustain specific anxiety responses. Consistent with this view, studies find that a substantial portion of people suffering from phobias can identify a traumatic conditioning experience that probably contributed to their anxiety disorder (McCabe & Antony, 2008). The acquisition of conditioned fears is far from automatic, however. For a variety of reasons, people vary in how easily they develop conditioned fears that may evolve into anxiety problems (Mineka, 2013).

The tendency to develop phobias of certain types of objects and situations may be explained by Martin Seligman's (1971) concept of *preparedness*. Like many theorists, Seligman believes that classical conditioning creates most phobic responses. *However, he suggests that people are biologically prepared by their evolutionary history to acquire some fears much more easily than others.* His theory would explain why people develop phobias of ancient sources of threat (such as snakes, spiders, and heights) much more readily than modern sources of threat (such as electrical outlets, hammers, or hot irons). Consistent with this view, researchers have found that phobic stimuli associated with evolutionary threats (snakes, spiders) tend to produce more rapid conditioning of fears and stronger fear responses than modern fear-relevant stimuli, such as guns and knives (Mineka & Öhman, 2002).

Cognitive Factors

Cognitive theorists maintain that certain styles of thinking make some people particularly vulnerable to anxiety disorders (Ferreri, Lapp, & Peretti, 2011). According to these theorists, some people are prone to suffer from problems with anxiety because they tend to (1) misinterpret harmless situations as threatening, (2) focus excessive attention on perceived threats, and (3) selectively recall information that seems threatening (Clark & Beck, 2010). In one intriguing test of the cognitive view, anxious and nonanxious subjects were asked to read thirty-two sentences that could be interpreted in either a threatening or a nonthreatening manner (Eysenck et al., 1991). For instance, one such sentence was "The doctor examined little Emma's growth," which could mean that the doctor checked her height or the growth of a tumor. The results showed that the anxious subjects interpreted the sentences in a threatening way more often than the nonanxious subjects did. Thus, the cognitive view holds that some people are prone to anxiety disorders and OCD because they see threat in every corner of their lives. Recently, researchers have also linked OCD to deficits in what is called *executive function*. Executive function refers to the basic cognitive processes that underlie self-regulation, planning, and decision making. In an influential meta-analysis of 110 relevant studies, Snyder et al. (2015) found broad impairments in executive function among OCD patients.

Stress

Finally, studies have supported the long-held suspicion that anxiety disorders are stress related. For instance, Faravelli and Pallanti (1989) found that patients with panic disorder had experienced a dramatic increase in stress in the month prior to the onset of their disorder. Other studies have found that stress levels are predictive of the severity of OCD patients' symptoms (Lin et al., 2007; Morgado et al., 2013). Thus, there is reason to believe that high stress often helps precipitate the onset of anxiety-related disorders.

Learning Objectives

- Distinguish between two types of dissociative disorders.
- Summarize what is known about the causes of dissociative disorders.

14.3 Dissociative Disorders

Dissociative disorders are probably the most controversial set of disorders in the diagnostic system, sparking heated debate among normally subdued researchers and clinicians. *Dissociative disorders* **are a class of disorders in which people lose contact with portions of** their consciousness or memory, resulting in disruptions in their sense of identity. Here we describe two dissociative syndromes—dissociative amnesia and dissociative identity disorder—both of which are relatively uncommon.

Description

Dissociative amnesia **is a sudden loss of memory for important personal information that is too extensive to be due to normal forgetting.** Memory losses may occur for a single traumatic event (such as an automobile accident or home fire) or for an extended period of time surrounding the event. Cases of amnesia have been observed after people have experienced disasters, accidents, combat stress, physical abuse, and rape, or after they have witnessed the violent death of a parent, among other things (Cardeña & Gleaves, 2007). In some cases, having forgotten their name, their family, where they live, and where they work, these people wander away from their home area. In spite of this wholesale forgetting, they remember matters unrelated to their identity, such as how to drive a car and how to do math.

Dissociative identity disorder (DID) **involves the coexistence in one person of two or more largely complete, and usually very different, personalities.** The name for this disorder used to be *multiple personality disorder*, which still enjoys some informal usage. The name for the disorder was changed because the old name seemed to imply that different people inhabited the same body, whereas the modern view is that these individuals fail to integrate incongruent aspects of their personality into a normal, coherent whole (Cardeña et al., 2013). In dissociative identity disorder, the divergences in behavior go far beyond those that people normally display in adapting to different roles in life. People with "multiple personalities" feel that they have more than one identity. Each personality has his or her own name, memories, traits, and physical mannerisms. Although it is relatively infrequent, this syndrome is often portrayed in novels, movies, and television shows, such as the satirical film *Me, Myself, and Irene*, a 2000 release starring Jim Carrey. In popular media portrayals, the syndrome is often mistakenly called *schizophrenia*. As you will see later, schizophrenic disorders are entirely different.

In dissociative identity disorder, the various personalities generally report that they are unaware of each other, although objective measures of memory suggest otherwise (Huntjens et al., 2006). The alternate personalities commonly display traits that are quite foreign to the original personality. For instance, a shy, inhibited person might develop a flamboyant, extraverted alternate personality. Transitions between identities often occur suddenly. The disparities between identities can be bizarre, as personalities may assert that they are different in age, race, gender, or sexual orientation (Kluft, 1996). Dissociative identity disorder is seen more in women than men (Simeon & Loewenstein, 2009).

Starting in the 1970s, a dramatic increase was seen in the diagnosis of DID. Only seventy-nine well-documented cases had accumulated up through 1970, but by the late-1990s about 40,000 cases were estimated to have been reported (Lilienfeld & Lynn, 2003). Some theorists believe that the disorder used to be underdiagnosed—that is, it often went undetected (Maldonado & Spiegel, 2014). However, other theorists argue that a handful of clinicians have begun overdiagnosing the condition and that some clinicians even contribute to the emergence of DID (Boysen & VanBergen, 2013). Consistent with this view, a survey of all the psychiatrists in Switzerland found that 90% of them had never seen a case of DID and 6 psychiatrists (out of 655 surveyed) accounted for two-thirds of the dissociative identity disorder diagnoses in Switzerland (Modestin, 1992).

Etiology of Dissociative Disorders

Dissociative amnesia is usually attributed to excessive stress. However, relatively little is known about why this extreme reaction occurs in a tiny minority of people but not in the vast majority who are subjected to similar stress.

The causes of dissociative identity disorder are the subject of some debate. Some skeptical theorists (Lilienfeld et al., 1999; Lynn et al., 2012) believe that people with multiple identities come to believe, thanks in part to book and movie portrayals of DID and reinforcement from their therapists, that independent entities within them are to blame for their peculiar behaviors, unpredictable moods, and ill-advised actions. Gradually, aided by subtle encouragement from their therapists and a tendency to fantasize, they come to attribute unique traits and memories to imaginary alternate personalities.

In contrast, many clinicians are convinced that DID is an authentic disorder (Dorahy et al., 2014; van der Hart & Nijenhuis, 2009). They argue that there is no incentive for either patients or therapists to manufacture cases of multiple personalities, which are often greeted with skepticism and outright hostility. They maintain that most cases of DID are rooted in severe emotional trauma that occurred during childhood (Maldonado & Spiegel, 2014). A substantial majority of people with DID report a history of disturbed home life, beatings and rejection from parents, and sexual abuse (Van der Hart & Nijenhuis, 2009). However, this abuse typically has not been independently verified (Ross & Ness, 2010). In the final analysis, little is known about the causes of dissociative identity disorder, which remains a controversial diagnosis.

Learning Objectives

- Describe depressive and bipolar disorders, discuss their prevalence, and explain their relation to suicide risk.
- Explain how genetic, neurochemical, and neuroanatomical factors contribute to the development of depressive and bipolar disorders.
- Discuss how cognitive processes, interpersonal factors, and stress contribute to the development of depressive and bipolar disorders.

14.4 Depressive and Bipolar Disorders

What might Abraham Lincoln, Marilyn Monroe, Kurt Cobain, Vincent van Gogh, Ernest Hemingway, Winston Churchill, Ted Turner, Alec Baldwin, Catherine Zeta-Jones, Sting, Jon Hamm, Ben Stiller, Demi Lovato, and Anne Hathaway have in common? Yes, they all achieved great prominence, albeit in different ways at different times. But, more pertinent to our interest, they all suffered from depression or bipolar disorder. Although these disorders can be terribly debilitating, people afflicted with them may still achieve greatness because such disorders tend to be *episodic*. In other words, depressive and bipolar disorders often come and go, interspersed among periods of normality.

In DSM-III and DSM-IV, *major depressive disorder* and *bipolar disorder* were lumped together in a category called mood disorders. In DSM-5 they each get their own chapter or

Many well-known people, such as Ben Stiller and Demi Lovato, have suffered from depressive and bipolar disorders. The episodic nature of these disorders means that they are not incompatible with effective work and success.

category, but we will discuss them together here. **Figure 14.5** depicts the main ways in which these disorders differ. People with major depressive disorder experience emotional extremes at just one end of the mood continuum as they experience periodic bouts of depression. People with bipolar disorders experience emotional extremes at both ends of the mood continuum, going through periods of both *depression* and *mania* (excitement and elation). Actually, although the name for the disorder suggests that all bipolar individuals experience both depression and mania, a small minority of people with bipolar disorder do not report episodes of depression (Johnson, Cuellar, & Peckham, 2014).

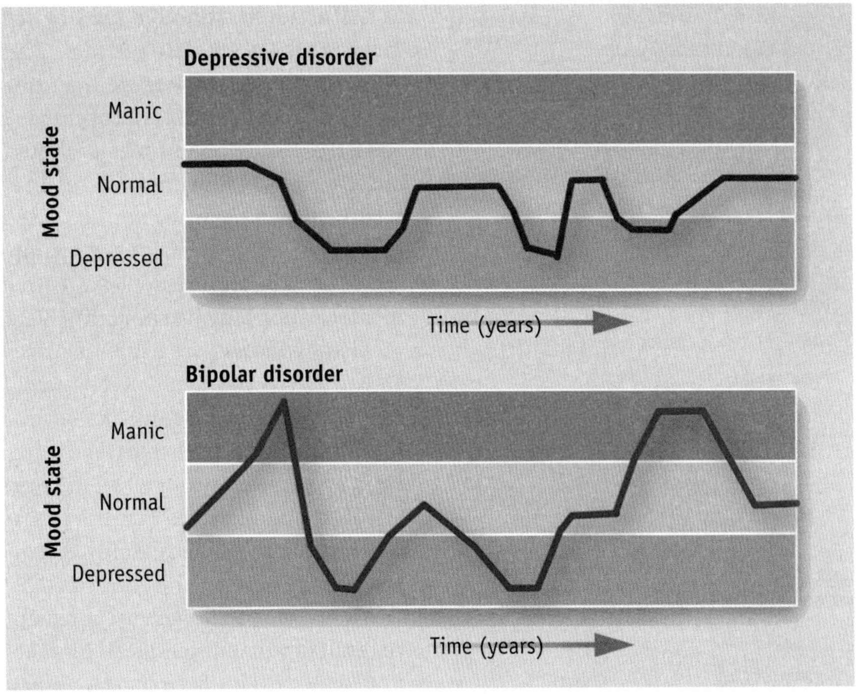

Major Depressive Disorder

The line between normal and abnormal depression can be difficult to draw (Bebbington, 2013). The *depressive disorders* category includes a number of milder syndromes, but the most common disorder in this domain is *major depressive disorder*. **In *major depressive disorder* people show persistent feelings of sadness and despair and a loss of interest in previous sources of pleasure.** **Figure 14.6** summarizes the most common symptoms of depressive episodes and compares them to the symptoms of manic episodes. A central feature of depression is *anhedonia*—**a diminished ability to experience pleasure.** Depressed people lack the energy or motivation to tackle the tasks of living, to the point where they often have trouble getting out of bed. Hence, they often give up things they used to find enjoyable, such as hobbies, favorite foods, or spending time with friends. Reduced appetite and insomnia are common. People with depression often lack energy. They tend to move sluggishly and talk slowly. Anxiety, irritability, and brooding are frequently observed. Self-esteem tends to sink as the depressed person begins to feel worthless.

The first onset of depression can occur at any point in the life span. However, a substantial majority of cases emerge before age 40. Depression occurs in children and adolescents,

Figure 14.5

Episodic patterns in depressive and bipolar disorders. Episodes of emotional disturbance come and go unpredictably in depressive and bipolar disorders. People with major depressive disorders suffer from bouts of depression only, while people with bipolar disorders experience both manic and depressive episodes. The time between episodes of disturbance varies greatly.

COMPARISON OF DEPRESSIVE AND MANIC SYMPTOMS		
Symptoms	**Depressive episode**	**Manic episode**
Emotional symptoms	Dysphoric, gloomy mood Diminished ability to experience pleasure Sense of hopelessness	Euphoric, enthusiastic mood Excessive pursuit of pleasurable activities Unwarranted optimism
Behavioral symptoms	Fatigue, loss of energy Insomnia Slowed speech and movement Social withdrawal	Energetic, tireless, hyperactive Decreased need for sleep Rapid speech and agitation Increased sociability
Cognitive symptoms	Impaired ability to think and make decisions Slowed thought processes Excessive worry, rumination Guilt, self-blame, unrealistic negative evaluations of one's worth	Grandiose planning, indiscriminate decision making Racing thoughts, easily distracted Impulsive behavior Inflated self-esteem and self-confidence

Figure 14.6

Common symptoms in manic and depressive episodes. The emotional, cognitive, and motor symptoms exhibited in manic and depressive episodes are largely the opposite of each other.

Susan Nolen-Hoeksema was renowned for her research on rumination and gender differences in depression.

as well as adults, although rates of depression are notably lower in children and somewhat lower in adolescents (Rohde et al., 2013). The vast majority of people who suffer from major depression experience more than one episode over the course of their lifetime (McInnis, Riba, & Greden, 2014). The average number of depressive episodes is five to six. The average length of these episodes is about 5 to 7 months (Keller et al., 2013). An earlier age of onset is associated with more recurrences, more severe symptoms, and a worse prognosis (Hammen & Keenan-Miller, 2013). Although depression tends to be episodic, some people suffer from chronic major depression that may persist for many years (Klein & Allmann, 2014). Depression is associated with an elevated risk for a variety of health problems and increases mortality by about 50% (Cuijpers et al., 2014).

How common are depressive disorders? Lifetime prevalence is estimated to be around 13% to 16% (Hammen & Keenan-Miller, 2013). At the low end, that estimate suggests that roughly 40 million people in the United States have suffered or will suffer from depression! If that news isn't sufficiently depressing, there is new evidence that the prevalence of depression may be on the rise in recent birth cohorts (Twenge, 2014).

Research indicates that the prevalence of depression is about twice as high in women as it is in men (Gananca, Kahn, & Oquendo, 2014). The many possible explanations for this gender gap are the subject of considerable debate. The gap does *not* appear to be attributable to differences in genetic makeup (Franić et al., 2010). A portion of the disparity may be result of women's elevated vulnerability to depression at certain points in their reproductive life cycle (Hilt & Nolen-Hoeksema, 2014). Obviously, only women have to worry abut the phenomena of postpartum and postmenopausal depression. Susan Nolen-Hoeksema (2001) argues that women experience more depression than men because they are far more likely to be victims of sexual abuse and somewhat more likely to endure poverty, harassment, and role constraints. In other words, she attributes the higher prevalence of depression among women to their experience of greater stress and adversity. Nolen-Hoeksema also believes that women have a greater tendency than men to *ruminate* about setbacks and problems. Evidence suggests that this tendency to dwell on one's difficulties elevates vulnerability to depression, as we will discuss momentarily.

Bipolar Disorder

Bipolar disorder **is typically marked by the experience of both depressed and manic periods.** The symptoms seen in manic periods are generally the opposite of those seen in depression (see **Figure 14.6** for a comparison). In a manic episode, a person's mood becomes elevated to the point of euphoria. Self-esteem skyrockets as the person bubbles over with optimism, energy, and extravagant plans. Individuals become hyperactive and may go for days without sleep. They talk rapidly and shift topics wildly as their minds race at breakneck speed. Judgment is often impaired. Some people in manic periods gamble impulsively, spend money frantically, or become sexually reckless. Although manic episodes may have some positive aspects (increases in energy and optimism), bipolar disorder ultimately proves to be troublesome for most victims. Manic periods often have a paradoxical negative undertow of uneasiness and irritability (Goodwin & Jamison, 2007). Moreover, mild manic episodes often escalate to higher levels that become scary and disturbing. Impaired judgment leads many victims to do things that they greatly regret later, as illustrated in the following case:

Robert, a dentist, awoke one morning with the idea that he was the most gifted dental surgeon in his tri-state area. He decided to remodel his two-chair dental office, installing twenty booths so that he could simultaneously attend to twenty patients. Impatient to get going on his remodeling, he rolled up his sleeves, got himself a sledgehammer, and began to knock down the walls in his office. Annoyed when that didn't go so well, he smashed his dental tools, washbasins, and X-ray equipment. Later, Robert's wife became concerned about his behavior and summoned two of her adult daughters for assistance. The daughters responded quickly, arriving at the family home with their husbands. In the ensuing discussion, Robert—after bragging about his sexual prowess—made advances toward his daughters. (Adapted from Kleinmuntz, 1980, p. 309)

Although not rare, bipolar disorder is much less common than depression. Bipolar disorder affects about 1% of the population, and unlike depression, it is seen equally often in males and females (Jauhar & Cavanagh, 2013). The onset of bipolar disorder is strongly age related. The typical age of onset is in the late teens or early twenties (Ketter & Chang, 2014).

Mood Dysfunction and Suicide

A tragic, heartbreaking problem associated with depressive and bipolar disorders is suicide, which is the tenth leading cause of death in the United States, accounting for about 40,000 deaths annually. Official statistics may underestimate the scope of the problem (Pritchard & Hansen, 2015), as many suicides are disguised as accidents, either by the suicidal person or by the survivors who try to cover up afterward. Moreover, experts estimate that suicide attempts may outnumber completed suicides by a ratio of as much as twenty-five to one (Rothberg & Feinstein, 2014). Evidence suggests that women *attempt* suicide three times more often than men. But men are more likely to actually kill themselves in an attempt, so they *complete* four times as many suicides as women (Rothberg & Feinstein, 2014).

With the luxury of hindsight, it is recognized that about 90% of the people who complete suicide suffer from some type of psychological disorder, although in some cases this disorder may not be readily apparent beforehand (Nock et al., 2014). As you might expect, both bipolar disorder and depression are associated with dramatic elevations in suicide rates. These disorders account for about 50% to 60% of completed suicides (Nock et al., 2014). The likelihood of a suicide attempt increases as the severity of individuals' depression increases. Still, suicide is notoriously difficult to predict. Perhaps the best predictor is when one expresses a sense of hopelessness about the future, but even that can be difficult to gauge (MacLeod, 2013). Unfortunately, there is no foolproof way to prevent suicidal persons from taking their own life. But some useful tips are compiled in **Figure 14.7**.

Etiology of Depressive and Bipolar Disorders

We know quite a bit about the etiology of depressive and bipolar disorders, although the puzzle hasn't been assembled completely. There appear to be a number of routes into these disorders, involving intricate interactions between psychological and biological factors.

Genetic Vulnerability

The evidence strongly suggests that genetic factors influence the likelihood of developing major depression (Lau et al., 2014) and bipolar disorder (Macritchie & Blackwood, 2013). In studies that assess the impact of heredity on psychological disorders, investigators look at *concordance rates*. **A *concordance rate* indicates the percentage of twin pairs or other pairs of relatives who exhibit the same disorder.** If relatives who share more genetic similarity show higher concordance rates than relatives who share less genetic overlap, this finding supports the genetic hypothesis. Twin studies, which compare identical and fraternal twins (see Chapter 2), suggest that genetic factors *are* involved in depressive and bipolar disorders (Kelsoe, 2009). Concordance rates average around 65% to 72% for identical twins but only 14% to 19% for fraternal twins, who share less genetic similarity.

"*Those? Oh, just a few souvenirs from my bipolar-disorder days.*"

Tom Cheney/The New Yorker Collection/Cartoon Bank.com

SUICIDE PREVENTION TIPS

1. *Take suicidal talk seriously.* When people talk about suicide in vague generalities, it's easy to dismiss it as idle talk and let it go. However, people who talk about suicide are a high-risk group, and their veiled threats should not be ignored. The first step in suicide prevention is to directly ask such people if they're contemplating suicide.

2. *Provide empathy and social support.* It is important to show the suicidal person that you care. People often contemplate suicide because they see the world around them as indifferent and uncaring. Thus, you must demonstrate to the suicidal person that you are genuinely concerned. Suicide threats are often a last-ditch cry for help. It is therefore imperative that you offer to help.

3. *Identify and clarify the crucial problem.* The suicidal person is often confused and feels lost in a sea of frustration and problems. It is a good idea to try to help sort through this confusion. Encourage the person to try to identify the crucial problem. Once it is isolated, the problem may not seem quite so overwhelming.

4. *Do not promise to keep someone's suicidal ideation secret.* If you really feel like someone's life is in danger, don't agree to keep his or her suicidal plans secret to preserve your friendship.

5. *In an acute crisis, do not leave a suicidal person alone.* Stay with the person until additional help is available. Try to remove any guns, drugs, sharp objects, and so forth that might provide an available means to commit suicide.

6. *Encourage professional consultation.* Most mental health professionals have some experience in dealing with suicidal crises. Many cities have suicide prevention centers with 24-hour hotlines. These centers are staffed with people who have been specially trained to deal with suicidal problems. It is important to try to get a suicidal person to seek professional assistance.

Figure 14.7

Preventing suicide. As Sudak (2005) notes, "It is not possible to prevent all suicides or to totally and absolutely protect a given patient from suicide. What is possible is to reduce the likelihood of suicide" (p. 2449). Hence, the advice summarized here may prove useful if you ever have to help someone through a suicidal crisis. (Based on American Association of Suicidology, 2007; American Foundation for Suicide Prevention, 2007; Fremouw, de Perczel, & Ellis, 1990; Rosenthal, 1988; Shneidman, Farberow, & Litman, 1994)

Thus, evidence suggests that heredity can create a *predisposition* to these disorders. Environmental factors probably determine whether this predisposition is converted into an actual disorder.

Neurochemical and Neuroanatomical Factors

Heredity may influence susceptibility to depressive and bipolar disorders by creating a predisposition toward certain types of neurochemical abnormalities in the brain. Correlations have been found between these disorders and abnormal levels of two neurotransmitters in the brain: norepinephrine and serotonin, although other neurotransmitter disturbances may also contribute (Thase, Hahn, & Berton, 2014). The details remain elusive, but low levels of serotonin appear to be a crucial factor underlying most forms of depression. A variety of drug therapies can be helpful in the treatment of depressive disorders. Most of these drugs are known to affect the availability (in the brain) of the neurotransmitters that have been related to depressive disorders (Bhagwagar & Heninger, 2009). Since this effect is unlikely to be a coincidence, it bolsters the plausibility of the idea that neurochemical changes contribute to depressive and bipolar disturbances.

Studies have also found some interesting correlations between depressive disorders and a variety of structural abnormalities in the brain. Perhaps the best-documented correlation is the association between depression and *reduced hippocampal volume*, especially in the dentate gyrus of the hippocampus (Treadway et al., 2015; Schmaal et al., 2015; see **Figure 14.8**). A relatively new theory of the biological bases of depression may be able to account for this finding. The springboard for this theory is the discovery that the human brain continues to generate new neurons (*neurogenesis*) in adulthood, especially in the hippocampus (Kozorovitskiy & Gould, 2008). Recent evidence suggests that depression

Figure 14.8

The hippocampus and depression. This graphic shows the hippocampus in blue. The photo inset shows a brain dissected to reveal the hippocampus in both the right and left hemispheres. It has long been known that the hippocampus plays a key role in memory, but its possible role in depression has come to light only in recent years. Research suggests that shrinkage of the hippocampal formation due to suppressed neurogenesis may be a key causal factor underlying depressive disorders.

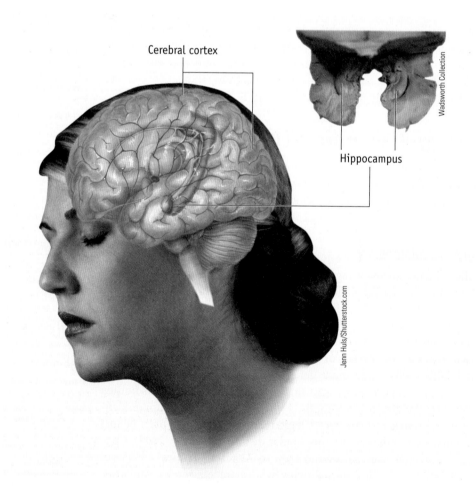

Cerebral cortex

Hippocampus

occurs when major life stress causes neurochemical reactions that suppress this neurogenesis, resulting in reduced hippocampal volume (Mahar et al., 2014). According to this view, the suppression of neurogenesis is the central cause of depression, and antidepressant drugs are successful because they promote neurogenesis (Boldrini et al., 2013). Other lines of research have implicated abnormally high reactivity in the *amygdala* as a factor in depression. The amygdala is a small structure in the brain that is known to play a key role in the learning of fear responses and may contribute to the regulation of other emotions (LeDoux & Damasio, 2013). Brain-imaging studies indicate that depressed subjects show heightened reactivity in the amygdala to negative emotional stimuli, which may contribute to vulnerability to depression (Swartz, Williamson, & Hairi, 2015).

Cognitive Factors

A variety of theories emphasize how cognitive factors contribute to depressive disorders (Clasen, Disner, & Beevers, 2013). We will discuss Aaron Beck's (1987) influential cognitive theory of depression in Chapter 15, where his approach to therapy is described. In this section, we examine Martin Seligman's *learned helplessness model* of depression. Based largely on animal research, Seligman (1974) proposed that depression is caused by *learned helplessness*—passive "giving up" behavior produced by exposure to unavoidable aversive events (such as uncontrollable shock in the laboratory). He originally considered learned helplessness to be a product of conditioning but eventually revised his theory, giving it a cognitive slant. The reformulated theory of learned helplessness postulates that the roots of depression lie in how people explain the setbacks and other negative events that they experience (Abramson, Seligman, & Teasdale, 1978). According to Seligman (1990), people who exhibit a *pessimistic explanatory style* are especially vulnerable to depression. These people tend to attribute their setbacks to their personal flaws instead of to situational factors, and they tend to draw global, far-reaching conclusions about their personal inadequacies based on these setbacks.

In accord with cognitive models of depression, Susan Nolen-Hoeksema (1991, 2000) has found that people who *ruminate* about their problems and setbacks have elevated rates of depression and tend to remain depressed longer than those who do not ruminate. People who tend to ruminate repetitively focus their attention on their depressing feelings, thinking constantly about how sad, lethargic, and unmotivated they are. Excessive rumination tends to foster and amplify episodes of depression by increasing negative thinking, impairing problem solving, and undermining social support (Lyubomirsky et al., 2015). Nolen-Hoeksema believes that women have a greater tendency to ruminate than men and that this disparity may be a major reason that depression is more prevalent in women.

In sum, cognitive models of depression maintain that negative thinking is what leads to depression in many people. The principal problem with cognitive theories is their difficulty in separating cause from effect. Does negative thinking cause depression? Or does depression cause negative thinking (see **Figure 14.9**)? Strong evidence favoring a causal role for negative thinking comes from a study by Alloy and colleagues (1999) who assessed explanatory style in first-year college students who were not depressed at the outset of the study, which followed students for 2.5 years. They found that a negative explanatory style was associated with increased occurrence of depression, as a major depressive disorder emerged in 17% of the students who exhibited a negative explanatory style in comparison to only 1% of the control students. These findings suggest that negative thinking makes people more vulnerable to depression.

Interpersonal Roots

Some theorists suggest that inadequate social skills put people on the road to depressive disorders (Ingram, Scott, & Hamill, 2009;

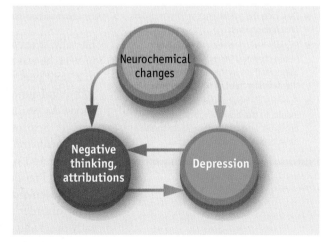

Figure 14.9

Interpreting the correlation between negative thinking and depression. Cognitive theories of depression assert that consistent patterns of negative thinking cause depression. Although these theories are highly plausible, depression could cause negative thoughts, or both could be caused by a third factor, such as neurochemical changes in the brain.

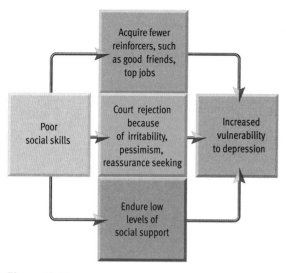

Figure 14.10

Interpersonal factors in depression. Interpersonal theories about the etiology of depression emphasize how inadequate social skills may contribute to the development of the disorder. Recent studies suggest that excessive reassurance seeking may play a particularly critical role in the social dynamics promoting depression.

see **Figure 14.10**). These theorists point out that depression-prone people lack the social finesse needed to acquire many important kinds of reinforcers, such as good friends, top jobs, and desirable spouses. This paucity of reinforcers could understandably lead to negative emotions and depression. Consistent with this theory, researchers have indeed found correlations between poor social skills and depression (Petty, Sachs-Ericsson, & Joiner, 2004).

Another interpersonal factor is that depressed people tend to be depressing (Joiner & Timmons, 2009). Individuals suffering from depression are often irritable and pessimistic. They complain a lot and aren't particularly enjoyable companions. They also alienate people by constantly asking for reassurances about their relationships and their worth. This excessive reassurance seeking ends up fostering rejection and is predictive of depression (Hames, Hagan, & Joiner, 2013). Yet another issue is that complicated and difficult social relations can greatly increase the level of stress in one's life. Insofar as depressed people are prone to experience awkward, tense, stormy, and frustrating interactions with family, friends, and colleagues, they are likely to generate chronic stress for themselves (Hammen & Shih, 2014), and as we will discuss next, stress can be a factor in mood dysfunction.

Precipitating Stress

Depressive and bipolar disorders sometimes appear mysteriously "out of the blue" in people who seem to be leading benign, nonstressful lives. For this reason, experts used to believe that these disorders were relatively uninfluenced by stress. However, advances in the measurement of personal stress have altered this picture. The evidence available today suggests the existence of a moderately strong link between stress and the onset of both major depression (Monroe, Slavich, & Georgiades, 2014) and bipolar disorder (Johnson et al., 2014). Of course, the vast majority of people who experience significant stress do not develop these disorders, so one's vulnerability to both stress and mood dysfunction must play a role (Bifulco, 2013). Unfortunately, vulnerability to depression seems to increase as people go through more recurrences of depressive episodes. Studies show that stress is less of a factor in triggering depression as episodes of depression accumulate over the years (Monroe et al., 2014).

14.5 Schizophrenic Disorders

Learning Objectives

- Describe the prevalence and symptoms of schizophrenia.
- Explain how genetic vulnerability, neurochemical factors, and structural abnormalities in the brain contribute to the development of schizophrenia.
- Summarize how neurodevelopmental insults to the brain, expressed emotion, and stress contribute to the development of schizophrenia.

Literally, *schizophrenia* means "split mind." However, when Eugen Bleuler coined the term in 1911, he was referring to the fragmenting of thought processes seen in the disorder—not to a "split personality." Unfortunately, writers in the popular media often assume that the split-mind notion refers to the syndrome in which a person manifests two or more personalities. As you have already learned, this syndrome is actually called *dissociative identity disorder.* Schizophrenia is a much more common, and altogether different, type of disorder.

Schizophrenia **is a disorder marked by delusions, hallucinations, disorganized thinking and speech, and deterioration of adaptive behavior.** How common is schizophrenia? Prevalence estimates suggest that about 1% of the population may suffer from schizophrenic disorders (Sadock, Sadock, & Ruiz, 2015). Schizophrenia is an extremely costly disorder for society because it is a severe, debilitating illness that tends to have an early onset and often requires lengthy hospital care. Moreover, individuals suffering from schizophrenia show an increased risk for suicide and for premature mortality (early death) from natural causes (Nielsen et al., 2013).

Symptoms

Schizophrenia is a severe disorder that wreaks havoc in victims' lives. Many of the key symptoms of schizophrenia are apparent in the following case history (adapted from

Sheehan, 1982). Sylvia was first diagnosed as schizophrenic at age 15. She has been in and out of many types of psychiatric facilities since then. During severe flare-ups of her disorder, her personal hygiene deteriorates. She rarely washes, wears clothes that neither fit nor match, and smears makeup on heavily but randomly. Sylvia occasionally hears voices talking to her. Sylvia tends to be argumentative, aggressive, and emotionally volatile. Her thoughts can be highly irrational, as is apparent from the following quotation:

"Mick Jagger wants to marry me. If I have Mick Jagger, I don't have to covet Geraldo Rivera. Mick Jagger is St. Nicholas and the Maharishi is Santa Claus. I want to form a gospel rock group called the Thorn Oil, but Geraldo wants me to be the music critic on Eyewitness News, so what can I do? Got to listen to my boyfriend. Teddy Kennedy cured me of my ugliness. I'm pregnant with the son of God. Creedmoor is the headquarters of the American Nazi Party. They're eating the patients here. I'm Joan of Arc. I'm Florence Nightingale. The door between the ward and the porch is the dividing line between New York and California. Divorce isn't a piece of paper, it's a feeling. Forget about Zip Codes. I need shock treatment." (Sheehan, 1982, pp. 104–105)

Sylvia's case clearly shows that schizophrenic thinking can be bizarre and that schizophrenia is a brutally disfiguring disorder. No single symptom is inevitably present, but the following symptoms are commonly seen in schizophrenia (Arango & Carpenter, 2011).

1. *Irrational thought.* Cognitive deficits and disturbed thought processes are the central, defining feature of schizophrenic disorders (Heinrichs et al., 2013). Various kinds of delusions are common. *Delusions* **are false beliefs that are maintained even though they clearly are out of touch with reality.** For example, one patient's delusion that he was a tiger (with a deformed body) persisted for 15 years (Kulick, Pope, & Keck, 1990). More typically, affected persons believe that their private thoughts are being broadcast to other people, that thoughts are being injected into their mind against their will, or that their thoughts are being controlled by some external force (Maher, 2001). In *delusions of grandeur*, people maintain that they are extremely famous or important. Sylvia expressed an endless array of grandiose delusions, such as thinking that Mick Jagger wanted to marry her and that she dictated the hobbit stories to Tolkien. In addition to delusions, the schizophrenic person's train of thought deteriorates. Thinking becomes chaotic rather than logical and linear. There is a "loosening of associations" as schizophrenic individuals shift topics in disjointed ways. The quotation from Sylvia illustrates this symptom dramatically. The entire passage involves a wild "flight of ideas."

2. *Deterioration of adaptive behavior.* Schizophrenia involves a noticeable deterioration in the quality of the person's routine functioning in work, social relations, and personal care (Harvey & Bowie, 2013). This deterioration is readily apparent in Sylvia's inability to get along with others and her neglect of personal hygiene.

3. *Distorted perception.* A variety of perceptual distortions may occur in schizophrenia, with the most common being auditory hallucinations, which are reported by about 75% of patients (Combs & Mueser, 2007). *Hallucinations* **are sensory perceptions that occur in the absence of a real external stimulus or that represent gross distortions of perceptual input.** Schizophrenics frequently report that they hear voices of nonexistent or absent people talking to them. Sylvia, for instance, heard messages from Paul McCartney. These voices often provide an insulting running commentary on the person's behavior ("You're an idiot for shaking his hand").

4. *Disturbed emotion.* Normal emotional tone can be disrupted in schizophrenia in a variety of ways. Although it may not be an accurate indicator of their underlying emotional experience, some victims show little emotional responsiveness, a symptom referred to as "blunted or flat affect." Others show inappropriate emotional responses that don't jell with the situation or with what they are saying. People with schizophrenia may also become emotionally volatile. This pattern was displayed by Sylvia, who often overreacted emotionally in erratic, unpredictable ways.

Traditionally, four subtypes of schizophrenic disorders were recognized: paranoid, catatonic, disorganized, and undifferentiated schizophrenia (Minzenberg, Yoon, & Carter, 2008). As its name implies, *paranoid schizophrenia* was thought to be dominated by delusions of persecution, along with delusions of grandeur. *Catatonic schizophrenia* was marked by striking motor disturbances, ranging from the muscular rigidity seen in a withdrawn state called a catatonic stupor to random motor activity seen in a state of catatonic excitement. *Disorganized schizophrenia* was viewed as a particularly severe syndrome marked by frequent incoherence, obvious deterioration in adaptive behavior, and virtually complete social withdrawal. People who were clearly schizophrenic but who could not be placed into any of the three previous categories were said to have *undifferentiated schizophrenia*, which involved idiosyncratic mixtures of schizophrenic symptoms.

However, in a radical departure from tradition, DSM-5 discarded the four subtypes of schizophrenia. Why? For many years researchers pointed out that there were not meaningful differences between the classic subtypes in etiology, prognosis, or response to treatment. The absence of such differences cast doubt on the value of distinguishing among the subtypes. Critics also noted that the catatonic and disorganized subtypes were rarely seen in contemporary clinical practice and that undifferentiated cases did not represent a subtype as much as a hodgepodge of "leftovers." Finally, researchers had stopped focusing their studies on the specific subtypes of schizophrenia (Braff et al., 2013).

Another approach to understanding and describing schizophrenia, advocated by Nancy Andreasen (1990) and others, is to distinguish between the *positive symptoms* and *negative symptoms* of the disorder (Stroup et al., 2014; see **Figure 14.11**). *Negative symptoms* involve behavioral deficits, such as flattened emotions, social withdrawal, apathy, impaired attention, poor grooming, lack of persistence at work or school, and poverty of speech. *Positive symptoms* involve behavioral excesses or peculiarities, such as hallucinations, delusions, incoherent thought, agitation, bizarre behavior, and wild flights of ideas. Most patients exhibit both types of symptoms but vary in the *degree* to which positive or negative symptoms dominate (Andreasen, 2009). A relative predominance of negative symptoms is associated with less effective social functioning (Robertson et al., 2014) and poorer overall treatment outcomes (Fervaha et al., 2014).

Schizophrenic disorders usually emerge during adolescence or early adulthood, with 75% of cases manifesting by the age of 30 (Perkins, Miller-Anderson, & Lieberman, 2006). Those who develop schizophrenia usually have a long history of peculiar behavior and cognitive and social deficits, although most do not manifest a full-fledged psychological disorder during childhood. The emergence of schizophrenia may be sudden, but it usually is insidious and gradual.

Etiology of Schizophrenia

Most of us can identify, at least to some extent, with people who suffer from depression, obsessive-compulsive disorders, and phobic disorders. You can probably imagine events that

Figure 14.11

Positive and negative symptoms in schizophrenia. Some theorists believe that schizophrenic disorders can be best understood by thinking in terms of two kinds of symptoms: positive symptoms (behavioral excesses) and negative symptoms (behavioral deficits). The percentages shown here, based on a sample of 111 schizophrenic patients studied by Andreasen (1987), provide an indication of how common each specific symptom is.

POSITIVE AND NEGATIVE SYMPTOMS IN SCHIZOPHRENIA			
Negative symptoms	Percent of patients	Positive symptoms	Percent of patients
Few friendship relationships	96	Delusions of persecution	81
Few recreational interests	95	Auditory hallucinations	75
Lack of persistence at work or school	95	Delusions of being controlled	46
Impaired grooming or hygiene	87	Derailment of thought	45
Paucity of expressive gestures	81	Delusions of grandeur	39
Social inattentiveness	78	Bizarre social, sexual behavior	33
Emotional nonresponsiveness	64	Delusions of thought insertion	31
Inappropriate emotion	63	Aggressive, agitated behavior	27
Poverty of speech	53	Incoherent thought	23

might leave you struggling with depression or grappling with anxiety. But what could account for Sylvia thinking that she was Joan of Arc or that she had dictated the hobbit novels to Tolkien? As mystifying as these delusions may seem, you'll see that the etiology of schizophrenic disorders is not all that different from the etiology of other disorders.

Genetic Vulnerability

Evidence is plentiful that hereditary factors play a role in the development of schizophrenic disorders (Riley & Kendler, 2011). For instance, in twin studies, concordance rates for schizophrenia average around 48% for identical twins, in comparison to about 17% for fraternal twins (Gottesman, 2001). Studies also indicate that a child born to two schizophrenic parents has about a 46% probability of developing a schizophrenic disorder (as compared to the probability of about 1% for the population as a whole). These and other findings that demonstrate the genetic roots of schizophrenia are summarized in **Figure 14.12**. Overall, the picture is similar to that seen for depressive and bipolar disorders. Several converging lines of evidence indicate that people inherit a genetically transmitted *vulnerability* to schizophrenia (Cornblatt et al., 2009). After years of inconsistent findings and difficulties in replicating results, genetic mapping studies are finally beginning to yield some promising insights regarding the specific combinations of genes and genetic mutations that increase individuals' risk for schizophrenia (Gelernter, 2015; Hall et al., 2015).

Recent research suggests that genetic vulnerability may be heightened when it is accompanied by relatively low general intelligence. A large-scale study in Sweden found that low IQ scores were associated with an increased prevalence of schizophrenia (Kendler et al., 2015). The data suggested that IQ moderated the effect of genetic vulnerability, as low IQ amplified genetic risk, whereas high IQ provided some protection against genetic risk.

Neurochemical Factors

Like depressive and bipolar disorders, schizophrenic disorders appear to be accompanied by changes in the activity of one or more neurotransmitters in the brain. Excess *dopamine* activity has been implicated as a likely cause of schizophrenia. This hypothesis makes sense because most of the drugs that are useful in the treatment of schizophrenia are known to dampen dopamine activity in the brain (Stroup et al., 2014). Recent research suggests that increased dopamine *synthesis* and *release* in specific regions of the brain may be the crucial factor that triggers schizophrenic illness in vulnerable individuals (Howes et al., 2011; Winton-Brown et al., 2014).

Studies have found that marijuana use during adolescence may help precipitate schizophrenia in young people who have a genetic vulnerability to the disorder (van Winkel & Kuepper, 2014). This unexpected finding has generated considerable debate about whether and how cannabis might contribute to the emergence of schizophrenia. Some critics have suggested that schizophrenia might lead to cannabis use rather than vice versa. In other words, emerging psychotic symptoms may prompt young people to turn to marijuana to self-medicate. However, recent, carefully controlled studies have not supported the self-medication explanation (van Winkel & Kuepper, 2014). The evidence suggests that there is a causal link between marijuana use and the emergence of schizophrenia, but the mechanism at work remains a mystery.

Structural Abnormalities in the Brain

Individuals with schizophrenia exhibit a variety of deficits in attention, perception, information processing, and short-term memory (Goldberg, David, & Gold, 2011). These cognitive deficits suggest that schizophrenic disorders may be caused by neurological

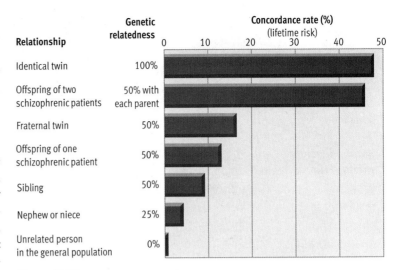

Figure 14.12

Genetic vulnerability to schizophrenic disorders. Relatives of schizophrenic patients have an elevated risk for schizophrenia. This risk is greater among closer relatives. Although environment also plays a role in the etiology of schizophrenia, the concordance rates shown here suggest that there must be a genetic vulnerability to the disorder. These concordance estimates are based on pooled data from forty studies.

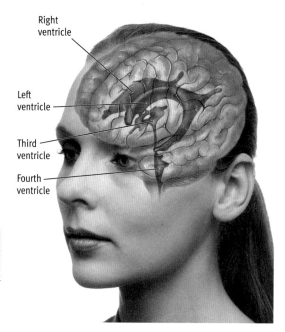

Right
ventricle

Left
ventricle

Third
ventricle

Fourth
ventricle

RimDream/Shutterstock.com

Figure 14.13

Schizophrenia and the ventricles of the brain.
Cerebrospinal fluid (CSF) circulates around the brain and spinal cord. The hollow cavities in the brain filled with CSF are called *ventricles*. The four ventricles in the human brain are depicted here. Studies with modern brain-imaging techniques suggest that an association exists between enlarged ventricles in the brain and the occurrence of schizophrenic disturbance.

defects. Brain imaging studies have yielded findings that support this idea. The most frequent finding is that there is an association between enlarged brain ventricles (the hollow, fluid-filled cavities in the brain depicted in **Figure 14.13**) and schizophrenic disturbance (Lawrie & Pantelis, 2011). Enlarged ventricles are assumed to reflect the degeneration of nearby brain tissue. Consistent with this assumption, a recent meta-analysis of MRI studies of more than 2000 schizophrenia patients found shrinkage in several crucial subcortical structures. The patients were found to have a smaller hippocampus, thalamus, and amygdala than comparable control subjects (van Erp et al., 2015). This structural deterioration could be a *consequence* of schizophrenia, or it could be a contributing *cause* of the illness.

The Neurodevelopmental Hypothesis

The *neurodevelopmental hypothesis* of schizophrenia asserts that schizophrenia is caused in part by various disruptions in the normal maturational processes of the brain before or at birth. According to this hypothesis, insults to the brain during sensitive phases of prenatal development or during birth can cause subtle neurological damage that elevates individuals' vulnerability to schizophrenia years later in adolescence and early adulthood (see **Figure 14.14**). What are the sources of these early insults? Thus far, research has focused mainly on viral infections or malnutrition during prenatal development and obstetrical complications during the birth process.

Quite a number of studies have found a link between exposure to influenza and other infections during prenatal development and increased prevalence of schizophrenia (Brown & Derkits, 2010), with inflammation thought to be the critical process that disrupts neural maturation (Miller et al., 2013). Additionally, a study that investigated the possible impact of prenatal malnutrition found an elevated incidence of schizophrenia in a cohort of people who were prenatally exposed to a severe famine in 1944–1945 because of a Nazi blockade of food deliveries in the Netherlands during World War II (Susser et al., 1996). Other research has shown that schizophrenic patients are more likely than control subjects to have a history of obstetrical complications (McGrath & Murray, 2011). Finally, research suggests that minor physical anomalies (slight anatomical defects of the head, hands, feet, and face) that would be consistent with prenatal neurological damage are more common in people with schizophrenia than in other people (Akabaliev, Sivkov, & Mantarkov, 2014). Collectively, these diverse studies argue for a relationship between early neurological trauma and a predisposition to schizophrenia (Rapoport, Giedd, & Gogtay, 2012).

Expressed Emotion

Studies of expressed emotion have primarily focused on how this element of family dynamics influences the *course* of schizophrenic illness after the onset of the disorder. *Expressed emotion (EE)* reflects the degree to which a relative of a schizophrenic patient displays highly critical or emotionally overinvolved attitudes toward the patient. Audiotaped interviews of relatives' communication are carefully evaluated for critical comments, hostility toward the patient, and excessive emotional involvement (overprotective, overconcerned attitudes).

Studies show that a family's expressed emotion is a good predictor of the course of a schizophrenic patient's illness. After release from a hospital, patients who return to a family high in

Prenatal viral infection

Prenatal malnutrition

Obstetrical complications

Other brain insults

Disruption of normal maturational processes before or at birth

Subtle neurological damage

Increased vulnerability to schizophrenia

Minor physical anomalies

Figure 14.14

The neurodevelopmental hypothesis of schizophrenia. Research suggests that insults to the brain sustained during prenatal development or at birth may disrupt crucial maturational processes in the brain, resulting in subtle neurological damage that gradually becomes apparent as youngsters develop. This neurological damage is believed to increase both vulnerability to schizophrenia and the incidence of minor physical anomalies.

expressed emotion show relapse rates two to three times those of patients who return to a family low in expressed emotion (Hooley, 2009). Part of the problem for patients returning to homes high in expressed emotion is that their families are probably sources of stress rather than of social support (Bebbington & Kuipers, 2011).

Stress

Many theories of schizophrenia assume that stress plays a role in triggering schizophrenic disorders. According to this notion, various biological and psychological factors influence individuals' *vulnerability* to schizophrenia. High stress may then serve to precipitate a schizophrenic disorder in someone who is vulnerable (Bebbington & Kuipers, 2011).

Until relatively recently, interest in the connection between stress and schizophrenia was limited to how adverse events in adolescence or early adulthood may contribute to provoking the onset of the disorder. However, in recent years there has been a surge of research on how severe stress in early childhood may increase individuals' vulnerability to schizophrenia 10 to 20 years later. In particular, quite a number of studies have reported a link between early childhood trauma and later psychotic disorders and symptoms (Bendall, Jackson, & Hulbert, 2010). For example, one recent study found an association between psychotic symptoms and exposure to sexual abuse, physical abuse, bullying, and institutional care during childhood (Bentall et al., 2012). It is not clear, however, whether the long-term negative effects of childhood trauma are specific to schizophrenia. For example, recent reviews have linked early childhood stress to a wide range of disorders, including depression, anxiety disorders, and eating disorders (Carr et al., 2013; Martins et al., 2011).

14.6 Autism Spectrum Disorder

Autism, or autism spectrum disorder (ASD), **is characterized by profound impairment of social interaction and communication and severely restricted interests and activities.** Originally called *infantile autism,* this disorder was first described by child psychiatrist Leo Kanner in the 1940s.

Symptoms

The central feature of autistic disorder is the child's lack of interest in other people. Children with autism act as though people in their environment are no different than nearby inanimate objects, such as toys, pillows, or chairs. They tend not to make eye contact with others or to need physical contact with their caregivers. They make no effort to connect with people and fail to bond with their parents or to develop normal peer relationships. Verbal communication can be very impaired, as about one-third of autistic children fail to develop speech (Wetherby & Prizant, 2005). Among those who do develop speech, their ability to initiate and sustain a conversation is very limited. And their use of language tends to be marked by peculiarities, such as *echolalia,* which involves rote repetition of others' words. Autistic children's interests are restricted in that they tend to become preoccupied with objects or repetitive body movements (spinning, body rocking, playing with their hands, and so forth). They can also be extremely inflexible, in that minor changes in their environment can trigger rages. Some autistic children exhibit self-injurious behavior, such as banging their heads, pulling their hair, or hitting themselves. About half of autistic children exhibit subnormal IQ scores (Volkmar et al., 2009).

Parents of autistic children typically become concerned about their child's development by about 15 to 18 months of age and usually seek professional consultation by about 24 months. The diagnosis of autism is usually made before affected children reach 3 years of age. More often than not, autism turns out to be a lifelong affliction requiring extensive family and institutional support throughout adulthood. However, with early and effective intervention, around 15% to 20% of autistic individuals are able to live independently in

Children with autism often fail to make eye contact with others and tend to find social attention unpleasant.

adulthood and another 20% to 30% approach this level of functioning (Volkmar et al., 2009). Moreover, recent research suggests that a small minority may experience a full recovery in adulthood (Fein et al., 2013).

Until relatively recently, the prevalence of autism was thought to be well under 1% (Newsschaffer, 2007). Since the mid-1990s, however, a dramatic (roughly fourfold) increase has occurred in the diagnosis of autism, with prevalence estimates approaching and even exceeding 1% (Idring et al., 2014; Zahorodny et al., 2014). Most experts believe that this surge in ASD is largely due to the result of greater awareness of the syndrome and the use of broader diagnostic criteria (Abbeduto et al., 2014). Contemporary prevalence estimates usually include related syndromes, such as *Asperger's disorder*, that are milder forms of the disorder that used to go uncounted, but are now included within the broadly defined DSM-5 version of autism *spectrum* disorder. Males account for about 80% of autism diagnoses, although curiously females tend to exhibit more severe impairments (Ursano, Kartheiser, & Barnhill, 2008).

Etiology of Autism Spectrum Disorder

Autism was originally blamed on cold, aloof parenting (Bettelheim, 1967), but that view was eventually discredited by research (Bhasin & Schendel, 2007). Given its appearance so early in life, most theorists today view autism as a disorder that originates in biological dysfunctions. Consistent with that viewpoint, twin studies and family studies have demonstrated that genetic factors make a major contribution to autistic disorders (Risch et al., 2014). Many theorists believe that autism must be due to some sort of brain abnormality, but until recently there was relatively little progress in pinpointing the nature of this abnormality. The most reliable finding has been that autism is associated with generalized brain enlargement that is apparent by age 2 (Hazlett et al., 2011). Children with autism appear to have 67% more neurons in the prefrontal cortex than other children (Courchesne et al., 2011). One recent study found evidence that this overgrowth may begin during prenatal development (Stoner et al., 2014). Theorists speculate that this overgrowth probably produces disruptions in neural circuits.

One hypothesis that has garnered a great deal of publicity is the idea that autism may be caused by the mercury used as a preservative in some childhood vaccines (Kirby, 2005). However, the 1998 study that first reported a link between vaccinations and autism has been discredited as fraudulent (Deer, 2011; Godlee, Smith, & Marcovitch, 2011). Moreover, independent efforts to replicate the purported association between vaccinations and autism have consistently failed (Paul, 2009; Wing & Potter, 2009), which brings us to our Spotlight on Research.

Spotlight on RESEARCH

Autism and Vaccinations

Source: Jain, A., Marshall, J., Buikema, A., Bancroft, T., Kelly, J. P., & Newschaffer, C. J. (2015). Autism occurrence by MMR vaccine status among U.S. children with older siblings with and without autism. *Journal of the American Medical Association, 313*(15), 1534–1540.

A number of studies have failed to find any correlation between measles mumps rubella (MMR) vaccinations and the incidence of autism spectrum disorder. However, due to all the "chatter" in popular media, many parents continue to believe that vaccines cause ASD. These concerns have led to reduced vaccination rates that appear to be responsible for several recent outbreaks of measles. The present study took another look at this controversial issue, using an exceptionally large sample, with a special focus on siblings of children with ASD, who are known to have an elevated risk for autism.

Method

The researchers analyzed data from a huge, national insurance claims database that tracks the health conditions of more than 34 million people in the United States, whose identities have been stricken from the database. The sample consisted of all children in the database born between 2001 and 2007 who were continuously enrolled in their health plans from birth to at least 5 years of age and had an older sibling. This approach yielded a sample of 95,727 children. Children (and their siblings) were classified as having autism if the database showed that they had two or more insurance claims on different dates citing ASD as the diagnostic code. The database also indicated whether the children had been administered either of the two recommended MMR vaccinations.

Results

Overall, 1.04% of the children received a diagnosis of ASD. Consistent with the evidence that ASD is partly genetic in origin, this rate was elevated (6.9%) among children who had an older sibling with ASD. In the sample as a whole, there were no significant differences between the vaccinated and unvaccinated children in their risk for autism. This finding also held for the high-risk children who had an older sibling with ASD. In fact, in this group, the relative risk for autism was slightly *lower* among those who were vaccinated.

Discussion

The results add to the building evidence that MMR vaccinations are not a factor in the emergence of autism. These findings are particularly reassuring given the large sample size and the focus on children who carry an elevated genetic risk for ASD.

Critical Thinking Questions

1. Why do you think that many people cling to the belief that vaccinations contribute to autism?
2. The conclusions of this study are based on insurance records. Can you think of any reasons why insurance records might be unreliable indicators of ASD or vaccination status?

14.7 Personality Disorders

Personality disorders **are a class of disorders marked by extreme, inflexible personality traits that cause subjective distress or impaired social and occupational functioning.** Personality disorders generally become recognizable during adolescence or early adulthood. One conservative estimate pegged the lifetime prevalence of personality disorders at around 12% (Caligor, Yeomans, & Levin, 2014).

DSM-5 lists ten personality disorders. They are grouped into three related clusters: anxious/fearful, odd/eccentric, and dramatic/impulsive. These disorders are described briefly in **Figure 14.15**. If you examine this figure, you will find a diverse collection of maladaptive

	PERSONALITY DISORDERS	
Cluster	**Disorder**	**Description**
Anxious/fearful	Avoidant personality disorder	Excessively sensitive to potential rejection, humiliation, or shame; socially withdrawn in spite of desire for acceptance from others
	Dependent personality disorder	Excessively lacking in self-reliance and self-esteem; passively allowing others to make all decisions; constantly subordinating own needs to others' needs
	Obsessive-compulsive personality disorder	Preoccupied with organization, rules, schedules, lists, trivial details; extremely conventional, serious, and formal; unable to express warm emotions
Odd/eccentric	Schizoid personality disorder	Defective in capacity for forming social relationships; showing absence of warm, tender feelings for others
	Schizotypal personality disorder	Showing social deficits and oddities of thinking, perception, and communication that resemble schizophrenia
	Paranoid personality disorder	Showing pervasive and unwarranted suspiciousness and mistrust of people; overly sensitive; prone to jealousy
Dramatic/impulsive	Histrionic personality disorder	Overly dramatic; tending to exaggerated expressions of emotion; egocentric, seeking attention
	Narcissistic personality disorder	Grandiosely self-important; preoccupied with success fantasies; expecting special treatment; lacking interpersonal empathy
	Borderline personality disorder	Unstable in self-image, mood, and interpersonal relationships; impulsive and unpredictable
	Antisocial personality disorder	Chronically violating the rights of others; failing to accept social norms, to form attachments to others, or to sustain consistent work behavior; exploitive and reckless

Figure 14.15

Personality disorders. There are ten personality disorders in DSM-5, which are described here. As you can see, these personality disorders are divided into three clusters: anxious/fearful, odd/eccentric, and dramatic/impulsive.

Source: Estimated gender ratios from Millon (1981).

personality syndromes. You may also notice that some personality disorders essentially are milder versions of more severe disorders that we have already covered. For example, the schizoid and schizotypal personality disorders are milder cousins of schizophrenic disorders. Although personality disorders tend to be relatively mild disorders in comparison to anxiety, mood, and schizophrenic disorders, they often are associated with significant impairments of social and occupational functioning (Trull, Carpenter, & Widiger, 2013).

Antisocial, Borderline, and Narcissistic Personality Disorders

Given the sheer number of personality disorders, we can only provide brief descriptions of a few of the more interesting syndromes in this category. Hence, we will take a quick look at the antisocial, borderline, and narcissistic personality disorders.

Antisocial Personality Disorder

People with this disorder are *antisocial* in the sense that they choose to *reject widely accepted social norms* regarding moral principles. People with antisocial personalities chronically exploit others. **The *antisocial personality disorder* is marked by impulsive, callous, manipulative, aggressive, and irresponsible behavior.** Since they haven't accepted the social norms they violate, people with antisocial personalities rarely feel guilty about their transgressions. Essentially, they lack an adequate conscience. The antisocial personality disorder occurs much more frequently among males than females (Torgersen, 2012). Many people with antisocial personalities get involved in illegal activities. However, some people with antisocial personalities keep their exploitive behavior channeled within the boundaries of the law. Such people may even enjoy high status in our society (Babiak & Hare, 2006). In other words, the concept of the antisocial personality disorder can apply to cutthroat business executives and scheming politicians, as well as to con artists, drug dealers, and petty thieves. People with antisocial personalities exhibit quite a variety of maladaptive traits (Hare & Neumann, 2008). Among other things, they rarely experience genuine affection for others. Sexually, they are predatory and promiscuous. They can tolerate little frustration, and they pursue immediate gratification. These characteristics make them unreliable employees, unfaithful spouses, inattentive parents, and undependable friends.

Borderline Personality Disorder

The *borderline personality disorder* is **marked by instability in social relationships, self-image, and emotional functioning.** This disorder appears to be somewhat more common in females than males (Tomko et al., 2014). These individuals tend to have turbulent interpersonal relationships marked by fears of abandonment (Hooley, Cole, & Gironde, 2012). They often switch back and forth between idealizing people and devaluing them. They tend to be intense, with frequent anger issues and poor control of their emotions. They tend to be moody, shifting between panic, despair, and feelings of emptiness. They are prone to impulsive behavior, such as reckless spending, drug use, or sexual behavior. Individuals with borderline personality disorder often exhibit fragile, unstable self-concepts, as their goals, values, opinions, and career plans shift suddenly. Borderline personality disorder is also associated with an elevated risk for self-injurious behavior, such as cutting or burning oneself, and with an increased risk for suicide (Caligor et al., 2014).

Narcissistic Personality Disorder

We discussed the personality trait of *narcissism* in Chapter 2. As you might guess, people with narcissistic personality disorder exhibit this trait to a very extreme degree. Hence, **the *narcissistic personality disorder* is marked by a grandiose sense of self-importance, a sense of entitlement, and an excessive need for attention and admiration.** This syndrome is more common in males (Trull et al., 2010). People with this disorder think they are unique and superior to others. They tend to be boastful and pretentious. Although they seem self-assured and confident, their self-esteem is actually quite fragile, leading them to fish for compliments and to be easily threatened by criticism. Their sense of entitlement manifests itself in arrogant expectations that they should merit special treatment and extra privileges. They routinely complain that others do not appreciate their accomplishments or give them the respect that they deserve. Some critics have argued that the current diagnostic criteria for narcissistic personality disorder focus too much on the overt, grandiose presentation of the disorder and too little on the covert, vulnerable side of the disorder (Skodol, Bender, & Morey, 2014).

Etiology of Personality Disorders

Like other disorders, the personality disorders all surely involve interactions between genetic predispositions and environmental factors, such as cognitive styles, coping patterns, and exposure to stress. As noted in Chapter 2, personality traits are shaped to a significant degree by heredity (South et al., 2013). Given that personality disorders consist of extreme manifestations of personality traits, it stands to reason that these disorders are also influenced by heredity, and the data from twin and family studies support this line of reasoning (Skodol et al., 2014). The environmental factors implicated in personality disorders vary considerably from one disorder to another, which makes sense given the diversity of the personality disorders. For example, contributing factors to antisocial personality disorder include dysfunctional family systems, erratic discipline, parental neglect, and parental modeling of exploitive, amoral behavior (Farrington, 2006; Sutker & Allain, 2001). In contrast, borderline personality disorder has been attributed primarily to a history of early trauma, including physical and sexual abuse (Ball & Links, 2009; Widom, Czaja, & Paris, 2009). Different constellations of environmental factors have been implicated for each of the other eight personality disorders.

APPLICATION

14.8 Understanding Eating Disorders

Learning Objectives

- Describe the subtypes, prevalence, and gender distribution of eating disorders.
- Explain how genetics, personality, culture, family dynamics, and disturbed thinking contribute to the development of eating disorders.

Answer the following "true" or "false."

____ **1.** Eating disorders are universal problems found in virtually all cultures.

____ **2.** People with anorexia nervosa are much more likely to recognize their eating behavior as pathological than are people suffering from bulimia nervosa.

____ **3.** The prevalence of eating disorders is twice as high in women as it is in men.

____ **4.** The binge-and-purge syndrome seen in bulimia nervosa is not common in anorexia nervosa.

All of these statements are false, as you will see in this Application. Although most people don't seem to take eating disorders as seriously as other types of psychological disorders, you will see that they are dangerous and debilitating. No psychological disorder is associated with a greater elevation in mortality (Striegel-Moore & Bulik, 2007).

Types of Eating Disorders

Eating disorders **are severe disturbances in eating behavior characterized by preoccupation with weight and unhealthy efforts to control weight.** The three syndromes are: *anorexia nervosa, bulimia nervosa*, and a new syndrome added to DSM-5 called *binge-eating disorder*.

Anorexia Nervosa

Anorexia nervosa **is characterized by intense fear of gaining weight, disturbed body image, refusal to maintain normal weight, and dangerous measures to lose weight.** Two subtypes have been distinguished. In *restricting type anorexia nervosa*, people drastically reduce their intake of food, sometimes literally starving themselves. In *binge-eating/purging type anorexia nervosa*, victims attempt to lose weight by forcing themselves to vomit after meals, by misusing laxatives and diuretics, and by engaging in excessive exercise.

Anorexics suffer from a disturbed body image. No matter how frail and emaciated the victims become, they insist that they are too fat. Their morbid fear of obesity means that they are never satisfied with their weight. If they gain a pound or two, they panic. The only thing that makes them happy is to lose more weight. The common result is a relentless decline in body weight. Because of their disturbed body image, people suffering from anorexia generally do *not* appreciate the maladaptive quality of their behavior and rarely seek treatment on their own. They are typically coaxed or coerced into treatment by friends or family members who are alarmed by their appearance.

Anorexia nervosa eventually leads to a cascade of medical problems, including *amenorrhea* (a loss of menstrual cycles in women), gastrointestinal problems, low blood pressure, *osteoporosis* (a loss of bone density), and metabolic disturbances that can lead to cardiac arrest or circulatory collapse (Mitchell & Wonderlich, 2014). Anorexia is associated with greatly elevated mortality rates (Franko et al., 2013).

Bulimia Nervosa

Bulimia nervosa **involves habitually engaging in out-of-control overeating followed by unhealthy compensatory efforts, such as self-induced vomiting, fasting, abuse of laxatives and diuretics, and excessive exercise.** The eating binges are usually carried out in secret and are followed by intense guilt and concern about gaining weight. These feelings motivate ill-advised strategies to undo the effects of the overeating. However, vomiting prevents the absorption of only about half of recently consumed food, and laxatives and diuretics have negligible impact on caloric intake, so people suffering from bulimia nervosa typically maintain a reasonably normal weight (Fairburn, Cooper, & Murphy, 2009). Medical problems associated with bulimia nervosa include cardiac arrythmias, dental problems, metabolic deficiencies, and gastrointestinal problems

Eating disorders have become distressingly common among young women in Western cultures. No matter how frail they become, people suffering from anorexia insist that they are too fat.

(Halmi, 2008). Like anorexia, bulimia is associated with elevated mortality rates, although this elevation is only about one-third as great as that seen for anorexia (Arcelus et al., 2011).

Obviously, bulimia nervosa shares many features with anorexia nervosa, such as a morbid fear of becoming obese, preoccupation with food, and rigid, maladaptive approaches to controlling weight that are grounded in naive all-or-none thinking. However, the syndromes also differ in crucial ways. First and foremost, bulimia is a much less life-threatening condition. Second, although their weight and appearance usually is more "normal" than that seen in anorexia, people with bulimia are much more likely to recognize that their eating behavior is pathological and are more prone to recognize their need for treatment (Guarda et al., 2007).

Binge-Eating Disorder

Binge-eating disorder **involves distress-inducing eating binges that are not accompanied by the purging, fasting, and excessive exercise seen in bulimia.** Obviously, this syndrome resembles bulimia, but it is less severe. Still, this disorder creates great distress, as binge eaters tend to be disgusted by their bodies and distraught about their overeating. People with binge-eating disorder are frequently overweight. Their excessive eating is often triggered by stress (Gluck, 2006).

Prevalence of Eating Disorders

Eating disorders are a product of modern, affluent Western culture, where food is generally plentiful and the desirability of being thin is widely endorsed. Until relatively recently, these problems were rarely seen outside of Western cultures. However, advances in communication have exported Western culture to far-flung corners of the globe, and eating disorders have started showing up in many non-Western societies, especially affluent Asian countries (Becker & Fay, 2006).

A huge gender gap exists in the likelihood of developing eating disorders. About 90% to 95% of individuals with anorexia nervosa and bulimia nervosa are female, and about 60% of those with binge-eating disorder are female (Devlin & Steinglass, 2014). The staggering gender disparities in the prevalence of the more serious eating disorders appears to be a result of cultural pressures rather than biological factors. Western standards of attractiveness emphasize being slender more for females than for males, and women generally experience heavier pressure to be physically attractive than men do (Strahan et al., 2008). Eating disorders mostly afflict *young* women. The typical age of

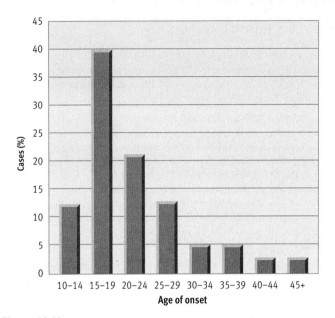

Figure 14.16

Age of onset for anorexia nervosa. Eating disorders emerge primarily during adolescence, as these data for anorexia nervosa show. This graph depicts how age of onset was distributed in a sample of 166 female patients from Minnesota. As you can see, more than half experienced the onset of their illness before the age of 20, with vulnerability clearly peaking between the ages of 15 and 19. (Data from Lucas, et al., 1991)

onset for anorexia is 14 to 18, and for bulimia it is 15 to 21 (see **Figure 14.16**).

How common are eating disorders in Western societies? Research suggests that among females about 1% develop anorexia nervosa, roughly 1.5% develop bulimia nervosa, and about 3.5% exhibit binge-eating disorder (Hudson et al., 2007). In some respects, these figures may only scratch the surface of the problem. Evidence suggests that another 2% to 4% of people may struggle with serious eating problems that do not quite qualify for a formal diagnosis (Swanson et al., 2011). And community surveys suggest that there may be more undiagnosed eating disorders among men than generally appreciated (Field et al., 2014).

Etiology of Eating Disorders

Like other types of psychological disorders, eating disorders are caused by multiple determinants that work interactively. Let's take a brief look at some of the factors that contribute to the development of anorexia nervosa and bulimia nervosa.

Genetic Vulnerability

The scientific evidence is not nearly as strong or complete for eating disorders as it is for many other types of psychopathology, but some people may inherit a genetic vulnerability to these problems (Thornton, Mazzeo, & Bulik, 2011). There is convincing evidence for a hereditary component in both anorexia nervosa and bulimia nervosa, with genetics probably playing a stronger role in anorexia (Trace et al., 2013).

Personality Factors

Genetic factors may exert their influence indirectly by fostering certain personality traits that make people more vulnerable to eating disorders. Although there are innumerable exceptions, victims of anorexia nervosa tend to be obsessive, rigid, neurotic, and emotionally restrained, whereas victims of bulimia nervosa tend to be impulsive, overly sensitive, and low in self-esteem (Wonderlich, 2002). Research also suggests that perfectionism is a risk factor for anorexia (Keel et al., 2012).

Cultural Values

The contribution of cultural values to the increased prevalence of eating disorders can hardly be overestimated. In Western society, young women are socialized to believe that they must be attractive and that to be attractive they must be as thin as the actresses and fashion models that dominate the media (Fox-Kales, 2011; Levine & Harrison, 2004). Thanks to this cultural milieu, many young women are dissatisfied with their weight because the societal ideals promoted by the media are unattainable for most of them (Thompson & Stice, 2001). Unfortunately, in a small portion of these women, the pressure to be thin, in combination with genetic vulnerability, family pathology, and other factors, leads to unhealthy efforts to control weight.

The Role of the Family

Many theorists emphasize how family dynamics can contribute to the development of anorexia nervosa and bulimia nervosa in young women. The principal issue appears to be that some mothers contribute to eating disorders simply by endorsing society's message that "you can never be too thin" and by modeling unhealthy dieting behaviors of their own (Francis & Birch, 2005). In conjunction with media pressures, this role modeling leads many daughters to internalize the idea that the thinner you are, the more attractive you are. Of course, peers can also endorse beliefs and model behaviors that promote eating disorders (Keel et al., 2013). Another potentially family-related issue is that there is an association between childhood sexual and physical abuse and an elevated risk for eating disorders (Steiger, Bruce, & Israel, 2013).

Cognitive Factors

Many theorists emphasize the role of disturbed thinking in the etiology of eating disorders. For example, anorexic patients' typical belief that they are fat when they are really wasting away is a dramatic illustration of how thinking goes awry. Patients with eating disorders display rigid, all-or-none thinking and many maladaptive beliefs (Roberts, Tchanturia, & Treasure, 2010). Such thoughts may include "I must be thin to be accepted," "If I am not in complete control, I will lose all control," "If I gain one pound, I'll go on to gain enormous weight." Additional research is needed to determine whether distorted thinking is a *cause* or merely a *symptom* of eating disorders.

CHAPTER 14　Review

Key Ideas

14.1 General Concepts
- The medical model views abnormal behavior as a disease. There are some problems with the medical model, but the disease analogy is useful. Some critics are concerned that medical diagnoses of abnormal behavior pin stigmatizing labels on people. The stigma associated with mental illness appears difficult to reduce. Three criteria are used in deciding whether people suffer from psychological disorders: deviance, personal distress, and maladaptive behavior.
- DSM-5 is the official psychodiagnostic classification system in the United States. The DSM has grown dramatically and now includes diagnoses for many syndromes that used to be considered everyday problems. Critics argue that this approach "medicalizes" everyday problems and casts the stigma of pathology on normal self-control issues.

14.2 Anxiety Disorders and Obsessive-Compulsive Disorder
- The anxiety disorders include generalized anxiety disorder, specific phobia, panic disorder, and agoraphobia. After decades of being lumped with the anxiety disorders, obsessive-compulsive disorder (OCD) was given its own category in DSM-5. These disorders have been linked to a genetic predisposition, an inhibited temperament, and neurochemical abnormalities in the brain at GABA synapses.
- Many anxiety responses, especially phobias, may be caused by classical conditioning and maintained by operant conditioning. Cognitive theorists maintain that some people are vulnerable to anxiety disorders because they see threats everywhere. Stress may also contribute to the onset of these disorders.

14.3 Dissociative Disorders
- Dissociative disorders include dissociative amnesia and dissociative identity disorder (DID). These disorders appear to be uncommon, although there is some controversy about the prevalence of DID. Stress and childhood trauma may contribute to DID, but overall, the causes of dissociative disorders are not well understood. Some theorists believe that people with DID come to believe, thanks in part to book and movie portrayals of DID and reinforcement from their therapists, that independent entities within them are to blame for their peculiar behaviors.

14.4 Depressive and Bipolar Disorders
- People with major depressive disorder show persistent feelings of sadness and despair, whereas as those with bipolar disorder usually experience both depressed and manic periods. Both of these disorders are associated with an elevated risk for suicide. People vary in their genetic vulnerability to depressive and bipolar disorders, which are accompanied by changes in neurochemical activity in the brain. Reduced hippocampal volume and suppressed neurogenesis may be factors in depression.
- Cognitive models posit that a pessimistic explanatory style, rumination, and other types of negative thinking contribute to depression. Depression is often rooted in interpersonal inadequacies, as people who lack social finesse often have difficulty acquiring life's reinforcers and their stormy social relations are a source of stress. Depressive and bipolar disorders are sometimes precipitated by stressful events.

14.5 Schizophrenic Disorders
- Schizophrenic disorders are characterized by deterioration of adaptive behavior, irrational thought, distorted perception, and disturbed mood. The distinction between positive and negative symptoms has proven useful, but most patients exhibit both types of symptoms. Schizophrenic disorders usually emerge gradually during adolescence or early adulthood.
- Research has linked schizophrenia to genetic vulnerability, changes in neurotransmitter activity at dopamine synapses, and enlarged ventricles in the brain. The neurodevelopmental hypothesis attributes schizophrenia to disruptions of normal maturational processes in the brain before or at birth. Patients who return to homes high in expressed emotion tend to have elevated relapse rates. Stress in early childhood may increase a person's vulnerability to schizophrenia. Precipitating stress in adolescence or adulthood may help to trigger the disorder in vulnerable individuals.

14.6 Autism Spectrum Disorder
- Autism is characterized by profound impairment of social interaction and communication and by severely restricted interests and activities. Since the mid-1990s there has been a dramatic increase in the diagnosis of autism. This increase is probably due to greater awareness of the syndrome and the use of broader diagnostic criteria.
- Genetic factors contribute to autistic disorders. Another factor is brain overgrowth, which may disrupt neural circuits. Research has failed to find an association between vaccinations and autism.

14.7 Personality Disorders
- Personality disorders are marked by extreme personality traits that cause distress and impaired functioning. There are ten personality disorders that are grouped into three clusters: anxious/fearful, odd/eccentric, and dramatic/impulsive. Antisocial personality disorder is characterized by manipulative, impulsive, exploitive, aggressive behavior.
- Borderline personality disorder is marked by instability in social relationships, self-concept, and emotional functioning. Narcissistic personality disorder involves a grandiose sense of self-importance, a sense of entitlement, and an excessive need for attention. Personality disorders are influenced by heredity and environmental factors.

14.8 Application: Understanding Eating Disorders
- The principal eating disorders are anorexia nervosa, bulimia nervosa, and binge-eating disorder. Anorexia and bulimia both lead to a cascade of medical problems, although anorexia is more dangerous. Eating disorders appear to be a product of modern, affluent, Westernized culture.
- Females account for 90% to 95% of anorexic and bulimic disorders. The typical age of onset is roughly 15 to 20. There appears to be a genetic vulnerability to eating disorders, which may be mediated by heritable personality traits. Cultural pressures on young women to be thin clearly help foster eating disorders. Some theorists emphasize how family dynamics and disturbed thinking can contribute to the development of eating disorders.

Key Terms

Agoraphobia p. 404
Anhedonia p. 409
Anorexia nervosa p. 423
Antisocial personality
　disorder p. 422
Anxiety disorders p. 402
Autism p. 419
Autism spectrum disorder
　(ASD) p. 419
Binge-eating disorder p. 424
Bipolar disorder p. 410
Borderline personality
　disorder p. 422
Bulimia nervosa p. 424
Concordance rate p. 411
Delusions p. 415
Diagnosis p. 400
Dissociative amnesia p. 407
Dissociative disorders p. 406

Dissociative identity disorder
　(DID) p. 407
Eating disorders p. 423
Etiology p. 400
Generalized anxiety
　disorder p. 403
Hallucinations p. 415
Major depressive disorder p. 409
Medical model p. 399
Narcissistic personality
　disorder p. 422
Neurotransmitters p. 405
Obsessive-compulsive disorder
　(OCD) p. 404
Panic disorder p. 404
Personality disorders p. 421
Prognosis p. 400
Schizophrenia p. 414
Specific phobia p. 403

Key People

Nancy Andreasen p. 416
Susan Nolen-Hoeksema
　pp. 410, 413

Martin Seligman pp. 406, 413
Thomas Szasz p. 400

1. Sergio has just entered treatment for bipolar disorder, and he is informed that most patients respond to drug treatment within a month. This information represents
   a. a prognosis.
   b. an etiology.
   c. a histology.
   d. a concordance.

2. Although Sue always feels high levels of dread, worry, and anxiety, she still meets her daily responsibilities. Sue's behavior
   a. should not be considered abnormal because her adaptive functioning is not impaired.
   b. should not be considered abnormal because everyone sometimes experiences worry and anxiety.
   c. can still be considered abnormal because she feels great personal distress.
   d. is both a and b.

3. People who repeatedly perform senseless rituals to overcome their anxiety are said to have a(n)
   a. generalized anxiety disorder.
   b. manic disorder.
   c. obsessive-compulsive disorder.
   d. specific phobia.

4. Which of the following has *not* been implicated in the etiology of anxiety-related disorders?
   a. Genetic vulnerability
   b. Hormonal dysfunctions
   c. Conditioning and learning
   d. Stress

5. Which of the following statements about dissociative identity disorder is true?
   a. The original personality is always aware of the alternate personalities.
   b. Dissociative identity disorder is an alternate name for schizophrenia.
   c. The multiple personalities are typically all quite similar to one another.
   d. Starting in the 1970s, there was a dramatic increase in the diagnosis of dissociative identity disorder.

6. After several months during which he was always gloomy and dejected, Mario has suddenly perked up. He feels elated and energetic and works around the clock on a writing project. He has also started to bet heavily on sporting events over the Internet, which he never did previously. Mario's behavior is consistent with
   a. schizophrenia.
   b. obsessive-compulsive disorder.
   c. bipolar disorder.
   d. dissociative identity disorder.

7. A concordance rate indicates the
   a. percentage of twin pairs or other relatives who exhibit the same disorder.
   b. percentage of people with a given disorder who are currently receiving treatment.
   c. prevalence of a given disorder in the general population.
   d. rate of cure for a given disorder.

8. Which of the following would be a negative symptom of schizophrenia?
   a. Auditory hallucinations
   b. Delusions of persecution
   c. Having virtually no friendships
   d. Delusions of grandeur

9. Research suggests that there is an association between schizophrenia and
   a. serotonin depletion.
   b. enlarged brain ventricles.
   c. degeneration in the medulla.
   d. abnormalities in the cerebellum.

10. About _____ of patients with anorexic and bulimic disorders are female.
    a. 40%
    b. 50% to 60%
    c. 75%
    d. 90% to 95%

Answers

1. a Page 400
2. c Pages 400–401
3. c Page 404
4. b Pages 405–406
5. d Page 407
6. c Page 410
7. a Page 411
8. c Page 416
9. b Page 418
10. d Page 424

Personal Explorations Workbook

Go to the *Personal Explorations Workbook* in the back of your textbook for exercises that can enhance your self-understanding in relation to issues raised in this chapter.

Exercise 14.1 *Self-Assessment:* Maudsley Obsessional-Compulsive Inventory

Exercise 14.2 *Self-Reflection:* What Are Your Attitudes on Mental Illness?

ULTRA F/Getty Images

What do you picture when you hear the term *psychotherapy*? If you're like most people, you probably envision a troubled patient lying on a couch in a therapist's office, with the therapist asking penetrating questions and providing sage advice. Typically, people believe that psychotherapy is only for those who are "sick" and that therapists have special powers that allow them to "see through" their clients. It is also widely believed that therapy requires years of deep probing into a client's innermost secrets. Many people further assume that therapists routinely tell their patients how to lead their lives. Like most stereotypes, this picture of psychotherapy is a mixture of fact and fiction, as you'll see in the upcoming pages.

In this chapter, we take a down-to-earth look at the process of *psychotherapy*, using the term in its broadest sense to refer to all the diverse approaches to the treatment of psychological problems. We start by discussing some general questions about the provision of treatment. Who seeks therapy? What kinds of professionals provide treatment? How many types of therapy are there? After considering these general issues, we examine some of the more widely used approaches to treating psychological maladies, analyzing their goals, techniques, and effectiveness. The Application at the end of the chapter focuses on practical issues involved in finding a therapist, in case you ever have to advise someone about seeking help. ■

15.1 Elements of the Treatment Process

Learning Objectives

■ Identify the three major categories of therapy and discuss patterns of treatment seeking.

■ Distinguish among the various types of mental health professionals involved in the provision of therapy.

In modern society people have a bewildering array of psychotherapy approaches to choose from. In fact, the immense diversity of therapeutic treatments makes defining the concept of *psychotherapy* difficult. But all psychotherapies have three key elements. They all involve a helping relationship (the treatment) between a professional with special training (the therapist) and another person in need of help (the client). Let's look at each of these elements.

Treatments: How Many Types Are There?

In their efforts to help people, mental health professionals use many methods of treatment, including discussion, emotional support, persuasion, conditioning procedures, relaxation training, role playing, drug therapy, biofeedback, and group therapy. Some therapists also use a variety of less-conventional procedures, such as rebirthing, poetry therapy, and primal therapy. No one knows exactly how many approaches to treatment there are. One expert (Kazdin, 1994) estimates that there may be more than 400 distinct types of psychotherapy! As varied as therapists' procedures are, approaches to treatment can be classified into three major categories.

1. *Insight therapies.* Insight therapy is "talk therapy" in the tradition of Freud's psychoanalysis. This is probably the approach to treatment that comes to mind when you think of psychotherapy. In insight therapies, clients engage in complex verbal interactions with their therapist. The goal in these discussions is to pursue increased insight regarding the nature of the client's difficulties and to sort through possible solutions.

2. *Behavior therapies.* Behavior therapies are based on the principles of learning and conditioning, which were introduced in Chapter 2. Instead of emphasizing personal insights, behavior therapists make direct efforts to alter problematic responses (phobic behaviors, for instance) and maladaptive habits (drug use, for instance).

3. *Biomedical therapies.* Biomedical approaches to therapy involve interventions into a person's physiological functioning. The most widely used procedures are drug therapy and electroconvulsive therapy. In recent decades, drug therapy has become the dominant mode of treatment for psychological disorders. As **Figure 15.1** shows, one large-scale study found that 57% of mental health patients were treated with medication only, up from 44% just 9 years earlier

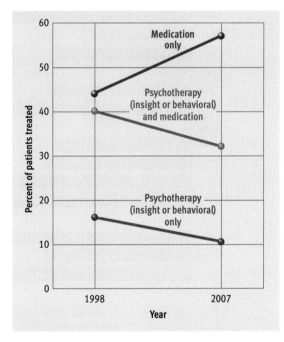

Figure 15.1

Escalating reliance on drug therapy. Using data from an ongoing national survey focusing on patterns of health care, Olfson and Marcus (2010) found some interesting trends in outpatient treatment for psychological disorders. Comparing treatment procedures in 1998 and 2007, they found that the percentage of patients treated with medication exclusively increased from 44% to 57%. During the same time period, the percentage of patients treated with insight or behavioral therapy alone, or in combination with drug therapy, declined.

(Olfson & Marcus, 2010). As the name bio*medical* therapies suggests, these treatments have traditionally been provided only by physicians with a medical degree (usually psychiatrists). This situation is changing, however, as psychologists have been campaigning for prescription privileges and have obtained prescription authority in three states.

Clients: Who Seeks Therapy?

People seeking mental health treatment show up with the full range of human problems: anxiety, depression, unsatisfactory interpersonal relations, troublesome habits, poor self-control, low self-esteem, marital conflicts, self-doubt, a sense of emptiness, and feelings of personal stagnation. Among adults, the two most common presenting problems are depression and anxiety disorders (Olfson & Marcus, 2010). A client in treatment does *not* necessarily have an identifiable psychological disorder. Some people seek professional help for everyday problems (career decisions, for instance) or vague feelings of discontent.

People vary considerably in their willingness to seek psychotherapy. Some people delay for many years before finally seeking treatment for their psychological problems. As you can see in **Figure 15.2**, women are more likely than men to receive treatment, and whites are more likely than blacks or Hispanics to obtain therapy. Treatment is also more likely when people have medical insurance and when they have more education (Olfson & Marcus, 2010).

Unfortunately, it appears that many people who need therapy don't receive it (Kazdin & Rabbitt, 2013). People who could benefit from therapy do not seek it for a variety of reasons. Lack of health insurance and cost concerns appear to be major barriers to obtaining needed care for many people. Perhaps the biggest roadblock is the stigma surrounding the receipt of mental health treatment (Corrigan, Druss, & Perlick, 2014). Unfortunately, many people equate seeking therapy with admitting personal weakness (Clement et al., 2015).

Therapists: Who Provides Professional Treatment?

Psychotherapy refers to *professional* treatment by someone with special training. Psychology and psychiatry are the principal professions involved in psychotherapy, providing the lion's share of mental health care. However, therapy is also provided by social workers, psychiatric nurses, counselors, and marriage and family therapists, as outlined in **Figure 15.3**.

Psychologists

Clinical psychologists and *counseling psychologists* **specialize in the diagnosis and treatment of psychological disorders and everyday behavioral problems.** In theory, the training of clinical psychologists emphasizes treatment of full-fledged disorders, whereas the training of counseling psychologists is slanted toward treatment of everyday adjustment problems in normal people. In practice, however, there is great overlap between clinical and counseling psychologists in training, in skills, and in the clientele they serve (Morgan & Cohen, 2008).

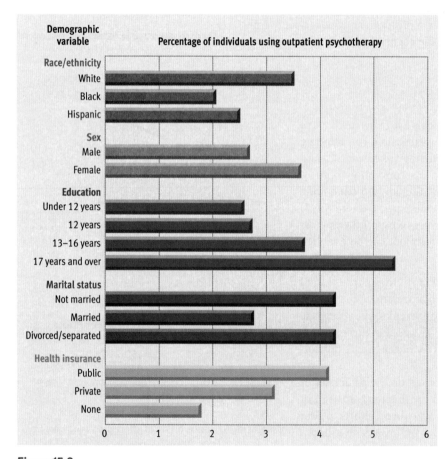

Figure 15.2

Therapy utilization rates. Olfson and Marcus (2010) analyzed data on the use of outpatient mental health services in the United States in relation to various demographic variables. In regard to marital status, utilization rates are particularly high among those who are divorced or not married. The use of therapy is also greater among those who have more education. Females are more likely to pursue therapy than males are, but utilization rates are relatively low among ethnic minorities and those who lack health insurance.

TYPES OF THERAPISTS			
Profession	**Degree**	**Education beyond bachelor's degree**	**Typical roles and activities**
Clinical psychologist	PhD or PsyD	5–7 years	Psychological testing, diagnosis, treatment with insight or behavior therapy
Counseling psychologist	PhD, PsyD or EdD	5–7 years	Similar to clinical psychologist, but more focus on work, career, and adjustment problems
Psychiatrist	MD	8 years	Diagnosis and treatment, primarily with biomedical therapies, but also insight therapies
Clinical social worker	MSW, DSW	2–5 years	Insight and behavior therapy, often help inpatients with their return to the community
Psychiatric nurse	RN, MA, or PhD	0–5 years	Inpatient care, insight and behavior therapy
Counselor	BA or MA	0–2 years	Vocational counseling, drug counseling, rehabilitation counseling
Marriage and family therapist	MA or PhD	2–5 years	Marital/couples therapy, family therapy

Figure 15.3

The principal mental health professions. Psychotherapists come from a variety of professional backgrounds. This chart provides an overview of various types of therapists' education and typical professional activities.

Both types of psychologists must earn a doctoral degree (Ph.D., Psy.D., or Ed.D.). A doctorate in psychology requires 5 to 7 years of training beyond a bachelor's degree. The process of gaining admission to a Ph.D. program in clinical psychology is highly competitive (about as competitive as for medical school). Psychologists receive most of their training on university campuses, although they also serve a 1- to 2-year internship in a clinical setting, such as a hospital. In providing therapy, psychologists use either insight or behavioral approaches. In comparison to psychiatrists, they are less likely to use psychoanalytic methods.

Psychiatrists

Psychiatrists **are physicians who specialize in the treatment of psychological disorders.** Many psychiatrists also treat everyday behavioral problems. However, in comparison to psychologists, psychiatrists devote more time to relatively severe disorders (schizophrenia, mood disorders) and less time to everyday marital, family, job, and school problems. Psychiatrists have an M.D. degree. Their graduate training requires 4 years of course work in medical school and a 4-year apprenticeship in a residency at an approved hospital. Their psychotherapy training occurs during their residency because the required course work in medical school is essentially the same for all students, whether they are going into surgery, pediatrics, or psychiatry. In comparison to psychologists, psychiatrists are more likely to use psychoanalysis and less likely to use group therapies or behavior therapies. That said, contemporary psychiatrists increasingly depend on medication as their principal mode of treatment (Olfson et al., 2014).

Other Mental Health Professionals

In hospitals and other institutions, *psychiatric social workers* and *psychiatric nurses* often work as part of a treatment team with a psychologist or psychiatrist. Psychiatric nurses, who may have a bachelor's or master's degree in their field, play a large role in hospital inpatient treatment. Psychiatric social workers generally have a master's degree and typically work with patients and their families to ease the patient's integration back into the community.

Many kinds of *counselors* also provide therapeutic services. Counselors are usually found working in schools, colleges, and human services agencies (youth centers, geriatric

Learn More Online

Online Dictionary of Mental Health
This thematically arranged "dictionary" comprises diverse links involving many forms of psychotherapy, the treatment of psychological disorders, and general issues of mental health. It is sponsored by the Centre for Psychotherapeutic Studies at the University of Sheffield's Medical School in the United Kingdom.

centers, family planning centers, and so forth). Counselors typically have a master's degree. They often specialize in particular types of problems, such as vocational counseling, marital counseling, rehabilitation counseling, and drug counseling.

Marriage and family therapists generally have a master's degree that prepares them to work with couples experiencing relationship problems or with dysfunctional families. Marital and family therapy has experienced enormous growth since the 1980s (Lebow, 2008).

Although clear differences exist among the helping professions in education and training, their roles in the treatment process overlap considerably. In this chapter, we refer to psychologists or psychiatrists as needed, but otherwise we use the terms *clinician, therapist,* and *mental health professional* to refer to psychotherapists of all kinds, regardless of their professional degree. Now that we have discussed the basic elements in psychotherapy, we can examine specific approaches to treatment in terms of their goals, procedures, and effectiveness. We begin with a few representative insight therapies.

Learning Objectives

- Understand the logic of psychoanalysis and describe the techniques used to probe the unconscious.
- Describe the role of therapeutic climate and process in client-centered therapy.
- Explain how group therapy, couples therapy, and family therapy are generally conducted.
- Assess the efficacy of insight therapies and discuss the importance of common factors.

15.2 Insight Therapies

Many schools of thought exist as to how to conduct insight therapy. Therapists with different theoretical orientations use different methods to pursue different kinds of insights. What these varied approaches have in common is that *insight therapies* **involve verbal interactions intended to enhance clients' self-knowledge and thus promote healthful changes in personality and behavior.** Although there may be hundreds of insight therapies, the leading eight or ten approaches appear to account for the lion's share of treatment. In this section, we delve into psychoanalysis, client-centered therapy, group therapy, and couples and family therapy.

Psychoanalysis

Sigmund Freud worked as a psychotherapist for almost 50 years in Vienna. Through a painstaking process of trial and error, he developed innovative techniques for the treatment of psychological disorders and distress. His system of *psychoanalysis* dominated psychiatry for more than half a century. Although this dominance has eroded in recent decades, a diverse array of psychoanalytic approaches to therapy continue to evolve and remain influential today (Luborsky, O'Reilly-Landry, & Arlow, 2011; Ursano & Carr, 2014).

Psychoanalysis **is an insight therapy that emphasizes the recovery of unconscious conflicts, motives, and defenses through techniques such as free association, dream analysis, and transference.** To appreciate the logic of psychoanalysis, we have to look at Freud's thinking about the roots of mental disorders. Freud treated mostly anxiety-dominated disturbances, such as phobic, panic, obsessive-compulsive, and conversion disorders, which were then called *neuroses*. He believed that neurotic problems are caused by unconscious conflicts left over from early childhood. As explained in Chapter 2, he thought that these inner conflicts involve battles among the id, ego, and superego, usually over sexual and aggressive impulses. Freud theorized that people depend on defense mechanisms to avoid confronting these conflicts, which remain hidden in the depths of the unconscious. However, he noted that defenses tend to be only partially successful in alleviating anxiety, guilt, and other distressing emotions. With this model in mind, let's take a look at the therapeutic procedures used in psychoanalysis.

Sigmund Freud's pioneering work on psychoanalysis paved the way for modern psychotherapy.

Probing the Unconscious

Given Freud's assumptions, we can see that the logic of psychoanalysis is very simple. The analyst attempts to probe the murky depths of the unconscious to discover the unresolved conflicts causing the client's neurotic behavior. In a sense, the analyst functions as a psychological detective. In this effort to explore the unconscious, he or she relies on two techniques: free association and dream analysis.

In *free association*, clients spontaneously express their thoughts and feelings exactly as they occur, with as little censorship as possible. Clients lie on a couch so they will be better able to let their minds drift freely. In free associating, clients expound on anything that comes to mind, regardless of how trivial, silly, or embarrassing it might be. Gradually, most clients begin to let everything pour out without conscious censorship. The analyst studies these free associations for clues about what is going on in the unconscious.

In *dream analysis*, **the therapist interprets the symbolic meaning of the client's dreams.** For Freud, dreams were the "royal road to the unconscious," the most direct means of access to patients' innermost conflicts, wishes, and impulses. Clients are encouraged and trained to remember their dreams, which they describe in therapy. The therapist then analyzes the symbolism in these dreams to interpret their meaning.

To better illustrate these matters, let's look at an actual case treated through psychoanalysis (adapted from Greenson, 1967, pp. 40–41). Mr. N was troubled by an unsatisfactory marriage. He claimed to love his wife, but he preferred sexual relations with prostitutes. Mr. N reported that his parents also endured lifelong marital difficulties. His childhood conflicts about their relationship appeared to be related to his problems. Both dream analysis and free association can be seen in the following description of a session in Mr. N's treatment:

Mr. N reports a fragment of a dream. All that he can remember is that he is waiting for a red traffic light to change when he feels that someone has bumped into him from behind. . . . The associations led to Mr. N's love of cars, especially sports cars. He loved the sensation, in particular, of whizzing by those fat, old, expensive cars. . . . His father always hinted that he had been a great athlete, but he never substantiated it. . . . Mr. N doubted whether his father could really perform. His father would flirt with a waitress in a cafe or make sexual remarks about women passing by, but he seemed to be showing off. If he were really sexual, he wouldn't resort to that.

As is characteristic of free association, Mr. N's train of thought meanders about with little direction. What did Mr. N's therapist extract from this session? The therapist saw sexual overtones in the dream fragment, where Mr. N was bumped from behind. The therapist also inferred that Mr. N had a competitive orientation toward his father, based on the free association about whizzing by fat, old, expensive cars. As you can see, analysts must *interpret* their clients' dreams and free associations. This is a critical process throughout psychoanalysis.

Interpretation

Interpretation **involves the therapist's attempts to explain the inner significance of the client's thoughts, feelings, memories, and behaviors.** Contrary to popular belief, analysts do not interpret everything, and they generally don't try to dazzle clients with startling revelations. Instead, analysts move forward inch by inch, offering interpretations that should be just out of the client's own reach (Samberg & Marcus, 2005). Mr. N's therapist eventually offered the following interpretations to his client:

I said to Mr. N near the end of the hour that I felt he was struggling with his feelings about his father's sexual life. He seemed to be saying that his father was sexually not a very potent man. . . . He also recalls that he once found a packet of condoms under his father's pillow when he was an adolescent and he thought "My father must be going to prostitutes." I then intervened and pointed out that the condoms under his father's pillow seemed to indicate more obviously that his father used the condoms with his mother, who slept in the same bed. However, Mr. N wanted to believe his wish-fulfilling fantasy: mother doesn't want sex with father and father is not very potent. The patient was silent and the hour ended.

As you may already have guessed, the therapist had concluded that Mr. N's difficulties were rooted in an Oedipal complex (see Chapter 2). Mr. N had unresolved sexual feelings toward his mother and hostile

In psychoanalysis, the therapist encourages the client to reveal thoughts, feelings, dreams, and memories that can then be interpreted in relation to the client's current problems.

feelings about his father. These unconscious conflicts, rooted in his childhood, were distorting his intimate relations as an adult.

Resistance

How would you expect Mr. N to respond to his therapist's suggestion that he was in competition with his father for the sexual attention of his mother? Obviously, most clients would have great difficulty accepting such an interpretation. Freud fully expected clients to display some resistance to therapeutic efforts. *Resistance* **involves largely unconscious defensive maneuvers intended to hinder the progress of therapy.** Resistance is assumed to be an inevitable part of the psychoanalytic process (Samberg & Marcus, 2005). Why do clients try to resist the helping process? Because they don't want to face up to the painful, disturbing conflicts they have buried in their unconscious. Although they have sought help, they are reluctant to confront their real problems.

Resistance may take many forms. Patients may show up late for their sessions, merely pretend to engage in free association, or express hostility toward the therapist. For instance, Mr. N's therapist noted that after the session just described, "The next day he began by telling me that he was furious with me." Analysts use a variety of strategies to deal with their clients' resistance. Often, a key consideration is the handling of *transference*, which we consider next.

Transference

Transference **occurs when clients start relating to their therapist in ways that mimic critical relationships in their lives.** Thus, a client might start relating to a therapist as if the therapist were an overprotective mother, rejecting brother, or passive spouse. In a sense, the client *transfers* conflicting feelings about important people onto the therapist (Høglend et al., 2011). For instance, in his treatment, Mr. N transferred some of the competitive hostility he felt toward his father onto his analyst. Psychoanalysts often encourage transference so that clients begin to reenact relations with crucial people in the context of therapy. These reenactments can help bring repressed feelings and conflicts to the surface, allowing the client to work through them.

Undergoing psychoanalysis is not easy. It can be a slow, painful process of self-examination that routinely requires 3 to 5 years of hard work. It tends to be a lengthy process because patients need time to gradually work through their problems and genuinely accept unnerving revelations (Williams, 2005). Ultimately, if resistance and transference can be handled effectively, the therapist's interpretations should lead the client to profound insights. For instance, Mr. N eventually admitted, "The old boy is probably right, it does tickle me to imagine that my mother preferred me and I could beat out my father. Later, I wondered whether this had something to do with my own screwed-up sex life with my wife." According to Freud, once clients recognize the unconscious sources of their conflicts, they can resolve these conflicts and discard their neurotic defenses.

Modern Psychodynamic Therapies

Although still available, classical psychoanalysis as done by Freud is not widely practiced anymore (Kay & Kay, 2008). Freud's psychoanalytic method was geared to a particular kind of clientele that he was seeing in Vienna a century ago. As his followers fanned out across Europe and America, many found that it was necessary to adapt psychoanalysis to different cultures, changing times, and new kinds of patients. Thus, many variations on Freud's original approach to psychoanalysis have developed over the years. These descendants of psychoanalysis are collectively known as *psychodynamic approaches* to therapy.

Today, we have a rich variety of psychodynamic approaches to therapy (Magnavita, 2008). Reviews of these treatments suggest that interpretation, resistance, and transference continue to play key roles in therapeutic efforts (Høglend et al., 2008). Other central features of modern psychodynamic therapies include (1) a focus on emotional experience, (2) exploration of efforts to avoid distressing thoughts and feelings, (3) identification of recurring patterns in patients' life experiences, (4) discussion of past experience, especially events in early childhood, (5) analysis of interpersonal relationships, (6) a focus on the therapeutic relationship itself, and (7) exploration of dreams and other aspects of fantasy life (Shedler, 2010; see **Figure 15.4**). Recent research suggests that psychodynamic approaches can be helpful in the treatment of a diverse array of disorders, including depression, anxiety disorders, personality disorders, and substance abuse (Josephs & Weinberger, 2013; Barber et al., 2013).

Client-Centered Therapy

You may have heard of people going into therapy to "find themselves" or to "get in touch with their real feelings." These now-popular phrases emerged out of the human potential movement, which was stimulated in part by the work of Carl Rogers (1951, 1986). Taking a humanistic perspective, Rogers devised *client-centered therapy* (also known as *person-centered therapy*) in the 1940s and 1950s. **Client-centered therapy is an insight therapy that emphasizes providing a supportive emotional climate for clients, who play a major role in determining the pace and direction of their therapy.**

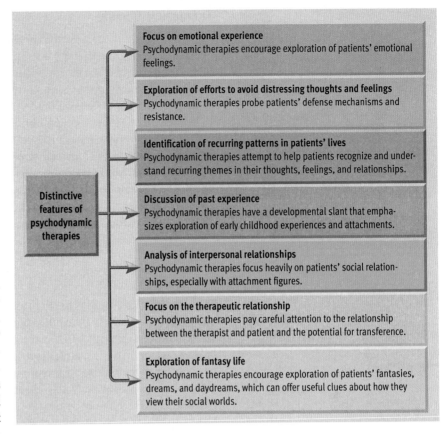

Figure 15.4

Core features of psychodynamic therapies. In an article on the efficacy of psychodynamic therapies, Jonathan Shedler (2010) outlined the distinctive aspects of modern psychodynamic techniques and processes. The seven features described here represent the core of contemporary psychodynamic treatment.

Rogers's theory about the principal causes of neurotic anxieties is quite different from the Freudian explanation. As discussed in Chapter 2, Rogers maintained that most personal distress is due to inconsistency, or "incongruence," between a person's self-concept and reality (see **Figure 15.5**). According to his theory, incongruence makes people prone to feel threatened by realistic feedback about themselves from others. According to Rogers, anxiety about such feedback often leads to reliance on defense mechanisms, distortions of reality, and stifled personal growth. Excessive incongruence is thought to be rooted in clients' overdependence on others for approval and acceptance.

Given Rogers's theory, client-centered therapists seek insights that are quite different from the repressed conflicts that psychoanalysts try to track down. Client-centered therapists help clients realize that they do not have to worry constantly about pleasing others and winning acceptance. They encourage clients to respect their own feelings and values. They help people restructure their self-concept to correspond better to reality. Ultimately, these therapists try to foster self-acceptance and personal growth.

Carl Rogers invented client-centered therapy, which emphasizes the importance of therapeutic climate.

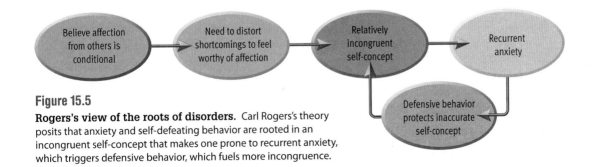

Figure 15.5

Rogers's view of the roots of disorders. Carl Rogers's theory posits that anxiety and self-defeating behavior are rooted in an incongruent self-concept that makes one prone to recurrent anxiety, which triggers defensive behavior, which fuels more incongruence.

Therapeutic Climate

Client-centered therapists emphasize the importance of a supportive emotional climate in therapy. They also work to clarify, rather than interpret, the feelings expressed by their patients.

In client-centered therapy, the *process* of therapy is not as important as the emotional *climate* in which the therapy takes place. According to Rogers, it is critical for the therapist to provide a warm, supportive, accepting climate in which clients can confront their shortcomings without feeling threatened. The lack of threat should reduce clients' defensive tendencies and thus help them to open up. To create this atmosphere of emotional support, Rogers believed that client-centered therapists must provide three conditions: (1) *genuineness* (honest communication), (2) *unconditional positive regard* (nonjudgmental acceptance of the client), and (3) *accurate empathy* (understanding of the client's point of view). Consistent with Rogers's view of the vital importance of therapeutic climate, research has found that measures of therapists' empathy and unconditional positive regard correlate with positive patient outcomes (Elliott et al., 2011; Farber & Doolin, 2011).

Therapeutic Process

In client-centered therapy, the client and therapist work together almost as equals. The therapist provides relatively little guidance and keeps interpretation and advice to a minimum (Raskin, Rogers, & Witty, 2011). So, just what does the client-centered therapist do, besides creating a supportive climate? The therapist's key task is *clarification*. Client-centered therapists try to function like a human mirror, reflecting statements back to their clients, but with enhanced clarity. They help clients become more aware of their true feelings by highlighting themes that may be obscure in the clients' rambling discourse. By working with clients to clarify their feelings, client-centered therapists hope to gradually build toward more far-reaching insights. In particular, they try to help clients become more aware of and comfortable with their genuine selves. Obviously, these are ambitious goals. Client-centered therapy resembles psychoanalysis in that both seek to achieve a major reconstruction of a client's personality.

Group Therapy

Although it dates back to the early part of the 20th century, group therapy came of age during World War II and its aftermath in the 1950s. During this period, the expanding demand for therapeutic services forced clinicians to use group techniques (Burlingame & Baldwin, 2011). **Group therapy** **is the simultaneous treatment of several or more clients in a group.** Most major insight therapies have been adapted for use with groups. Because of economic pressures in mental health care, the use of group therapy appears likely to grow in future years. Although group therapy can be conducted in a variety of ways, we can provide a general overview of the process as it usually unfolds (see Piper & Hernandez, 2013; Spitz, 2009; Stone, 2008).

A therapy group typically consists of four to twelve people, with six to eight participants regarded as an ideal number (Cox, Vinogradov, & Yalom, 2008). The therapist usually screens the participants, excluding anyone who seems likely to be disruptive. Some theorists maintain that judicious selection of participants is crucial to effective group treatment (Schlapobersky & Pines, 2009). In group treatment the therapist's responsibilities include selecting participants, setting goals for the group, initiating and maintaining the therapeutic process, and protecting clients from harm (Cox et al., 2008). The therapist often plays a relatively subtle role, staying in the background and focusing mainly on promoting group cohesiveness. The therapist always retains a special status, but the therapist and clients are on much more equal footing in group therapy than in individual therapy. The leader in group therapy expresses emotions, shares feelings, and copes with challenges from group members.

Group therapies have proven particularly helpful when members share similar problems, such as alcoholism, drug abuse, overeating, or depression.

In group therapy, participants essentially function as therapists for one another (Schachter, 2011). Group members describe their problems, trade viewpoints, share experiences, and discuss coping strategies. Most important, they provide acceptance and emotional support for one another. In this supportive atmosphere, group members work at peeling away the social masks that cover their insecurities. Once their problems are exposed, members work at correcting them. As members come to value one another's opinions, they work hard to display healthy changes to win the group's approval.

Group therapies obviously save time and money, which can be critical in understaffed mental hospitals and other institutional settings. However, group therapy is *not* just a less costly substitute for individual therapy. For many types of patients and problems, group therapy can be just as effective as individual treatment (Knauss, 2005; Stone, 2008). Moreover, group therapy has unique strengths of its own. For example, in group therapy participants often come to realize that their misery is not unique. They are reassured to learn that many other people have similar or even worse problems. Another advantage is that group therapy provides an opportunity for participants to work on their social skills in a safe environment. Group treatments are being used successfully for an increasingly diverse collection of problems and disorders in contemporary clinical practice (Burlingame, Strauss, & Joyce, 2013).

Couples and Family Therapy

Like group therapy, marital and family therapy rose to prominence after World War II. As their names suggest, these interventions are defined in terms of who is being treated. *Couples* or *marital therapy* **involves the treatment of both partners in a committed, intimate relationship, in which the main focus is on relationship issues.** Couples therapy is not limited to married couples. It is frequently provided to cohabiting couples, including gay couples. *Family therapy* **involves the treatment of a family unit as a whole, in which the main focus is on family dynamics and communication.** Family therapy often emerges out of efforts to treat children or adolescents with individual therapy. A child's therapist, for instance, might come to the realization that treatment is likely to fail because the child returns to a home environment that contributes to the child's problems and thus propose a broader family intervention.

As with other forms of insight therapy, there are different schools of thought about how to conduct couples and family therapy (Goldenberg, Goldenberg, & Pelavin, 2011). Some of these diverse systems are extensions of influential approaches to individual therapy, including psychodynamic, humanistic, and behavioral treatments. Other approaches are based on innovative models of families as complex systems and explicit rejection of individual models of treatment. Although the various approaches to couples and family therapy differ in terminology and their theoretical models of relationship and family dysfunction, they tend to share common goals. First, they seek to understand the entrenched patterns of interaction that produce distress. In this endeavor they view individuals as parts of a family ecosystem, and they assume that people behave as they do because of their role in the system (Lebow & Stroud, 2013). Second, they seek to help couples and families improve their communication and move toward healthier patterns of interaction.

What kinds of problems bring partners in for couples therapy? The full range of relationship problems, such as constant arguments without resolution, resentment about power imbalances, perceptions of emotional withdrawal, the discovery or disclosure of affairs, sexual difficulties, the threat of relationship dissolution, and concern about how relationship issues are affecting the couple's children (Spitz & Spitz, 2009). What are some of the indications for family therapy? It is likely to be helpful when a youngster's psychological difficulties appear to be rooted in family pathology, when families are buffeted by severe stress such as a serious illness or a

iStockphoto.com/101dalmatians

Marital therapists attempt to help partners to clarify their needs and desires in the relationship, appreciate their mutual contribution to problems, enhance their communication patterns, increase role flexibility and tolerance of differences, work out their balance of power, and learn to deal with conflict more constructively.

major transition, when blended families experience adjustment problems, when sibling conflicts spin out of control, or when someone tries to sabotage another family member's individual therapy (Bloch & Harari, 2009; Spitz & Spitz, 2009).

How Effective Are Insight Therapies?

Evaluating the effectiveness of any approach to treatment is a complex challenge (Comer & Kendall, 2013; Lilienfeld et al., 2014; Ogles, 2013). Evaluating treatment results is especially complicated for insight therapies. If you were to undergo insight therapy, how would you judge its effectiveness? By how you felt? By looking at your behavior? By asking your therapist? By consulting your friends and family? What would you be looking for? Various schools of therapy pursue entirely different goals. And clients' ratings of their progress are likely to be slanted toward a favorable evaluation because they want to justify their effort, their heartache, their expense, and their time. Even evaluations by professional therapists can be highly subjective. Moreover, people enter therapy with diverse problems of varied severity, creating huge confounds in efforts to assess the effectiveness of therapeutic interventions.

Despite these difficulties, thousands of outcome studies have been conducted to evaluate the effectiveness of insight therapy. These studies have examined a broad range of clinical problems and used diverse methods to assess therapeutic outcomes, including scores on psychological tests and ratings by family members, as well as therapists' and clients' ratings. These studies consistently indicate that insight therapy *is* superior to no treatment or to placebo treatment and that the effects of therapy are reasonably durable (Lambert, 2011; 2013). And when insight therapies are compared head to head against drug therapies, they usually show roughly equal efficacy (Arkowitz & Lilienfeld, 2007; Wampold, 2013). Studies generally find the greatest improvement early in treatment (roughly the first ten to twenty weekly sessions), with further gains gradually diminishing over time (Lambert, 2013), as the data from one study show in **Figure 15.6**. Of course, these broad generalizations mask considerable variability in outcome, but the general trends are encouraging.

Figure 15.6

Recovery as a function of number of therapy sessions. Based on a national sample of more than 6000 patients, Lambert, Hansen, and Finch (2001) mapped out the relationship between recovery and the duration of treatment. These data show that about half of the patients had experienced a clinically significant recovery after twenty weekly sessions of therapy. After forty-five sessions of therapy, about 70% had recovered.

Source: Adapted from Lambert, M. J., Hansen, N. B., & Finch, A. E. (2001). Patient-focused research: Using patient outcome data to enhance treatment effects. *Journal of Consulting and Clinical Psychology, 69*, 159–172.

How Do Insight Therapies Work?

Although there is considerable evidence that insight therapy tends to produce positive effects for a sizable majority of clients, vigorous debate continues about the *mechanisms of action* underlying these positive effects (Duncan & Reese, 2013). The advocates of various therapies tend to attribute the benefits of therapy to the particular methods used by each specific approach. In essence, they argue that different therapies achieve similar benefits through different processes. An alternative view espoused by many theorists is that the diverse approaches to therapy share certain *common factors* that account for much of the improvement experienced by clients (Wampold, 2001). Evidence supporting the common factors view has mounted in recent years (Lambert & Ogles, 2014).

What are the common denominators that lie at the core of diverse approaches to therapy? The models proposed to answer to this question vary considerably, but the most widely cited common factors include (1) the development of a therapeutic alliance with a professional helper, (2) the provision of emotional support and empathy, (3) the cultivation of hope and positive expectations in the client, (4) the provision of a rationale for the client's problems and a plausible method for reducing them, and (5) the opportunity to express feelings, confront problems, and gain new insights (Laska, Gurman, & Wampold, 2014; Weinberger, 1995). How important are these factors in therapy? Some theorists argue that common factors account for virtually *all* of the progress that clients make in therapy (Wampold, 2001). It seems more likely that the benefits of therapy represent the combined effects of common factors and specific procedures. One recent study attempted to quantify the influence of common factors in an analysis of thirty-one studies that focused on the treatment of depression. When the variance in patient outcomes was partitioned among various influences, the researchers estimated that 49% of this variance was attributable to common factors (Cuijpers et al., 2012). Admittedly, this is just one estimate based on one form of treatment for one specific disorder, so it does not provide a definitive answer regarding the importance of common factors. But it certainly suggests that common factors play a significant role in insight therapy.

15.3 Behavior Therapies

Behavior therapy is different from insight therapy in that behavior therapists make no attempt to help clients achieve grand insights about themselves. Why not? Because behavior therapists believe that such insights aren't necessary in order to produce constructive change. Consider a client troubled by compulsive gambling. The behavior therapist doesn't care whether this behavior is rooted in unconscious conflicts or parental rejection. What the client needs is to get rid of the maladaptive behavior. Consequently, the therapist simply designs a program to eliminate the compulsive gambling. The crux of the difference between insight therapy and behavior therapy lies in how each views symptoms. Insight therapists treat pathological symptoms as signs of an underlying problem. In contrast, behavior therapists think that the symptoms *are* the problem.

Behavior therapies **involve the application of the principles of learning to direct efforts to change clients' maladaptive behaviors.** Behavior therapies are based on two main assumptions (Stanley & Beidel, 2009). *First, it is assumed that behavior is a product of learning.* No matter how self-defeating or pathological a client's behavior might be, the behaviorist believes that it is the result of past conditioning. *Second, it is assumed that what has been learned can be unlearned.* The same learning principles that explain how the maladaptive behavior was acquired can be used to get rid of it. Thus, behavior therapists attempt to change clients' behavior by applying the principles of classical conditioning, operant conditioning, and observational learning.

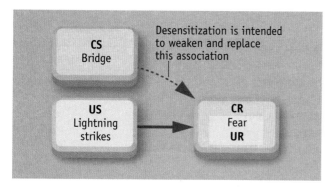

Figure 15.7

The logic underlying systematic desensitization.
Behaviorists argue that many phobic responses are acquired through classical conditioning, as in the example diagrammed here. Systematic desensitization targets the conditioned associations between phobic stimuli and fear responses.

Systematic Desensitization

Devised by Joseph Wolpe (1958, 1987), systematic desensitization revolutionized psychotherapy by giving therapists their first useful alternative to traditional "talk therapy" (Fishman, Rego, & Muller, 2011). *Systematic desensitization* **is a behavior therapy used to reduce clients' anxiety responses through counterconditioning.** The treatment assumes that most anxiety responses are acquired through classical conditioning (as we discussed in Chapter 14). According to this model, a harmless stimulus (for instance, a bridge) may be paired with a frightening event (lightning striking it), so that it becomes a conditioned stimulus eliciting anxiety. The goal of systematic desensitization is to weaken the association between the conditioned stimulus (the bridge) and the conditioned response of anxiety (see **Figure 15.7**).

Systematic desensitization involves three steps. *In the first step, the therapist helps the client build an anxiety hierarchy.* This is a list of anxiety-arousing stimuli related to the specific source of anxiety, such as flying, academic tests, or snakes. The client ranks the stimuli from the least anxiety arousing to the most anxiety arousing. *The second step involves training the client in deep muscle relaxation.* This second phase may begin during early sessions while the therapist and client are still constructing the anxiety hierarchy. *In the third step, the client tries to work through the hierarchy, learning to remain relaxed while imagining each stimulus.* Starting with the least anxiety-arousing stimulus, the client imagines the situation as vividly as possible while relaxing. If the client experiences strong anxiety, he or she drops the imaginary scene and concentrates on relaxation. The client keeps repeating this process until he or she can imagine a scene with little or no anxiety. Once a particular scene is conquered, the client moves on to the next stimulus situation in the anxiety hierarchy. Gradually, over a number of therapy sessions, the client progresses through the hierarchy, unlearning troublesome anxiety responses.

The effectiveness of systematic desensitization in reducing phobic responses is well documented (Spiegler, 2016). That said, interventions emphasizing direct exposures to anxiety-arousing situations have become behavior therapists' treatment of choice for phobic and other anxiety disorders (Rachman, 2009). **In** *exposure therapies* **clients are confronted with situations that they fear so they learn that these situations are really harmless.** The exposures take place in a controlled setting and often involve a gradual progression from less-feared to more-feared stimuli. These real-life exposures to anxiety-arousing situations usually prove harmless, and individuals' anxiety responses decline. In recent decades, some therapists have resorted to highly realistic virtual-reality presentations of feared situations via computer-generated imagery (Reger et al., 2011). Exposure therapies are versatile in that they can be used with the full range of anxiety disorders, including obsessive compulsive disorder, posttraumatic stress disorder, and panic disorder.

Social Skills Training

Many psychological problems grow out of interpersonal difficulties. Behavior therapists point out that humans are not born with social finesse. They acquire their social skills through learning. Unfortunately, some people have not learned how to be friendly, how to make conversation, how to express anger appropriately, and so forth. Social ineptitude can contribute to anxiety, feelings of inferiority, and various kinds of disorders. In light of these findings, therapists are increasingly using social skills training in efforts to improve clients' social abilities. This approach to therapy has yielded promising results in the treatment of social anxiety (Bögels & Voncken, 2008), depression (Thase, 2012), autism (Otero et al., 2015), and schizophrenia (Mueser et al., 2013).

Social skills training **is a behavior therapy designed to improve interpersonal skills that emphasizes modeling, behavioral rehearsal, and shaping.** This type of behavior therapy can be conducted with individual clients or in groups. Social skills training depends on the principles of operant conditioning and observational learning. The therapist makes use of *modeling* by encouraging clients to watch socially skilled friends and colleagues, so that the clients can acquire responses (eye contact, active listening, and so on) through observation.

In *behavioral rehearsal*, the client tries to practice social techniques in structured role-playing exercises. The therapist provides corrective feedback and uses approval to reinforce progress. Eventually, clients try their newly acquired skills in real-world interactions. Usually, they are given specific homework assignments. *Shaping* is used in that clients are gradually asked to handle more complicated and delicate social situations. For example, a nonassertive client may begin by working on making requests of friends. Only much later will the client be asked to tackle standing up to his or her boss.

Cognitive-Behavioral Treatments

In Chapter 3 we saw that people's cognitive interpretations of events make all the difference in the world in how well they handle stress. In Chapter 14 we learned that cognitive factors play a key role in the development of depression and other disorders. Citing the importance of findings such as these, behavior therapists started to focus more attention on their clients' cognitions in the 1970s (Hollon & Digiuseppe, 2011). **Cognitive-behavioral treatments use varied combinations of verbal interventions and behavior modification techniques to help clients change maladaptive patterns of thinking.** Some of these treatments, such as Albert Ellis's (1973) *rational-emotive behavior therapy* and Aaron Beck's (1976) *cognitive therapy* have proven extremely influential. Since we covered the main ideas underlying Ellis's approach in our discussion of coping strategies in Chapter 4, we focus here on Beck's system of cognitive therapy (Beck, 1987; Newman & Beck, 2009).

Cognitive therapy uses specific strategies to correct habitual thinking errors that underlie various types of disorders. Cognitive therapy was originally devised as a treatment for depression, but in recent years it has been applied fruitfully to a wide range of disorders (Hollon & Beck, 2013; Wright, Thase, & Beck, 2014). According to cognitive therapists, depression is caused by "errors" in thinking (see **Figure 15.8**). They assert that depression-prone people tend to (1) blame their setbacks on personal inadequacies without considering circumstantial explanations, (2) focus selectively on negative events while ignoring positive ones, (3) make unduly pessimistic projections about the future, and (4) draw negative conclusions about their worth as a person based on insignificant events. For instance, imagine that you got a low grade on a minor quiz in a class. If you made the kinds of errors in thinking just described, you might blame the grade on your woeful stupidity, dismiss comments from a classmate that it was an unfair test, gloomily predict that you will surely flunk the course, and conclude that you are not genuine college material.

The goal of cognitive therapy is to change clients' negative thoughts and maladaptive beliefs (Wright, Thase, & Beck, 2014). To begin, clients are taught to detect their automatic negative thoughts, the sorts of self-defeating statements that people are prone to make when analyzing problems. Examples might include "I'm just not smart enough," "No one really likes me," or "It's all my fault." Clients are then trained to subject these automatic thoughts to reality testing. The therapist helps them to see how unrealistically negative the thoughts are.

Cognitive therapy uses a variety of behavioral techniques, including modeling, systematic monitoring of one's behavior, and behavioral rehearsal (Beck & Weishaar, 2011). Clients are given "homework assignments" that focus on changing their overt behaviors. They may be instructed to engage in responses on their own, outside of the clinician's office. For example, one shy, insecure young man in cognitive therapy was told to go to a bar and engage three different women in conversations for up to 5 minutes each (Rush, 1984). He was instructed to record his thoughts before and after each of the conversations. This assignment revealed various maladaptive patterns of thought that gave the young man and his therapist plenty to work on in subsequent sessions.

Aaron Beck devised cognitive therapy, which focuses on changing clients' automatic negative thoughts.

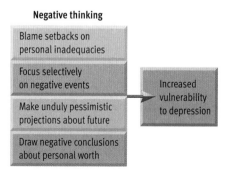

Figure 15.8

Beck's cognitive theory of depression. Beck's theory initially focused on the causes of depression, although it was gradually broadened to explain other disorders. According to Beck, depression is caused by the types of negative thinking shown here.

This book will make you feel outraged. This book will make you cry. Above all else, this book will educate you about how incredibly difficult it can be to get effective mental health care for people troubled by severe disturbances such as schizophrenia and bipolar disorder. You will learn that the American mental health system sometimes seems insane.

The author is a former *Washington Post* investigative reporter who was suddenly drawn into the quagmire of America's mental health system when his son, Mike, developed bipolar disorder at the age of 23. Mike became seriously psychotic—at one point he wrapped aluminum foil around his head so people wouldn't be able to read his thoughts. His behavior became erratic. He crashed his car while trying to drive with his eyes closed, informed strangers at a coffee shop that he had supernatural powers, and broke into a residence where he ignored a wailing burglar alarm and proceeded to pee on the carpet, turn on all the water faucets thereby flooding the home, and give himself a bubble bath—until the police arrived to detain him. In his disoriented state, Earley's son was not willing to voluntarily cooperate with treatment. So the family repeatedly found themselves in hospital emergency rooms where they were told that their son could not be admitted because—as an adult—he had the right to refuse treatment, even though his judgment was obviously severely impaired.

This frustrating experience motivated Earley to conduct a wide-ranging investigation of mental health care in the United States today. His journey took him to mental hospitals, prisons, courts, alternative facilities for the mentally ill, meetings of mental health advocacy groups, and street corners where the homeless mentally ill congregated. He learned that "What was happening to Mike was not an oddity. It was a tiny piece in a bigger story. A major shift had occurred in our country. The mentally ill, who used to be treated in state mental hospitals, were now being arrested. Our nation's jails and prisons were our new asylums" (p. 2).

This book tells two intertwined stories—Earley's personal battle to obtain meaningful treatment for his son and his investigative analysis of modern mental health care. Both stories are compelling, heart-wrenching, and enlightening. And both stories demonstrate that American society is not providing adequate care for a sizable segment of the mentally ill population.

How Effective Are Behavior Therapies?

Behavior therapists have historically placed more emphasis than insight therapists on the importance of measuring therapeutic outcomes. As a result, there is ample research on the effectiveness of behavior therapy (Stanley & Beidel, 2009). Of course, behavior therapies are not well suited to the treatment of some types of problems (vague feelings of discontent, for instance). Furthermore, it's misleading to make global statements about the effectiveness of behavior therapies because they include a variety of procedures designed for different purposes. For example, the value of systematic desensitization for phobias has no bearing on the value of aversion therapy for sexual deviance. For our purposes, it is sufficient to note that there is favorable evidence on the efficacy of most of the widely used behavioral interventions (Zinbarg & Griffith, 2008). Behavior therapies can make significant contributions to the treatment of depression, anxiety problems, phobias, obsessive-compulsive disorders, sexual dysfunction, schizophrenia, drug-related problems, eating disorders, hyperactivity, autism, and mental retardation (Craighead et al., 2013; Emmelkamp, 2013).

15.4 Biomedical Therapies

In the 1950s, a French surgeon was looking for a drug that would reduce patients' autonomic response to surgical stress. The surgeon noticed that chlorpromazine produced a mild sedation. Based on this observation, Delay and Deniker (1952) decided to give chlorpromazine to hospitalized schizophrenic patients to see whether it would have a calming effect on them. Their experiment was a dramatic success. Chlorpromazine became the first effective antipsychotic drug—and a revolution in psychiatry had begun. Hundreds of thousands of severely disturbed patients—patients who had appeared doomed to lead the remainder of their lives in mental hospitals—were gradually sent home thanks to the therapeutic effects of antipsychotic drugs. Today, biomedical therapies, such as drug treatment, lie at the core of psychiatric practice.

Biomedical therapies **are physiological interventions intended to reduce symptoms associated with psychological disorders.** These therapies assume that psychological disorders are caused, at least in part, by biological malfunctions. As we discussed in Chapter 14, this assumption clearly has merit for many disorders, especially the more severe ones. We will discuss two biomedical approaches to psychotherapy: drug therapy and electroconvulsive therapy (ECT).

Drug Therapy

Therapeutic drugs for mental disorders fall into four major groups: antianxiety drugs, antipsychotic drugs, antidepressant drugs, and mood stabilizers. As you can see in **Figure 15.9**, the rate at which psychiatrists prescribe these drugs has increased since the mid-1990s for all four of these drug classes (Olfson et al., 2014).

Antianxiety Drugs

Antianxiety drugs **reduce tension, apprehension, and nervousness.** The most popular of these drugs are Valium and Xanax, which are the trade names (the proprietary names that pharmaceutical companies use in marketing drugs) for diazepam and alprazolam, respectively. The drugs in this category are often referred to informally as *tranquilizers*. Antianxiety drugs exert their effects almost immediately. They can be fairly effective in alleviating feelings of anxiety (Dubovsky, 2009). However, their effects are measured in hours, so their impact is relatively short-lived. Common side effects of antianxiety drugs include drowsiness, depression, nausea, and confusion. These drugs also have some potential for abuse, dependency, and overdose, although the prevalence of these problems has been exaggerated (Martinez, Marangell, & Martinez, 2008). Another drawback is that patients who have been on antianxiety drugs for a while often experience withdrawal symptoms when their drug treatment is stopped (Ferrando, Owen, & Levenson, 2014).

Antipsychotic Drugs

Antipsychotic drugs are used primarily in the treatment of schizophrenia. They are also given to people with severe mood disorders who become delusional. The trade names (and generic names) of some prominent, first-generation drugs in this category are Thorazine (chlorpromazine), Mellaril (thioridazine), and Haldol (haloperidol). *Antipsychotic drugs* **are used to gradually reduce psychotic symptoms, including hyperactivity, mental confusion, hallucinations, and delusions.**

Studies suggest that antipsychotics reduce symptoms in about 70% of patients, albeit in varied degrees (Kane, Stroup, & Marder, 2009). When antipsychotic drugs are effective, they work their magic gradually, as shown in **Figure 15.10**. Patients usually begin to respond within 2 to 7 days. Further improvement may occur for several months. Many schizophrenic patients are placed on antipsychotics indefinitely because these drugs can reduce the likelihood of a relapse into an active schizophrenic episode.

Antipsychotic drugs undeniably make a major contribution to the treatment of severe mental disorders, and psychiatrists' reliance on antipsychotic medications has increased dramatically in recent decades (Olfson et al., 2012). However, antipsychotic drugs present their share of problems. They have many unpleasant side effects (Ferrando, Owen, & Levenson, 2014). Drowsiness, constipation, and cotton mouth are common. Patients may also experience tremors, muscular rigidity, and impaired coordination. After being released from a hospital, many schizophrenic patients, supposedly placed on antipsychotics indefinitely, discontinue their drug regimen because of the disagreeable side effects. Unfortunately, after patients stop taking their medication, about 70% relapse within a year (van Kammen et al., 2009). In addition to minor side effects, antipsychotics may cause a severe and lasting problem called *tardive dyskinesia*, which is seen in about 15% to 25%

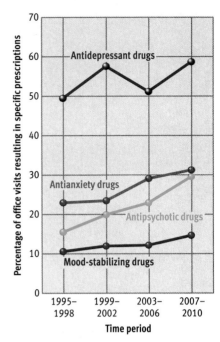

Figure 15.9

Increasing prescription of psychiatric drugs. Olfson et al. (2014) tracked prescription trends for psychiatric drugs over a period of 15 years. These data show the percentage of office visits to psychiatrists that resulted in the prescription of various types of drugs. As you can see, reliance on all four categories of psychiatric drugs has increased over this time period. (Based on data from Olfson, Kroenke, Wang, & Blanco, 2014)

Psychopharmacology Tips by Dr. Bob
University of Chicago physician and pharmacology specialist Robert Hsiung provides both broad and specific references about the interface of drugs and the human mind, including a searchable archive of professional information and tips about the field.

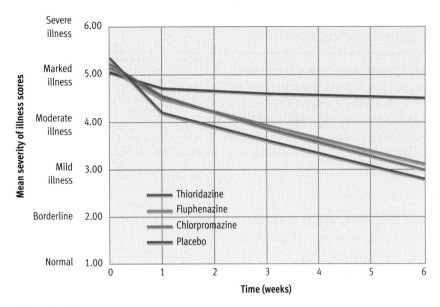

Figure 15.10

The time course of antipsychotic drug effects. Antipsychotic drugs reduce psychotic symptoms gradually, over a span of weeks, as graphed here. In contrast, patients given placebo pills show little improvement.

Source: From Cole, J. O., Goldberg, S. C., & Davis, J. M. (1966). Drugs in the treatment of psychosis. In P. Solomon (Ed.), *Psychiatric drugs*. New York: Grune & Stratton. From data in the NIMH-PSC Collaborative Study I. Reprinted by permission of J. M. Davis.

of patients who receive long-term treatment with traditional antipsychotics (Stewart, Russakoff, & Stewart, 2014). *Tardive dyskinesia* **is a neurological disorder marked by chronic tremors and involuntary spastic movements.** Once this debilitating syndrome emerges, there is no cure, although spontaneous remission sometimes occurs after the discontinuation of antipsychotic medication.

Psychiatrists currently rely primarily on a newer class of antipsychotic agents called *second-generation antipsychotic drugs*, such as clozapine, olanzapine, and quetiapine (Marder, Hurford, & van Kammen, 2009). These drugs appear to be roughly similar to the first-generation antipsychotics in therapeutic effectiveness, but they offer some advantages over the older drugs. For instance, they can help some treatment-resistant patients who do not respond to traditional antipsychotics. And the second-generation antipsychotics produce fewer unpleasant side effects and carry less risk for tardive dyskinesia. Of course, like all powerful drugs, they carry some risks. This drug class appears to increase patients' vulnerability to diabetes and cardiovascular problems. In the hopes of reducing drug discontinuation by patients and associated high relapse rates, psychiatrists are experimenting with long-acting, injectable antipsychotic medications that need to be administered on only a monthly basis. However, the early research results on this new approach to treatment have not yielded the increases in efficacy that clinicians hoped to see (Goff, 2014; McEvoy et al., 2014).

Antidepressant Drugs

As their name suggests, *antidepressant drugs* **gradually elevate mood and help bring people out of a depression.** Reliance on antidepressants has increased dramatically in the last 15 to 20 years, as they have become the most frequently prescribed class of medication in the United States (Olfson & Marcus, 2009). Today, the most widely prescribed antidepressants are the *selective serotonin reuptake inhibitors (SSRIs)*, which slow the reuptake process at serotonin synapses. The drugs in this class, which include Prozac (fluoxetine), Paxil (paroxetine), and Zoloft (sertraline), seem to yield rapid therapeutic gains in the treatment of depression while producing fewer unpleasant or dangerous side effects than previous generations of antidepressants (Sussman, 2009). SSRIs also have value in the treatment of obsessive-compulsive disorders, panic disorders, and other anxiety disorders (Mathew, Hoffman, & Charney, 2009; Ravindran & Stein, 2009). Although the SSRIs present far fewer problems than earlier antidepressants, they are not without side effects. Adverse effects include nausea, dry mouth, drowsiness, sexual difficulties, weight gain, feeling emotionally numb, agitation, and increases in suicidal thinking (Read, Cartwright, & Gibson, 2014).

Like antipsychotic drugs, antidepressants exert their effects gradually over a period of weeks, but about 60% of patients' improvement tends to occur in the first 2 weeks (Gitlin, 2014). A research review that looked carefully at the *severity* of patients' depression when medication was initiated found that people with serious depression benefit the most from antidepressants, whereas antidepressants appear to provide a relatively modest benefit for patients with mild to moderate depression. (Fournier et al, 2010).

A major concern in recent years has been evidence from a number of studies that SSRIs may increase the risk for suicide, primarily among adolescents and young adults (Healy & Whitaker, 2003; Holden, 2004). The challenge of collecting definitive data on this issue is much more daunting than one might guess, in part because suicide rates are already elevated among people who exhibit the disorders for which SSRIs are prescribed. The research findings on this issue are complicated and contradictory. One influential meta-analysis concluded that antidepressants lead to a slight elevation in the risk of suicidal behavior (Bridge et al., 2007). However, a more recent analysis of forty-one antidepressant drug trials failed to find an increase in suicidal risk (Gibbons et al., 2012).

Regulatory warnings from the U.S. Food and Drug Administration (FDA) have led to a decline in the prescription of SSRIs for adolescents. This trend has prompted concern that increases in suicide may occur among untreated individuals (Dudley et al., 2008). A recent study yielded disturbing evidence that bolsters this concern. Lu and colleagues (2014) found that in the second year after the FDA warnings antidepressant use declined by 31% among adolescents and by 24% among young adults, while apparent suicide attempts via drug overdose (a method of suicide that was relatively easy to track in medical data bases) increased by 22% among adolescents and by 34% among young adults. The association between reduced antidepressant

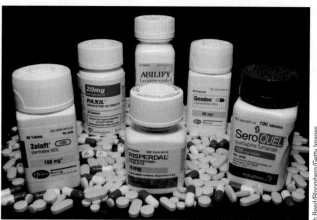

Psychiatric drugs can be helpful in the treatment of many types of disorders. However, critics of drug therapy are concerned that these drugs are overprescribed and that their negative side effects are underappreciated.

use and increased suicide may not reflect a causal relationship, but the findings are worrisome. Clearly, the risks of putting young patients on antidepressants needs to be weighed against the risks of not putting them on antidepressants. This is a complex issue, but the one thing experts seem to agree on is that adolescents starting on SSRIs should be monitored closely. Another recent, large-scale study found that the dose level administered may be a critical consideration. In this study, adolescents and young adults who started on a higher dose of an antidepressant than the modal (typical) dose were roughly twice as likely to engage in self-injurious behavior as those on lower doses (Miller et al, 2014). These data suggest that clinicians should take a conservative approach in prescribing antidepressants to adolescents and young adults.

Mood Stabilizers

Mood stabilizers **are drugs used to control mood swings in patients with bipolar mood disorders.** The principal drugs in this category are *lithium* and *valproate*. Both have proven valuable in preventing *future* episodes of both mania and depression in patients with bipolar illness (Miklowitz, 2014; Post & Altshuler, 2009). They can also be used in efforts to bring patients with bipolar illness out of *current* manic or depressive episodes. On the negative side of the ledger, lithium does have some dangerous side effects if its use isn't managed skillfully (Ferrando, Owen, & Levenson, 2014). Lithium levels in the patient's blood must be monitored carefully because high concentrations can be toxic and even fatal. Kidney and thyroid gland complications are the other major problems associated with lithium therapy.

Evaluating Drug Therapies

Drug therapies can produce clear therapeutic gains for many kinds of patients. What's especially impressive is that they can be effective in severe disorders that otherwise defy therapeutic endeavors. Nonetheless, drug therapies are controversial. Critics of drug therapy have raised a number of issues (Andrews et al., 2012; Bentall, 2009; Breggin, 2008; Kirsch, 2010; Spielmans & Kirsch, 2014). First, some critics argue that drug therapies often produce superficial curative effects. For example, Valium does not really solve problems with anxiety—it merely provides temporary relief from an unpleasant symptom. Moreover, this temporary relief may lull patients into complacency about their problem and prevent them from working toward a more lasting solution.

Second, critics charge that many drugs are overprescribed and many patients overmedicated. According to these critics, many physicians habitually hand out prescriptions without giving adequate consideration to more complicated and difficult interventions. Consistent with this line of criticism, a recent study of office visits to psychiatrists found

that they increasingly prescribe two and even three medications to patients, even though relatively little is known about the interactive effects of psychiatric drugs (Mojtabai & Olfson, 2010). Moreover, the growing reliance on medication has undermined the provision of insight and behavioral interventions. Although the empirical evidence on the value of insight and behavioral therapies has never been greater, the medicalization of psychological disorders has led to a decline in the utilization of psychosocial interventions that often may be just as effective, and probably safer than, drug therapies (Gaudiano & Miller, 2013).

Third, some critics charge that the side effects of therapeutic drugs are worse than the illnesses the drugs are supposed to cure. Citing problems such as tardive dyskinesia, lithium toxicity, and addiction to antianxiety agents, these critics argue that the risks of therapeutic drugs aren't worth the benefits. Some critics have also argued that psychiatric drugs may be helpful in the short term but that they disrupt neurotransmitter systems in ways that actually *increase* patients' vulnerability to psychological disorders in the long term (Andrews et al., 2011).

Critics maintain that the negative effects of psychiatric drugs are not fully appreciated because the pharmaceutical industry has managed to gain undue influence over the research enterprise as it relates to drug testing (Angell, 2004; Insel, 2010). Today, most researchers who investigate the benefits and risks of medications and craft diagnostic criteria and treatment guidelines have lucrative financial arrangements with the pharmaceutical industry, which they often fail to disclose (Cosgrove & Krimsky, 2012). Their studies are funded by drug companies and they often receive substantial consulting fees. Unfortunately, these financial ties appear to undermine the objectivity required in scientific research, as studies funded by pharmaceutical and other biomedical companies are far more likely to report favorable results than nonprofit-funded studies (Bekelman, Li, & Gross, 2003; Perlis et al., 2005).

Industry-financed drug trials also tend to be too brief to detect the long-term risks associated with new drugs (Vandenbroucke & Psaty, 2008), and when unfavorable results emerge, the data are often withheld from publication (Spielmans & Kirsch, 2014). Also, research designs are often slanted in a multitude of ways so as to exaggerate the positive effects and minimize the negative effects of the drugs under scrutiny (Carpenter, 2002; Spielmans & Kirsch, 2014). The conflicts of interest that appear to be pervasive in contemporary drug research raise grave concerns that require attention from researchers, universities, and federal agencies.

Electroconvulsive Therapy (ECT)

In the 1930s, a Hungarian psychiatrist named Ladislas Meduna speculated that epilepsy and schizophrenia could not coexist in the same body. On the basis of this observation, which turned out to be inaccurate, Meduna theorized that it might be useful to induce epileptic-like seizures in schizophrenic patients. Initially, a drug was used to trigger these seizures. However, by 1938, a pair of Italian psychiatrists (Cerletti & Bini, 1938) demonstrated that it was safer to elicit the seizures with electric shock. Thus, modern electroconvulsive therapy was born.

Electroconvulsive therapy (ECT) **is a biomedical treatment in which electric shock is used to produce a cortical seizure accompanied by convulsions.** In ECT, electrodes are attached to the skull over one or both temporal lobes of the brain. A light anesthesia is induced, and an electric current is then applied either to the right side or to both sides of the brain for about a second. Unilateral shock delivered to the right hemisphere is the preferred method of treatment today (Sackeim et al., 2009). The current triggers a brief (5–20 seconds) convulsive seizure, during which the patient usually loses consciousness. Patients normally awaken in an hour or two. People typically receive three treatments a week over a period of 2 to 7 weeks (Fink, 2009).

The clinical use of ECT peaked in the 1940s and 1950s, before effective drug therapies were widely available. ECT is not a rare treatment today, but its use has been declining. A recent study reported that the portion of hospitals with psychiatric units that offered ECT declined from 55% in 1993 to 35% in 2009 (Case et al., 2013). During the same period the number of patients treated with ECT decreased 43%. ECT advocates argue that ECT is underutilized because the public harbors many misconceptions about its risks and side effects (Fink, Kellner, & McCall, 2014; Kellner et al., 2012). Conversely, some critics of ECT have argued that it is overused because it is a lucrative procedure that boosts psychiatrists' income while consuming relatively little of their time in comparison to insight therapy (Frank, 1990).

Effectiveness of ECT

The evidence on the therapeutic efficacy of ECT is open to varied interpretations. Proponents of ECT maintain that it is a remarkably effective treatment for major depression (Fink, 2014; Prudic, 2009). However, opponents of ECT argue that the available studies are flawed and inconclusive and that ECT is probably no more effective than a placebo (Rose et al., 2003). Overall, enough favorable evidence seems to exist to justify *conservative* use of ECT in treating severe mood disorders in patients who have not responded to medication (Kellner et al., 2012). ECT patients who recover from their depression and do not relapse report great improvements in the quality of their lives (McCall et al., 2013). Unfortunately, relapse rates after ECT are distressingly high. A review of thirty-two studies found that the risk of relapse into depression was 38% after 6 months and 51% after 1 year (Jelovac, Kolshus, & McLoughlin, 2013). However, these high relapse rates may occur because ECT is largely reserved for patients who have severe, chronic depression that has not responded to drug treatment (Fekadu et al., 2009). In other words, if ECT is used only for the toughest cases, high relapse rates are to be expected.

Risks Associated with ECT

Even ECT proponents acknowledge that memory loss, impaired attention, and other cognitive deficits are common short-term side effects of electroconvulsive therapy (Nobler & Sackeim, 2006; Rowny & Lisanby, 2008). However, ECT proponents assert that these deficits are mild and usually disappear within a month or two (Fink, 2004). In contrast, ECT critics maintain that ECT-induced cognitive deficits are often significant and sometimes permanent (Breggin, 1991; Rose et al., 2003). A recent, thorough review of the evidence concluded that retrograde amnesia for autobiographical information is a common side effect of ECT and that these memory losses can be persistent and sometimes permanent (Sackeim, 2014). Given the concerns about the risks of ECT and the doubts about its efficacy, it appears that the use of ECT will remain controversial for some time to come.

Learning Objectives

- Describe the merits of blending approaches to therapy.
- Understand why therapy is underutilized by ethnic minorities and identify possible solutions.
- Explain how technology is being used to increase access to clinical services.

15.5 Current Trends and Issues in Treatment

The controversy about ECT is only one of many contentious issues and shifting trends in the world of mental health care. In this section, we discuss the continuing trend toward blending various approaches to therapy, efforts to respond more effectively to increasing cultural diversity in Western societies, and innovations in how treatment is delivered.

Blending Approaches to Treatment

In this chapter we have reviewed many approaches to treatment. However, there is no rule that a client must be treated with just one approach. Often, a clinician will use several techniques in working with a client. For example, a depressed person might receive group therapy (an insight therapy), social skills training (a behavior therapy), and antidepressant medication (a biomedical therapy). Studies suggest that combining approaches to treatment has merit (Szigethy & Friedman, 2009). In particular, combining medication with insight or behavioral treatments tends to yield modest improvements in outcomes, although not for all types of disorders (Forand, DeRubeis, & Amsterdam, 2013).

The value of multiple approaches may explain why a significant trend seems to have crept into the field of psychotherapy: a movement away from strong loyalty to individual schools of thought and a corresponding move toward integrating various approaches to therapy (Gold & Stricker, 2013). Most clinicians used to depend exclusively on one system of therapy while rejecting the utility of all others. This era of fragmentation may be drawing to a close. One survey of psychologists' theoretical orientations, summarized in **Figure 15.11**, found that 36% of the respondents described themselves as *eclectic* in approach (Norcross, Hedges, & Castle, 2002). *Eclecticism* involves drawing ideas from two or more systems of therapy, instead of committing to just one system. Eclectic therapists borrow ideas, insights, and techniques from a variety of sources while tailoring their intervention strategy to the unique needs of each client. Advocates of eclecticism, such as Arnold Lazarus (1995, 2008), maintain that therapists should ask themselves, "What is the best approach for this specific client, problem, and situation?" and then adjust their strategy accordingly.

Increasing Multicultural Sensitivity in Treatment

Research on how cultural factors influence the process and outcome of psychotherapy has burgeoned in recent years, motivated in part by the need to improve mental health services for ethnic minority groups in American society (Gunthert, 2014; Worthington, Soth-McNett, & Moreno, 2007). Studies suggest that American minority groups generally underutilize therapeutic services (Lopez et al., 2012; Snowden, 2012; Sue et al., 2012). Why? A variety of barriers appear to contribute to this problem (Lu et al., 2014; Zane et al., 2004). One major consideration is that many members of minority groups have a history of frustrating interactions with American bureaucracies. Therefore, they are distrustful of large, intimidating institutions, such as hospitals and community mental health centers (Henderson et al., 2014). Another issue is that most hospitals and mental health agencies are not

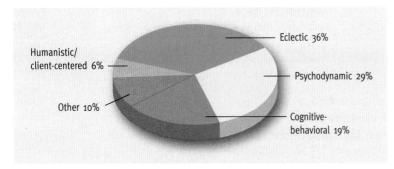

Figure 15.11

The leading approaches to therapy among psychologists. These data, from a survey of 531 psychologists who belong to the American Psychological Association's Division of Psychotherapy, provide some indication of how common an eclectic approach to therapy has become. The findings suggest that the most widely used approaches to therapy are eclectic, psychodynamic, and cognitive-behavioral treatments. (Based on data from Norcross, Hedges, & Castle, 2002)

adequately staffed with therapists who speak the languages used by minority groups in their service areas.

Yet another problem is that the vast majority of therapists have been trained almost exclusively in the treatment of white middle-class Americans. As a result, they are not familiar with the cultural backgrounds and unique characteristics of various ethnic groups. This culture gap often leads to misunderstandings, ill-advised treatment strategies, and reduced rapport. Consistent with this assertion, one study found that psychiatrists spent less time with African American patients than white patients (Olfson, Cherry, & Lewis-Fernández, 2009). Another study of more than 15,000 people suffering from depression found that Mexican Americans and African Americans were notably less likely to receive treatment than whites, as can be seen in **Figure 15.12** (González et al., 2010).

What can be done to improve mental health services for American minority groups? Researchers in this area have offered a variety of suggestions (Berger, Zane, & Hwang, 2014; Hansen et al., 2013; Miranda et al., 2005). Discussions of possible solutions usually begin with the need to recruit and train more ethnic minority therapists. Studies show that ethnic minorities are more likely to go to mental health facilities that are staffed by a higher proportion of people who share their ethnic background (Sue, Zane, & Young, 1994). Research has also shown that outcomes tend to be better and client satisfaction higher when clients see a therapist of similar ethnicity (Meyer, Zane, & Cho, 2011). Therapists who are similar in ethnicity are perceived as having more similar experiences and greater credibility. White therapists working with non-white clients have been urged to work harder at building a vigorous *therapeutic alliance* (a strong supportive bond) with their ethnic clients. A strong therapeutic alliance is associated with better therapeutic outcomes regardless of ethnicity (Crits-Christoph, Gibbons, & Mukherjee, 2013), but some studies suggest that it is especially crucial for minority clients (Bender et al., 2007). Finally, most authorities urge further investigation of how traditional approaches to therapy can be modified and tailored to be more compatible with specific cultural groups' attitudes, values, norms, and traditions. A recent review of research that has examined the effects of culturally adapted interventions found evidence that this tailoring process often seems to yield positive effects, although the evidence was mixed (Huey et al., 2014).

The concerns just discussed about providing culturally sensitive treatment for ethnic minorities also extend to sexual minorities. Lesbian, gay, bisexual, and transgender clients also need mental health services that are sensitive to their unique experiences and challenges (Strassberg & Mackaronis, 2014). One recent study of gay and lesbian clients found that 21% reported that they had worked with a therapist who they viewed as dismissive or unsupportive of their sexual identity (Kelley, 2015). Many of these clients indicated that they would prefer to work with a lesbian or gay therapist, or at least a gay-friendly therapist. Research on culturally competent treatment for sexual minorities is in its infancy, and much remains to be learned.

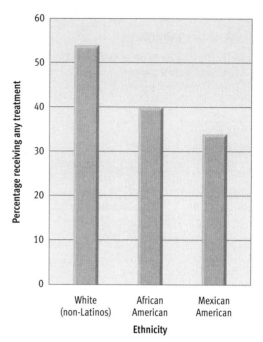

Figure 15.12

Ethnicity and treatment for depression. In a nationally representative sample of almost 16,000 subjects, Gonzáles and colleagues (2010), identified participants suffering from depression and ascertained what types of treatment they had received. When they analyzed these data in relation to ethnicity, they found that members of minority groups were less likely than whites to get treatment. The data graphed here show the percentage of patients receiving treatment of any kind.

Research indicates that ethnic minorities tend to feel more comfortable with therapists who share their ethnicity. Unfortunately, there is a shortage of minority therapists in the United States.

Using Technology to Expand the Delivery of Clinical Services

Although the problem is especially acute among ethnic minorities, inadequate availability of mental health care is a broad problem that reaches into every corner of our society. In an influential article, Alan Kazdin and Stacey Blase (2011) argue that there are just not enough clinicians and treatment facilities available to meet America's mental health needs. This shortage is particularly serious in small towns and rural areas. Moreover, Kazdin and Blase note that the traditional model of one-on-one therapy imposes constraints on the availability of treatment. The substantial costs of traditional treatments also contribute to the underutilization of psychotherapy services and the growing burden of mental illness. To address these problems, clinicians are increasingly attempting to harness technology to expand the delivery of mental health services and to reduce the costs of therapy.

Efforts to use technology to create new platforms for the delivery of therapeutic services have taken many forms. One of the simpler approaches is to deliver both individual and group therapy over the phone. This method has been used in the treatment of elderly clients with anxiety problems (Brenes, Ingram, & Danhauer, 2012) and veterans suffering from loneliness and depression (Davis, Guyker, & Persky, 2012). Another relatively simple innovation has been to use videoconferencing technology to provide both individual and group therapy. A recent review of research on this approach to treatment concluded that clinical outcomes are about the same as for face-to-face therapy and that clients tend to report high satisfaction (Backhaus et al., 2012).

Interventions delivered via the Internet hold even more promise for reaching large swaths of people who might otherwise go untreated. For example, software programs have been created for the treatment of substance abuse (Campbell et al., 2014), depression (Eells et al., 2014), generalized anxiety disorder (Amir & Taylor, 2012), obsessive-compulsive disorder (Andersson et al., 2011), and phobic disorders (Opris et al., 2012). Most of these treatments involve online, interactive, multimedia adaptations of cognitive-behavioral therapies. The computerized treatments typically consist of a series of modules that educate individuals about the nature and causes of their disorder and offer cognitive strategies for ameliorating their problems, along with practice exercises and homework assignments. In most cases the interventions include limited access to an actual therapist through the Internet, but some programs are fully automated with no therapist contact. Studies of computerized therapies suggest that they can be effective for many types of disorders, but more research and higher-quality research are needed before solid conclusions can be drawn on their value (Kiluk et al., 2011). This observation brings us to our Spotlight on Research for the chapter.

Spotlight on RESEARCH

Testing the Efficacy of Internet Therapy

Source: Wagner, B., Horn, A. B., & Maercker, A. (2014). Internet-based versus face-to-face cognitive behavioral intervention for depression: A randomized controlled non-inferiority trial. *Journal of Affective Disorders, 152–154,* 113–121.

As just noted, the movement toward delivering therapeutic services via the Internet creates a need for high-quality research that can evaluate the effectiveness of online interventions. A number of studies have used pretest-posttest designs to assess whether participants in computerized treatment showed improvements over time and reported promising results. However, this method provides no insight about whether Internet treatments are as effective as traditional in-person treatments. Thus, the present study set out to make the first randomized, controlled head-to-head comparison of Internet and traditional delivery methods for a widely used treatment—cognitive-behavioral therapy for depression.

Method

The participants were sixty-two depressed individuals recruited from the Zurich, Switzerland, area who were not currently in any treatment. Their baseline symptoms were assessed with online questionnaires prior to treatment, and then they were randomly assigned to either face-to-face or online treatment. The two groups were exposed to the same 8-week treatment regimen, with the same homework assignments. Face-to-face clients attended weekly therapy meetings, whereas the Internet clients were exposed to the same psychoeducational information through online modules. The Internet clients had online access to a therapist and received feedback on their homework from this therapist. Symptom levels for all participants were reassessed with self-report scales at the end of the 8-week intervention and 3 months after the completion of therapy.

Results

At the end of the therapy trial, both groups showed significant reductions in depression, anxiety, and feelings of hopelessness. There were no significant differences between the groups in the magnitude of these improvements. However, at the 3-month follow-up, a significant difference was observed between the groups in their level of depression, as the Internet group showed a *lower* level of depression than the face-to-face group (see **Figure 15.13**).

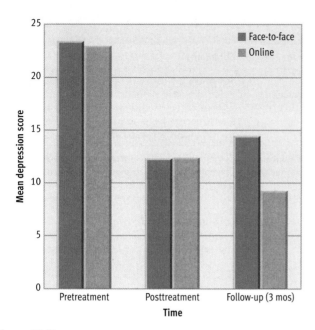

Figure 15.13

Internet versus face-to-face therapy for depression. Wagner, Horn, and Maercker (2014) measured participants' depression with the Beck Depression Inventory at three points in time: prior to treatment, at the end of the 8-week treatment, and 3 months after treatment was completed. As you can see, the two groups showed very similar pretreatment and posttreatment depression scores. But at the 3-month follow-up the online group showed further improvement, whereas the face-to-face group did not fully maintain its previous improvement. (Based on data from Wagner, Horn, & Maercker, 2014)

Discussion

The findings at the end of treatment suggest that Internet versions of cognitive-behavioral therapy can be just as effective as in-person therapy in the treatment of depression. Given the way Internet interventions can extend the availability of treatment, these results were viewed as very encouraging. The finding that the Internet group manifested greater improvement 3 months after the end of treatment was a surprise. The investigators speculate that the online group had less personal guidance from their therapists and hence felt more responsibility for their improvement and more confident about their ability to control their negative thoughts. This was only a small study, but this unexpected result suggests that Internet-based treatments may even have some advantages when compared to traditional modes of treatment.

Critical Thinking Questions

1. Although this was a well-crafted study, pragmatic considerations (cost, time, etc.) often limit what researchers can do. Can you think of some ways in which this study could be made stronger?

2. This study was conducted because researchers worry that Internet-based therapies may not be as effective as traditional therapies. Although that was not the finding in this particular study, outline some reasons why Internet treatment might be inferior to face-to-face treatment.

APPLICATION

15.6 Looking For a Therapist

Learning Objectives

■ Discuss where to seek therapy and the importance of a therapist's gender and professional background.

■ Evaluate the importance of a therapist's theoretical approach and understand what one should expect from therapy.

Answer the following "true" or "false."

_____ **1.** Psychotherapy is an art as well as a science.

_____ **2.** The type of professional degree that a therapist holds is relatively unimportant.

_____ **3.** Psychotherapy can be harmful or damaging to a client.

_____ **4.** Psychotherapy does not have to be expensive.

All of these statements are true. Do any of them surprise you? If so, you're in good company. Many people know relatively little about the practicalities of selecting a therapist. The task of finding an appropriate therapist is no less complex than shopping for any other major service. Should you see a psychologist or a psychiatrist? Should you opt for individual or group therapy? Should you see a client-centered therapist or a behavior therapist? The unfortunate part of this decision process is that people seeking psychotherapy often feel overwhelmed by personal problems. The last thing they need is to be confronted by yet another complex problem.

Nonetheless, the importance of finding a good therapist cannot be overestimated. Therapy can sometimes have harmful rather than helpful effects. We have already discussed how drug therapies and ECT can sometimes be damaging, but problems are not limited to these interventions. Talking about your problems with a therapist may sound pretty harmless, but studies indicate that insight therapies can also backfire (Lambert, 2013; Lilienfeld, 2007). Although a great many talented therapists are available, psychotherapy, like any other profession, has incompetent practitioners as well. Therefore, you should shop for a skilled therapist, just as you would for a good attorney or a good mechanic.

In this Application, we present some information that should be helpful if you ever have to look for a therapist for yourself or for a friend or family member (based on Beutler, Bongar, & Shurkin, 2001; Ehrenberg & Ehrenberg, 1994; Zimmerman & Strouse, 2002).

Where Do You Find Therapeutic Services?

Psychotherapy can be found in a variety of settings. Contrary to general belief, most therapists are not in private practice. Many work in institutional settings such as community mental health centers, hospitals, and human service agencies. The principal sources of therapeutic services are described in **Figure 15.14**. The exact configuration of therapeutic services available will vary from one community to another. To find out what your community has to offer, it is a good idea to consult your friends, your local phone book, or your local community mental health center.

Is the Therapist's Profession or Sex Important?

Psychotherapists may be trained in psychology, psychiatry, social work, counseling, psychiatric nursing, or marriage and family therapy. Researchers have *not* found any reliable associations between therapists' professional background and therapeutic efficacy (Beutler et al., 2004), probably because many talented therapists can be found in all of these professions. Thus, the kind of degree that a therapist holds doesn't need to be a crucial consideration in your selection process. It *is* true that currently only psychiatrists can prescribe drugs in most states. However, critics argue that many psychiatrists are too quick to use drugs to solve problems (Breggin, 2008; Whitaker, 2009). In any case, other types of therapists can refer you to a psychiatrist if they think that drug therapy would be helpful.

Whether a therapist's sex is important depends on your attitude (Nadelson, Notman, & McCarthy, 2005). If *you* feel that the therapist's sex is important, then for you it is. The therapeutic relationship must be characterized by trust and rapport. Feeling uncomfortable with a therapist of one sex or the other could inhibit the therapeutic process. Hence, you should feel free to look for a male or female therapist if you prefer to do so.

PRINCIPAL SOURCES OF THERAPEUTIC SERVICES

Source	Comments
Private practitioners	Self-employed therapists are listed in the Yellow Pages under their professional category, such as psychologists or psychiatrists. Private practitioners tend to be relatively expensive, but they also tend to be highly experienced therapists.
Community mental health centers	Community mental health centers have salaried psychologists, psychiatrists, and social workers on staff. The centers provide a variety of services and often have staff available on weekends and at night to deal with emergencies.
Hospitals	Several kinds of hospitals provide therapeutic services. There are both public and private mental hospitals that specialize in the care of people with psychological disorders. Many general hospitals have a psychiatric ward, and those that do not will usually have psychiatrists and psychologists on staff and on call. Although hospitals tend to concentrate on inpatient treatment, many provide outpatient therapy as well.
Human services agencies	Various social service agencies employ therapists to provide short-term counseling. Depending on your community, you may find agencies that deal with family problems, juvenile problems, drug problems, and so forth.
Schools and workplaces	Most high schools and colleges have counseling centers where students can get help with personal problems. Similarly, some large businesses offer in-house counseling to their employees.

Figure 15.14

Sources of therapeutic services. Therapists work in a variety of organizational settings. Foremost among them are the five described here.

Is Therapy Always Expensive?

Psychotherapy does not have to be prohibitively expensive. Private practitioners tend to be the most expensive, charging between $25 and $140 per (50-minute) hour. These fees may seem high, but they are in line with those of similar professionals, such as dentists and attorneys. Community mental health centers and social service agencies are usually supported by tax dollars. Hence, they can charge lower fees than most therapists in private practice. Many of these organizations use a sliding scale, so that clients are charged according to how much they can afford. Thus, most communities have inexpensive opportunities for psychotherapy. Moreover, many health insurance plans provide at least partial reimbursement for the cost of treatment.

Is the Therapist's Theoretical Approach Important?

Logically, you might expect that the diverse approaches to therapy vary in effectiveness. For the most part, that is *not* what researchers find, however. After reviewing the evidence, Jerome Frank (1961) and Lester Luborsky and his colleagues

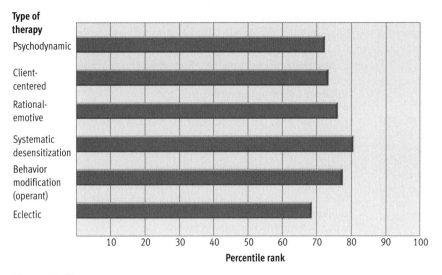

Type of therapy

(bar chart, x-axis: Percentile rank)

- Psychodynamic
- Client-centered
- Rational-emotive
- Systematic desensitization
- Behavior modification (operant)
- Eclectic

Figure 15.15

Efficacy of various approaches to therapy. Smith and Glass (1977) reviewed nearly 400 studies in which clients who were treated with a specific type of therapy were compared with a control group made up of people with similar problems who went untreated. The bars indicate the percentile rank (on outcome measures) attained by the average client treated with each type of therapy when compared to control subjects. The higher the percentile, the more effective the therapy was. As you can see, the different approaches were fairly close in their apparent effectiveness.

Source: Adapted from Smith, M. L., & Glass, G. V. (1977). Meta-analysis of psychotherapy outcome series. *American Psychologist, 32,* 752–760. Copyright © 1977 by the American Psychological Association. Adapted by permission of the authors.

(1975) both quote the dodo bird who has just judged a race in *Alice in Wonderland*: "Everybody has won, and *all* must have prizes." Improvement rates for various theoretical orientations usually come out pretty close in most studies (Lambert, 2013; Laska, Gurman, & Wampold, 2014). In their landmark review of outcome studies, Smith and Glass (1977) estimated the effectiveness of many major approaches to therapy. As **Figure 15.15** shows, the estimates cluster together closely.

However, these findings are a little misleading, as they have been averaged across many types of patients and many types of problems. Most experts seem to think that *for certain types of problems, some approaches to therapy are more effective than others* (Beutler, 2002; Barlow et al., 2013; Hofmann & Barlow, 2014). It is also important to point out that the finding that various approaches to therapy are roughly equal in overall efficacy does not mean that all *therapists* are created equal. Some therapists unquestionably are more effective than others and the differences can be sizable (Baldwin & Imel, 2013; Castonguay et al., 2013). However, these variations in effectiveness appear to depend on individual therapists' personal skills rather than on their theoretical orientation (Beutler et al., 2004). Good, bad, and mediocre therapists are found within each school of thought. Indeed, the tremendous variation among individual therapists in skills may be one of the main reasons that it is hard to find efficacy differences among theoretical approaches to therapy (Staines, 2008).

The key point is that effective therapy requires skill and creativity. Arnold Lazarus (1989), who devised an approach to treatment called multimodal therapy, emphasizes that therapists "straddle the fence between science and art." Therapy is scientific in that interventions are based on extensive theory and empirical research. Ultimately, though, each client is a unique human being. The therapist has to creatively fashion a treatment program that will help that individual (Goodheart, 2006).

What Is Therapy Like?

It is important to have realistic expectations about therapy, or you may be unnecessarily disappointed. Some people expect miracles. They think they will turn their life around quickly with little effort. Others expect their therapist to run their lives for them. These are unrealistic expectations.

Therapy is usually a slow process. Your problems are not likely to melt away quickly. Moreover, therapy is hard work, and your therapist is only a facilitator. Ultimately, *you* have to confront the challenge of changing your behavior, your feelings, or your personality. This process may not be pleasant. You may have to face up to some painful truths about yourself. As Ehrenberg and Ehrenberg (1994) point out, psychotherapy takes time, effort, and courage.

Therapy is both a science and an art. It is scientific in that practitioners are guided in their work by a huge body of empirical research. It is an art in that therapists often have to be creative in adapting their treatment procedures to individual patients and their idiosyncrasies.

CHAPTER 15 Review

Key Ideas

15.1 Elements of the Treatment Process
• Psychotherapy involves three elements: treatments, clients, and therapists. Approaches to treatment are diverse, but they can be grouped into three categories: insight therapies, behavior therapies, and biomedical therapies. People vary considerably in their willingness to seek psychotherapy, and many people who need therapy do not receive it.
• Therapists come from a variety of professional backgrounds. Clinical and counseling psychologists, psychiatrists, social workers, psychiatric nurses, counselors, and marriage and family therapists are the principal providers of therapeutic services.

15.2 Insight Therapies
• Insight therapies involve verbal interactions intended to enhance self-knowledge. In psychoanalysis, free association and dream analysis are used to explore the unconscious. When an analyst's probing hits sensitive areas, resistance can be expected. The transference relationship may be used to overcome this resistance. Classical psychoanalysis is not widely practiced anymore, but Freud's legacy lives on in a rich diversity of modern psychodynamic therapies.
• Rogers pioneered client-centered therapy, which is intended to provide a supportive climate in which clients can restructure their self-concepts. This therapy emphasizes clarification of the client's feelings and self-acceptance.
• Most theoretical approaches to insight therapy have been adapted for use with groups. Group therapy has its own unique strengths and is not merely a cheap substitute for individual therapy. Marital and family therapists seek to understand the entrenched patterns of interaction that produce distress for their clients, view individuals as parts of a family ecosystem, and attempt to help couples and families improve their communication.
• The weight of the evidence suggests that insight therapies can be effective. Studies generally find the greatest improvement early in treatment. Some theorists argue that the beneficial effects of diverse approaches to insight therapies are due to the operation of common factors that they share, such as provision of empathy, cultivation of hope, and the opportunity to express feelings. Research suggests that common factors play an important role in therapy.

15.3 Behavior Therapies
• Behavior therapies use the principles of learning in direct efforts to change specific aspects of behavior. Wolpe's systematic desensitization is a treatment for phobias. It involves the construction of an anxiety hierarchy, relaxation training, and step-by-step movement through the hierarchy. In exposure therapies clients are confronted with situations that they fear so they learn that these situations are really harmless.
• Social skills training can improve clients' interpersonal skills through modeling, behavioral rehearsal, and shaping. Beck's cognitive therapy concentrates on changing the way clients think about events in their lives. Ample evidence shows that behavior therapies are effective.

15.4 Biomedical Therapies
• Biomedical therapies involve physiological interventions for psychological problems. The principal biomedical treatments are drug therapy and electroconvulsive therapy. A great variety of disorders are treated with drugs. The principal types of therapeutic drugs are antianxiety drugs, antipsychotic drugs, antidepressant drugs, and mood stabilizers.
• Drug therapies can be effective, but they have their pitfalls. Many drugs produce problematic side effects, and some are overprescribed.

Critics argue that the negative effects of psychiatric drugs are not fully appreciated because the pharmaceutical industry has gained undue influence over drug testing research.
• Electroconvulsive therapy (ECT) is used to trigger a cortical seizure that is believed to have therapeutic value for depression. There is contradictory evidence and heated debate about the effectiveness of ECT and about possible risks associated with its use.

15.5 Current Trends and Issues in Treatment
• Combinations of insight, behavioral, and biomedical therapies are often used fruitfully in the treatment of psychological disorders. Many modern therapists are eclectic, using ideas and techniques gleaned from a number of theoretical approaches.
• Because of cultural, language, and access barriers, therapeutic services are underutilized by ethnic minorities in America. The crux of the problem is the failure of institutions to provide culturally sensitive forms of treatment for ethnic minorities. This is also an issue for sexual minorities.
• Clinicians are increasingly attempting to harness technology to expand the delivery of mental health services and to reduce the costs of therapy. These efforts to employ technology have included interventions via videoconferencing, telephone, and the Internet. The Spotlight on Research comparing Internet and face-to-face delivery of cognitive behavioral therapy provided promising evidence on the efficacy of these innovative approaches.

15.6 Application: Looking for a Therapist
• Therapeutic services are available in many settings, and such services do not have to be expensive. Excellent and mediocre therapists can be found in all of the mental health professions. Thus, therapists' personal skills are more important than their professional degree. In selecting a therapist, it is reasonable to insist on a therapist of one gender or the other.
• The various theoretical approaches to treatment appear to be fairly similar in overall effectiveness. However, for certain types of problems, some approaches to therapy may be more effective than others. Therapy requires time, hard work, and the courage to confront your problems.

Key Terms

Key People

1. Which of the following approaches to psychotherapy is based on the theories of Sigmund Freud and his followers?
   a. Behavior therapies
   b. Client-centered therapy
   c. Biomedical therapies
   d. Psychoanalytic therapy

2. Miriam is seeing a therapist who encourages her to let her mind ramble and say whatever comes up, regardless of how trivial or irrelevant it may seem. The therapist explains that she is interested in probing the depths of Miriam's unconscious mind. This therapist appears to practice _____ and the technique in use is _____.
   a. psychoanalysis; transference
   b. psychoanalysis; free association
   c. cognitive therapy; free association
   d. client-centered therapy; clarification

3. Because Suzanne has an unconscious sexual attraction to her father, she behaves seductively toward her therapist. Suzanne's behavior is most likely a form of
   a. resistance.
   b. transference.
   c. misinterpretation.
   d. spontaneous remission.

4. In terms of process, client-centered therapy emphasizes
   a. interpretation.
   b. probing the unconscious.
   c. clarification.
   d. all of the above.

5. With regard to studies of the efficacy of various treatments, research suggests that
   a. insight therapy is superior to no treatment or placebo treatment.
   b. individual insight therapy is effective, but group therapy is not.
   c. group therapy is effective, but individual insight therapy rarely works.
   d. insight therapy is effective, but only if patients remain in therapy for at least 3 years.

6. According to behavior therapists, pathological behaviors
   a. are signs of an underlying emotional or cognitive problem.
   b. should be viewed as the expression of an unconscious sexual or aggressive conflict.
   c. can be modified directly through the application of established principles of conditioning.
   d. both a and b.

7. In _____ clients learn how to change their automatic negative thoughts and maladaptive beliefs.
   a. systematic desensitization
   b. cognitive therapy
   c. aversion therapy
   d. psychoanalysis

8. Bryce's psychiatrist has prescribed both an antidepressant and lithium for him. Bryce's diagnosis is probably
   a. schizophrenia.
   b. obsessive-compulsive disorder.
   c. bipolar disorder.
   d. dissociative disorder.

9. Drug therapies have been criticized on the grounds that
   a. they are ineffective in most patients.
   b. they temporarily relieve symptoms without addressing the real problem.
   c. many drugs are overprescribed and many patients are overmedicated.
   d. both b and c.

10. A therapist's theoretical approach is not nearly as important as his or her
    a. age.
    b. appearance.
    c. personal characteristics and skills.
    d. type of professional training.

Answers
1. d Page 432
2. b Pages 432–433
3. b Page 434
4. c Page 436
5. a Page 438
6. c Page 439
7. b Page 441
8. c Page 445
9. d Pages 445–446
10. c Pages 452–453

Personal Explorations Workbook

Go to the *Personal Explorations Workbook* in the back of your textbook for exercises that can enhance your self-understanding in relation to issues raised in this chapter.

Exercise 15.1 *Self-Assessment:* Attitudes toward Seeking Professional Psychological Help

Exercise 15.2 *Self-Reflection:* Thinking about Therapy

CHAPTER 16 Positive Psychology

oliveromg/Shutterstock.com

On January 15, 2009, an unprecedented event galvanized the American public's attention and imbued people with feelings of joy. A passenger plane made a miraculous landing on the Hudson River in New York City. After the plane took off from LaGuardia Airport, the pilot, Chesley "Sully" Sullenberger, reported that a flock of birds had flown into the plane's engines, causing it to quickly lose power and altitude. Such bird strikes are perilous because they usually shut down one of the engines on an aircraft. This incident was much worse because the pilot believed that both engines were affected. Disaster was imminent, but moments later the pilot executed a near-perfect water landing, and all 155 on board were rescued from the icy waters. Images of the plane and the rescue of its passengers and crew by air and by boat flashed throughout the news media.

In addition to relief, elation was a common reaction to the plane's miraculous maneuver, which was quickly dubbed the "miracle on the Hudson" (Prochnau & Parker, 2010). The event elevated the spirits of those who witnessed it, heard about it, or watched it on television or via the Internet. The pilot, a modest man who claimed that his training served him well, became an instant hero, one whose actions generated a sense of appreciative wonder in observers. What people shared in the aftermath of this event might be called a sense of *awe*, a state some psychologists refer to as a moral, spiritual, or even an aesthetic emotion (Schurtz et al., 2012). People who feel elation or a sense of awe report experiencing a warm feeling in their chests, an expansion of their hearts,

The miraculous safe landing by US Air 1549 evoked feelings of awe that elevated the spirits of observers around the world.

and a strong and sure sense of connection to other people. We will review a Spotlight on Research regarding awe later in this chapter, when we discuss emotions.

This chapter is devoted to exploring the impact of such upbeat phenomena by presenting one of psychology's newest areas of inquiry: positive psychology. We define this new field and the three areas of research that compose it. We then discuss representative topics within each area in some detail. Our study of positive psychology concludes by considering the prospects and problems of studying how and why people thrive. This chapter's Application offers some simple exercises you can use to boost your own level of happiness. ■

16.1 The Scope of Positive Psychology

Learning Objectives

■ Define *positive psychology* and explain why it is a counterweight to the historic and dominant negative focus in the discipline.

■ Explain why positive psychology provides a framework for new as well as older research on well-being.

■ Identify positive psychology's three lines of inquiry.

You may have seen the popular bumper sticker suggesting that people "commit random acts of kindness and senseless acts of beauty." Seeing a car sporting this sentiment, you might conclude that the driver or owner is some sort of idealist or wide-eyed optimist. Perhaps the individual is someone who sees the proverbial glass as half-full rather than half-empty. But what if some serious psychological substance underlies the bumper sticker's message? Let's explore how a focus on what's good in life can be good for people.

Defining *Positive Psychology* and Its Brief History

Positive psychology **is a social and intellectual movement within the discipline of psychology that focuses on human strengths and how people can flourish and be successful** (Csikszentmihalyi & Nakamura, 2011). In part, the emergence of positive psychology was a reaction to the predominantly negative focus found in most other areas of the discipline. Think about your own perceptions of psychology. If you are like most students, you probably view psychology as a helping profession more than anything else. But consider how much of that "help" is based primarily on the study of weaknesses and problems—social, emotional, cognitive, and behavioral—that people exhibit (Seligman, 2002). Psychology's language is rooted in the negative, with words like *depression, anxiety*, and *disorder*.

Until 15 or so years ago, the study of positive qualities and their impact on people's health and well-being occurred entirely outside of the discipline's mainstream. Advocates of positive psychology argue that it provides a needed balance in the discipline. Note that research in positive psychology does not deny the importance of negative states, experiences, feelings, and emotions. Failing to recognize the complex range of human experience would make the approach incomplete (Brown & Holt, 2011). Though not always pleasant, for example, experiencing negative emotions can promote self-understanding and direct personal growth (Algoe, Fredrickson, & Chow, 2011; Shmotkin, 2005). We learn to appreciate life's richness by recognizing its tragic elements (Woolfolk, 2002). So, let's be very clear: Positive psychology is not "happiology" (Seligman, 2011); rather, it represents a new direction of inquiry for the field, one with an empirical literature that is growing by leaps and bounds (Donaldson, Dollwet, & Rao, 2015).

Such a shift in perspective requires more than just donning the equivalent of rose-colored glasses or acting like a "Pollyanna," someone who is encumbered by foolish or even blind optimism. Advocates of positive psychology (including some who actually call themselves "positive psychologists") want to discover how to harness people's strengths, virtues, and other good qualities to help them enhance their lives (Hone, Jarden, & Schofield, 2015). One of positive psychology's primary aims is to create tools and techniques for promoting and regulating well-being, emotions, and psychological health, which have an impact on individuals, their connections with others, and physical health (Quoidbach, Mikolajczak, & Gross, 2015). A good way to think of positive psychology is as an arm of psychology with potentially beneficial side effects, including the opportunity to prevent mental illness and reduce discontent by cultivating human strengths, such as courage, hope, and resilience, and helping people flourish in their lives (Seligman, 2011).

What led psychologists to consider developing this new subfield? As a researchable and teachable topic, positive psychology was not identified until 1998. During his year as president of the American Psychological Association (APA), Martin Seligman developed positive psychology as a counterweight to the discipline's negatively oriented history (Seligman, 1999). He was well known for his research on learned helplessness, depression, and the acquisition of phobias—downbeat topics that fit comfortably within psychology's traditional emphasis on the negative. So what prompted his sudden interest in the potential power of people's positive natures? Seligman (2002) reported that an exchange with his 5-year-old daughter Nikki triggered a chain of events that led to the founding of positive psychology. Quite simply, Nikki told her father that he was being a grump while the two of them were gardening. Seligman recalled:

Martin E. P. Seligman championed positive psychology during his year as president of the American Psychological Association.

Nikki . . .was throwing weeds into the air and dancing around. I yelled at her. She walked away, came back, and said . . . "Daddy, do you remember before my fifth birthday? From the time I was three to the time I was five, I was a whiner. I whined every day. When I turned five, I decided not to whine anymore. That was the hardest thing I've ever done. And if I can stop whining, you can stop being such a grouch." (2002, pp. 3–4)

By speaking some "truth to power," Nikki led her dad to experience something of an epiphany, a sudden flash of insight into an event. Raising children, for example, is not about telling them what to do (let alone yelling at them); rather, it is really about identifying and nurturing their good qualities and strengths. By extension, Seligman began to think about how the psychology of the past generations could have—*should* have—been about much more than negative, pathological states and human suffering (Seligman, 2003).

But this is recent history—what about other events in psychology's past that led to present-day positive psychology? Since World War II, psychology has focused on treating an increasing variety of psychological disorders (see Chapter 15). Indeed, clinical psychology was born out of the need to deal with the rise of pathology and psychological maladies linked to life in the modern world. Progress creates all kinds of stress, strain, and conflict. Consider the stressors found in daily life—work, money, love (or the lack thereof), family, purpose, and the need to find some meaning in all of them. Since the mid-20th century, the psychological community has responded to these changes and pressures by adhering to a disease model, where emphasis is on repairing damage rather than preventing it or inoculating people in advance against psychological distress (Maddux, 2009).

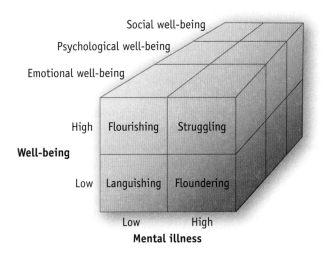

Social well-being
Psychological well-being
Emotional well-being

Well-being

High	Flourishing	Struggling
Low	Languishing	Floundering

Low — High

Mental illness

Figure 16.1

A proposed model of complete mental health based on positive psychological concepts. Keyes and Lopez (2002) proposed a model of complete mental health where psychological assessments of flourishing, struggling, languishing, and floundering are considered across each of three levels of well-being (emotional, psychological, social), which leads to twelve classifications of mental health. The ideal state of complete mental health, flourishing, is marked by a low level of mental illness and high levels of emotional, psychological, and social well-being.

Source: Adapted from Compton, W. C., & Hoffman, E. (2013). *Positive psychology: The science of happiness and flourishing.* Belmont, CA: Wadsworth/Cengage.

Seligman and like-minded researchers felt that the time was right to mount a campaign for change so that psychologists and the people they study, treat, and teach would learn to see their lives as fulfilling rather than as stress-ridden and dysfunctional (Keyes & Haidt, 2003). Gatherings were held, plans were laid, and then conferences and workshops were conducted where junior and senior psychologists met to develop a philosophy and identify goals for what became known as positive psychology. Soon after, scholarly articles, books, and journals dealing with positive psychology appeared (Linley, 2009). As Seligman and Mihaly Csikszentmihalyi (2000), another founder of the movement, claimed, "The aim of positive psychology is to begin to catalyze a change in the focus of psychology from preoccupation with only repairing the worst things in life to also building positive qualities" (p. 5).

If nothing else, positive psychology wants to change the traditional conception of mental health by helping people *flourish*—that is, to have high levels of well-being and low levels of mental illness (Keyes, 2009). Individuals who are *struggling* have high levels of both well-being and mental illness. Those who are *floundering* tend to have low levels of well-being but high levels of mental illness. Finally, a person who has low well-being and low mental health is said to be *languishing*. **Figure 16.1** presents this combination in an alternative model of complete mental health. Note that when individuals truly flourish (possess high well-being and low mental illness), they also display a combination of high emotional well-being, high psychological well-being, and high social well-being (Keyes & Lopez, 2002).

What about you? Are you flourishing in your daily life? To flourish is to be successful in important areas of your life, including enjoying good relationships with others, having a favorable level of self-esteem, and experiencing feelings of purpose and optimism. **Figure 16.2** shows a scale that measures flourishing in daily life that was developed by positive psychologist Ed Diener and his colleagues (Diener, Oishi, & Lucas, 2009). Complete this brief self-assessment to assess your current level of flourishing.

Reconsidering Older Research in Light of the New Positive Psychology

Positive psychology represents a turning point, even a change in the zeitgeist, for the discipline of psychology. The term *zeitgeist* refers to a

---

THE FLOURISHING SCALE

Below are eight statements with which you may agree or disagree. Using the 1–7 scale below, indicate your agreement with each item by indicating that response for each statement.

7 = Strongly agree
6 = Agree
5 = Slightly agree
4 = Neither agree nor disagree
3 = Slightly disagree
2 = Disagree
1 = Strongly disagree

_____ **1.** I lead a purposeful and meaningful life.

_____ **2.** My social relationships are supportive and rewarding.

_____ **3.** I am engaged and interested in my daily activities.

_____ **4.** I actively contribute to the happiness and well-being of others.

_____ **5.** I am competent and capable in the activities that are important to me.

_____ **6.** I am a good person and live a good life.

_____ **7.** I am optimistic about my future.

_____ **8.** People respect me.

Scoring: Add the responses, varying from 1 to 7, for all eight items. The possible range of scores is from 8 (lowest possible) to 56 (highest possible). A high score represents a person with many psychological resources and strengths.

Figure 16.2

The Flourishing Scale. This brief scale assesses an individual's self-perceptions of success in various important areas of daily life, including relationships, optimism, purpose, and self-esteem. By completing the scale, you will receive a summary representing your current level of well-being.

Source: Adapted from Diener, E., Wirtz, D., Tov, W., Kim-Prieto, C., Choi, D., Oishi, S., & Biswas-Diener, R. (2009). New measures of well-being: Flourishing and positive and negative feelings. *Social Indicators Research, 39,* 247–266.

timely intellectual state of mind that many people contribute to and share. Positive psychology's emergence seems to fit this description, but can we really conclude that this subdiscipline just "appeared" once Seligman and others began to communicate, organize, conceive, and publish relevant research?

The answer is probably not, and here's why: Good ideas are often "in the air" before someone studies them or before a topical area is formally named. Thus, as an organized effort, the positive psychology movement *is* new, but many of the questions being studied are not; in fact, quite a few have been examined by psychologists for decades outside of the discipline's mainstream (Downey & Chang, 2014). Various theories, hypotheses, and research results pertaining to beneficial qualities and psychological themes in human experience have been around since the 1950s and 1960s (e.g., Rogers, 1961). Indeed, humanistic psychology, another subdiscipline, has long pursued questions that seem similar to those now asked by positive psychologists (Linley, 2009). In fact, some humanistic psychologists have identified a tension between the two fields (Medlock, 2012), while others argue that positive psychology is overlooking, even neglecting, established scholarly work in humanistic psychology (Friedman & Robbins, 2012). And as advocates of positive psychology are quick to acknowledge, questions regarding what constitutes "the good life" have been pursued by philosophers since Plato and Aristotle (Huta, 2013).

As you read this chapter, you will notice that older research and references are routinely mixed in with newer ones (those appearing after positive psychology's "birth" in 1998). Juxtaposing old with new research should not seem odd, as the questions asked and answers obtained earlier can now be examined fruitfully in light of new data linked to positive psychology's three areas of inquiry.

Introducing Positive Psychology's Three Lines of Inquiry

Positive psychology pursues three lines of inquiry, which make up the "three legs" on which positive psychology stands (Seligman & Csikszentmihalyi, 2000). First, positive psychology is interested in *positive subjective experiences*. Such experiences include good moods, positive emotions, happiness, love, and other psychological processes that promote or maintain feelings of well-being in individuals. The second area is *positive individual traits* that enable people to thrive. The traits falling under this heading are character strengths and virtues, including such qualities as hope, resilience, and gratitude. The third line of inquiry focuses on *positive institutions*, the settings and organizations that promote civil discourse and enhance people's positive subjective experiences and positive personal traits collectively. Positive institutions include close-knit families, quality schools, good work environments, and safe, supportive neighborhoods and communities.

Each area of inquiry seeks to understand the ways people can flourish daily. The next three sections in the chapter review concepts and illustrative research representing these areas. We begin with people's private feelings of well-being: positive subjective experiences.

Learning Objectives

- Distinguish between moods and emotions, and discuss how thought speed and the broaden-and-build model are linked to positive states.
- Explain the flow experience and typical activities that trigger it.
- Outline the advantages of mindfulness over mindlessness, describe the Spotlight on Research regarding awe and prosocial behavior, and define *savoring*.

16.2 Positive Subjective Experiences

Some positive psychologists focus on the study of *positive subjective experiences*, **or the positive but private feelings and thoughts people have about themselves and the events in their lives.** The frequency of positive subjective experiences is linked to people's success in marriage, friendship, income, and health, among other areas of daily life; such personal accomplishments lead to good feelings and make people more successful (Lyubomirsky, King, & Diener, 2005).

Subjective experiences are present focused. In fact, considerable research has examined the most common positive subjective state, happiness, as discussed in Chapter 1 (see also David, Boniwell, & Conley Ayers, 2013; Lyubomirsky, 2013). Sensual pleasures—pleasant tastes (chocolate) and smells (fresh-baked bread), for example, as well as touch (a friendly caress)—can trigger positive subjective states in people.

But subjective states are not just in the present. People can recall past experiences that conjure up feelings of contentment or satisfaction. Reviewing childhood memories, such as holidays, birthdays, or vacations, can be especially gratifying. Events need not be based in the distant past, either. An office worker can call up feelings of satisfaction by recalling a successful performance review she received from her boss a month before or by remembering the goal her soccer-playing daughter made the previous week. Whether you reflect on a distant, recent, or current moment that was favorable, you can experience a change in mood from a neutral state to a more positive one.

"I don't sing because I am happy. I am happy because I sing."

Positive Moods

When someone reports being in a "good mood," the person is not usually referring to emotion per se. Emotions are stronger subjective experiences, much more distinct than moods. Moods are global responses to experience and tend to be more diffuse and pervasive, lasting much longer than emotions (Morris, 1999). Think about someone you know who is always cheerful and upbeat—that is, she is usually in a good mood. Imagine this friend returning to her parked car only to discover a parking ticket on her windshield. How does she react? She may become angry at herself for forgetting to put change in the meter, but later, she has forgotten the costly ticket, returning to her usual smiling and placid self. In other words, she is again experiencing a relatively good mood.

When people are in good moods, they anticipate that good things will happen to them; as a consequence, they often make good things happen. Being in a positive mood has several beneficial effects, including making people more agreeable, more helpful, less aggressive, and even better at decision making (Isen, 2002).

Positive Moods Can Promote Creative Solutions

We know that being in a positive mood can enhance people's creativity (Hoffman, 2013; Kaufman, 2015). For example, Isen and her colleagues hypothesized that positive mood would promote creative problem solving (Isen, Daubman, & Nowicki, 1987). For 5 minutes, groups of men and women watched either a funny "blooper" reel or an emotionally neutral film. Afterward, each participant was introduced to the "candle task," a measure of creative problem solving (Duncker, 1945). An experimenter read these instructions aloud:

On the table [in front of you] are a book of matches, a box of tacks, and a candle. Above the table on the wall is a corkboard. Your task is to affix the candle to the corkboard in such a way that it will burn without dripping wax on the table or the floor beneath. You will be given 10 minutes to work on the problem.

Do you see the quick and correct solution? By pouring out the contents of the box and then tacking it to the corkboard, it becomes a candleholder (see **Figure 16.3**). The lit candle can then be placed upright on the box while being connected to the wall. This solution prevents wax from dripping onto the floor. Once you recognize the solution, it seems obvious, yet many participants fail to identify the correct solution before the 10 minutes is up.

What was the impact of the mood manipulation (viewing one of the two films) on creativity and solving the candle task? As Isen and colleagues (1987) anticipated, participants viewing the funny film were more

Problem

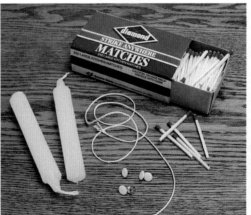

Solution

Figure 16.3

The Duncker candle task for demonstrating creativity: problem and solution. Problem solvers are given a candle, a book of matches, and a box of tacks (left). They are then told to attach the candle to the wall in such a way that wax will not drip onto the table top. The correct solution—tacking the box to the wall so it can serve as a base to hold the lit candle (with no dripping onto the table) is shown on the right.

likely to solve the problem correctly in the allotted time than those who watched the neutral film. Related studies support the finding that good moods as well as positive emotions help people to be more creative in their thinking (e.g., To et al., 2012). One way to think about positive affect (feelings)—whether in the guise of milder moods or stronger emotions—is that it helps people see things in new, unconventional ways.

We have considered how positive mood can lead to particular outcomes, such as creative thinking. What if we reverse the process: Are there qualities associated with thinking that can lead to particular moods, especially positive ones? To answer that, let's take a look at some fascinating new research.

Positive Moods Are Linked with Quick Thoughts

When was the last time you felt your thoughts racing—that is, moving at a faster-than-usual rate? Thought speed turns out to have an impact on both feeling and behavior (Pronin, 2013). Chances are that if your thoughts were racing along at a brisk pace, you were probably in a good mood.

Pronin and Jacobs (2008) argue that faster thinking generally leads to a more positive mood (see also Pronin, Jacobs, & Wegner, 2008). However, when thoughts are too fast, they can be associated with feelings of *mania*, an abnormally elevated mood. What about slower thoughts? As you may have already surmised, they are often linked with negative moods. And very slow or sluggish thoughts can lead to depressive feelings. Thought speed is one property of a more general concept that Pronin and Jacobs call *mental motion*.

Besides thought speed, mental motion also involves thought variability (Pronin & Jacobs, 2008). When one's thought is varied—thinking about many different things, not just one or two—one's mood is usually positive. Repetitive thoughts on the same topic, or what is sometimes referred to as *rumination*, are associated with negative affect. At the positive extreme of thought variation, people can experience mania or even a reverie or dreamlike state. Approaching the negative extreme, however, thoughts can become depressive or anxiety ridden. When quick thoughts and varied thinking meet, people feel elated; when thoughts are plodding and repetitive, however, people experience dejection. Naturally, thought speed and variability can oppose each other—when one is fast (or slow), the other can be varied (or repetitive). The consequences for various possible combinations of mental motion's properties for mood are shown in **Figure 16.4** (note where normal mood lies compared to the predictable deviations surrounding it as thought speed and variability change).

Finally, Pronin and Jacobs (2008) argue that thought speed and variability operate independently of the *content* of thought. In other words, you might assume that slow thoughts are necessarily negative thoughts, but that is not always so. Although emotional problems such as depression and anxiety have been linked to nonrational or dysfunctional thinking (Beck, 2008), the arguments for mental motion's impact on mood do not require that thoughts have any particular content.

Let's review a simple experiment that illustrates the relationship between basic speed of thought and mood, as well as some of its psychological consequences. Pronin, Jacobs, and Wegner (2008) had a group of college students spend 10 minutes writing down solutions to a hypothetical problem (how to earn 1 year's private college tuition in a summer). Participants in the *fast-thought* group were told to produce "every idea you possibly can," whereas those in the *slow-thought* condition were asked to develop "as many good ideas as you can." The findings are summarized in **Figure 16.5**. People in the fast-thought group generated more ideas and felt themselves to be thinking at a faster rate compared to those in the other group (see the left side of **Figure 16.5**). Further, the fast-thought group experienced more positive mood levels and reported higher levels of energy

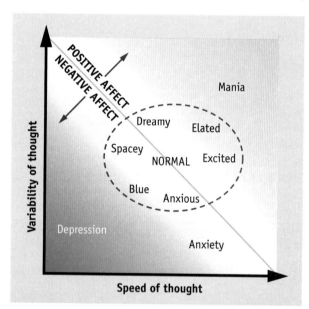

Figure 16.4

Mental motion and mood: The consequences of thought speed and variability for how people may feel. This diagram illustrates the theorized relationships between the speed and variability of thought and moods. Varied but fast thinking leads to feelings of elation, while slow repetitive thinking causes feelings of dejection. When thought variability and speed oppose each other (one is low while the other is high), people's moods may depend upon which of the two factors is more extreme. The mood states created by these combinations vary apart from their positive or negative valence. For example, repetitive thinking can create feelings of anxiety rather than depression if the thinking is rapid; indeed, anxious states of being are generally linked with more rapid thought than depressive states.

Source: Adapted from Pronin, E., & Jacobs, E. (2008). Thought speed, mood, and the experience of mental motion. *Perspectives on Psychological Science, 3*, 461–485.

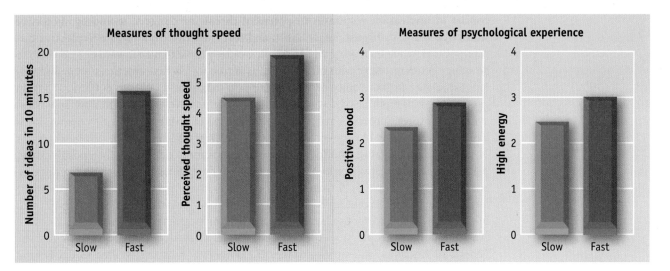

Figure 16.5

Results of the self-generated ideas, speed of thought, and mood experiment. Participants in the fast-thinking condition of the experiment generated more ideas in the allotted time than did their peers (see the graph on the far left). The crucial results are shown in the two graphs on the right. As you can see, those in the fast-thinking group reported having a more positive mood and higher levels of energy than those in the slow-thinking group.

Source: Adapted from Pronin, E., & Jacobs, E. (2008). Thought speed, mood, and the experience of mental motion. *Perspectives on Psychological Science, 3,* 461–485.

than the slow-thought group (see the right side of **Figure 16.5**). Though preliminary, these findings suggested beneficial implications for developing thought-speed-based interventions for treating mood disorders (Pronin & Wegner, 2006).

Positive mood and speed of thoughts are usually quite low and slow for people who are experiencing depression. Recent research by Yang, Friedman-Wheeler, and Pronin (2014) found that the mood of people with mild to moderate depressive symptoms could be enhanced when the speed of their thoughts was accelerated. To create this "mood boost," participants read a streaming text that was shown at a controlled rate (paced either fast or at a neutral speed). In two experiments, people with mild to moderate depressive symptoms who were led to think faster reported more positive moods than those whose thoughts proceeded at a more neutral pace. The positive mood group also reported higher levels of positive mood at the study's end compared to a pretest assessment, a result that points to the efficacy of the mood boost following the thought acceleration manipulation. People with minimal or no depressive symptoms displayed similar mood reports in both conditions, however, individuals with more severe depressive symptoms were not influenced by the mood manipulation. Future efforts should determine whether there are long-lasting benefits associated with inducing fast thinking and, if so, more therapeutic interventions could be designed.

Positive Emotions

Whereas moods are low-level feelings that last for lengthy periods of time ("I was grumpy all week"), emotions are stronger but shorter-lived feelings, acute responses to some particular event ("I was overjoyed when I won the dance contest"). As noted in Chapter 3, *emotions* **are powerful, largely uncontrollable feelings, accompanied by physiological changes.** When psychologists speak of emotions, they usually divide them into two categories: positive and negative. *Positive emotions* **consist of pleasant responses to events that promote connections with others, including subjective states such as happiness, joy, euphoria, gratitude, and contentment.** When individuals experience positive emotions, they feel good about themselves, about other people, and often about whatever they are doing or thinking. Interestingly, some people are more prone to experiencing positive emotions than others are (Cohn & Frederickson, 2009; Tugade, Shiota, & Kirby, 2014). In contrast, *negative emotions*

consist of unpleasant responses to potential threats or dangers, including subjective states like sadness, disgust, anger, guilt, and fear. Negative emotions are unpleasant disruptions that, while increasing vigilance, often cause people to turn inward or lead them to be snippy or disagreeable with others. And, as is true for positive emotions, some individuals experience negative emotions more routinely than others (Watson & Clark, 1984). In general, negative emotions draw more attention than positive ones, and this predisposition is likely an evolved process (Froh, 2009). The division of positive and negative emotions is basic, a structural fact of people's normal emotional lives (Watson, 2002).

Historically, negative emotions have been studied more extensively than positive ones, perhaps because negative emotions have evolutionary significance (experiencing negative emotions alerts people to threats). These emotions make people wary, narrowing their focus of attention (Derryberry & Tucker, 1994). Second, negative emotions are implicated in the "flight or fight response," which occurs when an organism feels threatened. Negative emotions compel people to act through emotionally linked *specific action tendencies*, or behavioral reactions with survival value. The automatic response is often to flee from a perceived threat (a mugger, a bully) or to fight off an attacker. Another reason that negative emotions receive so much attention is their sheer quantity; they outnumber positive emotions by about three to one (Ellsworth & Smith, 1988), which may have contributed to the bias among psychologists to study them.

But what about positive emotions—what value do they have? Some intriguing answers to this question have come from Barbara Fredrickson, a social and positive psychologist who asserts that positive emotions play particular roles in people's mental and physical lives (Sekerka, Vacharkulksemsuk, & Fredrickson, 2012). Fredrickson (Conway et al., 2013; Tugade, Devlin, & Fredrickson, 2014) developed the *broaden-and-build model* of positive emotions to explain how they benefit human beings. In contrast to negative emotions, positive ones spawn *nonspecific action tendencies* that nonetheless lead to adaptive responses. For example, when adults experience positive emotions, they are more likely to aid people in need, engage others in social interaction, perform some creative activity, or try out some new experience (e.g., Isen, 2004). Positive emotions also serve as beneficial counterweights to the dysphoric or fearful feelings associated with emotional dysfunction and psychopathology (Garland et al., 2010). Put simply, positive emotions open people up to a variety of new behavioral options that promote and maintain psychosocial well-being.

Positive emotions also broaden people's cognitive responses by promoting new and beneficial *thought-action tendencies*, where established ways of positive thinking are associated with particular acts or behaviors. For example, when children are feeling joy, they become more playful and imaginative, often investigating their environments (Fredrickson, 1998). This joyful exploration allows them to learn new things about the world and about themselves.

In one study, Fredrickson and Branigan (2005) demonstrated that the experience of joy did indeed broaden people's thought-action tendencies. After watching one of five emotion-eliciting film clips (joy, contentment, anger, fear, or a neutral condition), research participants wrote down lists of everything they would like to have done at that moment. As shown in **Figure 16.6**, the participants who felt either joy or contentment listed significantly

Barbara Fredrickson developed the broaden-and-build theory of positive emotions.

Figure 16.6

The broadening effects of positive emotions compared to neutral or negative emotions. Experiencing an emotional state of joy or contentment led research participants to list a greater number of activities they might like to engage in at that moment than did individuals experiencing a neutral or negative emotional state.

Source: Adapted from Fredrickson, B. L. (2002). Positive emotions. In C. R. Snyder & S. J. Lopez (Eds.), *Handbook of positive psychology* (pp. 120–134). New York: Oxford University Press.

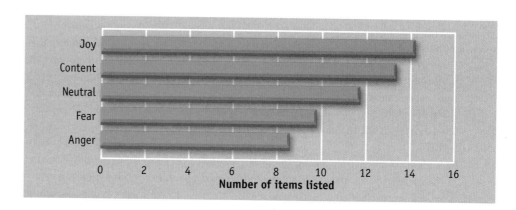

more desired possible actions than the individuals in the negative or neutral emotion groups. Being joyful or contented apparently leads people to think of future possible activities they might engage in, whereas a negative or even neutral emotional state narrows people's thoughts and reduces the range of possible subsequent actions.

Thus, the broaden-and-build model proposes that positive emotions *broaden* people's outlooks, and then they *build on* subsequent learning to develop future emotional and intellectual resources. Positive emotions create "bankable" social, cognitive, and affective resources that can be drawn on with emotional interest in the future. **Figure 16.7** illustrates the broaden-and-build model. Fredrickson postulates that broader thought-action repertoires lead to increased well-being, which in turn triggers more positive emotions leading to happiness and what Fredrickson (2002) refers to as upward spirals of health. These spirals promote both mental and physical health (Kok et al., 2013).

Recently, Fredrickson and her colleagues argued that physical activity, such as routine exercise, not only enhances emotional experiences but also appears to develop the aforementioned psychosocial resources (Hogan et al., 2015). In a series of studies, these researchers looked at the benefits of physical activity as well as the downside of sedentary behavior (being a "couch potato"). They suggest that sedentary behavior, such as watching television rather than performing physical activities, not only negatively impacts emotional experiences but also erodes available psychosocial resources. People often view exercise as an obligation rather than a pleasure; perhaps one way to get them to think and act differently is to focus on the good feelings routine physical activities generate, as well as the mental and physical health resources they develop.

What else do positive emotions accomplish besides broadening thought-action repertoires? Fredrickson advanced **the *undoing hypothesis*, which posits that positive emotions aid the mind and the body by recovering a sense of balance and flexibility following an episode experiencing negative emotion** (Fredrickson & Joiner, 2002). When people are stressed, such as when a group of students take an unexpectedly difficult exam, the presence of positive emotions triggered by the shared experience (e.g., the students meet after the test, discuss it, and share their anxieties) undo the stressor's aftereffects more quickly. The students are likely to feel better once they realize they all felt the same way about the exam. They will smile at one another, roll their eyes, possibly even laugh at how absurdly difficult the questions were, leading to positive emotions that effectively wipe out the physiological and biochemical effects caused by the stressful test-taking experience. Additionally, the resulting positive emotions reestablish flexible and open thinking after the narrowed perspective caused by the negative (stressful) emotions felt during the tough test.

Many times positive emotions are responses to events—that is, they are caused by good things that happen. We also need to consider the consequences of positive emotions that people intentionally create by pursuing particular activities or by learning to self-generate them (Fredrickson, 2013).

Flow

Do you ever find yourself so happily engaged in a challenging or interesting activity that you "lose yourself" in it? If you are an athlete, for example, you may describe the experience as "being in the zone" when you are playing basketball or tennis. Of course, the activity does not have to be particularly physical; video gamers routinely report losing all sense of time while engaged in a game. Likewise, surgeons report that the physical and intellectual challenges of doing an operation can place them into a zone for optimal performance. Musicians say the same thing about playing an instrument and performing for others. Psychologist Mihaly Csikszentmihalyi named this psychological phenomenon

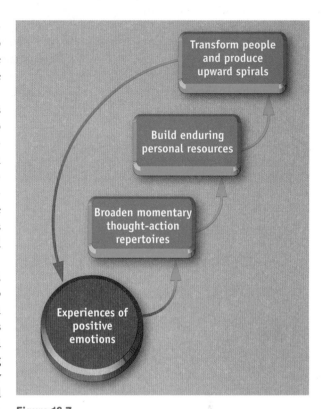

Figure 16.7

The broaden-and-build theory of positive emotions. According to Fredrickson (2002), the personal resources people gain during positive emotional states last for some time. This figure illustrates the three hypothesized sequential effects of positive emotions. First, positive emotions broaden people's range of thought-action sequences, which in turn builds personal resources, and culminates by producing upward spirals of positive emotions. The cycle then repeats itself.

"flow." *Flow* **is the state of being in which a person becomes fully involved and engaged in the present time by some interesting, challenging, and intrinsically rewarding activity.**

Csikszentmihalyi recognized the pull of flow experiences in his own life when he played chess or went rock or mountain climbing (Diener & Biswas-Diener, 2008). He refers to *flow* as an optimal state (Csikszentmihalyi, 2014a). To Csikszentmihalyi (1975):

Flow denotes the holistic sensation present when we act with total involvement . . . It is the state in which action follows upon action according to an internal logic which seems to need no conscious intervention on our part. We experience it as a unified flowing from one moment to the next, in which we feel in control of our actions, and in which there is little distinction between self and environment; between stimulus and response; or between past, present, and future. (p. 43)

When entering this "optimal experience," people become less self-aware, lose all track of time, and focus their energies and attention on doing some engaging activity where skill and challenge are in balance. The flow experience is multifaceted (Delle Fave, 2009). Individuals who experience flow rarely worry about losing control over what they are doing, which, paradoxically, provides them with a sense of control. They often concentrate so deeply on what they are doing that they become oblivious to their surroundings and the people in them (Nakamura & Csikszentmihalyi, 2009). In Csikszentmihalyi's (1990) view, people's quality of life is partially determined by how well they are able to control their consciousness; more control promotes order and well-being, while less leads to psychological disorder and dissatisfaction (Csikszentmihalyi, 2014b).

Finding Flow

Virtually anyone can find flow. According to Csikszentmihalyi, flow was originally conceived as a phenomenon falling between the opposite experiences of boredom and anxiety, and he believes that people experience flow when they find a balanced, meaningful place between these poles of experience. He also suggested that flow can be characterized as a balance between a person's current skill level and a situation's challenges (Abuhamdeh & Csikszentmihalyi, 2012). Indeed, flow occurs where challenges are just manageable. This argument makes sense: When the level of challenge in a task is right, people rise to the occasion to meet it. But if the challenge level is too high, people often begin to feel anxious about what they are doing—worrying about their performance, questioning their own competence—and, consequently, do not experience flow because they are distracted.

Similarly, if a task is monotonous or repetitive, people quickly become bored; it is not possible to achieve the flow state if one is not engaged in what one is doing. Think about a mundane task, such as stuffing envelopes. If you had to do it all day, every day, you would become fidgety, annoyed, and frustrated, as well as undeniably bored, because the task would be too easy (and tiresome) for you. Once mastered, there would be no change in it and nothing new to learn in order to perform it.

Thus, to find flow and develop your creative potential, you must find a challenging activity that matches your skill level. Once an activity is chosen and the requisite challenge and skill levels are met, you can have a flow experience virtually whenever you wish.

A key element of a flow experience is that even if it is initially undertaken for other reasons, it becomes intrinsically rewarding. Thus, a child may be enrolled in a dance class by her parents, who tell her that the exercise will keep her weight down, give her poise, and keep her healthy. But once she begins to enjoy the challenge of learning new steps and routines, dancing becomes an activity worth doing for its own sake—her parents' reasons, though still true in one sense, have nothing to do with her reason for dancing. As William Butler Yeats put it in his 1928 poem "Among School Children":

O body swayed to music, O brightening glance,
How can we know the dancer from the dance?

When experiencing flow, people have the pleasure of stretching themselves and their talents in new directions. For this reason, flow often occurs when people pursue creative or stimulating work, including aesthetic efforts (art, dance, music, drama, writing), hobbies, or sports, among other possibilities (Nakamura & Csikszentmihalyi, 2009). Further, anyone in almost any situation can experience flow. Factors such as social class, gender, culture, and age have no influence on its occurrence.

Aside from the obvious fact that people find it to be a reinforcing state, why seek flow? For one thing, flow feels good and becomes motivational. Besides enhancing certain skills, flow provides positive emotions, staves off negative affect, and promotes goal commitment and achievement (Nakamura & Csikszentmihalyi, 2009).

If flow feels good and is reinforcing, shouldn't it be most likely to occur when people are having fun? Perhaps, but that all depends on how one defines *fun*. For many, their work

Flow occurs when people are engaged in challenging activities that match their skill levels, such as creating a work of art or playing a musical instrument.

is their play. Thus, there may be a somewhat paradoxical side to flow—namely, that people are most likely to experience this absorbing state when they are at work rather than play. Individuals who enjoy their work report being in flow quite often, and, not surprisingly, flow may be linked to job satisfaction (Csikszentmihalyi & LeFevre, 1989). Why does this happen? Presumably because work often presents a good balance between challenge and skill. Of course, work is also something nearly everyone does and does quite often, as compared to hobbies or recreational sports, for example.

Flow is found in all sorts of situations besides work and the workplace. We already mentioned sports. Participating in a psychotherapy session (Grafanaki et al., 2007) or a religious ritual can lead to flow (Han, 1998), as can teaching (Beard, Stansbury, & Wayne, 2010), taking part in online learning (Shin, 2006), driving a car (Csikszentmihalyi, 1997), reading for pleasure (McQuillan & Conde, 1996), engaging with one's family (Rathunde, 1988), and—surprisingly—cramming for a test (Brinthaupt & Shin, 2001). Even using a computer can lead to a flow state (Ghani & Deshpande, 1994). Oddly, perhaps, military combat can lead to flow as well (Harari, 2008). Boring tasks, such as housework, appear to prevent flow (Csikszentmihalyi, 1997) unless the situation is changed (listening to music while waxing the floor or scrubbing the tub can often do the trick).

Does Everyone Find Flow?

Csikszentmihalyi found that about 20% of respondents in American and European samples said they experienced flow quite frequently, usually several times a day. Very intense flow experiences were felt by a smaller percentage of respondents, however. Around 15% of a given sample will report that they have never had such an experience.

Are there any personality characteristics linked with the likelihood to experience flow? Ullén et al. (2012) explored whether the tendency to experience flow was associated with the Big Five personality traits (recall our discussion in Chapter 2). The investigators predicted and found that flow was negatively correlated with neuroticism, presumably because the anxiety and negative affect linked to this trait interferes with flow's emotional qualities. Flow was also positively associated with conscientiousness.

Mindfulness

Active engagement with a challenging and interesting activity—the flow experience—is one way to promote well-being. Surprisingly, there is another, simpler way to do so: by actively and mindfully noticing new things and drawing distinctions among them. Social psychologist Ellen Langer created the term *mindfulness* **to refer to a cultivated perspective in which people are sensitive to context and focused on the present.** People in a state of mindfulness notice novel features and readily attend to them, just as they draw novel distinctions in what they see. According to Langer (Ie, Ngnoumen, & Langer, 2014), to become more mindful people need to (1) resist the impulse to reduce or control the uncertainty found in daily living; (2) become less prone to evaluate themselves, others, and the situations they encounter; and (3) try to override their propensity to perform automatic ("stereotyped" or "scripted") behavior. To Langer, mindfulness "is a flexible state of mind—an openness to novelty, a process of actively drawing novel distinctions" (p. 214).

Ellen J. Langer studies the benefits of mindfulness on health and well-being.

Mindfulness has been found to promote or enhance well-being in a variety of situations. Children prefer to interact with mindful adults (Langer, Cohen, & Djikic, 2012) and, in classroom settings, mindfulness can improve student learning (Ritchart & Perkins, 2002), including helping young girls overcome gender differences when learning math (Anglin, Pirson, & Langer, 2008). People who are more mindful are also less judgmental of others (Adair & Fredrickson, 2015). Mindfulness can reduce the negative feelings associated with experiencing discrimination as well as the depressive symptoms that accompany being the target of prejudice (Brown-Iannuzzi et al., 2014). People in mindfully based marriages are more satisfied (Burpee & Langer, 2005), and a mindful perspective can even reduce the tendency to use aging stereotypes (Djikie, Langer, & Stapleton, 2008) and can promote well-being in older adults (Hsu & Langer, 2013).

Mindfulness is also found to have decided implications for physical health. Langer and her colleagues recruited 197 participants with amyotrophic lateral sclerosis (ALS), an infrequent, progressive, and fatal neurodegenerative disease (Pagnini et al., 2015). Participants completed online assessments twice, 4 months apart. The assessments included measures of mindfulness as a trait, physical impairment, quality of life, anxiety, and depression. Participants who displayed mindfulness positively affected changes in their physical symptoms. Those higher in mindfulness showed a slower progression of ALS after 4 months, and the first assessment of mindfulness predicted higher quality of life and well-being at the second assessment. Langer and colleagues argue that mindfulness is a powerful psychological construct, one that may be able to slow the progress of a fatal disease that is viewed as exclusively biological in nature.

One way to understand mindfulness's benefits is to compare and contrast it with its problematic counterpart, mindlessness. Langer (1998) argues that people slip into a state of *mindlessness* **by engaging in rote behavior—performing familiar, scripted actions without much cognition, as if on autopilot.** When individuals are mindless, they are not doing much active thinking. Sometimes, mindlessness can be adaptive; it frees up conscious attention and awareness when a task is familiar. Think back to when you learned to drive a car and how you had to pay rapt attention to what you were doing; by comparison, driving is likely to be a veritable breeze now. There is a down side to such mindless adaptation, however; you miss a great deal of information when you behave mindlessly. Sudden changes and novelties that appear in the environment are overlooked, for example, as are fine details. When driving mindlessly, you might miss a stop sign and drive right through it (or you might hit the car that stopped suddenly in front of you because you never saw it slow down). So, there are potential costs when attention and awareness are too free or loose. It's almost as if one is not really "there" to mentally follow what's happening. People are much better off when they take note of new information whatever the context happens to be.

Practically speaking, how can you become more mindful? You can do so by treating the facts you learn as conditional—that is, as linked to one and not necessarily other situations (cultivating fresh perspectives on experiences). Mindfulness researchers suggest another way: becoming aware of novelty and creating new distinctions by using *meditation*, or the disciplined, continuous, and focused contemplation of some subject or object (see Chapter 4). With regular meditation, people learn to train and direct their attention in nonanalytical and unemotional ways, subsequently becoming more mindful as a result (Marchand, 2012). Shapiro, Schwartz, and Santerre (2002) suggest that when people experience moments of mindfulness when engaging in *mindfulness meditation*, some related qualities of this psychological state enter their consciousness. Some of these mindfulness qualities are shown in **Figure 16.8**. Note how well many match up with the overall focus and goals of positive psychology. If you

SOME QUALITIES ASSOCIATED WITH MINDFULNESS MEDITATION	
Quality	**Description**
Nonjudging	Impartial witnessing, observing the present moment by moment without explanation and categorization
Acceptance	Open to seeing things as they really are in the present moment with a clear understanding
Loving kindness	Being benevolent, compassionate, and forgiving, and demonstrating unconditional love
Patience	Allowing things to unfold in their time, bringing patience to oneself, to others, and to the present moment
Openness	Seeing things as if for the first time, creating possibility by paying attention to all feedback in the present moment
Nonstriving	Non-goal oriented, remaining unattached to outcome or achievement, not forcing things
Trust	Trusting the self, as well as one's body, intuitions, and emotions, and that life is unfolding as it is supposed to
Gentleness	Having a soft, tender, and considerate quality, but neither passive nor undisciplined
Gratitude	The quality of reverence, appreciating and being thankful for the present moment
Empathy	The quality of both feeling and understanding the situation of another person in the present time; communicating knowledge of the person's state to the person
Generosity	Giving in the present moment within a context of love and compassion, without attachment to gain or thought of return
Letting go	Demonstrating nonattachment or holding on to feelings, thoughts, or experiences; letting go does not refer to suppressing these states

Figure 16.8

Some qualities associated with mindfulness meditation. People who learn mindfulness meditation can expect to derive some benefits from the activity. As you can see, the qualities listed here fit well with established themes in positive psychology.

Source: Adapted from Shapiro, S. J., Schwartz, G.E.R., & Santerre, C. (2002). Meditation and positive psychology. In C. R. Snyder & S. J. Lopez (Eds.), *The handbook of positive psychology* (pp. 632–645). New York: Oxford University Press.

Encountering nature provides restorative benefits, including enhanced attention, lowered stress, and improved emotional function.

were to take up mindfulness meditation, which qualities would you hope to achieve or experience as a result?

If mindfulness meditation does not seem to be a likely course of action for you anytime soon, there is a simpler way for you to increase your attention, reduce your stress, and improve your subjective well-being: Go outside and experience nature. Research suggests that spending even a modest amount of time in natural surroundings—the forest or woods, a park, perhaps a garden—has restorative effects that make people more cognitively attentive and function better emotionally (Berman et al., 2012). In one study, for example, nineteen undergraduates spent half an hour walking around an arboretum near the University of Michigan's campus, while an equal number of students ambled around downtown Ann Arbor (Berman, Jonides, & Kaplan, 2008). When everyone returned to the lab to complete a battery of stress and short-term memory measures, the researchers found that the individuals who strolled in the arboretum had lower stress levels and heightened attention compared to the control group who ventured downtown. The explanation? Natural environments are much less mentally taxing than urban settings. Intuitively, individuals know that green and leafy settings are peaceful places that encourage them to relax and renew themselves. In contrast, even medium-sized cities are full of noise and busy distractions made by traffic, crowds, and the like. Clearly, city dwellers can restore their peace of mind by seeking out green spaces (Reynolds, 2015).

If experiencing nature can have a restorative influence by enhancing mindfulness and emotional well-being, can there be any accompanying behavioral consequences? This question is at the heart of our Spotlight on Research, which explores awe and the potential for promoting prosocial or helping behavior.

Spotlight on RESEARCH

Experiencing Awe Promotes Prosocial Action

Source: Piff, P. K., Dietze, P., Feinberg, M., Stancato, D. M., & Keltner, D. (2015). Awe, the small self, and prosocial behavior. *Journal of Personality and Social Psychology, 108,* 883–889.

Awe is an emotional response people feel when encountering something larger than themselves, such as a beautiful moment, art, the natural world, transcendent music, or something spiritual. Moments of awe are said to be marked by two qualities: the feeling of being diminished in the presence of the awesome event or thing and the accompanying desire to be good or kind to others. Piff et al. conducted five studies examining awe. We will focus on the fifth and final study, which examined whether a naturalistic induction of awe—looking upward at a grove of tall trees for 1 minute—increased prosocial behavior compared to a control condition where participants gazed up at a tall, if unremarkable, college building for a similar amount of time. The researchers predicted that compared to the control condition, the awe-inspired participants would be more helpful toward an experimenter in a staged pratfall.

Method

Participants. Ninety undergraduate students participated as part of a psychology course requirement (28% European American; 40% Asian American; 29% African American; Latino/a, Native American or other; and 3% declined to report their ethnicity). They were told that the study dealt with visual perception.

Materials and procedure. At the lab, participants completed demographic measures and were then directed to another part of the campus, where an experimenter randomly assigned half to the experimental (awe) group and the remainder to a control condition. Participants in the awe condition were directed to look upward at a grove of Tasmanian eucalyptus trees, most of which are 200 feet tall or taller, for 1 minute. Control participants looked at a tall campus building adjacent to but visually away from the grove for 1 minute. A separate sample of participants had previously gazed upward at the trees or building and then completed scales assessing various emotions, including awe, thereby demonstrating that the trees were more awe inducing than the building. The main dependent measure was then delivered when the experimenter approached each participant with a questionnaire and a box of eleven pens. The experimenter deliberately staged an accident by dropping the pens in front of the participant. The number of pens a participant gathered up was the measure of helpfulness.

Results

Did gazing at a grove of tall trees induce awe and greater helping compared to looking at a typical tall building? As expected, participants in the awe condition picked up more pens compared to the control group. The difference between the two groups was statistically reliable.

Discussion

Two important findings were obtained in this elegantly simple study. First, awe can be induced quickly. Here, gazing at very tall trees elicited the emotion after only 1 minute. Second, even a brief, modest induction of awe is sufficient to encourage people to be more helpful than individuals who are not experiencing this elevating emotion. Future research should explore the processes linked to awe that promote prosocial behavior.

Critical Thinking Questions

1. When have you experienced awe? Can you recall whether this emotion influenced your actions, whether prosocial or otherwise?
2. Why did the investigators use a separate group of participants to test whether the awe induction (looking at the trees or the building) was successful? Why didn't they simply have the experimental and control groups who took part in the fifth study complete the emotion assessments?
3. Can you think of some other features in the world that could elicit awe the ways the trees did? Do you think an awe-inspiring stimulus must be natural or are their some human creations that might also elicit this emotion?

Savoring: Deliberately Making Pleasures Last

How often do people slow down enough to really reflect on what they are doing and experiencing at that moment in time? Why don't people savor more of their daily experiences?

Savoring is a new concept in positive psychology but, as you will see, it has an excellent conceptual fit with the field and its goals. *Savoring* **refers to the power to focus on, value, and even boost the enjoyment of almost any experience, whether great or small** (Bryant & Veroff, 2007). To savor is to enjoy subjective states related to some current experience, one rooted in process and not outcome; the journey, if you will, is more important than arriving at the destination. You can savor a good, strong cup of coffee, a well-performed piece of music, or even the scarlet, orange, and yellow foliage of autumn in New England. Researchers who study savoring claim it is an active process, more than mere pleasure or the enjoyment of something or some activity. When you savor reading a book or watching a play or film, for example, a reflective quality is involved: Whether reader or viewer, you must attend to and consciously appreciate what is engaging your attention.

What factors affect the intensity of savoring? Bryant and Veroff (2007) suggest several, including:

1. *Duration.* The more time available for the experience, the greater the chance to savor it. Dedicated time like that reserved for exercise or socializing should be set aside for enjoying particular pleasures.
2. *Stress reduction.* When distracting stress departs (you stop dwelling on all the homework you have to do over the weekend), savoring becomes possible (you can enjoy spending Friday evening with friends).
3. *Complexity.* More complex experiences produce greater quality and intensity of savoring. Examining a detailed work of art—an intricate painting—can lead to more sustained delight than perusing a simple drawing. Experts—individuals with deep knowledge in a subject—can experience more complex savoring when encountering a stimulus than can neophytes. Expert coffee, wine, or tea tasters, for instance, are likely to savor particular examples of these beverages more than the rest of us.
4. *Balanced self-monitoring.* If you think too much about what you are doing or become too self-focused, you can distort your ability to savor an experience.
5. *Social connection.* You might believe that savoring is a solitary pursuit. However, research reveals that savoring is that much more pleasurable if you have other people with whom to share the experience. Concerts, for example, are more enjoyable if you attend with a friend.

Literally taking time to "smell the roses" is an opportunity to savor nature's beauty.

Figure 16.9

A Savoring Scale. People who savor things—special experiences, tastes, smells, views, and so on—have the ability to focus, value, and boost their enjoyment in the moment. To determine whether you tend to savor such moments, take the scale shown here.

Source: Adapted from page 782 in Bryant, F. (1989) A four-factor model of perceived control: Avoiding, coping, obtaining, and savoring. *Journal of Personality, 57,* 773–797.

THE SAVORING SCALE
Assess each question by selecting the number that best describes your response. To what degree do you savor the present moment?
1. When good things have happened in your life, how much do you feel you have typically been able to appreciate or enjoy them? 1 = Not at all   2 = A little bit   3 = Some   4 = A lot   5 = A great deal
2. Compared to most other people you know, how much pleasure have you typically gotten from good things that have happened to you? 1 = Not at all   2 = A little bit   3 = Some   4 = A lot   5 = A great deal
3. When something good happens to you, compared to most other people you know, how long does it usually affect the way you feel? Provide a number ranging from 1 (not for very long) to 7 (for a very long time): _____
4. When good things have happened to you, have there ever been times when you felt like everything was really going your way; that is, when you felt on top of the world, or felt a great deal of joy in life, or found it hard to contain your positive feelings? How often would you say you felt like that? 1 = Many times   2 = Sometimes   3 = Once in a while   4 = Never
5. How often would you say that you feel like jumping for joy? 1 = Never   2= Rarely   3 = Sometimes   4 = Often
Scoring: Reverse the number you gave to question 4 (i.e., 1 = 4, 2 = 3, 3 = 2, 4 =1) and then total your numbers for the five items. Scores can range from 5 to 25, with higher scores reflecting greater savoring of positive outcomes. Undergraduates in an introductory psychology course scored a mean of 18.76.

In sum, it pays to make time to savor the pleasures encountered in daily life. Research suggests that savoring may reduce depressive symptoms and negative emotions (Hurley & Kwon, 2012), as well as to help people to be happier and more relaxed (Jose, Lim, & Bryant, 2012). What about you? Are you prone to savor the moment? Answer the questions found in the Savoring Scale shown in **Figure 16.9** to find out.

Learning Objectives

- Explain the concept of positive individual traits.
- Define *hope, resilience, posttraumatic growth,* and *grit* as beneficial qualities.
- Clarify why gratitude is a character strength.

16.3 Positive Individual Traits

Whereas subjective states account for people's positive feelings, *positive individual traits* **are dispositional qualities that account for why some people are happier and psychologically healthier than others.** Traits sway the interpretations people use to find meaning in events, influence their choices, help them select goals, and ultimately drive what they do behaviorally. Think about someone you know who gets along well with other people. The fact that you see this person as being highly agreeable or cooperative represents what psychologists call a *trait*, an individual difference that makes your friend stand out from your other acquaintances (see Chapter 2). Another friend of yours might come across as reliable—that is, very organized and high in self-control, someone who takes few risks and works rather deliberately to achieve particular ends. An important quality of positive traits like these is the assumption that they can be taught (Peterson & Seligman, 2004). Positive traits can also emerge as a response or reaction to life situations people experience. Here we discuss four examples of positive individual traits: hope, resilience, grit, and gratitude.

Hope: Achieving Future Goals

Positive psychology is keenly interested in positive individual traits that encourage people to anticipate good rather than bad outcomes. Consider *hope,* **which refers to people's expectations that their goals can be achieved in the future** (Cheavens & Ritschel, 2014). People become more excited by goals they can actually achieve than those that seem too much of a challenge. Given its future directedness, hope is related to optimism, which is discussed in Chapters 3 and 5.

The late C. R. Snyder (2002), a social and clinical psychologist, argued that these goal-directed expectations have two components: agency and pathways. *Agency* involves a person's judgment that his or her goals can be achieved (Feldman, Rand, & Kahle-Wrobleski, 2009). For example, a college student might determine whether obtaining a high grade in a required course is possible. In other words, does Hannah expect that she can obtain the desired grade because she possesses the necessary drive or organizational skills? Agency, then, represents one's motivation to seek desired goals, and it appears to be linked with life satisfaction (Bailey et al., 2007). The second component in Snyder's theory, *pathways*, refers to Hannah's beliefs that successful plans can be crafted to reach the goal of a high grade. Pathways represent the realistic road map to achieving the goal. A hopeful outlook would identify several paths to the goal (more hours of study, completing assigned readings in advance, faithfully attending class, doing homework, and so on), not merely one (Rand & Cheavens, 2009). A person's pathways complement his or her agency by serving as what Snyder (1994) called "waypower."

Snyder and colleagues (1991) developed the Trait Hope Scale to assess both agency and pathways (see **Figure 16.10**). Respondents rate how true each statement on the scale appears to be for them. A summary score of the agency and pathway items indicates a person's degree of hope (scores can range between 8 and 64; see **Figure 16.10**). Separate scales also measure state hope (how a person feels at a single moment in time) (Snyder et al., 1996) and children's hope (Edwards & McClintock, 2013), as well.

Why should anyone try to be a hopeful person? For several reasons, actually (Snyder, Rand, & Sigmon, 2002). Not surprisingly, hopeful people experience more positive emotions than those who have a more despairing outlook, and, as we have discussed, such emotions can be beneficial for a variety of reasons. Individuals who have hope expect to be better off in the future, just as they believe they will be better prepared than others to deal with any stressful circumstances that arise. Why might this be the case? Hopeful people are likely to be flexible thinkers, always on the lookout for alternative pathways to attain their goals or to get around obstacles. They are also likely to be buoyed up by the positive social support they receive from those who are drawn to their encouraging, upbeat natures (Snyder, Rand & Sigmon, 2002). For example, hope has been shown to help individuals with spinal cord injuries pursue goals, which were in turn linked to participation in daily life and life satisfaction (Smedema, Chan, & Phillips, 2014).

A MEASURE OF HOPE AS A TRAIT
Read each item carefully. Using the scale shown below, please select the number that best describes YOU and put that number in the blank provided.

1 = Definitely false	5 = Slightly true
2 = Mostly false	6 = Somewhat true
3 = Somewhat false	7 = Mostly true
4 = Slightly false	8 = Definitely true

_____ **1.** I can think of many ways to get out of a jam.

_____ **2.** I energetically pursue my goals.

_____ **3.** I feel tired most of the time.

_____ **4.** There are lots of ways around any problem.

_____ **5.** I am easily downed in an argument.

_____ **6.** I can think of many ways to get the things in life that are important to me.

_____ **7.** I worry about my health.

_____ **8.** Even when others get discouraged, I know I can find a way to solve the problem.

_____ **9.** My past experiences have prepared me well for my future.

_____ **10.** I've been pretty successful in life.

_____ **11.** I usually find myself worrying about something.

_____ **12.** I meet the goals I set for myself.

Figure 16.10

Snyder's Trait Hope Scale. According to C. R. Snyder, as a trait, hope has two characteristics: agency and pathways. To determine your Agency subscale score, add items 2, 9, 10, and 12; your Pathways subscale score is derived by adding items 1, 4, 6, and 8. The total Hope Scale Score is the total of the four Agency and the four Pathway items. A higher total score reflects a greater degree of hope for the future. Scores can range from 8 to 64. In six samples of college students studied by Snyder et al. (1991), the average score was 25.

Source: From Snyder, C. R., Harris, C., Anderson, J. R., Holeran, S. A., Irving, L. M., Sigmon, S. T., Yoshinobu, L., Gibb, J., Langelle, C., & Harney, P. (1991). The will and the ways: Development and validation of an individual-differences measure of hope. *Journal of Personality and Social Psychology, 60*, 570–585.

Resilience: Reacting Well to Life's Challenges

Another important positive trait is *resilience*, **a person's ability to recover and often prosper following some consequential life event.** Such events are often traumatic—an accident, loss, or catastrophe causes an individual to cope with a situation that can leave psychological scars. Resilient people cope with threats, maintaining, recovering, or even improving mental and physical health in the process of doing so (Ryff & Singer, 2003).

Resilience research examines various tumultuous events, including how people deal with threats such as aging, natural disasters, war, divorce, traumatic brain injury, alcoholism and mental illness in parents, family violence, the demands of single parenting, and, of course, the loss of a loved one (Bonanno, 2009; Godwin, Lukow, & Lichiello, 2015; Masten & Reed, 2002; Moore et al., 2015; Ryff & Singer, 2003). These threats range from extreme but rare events (war) to those that are tragically commonplace (family problems). Whatever

TEN WAYS TO CULTIVATE RESILIENCE
1. Foster connections with family members, friends, and people in the community
2. Try not to catastrophize when a crisis happens; don't see an event as insurmountable
3. Realize and accept that change is a part of life
4. Move forward towards your goals
5. Whenever possible be decisive but rely on problem-and-task-focused coping strategies
6. Keep on the lookout for opportunities for self-discovery
7. Develop and maintain a positive view of yourself
8. Keep events, especially troubling ones, in perspective
9. Maintain a hopeful outlook
10. Take good care of yourself, paying special attention to your needs and feelings

Figure 16.11

Ten ways to cultivate resilience. There are concrete things you can do in your life to develop resilience. The key is to select those that are likely to work well for you.

Source: Adapted from American Psychological Association. (2012). The Road to Resilience: 10 Ways to Build Resilience. Retrieved from www.apa.org/helpcenter/road-resilience.aspx

its qualities, the threat is usually so severe and potentially damaging, if not life threatening, that most observers would expect negative rather than positive outcomes. Yet in spite of these traumatic "perfect storms," some people persevere and emerge psychologically resilient.

For example, imagine the future lives of children who are raised in abusive or neglectful households or in communities wracked by poverty, illness, and disease. Individuals born into such environments are said to be at higher risk than others for various mental, physical, social, and economic problems (Masten & Reed, 2002). Would anyone predict that children reared in such settings would eventually thrive and lead productive and happy lives? The surprising reality is that the resilient ones do.

The good news is that a resilient outlook can be cultivated by anyone because it is not a trait but a way of coping with adverse situations. Indeed, each person can be resilient in a different way. **Figure 16.11** lists ten factors that are believed to be important when cultivating resilience. How many of them do you already incorporate into your life? Which of the others can you learn?

In addition to resilience, some people display growth following a trauma such as an accident, a serious illness, or the onset of a disability. ***Posttraumatic growth* refers to enhanced personal strength, realization of what is truly important in life, and increased appreciation for life, friends, and family following trauma.** Posttraumatic growth provides empirical evidence that sometimes personal suffering can lead to positive insights (Davis & Nolen-Hoeksema, 2009; Groleau et al., 2012). Whereas resilience can help people rebound to their pretrauma levels, posttraumatic growth implies that people can also psychologically exceed those original levels by displaying enhanced functioning and positive changes, sometimes with the aid of some intervention (Roepke, 2015). In fact, a surprising number of people actually claim that trauma "was the best thing that ever happened" to them (Park, 1998).

Figure 16.12 lists a variety of positive changes that are attributed to posttraumatic growth (Ryff & Singer, 2003). These changes can be categorized as being perceptual, relationship based, or a life priority. Advocates of positive psychology have helped reduce the skepticism associated with claims of posttraumatic growth and related coping strategies. Although verifying documented positive growth can be difficult, psychologists are now less likely to assume such change is a convenient rationalization, factual distortion, or unfounded self-report (Lechner, Tennen, & Affleck, 2009).

Learn More Online

VIA Institute on Character

To learn about your own signature character strengths, you may want to complete the Values in Action (VIA) survey, available at this site. The survey is a psychometrically sound instrument that is based on twenty-four personality elements linked to positive behavior and well-being.

Grit: Harnessing Effort over the Long Term

What makes some people try harder to succeed at challenges than others? Casual observation reveals that some people are apt to accomplish more than others, even when both have equal levels of intelligence. Positive psychologist Angela Duckworth and her colleagues (2007; Duckworth, 2013) propose that some people have higher levels of a noncognitive trait they call grit. ***Grit* is defined as possessing perseverance and passion for achieving long-term goals.** People who have higher levels of grit are apt to demonstrate serious effort and attention to accomplishing a goal despite setbacks, adversity, and slowdowns that impede their progress. According to Duckworth and colleagues, "The gritty individual approaches achievement as a marathon; his or her advantage is stamina" (p. 1088). Although both constructs can lead to an individual's success, grit has been shown to be independent of self-control (Duckworth & Gross, 2014).

How does grit affect people's behavioral success? In one study, Duckworth and colleagues (2007) examined whether grit predicted the grade point averages (GPAs) of students attending an elite university. A group of 139 men and women completed the Grit Scale and reported their GPAs. As expected, gritty students had significantly higher GPAs than their less gritty counterparts. Another study explored grit's impact on the performance of child finalists in the 2005 Scripps National Spelling Bee. Duckworth and colleagues had the finalists complete the Grit Scale and other measures before the spelling competition began. They found that grittiness predicted who advanced to higher rounds in the competition. Why did those high on grit do so well in concrete terms? Gritty contestants were apt to stay in the competition longer because they studied longer, a factor attesting to their drive and stamina. The grittiest spellers were not necessarily the smartest or best spellers—they just stuck with and worked harder at preparing for the spelling bee.

More recent research found that novice teachers with grit have greater career success than their peers (Robertson-Kraft & Duckworth, 2014). They were found to be more effective in their classrooms and were much less likely to quit their teaching positions prior to the end of their first year. Grit has also been linked with higher retention rates in samples of people in the military, workers in job settings, and married couples (Eskreis-Winkler et al., 2014). Why do people vary in their level of grit or whether they possess the trait at all? Some evidence suggests that individual differences in grit may be at least partially due to the differences in what activities make people happy (Von Culin, Tsukayama, & Duckworth, 2014).

Gratitude: The Power of Being Thankful

One of the most promising positive individual traits receiving considerable research attention is gratitude, or being grateful for what you have or others have done for you (Ahrens & Forbes, 2014). As a human strength, *gratitude* **entails recognizing and concentrating on the good things in one's life and being thankful for them.** Gratitude, which is assumed to be part of the good life (Watkins, 2014), is often considered within a moral context, related to but distinct from other moral emotions, like elevation (Siegel, Thomson, & Navarro, 2014). In fact, being ungrateful—that is, expressing *in*gratitude—is considered a vice (Bono, Emmons, & McCullough, 2004). Expressing gratitude toward others in response to their helpful actions is a social norm (Eibach, Wilmot, & Libby, 2015). Experiencing gratitude (being thankful) and expressing it (thanking someone for being gracious to you) are among the most common ways to experience this beneficial, positive emotion (Emmons, 2005). Other research indicates that gratitude can be personality related, so that some people are more likely to express and experience it than others (Bhullar, Surman, & Schutte, 2015).

What are the psychosocial consequences of expressing gratitude? As might be expected, doing so enhances social connections with others (Algoe, Fredrickson, & Gable, 2013), including fostering new relationships and promoting interpersonal warmth (Williams & Bartlett, 2015). More than that, however, expressing gratitude appears to extend the time people feel positive emotions linked to being thankful. Where negative affect lingers, positive moods tend to be shorter (Larsen & Prizmic, 2008). Besides benefiting others, conveying gratitude benefits the self, too. Feelings of gratitude make one feel happy, at times joyful, and can be a source of contentment (Wood, Froh, & Geraghty, 2010). As author G. K. Chesterton (Chesterton & Schall, 2001) suggested, "Thanks are the highest form of thought, and that gratitude is happiness doubled by wonder (p. 463)."

Perhaps the best part of gratitude is that it is so easy to express, and, as a virtue, it can be performed almost anytime or anywhere. So, the next time someone does something nice for you, whether great or small, be sure to acknowledge the help or kindness by saying "thank-you" and expressing your appreciation in greater detail. Both you and your recipient will benefit psychologically from your simple act (see the Application section of this chapter for a gratitude-related exercise).

ASPECTS OF POSTTRAUMATIC GROWTH
Perceptual changes
Self is perceived as a survivor and not a victim
Increased feelings of personal strength, self-reliance, and self-confidence
Enhanced appreciation for life's fragile nature, including one's own
Relationship changes
Increased compassion for and willingness to give to others
Closer bonds with family
Feelings of closeness with others and greater willingness to disclose emotions
Life priority changes
Reduced concern with possessions, money, and social status
Greater willingness to take life easier
Enhanced clarity regarding what really matters in life
A deeper and more spiritual sense of the meaning of life

Figure 16.12

Positive changes attributed to posttraumatic growth. After experiencing a trauma, some people respond by exhibiting positive changes that generally fall into three areas: perceptual changes, relationship changes, and life priority changes. This figure illustrates examples of growth within each area.

Source: Adapted from Baumgardner, S. R., & Crothers, M. K. (2009). *Positive psychology.* Upper Saddle River, NJ: Prentice-Hall.

Positive subjective experiences and positive individual traits both benefit the individual. What does positive psychology have to offer the community? Broader than the other two areas of inquiry, the third defining area of positive psychology encompasses the group level of analysis by examining positive institutions. *Positive institutions* **are those organizations that cultivate civic virtues, encouraging people to behave like good citizens while promoting the collective good.** Positive institutions, including workplaces, schools, families, and organizations, help build and maintain a beneficial society in which to live (Rich, 2014). What qualities are fostered by positive institutions? When positive psychological socialization occurs, people who pass through and learn from positive institutions are focused on being nurturing, altruistic, tolerant, and responsible. Individuals who "graduate" from positive institutions tend to have a good work ethic.

Positive Workplaces

Some positive psychologists are interested in developing and maintaining organizations that provide a pleasant workplace and allow workers to thrive (Gilbert & Kelloway, 2014; Luthans & Youssef, 2009). In fact, a new movement known as *positive organizational behavior (POB)* is dedicated to studying beneficial human strengths and competencies and how they can be advanced, evaluated, and managed as a means to improve worker performance in businesses and organizations (Nelson & Cooper, 2007). Within POB, there is a related emphasis on supporting organizational accomplishments and development of individuals by improving the quality of the relationships between co-workers (Harter, 2008), thereby creating happier organizations (Caza & Cameron, 2013).

As noted in Chapter 13, a good way to think about the sorts of careers that positive organizations or workplaces spawn is by thinking about the distinction between a job and a calling. While studying people who worked in jobs ranging from clerical to professional, Wrzesniewski et al. (1997) found that workers viewed their chosen occupations in one of three ways.

- *Just a "job."* Money is necessary for survival, so work is done for pay. Individuals with this view often think of themselves as primary providers for their families.
- *A career.* Work satisfies this second group's desire and need to achieve, compete, and acquire status or prestige. Personal pride is clearly at stake here.
- *A "calling."* The third group view their work as a means for personal fulfillment and social purpose. Work is a service for themselves as well as to other people. Thus, work provides community service and personal fulfillment.

Try putting these distinctions in more personal terms for yourself: Will you seek work that simply satisfies financial necessity (paying bills, providing security), or do you aspire to work that is personally fulfilling or even that "gives back" to your community?

Positive workplaces can help to make work engaging, interesting, and even a pleasure.

iStockphoto.com/David Newton

Blend Images/Ariel Skelley/Getty Images

Positive Schools

Most research on students' experiences within schools has focused on the negative, emphasizing problems with educational efforts (Alford & White, 2015). Recently, however, some psychologists focused on what they call school satisfaction, or students' judgments about their holistic school experiences (Huebner et al., 2009). Representing individual differences, *school satisfaction* is composed of both cognition (what students believe regarding educational experiences) and affect (students' reported frequency of positive and negative emotions in educational settings).

Thus far, a few findings regarding school satisfaction have emerged. First, school satisfaction is a good predictor of student engagement and academic progress as early as kindergarten (Ladd, Buhs, & Seid, 2000). Students who are high in school satisfaction tend to have higher GPAs than other students, as well as fewer reported psychological symptoms and a heightened sense of agency (Huebner & Gillman, 2006). It's no surprise that students who are more engaged and performing well academically are also less likely to display adolescent problem behaviors (DeSantis et al., 2006). Thus, school satisfaction appears to be a promising, positive variable for the study of positive academic achievement in schools. The very good news for educators, parents, and students is that, with planning, positive schools can be designed (White & Murray, 2015).

Virtuous Institutions?

Can positive institutions be like people? That is, can institutions both possess and promote positive virtues? Peterson (2006) notes that qualities that are intrinsically good can be found in everyday institutions like those we discussed in this section, as well as clubs, sports teams, government agencies, and organizations found throughout society. **Figure 16.13** lists the virtues that Peterson suggests make institutions positive contributors to people's lives. As you examine the figure, think about the institutions you come into contact with regularly: How many of them display or enact these virtues?

THE VIRTUES OF POSITIVE INSTITUTIONS	
Virtue	**Description**
Purpose	The institution provides a shared vision of the moral goals promoted by the institution; these goals are routinely remembered and celebrated.
Fairness	Rules exist and are known; rewards and punishments are administered consistently.
Humanity	The institution cares for its members, and vice versa.
Safety	The institution protects its members from threats, dangers, and exploitation.
Dignity	No matter what their status, all members of the institution are treated with respect.

Figure 16.13

Virtues found in positive institutions. Positive institutions are thought to offer a variety of benefits to the individuals who work within them, as well as to the communities in which they reside. This figure lists some of the basic virtues such institutions provide. Can you think of any others?

Source: Adapted from Peterson, C. (2006). *A primer in positive psychology.* New York: Oxford University Press.

Learning Objectives

- Identify some criticisms concerning positive psychology.
- Outline some opportunities for positive psychology's future.

16.5 Positive Psychology: Problems and Prospects

Positive psychology has come a long way in a fairly short time, but is it here for the long run? Will this new subfield continue to attract interested students and researchers? Is it more of a fad or psychological fashion than a genuinely new area of empirical inquiry? To paraphrase two of its midwives, Christopher Peterson and Martin Seligman (2003), will it have the evergreen popularity of the Beatles—or suffer the "has-been" fate of Duran Duran?

Problems

Positive psychology has not been without critics and skeptics (Richardson & Guignon, 2008). For example, the late Richard Lazarus (2003), a renowned psychologist and stress researcher, wondered whether its message is not only *not* very new but destined to be a fad that will pass, later return, and pass again. Why? Because many important conceptual and empirical issues will likely be left unresolved while new disciplinary fads will appear. Lazarus also questioned whether parsing the discipline of psychology into positive and negative spheres is not only an oversimplification but a way to introduce theoretical as well as practical problems into psychological research. As Lazarus (2003a) humorously but effectively posed it:

God needs Satan, and vice versa. One would not exist without the other. We need the bad which is part of life, to fully appreciate the good. (p. 94)

More recently, there have been some intellectual skirmishes between humanistic psychology and positive psychology (Friedman, 2014; Schneider, 2011; Waterman, 2014). Waterman (2013), for example, suggested that the two subfields are divided from and ambivalent toward each other due to distinct perspectives on the nature of humanity and well-being, methods and approaches to research, and philosophical differences regarding therapies and interventions. Others believe reconciliation is possible (Friedman, 2013).

As you read this chapter, you might have wondered whether this new area is really all that new. For example, perhaps positive psychology is little more than the repackaging of "old wine in new bottles." Or, more charitably, perhaps the framework of positive psychology is useful for reorganizing how we think about positive events, thoughts, feelings, and even behaviors, but it might not be the paradigm shift its creators hoped it would be. As partisans on either side of the positive psychology debate will agree, only time will tell whether it has both staying power and ongoing influence in the wider discipline. That being the case, what should we look for, and forward to, if positive psychology is to flourish?

Prospects

The late Christopher Peterson (2006) offers what may be the most telling indicator of success: Will there be needed balance between the positive and negative aspects of psychology? Perhaps survival of the label "positive psychology" will matter less if this desired and needed balance occurs. A close second criterion is whether research can address why people don't seek out those qualities of life that make them truly happy. In other words, if research identifies which activities enable people to lead a good life (Music, 2014), will they apply these findings to their own lives? As research evidence and intervention studies appear, it will be exciting to see whether people do indeed change the ways they live (the exercises in this next section may provide you with an opportunity to see how easy it is to introduce new, positive routines into you own life).

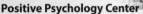

16.6 Boosting Your Own Happiness

Answer the following "true" or "false."

____ **1.** Writing a sincere thank-you note can enhance well-being in you as well as the recipient.

____ **2.** Sharing good things that happen to you with an interested other person (and vice versa) can generate beneficial positive emotions.

____ **3.** Sometimes spending money can make you happy.

If you answered "false" to any or all of these questions because you concluded that the described activities were too simple, there is still more you can learn about the nature of happiness. Enhancing your own well-being may be easier than you believe. You spent this chapter reading and thinking about how positive psychological insights affect and benefit the lives of others. Now it's your turn: How can positive psychology be used to improve your own life? This Application contains four simple exercises, each of which can pay some serious psychosocial dividends (Mongrain & Anselmo-Matthews, 2012). Give them a try. Good luck.

Writing and Delivering a Gratitude Letter

Most of us are good at saying thank-you to folks who have done something nice for us, but expressing gratitude is tougher. Take a few minutes and think of all the people who have gone out of their way to help you so far in your life. Your parents, siblings, and grandparents are likely candidates, as are some of your teachers or coaches, roommates, close friends, perhaps some neighbors, and select others. Pick one of these people, the one you believe did you the greatest kindness to date. If you have never properly expressed gratitude to that individual, here's your chance.

Write a personal letter to your chosen individual—an email won't do because such messages are usually brief and can seem impersonal—and explain in clear terms how he or she helped you and why you are so very grateful. Better yet, make your letter more spontaneous by writing it by hand instead of typing it. Make the letter as rich and detailed as possible. In the ideal case, visit the person, hand-deliver your letter, and have the individual read it while you are there (Peterson, 2006). If this face-to-face encounter is not possible, you can mail the letter (or email if you absolutely must—but no texting, please!), then later speak to the person by phone.

What will happen once your letter is read? You will move the recipient (possibly to tears), but your expression of gratitude will also gratify him or her. Although both of you are likely to feel happy (Seligman et al., 2005), your life satisfaction will likely rise and any depressive symptoms will dissipate (Toepfer, Cichy, & Peters, 2012). Such letters are more life affirming in the moment than they are life changing in the long run (that is, unless you decide to write a gratitude letter every so often for the foreseeable future!). Still, being grateful is a good thing because those who feel gratitude turn out to be much happier than those who don't (Park, Peterson, & Seligman, 2004).

What about people who are no longer with us, such as loved ones who have died? Is it possible to express gratitude for

The expression of sincere gratitude benefits the person being thanked as well as the person doing the thanking.

the kindness they gave when they were alive? Yes. If you wish, you can use these directions as a model for writing a gratitude letter to a departed friend or loved one. You may not be able to directly share the letter with the person, but you are apt to bring up pleasant memories to reflect on as you express your gratitude in words on paper. These memories may allow you to once again have a "conversation" with a person to whom you owe a great deal.

As an alternative to writing a letter, you could keep a gratitude journal wherein you record those things you are thankful for on a regular basis. Where the gratitude letter strengthens your relationship with another person, the act of journaling turns out to cultivate positive, appreciative feelings for what one has (Kaczmarek et al., 2015).

Sharing a Story Illustrating the Best in You

Most of people avoid blowing their own horns, but they can all remember times when they did things that brought out the best in them. Because people really don't like to brag, they often keep these stories to themselves. Although such modesty is admirable, there may be times when telling others about one's exemplary acts can serve as an example or even a source of inspiration. As you consider this activity, let this be one of these rare times when you disclose an act of private goodness to others.

What are the ground rules? Well, you should be honest and err on the side of modesty (again, no bragging) unless what you did was truly selfless and self-defining. Once you recall your example, be prepared to share it with others, probably members of the class in which you are using this book. You might ask the course instructor whether a class could be devoted to having people share their stories with one another. Alternatively, you could write a brief, one-page essay telling your tale. Your essay could then be posted on an online site where only other members of your class could access and read it. Or copies could be made of everyone's stories and assigned as reading for a future class meeting. This last option lacks the passion and punch of hearing people tell their "personal best" stories, but this is one assignment that is likely to be read by all. If this exercise is not done in the context of your class, you could agree to swap stories with a classmate or two, which is a great way to make new friends as you explore the course material.

One last thing: Remember the golden rule of doing unto others what you'd have them do unto you. When people listen politely and with interest to your story, be sure to do the same for them (see the next exercise).

Sharing Good News and Capitalizing with Others

The humorist Fran Lebowitz (1982) once wrote that "the opposite of talking isn't listening. The opposite of talking is waiting" (p. 17). Is that how you often treat those who are close to you when they vie for your attention? Do you really listen closely to what they say and respond accordingly, especially when the news they are imparting is good? Do you focus more on wanting to tell the other person what good thing happened to you rather than celebrating his or her achievement? You, of course, want friends and loved ones to revel in your good fortune, but unless you do the same for them, you may not get the response you seek—or as we will see—any positive psychosocial benefits.

Positive psychologist Shelly Gable and her colleagues discovered that how people give and respond to good news from others has profound consequences for both the self and others (Gable et al., 2004). Specifically, sharing good news with those close to us can lead to "capitalization" when they respond with sincere interest and enthusiasm to what we say. *Capitalization* **refers to telling other people about whatever good things are happening in our own lives.** The term is admittedly unusual in this context, but one of the word's meanings is to "turn something into an advantage," which is what people do when they share good things with others. How so? Well, others' positive responses to sharing creates positive emotions in the sharer, which capitalizes or builds on his or her already good feelings. These feelings of mutual respect, delight, and acknowledgment appear to enhance the qualities of the shared relationship. In short, both parties benefit socially and emotionally when good news is received and responded to in favorable ways (Conoley et al., 2015).

What happens when people don't respond favorably to the good news of others? (Note that we are not talking about situations that trigger envy for a friend's career success, say, or jealousy at her new romance—we are considering those times when people ignore sharing in some modest, if still happy, event.) Nothing happens: No positive emotions result, so

Capitalization occurs when people share news about the good things happening in their lives with others.

neither self-reported well-being nor relationship improves. Keep this in mind the next time you are tired at the end of the day and a friend or significant other wants to share some modest successes since you last talked. Rustling up some smiles and congratulations really won't take much effort on your part, and you are more likely to have the attention repaid to you sometime soon. Better still, you will focus less on your fatigue (always a good thing) and potentially improve your bonds with your pal or partner. Isn't that worth celebrating? This simple form of "paying it forward" can benefit everyone.

Prosocial Spending to Make You Happy

Let's close this Application with an interesting, if somewhat ironic, activity. Based on the research cited in Chapter 1, we know that money and material goods don't buy happiness, right (Diener & Biswas-Diener, 2008)? Although many people believe that spending money on themselves will lead to happiness, there is ample evidence that such self-indulgence rarely leads to positive feelings. Can spending money ever make us happy? Well, it appears that under certain circumstances it can make us happier people. According to Dunn and Norton (2013), there are ways consumers can actually get more happiness when they choose to spend money. These include:

- Buying more experiences (plays, movies, concerts) rather than material goods (clothes, gadgets).
- Making something a treat by buying it (a triple mocha latte) once in a while rather than daily.
- Buying more small pleasures (a chocolate sundae) and fewer large ones (a new car).
- Buying more free or leisure time by working less or by hiring others to perform less desirable tasks (cleaning, doing laundry, or yard maintenance).

- Paying in advance (buying an all-expenses included vacation) and then enjoying later (anticipation makes the event more enjoyable, as does not having to lay out further funds for it).
- Using money to benefit others rather than oneself.

This last possibility is intriguing: Can we spend money on behalf of others and make ourselves happy in the process?

Dunn, Aknin, and Norton (2008) gave research participants either $5 or $20 to spend on themselves or on another person. Those who spent the money on others were happier than those who spent it on themselves. Dunn and colleagues also found that people who spend a greater portion of their incomes on others or on charitable donations are much happier than those who simply spend their earnings on themselves. A related study by Aknin et al. (2010) found that when Ugandan and Canadian students reflected back on times they had been generous to others, they reported higher levels of happiness than students who thought back to times they had spent money on themselves (see also, Aknin et al., 2013; Dunn, Aknin, & Norton, 2014).

Why does spending on others—what researchers refer to as *prosocial spending*—heighten happiness? Giving to others makes us feel we are responsible, giving, and caring individuals. The act of giving makes us feel good about ourselves. When we spend our funds on others, we are also strengthening our social ties with them, and people with stronger social relationships are generally happier. Engaging in prosocial spending on others allows us to feel good about ourselves (Anik et al., 2011a).

So, the next time you and a friend meet for coffee, go to a movie, or grab a quick bite, why not offer to pay? Or, if you see some small gift that you know will brighten a friend or loved one's day—a book, some chocolate, a flower, a charitable contribution, whatever—consider making the modest purchase in the interest of prosocial relations. You and your pal will be both very happy that you did (Aknin, Dunn, & Norton, 2012).

"*Who says you can't buy happiness!*"

CHAPTER 16 Review

Key Ideas

16.1 The Scope of Positive Psychology
- Positive psychology is a new area of psychology dedicated to the study of human strengths and how people can flourish in daily life. This subfield emerged as a reaction to the larger discipline's predominant focus on psychological problems. By providing needed balance, positive psychology can encourage people to focus on the positive aspects of daily living.
- Although it is a new area, many of the issues positive psychology explores have been studied outside the mainstream areas of the discipline for some time. Positive psychology provides an organizing framework for older and newer concepts related to well-being and the good life.
- Positive psychology explores three related lines of behavioral research: positive subjective experiences (such as good mood and positive emotions), positive individual traits (including hope, resilience, and gratitude), and positive institutions (such as beneficial work environments, good schools, and solid families).

16.2 Positive Subjective Experiences
- Positive subjective experiences entail the positive but usually private thoughts and feelings people have about their lives. Positive moods are global, longlasting reactions to events, whereas positive emotions are accute, distinct responses that last for shorter periods of time. Positive moods and emotions promote particular thoughts, feelings, and behaviors.
- Fredrickson's broaden-and-build model explains why positive emotions lead to new and beneficial ways of thinking and acting. Whereas negative emotions narrow people's thoughts, positive ones widen people's perspectives, creating future emotional and intellectual resources in the process.
- Flow is a psychological state marked by complete involvement and engagement with interesting, challenging, and intrinsically rewarding activities. Flow occurs when a person's skills are balanced by challenges that are just manageable.
- Mindful behavior is marked by attention and response to novel features of daily experience, whereas mindlessness occurs when individuals engage in familiar or rote actions that require little active thought.

16.3 Positive Individual Traits
- Positive individual traits are qualities of character, some of which are learned while others are inherited. These positive dispositions explain why some people are happier and psychologically healthier than others.
- People who display hope anticipate that their desired goals can be met in the future. According to Snyder, hope consists of agency and pathways. The trait of hope is associated with the experience of positive emotions.
- Resilient people recover their psychological well-being following traumatic experiences better and faster than less-resilient people do. As evidence for such resilience, posttraumatic growth is marked by people's recogntion of what things truly matter, including enhanced appreciation for friends, loved ones, and life in general.
- Grit is a trait linked to perseverance and passion for successfully completing a long-term goal. People who have high levels of grit display stamina and a drive to achieve in spite of impediments.
- Gratitude occurs when people are thankful for the good things in their lives, particularly expressing appreciation for what others have done for them.

16.4 Positive Institutions
- Positive institutions are organizations promoting civic virtues that help people act like good citizens who care about the general welfare. Schools can fall under this heading as well. Positive institutions promote purpose, fairness, humility, safety, and dignity.

16.5 Positive Psychology: Problems and Prospects
- Some critics argue that positive psychology is nothing more than old or exisiting ideas repackaged in a new, if positive, framework. Positive psychology's defenders counter that this subfield will achieve its goals if the larger discipline becomes more balanced where positive and negative psychological processes are concerned.

16.6 Application: Boosting Your Own Happiness
- Feelings of happiness can be achieved if people express sincere gratitude to someone who helped them in the past, and share stories illustrating their own good actions that benefitted other people.
- There are psychologically beneficial qualities to sharing one's good news with others, enthusiastically listening to positive information other people share, and spending money on others rather than oneself.

Key Terms

Capitalization p. 480	Positive individual
Emotions p. 463	traits p. 472
Flow p. 466	Positive institutions p. 476
Gratitude p. 475	Positive psychology p. 457
Grit p. 474	Positive subjective experiences
Hope p. 472	p. 460
Mindlessness p. 469	Posttraumatic growth p. 474
Mindfulness p. 468	Resilience p. 473
Negative emotions p. 463	Savoring, p. 471
Positive emotions p. 463	Undoing hypothesis p. 465

Key People

Mihaly Csikszentmihalyi pp. 465–468	Ellen J. Langer p. 468
Barbara Fredrickson pp. 464–466	Martin Seligman p. 458
	C. R. Snyder p. 473

CHAPTER 16   Practice Test

1. As a social and intellectual movement within the larger discipline of psychology, positive psychology is concerned with
   a. human strengths.
   b. how people can flourish.
   c. creating a balance between the challenges and pleasures of daily life.
   d. all of the above.

2. Of positive psychology's three lines of inquiry, which one deals with psychological processes that promote favorable moods and emotions?
   a. Positive subjective experiences
   b. Positive individual traits
   c. Positive resilience
   d. Positive institutions

3. Being placed in a positive mood has been shown to make people
   a. less alert.
   b. more creative.
   c. more wary.
   d. think slowly.

4. Flow is a state of being in which a person
   a. perceives a sense of balance and well-being following a negative emotion.
   b. has positive thoughts linked with a broad range of subsequent actions.
   c. is fully engaged in an interesting, challenging, and rewarding activity.
   d. behaves in ways that have survival value.

5. A beneficial change in personal relations following some stressful event, such as developing closer bonds with one's family, is an example of
   a. postraumatic growth.
   b. capitalization.
   c. hope.
   d. mindfulness.

6. The human expectation that goals can be met in the future is primarily associated with
   a. hope.
   b. mindfulness.
   c. postraumatic growth.
   d. resilience.

7. Which of the following is *not* a virtue found within positive institutions?
   a. Dignity
   b. Thrift
   c. Fairness
   d. Humanity

8. Critics and skeptics of positive psychology sometimes argue that
   a. positive psychological research is unscientific.
   b. positive psychological processes are difficulty to demonstrate empirically.
   c. positive psychology's message is not new and may be nothing but a fad.
   d. positive psychology is misguided and that mainstream psychology should focus exclusively on the negative aspects of daily life.

9. Which of the following was *not* among the suggestions for prosocial spending to enhance happiness?
   a. Buying more free or leisure time
   b. Spending money to benefit others rather than oneself.
   c. Buying more large pleasures and fewer small ones
   d. Buying more experiences and fewer material goods

10. Sharing good news about our lives with those we are close to is known as
    a. capitalization.
    b. savoring.
    c. resilience.
    d. mindfulness.

Answers
1. d Pages 457–459
2. a Pages 460–461
3. b Pages 461–462
4. c Pages 465–466
5. a Page 474
6. a Pages 472–473
7. b Page 477
8. c Pages 477–478
9. c Pages 480–481
10. a Page 480

Personal Explorations Workbook

Go to the *Personal Explorations Workbook* in the back of your textbook for exercises that can enhance your self-understanding in relation to issues raised in this chapter.

Exercise 16.1 *Self-Assessment:* What Is Your Happiness Profile?

Exercise 16.2 *Self-Reflection:* Thinking about How You Construe Happiness

Glossary

acculturation Changing to adapt to a new culture.

acquired immune deficiency syndrome (AIDS) A disorder in which the immune system is gradually weakened and eventually disabled by the human immunodeficiency virus (HIV).

acute stressors Threatening events that have a relatively short duration and a clear endpoint.

adjustment The psychological processes through which people manage or cope with the demands and challenges of everyday life.

affective forecasting Efforts to predict one's emotional reactions to future events.

aggression Any behavior intended to hurt someone, either physically or verbally.

agoraphobia A fear of going out to public places.

alcohol dependence (alcoholism) A chronic, progressive disorder marked by a growing compulsion to drink and impaired control over drinking that eventually interferes with health and social behavior.

alcoholism *See* alcohol dependence.

ambient stress Chronic environmental conditions that, although not urgent, are negatively valued and place adaptive demands on people.

anal intercourse The insertion of the penis into a partner's anus and rectum.

androcentrism The belief that the male is the norm.

androgens The principal class of male sex hormones.

androgyny The coexistence of both masculine and feminine personality traits in a single person.

anhedonia A diminished ability to experience pleasure.

anorexia nervosa An eating disorder characterized by intense fear of gaining weight, disturbed body image, refusal to maintain normal weight, and use of dangerous measures to lose weight.

antecedents Events that typically precede a target response.

antianxiety drugs Drugs that relieve tension, apprehension, and nervousness.

anticipatory stressors Upcoming or future events that are perceived to be threatening.

antidepressant drugs Drugs that gradually elevate mood and help to bring people out of a depression.

antipsychotic drugs Drugs used to gradually reduce psychotic symptoms, including hyperactivity, mental confusion, hallucinations, and delusions.

antisocial personality disorder A disorder marked by impulsive, callous, manipulative, aggressive, and irresponsible behavior.

anxiety disorders A class of disorders marked by feelings of excessive apprehension and anxiety.

approach-approach conflict A conflict in which a choice must be made between two attractive goals.

approach-avoidance conflict A conflict in which a choice must be made about whether to pursue a single goal that has both attractive and unattractive aspects.

archetypes Emotionally charged images and thought forms that have universal meaning.

asexuals People who feel little need for emotional-sexual relationships with either gender.

assertiveness Acting in one's own best interests by expressing one's thoughts and feelings directly and honestly.

atherosclerosis A disease characterized by gradual narrowing of the coronary arteries.

attachment styles Typical ways of interacting in close relationships.

attitudes Beliefs and feelings about people, objects, and ideas.

attributions Inferences that people draw about the causes of their own behavior, others' behavior, and events.

autism/autism spectrum disorder (ASD) A psychological disorder characterized by profound impairment of social interaction and communication and severely restricted interests and activities.

autonomic nervous system (ANS) That portion of the peripheral nervous system made up of the nerves that connect to the heart, blood vessels, smooth muscles, and glands.

avoidance-avoidance conflict A conflict in which a choice must be made between two unattractive goals.

basking in reflected glory The tendency to enhance one's image by publicly announcing one's association with those who are successful.

behavior modification A systematic approach to changing behavior through the application of the principles of conditioning.

behavior therapies The application of the principles of learning to direct efforts to change clients' maladaptive behaviors.

behavior Any overt (observable) response or activity by an organism.

behavioral contract A written agreement outlining a promise to adhere to the contingencies of a behavior modification program.

behaviorism A theoretical orientation based on the premise that scientific psychology should study observable behavior.

binge-eating disorder An eating disorder that involves distress-inducing eating binges that are not accompanied by the purging, fasting, and excessive exercise seen in bulimia.

biomedical therapies Physiological interventions intended to reduce symptoms associated with psychological disorders.

biopsychosocial model The idea that physical illness is caused by a complex interaction of biological, psychological, and sociocultural factors.

bipolar disorder Disorder typically marked by the experience of both depressed and manic periods.

bisexuals People who seek emotional-sexual relationships with members of both genders.

body image One's attitudes, beliefs, and feelings about one's body.

body mass index (BMI) Weight (in kilograms) divided by height (in meters) squared (kg/m^2).

borderline personality disorder A disorder marked by instability in social relationships, self-image, and emotional functioning.

brainstorming Generating as many ideas as possible while withholding criticism and evaluation.

bulimia nervosa An eating disorder characterized by habitually engaging in out-of-control overeating followed by unhealthy compensatory efforts, such as self-induced vomiting, fasting, abuse of laxatives and diuretics, and excessive exercise.

burnout Syndrome of physical and emotional exhaustion, cynicism, and a lowered sense of self-efficacy that is attributable to work-related stress.

bystander effect The tendency for individuals to be less likely to provide help when others are present than when they are alone.

cancer Malignant cell growth, which may occur in many organ systems in the body.

cannabis The hemp plant from which marijuana, hashish, and THC are derived.

capitalization Telling other people about whatever good things are happening in our own lives.

case study An in-depth investigation of an individual subject.

catastrophic thinking Unrealistic appraisals of stress that exaggerate the magnitude of one's problems.

catharsis The release of emotional tension.

cerebral hemispheres The right and left halves of the cerebrum, which is the convoluted outer layer of the brain.

channel The medium through which a message is sent.

chronic stressors Threatening events that have a relatively long duration and no readily apparent time limit.

classical conditioning A type of learning in which a neutral stimulus acquires the capacity to evoke a response that was originally evoked by another stimulus.

client-centered therapy An insight therapy that emphasizes providing a supportive emotional climate for clients, who play a major role in determining the pace and direction of their therapy.

clinical psychologists Psychologists who specialize in the diagnosis and treatment of psychological disorders and everyday behavioral problems.

clinical psychology The branch of psychology concerned with the diagnosis and treatment of psychological problems and disorders.

close relationships Those relationships that are important, interdependent, and long lasting.

cognitive therapy An insight therapy that uses specific strategies to correct habitual thinking errors that underlie various types of disorders.

cognitive-behavioral treatments Therapy approach that uses varied combinations of verbal interventions and behavior modification techniques to help clients change maladaptive patterns of thinking.

cohabitation Living together in a sexually intimate relationship without the legal bonds of marriage.

coitus The insertion of the penis into the vagina and (typically) pelvic thrusting.

collective unconscious According to Jung, a storehouse of latent memory traces inherited from people's ancestral past that is shared with the entire human race.

collectivism Putting group goals ahead of personal goals and defining one's identity in terms of the groups to which one belongs.

commitment The decision and intent to maintain a relationship in spite of the difficulties and costs that may arise.

communication apprehension The anxiety caused by having to talk with others.

comparison level for alternatives One's estimation of the available outcomes from alternative relationships.

comparison level One's personal standard of what constitutes an acceptable balance of rewards and costs in a relationship.

compensation A defense mechanism characterized by efforts to overcome imagined or real inferiorities by developing one's abilities.

compliance When people yield to social pressure in their public behavior, even though their private beliefs have not changed.

concordance rate A statistic that indicates the percentage of twin pairs or other pairs of relatives who exhibit the same disorder.

conditioned response (CR) A learned reaction to a conditioned stimulus that occurs because of previous conditioning.

conditioned stimulus (CS) A previously neutral stimulus that has acquired the capacity to evoke a conditioned response through conditioning.

confirmation bias The tendency to seek information that supports one's beliefs while not pursuing disconfirming information.

conformity When people yield to real or imagined social pressure.

conscious According to Freud, whatever one is aware of at a particular point in time.

conservation psychology The study of the interactive relationships between humans and the rest of nature, with a particular focus on how to enhance conservation of natural resources.

constructive coping Efforts to deal with stressful events that are judged to be relatively healthful.

context The environment in which communication takes place.

control group Subjects in an experiment who do not receive the special treatment given to the experimental group.

coping Efforts to master, reduce, or tolerate the demands created by stress.

coronary heart disease A chronic disease that results from a reduction in blood flow from the coronary arteries, which supply the heart with blood.

corpus callosum The band of fibers connecting the two hemispheres of the brain.

correlation coefficient A numerical index of the degree of relationship that exists between two variables.

correlation The extent to which two variables are related to each other.

counseling psychologists Psychologists who specialize in the diagnosis and treatment of psychological disorders and everyday behavioral problems.

couples therapy The treatment of both partners in a committed, intimate relationship, in which the main focus is on relationship issues.

cunnilingus The oral stimulation of the female genitals.

date rape Forced and unwanted intercourse in the context of dating.

defense mechanisms Largely unconscious reactions that protect a person from unpleasant emotions such as anxiety and guilt.

defensive attribution The tendency to blame victims for their misfortune, so that one feels less likely to be victimized in a similar way.

defensiveness An excessive concern with protecting oneself from being hurt.

delusions False beliefs that are maintained even though they clearly are out of touch with reality.

dependent variable In an experiment, the variable that is thought to be affected by manipulations of the independent variable.

diagnosis Distinguishing one illness from another.

discrimination Behaving differently, usually unfairly, toward members of a group.

displaced workers Individuals who are unemployed because their jobs have disappeared.

displacement Diverting emotional feelings (usually anger) from their original source to a substitute target.

display rules Norms that govern the appropriate display of emotions in a culture.

dissociative amnesia A sudden loss of memory for important personal information that is too extensive to be due to normal forgetting.

dissociative disorders A class of disorders in which people lose contact with portions of their consciousness or memory, resulting in disruptions in their sense of identity.

dissociative identity disorder (DID) Dissociative disorder that involves the coexistence in one person of two or more largely complete, and usually very different, personalities.

divorce The legal dissolution of a marriage.

door-in-the-face (DITF) technique Making a large request that is likely to be turned down in order to increase the chances that people will agree to a smaller request later.

downward social comparison A defensive tendency to compare oneself with someone whose troubles are more serious than one's own.

dream analysis A psychotherapeutic technique in which the therapist interprets the symbolic meaning of the client's dreams.

dual-earner households Households in which both partners are employed.

eating disorders Severe disturbances in eating behavior characterized by preoccupation with weight and unhealthy efforts to control weight.

ecstasy *See* MDMA.

ego According to Freud, the decision-making component of personality that operates according to the reality principle.

elaboration likelihood model The idea that an individual's thoughts about a persuasive message (rather than the message itself) determine whether attitude change will occur.

electroconvulsive therapy (ECT) A biomedical treatment in which electric shock is used to produce a cortical seizure accompanied by convulsions.

electronically mediated communication Interpersonal communication that takes place via technology.

emotional intelligence Ability to perceive and express emotion, use emotions to facilitate thought, understand and reason with emotion, and regulate emotion.

emotions Powerful, largely uncontrollable feelings, accompanied by physiological changes.

empiricism The premise that knowledge should be acquired through observation.

endocrine system Glands that secrete chemicals called hormones into the bloodstream.

endogamy The tendency of people to marry within their own social group.

environmental psychologists Psychologists who study how individuals are affected by, and interact with, their physical environments.

erectile difficulties The male sexual dysfunction characterized by the persistent inability to achieve or maintain an erection adequate for intercourse.

erogenous zones Areas of the body that are sexually sensitive or responsive.

estrogens The principal class of female sex hormones.

etiology The apparent causation and developmental history of an illness.

evolutionary psychology A field of psychology that examines behavioral processes in terms of their adaptive value for members of a species over the course of many generations.

experiment A research method in which the investigator manipulates an one (independent) variable under carefully controlled conditions and observes whether there are changes in a second (dependent) variable as a result.

experimental group The subjects in an experiment who receive some special treatment in regard to the independent variable.

explanatory style The tendency to use similar causal attributions for a wide variety of events in one's life.

exposure therapies An approach to behavior therapy in which clients are confronted with situations that they fear so they learn that these situations are really harmless.

expressiveness An orientation toward emotion and relationships.

external attributions Ascribing the causes of behavior to situational demands and environmental constraints.

extinction The gradual weakening and disappearance of a conditioned response tendency.

factor analysis Technique of analyzing correlations among many variables to identify closely related clusters of variables.

family life cycle An orderly sequence of developmental stages that families tend to progress through.

family therapy The treatment of a family unit as a whole, in which the main focus is on family dynamics and communication.

fellatio The oral stimulation of the penis.

fight-or-flight response A physiological reaction to threat that mobilizes an organism for attacking (fight) or fleeing (flight) an enemy.

fixation In Freud's theory, a failure to move forward from one stage to another as expected.

flow The state of being in which a person becomes fully involved and engaged in the present time by some interesting, challenging, and intrinsically rewarding activity.

foot-in-the-door (FITD) technique Getting people to agree to a small request to increase the chances that they will agree to a larger request later.

forgiveness Counteracting the natural tendencies to seek vengeance or avoid an offender, thereby releasing this person from further liability for his or her transgression.

free association A psychotherapeutic technique in which clients spontaneously express their thoughts and feelings exactly as they occur, with as little censorship as possible.

frustration The feelings that occur in any situation in which the pursuit of some goal is thwarted.

fundamental attribution error The tendency to explain other people's behavior as the result of personal, rather than situational, factors.

gender roles Cultural expectations about what is appropriate behavior for each gender.

gender schemas Cognitive structures that guide the processing of gender-relevant information.

gender stereotypes Widely shared beliefs about males' and females' abilities, personality traits, and social behavior.

gender The state of being male or female.

gender-role identity A person's identification with the qualities regarded as masculine or feminine.

gender-role transcendence perspective The idea that to be fully human, people need to move beyond gender roles as a way of organizing their perceptions of themselves and others.

general adaptation syndrome A model of the body's stress response, consisting of three stages: alarm, resistance, and exhaustion.

generalized anxiety disorder A disorder marked by a chronic high level of anxiety that is not tied to any specific threat.

glass ceiling An invisible barrier that prevents most women and ethnic minorities from advancing to the highest levels of occupations.

gonads The sex glands.

gratitude Recognizing and concentrating on the good things in one's life and being thankful for them.

grit Possessing perseverance and passion for achieving long-term goals.

group therapy The simultaneous treatment of several or more clients in a group.

hallucinations Sensory perceptions that occur in the absence of a real external stimulus or that represent gross distortions of perceptual input.

hallucinogens A diverse group of drugs that have powerful effects on mental and emotional functioning, marked most prominently by distortions in sensory and perceptual experience.

hardiness A disposition marked by commitment, challenge, and control that is purportedly associated with strong stress resistance.

health psychology The subfield of psychology concerned with how psychosocial factors relate to the promotion and maintenance of health, and with the causation, prevention, and treatment of illness.

hedonic adaptation The phenomenon that occurs when the mental scale that people use to judge pleasantness-unpleasantness of their experiences shifts so that their neutral point, or baseline for comparison, is changed.

heritability ratio An estimate of the proportion of trait variability in a population that is determined by variations in genetic inheritance.

heterosexism The assumption that all individuals and relationships are heterosexual.

heterosexuals People who seek emotional-sexual relationships with members of the other gender.

hierarchy of needs A systematic arrangement of needs, according to priority, in which basic needs must be met before less basic needs are aroused.

hindsight bias The common tendency to mold one's interpretation of the past to fit how events actually turned out.

homogamy The tendency of people to marry others who have similar personal characteristics.

homophobia The intense fear and intolerance of homosexuals.

homosexuals People who seek emotional-sexual relationships with members of the same gender.

hope People's expectations that their goals can be achieved in the future.

hormones Chemical substances released into the bloodstream by the endocrine glands.

hostility A persistent negative attitude marked by cynical, mistrusting thoughts, feelings of anger, and overtly aggressive actions.

humanism A theoretical orientation that emphasizes the unique qualities of humans, especially their free will and their potential for personal growth.

hypoactive sexual desire Lack of interest in sexual activity.

id In Freud's theory, the primitive, instinctive component of personality that operates according to the pleasure principle.

identification Bolstering self-esteem by forming an imaginary or real alliance with some person or group.

immune response The body's defensive reaction to invasion by bacteria, viral agents, or other foreign substances.

impression management Usually conscious efforts by people to influence how others think of them.

incongruence The disparity between one's self-concept and one's actual experience.

independent variable In an experiment, a condition or event that an experimenter varies in order to see its impact on another variable.

individualism Putting personal goals ahead of group goals and defining one's identity in terms of personal attributes rather than group memberships.

industrial/organizational (I/O) psychology The study of human behavior in the workplace.

informational influence When people look to others for how to behave in ambiguous situations.

ingratiation Behaving in ways to make oneself likable to others.

insight therapies A group of psychotherapies in which verbal interactions are intended to enhance clients' self-knowledge and thus promote healthful changes in personality and behavior.

instrumentality An orientation toward action and accomplishment.

interdependence theory The idea that interpersonal relationships are governed by perceptions of the rewards and costs exchanged in interactions.

internal attributions Ascribing the causes of behavior to personal dispositions, traits, abilities, and feelings.

internal conflict The struggle that occurs when two or more incompatible motivations or behavioral impulses compete for expression.

Internet addiction Spending an inordinate amount of time on the Internet and an inability to control online use.

interpersonal communication An interactional process in which one person sends a message to another.

interpersonal conflict When two or more people disagree.

interpretation A therapist's attempts to explain the inner significance of the client's thoughts, feelings, memories, and behaviors.

intimacy Warmth, closeness, and sharing in a relationship.

intimate partner violence Aggression toward those who are in close relationships to the aggressor.

investments Things that people contribute to a relationship that they can't get back if the relationship ends.

kinesics The study of communication through body movements.

labor force All people who are employed, as well as those who are currently unemployed but are looking for work.

learned helplessness Passive behavior produced by exposure to unavoidable aversive events.

leisure Unpaid activities people choose to engage in because the activities are personally meaningful.

life changes Any noticeable alterations in one's living circumstances that require readjustment.

listening A mindful activity and complex process requiring one to select and organize information, interpret and respond to communications, and recall what one has heard.

loneliness The emotional state that occurs when a person has fewer interpersonal relationships than desired or when these relationships are not as satisfying as desired.

lowball technique Getting someone to commit to an attractive proposition before its hidden costs are revealed.

major depressive disorder Disorder characterized by persistent feelings of sadness and despair and a loss of interest in previous sources of pleasure.

manic-depressive disorder See bipolar disorder.

marital therapy The treatment of both partners in a committed, intimate relationship, in which the main focus is on relationship issues.

marriage The legally and socially sanctioned union of sexually intimate adults.

masturbation The stimulation of one's own genitals.

matching hypothesis The idea that people of similar levels of physical attractiveness gravitate toward each other.

MDMA A compound related to both amphetamines and hallucinogens, especially mescaline; it produces a high that typically lasts a few hours or more.

medical model The idea that it is useful to think of abnormal behavior as a disease.

meditation A family of mental exercises in which a conscious attempt is made to focus attention in a nonanalytical way.

menarche The first occurrence of menstruation.

mere exposure effect An increase in positive feelings toward a novel stimulus (such as a person) based on frequent exposure to it.

message The information transmitted by the sender or source of persuasion.

meta-analysis Combines the statistical results of many studies on the same question, yielding an estimate of the size and consistency of a variable's effects.

mindfulness A cultivated perspective in which people are sensitive to context and focused on the present.

mindlessness Engaging in rote behavior, performing familiar, scripted actions without much cognition, as if on autopilot.

mnemonic devices Strategies for enhancing memory.

monogamy The practice of having only one spouse at a time.

mood stabilizers Drugs used to control mood swings in patients with bipolar mood disorders.

multiple-personality disorder See dissociative identity disorder (DID).

narcissism A personality trait marked by an inflated sense of importance, a need for attention and admiration, a sense of entitlement, and a tendency to exploit others.

narcissistic personality disorder A disorder marked by a grandiose sense of self-importance, a sense of entitlement, and an excessive need for attention and admiration.

narcotics Drugs derived from opium that are capable of relieving pain.

naturalistic observation An approach to research in which the researcher engages in careful observation of behavior without intervening directly with the subjects.

need for cognition The tendency to seek out and enjoy effortful thought, problem-solving activities, and in-depth analysis.

need for self-actualization The need to fulfill one's potential; the highest need in Maslow's motivational hierarchy.

negative emotions Unpleasant responses to potential threats or dangers, including subjective states like sadness, disgust, anger, guilt, and fear.

negative reinforcement The strengthening of a response (increases in frequency) because it is followed by the removal of a (presumably) unpleasant stimulus.

neuroticism A broad personality trait associated with chronic anxiety, insecurity, and self-consciousness.

neurotransmitters Chemicals that carry signals from one neuron to another.

noise Any stimulus that interferes with accurately expressing or understanding a message.

nonverbal communication The transmission of meaning from one person to another through means or symbols other than words.

nonverbal sensitivity The ability to accurately encode (express) and decode (understand) nonverbal cues.

normative influence When people conform to social norms for fear of negative social consequences.

nutrition A collection of processes (mainly food consumption) through which an organism utilizes the materials (nutrients) required for survival and growth.

obedience A form of compliance that occurs when people follow direct commands, usually from someone in a position of authority.

observational learning Learning that occurs when an organism's responding is influenced by the observation of others, who are called models.

obsessive-compulsive disorder (OCD) A disorder marked by persistent, uncontrollable intrusions of unwanted thoughts (obsessions) and urges to engage in senseless rituals (compulsions).

occupational interest inventories Tests that measure one's interests as they relate to various jobs or careers.

Oedipal complex According to Freud, children erotically manifest tinged desires for the other-sex parent, accompanied by feelings of hostility toward the same-sex parent.

operant conditioning A form of learning in which voluntary responses come to be controlled by their consequences.

optimism A general tendency to expect good outcomes.

orgasm The release that occurs when sexual arousal reaches its peak intensity and is discharged in a series of muscular contractions that pulsate through the pelvic area.

orgasmic difficulties Sexual disorders characterized by the ability to experience sexual arousal but persistent problems in achieving orgasm.

overdose An excessive dose of a drug that can seriously threaten one's life.

overlearning Continued rehearsal of material after one has first appeared to have mastered it.

panic disorder Recurrent attacks of overwhelming anxiety that usually occur suddenly and unexpectedly.

paralanguage All vocal cues other than the content of the verbal message itself.

parental investment theory The idea that a species' mating patterns depend on what each sex has to invest—in the way of time, energy, and survival risk—to produce and nurture offspring.

passion The intense feelings (both positive and negative) experienced in love relationships, including sexual desire.

person perception The process of forming impressions of others.

personal space A zone of space surrounding a person that is felt to "belong" to that person.

personality An individual's unique constellation of consistent behavioral traits.

personality disorders A class of disorders marked by extreme, inflexible personality traits that cause subjective distress or impaired social and occupational functioning.

personality trait A durable disposition to behave in a particular way in a variety of situations.

persuasion The communication of arguments and information intended to change another person's attitudes.

physical dependence The need to continue to take a drug to avoid withdrawal illness (which occurs when drug use is terminated).

polygamy Having more than one spouse at one time.

polygraph A device that records fluctuations in physiological arousal as a person answers questions.

positive emotions Pleasant responses to events that promote connections with others, including subjective states such as happiness, joy, euphoria, gratitude, and contentment.

positive individual traits Dispositional qualities that account for why some people are happier and psychologically healthier than others.

positive institutions Those organizations that cultivate civic virtues, encouraging people to behave like good citizens while promoting the collective good.

positive psychology A social and intellectual movement within the discipline of psychology that focuses on human strengths and how people can flourish and be successful.

positive reinforcement The strengthening of a response (increases in frequency) because it is followed by the arrival of a (presumably) pleasant stimulus.

positive subjective experiences The positive but private feelings and thoughts people have about themselves and the events in their lives.

possible selves One's conceptions about the kind of person one might become in the future.

posttraumatic growth Enhanced personal strength, realization of what is truly important in life, and increased appreciation for life, friends, and family following trauma.

posttraumatic stress disorder (PTSD) Enduring psychological disturbance attributed to the experience of a major traumatic event.

preconscious According to Freud, material just beneath the surface of awareness that can be easily retrieved.

prejudice A negative attitude toward members of a group.

premature ejaculation Impaired sexual relations because a man consistently reaches orgasm too quickly.

pressure Expectations or demands that one behave in a certain way.

primacy effect The fact that initial information carries more weight than subsequent information.

primary appraisal An initial evaluation of whether an event is (1) irrelevant to one, (2) relevant, but not threatening, or (3) stressful.

procrastination The tendency to delay tackling tasks until the last minute.

prognosis A forecast about the probable course of an illness.

projection Attributing one's own thoughts, feelings, or motives to another person.

projective tests Personality tests that ask subjects to respond to vague, ambiguous stimuli in ways that may reveal the respondents' needs, feelings, and personality traits.

proxemics The study of people's use of interpersonal space.

proximity Geographic, residential, and other forms of spatial closeness.

psychiatrists Physicians who specialize in the treatment of psychological disorders.

psychoanalysis An insight therapy that emphasizes the recovery of unconscious conflicts, motives, and defenses through techniques such as free association, dream analysis, and transference.

psychodynamic theories All the diverse theories descended from the work of Sigmund Freud that focus on unconscious mental forces.

psychological dependence When a person must continue to take a drug to satisfy intense mental and emotional craving for it.

psychological test A standardized measure of a sample of a person's behavior.

psychology The science that studies behavior and the physiological and mental processes that underlie it and the profession that applies the accumulated knowledge of this science to practical problems.

psychosexual stages In Freud's theory, developmental periods with a characteristic sexual focus that leave their mark on adult personality.

psychosomatic diseases Genuine physical ailments thought to be caused in part by stress and other psychological factors.

public self An image presented to others in social interactions.

punishment The weakening (decrease in frequency) of a response because it is followed by the arrival of a (presumably) unpleasant stimulus.

rational-emotive behavior therapy An approach to therapy that focuses on altering clients' patterns of irrational thinking to reduce maladaptive emotions and behavior.

rationalization Creating false but plausible excuses to justify unacceptable behavior.

reaction formation Behaving in a way that is exactly the opposite of one's true feelings.

receiver The person to whom a message is sent.

reciprocal liking Liking those who show that they like you.

reciprocity principle The rule that one should pay back in kind what one receives from others.

reference group A set of people who are used as a gauge in making social comparisons.

refractory period A time following orgasm during which males are largely unresponsive to further stimulation.

regression A reversion to immature patterns of behavior.

relationship maintenance The actions and activities used to sustain the desired quality of a relationship.

reliability The measurement consistency of a test.

repression Keeping distressing thoughts and feelings buried in the unconscious.

resilience A person's ability to recover and often prosper following some consequential life event.

resistance Largely unconscious defensive maneuvers intended to hinder the progress of therapy.

savoring The power to focus on, value, and even boost the enjoyment of almost any experience, whether great or small.

schizophrenia A disorder marked by delusions, hallucinations, disorganized thinking and speech, and deterioration of adaptive behavior.

secondary appraisal An evaluation of one's coping resources and options for dealing with stress.

sedatives Sleep-inducing drugs that tend to decrease central nervous system and behavioral activity.

self-actualization *See* need for self-actualization.

self-attributions Inferences that people draw about the causes of their own behavior.

self-concept A collection of beliefs about one's own basic nature, unique qualities, and typical behavior.

self-defeating behaviors Seemingly intentional acts that thwart a person's self-interest.

self-disclosure The voluntary act of sharing personal information about yourself with another person.

self-discrepancy A mismatch between the self-perceptions that make up the actual self, ideal self, and ought self.

self-efficacy One's belief about one's ability to perform behaviors that should lead to expected outcomes.

self-enhancement The tendency to seek positive (and reject negative) information about oneself.

self-esteem One's overall assessment of one's worth as a person.

self-fulfilling prophecy The process whereby expectations about a person cause him or her to behave in ways that confirm the expectations.

self-handicapping The tendency to sabotage one's performance to provide an excuse for possible failure.

self-monitoring The degree to which people attend to and control the impressions they make on others.

self-regulation The process of directing and controlling one's behavior to achieve desired goals.

self-report inventories Personality scales that ask individuals to answer a series of questions about their characteristic behavior.

self-serving bias The tendency to attribute one's successes to personal factors and one's failures to situational factors.

sender The person who initiates a message.

sensate focus A sex-therapy exercise in which partners take turns pleasuring each other with guided verbal feedback and in which certain kinds of stimulation are temporarily forbidden.

set-point theory Theory that proposes that the body monitors fat-cell levels to keep them (and weight) fairly stable.

settling-point theory Theory that proposes that weight tends to drift around the level at which the constellation of factors that determine food consumption and energy expenditure achieve an equilibrium.

sex therapy The professional treatment of sexual dysfunctions.

sexism Discrimination against people on the basis of their gender.

sexual dysfunction Impairments in sexual functioning that cause subjective distress.

sexual harassment Unwelcome conduct on the basis of gender.

sexual identity The complex set of personal qualities, self-perceptions, attitudes, values, and preferences that guide one's sexual behavior.

sexual orientation A person's preference for emotional and sexual relationships with individuals of the same gender, the other gender, or either gender.

sexually transmitted disease (STD) A disease or infection transmitted primarily through sexual contact.

shaping Modifying behavior by reinforcing closer and closer approximations of the desired response.

shyness Discomfort, inhibition, and excessive caution in interpersonal relations.

social comparison theory The idea that individuals compare themselves with others in order to assess their abilities and opinions.

social constructionism The assertion that individuals construct their own reality based on societal expectations, conditioning, and self-socialization.

social exchange theory The idea that interpersonal relationships are governed by perceptions of the rewards and costs exchanged in interactions.

social role theory The assertion that minor gender differences are exaggerated by the different social roles that males and females occupy.

social skills training A behavior therapy designed to improve interpersonal skills that emphasizes modeling, behavioral rehearsal, and shaping.

social support Aid and succor provided by members of one's social networks.

socialization The acquisition of the norms and roles expected of people in a particular society.

source The person who sends a persuasive communication.

specific phobia A phobia marked by a persistent and irrational fear of an object or situation that presents no realistic danger.

spermarche An adolescent male's first ejaculation.

standardization The uniform procedures used to administer and score a test.

stereotypes Widely held beliefs that people have certain characteristics simply because of their membership in a particular group.

stimulants Drugs that tend to increase central nervous system and behavioral activity.

stress Any circumstances that threaten or are perceived to threaten one's well-being and thereby tax one's coping abilities.

subjective well-being Individuals' personal assessments of their overall happiness or life satisfaction.

superego According to Freud, the moral component of personality that incorporates social standards about what represents right and wrong.

surveys Structured questionnaires or interviews designed to solicit information about specific aspects of participants' behavior, attitudes, and beliefs.

sustainable world A world in which human activities and needs are balanced with those of other species and future generations, taking into account ecological as well as social and economic factors.

systematic desensitization A behavior therapy used to reduce clients' anxiety responses through counterconditioning.

tardive dyskinesia A neurological disorder marked by chronic tremors and involuntary spastic movements.

test norms Statistics that provide information about where a score on a psychological test ranks in relation to other scores on that test.

token economy A system for doling out symbolic reinforcers that are exchanged later for a variety of genuine reinforcers.

token A symbol of all the members of that group.

tolerance A progressive decrease in responsiveness to a drug with continued use.

transference A phenomenon that occurs when clients start relating to their therapist in ways that mimic critical relationships in their lives.

twin studies A research method in which researchers assess hereditary influence by comparing the resemblance of identical twins and fraternal twins on a trait.

Type A personality A personality style marked by a strong competitive orientation, impatience and urgency, and anger and hostility.

Type B personality A personality style marked by relatively relaxed, patient, easygoing, amicable behavior.

unconditioned response (UCR) An unlearned reaction to an unconditioned stimulus that occurs without previous conditioning.

unconditioned stimulus (UCS) A stimulus that evokes an unconditioned response without previous conditioning.

unconscious According to Freud, thoughts, memories, and desires that are well below the surface of conscious awareness but that nonetheless exert great influence on one's behavior.

underemployment Settling for a job that does not fully utilize one's skills, abilities, and training.

undoing hypothesis The idea that positive emotions aid the mind and the body by recovering a sense of balance and flexibility following an episode experiencing negative emotion.

unrealistic optimism Awareness that certain health-related behaviors are dangerous but erroneously viewing those dangers as risks for others rather than oneself.

validity The ability of a test to measure what it was designed to measure.

variables *See* dependent variable; independent variable.

vasocongestion Engorgement of blood vessels.

work An activity that produces something of value for others.

work-family conflict The feeling of being pulled in multiple directions by competing demands from job and family.

workforce *See* labor force.

References

Aamodt, M. (2010). *Industrial/organizational psychology: An applied approach.* Belmont, CA: Wadsworth/Cengage.

Abbeduto, L., Ozonoff, S., Thurman, A. J., McDuffie, A., & Schweitzer, J. (2014). Neurodevelopmental disorders. In R. E. Hales, S. C. Yudofsky, & L. W. Roberts (Eds.), The American Psychiatric Publishing textbook of psychiatry (6th ed.). Washington, DC: American Psychiatric Publishing.

Abbey, A. (2009). Alcohol and sexual assault. In H. T. Reis & S. Sprecher (Eds.), *Encyclopedia of human relationships, Vol. 1.* Los Angeles: Sage Reference.

Abel, E. L., & Kruger, M. L. (2010). Smile intensity in photographs predicts longevity. *Psychological Science, 21*(4), 542–544. doi:10.1177/0956797610363775

Abi-Saleh, B., Iskanadar, S. B., Elgharib, N., & Cohen, M. V. (2008). C-reactive protein: The harbinger of cardiovascular diseases. *Southern Medical Journal, 101,* 525–533.

Abma, J. C., & Martinez, G. M. (2006). Childlessness among older women in the United States: Trends and profiles. *Journal of Marriage and Family, 68,* 1045–1056.

Abramowitz, J. S., & Jacoby, R. J. (2015). Obsessive-compulsive and related disorders: A critical review of the new diagnostic class. *Annual Review of Clinical Psychology, 11,* 165–186. doi:10.1146/annurev-clinpsy-032813-153713

Abrams, D., Viki, G. T., Masser, B., & Bohner, G. (2003). Perceptions of stranger acquaintance rape: The role of benevolent and hostile sexism in victim blame and rape proclivity. *Journal of Personality and Social Psychology, 84,* 111–125.

Abramson, L. Y., Seligman, M. E. P., & Teasdale, J. D. (1978). Learned helplessness in humans: Critique and reformulation. *Journal of Abnormal Psychology, 87,* 49–74.

Abuhamdeh, S., & Csikszentmihalyi, M. (2012). The importance of challenge for the enjoyment of intrinsically motivated, goal-directed activities. *Personality and Social Psychology Bulletin, 38*(3), 317–330. doi:10.1177/0146167211427147

Achtziger, A., Hubert, M., Kenning, P., Raab, G., & Reisch, L. (2015). Debt out of control: The links between self-control, compulsive buying, and real debts. *Journal of Economic Psychology, 49,* 141–149. doi:10.1016/j.joep.2015.04.003

Ackerman, J. M., Griskevicius, V., & Li, N. P. (2011). Let's get serious: Communicating commitment in romantic relationships. *Journal of Personality and Social Psychology, 100*(6), 1079–1094. doi:10.1037/a0022412

Ackerman, J. M., Shapiro, J. R., Neuberg, S. L., Kenrick, D. T., Becker, D. V., Griskevicius, V., Maner, J. K., & Schaller, M. (2006). They all look the same to me (unless they're angry): From out-group homogeneity to out-group heterogeneity. *Psychological Science, 17,* 836–840.

Adair, K. C., & Fredrickson, B. L. (2015). Be open: Mindfulness predicts reduced motivated perception. *Personality and Individual Differences, 83,* 198–201. doi:10.1016/j.paid.2015.04.008

Adams, G. (2012). Context in person, person in context: A cultural psychology approach to social-personality psychology. In K. Deaux & M. Snyder (Eds.), *The Oxford handbook of personality and social psychology* (pp. 182–208). New York: Oxford University Press.

Adams, S. (2013). Half of college grads are working jobs that don't require a degree. Retrieved from www.forbes.com /sites/susanadams/2013/05/28/half-of-college-grads-are -working-jobs-that-dont-require-a-degree

Adler, A. (1917). *Study of organ inferiority and its psychical compensation.* New York: Nervous and Mental Diseases Publishing.

Adler, A. (1927). *Practice and theory of individual psychology.* New York: Harcourt, Brace & World.

Adorno, T. W., Frenkel-Brunswik, E., Levinson, D. J., & Sanford, B. W. (1950). *The authoritarian personality.* New York: Harper & Row.

Aggarwal, P., Jun, S., & Huh, J. (2011). Scarcity messages: A consumer competition perspective. *Journal of Advertising, 40*(3), 19–30. doi:10.2753/JOA0091-3367400302

Agnew, C. R., & VanderDrift, L. E. (2015). Relationship maintenance and dissolution. In M. Mikulincer, P. R. Shaver, J. A. Simpson, & J. F. Dovidio (Eds.), *APA handbook of personality and social psychology, Vol. 3: Interpersonal relations* (pp. 581–604). Washington, DC: American Psychological Association. doi:10.1037/14344-021

Agocha, V. B., Asencio, M., & Decena, C. U. (2014). Sexuality and culture. In D. L. Tolman, L. M. Diamond, J. A. Bauermeister, W. H. George, J. G. Pfaus, & L. M. Ward (Eds.), *APA handbook of sexuality and psychology* (pp. 183–228). Washington, DC: American Psychological Association. doi:10.1037/14194-006

Ahern, A. L., Bennett, K. M., & Hetherington, M. M. (2008). Internalization of the ultra-thin ideal: Positive implicit associations with underweight fashion models are associated with drive for thinness in young women. *Eating Disorders, 16,* 294–307.

Ahrens, A. H., & Forbes, C. N. (2014). Gratitude. In M. M. Tugade, M. N. Shiota, L. D. Kirby, M. M. Tugade, M. N. Shiota, & L. D. Kirby (Eds.), *Handbook of positive emotions* (pp. 342–361). New York: Guilford.

Aikawa, A., Fujita, M., & Tanaka, K. (2007). The relationship between social skills deficits and depression, loneliness, and social anxiety: Rethinking a vulnerability model of social skills deficits. *The Japanese Journal of Social Psychology, 23,* 95–103.

Ainsworth, M. D. S., Blehar, M. C., Waters, E., & Wall, S. (1978). *Patterns of attachment: A psychological study of the strange situation.* Hillsdale, NJ: Erlbaum.

Ajzen, I. (2012). Attitudes and persuasion. In K. Deaux, M. Snyder, K. Deaux, & M. Snyder (Eds.), *The Oxford handbook of personality and social psychology* (pp. 367–393). New York: Oxford University Press.

Akabaliev, V. H., Sivkov, S. T., & Mantarkov, M. Y. (2014). Minor physical anomalies in schizophrenia and bipolar I disorder and the neurodevelopmental continuum of psychosis. *Bipolar Disorders, 16,* 633–641. doi:10.1111/bdi.12211

Akerstedt, T., Kecklund, G., & Axelsson, J. (2007). Impaired sleep after bedtime stress and worries. *Biological Psychology, 76*(3), 170–173.

Akhtar, S. (2007). *Listening to others: Developmental and clinical aspects of empathy and attunement.* Lanham, MD: Jason Aronson.

Aknin, L. B., Barrington-Leigh, C. P., Dunn, E. W., Helliwell, J. F., Biswas-Diener, R., Kemeza, I., Nyende, P., Ashton-James, C. E., & Norton, M. I. (2010). *Prosocial spending and well-being: Cross-cultural evidence for a psychological universal,* No. 16415, NBER Working Papers, National Bureau of Economic Research.

Aknin, L. B., Barrington-Leigh, C. P., Dunn, E. W., Helliwell, J. F., Burns, J., Biswas-Diener, R., Kemeza, I., Nyende, P., Ashton-James, C., & Norton, M. I. (2013). Prosocial spending and well-being: Cross-cultural evidence for a psychological universal. *Journal Of Personality And Social Psychology, 104*(4), 635–652. doi:10.1037/a0031578

Aknin, L. B., Dunn, E. W., & Norton, M. I. (2012). Happiness runs in a circular motion: Evidence for a positive feedback loop between prosocial spending and happiness. *Journal of Happiness Studies, 13*(2), 347–355. doi:10.1007 /s10902-011-9267-5

Aknin, L. B., Sandstrom, G. M., Dunn, E. W., & Norton, M. I. (2011). It's the recipient that counts: Spending money on strong social ties leads to greater happiness than spending on weak social ties. *Plos ONE, 6*(2). doi:10.1371/journal.pone.0017018

Akpan, J., & Notar, C. E. (2012). How to write a professional knockout resume to differentiate yourself. *College Student Journal, 46*(4), 880–891.

Al Ramiah, A., & Hewstone, M. (2013). Intergroup contact as a tool for reducing, resolving, and preventing intergroup conflict: Evidence, limitations, and potential. *American Psychologist, 68*(7), 527–542. doi:10.1037/a0032603

Alan Guttmacher Institute (2012a). Contraception use in the United States. Fact sheet. Retrieved from www.guttmacher.org/pubs/fb_contr_use.html

Alan Guttmacher Institute (2012b). Facts on American teens' sexual and reproductive health. Retrieved from www.guttmacher.org/pubs/FB-Teen-SexEd.html

Alan Guttmacher Insitute (2015). Sex and HIV education. Retrieved from www.guttmacher.org/statecenter/spibs /spib_SE.pdf

Alanko, K., Santtila, P., Harlaar, N., Witting, K., Varjonen, M., Jern, P., Johansson, A., von der Pahlen, B., & Sandnabba, N. K. (2008). The association between childhood gender atypical behavior and adult psychiatric symptoms is moderated by parenting style. *Sex Roles, 58,* 837–847.

Albert, P., Rice, K. G., & Caffee, L. (2014). Perfectionism affects blood pressure in response to repeated exposure to stress. *Stress and Health: Journal of the International Society for the Investigation of Stress.* doi:10.1002/smi.2591

Alberti, R. E., & Emmons, M. L. (2001). *Your perfect right.* San Luis Obispo, CA: Impact Publishers.

Aldwin, C. M. (2007). *Stress, coping, and development: An integrative perspective.* New York: Guilford.

Aldwin, C. M., Jeong, Y., Igarashi, H., Choun, S., & Spiro III, A. (2014). Do hassles mediate between life events mortality in older men? Longitudinal findings from the VA Normative Aging Study. *Experimental Gerontology, 59,* 74–80.

Alessandri, G., Borgogni, L., Schaufeli, W. B., Caprara, G. V., & Consiglio, C. (2015). From positive orientation to job performance: The role of work engagement and self-efficacy beliefs. *Journal of Happiness Studies, 16*(3), 767–788. doi:10.1007/s10902-014-9533-4

Alford, Z., & White, M. A. (2015). Positive school psychology. In M. A. White, A. S. Murray, M. A. White, & A. S. Murray (Eds.), *Evidence-based approaches in positive education: Implementing a strategic framework for well-being in schools* (pp. 93–109). New York: Springer Science + Business Media. doi:10.1007/978-94-017-9667-5_5

Algoe, S. B., Fredrickson, B. L., & Chow, S. (2011). The future of emotions research within positive psychology. In K. M. Sheldon, T. B. Kashdan, & M. F. Steger (Eds.), *Designing positive psychology: Taking stock and moving forward* (pp. 115-132). New York: Oxford University Press. doi:10.1093/acprof:oso/9780195373585.003.0008

Algoe, S. B., Fredrickson, B. L., & Gable, S. L. (2013). The social functions of the emotion of gratitude via expression. *Emotion, 13*(4), 605-609. doi:10.1037/a0032701

Allan, R. (2011). Type A behavior pattern. In R. Allen & J. Fisher (Ed.), *Heart and mind: The practice of cardiac psychology* (2nd ed., pp. 287–290). Washington, DC: American Psychological Association.

Allen, E. S., Rhoades, G. K., Stanley, S. M., Markman, H. J., Williams, T., Melton, J., & Clements, M. L. (2008). Premarital precursors of marital infidelity. *Family Process, 47,* 243–259.

Allen, T. D. (2013). The work-family role interface: A synthesis of the research from industrial and organizational psychology. In N. W. Schmitt, S. Highhouse, I. B. Weiner, N. W. Schmitt, S. Highhouse, & I. B. Weiner (Eds.), *Handbook of psychology, Vol. 12: Industrial and organizational psychology* (2nd ed., pp. 698–718). Hoboken, NJ: Wiley.

Allison, D. B., Heshka, S., Neale, M. C., Lykken, D. T., & Heymsfield, S. B. (1994). A genetic analysis of relative weight among 4,020 twin pairs, with an emphasis on sex effects. *Health Psychology, 13,* 362–365.

Alloy, L. B., Abramson, L. Y., Whitehouse, W. G., Hogan, M. E., Tashman, N. A., Steinberg, D. L., Rose, D. T., & Donovan, P. (1999). Depressogenic cognitive styles: Predictive validity, information processing and personality characteristics, and developmental origins. *Behavioral Research and Therapy, 37,* 503–531.

Alston, L. L., Kratchmer, C., Jeznach, A., Bartlett, N. T., Davidson, P. S. R., & Fujiwara, E. (2013). Self-serving episodic memory biases: Findings in the repressive coping style. *Frontiers In Behavioral Neuroscience, 7.* doi:10.3389 /fnbeh.2013.00117

Altemeyer, B. (1988a). *Enemies of freedom: Understanding right-wing authoritarianism.* San Francisco: Jossey-Bass.

Altemeyer, B. (1988b). The good soldier, marching in step: A psychological explanation of state terror. *Sciences,* March/ April, 30–38.

Altemeyer, B. (1998). The other "authoritarian personality." *Advances in Experimental Social Psychology, 30,* 47–92.

Altman, I., & Taylor, D. A. (1973). *Social penetration: The development of interpersonal relationships.* New York: Irvington.

Amato, P. R. (1999). Children of divorced parents as young adults. In E. M. Hetheringon (Ed.), *Coping with divorce, single parenting, and remarriage: A risk and resiliency perspective.* Mahwah, NJ: Erlbaum.

Amato, P. R. (2001). The consequences of divorce for adults and children. In R. M. Milardo (Ed.), *Understanding families into the new millennium: A decade in review.* Minneapolis, MN: National Council on Family Relations.

Amato, P. R. (2003). Reconciling divergent perspectives: Judith Wallerstein, quantitative family research, and children of divorce. *Family Relations: Interdisciplinary Journal of Applied Family Studies, 52*(4), 332–339.

Amato, P. R. (2010). Research on divorce: Continuing trends and new developments. *Journal of Marriage and Family, 72*(3), 650–666. doi:10.1111/j.1741-3737.2010.00723.x

Amato, P. R., & Anthony, C. J. (2014). Estimating the effects of parental divorce and death with fixed effects models. *Journal of Marriage and Family, 76*(2), 370–386.

Amato, P. R., & Previti, D. (2003). People's reasons for divorcing: Gender, social class, the life course, and adjustment. *Journal of Family Issues, 24*(5), 602–626.

American Association of Suicidology. (2007). Understanding and helping the suicidal individual. Retrieved from www.suicidology.org/associations/1045/files/Understanding.pdf

American Association of University Women (AAUW). (2015). *The simple truth about the gender pay gap.* Washington, DC: AAUW.

American Cancer Society. (2008). *Cancer facts and figures 2008.* Atlanta, GA: American Cancer Society.

American Foundation for Suicide Prevention. (2007). When you fear someone may take their own life. Retrieved from www.afsp.org/index.cfm?page_id=F2F25092-7E90 -9BD4-C4658F1D2B5D19A0

American Heart Association. (2012). Executive summary: Heart disease and stroke statistics—2012. Update: A report from the American Heart Association. *Circulation, 125,* 188-197. doi: 10.1161/CIR.0b013e3182456d46

American Psychiatric Association. (2013). Diagnostic and statistical manual of mental disorders: DSM-5. Washington, DC: American Psychiatric Association.

American Psychological Association. (2010). *Stress in America Findings.* Washington, DC: American Psychological Association

American Psychological Association. (2015). *Stress in America Findings.* Washington, DC: American Psychological Association.

American Psychological Association. (2015, February 4). Stress in America: Paying with our health. Retrieved from www.apa.org/news/press/releases/stress/2014/stress-report.pdf

American Society for Aesthetic Plastic Surgery (2015). The American Society for Aesthetic Plastic Surgery reports Americans spent more than 12 billion in 2014; Procedures for men up 43% over five year period. Retrieved from www.surgery.org/media/news-releases/the-american -society-for-aesthetic-plastic-surgery-reports-americans -spent-more-than-12-billion-in-2014--pro

Amir, N., & Taylor, C. T. (2012). Combining computerized home-based treatments for generalized anxiety disorder: An attention modification program and cognitive behavioral therapy. *Behavior Therapy, 43,* 546–559. doi:10.1016/j.beth .2010.12.008

Anacker, C. (2014). Adult hippocampal neurogenesis in depression: Behavioral implications and regulation by the stress system. In C. M. Pariante & M. D. Lapiz-Bluhm (Eds.), *Behavioral neurobiology of stress-related disorders.* New York: Springer-Verlag.

Andersen, P., Gannon, J., & Kalchik, J. (2013). Proxemic and haptic interaction: The closeness continuum. In J. A. Hall, M. L. Knapp, J. A. Hall, & M. L. Knapp (Eds.), *Nonverbal communication* (pp. 295–329). Boston: De Gruyter Mouton. doi:10.1515/9783110238150.295

Andersen, S. M., & Przybylinski, E. (2014). Cognitive distortion in interpersonal relations: Clinical implications of social cognitive research on person perception. *Journal of Psychotherapy Integration, 24*(1), 13–24. doi:10.1037 /a0035968

Andersen, S. M., Reznik, I., & Manzella, L. M. (1996). Eliciting facial affect, motivation, and expectancies in transference: Significant-other representations in social relations. *Journal of Personality and Social Psychology, 71,* 1108–1129.

Anderson, B., Wethington, E., & Kamarck, T. W. (2011). Interview assessment of stressor exposure. In R. J. Contrada & A. Baum (Eds.), *The handbook of stress science: Biology, psychology, and health* (pp. 1–9). New York: Springer.

Anderson, C., Srivastava, S., Beer, J. S., Spataro, S. E., & Chapman, J. A. (2006). Knowing your place: Self-perceptions of status in face-to-face groups. *Journal of Personality and Social Psychology, 91,* 1094–1110.

Anderson, C. A., & Bushman, B. J. (2001). Effects of violent video games on aggressive behavior, aggressive cognition, aggressive affect, physiological arousal, and prosocial behavior: A meta-analytic review of the scientific literature. *Psychological Science, 12,* 353–359.

Anderson, C. A., Shibuya, A., Ihori, N., Swing, E. L., Bushman, B. J., Sakamoto, A., . . . Saleem, M. (2010). Violent video game effects on aggression, empathy, and prosocial behavior in Eastern and Western countries: A meta-analytic review. *Psychological Bulletin, 136*(2), 151–173. doi:10.1037/a0018251

Anderson, S., & Winefield, A. H. (2011). The impact of underemployment on psychological health, physical health, and work attitudes. In D. C. Maynard & D. C. Feldman (Eds.), *Underemployment: Psychological, economic, and social challenges* (pp. 165–185). New York: Springer Science + Business Media.

Andersson, E., Ljótsson, B., Hedman, E., Kaldo, V., Paxling, B., Andersson, G., . . . Rück, C. (2011). Internet-based cognitive behavior therapy for obsessive compulsive disorder: A pilot study. *BMC Psychiatry, 11*(125), 1–10. doi:10.1186/1471-244X-11-125

Andreasen, N. C. (1987). Creativity and mental illness: Prevalence rates in writers and their first-degree relatives. *American Journal of Psychiatry, 144,* 1288–1292.

Andreasen, N. C. (1990). Positive and negative symptoms: Historical and conceptual aspects. In N. C. Andreasen (Ed.), *Modern problems of pharmacopsychiatry: Positive and negative symptoms and syndromes.* Basel: Karger.

Andreasen, N. C. (2009). Schizophrenia: A conceptual history. In M. C. Gelder, N. C. Andreasen, J. J. López-Ibor, Jr., & J. R. Geddes (Eds.), *New Oxford textbook of psychiatry, Vol. 1* (2nd ed.). New York: Oxford University Press.

Andreassen, C. S. (2015). Workaholism: The concept and its assessment. In I. Harpaz, R. Snir, I. Harpaz, & R. Snir (Eds.), *Heavy work investment: Its nature, sources, outcomes, and future directions* (pp. 68–97). New York: Routledge/Taylor & Francis Group.

Andrews, P. W., Kornstein, S. G., Halberstadt, L. J., Gardner, C. O., & Neale, M. C. (2011). Blue again: Perturbational effects of antidepressants suggest monoaminergic homeostasis in major depression. *Frontiers in Psychology, 2*(159), 1–24. doi:10.3389/fpsyg.2011.00159

Andrews, P. W., Thomson, J. A., Jr., Amstadter, A., & Neale, M. C. (2012). *Primum non nocere:* An evolutionary analysis of whether antidepressants do more harm than good. *Frontiers in Psychology, 3*(117), 1–19. doi:10.3389 /fpsyg.2012.00117

Angelakis, I., Gooding, P., Tarrier, N., & Panagioti, M. (2015). Suicidality in obsessive compulsive disorder (OCD): A systematic review and meta-analysis. *Clinical Psychology Review, 39,* 1–15. doi:10.1016/j.cpr.2015.03.002

Angell, M. (2004). *The truth about the drug companies: How they deceive us and what to do about it.* New York: Random House.

Anglin, L. P., Pirson, M., & Langer, E. (2008). Mindful learning: A moderator of gender differences in mathematics performance. *Journal of Adult Development, 15*(3–4), 132–139.

Angulo, S., Brooks, M. L., & Swann, Jr., W. (2011). Swimming serenely in a sea of words: Sexism, communication, and precarious couples. *Personal Relationships, 18*(4), 604–616. doi:10.1111/j.1475-6811.2010.01322.x

Ansbacher, H. (1970, February). Alfred Adler, individual psychology. *Psychology Today,* pp. 42–44, 66.

Antecol, H., Jong, A., & Steinberger, M. (2008). The sexual orientation wage gap: The role of occupational sorting and human capital. *Industrial & Labor Relations Review, 61,* 518–543.

Antoni, M. H., & Carrico, A. W. (2012). Psychological and biobehavioral processes in HIV disease. In A. Baum, T. A. Revenson, & J. Singer (Eds.), *Handbook of health psychology* (pp. 755–770). New York: Guilford.

Antoniou, A. G., & Cooper, C. L. (2005). *Research companion to organizational health psychology.* Northampton, MA: Edward Elgar.

App, B., McIntosh, D. N., Reed, C. L., & Hertenstein, M. J. (2011). Nonverbal channel use in communication of emotion: How may depend on why. *Emotion, 11*(3), 603–617. doi:10.1037/a0023164

Arango, C., & Carpenter, W. T. (2011). The schizophrenia construct: Symptomatic presentation. In D. R. Weinberger & P. Harrison (Eds.), *Schizophrenia* (3rd ed.). Malden, MA: Wiley-Blackwell.

Arbona, C. (2005). Promoting the career development and academic achievement of at-risk youth: College access programs. In S. D. Brown & R. W. Lent (Eds.), *Career development and counseling: Putting theory and research to work.* New York: Wiley.

Arcelus, J., Mitchell, A. J., Wales, J., & Nielsen, S. (2011). Mortality rates in patients with anorexia nervosa and other eating disorders: A meta-analysis of 36 studies. *Archives of General Psychiatry, 68,* 724–731. doi:10.1001 /archgenpsychiatry.2011.74

Archer, J. (2005). Are women or men the more aggressive sex? In S. Fein, G. R. Goethals, & M. J. Sandstrom (Eds.), *Gender and aggression: Interdisciplinary perspectives.* Mahwah, NJ: Erlbaum.

Argyle, M. (1999). Causes and correlates of happiness. In D. Kahneman, E. Diener, & N. Schwarz (Eds.), *Well-being: The foundations of hedonic psychology.* New York: Sage.

Argyle, M., & Henderson, M. (1984). The rules of friendship. *Journal of Social and Personal Relationships, 1,* 211–237.

Aries, E. (1998). Gender differences in interaction: A reexamination. In D. J. Canary & K. Dindia (Eds.), *Sex differences and similarities in communication: Critical essays and empirical investigations of sex and gender in interaction.* Mahwah, NJ: Erlbaum.

Arkowitz, H., & Lilienfeld, S. O. (2007). The best medicine? How drugs stack up against talk therapy for the treatment of depression. *Scientific American Mind, 18*(5), 80–83.

Arkowitz, H., & Lilienfeld, S. O. (2010, September/ October). The "Just do it!" trap: Why Dr. Phil and Dr. Laura won't solve your problems. *Scientific American Mind,* 64–65.

Armbruster, B. B. (2000). Taking notes from lectures. In R. F. Flippo & D. C. Caverly (Eds.), *Handbook of college reading and study strategy research.* Mahwah, NJ: Erlbaum.

Armour, S. (2004, May 4). Some moms quit as offices scrap family-friendliness. *USA Today,* pp. 1A–2A.

Aronson, J. M., Cohen, G., & Nail, P. R. (1999). *Cooperation in the classroom: The jigsaw method.* New York: Longman.

Arpino, B., & Bordone, V. (2014). Does grandparenting pay off? The effect of child care on grandparents' cognitive functioning. *Journal of Marriage And Family, 76*(2), 337–351.

Arriaga, P., Esteves, F., Carneiro, P., & Monteiro, M. B. (2006). Violent computer games and their effects on state hostility and physiological arousal. *Aggressive Behavior, 32,* 358–371.

Artham, S. M., Lavie, C. J., & Milani, R. V. (2008). Cardiac rehabilitation programs markedly improve high-risk profiles in coronary patients with high psychological distress. *Southern Medical Journal, 101,* 262–267.

Asbury, K., & Plomin, R. (2014). *G is for genes: The impact of genetics on education and achievement.* Malden, MA: Wiley-Blackwell.

Asch, S. E. (1955). Opinions and social pressures. *Scientific American, 193*(5), 31–35.

Asch, S. E. (1956). Studies of independence and conformity: A minority of one against a unanimous majority. *Psychological Monographs, 70* (9, Whole No. 416).

Ashcraft, K. A., & Bonneau, R. H. (2008). Psychological stress exacerbates primary vaginal herpes simplex virus type 1 (HSV-1) infection by impairing both innate and adaptive immune responses. *Brain, Behavior, and Immunity, 22*(8),1231–1240. doi: 10.1016/j.bbi.2008.06.008

Asmundson, G. G., Taylor, S., & Smits, J. J. (2014). Panic disorder and agoraphobia: An overview and commentary on DSM-5 changes. *Depression and Anxiety, 31*(6), 480–486. doi:10.1002/da.22277

Assawasuwannakit, P., Braund, R., & Duffull, S. B. (2015). A model-based meta-analysis of the influence of factors that impact adherence to medications. *Journal of Clinical Pharmacy And Therapeutics, 40*(1), 24–31. doi:10.1111/jcpt.12219

Aubin, S., & Heiman, J. R. (2004). Sexual dysfunction from a relationship perspective. In J. H. Harvey, A. Wenzel, & S. Sprecher (Eds.), *The handbook of sexuality in close relationships.* Mahwah, NJ: Lawrence Erlbaum.

Aubrey, J. S., & Harrison, K. (2004). The gender-role content of children's favorite television programs and its links to their gender-related perceptions. *Media Psychology, 6,* 11–146.

Auster, C. J., & Ohm, S. C. (2000). Masculinity and femininity in contemporary American society: A reevaluation using the Bem Sex-Role Inventory. *Sex Roles, 43,* 499–528.

Awasthi, A., & Mandal, M. K. (2015). Facial expressions of emotions: Research perspectives. In M. K. Mandal, A. Awasthi, M. K. Mandal, & A. Awasthi (Eds.), *Understanding facial expressions in communication: Cross-cultural and multidisciplinary perspectives* (pp. 1–18). New York: Springer Science + Business Media. doi:10.1007/978-81-322-1934-7_1

Ayoola, A. B., Nettleman, M., & Brewer, J. (2007). Reasons for unprotected intercourse in adult women. *Journal of Women's Health, 16,* 302–310.

Ayotte, B. J., Margrett, J. A., & Hicks-Patrick, J. (2010). Physical activity in middle-aged and young-old adults: The roles of self-efficacy, barriers, outcome expectancies, self-regulatory behaviors and social support. *Journal of Health Psychology, 15*(2), 173–185. doi:10.1177/1359105309342283

Ayres, J., Hopf, T., & Ayres, D. M. (1994). An examination of whether imaging ability enhances the effectiveness of an intervention designed to reduce speech anxiety. *Communication Education, 43*(3), 252–258.

Aziz, S., & Burke, R. J. (2015). Personality factors, workaholism, and heavy work investment. In I. Harpaz, R. Snir, I. Harpaz, R. Snir (Eds.), *Heavy work investment: Its nature, sources, outcomes, and future directions* (pp. 31–46). New York: Routledge/Taylor & Francis Group.

Aziz, S., & Zickar, M. J. (2006). A cluster analysis investigation of workaholism as a syndrome. *Journal of Occupational Health Psychology, 11*(1), 52–62.

Azizli, N., Atkinson, B. E., Baughman, H. M., & Giammarco, E. A. (2015). Relationships between general self-efficacy, planning for the future, and life satisfaction. *Personality and Individual Differences, 82,* 58–60. doi:10.1016/j.paid.2015.03.006

Babiak, P., & Hare, R. D. (2006). *Snakes in suits: When psychopaths go to work.* New York: Regan/HarperCollins.

Bachman, J. G., O'Malley, P. M., Freedman-Doan, P., Trzesniewski, K. H., & Donnellan, M. B. (2011). Adolescent self-esteem: Differences by race/ethnicity, gender, and age. *Self and Identity, 10*(4), 445–473. doi:10.1080/15298861003794538

Back, M. D., Schmukle, S. C., & Egloff, B. (2008). Becoming friends by chance. *Psychological Science, 19*(5), 439–440. doi:10.1111/j.1467-9280.2008.02106.x

Back, M. D., Schmukle, S. C., & Egloff, B. (2010). Why are narcissists so charming at first sight? Decoding the narcissism-popularity link at zero acquaintance. *Journal of Personality and Social Psychology, 98*(1), 132–145. doi:10.1037/a0016338

Backhaus, A., Agha, Z., Maglione, M. L., Repp, A., Ross, B., Zuest, D., . . . Thorp, S. R. (2012). Videoconferencing psychotherapy: A systematic review. *Psychological Services, 9,* 111–131. doi:10.1037/a0027924

Badgett, M. V. L. (2003). Employment and sexual orientation: Disclosure and discrimination in the workplace. In L. D. Garnets & D. C. Kimmel (Eds.), *Psychological perspectives on lesbian, gay, and bisexual experiences* (2nd ed.). New York: Columbia University Press.

Baek, Y. M., Kim, E., & Bae, Y. (2014). My privacy is okay, but theirs is endangered: Why comparative optimism matters in online privacy concerns. *Computers in Human Behavior, 31,* 48–56. doi:10.1016/j.chb.2013.10.010

Bailey, J. M., & Pillard, R. C. (1991). A genetic study of male sexual orientation. *Archives of General Psychiatry, 48,* 1089–1096.

Bailey, J. M., Pillard, R. C., Neale, M. C., & Agyei, Y. (1993). Heritable factors influence sexual orientation in women. *Archives of General Psychiatry, 50,* 217–223.

Bailey, T. C., Eng, W., Frisch, M. B., & Snyder, C. R. (2007). Hope and optimism as related to life satisfaction. *The Journal of Positive Psychology, 2*(3), 168–175. doi:10.1080/17439760701409546

Baillargeon, R. H., Zoccolillo, M., Keenan, K., Cote, S., Persusse, D., Wu, H., Boivin, M., & Tremblay, R. E. (2007). Gender differences in physical aggression: A prospective population-based survey of children before and after 2 years of age. *Developmental Psychology, 43,* 13–26.

Baker, F., Ainsworth, S. R., Dye, J. T., Crammer, C., Thun, M. J., Hoffmann, D., Repace, J. L., Henningfield, J. E., Slade, J., Pinney, J., Shanks, T., Burns, D. M., Connolly, G. N., & Shopland, D. R. (2000). Health risks associated with cigar smoking. *Journal of the American Medical Association, 284,* 735–740.

Balducci, C., Cecchin, M., Fraccaroli, F., & Schaufeli, W. B. (2012). Exploring the relationship between workaholism and workplace aggressive behaviour: The role of job-related emotion. *Personality and Individual Differences.* doi:10.1016/j.paid.2012.05.004

Baldwin, S. A., & Imel, Z. E. (2013). Therapist effects: Findings and methods. In M. J. Lambert (Ed.). *Bergin and Garfield's handbook of psychotherapy and behavior change* (6th ed.). New York: Wiley.

Ball, J. S., & Links, P. S. (2009). Borderline personality disorder and childhood trauma: Evidence for a causal relationship. *Current Psychiatry Reports, 11*(1), 63–68. doi:10.1007/s11920-009-0010-4

Balsam, K. F., Beauchaine, T. P., Mickey, R. M., & Rothblum, E. D. (2005). Mental health of lesbian, gay, bisexual, and heterosexual siblings: Effects of gender, sexual orientation, and family. *Journal of Abnormal Psychology, 114,* 471–476.

Baltazar, M., Hazem, N., Vilarem, E., Beaucousin, V., Picq, J., & Conty, L. (2014). Eye contact elicits bodily self-awareness in human adults. *Cognition, 133*(1), 120–127. doi:10.1016/j.cognition.2014.06.009

Bandura, A. (1986). *Social foundations of thought and action: A social-cognitive theory.* Englewood Cliffs, NJ: Prentice-Hall.

Bandura, A. (1997). *Self-efficacy: The exercise of control.* New York: Freeman.

Bandura, A. (2000). Social cognitive theory: An agentic perspective. *Annual Review of Psychology, 52,* 1–26.

Bandura, A. (2004). Health promotion by social cognitive means. *Health Education & Behavior, 31*(2), 143–164.

Bandura, A. (2012). On the functional properties of perceived self-efficacy revisited. *Journal of Management, 38*(1), 9–44. doi:10.1177/0149206311410606

Bandura, A. (2012). Social cognitive theory. In P. A. Van Lange, A. W. Kruglanski, & E. T. Higgins (Eds.), *Handbook of theories of social psychology, Vol. 1.* Los Angeles: Sage.

Bandura, A. (2013). The role of self-efficacy in goal-based motivation. In E. A. Locke, G. P. Latham (Eds.), *New developments in goal setting and task performance* (pp. 147–157). New York: Routledge/Taylor & Francis Group.

Banks, S., & Dinges, D. F. (2011). Chronic sleep deprivation. In M. H. Kryger, T. Roth, & W. C. Dement (Eds.), *Principles and practice of sleep medicine.* Philadelphia: Elsevier Saunders.

Bänziger, T., Scherer, K. R., Hall, J. A., & Rosenthal, R. (2011). Introducing the MiniPONS: A short multichannel version of the Profile of Nonverbal Sensitivity (PONS). *Journal of Nonverbal Behavior, 35*(3), 189–204. doi:10.1007/s10919-011-0108-3

Barber, B. K. (1994). Cultural, family, and personal contexts of parent-adolescent conflict. *Journal of Marriage and the Family, 56,* 375–386.

Barber, J. P., Muran, C., McCarthy, K. S., & Keefe, J. R. (2013). Research on dynamic therapies. In M. J. Lambert (Ed.). *Bergin and Garfield's handbook of psychotherapy and behavior change* (6th ed.). New York: Wiley.

Barden, J., Rucker, D., & Petty, R. E. (2005). "Saying one thing and doing another": Examining the impact of event order on hypocrisy judgments of others. *Personality and Social Psychology Bulletin, 31,* 1463–1474.

Bargh, J. A. (1997). The automaticity of everyday life. In R. S. Wyer Jr. (Ed.), *Advances in social cognition, Vol. 10.* Mahwah, NJ: Erlbaum.

Bargh, J. A. (1999). The cognitive monster: The case against the controllability of automatic stereotype effects. In S. Chaiken & Y. Trope (Eds.), *Dual process theories in social psychology.* New York: Guilford.

Bargh, J. A., Chen, M., & Burrows, L. (1996). Automaticity of social behavior: Direct effects of trait construct and stereotype activation on action. *Journal of Personality and Social Psychology, 71,* 230–244.

Bargh, J. A., & McKenna, K. Y. A. (2004). The Internet and social life. *Annual Review of Psychology, 55,* 573–590.

Barker, M. J., & Richards, C. (2015). Further genders. In M. J. Barker, C. Richards, C. Richards, M. J. Barker (Eds.), *The Palgrave handbook of the psychology of sexuality and gender* (pp. 166–182). New York: Palgrave Macmillan.

Barlett, D. L., & Steele, J. B. (1979). *Empire: The life, legend and madness of Howard Hughes.* New York: Norton.

Barlow, D. H., Bullis, J. R., Comer, J. S., & Ametaj, A. A. (2013). Evidence-based psychological treatments: an update and a way forward. *Annual Review of Clinical Psychology, 9,* 1–27. doi:10.1146/annurev-clinpsy-050212-185629

Barnes, V. A., Treiber, F., & Davis, H. (2001). The impact of Transcendental Meditation on cardiovascular function at rest and during acute stress in adolescents with high norspeed in old age. *Current Directions in Psychological Science, 6,* 163–169.

Barnett, H. L., Keel, P. K., & Conoscenti, L. M. (2001). Body type preferences in Asian and Caucasian college students. *Sex Roles, 45* (11–12), 867–878.

Barnett, O. W., & LaViolette, A. D. (1993). *It could happen to anyone: Why battered women stay.* Thousand Oaks, CA: Sage.

Barnett, R. C., & Hyde, J. S. (2001). Women, men, work, and family: An expansionist theory. *American Psychologist, 56*(10), 781–796.

Barreto, M., & Ellemers, N. (2013). Sexism in contemporary societies: How it is expressed, perceived, confirmed, and resisted. In M. K. Ryan & N. R Branscombe (Eds.), *The Sage handbook of gender and psychology* (pp. 289–305). Thousand Oaks, CA: Sage.

Barreto, M., Ryan, M. K., & Schmitt, M. T. (2009). *The glass ceiling in the 21st century: Understanding barriers to gender equality.* Washington, DC: American Psychological Association. doi:10.1037/11863-000

Barron, L. G., & Hebl, M. (2011). Sexual orientation: A protected and unprotected class. In M. A. Paludi, C. J. Paludi, E. R. DeSouza, M. A. Paludi, C. J. Paludi, E. R. DeSouza (Eds.), *Praeger handbook on understanding and preventing workplace discrimination, Vols. 1 and 2* (pp. 251–273). Santa Barbara, CA: Praeger/ABC-CLIO.

Barry, B., & Friedman, R. A. (1998). Bargainer characteristics in distributive and integrative negotiation. *Journal of Personality and Social Psychology, 74,* 345–359.

Barsky, A. J. (1988). The paradox of health. *New England Journal of Medicine, 318,* 414–418.

Bartholomew, K. (1990). Avoidance of intimacy: An attachment perspective. *Journal of Social and Personal Relationships, 7,* 47–178.

Bartholomew, K., Cobb, R. J., & Dutton, D. G. (2015). Established and emerging perspectives on violence in intimate relationships. In M. Mikulincer, P. R. Shaver, J. A. Simpson, & J. F. Dovidio (Eds.), *APA handbook of personality and social psychology, Vol. 3: Interpersonal relations* (pp. 605–630). Washington, DC: American Psychological Association. doi:10.1037/14344-022

Bartholow, B. D., Bushman, B. J., & Sestir, M. A. (2006). Chronic violent video game exposure and desensitization to violence: Behavioral and event-related brain potential data. *Journal of Experimental Social Psychology, 42,* 532–539.

Bartone, P., Roland, R., Picano, J., & Williams, T. (2008). Psychological hardiness predicts success in U.S. Army Special Forces candidates. *International Journal of Selections and Assessment, 16*(1), 78–81.

Baruch, Y. (2011). The positive well-being aspects of workaholism in cross cultural perspective: The chocoholism metaphor. *The Career Development International, 16*(6), 572–591. doi:10.1108/13620431111178335

Barutçu Yıldırım, F., & Demir, A. (2015). Breakup adjustment in young adulthood. *Journal of Counseling and Development, 93*(1), 38–44. doi:10.1002/j.1556-6676.2015.00179.x

Bassuk, S. S., & Manson, J. E. (2010). Physical activity and cardiovascular disease prevention in women: A review of the epidemiologic evidence. *Nutrition, Metabolism, and Cardiovascular Disease, 20,* 467–473.

Batalha, L., & Reynolds, K. J. (2013). Gender and personality: Beyond gender stereotypes to social identity and the dynamics of social change. In M. K. Ryan & N. R Branscombe (Eds.), *The Sage handbook of gender and psychology* (pp. 165–182). Thousand Oaks, CA: Sage.

Baucom, D. H., Snyder, D. K., & Abbott, B. V. (2014). Infidelity. In L. Grossman, S. Walfish (Ed.), *Translating psychological research into practice* (pp. 419–426). New York: Springer.

Bauer, I., & Wrosch, C. (2011). Making up for lost opportunities: The protective role of downward social comparisons for coping with regrets across adulthood. *Personality and Social Psychology Bulletin, 37*(2), 215–228. doi:10.1177/0146167210393256

Bauermeister, J. A., Johns, M. M., Pingel, E., Eisenberg, A., Santana, M., & Zimmerman, M. (2011). Measuring love: Sexual minority male youths' ideal romantic characteristics. *Journal of LGBT Issues in Counseling, 5*(2), 102–121. doi:10.1080/15538605.2011.574573

Bauman, S. (2015). Cyberbullying and sexting: School mental health concerns. In R. H. Witte, G. S. Mosley-Howard, R. H. Witte, & G. S. Mosley-Howard (Eds.), Mental health practice in today's schools: Issues and interventions (pp. 241–263). New York: Springer.

Baumeister, R. F. (1984). Choking under pressure: Self-consciousness and paradoxical effects of incentives on skillful performance. *Journal of Personality and Social Psychology, 46*, 610–620.

Baumeister, R. F. (1989). The optimal margin of illusion. *Journal of Social and Clinical Psychology, 8*, 176–189.

Baumeister, R. F. (1995). Disputing the effects of championship pressures and home audiences. *Journal of Personality and Social Psychology, 68*, 644–648.

Baumeister, R. F. (1997). Esteem threat, self-regulatory breakdown, and emotional distress as factors in self-defeating behavior. *Review of General Psychology, 1*, 145–174.

Baumeister, R. F. (1998). The self. In D. T. Gilbert, S. T. Fiske, & G. Lindzey (Eds.), *The handbook of social psychology*. Boston: McGraw-Hill.

Baumeister, R. F., & Alquist, J. L. (2009). Self-regulation as a limited resource: Strength model of control and depletion. In J. P. Forgas, R. F. Baumeister, D. M. Tice, J. P. Forgas, R. F. Baumeister, & D. M. Tice (Eds.), *Psychology of self-regulation: Cognitive, affective, and motivational processes* (pp. 21–33). New York: Psychology Press.

Baumeister, R. F., Bratslavsky, E., Muraven, M., & Tice, D. M. (1998). Ego depletion: Is the active self a limited resource? *Journal of Personality and Social Psychology, 74*(5), 1252–1265.

Baumeister, R. F., & Bushman, B. C. (2011). *Social psychology and human nature* (2nd ed.). Belmont, CA: Wadsworth/Cengage.

Baumeister, R. F., Campbell, J. D., Krueger, J. I., & Vohs, K. D. (2003). Does high self-esteem cause better performance, interpersonal success, happiness, or healthier lifestyles? *Psychological Science in the Public Interest, 4*(1), 1–44.

Baumeister, R. F., Gailliot, M., DeWall, M., & Oaten, M. (2006). Self-regulation and personality: How interventions increase regulatory success, and how depletion moderates the effects of traits on behavior. *Journal of Personality, 74*, 1773–1801.

Baumeister, R. F., Masicampo, E. J., & Twenge, J. M. (2013). The social self. In H. Tennen, J. Suls, I. B. Weiner, H. Tennen, J. Suls, & I. B. Weiner (Eds.), *Handbook of psychology, Vol. 5: Personality and social psychology* (2nd ed., pp. 247–273). Hoboken, NJ: Wiley.

Baumeister, R. F., & Steinhilber, A. (1984). Paradoxical effects of supportive audiences on performance under pressure: The home field disadvantage in sports championships. *Journal of Personality and Social Psychology, 47*, 85–93.

Baumeister, R. F., & Twenge, J. M. (2003). The social self. In T. Millon & M. J. Lerner (Eds.) *Handbook of psychology, Vol. 5: Personality and social psychology.* New York: Wiley.

Baumeister, R. F., & Vonasch, A. J. (2015). Uses of self-regulation to facilitate and restrain addictive behavior. *Addictive Behaviors, 44*, 3–8. doi:10.1016/j.addbeh.2014.09.011

Baumrind, D. (2013). Authoritative parenting revisited: History and current status. In R. E. Larzelere, A. S. Morris, A. W. Harrist, R. E. Larzelere, A. S. Morris, & A. W. Harrist (Eds.), *Authoritative parenting: Synthesizing nurturance and discipline for optimal child development* (pp. 11–34). Washington, DC: American Psychological Association. doi:10.1037/13948-002

Bavelas, J. B., Coates, L., & Johnson, T. (2002). Listener responses as a collaborative process: The role of gaze. *Journal of Communication, 52*(3), 566–580.

Bay-Hinitz, A. K., Peterson, R. F., & Quilitch, H. R. (1994). Cooperative games: A way to modify aggressive and cooperative behaviors in young children. *Journal of Applied Behavior Analysis, 27*, 435–446.

Beall, A. T., & Tracy, J. L. (2013). Women are more likely to wear red or pink at peak fertility. *Psychological Science, 24*(9), 1837–1841. doi:10.1177/0956797613476045

Beaman, R., Wheldall, K., & Kemp, C. (2006). Differential teacher attention to boys and girls in the classroom. *Educational Review, 58*, 339–366.

Beard, K., Stansberry, H., & Wayne, K. (2010). The nature, meaning and measure of teacher flow in elementary schools: A test of rival hypotheses. *Educational Administration Quarterly, 46*(3), 426–458.

Bebbington, P. (2013). The classification and epidemiology of unipolar depression. In M. Power (Ed.), *The Wiley-Blackwell handbook of mood disorders* (2nd ed.). Malden, MA: Wiley-Blackwell.

Bebbington, P. E., & Kuipers, E. (2011). Schizophrenia and psychosocial stress. In D. R. Weinberger & P. Harrison (Eds.), *Schizophrenia* (3rd ed.). Malden, MA: Wiley-Blackwell.

Beck, A. T. (1976). *Cognitive therapy and the emotional disorders.* New York: International Universities Press.

Beck, A. T. (1987). Cognitive therapy. In J. K. Zeig (Ed.), *The evolution of psychotherapy.* New York: Brunner/Mazel.

Beck, A. T. (1997). Cognitive therapy: Reflections. In J. K. Zeig (Ed.), *The evolution of psychotherapy: The third conference*. New York: Brunner/Mazel.

Beck, A. T. (2008). The evolution of the cognitive model of depression and its neurobiological correlates. *American Journal of Psychiatry, 165*, 969–977.

Beck, A. T., & Weishaar, M. E. (2011). Cognitive therapy. In R. J. Corsini & D. Wedding (Eds.), *Current psychotherapies* (9th ed.). Belmont, CA: Brooks/Cole.

Becker, A., & Fay, K. (2006). Sociocultural issues and eating disorders. In S. Wonderlich, J. Mitchell, M. de Zwaan, & H. Steiger (Eds.), *Annual review of eating disorders*. Oxon, England: Radcliffe.

Behar, R. (1991, May 6). The thriving cult of greed and power. *Time*, pp. 50–77.

Behrens, E. L., & Nauta, M. M. (2014). The self-directed search as a stand-alone intervention with college students. *The Career Development Quarterly, 62*(3), 224–238. doi:10.1002/j.2161-0045.2014.00081.x

Beilock, S. (2010). *Choke: What the secrets of the brain reveal about getting it right when you have to.* New York: Free Press.

Bekelman, J. E., Li, Y., & Gross, C. P. (2003). Scope and impact of financial conflicts of interests in biomedical research. *Journal of the American Medical Association, 289*, 454–465.

Bell, A. P., Weinberg, M. S., & Hammersmith, K. S. (1981). *Sexual preference—Its development in men and women.* Bloomington: Indiana University Press.

Bell, B. G., & Grubin, D. (2010). Functional magnetic resonance imaging may promote theoretical understanding of the polygraph test. *Journal of Forensic Psychiatry & Psychology, 21*(1), 52–65. doi:10.1080/14789940903220676

Belmore, S. M. (1987). Determinants of attention during impression formation. *Journal of Experimental Psychology: Learning, Memory, and Cognition, 13*, 480–489.

Belsky, J. (2009). Parenthood, transition to. In H. T. Reis & S. Sprecher (Eds.), *Encyclopedia of human relationships: Vol. 3* (pp. 1204–1207). Los Angeles: Sage Reference.

Bem, S. L. (1975, September). Androgyny vs. the tight little lives of fluffy women and chesty men. *Psychology Today*, pp. 58–62.

Bem, S. L. (1983). Gender schema theory and its implications for child development: Raising gender-aschematic children in a gender-schematic society. *Signs, 8*, 598–616.

Bem, S. L. (1993). The lenses of gender: *Transforming the debate on sexual inequality.* New Haven, CT: Yale University Press.

Bendall, S., Jackson, H. J., & Hulbert, C. A. (2010). Childhood trauma and psychosis: Review of the evidence and directions for psychological interventions. *Australian Psychologist, 45*, 299–306. doi:10.1080/00050060903443219

Bender, D. S., Skodol, A. E., Dyck, I. R., Markowitz, J. C., Shea, M. T., Yen, S., . . . Grilo, C. M. (2007). Ethnicity and mental health treatment utilization by patients with personality disorders. *Journal of Consulting and Clinical Psychology, 75*, 992–999.

Ben-Ezra, M. (2004). Trauma in antiquity: 4000 year old post-traumatic reactions? *Stress and Health, 20*, 121–125.

Benka, J., Nagyova, I., Rosenberger, J., Macejova, Z., Lazurova, I., Van der Klink, J., Groothoff, J., & Van Dijk, J. (2014). Is coping self-efficacy related to psychological distress in early and established rheumatoid arthritis patients? *Journal of Developmental and Physical Disabilities, 26*(3), 285–297. doi:10.1007/s10882-013-9364-y

Benson, H. (1975). *The relaxation response* (1st ed.). New York: Morrow.

Benson, L. S., Martins, S. L., & Whitaker, A. K. (2015). Correlates of heterosexual anal intercourse among women in the 2006–2010 National Survey of Family Growth. *Journal Of Sexual Medicine, 12*(8), 1746–1752. doi:10.1111/jsm.12961

Bentall, R. P. (2009). *Doctoring the mind: Is our current treatment of mental illness really any good?* New York: New York University Press.

Bentall, R. P., Wickham, S., Shevlin, M., & Varese, F. (2012). Do specific early-life adversities lead to specific symptoms of psychosis? A study from the 2007 Adult Psychiatric Morbidity Survey. *Schizophrenia Bulletin, 38*, 734–740. doi:10.1093/schbul/sbs049

Berdahl, J. L. (2007). The sexual harassment of uppity women. *Journal of Applied Psychology, 92*, 425–437.

Berdahl, J. L., & Moore, C. (2006). Workplace harassment: Double jeopardy for minority women. *Journal of Applied Psychology, 91*, 426–436.

Berg, J. M., Dutton, J. E., & Wrzesniewski, A. (2013). Job crafting and meaningful work. In B. J. Dik, Z. S. Byrne, M. F. Steger (Eds.), *Purpose and meaning in the workplace* (pp. 81–104). Washington, DC: American Psychological Association. doi:10.1037/14183-005

Berg, V., Lummaa, V., Lahdenperä, M., Rotkirch, A., & Jokela, M. (2014). Personality and long-term reproductive success measured by the number of grandchildren. *Evolution and Human Behavior, 35*, 533-539. doi:10.1016/j.evolhumbehav.2014.07.006

Berger, L. K., Zane, N., & Hwang, W. (2014). Therapist ethnicity and treatment orientation differences in multicultural counseling competencies. *Asian American Journal of Psychology, 5*(1), 53–65. doi:10.1037/a0036178

Berger, R. (1998). The experience and issues of gay step families. *Journal of Divorce and Remarriage, 29*(3–4), 93–102. doi:10.1300/J087v29n03_06

Bergsma, A. (2008). Do self-help books help? *Journal of Happiness Studies, 9*(3), 341–360. doi:10.1007/s10902-006-9041-2

Berkowitz, L. (1989). Frustration-aggression hypothesis: Examination and reformulation. *Psychological Bulletin, 106*, 59–73.

Berman, M. G., Jonides, J., & Kaplan, S. (2008). The cognitive benefits of interacting with nature. *Psychological Science, 19*, 1207–1212.

Berman, M. G., Kross, E., Krpan, K. M., Askren, M. K., Burson, A., Deldin, P. J., . . . Jonides, J. (2012). Interacting with nature improves cognition and affect for individuals with depression. *Journal of Affective Disorders.* doi:10.1016/j.jad.2012.03.012

Bernieri, F. J., & Petty, K. N. (2011). The influence of handshakes on first impression accuracy. *Social Influence, 6*(2), 78–87. doi:10.1080/15534510.2011.566706

Berry, D., Sheehan, R., Heschel, R., Knafl, K., Melkus, G., & Grey, M. (2004). Family-based interventions for childhood obesity: A review. *Journal of Family Nursing, 10*, 429–449.

Berscheid, E., Dion, K., Walster, E., & Walster, G. (1971). Physical attractiveness and dating choice: A test of the matching hypothesis. *Journal of Personality and Social Psychology, 7*, 173–189.

Berthoud, H., & Morrison, C. (2008). The brain, appetite, and obesity. *Annual Review of Psychology, 59*, 55–92.

Bertrams, A., Englert, C., Dickhäuser, O., & Baumeister, R. F. (2013). Role of self-control strength in the relation between anxiety and cognitive performance. *Emotion, 13*(4), 668–680. doi:10.1037/a0031921

Berzon, B. (2004). *Permanent partners: Building gay and lesbian relationships that last.* New York: The Penguin Group.

Betensky, J. D., Contrada, R. J., & Glass, D. C. (2012). Psychosocial factors in cardiovascular disease: Emotional states, conditions, and attributes. In A. Baum, T. A Revenson, & J. Singer (Eds.), *Handbook of health psychology* (pp. 637–662). New York: Guilford.

Bettelheim, B. (1967). *The empty fortress.* New York: Free Press.

Betz, N. E. (1993). Women's career development. In F. L. Denmark & M. A. Paludi (Eds.), *Psychology of women: A handbook of issues and theories.* Westport, CT: Greenwood Press.

Betz, N. E. (2006). Women's career development. In J. Worell & C. D. Goodheart (Eds.), *Handbook of girls' and women's psychological health.* New York: Oxford University Press.

Betz, N. E. (2008). Women's career development. In F. L. Denmark, M. A. Paludi, F. L. Denmark, M. A. Paludi (Eds.), *Psychology of women: A handbook of issues and theories* (2nd ed., pp. 717–752). Westport, CT: Praeger/Greenwood.

Betz, N. E., & Klein, K. L. (1996). Relationships among measures of career self-efficacy, generalized self-efficacy, and global self-esteem. *Journal of Career Assessment, 4*(3), 285–298.

Beusterien, K. M., Davis, E. A., Flood, R., Howard, K., & Jordan, J. (2008). HIV patient insight on adhering to medication: A qualitative analysis. *AIDS Care, 20,* 251–259.

Beutler, L. E. (2002). The dodo bird is extinct. *Clinical Psychology: Science & Practice, 9*(1), 30–34.

Beutler, L. E., Bongar, B., & Shurkin, J. N. (2001). *A consumers guide to psychotherapy.* New York: Oxford University Press.

Beutler, L. E., Malik, M., Alimohamed, S., Harwood, T. M., Talebi, H., Noble, S., & Wong, E. (2004). Therapist variables. In M. J. Lambert (Ed.), *Bergin and Garfield's handbook of psychotherapy and behavior change.* New York: Wiley.

Bhagwagar, Z., & Heninger, (2009). Antidepressants. In M. C. Gelder, N. C. Andreasen, J. J. López-Ibor, Jr., & J. R. Geddes (Eds.), *New Oxford textbook of psychiatry, Vol. 1* (2nd ed.). New York: Oxford University Press.

Bhargava, S., Kassam, K. S., & Loewenstein, G. (2014). A reassessment of the defense of parenthood. *Psychological Science, 25,* 299–302. doi:10.1177/0956797613503348

Bhasin, T., & Schendel, D. (2007). Sociodemographic risk factors for autism in a U.S. metropolitan area. *Journal of Autism and Developmental Disorders, 37,* 667–677.

Bhullar, N., Surman, G., & Schutte, N. S. (2015). Dispositional gratitude mediates the relationship between a past-positive temporal frame and well-being. *Personality and Individual Differences, 76,* 52–55. doi:10.1016/j.paid.2014.11.025

Bianchi, S., Milkie, M. A., Sayer, L. C., & Robinson, J. P. (2000). Is anyone doing the housework? Trends in the gender division of household labor. *Social Forces, 79*(1), 191–228.

Biernat, M., & Billings, L. S. (2001). Standards, expectancies and social comparison. In A. Tesser & N. Schwarz (Eds.), *Blackwell handbook of social psychology: Intraindividual processes.* Malden, MA: Blackwell.

Bifulco, A. (2013). Psychosocial models and issues in major depression. In M. Power (Ed.), *The Wiley-Blackwell handbook of mood disorders* (2nd ed.). Malden, MA: Wiley-Blackwell.

Billedo, C. J., Kerkhof, P., & Finkenauer, C. (2015). The use of social networking sites for relationship maintenance in long-distance and geographically close romantic relationships. *Cyberpsychology, Behavior, and Social Networking, 18*(3), 152–157. doi:10.1089/cyber.2014.0469

Birtel, M. D., & Crisp, R. J. (2012). 'Treating' prejudice: An exposure-therapy approach to reducing negative reactions toward stigmatized groups. *Psychological Science, 23*(11), 1379-1386. doi:10.1177/0956797612443838

Bjork, R. A., Dunlosky, J., & Kornell, N. (2013). Self-regulated learning: Beliefs, techniques, and illusions. *Annual Review of Psychology, 64,* 417–444.

Blaine, B., & Crocker, J. (1993). Self-esteem and self-serving biases in reaction to positive and negative events: An integrative review. In R. F. Baumeister (Ed.), *Self-esteem: The puzzle of low self-regard.* New York : Plenum.

Blair, C., Granger, D. A., Willoughby, M., Mills-Koonce, R., Cox, M., Greenberg, M. T., . . . Fortunato, C. K. (2011). Salivary cortisol mediates effects of poverty and parenting on executive functions in early childhood. *Child Development, 82*(6), 1970–1984. doi:10.1111/j.1467-8624.2011.01643.x

Blair, S. L. (2013). The division of household labor. In G. W. Peterson, K. R. Bush, G. W. Peterson, K. R. Bush (Eds.), *Handbook of marriage and the family* (3rd ed., pp. 613–635). New York: Springer Science + Business Media. doi:10.1007/978-1-4614-3987-5_25

Blair, S. N., Kohl, H. W., Paffenbarger, R. S., Clark, D. G., Cooper, K. H., & Gibbons, L. W. (1989). Physical fitness and all-cause mortality: A prospective study of healthy men and women. *Journal of the American Medical Association, 262,* 2395–2401.

Blair-Loy, M., & DeHart, G. (2003). Family and careeer trajectories among African American female attorneys. *Journal of Family Issues, 24,* 908–933.

Blakemore, J. E. O. (2003). Children's beliefs about violating gender norms: Boys shouldn't look like girls, and girls shouldn't act like boys. *Sex Roles, 48*(9/10), 411–419.

Blankenship, K. L., & Wegener, D. T. (2008). Opening the mind to close it: Considering a message in light of important values increases message processing and later resistance to change. *Journal of Personality and Social Psychology, 94*(2), 196–213.

Blanton, H., Buunk, B. P., Gibbons, F. X., & Kuyper, H. (1999). When better-than-others compare upward: Choice of comparison and comparative evaluation as independent predictors of academic performance. *Journal of Personality and Social Psychology, 76,* 420–430.

Blashfield, R. K., Keeley, J. W., Flanagan, E. H., & Miles, S. R. (2014). The cycle of classification: DSM-I through DSM-5. *Annual Review of Clinical Psychology, 10,* 25–51. doi:10.1146/annurev-clinpsy-032813-153639

Blass, T. (2012). A cross-cultural comparison of studies of obedience using the Milgram paradigm: A review. *Social and Personality Psychology Compass, 6*(2), 196–205. doi:10.1111/j.1751-9004.2011.00417.x

Bleakley, A., Hennessy, M., & Fishbein, M. (2011). A model of adolescents' seeking of sexual content in their media choices. *Journal of Sex Research, 48*(4), 309-315. doi:10.1080/00224499.2010.497985

Bloch, S., & Harari, E. (2009). Family therapy in the adult psychiatric setting. In M. C. Gelder, N. C. Andreasen, J. J. López-Ibor, Jr., & J. R. Geddes (Eds.), *New Oxford textbook of psychiatry, Vol. 1* (2nd ed.). New York: Oxford University Press.

Blume, B. D., Baldwin, T. T., & Ryan, K. C. (2013). Communication apprehension: A barrier to students' leadership, adaptability, and multicultural appreciation. *Academy of Management Learning & Education, 12*(2), 158–172.

Blume, B. D., Dreher, G. F., & Baldwin, T. T. (2010). Examining the effects of communication apprehension within assessment centres. *Journal of Occupational and Organizational Psychology, 83*(3), 663–671. doi:10.1348/096317909X463652

Blustein, D. L., Coutinho, M. N., Murphy, K. A., Backus, F., & Catraio, C. (2011). Self and social class in career theory and practice. In P. J. Hartung, L. M. Subich, P. J. Hartung, L. M. Subich (Eds.), *Developing self in work and career: Concepts, cases, and contexts* (pp. 213–229). Washington, DC: American Psychological Association. doi:10.1037/12348-013

Blustein, D. L., Kozan, S., Connors-Kellgren, A., & Rand, B. (2015). Social class and career intervention. In P. J. Hartung, M. L. Savickas, W. B. Walsh, P. J. Hartung, M. L. Savickas, W. B. Walsh (Eds.), *APA handbook of career intervention, Vol. 1: Foundations* (pp. 243–257). Washington, DC: American Psychological Association. doi:10.1037/14438-014

Boase, J., & Wellman, B. (2006). Personal relationships: On and off the internet. In A. L. Vangelisti & D. Perlman (Eds.), *The Cambridge handbook of personal relationships.* New York: Cambridge University Press.

Bobek, B. L., & Robbins, S. B. (2005). Counseling for career transition: Career pathing, job loss, and reentry. In S. D. Brown & R. W. Lent (Eds.), *Career development and counseling: Putting theory and research to work.* New York: Wiley.

Bockting, W. O. (2014). Transgender identity development. In D. L. Tolman, L. M. Diamond, J. A. Bauermeister, W. H. George, J. G. Pfaus, & L. M. Ward (Eds.), *APA handbook of sexuality and psychology* (pp. 739–758). Washington, DC: American Psychological Association. doi:10.1037/14193-024

Bodenhausen, G. V., & Richeson, J. A. (2010). Prejudice, stereotyping, and discrimination. In R. F. Baumeister & E. J. Finkel (Eds.), *Advanced social psychology: The state of the science* (pp. 341–383). New York: Oxford University Press.

Bodenmann, G., Charvoz, L., Bradbury, T. N., Bertoni, A., Iafrate, R., Giuliani, C., . . . Behling, J. (2007). The role of stress in divorce: A three-nation retrospective study. *Journal of Social and Personal Relationships, 24*(5), 707–728. doi:10.1177/0265407507081456

Bogaert, A. F., & Skorska, M. (2011). Sexual orientation, fraternal birth order, and the maternal immune hypothesis: A review. *Frontiers in Neuroendocrinology, 32*(2), 247–254. doi:10.1016/j.yfrne.2011.02.004

Bögels, S. M., & Voncken, M. (2008). Social skills training versus cognitive therapy for social anxiety disorder characterized by fear of blushing, trembling, or sweating. *International Journal of Cognitive Therapy, 1*(2), 138–150. doi:10.1521/ijct.2008.1.2.138

Boldrini, M., Santiago, A. N., Hen, R., Dwork, A. J., Rosoklija, G. B., Tamir, H., Arango, V., & Mann, J. J. (2013). Hippocampal granule neuron number and denate gyrus volume in antidepressant-treated and untreated major depression. *Neuropsychopharmacology, 38,* 1068–1077. doi:10.1038/npp.2013.5

Boles, D. B. (2005). A large-sample study of sex differences in functional cerebral lateralization. *Journal of Clinical and Experimental Neuropsychology, 27,* 759–768.

Bolger, N. (1990). Coping as a personality process: A prospective study. *Journal of Personality and Social Psychology, 59,* 525–537.

Bolino, M. C., & Turnley, W. H. (2005). The personal costs of citizenship behavior: The relationship between individual initiative and role overload, job stress, and work-family conflict. *Journal of Applied Psychology, 90*(4), 740–748.

Bolino, M. C., Klotz, A. C., & Daniels, D. (2014). The impact of impression management over time. *Journal of Managerial Psychology, 29*(3), 266–284. doi:10.1108/JMP-10-2012-0290

Bolkan, C., Hooker, K., & Coehlo, D. (2015). Possible selves and depressive symptoms in later life. *Research on Aging, 37*(1), 41–62. doi: 10.1177/0164027513520557

Bolles, R. N. (2007). *The 2007 what color is your parachute? A practical manual for job-hunters and career-changers.* Berkeley, CA: Ten Speed Press.

Bolles, R. N. (2014). *What color is your parachute? 2015: A practical manual for job-hunters and career-changers.* New York: Ten Speed Press.

Bonanno, G. A. (2009). *The other side of sadness: What the new science of bereavement tells us about life after loss.* New York: Basic Books.

Bonanno, G. A., & Burton, C. L. (2013). Regulatory flexibility: An individual differences perspective on coping and emotion regulation. *Perspectives on Psychological Science, 8*(6), 591–612. doi:10.1177/1745691613504116

Bond, J. T., Thompson, C., Galinsky, E., & Prottas, D. (2003). *The 2002 national study of the changing workforce.* New York: Families and Work Institute.

Bonebright, C. A., Clay, D. L., & Ankenmann, R. D. (2000). The relationship of workaholism with work-life conflict, life satisfaction, and purpose in life. *Journal of Counseling Psychology, 47,* 469–477.

Bonetti, L., Campbell, M., & Gilmore, L. (2010). The relationship of loneliness and social anxiety with children's and adolescents' online communication. *Cyberpsychology, Behavior, and Social Networking, 13*(3), 279–285. doi:10.1089/cyber.2009.0215

Bono, G., Emmons, R. A., & McCullough, M. E. (2004). Gratitude in practice and the practice of gratitude. In P. A. Linley & S. Joseph (Eds.), *Positive psychology in practice* (pp. 464–484). Hoboken, NJ: Wiley.

Bookwala, J. (2009). Couples in middle age. In H. T. Reis & S. Sprecher (Eds.), *Encyclopedia of human relationships: Vol. 2* (pp. 340–343). Los Angeles: Sage Reference.

Boren, J. P. (2014). The relationships between co-rumination, social support, stress, and burnout among working adults. *Management Communication Quarterly, 28*(1), 3–25. doi:10.1177/0893318913509283

Bornstein, M. H., Jager, J., & Steinberg, L. D. (2013). Adolescents, parents, friends/peers: A relationships model. In R. M. Lerner, M. A. Easterbrooks, J. Mistry, & I. B. Weiner (Eds.), *Handbook of psychology, Vol. 6: Developmental psychology.* New York: Wiley.

Bornstein, R. F., Denckla, C. A., & Chung, W.-J. (2013). Psychodynamic models of personality. In H. Tennen, J. Suls, & I. B. Weiner (Eds.), *Handbook of psychology, Vol. 5: Personality and social psychology* (2nd ed., pp. 43–64). Hoboken, NJ: Wiley.

Borys, S., & Perlman, D. (1985). Gender differences in loneliness. *Personality and Social Psychology Bulletin, 11,* 63–74.

Bosker, Bianca. (2012). Fortune 500 list boasts more female CEOs than ever before. Retrieved from www.huffingtonpost.com/2012/05/07/fortune-500-female-ceos_n_1495734.html

Bosson, J. K., Vandello, J. A., & Caswell, T. A. (2013). Precious manhood. In M. K. Ryan & N. R Branscombe (Eds.), *The Sage handbook of gender and psychology* (pp. 115–130). Thousand Oaks, CA: Sage.

Bouchard, C. (2002). Genetic influences on body weight. In C. G. Fairburn & K. D. Brownell (Eds.), *Eating disorders and obesity: A comprehensive handbook* (2nd ed., pp. 16–21). New York: Guilford.

Bouchard, G. (2014). How do parents react when their children leave home? An integrative review. *Journal of Adult Development, 21*(2), 69–79. doi:10.1007/s10804-013-9180-8

Bovornusvakool, W., Vodanovich, S. J., Ariyabuddhiphongs, K., & Ngamake, S. T. (2012). Examining the antecedents and consequences of workaholism. *The Psychologist-Manager Journal, 15*(1), 56–70. doi:10.1080/10887156.2012.649994

Bower, G. H. (1970). Analysis of a mnemonic device. *American Scientist, 58,* 496–499.

Bower, S. A., & Bower, G. H. (1991). *Asserting yourself: A practical guide for positive change* (2nd ed.). Reading, MA: Addison-Wesley.

Bower, S. A., & Bower, G. H. (2004). *Asserting yourself: A practical guide for positive change* (updated ed.). Cambridge, MA: Da Capo Press/Perseus.

Bowes-Sperry, L., & Tata, J. (1999). A multiperspective framework of sexual harassment. In G. N. Powell (Ed.), *Handbook of gender and work.* Thousand Oaks, CA: Sage.

Bowlby, J. (1980). *Attachment and loss, Vol. 3: Loss: Sadness and depression.* New York: Basic Books.

Boyce, C. J., Brown, G. A., & Moore, S. C. (2010). Money and happiness: Rank of income, not income, affects life satisfaction. *Psychological Science, 21*(4), 471–475.

Boyczuk, A. M., & Fletcher, P. C. (2015). The ebbs and flows: Stresses of sandwich generation caregivers. *Journal of Adult Development.* doi:10.1007/s10804-015-9221-6

Boyer, S. L., Edmondson, D. R., Artis, A. B., & Fleming, D. (2014). Self-directed learning: A tool for lifelong learning. *Journal of Marketing Education, 36*(1), 20–32. doi:10.1177/0273475313494010

Boyle, M. (2007). The problem with diagnosis. *The Psychologist, 20,* 290–292.

Boysen, G. A., & VanBergen, A. (2013). A review of published research on adult dissociative identity disorder: 2000–2010. *Journal of Nervous and Mental Disease, 201*(1), 5–11. doi:10.1097/NMD.0b013e31827aaf81

Bradbury, T. N., Campbell, S. M., & Fincham, F. D. (1995). Longitudinal and behavioral analysis of masculinity and femininity in marriage. *Journal of Personality and Social Psychology, 68*(2), 328–341.

Bradfield, J., Taal, H., Timpson, N., Scherag, A., Lecoeur, C., Warrington, N., . . . Early Growth Genetics Consortium. (2012). A genome-wide association meta-analysis identifies new childhood obesity loci. *Nature Genetics, 44*(5), 526–531. doi: 10.1038/ng.2247

Bradford, A., & Schwartz, L. (2014). Inhibited sexual desire in women. In L. Grossman, S. Walfish, (Eds.), *Translating psychological research into practice* (pp. 427–433). New York: Springer.

Braff, D. L., Ryan, J., Rissling, A. J., & Carpenter, W. T. (2013). Lack of use in the literature from the last 20 years supports dropping traditional schizophrenia subtypes from DSM-5 and ICD-11. *Schizophrenia Bulletin, 39,* 751–753. doi:10.1093/schbul/sbt068

Brajša-Žganec, A., Merkaš, M., & Šverko, I. (2011). Quality of life and leisure activities: How do leisure activities contribute to subjective well-being? *Social Indicators Research, 102*(1), 81–91. doi:10.1007/s11205-010-9724-2

Brambilla, M., Ravenna, M., & Hewstone, M. (2012). Changing stereotype content through mental imagery: Imagining intergroup contact promotes stereotype change. *Group Processes & Intergroup Relations, 15*(3), 305–315. doi:10.1177/1368430211427574

Bramlett, M. D., & Mosher, W. D. (2002). Cohabitation, marriage, divorce, and remarriage in the United States. *Vital Health Statistics, 23*(22).

Brandt, M. J. (2011). Sexism and gender inequality across 57 societies. *Psychological Science, 22*(11), 14131418. doi:10.1177/0956797611420445

Brandts, J., Groenert, V., & Rott, C. (2015). The impact of advice on women's and men's selection into competition. *Management Science, 61*(5), 1018–1035. doi:10.1287/mnsc.2013.1877

Brannon, L. (2005). *Gender: Psychological perspectives.* Boston: Allyn & Bacon.

Brannon, R. (1976). The male sex role: Our culture's blueprint of manhood, and what it's done for us lately. In D. David & R. Brannon (Eds.), *The forty-nine percent majority.* Reading, MA: Addison-Wesley.

Brannon, T. N., Markus, H. R., & Taylor, V. J. (2015). "'Two souls, two thoughts,' two self-schemas: Double consciousness can have positive academic consequences for African Americans. *Journal of Personality And Social Psychology, 108*(4), 586–609. doi:10.1037/a0038992

Brassard, A., Péloquin, K., Dupuy, E., Wright, J., & Shaver, P. R. (2012). Romantic attachment insecurity predicts sexual dissatisfaction in couples seeking marital therapy. *Journal of Sex and Marital Therapy, 38*(3), 245–262. doi:10.1080/0092623X.2011.606881

Braunstein-Bercovitz, H., Benjamin, B. A., Asor, S., & Lev, M. (2012). Insecure attachment and career indecision: Mediating effects of anxiety and pessimism. *Journal of Vocational Behavior, 81*(2), 236–244. doi:10.1016/j.jvb.2012.07.009

Braver, S. L., & Lamb, M. E. (2013). Marital dissolution. In G. W. Peterson, K. R. Bush, G. W. Peterson, K. R. Bush (Eds.), *Handbook of marriage and the family* (3rd ed., pp. 487–516). New York: Springer Science + Business Media. doi:10.1007/978-1-4614-3987-5_21

Bray, J. H. (2009). Remarriage. In H. T. Reis & S. Sprecher (Eds.), *Encyclopedia of human relationships: Vol. 3* (pp. 1359–1363). Los Angeles: Sage Reference.

Bredt, B. M., Higuera-Alhino, D., Hebert, S. J., McCune, J. M., & Abrams, D. I. (2002). Short-term effects of cannabinoids on immune phenotype and function in HIV-1-infected patients. *Journal of Clinical Pharmacology, 42,* 90S–96S.

Breggin, P. R. (1991). *Toxic psychiatry.* New York: St. Martin's Press.

Breggin, P. R. (2008). *Medication madness: A psychiatrist exposes the dangers of mood-altering medications.* New York: St. Martin's Press.

Brehm, J. W. (1956). Postdecision changes in the desirability of alternatives. *Journal of Abnormal and Social Psychology, 52,* 384–389.

Brenes, G. A., Ingram, C. W., Danhauer, S. C. (2012). Telephone-delivered psychotherapy for late-life anxiety. *Psychological Services, 9,* 219–220. doi:10.1037/a0025950

Brennan, K. A., Clark, C. L., & Shaver, P. R. (1998). Self-report measurement of adult attachment: An integrative overview. In J. A. Simpson & W. S. Rholes (Eds.), *Attachment theory and close relationships.* New York: Guilford.

Breslin, F. C., & Mustard, C. (2003). Factors influencing the impact of unemployment on mental health among young and older adults in a longitudinal, population-based survey. *Scandinavian Journal of Work, Environment & Health, 29*(1), 5–14.

Brewer, M. B. (2007). The importance of being we: Human nature and intergroup relations. *American Psychologist, 62,* 726–738.

Brewer, M. B., & Brown, R. J. (1998). Inter-group relations. In D. T. Gilbert, S. T. Fiske, & G. Lindzey (Eds.), *The handbook of social psychology, Vol. 2* (4th ed.). New York: McGraw-Hill.

Brickman, P., Coates, D., & Janoff-Bulman, R. (1978). Lottery winners and accident victims: Is happiness relative? *Journal of Personality and Social Psychology, 36,* 917–927.

Bridge, J. A., Iyengar, S., Salary, C. B., Barbe, R. P., Birmaher, B., Pincus, H. A., . . . Brent, D. A. (2007). Clinical response and risk for reported suicidal ideation and suicide attempts in pediatric antidepressant treatment: A meta-analysis of randomized controlled trials. *Journal of the American Medical Association, 297,* 1683–1969.

Bridges, K. R., & Roig, M. (1997). Academic procrastination and irrational thinking: A re-examination with context controlled. *Personality & Individual Differences, 22,* 941–944.

Bridgett, D. J., Burt, N. M., Edwards, E. S., & Deater-Deckard, K. (2015). Intergenerational transmission of self-regulation: A multidisciplinary review and integrative conceptual framework. *Psychological Bulletin, 141*(3), 602–654. doi:10.1037/a0038662

Brinthaupt, T. M., & Shin, C. M. (2001). The relationship of academic cramming to the flow experience. *College Student Journal, 35,* 457–471.

Briton, N. J., & Hall, J. A. (1995). Beliefs about female and male nonverbal communication. *Sex Roles, 32*(1-2), 79–90.

Britton, B. K., & Tesser, A. (1991). Effects of time-management practices on college grades. *Journal of Educational Psychology, 83,* 405–410.

Brody, L. R., & Hall, J. A. (2010). Gender, emotion, and socialization. In J. C. Chrisler & D. R. McCreary (Eds.), *Handbook of gender research in psychology, Vol. 1* (pp. 429–454). New York: Springer.

Brody, S., & Costa, R. M. (2009). Satisfaction (sexual, life, relationship, and mental health) is associated directly with penile and vaginal intercourse, but inversely with other sexual behavior frequencies. *Journal of Sexual Medicine, 6,* 1947–1954.

Brondolo, E., ver Halen, N. B., Libby, D., & Pencille, M. (2011). Racism as a psychosocial stressor. In R. J. Contrada & A. Baum (Eds.), *The handbook of stress science: Biology, psychology, and health* (pp. 167–184). New York: Springer.

Brookes, R., Lehman, T. C., Maguire, S., Mitchell, P., Mejia, V. A., Johnson Aramaki, T., & Raboni, E. M. (2010). Real life. Real talk. Creating engagement in sexual and reproductive health among parents, teens, families, and communities. *Social Marketing Quarterly, 16*(1), 52–69. doi:10.1080/15245000903551839

Brooks, G. (2010). The crisis of masculinity. In *Beyond the crisis of masculinity: A transtheoretical model for male-friendly therapy* (pp. 13–22). Washington, DC: American Psychological Association. doi:10.1037/12073-001

Brotheridge, C. M., & Grandey, A. A. (2002). Emotional labor and burnout: Comparing two perspectives of "people work." *Journal of Vocational Behavior, 60,* 17–39.

Brotto, L. A., & Smith, K. B. (2014). Sexual desire and pleasure. In D. L. Tolman, L. M. Diamond, J. A. Bauermeister, W. H. George, J. G. Pfaus, L. M. Ward (Eds.), *APA handbook of sexuality and psychology* (pp. 205–244). Washington, DC: American Psychological Association. doi:10.1037/14193-008

Brotto, L. A., Bitzer, J., Laan, E., Leiblum, S., & Luria, M. (2010). Women's sexual desire and arousal disorders. *Journal of Sexual Medicine, 7,* 586–614. doi:10.1111.j.17436109.2009.01630.x

Brown, A. S., & Derkits, E. J. (2010). Prenatal infection and schizophrenia: A review of epidemiologic and translational studies. *American Journal of Psychiatry, 167*(3), 261–280. doi:10.1176/appi.ajp.2009.09030361

Brown, B. (2015). *Rising strong.* New York: Spiegel & Grau.

Brown, C. G. (2012). A systematic review of the relationship between self-efficacy and burnout in teachers. *Educational and Child Psychology, 29*(4), 47–63.

Brown, J. D. (2012). Understanding the better than average effect: Motives (still) matter. *Personality And Social Psychology Bulletin, 38*(2), 209–219. doi:10.1177/0146167211432763

Brown, J. D., & Marshall, M. A. (2006). The three faces of self-esteem. In M. H. Kernis (Ed.), *Self-esteem issues and answers: A sourcebook of current perspectives* (pp. 4–9). New York: Psychology Press.

Brown, J. M., Stewart, J. C., Stump, T. E., & Callahan, C. M. (2011). Risk of coronary heart disease events over 15 years among older adults with depressive symptoms. *The American Journal of Geriatric Psychiatry, 19*(8), 721–729.

Brown, K., & Holt, M. (2011). Experiential processing and the integration of bright and dark sides of the human psyche. In K. M. Sheldon, T. B. Kashdan & M. F. Steger (Eds.), *Designing positive psychology: Taking stock and moving forward* (pp. 147–159). New York: Oxford University Press. doi:10.1093/acprof:oso/9780195373585.003.0010

Brown, T. T., & Dobs, A. S. (2002). Endocrine effects of marijuana. *Journal of Clinical Pharmacology, 42,* 97S–102S.

Browne, A. (1993a). Family violence and homelessness: The relevance of trauma histories in the lives of homeless women. *American Journal of Orthopsychiatry, 63,* 370–384.

Brownell, K. D., & Wadden, T. A. (2000). Obesity. In B. J. Sadock & V. A. Sadock (Eds.), *Kaplan and Sadock's comprehensive textbook of psychiatry* (7th ed.). Philadelphia: Lippincott/Williams & Wilkins.

Brown-Iannuzzi, J. L., Adair, K. C., Payne, B. K., Richman, L. S., & Fredrickson, B. L. (2014). Discrimination hurts, but mindfulness may help: Trait mindfulness moderates the relationship between perceived discrimination and depressive symptoms. *Personality and Individual Differences, 56,* 201–205. doi:10.1016/j.paid.2013.09.015

Brunet, P. M., Schmidt, L. A. (2007). Is shyness context specific? Relation between shyness and online disclosure. *Journal of Research in Personality, 41,* 938–945.

Bryant, F. (1989) A four-factor model of perceived control: Avoiding, coping, obtaining, and savoring. *Journal of Personality, 57,* 773–797.

Bryant, F. B., & Veroff, J. (2007). *Savoring: A new model of positive experience.* Mahwah, NJ: Erlbaum.

Buchanan, C. M., & Hughes, J. L. (2009). Construction of social reality during early adolescence: Can expecting storm and stress increase real or perceived storm and stress? *Journal of Research on Adolescence, 19*(2), 261–285.

Buchwald, H., Avidor, Y., Braunwald, E., Jensen, M. D., Pories, W., Fahrbach, K., & Schoelles, K. (2004). Bariatric surgery: A systematic review and meta-analysis. *Journal of the American Medical Association, 292,* 1724–1737.

Buck, A. A., & Neff, L. A. (2012). Stress spillover in early marriage: The role of self-regulatory depletion. *Journal of Family Psychology, 26*(5), 698–708. doi:10.1037/a0029260

Buck, R., & Miller, M. (2015). Beyond facial expression: Spatial distance as a factor in the communication of discrete emotions. In A. Kostić, D. Chadee, A. Kostić, & D. Chadee (Eds.), *The social psychology of nonverbal communication* (pp. 173–197). New York: Palgrave Macmillan.

Buckingham, J. T., & Alicke, M. D. (2002). The influence of individual versus aggregate social comparison and the presence of others on self–evaluations. *Journal of Personality and Social Psychology, 83*(5), 1117–1130.

Budney, A. J., Vandrey, R. L., & Fearer, S. (2011). Cannabis. In P. Ruiz & E. C. Strain (Eds.), *Lowinson and Ruiz's substance abuse: A comprehensive textbook* (5th ed., pp. 214–237). Philadelphia: Lippincott Williams & Wilkins.

Buehlman, K. T., Gottman, J. M., & Katz, L. F. (1992). How a couple views their past predicts their future: Predicting divorce from an oral history interview. *Journal of Family Psychology, 5,* 295–318.

Buhi, E. R., Blunt, H., Wheldon, C., & Bull, S. S. (2014). Sexuality and new technologies. In D. L. Tolman & L. M. Diamond, *APA handbook of sexuality and psychology* (pp. 77–101). Washington, DC: American Psychological Association. doi:10.1037/14194-003

Bulik, C. M. (2004). Genetic and biological risk factors. In J. K. Thompson (Ed.), *Handbook of eating disorders and obesity.* New York: Wiley.

Bunker, S. J., Colquhoun, D. M., Esler, M. D., Hickie, I. B., Hunt, D., Jelinek, V. M., Oldenberg, B. F., Peach, H. G., Ruth, D., Tennant, C. C., & Tonkin, A. M. (2003). "Stress" and coronary heart disease: psychosocial risk factors. *Medical Journal of Australia, 178*(6), 272–276.

Burger, J. M. (2009). Replicating Milgram: Would people still obey today? *American Psychologist, 64*(1), 1–11.

Burger, J. M. (2014). Situational features in Milgram's experiment that kept his participants shocking. *Journal of Social Issues, 70*(3), 489–500. doi:10.1111/josi.12073

Burger, J. M. (2015). *Personality* (9th ed.). San Francisco, CA: Cengage.

Burger, J. M., & Cornelius, T. (2003). Raising the price of agreement: Public commitment and the lowball compliance procedure. *Journal of Applied Social Psychology, 33*(5), 923–934.

Burger, J. M., & Guadagno, R. E. (2003). Self-concept clarity and the foot-in-the-door procedure. *Basic and Applied Social Psychology, 25*(1), 79–86.

Burgess, M. C. R., & Burpo, S. (2012). The effect of music videos on college students' perceptions of rape. *College Student Journal, 46*(4), 748–763.

Burgoon, J. K. (1994). Nonverbal signals. In M. L. Knapp & G. R. Miller (Eds.), *Handbook of interpersonal communication* (2nd ed.). Thousand Oaks, CA: Sage.

Burhans, K. K., & Dweck, C. S. (1995). Helplessness in early childhood: The role of contingent worth. *Child Development, 66,* 1719–1738.

Burke, B. L., Martens, A., & Faucher, E. H. (2010). Two decades of terror management theory: A meta-analysis of mortality salience research. *Personality and Social Psychology Review, 14*(2), 155–195. doi:10.1177/1088868309352321

Burke, R. J. (2001). Workaholism in organizations: The role of organizational values. *Personnel Review, 30,* 637–645.

Burke, W. W. (2011). *Organizational change: Theory and practice* (3rd ed.). Thousand Oaks, CA: Sage.

Burkley, E., Curtis, J., Burkley, M., & Hatvany, T. (2015). Goal fusion: The integration of goals within the self-concept. *Self And Identity, 14*(3), 348–368. doi:10.1080/15298868.2014.1000959

Burlingame, G. M., & Baldwin, S. (2011). Group therapy. In J. C. Norcross, G. R. Vandenbos, & D. K. Freedheim (Eds.), *History of psychotherapy: Continuity and change* (2nd ed.). Washington, DC: American Psychological Association.

Burlingame, G. M., Strauss, B., & Joyce, A. S. (2013). Change mechanisms and effectiveness of small group treatments. In M. J. Lambert (Ed.). *Bergin and Garfield's handbook of psychotherapy and behavior change* (6th ed.). New York: Wiley.

Burns, S. T. (2015). Person matching for career exploration and choice. In P. J. Hartung, M. L. Savickas, W. B. Walsh, P. J. Hartung, M. L. Savickas, W. B. Walsh (Eds.), *APA handbook of career intervention, Vol. 2: Applications* (pp. 11–23). Washington, DC: American Psychological Association. doi:10.1037/14439-002

Burpee, L., & Langer, E. (2005). Mindfulness and marital satisfaction. *Journal of Adult Development, 12*(1), 43–51.

Burton, C., Campbell, P., Jordan, K., Strauss, V., & Mallen, C. (2013). The association of anxiety and depression with future dementia diagnosis: A case-control study in primary care. *Family Practice, 30*(1), 25–30. doi:10.1093/fampra/cms044

Bush, K. R., & Peterson, G. W. (2013). Parent-child relationships in diverse contexts. In G. W. Peterson, K. R. Bush, G. W. Peterson, K. R. Bush (Eds.), *Handbook of marriage and the family* (3rd ed.; pp. 275–302). New York: Springer Science + Business Media. doi:10.1007/978-1-4614-3987-5_13

Bushman, B. J., & Anderson, C. A. (2001). Media violence and the American public. *American Psychologist, 56,* 477–489.

Bushman, B. J., & Baumeister, R. F. (1998). Threatened egotism, narcissism, self-esteem, and direct and displaced aggression: Does self-love or self-hate lead to violence? *Journal of Personality and Social Psychology, 75*(1), 219–229.

Bushman, B. J., Baumeister, R. F., Thomaes, S., Ryu, E., Begeer, S., & West, S. G. (2009). Looking again, and harder, for a link between self-esteem and aggression. *Journal of Personality, 77*(2), 427–446.

Bushman, B. J., Bonacci, A. M., van Dijk, M., & Baumeister, R. F. (2003). Narcissism, sexual refusal, and aggression: Testing a narcissistic reactance model of sexual coercion. *Journal of Personality and Social Psychology, 84,* 1027–1040.

Bushman, B. J., & Huesmann, L. (2012). Effects of violent media on aggression. In D. G. Singer & J. L. Singer (Eds.), *Handbook of children and the media* (2nd ed., pp. 231–248). Thousand Oaks, CA: Sage.

Bushman, B. J., Moeller, S. J., & Crocker, J. (2011). Sweets, sex, or self-esteem? Comparing the value of self-esteem boosts with other pleasant rewards. *Journal of Personality, 79*(5), 993–1012. doi:10.1111/j.1467-6494.2011.00712.x

Bushman, B. J., & Whitaker, J. L. (2010). Like a magnet: Catharsis beliefs attract angry people to violent video games. *Psychological Science, 21*(6), 790–792. doi:10.1177/0956797610369494

Buss, A. H. (2012). Self II: Self-esteem and identity. In *Pathways to individuality: Evolution and development of personality traits* (pp. 141–168). Washington, DC: American Psychological Association. doi:10.1037/13087-007

Buss, D. M. (1988). The evolution of human intrasexual competition: Tactics of mate attraction. *Journal of Personality and Social Psychology, 54,* 616–628.

Buss, D. M. (1989). Sex differences in human mate preferences: Evolutionary hypotheses tested in 37 cultures. *Behavioral and Brain Sciences, 12,* 1–14.

Buss, D. M. (1991). Evolutionary personality psychology. *Annual Review of Psychology, 42,* 459–491.

Buss, D. M. (1995). Evolutionary psychology: A new paradigm for psychological science. *Psychological Inquiry, 6,* 1–30.

Buss, D. M. (2009). The great struggles of life: Darwin and the emergence of evolutionary psychology. *American Psychologist, 64*(2), 140–148. doi:10.1037/a0013207

Buss, D. M., & Kenrick, D. T. (1998). Evolutionary social psychology. In D. T. Gilbert, S. T. Fiske, & G. Lindzey (Eds.), *The handbook of social psychology.* New York: McGraw-Hill.

Buss, D. M., & Penke, L. (2015). Evolutionary personality psychology. In M. Mikulincer, P. R. Shaver, M. L. Cooper, & R. J. Larsen (Eds.), *APA handbook of personality and social psychology, Vol. 4: Personality processes and individual differences.* Washington, DC: American Psychological Association.

Buss, D. M., Shackelford, T. K., Kirkpatrick, L. A., & Larsen, R. J. (2001). A half century of mate preferences: The cultural evolution of values. *Journal of Marriage and Family, 63,* 491–503.

Bussey, K. (2013). Gender development. In M. K. Ryan & N. R Branscombe (Eds.), *The Sage handbook of gender and psychology* (pp. 81–99). Thousand Oaks, CA: Sage.

Bussey, K., & Bandura, A. (1984). Influence of gender constancy and social power on sex-linked modeling. *Journal of Personality and Social Psychology, 47,* 1292–1302.

Bussey, K., & Bandura, A. (2004). Social cognitive theory of gender development and functioning. In A. H. Eagly, A. E. Beall, & R. J. Sternberg (Eds.), *The psychology of gender.* New York: Guilford.

Butcher, J. N., Bubany, S., & Mason, S. N. (2013). Assessment of personality and psychopathology with self-report inventories. In K. F. Geisinger, B. A. Bracken, J. F. Carlson, J. C. Hansen, N. R. Kuncel, S. P. Reise, & M. C. Rodriguez, *APA handbook of testing and assessment in psychology, Vol. 2: Testing and assessment in clinical and counseling psychology.* Washington, DC: American Psychological Association. doi:10.1037/14048-011

Butler, E. A., Egloff, B., Wlhelm, F. H., Smith, N. C., Erickson, E. A., & Gross, J. J. (2003). The social consequences of expressive suppression. *Emotion, 3*(1), 48–67.

Buunk, A. P., & Dijkstra, P. (2006). Temptation and threat: Extradyadic relations and jealousy. In A. L. Vangelisti & D. Perlman (Eds.), *The Cambridge handbook of personal relationships.* New York: Cambridge University Press.

Byers, E. (2011). Beyond the birds and the bees and was it good for you? Thirty years of research on sexual communication. *Canadian Psychology/Psychologie Canadienne, 52*(1), 20–28. doi:10.1037/a0022048

Byers, E. S., & Rehman, U. S. (2014). Sexual well-being. In D. L. Tolman, L. M. Diamond, J. A. Bauermeister, W. H. George, J. G. Pfaus, L. M. Ward (Eds.), *APA handbook of sexuality and psychology* (pp. 317–337). Washington, DC: American Psychological Association. doi:10.1037/14193-011

Byrd-Craven, J., & Geary, D. C. (2013). An evolutionary understanding of sex differences. In M. K. Ryan & N. R Branscombe (Eds.), *The Sage handbook of gender and psychology* (pp. 100–114). Thousand Oaks, CA: Sage.

Byrm, R. J., & Lenton, R. L. (2001). Love online: A report on digital dating in Canada. Retrieved from www.nelson.com/nelson/harcourt/sociology/newsociety3e/loveonline.pdf

Byrne, R. (2006). *The secret.* New York: Atria Books.

Byrne, S., Barry, D., & Petry, N. M. (2012). Predictors of weight loss success. Exercise vs. dietary self-efficacy and treatment attendance. *Appetite, 58,* 695–698. doi:10.1016/j.appet.2012.01.005

Cable, N., Bartley, M., Chandola, T., & Sacker, A. (2013). Friends are equally important to men and women, but family matters more for men's well-being. *Journal of Epidemiology and Community Health, 67*(2), 166–171. doi:10.1136/jech-2012-201113

Cabral, G. A., & Petit, D. A. D. (1998). Drugs and immunity: Cannabinoids and their role in decreased resistance to infectious disease. *Journal of Neuroimmunology, 83,* 116–123.

Cacioppo, J. T., & Cacioppo, S. (2014). Social relationships and health: The toxic effects of perceived social isolation. *Social and Personality Psychology Compass, 8,* 58–72. doi:10.1111/spc3.12087

Cacioppo, J. T., Cacioppo, S., Cole, S. W., Capitanio, J. P., Goossens, L., & Boomsma, D. I. (2015a). Loneliness across phylogeny and a call for comparative studies and animal models. *Perspectives on Psychological Science, 10*(2), 202–212. doi:10.1177/1745691614564876

Cacioppo, S., Grippo, A. J., London, S., Goossens, L., & Cacioppo, J. T. (2015b). Loneliness: Clinical import and interventions. *Perspectives on Psychological Science, 10*(2), 238–249. doi:10.1177/1745691615570616

Cacioppo, J. T., & Patrick, W. (2008). *Loneliness.* New York: Norton.

Cahn, D. D. (2009). Friendship, conflict and dissolution. In H. T. Reis & S. Sprecher (Eds.), *Encyclopedia of human relationships: Vol. 1* (pp. 703–706). Los Angeles: Sage Reference.

Calhoun, L. G., & Tedeschi, R. G. (2013). *Posttraumatic growth in clinical practice.* New York: Routledge/Taylor & Francis Group.

Caligor, E., Yeomans, F., & Levin, Z. (2014). Feeding and eating disorders. In J. L. Cutler (Ed.), *Psychiatry* (3rd ed.). New York: Oxford University Press.

Calvo, M. G., Gutiérrez-García, A., Fernández-Martín, A., & Nummenmaa, L. (2014). Recognition of facial expressions of emotion is related to their frequency in everyday life. *Journal of Nonverbal Behavior, 38*(4), 549–567. doi:10.1007/s10919-014-0191-3

Cameron, D. (2007). *The myth of Mars and Venus: Do men and women really speak different languages?* Oxford, UK: Oxford University Press.

Cameron, H. A., & Glover, L. R. (2015). Adult neurogenesis: Beyond learning and memory. *Annual Review of Psychology, 66,* 53–81. doi:10.1146/annurev-psych-010814-015006

Cameron, L. D., Booth, R. J., Schlatter, M., Ziginaskas, D., & Harman, J. E. (2007). Changes in emotion regulation and psychological adjustment following use of a group psychosocial support program for women recently diagnosed with breast cancer. *Psycho-Oncology, 16,* 171–180.

Campbell, A. C., Nunes, E. V., Matthews, A. G., Stitzer, M., Miele, G. M., Polsky, D., . . . Ghitza, U. E. (2014). Internet-delivered treatment for substance abuse: A multisite randomized controlled trial. *The American Journal of Psychiatry, 171,* 683–690. doi:10.1176/appi.ajp.2014.13081055

Campbell, J. D. (1990). Self-esteem and clarity of the self-concept. *Journal of Personality and Social Psychology, 59,* 538–549.

Campbell, J. D., Assanand, S., & DiPaula, A. (2000). Structural features of the self-concept and adjustment. In A. Tesser, R. B. Felson, & J. M. Suls (Eds.), *Psychological perspectives on self and identity*. Washington, DC: American Psychological Association.

Campbell, J. D., Chew, B., & Scratchley, L. S. (1991). Cognitive and emotional reactions to daily events: The effects of self-esteem and self-complexity. *Journal of Personality, 59,* 473–505.

Campbell, J. D., & Lavallee, L. F. (1993). Who am I? The role of self-concept confusion in understanding the behavior of people with low self-esteem. In R. Baumeister (Ed.), *Self-esteem: The puzzle of low self-regard.* New York: Plenum.

Campbell, K., Wright, D. W., & Flores, C. G. (2012). Newlywed women's marital expectations: Lifelong monogamy? *Journal of Divorce and Remarriage, 53*(2), 108–125. doi:10.1080/10502556.2012.651966

Campbell, W. K. (2005). *When you love a man who loves himself.* Naperville, IL: Sourcebooks.

Canary, D. J., & Stafford, L. (1994). *Maintaining relationships through strategic and routine interaction.* In D. J. Canary & L. Stafford (Eds.), Communication and relationship maintenance (pp. 3–22). San Diego, CA: Academic Press.

Cannon, W. B. (1929). *Bodily changes in pain, hunger, fear, and rage.* Oxford, UK: Appleton.

Cantor, J. R., & Venus, P. (1980). The effects of humor on recall of a radio advertisement. *Journal of Broadcasting and Electronic Media, 24,* 13–22.

Cardeña, E., & Gleaves, D. H. (2007). Dissociative disorders. In M. Hersen, S. M. Turner, & D. C. Beidel (Eds.), *Adult psychopathology and diagnosis.* New York: Wiley.

Cardeña, E., Butler, L. D., Reijman, S., & Spiegel, D. (2013). Disorders of extreme stress. In T. A. Widiger, G. Stricker, I. B. Weiner, G. Stricker, T. A. Widiger, & I. B. Weiner (Eds.), *Handbook of psychology, Vol. 8: Clinical psychology* (2nd ed.). New York: Wiley.

Cardoso, C., Ellenbogen, M. A., Serravalle, L., & Linnen, A. (2013). Stress-induced negative mood moderates the relation between oxytocin administration and trust: Evidence for the tend-and-befriend response to stress? *Psychoneuroendocrinology, 38*(11), 2800–2804. doi:10.1016/j.psyneuen.2013.05.006

Carducci, B. J. (1999). *The pocket guide to making successful small talk.* New Albany, IN: Pocket Guide Publications.

Carey, K. B., Durney, S. E., Shepardson, R. L., & Carey, M. P. (2015a). Incapacitated and forcible rape of college women: Prevalence across the first year. *Journal of Adolescent Health, 56*(6), 678–680. doi:10.1016/j.jadohealth.2015.02.018

Carey, K. B., Durney, S. E., Shepardson, R. L., & Carey, M. P. (2015b). Precollege predictors of incapacitated rape among female students in their first year of college. *Journal of Studies on Alcohol and Drugs, 76*(6), 829–837. doi:10.15288/jsad.2015.76.829

Carey, M. P., & Vanable, P. A. (2003). AIDS/HIV. In A. M. Nezu, C. M. Nezu, & P. A. Geller (Eds.), *Handbook of psychology, Vol. 9: Health psychology.* New York: Wiley.

Carli, L. L. (2013). Gendered communication and social influence. In M. K. Ryan & N. R Branscombe (Eds.), *The Sage handbook of gender and psychology* (pp. 199–215). Thousand Oaks, CA: Sage.

Carlson, E. N., & Furr, R. M. (2009). Evidence of differential meta-accuracy: People understand the different impressions they make. *Psychological Science, 20*(8), 1033–1039.

Carlson, R. (1997). *Don't sweat the small stuff . . . and it's all small stuff: Simple ways to keep the little things from taking over your life.* New York: Hyperion.

Carlston, D. E., & Schneid, E. D. (2015). When literatures collide: Synergies between stereotyping and impression formation. In S. J. Stroessner, J. W. Sherman, S. J. Stroessner, & J. W. Sherman (Eds.), *Social perception from individuals to groups* (pp. 93–124). New York: Psychology Press.

Carmer, P. (2008). Seven pillars of defense mechanism theory. *Social and Personality Psychology Compass, 2,* 1963–1981. doi: 10.1111/j.1751-9004.2008.00135.x

Carmody, J., & Baer, R. A. (2008). Relationships between mindfulness practice and levels of mindfulness, medical and psychological symptoms and well-being in a mindfulness-based stress reduction program. *Journal of Behavioral Medicine, 31*(1), 23–33. doi:10.1007/s10865-007-9130-7

Carothers, B. J., & Reis, H. T. (2013). Men and women are from Earth: Examining the latent structure of gender. *Journal of Personality and Social Psychology, 104*(2), 385–407. doi:10.1037/a0030437

Carpenter, C. J. (2012). Narcissism on Facebook: Self-promotional and anti-social behavior. *Personality and Individual Differences, 52,* 482–486. doi:10.1016/j.paid.2011.11.011

Carpenter, S. K. (2012). Testing enhances the transfer of learning. *Current Directions in Psychological Science, 21,* 279–283. doi:10.1177/0963721412452728

Carpenter, S. K. (2014). Spacing and interleaving of study and practice. In V. A. Benassi, C. E. Overson, & C. M. Hakala (Eds.), *Applying science of learning in education: Infusing psychological science into the curriculum.* Washington, DC: Society for the Teaching of Psychology.

Carpenter, W. T. (2002). From clinical trial to prescription. *Archives of General Psychology, 59,* 282–285.

Carr, C. P., Martins, C. S., Stingel, A. M., Lemgruber, V. B., & Juruena, M. F. (2013). The role of early life stress in adult psychiatric disorders: A systematic review according to childhood trauma subtypes. *Journal of Nervous and Mental Disease, 201,* 1007–1020. doi:10.1097/NMD.0000000000000049

Carr, D., Freedman, V. A., Cornman, J. C., & Schwarz, N. (2014). Happy marriage, happy life? Marital quality and subjective well-being in later life. *Journal of Marriage and Family, 76*(5), 930–948. doi:10.1111/jomf.12133

Carroll, J. L. (2007). *Sexuality now: Embracing diversity.* Belmont, CA: Wadsworth.

Carroll, L. J., & Rothe, J. P. (2014). Viewing vehicular violence through a wide angle lens: Contributing factors and a proposed framework. *Canadian Journal of Criminology and Criminal Justice, 56*(2), 149–166. doi:10.3138/cjccj.2014.ES01

Carson, E. A. (2015). Prisoners in 2014. Retrieved from www.bjs.gov/index.cfm?ty=pbdetail&iid=5387

Carson, S. H., & Langer, E. J. (2006). Mindfulness and self-acceptance. *Journal of Rational-Emotive & Cognitive Behavior Therapy, 24,* 29–43.

Carter, B., & McGoldrick, M. (1988). Overview: The changing family life cycle—A framework for family therapy. In E. A. Carter & M. McGoldrick (Eds.), *The changing family life cycle: A framework for family therapy* (2nd ed.). New York: Gardner Press.

Carter, B., & McGoldrick, M. (1999). Overview: The expanded family life cycle: Individual, family, and social perspectives. In B. Carter & M. McGoldrick (Eds.), *The expanded family life cycle: Individual, family, and social perspectives* (3rd ed.). Boston: Allyn & Bacon.

Carter, T. J., & Dunning, D. (2008). Faulty self-assessment: Why evaluating one's own competence is an intrinsically difficult task. *Social and Personality Psychology Compass, 2*(1), 346–360.

Carter-Sowell, A. R., Chen, Z., & Williams, K. D. (2008). Ostracism increases social susceptibility. *Social Influence, 3*(3),143–153.

Carvalho, J., & Nobre, P. (2011). Biopsychosocial determinants of men's sexual desire: Testing an integrative model. *Journal of Sexual Medicine, 8*(3), 754–763. doi:10.1111/j.1743-6109.2010.02156.x

Carver, C. S. (2011). Coping. In R. J. Contrada & A. Baum (Eds.), *The handbook of stress science: Biology, psychology, and health* (pp. 221–229). New York: Springer.

Carver, C. S., & Connor-Smith, J. (2010). Personality and coping. *Annual Review of Psychology, 61,* 679–704. doi:10.1146/annurev.psych.093008.100352

Carver, C. S., & Scheier, M. F. (2014). Dispositional optimism. *Trends in Cognitive Sciences, 18,* 293–299. doi:10.1016/j.tics.2014.02.003

Carver, C. S., Pozo, C., Harris, S. D., Noriega, V., Scheier, M. F., Robinson, D. S., Ketcham, A. S., Moffat, F. L., Jr., & Clark, K. C. (1993). How coping mediates the effect of optimism on distress: A study of women with early-stage breast cancer. *Journal of Personality and Social Psychology, 65,* 375–390.

Carver, C. S., Scheier, M. F., & Weintraub, J. K. (1989). Assessing coping strategies: A theoretically based approach. *Journal of Personality and Social Psychology, 56,* 267–283.

Case, B. G., Bertollo, D. N., Laska, E. M., Price, L. H., Siegel, C. E., Olfson, M., & Marcus, S. C. (2013). Declining use of electroconvulsive therapy in United States general hospitals. *Biological Psychiatry, 73,* 119–126.

Cashdan, E. (1998). Smiles, speech, and body posture: How women and men display sociometric status and power. *Journal of Nonverbal Behavior, 22,* 209–228.

Castano, E. (2012). Antisocial behavior in individuals and groups: An empathy-based approach. In K. Deaux & M. Snyder (Eds.), *The Oxford handbook of personality and social psychology* (pp. 419–445). New York: Oxford University Press.

Castonguay, L., Barkham, M., Lutz, W., & McAleavey, A. (2013). Practice-oriented research: Approaches and applications. In M. J. Lambert (Ed.). *Bergin and Garfield's handbook of psychotherapy and behavior change* (6th ed.). New York: Wiley.

Catalyst. (2007). Catalyst releases 2006 census of women in Fortune 500 corporate officer and board positions. Retrieved from www.catalyst.org/pressroom/press_releases/2006_Census_Release.pdf

Catalyst. (2012). Sex discrimination and sexual harassment. Retreived from www.catalyst.org/publication/213/sex-discrimination-and-sexual-harrassment

Catalyst. (2014). Statistical overview of women in the workplace. Retrieved from www.catalyst.org/knowledge/statistical-overview-women-workplace

Cate, R. M., & Lloyd, S. A. (1988). Courtship. In S. Duck (Ed.), *Handbook of personal relationships.* New York: Wiley.

Cattell, R. B., Eber, H. W., & Tatsuoka, M. M. (1970). *Handbook of the Sixteen Personality Factor Questionnaire* (16PF). Champaign, IL: Institute for Personality and Ability Testing.

Caza, A., & Cameron, K. S. (2013). An introduction to happiness and organizations. In S. A. David, I. Boniwell, A. Conley Ayers, S. A. David, I. Boniwell, & A. Conley Ayers (Eds.), *The Oxford handbook of happiness* (pp. 671–675). New York: Oxford University Press.

Ceci, S. J., Ginther, D. K., Kahn, S., & Williams, W. M. (2014). Women in academic science: A changing landscape. *Psychological Science in the Public Interest, 15*(3), 75–141. doi:10.1177/1529100614541236

Ceci, S. J., Williams, W. M., & Barnett, S. M. (2009). Women's underrepresentation in science: Sociocultural and biological considerations. *Psychological Bulletin, 135*(2), 218–261. doi:10.1037/a0014412

Centers for Disease Control and Prevention (2006). Update: Trends in AIDS incidence-United States. *MMWR, 46*(37), 861–867.

Centers for Disease Control and Prevention (2009). Sexual and reproductive health of persons aged 10–24 years: United States, 2002–2007. Retrieved from www.cdc.gov/mmwr/preview/mmwrhtml/ss5806al.htm?s

Centers for Disease Control and Prevention (2011a). Sexual violence, stalking, and intimate partner violence widespread in the U.S. Retrieved from www.cdc.gov/media/releases/2011/p1214_sexual_violence.html

Centers for Disease Control and Prevention (2011b). Quitting Smoking Among Adults: United States, 2001–2010. *Morbidity and Mortality Weekly Report 2011, 60*(44), 1513–1519.

Centers for Disease Control and Prevention (2012a). HIV in the United States. Retrieved from www.cdc.gov/hiv/resources/factsheets/us.htm

Centers for Disease Control and Prevention (2012b). Sexual risk behavior: HIV, STD, & teen pregnancy prevention. Retrieved from www.cdc.gov/healthyyouth/sexualbehaviors/index.htm

Centers for Disease Control and Prevention (2013). Current cigarette smoking among adults in the United States. Retrieved from www.cdc.gov/tobacco/data_statistics/fact_sheets/adult_data/cig_smoking

Centers for Disease Control and Prevention (2014a). Genital HPV infection. Fact sheet. Retrieved from www.cdc.gov/std/hpv/stdfact-hpv.htm

Centers for Disease Control and Prevention (2014b). Health effects of cigarette smoking. Retrieved from www.cdc.gov/tobacco/data_statistics/fact_sheets/health_effects/effects_cig_smoking/

Centers for Disease Control and Prevention (2015a). HIV among women. Retrieved from www.cdc.gov/hiv/group/gender/women/index.html#refd

Centers for Disease Control and Prevention (2015b). Reproductive health. Retrieved from www.cdc.gov/reproductivehealth/depression

Cepeda, N. J., Pashler, H., Vul, E., Wixted, J. T., & Roher, D. (2006). Distributed practice in verbal recall tasks: A review and quantitative synthesis. *Psychological Bulletin, 132,* 354–380.

Cerletti, U., & Bini, L. (1938). Un nuevo metodo di shock-terapie "L'elettro-shock." *Bolletino Accademia Medica Roma, 64,* 136–138.

Chaiken, S. (1979). Communicator's physical attractiveness and persuasion. *Journal of Personality and Social Psychology, 37,* 1387–1397.

Chang, C. H., Rosen, C. C., & Levy, P. E. (2009). The relationship between perceptions of organizational politics and employee attitudes, strain, and behavior: A meta-analysis. *Academy of Management Journal, 52,* 779–801.

Chang, J. (2015). The interplay between collectivism and social support processes among Asian and Latino American college students. *Asian American Journal of Psychology, 6*(1), 4–14. doi:10.1037/a0035820

Chang, R. Y., & Kelly, P. K. (1993). *Step-by-step problem solving: A practical guide to ensure problems get (and stay) solved.* Irvine, CA: Richard Chang Associates.

Chaplin, T. M., Cole, P. M., & Zahn-Waxler, C. (2005). Parental socialization of emotion expression: Gender differences and relations to child adjustment. *Emotion, 5*(1), 80–88. doi:10.1037/1528-3542.5.1.80

Charles, S. T., Gatz, M., Kato, K., & Pedersen, N. L. (2008). Physical health 25 years later: The predictive ability of neuroticism. *Health Psychology, 27,* 369–378.

Charles, S. T., Piazza, J. R., Mogle, J., Sliwinski, M. J., & Almeida, D. M. (2013). The wear and tear of daily stressors on mental health. *Psychological Science, 24,* 733–741. doi: 10.1177/0956797612462222

Cheavens, J. S., & Ritschel, L. A. (2014). Hope theory. In M. M. Tugade, M. N. Shiota, L. D. Kirby, M. M. Tugade, M. N. Shiota, & L. D. Kirby (Eds.), *Handbook of positive emotions* (pp. 396–410). New York: Guilford.

Chen, C., Boucher, H., & Tapias, M. P. (2006). The relational self revealed: Integrative conceptualization and implications for interpersonal life. *Psychological Bulletin, 132*(2), 151–179.

Chen, G., & Martin, R. A. (2007). A comparison of humor styles, coping humor, and mental health between Chinese and Canadian university students. *Humor, 20,* 215–234.

Chen, S., Gau, S. F., Pikhart, H., Peasey, A., Chen, S., & Tsai, M. (2014). Work stress and subsequent risk of internet addiction among information technology engineers in Taiwan. *Cyberpsychology, Behavior, and Social Networking, 17,* 542–550. doi: 10.1089/cyber.2013.0686

Cheng, C. (2001). Assessing coping flexibility in real-life and laboratory settings: A multimethod approach. *Journal of Personality and Social Psychology, 80*(5), 814–833.

Cheng, C. (2003). Cognitive and motivational processes underlying coping flexibility: A dual-process model. *Journal of Personality and Social Psychology, 84,* 425–438.

Cheng, C., & Yee-Iam Li, A. (2014). Internet addiction prevalence and quality of (real) life: A meta-analysis of 31 nations across seven world regions. *Cyberpsychology, Behavior, and Social Networking, 17,* 755–760. doi: 10.1089/cyber.2014.0317

Cherlin, A. J. (1999). Going to extremes: Family structure, children's well-being, and social science. *Demography, 36,* 421–428.

Chernev, A., Böckenholt, U., & Goodman, J. (2015). Choice overload: A conceptual review and meta-analysis. *Journal of Consumer Psychology, 25*(2), 333–358. doi:10.1016/j.jcps.2014.08.002

Cherney, I. D., Bersted, K., & Smetter, J. (2014). Training spatial skills in men and women. *Perceptual and Motor Skills, 119*(1), 82–99. doi:10.2466/23.25.PMS.119c12z0

Chesterton, G. K., & Schall, J.V. (2001). *The collected works of G. K. Chesterton, Vol. 20: Christendom in Dublin, Irish impressions, the new Jerusalem, a short history of England* (p. 463). San Francisco, CA. Ignatius Press.

Chew, S. L. (2014). Helping students to get the most out of studying. In V. A. Benassi, C. E. Overson, & C. M. Hakala (Eds.), *Applying science of learning in education: Infusing psychological science into the curriculum.* Washington, DC: Society for the Teaching of Psychology.

Chia, R. C., Moore, J. L., Lam, K. N., Chuang, C. J., & Cheng, B. S. (1994). Cultural differences in gender role attitudes between Chinese and American students. *Sex Roles, 31,* 23–29.

Chida, Y., & Steptoe, A. (2009). The association of anger and hostility with future coronary heart disease: A meta-analytic review of prospective evidence. *Journal of the American College of Cardiology, 53,* 936–946.

Chin, H. B., Sipe, T., Elder, R., Mercer, S. L., Chattopadhyay, S. K., Jacob, V., . . . Santelli, J. (2012). The effectiveness of group-based comprehensive risk-reduction and abstinence education interventions to prevent or reduce the risk of adolescent pregnancy, human immunodeficiency virus, and sexually transmitted infections: Two systematic reviews for the Guide to Community Preventive Services. *American Journal of Preventive Medicine, 42*(3), 272–294. doi:10.1016/j.amepre.2011.11.006

Chiu, C.-Y., Kim, Y. –H., & Wan, W. W. N. (2008). Personality: Cross-cultural perspectives. In G. J. Boyle, G. Matthews, & D. H. Saklofske (Eds.), *The Sage handbook of personality theory and assessment* (pp. 124–144). Los Angeles: Sage.

Chivers, M. L., Suschinsky, K. D., Timmers, A. D., & Bossio, J. A. (2014). Experimental, neuroimaging, and psychophysiological methods in sexuality research. In D. L. Tolman, L. M. Diamond, J. A. Bauermeister, W. H. George, J. G. Pfaus, L. M. Ward (Eds.), *APA handbook of sexuality and psychology* (pp. 99–119). Washington, DC: American Psychological Association. doi:10.1037/14193-005

Choi, O. (2015). Using fMRI for lie detection: Ready for court. In K. J. Weiss, C. Watson, K. J. Weiss, C. Watson (Eds.), *Psychiatric expert testimony: Emerging applications* (pp. 84–101). New York: Oxford University Press. doi:10.1093/med/9780199346592.003.0006

Chopra, D. (1993). *Ageless body, timeless mind.* New York: Crown.

Chou, F., Holzemer, W. L., Portillo, C. J., & Slaughter, R. (2004). Self-care strategies and sources of information for HIV/AIDS symptom management. *Nursing Research, 53,* 332–339.

Chow, H. H. (2011). Procrastination among undergraduate students: Effects of emotional intelligence, school life, self-evaluation, and self- efficacy. *Alberta Journal of Educational Research, 57*(2), 234–240.

Chow, J. T., & Lau, S. (2015). Nature gives us strength: Exposure to nature counteracts ego-depletion. *The Journal of Social Psychology, 155*(1), 70–85. doi:10.1080/00224545.2014.972310

Chudzikowski, K. (2011). Career transitions and career success in the "new" career era. *Journal of Vocational Behavior.* doi:10.1016/j.jvb.2011.10.005

Church, A. T. (2010). Current perspectives in the study of personality across cultures. *Perspectives on Psychological Science, 5,* 441–449. doi:10.1177/1745691610375559

Church, A. T., Alvarez, J. M., Mai, N. T. Q., French, B. F., Katigbak, M. S., & Ortiz, F. A. (2011). Are cross-cultural comparisons of personality profiles meaningful? Differential item and facet functioning in the Revised NEO Personality Inventory. *Journal of Personality and Social Psychology, 101,* 1068–1089. doi:10.1037/a0025290

Church, T. S., Earnest, C. P., Skinner, J. S., & Blair, S. N. (2007). Effects of different doses of physical activity on cardiorespiratory fitness among sedentary, overweight or obese postmenopausal women with elevated blood pressure: A randomized control trial. *Journal of the American Medical Association, 297,* 2081–2091.

Cialdini, R. B. (2001). *Influence: Science and practice* (4th ed.). Boston: Allyn & Bacon.

Cialdini, R. B. (2007). *Influence: Science and practice.* New York: HarperCollins.

Cialdini, R. B., Borden, R. J., Thorne, A., Walker, M. R., Freeman, S., & Sloan, L. R. (1976). Basking in reflected glory: Three (football) field studies. *Journal of Personality and Social Psychology, 34,* 366–375.

Cialdini, R. B., & Sagarin, B. J. (2005). Interpersonal influence. In T. Brock & M. Green (Eds.), *Persuasion: Psychological insights and perspectives* (pp. 143–169). Newbury Park, CA: Sage.

Ciraulo, D. A., & Knapp, C. (2011). Sedative-hypnotics. In P. Ruiz & E. C. Strain (Eds.), *Lowinson and Ruiz's substance abuse : A comprehensive textbook* (5th ed.; pp. 255–266). Philadelphia: Lippincott Williams & Wilkins.

Clark, D. A., & Beck, A. T. (2010). *Cognitive therapy of anxiety disorders: Science and practice.* New York: Guilford.

Clark, D. A., Abramowitz, J., Alcolado, G. M., Alonso, P., Belloch, A., Bouvard, M., . . . Wong, W. (2014). Part 3: A question of perspective: The association between intrusive thoughts and obsessionality in 11 countries. *Journal of Obsessive-Compulsive and Related Disorders, 3*(3), 292–299. doi:10.1016/j.jocrd.2013.12.006

Clark, J. K., Evans, A. T., & Wegener, D. T. (2011). Perceptions of source efficacy and persuasion: Multiple mechanisms for source effects on attitudes. *European Journal of Social Psychology, 41*(5), 596–607. doi:10.1002/ejsp.787

Clark, J. K., Wegener, D. T., Habashi, M. M., & Evans, A. T. (2012). Source expertise and persuasion: The effects of perceived opposition or support on message scrutiny. *Personality and Social Psychology Bulletin, 38*(1), 90–100. doi:10.1177/0146167211420733

Clark, M. S., & Mills, J. (1993). The difference between communal and exchange relationships: What it is and is not. *Journal of Personality and Social Psychology Bulletin, 19,* 684–691.

Clark, R. (2003). Self-reported racism and social support predict blood pressure reactivity in Blacks. *Annals of Behavioral Medicine, 25,* 127–136.

Clarke, V. A., Lovegrove, H., Williams, A., & Machperson, M. (2000). Unrealistic optimism and the health belief model. *Journal of Behavioral Medicine, 23,* 367–376.

Clasen, P. C., Disner, S. G., & Beevers, C. G. (2013). Cognition and depression: Mechanisms associated with the onset and maintenance of emotional disorder. In M. D. Robinson, E. Watkins, & E. Harmon-Jones (Eds.), *Handbook of cognition and emotion.* New York: Guilford.

Classen, T. J., & Dunn, R. A. (2012). The effect of job loss and unemployment duration on suicide risk in the United States: A new look using mass-layoffs and unemployment duration. *Health Economics, 21,* 338–350. doi:10.1002/hec.1719

Clay, R. R. (2011). Is stress getting to you? *Monitor on Psychology, 42*(1), 58–63.

Clement, S., Schauman, O., Graham, T., Maggioni, F., Evans-Lacko, S., Bezborodovs, N., . . . Thornicroft, G. (2015). What is the impact of mental health-related stigma on help-seeking? A systematic review of quantitative and qualitative studies. *Psychological Medicine, 45*(1), 11–27. doi:10.1017/S0033291714000129

Clements, A. M., Rimrodt, S. L., Abel, J. R., Blankner, J. G., Mostofsky, S. H., Pekar, J. J., . . . Cutting, L. E. (2006). Sex differences in cerebral laterality of language and visuospatial processing. *Brain and Language, 98*(2), 150–158.

Clements, M. L., Stanley, S. M., & Markman, H. J. (2004). Before they said "I do": Discriminating among marital outcomes over 13 years. *Journal of Marriage and Family, 66,* 613–626.

Clifford, S., Barber, N., & Horne, R. (2008). Understanding different beliefs held by adherers, unintentional nonadherers, and intentional nonadherers: Application of the Necessity-Concerns Framework. *Journal of Psychosomatic Research, 64,* 41–46.

Cochran, S. D., & Mays, V. M. (2013). Sexual orientation and mental health. In C. J. Patterson & A. R. D'Augelli (Eds.), *Handbook of psychology and sexual orientation* (pp. 204–222). New York: Oxford University Press.

Cohan, C. L. (2013). The cohabitation conundrum. In M. A. Fine & F. D. Fincham (Eds.), *Handbook of family theories: A content-based approach* (pp. 105–122). New York: Routledge/Taylor & Francis Group.

Cohen, C. E. (1981). Person categories and social perception: Testing some boundaries of the processing effects of prior knowledge. *Journal of Personality and Social Psychology, 40,* 441–452.

Cohen, F., & Solomon, S. (2011). The politics of mortal terror. *Current Directions in Psychological Science, 20,* 316–320. doi:10.1177/0963721411416570

Cohen, S. (2005). Keynote presentation at the eight international congress of behavioral medicine: the pittsburgh common cold studies: Psychosocial predictors of susceptibility to respiratory infectious illness. *International Journal Of Behavioral Medicine, 12*(3), 123–131. doi:10.1207/s15327558ijbm1203_1

Cohen, S., Doyle, W. J., Turner, R., Alper, C. M., & Skoner, D. P. (2003). Sociability and susceptibility to the common cold. *Psychological Science, 14*(5), 389–395.

Cohen, S., Frank, E., Doyle, W. J., Skoner, D. P., Rabin, B. S., & Gwaltney, Jr., J. M. (1998). Types of stressors that increase susceptibility to the common cold in healthy adults. *Health Psychology, 17,* 214–223.

Cohen, S., Janicki-Deverts, D., Turner, R. B., & Doyle, W. J. (2015). Does hugging provide stress-buffering social support? A study of susceptibility to upper respiratory infection and illness. *Psychological Science, 26*(2), 135–147. doi:10.1177/0956797614559284

Cohen, S., Lichtenstein, E., Prochaska, J. O., Rossi, J. S., Gritz, E. R., Carr, C. R., . . . Ossip-Klein, D. (1989). Debunking myths about self-quitting: Evidence from 10 prospective studies of persons who attempt to quit smoking by themselves. *American Psychologist, 44,* 1355–1365.

Cohn, M. A., & Fredrickson, B. L. (2009). Positive emotions. In S. J. Lopez & C. R. Snyder (Eds.), *Oxford handbook of positive psychology* (2nd ed., pp. 13–24). New York: Oxford University Press.

Cohn, V., Passel, J., Wang, W., & Livingston, G. (2011). Barely half of U.S. adults are married—a record low. Pew Research Center. Retrieved from www.pewsocialtrends.org/2011/12/14/barely-half-of-u-s-adults-are-married-a-record-low/?src=sdt-carousel

Coles, M. E., Schofield, C. A., & Pietrefesa, A. S. (2006). Behavioral inhibition and obsessive-compulsive disorder. *Journal of Anxiety Disorders, 20,* 1118–1132.

Collaer, M. L., & Hines, M. (1995). Human behavioral sex differences: A role for gonadal hormones during early development? *Psychological Bulletin, 118,* 55–107.

CollegeBoard (2015). Total group profile report. Retrieved from https://secure-media.collegeboard.org/digitalServices/pdf/sat/total-group-2015.pdf

Colligan, T. W., & Higgins, E. M. (2005). Workplace stress: Etiology and consequences. *Journal of Workplace Behavioral Health, 21*(2), 89–97.

Coltrane, S. (2001). Marketing the marriage "solution": Misplaced simplicity in the politics of fatherhood. *Sociological Perspectives, 44*(4), 387–418.

Coltrane, S., & Shih, K. Y. (2010). Gender and the division of labor. In J. C. Chrisler & D. R. McCreary (Eds.), *Handbook of gender research in psychology, Vol 2: Gender research in social and applied psychology* (pp. 401–422). New York: Springer Science + Business Media. doi:10.1007/978-1-4419-1467-5_17

Colvin, C. R., & Block, J. (1994). Do positive illusions foster mental health? An examination of the Taylor and Brown formulation. *Psychological Bulletin, 116,* 3–20.

Colvin, C. R., Block, J., & Funder, D. C. (1995). Overly positive self-evaluations and personality: Negative implications for mental health. *Journal of Personality and Social Psychology, 68,* 1152–1162.

Comas-Diaz, L. (1987). Feminist therapy with mainland Puerto Rican women. *Psychology of Women Quarterly, 11,* 461–474.

Combs, D. R., & Mueser, K. T. (2007). Schizophrenia. In M. Hersen, S. M. Turner, & D. C. Beidel (Eds.), *Adult psychopathology and diagnosis.* New York: Wiley.

Comer, J. S., & Kendall, P. C. (2013). Methodology, design, and evaluation in psychotherapy research. In M. J. Lambert (Ed.). *Bergin and Garfield's handbook of psychotherapy and behavior change* (6th ed.). New York: Wiley.

Commerce Clearing House. (2007). *2007 CCH unscheduled absenteeism survey.* Riverwoods, IL: Commerce Clearning House.

Compton, M. T., Goulding, S. M., & Walker, E. F. (2007). Cannabis use, first-episode psychosis, and schizotypy: A summary and synthesis of recent literature. *Current Psychiatry Reviews, 3,* 161–171.

Condon, P., Desbordes, G., Miller, W. B., & DeSteno, D. (2013). Meditation increases compassionate responses to suffering. *Psychological Science, 24*(10), 2125–2127. doi:10.1177/0956797613485603

Confer, J. C., Perilloux, C., & Buss, D. M. (2010). More than just a pretty face: Men's priority shifts toward bodily attractiveness in short-term versus long-term mating contexts. *Evolution and Human Behavior, 31*(5), 348–353. doi:10.1016/j.evolhumbehav.2010.04.002

Conley, K. M., & Lehman, B. J. (2012). Test anxiety and cardiovascular responses to daily academic stressors. *Stress and Health: Journal of The International Society for the Investigation of Stress, 28*(1), 41–50. doi:10.1002/smi.1399

Connor Snibe, A., & Markus, H. R. (2005). You can't always get what you want: Educational attainment, agency, and choice. *Journal of Personality and Social Psychology, 88,* 703–720.

Conoley, C. W., Vasquez, E., Del Carmen Bello, B., Oromendia, M. F., & Jeske, D. R. (2015). Celebrating the accomplishments of others: Mutual benefits of capitalization. *The Counseling Psychologist, 43*(5), 734–751. doi:10.1177/0011000015584066

Conrad, K., Dixon, T., & Zhang, Y. (2009). Controversial rap themes, gender portrayals and skin tone distortion: A content analysis of rap music videos. *Journal of Broadcasting and Electronic Media, 53,* 134–156.

Converse, P. D., Pathak, J., DePaul-Haddock, A., Gotlib, T., & Merbedone, M. (2012). Controlling your environment and yourself: Implications for career success. *Journal of Vocational Behavior, 80*(1), 148–159. doi:10.1016/j.jvb.2011.07.003

Conway, A. M., Tugade, M. M., Catalino, L. I., & Fredrickson, B. L. (2013). The broaden-and-build theory of positive emotions: Form, function, and mechanisms. In S. A. David, I. Boniwell, & A. Conley Ayers (Eds.), *The Oxford handbook of happiness* (pp. 17–34). New York: Oxford University Press.

Cook, T., Church, M., Ajanaku, S., & Shadish, W. (1996). The development of occupational aspirations and expectations among inner-city boys. *Child Development, 67*(6), 3368–3385.

Cooper, C., Bebbington, P., King, M., Jenkins, R., Farrell, M., Brugha, T., . . . Livingston, G. (2011). Happiness across age groups: Results from the 2007 National Psychiatric Morbidity Survey. *International Journal of Geriatric Psychiatry, 26,* 608–614. doi:10.1002/gps.2570

Cope, M. B., Fernández, J. R., & Allison, D. B. (2004). Genetic and biological risk factors. In J. K. Thompson (Ed.), *Handbook of eating disorders and obesity.* New York: Wiley.

Copen, C. E., Chandra, A., & Martinez, G. (2012). Prevalence and timing of oral sex with opposite-sex partners among females and males aged 15–24 years: United States, 2007–2010. *National health statistics reports; No. 56.* Hyattsville, MD: National Center for Health Statistics.

Copen, C. E., Daniels, K., Vespa, J., & Mosher, W. D. (2012). First marriages in the United States: Data from the 2006–2010 National Survey of Family Growth. *National Health Statistics Reports; No. 49.* Hyattsville, MD: National Center for Health Statistics.

Corcoran, K. (2013). The efficiency of similarity-focused comparisons in person perception. *The Journal of Social Psychology, 153*(2), 127–130. doi:10.1080/00224545.2012.725111

Cordova, J. V., & Harp, A. G. (2009). Deteriorating relationships. In H. T. Reis & S. Sprecher (Eds.), *Encyclopedia of human relationships, Vol. 2* (pp. 402–407). Los Angeles: Sage Reference.

Cornblatt, B. A., Green, M. F., Walker, E. F., & Mittal, V. A. (2009). Schizophrenia: Etiology and neurocognition. In P. H. Blaney & T. Millon (Eds.), *Oxford textbook of psychopathology* (pp. 298–332). New York: Oxford University Press.

Cornell, D. G. (1997). Post hoc explanation is not prediction. *American Psychologist, 52,* 1380.

Correia, I., Vala, J., & Aguiar, P. (2007). Victim's innocence, social categorization, and the threat to the belief in a just world. *Journal of Experimental Social Psychology, 43,* 31–38.

Correll, J., Wittenbrink, B., Crawford, M. T., & Sadler, M. S. (2015). Stereotypic vision: How stereotypes disambiguate visual stimuli. *Journal of Personality and Social Psychology, 108*(2), 219–233. doi:10.1037/pspa0000015

Corrigan, P. W., Druss, B. G., & Perlick, D. A. (2014). The impact of mental illness stigma on seeking and participating in mental health care. *Psychological Science in the Public Interest, 15*(2), 37–70. doi:10.1177/1529100614531398

Corty, E. W., & Guardiani, J. M. (2008). Canadian and American sex therapists' perceptions of normal and abnormal ejaculatory latencies: How long should intercourse last? *Journal of Sexual Medicine, 5,* 1251–1256.

Cosgrove, L., & Krimsky, S. (2012). A comparison of DSM-IV and DSM-5 panel members' financial associations with industry: A pernicious problem persists. *PLoS Medicine, 9,* e1001190. doi:10.1371/journal.pmed.1001190

Costa, P. T., Jr., & McCrae, R. R. (1992). *Revised NEO Personality Inventory: NEO PI and NEO Five-Factor Inventory (Professional Manual).* Odessa, FL: Psychological Assessment Resources.

Costa, P. T., Jr., & McCrae, R. R. (2008). The revised NEO Personality Inventory (NEO-PI-R). In G. J. Boyle, G. Matthews, & D. H. Saklofske (Eds.), *The Sage handbook of personality theory and assessment, Vol. 2* (pp.179–198). Los Angeles: Sage.

Courchesne, E., Mouton, P. R., Calhoun, M. E., Semendeferi, K., Ahrens-Barbeau, C., Hallet, M. J., . . . Pierce, K. (2011). Neuron number and size in prefrontal cortex of children with autism. *JAMA: Journal of The American Medical Association, 306,* 2001–2010. doi:10.1001/jama.2011.1638

Cowan, C. P., & Cowan, P. A. (2000). *When partners become parents.* Mahwah, NJ: Erlbaum.

Cox, P. D., Vinogradov, S., & Yalom, I. D. (2008). Group therapy. In R. E. Hales, S. C. Yudofsky, & G. O. Gabbard (Eds.), *The American Psychiatric Publishing textbook of psychiatry* (pp. 1329–1376). Washington, DC: American Psychiatric Publishing.

Crabb, P. B., & Marciano, D. L. (2011). Representations of material culture and gender in award-winning children's books: A 20-year follow-up. *Journal of Research in Childhood Education, 25*(4), 390–398. doi:10.1080/02568543.2011.605209

Crafford, A., Adams, B. G., Saayman, T., & Vinkenburg, C. (2015). The process of identity work: Negotiating a work identity. In P. W. Jansen, G. Roodt, P. W. Jansen, & G. Roodt (Eds.), *Conceptualising and measuring work identity: South-African perspectives and findings* (pp. 53–86). New York: Springer Science + Business Media. doi:10.1007/978-94-017-9242-4_3

Craighead, W. E., Craighead, L. W., Ritschel, L. A., & Zagoloff, A. (2013). Behavior therapy and cognitive-behavioral therapy. In G. Stricker & T. A. Widiger (Eds.), *Handbook of psychology, Vol. 8: Clinical psychology* (2nd ed.). New York: Wiley.

Crain, T. L., Hammer, L. B., Bodner, T., Kossek, E. E., Moen, P., Lilienthal, R., & Buxton, O. M. (2014). Work-family conflict, family-supportive supervisor behaviors (FSSB) and sleep outcomes. *Journal of Occupational Health Psychology, 19*(2), 155–167. doi: 10.1037/a0036010

Cramer, P. (2008). Seven pillars of defense mechanism theory. *Social and Personality Psychology Compass, 2*(5), 1963–1981. doi:10.1111/j.1751-9004.2008.00135.x

Cramer, P. (2015). Defense mechanisms: 40 years of empirical research. *Journal of Personality Assessment, 97*(2), 114-122. doi:10.1080/00223891.2014.947997

Cramer, R. J., Miller, A. K., Amacker, A. M., & Burks, A. C. (2013). Openness, right-wing authoritarianism, and antigay prejudice in college students: A mediational model. *Journal of Counseling Psychology, 60*(1), 64–71. doi:10.1037/a0031090

Crano, W. D., & Prislin, R. (Eds.). (2008). *Attitudes and attitude change.* New York: Psychology Press.

Crary, J. (2013). *24/7: Late capitalism and the ends of sleep.* London: Verso.

Crawford, S. A., & Caltabiano, N. J. (2011). Promoting emotional well-being through the use of humour. *The Journal of Positive Psychology, 6*(3), 237–252. doi:10.1080/17439760.2011.577087

Crede, M., & Kuncel, N. R. (2008). Study habits, skills, and attitudes: The third pillar supporting collegiate academic performance. *Perspectives on Psychological Science, 3*(6), 425–453. doi:10.1111/j.1745-6924.2008.00089.x

Creed, P., Lehmann, K., & Hood, M. (2009). The relationship between core self-evaluations, employment commitment, and well-being in the unemployed. *Personality and Individual Differences, 47*(4), 310–315.

Creed, P., Prideaux, L., & Patton, W. (2005). Antecedents and consequences of career decisional states in adolescence. *Journal of Vocational Behavior, 67,* 397–412.

Crews, F. (2006). *Follies of the wise: Dissenting essays.* Emeryville, CA: Shoemaker Hoard.

Crisp, R. J., & Birtel, M. D. (2014). Reducing prejudice through mental imagery: Notes on replication, interpretation, and generalization. *Psychological Science, 25*(3), 840–841. doi:10.1177/0956797613520169

Crisp, R. J., & Hewstone, M. E. (2006). *Multiple social categorization: Processes, models, and applications.* New York: Psychology Press.

Crisp, R. J., & Turner, R. N. (2013). Imagined intergroup contact: Refinements, debates, and clarifications. In G. Hodson, M. Hewstone, G. Hodson, & M. Hewstone (Eds.), *Advances in intergroup contact* (pp. 135–151). New York: Psychology Press.

Crits-Christoph, P., Gibbons, M. B., & Mukherjee, D. (2013). Psychotherapy process-outcome research. In M. J. Lambert (Ed.). *Bergin and Garfield's handbook of psychotherapy and behavior change* (6th ed.). New York: Wiley.

Crocetti, D. (2013). Genes and hormones: What make up an individual's sex. In M. Ah-King, M. Ah-King (Eds.), *Challenging popular myths of sex, gender and biology* (pp. 23–32). New York: Springer Science + Business Media. doi:10.1007/978-3-319-01979-6_3

Crocker, J., & Luhtanen, R. (1990). Collective self-esteem and ingroup bias. *Journal of Personality and Social Psychology, 58,* 60–67.

Crocker, J., & McGraw, K. M. (1984). What's good for the goose is not good for the gander: Solo status as an obstacle to occupational achievement for males and females. *American Behavioral Scientist, 27,* 357–370.

Crooks, R., & Baur, K. (2008). *Our sexuality.* Belmont, CA: Wadsworth.

Cross, P. (1977). Not can but will college teaching be improved? *New Directions for Higher Education, 17,* 1–15.

Cross, S. E., & Gore, J. S. (2003). Cultural models of the self. In M. R. Leary & J. P. Tangney (Eds.), *Handbook of self and identity.* New York: Guilford.

Crouter, A. C., Bumpus, M. F., Maguire, M. C., & McHale, S. M. (1999). Linking parents' work pressure and adolescents' well-being: Insights into dynamics in dual-earner families. *Developmental Psychology, 35,* 1453–1461.

Crowell, J. A., Treboux, D., & Waters, E. (2002). Stability of attachment representations: The transition to marriage. *Developmental Psychology, 38,* 467–479.

Crowl, A., Ahn, S., & Baker, J. (2008). A meta-analysis of developmental outcomes for children of same-sex and heterosexual parents. *Journal of GLBT Family Studies, 4,* 385–407.

Crowley, A. E., & Hoyer, W. D. (1994). An integrative framework for understanding two-sided persuasion. *Journal of Consumer Research, 20,* 561–574.

Crum, A., & Lyddy, C. (2014). De-stressing stress: The power of mindsets and the art of stressing mindfully. In A. Ie, C. T. Ngnoumen, E. J. Langer, A. Ie, C. T. Ngnoumen, & E. J. Langer (Eds.), *The Wiley Blackwell handbook of mindfulness, Vols. I and II* (pp. 948–963). Wiley-Blackwell.

Crum, A. J., Salovey, P., & Achor, S. (2013). Rethinking stress: The role of mindsets in determining stress response. *Journal of Personality and Social Psychology, 104,* 716–733. doi: 10.1037/a0031201

Csikszentmihalyi, M. (1975). Play and intrinsic rewards. *Journal of Humanistic Psychology, 15,* 41–63.

Csikszentmihalyi, M. (1990). *Flow: The psychology of optimal experience.* New York: HarperCollins.

Csikszentmihalyi, M. (1997). *Finding flow.* New York: Basic Books.

Csikszentmihalyi, M. (2014a). *Applications of flow in human development and education: The collected works of Mihaly Csikszentmihalyi.* New York: Springer Science + Business Media. doi:10.1007/978-94-017-9094-9

Csikszentmihalyi, M. (2014b). The politics of consciousness. In T. J. Hämäläinen, J. Michaelson, T. J. Hämäläinen, & J. Michaelson (Eds.), *Well-being and beyond: Broadening the public and policy discourse* (pp. 271–282). Northampton, MA: Edward Elgar.

Csikszentmihalyi, M., & LeFevre, J. (1989). Optimal experience in work and leisure. *Journal of Personality and Social Psychology, 56,* 815–822.

Csikszentmihalyi, M., & Nakamura, J. (2011). Positive psychology: Where did it come from, where is it going? In K. M. Sheldon, T. B. Kashdan, & M. F. Steger (Eds.), *Designing positive psychology: Taking stock and moving forward* (pp. 3–8). New York: Oxford University Press.

Cuddy, A. C., Wolf, E. B., Glick, P., Crotty, S., Chong, J., & Norton, M. I. (2015). Men as cultural ideals: Cultural values moderate gender stereotype content. *Journal of Personality and Social Psychology, 109*(4), 622–635. doi:10.1037/pspi0000027

Cuijpers, P., Driessen, E., Hollon, S. D., van Oppen, P., Barth, J., & Andersson, G. (2012). The efficacy of non-directive supportive therapy for adult depression: A meta-analysis. *Clinical Psychology Review, 32*(4), 280–291. doi:10.1016/j.cpr.2012.01.003

Cuijpers, P., Vogelzangs, N., Twisk, J., Kleiboer, A., Li, J., & Penninx, B. W. (2014). Comprehensive meta-analysis of excess mortality in depression in the general community versus patients with specific illnesses. *The American Journal of Psychiatry, 171,* 453–462. doi:10.1176/appi.ajp.2013.13030325

Cullen, B. A., McGinty, E. E., Zhang, Y., Dosreis, S. C., Steinwachs, D. M., Guallar, E., & Daumit, G. L. (2013). Guideline-concordant antipsychotic use and mortality in schizophrenia. *Schizophrenia Bulletin, 39,* 1159–1168. doi:10.1093/schbul/sbs097

Cullen, L. T. (2007, February 22). It's a wrap. You're hired! *Time,* p. 57.

Cuming, S., & Rapee, R. M. (2010). Social anxiety and self-protective communication style in close relationships. *Behaviour Research and Therapy, 48*(2), 87–96. doi:10.1016/j.brat.2009.09.010

Cunningham, C. O., & Selwyn, P. A. (2005). HIV-related medical complications and treatment. In J. H. Lowinson, P. Ruiz, R. B. Millman, & J. G. Langrod (Eds.), *Substance abuse: A comprehensive textbook.* Philadelphia: Lippincott/Williams & Wilkins.

Cunningham, M. R. (2009a). Physical attractiveness, defining characteristics. In H. T. Reis & S. Sprecher (Eds.), *Encyclopedia of human relationships, Vol. 3* (pp. 1237–1242). Los Angeles: Sage Reference.

Cunningham, M. R. (2009b). Polygamy. In H. T. Reis & S. Sprecher (Eds.), *Encyclopedia of human relationships, Vol. 3* (pp. 1256–1259). Los Angeles: Sage Reference.

Cunningham, M. R., Barbee, A. P., & Pike, C. L. (1990). What do women want? Facialmetric assessment of multiple motives in the perception of male facial physical attractiveness. *Journal of Personality and Social Psychology, 59,* 61–72.

Cunningham, M. R., Druen, P. B., & Barbee, A. P. (1997). Angels, mentors, and friends: Trade-offs among evolutionary, social, and individual variables in physical appearance. In J. A. Simpson & D. T. Kenrick (Eds.), *Evolutionary Social Psychology.* Mahwah, NJ: Erlbaum.

Curci, A., Lanciano, T., Soleti, E., Zammuner, V. L., & Salovey, P. (2013). Construct validity of the italian version of the Mayer–Salovey–Caruso emotional intelligence test (MSCEIT) v2.0. *Journal of Personality Assessment, 95*(5), 486–494. doi:10.1080/00223891.2013.778272

Curioni, C. C., & Lourenco, P. M. (2005). Long-term weight loss after diet and exercise: A systematic review. *International Journal of Obesity, 29,* 1168–1174.

Cushing-Daniels, B., & Tsz-Ying, Y. (2009). Wage penalties and sexual orientation: An update using the general social survey. *Contemporary Economic Policy, 27*(2), 164–175.

Dai, X., Dong, P., & Jia, J. S. (2014). When does playing hard to get increase romantic attraction? *Journal of Experimental Psychology: General, 143*(2), 521–526. doi:10.1037/a0032989; 10.1037/a0032989.supp (Supplemental)

Dallman, M. F., Bhatnagar, S., & Viau, V. (2007). Hypothalamic-pituitary-adrenal axis. In G. Fink (Ed.), *Encyclopedia of stress.* San Diego, CA: Elsevier Academic Press.

Dallman, M. F., Pecoraro, N. C., & la Fleur, S. E. (2005). Chronic stress and comfort foods: Self-medication and abdominal obesity. *Brain, Behavior, and Immunity, 19*(4), 275–280. doi:10.1016/j.bbi.2004.11.004

Dalton, S. O., & Johansen, C. (2005). Stress and cancer: The critical research. In C. L. Cooper (Ed.), *Handbook of stress medicine and health.* Boca Raton, FL: CRC Press.

Danaher, K., & Branscombe, N. R. (2010). Maintaining the system with tokenism: Bolstering individual mobility beliefs and identification with a discriminatory organization. *British Journal of Social Psychology, 49*(2), 343–362. doi:10.1348/014466609X457530

Darke, S., Kaye, S., & Duflou, J. (2006). Comparative cardiac pathology among deaths due to cocaine toxicity, opioid toxicity and non-drug related causes. *Addiction, 101,* 1771–1777.

David, D. H., & Lyons-Ruth, K. (2005). Differential attachment responses of male and female infants to frightening maternal behavior: Tend or befriend versus fight of flight? *Infant Mental Health Journal, 26*(1), 1–18.

David, S. A., Boniwell, I., & Conley Ayers, A. (Eds.). (2013). *The Oxford handbook of happiness.* New York: Oxford University Press.

Davidson, K. W., & Motofsky, E. (2010). Anger expression and the risk of coronary heart disease: Evidence from the Nova Scotia Health Survey. *American Heart Journal, 159,* 199–206.

Davidson, M. J., & Fielden, S. (1999). Stress and the working woman. In G. N. Powell (Ed.), *Handbook of gender and work.* Thousand Oaks, CA: Sage.

Davis, C. G., & Nolen-Hoeksema, S. (2009). Making sense of loss, perceiving benefits, and posttraumatic growth. In S. J. Lopez & C. R. Snyder (Eds.), *Oxford handbook of positive psychology* (2nd ed., pp. 641–649). New York: Oxford University Press.

Davis, D. E., Ho, M. Y., Griffin, B. J., Bell, C., Hook, J. N., Van Tongeren, D. R., . . . Westbrook, C. J. (2015). Forgiving the self and physical and mental health correlates: A meta-analytic review. *Journal of Counseling Psychology, 62*(2), 329–335. doi:10.1037/cou0000063; 10.1037/cou0000063.supp (Supplemental)

Davis, M., Guyker, W., & Persky, I. (2012). Uniting veterans across distance through telephone-based reminiscence group therapy intervention. *Psychological Services, 9,* 206–208. doi:.10.1037/a0026117

Davis, M. C., Burke, H. M., Zautra, A. J., & Stark, S. (2013). Arthritis and musculoskeletal conditions. In A. M. Nezu, C. M. Nezu, & P. A. Geller (Eds.), *Handbook of Psychology, Vol. 9: Health Psychology* (pp. 182–199). Hoboken, NJ: Wiley.

de Bloom, J., Geurts, S. E., Sonnentag, S., Taris, T., de Weerth, C., & Kompier, M. J. (2011). How does a vacation from work affect employee health and well-being? *Psychology and Health, 26*(12), 1606–1622. doi:10.1080/08870446.2010.546860

de Bloom, J., Geurts, S. E., Taris, T. W., Sonnentag, S., de Weerth, C., & Kompier, M. J. (2010). Effects of vacation from work on health and well-being: Lots of fun, quickly gone. *Work & Stress, 24*(2), 196–216. doi:10.1080/02678373.2010.493385

de Calvo, M. P. C., & Reich, D. A. (2009). Detecting perceiver expectancies: The role of perceiver distraction in spontaneously triggering identity negotiation. *Basic and Applied Social Psychology, 31*(2), 174–187.

De Dreu, C. K., W., Beersma, B. Stroebe, K., & Euwema, M. C. (2006). Motivated information processing, strategic choice, and the quality of negotiated agreement. *Journal of Personality and Social Psychology, 90,* 927–943.

de França, D. X., & Monteiro, M. B. (2013). Social norms and the expression of prejudice: The development of aversive racism in childhood. *European Journal Of Social Psychology, 43*(4), 263–271. doi:10.1002/ejsp.1965

de Graaf, J. (Ed.). (2003). *Take back your time: Fighting overwork and time poverty in America.* San Francisco, CA: Berrett-Koehler.

de Graaf, J., Wann, D., & Naylor, T. H. (2014). *Affluenza: How overconsumption is killing us, and how we can fight back* (3rd ed.). San Francisco, CA: Berrett-Koehler.

De Hoog, N., Stroebe, W., & De Wit, J. B. F. (2007). The impact of vulnerability to and severity of a health risk on processing and acceptance of fear-arousing communications: A meta-analysis. *Review of General Psychology, 11*(3), 258–285.

De Witte, H., Vander Elst, T., & De Cuyper, N. (2015). Job insecurity, health and well-being. In J. Vuori, R. Blonk, R. H. Price, J. Vuori, R. Blonk, & R. H. Price (Eds.), *Sustainable working lives: Managing work transitions and health throughout the life course* (pp. 109–128). New York: Springer Science + Business Media. doi:10.1007/978-94-017-9798-6_7

Deacon, B. J. (2013). The biomedical model of mental disorder: A critical analysis of its validity, utility, and effects on psychotherapy research. *Clinical Psychology Review, 33,* 846–861. doi:10.1016/j.cpr.2012.09.007

Dean, L. R., Carroll, J. S., & Yang, C. (2007). Materialism, perceived financial problems, and marital satisfaction. *Family and Consumer Sciences Research Journal, 35,* 260–281.

DeAndrea, D. C., Tong, S., & Walther, J. B. (2011). Dark sides of computer-mediated communication. In W. R. Cupach & B. H. Spitzberg (Eds.), *The dark side of close relationships II* (pp. 95–118). New York, N: Routledge/Taylor & Francis Group.

DeAngelis, T. (2001, December). Are men emotional mummies? *Monitor on Psychology,* pp. 40–41.

DeAngelis, T. (2004). What's to blame for the surge in super-size Americans? *Monitor on Psychology, 35*(1), 46, 62.

Debatin, B., Lovejoy, J. P., Horn, A., & Hughes, B. N. (2009). Facebook and online privacy: Attitudes, behaviors, and unintended consequences. *Journal of Computer-Mediated Communication, 15*(1), 83–108. doi:10.1111/j.1083-6101.2009.01494.x

Deer, B. (2011). How the case against the MMR vacine was fixed. *BMJ, 342,* 77–82.

Delay, J., & Deniker, P. (1952). *Trente-huit cas de psychoses traitees par la cure prolongee et continue de 4560 RP.* Paris: Masson et Cie.

Delle Fave, A. (2009). Optimal experience and meaning: Which relationship? *Psychological Topics, 18*(20), 284–302.

DeMaris, A., Benson, M. L., Fox, G. L., Hill, T., & Van Wyk, J. (2003). Distal and proximal factors in domestic violence: A test of an integrated model. *Journal of Marriage and Family, 65,* 652–667.

Demir, M., & Özdemir, M. (2010). Friendship, need satisfaction and happiness. *Journal of Happiness Studies, 11*(2), 243–259. doi:10.1007/s10902-009-9138-5

Demir, M., Orthel, H., & Andelin, A. K. (2013). Friendship and happiness. In S. A. David, I. Boniwell & A. Conley Ayers (Eds.), *The Oxford handbook of happiness.* New York: Oxford University Press.

Demo, D. H. (1992). Parent-child relations: Assessing recent changes. *Journal of Marriage and the Family, 54,* 104–117.

Demo, D. H., & Fine, M. A. (2009). Children and divorce. In H. T. Reis & S. Sprecher (Eds.), *Encyclopedia of human relationships, Vol. 2* (pp. 453–458). Los Angeles: Sage Reference.

Deniz, O., Aygül, R., Koçak, N., Orhan, A., & Kaya, M. D. (2004). Precipitating factors of migraine attacks in patients with migraine with and without aura. *Pain Clinic, 16,* 451–456.

Denmark, F. L., German, S. T., & Brodsky, J. B. (2011). Sex discrimination. In M. A. Paludi, C. R. Paludi, & E. R. DeSouza (Eds.), *Praeger handbook on understanding and preventing workplace discrimination* (pp. 195–226). Santa Barbara, CA: Praeger/ABC-CLIO.

DePaulo, B. (2014). Single in a society preoccupied with couples. In R. J. Coplan, J. C. Bowker, R. J. Coplan, J. C. Bowker (Eds.), *The handbook of solitude: Psychological perspectives on social isolation, social withdrawal, and being alone* (pp. 302–316). Wiley-Blackwell.

DePaulo, B. M. (1994). Spotting lies: Can humans learn to do better? *Current Directions in Psychological Science, 3*(3), 83–86.

DePaulo, B. M. (2004). The many faces of lies. In A. G. Miller (Ed.), *The social psychology of good and evil* (pp. 303–326). New York: Guilford.

DePaulo, B. M. (2011). Living single: Lightening up those dark, dopey myths. In W. R. Cupach & B. H. Spitzberg (Eds.), *The dark side of close relationships II* (pp. 409–439). New York: Routledge/Taylor & Francis Group.

DePaulo, B. M., Ansfield, M. E., Kirkendol, S. E., & Boden, J. M. (2004). Serious lies. *Basic and Applied Social Psychology, 6,* 147–167.

DePaulo, B. M., Charlton, K., Cooper, H., Lindsay, J. J., & Muhlenbruck, L. (1997). The accuracy-confidence correlation in the detection of deception. *Personality and Social Psychology Review, 1*(4), 346–357.

DePaulo, B. M., & Friedman, H. (1998). Nonverbal communication. In D. T. Gilbert, S. T. Fiske, & G. Lindzey (Eds.), *The handbook of social psychology, Vol. 2.* Boston: McGraw-Hill.

DePaulo, B. M., Lindsay, J. J., Malone, B. E., Muhlenbruck, L., Charlton, K., & Cooper, H. (2003). Cues to deception. *Psychological Bulletin, 129*(1), 74–118.

DePaulo, B. M., Stone, J., & Lassiter, G. D. (1985). Deceiving and detecting deceit. In B. R. Schlenker (Ed.), *The self and social life.* New York: McGraw-Hill.

DePrince, A. P., Chu, A. T., & Pineda, A. S. (2011). Links between specific posttrauma appraisals and three forms of trauma-related distress. *Psychological Trauma: Theory, Research, Practice, and Policy, 3*(4), 430-441. doi:10.1037/a0021576

Derks, B., Ellemers, N., van Laar, C., & de Groot, K. (2011). Do sexist organizational cultures create the Queen Bee. *British Journal of Social Psychology, 50*(3), 519–535. doi:10.1348/014466610X525280

Derks, B., Van Laar, C., & Ellemers, N. (2016). The queen bee phenomenon: Why women leaders distance themselves from junior women. *The Leadership Quarterly.* doi:10.1016/j.leaqua.2015.12.007

Derks, B., Van Laar, C., Ellemers, N., & de Groot, K. (2011). Gender-bias primes elicit queen-bee responses among senior policewomen. *Psychological Science, 22*(10), 1243–1249. doi:10.1177/0956797611417258

Derlega, V. J., Winstead, B. A., & Greene, K. (2008). Self-disclosure and starting a close relationship. In S. Sprecher, A. Wenzel, J. Harvey, S. Sprecher, A. Wenzel, J. Harvey (Eds.), *Handbook of relationship initiation* (pp. 153–174). New York: Psychology Press.

Derlega, V. J., Winstead, B. A., Wong, P. T. P., & Hunter, S. (1985). Gender effects in an initial encounter: A case where men exceed women in disclosure. *Journal of Social and Personal Relationships, 2,* 25–44.

Derry, H. M., Fagundes, C. P., Andridge, R., Glaser, R., Malarkey, W. B., & Kiecolt-Glaser, J. K. (2013). Lower subjective social status exaggerates interleukin-6 responses to a laboratory stressor. *Psychoneuroendocrinology, 38*(11), 2676–2685. doi:10.1016/j.psyneuen.2013.06.026

Derryberry, D., & Tucker, D. M. (1994). Motivating the focus of attention. In P. M. Neidenthal & S. Kitayama (Eds.), *The heart's eye: Emotional influences in perception and attention* (pp. 167–196). San Diego, CA: Academic Press.

DeSantis King, A., Huebner, E. S., Suldo, S. M., & Valois, R. F. (2006). An ecological view of school satisfaction in adolescence: Linkages between social support and behavior problems. *Applied Research in Quality of Life, 1,* 279–295.

Destin, M., & Oyserman, D. (2009). From assets to school outcomes: How finances shape children's perceived possibilities and planned effort. *Psychological Science, 20,* 414–418.

Deutsch, M. (2011). Constructive conflict management for the world today. In P. T. Coleman (Ed.), *Conflict, interdependence, and justice: The intellectual legacy of Morton Deutsch* (pp. 289–307). New York: Springer Science + Business Media.

Devine, P. G. (1989). Stereotypes and prejudice: Their automatic and controlled components. *Journal of Personality and Social Psychology, 56,* 5–18.

Devlin, M. J., & Steinglass, J. E. (2014). Feeding and eating disorders. In J. L. Cutler (Ed.), *Psychiatry* (3rd ed. pp. 291–322). New York: Oxford University Press.

DeWall, C. N., Baumeister, R. F., Gailliot, M. T., & Maner, J. K. (2008). Depletion makes the heart grow less helpful: Helping as a function of self-regulatory energy and genetic relatedness. *Personality and Social Psychology Bulletin, 34,* 1653–1662.

Dey, J. G., & Hill, C. (2007). *Behind the pay gap.* Washington, DC: American Association of University Women Educational Foundation.

DeYoung, C. G. (2015). Openness/intellect: A dimension of personality reflecting. In M. Mikulincer, P. R. Shaver, M. L. Cooper, & R. J. Larsen (Eds.), *APA handbook of personality and social psychology, Vol. 4: Personality processes and individual differences.* Washington, DC: American Psychological Association.

Dhont, K., & Van Hiel, A. (2012). Intergroup contact buffers against the intergenerational transmission of authoritarianism and racial prejudice. *Journal of Research in Personality, 46*(2), 231–234. doi:10.1016/j.jrp.2011.12.008

Diamond, L. M. (2007). "Having a girlfriend without knowing it": Intimate friendships among adolescent sexual-minority women. In K. E. Lovaas & M. M. Jenkins (Eds.), *Sexualities & communication in everyday life* (pp. 107–115). Thousand Oaks, CA: Sage.

Diamond, L. M. (2013a). Concepts of female sexual orientation. In C. J. Patterson, A. R. D'Augelli (Eds.), *Handbook of psychology and sexual orientation* (pp. 3–17). New York: Oxford University Press.

Diamond, L. M. (2013b). Sexuality in relationships. In J. A. Simpson, L. Campbell, J. A. Simpson, L. Campbell (Eds.), *The Oxford handbook of close relationships* (pp. 589–614). New York: Oxford University Press.

Diamond, L. M. (2014). Gender and same-sex sexuality. In D. L. Tolman, L. M. Diamond, J. A. Bauermeister, W. H. George, J. G. Pfaus, L. M. Ward (Eds.), *APA handbook of sexuality and psychology* (pp. 629–652). Washington, DC: American Psychological Association. doi:10.1037/14193-020

Diamond, L. M. (2015). Sexuality and same-sex sexuality in relationships. In M. Mikulincer, P. R. Shaver, J. A. Simpson, & J. F. Dovidio (Eds.), *APA handbook of personality and social psychology, Vol. 3: Interpersonal relations* (pp. 523–553). Washington, DC: American Psychological Association. doi:10.1037/14344-019

Diamond, L. M., & Lucas, S. (2004). Sexual-minority and heterosexual youths' peer relationships: Experiences, expectations, and implications for well-being. *Journal of Research on Adolescence, 14*(3), 313–340. doi:10.1111/j.1532-7795.2004.00077.x

Dickerson, C. A., Thibodeau, R., Aronson, E., & Miller, D. (1992). Using cognitive dissonance to encourage water conservation. *Journal of Applied Social Psychology, 22*(11), 841–854. doi:10.1111/j.1559-1816.1992.tb00928.x

Dickey, J. (2015, June 1). Save our vacation, *Time, 185*(20), 44–49.

Diehl, C., Glaser, T., & Bohner, G. (2014). Face the consequences: Learning about victim's suffering reduces sexual harassment myth acceptance and men's likelihood to sexually harass. *Aggressive Behavior, 40*(6), 489–503. doi:10.1002/ab.21553

Diekman, A. B., & Murnen, S. K. (2004). Learning to be little women and little men: The inequitable gender equality of nonsexist children's literature. *Sex Roles, 50*(5/6), 373–385.

Diener, E., & Biswas-Diener, R. (2008). *Happiness: Unlocking the mysteries of psychological wealth* London: Wiley-Blackwell.

Diener, E., & Chan, M. Y. (2011). Happy people live longer: Subjective well-being contributes to health and longevity. *Applied Psychology: Health and Well-Being, 3*(1), 1–43. doi:10.1111/j.1758-0854.2010.01045.x

Diener, E., & Diener, C. (1996). Most people are happy. *Psychological Science, 7,* 181–185.

Diener, E., & Diener, M. (1995). Cross-cultural correlates of life-satisfaction and self-esteem. *Journal of Personality and Social Psychology, 68,* 653–663.

Diener, E., Kesebir, P., & Tov, W. (2009). Happiness. In M. R. Leary & R. H. Hoyle (Eds.), Handbook of individual differences in social behavior (pp. 147–160). New York: Guilford.

Diener, E., Oishi, S., & Lucas, R. E. (2009). Subjective well-being: The science of life satisfaction. In S. J. Lopez & C. R. Snyder (Eds.), *Oxford handbook of positive psychology* (2nd ed., pp. 187–194). New York: Oxford University Press.

Diener, E., Oishi, S., & Lucas, R. E. (2015). National accounts of subjective well-being. *American Psychologist, 70*(3), 234–242. doi:10.1037/a0038899

Diener, E., & Seligman, M. E. P. (2004). Beyond money: Toward an economy of well-being. *Psychological Science in the Public Interest, 5*(1), 1–31.

Diener, E., Tay, L., & Myers, D. G. (2011). The religion paradox: If religion makes people happy, why are so many dropping out? *Journal of Personality and Social Psychology, 101,* 1278–1290. doi:10.1037/a00224402

Diener, E., Wolsic, B., & Fujita, F. (1995). Physical attractiveness and subjective well-being. *Journal of Personality and Social Psychology, 69,* 120–129.

Dijkstra, P., Gibbons, F. X., & Buunk, A. P. (2010). Social comparison theory. In J. E. Maddux & J. P. Tangney (Eds.), *Social psychological foundations of clinical psychology* (pp. 195–211). New York: Guilford.

DiMatteo, M. R. (1997). Health behaviors and care decisions: An overview of professional-patient communication. In D. S. Gochman (Ed.), *Handbook of health behavior research II: Provider determinants.* New York: Plenum.

DiMatteo, M. R., Giordani, P. J., Lepper, H. S., & Croghan, T. W. (2002). Patient adherence and medical treatment outcomes: A meta-analysis. *Medical Care, 40,* 794–811.

Din, J. N., Newby, D. E., & Flapan, A. D. (2004). Omega 3 fatty acids and cardiovascular disease—fishing for a natural treatment. *British Medical Journal, 328,* 30–35.

Dindia, K. (2006). Men are from North Dakota, women are from South Dakota. In K. Dindia (Ed.), *Sex differences and similarities in communication* (2nd ed., pp. 3–20). Mahwah, NJ: Lawrence Erlbaum.

Dion, K. (1973). Young children's stereotyping of facial attractiveness. *Developmental Psychology, 9,* 183–188.

Dion, K. K., Berscheid, E., & Walster, E. (1972). What is beautiful is good. *Journal of Personality and Social Psychology, 24,* 285–290.

Dion, K. L. (2003). Prejudice, racism and discrimination. In T. Millon & M. J. Lerner (Eds.), *Handbook of psychology, Vol. 5: Personality and social psychology.* New York: Wiley.

Dir, A. L., & Cyders, M. A. (2015). Risks, risk factors, and outcomes associated with phone and Internet sexting among university students in the united states. *Archives of Sexual Behavior, 44*(6), 1675–1684. doi:10.1007/s10508-014-0370-7

Dittmar, H., Bond, R., Hurst, M., & Kasser, T. (2014). The relationship between materialism and personal well-being: A meta-analysis. *Journal of Personality and Social Psychology, 107*(5), 879–924. doi:10.1037/a0037409

Dittner, A. J., Rimes, K., & Thorpe, S. (2011). Negative perfectionism increases the risk of fatigue following a period of stress. *Psychology and Health, 26*(3), 253–268. doi:10.1080/08870440903225892

Diwadkar, V. A., Bustamante, A., Ral, H., & Uddin, M. (2014). Epigenetics, stress, and their potential impact on brain network function: A focus on the schizophrenia diatheses. *Frontiers in Psychiatry, 5,* 71. doi:10.3389/fpsyt.2014.00071

Djamba, Y. K., & Kimuna, S. R. (2014). Are Americans really in favor of interracial marriage? A closer look at when they are asked about black-white marriage for their relatives. *Journal of Black Studies, 45*(6), 528–544. doi:10.1177/0021934714541840

Djikic, M., Langer, E. J., & Stapleton, S. F. (2008). Reducing stereotyping through mindfulness: Effects on automatic stereotype-activated behaviors. *Journal of Adult Development, 15*(2), 106–111.

Dodge, B., Jeffries, W. L., & Sandfort, T. G. M. (2008). Beyond the down low: Sexual risk, protection, and disclosure among at risk Black men who have sex with both men and women (MSMW). *Archive of Sexual Behavior, 37,* 683–696.

Doerr, C. E., & Baumeister, R. F. (2010). Self-regulatory strength and psychological adjustment: Implications of the limited resource model of self-regulation. In J. E. Maddux & J. Tangney (Eds.), *Social psychological foundations of clinical psychology* (pp. 71–83). New York: Guilford.

Dohm, A., & Wyatt, I. (2002). College at work: Outlook and earnings for college graduates, 2000–10. *Occupational Outlook Quarterly, 46*(3), 3–15.

Dohrenwend, B. P., Yager, T. J., Wall, M. M., & Adams, B. G. (2013). The roles of combat exposure, personal vulnerability, and involvement in harm to civilians or prisoners in Vietnam War–related posttraumatic stress disorder. *Clinical Psychological Science, 1*(3), 223–238.

Dolby, S. K. (2005). *Self-help books: Why Americans keep reading them.* Urbana, IL: University of Illinois Press.

Dollard, J., Doob, L. W., Miller, N. E., Mowrer, O. H., & Sears, R. R. (1939). *Frustration and aggression.* New Haven, CT: Yale University Press.

Dollard, M. F., & Karasek, R. A. (2010). Building psychosocial safety climate: Evaluation of a socially coordinated PAR risk management stress prevention study. In J. Houdmont, S. Leka, J. Houdmont, & S. Leka (Eds.), *Contemporary occupational health psychology: Global perspectives on research and practice, Vol. 1* (pp. 208–233). Wiley-Blackwell. doi:10.1002/9780470661550.ch11

Donahey, K. M. (2010). Female orgasmic disorder. In S. B. Levine (Ed.), *Handbook of clinical sexuality for mental health professionals* (2nd ed., pp. 351–368). New York: Routledge/Taylor & Francis Group.

Donaldson, S. I., Dollwet, M., & Rao, M. A. (2015). Happiness, excellence, and optimal human functioning revisited: Examining the peer-reviewed literature linked to positive psychology. *The Journal of Positive Psychology, 10*(3), 185–195. doi:10.1080/17439760.2014.943801

Donnellan, M. B., Trzesniewski, K. H., Robins, R. W., Moffitt, T. E., & Caspi, A. (2005). Low self-esteem is related to aggression, antisocial behavior, and delinquincy. *Psychological Science, 16,* 328–335.

Dorahy, M. J., Brand, B. L., _ar, V., Krüger, C., Stavropoulos, P., Martínez-Taboas, A., . . . Middleton, W. (2014). Dissociative identity disorder: An empirical overview. *Australian and New Zealand Journal of Psychiatry, 48,* 402–417. doi:10.1177/0004867414527523

Dornelas, E. A., Gallagher, J., & Burg, M. M. (2014). Reducing stress to improve health. In K. A. Riekert, J. K. Ockene, L. Pbert, K. A. Riekert, J. K. Ockene, & L. Pbert (Eds.), *The handbook of health behavior change* (4th ed.; pp. 229–244). New York: Springer.

Dougherty, D. D., Wilhelm, S., & Jenike, M. A. (2014). Obsessive-compulsive and related disorders. In R. E. Hales, S. C. Yudofsky, & L. W. Roberts (Eds.), *The American Psychiatric Publishing textbook of psychiatry* (6th ed.). Washington, DC: American Psychiatric Publishing.

Douglas, J. H., & Steinberger, M. D. (2015). The sexual orientation wage gap for racial minorities. *Industrial Relations: A Journal of Economy & Society, 54*(1), 59–108. doi:10.1111/irel.12077

Dovidio, J. F., Ellyson, S. L., Keating, C. F., Heltman, K., & Brown, C. E. (1988). The relationship of social power to visual display of dominance between men and women. *Journal of Personality and Social Psychology, 54,* 233–242.

Dovidio, J. F., Gaertner, S. L., Esses, V. M., & Brewer, M. B. (2003). Social conflict, harmony, and integration. In T. Millon & M. J. Lerner (Eds.) *Handbook of psychology, Vol. 5: Personality and social psychology.* New York: Wiley.

Downey, C. A., & Chang, E. C. (2014). History of cultural context in positive psychology: We finally come to the start of the journey. In J. Teramoto Pedrotti, L. M. Edwards, J. Teramoto Pedrotti, & L. M. Edwards (Eds.), *Perspectives on the intersection of multiculturalism and positive psychology* (pp. 3–16). New York: Springer Science + Business Media. doi:10.1007/978-94-017-8654-6_1

Downey, L. A., Sands, H., Jones, L., Clow, A., Evans, P., Stalder, T., & Parrott, A. C. (2015). Reduced memory skills and increased hair cortisol levels in recent Ecstasy/MDMA users: Significant but independent neurocognitive and neurohormonal deficits. *Human Psychopharmacology: Clinical and Experimental, 30*(3), 199–207.

Drago, R. W. (2007). *Striking a balance: Work, family, life.* Boston: Dollars & Sense.

Dreu, C. d., Aaldering, H., & Saygi, Ö. (2015). Conflict and negotiation within and between groups. In M. Mikulincer, P. R. Shaver, J. F. Dovidio, J. A. Simpson, (Eds.), *APA handbook of personality and social psychology, Vol. 2: Group processes* (pp. 151–176). Washington, DC: American Psychological Association. doi:10.1037/14342-006

Drigotas, S. M. (2002). The Michelangelo phenomenon and personal well-being. *Journal of Personality, 70,* 59–77.

Drouin, M., Ross, J., & Tobin, E. (2015). Sexting: A new, digital vehicle for intimate partner aggression? *Computers in Human Behavior, 50,* 197–204. doi:10.1016/j.chb.2015.04.001

Dubovsky, S. L. (2009). Benzodiazepine receptor agonists and antagonists. In B. J. Sadock, V. A. Sadock, & P. Ruiz (Eds.), *Kaplan & Sadock's comprehensive textbook of psychiatry* (pp. 3044–3055). Philadelphia: Lippincott Williams & Wilkins.

Duck, S., & Usera, D. A. (2014). Language and interpersonal relationships. In T. M. Holtgraves & T. M. Holtgraves (Eds.), *The Oxford handbook of language and social psychology* (pp. 188–200). New York: Oxford University Press.

Duck, S. W. (1982). A topography of relationship disengagement and dissolution. In S. W. Duck (Ed.), *Personal relationship 4: Dissolving personal relationships* (pp. 1–30). London: Academic Press.

Duck, S. W. (2006). *Human relationships* (4th ed.). London: Sage.

Duck, T., Middleton, J., Simpson, D., Thibodeaux, J., McDaniel, J., & Buboltz, W. (2013). Family of origin and career development. In A. Di Fabio (Ed.), *Psychology of counseling* (pp. 125–169). Hauppauge, NY: Nova Biomedical Books.

Duckworth, A. L. (2013). True grit. *The Observer, 26*(4), 1–3.

Duckworth, A.L., & Gross, J.J. (2014). Self-control and grit: Related but separable determinants of success. *Current Directions in Psychological Science, 23,* 319–325.

Duckworth, A. L., Peterson, C., Matthews, M. D., & Kelly, D. R. (2007). Grit: Perseverance and passion for long-term goals. *Journal of Personality and Social Psychology, 92*(6), 1087–1101. doi:10.1037/0022-3514.92.6.1087

Dudley, M., Hadzi-Pavlovic, D., Andrews, D., & Perich, T. (2008). New-generation antidepressants, suicide and depressed adolescents: How should clinicians respond to changing evidence? *Australian and New Zealand Journal of Psychiatry, 42*(6), 456–466. doi:10.1080/00048670802050538

Duffy, R. D., Autin, K. L., & Bott, E. M. (2015). Work volition and job satisfaction: Examining the role of work meaning and person–environment fit. *The Career Development Quarterly, 63*(2), 126–140. doi:10.1002/cdq.12009

Duhigg, C. (2012). *The power of habit: Why we do what we do in life and business.* New York: Random House.

Dunbar-Jacob, J., & Schlenk, E. (2001). Patient adherence to treatment regimen. In A. Baum, T. A. Revenson & J. E. Singer (Eds.), *Handbook of health psychology.* Mahwah, NJ: Erlbaum.

Duncan, B. L., & Reese, R. J. (2013). Empirically supported treatments, evidence-based treatments, and evidence-based practice. In G. Stricker & T. A. Widiger (Eds.), *Handbook of psychology, Vol. 8: Clinical psychology* (2nd ed.). New York: Wiley.

Duncan, C. P., & Nelson, J. E. (1985). Effects of humor in a radio advertising experiment. *Journal of Advertising, 14,* 33–40, 64.

Duncker, K. (1945). On problem solving. *Psychological Monographs, 58*(5, i–113).

Dunlosky, J., Rawson, K. A., Marsh, E. J., Nathan, M. J., & Willingham, D. T. (2013). Improving students' learning with effective learning techniques: Promising directions from cognitive and educational psychology. *Psychological Science in the Public Interest, 14*(1), 4–58. doi:10.1177/1529100612453266

Dunn, A. L., Trivedi, M. H., & O'Neal, H. A. (2001). Physical activity dose-response effects on outomes of depression and anxiety. *Medicine and Science in Sports and Exercise, 33,* S587–S597.

Dunn, E., & Norton, M. (2013). *Happy money: The science of happier spending.* New York: Simon & Schuster.

Dunn, E. W., Aknin, L. B., & Norton, M. I. (2008). Spending money on others promotes happiness. *Science, 319*(5870), 1687–1688. doi:10.1126/science.1150952

Dunn, E. W., Aknin, L. B., & Norton, M. I. (2014). Prosocial spending and happiness: Using money to benefit others pays off. *Current Directions in Psychological Science, 23*(1), 41–47. doi:10.1177/0963721413512503

Dunn, E. W., Gilbert, D. T., & Wilson, T. D. (2011). If money doesn't make you happy, then you probably aren't spending it right. *Journal of Consumer Psychology, 21*(2), 115–125. doi:10.1016/j.jcps.2011.02.002

Dunn, E. W., Wilson, T. D., & Gilbert, D. T. (2003). Location, location, location: The misprediction of satisfaction in housing lotteries. *Personality and Social Psychology Bulletin, 29,* 1421–1432.

Dunning, D. (2006). Strangers to ourselves? *The Psychologist, 19*(10), 600–603.

Dunning, D. (2011). The Dunning-Kruger effect: On being ignorant of one's own ignorance. In J. M. Olson, M. P. Zanna, J. M. Olson, & M. P. Zanna (Eds.), *Advances in experimental social psychology, Vol. 44* (pp. 247–296). San Diego, CA: Academic Press. doi:10.1016/B978-0-12-385522-0.00005-6

Dunning, D., & Sherman, D. A. (1997). Stereotypes and tacit inference. *Journal of Personality and Social Psychology, 73*(3), 459–471.

Dweck, C. S. (2007). Is math a gift? Beliefs that put females at risk. In S. J. Ceci & W. M. Williams (Eds.), *Why aren't more women in science?* (pp. 47–56). Washington, DC: American Psychological Association.

Dykstra, P. A., & Fokkema, T. (2007). Social and emotional loneliness among divorced and married men and women: Comparing the deficit and cognitive perspectives. *Basic and Applied Social Psychology, 29,* 1–12.

Eagly, A. H. (1987). *Sex differences in social behavior: A social-role interpretation.* Hillsdale, NJ: Erlbaum.

Eagly, A. H. (2013). The science and politics of comparing women and men: A reconsideration. In M. K. Ryan & N. R Branscombe (Eds.), *The Sage handbook of gender and psychology* (pp. 11–28). Thousand Oaks, CA: Sage.

Eagly, A. H., & Chaiken, S. (1998). Attitude structure and function. In D. T. Gilbert, S. T. Fiske, & G. Lindzey (Eds.), *Handbook of social psychology.* New York: McGraw-Hill.

Eagly, A. H., & Sczesny, S. (2009). Stereotypes about women, men, and leaders: Have times changed? In M. Barreto, M. K. Ryan, & M. T. Schmitt (Eds.), *The glass ceiling in the 21st century: Understanding barriers to gender equality* (pp. 21–47). Washington, DC: American Psychological Association.

Eagly, A. H., & Wood, W. (1999). The origins of sex differences in human behavior: Evolved dispositions versus social roles. *American Psychologist, 54*(6), 408–423.

Eagly, A. H., & Wood, W. (2012). Social role theory. In P. M. Van Lange, A. W. Kruglanski, E. T. Higgins, P. M. Van Lange, A. W. Kruglanski, & E. T. Higgins (Eds.), *Handbook of theories of social psychology* (Vol. 2; pp. 458–476). Thousand Oaks, CA: Sage. doi:10.4135/9781446249222.n49

Eagly, A. H., & Wood, W. (2013). The nature–nurture debates: 25 years of challenges in understanding the psychology of gender. *Perspectives on Psychological Science, 8*(3), 340–357. doi:10.1177/1745691613484767

Easterbrook, G. (2003). *The progress paradox: How life gets better while people feel worse.* New York: Random House.

Eastwick, P. W. (2013). Cultural influences on attraction. In J. A. Simpson, L. Campbell (Eds.), Oxford handbook of close relationships (pp. 161–182). New York: Oxford University Press.

Eccles, J. S. (2001). Achievement. In J. Worrell (Ed.), *Encyclopedia of women and gender.* San Diego, CA: Academic Press.

Eccles, J. S. (2007). Where are all the women? Gender differences in participation in physical science and engineering. In S. J. Ceci & W. M. Williams (Eds.), *Why aren't more women in science?* (pp. 199–210). Washington, DC: American Psychological Association.

Eccles, J. S. (2014). Gender and achievement choices. In E. T. Gershoff, R. S. Mistry, D. A. Crosby, E. T. Gershoff, R. S. Mistry, & D. A. Crosby (Eds.), *Societal contexts of child development: Pathways of influence and implications for practice and policy* (pp. 19–34). New York: Oxford University Press.

Eckert, P., & McConnell-Ginet, S. (2003). *Language and gender.* Cambridge, UK: Cambridge University Press.

Eckhardt, C. I., Sprunger, J. G., & Hamel, J. (2014). Intimate partner violence perpetrators. In L. Grossman, S. Walfish, L. Grossman, & S. Walfish (Eds.), *Translating psychological research into practice* (pp. 443–451). New York: Springer.

Edwards, A. G. K., Hulbert-Williams, N., & Neal, R. D. (2008). Psychological interventions for women with metastatic breast cancer. *Cochrane Database of Systematic Reviews,* Cochrane Art. No.: CD004253. doi: 10.1002/14651858. CD004253.pub3.

Edwards, K., & Smith, E. E. (1996). A disconfirmation bias in the evaluation of arguments. *Journal of Personality and Social Psychology, 71,* 5–24.

Edwards, L. M., & McClintock, J. B. (2013). Promoting hope among youth: Theory, research, and practice. In C. Proctor, P. A. Linley, C. Proctor, P. A. Linley (Eds.), *Research, applications, and interventions for children and adolescents: A positive psychology perspective* (pp. 43–55). New York: Springer Science + Business Media. doi:10.1007/978-94-007-6398-2_4

Eells, T. D., Barrett, M. S., Wright, J. H., & Thase, M. (2014). Computer-assisted cognitive–behavior therapy for depression. *Psychotherapy, 51*(2), 191–197. doi:10.1037/a0032406

Ehrenberg, O., & Ehrenberg, M. (1994). *The psychotherapy maze: A consumer's guide to getting in and out of therapy.* Northvale, NJ: Jason Aronson.

Eibach, R. P., Wilmot, M. O., & Libby, L. K. (2015). The system-justifying function of gratitude norms. *Social and Personality Psychology Compass, 9*(7), 348–358. doi:10.1111/spc3.12184

Einarsdóttir, S., & Rounds, J. (2009). Gender bias and construct validity in vocational interest measurement: Differential item functioning in the Strong Interest Inventory. *Journal of Vocational Behavior, 74*(3), 295–307. doi:10.1016/j.jvb.2009.01.003

Einstein, G. O., & McDaniel, M. A. (2004). *Memory fitness: A guide for successful aging.* New Haven, CT: Yale University Press.

Eisenberger, N. I. (2012). Broken hearts and broken bones: A neural perspective on the similarities between social and physical pain. *Current Directions in Psychological Science, 21*(1), 42–47. doi:10.1177/0963721411429455

Eisenbruch, A. B., Simmons, Z. L., & Roney, J. R. (2015). Lady in red: Hormonal predictors of women's clothing choices. *Psychological Science, 26*(8), 1332–1338. doi:10.1177/0956797615586403

Ekman, P. (1972). Universals and cultural differences in facial expressions of emotion. In J. Cole (Ed.), *Nebraska symposium on motivation, 1971.* Lincoln, NE: University of Nebraska Press.

Ekman, P. (1975, September). The universal smile: Face muscles talk every language. *Psychology Today,* pp. 35–39.

Ekman, P. (1994). Strong evidence for universals in facial expressions: A reply to Russell's mistaken critique. *Psychological Bulletin, 115,* 268–287.

Ekman, P. (2009). *Telling lies: Clues to deceit in the marketplace, politics, and marriage* (Rev. ed.). New York: Norton.

Ekman, P., & Friesen, W. V. (1984). *Unmasking the face.* Palo Alto, CA: Consulting Psychologists Press.

Ekman, P., & Matsumoto, D. (2011). Reading faces: The universality of emotional expression. In M. A. Gernsbacher, R. W. Pew, L. M. Hough, J. R. Pomerantz, (Eds.), *Psychology and the real world: Essays illustrating fundamental contributions to society* (pp. 140–146). New York: Worth.

Ekman, P., & O'Sullivan, M. (1991). Who can catch a liar? *American Psychologist, 44*(9), 913–920.

Ekman, P., O'Sullivan, M., & Frank, M. G. (1999). A few can catch a liar. *Psychological Science, 10*(3), 263–266.

Elfenbein, H. A., & Ambady, N. (2002). Universals and cultural differences in recognizing emotions of a different cultural group. *Current Directions in Psychological Science, 12*(5), 159–164.

Elias, S. M., Gibson, L. A., & Barney, C. E. (2013). The role of social power in sexual harassment and job discrimination. In S. M. Elias(Ed.), *Deviant and criminal behavior in the workplace* (pp. 178–194). New York: New York University Press.

Ellemers, N., & Haslam, S. (2012). Social identity theory. In P. M. Van Lange, A. W. Kruglanski, & E. Higgins (Eds.), *Handbook of theories of social psychology, Vol. 2* (pp. 379–398). Thousand Oaks, CA: Sage.

Ellington, L., & Wiebe, D. J. (1999). Neuroticism, symptom presentation, and medical decision making. *Health Psychology, 18*(6), 634–643.

Elliot, A. J., & Niesta, D. (2008). Romantic red: Red enhances men's attraction to women. *Journal of Personality and Social Psychology, 95*(5), 1150–1164. doi:10.1037/0022-3514.95.5.1150

Elliot, A. J., Niesta Kayser, D., Greitemeyer, T., Lichtenfeld, S., Gramzow, R. H., Maier, M. A., & Liu, H. (2010). Red, rank, and romance in women viewing men. *Journal of Experimental Psychology: General, 139*(3), 399–417. doi:10.1037/a0019689

Elliott, R., Bohart, A. C., Watson, J. C., & Greenberg, L. S. (2011). Empathy. *Psychotherapy, 48*(1), 43–49.

Ellis, A. (1973). *Humanistic psychotherapy: The rational-emotive approach.* New York: Julian Press.

Ellis, A. (1977). *Reason and emotion in psychotherapy.* Seacaucus, NJ: Lyle Stuart.

Ellis, A. (1985). *How to live with and without anger.* New York: Citadel Press.

Ellis, A. (1987). The evolution of rational-emotive therapy (RET) and cognitive behavior therapy (CBT). In J. K. Zeig (Ed.), *The evolution of psychotherapy.* New York: Brunner/Mazel.

Ellis, A. (1996). How I learned to help clients feel better and get better. *Psychotherapy, 33,* 149–151.

Ellis, A. (2001). *Overcoming destructive beliefs, feelings, and behaviors: New directions for Rational Emotive Behavior Therapy.* Amherst, NY: Prometheus Books.

Ellis, J. (2006a, January 28). "IM-speak" struggle for teachers. *Statesboro Herald,* pp. 1A, 14A.

Ellsworth, P. C., & Smith, C. A. (1988). Shades of joy: Patterns of appraisal differentiating pleasant emotions. *Cognition and Emotion, 2,* 301–331.

Elman, I., Tschibelu, E., & Borsook, D. (2010). Psychosocial stress and its relationship to gambling urges in individuals with pathological gambling. *The American Journal on Addictions, 19,* 332–339.

Else-Quest, N. M., Hyde, J. S., & Linn, M. C. (2010). Cross-national patterns of gender differences in mathematics: A meta-analysis. *Psychological Bulletin, 136,* 103–127.

Elst, T. V., Van den Broeck, A., De Witte, H., & De Cuyper, N. (2012). The mediating role of frustration of psychological needs in the relationship between job insecurity and work-related well-being. *Work & Stress, 26*(3), 252–271. doi:10.1080/02678373.2012.703900

Emanuel, H. M. (1987). Put time on your side. In A. D. Timpe (Ed.), *The management of time.* New York: Facts on File.

Emery, C. F., Anderson, D. R., & Goodwin, C. L. (2012). Coronary heart disease and hypertension. In A. M. Nezu, C. M. Nezu, P. A. Geller, & I. B. Weiner (Eds.), *Handbook of psychology, Vol. 9: Health psychology* (2nd ed.). New York: Wiley.

Emmelkamp, P. M. (2013). Behavior therapy with adults. In M. J. Lambert (Ed.), *Bergin and Garfield's handbook of psychotherapy and behavior change* (6th ed.). New York: Wiley.

Emmons, R. A. (2003). Personal goals, life meaning, and virtue: Wellsprings of a positive life. In C. L. M. Keyes & J. Haidt (Eds.), *Flourishing: Positive psychology and the life well-lived.* Washington, DC: American Psychological Association.

Emmons, R.A. (2005). Giving thanks: Psychological research on gratitude and praise. In C. L. Harper, Jr. (Ed.), *Spiritual information: 100 perspectives* (pp. 451–456). Philadelphia: Templeton Foundation Press.

Endendijk, J. J., Groeneveld, M. G., van der Pol, L. D., van Berkel, S. R., Hallers-Haalboom, E. T., Mesman, J., & Bakermans-Kranenburg, M. J. (2014). Boys don't play with dolls: Mothers' and fathers' gender talk during picture book reading. *Parenting: Science and Practice, 14*(3–4), 141–161. doi:10.1080/15295192.2014.972753

Ent, M. R., & Baumeister, R. F. (2014). Obedience, self-control, and the voice of culture. *Journal of Social Issues, 70*(3), 574-586. doi:10.1111/josi.12079

Epley, N., & Dunning, D. (2000). Feeling "holier than thou": Are self-serving assessments produced by errors in self- or social prediction? *Journal of Personality and Social Psychology, 79*(6), 861–875. doi:10.1037/0022-3514.79.6.861

Epstein, D. H., Phillips, K. A., & Preston, K. L. (2011). Opioids. In P. Ruiz & E. C. Strain (Eds.), *Lowinson and Ruiz's substance abuse: A comprehensive textbook* (5th ed.; pp. 161–190). Philadelphia: Lippincott Williams & Wilkins.

Epstein, R. (2001). Physiologist Laura. *Psychology Today, 34* (4), 5.

Epstein, R. (2007, February–March). The truth about online dating. *Scientific American Mind, 18,* pp. 28–35.

Equal Employment Opportunity Commission. (2007). Occupational employment in private industry by race/ethnic group/sex, and by industry, United States, 2005. Retrieved from www.eeoc.gov/stats/jobpat/2005/national.html

Erickson, K. I., Creswell, J. D., Verstynen, T. D., & Gianaros, P. J. (2014). Health neuroscience: Defining a new field. *Current Directions In Psychological Science, 23*(6), 446–453. doi:10.1177/0963721414549350

Erikson, C. K. (2007). *The science of addiction: From neurobiology to treatment.* New York: Norton.

Escolas, S. M., Pitts, B. L., Safer, M. A., & Bartone, P. T. (2013). The protective value of hardiness on military posttraumatic stress symptoms. *Military Psychology, 25*(2), 116–123. doi:10.1037/h0094953

Eshbaugh, E. M., & Gute, G. (2008). Hookups and sexual regret among college women. *Journal of Social Psychology, 148,* 77–89.

Eskreis-Winkler, L., Shulman, E., Beal, S., & Duckworth, A.L. (2014). The grit effect: Predicting retention in the military, the workplace, school and marriage. *Frontiers in Personality Science and Individual Difference, 5,* 36. Retrieved from www.ncbi.nlm.nih.gov/pmc/articles/PMC3910317

Esterson, A. (2001). The mythologizing of psychoanalytic history: Deception and self-deception in Freud's accounts of the seduction theory episode. *History of Psychiatry, 7,* 329–352.

Evans, G. W., Becker, F. D., Zahn, A., Bilotta, E., & Keesee, A. M. (2012). Capturing the ecology of workplace stress with cumulative risk assessment. *Environment and Behavior, 44*(1), 136–154. doi:10.1177/0013916510389981

Evans, G. W., & Cassells, R. C. (2014). Childhood poverty, cumulative risk exposure, and mental health in emerging adults. *Clinical Psychological Science, 2*(3), 287–296. doi:10.1177/2167702613501496

Evans, G. W., & Kim, P. (2013). Childhood poverty, chronic stress, self-regulation, and coping. *Child Development Perspectives, 7*(1), 43–48. doi:10.1111/cdep.12013

Evans, G. W., & Stecker, R. (2004). Motivational consequences of environmental stress. *Journal of Environmental Psychology, 24*(2), 143–165.

Evans, G. W., & Wener, R. E. (2007). Crowding and personal space invasion on the train: Please don't make me sit in the middle. *Journal of Environmental Psychology, 27,* 90–94. doi:10.1016/j.jenvp.2006.10.002

Everett, M. D., Kinser, A. M., & Ramsey, M. W. (2007). Training for old age: Production functions for the aerobic exercise inputs. *Medicine and Science in Sports and Exercise, 39,* 2226–2233.

Everson, S. A., Kauhanen, J., Kaplan, G. A., Goldberg, D. E., Julkunen, J., Tuomilehto, J., & Salonen, J. T. (1997). Hostility and increased risk of mortality and acute myocardial infarction: The mediating role of behavioral risk factors. *American Journal of Epidemiology, 146*(2), 142–152.

Eyal, K, & Finnerty, K. (2009). The portrayal of sexual intercourse on television: How, who, and with what consequence? *Mass Communication & Society, 12,* 143–169.

Eysenck, H. J. (1967). *The biological basis of personality.* Springfield, IL: Charles C Thomas.

Eysenck, H. J. (1982). *Personality, genetics and behavior: Selected papers.* New York: Praeger.

Eysenck, M. W., Mogg, K., May, J., Richards, A., & Mathews, A. (1991). Bias in interpretation of ambiguous sentences related to threat in anxiety. *Journal of Abnormal Psychology, 100,* 144–150.

Fabes, R. A., Hanish, L. D., & Martin, C.L. (2003). Children at play: The role of peers in understanding the effects of child care. *Child Development, 74,* 1039–1043.

Facebook. (2011). Statistics. Retrieved from www.facebook.com/press/info.php?statistics

Fagundes, C. P., & Way, B. (2014). Early-life stress and adult inflammation. *Current Directions in Psychological Science, 23*(4), 277–283. doi:10.1177/0963721414535603

Fagundes, C. P., Bennett, J. M., Derry, H. M., & Kiecolt-Glaser, J. K. (2011). Relationships and inflammation across the lifespan: Social developmental pathways to disease. *Social and Personality Psychology Compass, 5*(11), 891–903. doi:10.1111/j.1751-9004.2011.00392.x

Fagundes, C. P., Glaser, R., Hwang, B. S., Malarkey, W. B., & Kiecolt-Glaser, J. K. (2013). Depressive symptoms enhance stress-induced inflammatory responses. *Brain, Behavior, and Immunity, 31,* 172–176. doi:10.1016/j.bbi.2012.05.006

Fairbrother, K., & Warn, J. (2003). Workplace dimensions, stress, and job satisfaction. *Journal of Managerial Psychology, 18*(1), 8–21.

Fairburn, C. G., Cooper, Z., & Murphy, R. (2009). Bulimia nervosa. In M. C. Gelder, N. C. Andreasen, J. J. López-Ibor, Jr., & J. R. Geddes (Eds.), *New Oxford textbook of psychiatry, Vol. 1* (2nd ed.). New York: Oxford University Press.

Falconier, M. K., Nussbeck, F., Bodenmann, G., Schneider, H., & Bradbury, T. (2015). Stress from daily hassles in couples: Its effects on intradyadic stress, relationship satisfaction, and physical and psychological well-being. *Journal of Marital and Family Therapy, 41*(2), 221–235. doi:10.1111/jmft.12073

Falomir-Pichastor, J. M., & Frederic, N. S. (2013). The dark side of heterogeneous ingroup identities: National identification, perceived threat, and prejudice against immigrants. *Journal of Experimental Social Psychology, 49*(1), 72–79. doi:10.1016/j.jesp.2012.08.016

Falsetti, S. A., & Ballenger, J. C. (1998). Stress and anxiety disorders. In J. R. Hubbard & E. A. Workman (Eds.), *Handbook of stress medicine: An organ system approach.* New York: CRC Press.

Falvo, R., Capozza, D., Di Bernardo, G. A., & Pagani, A. F. (2015). Can imagined contact favor the "humanization" of the homeless? *TPM-Testing, Psychometrics, Methodology in Applied Psychology, 22*(1), 23–30.

Families and Work Institute. (2004). *Generation and gender in the workplace.* New York: Families and Work Institute.

Faravelli, C., & Pallanti, S. (1989). Recent life events and panic disorders. *American Journal of Psychiatry, 146,* 622–626.

Farber, B. A., & Doolin, E. M. (2011). Positive regard and affirmation. In J. C. Norcross (Ed.), *Psychotherapy relationships that work: Evidence-based responsiveness* (2nd ed.). New York: Oxford University Press. doi:10.1093/acprof:oso/9780199737208.003.0008

Farrington, D. P. (2006). Family Background and Psychopathy. In C. J. Patrick (Ed.), *Handbook of psychopathy* (pp. 229-250). New York: Guilford.

Federal Bureau of Investigation (2011). Crime in the United States 2011. Retrieved from https://www.fbi.gov/about-us/cjis/ucr/crime-in-the-u.s/2011/crime-in-the-u.s.-2011/tables/table_66_arrests_suburban_areas_by_sex_2011.xls

Federal Bureau of Investigation (2013). 2013 Hate Crime Statistics. Retrieved from https://www.fbi.gov/about-us/cjis/ucr/hate-crime/2013

Feeny, N. C., Stines, L. R., & Foa, E. B. (2007). Posttraumatic stress disorder-clinical. In G. Fink (Ed.), *Encyclopedia of stress: Vols. 1–4* (2nd ed., pp. 135–139). San Diego, CA: Elsevier Academic Press.

Fehr, B. (1996). *Friendship processes.* Thousand Oaks, CA: Sage.

Fehr, B. (2000). The life cycle of friendship. In C. Hendrick & S. S. Hendrick (Eds.), *Close relationships: A sourcebook.* Thousand Oaks, CA: Sage.

Fehr, B. (2004). Intimacy expectations in same-sex friendships: A prototype interaction-pattern model. *Journal of Personality and Social Psychology, 86*(2), 265–284.

Fehr, B. (2015). Love: Conceptualization and experience. In M. Mikulincer, P. R. Shaver, J. A. Simpson, & J. F. Dovidio (Eds.), *APA handbook of personality and social psychology, Vol. 3: Interpersonal relations* (pp. 495–522). Washington, DC: American Psychological Association. doi:10.1037/14344-018

Fein, D., Barton, M., Eigsti, I., Kelley, E., Naigles, L., Schultz, R. T., . . . Tyson, K. (2013). Optimal outcome in individuals with a history of autism. *Journal of Child Psychology and Psychiatry, 54*(2), 195–205. doi:10.1111/jcpp.12037

Fein, S. (1996). Effects of suspicion on attributional thinking and the correspondence bias. *Journal of Personality and Social Psychology, 70,* 1164–1184.

Feingold, A. (1988). Matching for attractiveness in romantic partners and same-sex friends: A meta-analysis and theoretical critique. *Psychological Bulletin, 104,* 226–235.

Feingold, A. (1992). Good-looking people are not what we think. *Psychological Bulletin, 111,* 304–341.

Fekadu, A., Wooderson, S. C., Markopoulo, K., Donaldson, C., Papadopoulos, A., & Cleare, A. J. (2009). What happens to patients with treatment-resistant depression? A systematic review of medium to long term outcome studies. *Journal of Affective Disorders, 116*(1–2), 4–11. doi:10.1016/j.jad.2008.10.014

Feldman, D. B., Rand, K. L., & Kahle-Wrobleski, K. (2009). Hope and goal attainment: Testing a basic prediction of hope theory. *Journal of Social and Clinical Psychology, 28*(4), 479–497. doi:10.1521/jscp.2009.28.4.479

Felmlee, D. H., Hilton, K., & Orzechowicz, D. (2012). Romantic attraction and stereotypes of gender and sexuality. In M. A. Paludi (Ed.), *The psychology of love* (pp. 171–186). Santa Barbara, CA: Praeger/ABC-CLIO.

Feng, B., & MacGeorge, E. L. (2010). The influences of message and source factors on advice outcomes. *Communication Research, 37*(4), 553–575. doi:10.1177/0093650210368258

Ferguson, J. Bauld, L., Chesterson, J., & Judge, K. (2005). The English smoking treatment services: One-year outcomes. *Addiction, 100* (Suppl. 2), 59–69.

Ferrando, S. J., Owen, J. A., & Levenson, J. L. (2014). Psychopharmacology. In R. E. Hales, S. C. Yudofsky, & L. W. Roberts (Eds.), *The American Psychiatric Publishing textbook of psychiatry* (6th ed.). Washington, DC: American Psychiatric Publishing.

Ferrari, J. R. (1992). Psychometric validation of two adult measures of procrastination: Arousal and avoidance measures. *Journal of Psychopathology & Behavioral Assessment, 14,* 97–100.

Ferrari, J. R. (2001). Getting things done on time: Conquering procrastination. In C. R. Snyder (Ed.), *Coping with stress: Effective people and processes.* New York: Oxford University Press.

Ferrari, J. R., Diaz-Morales, J. F., O'Callaghan, J., Diaz, K., & Argumedo, D. (2007). Frequent behavioral delay tendencies by adults: International prevalence rates of chronic procrastination. *Journal of Cross-Cultural Psychology, 38,* 458–464.

Ferrari, J. R., Johnson, J. L., & McCown, W. G. (1995). *Procrastination and task avoidance: Theory research and treatment.* New York: Plenum.

Ferreri, F., Lapp, L. K., & Peretti, C. (2011). Current research on cognitive aspects of anxiety disorders. *Current Opinion in Psychiatry, 24*(1), 49–54. doi:10.1097/YCO.0b013e32833f5585

Fervaha, G., Foussias, G., Agid, O., & Remington, G. (2014). Impact of primary negative symptoms on functional outcomes in schizophrenia. *European Psychiatry, 29,* 449–455. doi:10.1016/j.eurpsy.2014.01.007

Festinger, L. (1954). A theory of social comparison processes. *Human Relations, 7,* 117–140.

Fichter, M., Quadflieg, N., & Fisher, U. (2011). Severity of alcohol-related problems and mortality: Results from a 20-year prospective epidemiological community study. *European Archives of Psychiatry & Clinical Neuroscience, 261*(4), 293–302.

Field, A. E., Sonneville, K. R., Crosby, R. D., Swanson, S. A., Eddy, K. T., Camargo, C. A., . . . Micali, N. (2014). Prospective associations of concerns about physique and the development of obesity, binge drinking, and drug use among adolescent boys and young adult men. *JAMA Pediatrics, 168*(1), 34–39. doi:10.1001/jamapediatrics.2013.2915

Field, T. (2014). *Touch* (2nd ed.). Cambridge, MA: MIT Press.

Figueredo, A. J., Gladden, P., Vásquez, G., Wolf, P. S. A., & Jones, D. N. (2009). Evolutionary theories of personality. In P. J. Corr & G. Matthews (Eds.), *The Cambridge handbook of personality psychology* (pp. 265–274). New York: Cambridge University Press.

Finder, A. (2006, June 11). For some, online persona undermines a resume. *New York Times.* Retrieved from www.nytimes.com/2006/06/11/us/11recruit.hymlhtml

Fine, C. (2010). From scanner to sound bite: Issues in interpreting and reporting sex differences in the brain. *Current Directions in Psychological Science, 19*(5), 280–283. doi:10.1177/0963721410383248

Fine, C. (2013). Neurosexism in functional neuroimaging: From scanner to pseudo-science to psyche. In M. K. Ryan & N. R Branscombe (Eds.), *The Sage handbook of gender and psychology* (pp. 45–60). Thousand Oaks, CA: Sage.

Finer, L. B., & Zolna, M.R. (2014). Shifts in intended and unintended pregnancies in the United States, 2001–2008, *American Journal of Public Health, 2014, 104*(S1):S44–S48.

Fingerhut, A. W. (2011). Straight allies: What predicts heterosexuals' alliance with the LGBT community? *Journal of Applied Social Psychology, 41*(9), 2230–2248. doi:10.1111/j.1559-1816.2011.00807.x

Fingerhut, A. W., & Peplau, L. A. (2013). Same-sex romantic relationships. In C. J. Patterson & A. R. D'Augelli, (Eds.), *Handbook of psychology and sexual orientation* (pp. 165–178). New York: Oxford University Press.

Fink, M. (2004). *Electroshock: Healing mental illness.* New York: Oxford University Press.

Fink, M. (2014). What was learned: Studies by the consortium for research in ECT (CORE) 1997–2011. *Acta Psychiatrica Scandinavica 129*(6), 417–426. doi:10.1111/acps.12251

Fink, M., Kellner, C. H., & McCall, W. V. (2014). The role of ECT in suicide prevention. *The Journal of ECT, 30*(1), 5–9. doi:10.1097/YCT.0b013e3182a6ad0d

Fink, M. F. (2009). Nonpharmacological somatic treatments: Electroconvulsive therapy. In M. C. Gelder, N. C. Andreasen, J. J. López-Ibor, Jr., & J. R. Geddes (Eds.), *New Oxford textbook of psychiatry, Vol. 1* (2nd ed.). New York: Oxford University Press.

Finkel, E. J., Cheung, E. O., Emery, L. F., Carswell, K. L., & Larson, G. M. (2015). The suffocation model: Why marriage in America is becoming an all-or-nothing institution. *Current Directions in Psychological Science, 24*(3), 238–244. doi:10.1177/0963721415569274

Finkel, E. J., & Eastwick, P. W. (2015). Interpersonal attraction: In search of a theoretical Rosetta stone. In M. Mikulincer, P. R. Shaver, J. A. Simpson, & J. F. Dovidio (Eds.), *APA handbook of personality and social psychology, Vol. 3: Interpersonal relations* (pp. 179–210). Washington, DC: American Psychological Association. doi:10.1037/14344-007

Finkel, E. J., Eastwick, P. W., Karney, B. R., Reis, H. T., & Sprecher, S. (2012). Online dating: A critical analysis from the perspective of psychological science. *Psychological Science in the Public Interest, 13*(1), 3–66. doi:10.1177/1529100612436522

Finkel, E. J., & Eckhardt, C. I. (2013). Intimate partner violence. In J. A. Simpson & L. Campbell (Eds.), *The Oxford*

handbook of close relationships (pp. 452–474). New York: Oxford University Press.

Finkel, E. J., Norton, M. I., Reis, H. T., Ariely, D., Caprariello, P. A., Eastwick, P. W., . . . Maniaci, M. R. (2015). When does familiarity promote versus undermine interpersonal attraction? A proposed integrative model from erstwhile adversaries. *Perspectives on Psychological Science, 10*(1), 3–19. doi:10.1177/1745691614561682

Fischer, A., & Evers, C. (2013). The social basis of emotion in men and women. In M. K. Ryan & N. R Branscombe (Eds.), *The Sage handbook of gender and psychology* (pp. 181–198). Thousand Oaks, CA: Sage.

Fischer, P., Greitemeyer, T., Kastenmüller, A., Vogrincic, C., & Sauer, A. (2011). The effects of risk-glorifying media exposure on risk-positive cognitions, emotions, and behaviors: A meta-analytic review. *Psychological Bulletin, 137*(3), 367–390. doi:10.1037/a0022267

Fischer, P., Greitemeyer, T., & Pollozek, F. (2006). The unresponsive bystander: Are bystanders more responsive in dangerous emergencies? *European Journal of Social Psychology, 36*, 267–278.

Fischer, P., Krueger, J. I., Greitemeyer, T., Vogrincic, C., Kastenmüller, A., Frey, D., . . . Kainbacher, M. (2011). The bystander-effect: A meta-analytic review on bystander intervention in dangerous and non-dangerous emergencies. *Psychological Bulletin, 137*(4), 517–537. doi:10.1037/a0023304

Fischer, R., Ferreira, M. C., Assmar, E., Redford, P., Harb, C., Glazer, S., Cheng, B.-S., Jiang, D.-Y., Wong, C. C., Kumar, N., Kärtner, J., Hofer, J., & Achoui, M. (2009). Individualism-collectivism as descriptive norms: Development of a subjective norm approach to cultural measurement. *Journal of Cross-Cultural Psychology, 40*(2), 187–213.

Fishman, D. B., Rego, S. A., & Muller, K. L. (2011). Behavioral theories of psychotherapy. In J. C. Norcross, G. R. Vandenbos, & D. K. Freedheim (Eds.), *History of psychotherapy: Continuity and change* (2nd ed.). Washington, DC: American Psychological Association.

Fiske, S. T. (1993). Social cognition and social perception. *Annual Review of Psychology, 44*, 155–194.

Fiske, S. T. (2002). What we know now about bias and intergroup conflict, the problem of the century. *Current Directions in Psychological Science, 11*(4), 123–128.

Fiske, S. T. (2004). *Social beings: A core motives approach to social psychology.* New York: Wiley.

Fiske, S. T., & Taylor, S. E. (2013). *Social cognition: From brains to culture* (2nd ed.). Thousand Oaks, CA: Sage.

Flegal, K. M., Carroll, M. D., Kit, B. K., & Ogden, C. L. (2012). Prevalence of obesity and trends in the distribution of body mass index among US Adults, 1999–2010. *JAMA: Journal of the American Medical Association, 307*(5), 491–497. doi: 10.1001/jama.2012.39

Fletcher, G. J. O. (2002). *The new science of intimate relationships.* Malden, MA: Blackwell. doi:10.1002/9780470773390

Fletcher, G. J. O., Tither, J. M., O'Loughlin, C., Friesen, M., & Overall, N. (2004). Warm and homely or cold and beautiful? Sex differences in trading off traits in mate selection. *Personality and Social Psychology Bulletin, 30*, 659–672.

Flett, G. L., Hewitt, P. L., & Martin, T. R. (1995). Dimensions of perfectionism and procrastination. In J. R. Ferrari, J. L. Johnson, & W. G. McCown (Eds.), *Procrastination and task avoidance: Theory, research, and treatment.* New York: Plenum.

Fleuriet, C., Cole, M., & Guerrero, L. K. (2014). Exploring Facebook: Attachment style and nonverbal message characteristics as predictors of anticipated emotional reactions to Facebook postings. *Journal of Nonverbal Behavior, 38*(4), 429–450. doi:10.1007/s10919-014-0189-x

Floyd, K., Boren, J. P., Hannawa, A. F., Hesse, C., McEwan, B., & Veksler, A. E. (2009). Kissing in marital and cohabiting relationships: Effects on blood lipids, stress, and relationship satisfaction. *Western Journal of Communication, 73*, 113–133.

Folkman, S. (2008). The case for positive emotions in the stress process. *Anxiety, Stress, Coping, 21*, 3–14.

Folkman, S., Moskowitz, J. T., Ozer, E. M., & Park, C. L. (1997). Positive meaningful events and coping in the context of HIV/AIDS. In B. H. Gottlieb (Ed.), *Coping with chronic stress.* New York: Plenum.

Forand, N. R., DeRubeis, R. J., & Amsterdam, J. D. (2013). Combining medication and psychotherapy in the treatment of major mental disorders. In M. J. Lambert (Ed.). *Bergin*

and Garfield's handbook of psychotherapy and behavior change (6th ed.). New York: Wiley.

Forest, A. L., & Wood, J. V. (2012). When social networking is not working: Individuals with low self-esteem recognize but do not reap the benefits of self-disclosure on Facebook. *Psychological Science, 23*(3), 295–302. doi:10.1177/0956797611429709

Forgas, J. P. (2011). Can negative affect eliminate the power of first impressions? Affective influences on primacy and recency effects in impression formation. *Journal of Experimental Social Psychology, 47*(2), 425–429. doi:10.1016/j.jesp .2010.11.005

Forgas, J. P., & Williams, K. D. (Eds.). (2002). *The social self: Cognitive, interpersonal, and intergroup perspectives.* New York: Psychology Press.

Forsyth, D. R. (2013). Social influence and group behavior. In H. Tennen, J. Suls, & I. B. Weiner (Eds.), *Handbook of psychology, Vol. 5: Personality and social psychology* (2nd ed.; pp. 305–328). Hoboken, NJ: Wiley.

Forsyth, D. R., Lawrence, N. K., Burnette, J. L., & Baumeister, R. F. (2007). Attempting to improve the academic performance of struggling college students by bolstering self-esteem: An intervention that backfired. *Journal of Social and Clinical Psychology, 26*, 447–459.

Fortenberry, J. D., Schick, V., Herbenick, D., Sanders, S. A., Dodge, B., & Reece, M. (2010). Sexual behaviors and condom use at last vaginal intercourse: A national sample of adolescents ages 14 to 17 years. *Journal of Sexual Medicine, 7*(5), 305–314.

Fortune, J. L., & Newby-Clark, I. R. (2008). My friend is embarrassing me: Exploring the guilty by association effect. *Journal of Personality and Social Psychology, 95*(6), 1440–1449.

Fournier, J. C., DeRubeis, R. J., Hollon, S. D., Dimidjian, S., Amsterdam, J. D., Shelton, R. C., & Fawcett, J. (2010). Antidepressant drug effects and depression severity: A patient-level meta-analysis. *Journal of the American Medical Association, 303*(1), 47–53.

Fowers, B. J., Applegate, B., Olson, D. H., & Pomerantz, B. (1994). Marital conventionalization as a measure of marital satisfaction: A confirmatory factor analysis. *Journal of Family Psychology, 8*, 98–103.

Fox, G. L., Bruce, C., & Combs-Orme, T. (2000). Parenting expectations and concerns of fathers and mothers of newborn infants. *Family Relations, 49*(2), 123–131.

Fox-Kales, E. (2011). *Body shots: Hollywood and the culture of eating disorders.* Albany, NY: State University of New York Press.

Fragale, A. R., & Grant, A. M. (2015). Busy brains, boasters' gains: Self-promotion effectiveness depends on audiences cognitive resources. *Journal of Experimental Social Psychology, 58*, 63–76. doi:10.1016/j.jesp.2014.12.002

Fraley, R. C. (2002). Attachment stability from infancy to adulthood: Meta-analysis and dynamic modeling of developmental mechanisms. *Personality and Social Psychology Review, 6*(2), 123–151.

Fraley, R., & Shaver, P. R. (2000). Adult romantic attachment: Theoretical developments, emerging controversies, and unanswered questions. *Review of General Psychology, 4*(2), 132–154. doi:10.1037/1089-2680.4.2.132

Frame, L. E., Mattson, R. E., & Johnson, M. D. (2009). Predicting success or failure of marital relationships. In H. T. Reis & S. Sprecher (Eds.), *Encyclopedia of human relationships, Vol. 3* (pp. 1275–1279). Los Angeles: Sage Reference.

Frances, A. (2013). *Saving normal: An insider's revolt against out-of-control psychiatric diagnosis, DSM-5, Big Pharma, and the medicalization of ordinary life.* New York: Morrow.

Frances, A. J., & Widiger, T. (2012). Psychiatric diagnosis: Lessons from the DSM-IV past and cautions for the DSM-5 future. *Annual Review of Clinical Psychology, 8*109-130. doi:10.1146/annurev-clinpsy-032511-143102

Francis, L. A., & Birch, L. L. (2005). Maternal influences on daughters' restrained eating behavior. *Health Psychology, 24*, 548–554.

Francoeur, R. T. (2007). Catholic culture and sexual health. In M. S. Tepper & A. F. Owens (Eds.), *Sexual health, Vol 3: Moral and cultural foundations* (pp. 43–77). Westport, CT: Praeger/Greenwood.

Franić, S., Middeldorp, C. M., Dolan, C. V., Ligthart, L., & Boomsma, D. I. (2010). Childhood and adolescent anxiety and depression: beyond heritability. *Journal of the American Academy of Child & Adolescent Psychiatry, 49*, 820–829.

Frank, J. D. (1961). *Persuasion and healing.* Baltimore: John Hopkins University Press.

Frank, L. R. (1990). Electroshock: Death, brain damage, memory loss, and brainwashing. *The Journal of Mind and Behavior, 11*, 489–512.

Frankenhuis, W. E., & de Weerth, C. (2013). Does early-life exposure to stress shape or impair cognition? *Current Directions in Psychological Science, 22*(5), 407–412. doi:10.1177/0963721413484324

Franko, D. L., & Roehrig, J. P. (2011). African American body images. In T. F. Cash & L. Smolak (Eds.), *Body image: A handbook of science, practice, and prevention* (2nd ed., pp. 221–228). New York: Guilford.

Franko, D. L., Keshaviah, A., Eddy, K. T., Krishna, M., Davis, M. C., Keel, P. K., & Herzog, D. B. (2013). A longitudinal investigation of mortality in anorexia nervosa and bulimia nervosa. *The American Journal of Psychiatry, 170*, 917–925. doi:10.1176/appi.ajp.2013.12070868

Franzoi, S. L., & Kern, K. (2009). Body image, relationship implications. In H. T. Reis & S. Sprecher (Eds.), *Encyclopedia of human relationships, Vol. 1* (pp. 181–183). Los Angeles: Sage Reference.

Frauendorfer, D., & Mast, M. S. (2015). The impact of nonverbal behavior in the job interview. In A. Kostić & D. Chadee (Eds.), *The social psychology of nonverbal communication* (pp. 220–247). New York: Palgrave Macmillan.

Frazier, P. A. (2009). Rape. In H. T. Reis & S. Sprecher (Eds.), *Encyclopedia of human relationships, Vol. 3* (pp. 1325–1328). Los Angeles: Sage Reference.

Frederick, S., & Loewenstein, G. (1999). Hedonic adaptation. In D. Kahneman, E. Diener, & N. Schwarz (Eds.), *Well-being: The foundations of hedonic psychology.* New York: Sage.

Fredrickson, B. L. (1998). What good are positive emotions? *Review of General Psychology, 2*, 300–319.

Fredrickson, B. L. (2002). Positive emotions. In C. R. Snyder & S. J. Lopez (Eds.), *Handbook of positive psychology* (pp. 120–134). New York: Oxford University Press.

Fredrickson, B. L. (2006). The broaden-and-build theory of positive emotions. In M. Csikszentmihalyi & I. S. Csikszentmihalyi (Eds.), *A life worth living: Contributions to positive psychology.* New York: Oxford University Press.

Fredrickson, B. L. (2013). Learning to self-generate positive emotions. In D. Hermans, B. Rimé, & B. Mesquita (Eds.), *Changing emotions* (pp. 151–156). New York: Psychology Press.

Fredrickson, B. L., & Branigan, C. (2005). Positive emotions broaden the scope of attention and thought-action repertoires. *Cognition and Emotion, 19*, 313–332.

Fredrickson, B. L., & Joiner, T. (2002). Positive emotions trigger upward spirals toward emotional well-being. *Psychological Science, 13*, 172–175.

Fredrickson, B. L., Tugade, M. M., Waugh, C. E., & Larkin, G. R. (2003). What good are positive emotions in crises? A prospective study of resilience and emotions following the terrorist attacks on the United States on September 11th, 2001. *Journal of Personality and Social Psychology, 84*(2), 365–376.

Freedman, J. L., & Fraser, S. C. (1966). Compliance without pressure: The foot-in-the-door technique. *Journal of Personality and Social Psychology, 4*, 195–202.

Fremouw, W. J., de Perczel, M., & Ellis, T. E. (1990). *Suicide risk: Assessment and response guidelines.* New York: Pergamon.

French, S. A., Harnack, L., & Jeffrey, R. W. (2000). Fast food restaurant use among women in the Pound of Prevention study: Dietary, behavioral and demographic correlates. *International Journal of Obesity, 24*, 1353–1359.

Freud, S. (1920/1924). *A general introduction to psychoanalysis.* New York: Boni and Liveright.

Freud, S. (1923). The ego and the id. In J. Strachey (Ed., Trans.), *The standard edition of the complete psychological works of Sigmund Freud, Vol. 19.* London: Hogarth.

Friedan, B. (1964). *The feminine mystique.* New York: Dell.

Friedman, H. (2014). Are humanistic and positive psychology really incommensurate? *American Psychologist, 69*(1), 89–90. doi:10.1037/a0034865

Friedman, H. L. (2013). Reconciling humanistic and positive psychology: Bridging the cultural rift. In R. House, D. Kalisch, J. Maidman, R. House, D. Kalisch, J. Maidman (Eds.), *The future of humanistic psychology* (pp. 17–22). Ross-on-Wye, England: PCCS Books.

Friedman, H. L., & Robbins, B. (2012). The negative shadow cast by positive psychology: Contrasting views and implications of humanistic and positive psychology on resiliency. *The Humanistic Psychologist, 40*(1), 87–102. doi:10.1080/08873267.2012.643720

Friedman, H. S. (2007). Personality, disease, and self-healing. In H. S. Friedman & R. C. Silver (Eds.), *Foundations of health psychology*. New York: Oxford University Press.

Friedman, H. S., & Kern, M. L. (2014). Personality, well-being, and health. *Annual Review of Psychology, 65,* 719–742. doi:10.1146/annurev-psych-010213-115123

Friedman, H. S., & Martin, L. R. (2011). *The longevity project: Surprising discoveries for health and long life from the landmark eight-decade study*. New York: Hudson Street/Penguin.

Friedman, M. (1996). *Type A behavior: Its diagnosis and treatment.* New York: Plenum.

Friedman, M., & Rosenman, R. F. (1974). *Type A behavior and your heart.* New York: Knopf.

Frieze, I. H., & Ciccocioppo, M. (2009). Gender-role attitudes. In H. T. Reis & S. Sprecher (Eds.), *Encyclopedia of human relationships, Vol. 1* (pp. 751–754). Los Angeles: Sage Reference.

Frieze, I. H., & Yu Li, M. (2010.) Gender, aggression, and prosocial behavior. In J. C. Chrisler & D. R. McCreary (Eds.), *Handbook of gender research in psychology, Vol. 2* (pp. 311–335). New York: Springer.

Frisby, B. N., Booth-Butterfield, M., Dillow, M. R., Martin, M. M., & Weber, K. D. (2012). Face and resilience in divorce: The impact on emotions, stress, and post-divorce relationships. *Journal of Social and Personal Relationships, 29*(6), 715–735. doi:10.1177/0265407512443452

Froh, J. J. (2009). Positive emotions. In S. J. Lopez (Ed.), *The encyclopedia of positive psychology, Vol. II* (pp. 711–717). Malden, MA: Wiley-Blackwell.

Frost, J. J., Lindberg, L. D., & Finer, L. B. (2012). Young adults' contraceptive knowledge, norms and attitudes: Associations with risk of unintended pregnancy. *Perspectives on Sexual and Reproductive Health, 44*(2), 107–116. doi:10.1363/4410712

Fruhauf, C. A. (2009). Caregiver role. In H. T. Reis & S. Sprecher (Eds.), *Encyclopedia of human relationships, Vol. 2* (pp. 195–197). Los Angeles: Sage Reference.

Fry, R. (2012). The Pew Research Center. No reversal in decline of marriage. Retrieved from www.pewsocialtrends.org/2012/11/20/no-reversal-in-decline-of-marriage

Fry, R. (2015). The Pew Research Center. Record share of young women are living with their parents, relatives. Retrieved from www.pewresearch.org/fact-tank/2015/11/11/record-share-of-young-women-are-living-with-their-parents-relatives

Fuertes, J. N., Mislowack, A., Bennett, J., Paul, L., Gilbert, T. C., Fontan, G., & Boylan, L. S. (2007). The physician-patient working alliance. *Patient Education and Counseling, 66,* 29–36.

Fuglestad, P. T., & Snyder, M. (2009). Self-monitoring. In M. R. Leary & R. H. Hoyle (Eds.), *Handbook of individual differences in social behavior* (pp. 574–591). New York: Guilford.

Fuglestad, P. T., & Snyder, M. (2010). Status and the motivational foundations of self-monitoring. *Social and Personality Psychology Compass, 4*(11), 1031–1041. doi:10.1111/j.1751-9004.2010.00311.x

Fukushima, Y., Ohmura, H., Mokuno, H., Kajimoto, K., Kasai, T., Hirayama, S., . . . Daida, H. (2012). Non-high-density lipoprotein cholesterol is a practical predictor of long-term cardiac death after coronary artery bypass grafting. *Atherosclerosis, 221*(1), 206–211. doi: 10.1016/j.atherosclerosis.2011.12.012

Furnham, A., & Cheng, H. (2000). Perceived parental behavior, self-esteem and happiness. *Social Psychiatry and Psychiatric Epidemiology, 35*(10), 463–470.

Fyer, A. J. (2009). Anxiety disorders: Genetics. In B. J. Sadock, V. A. Sadock, & P. Ruiz (Eds.), *Kaplan & Sadock's comprehensive textbook of psychiatry* (pp. 1898–1905). Philadelphia: Lippincott Williams & Wilkins.

Gable, S. L., Gonzaga, G. C., & Strachman, A. (2006). Will you be there for me when things go right? Supportive responses to positive event disclosures. *Journal of Personality and Social Psychology, 91,* 904–917.

Gable, S. L., Reis, H. T., Impett, E. A., & Asher, E. R. (2004). What do you do when things go right? The intrapersonal and interpersonal benefits of sharing positive events. *Journal of Personality and Social Psychology, 87,* 228–245.

Gabriel, M. T., Critelli, J. W., & Ee, J. S. (1994). Narcissistic illusions in self-evaluation of intelligence and attractiveness. *Journal of Personality, 62,* 143–155.

Gaertner, S. L., & Dovidio, J. F. (2005). Understanding and addressing contemporary racism: From aversive racism to the common ingroup identity model. *Journal of Social Issues, 61,* 615–639.

Gailliot, M. T., Baumeister, R. F., DeWall, C. N., Maner, J. K., Plant, E. A., Tice, D. M., . . . Schmeichel, B. J. (2007). Self-control relies on glucose as a limited energy source: Willpower is more than a metaphor. *Journal of Personality and Social Psychology, 92*(2), 325-336. doi:10.1037/0022-3514.92.2.325

Gaines, Jr., S. O. (2009). Interracial and interethnic relationships. In H. T. Reis & S. Sprecher (Eds.), *Encyclopedia of human relationships, Vol. 1* (pp. 905–907). Los Angeles: Sage Reference.

Gajendran, R. S., & Harrison, D. A. (2007). The good, the bad, and the unknown about telecommuting: Meta-analysis of psychological mediators and individual consequences. *Journal of Applied Psychology, 92*(6), 1524–1541.

Galatzer-Levy, I., Burton, C. L., & Bonanno, G. A. (2012). Coping flexibility, potentially traumatic life events, and resilience: A prospective study of college student adjustment. *Journal of Social and Clinical Psychology, 31*(6), 542–567. doi:10.1521/jscp.2012.31.6.542

Galdas, P. M., Cheater, F., & Marshall, P. (2005). Men and health-seeking behavior: Literature review. *Journal of Advanced Nursing, 49,* 616–623.

Galdi, S., Maass, A., & Cadinu, M. (2014). Objectifying media: Their effect on gender role norms and sexual harassment of women. *Psychology of Women Quarterly, 38*(3), 398–413. doi:10.1177/0361684313515185

Gale, C. R., Booth, T., Mõttus, R., Kuh, D., & Deary, I. J. (2013). Neuroticism and extraversion in youth predict mental wellbeing and life satisfaction 40 years later. *Journal of Research in Personality, 47,* 687–697. doi:10.1016/j.jrp.2013.06.005

Gallagher, D. T., Hadjiefthyvoulou, F., Fisk, J. E., Montgomery, C., Robinson, S. J., & Judge, J. (2014). Prospective memory deficits in illicit polydrug users are associated with the average long-term typical dose of ecstasy typically consumed in a single session. *Neuropsychology, 28*(1), 43–54.

Gallagher, M. W., Lopez, S. J., Pressman, S. D. (2013). Optimism is universal: Exploring the presence and benefits of optimism in a representative sample of the world. *Journal of Personality, 81,* 429–440. doi: 10.1111/jopy.12026

Gallo, K. P., Thompson-Hollands, J., Pincus, D. B., & Barlow, D. H. (2013). Anxiety disorders. In T. A. Widiger, G. Stricker, I. B. Weiner (Eds.), *Handbook of psychology, Vol. 8: Clinical psychology* (2nd ed.). New York: Wiley.

Gamer, M. (2014). Mind reading using neuroimaging: Is this the future of deception detection? *European Psychologist, 19*(3), 172–183. doi:10.1027/1016-9040/a000193

Gananca, L., Kahn, D. A., & Oquendo, M. A. (2014). Mood disorders. In J. L. Cutler (Ed.), *Psychiatry* (3rd ed.). New York: Oxford University Press.

Gangestad, S. W., & Snyder, M. (2000). Self-monitoring appraisal and reappraisal. *Psychological Bulletin, 126*(4), 530–555.

Ganzach, Y. (1998). Intelligence and job satisfaction. *Academy of Management Journal, 41,* 526–539.

Ganzach, Y., & Fried, I. (2012). The role of intelligence in the formation of well-being: From job rewards to job satisfaction. *Intelligence, 40*(4), 333–342. doi:10.1016/j.intell.2012.03.004

Gao, G. (2015). Most Americans now say learning their child is gay wouldn't upset them. Retrieved from www.pewresearch.org/fact-tank/2015/06/29/most-americans-now-say-learning-their-child-is-gay-wouldnt-upset-them

Garcia, J. R., Reiber, C., Massey, S. G., & Merriwether, A. M. (2012). Sexual hookup culture: A review. *Review of General Psychology, 16*(2), 161–176. doi:10.1037/a0027911

Garland, E. L., Fredrickson, B., Kring, A. M., Johnson, D. P., Meyer, P. S., & Penn, D. L. (2010). Upward spirals of positive emotions counter downward spirals of negativity: Insights from the broaden-and-build theory and affective neuroscience on the treatment of emotion dysfunctions and deficits in psychopathology. *Clinical Psychology Review, 30*(7), 849–864. doi:10.1016/j.cpr.2010.03.002.

Garland, E. L., Gaylord, S. A., & Fredrickson, B. L. (2011). Positive reappraisal mediates the stress-reductive effects of mindfulness: An upward spiral process. *Mindfulness, 2*(1), 59–67. doi:10.1007/s12671-011-0043-8

Garnets, L. D., & Kimmel, D. C. (1991). Lesbian and gay male dimensions in the psychological study of human diversity. In J. D. Goodchilds (Ed.), *Psychological perspectives on human diversity in America.* Washington, DC: American Psychological Association.

Gaudiano, B. A., & Miller, I. W. (2013). The evidence-based practice of psychotherapy: Facing the challenges that lie ahead. *Clinical Psychology Review, 33,* 813–824. doi:10.1016/j.cpr.2013.04.004

Gavazzi, S. (2013). Theory and research pertaining to families with adolescents. In G. W. Peterson & K. R. Bush (Eds.), *Handbook of marriage and the family* (3rd ed.; pp. 303–327). New York: Springer Science + Business Media. doi:10.1007/978-1-4614-3987-5_14

Gawronski, B., Brochu, P. M., Sritharan, R., & Strack, F. (2012). Cognitive consistency in prejudice-related belief systems: Integrating old-fashioned, modern, aversive, and implicit forms of prejudice. In B. Gawronski & F. Strack (Eds.), *Cognitive consistency: A fundamental principle in social cognition* (pp. 369–389). New York: Guilford.

Gecas, V., & Seff, M. A. (1990). Families and adolescents: A review of the 1980s. *Journal of Marriage and the Family, 52,* 941–958.

Geisinger, K. F. (2013). Reliability. In K. F. Geisinger, B. A. Bracken, J. F. Carlson, J. C. Hansen, N. R. Kuncel, S. P. Reise, & M. C. Rodriguez (Eds.), *APA handbook of testing and assessment in psychology, Vol. 1: Test theory and testing and assessment in industrial and organizational psychology*. Washington, DC: American Psychological Association. doi:10.1037/14047-002

Gelernter, J. (2015). Genetics of complex traits in psychiatry. *Biological Psychiatry, 77*(1), 36–42. doi:10.1016/j.biopsych.2014.08.005

Gellad, W. F., Grenard, J. L., & Marcum, Z. A. (2011). A systematic review of barriers to medication adherence in the elderly: Looking beyond cost and regimen complexity. *American Journal of Geriatric Pharmacotherapy (AJGP), 9*(1), 11–23. doi:10.1016/j.amjopharm.2011.02.004

Gentile, B., Grabe, S., Dolan-Pascoe, B., Twenge, J. M., Wells, B. E., & Maitino, A. (2009). Gender differences in domain-specific self-esteem: A meta-analysis. *Review of General Psychology, 13*(1), 34–45.

Geraerts, E., Dritschel, B., Kreplin, U., Miyagawa, L., & Waddington, J. (2012). Reduced specificity of negative autobiographical memories in repressive coping. *Journal of Behavior Therapy and Experimental Psychiatry, 43*(Suppl. 1), S32–S36. doi:10.1016/j.jbtep.2011.05.007

Gerding, A., & Signorielli, N. (2014). Gender roles in tween television programming: A content analysis of two genres. *Sex Roles, 70*(1–2), 43–56. doi:10.1007/s11199-013-0330-z

Geurts, T., van Tilburg, T., Poortman, A., & Dykstra, P. A. (2015). Child care by grandparents: Changes between 1992 and 2006. *Ageing & Society, 35*(6), 1318–1334. doi:10.1017/S0144686X14000270

Ghani, J. A., & Deshpande, S. P. (1994). Task characteristics and the experience of optimal flow in human-computer interaction. *The Journal of Psychology, 128*(4), 381–391.

Ghosh, T. S., Van Dyke, M., Maffey, A., Whitley, E., Erpelding, D., & Wolk, L. (2015). Medical marijuana's public health lessons: Implication for retail marijuana in Colorado. *The New England Journal of Medicine, 372*(11), 991–993.

Gibbons, A. M., Cleveland, J. N., & Marsh, R. (2014). Sexual harassment and bullying at work. In J. Lipinski, L. M. Crothers, J. Lipinski, & L. M. Crothers (Eds.), *Bullying in the workplace: Causes, symptoms, and remedies* (pp. 193–222). New York: Routledge/Taylor & Francis Group.

Gibbons, M. B. C., Crits-Christoph, P., & Hearon, B. (2008). The empirical status of psychodynamic therapies. *Annual Review of Clinical Psychology, 4,* 93–108.

Gibbons, R., D., Brown, C. H., Hur, K., Davis, J. M., & Mann, J. J. (2012). Suicidal thoughts and behavior with antidepressant treatment: Reanalysis of the randomized placebo-controlled studies of fluoxetine and venlafaxine. *Archives of General Psychiatry, 69,* 580–587. doi:10.1001/archgenpsychiatry.2011.2048

Gibbs, J. L., Ellison, N. B., & Heino, R. D. (2006). Self-presentation in online personals: The role of anticipated future interaction, self-disclosure, and perceived success in Internet dating. *Communication Research, 33*(2), 152–177.

Gilbert, D. T. (2006). *Stumbling on happiness.* New York: Knopf.

Gilbert, D. T., & Malone, P. S. (1995). The correspondence bias. *Psychological Bulletin, 117,* 21–38.

Gilbert, S., & Kelloway, E. K. (2014). Positive psychology and the healthy workplace. In A. Day, E. K. Kelloway, J. J. Hurrell, A. Day, E. K. Kelloway, & J. J. Hurrell (Eds.), *Workplace well-being: How to build psychologically healthy workplaces* (pp. 50–71). Hoboken, NJ: Wiley-Blackwell.

Gillham, J., & Reivich, K. (2007). Cultivating optimism in childhood and adolescence. In A. Monat, R. S. Lazarus, & G. Reevy (Eds.), *The Praeger handbook on stress and coping* (pp. 309–326). Westport, CT: Praeger.

Gillham, J., & Seligman, M. E. P. (1999). Footsteps on the road to positive psychology. *Behaviour Research and Therapy, 37,* S163–S173.

Gilovich, T., Kruger, J., & Medvec, V. H. (2002). The spotlight effect revisited: Overestimating the manifest variability of our actions and appearance. *Journal of Experimental Social Psychology, 38,* 93–99.

Gilovitch, T., Medvec, V. H., & Savitsky, K. (2000). The spotlight effect in social judgment: An egocentric bias in estimates of one's own actions and appearance. *Journal of Personality and Social Psychology, 78,* 211–222.

Gilson, T. A., Chow, G. M., & Feltz, D. L. (2012). Self-efficacy and athletic squat performance: Positive or negative influences at the within- and between-levels of analysis. *Journal of Applied Social Psychology, 42,* 1467–1485. doi:10.1111/j.1559-1816.2012.00908.x

Gitlin, M. J. (2014). Pharmacotherapy and other somatic treatments for depression. In I. H. Gotlib & C. L. Hammen, (Eds.), *Handbook of depression* (3rd ed). New York: Guilford.

Glascock, J. (2001). Gender roles on prime-time network television: Demograhics and behaviors. *Journal of Broadcasting and Electronic Media, 45*(4), 656–669.

Glassman, A., Maj, M., & Sartorius, N. (2011). *Depression and heart disease.* Hoboken, NJ: Wiley.

Glassman, A., Shapiro, P. A., Ford, D. E., Culpepper, L., Finkel, M. S., Swenson, J. R., Bigger, J. T., Rollman, B. L., & Wise, T. N. (2003). Cardiovascular health and depression. *Journal of Psychiatric Practice, 9*(6), 409–421.

Gleason, M. E. J., & Masumi, I. (2014). Social support. In M. Mikulincer, P. R. Shaver, E. Borgida, & J. A. Bargh (Eds.), *APA handbook of personality and social psychology, Vol. 3: Interpersonal relations.* Washington, DC: American Psychological Association.

Gloria, C. T., & Steinhardt, M. A. (2014). Relationships among positive emotions, coping, resilience, and mental health. *Stress and Health: Journal of the International Society for the Investigation of Stress.* doi: 10.1002/smi.2589

Gluck, M. E. (2006). Stress response and binge eating disorder. *Appetite, 46*(1), 26–30.

Gluszek, A., & Dovidio, J. F. (2010). The way *they* speak: A social psychological perspective on the stigma of nonnative accents in communication. *Personality and Social Psychology Review, 14,* 214–237.

Gmel, G., & Rehm, J. (2003). Harmful alcohol use. *Alcohol Research & Health, 27,* 52–62.

Godlee, F., Smith, J., & Marcovitch, H. (2011). Wakefield's article linking MMR vacine and autism was fraudulent. *BMJ, 342,* 64–66.

Godwin, E. E., Lukow, H. I., & Lichiello, S. (2015). Promoting resilience following traumatic brain injury: Application of an interdisciplinary, evidence-based model for intervention. *Family Relations: An Interdisciplinary Journal of Applied Family Studies, 64*(3), 347–362. doi:10.1111/fare.12122

Goetz, T., Bieg, M., Lüdtke, O., Pekrun, R., & Hall, N. C. (2013). Do girls really experience more anxiety in mathematics? *Psychological Science, 24*(10), 2079–2087. doi:10.1177/0956797613486989

Goff, D. C. (2014). Maintenance treatment with long-acting injectable antipsychotics: Comparing old with new. *Journal of the American Medical Association, 311,* 1973–1974.

Goffman, E. (1959). *The presentation of self in everyday life.* Garden City, NJ: Doubleday.

Goforth, H. W., Caram, L. B., Maldonado, J., Ruiz, P., & Fernandez, F. (2011). Psychiatric complications of HIV-1 infection and drug abuse. In P. Ruiz & E. C. Strain (Eds.), *Lowinson and Ruiz's substance abuse: A comprehensive textbook* (5th ed.; pp. 682–694). Philadelphia: Lippincott Williams & Wilkins.

Gold, J., & Stricker, G. (2013). Psychotherapy integration and integrative psychotherapies. In G. Stricker & T. A. Widiger (Eds.), *Handbook of psychology, Vol. 8: Clinical psychology* (2nd ed.). New York: Wiley.

Goldberg, A. E., & Perry-Jenkins, M. (2004). Division of labor and working-class women's well-being across the transition to parenthood. *Journal of Family Psychology, 18*(1), 225–236.

Goldberg, C., & Zhang, L. (2004). Simple and joint effects of gender and self-esteem on responses to same-sex sexual harrassment. *Sex Roles, 50*(11/12), 823–833.

Goldberg, T. E., David, A., & Gold, J. M. (2011). Neurocognitive impairments in schizophrenia: Their character and their role in symptom formation. In D. R. Weinberger & P. Harrison (Eds.), *Schizophrenia* (3rd ed.). Malden, MA: Wiley-Blackwell.

Goldenberg, I., Goldenberg, H., & Pelavin, E. G. (2011). Family therapy. In R. J. Corsini & D. Wedding (Eds.), *Current psychotherapies* (9th ed.). Belmont, CA: Brooks/Cole.

Goldin-Meadow, S. (2003). *Hearing gesture: How our hands help us think.* Cambridge, MA: Belknap Press of Harvard University Press.

Goldzweig, C. L., Balekian, T. M., Rolon, C., Yano, E. M., & Shekelle, P. G. (2006). The state of women veterans' health research: Results of a systematic literature review. *Journal of General Internal Medicine, 21*(Suppl. 3), S82–S92.

Goleman, D. (2011). *Leadership: The power of social intelligence.* Florence, MA: More Than Sound.

Gomez, A., Brooks, M. L., Buhrmeister, M. D., Vaquez, A., Jetten, J., & Swann, Jr., W. B. (2011). On the nature of identity fusion: Insights into the construct and a new measure. *Journal of Personality and Social Psychology, 100,* 918–933.

Gonzaga, G. C. (2009). Similarity in ongoing relationships. In H. T. Reis & S. Sprecher (Eds.), *Encyclopedia of human relationships, Vol. 3* (pp. 1496–1499). Los Angeles: Sage Reference.

Gonzaga, G. C., Campos, B, & Bradbury, T. (2007). Similarity, convergence, and relationship satisfaction in dating and married couples. *Journal of Personality and Social Psychology, 93,* 34–48.

González, H. M., Vega, W. A., Williams, D. R., Tarraf, W., West, B. T., & Neighbors, H. W. (2010). Depression care in the United States: Too little for too few. *Archives of General Psychiatry, 67*(1), 37–46.

Goodall, K. (1972, November). Field report: Shapers at work. *Psychology Today,* pp. 53–63, 132–138.

Goode-Cross, D. T., Good, G. E. (2008). African American men who have sex with men: Creating safe spaces through relationships. *Psychology of Men & Masculinity, 9,* 221–234.

Gooden, A. M., & Gooden, M. A. (2001). Gender representation in notable children's picture books: 1995–1999. *Sex Roles, 45*(1/2), 89–101.

Goodfriend, W. (2009). Proximity and attraction. In H. T. Reis & S. Sprecher (Eds.), *Encyclopedia of human relationships, Vol. 3* (pp. 1297–1299). Los Angeles: Sage Reference.

Goodheart, C. D. (2006). Evidence, endeavor, and expertise in psychology practice. In C. D. Goodheart, A. E. Kazdin, & R. J. Sternberg (Eds.), *Evidence-based psychotherapy: Where practice and research meet* (pp. 37–62). Washington, DC: American Psychological Association.

Goodrick, G. K., Pendleton, V. R., Kimball, K. T., Poston, W. S., Carlos, R., Rebecca, S., & Foreyt, J. P. (1999). Binge eating severity, self-concept, dieting self-efficacy and social support during treatment of binge eating disorder. *International Journal of Eating Disorders, 26*(3), 295–300.

Goodwin, F. K., & Jamison, K. R. (2007). *Manic-depressive illness: Bipolar disorders and recurrent depression.* New York: Oxford University Press.

Goossens, L., van Roekel, E., Verhagen, M., Cacioppo, J. T., Cacioppo, S., Maes, M., & Boomsma, D. I. (2015). The genetics of loneliness: Linking evolutionary theory to genome-wide genetics, epigenetics, and social science. *Perspectives on Psychological Science, 10*(2), 213–226. doi:10.1177/1745691614564878

Gorchoff, S. M., John, O. P., & Helson, R. (2008). Contextualizing change in marital satisfaction during middle age: An 18-year longitudinal study. *Psychological Science, 19*(11), 1194–1200. doi:10.1111/j.1467-9280.2008.02222.x

Gordon, R. A. (2008). Attributional style and athletic performance: Strategic optimism and defensive pessimism. *Psychology of Sport and Exercise, 9*(3), 336–350.

Gordon, R. M. (2005). The doom and gloom of divorce research: Comment on Wallerstein and Lewis (2004). *Psychoanalytic Psychology, 22,* 450–451.

Gortner, E.M., Rude, S.S., & Pennebaker, J.W. (2006). Benefits of expressive writing in lowering rumination and depressive symptoms. *Behavior Therapy, 37,* 292–303.

Gottdiener, J. S., Krantz, D. S., & Howell, R. H., Hecht, G. M., Klein, J., Falconer, J. J., & Rozanski, A. (1994). Induction of silent myocardial ischemia with mental stress testing: Relationship to the triggers of ischemia during daily life activities and to ischemic functional severity. *Journal of the American College of Cardiology, 24,* 1645–1651.

Gottesman, I. I. (2001). Psychopathology through a life span–genetic prism. *American Psychologist, 56,* 867–878.

Gottfried, A. E., & Gottfried, A. W. (2008). The upside of maternal and dual-earner employment: A focus on positive family adaptations, home environments, and child development in the Fullerton longitudinal study. In A. Marcus-Newhall, D. F. Halpern, & S. J. Tan (Eds.), *The changing realities of work and family* (pp. 25–42). Malden, MA: Wiley-Blackwell.

Gottman, J. M. (1994). *What predicts divorce?* Hillsdale, NJ: Erlbaum.

Gottman, J. M. (2011). *The science of trust: Emotional attunement for couples.* New York: Norton.

Gottman, J. M., & Gottman, J. S. (2008). Gottman method couple therapy. In A. S. Gurman (Ed.), *Clinical handbook of couple therapy* (4th ed., pp. 138–164). New York: Guilford.

Gottman, J. M., Gottman, J. S., & DeClaire, J. (2006). *Ten lessons to transform your marriage.* New York: Three Rivers Press.

Gottman, J., Gottman, J. S., Greendorfer, A., & Wahbe, M. (2014). An empirically based approach to couples' conflict. In P. T. Coleman, M. Deutsch, E. C. Marcus, P. T. Coleman, M. Deutsch, E. C. Marcus (Eds.), *The handbook of conflict resolution: Theory and practice* (3rd ed.; pp. 898–920). San Francisco, CA: Jossey-Bass.

Grafanaki, S., Brennan, M., Holmes, S., Tang, K., & Alvarez, S. (2007). In search of flow in counseling and psychotherapy: Identifying the necessary ingredients of peak moments of therapy interaction. *Person-Centered and Experiential Psychotherapies, 6*(4), 240–255.

Granhag, P. A., Vrij, A., & Verschuere, B. (2015). *Detecting deception: Current challenges and cognitive approaches.* Hoboken, NJ: Wiley-Blackwell.

Granic, I., Lobel, A., & Engels, R. E. (2014). The benefits of playing video games. *American Psychologist, 69*(1), 66–78. doi:10.1037/a0034857

Gray, A. W., Parkinson, B., & Dunbar, R. I. (2015). Laughter's influence on the intimacy of self-disclosure. *Human Nature, 26*(1), 28–43. doi:10.1007/s12110-015-9225-8

Graziano, W. G., & Tobin, R. M. (2009). Agreeableness. In M. R. Leary & R. H. Hoyle (Eds.), *Handbook of individual differences in social behavior* (pp. 46–61). New York: Guilford.

Grearson, J, & Smith, L. (2009). The luckiest girls in the world. In T. A. Karis & K. D. Killian, *Intercultural couples: Exploring diversity in intimate relationships* (pp. 71–87). New York: Routledge/Taylor & Francis Group.

Green, J. D., Sedikides, C., & Gregg, A. P. (2008). Forgotten but not gone: The recall and recognition of self-threatening memories. *Journal of Experimental Social Psychology, 44,* 547–561.

Green, L. (2013). Integral diversity in action: Implementing an integral diversity program in a workplace environment. *Journal of Integral Theory and Practice, 8*(3–4), 56–65.

Green, L. R., Richardson, D. S., Lago, T., & Schatten-Jones, E. C. (2001). Network correlates of social and emotional loneliness in young and older adults. *Personality and Social Psychol Bulletin, 27*(3), 281–288.

Greenaway, K. H., Louis, W. R., Hornsey, Mogy. J., & Jones, J. M. (2014). Perceived control qualifies the effects of threat on prejudice. *British Journal of Social Psychology, 53*(3), 422–442. doi:10.1111/bjso.12049

Greenberg, J., Landau, M., Kosloff, S., & Solomon, S. (2009). How our dreams of death transcendence breed prejudice, stereotyping, and conflict: Terror management theory. In T. D. Nelson (Ed.), *Handbook of prejudice, stereotyping, and discrimination* (pp. 309–332). New York: Psychology Press.

Greenberg, J. S. (2002). *Comprehensive stress management: Health and human performance.* New York: McGraw-Hill.

Greene, K., Derlega, V., & Mathews, A. (2006). Self-disclosure in personal relationships. In A. L. Vangelisti & D. Perlman (Eds.), *Cambridge handbook of personal relationships.* Cambridge, MA: Cambridge University Press.

Greenhaus, J. H. (2003). Career dynamics. In W. C. Borman, D. R. Ilgen, & R. J. Klimoski (Eds.), *Handbook of psychology, Vol. 12: Industrial and organizational psychology*. New York: Wiley.

Green McDonald, P., O'Connell, M., & Suls, J. (2015). Cancer control falls squarely within the province of the psychological sciences. *American Psychologist 70*(2), 61–74. doi: 10.1037/a00038873.

Greenson, R. R. (1967). *The technique and practice of psychoanalysis, Vol. 1*. New York: International Universities Press.

Greenwald, A. G., Poehlman, T. A., Uhlmann, E. L., & Banaji, M. R. (2009). Understanding and using the Implicit Association Test: III. Meta-analysis of predictive validity. *Journal of Personality And Social Psychology, 97*(1), 17–41. doi:10.1037/a0015575

Greenwood, D. N., & Lippman, J. R. (2010). Gender and media: Content, uses, and impact. In J. C. Chrisler & D. R. McCreary (Eds.), *Handbook of gender research in psychology, Vol. 2* (pp. 643–669). New York: Springer.

Greitemeyer, T., & Mügge, D. O. (2015). When bystanders increase rather than decrease intentions to help. *Social Psychology, 46*(2), 116–119. doi:10.1027/1864-9335/a000215

Grekin, E. R., & Ayna, D. (2012). Waterpipe smoking among college students in the United States: A review of the literature. *Journal of American College Health, 60*(3), 244–249. doi:10.1080/07448481.2011.589419

Griffeth, R. W., Hom, P. W., & Gaertner, S. (2000). A meta-analysis of antecedents and correlates of employee turnover: Update, moderator tests, and research implications for the next millennium. *Journal of Management, 26*, 463–488.

Griffith, K. H., & Hebl, M. R. (2002). The disclosure dilemma for gay men and lesbians: "Coming out" at work. *Journal of Applied Psychology, 87*(6), 1191–1199.

Griffiths, M. (2011). Workaholism—a 21st-century addiction. *The Psychologist, 24*(10), 740–744.

Grijalva, E., Newman, D. A., Tay, L., Donnellan, M. B., Harms, P. D., Robins, R. W., & Yan, T. (2015). Gender differences in narcissism: A meta-analytic review. *Psychological Bulletin, 141*(2), 261–310. doi:10.1037/a0038231

Griskevicius, V., Haselton, M. G., & Ackerman, J. M. (2015). Evolution and close relationships. In M. Mikulincer, P. R. Shaver, J. A. Simpson, & J. F. Dovidio (Eds.), *APA handbook of personality and social psychology, Vol. 3: Interpersonal relations* (pp. 3–32). Washington, DC: American Psychological Association. doi:10.1037/14344-001

Groleau, J. M., Calhoun, L. G., Cann, A., & Tedeschi, R. G. (2012). The role of centrality of events in posttraumatic distress and posttraumatic growth. *Psychological Trauma: Theory, Research, Practice, and Policy*. doi:10.1037/a0028809

Gross, A. L., Brandt, J., Bandeen-Roche, K., Carlson, M. C., Stuart, E. A., Marsiske, M., & Rebok, G. W. (2014). Do older adults use the method of loci? Results from the active study. *Experimental Aging Research, 40*, 140–163. doi:10.1080/0361073X.2014.882204

Gross, J. J. (2001). Emotion regulation in adulthood: Timing is everything. *Current Directions in Psychological Science, 10*, 214–219.

große Deters, F., Mehl, M. R., & Eid, M. (2014). Narcissistic power poster? On the relationship between narcissism and status updating activity on Facebook. *Journal of Research in Personality, 53*, 165–174. doi:10.1016/j.jrp.2014.10.004

Grothues, C. A., & Marmion, S. L. (2006). Dismantling the myths about intimate violence against women. In P. K. Lundberg-Love & S. L. Marmion (Eds.), *"Intimate" violence against women: When spouses, partners, or lovers attack*. Westport, CT: Praeger.

Gruber, J., & Moskowitz, J. T. (2014). *Positive emotion: Integrating the light sides and dark sides*. New York: Oxford University Press.

Grunberg, N. E., Berger, S. S., & Hamilton, K. R. (2011). Stress and drug use. In R. J. Contrada & A. Baum (Eds.), *The handbook of stress science: Biology, psychology, and health* (pp. 286–300). New York: Springer.

Grunberg, N. E., Faraday, M. M., & Rahman, M. A. (2001). The psychobiology of nicotine self-administration. In A. Baum, T. A. Revenson, & Singer, J. E. (Eds.), *Handbook of health psychology* (pp. 249–261). Mahwah, NJ: Erlbaum.

Grusec, J. E., & Davidov, M. (2015). Analyzing socialization from a domain-specific perspective. In J. E. Grusec, P. D. Hastings, J. E. Grusec, & P. D. Hastings (Eds.), *Handbook of socialization: Theory and research* (2nd ed.; pp. 158–181). New York: Guilford.

Guadagno, R. E., & Cialdini, R. B. (2010). Preference for consistency and social influence: A review of current research findings. *Social Influence, 5*(3), 152–163. doi:10.1080/15534510903332378

Guarda, A. S., Pinto, A. M., Coughlin, J. W., Hussain, S., Haug, N. A., & Heinberg, L. J. (2007). Perceived coercion and change in perceived need for admission in patients hospitalized for eating disorders. *American Journal of Psychiatry, 164*, 108–114.

Guéguen, N. (2002). Status, apparel and touch: Their joint effects on compliance to a request. *North American Journal of Psychology, 4*(2), 279–286.

Guéguen, N., & Pascual, A. (2014). Low-ball and compliance: Commitment even if the request is a deviant one. *Social Influence, 9*(3), 162–171. doi:10.1080/15534510.2013.798243

Guéguen, N., Bougeard-Delfosse, C., & Jacob, C. (2015). The positive effect of the mere presence of a religious symbol on compliance with an organ donation request. *Social Marketing Quarterly, 21*(2), 92–99. doi:10.1177/1524500415582070

Guéguen, N., Fischer-Lokou, J., Lefebvre, L., & Lamy, L. (2008). Women's eye contact and men's later interest: Two field experiments. *Perceptual and Motor Skills, 106*(1), 63–66.

Guéguen, N., Jacob, C., & Meineri, S. (2011). Effects of the door-in-the-face technique on restaurant customers' behavior. *International Journal of Hospitality Management, 30*(3), 759–761. doi:10.1016/j.ijhm.2010.12.010

Guéguen, N., Joule, R., Courbert, D., Halimi- Falkowicz, S., & Marchand, M. (2013). Repeating "yes" in a first request and compliance with a later request: The four walls technique. *Social Behavior And Personality, 41*(2), 199–202. doi:10.2224/sbp.2013.41.2.199

Gull, M., & Rana, S. A. (2013). Manifestation of forgiveness, subjective well being and quality of life. *Journal of Behavioural Sciences, 23*(2), 18–36.

Günaydin, G., Zayas, V., Selcuk, E., & Hazan, C. (2012). I like you but I don't know why: Objective facial resemblance to significant others influences snap judgments. *Journal of Experimental Social Psychology, 48*(1), 350–353. doi:10.1016/j.jesp.2011.06.001

Gunthert, K. (2014). Special series: Part I. Cultural competence at the intersection of research, practice, and training. *The Behavior Therapist, 37*(5), 100–101.

Gupta, U., & Singh, P. (1982). Exploratory study of love and liking type of marriages. *Indian Journal of Applied Psychology, 19*, 92–97.

Gustafsson Sendén, M., Sikström, S., & Lindholm, T. (2015). "She" and "he" in news media messages: Pronoun use reflects gender biases in semantic contexts. *Sex Roles, 72*(1–2), 40–49. doi:10.1007/s11199-014-0437-x

Gutman, D. A., & Nemeroff, C. B. (2011). Stress and depression. In R. J. Contrada & A. Baum (Eds.), *The handbook of stress science: Biology, psychology, and health* (pp. 345–357). New York: Springer.

Guttmacher Insitute (2015). Sex and HIV education. Retrieved from www.guttmacher.org/statecenter/spibs/spib_SE.pdf

Haas, L. (1999). Families and work. In M. B. Sussman, S. K. Steinmetz, & G. W. Peterson (Eds.), *Handbook of marriage and the family*. New York: Plenum.

Hadjikhani, N., Hoge, R., Snyder, J., & de Gelder, B. (2008). Pointing with the eyes: The role of gaze in communicating danger. *Brain and Cognition, 68*(1), 1–8.

Hafer, C. L. (2000). Do innocent victims threaten the belief in a just world? Evidence from a modified Stroop task. *Journal of Personality and Social Psychology, 79*(2), 165–173.

Haglund, K. A., & Fehring, R. J. (2010). The association of religiosity, sexual education, and parental factors with risky sexual behaviors among adolescents and young adults. *Journal of Religion and Health, 49*(4), 460–472. doi:10.1007/s10943-0099267-5

Hahn-Holbrook, J., & Haselton, M. (2014). Is postpartum depression a disease of modern civilization? *Current Directions In Psychological Science, 23*(6), 395–400. doi:10.1177/0963721414547736

Hale, W. J., Perrotte, J. K., Baumann, M. R., & Garza, R. T. (2015). Low self-esteem and positive beliefs about smoking: A destructive combination for male college students. *Addictive Behaviors, 46*, 94–99. doi:10.1016/j.addbeh.2015.03.007

Halim, M. L., & Ruble, D.. (2010). Gender identity and stereotyping in early and middle childhood. In J. C. Chrisler & D. R. McCreary (Eds.), *Handbook of gender research in psychology, Vol. 1* (pp. 495–525). New York: Springer.

Hall, D. T., Feldman, E., & Kim, N. (2013). Meaningful work and the protean career. In B. J. Dik, Z. S. Byrne, & M. F. Steger (Eds.), *Purpose and meaning in the workplace* (pp. 57–78). Washington, DC: American Psychological Association. doi:10.1037/14183-004

Hall, E. T. (1966) *The hidden dimension*. Garden City, NY: Doubleday.

Hall, E. T. (2008). Adumbration as a feature of intercultural communication. In C. D. Mortensen (Ed.), *Communication theory* (2nd ed., pp. 420–432). New Brunswick, NJ: Transaction Publishers.

Hall, E. T., & Whyte, W. (2008). Intercultural communication. In C. Mortensen (Ed.), *Communication theory* (2nd ed., pp. 403-419). Piscataway, NJ: Transaction Publishers.

Hall, H. I., Song, R., Rhodes, P., Prejean, J., An, Q., Lee, L. M., . . . Janssen, R. S. (2008). Estimation of HIV incidence in the United States. *JAMA: Journal of the American Medical Association, 300*(5), 520–529. doi:10.1001/jama.300.5.520

Hall, J., Trent, S., Thomas, K. L., O'Donovan, M. C., & Owen, M. J. (2015). Genetic risk for schizophrenia: Convergence on synaptic pathways involved in plasticity. *Biological Psychiatry, 77*(1), 52–58. doi:10.1016/j.biopsych.2014.07.011

Hall, J. A. (2006a). How big are nonverbal sex differences? The case of smiling and nonverbal sensitivity. In K. Dindia & D. Canary (Eds.), *Sex differences and similarities in communication* (pp. 59–81). Mahwah, NJ: Erlbaum.

Hall, J. A. (2006b). Women's and men's nonverbal communication: Similarities, differences, stereotypes, and origins. In V. Manusov & M. L. Patterson (Eds.), *The Sage handbook of nonverbal communication* (pp. 201–218). Thousand Oaks, CA: Sage.

Hall, J. A. (2011). Sex differences in friendship expectations: A meta-analysis. *Journal of Social and Personal Relationships, 28*(6), 723–747. doi:10.1177/0265407510386192

Hall, J. A. (2012). Friendship standards: The dimensions of ideal expectations. *Journal of Social and Personal Relationships, 29*(7), 884–907. doi:10.1177/0265407512448274

Hall, J. A., Blanch-Hartigan, D., & Roter, D. L. (2011). Patients' satisfaction with male versus female physicians: A meta-analysis. *Medical Care, 49*, 611–617.

Hall, J. A., Coats, E., & Smith-LeBeau, L. (2005). Nonverbal behavior and the vertical dimension of social relations: A meta-analysis. *Psychological Bulletin, 131*, 898–924.

Hall, J. A., Larson, K. A., & Watts, A. (2011). Satisfying friendship maintenance expectations: The role of friendship standards and biological sex. *Human Communication Research, 37*(4), 529–552. doi:10.1111/j.1468-2958.2011.01411.x

Hall, J. A., & Matsumoto, D. (2004). Gender differences in judgments of multiple emotions from facial expressions. *Emotion, 4*(2), 201–206.

Hall, P., West, J. H., & Hill, S. (2012). Sexualization in lyrics of popular music from 1959 to 2009: Implications for sexuality educators. *Sexuality and Culture: An Interdisciplinary Quarterly, 16*(2), 103–117. doi:10.1007/s12119-011-9103-4

Hallowell, E. M. (2006*). Crazy busy: Overstretched, overbooked, and about to snap! Strategies for handling your fast-paced life*. New York: Ballantine.

Halmi, K. A. (2008). Eating disorders: Anorexia nervosa, bulimia nervosa, and obesity. In R. E. Hales, S. C. Yudofsky, & G. O. Gabbard (Eds.), *The American Psychiatric Publishing textbook of psychiatry* (pp. 971–998). Washington, DC: American Psychiatric Publishing.

Halpern, D. F. (1997). Sex differences in intelligence: Implications for education. *American Psychologist, 52*, 1091–1102.

Halpern, D. F. (2000). *Sex differences in cognitive abilities* (3rd ed.). Mahwah, NJ: Erlbaum.

Halpern, D. F. (2004). A cognitive-process taxonomy for sex differences in cognitive abilities. *Current Directions in Psychological Science, 13*(4), 135–139.

Halpern, D. F. (2005). Psychology at the intersection of work and family: Recommendations for employers, working families, and policymakers. *American Psychologist, 60*, 397–409.

Halpern, S. D., French, B., Small, D. S., Saulsgiver, K., Harhay, M. O., Audrain-McGovern, J., Loewenstein, G., Brennan, T. A., Asch, D. A., & Volpp, K. G. (2015). Randomized trial of four financial-incentive programs for smoking cessation. *The New England Journal of Medicine, 372*(22), 2108–2117. doi: 10.1056/NEJMoa1414293

Ham, J., & Vonk, R. (2011). Impressions of impression management: Evidence of spontaneous suspicion of ulterior motivation. *Journal of Experimental Social Psychology, 47*(2), 466–471. doi:10.1016/j.jesp.2010.12.008

Hames, J. L., Hagan, C. R., & Joiner, T. E. (2013). Interpersonal processes in depression. *Annual review of clinical psychology, 9,* 355–377. doi:10.1146/annurev-clinpsy-050212-185553

Hamilton, A. (1999). You've got mail! *Time,* 83.

Hamilton, B. E., Martin, J. A., Osterman, M. J. K., & Curtin, S. C. (2015). Births: Final data for 2013. Hyattsville, MD: National Center for Health Statistics. Retrieved from www.cdc.gov/nchs/data/nvsr/nvsr64/nvsr64_01.pdf

Hamilton, J. C., Deemer, H. N., & Janata, J. W. (2003). Feeling sad but looking good: Sick role features that lead to favorable interpersonal judgments. *Journal of Social and Clinical Psychology, 22*(3), 253–274.

Hammen, C. L., & Shih, J. (2014). Depression and interpersonal processes. In I. H. Gotlib & C. L. Hammen (Eds.), *Handbook of depression* (3rd ed.). New York: Guilford.

Hammen, C., & Keenan-Miller, D. (2013). Mood disorders. In T. A. Widiger, G. Stricker, & I. B. Weiner (Eds.), *Handbook of psychology, Vol. 8: Clinical psychology* (2nd ed.). New York: Wiley.

Han, S. (1998). The relationship between life satisfaction and flow in elderly Korean immigrants. In M. Csikszentmihalyi & I. S. Csikszentmihalyi (Eds.), *Optimal experiences: Psychological studies of flow in consciousness* (pp. 138–149). New York: Cambridge University Press

Hanayama, A., & Mori, K. (2011). Conformity of six-year-old children in the Asch experiment without using confederates. *Psychology, 2*(7), 661–664. doi:10.4236/psych.2011.27100

Hand, M. M., Thomas, D., Buboltz, W. C., Deemer, E. D., & Buyanjargal, M. (2013). Facebook and romantic relationships: Intimacy and couple satisfaction associated with online social network use. *Cyberpsychology, Behavior, and Social Networking, 16*(1), 8–13. doi:10.1089/cyber.2012.0038

Hanna, S. L., Suggett, R., & Radtke, D. (2008). *Person to person: Positive relationships don't just happen.* Upper Saddle River, NJ: Pearson/Prentice Hall.

Hansen, H., Dugan, T. M., Becker, A. E., Lewis-Fernández, R., Lu, F. G., Oquendo, M. A., . . . Trujillo, M. (2013). Educating psychiatry residents about cultural aspects of care: A qualitative study of approaches used by U.S. expert faculty. *Academic Psychiatry, 37,* 412–416. doi:10.1176/appi.ap.12080141

Hansen, J. C. (2005). Assessment of interests. In S. D. Brown & R. W. Lent (Eds.), *Career development and counseling: Putting theory and research to work.* Hoboken, NJ: Wiley.

Hansen, P. E., Floderus, B., Fredrickson, K., & Johansen, C. B. (2005). Personality traits, health behavior, and risk for cancer: A prospective study of a twin cohort. *Cancer, 103,* 1082–1091.

Happonen, P., Voutilainen, S., & Salonen, J. T. (2004). Coffee drinking is dose dependently related to the risk of acute coronary events in middle-aged men. *Journal of Nutrition, 134*(9), 2381–2386.

Harari, Y. N. (2008). Combat flow: Military, political, and ethical dimensions of subjective well-being in war. *Review of General Psychology, 12*(3), 253–264.

Harasymchuk, C., & Fehr, B. (2010). A script analysis of relational boredom: Causes, feelings, and coping strategies. *Journal of Social and Clinical Psychology, 29*(9), 988–1019. doi:10.1521/jscp.2010.29.9.988

Harber, K. D., Zimbardo, P. G., & Boyd, J. N. (2003). Participant self-selection bias as a function of individual differences in time perspective. *Basic and Applied Social Psychology, 25,* 255–264.

Hardin, E. E., & Lakin, J. L. (2009). The Integrated Self-Discrepancy Index: A valid and reliable measure of self-discrepancies. *Journal of Personality Assessment, 91*(3), 245–253.

Hare, R. D., & Neumann, C. S. (2008). Psychopathy as a clinical and empirical construct. *Annual Review of Clinical Psychology, 4,* 217–246. doi:10.1146/annurev.clinpsy.3.022806.091452

Hargie, O. (2011). *Skilled interpersonal communication: Research, theory, and practice* (5th ed.). New York: Routedge/Taylor & Francis.

Hariharan, M., Swain, S., & Chivukula, U. (2014). Childhood stress and its impact on learning and academic performance. In A. J. Holliman, A. J. Holliman (Eds.), *The Routledge international companion to educational psychology* (pp. 127–139). New York: Routledge/Taylor & Francis Group.

Haring, M., Hewitt, P. L., & Flett, G. L. (2003). Perfectionism, coping, and quality of intimate relationships. *Journal of Marriage & Family, 65*(1), 143–158.

Harrigan, J. A., Lucic, K. S., Kay, D., McLaney, A., & Rosenthal, R. (1991). Effect of expresser role and type of self-touching on observers' perceptions. *Journal of Applied Psychology, 21,* 585–609.

Harrington, T., & Long, J. (2013). The history of interest inventories and career assessments in career counseling. *The Career Development Quarterly, 61*(1), 83–92. doi:10.1002/j.2161-0045.2013.00039.x

Harris, C., & Wagner, D. (2009, October 23). Business has grown for sweat-lodge guru: Cracks form in motivational mogul's empire. *The Arizona Republic.* Retrieved from www.azcentral.com/12news/news/articles/2009/10/23/20091023rayprofile1023-CP.html

Harris, J. B., Schwartz, S. M., & Thompson, B. (2008). Characteristics associated with self-identification as a regular smoker and desire to quit among college students who smoke cigarettes. *Nicotine and Tobacco Research, 10,* 69–76.

Harris, T. (1967). *I'm OK—You're OK.* New York: HarperCollins.

Harrison, D. A., Kravitz, D. A., Mayer, D. M., Leslie, L. M., & Lev-Arey, D. (2006). Understanding attitudes towards affirmative action programs in employment: Summary and meta-analyses of 35 years of research. *Journal of Applied Psychology, 91,* 1013–1036.

Harrison, J. A., & Wells, R. B. (1991). Bystander effects on male helping behavior: Social comparison and diffusion of responsibility. *Representative Research in Social Psychology, 19*(1), 53–63.

Harter, J. K. (2008). Employee engagement: How great managing drives performance. In S. J. Lopez (Ed.), *Positive psychology: Exploring the best in people, Vol. 4* (pp. 99–110). Westport, CT: Praeger.

Harter, S. (1998). The development of self-representations. In N. Eisenberg (Ed.), *Handbook of child psychology, Vol. 3: Social, emotional, and personality development.* New York: Wiley.

Harter, S. (2003). The development of self-representations during childhood and adolescence. In M. R. Leary & J. P. Tangney (Eds.), *Handbook of self and identity.* New York: Guilford.

Harter, S. (2012). Emerging self-processes during childhood and adolescence. In M. R. Leary & J. P. Tangney (Eds.), *Handbook of self and identity* (2nd ed., pp. 680–715). New York: Guilford.

Hartl, A. C., Laursen, B., & Cillessen, A. N. (2015). A survival analysis of adolescent friendships: The downside of dissimilarity. *Psychological Science, 26*(8), 1304–1315. doi:10.1177/0956797615588751

Hartmann, E., & Hartmann, T. (2014). The impact of exposure to Internet-based information about the Rorschach and the MMPI–2 on psychiatric outpatients' ability to simulate mentally healthy test performance. *Journal of Personality Assessment, 96,* 432–444. doi:10.1080/00223891.2014.882342

Hartung, P. J., & Niles, S. G. (2000). Established career theories. In D. A. Luzzo (Ed.), *Career counseling of college students: An empirical guide to strategies that work* (pp. 3–21). Washington, DC: American Psychological Association. doi:10.1037/10362-001

Harvard Crimson. (2005, January 14). Full transcript: President Summers' remarks at the National Bureau of Economic Research. *Harvard Crimson,* Retrieved from www.thecrimson.com/article.aspx?ref=505844

Harvey, J. H., & Omarzu, J. (1999). *Minding the close relationship: A theory of relationship enhancement.* New York: Cambridge University Press.

Harvey, P. D., & Bowie, C. R. (2013). Schizophrenia spectrum disorders. In T. A. Widiger, G. Stricker, & I. B. Weiner, (Eds.), *Handbook of psychology, Vol. 8: Clinical psychology* (2nd ed.). New York: Wiley.

Hasan, Y., Bègue, L., & Bushman, B. J. (2012). Viewing the world through "blood-red tinted glasses": The hostile expectation bias mediates the link between violent video game exposure and aggression. *Journal of Experimental Social Psychology, 48*(4), 953–956.

Hasan, Y., Bègue, L., & Bushman, B. J. (2013). Violent video games stress people out and make them more aggressive. *Aggressive Behavior, 39*(1), 64–70. doi:10.1002/ab.21454

Haskell, W. L., Lee, I., Pate, R. R., Powell, K. E., Blair, S. N., Franklin, B. A., . . . Bauman, A. (2007). Physical activity and public health: Updated recommendations from the American College of Sports Medicine and the American Heart Association. *Medical Science Sports Exercise, 39,* 1423–1434.

Hass, N. (2006. January 8). In your Facebook. Retrieved from www.nytimes.com/2006/01/08/education/edlife/facebooks.html

Hatch, A. (2009). Alternative relationship lifestyles. In H. T. Reis & S. Sprecher (Eds.), *Encyclopedia of human relationships, Vol. 2* (pp. 85–88). Los Angeles: Sage Reference.

Hatcher, R. A., Trussell, J., Stewart, F. H., Nelson, A. L., Cates, W. Jr., Guest, F., & Kowal, D. (2004). *Contraceptive technology.* New York: Ardent Media.

Hatfield, E., & Rapson, R. L. (1993). *Love, sex, and intimacy: Their psychology, biology, and history.* New York: HarperCollins.

Hatfield, E., & Sprecher, S. (2009). Matching hypothesis. In H. T. Reis & S. Sprecher (Eds.), *Encyclopedia of human relationships, Vol. 2* (pp. 1065–1067). Los Angeles: Sage Reference.

Hatzenbuehler, M. L., Hilt, L. M., & Nolen-Hoeksema, S. (2010). Gender, sexual orientation, and vulnerability to depression. In J. C. Chrisler & D. R. McCreary (Eds.), *Handbook of gender research in psychology, Vol. 2* (pp. 133–151). New York: Springer.

Haushofer, J., & Fehr, E. (2014). On the psychology of poverty. *Science, 344*(6186), 862–867. doi:10.1126/science.1232491

Havas, S., Dickinson, B. D., & Wilson, M. (2007). The urgent need to reduce sodium consumption. *Journal of the American Medical Association, 298,* 1439–1441.

Hawkins, D. N., & Booth, A. (2005). Unhappily ever after: Effects of long-term, low-quality marriages on well-being. *Social Forces, 84,* 451–471.

Hayati, A. M., & Shariatifar, S. (2009). Mapping strategies. *Journal of College Reading and Learning, 39,* 53–67.

Haynes, G. A., & Olson, J. M. (2006). Coping with threats to just-world beliefs: Derogate, blame, or help? *Journal of Applied Social Psychology, 36*(3), 664–682.

Hays, P. A. (2014). *Creating well-being: Four steps to a happier, healthier life* (pp. 153–165). Washington, DC: American Psychological Association.

Hazan, C., & Shaver, P. (1986). *Parental caregiving style questionnaire.* Unpublished questionnaire.

Hazan, C., & Shaver, P. (1987). Romantic love conceptualized as an attachment process. *Journal of Personality and Social Psychology, 52,* 511–524.

Hazlett, H. C., Poe, M. D., Gerig, G., Styner, M., Chappell, C., Smith, R. G., . . . Piven, J. (2011). Early brain overgrowth in autism associated with an increase in cortical surface area before age 2 years. *Archives of General Psychiatry, 68,* 467–476. doi:10.1001/archgenpsychiatry.2011.39

He, Q., Glas, C. W., Kosinski, M., Stillwell, D. J., & Veldkamp, B. P. (2014). Predicting self-monitoring skills using textual posts on facebook. *Computers In Human Behavior, 33,* 69–78. doi:10.1016/j.chb.2013.12.026

Healy, D., & Whitaker, C. (2003). Antidepressants and suicide: Risk-benefit conundrums. *Journal of Psychiatry & Neuroscience, 28*(5), 340–347.

Heatherton, T. F., & Polivy, J. (1991). Development and validation of a scale for measuring state self-esteem. *Journal of Personality and Social Psychology, 60,* 895–910.

Hegarty, P., & Buechel, C. (2006). Androcentric reporting of gender differences in APA journals: 1965–2004. *Review of General Psychology, 10,* 377–389.

Hegarty, P., Parslow, O., Ansara, Y. G., & Quick, F. (2013). Androcentrism: Changing the landscape without leveling the playing field? In M. K. Ryan & N. R Branscombe (Eds.), *The Sage handbook of gender and psychology* (pp. 29–44). Thousand Oaks, CA: Sage.

Heider, F. (1958). *The psychology of interpersonal relations*. New York: Wiley.

Heilman, M. E., & Okimoto, T. G. (2007). Why are women penalized for success at male tasks? The implied community deficit. *Journal of Applied Psychology, 92*, 81–92.

Heimpel, S. A., Wood, J. V., Marshall, M. A., & Brown, J. D. (2002). Do people with low self-esteem really want to feel better? Self-esteem differences in motivation to repair negative moods. *Journal of Personality and Social Psychology, 82*, 128–147.

Heine, S. J., Buchtel, E. E., & Norenzayan, A. (2008). What do cross-national comparisons of personality traits tell us? The case of conscientiousness. *Psychological Science, 19*(4), 309–313. doi:10.1111/j.1467-9280.2008.02085.x

Heine, S. J., & Hamamura, T. (2007). In search of East Asian self-enhancement. *Personality and Social Psychology Review, 11*(1), 1–24. doi:10.1177/1088868306294587

Heinrichs, R. W., Miles, A. A., Ammari, N., & Muharib, E. (2013). Cognition as a central illness feature in schizophrenia. In P. D. Harvey (Ed.), *Cognitive impairment in schizophrenia: Characteristics, assessment and treatment*. New York: Cambridge University Press. doi:10.1017/CBO9781139003872.002

Helgeson, V. S., Snyder, P., & Seltman, H. (2004). Psychological and physical adjustment of breast cancer over 4 years: Identifying distinct trajectories of change. *Health Psychology, 23*, 3–15.

Helms, H. M. (2013). Marital relationships in the twenty-first century. In G. W. Peterson, K. R. Bush, G. W. Peterson, K. R. Bush (Eds.), *Handbook of marriage and the family* (3rd ed.; pp. 233–254). New York: Springer Science + Business Media. doi:10.1007/978-1-4614-3987-5_11

Helwig, A. (2008). From childhood to adulthood: A 15-year longitudinal career development study. *Career Development Quarterly, 57*(1), 38–50.

Helzer, J. E., Wittchen, H., Krueger, R. F., & Kraemer, H. C. (2008a). Dimensional options for DSM-V: The way forward. In J. E. Helzer, H. C. Kraemer, R. F. Krueger, H. Wittchen, P. J. Sirovatka, & D. A. Regier (Eds.), *Dimensional approaches in diagnostic classification: Refining the research agenda for DSM-V* (pp. 115–127). Washington, DC: American Psychiatric Association.

Henderson, K. E., & Brownell, K. D. (2004). The toxic environment and obesity: Contribution and cure. In J. K. Thompson (Ed.), *Handbook of eating disorders and obesity*. New York: Wiley.

Henderson, R. C., Williams, P., Gabbidon, J., Farrelly, S., Schauman, O., Hatch, S., . . . Clement, S. (2014, March). Mistrust of mental health services: Ethnicity, hostpital admission and unfair treatment. *Epidemiological and Psychiatric Sciences*, 1–8.

Hendriks, H. F. J. (2007). Moderate alcohol consumption and insulin sensitivity: Observations and possible mechanisms. *Annals of Epidemiology, 17*(Suppl.), S40–S42.

Henley, N. M. (1986). *Body politics: Power, sex, and nonverbal communication* (2nd ed.). New York: Simon & Schuster.

Henley, N. M., & Freeman, J. (1995). The sexual politics of interpersonal behavior. In J. Freeman (Ed.), *Women: A feminist perspective* (5th ed.). Mountain View, CA: Mayfield.

Henry, R. G., Miller, R. B., & Giarrusso, R. (2005). Difficulties, disagreements, and disappointments in late-life marriages. *International Journal of Aging and Human Development, 61*, 243–264.

Heppner, E. G., Hart, C. M., & Sedikides, C. (2014). Moving narcissus: Can narcissists be empathic? *Personality and Social Psychology Bulletin, 40*, 1079–1091. doi:10.1177/0146167214535812

Heppner, P. P., & Lee, D. (2005). Problem-solving appraisal and psychological adjustment. In C. R. Snyder & S. J. Lopez (Eds.), *Handbook of positive psychology*. New York: Oxford University Press.

Herbenick, D., Mullinax, M., & Mark, K. (2014). Sexual desire discrepancy as a feature, not a bug, of long-term relationships: Women's self-reported strategies for modulating sexual desire. *Journal of Sexual Medicine, 11*(9), 2196–2206. doi:10.1111/jsm.12625

Herbenick, D., Reece, M., Sanders, S., Dodge, B., Ghassemi, A., & Fortenberry, J. D. (2009). Prevalence and characteristics of vibrator use by women in the United States: Results from a nationally representative study. *Journal of Sexual Medicine, 6*, 1857–1866.

Herbenick, D., Reece, M., Schick, V., Sanders, S. A., Dodge, B., & Fortenberry, J. D. (2010a). An event-level analysis of the sexual characteristics and composition among adults ages 18 to 59: Results from a national probability sample in the United States. *Journal of Sexual Medicine, 7*(5), 346–361.

Herbenick, D., Reece, M., Schick, V., Sanders, S. A., Dodge, B., & Fortenberry, J. D. (2010b). Sexual behavior in the United States: Results from a national probability sample of men and women ages 14–94. *Journal of Sexual Medicine, 7*(5), 255–265.

Herbenick, D., Reece, M., Schick, V., Sanders, S. A., Dodge, B., & Fortenberry, J. D. (2010c). Sexual behaviors, relationships, and perceived health status among adult women in the United States: Results from a national probability sample. *Journal of Sexual Medicine, 7*(5), 277–290.

Herbenick, D., Reece, M., Sanders, S. A., Dodge, B., Ghassemi, A., & Fortenberry, J. (2010d). Women's vibrator use in sexual partnerships: Results from a nationally representative survey in the United States. *Journal of Sex and Marital Therapy, 36*(1), 49–65. doi:10.1080/00926230903375677

Herbenick, D., Schick, V., Sanders, S. A., Reece, M., & Fortenberry, J. D. (2015). Pain experienced during vaginal and anal intercourse with other-sex partners: Findings from a nationally representative probability study in the United States. *Journal of Sexual Medicine, 12*(4), 1040–1051. doi:10.1111/jsm.12841

Herbert, J. D., & Brandsma L.L. (2015). Understanding and enhancing psychological acceptance. In S. J. Lynn, W. T. O'Donohue, & S. O. Lilienfeld (Eds.), *Health, happiness and well-being: Better living through psychological science* (pp. 62–88). Los Angeles: Sage.

Herek, G. M. (2006). Legal recognition of same-sex relationships in the United States: A social science perspective. *American Psychologist, 61*, 607–621.

Herek, G. M. (2009). Hate crimes and stigma-related experiences among sexual minority adults in the United States: Prevalence estimates from a national probability sample. *Journal of Interpersonal Violence, 24*, 54–74.

Herek, G. M., & Capitanio, J. (1996). "Some of my best friends": Intergroup contact concealable stigma, and heterosexuals' attitudes toward gay men and lesbians. *Personality and Social Psychology Bulletin, 22*, 412–424.

Herman, C. P., & Polivy, J. (2010). Sex and gender differences in eating behavior. In J. C. Chrisler & D. R. McCreary (Eds.), *Handbook of gender research in psychology, Vol. 1* (pp. 455–469). New York: Springer.

Hermann, D., Raybeck, D., & Gruneberg, M. (2002). *Improving memory and study skills: Advances in theory and practice*. Ashland, OH: Hogrefe & Huber.

Hernandez, I., & Preston, J. L. (2013). Disfluency disrupts the confirmation bias. *Journal of Experimental Social Psychology, 49*(1), 178–182. doi:10.1016/j.jesp.2012.08.010

Hernandez, K. M., Mahoney, A., & Pargament, K. I. (2011). Sanctification of sexuality: Implications for newlyweds' marital and sexual quality. *Journal of Family Psychology, 25*(5), 775–780. doi:10.1037/a0025103

Hernandez, K. M., Mahoney, A., & Pargament, K. I. (2014). Sexuality and religion. In D. L. Tolman, L. M. Diamond, J. A. Bauermeister, W. H. George, J. G. Pfaus, & L. M. Ward (Eds.), *APA handbook of sexuality and psychology* (pp. 425–447). Washington, DC: American Psychological Association. doi:10.1037/14194-013

Hernandez, R., Kershaw, K. N., Siddique, J., Boehm, J. K., Kubzansky, L. D., Diez-Roux, A., Ning, H., & Lloyd-Jones, D. M. (2015). Optimism and cardiovascular health: Multi-ethnic study of atherosclerosis (MESA). *Health Behavior and Policy Review, 2*, 62–73.

Hertenstein, M. J. (2011). The communicative functions of touch in adulthood. In M. J. Hertenstein & S. J. Weiss (Eds.), *The handbook of touch: Neuroscience, behavioral, and health perspectives* (pp. 299–327). New York: Springer.

Hertenstein, M. J., Hansel, C. A., Butts, A. M., & Hile, S. N. (2009). Smile intensity in photographs predicts divorce later in life. *Motivation and Emotion, 33*, 99–105.

Hetherington, E. M. (1993). An overview of the Virginia longitudinal study of divorce and remarriage with a focus on early adolescence. *Journal of Family Psychology, 7*, 1–18.

Hetherington, E. M. (1999). Should we stay together for the sake of the children? In E. M. Hetherington (Ed.), *Coping with divorce, single parenting, and remarriage: A risk and resiliency perspective*. Mahwah, NJ: Erlbaum.

Hetherington, E. M. (2003). Intimate pathways: Changing patterns in close personal relationships across time. *Family Relations: Interdisciplinary Journal of Applied Family Studies, 52*(4), 318–331.

Hettich, P. I., & Landrum, R. E. (2014). *Your undergraduate degree in psychology: From college to career*. Thousand Oaks, CA: Sage.

Heyder, A., & Kessels, U. (2015). Do teachers equate male and masculine with lower academic engagement? How students' gender enactment triggers gender stereotypes at school. *Social Psychology of Education, 18*(3), 467–485. doi:10.1007/s11218-015-9303-0

Heyman, R. E., Lorber, M. F., Eddy, J. M., & West, T. V. (2014). Behavioral observation and coding. In H. T. Reis & C. M. Judd (Eds.), *Handbook of research methods in social and personality psychology* (2nd ed.). New York: Cambridge University Press.

Hicks, T. V., & Leitenberg, H. (2001). Sexual fantasies about one's partner versus someone else: Gender differences in incidence and frequency. *Journal of Sex Research, 38*(1), 43–50.

Hidalgo, M. A., Ehrensaft, D., Tishelman, A. C., Clark, L. F., Garofalo, R., Rosenthal, S. M., . . . Olson, J. (2013). The gender affirmative model: What we know and what we aim to learn. *Human Development, 56*(5), 285–290.

Higgins, E. T. (1987). Self-discrepancy: A theory relating self and affect. *Psychological Review, 94*(3), 319–340.

Higgins, E. T. (1989). Self-discrepancy theory: What patterns of self-beliefs cause people to suffer? In L. Berkowitz, L. Berkowitz (Eds.), *Advances in experimental social psychology, Vol. 22* (pp. 93–136). San Diego, CA: Academic Press. doi:10.1016/S0065-2601(08)60306-8

Higgins, E. T. (1999). When do self-descrepancies have specific relations to emotions? The second-generation question of Tangney, Niedenthal, Covert, and Barlow (1998). *Journal of Personality and Social Psychology, 77*(6), 1313–1317.

Higgins, C. A., & Judge, T. A. (2004). The effect of applicant influence tactics on recruiter perceptions of fit and hiring recommendations: a field study. *Journal of Applied Psychology, 89*(4), 622–632.

Higgins, E. T., Shah, J., & Friedman, R. (1997). Emotional responses to goal attainment: Strength of regulatory focus as a moderator. *Journal of Personality and Social Psychology, 72*(3), 515–525.

Hill, A. J. (2002). Prevalence and demographics of dieting. In C. G. Fairburn & K. D. Brownell (Eds.), *Eating disorders and obesity: A comprehensive handbook*. New York: Guilford.

Hill, C. T., Rubin, Z., & Peplau, L. A. (1976). Breakups before marriage: The end of 103 affairs. *Journal of Social Issues, 32*, 147–168.

Hill, E. M., & Gick, M. L. (2011). The big five and cervical cancer screening barriers: Evidence for the influence of conscientiousness, extraversion, and openness. *Personality and Individual Differences, 50*(5), 662–667. doi: 10.1016/j.paid.2010.12.013

Hill, J. O., & Wyatt, H. R. (2005). Role of physical activity in preventing and treating obesity. *Journal of Applied Physiology, 99*, 765–770.

Hill, K. P., & Weiss, R. D. (2011). Amphetamines and other stimulants. In P. Ruiz & E. C. Strain (Eds.), *Lowinson and Ruiz's substance abuse: A comprehensive textbook* (5th ed.; pp. 238–254). Philadelphia: Lippincott Williams & Wilkins.

Hilt, L. M., & Nolen-Hoeksema, S. (2014). Gender differences in depression. In I. H. Gotlib & C. L. Hammen (Eds.), *Handbook of depression* (3rd ed.). New York: Guilford.

Hines, M. (1990). Gonadal hormones and human cognitive development. In J. Balthazart (Ed.), *Hormones, brain and behavior in vertebrates: 1. Sexual differentiation, neuroanatomical aspects, neurotransmitters and neuropeptides*. Basel: Karger.

Hines, M. (2010). Sex-related variation in human behavior and the brain. *Trends in Cognitive Sciences, 14*(10), 448–456. doi:10.1016/j.tics.2010.07.005

Hines, M. (2011). Gender development and the human brain. *Annual Review of Neuroscience, 34*, 69–88. doi:10.1146/annurev-neuro-061010-113654

Hinic, D. (2011). Problems with "internet addiction" diagnosis and classification. *Psychiatria Danubina, 23*, 145–151.

Hiroto, D. S., & Seligman, M. E. P. (1975). Generality of learned helplessness in man. *Journal of Personality and Social Psychology, 31*, 311–327.

Hirt, E. R., Zillman, D., Erikson, G. A., & Kennedy, C. (1992). Costs and benefits of allegiance: Changes in fans' self-ascribed competence after team victory versus defeat. *Journal of Personality and Social Psychology, 63,* 724–738.

Ho, A. K., Sidanius, J., Pratto, F., Levin, S., Thomsen, L., Kteily, N., & Sheehy-Skeffington, & J. (2012). Social dominance orientation: Revisiting the structure and function of a variable predicting social and political attitudes. *Personality and Social Psychology Bulletin, 38*(5), 583–606. doi:10.1177/0146167211432765

Ho, R. C., Zhang, M. W. B., Tsang, T. Y., Toh, A. H., Pan, F., Lu, Y., . . . Mak, K. (2014). The association between internet addiction and psychiatric co-morbidity: A meta-analysis. *BMC Psychiatry, 14,* 183.

Hochschild, A. R. (2003). *The managed heart: Commercialization of human feeling.* Berleley, CA: University of California Press.

Hodson, G., Dovidio, J. F., & Gaertner, S. L. (2010). The aversive form of racism. In J. Chin (Ed.), *The psychology of prejudice and discrimination: A revised and condensed edition* (pp. 1–13). Santa Barbara, CA: Praeger/ABC-CLIO.

Hoffmann, J. D. (2013). Emotions and creativity. In C. Mohiyeddini, M. Eysenck, S. Bauer, C. Mohiyeddini, M. Eysenck, & S. Bauer (Eds.), *Handbook of psychology of emotions, Vol. 1: Recent theoretical perspectives and novel empirical findings* (pp. 377–405). Hauppauge, NY: Nova Science Publishers.

Hofmann, S. G., & Barlow, D. H. (2014). Evidence-based psychological interventions and the common factors approach: The beginnings of a rapprochement? *Psychotherapy, 51,* 510–513. doi:10.1037/a0037045

Hofmann, S. G., Sawyer, A. T., Witt, A. A., & Oh, D. (2010). The effect of mindfulness-based therapy on anxiety and depression: A meta-analytic review. *Journal of Consulting and Clinical Psychology, 78*(2), 169–183. doi:10.1037/a0018555

Hofstede, G. (1983). Dimensions of national cultures in fifty countries and three regions. In J. Deregowski, S. Dzuirawiec, & R. Annis (Eds.), *Explications in cross-cultural psychology.* Lisse: Swets and Zeitlinger.

Hofstede, G. (2001). *Culture's consequences: Comparing values, behaviors, institutions, and organizations across nations.* Thousand Oaks, CA: Sage.

Hogan, B. F., & Linden, W. (2004). Anger response styles and blood pressure: At least don't ruminate about it! *Annals of Behavioral Medicine, 27,* 38–49.

Hogan, C. L., Catalino, L. I., Mata, J., & Fredrickson, B. L. (2015). Beyond emotional benefits: Physical activity and sedentary behaviour affect psychosocial resources through emotions. *Psychology & Health, 30*(3), 354–369. doi:10.1080/08870446.2014.973410

Høgh-Olesen, H. (2008). Human spatial behaviour: The spacing of people, objects, and animals in six cross-cultural samples. *Journal of Cognition and Culture, 8*(3–4), 245–280. doi:10.1163/156853708X358173

Høglend, P., Bøgwald, K. -P., Amlo, S., Marble, A., Ulberg, R., Sjaastad, M. C., . . . Johansson, P. (2008). Transference interpretations in dynamic psychotherapy: Do they really yield sustained effects? *American Journal of Psychiatry, 165,* 763–771.

Høglend, P., Hersoug, A., Bøgwald, K., Amlo, S., Marble, A., Sørbye, Ø., . . . Crits-Christoph, P. (2011). Effects of transference work in the context of therapeutic alliance and quality of object relations. *Journal of Consulting and Clinical Psychology, 79*(5), 697–706. doi:10.1037/a0024863

Holahan, C. J., Moos, R. H., Holahan, C. K., Brennan, P. L., & Schutte, K. K. (2005). Stress generation, avoidance coping and depressive symptoms: A 10-year model. *Journal of Consulting and Clinical Psychology, 73,* 658–666.

Holden, C. (2004). FDA weighs suicide risk in children on antidepressants. *Science, 303,* 745.

Holland, J. L. (1985). *Making vocational choices: A theory of vocational personalities and work environments.* Englewood Cliffs, NJ: Prentice-Hall.

Holland, J. L. (1996). Exploring careers with a typology: What we have learned and some new directions. *American Psychologist, 51,* 397–406.

Holland, J. L. (1997). *Making vocational choices* (3rd ed.). Odessa, FL: Psychological Assessment Resources.

Holland, R. W., Roeder, U., van Baaren, R. B., Brandt, A. C., & Hannover, B. (2004). Don't stand so close to me: The effects of self-construal on interpersonal closeness. *Psychological Science, 15,* 237–242.

Hollenbaugh, E. E., & Ferris, A. L. (2015). Predictors of honesty, intent, and valence of Facebook self-disclosure. *Computers in Human Behavior, 50,* 456–464. doi:10.1016/j.chb.2015.04.030

Hollon, S. D., & Beck, A. T. (2013). Cognitive and cognitive-behavioral therapies. In M. J. Lambert (Ed.), *Bergin and Garfield's handbook of psychotherapy and behavior change* (6th ed.). New York: Wiley.

Hollon, S. D., & DiGiuseppe, R. (2011). Cognitive theories of psychotherapy. In J. C. Norcross, G. R. Vandenbos, & D. K. Freedheim (Eds.), *History of psychotherapy: Continuity and change* (2nd ed.). Washington, DC: American Psychological Association.

Holmes, T. H., & Rahe, R. H. (1967). The Social Readjustment Rating Scale. *Journal of Psychosomatic Research, 11,* 213–218.

Holt-Lunstad, J., Smith, T. B., Baker, M., Harris, T., & Stephenson, D. (2015). Loneliness and social isolation as risk factors for mortality: A meta-analytic review. *Perspectives on Psychological Science, 10*(2), 227–237. doi:10.1177/1745691614568352

Holt-Lunstad J., Smith T. B., Layton J. B. (2010). Social relationships and mortality risk: A meta-analytic review. *PLoS Medicine, 7*(7): e1000316. doi:10.1371/journal.pmed.1000316

Holt-Lunstad, J., Smith, T., & Uchino, B. (2008). Can hostility interfere with the health benefits of receiving social support? The impact of cynical hostility on cardiovascular reactivity during social support interactions with friends. *Annals of Behavioral Medicine: A Publication of the Society of Behavioral Medicine, 35*(3), 319–330.

Hone, L. C., Jarden, A., & Schofield, G. M. (2015). An evaluation of positive psychology intervention effectiveness trials using the re-aim framework: A practice-friendly review. *The Journal of Positive Psychology, 10*(4), 303–322. doi:10.1080/17439760.2014.96526

Honts, C. R., Raskin, D. C., & Kircher, J. C. (2002). The scientific status of research on polygraph testing. In D. L. Faigman, D. H. Kaye, M. J. Saks, & J. Sanders (Eds.), *Modern scientific evidence: The law and science of expert testimony, Vol. 2.* St. Paul, MN: West Publishing.

Hoobler, J. M., Lemmon, G., & Wayne, S. J. (2011). Women's underrepresentation in upper management: New insights on a persistent problem. *Organizational Dynamics, 40*(3), 151–156. doi:10.1016/j.orgdyn.2011.04.001

Hood, K. E., Draper, P., Crockett, L. J., & Petersen, A. C. (1987). The ontogeny and phylogeny of sexual differences in development: A biopsychosocial synthesis. In B. Carter (Ed.), *Current conceptions of sex roles and sex typing: Theory and research.* New York: Praeger.

Hooley, J. M. (2009). Schizophrenia: Interpersonal functioning. In P. H. Blaney & T. Millon (Eds.), *Oxford textbook of psychopathology* (pp. 333–360). New York: Oxford University Press.

Hooley, J. M., Cole, S. H., & Gironde, S. (2012). Borderline personality disorder. In T. A. Widiger (Ed.), *The Oxford handbook of personality disorders.* New York: Oxford University Press. doi:10.1093/oxfordhb/9780199735013.013.0020

Hopwood, C. J., & Wright, A. C. (2012). A comparison of passive-aggressive and negativistic personality disorders. *Journal of Personality Assessment, 94*(3), 296–303. doi:10.1080/00223891.2012.655819

Horn, S. S. (2013). Attitudes about sexual orientation. In C. J. Patterson, A. R. D'Augelli (Eds.), *Handbook of psychology and sexual orientation* (pp. 239–251). New York: Oxford University Press.

Horvath, S., & Morf, C. C. (2010). To be grandiose or not to be worthless: Different routes to self-enhancement for narcissism and self-esteem. *Journal of Research in Personality, 44*(5), 585–592. doi:10.1016/j.jrp.2010.07.002

Horvath, T. L. (2005). The hardship of obesity: A soft-wired hypothalamus. *Nature Neuroscience, 8,* 561–565.

Hoscheidt, S. M., Dongaonkar, B., Payne, J., & Nadel, L. (2013). Emotion, stress, and memory. In D. Reisberg (Ed.), *The Oxford handbook of cognitive psychology* (pp. 557–570). New York: Oxford University Press. doi:10.1093/oxfordhb/9780195376746.013.0035

Houlcroft, L., Bore, M., & Munro, D. (2012). Three faces of narcissism. *Personality and Individual Differences, 53*(3), 274–278. doi:10.1016/j.paid.2012.03.036

Hovland, C. I., & Weiss, W. (1951). The influence of source credibility on communication effectiveness. *Public Opinion Quarterly, 15,* 635–650.

Howes, O. D., Bose, S. K., Turkheimer, F., Valli, I., Egerton, A., Valmaggia, L. R., . . . McGuire, P. (2011). Dopamine synthesis capacity before onset of psychosis: A prospective [^{18}F]-DOPA PET imaging study. *The American Journal of Psychiatry, 168*(12), 1311–1317.

Hsu, L. M., & Langer, E. J. (2013). Mindfulness and cultivating well-being in older adults. In S. A. David, I. Boniwell, & A. Conley Ayers (Eds.), *The Oxford handbook of happiness* (pp. 1026–1036). New York: Oxford University Press.

Hu, F. B., & Willett, W. C. (2002). Optimal diets for prevention of coronary heart disease. *Journal of the American Medical Association, 288*(20), 2569–2578.

Huan, V. S., Ang, R. P., Chong, W. H., & Chye, S. (2014). The impact of shyness on problematic internet use: The role of loneliness. *The Journal of Psychology: Interdisciplinary and Applied, 148*(6), 699–715. doi:10.1080/00223980.2013.825229

Hudson, J. I., Hiripi, E., Pope, H. G., & Kessler, R. C. (2007). The prevelance and correlates of eating disorders in the national comorbidity survey replication. *Biological Psychiatry, 61,* 348–358.

Huebner, E. S., & Gilman, R. (2006). Students who like and dislike school. *Applied Research in Quality of Life, 2,* 139–150.

Huebner, E. S., Gilman, R., Reschly, A. L., & Hall, R. (2009). Positive schools. In S. J. Lopez & C. R. Snyder (Eds.), *Oxford handbook of positive psychology* (2nd ed., pp. 561–568). New York: Oxford.

Huey, S. J., Tilley, J. L., Jones, E. O., & Smith, C. A. (2014). The contribution of cultural competence to evidence-based care for ethnically diverse populations. *Annual Review of Clinical Psychology, 10,* 305–338. doi:10.1146/annurev-clinpsy-032813-153729

Hughes, E., & Parkes, K. (2007). Work hours and well-being: The roles of work-time control and work-family interference. *Work & Stress, 21*(3), 264–278.

Hultin, M. (2003). Some take the glass escalator, some hit the glass ceiling? Career consequences of occupational sex segregation. *Work and Occupations, 30*(1), 30–61.

Human, R., Thomas, K. F., Dreyer, A., Amod, A. R., Wolf, P. A., & Jacobs, W. J. (2013). Acute psychosocial stress enhances visuospatial memory in healthy males. *South African Journal of Psychology, 43*(3), 300–313. doi:10.1177/0081246313496913

Hunt, D. S., Lin, C. A., & Atkin, D. J. (2014). Communicating social relationships via the use of photo-messaging. *Journal of Broadcasting and Electronic Media, 58*(2), 234-252. doi:10.1080/08838151.2014.906430

Hunter, J. E., & Hunter, R. F. (1984). Validity and utility of alternative predictors of job performance. *Psychological Bulletin, 96*(1), 72–98.

Huntjens, R. C., Peters, M. L., Woertman, L., Bovenschen, L. M., Martin, R. C., & Postma, A. (2006). Inter-identity amnesia in dissociative identity disorder: A simulated memory impairment? *Psychological Medicine, 36,* 857–863. doi:10.1017/S0033291706007100

Huq, F. (2007). Molecular modeling analysis of the metabolism of cocaine. *Journal of Pharmacology and Toxicology, 2,* 114–130.

Hurley, D. B., & Kwon, P. (2012). Results of a study to increase savoring the moment: Differential impact on positive and negative outcomes. *Journal of Happiness Studies, 13*(4), 579–588. doi:10.1007/s10902-011-9280-8

Hurrell, J. J., & Sauter, S. L. (2012). Occupational stress: Causes, consequences, prevention and intervention. In A. M. Rossi, P. L. Perrewé, J. A. Meurs, A. M. Rossi, P. L. Perrewé, & J. A. Meurs (Eds.), *Coping and prevention* (pp. 231–247). Charlotte, NC: IAP Information Age Publishing.

Huston, T. L., Niehuis, S., & Smith, S. E. (2001). The early marital roots of conjugal distress and divorce. *Current Directions in Psychological Science, 10*(4), 116–119.

Huta, V. (2013). Eudaimonia. In S. A. David, I. Boniwell, A. Conley Ayers, S. A. David, I. Boniwell, & A. Conley Ayers (Eds.), *The Oxford handbook of happiness* (pp. 201–213). New York: Oxford University Press.

Hyde, A. L., Conroy, D. E., Pincus, A. L., & Ram, N. (2011). Unpacking the feel-good effect of free-time physical activity: Between- and within-person associations with pleasant-activated feeling states. *Journal of Sport & Exercise Psychology, 33*(6), 884–902.

Hyde, J. S. (1996). Where are the gender differences? Where are the gender similarities? In D. M. Buss & N. M. Malamuth (Eds.), *Sex, power, conflict: Evolutionary and feminist perspectives.* New York: Oxford University Press.

Hyde, J. S. (2004). *Half the human experience: The psychology of women.* Boston: Houghton Mifflin.

Hyde, J. S. (2007). New directions in the study of gender similarities and differences. *Current Directions in Psychological Science, 16,* 259–263.

Hyde, J. S. (2014). Gender similarities and differences. *Annual Review of Psychology, 65,* 373–398. doi:10.1146/annurev-psych-010213-115057

Hynes, K. H., & Clarkberg, M. (2005). Women's employment patterns during early parenthood: A group-based trajectory analysis. *Journal of Marriage and Family, 67,* 222–239.

Iaccino, J. F. (1996). A further examination of the bizarre imagery mnemonic: Its effectiveness with mixed context and delayed testing. *Perceptual & Motor Skills, 83,* 881–882.

Iacono, W. G. (2008). Accuracy of polygraph techniques: Problems using confessions to determine the truth. *Physiology & Behavior, 95*(1–2), 24–26.

Iacono, W. G. (2009). Psychophysiological detection of deception and guilty knowledge. In K. S. Douglas, J. L. Skeem, & S. O. Lilienfeld (Eds.), *Psychological science in the courtroom: Consensus and controversy* (pp. 224–241). New York: Guilford.

Ickovics, J. R., Thayaparan, B., & Ethier, K. A. (2001). Women and AIDS: A contextual analysis. In A. Baum, T. A. Revenson, & J. E. Singer (Eds.), *Handbook of health psychology.* Mahwah, NJ: Erlbaum.

Idring, S., Lundberg, M., Sturm, H., Dalman, C., Gumpert, C., Rai, D., . . . Magnusson, C. (2014). Changes in prevalence of autism spectrum disorders in 2001–2011: Findings from the Stockholm youth cohort. *Journal of Autism and Developmental Disorders.* doi:10.1007/s10803-014-2336-y

Ie, A., Ngnoumen, C. T., & Langer, E. J. (Eds.). (2014). *The Wiley Blackwell handbook of mindfulness* (Vols. I and II). Hoboken, NJ: Wiley-Blackwell.

Ignatius, E., & Kokkonen, M. (2007). Factors contributing to verbal self-disclosure. *Nordic Psychology, 59*(4), 362–391.

Ihle-Helledy, K., Zytowski, D. G., & Fouad, N. A. (2004). Kuder career search: Test-retest reliability and consequential validity. *Journal of Career Assessment, 12*(3), 285–297. doi:10.1177/1069072703257752

Ikovics, J. R., Milan, S., Boland, R., Schoenbaum, E., Schuman, P., & Vladhov, D. (2006). Psychological resources protect health: 5-year survival and immune function among HIV-infected women from four US cities. *AIDS, 20,* 1851–1860.

Ilies, R., Hauserman, N., Schwochau, S., & Stibal, J. (2003). Reported incidents of rates of work-related sexual harassment in the United States: Using meta-analysis to explain reported rate disparities. *Personnel Psychology, 56,* 607–631.

Iliescu, D., Ilie, A., Ispas, D., & Ion, A. (2013). Examining the psychometric properties of the Mayer-Salovey-Caruso Emotional Intelligence Test: Findings from an eastern European culture. *European Journal of Psychological Assessment, 29*(2), 121-128. doi:10.1027/1015-5759/a000132

Imada, T. (2012). Cultural narratives of individualism and collectivism: A content analysis of textbook stories in the United States and Japan. *Journal of Cross-Cultural Psychology, 43*(4), 576–591. doi:10.1177/0022022110383312

Impett, E. A., & Peplau, L. A. (2006). "His" and "her" relationships? A review of the empirical evidence. In A. L. Vangelisti & D. Perlman (Eds.), *The Cambridge handbook of personal relationships.* New York: Cambridge University Press.

Infante, J. R., Torres-Avisbal, M., Pinel, P., Vallejo. J. A., Peran, F., Gonzalez, F., Contreras, P., Pacheco, C., Roldan, A., & Latre, J. M. (2001). Catecholamine levels in practitioners of the transcendental meditation technique. *Physiology & Behavior, 72*(1–2), 141–146.

Ingram, R. E., Scott, W. D., & Hamill, S. (2009). Depression: Social and cognitive aspects. In P. H. Blaney & T. Millon (Eds.), *Oxford textbook of psychopathology* (pp. 230–252). New York: Oxford University Press.

Insel, T. R. (2010). Psychiatrists' relationships with pharmaceutical companies: Part of the problem or part of the solution? *Journal of the American Medical Association, 303*(12), 1192–1193. doi:10.1001/jama.2010.317

Insko, C. A., Smith, R. H., Alicke, M. D., Wade, J., & Taylor, S. (1985). Conformity and group size: The concern with being right and the concern with being liked. *Personality and Social Psychology Bulletin, 11,* 41–50.

Institute for Women's Policy Research. (2012). The gender wage gap by occupation. Retrieved from www.iwpr.org/publications/pubs/the-gender-wage-gap-by-occupation-1

Internet World Stats (2015). Internet usage and population statistics. Retrieved from www.internetworldstats.com/stats.htm

Iqbal, R., Anand, S., Ounpuu, S., Islam, S., Zhang, X., Rangarajan, S., . . . INTERHEART Study Investigators. (2008). Dietary patterns and the risk of acute myocardial infarction in 52 countries: Results of the INTERHEART study. *Circulation, 118,* 1929–1937.

Isen, A. M. (2002). A role for neuropsychology in understanding the facilitating influence of positive affect on social behavior and cognitive processes. In C. R. Snyder & S. J. Lopez (Eds.), *Handbook of positive psychology* (pp. 528–540). New York: Oxford University Press.

Isen, A. M. (2004). Some perspectives on positive feelings and emotions: Positive affect facilitates thinking and problem solving. In A. S. R. Manstead, N. Frijda, & A. Fischer (Eds.), *Feelings and emotions: The Amsterdam symposium* (pp. 263–281). New York: Cambridge University Press.

Isen, A. M., Daubman, K. A., & Nowicki, G. P. (1987). Positive affect facilitates creative problem solving. *Journal of Personality and Social Psychology, 52,* 1121–1131.

Isley, M. M., Edelman, A., Kaneshiro, B., Peters, D., Nichols, M. D., & Jensen, J. T. (2010). Sex education and contraceptive use at coital debut in the United States: Results from Cycle 6 of the National Survey of Family Growth. *Contraception, 82*(3), 236–242.

Ito, T. A. (2011). Perceiving social category information from faces: Using ERPs to study person perception. In A. Todorov, S. T. Fiske, & D. A. Prentice (Eds.), *Social neuroscience: Toward understanding the underpinnings of the social mind* (pp. 85–100). New York: Oxford University Press.

Ito, T. A., Chiao, K. W., Devine, P. G., Lorig, T., & Cacioppo, J. T. (2006). The influence of facial feedback on race bias. *Psychological Science, 17,* 256–261.

Ivan, L. (2013). Nonverbal sensitivity: Evidence for different accuracy on face and voice channels using static or dynamic items. In A. Freitas-Magalhães (Ed.), *Emotional expression: The brain and the face, Vol. 4* (pp. 175–193). Porto, Portugal: Edições Universidade Fernando Pessoa.

Ivancevich, J. M., Matteson, M. T., Freedman, S. M., & Phillips, J. S. (1990). Worksite stress management interventions. *American Psychologist, 45,* 252–261.

Izard, C., Fine, S., Schultz, D., Mostow, A., Ackerman, B., & Youngstrom, E. (2001). Emotion knowledge as a predictor of social behavior and academic competence in children at risk. *Psychological Science, 12*(1), 18–23.

Jacks, J. Z., & Cameron, K. A. (2003). Strategies for resisting persuasion. *Basic and Applied Social Psychology, 25*(2), 145–161. http://dx.doi.org/10.1207/S15324834BASP2502_5

Jacks, J. Z., & Lancaster, L. C. (2015). Fit for persuasion: The effects of nonverbal delivery style, message framing, and gender on message effectiveness. *Journal of Applied Social Psychology, 45*(4), 203–213. doi:10.1111/jasp.12288

Jackson, L. A., Hunter, J. E., & Hodge, C. N. (1995). Physical attractiveness and intellectual competence: A meta-analytic review. *Social Psychology Quarterly, 58,* 108–122.

Jackson, L. M. (2011). Intergroup relations and prejudice. In *The psychology of prejudice: From attitudes to social action* (pp. 103–116). Washington, DC: American Psychological Association. doi:10.1037/12317-006

Jackson, T., Fritch, A., Nagasaka, T., & Gunderson, J. (2002). Towards explaining the association between shyness and loneliness: A path analysis with American college students. *Social Behavior and Personality, 30*(3), 263–270.

Jacob, C., & Guéguen, N. (2012). The effect of physical distance between patrons and servers on tipping. *Journal of Hospitality & Tourism Research, 36*(1), 25–31. doi:10.1177/1096348010388660

Jadva, V., Hines, M., & Golombok, S. (2010). Infants' preferences for toys, colors, and shapes: Sex differences and similarities. *Archives of Sexual Behavior, 39*(6), 1261–1273. doi:10.1007/s10508-010-9618-z

Jain, A., Marshall, J., Buikema, A., Bancroft, T., Kelly, J. P., & Newschaffer, C. J. (2015). Autism occurrence by MMR vaccine status among US children with older siblings with and without autism. *JAMA: Journal of the American Medical Association, 313*(15), 1534–1540. doi:10.1001/jama.2015.3077

Jakicic, J. M., & Gallagher, K. I. (2002). Physical activity considerations for management of body weight. In D. H. Bessesen & R. Kushner (Eds.), *Evaluation & Management of Obesity.* Philadelphia: Hanley & Belfus.

Jakupcak, M., Salters, K., Gratz, K. L., & Roemer, L. (2003). Masculinity and emotionality: An investigation of men's primary and secondary emotional responding. *Sex Roles, 49*(3–4), 111–120.

James, J. E. (2004). Critical review of dietary caffeine and blood pressure: A relationship that should be taken more seriously. *Psychosomatic Medicine, 66*(1), 63–71.

Jamieson, J. P., Mendes, W. B., & Nock, M. K. (2013). Improving acute stress responses: The power of reappraisal. *Current Directions in Psychological Science, 22*(1), 51–56.

Jamieson, J. P., Nock, M. K., & Mendes, W. B. (2012). Mind over matter: Reappraising arousal improves cardiovascular and cognitive responses to stress. *Journal of Experimental Psychology: General, 141*(3), 417–422. doi:10.1037/a0025719

Janiszewski, P. M., Janssen, I., & Ross, R. (2009). Abdominal obesity and physical inactivity are associated with erectile dysfunction independent of body mass index. *Journal of Sexual Medicine, 6,* 1990–1998.

Jansz, J. (2000). Masculine identity and restrictive emotionality. In A. H. Fischer (Ed.), *Gender and emotion: Social psychological perspectives.* Cambridge, UK: Cambridge University Press.

Jaremka, L. M., Fagundes, C. P., Glaser, R., Bennett, J. M., Malarkey, W. B., & Kiecolt-Glaser, J. K. (2013). Loneliness predicts pain, depression, and fatigue: Understanding the role of immune dysregulation. *Psychoneuroendocrinology, 38,* 1310–1317. doi: 10.1016/j.psyneuen.2012.11.016

Jaremka, L. M., Fagundes, C. P., Peng, J., Bennett, J. M., Glaser, R., Malarkey, W. B., & Kiecolt-Glaser, J. K. (2013a). Loneliness promotes inflammation during acute stress. *Psychological Science, 24*(7), 1089–1097. doi:10.1177/0956797612464059

Jaremka, L. M., Glaser, R., Malarkey, W. B., & Kiecolt-Glaser, J. K. (2013b). Marital distress prospectively predicts poorer cellular immune function. *Psychoneuroendocrinology, 38*(11), 2713–2719. doi:10.1016/j.psyneuen.2013.06.031

Jauhar, S., & Cavanagh, J. (2013). Classification and epidemiology of bipolar disorder. In M. Power (Ed.), *The Wiley-Blackwell handbook of mood disorders* (2nd ed.). Malden, MA: Wiley-Blackwell.

Jeffery, R. W., Epstein, L. H., Wilson, G. T., Drewnowski, A., Stunkard, A. J., Wing, R. R., & Hill, D. R. (2000). Long-term maintenance of weight loss: Current status. *Health Psychology, 19*(1), 5–16.

Jeffery, R. W., Kelly, K. M., Rothman, A. J., Sherwood, N. E., & Boutelle, K. N. (2004). The weight-loss experience: A descriptive analysis. *Annals of Behavioral Medicine, 27,* 100–106.

Jehn, K. A. (2014). Types of conflict: The history and future of conflict definitions and typologies. In O. B. Ayoko, N. M. Ashkanasy, K. A. Jehn, O. B. Ayoko, N. M. Ashkanasy, K. A. Jehn (Eds.), *Handbook of conflict management research* (pp. 3–18). Northampton, MA: Edward Elgar. doi:10.4337/9781781006948.00007

Jelovac, A., Kolshus, E., & McLoughlin, D. M. (2013). Relapse following successful electroconvulsive therapy for major depression: A meta-analysis. *Neuropsychopharmacology, 38,* 2467–2474. doi:10.1038/npp.2013.149

Jenks, R. A., & Higgs, S. (2007). Associations between dieting and smoking-related behaviors in young women. *Drug and Alcohol Dependence, 88,* 291–299.

Jetten, J., Branscombe, N. R., Iyer, A., & Asai, N. (2013). Appraising gender discrimination as legitimate or illegitimate: Antecedents and consequences. In M. K. Ryan & N. R. Branscombe (Eds.), *The Sage handbook of gender and psychology* (pp. 306–322). Thousand Oaks, CA: Sage.

Jiang, Z., Heng, C. S., & Choi, B. F. (2013). Privacy concerns and privacy-protective behavior in synchronous online social interactions. *Information Systems Research, 24*(3), 579–595. doi:10.1287/isre.1120.0441

Johansen, C. (2010). Psychosocial factors. In J. C. Holland, W. S. Breitbart, P. B. Jacobsen, M. S. Lederberg, M. J. Loscalzo, &

R. McCorkle (Eds.), *Psycho-oncology* (2nd ed., pp. 57–61). New York: Oxford University Press.

Johnson, A., Sandford, J., & Tyndall, J. (2007). Written and verbal information versus verbal information only for patients being discharged from acute settings to home. *Cochrane Database of Systematic Reviews,* Cochrane Art. No.: CD003716. doi: 10.1002/14651858.CD003716

Johnson, A. J., Haigh, M. M., Becker, J. A. H., Craig, E. A., & Wigley, S. (2008). College students' use of relational management strategies in email in long-distance and geographically close relationships. *Journal of Computer-Mediated Communication, 13,* 381–404.

Johnson, B. A., & Ait-Daoud, N. (2005). Alcohol: Clinical aspects. In J. H. Lowinson, P. Ruiz, R. B. Millman, & J. G. Langrod (Eds.), *Substance abuse: A comprehensive textbook.* Philadelphia: Lippincott/Williams & Wilkins.

Johnson, M. D., & Chen, J. (2015). Blame it on the alcohol: The influence of alcohol consumption during adolescence, the transition to adulthood, and young adulthood on one-time sexual hookups. *Journal of Sex Research, 52*(5), 570–579. doi:10.1080/00224499.2014.913281

Johnson, M. P., & Ferraro, K. J. (2001). Research on domestic violence in the 1990's: Making distinctions. In R. M. Milardo (Ed.), *Understanding families into the new millennium: A decade in review.* Minneapolis, MN: National Council on Family Relations.

Johnson, S., Gur, R. M., David, Z., & Currier, E. (2015). One-session mindfulness meditation: A randomized controlled study of effects on cognition and mood. *Mindfulness, 6*(1), 88–98. doi:10.1007/s12671-013-0234-6

Johnson, S. B., & Carlson, D. N. (2004). Medical regimen adherence: Concepts, assessment, and interventions. In J. M. Raczynski & L. C. Leviton (Eds.), *Handbook of clinical health psychology, Vol. 2: Disorders of behavior and health.* Washington, DC: American Psychological Association.

Johnson, S. L., Cuellar, A. K., & Peckham, A. D. (2014). Risk factors for bipolar disorder. In I. H. Gotlib & C. L. Hammen (Eds.), *Handbook of depression* (3rd ed.). New York: Guilford.

Johnson, W. (2010). Understanding the genetics of intelligence: Can height help? Can corn oil? *Current Directions in Psychological Science, 19,* 177–182. doi:10.1177/0963721410370136

Johnson, W., & Krueger, R. F. (2006). How money buys happiness: Genetic and environmental processes linking finances and life satisfaction. *Journal of Personality and Social Psychology, 90,* 680–691.

Johnston, L. D., O'Malley, P. M., Bachman, J. G., & Schulenberg, J. E. (2007). *Monitoring the future: National survey results on drug use, 1975–2006, Vol. 2: College students and adults ages 19–45* (NIH Publication No. 07–6206). Bethesda, MD: National Institute on Drug Abuse.

Johnston, L. D., O'Malley, P. M., Bachman, J. G., & Schulenberg, J. E. (2008). *Monitoring the future: National results on adolescent drug use: Overview of key findings* (NIH Publication No. 08–6418). Bethesda, MD: National Institute on Drug Abuse.

Johnston, L. D., O'Malley, P. M., Bachman, J. G., & Schulenberg, J. E. (2009). *Monitoring the future: National survey on drug use, 1975–2008, Vol. 2: College students and adults ages 19–50* (NIH Publication No. 09-7403). Bethesda, MD: National Institute on Drug Abuse.

Joiner, T. E., & Timmons, K. A. (2009). Depression in its interpersonal context. In I. H. Gotlib & C. L. Hammen (Eds.), *Handbook of depression* (pp. 322–339). New York: Guilford.

Jokela, M. (2012). Birth-cohort effects in the association between personality and fertility. *Psychological Science, 23*(8), 835–841. doi:10.1177/0956797612439067

Jokela, M., Alvergne, A., Pollet, T. V., & Lummaa, V. (2011). Reproductive behavior and personality traits of the Five Factor Model. *European Journal of Personality, 25*(6), 487–500. doi:10.1002/per.822

Jonason, P. K., Foster, J. D., McCain, J., & Campbell, W. K. (2015). Where birds flock to get together: The who, what, where, and why of mate searching. *Personality and Individual Differences, 80,* 76–84. doi:10.1016/j.paid.2015.02.018

Jones, E. E. (1990). *Interpersonal perception.* New York: Freeman.

Jones, E. E., & Davis, K. (1965). From acts to dispositions: The attribution process in person perception. In L. Berkowitz (Ed.), *Advances in experimental social psychology, Vol. 2.* New York: Academic Press.

Jones, R. A., & Brehm, J. W. (1970). Persuasiveness of one- and two-sided communications as a function of awareness there are two sides. *Journal of Experimental Social Psychology, 6,* 47–56.

Jones, R. K., Zolna, M. R. S., Henshaw, S. K., & Finer, L. B. (2008). Abortion in the United States: Incidence and access to services, 2005. *Perspectives on Sexual and Reproductive Health, 40*(1), 6–16. doi:10.1363/4000608

Jorgensen, R. S., & Kolodziej, M. E. (2007). Suppressed anger, evaluative threat, and cardiovascular reactivity: A tripartite profile approach. *International Journal of Psychophysiology, 66,* 102–108.

Jose, P. E., Lim, B. T., & Bryant, F. B. (2012). Does savoring increase happiness? A daily diary study. *The Journal of Positive Psychology, 7*(3), 176–187. doi:10.1080/17439760.2012.671345

Josephs, L., & Weinberger, J. (2013). Psychodynamic psychotherapy. In G. Stricker & T. A. Widiger (Eds.), *Handbook of psychology, Vol. 8: Clinical psychology* (2nd ed.). New York: Wiley.

Joyal, C. C., Cossette, A., & Lapierre, V. (2015). What exactly is an unusual sexual fantasy? *Journal of Sexual Medicine, 12*(2), 328–340. doi:10.1111/jsm.12734

Joyner, T. (1999, November 14). All-work is American way: Atlanta poll finds 21 percent work 50-plus hours a week. *The Atlanta Journal-Constitution,* pp. R1, R5.

Judge, T. A., & Klinger, R. (2008). Job satisfaction: Subjective well-being at work. In M. Eid & R. J. Larsen (Eds.), *The science of subjective well-being* (pp. 393–413). New York: Guilford.

Judge, T. A., Livingston, B. A., & Hurst, C. (2012). Do nice guys—and gals—really finish last? The joint effects of sex and agreeableness on income. *Journal of Personality and Social Psychology, 102,* 390–407. doi:10.1037/a0026021

Julien, R. M., Advokat, C. D., & Comaty, J. E. (2011). *A primer of drug action: A comprehensive guide to the actions, uses, and side effects of psychoactive drugs* (12th ed.). New York: Worth.

Jung, C. G. (1921). Psychological types. In *Collected Works, Vol. 6.* Princeton, NJ: Princeton University Press.

Jung, C. G. (1933). *Modern man in search of a soul.* New York: Harcourt, Brace & World.

Justman, S. (2005). *Fool's paradise: The unreal world of pop psychology.* Chicago: Ivan R. Dee.

Kaczmarek, L. D., Kashdan, T. B., Drążkowski, D., Enko, J., Kosakowski, M., Szäefer, A., & Bujacz, A. (2015). Why do people prefer gratitude journaling over gratitude letters? The influence of individual differences in motivation and personality on web-based interventions. *Personality and Individual Differences, 75,* 1–6. doi:10.1016/j.paid.2014.11.004

Kagan, J., Snidman, N., & Arcus, D. M. (1992). Initial reactions to unfamiliarity. *Current Directions in Psychological Science, 1*(6), 171–174.

Kahlenberg, S. G., & Hein, M. M. (2010). Progression on Nickelodeon? Gender-role stereotypes in toy commercials. *Sex Roles, 62*(11–12), 830–847. doi:10.1007/s11199-009-9653-1

Kahn, A. S., & Andreoli Mathie, V. (1999). Sexuality, society, and feminism: Psychological perspectives on women. In C. B. Travis & J. W. White (Eds.), *Sexuality, society, and feminism: Psychological perspectives on women.* Washington, DC: American Psychological Association.

Kahneman, D. (1999). Objective happiness. In D. Kahneman, E. Diener, & N. Schwarz (Eds.), *Well-being: The foundations of hedonic psychology.* New York: Sage.

Kahneman, D. (2011). *Thinking, fast and slow.* New York: Farrar, Straus, & Giroux.

Kahneman, D., & Deaton, A. (2010). High income improves evaluation of life but not emotional well-being. *Proceedings of the National Academy of Sciences of the United States of America, 107*(38), 16489–16493. doi:10.1073/pnas.1011492107

Kaiser, A., Haller, S., Schmitz, S., & Nitsch, C. (2009). On sex/gender related similarities and differences in fMRI language research. *Brain Research Reviews, 61,* 49–59.

Kalant, H. (2004). Adverse effects of cannabis on health: An update of the literature since 1966. *Progress in Neuro-Psychopharmocology and Biological Psychiatry, 28,* 849–863.

Kalichman, S. C. (1995). *Understanding AIDS: A guide for mental health professionals.* Washington, DC: American Psychological Association.

Kalichman, S. C., Eaton, L., & Cherry, C. (2010). "There is no proof that HIV causes AIDS": AIDS denialism beliefs among people living with HIV/AIDS. *Journal of Behavioral Medicine, 33*(6), 432–440. doi:10.1007/s10865-010-9275-7

Kana, R. K., & Travers, B. G. (2012). Neural substrates of interpreting actions and emotions from body postures. *Social Cognitive and Affective Neuroscience, 7*(4), 446–456. doi:10.1093/scan/nsr022

Kane, E. W. (2000). Racial and ethnic variations in gender-related attitudes. *Annual review of sociology, 26,* 419–439.

Kane, J. M., Stroup, T. S., & Marder, S. R. (2009). Schizophrenia: Pharmacological treatment. In B. J. Sadock, V. A. Sadock, & P. Ruiz (Eds.), *Kaplan & Sadock's comprehensive textbook of psychiatry* (pp. 1547–1555). Philadelphia: Lippincott Williams & Wilkins.

Kanno, T., Iijima, K., Abe, Y., Koike, T., Shimada, N., Hoshi, T., Sano, N., Ohyauchi, M., Ito, H., Atsumi, T., Konishi, H., Asonuma, S., & Shimosegawa, T. (2013). Peptic ulcers after the Great East Japan Earthquake and tsunami: Possible existence of psychosocial stress ulcers in humans. *Journal of Gastroenterology, 48*(4), 483–490. doi: 10.1007/s00535-012-0681-1

Kant, A. K., Schatzkin, A., Graubard, B. I., & Schairer, C. (2000). A prospective study of diet quality and mortality in women. *Journal of the American Medical Association, 283,* 2109–02115.

Kantamneni, N. (2014). Vocational interest structures for Asian Americans, Middle-Eastern Americans and Native Americans on the 2005 Strong Interest Inventory. *Journal of Vocational Behavior, 84*(2), 133–141. doi:10.1016/j.jvb.2013.11.003

Kaplan, H. S. (1979). *Disorders of sexual desire.* New York: Simon & Schuster.

Karam, E., Kypri, K., & Salamoun M. (2007). Alcohol use among college students: An international perspective. *Current Opinion in Psychiatry, 20,* 213–221.

Karlsen, E., Dybdahl, R., & Vitterso, J. (2006). The possible benefits of difficulty: How stress can increase and decrease subjective well-being. *Scandinavian Journal of Psychology, 47,* 411–417.

Karremans, J. C., Pronk, T. M., & van der Wal, R. C. (2015). Executive control and relationship maintenance processes: An empirical overview and theoretical integration. *Social and Personality Psychology Compass, 9*(7), 333–347. doi:10.1111/spc3.12177

Kashdan, T. B., Barrett, L. F., & McKnight, P. E. (2015). Unpacking emotion differentiation: Transforming unpleasant experience by perceiving distinctions in negativity. *Current Directions in Psychological Science, 24*(1), 10–16. doi:10.1177/0963721414550708

Kassin, S. M., Fein, S., & Markus, H. (2011). *Social psychology* (8th ed.). Belmont, CA: Wadsworth/Cengage.

Kath, L., Swody, C., Magley, V., Bunk, J., & Gallus, J. (2009). Cross-level, three-way interactions among work-group climate, gender, and frequency of harassment on morale and withdrawal outcomes of sexual harassment. *Journal of Occupational & Organizational Psychology, 82*(1), 159–182.

Kato, T. (2012). Development of the Coping Flexibility Scale: Evidence for the coping flexibility hypothesis. *Journal of Counseling Psychology, 59*(2), 262–273. doi:10.1037/a0027770

Katz-Wise, S., & Hyde, J. S. (2014). Sexuality and gender: The interplay. In D. L. Tolman, L. M. Diamond, J. A. Bauermeister, W. H. George, J. G. Pfaus, & L. M. Ward (Eds.), *APA handbook of sexuality and psychology* (pp. 29–62). Washington, DC: American Psychological Association. doi:10.1037/14193-002

Kaufmann, G. (2015). The mood and creativity puzzle. In C. E. Shalley, M. A. Hitt, J. Zhou, C. E. Shalley, M. A. Hitt, & J. Zhou (Eds.), *The Oxford handbook of creativity, innovation, and entrepreneurship* (pp. 141–158). New York: Oxford University Press.

Kawachi, I., Colditz, G. A., Stampfer, M. J., Willett, W. C., Manson, J. E., Rosner, B., . . . Hennekens, C. H. (1994). Smoking cessation and time course of decreased risks of coronary heart disease in middle-aged women. *Archives of Internal Medicine, 154,* 169–175.

Kay, J., & Kay, R. L. (2008). Individual psychoanalytic psychotherapy. In A. Tasman, J. Kay, J. A. Lieberman, M. B. First, & M. Maj (Eds.), *Psychiatry* (3rd ed.). New York: Wiley-Blackwell.

Kayser, D. N., Elliot, A. J., & Feltman, R. (2010). Red and romantic behavior in men viewing women. *European Journal of Social Psychology, 40*(6), 901–908. doi:10.1002/ejsp.757

Kazdin, A. E. (1994). Methodology, design, and evaluation in psychotherapy research. In A. E. Bergin & S. L. Garfield (Eds.), *Handbook of psychotherapy and behavior change* (4th ed.). New York: Wiley.

Kazdin, A. E. (2001). *Behavior modification in applied settings.* Belmont, CA: Wadsworth.

Kazdin, A. E., & Blase, S. L. (2011). Rebooting psychotherapy research and practice to reduce the burden of mental illness. *Perspectives on Psychological Science, 6,* 21–37. doi:10.1177/1745691610393527

Kazdin, A. E., & Rabbitt, S. M. (2013). Novel models for delivering mental health services and reducing the burdens of mental illness. *Clinical Psychological Science, 1*(2), 170–191. doi:10.1177/2167702612463566

Keel, P. K., Brown, T. A., Holland, L. A., & Bodell, L. P. (2012). Empirical classification of eating disorders. *Annual Review of Clinical Psychology, 8,* 381–404. doi:10.1146/annurev-clinpsy-032511-143111

Keel, P. K., Forney, K. J., Brown, T. A., & Heatherton, T. F. (2013). Influence of college peers on disordered eating in women and men at 10-year follow-up. *Journal of Abnormal Psychology, 122,* 105–110. doi:10.1037/a0030081

Keesey, R. E. (1995). A set-point model of body weight regulation. In K. D. Brownell & C. G. Fairburn (Eds.), *Eating disorders and obesity: A comprehensive handbook.* New York: Guilford.

Kegan, R. (1994). *In over our heads: The mental demands of modern life.* Cambridge, MA: Harvard University Press.

Keinan, G. (1987). Decision making under stress: Scanning of alternatives under controllable and uncontrollable threats. *Journal of Personality and Social Psychology, 52,* 639–644.

Keller, M. B., Boland, R., Leon, A., Solomon, D., Endicott, J., & Li, C. (2013). Clinical course and outcome of unipolar major depression. In M. B. Keller, W. H. Coryell, J. Endicott, J. D. Maser, & P. J. Schettler (Eds.), *Clinical guide to depression and bipolar disorder: Findings from the Collaborative Depression Study.* Washington, DC: American Psychiatric Press.

Kelley, F. A. (2015). The therapy relationship with lesbian and gay clients. *Psychotherapy, 52*(1), 113–118. doi:10.1037/a0037958

Kelley, H. H. (1950). The warm-cold dimension in first impressions of persons. *Journal of Personality, 18,* 431–439.

Kelley, H. H. (1967). Attribution theory in social psychology. In D. Levine (Ed.), *Nebraska Symposium on Motivation, Vol. 15.* Lincoln: University of Nebraska Press.

Kelley, H. H., & Thibaut, J. W. (1978). *Interpersonal relations: A theory of interdependence.* New York: Wiley-Interscience.

Kellner, C. H., Greenberg, R. M., Murrough, J. W., Bryson, E. O., Briggs, M. C., & Pasculli, R. M. (2012). ECT in treatment-resistant depression. *American Journal of Psychiatry, 169,* 1238–1244. doi:10.1176/appi.ajp.2012.12050648

Kelsoe, J. R. (2009). Mood disorders: Genetics. In B. J. Sadock, V. A. Sadock, & P. Ruiz (Eds.), *Kaplan & Sadock's comprehensive textbook of psychiatry* (pp. 1653–1663). Philadelphia: Lippincott Williams & Wilkins.

Kendall, N. (2014). Sexuality education. In D. L. Tolman, L. M. Diamond, J. A. Bauermeister, W. H. George, J. G. Pfaus & L. M. Ward (Eds.), *APA handbook of sexuality and psychology* (pp. 339–371). Washington, DC: American Psychological Association. doi:10.1037/14194-011

Kendler, K. S., Myers, J., & Prescott, C. A. (2005). Sex differences in the relationship between social support and risk for major depression: A longitudinal study of opposite-sex twin pairs. *American Journal of Psychiatry, 162,* 250–256.

Kendler, K. S., Ohlsson, H., Sundquist, J., & Sundquist, K. (2015). IQ and schizophrenia in a Swedish national sample: Their causal relationship and the interaction of IQ with genetic risk. *The American Journal of Psychiatry, 172*(3), 259–265. doi:10.1176/appi.ajp.2014.14040516

Kenfield, S. A., Stampfer, M. J., Rosner, B. A., & Colditz, G. A. (2008). Smoking and smoking cessation in relation to mortality in women. *Journal of the American Medical Association, 299,* 2037–2047.

Kennedy, G. J., Martinez, M. M., & Garo, N. (2010). Sex and mental health in old age. *Primary Psychiatry, 17*(1), 22–30.

Kennedy, S. (2007). Psychological factors and immunity in HIV infections: Stress, coping, social support, and intervention outcomes. In A. Monat, R. S. Lazarus, & G. Reevy (Eds.), *The Praeger handbook on stress and coping* (pp. 199–215). Westport, CT: Praeger.

Kenrick, D. T., Neuberg, S. L., & White, A. E. (2013). Relationships from an evolutionary life history perspective. In J. A. Simpson, L. Campbell, J. A. Simpson, L. Campbell (Eds.), *The Oxford handbook of close relationships* (pp. 13–38). New York: Oxford University Press

Kern, M. L., & Friedman, H. S. (2011a). Personality and pathways of influence on physical health. *Social and Personality Psychology Compass, 5*(1), 76–87. doi:10.1111/j.1751-9004.2010.00331.x

Kern, M. L., & Friedman, H. S. (2011b). Personality and differences in health and longevity. In T. Chamorro-Premuzic, S. von Stumm, & A. Furnham (Eds.), *The Wiley-Blackwell handbook of individual differences* (pp. 461–489). Wiley-Blackwell.

Kernis, M. H. (2003a). Optimal self-esteem and authenticity: Separating fantasy from reality. *Psychological Inquiry, 14*(1), 83–89.

Kernis, M. H. (2003b). Toward a conceptualization of optimal self-esteem. *Psychological Inquiry, 14*(1), 1–26.

Kernis, M. H., & Goldman, B. M. (2003). Stability and variability in self-concept and self-esteem. In M. R. Leary and J. P. Tangney (Eds.), *Handbook of self and identity.* New York: Guilford.

Ketter, T. A., & Chang, K. D. (2014). Bipolar and related disorders. In R. E. Hales, S. C. Yudofsky, & L. W. Roberts (Eds.), *The American Psychiatric Publishing textbook of psychiatry* (6th ed.). Washington, DC: American Psychiatric Publishing.

Keyes, C. M. (2009). Toward a science of mental health. In S. J. Lopez & C. R. Snyder (Eds.), *Oxford handbook of positive psychology* (2nd ed., pp. 89–95). New York: Oxford University Press.

Keyes, C. M., & Haidt, J. (Eds.). (2003). *Flourishing: Positive psychology and the life well-lived.* Washington, DC: American Psychological Association.

Keyes, C. M., & Lopez, S. J. (2002). Toward a science of mental health: Positive directions in diagnosis and interventions. In C. R. Snyder & S. J. Lopez (Eds.), *Handbook of positive psychology* (pp. 45–59). New York: Oxford University Press.

Keysar, B., & Henly, A. S. (2002). Speakers' overestimation of their effectiveness. *Psychological Science, 13,* 207–212.

Kiecolt-Glaser, J. K. (2009). Psychoneuroimmunology: Psychology's gateway to biomedical future. *Perspectives on Psychological Science, 4*(4), 367–369. doi:10.1111/j.1745-6924.2009.01139.x

Kiecolt-Glaser, J. K., Garner, W., Speicher, C., Penn, G. M., Holliday, J., & Glaser, R. (1984). Psychosocial modifiers of immunocompetence in medical students. *Psychosomatic Medicine, 46,* 7–14.

Kiernan, K. (2004). Redrawing the boundaries of marriage. *Journal of Marriage and Family, 66,* 980–987.

Killian, K. D. (2012). Resisting and complying with homogamy: Interracial couples' narratives about partner differences. *Counselling Psychology Quarterly, 25*(2), 125–135. doi:10.1080/09515070.2012.680692

Kilmartin, C. T. (2000). *The masculine self* (2nd ed.). Boston: McGraw-Hill.

Kilmartin, C. T. (2007). *The masculine self.* Cornwall-on-Hudson, New York: Sloan.

Kiluk, B. D., Sugarman, D. E., Nich, C., Gibbons, C. J., Martino, S., Rounsaville, B. J., & Carroll, K. M. (2011). A methodological analysis of randomized clinical trials of computer-assisted therapies for psychiatric disorders: Toward improved standards for an emerging field. *The American Journal of Psychiatry, 168,* 790–799. doi:10.1176/appi.ajp.2011.10101443

Kim, A., & Berry, C. M. (2015). Individual differences in social dominance orientation predict support for the use of cognitive ability tests. *Journal of Personality, 83*(1), 14–25. doi:10.1111/jopy.12078

Kim, H. S., Sherman, D. K., Ko, D., & Taylor, S. E. (2006). Pursuit of comfort and pursuit of harmony: Culture, relationships, and social support seeking. *Personality and Social Psychology Bulletin, 32,*1595–1607.

Kim, J., & Gray, K. (2008). Leave or stay? Battered women's decision after intimate partner violence. *Journal of Interpersonal Violence, 23,* 1465–1482.

Kim, K. R., & Seo, E. H. (2015). The relationship between procrastination and academic performance: A meta-analysis. *Personality and Individual Differences, 82,* 26–33. doi:10.1016/j.paid.2015.02.038

Kim, S., Plumb, R., Gredig, Q., Rankin, L., & Taylor, B. (2008). Medium-term post-Katrina health sequelae among New Orleans residents: Predictors of poor mental and physical health. *Journal of Clinical Nursing, 17,* 2335–2342.

King, E. B., Hebl, M. R., George, J. M., & Matusik, S. F. (2010). Understanding tokenism: Antecedents and consequences of a psychological climate of gender inequity. *Journal of Management, 36*(2), 482–510. doi:10.1177/0149206308328508

King, L. A., & Emmons, R. A. (1990). Conflict over emotional expression: Psychological and physical correlates. *Journal of Personality and Social Psychology, 58,* 864–877.

King, L. A., & Emmons, R. A. (1991). Psychological, physical, and interpersonal correlates of emotional expressiveness, conflict and control. *European Journal of Personality, 5,* 131–150.

King, L. A., King, D. W., Fairbank, J. A., Keane, T. M., & Adams, G. A. (1998). Resilience-recovery factors in post-traumatic stress disorder among female and male Vietnam veterans: Hardiness, postwar social support, and additional stressful life events. *Journal of Personality and Social Psychology, 74,* 420–434.

Kinsey, A. C., Pomeroy, W. B., & Martin, C. E. (1948). *Sexual behavior in the human male.* Philadelphia: Saunders.

Kirby, D. (2005). *Evidence of harm: Mercury in vaccines and the autism epidemic: A medical controversy.* New York: St. Martin's Press.

Kirk, S. A., Gomory, T., & Cohen, D. (2013). *Mad science: Psychiatric coercion, diagnosis, and drugs.* New Brunswick, NJ: Transaction Publishers.

Kirsch, I. (2010). *The emperor's new drugs: Exploding the antidepressant myth.* New York: Basic Books.

Kistler, M. E., & Lee, M. J. (2010). Does exposure to sexual hip-hop music videos influence the sexual attitudes of college students? *Mass Communication and Society, 13*(1), 67–86. doi:10.1080/15205430902865336

Kitayama, S. (1996). *The mutual constitution of culture and the self: Implications for emotions.* Paper presented at the Annual Meeting of the American Psychological Society.

Klassen, M. (1987). How to get the most out of your time. In A. D. Timpe (Ed.), *The management of time.* New York: Facts on File.

Klatsky, A. L. (2008). Alcohol, wine, and vascular diseases: An abundance of paradoxes. *American Journal of Physiology: Heart and Circulatory Physiology, 63,* 582–583.

Klatzky, R. L., & Lederman, S. J. (2013). Touch. In A. F. Healy, R. W. Proctor, I. B. Weiner, A. F. Healy, R. W. Proctor, & I. B. Weiner (Eds.), *Handbook of psychology, Vol. 4: Experimental psychology* (2nd ed.; pp. 152–178). Hoboken, NJ: Wiley.

Klein, D. N., & Allmann, A. E. (2014). Course of depression: Persistence and recurrence. In I. H. Gotlib & C. L. Hammen (Eds.), *Handbook of depression* (3rd ed.). New York: Guilford.

Klein, O., Snyder, M., & Livingston, R. W. (2004). Prejudice on the stage: Self-monitoring and the public expression of group attitudes. *British Journal of Social Psychology, 43*(2), 299–314. doi:10.1348/0144666041501697

Klein, S. B. (2012). The self and science: Is it time for a new approach to the study of human experience? *Current Directions in Psychological Science, 21,* 253–257.

Kleinke, C. L. (1986). Gaze and eye contact: A research review. *Psychological Bulletin, 100,* 78–100.

Kleinke, C. L. (2007). What does it mean to cope? In A. Monat, R. S. Lazarus, & G. Reevy (Eds.), *The Praeger handbook on stress and coping* (pp. 289–308). Westport, CT: Praeger.

Kleinmuntz, B. (1980). *Essentials of abnormal psychology.* San Francisco: Harper & Row.

Kleinplatz, P. J., & Diamond, L. M. (2014). Sexual diversity. In D. L. Tolman, L. M. Diamond, J. A. Bauermeister, W. H. George, J. G. Pfaus, & L. M. Ward (Eds.), *APA handbook of sexuality and psychology,* (pp. 245–267). Washington, DC: American Psychological Association. doi:10.1037/14193-009

Klettke, B., Hallford, D. J., & Mellor, D. J. (2014). Sexting prevalence and correlates: A systematic literature review. *Clinical Psychology Review, 34*(1), 44–53. doi:10.1016/j.cpr.2013.10.007

Kline, G. H., Pleasant, N. D., Whitton, S. W., & Markman, H. J. (2006). Understanding couple conflict. In A. L. Vangelisti & D. Perlman (Eds.), *The Cambridge handbook of personal relationships*. New York: Cambridge University Press.

Klinesmith, J., Kasser, T., & McAndrew, F. T. (2006). Guns, testosterone, and aggression: An experimental test of a mediational hypothesis. *Psychological Science, 17,* 568–571.

Kling, K. C., Hyde, J. S., Showers, C. J., & Buswell, B. N. (1999). Gender differences in self-esteem: A meta-analysis. *Psychological Bulletin, 125*(4), 470–500.

Kloth, N., Altmann, C. S., & Schweinberger, S. R. (2011). Facial attractiveness biases the perception of eye contact. *The Quarterly Journal of Experimental Psychology, 64*(10), 1906–1918. doi:10.1080/17470218.2011.587254

Kluft, R. P. (1996). Dissociative identity disorder. In L. K. Michelson & W. J. Ray (Eds.), *Handbook of dissociation: Theoretical, empirical, and clinical perspectives.* New York: Plenum.

Kluger, R. (1996). *Ashes to ashes: America's hundred-year cigarette war, the public health and the unabashed triumph of Philip Morris.* New York: Knopf.

Knapp, M. L., Hall, J. A., & Horgan, T. G. (2014). *Nonverbal communication in human interaction* (8th ed.). Belmont, CA: Wadsworth.

Knaus, W. (2000). Procrastination, blame, and change. *Journal of Social Behavior and Personality, 15,* 153–166.

Knauss, W. (2005). Group psychotherapy. In G. O. Gabbard, J. S. Beck, & J. Holmes (Eds.), *Oxford textbook of psychotherapy*. New York: Oxford University Press.

Knox, D., Vail-Smith, K., & Zusman, M. (2007). The lonely college male. *International Journal of Men's Health, 6*(3), 273–279. doi:10.3149/jmh.0603.273

Knox, D., Vail-Smith, K., & Zusman, M. (2008). "Men are dogs": Is the stereotype justified? Data on the cheating college male. *College Student Journal, 42,* 1015–1022.

Kobasa, S. C. (1979). Stressful life events, personality, and health: An inquiry into hardiness. *Journal of Personality and Social Psychology, 37,* 1–11.

Kobasa, S. C. (1984, September). How much stress can you survive? *American Health,* pp. 64–77.

Koch, A. J., D'Mello, S. D., & Sackett, P. R. (2015). A meta-analysis of gender stereotypes and bias in experimental simulations of employment decision making. *Journal of Applied Psychology, 100*(1), 128–161. doi:10.1037/a0036734

Kochanek, K. D., Xu, J., Murphy, S. L., Minino, A. M., & Kung, H.-C. (2011). Deaths: Preliminary data for 2009. *National Vital Statistics Reports, 59*(4), 1–68.

Koenig, H. G. (2004). Religion, spirituality, and medicine: Research findings and implications for clinical practice. *South Medical Journal, 97,* 1194 –1200.

Koenig, H. G. (2010). Spirituality and mental health. *International Journal of Applied Psychoanalytic Studies, 7*(2), 116–122.

Koenig, H. G. (2013). Religion and spirituality in coping with acute and chronic illness (pp. 275–295). Washington, DC: American Psychological Association. doi:10.1037/14046-014

Kok, B. E., Coffey, K. A., Cohn, M. A., Catalino, L. I., Vacharkulksemsuk, T., Algoe, S. B., . . . Fredrickson, B. L. (2013). How positive emotions build physical health: Perceived positive social connections account for the upward spiral between positive emotions and vagal tone. *Psychological Science, 24*(7), 1123–1132. doi:10.1177/0956797612470827

Kolodny, A., Courtwright, D. T., Hwang, C. S., Kreiner, P., Eadie, J. L., Clark, T. W., & Alexander, G. C. (2015). The prescription opioid and heroin crisis: A public health approach to an epidemic of addiction. *Annual Review of Public Health, 36,* 559–574.

Konrath, S. H., O'Brien, E. H., & Hsing, C. (2011). Changes in dispositional empathy in American college students over time: A meta-analysis. *Personality and Social Psychology Review, 15,* 180–198.

Konyu-Fogel, G. (2015). Career management and human resource development of a global, diverse workforce. In C. Hughes (Eds.), *Impact of diversity on organization and career development* (pp. 80–104). Hershey, PA: Business Science Reference/IGI Global. doi:10.4018/978-1-4666-7324-3.ch004

Koopmann-Holm, B., & Matsumoto, D. (2011). Values and display rules for specific emotions. *Journal of Cross-Cultural Psychology, 42*(3), 355–371. doi:10.1177/0022022110362753

Koopmans, G. T., & Lamers, L. M. (2007). Gender and health care utilization: The role of mental distress and help-seeking propensity. *Social Science & Medicine, 64,* 1216–1230.

Koordeman, R., Anschutz, D., & Engels, R. (2012). The effect of alcohol advertising on immediate alcohol consumption in college students: An experimental study. *Alcoholism, Clinical, and Experimental Research, 36*(5), 874–880. doi: 10.1111/j.1530-0227.2011.01655.x

Koriat, A., & Bjork, R. A. (2005). Illusions of competence in monitoring one's knowledge during study. *Journal of Experimental Psychology: Learning, Memory, and Cognition, 31,* 187–194.

Kornell, N., & Metcalfe, J. (2014). The effects of memory retrieval, errors and feedback on learning. In V. A. Benassi, C. E. Overson, & C. M. Hakala (Eds.), *Applying science of learning in education: Infusing psychological science into the curriculum.* Washington, DC: Society for the Teaching of Psychology.

Kornell, N., Rhodes, M. G., Castel, A. D., & Tauber, S. K. (2011). The ease-of-processing heuristic and the stability bias: Dissociating memory, memory beliefs, and memory judgments. *Psychological Science, 22,* 787–794. doi:10.1177/0956797611407929

Korotkov, D., Perunovic, M., Claybourn, M., Fraser, I., Houlihan, M., Macdonald, M., & Korotkov, K. (2011). The Type B behavior pattern as a moderating variable of the relationship between stressor chronicity and health behavior. *Journal of Health Psychology, 16*(3), 397–409. doi:10.1177/1359105310380082

Kosic, A., Phalet, K., & Mannetti, L. (2012). Ethnic categorization: The role of epistemic motivation, prejudice, and perceived threat. *Basic and Applied Social Psychology, 34*(1), 66–75. doi:10.1080/01973533.2011.637724

Koslowsky, M., & Pindek, S. (2011). Impression management: Influencing perceptions of self. In D. Chadee (Ed.), *Theories in social psychology* (pp. 280–296). Wiley-Blackwell.

Kostić, A., & Chadee, D. (2015). Emotional recognition, fear, and nonverbal behavior. In A. Kostić & D. Chadee (Eds.), *The social psychology of nonverbal communication* (pp. 134–150). New York: Palgrave Macmillan.

Kouabenan, D. R., Gilibert, D., Médina, M., & Bouzon, F. (2001). Hierarchical position, gender, accident severity, and causal attribution. *Journal of Applied Social Psychology, 31*(3), 553–575. doi:10.1111/j.1559-1816.2001.tb02056.x

Kowalski, R. M. (1993). Inferring sexual interest from behavioral cues: Effects of gender and sexually relevant attitudes. *Sex Roles, 29,* 13–36.

Kozlowski, S. W. J., & Bell, B. S. (2003). Work groups and teams in organizations. In W. C. Borman, D. R. Ilgen, & R. J. Klimoski (Eds.), *Handbook of psychology, Vol. 12: Industrial and organizational psychology.* New York: Wiley.

Kozorovitskiy, Y., & Gould, E. (2008). Adult neurogenesis in the hippocampus. In C. A. Nelson & M. Luciana (Eds.), *Handbook of developmental cognitive neuroscience* (2nd ed., pp. 51–61). Cambridge, MA: MIT Press.

Kraaij, V., & Garnefski, N. (2006). The role of intrusion, avoidance, and cognitive coping strategies more then 50 years after war. *Anxiety, Stress, & Coping, 19*(1), 1–14.

Kraft, S. (2009, October 22). Sweat lodge deaths a new test for self-help guru. *Los Angeles Times.* Retrieved from www.latimes.com/news/nationworld/nation/la-na-guru22-2009oct22,0,6180058.story

Kramer, P. D. (2006). *Freud: Inventor of the modern mind.* New York: HarperCollins.

Krause, K., & Freund, A. M. (2014). How to beat procrastination: The role of goal focus. *European Psychologist, 19*(2), 132–144. doi:10.1027/1016-9040/a000153

Kreider, R. M. (2005). *Number, timing, and duration of marriages and divorces: 2001. U.S. Census Bureau, Household Economic Studies.* Washington DC: Department of Commerce.

Kreider, R. M., & Ellis, R. (2011). Number, timing, and duration of marriages and divorces: 2009. Current Population Reports, P70–P125, U.S. Census Bureau, Washington, DC.

Krejtz, I., Nezlek, J. B., Michnicka, A., Holas, P., & Rusanowska, M. (2014). Counting one's blessings can reduce the impact of daily stress. *Journal of Happiness Studies.* doi:10.1007/s10902-014-9578-4

Krendl, A. C., Ambady, N., & Kensinger, E. A. (2015). The dissociable effects of stereotype threat on older adults' memory encoding and retrieval. *Journal of Applied Research in Memory and Cognition, 4*(2), 103–109. doi:10.1016/j.jarmac.2015.02.001

Kring, A. M., & Gordon, A. H. (1998). Sex differences in emotion: Expression, experience, and physiology. *Journal of Personality and Social Psychology, 74*(3), 686–703.

Krizan, Z., & Johar, O. (2015). Narcissistic rage revisited. *Journal of Personality and Social Psychology, 108*(5), 784–801. doi:10.1037/pspp0000013

Krosnick, J. A. Lavrakas, P. J., & Kim, N. (2014). Survey research. In H. T. Reis & C. M. Judd (Eds.), *Handbook of research methods in social and personality psychology* (2nd ed.). New York: Cambridge University Press.

Krueger, J. I., & DiDonato, T. E. (2008). Social categorization and the perception of groups and group differences. *Social and Personality Psychology Compass, 2,* 733–750.

Krueger, J. I., Vohs, K. D., & Baumeister, R. F. (2009). Is the allure of self-esteem a mirage after all? *American Psychologist, 63,* 64–65.

Krueger, W. C. F. (1929). The effect of overlearning on retention. *Journal of Experimental Psychology, 12,* 71–78.

Kruger, J., Galuska, D. A, Serdula, M. K., & Jones, D. A. (2004). Attempting to lose weight: Specific practices among U.S. adults. *American Journal of Preventive Medicine, 26,* 402–406.

Krumrei, E, Coit, C., Martin, S., Fogo, W., & Mahoney, A. (2007). Post-divorce adjustment and social relationships: A meta-analytic review. *Journal of Divorce and Remarriage, 46,* 145–166.

Krusemark, E. A., Campbell, W. K., & Clementz, B. A. (2008). Attributions, deception, and event related potentials: An investigation of the self-serving bias. *Psychophysiology, 45*(4), 511–515.

Kteily, N., Ho, A. K., & Sidanius, J. (2012). Hierarchy in the mind: The predictive power of social dominance orientation across social contexts and domains. *Journal of Experimental Social Psychology, 48*(2), 543–549. doi:10.1016/j.jesp.2011.11.007

Kulick, A. R., Pope, H. G., & Keck, P. E. (1990). Lycanthropy and self-identification. *Journal of Nervous and Mental Disease, 178,* 134–137.

Kulik, L. (2000). Jobless men and women: A comparative analysis of job search intensity, attitudes toward unemployment and related responses. *Journal of Occupational and Behavioral Psychology, 73*(4), 487–500.

Kung, H. C., Hoyert, D. L., Xu, J. Q., & Murphy, S. L. (2008). Deaths: Final data for 2005. *National Vital Statistics Reports, 56*(10), 1–66.

Kunkel, D., Eyal, K., Donnerstein, E., Farrar, K. M., Biely, E., & Rideout, V. (2007). Sexual socialization messages on entertainment television: Comparing content trends 1997–2002. *Media Psychology, 9*(3), 595–622. doi:10.1080/15213260701283210

Kunkel, D., Farrar, K. M., Eyal, K., Biely, E., Donnerstein, E., & Rideout, V. (2007). Sexual socialization messages on entertainment television: Comparing content trends, 1997–2002. *Media Psychology, 10,* 595–622.

Kupfer, D. J., Kuhl, E. A., & Regier, D. A. (2013). DSM-5—The future arrived. *JAMA: Journal of the American Medical Association, 309,* 1691–1692.

Kurdek, L. A. (2004). Gay men and lesbians: The family context. In M. Coleman & L. H. Ganong (Eds.), *Handbook of contemporary families: Considering the past, contemplating the future.* Thousand Oaks, CA: Sage.

Kurdek, L. A. (2005). What do we know about gay and lesbian couples? *Current Directions in Psychological Science, 14*(5), 251–254.

Kurdek, L. A., & Schmitt, J. P. (1986). Interaction of sex role self-concept with relationship quality and relationship beliefs in married, heterosexual cohabiting, gay, and lesbian couples. *Journal of Personality and Social Psychology, 51,* 365–370.

Kuroki, T., Ohta, A., Sherriff-Tadano, R., Matsuura, E., Takashima, T., Iwakiri, R., & Fujimoto, K. (2011). Imbalance in the stress-adaptation system in patients with inflammatory bowel disease. *Biological Research for Nursing, 13,* 391–398.

Kuyper, H., & Dijkstra, P. (2009). Better-than-average effects in secondary education: A 3-year follow-up. *Educational Research and Evaluation, 15*(2), 167–184.

Kwan, V. S., & Herrmann, S. D. (2015). The interplay between culture and personality. In M. Mikulincer, P. R. Shaver, M. L. Cooper, & R. J. Larsen (Eds.), *APA handbook of personality and social psychology, Vol. 4: Personality processes and individual differences.* Washington, DC: American Psychological Association.

Ladd, G. W., Buhs, E. S., & Seid, M. (2000). Children's initial sentiments about kindergarten: Is liking school an antecedent of early classroom participation and achievement? *Merrill-Palmer Quarterly, 46,* 255–278.

La Greca, A. M. (2007). Posttraumatic stress disorder in children. In G. Fink (Ed.), *Encyclopedia of stress: Vols. 1–4* (2nd ed., pp. 145–149). San Diego, CA: Elsevier Academic Press.

Lakein, A. (1996). *How to get control of your time and your life.* New York: New American Library.

Lakey, B. (2013). Perceived social support and happiness: The role of personality and relational processes. In S. A. David, I. Boniwell & A. Conley Ayers (Eds.), *The Oxford handbook of happiness.* New York: Oxford University Press.

Lambert, A. J., Burroughs, T., & Nguyen, T. (1999). Perceptions of risk and the buffering hypothesis: The role of just world beliefs and right wing authoritarianism. *Personality and Social Psychology Bulletin, 25,* 643–656.

Lambert, M. J. (2011). Psychotherapy research and its achievements. In J. C. Norcross, G. R. Vandenbos, & D. K. Freedheim (Eds.), *History of psychotherapy: Continuity and change* (2nd ed.). Washington, DC: American Psychological Association.

Lambert, M. J. (2013). The efficacy and effectiveness of psychotherapy. In M. J. Lambert (Ed.), *Bergin and Garfield's handbook of psychotherapy and behavior change* (6th ed.). New York: Wiley.

Lambert, M. J., Hansen, N. B., & Finch, A. E. (2001). Patient-focused research: Using patient outcome data to enhance treatment effects. *Journal of Consulting and Clinical Psychology, 69,* 159–172.

Lambert, M. J., & Ogles, B. M. (2014). Common factors: Post hoc explanation or empirically based therapy approach? *Psychotherapy, 51,* 500–504. doi:10.1037/a0036580

Lamkin, J., Clifton, A., Campbell, W. K., & Miller, J. D. (2014). An examination of the perceptions of social network characteristics associated with grandiose and vulnerable narcissism. *Personality Disorders: Theory, Research, and Treatment, 5*(2), 137–145. doi:10.1037/per0000024

Lammers, J., Stoker, J. I., Jordan, J., Pollmann, M., & Stapel, D. A. (2011). Power increases infidelity among men and women. *Psychological Science, 22*(9), 1191–1197. doi:10.1177/0956797611416252

Lamont, R. A., Swift, H. J., & Abrams, D. (2015). A review and meta-analysis of age-based stereotype threat: Negative stereotypes, not facts, do the damage. *Psychology and Aging, 30*(1), 180–193. doi:10.1037/a0038586

Lampert, R. (2010). Anger and ventricular arrhythmias. *Current Opinion in Cardiology, 25*(1), 46–52.

Landau, M. J., Oyserman, D., Keefer, L. A., & Smith, G. C. (2014). The college journey and academic engagement: How metaphor use enhances identity-based motivation. *Journal of Personality and Social Psychology, 106*(5), 679–698. doi:10.1037/a0036414

Landau, M. J., & Sullivan, D. (2015). Terror management motivation at the core of personality. In M. Mikulincer, P. R. Shaver, M. L. Cooper, & R. J. Larsen (Eds.), *APA handbook of personality and social psychology, Vol. 4: Personality processes and individual differences.* Washington, DC: American Psychological Association.

Landrum, R. E., & Davis, S. F. (2013). *The psychology major: Career options and strategies for success* (5th ed.). New York: Pearson.

Lane S. D., Cherek, D. R., Tcheremissine, O. V., Lieving, L. M., & Pietras, C. J. (2005). Acute marijuana effects on human risk taking. *Neuropsychopharmocology, 30,* 800–809.

Langer, E. J. (1989). *Mindfulness.* New York: Addison-Wesley.

Langer, E. J. (1998). *The power of mindful learning.* Cambridge, MA: Da Capo Press.

Langer, E. J. (2009). Mindfulness. In S. J. Lopez (Ed.), *The encyclopedia of positive psychology, Vol. II* (pp. 618–622). Malden, MA: Wiley-Blackwell.

Langer, E. J., Cohen, M., & Djikic, M. (2012). Mindfulness as a psychological attractor: The effect on children. *Journal of Applied Social Psychology, 42*(5), 1114–1122. doi:10.1111/j.1559-1816.2011.00879.x

Langlois, J. H., Kalakanis, L., Rubenstein, A. J., Larson, A., Hallam, M., & Smoot, M. (2000). Maxims or myths of beauty? A meta-analytic and theoretical review. *Psychological Bulletin, 126*(3), 390–423.

Lansford, J. E. (2009). Parental divorce and children's adjustment. *Perspectives on Psychological Science, 4,* 140–152.

LaPiere, R. T. (1934). Attitudes vs. actions. *Social Forces, 13,* 230–237.

LaRose, R., & Rifon, N. A. (2007). Promoting *i*-safety: Effects of privacy warnings and privacy seals on risk assessment and online privacy behavior. *The Journal of Consumer Affairs, 41*(1), 127–149.

Larsen, R. J., & Prizmic, Z. (2008). Regulation of emotional well-being: Overcoming the hedonic tredmill. In M. Eid & R. J. Larsen (Eds.), *The science of subjective well-being* (pp. 258–289). New York: Guilford.

Laska, K. M., Gurman, A. S., & Wampold, B. E. (2014). Expanding the lens of evidence-based practice in psychotherapy: A common factors perspective. *Psychotherapy, 51,* 467–481. doi:10.1037/a0034332

Laskoff, M. B. (2004). *Landing on the right side of your ass: A survival guide for the recently unemployed.* New York: Three Rivers Press.

Lau, J. Y., Lester, K. J., Hodgson, K., & Eley, T. C. (2014). The genetics of mood disorders. In I. H. Gotlib & C. L. Hammen (Eds.), *Handbook of depression* (3rd ed.). New York: Guilford.

Lauer, J., & Lauer, R. (1985, June). Marriages made to last. *Psychology Today,* pp. 22–26.

Laughlin, H. (1967). *The neuroses.* Washington, DC: Butterworth.

Laughlin, H. (1979). *The ego and its defenses.* New York: Aronson.

Laurenceau, J. P., Barrett, L. F., & Rovine, M. J. (2005). The interpersonal process model of intimacy in marriage: A daily-diary and multilevel modeling approach. *Journal of Family Psychology, 19,* 314–323.

Laurenceau, J. P., & Kleinman, B. M. (2006). Intimacy in personal relationships. In A. L. Vangelisti & D. Perlman (Eds.), *The Cambridge handbook of personal relationships.* New York: Cambridge University Press.

Lautsch, B. A., Kossek, B. A., & Ernst, E. (2011). Managing a blended workforce: Telecommuters and non-telecommuters. *Organizational Dynamics, 40*(1), 10–17. doi:10.1016/j.orgdyn.2010.10.005

Lavee, Y. (2013). Stress processes in families and couples. In G. W. Peterson & K. R. Bush (Eds.), *Handbook of marriage and the family* (3rd ed.; pp. 159-176). New York: Springer Science + Business Media. doi:10.1007/978-1-4614-3987-5_8

Lawrence, E., Rothman, A. D., Cobb, R. J., Rothman, M. T., & Bradbury, T. N. (2008). Marital satisfaction across the transition to parenthood. *Journal of Family Psychology, 22,* 41–50.

Lawrie, S. M., & Pantelis, C. (2011). Structural brain imaging in schizophrenia and related populations. In D. R. Weinberger & P. Harrison (Eds.), *Schizophrenia* (3rd ed.). Malden, MA: Wiley-Blackwell.

Lawson, T. J. (2010). The social spotlight increases blindness to change blindness. *Basic and Applied Social Psychology, 32,* 360–368.

Lay, C. H. (1995). Trait procrastination, agitation, dejection, and self-discrepancy. In J. R. Ferrari, J. L. Johnson, & W. G. McCown (Eds.), *Procrastination and task avoidance: Theory, research, and treatment.* New York: Plenum.

Lazarus, A. A. (1989). Multimodal therapy. In R. J. Corsini & D. Wedding (Eds.), *Current psychotherapies.* Itasca, IL: F. E. Peacock.

Lazarus, A. A. (1995). Different types of eclecticism and integration: Let's be aware of the dangers. *Journal of Psychotherapy Integration, 5,* 27–39.

Lazarus, A. A. (2008). Technical eclecticism and multimodal therapy. In J. L. Lebow (Ed.), *Twenty-first century psychotherapies: Contemporary approaches to theory and practice.* New York: Wiley.

Lazarus, R. S. (1993). Why we should think of stress as a subset of emotion. In L. Goldberger & S. Breznitz (Eds.), *Handbook of stress: Theoretical and clinical aspects* (2nd ed.). New York: Free Press.

Lazarus, R. S. (2003). Does the positive psychology movement have legs? *Psychological Inquiry, 14,* 93–109.

Lazarus, R. S., & Folkman, S. (1984). *Stress, appraisal and coping.* New York: Springer.

Le, B., Dove, N. L., Agnew, C. R., Korn, M. S., & Mutso, A. A. (2010). Predicting nonmarital romantic relationship dissolution: A meta-analytic synthesis. *Personal Relationships, 17*(3), 377–390. doi:10.1111/j.1475-6811.2010.01285.x

Leal, S., & Vrij, A. (2008). Blinking during and after lying. *Journal of Nonverbal Behavior, 32,* pp. 187–194.

Leaper, C. R., Breed, L., Hoffman, L., & Perlman, C. A. (2002). Variations in the gender-stereotyped content of children's television cartoons across genres. *Journal of Applied Social Psychology, 32,* 1653–1662.

Leaper, C., & Farkas, T. (2015). The socialization of gender during childhood and adolescence. In J. E. Grusec & P. D. Hastings (Eds.), *Handbook of socialization: Theory and research* (2nd ed.; pp. 541–565). New York: Guilford.

Leaper, C., & Robnett, R. D. (2011). Women are more likely than men to use tentative language, aren't they? A meta-analysis testing for gender differences and moderators. *Psychology of Women Quarterly, 35*(1), 129–142. doi:10.1177/0361684310392728

Leary, M. R., & Guadagno, J. (2011). The sociometer, self-esteem, and the regulation of interpersonal behavior. In K. D. Vohs & R. F. Baumeister (Eds.), *Handbook of self-regulation: Research, theory, and applications* (2nd ed.; pp. 339–354). New York: Guilford.

Lebow, J., & Stroud, C. B. (2013). Family therapy. In G. Stricker & T. A. Widiger (Eds.), *Handbook of psychology, Vol. 8: Clinical psychology* (2nd ed.). New York: Wiley.

Lebow, J. L. (2008). Couple and family therapy. In J. L Lebow (Ed.), *Twenty-first century psychotherapies: Contemporary approaches to theory and practice* (pp. 307–346). New York: Wiley.

Lebowitz, F. (1982). *Social studies.* New York: Pocket Books.

Lechner, S. C., Tennen, H., & Affleck G. (2009). Benefit-finding and growth. In S. J. Lopez & C. R. Snyder (Eds.), *Oxford handbook of positive psychology* (2nd ed., pp. 633–640). New York: Oxford University Press.

Ledbetter, A. M., Griffin, E., & Sparks, G. G. (2007). Forecasting "friends forever": A longitudinal investigation of sustained closeness between best friends. *Personal Relationships, 14,* 343–350.

Ledermann, T., Bodenmann, G., Rudaz, M., & Bradbury, T. N. (2010). Stress, communication, and marital quality in couples. *Family Relations: An Interdisciplinary Journal of Applied Family Studies, 59*(2), 195–206.

Ledgerwood, A. (2014). Evaluations in their social context: Distance regulates consistency and context dependence. *Social and Personality Psychology Compass, 8*(8), 436–447. doi:10.1111/spc3.12123

LeDoux, J. E., & Damasio, A. R. (2013). Emotions and feelings. In E. R. Kandel, J. H. Schwartz, T. M. Jessel, S. A. Siegelbaum & A. J. Hudspet (Eds.), *Principles of neural science* (5th ed., pp. 1079–1093). New York: McGraw-Hill.

Lee, I. M., & Buchner, D. M. (2008). The importance of walking to public health. *Medicine and& Science in Sports and Exercise, 40,* S512–S518.

Lee, I.-M., & Skerrett, P. J. (2001). Physical activity and all-cause mortality. What is the dose-response relation? *Medicine and Science in Sports and Exercise, 33,* S459–S471.

Lee, J. D., McNeely, J., & Gourevitch, M. N. (2011). Medical complications of drug use/dependence. In P. Ruiz & E. C. Strain (Eds.), *Lowinson and Ruiz's substance abuse: A comprehensive textbook* (5th ed.) (pp. 663–681). Philadelphia: Lippincott Williams & Wilkins.

Lee, S., & Oyserman, D. (2009). Expecting to work, fearing homelessness: The possible selves of low-income mothers. *Journal of Applied Social Psychology, 39*(6), 1334–1355.

Lee, S. Y., Gregg, A. P., & Park, S. H. (2013). The person in the purchase: Narcissistic consumers prefer products that positively distinguish them. *Journal of Personality and Social Psychology, 105,* 335–352. doi:10.1037/a0032703

Leeds, E. M., & Maurer, R. A. (2009). Using digital video technology to reduce communication apprehension in business education. *INFORMS Transactions on Education, 9*(2), 84–92. doi:10.1287/ited.1090.0023

Lefcourt, H. M. (2005). Humor. In C. R. Snyder & S. J. Lopez (Eds.), *Handbook of positive psychology.* New York: Oxford University Press.

Lefcourt, H. M., Davidson, K., Shepherd, R., Phillips, M., Prkachin, K., & Mills, D. (1995). Perspective-taking humor: Accounting for stress moderation. *Journal of Social and Clinical Psychology, 14,* 373–391.

Leibel, R. L., Rosenbaum, M., & Hirsch, J. (1995). Changes in energy expenditure resulting from altered body weight. *New England Journal of Medicine, 332,* 621–629.

Leitenberg, H., Detzer, M. J., & Srebnik, D. (1993). Gender differences in masturbation and the relation of masturbation experience in preadolescence and/or early adolescence to sexual behavior and sexual adjustment in young adulthood. *Archives of Sexual Behavior, 22,* 87–98.

Leiter, M. P., Bakker, A. B., & Maslach, C. (2014). *Burnout at work: A psychological perspective.* New York: Psychology Press.

Leiter, M. P., & Maslach, C. (2014). Interventions to prevent and alleviate burnout. In M. P. Leiter, A. B. Bakker, & C. Maslach (Eds.), *Burnout at work: A psychological perspective* (pp. 145–167). New York: Psychology Press.

Lemay, E. J., Clark, M. S., & Greenberg, A. (2010). What is beautiful is good because what is beautiful is desired: Physical attractiveness stereotyping as projection of interpersonal goals. *Personality and Social Psychology Bulletin, 36*(3), 339–353. doi:10.1177/0146167209359700

Lengua, L. J., Long, A. C., & Meltzoff, A. N. (2006). Pre-attack stress-load, appraisals, and coping in children's responses to the 9/11 terrorist attacks. *Journal of Child Psychology and Psychiatry, 47,* 1219–1227.

Leonard, N. H., & Harvey, M. (2008). Negative perfectionism: Examining negative excessive behavior in the workplace. *Journal of Applied Social Psychology, 38,* 585–610.

Leondari, A., & Gonida, E. N. (2008). Adolescents' possible selves, achievement goal orientations, and academic achievement. *Hellenic Journal of Psychology, 5*(2), 179–198.

Leonhardt, D. (2014, May 27). Is college worth it? Clearly, new data say. *New York Times.* Retrieved from www.nytimes.com/2014/05/27/upshot/is-college-worth-it-clearly-new-data-say.html

Leslie, L. A., & Letiecq, B. L. (2004). Marital quality of African American and white partners in interracial couples. *Personal Relationships, 11,* 559–574.

Lett, H. S., Blumenthal, J. A., Babyak, M. A., Sherwood, A., Strauman, T., Robins, C., & Newman, M. F. (2004). Depression as a risk factor for coronary artery disease: Evidence, mechanisms, and treatment. *Psychosomatic Medicine, 66*(3), 305–315.

Leutner, F., Ahmetoglu, G., Akhtar, R., & Chamorro-Premuzic, T. (2014). The relationship between the entrepreneurial personality and the Big Five personality traits. *Personality and Individual Differences, 63,* 58–63. doi:10.1016/j.paid.2014.01.042

Levant, R. F. (2011). Research in the psychology of men and masculinity using the gender role strain paradigm as a framework. *American Psychologist, 66*(8), 765–776. doi:10.1037/a0025034

Levant, R. F., & Richmond, K. (2016). The gender role strain paradigm and masculinity ideologies. In Y. J. Wong & S. R. Wester (Eds.), *APA handbook of men and masculinities* (pp. 23–49). Washington, DC: American Psychological Association. doi:10.1037/14594-002

Levenson, R. W., Carstensen, L. L., & Gottman, J. M. (1993). Long-term marriage: Age, gender, and satisfaction. *Psychology and Aging, 8,* 301–313.

Leventhal, H., Cameron, L., & Leventhal, E. A. (2005). Do messages from your body, your friends, your doctor, or the media shape your health behavior? In T. C. Brock & M. C. Green (Eds.), *Persuassion: Psychological insights and perspectives.* Thousand Oaks, CA: Sage.

Leventhal, H., Musumeci, T., & Leventhal, E. (2006). Psychological approaches to the connection of health and behavior. *South African Journal of Psychology, 36,* 666–682.

Leventhal, H., Weinman, J., Leventhal, E. A., & Phillips, L. A. (2008). Health psychology: The search for pathways between behavior and health. *Annual Review of Psychology, 59,* 477–505.

Levin, A. R., & Rotter, M. (2014). Sexual harassment. In E. Ford & M. Rotter (Eds.), *Landmark cases in forensic psychiatry* (pp. 112–114). New York: Oxford University Press.

Levin, T., & Kissane, D. W. (2006). Psychooncology: The state of its development in 2006. *European Journal of Psychiatry, 20,* 183–197.

Levine, J. M., & Tindale, R. S. (2015). Social influence in groups. In M. Mikulincer, P. R. Shaver, J. F. Dovidio, & J. A. Simpson (Eds.), *APA handbook of personality and social psychology, Vol. 2: Group processes* (pp. 3–34). Washington, DC: American Psychological Association. doi:10.1037/14342-001

Levine, M. P., & Harrison, K. (2004). Media's role in the perpetuation and prevention of negative body image and disordered eating. In J. K. Thompson (Ed.), *Handbook of eating disorders and obesity.* New York: Wiley.

Levinthal, C. F. (2014). *Drugs, behavior, and modern society* (8th ed.). Boston: Pearson.

Levy, D., & Brink, S. (2005). *A change of heart: How the people of Framingham, Massachusetts, helped unravel the mysteries of cardiovascular disease.* New York: Knopf.

Levy, I., & Ben-David, S. (2015). Mechanism of bystander-blaming: Defensive attribution, counterfactual thinking, and gender. *International Journal of Offender Therapy and Comparative Criminology, 59*(1), 96–113. doi:10.1177/0306624X13503297

Levy, S. R., Stroessner, S. J., & Dweck, C. S. (1998). Stereotype formation and endorsement: The role of implicit theories. *Journal of Personality and Social Psychology, 74*(6), 1421–1436.

Lewin, K. (1935). *A dynamic theory of personality.* New York: McGraw-Hill.

Lewis, K., Kaufman, J., & Christakis, N. (2008). The taste for privacy: An analysis of college student privacy settings in an online social network. *Journal of Computer-Mediated Communication, 14,* 79–100.

Li, N. P., Yong, J. C., Tov, W., Sng, O., Fletcher, G. J. O., Valentine, K. A., . . . Balliet, D. (2013). Mate preferences do predict attraction and choices in the early stages of mate selection. *Journal of Personality and Social Psychology, 105*(5), 757–776. doi:10.1037/a0033777; 10.1037/a0033777.supp (Supplemental)

Li, S., & Li, Y-M. (2007). How far is enough? A measure of information privacy in terms of interpersonal distance. *Environment and Behavior, 39,* 317–331.

Li, T., & Chan, D. K. (2012). How anxious and avoidant attachment affect romantic relationship quality differently: A meta-analytic review. *European Journal of Social Psychology, 42*(4), 406–419. doi:10.1002/ejsp.1842

Liao, Y. (2014). Relationship between coping style and mental health: A meta-analysis. *Chinese Journal of Clinical Psychology, 22*(5), 897–900.

Lick, D. J., Durso, L. E., & Johnson, K. L. (2013). Minority stress and physical health among sexual minorities. *Perspectives on Psychological Science, 8*(5), 521–548. doi:10.1177/1745691613497965

Lieberman, M. D., Gaunt, R., Gilbert, D. T., & Trope, Y. (2004). Reflection and reflexion: A social cognitive neuroscience approach to attributional inference. In M. P. Zanna (Ed.), *Advances in experimental social psychology, Vol. 34.* San Diego, CA: Academic Press.

Liewer, L., Mains, D., Lykens, K., & René, A. (2008). Barriers to women's cardiovascular risk knowledge. *Health Care for Women International, 29*(1), 23–38.

Lilienfeld, S. O. (2007). Psychological treatments that cause harm. *Perspectives on Psychological Science, 2,* 53–70.

Lilienfeld, S. O., & Landfield, K. (2008). Science and pseudoscience in law enforcement: A user-friendly primer. *Criminal Justice and Behavior, 35*(10), 1215–1230.

Lilienfeld, S. O., & Lynn, S. J. (2003). Dissociative identity disorder: Multiple personalities, multiple controversies. In S. O. Lilienfeld, S. Lynn, S. Jay, & J. M. Lohr (Eds.), *Science and pseudoscience in clinical psychology.* New York: Guilford.

Lilienfeld, S. O., Lynn, S. J., Kirsch, I., Chaves, J. F., Sarbin, T. R., Ganaway, G. K., & Powell, R. A. (1999). Dissociative identity disorder and the sociocognitive model: Recalling the lessons of the past. *Psychological Bulletin, 125*(5), 507–523.

Lilienfeld, S. O., Ritschel, L. A., Lynn, S. J., Cautin, R. L., & Latzman, R. D. (2014). Why ineffective psychotherapies appear to work: A taxonomy of causes of spurious therapeutic effectiveness. *Perspectives on Psychological Science, 9,* 355–387. doi:10.1177/1745691614535216

Lilienfeld, S. O., Wood, J. M., & Garb, H. N. (2000). The scientific status of projective tests. *Psychological Science in the Public Interest, 1*(2), 27–66.

Lin, H., Katsovich, L., Ghebremichael, M., Findley, D. B., Grantz, H., Lombroso, P. J., . . . Leckman, J. F. (2007). Psychosocial stress predicts future symptom severities in children and adolescents with Tourette syndrome and/or obsessive-compulsive disorder. *Journal of Child Psychology and Psychiatry, 48*(2), 157–166. doi:10.1111/j.1469-7610.2006.01687.x

Lin, Y., & Huang, C. (2006). The process of transforming daily social interactions to relationship intimacy: A longitudinal study. *Chinese Journal of Psychology, 48*(1), 35–52.

Lindberg, S. M., Hyde, J., Petersen, J. L., & Linn, M. C. (2010). New trends in gender and mathematics performance: A meta-analysis. *Psychological Bulletin, 136*(6), 1123–1135. doi:10.1037/a0021276

Lindgren, H. C. (1969). *The psychology of college success: A dynamic approach.* New York: Wiley.

Linley, P. A. (2009). Positive psychology (history). In S. J. Lopez (Ed.), *The encyclopedia of positive psychology, Vol. II* (pp. 742–746). Malden, MA: Wiley-Blackwell.

Lippa, R. A. (2005). *Gender, nature, and nurture.* Mahwah, NJ: Erlbaum.

Lippa, R. A. (2007). The preferred traits of mates in a cross-national study of heterosexual and homosexual men and women: An examination of biological and cultural influences. *Archives of Sexual Behavior 36,* 193–208.

Lippa, R. A. (2010). Sex differences in personality traits and gender-related occupational preferences across 53 nations: Testing evolutionary and social-environmental theories. *Archives of Sexual Behavior, 39*(3), 619–636. doi:10.1007/s10508-008-9380-7

Lips, H. M. (2013). The gender pay gap: Challenging the rationalizations. Perceived equity, discrimination, and the limits of human capital models. *Sex Roles, 68*(3–4), 169–185. doi:10.1007/s11199-012-0165-z

Liptak, A. (2015). Supreme court ruling makes same-sex marriage a right nationwide. *New York Times.* Retrieved from www.nytimes.com/2015/06/27/us/supreme-court-same-sex-marriage.html

Little, A. C., DeBruine, L. M., & Jones, B. C. (2014). Sex differences in attraction to familiar and unfamiliar opposite-sex faces: Men prefer novelty and women prefer familiarity. *Archives of Sexual Behavior, 43*(5), 973–981. doi:10.1007/s10508-013-0120-2

Littlefield, M. B. (2003). Gender role identity and stress in African American women. *Journal of Human Behavior in the Social Environment, 8*(4), 93–104.

Liu, H., & Wang H. (2009). Relationship between loneliness, friendship quality and peer acceptance in 209 primary school children. *Chinese Mental Health Journal, 23,* 44–47.

Livingston, G. (2013). The Pew Research Center. At Grandmother's house we stay: One-in-ten children are living with a grandparent. Retrieved from www.pewsocialtrends.org/2013/09/04/at-grandmothers-house-we-stay

Livingston, G. (2014a). Pew Research Center. In terms of childlessness, U.S. ranks near the top worldwide. Retrieved from www.pewresearch.org/fact-tank/2014/01/03/in-terms-of-childlessness-u-s-ranks-near-the-top-worldwide

Livingston, G. (2014b). Pew Research Center. Four-in-ten couples are saying "I do," again. Retrieved from www.pewsocialtrends.org/2014/11/14/four-in-ten-couples-are-saying-i-do-again

Livingston, G. (2014c). Pew Research Center. Fewer than half of U.S. kids today live in a "traditional" family. Retrieved from www.pewresearch.org/fact-tank/2014/12/22/less-than-half-of-u-s-kids-today-live-in-a-traditional-family

Livingston, G. (2015). Pew Research Center. Childlessness. Retrieved from www.pewsocialtrends.org/2015/05/07/childlessness

Llorca, P. (2008). Monitoring patients to improve physical health and treatment outcome. *European Neuropsychopharmacology, 18,* S140–S145.

Lloyd, S. A. (2013). Family violence. In G. W. Peterson, K. R. Bush, G. W. Peterson, K. R. Bush (Eds.), *Handbook of marriage and the family (3rd ed.)* (pp. 449-485). New York: Springer Science + Business Media. doi:10.1007/978-1-4614-3987-5_20

Lock, R. D. (2005a). *Taking charge of your career direction: Career planning guide, Book 1.* Belmont, CA: Wadsworth.

Lock, R. D. (2005b). *Job Search: Career Planning Guide, Book 2.* Belmont, CA: Wadsworth.

Lockwood, P. (2002). Could it happen to you? Predicting the impact of downward social comparisons on the self. *Journal of Personality and Social Psychology, 82,* 343–358.

Loflin, M., & Earleywine, M. (2015). The case for medical marijuana use: An issue of relief. *Drug and Alcohol, 149,* 293–297.

Lofquist, D., Lugaila, T., O'Connell, M., & Feliz, S. (2012). Households and families: 2010. *2010 Census briefs.* Retrieved from www.census.gov/prod/cen2010/briefs/c2010br-14.pdf

Lohmer, M. (2012). Different organizations—different burnouts: Burnout as interplay between personality pattern and organizational structure. In H. Brunning (Ed.), *Psychoanalytic reflections on a changing world* (pp. 51–65). London: Karnac Books.

Lohoff, F. W., & Berrettini, W. H. (2009). Genetics of mood disorders. In D. S. Charney & E. J. Nestler (Eds.), *Neurobiology of mental illness* (pp. 360–377). New York: Oxford University Press.

Longmore, M. A., Manning, W. D., & Giordano, P. C. (2013). Parent-child relationships in adolescence. In M. A. Fine & F. D. Fincham (Eds.), *Handbook of family theories: A content-based approach* (pp. 28–50). New York: Routledge/Taylor & Francis Group.

Lopes, P. N., Brackett, M. A., Nezlek, J. B., Schutz, A., Sellin, I., & Salovey, P. (2004). Emotional intelligence and social interaction. *Personality and Social Psychology Bulletin, 30*(8), 1018–1034.

López, S. R., Barrio, C., Kopelowicz, A., & Vega, W. A. (2012). From documenting to eliminating disparities in mental health care for Latinos. *American Psychologist, 67,* 511–523. doi:10.1037/a0029737

Loth, K., van den Berg, P., Eisenberg, M., & Neumark-Sztainer, D. (2008). Stressful life events and disordered eating behaviors: Findings from Project EAT. *Journal of Adolescent Health, 43,* 514–516.

Loving, T. J., & Sbarra, D. A. (2015). Relationships and health. In M. Mikulincer, P. R. Shaver, J. A. Simpson, & J. F. Dovidio, (Eds.), *APA handbook of personality and social psychology, Vol. 3: Interpersonal relations* (pp. 151–176). Washington, DC: American Psychological Association. doi:10.1037/14344-006

Loving, T. J., & Slatcher, R. B. (2013). Romantic relationships and health. In J. A. Simpson, L. Campbell, J. A. Simpson, L. Campbell (Eds.), *The Oxford handbook of close relationships* (pp. 617–637). New York: Oxford University Press.

Lozano, B. E., Stephens, R. S., & Roffman, R. A. (2006). Abstinence and moderate use goals in the treatment of marijuana dependence. *Addiction, 101,* 1589–1597.

Lu, F. G., Lewis-Fernandez, R., Primm, A. B., Lim, R. F., & Aggarwal, N. K. (2014). Treatment of culturally diverse populations. In R. E. Hales, S. C. Yudofsky, & L. W. Roberts (Eds.), *The American Psychiatric Publishing textbook of psychiatry* (6th ed.). Washington, DC: American Psychiatric Publishing.

Lu, S. (October 2014). How chronic stress is harming our DNA. *APA Monitor, 45*(9), 28.

Luborsky, E. B., O'Reilly-Landry, M., & Arlow, J. A. (2011). Psychoanalysis. In R. J. Corsini & D. Wedding (Eds.), *Current psychotherapies* (9th ed.). Belmont, CA: Brooks/Cole.

Luborsky, L., Singer, B., & Luborsky, L. (1975). Comparative studies of psychotherapies: Is it true that everyone has won and all must have prizes? *Archives of General Psychiatry, 32,* 995–1008.

Lucas, A. R., Beard, C. M., O'Fallon, W. M., & Kurland, L. T. (1991). 50-year trends in the incidence of anorexia nervosa in Rochester, Minn.: A population-based study. *American Journal of Psychiatry, 148,* 917–922.

Lucas, R. E. (2007). Adaptation and the set-point model of subjective well-being: Does happiness change after major life events? *Current Directions in Psychological Science, 16,* 75–79.

Lucas, R. E., & Diener, E. (2015). Personality and subjective well-being: Current issues and controversies. In M. Mikulincer, P. R. Shaver, M. L. Cooper, & R. J. Larsen (Eds.), *APA handbook of personality and social psychology, Vol. 4: Personality processes and individual differences.* Washington, DC: American Psychological Association.

Lucassen, P. J., Pruessner, J., Sousa, N., Almeida, O. X., Van Dam, A. M., Rajkowska, G., . . . Czéh, B. (2014). Neuropathology of stress. *Acta Neuropathologica, 127*(1), 109–135. doi:10.1007/s00401-013-1223-5

Lucas-Thompson, R. G., Goldberg, W. A., & Prause, J. (2010). Maternal work early in the lives of children and its distal associations with achievement and behavior problems: A meta-analysis. *Psychological Bulletin, 136*(6), 915–942. doi:10.1037/a0020875

Lueders, A., Hall, J. A., Pennington, N. R., & Knutson, K. (2014). Nonverbal decoding on Facebook: Applying the IPT-15 and the SSI to personality judgments. *Journal of Nonverbal Behavior, 38*(4), 413–427. doi:10.1007/s10919-014-0195-z

Lulofs, R. S. (1994). *Conflict: From theory to action.* Scottsdale, AZ: Gorsuch Scarisbuck Publishers.

Lulofs, R. S., & Cahn, D. D. (2000). *Conflict: From theory to action* (2nd ed.). Boston: Allyn & Bacon.

Lundberg-Love, P. K., & Wilkerson, D. K. (2006). Battered women. In P. K. Lundberg-Love & S. L. Marmion (Eds.), *"Intimate" violence against women: When spouses, partners, or lovers attack.* Westport, CT: Praeger.

Luthans, F., & Youssef, C. M. (2009). Positive workplaces. In S. J. Lopez & C. R. Snyder (Eds.), *Oxford handbook of positive psychology* (2nd ed., pp. 579–588). New York: Oxford University Press.

Lutz, C. J., & Ross, S. R. (2003). Elaboration versus fragmentation: Distinguishing between self-complexity and self-concept differentiation. *Journal of Social and Clinical Psychology, 22*(5), 537–559.

Lydon, J. E., & Quinn, S. K. (2013). Relationship maintenance processes. In J. A. Simpson & L. Campbell (Eds.), *The Oxford handbook of close relationships* (pp. 573–588). New York: Oxford University Press.

Lyness, K. S., & Heilman, M. E. (2006). When fit is fundamental: Performance evaluations and promotions of upper-level female and male managers. *Journal of Applied Psychology, 91,* 777–785.

Lynn, S. J., Lilienfeld, S. O., Merckelbach, H., Giesbrecht, T., & van der Kloet, D. (2012). Dissociation and dissociative disorders: Challenging conventional wisdom. *Current Directions in Psychological Science, 21*(1), 48–53. doi:10.1177/0963721411429457

Lyons, H., Giordano, P. C., Manning, W. D., & Longmore, M. A. (2011). Identity, peer relationships, and adolescent girls' sexual behavior: An exploration of the contemporary double standard. *Journal of Sex Research, 48*(5), 437–449. doi:10.1080/00224499.2010.506679

Lytton, H., & Romney, D. M. (1991). Parents' differential socialization of boys and girls: A meta-analysis. *Psychological Bulletin, 109,* 267–296.

Lyubomirsky, S. (2013). *The myths of happiness: What should make you happy, but doesn't, what shouldn't make you happy, but does.* New York: Penguin Press.

Lyubomirsky, S., King, L., & Diener, E. (2005). The benefits of frequent positive affect: Does happiness lead to success? *Psychological Bulletin, 131,* 803–855.

Lyubomirsky, S., Layous, K., Chancellor, J., & Nelson, S. K. (2015). Thinking about rumination: The scholarly contributions and intellectual legacy of Susan Nolen-Hoeksema. *Annual Review of Clinical Psychology, 11,* 1–22. doi:10.1146/annurev-clinpsy-032814-112733

Lyubomirsky, S., Sheldon, K. M., & Schkade, D. (2005). Pursuing happiness: The architecture of sustainable change. *Review of General Psychology, 9*(2), 111–131.

Maass, A., Cadinu, M., & Galdi, S. (2013). Sexual harassment: Motivations and consequences. In M. K. Ryan & N. R. Branscombe (Eds.) *The Sage handbook of gender and psychology* (pp. 341–358). London: Sage.

Maccoby, E. E. (1998). *The two sexes: Growing up apart, coming together.* Cambridge, MA: Belknap Press.

Maccoby, E. E. (2002). Gender and group processes: A developmental perspective. *Current Direction in Psychological Science, 11*(2), 54–58.

MacGregor, J. D., & Holmes, J. G. (2011). Rain on my parade: Perceiving low self-esteem in close others hinders positive self-disclosure. *Social Psychological and Personality Science, 2*(5), 523–530. doi:10.1177/1948550611400098

Mack, A. H., Franklin Jr., J. E., & Frances, R. J. (2003). Substance use disorders. In R. E. Hales & S. C. Yudofsky (Eds.), *Textbook of clinical psychiatry.* Washington, DC: American Psychiatric Publishing.

Mackenzie, R. A. (1997). *The time trap.* New York: AMACOM.

Mackie, D. M., Worth, L. T., & Asuncion, A. G. (1990). Processing of persuasive in-group messages. *Journal of Personality and Social Psychology, 58,* 812–822.

MacLeod, A. K. (2013). Suicide and attempted suicide. In M. Power (Ed.), *The Wiley-Blackwell handbook of mood disorders* (2nd ed.). Malden, MA: Wiley-Blackwell.

Macritchie, K., & Blackwood, D. (2013). Neurobiological theories of bipolar disorder. In M. Power (Ed.), *The Wiley-Blackwell handbook of mood disorders* (2nd ed.). Malden, MA: Wiley-Blackwell.

Madathil, J., & Benshoff, J. M. (2008). Importance of marital characteristics and marital satisfaction: A comparison of Asian Indians in arranged marriages and Americans in marriages of choice. *The Family Journal, 16,* 222–230.

Madden, M., & Lenhart, A. (2006). Online dating. Retrieved from www.pewinternet.org/pdfs/PIP_Online_Dating.pdf

Maddi, S. R. (2007). The story of hardiness: Twenty years of theorizing, research, and practice. In A. Monat, R. S. Lazarus, & G. Reevy (Eds.), *The Praeger handbook on stress and coping* (pp. 327–340). Westport, CT: Praeger.

Maddi, S. R. (2013). *Hardiness: Turning stressful circumstances into resilient growth.* New York: Springer Science + Business Media.

Maddux, J. E. (2009). Stopping the "madness": Positive psychology and deconstructing the illness ideology and the DSM. In S. J. Lopez & C. R. Snyder (Eds.), *Oxford handbook of positive psychology* (2nd ed., pp. 61–69). New York: Oxford University Press.

Maddux, J. E., & Gosselin, J. T. (2003). Self-efficacy. In M. R. Leary & J. P. Tangney (Eds.), *Handbook of self and identity.* New York: Guilford.

Madey, S. F., & Jilek, L. (2012). Attachment style and dissolution of romantic relationships: Breaking up is hard to do, or is it? *Individual Differences Research, 10*(4), 202–210.

Madey, S. F., & Rodgers L. (2009). The effect of attachment and Sternberg's triangular theory of love on relationship satisfaction. *Individual Differences Research, 7,* 76–84.

Madon, S., Willard, J., Guyll, M., & Scherr, K. C. (2011). Self-fulfilling prophecies: Mechanisms, power, and links to social problems. *Social and Personality Psychology Compass, 5*(8), 578–590. doi:10.1111/j.1751-9004.2011.00375.x

Madsen, O. J. (2015). *Optimizing the self: Social representations of self-help.* New York: Routledge/Taylor & Francis Group.

Magnavita, J. J. (2008). Psychoanalytic psychotherapy. In J. L. Lebow (Ed.), *Twenty-first century psychotherapies: Contemporary approaches to theory and practice.* New York: Wiley.

Magnavita, N., Elovaino, M., Heponiemi, T., Magnavita, A. M., & Bergamaschi, A. (2011). Are skin disorders related to work strain in hospital workers? A cross-sectional study. *BMC Public Health, 11,* 600. Retrieved from www.biomedcentral.com/1471-2458/11/600

Mahar, I., Bambico, F. R., Mechawar, N., & Nobrega, J. N. (2014). Stress, serotonin, and hippocampal neurogenesis in relation to depression and antidepressant effects. *Neuroscience and Biobehavioral Reviews, 38,* 173–192. doi:10.1016/j.neubiorev.2013.11.009

Maher, B. A. (2001). Delusions. In P. B. Sutker & H. E. Adams (Eds.), *Comprehensive handbook of psychopathology* (3rd ed.). New York: Kluwer Academic/Plenum.

Mahoney, M. J. (1979). *Self-change: Strategies for solving personal problems.* New York: Norton.

Maisel, N. C., Gable, S. L., & Strachman, A. (2008). Responsive behaviors in good times and in bad. *Personal Relationships, 15,* 317–338.

Major, B., Barr, L., Zubeck, J., & Babey, S. H. (1999). Gender and self-esteem: A meta-analysis. In W. B. Swann, Jr., J. H. Langlois, & L. A. Gilbert (Eds.), *Sexism and stereotypes in modern society: The gender science of Janet Taylor Spence.* Washington, DC: American Psychological Association.

Major, B., Schmidlin, A. M., & Williams, L. (1990). Gender patterns in social touch: The impact of setting and age. *Journal of Personality and Social Psychology, 58,* 634–643.

Major, D. A., & Morganson, V. J. (2011). Applying industrial-organizational psychology to help organizations and individuals balance work and family. *Industrial and Organizational Psychology: Perspectives on Science and Practice, 4*(3), 398–401. doi:10.1111/j.1754-9434.2011.01360.x

Maldonado, J. R., & Spiegel, D. (2014). Dissociative disorders. In R. E. Hales, S. C. Yudofsky, & L. W. Roberts (Eds.), *The American Psychiatric Publishing textbook of psychiatry* (6th ed.). Washington, DC: American Psychiatric Publishing.

Malle, B. F. (2004). *How the mind explains behavior: Folk explanations, meaning, and social interaction.* Cambridge, MA: MIT Press.

Malle, B. F. (2011a). Attribution theories: How people make sense of behavior. In D. Chadee (Ed.), *Theories in social psychology* (pp. 72–95). Wiley-Blackwell.

Malle, B. F. (2011b). Time to give up the dogmas of attribution: An alternative theory of behavior explanation. *Advances in experimental social psychology, 44,* 297–352.

Mandal, M. K., & Awasthi, A. (2015). *Understanding facial expressions in communication: Cross-cultural and multidisciplinary perspectives.* New York: Springer Science + Business Media. doi:10.1007/978-81-322-1934-7

Mandel, H., & Young, J. (2009). *Here's the deal: Don't touch me.* New York: Bantam.

Mann, S., Ewens, S., Shaw, D., Vrij, A., Leal, S., & Hillman, J. (2013). Lying eyes: Why liars seek deliberate eye contact. *Psychiatry, Psychology and Law, 20*(3), 452–461. doi:10.1080/13218719.2013.791218

Manning, J. (2015). Positive and negative communicative behaviors in coming-out conversations. *Journal of Homosexuality, 62*(1), 67–97. doi:10.1080/00918369.2014.957127

Manning, W. D., & Cohen, J. A. (2012). Premarital cohabitation and marital dissolution: An examination of recent marriages. *Journal of Marriage and Family, 74*(2), 377–387. doi:10.1111/j.1741-3737.2012.00960.x

Manning, W. D., Brown, S. L., & Payne, K. K. (2014). Two decades of stability and change in age at first union formation. *Journal of Marriage and Family, 76,* 247–260. doi: 10.1111/jomf.12090

Manson, J. E., Skerrett, P. J., Greenland, P., & VanItallie, T. B. (2004). The escalating pandemics of obesity and sedentary lifestyles: A call to action for clinicians. *Archives of Internal Medicine, 164,* 249–258.

Mantell, J. E., Stein, Z. A., & Susser, I. (2008). Women in the time of AIDS: Barriers, bargains, and benefits. *AIDS Education and Prevention, 20,* 91–106.

Marchand, W. R. (2012). Mindfulness-based stress reduction, mindfulness-based cognitive therapy, and Zen mediation for depression, anxiety, pain, and psychological distress. *Journal of Psychiatric Practice, 18*(4), 233–252. doi:10.1097/01.pra.0000416014.53215.86

Marder, S. R., Hurford, I. M., & van Kammen, D. P. (2009). Second-generation antipsychotics. In B. J. Sadock, V. A. Sadock, & P. Ruiz (Eds.), *Kaplan & Sadock's comprehensive textbook of psychiatry* (pp. 3206–3240). Philadelphia: Lippincott Williams & Wilkins.

Maricchiolo, F., Gnisci, A., Bonaiuto, M., & Ficca, G. (2009). Effects of different types of hand gestures in persuasive speech on receivers' evaluations. *Language and Cognitive Processes, 24*(2), 239–266.

Mark, K. P., Janssen, E., & Milhausen, R. R. (2011). Infidelity in heterosexual couples: Demographic, interpersonal, and personality-related predictors of extradyadic sex. *Archives of Sexual Behavior, 40*(5), 971–982. doi:10.1007/s10508-011-9771-z

Markman, A. B., Maddox, W., & Worthy, D. A. (2006). Choking and excelling under pressure. *Psychological Science, 17*(11), 944–948. doi:10.1111/j.1467-9280.2006.01809.x

Markus, H., & Cross, S. (1990). The interpersonal self. In L. A. Pervin (Ed.), *Handbook of personality: Theory and research* (pp. 576–608). New York: Guilford.

Markus, H., & Kitayama, S. (2004). Models of agency: Sociocultural diversity in the construction of action. In V. Murphy-Berman & J. Berman (Eds.), *Nebraska Symposium on Motivation: Cross-cultural differences in perspectives on the self.* Lincoln: University of Nebraska Press.

Marsh, J. M., & Butler, A. C. (2013). Memory in educational settings, In D. Reisberg (Ed.), *Oxford handbook of cognitive psychology.* New York: Oxford University Press.

Marshall, T. C., Lefringhausen, K., & Ferenczi, N. (2015). The Big Five, self-esteem, and narcissism as predictors of the topics people write about in Facebook status updates. *Personality and Individual Differences, 85,* 35–40. doi:10.1016/j.paid.2015.04.039

Martin, A. J., Marsh, H. W., Williamson, A., & Debus, R. L. (2003). Self-handicapping, defensive pessimism, and goal orientation: A qualitative study of university students. *Journal of Educational Psychology, 95,* 617–628.

Martin, B. S. (2012). A stranger's touch: Effects of accidental interpersonal touch on consumer evaluations and shopping time. *Journal of Consumer Research, 39*(1), 174–184. doi:10.1086/662038

Martin, C. L., Ruble, D., & Szkrybalo, J. (2002). Cognitive theories of early gender development. *Psychological Bulletin, 128*(6), 903–933.

Martin, L. R., Haskard-Zolnierek, K. B., & DiMatteo, M. R. (2010). *Health behavior change and treatment adherence: Evidence-based guidelines for improving health care.* New York: Oxford University Press.

Martin, R. A., & Lefcourt, H. M. (1983). Sense of humor as a moderator of the relation between stressors and moods. *Journal of Personality and Social Psychology, 45,* 1313–1324.

Martinez, E. (2009, October 27). James Ray gives "laughable" 50 percent refund to Sweat Lodge victim's family. *CBS News,* Retrieved from www.cbsnews.com/blogs/2009/08/28/crimesider/entry5271390.shtml

Martinez, G., Abma, J., & Casey, C. (2010). Educating teenagers about sex in the United States. *NCHS Data Brief,* No. 44.

Martinez, M., Marangell, L. B., & Martinez, J. M. (2008). Psychopharmacology. In R. E. Hales, S. C. Yudofsky, & G. O. Gabbard (Eds.), *The American Psychiatric Publishing textbook of psychiatry* (pp. 1053–1132). Washington, DC: American Psychiatric Publishing.

Martins, A., Ramalho, N., & Morin, E. (2010). A comprehensive meta-analysis of the relationship between emotional intelligence and health. *Personality and Individual Differences, 49*(6), 554–564. doi:10.1016/j.paid.2010.05.029

Martins, C. S., de Carvalho Tofoli, S. M., Von Werne Baes, C., & Juruena, M. (2011). Analysis of the occurrence of early life stress in adult psychiatric patients: A systematic review. *Psychology & Neuroscience, 4*(2), 219–227. doi:10.3922/j.psns.2011.2.007

Martin-Uzzi, M., & Duval-Tsioles, D. (2013). The experience of remarried couples in blended families. *Journal of Divorce and Remarriage, 54*(1), 43–57. doi:10.1080/10502556.2012.743828

Maslach, C. (2003). Job burnout: New directions in research and intervention. *Current Directions in Psychological Science, 12*(5), 189–192.

Maslach, C. (2005). Understanding burnout: Work and family issues. In D. F. Halpern & S. E. Murphy (Eds.), *From work-family balance to work-family interaction: Changing the metaphor.* Mahwah, NJ: Erlbaum.

Maslach, C., & Leiter, M. P. (2007). *Burnout.* In G. Fink (Ed.), *Encyclopedia of stress: Vols. 1–4* (2nd ed., pp. 368–371). San Diego, CA: Elsevier Academic Press.

Maslach, C., & Leiter, M. P. (2014). Burnout in the workplace: A global problem in need of solution. In S. Cooper, K. Ratele, S. Cooper, & K. Ratele (Eds.), *Psychology serving humanity: Proceedings of the 30th International Congress of Psychology, Vol. 2: Western psychology* (pp. 116–126). New York: Psychology Press.

Maslow, A. H. (1968). *Toward a psychology of being.* New York: Van Nostrand.

Maslow, A. H. (1970). *Motivation and personality.* New York: Harper & Row.

Masten, A. S., & Reed, M. J. (2002). Resilience in development. In C. R. Snyder & S. J. Lopez (Eds.), *Handbook of positive psychology* (pp. 74–88). New York: Oxford University Press.

Masters, W. H., & Johnson, V. E. (1966). *Human sexual response.* Boston: Little, Brown.

Masters, W. H., & Johnson, V. E. (1970). *Human sexual inadequacy.* Boston: Little, Brown.

Masuda, T., & Nisbett, R. E. (2006). Culture and change blindness. *Cognitive Science, 30,* 381–399.

Matheson, K., & Foster, M. D. (2013). Coping with the stress of gender discrimination. In M. K. Ryan & N. R. Branscombe (Eds.) *The Sage Handbook of Gender and Psychology* (pp. 323–340). London: Sage.

Mathew, S. J., Hoffman, E. J., & Charney, D. S. (2009). Pharmacotherapy of anxiety disorders. In D. S. Charney & E. J. Nestler (Eds.), *Neurobiology of mental illness* (p. 731). New York: Guilford.

Matlin, M. W. (2004). *The psychology of women* (5th ed.). Belmont, CA: Wadsworth.

Matsumoto, D., & Hwang, H. C. (2013a). Culture and nonverbal communication. In J. A. Hall & M. L. Knapp (Eds.), *Nonverbal communication* (pp. 697–727). Boston, MA: De Gruyter Mouton. doi:10.1515/9783110238150.697

Matsumoto, D., & Hwang, H. S. (2013b). Cultural influences on nonverbal behavior. In D. Matsumoto, M. G. Frank, & H. S. Hwang (Eds.), *Nonverbal communication: Science and applications* (pp. 97–120). Thousand Oaks, CA: Sage.

Matthews, G., Emo, A. K., Funke, G., Zeidner, M., Roberts, R. D., Costa Jr., P. T., & Schulze, R. (2006). Emotional intelligence, personality, and task-induced stress. *Journal of Experimental Psychology: Applied, 12,* 96–107.

Matthews, K. A., & Gallo, L. C. (2011). Psychological perspectives on pathways linking socioeconomic status and physical health. *Annual Review of Psychology, 62,* 501–530.

Mayer, J. D., Perkins, D. M., Caruso, D. R., & Salovey, P. (2001). Emotional intelligence and giftedness. *Roeper Review, 23,* 131–137.

Mayer, J. D., Salovey, P., & Caruso, D. R. (2002). *Mayer-Salovey-Caruso Emotional Intelligence Test (MSCEIT): User's manual.* Toronto, Canada: Multi-Health Systems.

Mayer, J. D., Salovey, P., & Caruso, D. R. (2008). Emotional Intelligence: New ability or eclectic traits, *American Psychologist, 63,* 503–517.

Mayer, J. D., Salovey, P., & Caruso, D. R. (2012). The validity of the MSCEIT: Additional analyses and evidence. *Emotion Review, 4*(4), 403–408. doi:10.1177/1754073912445815

Mayeux, L. (2014). Understanding popularity and relational aggression in adolescence: The role of social dominance orientation. *Social Development, 23*(3), 502–517. doi:10.1111/sode.12054

Mayo Clinic. (2009). Premature ejaculation. Retrieved from www.mayoclinic.com/health/premature-ejaculation/DS00578

Mayordomo-Rodríguez, T., Meléndez-Moral, J. C., Viguer-Segui, P., & Sales-Galán, A. (2015). Coping strategies as predictors of well-being in youth adult. *Social Indicators Research, 122*(2), 479–489. doi:10.1007/s11205-014-0689-4

McAbee, S. T., & Oswald, F. L. (2013). The criterion-related validity of personality measures for predicting GPA: A meta-analytic validity competition. *Psychological Assessment, 25,* 532–544. doi:10.1037/a0031748

McCabe, J., Fairchild, E., Grauerholz, L., Pescosolido, B. A., & Tope, D. (2011). Gender in twentieth-century children's books: Patterns of disparity in titles and central characters. *Gender & Society, 25*(2), 197–226. doi:10.1177/0891243211398358

McCabe, R. E., & Antony, M. M. (2008). Anxiety disorders: Social and specific phobias. In A. Tasman, J. Kay, J. A. Lieberman, M. B. First, & M. Maj (Eds.), *Psychiatry* (3rd ed.). New York: Wiley-Blackwell.

McCall, W. V., Reboussin, D., Prudic, J., Haskett, R. F., Isenberg, K., Olfson, M., . . . Sackeim, H. A. (2013). Poor health-related quality of life prior to ECT in depressed patients normalizes with sustained remission after ECT. *Journal of Affective Disorders, 147*(1–3), 107–111. doi:10.1016/j.jad.2012.10.018

McCann, U. D. (2011). PCP/designer drugs/MDMA. In P. Ruiz & E. C. Strain (Eds.), *Lowinson and Ruiz's substance abuse: A comprehensive textbook* (5th ed.; pp. 277–283). Philadelphia: Lippincott Williams & Wilkins.

McCormack, S. A., & Levine, T. R. (1990). When lovers become leery: The relationship between suspiciousness and accuracy in detecting deception. *Communication Monographs, 57,* 219–230.

McCrae, R. R., Chan, W., Jussim, L., De Fruyt, F., Löckenhoff, C. E., De Bolle, M., . . . Terracciano, A. (2013). The inaccuracy of national character stereotypes. *Journal of Research in Personality– 47,* 831–842. doi:10.1016/j.jrp.2013.08.006

McCrae, R. R., & Costa, Jr., P. T. (1987). Validation of the five-factor model of personality across instruments and observers. *Journal of Personality and Social Psychology, 52,* 81–90.

McCrae, R. R., & Costa, Jr., P. T. (1997). Personality trait structure as a human universal. *American Psychologist, 52,* 509–516.

McCrae, R. R., & Costa, Jr., P. T. (2003). *Personality in adulthood: A five-factor theory perspective.* New York: Guilford.

McCrae, R. R., Gaines, J. F., & Wellington, M. A. (2013).The five-factor model in fact and fiction. In H. Tennen, J. Suls, & I. B. Weiner (Eds.), *Handbook of psychology, Vol. 5: Personality and social psychology* (2nd ed.). New York: Wiley.

McCrae, R. R., & Sutin, A. R. (2009). Openness to experience. In M. R. Leary & R. H. Hoyle (Eds.), *Handbook of individual differences in social behavior* (pp. 257–274). New York: Guilford.

McCrae, R. R., & Terracciano, A. (2006). National character and personality. *Current Direction in Psychological Science, 15*(4), 156–161.

McCrae, R. R., Terracciano, A., & 78 Members of the Personality Profiles of Cultures Project. (2005). Universal features of personality traits from the observer's perspective: Data from 50 cultures. *Journal of Personality and Social Psychology, 88*, 547–561.

McCullough, M. E. (2001). Forgiving. In C. R. Snyder (Ed.), *Coping with stress: Effective people and processes*. New York: Oxford University Press.

McCullough, M. E., & Witvliet, C. V. (2005). The psychology of forgiveness. In C. R. Snyder & S. J. Lopez (Eds.), *Handbook of positive psychology*. New York: Oxford University Press.

McDermott, K. B., Agarwal, P. K., D'Antonio, L., Roediger, H. I., & McDaniel, M. A. (2014). Both multiple-choice and short-answer quizzes enhance later exam performance in middle and high school classes. *Journal of Experimental Psychology: Applied, 20*(1), 3–21. doi:10.1037/xap0000004

McDonald, M. M., Donnellan, M. B., Lang, R., & Nikolajuk, K. (2014). Treating prejudice with imagery: Easier said than done? *Psychological Science, 25*(3), 837–839. doi:10.1177/0956797613516010

McDonald, P. G., O'Connell, M., & Suls, J. (2015). Cancer control falls squarely within the province of the psychological sciences. *American Psychologist, 70*(2), 61–74.

McDougle, L. G. (1987). Time management: Making every minute count. In A. D. Timpe (Ed.), *The management of time*. New York: Facts on File.

McElwee, R. O., & Haugh, J. A. (2010). Thinking clearly versus frequently about the future self: Exploring this distinction and its relation to possible selves. *Self and Identity, 9*(3), 298–321. doi:10.1080/15298860903054290

McEvoy, J. P., Byerly, M., Hamer, R. M., Dominik, R., Swartz, M. S., Rosenheck, R. A., . . . Stroup, T. S. (2014). Effectiveness of paliperidone palmitate vs haloperidol decanoate for maintenance treatment of schizophrenia: A randomized clinical trial. *Journal of the American Medical Association, 311*, 1978–1986. doi:10.1001/jama.2014.4310

McGee, M. (2005). *Self-help, Inc.: Makeover culture in American life*. New York: Oxford University Press.

McGoldrick, M., & Carter, B. (2003). The family life cycle. In F. Walsh (Ed.), *Normal family processes: Growing diversity and complexity* (3rd ed.) (pp. 375–398). New York: Guilford.

McGoldrick, M., & Shibusawa, T. (2012). The family life cycle. In F. Walsh, F. Walsh (Eds.), *Normal family processes: Growing diversity and complexity* (4th ed.; pp. 375–398). New York: Guilford.

McGrath, J. J., & Murray, R. M. (2011). Environmental risk factors for schizophrenia. In D. R. Weinberger & P. Harrison (Eds.), *Schizophrenia* (3rd ed.). Malden, MA: Wiley-Blackwell.

McGraw, A. P., Warren, C., Williams, L. E., & Leonard, B. (2012). Too close for comfort, or too far to care? Finding humor in distant tragedies and close mishaps. *Psychological Science, 23*(10), 1215-1223. doi:10.1177/0956797612443831

McGraw, A. P., Williams, L. E., & Warren, C. (2014). The rise and fall of humor: Psychological distance modulates humorous responses to tragedy. *Social Psychological and Personality Science, 5*(5), 566–572. doi:10.1177/1948550613515006

McGuire, W. J., & Padawer-Singer, A. (1978). Trait salience in the spontaneous self-concept. *Journal of Personality and Social Psychology, 33*, 743–754.

McHugh, J. E., McDonnell, R., O'Sullivan, C., & Newell, F. N. (2010). Perceiving emotion in crowds: The role of dynamic body postures on the perception of emotion in crowded scenes. *Experimental Brain Research, 204*(3), 361–372. doi:10.1007/s00221-009-2037-5

McHugh, M. C., & Hambaugh, J. (2010.) She said, he said: Gender, language and power. In J. C. Chrisler & D. R. McCreary (Eds.), *Handbook of gender research in psychology, Vol. 2* (pp. 379–410). New York: Springer.

McInnis, M. G., Ribia, M., & Greden, J. F. (2014). Anxiety disorders. In R. E. Hales, S. C. Yudofsky, & L. W. Roberts (Eds.), *The American Psychiatric Publishing textbook of psychiatry* (6th ed.). Washington, DC: American Psychiatric Publishing.

McKay, M., Davis, M., & Fanning, P. (1995). *Messages: The communications skills book*. Oakland, CA: New Harbinger.

McKay, M., Davis, M., & Fanning, P. (2009). *Messages: The communications skills book* (3rd ed.). Oakland, CA: New Harbinger.

McKay, M., & Fanning, P. (2000). *Self-esteem* (3rd ed.). Oakland, CA: New Harbinger.

McKeever, V. M., & Huff, M. E. (2003). A diathesis-stress model of posttraumatic stress disorder: Ecological, biological and residual stress pathways. *Review of General Psychology, 7*(3), 237–250.

McKenna, K. Y. A. (2009). Internet, attraction on. In H. T. Reis & S. Sprecher (Eds.), *Encyclopedia of human relationships, Vol. 2* (pp. 881–884). Los Angeles: Sage Reference.

McKenna, K. Y. A., Green, A., & Gleason, M. (2002). Relationship formation on the internet: What's the big attraction? *Journal of Social Issues, 58*, 9–31.

McKenna, M. C., Zevon, M. A., Corn, B., & Rounds, J. (1999). Psychosocial factors and the development of breast cancer: A meta-analysis. *Health Psychology, 18*(5), 520–531.

McManus, P. A., & DiPrete, T. (2001). Losers and winners: Financial consequences of separation and divorce for men. *American Sociological Review, 66*, 246–268.

McNally, R. J. (2007). Betrayal trauma theory: A critical appraisal. *Memory, 15*, 280–294.

McNulty, J. K., & Widman, L. (2014). Sexual narcissism and infidelity in early marriage. *Archives of Sexual Behavior, 43*(7), 1315–1325. doi:10.1007/s10508-014-0282-6

McQuillan, J., & Conde, G. (1996). The conditions of flow in reading: Two studies of optimal experience. *Reading Psychology: An International Quarterly, 17*, 109–135.

McQuillan, J., Greil, A. L., Shreffler, K. M., Wonch-Hill, P. A., Gentzler, K. C., & Hathcoat, J. D. (2012). Does the reason matter? Variations in childlessness concerns among U.S. women. *Journal of Marriage and Family, 74*(5), 1166–1181.

McWhirter, B. T. (1990). Loneliness: A review of current literature, with implications for counseling and research. *Journal of Counseling and Development, 68*, 417–422.

McWhorter, K. T. (2013). *College reading and study skills* (12th ed.). New York: Pearson.

McWilliams, S., & Barrett, A. E. (2014). Online dating in middle and later life: Gendered expectations and experiences. *Journal of Family Issues, 35*(3), 411–436. doi:10.1177/0192513X12468437

Medlock, G. (2012). The evolving ethic of authenticity: From humanistic to positive psychology. *The Humanistic Psychologist, 40*(1), 38–57. doi:10.1080/08873267.2012.643687

Meece, J. L., & Scantlebury, K. (2006). Gender and schooling: Progress and persistent barriers. In J. Worrell & C. D. Goodheart (Eds.), *Handbook of girls' and women's psychological health*. New York: Oxford University Press.

Mehta, N., & Atreja, A. (2015). Online social support networks. *International Review of Psychiatry, 27*(2), 118–123. doi:10.3109/09540261.2015.1015504

Miech, R. A., Johnston, L., O'Malley, P. M., Bachman, J. G., Schulenberg, J., & Patrick, M. E. (2015). Trends in use of marijuana and attitudes toward marijuana among youth before and after decriminalization: The case of California 2007–2013. *International Journal of Drug Policy, 26*(4), 336–344.

Meijer, A. M., & van den Wittenboer, G. L. H. (2007). Contribution of infants' sleep and crying to marital relationship of first-time parent couples in the 1st year after childbirth. *Journal of Family Psychology, 21*, 49–57.

Meijer, E. H., & Verschuere, B. (2015). The polygraph: Current practice and new approaches. In P. A. Granhag, A. Vrij, & B. Verschuere (Eds.), *Detecting deception: Current challenges and cognitive approaches* (pp. 59–80). Wiley-Blackwell.

Meisler, G. (2014). Exploring emotional intelligence, political skill, and job satisfaction. *Employee Relations, 36*(3), 280–293. doi:10.1108/ER-02-2013-0021

Meissner, C. A., & Brigham, J. C. (2001). Thirty years of investigating the own-race bias in memory for faces: A meta-analytic review. *Psychology, Public Policy, and Law, 7*, 3–35.

Melanson, K. J. (2007). Dietary factors in reducing risk of cardiovascular diseases. *American Journal of Lifestyle Medicine, 1*(1), 24–28.

Mellers, B. A., Richards, V., & Birnbaum, M. H. (1992). Distributional theories of impression formation. *Organizational Behavior and Human Decision Processes, 51*, 313–343.

Menkin, J. A., Robles, T. F., Wiley, J. F., & Gonzaga, G. C. (2015). Online dating across the life span: Users' relationship goals. *Psychology and Aging, 30*(4), 987–993. doi:10.1037/a0039722

Merali, N. (2012). Arranged and forced marriage. In M. A. Paludi (Ed.), *The psychology of love* (pp. 143–168). Santa Barbara, CA: Praeger/ABC-CLIO.

Merton, R. (1948). The self-fulfilling prophecy. *Antioch Review, 8*, 193–210.

Mesch, G. S., & Talmud, I. (2007). Similarity and the quality of online and offline social relationships among adolescents in Israel. *Journal of Research on Adolescence, 17*, 455–466.

Messineo, M. J. (2008). Does advertising on Black Entertainment Television portray more positive gender representation compared to broadcast networks? *Sex Roles, 59*, 752–764.

Metzger, J. A. (2014). Adaptive defense mechanisms: Function and transcendence. *Journal of Clinical Psychology, 70*(5), 478–488. doi:10.1002/jclp.22091

Meyer, D. D., Jones, M., Rorer, A., & Maxwell, K. (2015). Examining the associations among attachment, affective state, and romantic relationship quality. *The Family Journal, 23*(1), 18–25. doi:10.1177/1066480714547698

Meyer, G. J., Hsiao, W., Viglione, D. J., Mihura, J. L., & Abraham, L. M. (2013). Rorschach scores in applied clinical practice: A survey of perceived validity by experienced clinicians. *Journal of Personality Assessment, 95*, 351–365. doi:10.1080/00223891.2013.770399

Meyer, G. J., & Viglione, D. J. (2008). An introduction to Rorschach assessment. In R. P. Archer & S. R. Smith (Eds.), *Personality assessment*. New York: Routledge/Taylor & Francis Group.

Meyer, O., Zane, N., & Cho, Y. I. (2011). Understanding the psychological processes of the racial match effect in Asian Americans. *Journal of Counseling Psychology, 58*(3), 335–345. doi:10.1037/a0023605

Meyer-Griffith, K., Reardon, R. C., & Hartley, S. (2009). An examination of the relationship between career thoughts and communication apprehension. *The Career Development Quarterly, 58*(2), 171–180.

Mickelson, K. D., Kessler, R. C., & Shaver, P. R. (1997). Adult attachment in a nationally representative sample. *Journal of Personality and Social Psychology, 73*, 1092–1106.

Mihura, J. L., Meyer, G. J., Bombel, G., & Dumitrascu, N. (2015). Standards, accuracy, and questions of bias in Rorschach meta-analyses: Reply to Wood, Garb, Nezworski, Lilienfeld, & Duke (2015). *Psychological Bulletin, 141*(1), 250–260. doi:10.1037/a0038445

Mihura, J. L., Meyer, G. J., Dumitrascu, N., & Bombel, G. (2013). The validity of individual Rorschach variables: Systematic reviews and meta-analyses of the comprehensive system. *Psychological Bulletin, 139*(3), 548–605. doi:10.1037/a0029406

Miklowitz, D. J. (2014). Pharmacotherapy and psychosocial treatments. In I. H. Gotlib & C. L. Hammen, (Eds.), *Handbook of depression* (3rd ed.). New York: Guilford.

Mik-Meyer, N., & Obling, A. R. (2012). The negotiation of the sick role: General practitioners' classification of patients with medically unexplained symptoms. *Sociology of Health & Illness, 34*(7), 1025–1038. doi:10.1111/j.1467-9566.2011.01448.x

Mikulincer, M., & Shaver, P. R. (2011). An attachment perspective on interpersonal and intergroup conflict. In J. P. Forgas, A. W. Kruglanski, & K. D. Williams (Eds.), *The psychology of social conflict and aggression* (pp. 19–35). New York: Psychology Press.

Milgram, N., Marshevsky, S., & Sadeh, C. (1995). Correlates of academic procrastination: Discomfort, task aversiveness, and task capability. *Journal of Psychology, 129*, 145–155.

Milgram, S. (1963). Behavioral study of obedience. *Journal of Abnormal and Social Psychology, 67*, 371–378.

Miller Burke, J., & Attridge, M. (2011). Pathways to career and leadership success: Part 1: A psychosocial profile of $100k professionals. *Journal of Workplace Behavioral Health, 26*, 175–206. doi:10.1080/15555240.2011.589718

Miller, B. J., Culpepper, N., Rapaport, M. H., & Buckley, P. (2013). Prenatal inflammation and neurodevelopment in schizophrenia: A review of human studies. *Progress in Neuro-Psychopharmacology & Biological Psychiatry, 42*, 92–100. doi:10.1016/j.pnpbp.2012.03.010

Miller, C. B. (2009). Yes we did! Basking in reflected glory and cutting off reflected failure in the 2008 presidential election. *Analyses of Social Issues and Public Policy (ASAP), 9*(1), 283–296. doi:10.1111/j.1530-2415.2009.01194.x

Miller, G. P. (1978). *Life choices: How to make the critical decisions—about your education, career, marriage, family, life style.* New York: Thomas Y. Crowell.

Miller, J. D., Gentile, B., Wilson, L., & Campbell, W. K. (2013). Grandiose and vulnerable narcissism and the DSM-5 pathological personality trait model. *Journal of Personality Assessment, 95*(3), 284–290. doi:10.1080/00223891.2012.685907

Miller, K. S., Fasula, A. M., Lin, C. Y., Levin, M. L., Wyckoff, S. C., & Forehand, R. (2012). Ready, set, go: African American preadolescents' sexual thoughts, intentions, and behaviors. *The Journal of Early Adolescence, 32*(2), 293–307. doi:10.1177/0272431610393247

Miller, M., Swanson, S. A., Azrael, D., Pate, V., & Stürmer, T. (2014). Antidepressant dose, age, and the risk of deliberate self-harm. *JAMA Internal Medicine, 174*(6), 899–909.

Miller, N. E. (1944). Experimental studies of conflict. In J. McV. Hunt (Ed.), *Personality and the behavior disorders, Vol. 1.* New York: Ronald.

Miller, N. E. (1959). Liberalization of basic S-R concepts: Extension to conflict behavior, motivation, and social learning. In S. Koch (Ed.), *Psychology: A study of a science, Vol. 2.* New York: McGraw-Hill.

Miller, R. S., Perlman, D., & Brehm, S. S. (2007). *Intimate relationships.* Boston: McGraw-Hill.

Miller, S. L., & Maner, J. K. (2008). Coping with romantic betrayal: Sex differences in responses to partner infidelity. *Evolutionary Psychology, 6,* 413–426.

Millett, K. (1970). *Sexual politics.* Garden City, NY: Doubleday.

Millon, T. (1981). *Disorders of personality: DSM III, axis II.* New York: Wiley.

Mineka, S. (2013). Individual differences in the acquisition of fears. In D. Hermans, B. Rimé, & B. Mesquita (Eds.), *Changing emotions.* New York: Psychology Press.

Mineka, S., & Öhman, A. (2002). Phobias and preparedness: The selective, automatic and encapsulated nature of fear. *Biological Psychiatry, 52,* 927–937.

Mineka, S., & Zinbarg, S. (2006). A contemporary learning theory perspective on the etiology of anxiety disorders: It's not what you thought it was. *American Psychologist, 61,* 10–26.

Minzenberg, M. J., Yoon, J. H., & Carter, C. S. (2008). Schizophrenia. In R. E. Hales, S. C. Yudofsky, & G. O. Gabbard (Eds.), *The American Psychiatric Publishing textbook of psychiatry* (pp. 407–456). Washington, DC: American Psychiatric Publishing.

Miranda, J., Bernal, G., Lau, A., Kohn, L., Hwang, W., & LaFromboise, T. (2005). State of the science on psychosocial interventions for ethnic minorities. *Annual Review of Clinical Psychology, 1,* 113–142.

Mirecki, R. M., Chou, J. L., Elliott, M., & Schneider, C. M. (2013). What factors influence marital satisfaction? Differences between first and second marriages. *Journal of Divorce and Remarriage, 54*(1), 78–93. doi:10.1080/10502556.2012.743831

Mischel, W. (1973). Toward a cognitive social learning conceptualization of personality. *Psychological Review, 80,* 252–283.

Mischel, W., Shoda, Y., & Peake, P. K. (1988). The nature of adolescent competencies predicted by preschool delay of gratification. *Journal of Personality and Social Psychology, 54,* 687–696.

Mitchell, A. E., Castellani, A. M., Herrington, R. L., Joseph, J. I., Doss, B. D., & Snyder, D. K. (2008). Predictors of intimacy in couples' discussions of relationship injuries: An observational study. *Journal of Family Psychology, 22,* 21–29.

Mitchell, J. E., & Wonderlich, S. A. (2014). Feeding and eating disorders. In R. E. Hales, S. C. Yudofsky, & L. W. Roberts (Eds.), *The American Psychiatric Publishing textbook of psychiatry* (6th ed.). Washington, DC: American Psychiatric Publishing.

Mitchell, V. F. (1987). Rx for improving staff effectiveness. In A. D. Timpe (Ed.), *The management of time.* New York: Facts on File.

Miyamoto, Y., & Kitayama, S. (2002). Cultural variation in correspondence bias: The critical role of attitude diagnosticity of socially constrained behavior. *Journal of Personality and Social Psychology, 83*(5), 1239–1248.

Modestin, J. (1992). Multiple personality disorder in Switzerland. *American Journal of Psychiatry, 149,* 88–92.

Mohren, D. C. L., Swaen, G. M. H., Kant, I., van Schayck, C. P., & Galama, J. M. D. (2005). Fatigue and job stress as predictors for sickness absence during common infections. *International Journal of Behavioral Medicine, 12*(1), 11–20.

Mojtabai, R., & Olfson, M. (2010). National trends in psychotropic medication polypharmacy in office-based psychiatry. *Archives of General Psychiatry, 67*(1), 26–36.

Mokdad, A. H., Marks, J. S., Stroup, D. F., & Gerberding, J. L. (2004). Actual causes of death in the United States, 2000. *Journal of the American Medical Association, 291,* 1238–1245.

Moldovan, A. R., & David, D. (2011). Effect of obesity treatments on eating behavior: Psychosocial interventions versus surgical interventions: A systematic review. *Eating Behaviors, 12*(3), 161–167.

Mongrain, M., & Anselmo-Matthews, T. (2012). Do positive psychology exercises work? A replication of Seligman et al. (2005). *Journal of Clinical Psychology, 68*(4), 382–389. doi:10.1002/jclp.21839

Monninkhof, E. M., Elias, S. G., Vlems, F. A., Tweel van der, I., Schuit, A. J., Voskuil, D. W., & Leeuwen, F. E. (2007). Physical activity and breast cancer: A systematic review. *Epidemiology, 18,* 137–157.

Monroe, S. M., Slavich, G. M., & Georgiades, K. (2014). The social environment and depression: The roles of life stress. In I. H. Gotlib & C. L. Hammen (Eds.), *Handbook of depression* (3rd ed.). New York: Guilford.

Montoya, R. M., & Horton, R. S. (2012). The reciprocity of liking effect. In M. A. Paludi (Ed.), *The psychology of love, Vols. 1–4* (pp. 39–57). Santa Barbara, CA: Praeger/ABC-CLIO.

Montoya, R. M., & Horton, R. S. (2014). A two-dimensional model for the study of interpersonal attraction. *Personality and Social Psychology Review, 18*(1), 59–86. doi:10.1177/1088868313501887

Moore, D. S., & Johnson, S. P. (2008). Mental rotation in human infants. *Psychological Science, 19,* 1063–1066.

Moore, D. W. (2001, August 31). Most American workers satisfied with their job: One-third would be happier in another job. The Gallup Organization. Retrieved from www.gallup.com/poll/releases/pr010831.asp

Moore, D. W. (2003, January 3). Family, health most important aspects of life. Retrieved from www.gallup.com/poll/content/?Ci=7504.

Moore, M. R. (2008). Gendered power relations among women: A study of household decision making in Black, lesbian stepfamilies. *American Sociological Review, 73*(2), 335–356. doi:10.1177/000312240807300208

Moore, R. C., Eyler, L. T., Mausbach, B. T., Zlatar, Z. Z., Thompson, W. K., Peavy, G., . . . Jeste, D. V. (2015). Complex interplay between health and successful aging: Role of perceived stress, resilience, and social support. *The American Journal of Geriatric Psychiatry, 23*(6), 622–632. doi:10.1016/j.jagp.2014.08.004

Moore, R. L., & Wei, L. (2012). Modern love in China. In M. A. Paludi (Ed.), *The psychology of love* (pp. 27–42). Santa Barbara, CA: Praeger/ABC-CLIO.

Moos, R. H., & Billings, A. G. (1982). Conceptualizing and measuring coping resources and processes. In L. Goldberger & S. Breznitz (Eds.), *Handbook of stress: Theoretical and clinical aspects.* New York: Free Press.

Morahan-Martin, J., & Schumacher, P. (2003). Loneliness and social uses of the iInternet. *Computers in Human Behavior, 19*(6), 659–671.

Moran, C. M., Diefendorff, J. M., & Greguras, G. J. (2013). Understanding emotional display rules at work and outside of work: The effects of country and gender. *Motivation And Emotion, 37*(2), 323–334. doi:10.1007/s11031-012-9301-x

Moran, J. M., Eshin J., & Mitchell, J. P. (2014). Spontaneous mentalizing predicts the fundamental attribution error. *Journal of Cognitive Neuroscience, 26*(3), 569–576.

Moretti, M. M., & Higgins, E. T. (1990). Relating self-discrepancy to self-esteem: The contribution of discrepancy beyond actual-self ratings. *Journal of Experimental Social Psychology, 26,* 108–123.

Morgado, P., Freitas, D., Bessa, J. M., Sousa, N., & Cerqueira, J. J. (2013). Perceived stress in obsessive–compulsive disorder is related with obsessive but not compulsive symptoms. *Frontiers iIn Psychiatry, 4.*

Morgan, H. J., & Janoff-Bulman, R. (1994). Victims' responses to traumatic life events: An unjust world or an uncaring world? *Social Justice Research, 7,* 47–68.

Morgan, M. J. (2000). Ecstasy (MDMA): A review of its possible persistent psychological effects. *Psychopharmacology, 152*(3), 230–248.

Morgan, R. D., & Cohen, L. M. (2008). Clinical and counseling psychology: Can differences be gleaned from printed recruiting materials? *Training and Education in Professional Psychology, 2*(3), 156–164.

Morgenstern, J. (2000). *Time management from the inside out.* New York: Holt.

Mori, K., & Arai, M. (2010). No need to fake it: Reproduction of the Asch experiment without confederates. *International Journal of Psychology, 45*(5), 390–397. doi:10.1080/00207591003774485

Morris, C. E., Reiber, C., & Roman, E. (2015). Quantitative sex differences in response to the dissolution of a romantic relationship. *Evolutionary Behavioral Sciences.* doi:10.1037/ebs0000054

Morris, W. L., & DePaulo, B. M. (2009). Singlehood. In H. T. Reis & S. Sprecher (Eds.), *Encyclopedia of human relationships, Vol. 3* (pp. 1504–1507). Los Angeles: Sage Reference.

Morris, W. N. (1999). The mood system. In D. Kahneman, E. Diener, & N. Schwartz (Eds.), *Well-being: The foundations of hedonic psychology* (pp. 169–189). New York: Russell Sage Foundation.

Morrow, G. D. (2009). Exchange processes. In H. T. Reis & S. Sprecher (Eds.), *Encyclopedia of human relationships, Vol. 1* (pp. 551–555). Los Angeles: Sage Reference.

Moskowitz, D. S. (1994). Cross-situational generality and the interpersonal circumplex. *Journal of Personality and Social Psychology, 66,* 921–933.

Moskowitz, G. B., & Gill, M. J. (2013). Person perception. In D. Reisberg (Ed.) , *The Oxford handbook of cognitive psychology* (pp. 918–942). New York: Oxford University Press. doi:10.1093/oxfordhb/9780195376746.013.0058

Moskowitz, J. T. (2003). Positive affect predicts lower risk of AIDS mortality. *Psychosomatic Medicine, 65,* 620–626.

Moskowitz, J. T., & Saslow, L. R. (2014). Health and psychology: The importance of positive affect. In M. M. Tugade, M. N. Shiota, & L. D. Kirby (Eds.), *Handbook of positive emotions.* New York: Guilford.

Moskowitz, J. T., Shmueli-Blumberg, D., Acree, M., & Folkman, S. (2012). Positive affect in the midst of distress: Implications for role functioning. *Journal of Community and Applied Social Psychology, 22*(6), 502–518. doi:10.1002/casp.1133

Motel, S., & Dost, M. (2015). The Pew Research Center. Half of unmarried LGBT Americans say they would like to wed. Retrieved from www.pewresearch.org/fact-tank/2015/06/26/half-of-unmarried-lgbt-americans-say-they-would-like-to-wed

Mowrer, O. H. (1947). On the dual nature of learning: A reinterpretaton of "conditioning" and "problem-solving." *Harvard Educational Review, 17,* 102–150.

Moynihan, J. A., Heffner, K. L., Caserta, M. T., & O'Connor, T. G. (2014). Stress and immune function in humans: A life-course perspective. In A. W. Kusnecov & H. Anisman (Eds.), *The Wiley-Blackwell handbook of psychoneuroimmunology* (pp. 251–265). Wiley-Blackwell.

Muehlenhard, C. L. (2011). Examining stereotypes about token resistance to sex. *Psychology of Women Quarterly, 35*(4), 676–683. doi:10.1177/0361684311426689

Muehlenhard, C. L., & Shippee, S. K. (2010). Men's and women's reports of pretending orgasm. *Journal of Sex Research, 47*(6), 552–567. doi:10.1080/00224490903171794

Mueller, P. A., & Oppenheimer, D. M. (2014). The pen is mightier than the keyboard: Advantages of longhand over laptop note taking. *Psychological Science, 25*(6), 1159–1168. doi:10.1177/0956797614524581

Mueser, K. T., Deavers, F., Penn, D. L., & Cassisi, J. E. (2013). Psychosocial treatments for schizophrenia. *Annual Review of Clinical Psychology, 9,* 465–497. doi:10.1146/annurev-clinpsy-050212-185620

Mulhall, J., King, R., Glina, S., & Hvidsten, K. (2008). Importance of and satisfaction with sex among men and women worldwide: Results of the Global Better Sex Survey. *Journal of Sexual Medicine, 5,* 788–795.

Muller, K. W., Glaesmer, H., Brahler, E., Woelfling, K., & Beutel, M. E. (2014). Prevalence of internet addiction in the general population: Results from a German population-based survey. *Behaviour & Information Technology, 33,* 757–766. doi: 10.1080/0144929X.2013.810778

Mund, M., & Mitte, K. (2012). The costs of repression: A meta-analysis on the relation between repressive coping and somatic diseases. *Health Psychology, 31*(5), 640–649. doi:10.1037/a0026257

Murnen, S. K., & Don, B. P. (2012). Body image and gender roles. In T. F. Cash (Ed.), *Encyclopedia of body image and human appearance, Vol. 1* (pp. 128–134). San Diego, CA: Elsevier Academic Press. doi:10.1016/B978-0-12-384925-0.00019-5

Murrell, A. J., Dietz-Uhler, B. L., Dovidio, J. F., Gaertner, S. L., & Drout, E. (1994). Aversive racism and resistance to affirmative action: Perceptions of justice are not necessarily color blind. *Basic and Applied Social Psychology, 17*(1–2), 71–86.

Murry, V. M., Mayberry, L. S., & Berkel, C. (2013). Gender and family relations. In G. W. Peterson & K. R. Bush (Eds.), *Handbook of marriage and the family* (3rd ed.; pp. 401–422). New York: Springer Science + Business Media. doi:10.1007/978-1-4614-3987-5_18

Murtaugh, M. A. (2004). Meat consumption and the risk of colon and rectal cancers. *Clinical Nutrition, 13,* 61–64.

Music, G. (2014). *The good life: Well-being and the new science of altruism, selfishness, and immorality*. New York: Routledge/Taylor & Francis Group.

Musick, K., & Bumpass, L. (2012). Reexamining the case for marriage: Union formation and changes in well-being. *Journal of Marriage and Family, 74,* 1–18. doi:10.1111/j.1741-3737.2011.00873.x

Mussweiler, T., & Rütter, K. (2003). What are friends for! The use of routine standards in social comparison. *Journal of Personality and Social Psychology, 85,* 467–481.

Mustanski, B., Kuper, L., & Greene, G. J. (2014). Development of sexual orientation and identity. In D. L. Tolman, L. M. Diamond, J. A. Bauermeister, W. H. George, J. G. Pfaus, L. M. Ward (Eds.), *APA handbook of sexuality and psychology*, (pp. 597–628). Washington, DC: American Psychological Association. doi:10.1037/14193-019

Musto, D. F., & Wish, E. D. (2011). Historical perspectives. In P. Ruiz & E. C. Strain (Eds.), *Lowinson and Ruiz's substance abuse: A comprehensive textbook* (5th ed.; pp. 1–16). Philadelphia: Lippincott Williams & Wilkins.

Myers, D. G. (1980). *Inflated self: Human illusions and the biblical call to hope.* New York: Seabury Press.

Myers, D. G. (1992). *The pursuit of happiness: Who is happy—and why.* New York: Morrow.

Myers, D. G. (2013). Religious engagement and well-being. In S. A. David, I. Boniwell, & A. Conley Ayers (Eds.), *The Oxford handbook of happiness.* New York: Oxford University Press.

Nadal, K. L. (2008). Preventing racial, ethnic, gender, sexual minority, disability, and religious microaggressions: Recommendations for promoting positive mental health. *Prevention in Counseling Psychology: Theory, Research, Practice and Training, 2,* 22–27.

Nadal, K. L., & Haynes, K. (2012). The effects of sexism, gender microaggressions, and other forms of discrimination on women's mental health and development. In P. K. Lundberg-Love, K. L. Nadal, & M. A. Paludi (Eds.), *Women and mental disorders* (pp. 87–101). Santa Barbara, CA: Praeger/ABC-CLIO.

Nadelson, C. C., Notman, M. T., & McCarthy, M. K. (2005). Gender issues in psychotherapy. In G. O. Gabbard, J. S. Beck, & J. Holmes (Eds.), *Oxford textbook of psychotherapy*. New York: Oxford University Press.

Nakamura, J., & Csikszentmihalyi, M. (2009). Flow theory and research. In C. R. Snyder & S. Lopez (Eds)., *Oxford handbook of positive psychology* (2nd ed., pp. 195–206). New York: Oxford University Press.

National Association of Women Business Owners. (2010). New census data reinforces the economic power of women owned businesses in the U.S. says NAWBO. Retrieved from http://nawbo.org/content_11800.cfm

Naumann, L. P., Vazire, S., Rentfrow, P. J., & Gosling, S. D. (2009). Personality judgments based on physical appearance. *Personality and Social Psychology Bulletin, 35*(12), 1661–1671. doi:10.1177/0146167209346309

Near, C. E. (2013). Selling gender: Associations of box art representation of female characters with sales for teen- and mature-rated video games. *Sex Roles, 68*(3–4), 252–269. doi:10.1007/s11199-012-0231-6

Neff, K. D. (2011). Self-compassion, self-esteem, and well-being. *Social and Personality Psychology Compass, 5,* 1–12.

Neff, L. A. (2012). Putting marriage in its context: The influence of external stress on early marital development. In L. Campbell & T. J. Loving (Eds.), *Interdisciplinary research on close relationships: The case for integration* (pp. 179–203). Washington, DC: American Psychological Association. doi:10.1037/13486-008

Negy, C., Schwartz, S., & Reig-Ferrer, A. (2009). Violated expectations and acculturative stress among U.S. Hispanic immigrants. *Cultural Diversity and Ethnic Minority Psychology, 15,* 255–264.

Neilson Research Group (2014). An era of growth: The cross platform report. Retrieved from www.tvb.org/media/file/Nielsen-Cross-Platform-Report_Q4-2013.pdf

Nelson, D. L., & Cooper, C. L. (Eds.), (2007). *Positive organizational behavior.* London: Sage.

Nelson, S. K., Kushlev, K., English, T., Dunn, E. W., & Lyubomirsky, S. (2013). In defense of parenthood: Children are associated with more joy than misery. *Psychological Science, 24*(1), 3–10. doi:10.1177/0956797612447798

Nelson, S. K., Kushlev, K., & Lyubomirsky, S. (2014). The pains and pleasures of parenting: When, why, and how is parenthood associated with more or less well-being? *Psychological Bulletin, 140*(3), 846–895. doi:10.1037/a0035444

Neria, Y., DiGrande, L., & Adams, B. G. (2011). Posttraumatic stress disorder following the September 11, 2001, terrorist attacks: A review of the literature among highly exposed populations. *American Psychologist, 66*(6), 429–446. doi:10.1037/a0024791

Nesdale, D., De Vries Robbé, M., & Van Oudenhoven, J. (2012). Intercultural effectiveness, authoritarianism, and ethnic prejudice. *Journal of Applied Social Psychology, 42*(5), 1173–1191. doi:10.1111/j.1559-1816.2011.00882.x

Nettelhorst, S. C., & Brannon, L. A. (2012). The effect of advertisement choice, sex, and need for cognition on attention. *Computers in Human Behavior, 28*(4), 1315–1320. doi:10.1016/j.chb.2012.02.015

Nettle, D. (2006). The evolution of personality variation in humans and other animals. *American Psychologist, 61,* 622–631.

New Media Trend Watch. (2012) Demographics. Retrieved from www.newmediatrendwatch.com/markets-by-country/17-usa/123-demographics

Newcombe, N. S. (2007). Taking science seriously: Straight thinking about spatial sex differences. In S. J. Ceci & W. M. Williams (Eds.), *Why aren't more women in science?* (pp. 69–78). Washington, DC: American Psychological Association.

Newcombe, N. S. (2010). On tending our scientific knitting: Thinking about gender in the context of evolution. In J. C. Chrisler & D. R. McCreary (Eds.), *Handbook of gender research in psychology, Vol. 1* (pp. 259–274). New York: Springer.

Newmahr, S. (2011). Homosexuality. In C. D. Bryant (Ed.), *The Routledge handbook of deviant behavior* (pp. 253–259). New York: Routledge/Taylor & Francis Group.

Newman, C. F., & Beck, A. T. (2009). Cognitive therapy. In B. J. Sadock, V. A. Sadock, & P. Ruiz (Eds.), *Kaplan & Sadock's comprehensive textbook of psychiatry* (pp. 2857–2872). Philadelphia: Lippincott Williams & Wilkins.

Newman, D. B., Tay, L., & Diener, E. (2014). Leisure and subjective well-being: A model of psychological mechanisms as mediating factors. *Journal of Happiness Studies, 15*(3), 555–578. doi:10.1007/s10902-013-9435-x

Newman, M. G., & Llera, S. J. (2011). A novel theory of experiential avoidance in generalized anxiety disorder: A review and synthesis of research supporting a contrast avoidance model of worry. *Clinical Psychology Review, 31,* 371–382. doi:10.1016/j.cpr.2011.01.008

Newman, M. G., Llera, S. J., Erickson, T. M., Przeworski, A., & Castonguay, L. G. (2013). Worry and generalized anxiety disorder: A review and theoretical synthesis of evidence on nature, etiology, mechanisms, and treatment. *Annual Review of Clinical Psychology, 9,* 275–297. doi:10.1146/annurev-cinpsy-050212-185544

Nezu, A. M., & Nezu, C. M. (2014). Problem-solving strategies. In S. G. Hofmann, D. J. A. Dozois, W. Rief, & J. A. J. Smits (Eds.), (pp. 67–84) Wiley-Blackwell.

Nezu, A. M., Nezu, C. M., Felgoise, S. H., & Zwick, M. L. (2003). Psychosocial oncology. In A. M. Nezu, C. M. Nezu, & P. A. Geller (Eds.), *Handbook of psychology, Vol. 9: Health psychology.* New York: Wiley.

Nezu, A. M., Raggio, G., Evans, A. N., & Nezu, C. M. (2012). Diabetes mellitus. In A. M. Nezu, C. M. Nezu, P. A. Geller, & I. B. Weiner (Eds.), *Handbook of psychology, Vol. 9: Health psychology* (2nd ed.). New York: Wiley.

Nezu, U., Kamiyama, H., Kondo, Y., Sakuma, M., Morimoto, T., & Ueda, S. (2013). Effect of low-protein diet on kidney function in diabetic nephropathy: Meta-analysis of randomised controlled trials. *Britsh Medical Journal Open* 3(5), ii. doi: 10.1136/bmjopen-2013-002934

Ng, T. W., & Feldman, D. C. (2009). How broadly does education contribute to job performance? *Personnel Psychology, 62,* 89–134.

Ng, T. W., Sorenson, K. L., & Feldman, D. C. (2007). Dimensions, antecedents, and consequences of workaholism: A conceptual integration and extension. *Journal of Organizational Behavior, 28,* 111–136.

Nicholson, C. (2006). Freedom and choice, culture, and class. *APS Observer, 19*(8), 31, 45.

Nicholson, I. (2011). "Torture at Yale": Experimental subjects, laboratory torment and the "rehabilitation" of Milgram's "Obedience to Authority." *Theory & Psychology, 21*(6), 737–761. doi:10.1177/0959354311420199

Nickerson, R. S. (1998). Confirmation bias: A ubiquitous phenomenon in many guises. *Review of General Psychology, 2,* 175–220.

Niedenthal, P. M., Setterlund, M. B., & Wherry, M. B. (1992). Possible self-complexity and affective reactions to goal-relevant evaluation. *Journal of Personality and Social Psychology, 63,* 5–16.

Niederhoffer, K. G., & Pennebaker, J. W. (2005). Sharing one's story: On the benefits of writing or talking about emotional experience. In C. R. Snyder & S. J. Lopez (Eds.), *Handbook of positive psychology*. New York: Oxford University Press.

Nielsen, M. B., & Einarsen, S. S. (2012). Prospective relationships between workplace sexual harassment and psychological distress. *Occupational Medicine, 62*(3), 226–228. doi:10.1093/occmed/kqs010

Nielsen, M. B., & Knardahl, S. (2014). Coping strategies: A prospective study of patterns, stability, and relationships with psychological distress. *Scandinavian Journal of Psychology, 55*(2), 142–150. doi:10.1111/sjop.12103

Nielsen, R. E., Uggerby, A. S., Jensen, S. W., & McGrath, J. J. (2013). Increasing mortality gap for patients diagnosed with schizophrenia over the last three decades: A Danish nationwide study from 1980 to 2010. *Schizophrenia Research, 146*(1–3), 22–27. doi:10.1016/j.schres.2013.02.025

Nillni, Y. I., Rohan, K. J., & Mahon, J. N., Pineles, S. L., & Zvolensky, M. J. (2013). The role of anxiety sensitivity in the experience of menstrual-related symptoms reported via daily diary. *Psychiatry Research, 210*(2), 564–569. doi: 10.1016/j.psychres.2013.07.016

Nkomo, S. M., & Ariss, A. A. (2014). The historical origins of ethnic (white) privilege in US organizations. *Journal of Managerial Psychology, 29*(4), 389–404. doi:10.1108/JMP-06-2012-0178

Nobler, M. S., & Sackeim, H. A. (2006). Electroconvulsive therapy and transcranial magnetic stimulation. In D. J. Stein, D. J. Kupfer, & A. F. Schatzberg (Eds.), *Textbook of mood disorders*. Washington, DC: American Psychiatric Publishing.

Nobre, P. J., & Pinto-Gouveia, J. (2008). Cognitive and emotional predictors of female sexual dysfunctions: Preliminary findings. *Journal of Sex and Marital Therapy, 34*(4), 325–342. doi:10.1080/00926230802096358

Nock, M. K., Millner, A. J., Deming, C. A., & Glenn, C. R. (2014). Depression and suicide. In I. H. Gotlib & C. L. Hammen (Eds.), *Handbook of depression* (3rd ed.). New York: Guilford.

Noguchi, K., Kamada, A., & Shrira, I. (2014). Cultural differences in the primacy effect for person perception. *International Journal of Psychology, 49*(3), 208–210.

Nolen-Hoeksema, S. (1991). Responses to depression and their effects on the duration of depressive episodes. *Journal of Abnormal Psychology, 100,* 569–582.

Nolen-Hoeksema, S. (2000). The role of rumination in depressive disorders and mixed anxiety/depressive symptoms. *Journal of Abnormal Psychology, 109*(3), 504–511.

Nolen-Hoeksema, S. (2001). Gender differences in depression. *Current Directions in Psychological Science, 10,*173–176.

Nolen-Hoeksema, S. (2012). Emotion regulation and psychopathology: The role of gender. *Annual Review of Clinical Psychology,* 861–887. doi:10.1146/annurev-clinpsy-032511-143109

Nolen-Hoeksema, S. (2013). Gender differences. In P. M. Miller, S. A. Ball, M. E. Bates, A. W. Blume, K. M. Kampman, D. J. Kavanagh, et al. (Eds.), *Comprehensive addictive behaviors and disorders, Vol. 1: Principles of addiction* (pp. 141–147). San Diego, CA: Elsevier Academic Press.

Nolen-Hoeksema, S., & Davis, C. G. (2005). Positive responses to loss: Perceiving benefits and growth. In C. R. Snyder & S. J. Lopez (Eds.), *Handbook of positive psychology.* New York: Oxford University Press.

Nomaguchi, K., & Milkie, M. A. (2015). Gender, accuracy about partners' work-family conflict, and relationship quality. In M. J. Mills (Ed.), *Gender and the work-family experience: An intersection of two domains* (pp. 159–176). Cham, Switzerland: Springer International Publishing. doi:10.1007/978-3-319-08891-4_9

Nomaguchi, K. M. (2006). Maternal employment, nonparental care, mother-child interactions and child outcomes during preschool years. *Journal of Marriage and Family, 68,* 1341–1369.

Nomaguchi, K. M., & Milkie, M. A. (2003). Costs and rewards of children: The effects of becoming a parent on adults' lives. *Journal of Marriage and Family, 65,* 356–374.

Norcross, J. C., Campbell, L. F., Grohol, J. M., Santrock, J. W., Selagea, F., & Sommer, R. (2013). *Self-help that works: Resources to improve emotional health and strengthen relationships* (4th ed.). New York: Oxford University Press.

Norcross, J. C., Hedges, M., & Castle, P. H. (2002). Psychologists conducting psychotherapy in 2001: A study of the Division 29 membership. *Psychotherapy: Theory, Research, Practice, Training, 39,* 97–102.

North, M. S., & Fiske, S. T. (2014). Social categories create and reflect inequality: Psychological and sociological insights. In J. T. Cheng, J. L. Tracy, & C. Anderson (Eds.), *The psychology of social status* (pp. 243–265). New York: Springer Science + Business Media. doi:10.1007/978-1-4939-0867-7_12

Northrup, C., Schwartz, P., & Witte, J. (2012). *The Normal bar: The secrets of happy couples and what they reveal about creating a new normal in your relationship.* New York: Harmony Books.

Norton, P. G. W. (2004, February 1). Low-fat foods helped fuel obesity epidemic. *Family Practice News,* p. 22.

Norwood, K., & Duck, S. (2009). Dissolution of relationships, processes. In H. T. Reis & S. Sprecher (Eds.), *Encyclopedia of human relationships, Vol. 2* (pp. 445–449). Los Angeles: Sage Reference.

Nosek, B. A., Smyth, F. L., Hansen, J. J., Devos, T., Lindner, N. M., Ranganath, K. A., . . . Banaji, M. R. (2007). Pervasiveness and correlates of implicit attitudes and stereotypes. *European Review of Social Psychology, 18,* 36–88. doi:10.1080/10463280701489053

Novakova, B., Harris, P. R., Ponnusamy, A., & Reuber, M. (2013). The role of stress as a trigger for epileptic seizures: A narrative review of evidence from human and animal studies. *Epilepsia, 54,* 1866–1876. doi: 10.1111/epi.12377

Novelli, D., Drury, J., & Reicher, S. (2010). Come together: Two studies concerning the impact of group relations on "personal space." *British Journal of Social Psychology, 49*(2), 223–236. doi:10.1348/014466609X449377

Nurnberger, J. I., & Zimmerman, J. (1970). Applied analysis of human behavior: An alternative to conventional motivational inferences and unconscious determination in therapeutic programming. *Behavior Therapy, 1,* 59–69.

Nye, C. D., Su, R., Rounds, J., & Drasgow, F. (2011). *Vocational interests and performance: A quantitative summary of 60 years of research.* Paper presented at the annual meeting of the International Personnel Assessment Council, Washington, DC.

O'Connor, A. (2012, June 12). Really? Quitting smoking is harder for women. *New York Times,* D5.

O'Connor, D. B., & Conner, M.. (2011). Effects of stress on eating behavior. In R. J. Contrada & A. Baum (Eds.), *The handbook of stress science: Biology, psychology, and health* (pp. 275–286). New York: Springer.

O'Hara, M. W. (2009). Postpartum depression: What we know. *Journal of Clinical Psychology, 65,* 1258–1269.

O'Hara, R. E., Gibbons, F. X., Gerrard, M., Li, Z., & Sargent, J. D. (2012). Greater exposure to sexual content in popular movies predicts earlier sexual debut and increased sexual risk taking. *Psychological Science, 23*(9), 984–993. doi:10.1177/0956797611435529

O'Keefe, D. (2002). *Persuasion: Theory and research* (2nd ed.). Newbury Park, CA: Sage.

O'Keefe, D. J., & Hale, S. L. (2001). An odds-ratio based meta-analysis of research on the door-in-the-face influence strategy. *Communication Reports, 14*(1), 31–38.

O'Leary-Kelly, A. M., Bowes-Sperry, L., Bates, C. A., & Lean, E. R. (2009). Sexual harassment at work: A decade (plus) of progress. *Journal of Management, 35*(3), 503–536.

O'Sullivan, L. F., & Thompson, A. E. (2014). Sexuality in adolescence. In D. L. Tolman, L. M. Diamond, J. A. Bauermeister, W. H. George, J. G. Pfaus, & L. M. Ward (Eds.), *APA handbook of sexuality and psychology,* (pp. 433–486). Washington, DC: American Psychological Association. doi:10.1037/14193-015

Oakes, P. (2001). The root of all evil in intergroup relations? Unearthing the categorization process. In R. Brown & S. L. Gaertner (Eds.), *Blackwell handbook of social psychology: Intergroup processes.* London: Blackwell.

Oaten, M., & Cheng, K. (2006). Longitudinal gains in self-regulation from regular physical exercise. *British Journal of Health Psychology, 11,* 717–733.

Occupational Outlook Handbook. (2014). Bureau of Labor statistics: Fastest growing occupations, 2012–2022. Retrieved from www.bls.gov/ooh/fastest-growing.htm

Ogden, C. L., Carroll, M. D., & Flegal, K. M. (2008). High body mass index for age among US children and adolescents, 2003–2006. *Journal of the American Medical Association, 299,* 2401–2405.

Ogedegbe, G., Schoenthaler, A., & Fernandez, S. (2007). Appointment keeping behavior is not related to medication adherence in hypertensive African Americans. *Journal of General Internal Medicine, 22,* 1176–1179.

Ogle, C. M., Rubin, D. C., Berntsen, D., & Siegler, I. C. (2013). The frequency and impact of exposure to potentially traumatic events over the life course. *Clinical Psychological Science, 1*(4), 426–434. doi:10.1177/2167702613485076

Ogles, B. M. (2013). Measuring change in psychotherapy research. In M. J. Lambert (Ed.), *Bergin and Garfield's handbook of psychotherapy and behavior change* (6th ed.). New York: Wiley.

O'Keefe, D. J. (2013). The elaboration likelihood model. In J. P. Dillard & L. Shen (Eds.), *The Sage handbook of persuasion: Developments in theory and practice* (2nd ed.; pp. 137–149). Thousand Oaks, CA: Sage.

Olds, J., & Schwartz, R. S. (2009). *The lonely American: Drifting apart in the twenty-first century.* Boston: Beacon Press.

Olfson, M., Blanco, C., Liu, S.-M., Wang, S., & Correll, C. U. (2012). National trends in the office-based treatment of children, adolescents, and adults with antipsychotics. *JAMA Psychiatry, 69*(12), 1247–1256.

Olfson, M., Cherry, D. K., & Lewis-Fernández, R. (2009). Racial differences in visit duration of outpatient psychiatric visits. *Archives of General Psychiatry, 66,* 214–221.

Olfson, M., Kroenke, K., Wang, S., & Blanco, C. (2014). Trends in office-based mental health care provided by psychiatrists and primary care physicians. *Journal of Clinical Psychiatry, 75,* 247–253. doi:10.4088/JCP.13m08834

Olfson, M., & Marcus, S. C. (2009). National patterns in antidepressant medication treatment. *Archives of General Psychiatry, 66,* 848–856.

Olfson, M., & Marcus, S. C. (2010). National trends in outpatient psychotherapy. *The American Journal of Psychiatry, 167*(12), 1456–1463. doi:10.1176/appi.ajp.2010.10040570

Olivola, C. Y., & Todorov, A. (2010). Fooled by first impressions? Reexamining the diagnostic value of appearance-based inferences. *Journal of Experimental Social Psychology, 46*(2), 315–324. doi:10.1016/j.jesp.2009.12.002

Oppliger, P. A. (2007). Effects of gender stereotyping on socialization. In R. W. Preiss, B. M. Gayle, N. Burrell, M. Allen, & J. Bryant (Eds.), *Mass media effects research: Advances through meta-analysis* (pp. 199–214). Mahwah, NJ: Erlbaum.

Opris, D., Pintea, S., Garcia-Palacios, A., Botella, C., Szamosközi, S., & David, D. (2012). Virtual reality exposure therapy in anxiety disorders: A quantitative meta-analysis. *Depression and Anxiety, 29,* 85–93. doi:10.1002/da.20910

O'Reilly, J., & Peterson, C. C. (2014). Theory of mind at home: Linking authoritative and authoritarian parenting styles to children's social understanding. *Early Child Development and Care, 184*(12), 1934–1947. doi:10.1080/03004430.2014.894034

Orenstein, P. (1995). *Schoolgirls: Young women, self-esteem, and the confidence gap.* New York: Anchor Books.

Orth, U., Robins, R. W., & Widaman, K. F. (2012). Life-span development of self-esteem and its effects on important life outcomes. *Journal of Personality and Social Psychology, 102*(6), 1271–1288. doi:10.1037/a0025558

Ostafin, B., & Brooks, J. (2011). Drinking for relief: Negative affect increases automatic alcohol motivation in coping-motivated drinkers. *Motivation & Emotion, 35*(3), 285–295. doi: 10.1007/s11031-010-9194-5

Osteen, J. (2009). *Become a better you: 7 keys to improving your life every day.* New York: Free Press.

Ostrom, T. M., & Sedikides, C. (1992). Out-group homogeneity effects in natural and minimal groups. *Psychological Bulletin, 112,* 536–552.

Oswald, D. L., Clark, E. M., & Kelly, C. M. (2004). Friendship maintenance: An analysis of individual and dyad behaviors. *Journal of Social and Clinical Psychology, 23*(3), 413–441. doi:10.1521/jscp.23.3.413.35460

Otero, T. L., Schatz, R. B., Merrill, A. C., & Bellini, S. (2015). Social skills training for youth with autism spectrum disorders: A follow-up. *Child and Adolescent Psychiatric Clinics of North America, 24*(1), 99–115. doi:10.1016/j.chc.2014.09.002

Ouweneel, E., Schaufeli, W. B., & Le Blanc, P. M. (2013). Believe, and you will achieve: Changes over time in self-efficacy, engagement, and performance. *Applied Psychology: Health and Well-Being, 5*(2), 225–247.

Overton, S. L., & Medina, S. L. (2008). The stigma of mental illness. *Journal of Counseling & Development, 86*(2), 143–151.

Owen, J., & Fincham, F. D. (2011). Effects of gender and psychosocial factors on "friends with benefits" relationships among young adults. *Archives of Sexual Behavior, 40*(2), 311–320. doi:10.1007/s10508-010-9611-6

Owen, J., Fincham, F. D., & Manthos, M. (2013). Friendship after a friends with benefits relationship: Deception, psychological functioning, and social connectedness. *Archives of Sexual Behavior, 42*(8), 1443–1449. doi:10.1007/s10508-013-0160-7

Owens, E. W., Behun, R. J., Manning, J. C., & Reid, R. C. (2012). The impact of internet pornography on adolescents: A review of the research. *Sexual Addiction & Compulsivity, 19*(1–2), 99–122. doi:10.1080/10720162.2012.660431

Oyserman, D., Bybee, D., & Terry, K. (2006). Possible selves and academic outcomes: How and when possible selves impel action. *Journal of Personality and Social Psychology, 91,* 188–204.

Oyserman, D., Destin, M., & Novin, S. (2015). The context-sensitive future self: Possible selves motivate in context, not otherwise. *Self and Identity, 14*(2), 173–188. doi:10.1080/15298868.2014.965733

Oyserman, D., Elmore, K., & Smith, G. (2012). Self, self-concept, and identity. In M. R. Leary & J. P. Tangney (Eds.), *Handbook of self and identity* (2nd ed., pp. 69–104). New York: Guilford.

Ozer, E. J., Best, S. R., Lipsey, T. L., & Weiss, D. S. (2003). Predictors of posttraumatic stress disorder and symptoms in adults: A meta-analysis. *Psychological Bulletin, 129*(1), 52–73.

Ozer, E. M., & Bandura, A. (1990). Mechanisms governing empowerment effects: A self-efficacy analysis. *Journal of Personality and Social Psychology, 58,* 472–486.

Pacchiarotti, I., Bond, D. J., Baldessarini, R. J., Nolen, W. A., Grunze, H., Licht, R. W., . . . Vieta, E. (2013). The International Society for Bipolar Disorders (ISBD) task force report on antidepressant use in bipolar disorders. *The American Journal of Psychiatry, 170,* 1249–1262. doi:10.1176/appi.ajp.2013.13020185

Pachankis, J. E., Cochran, S. D., & Mays, V. M. (2015). The mental health of sexual minority adults in and out of the closet: A population-based study. *Journal of Consulting and Clinical Psychology, 83*(5), 890–901. doi:10.1037/ccp0000047

Paczynski, R. P., & Gold, M. S. (2011). Cocaine and crack. In P. Ruiz & E. C. Strain (Eds.), *Lowinson and Ruiz's substance abuse: A comprehensive textbook* (5th ed.; pp. 191–213). Philadelphia: Lippincott Williams & Wilkins.

Pagnini, F., Phillips, D., Bosma, C. M., Reece, A., & Langer, E. (2015). Mindfulness, physical impairment and psychological well-being in people with amyotrophic lateral sclerosis. *Psychology and Health, 30*(5), 503–517.

Palomares, N. A. (2009). Women are sort of more tentative than men, aren't they? How men and women use tentative language differently, similarly, and counterstereotypically as a function of gender salience. *Communication Research, 36*, 538–560.

Panagiotidis, P., Papadopoulou, M., Diakogiannis, I., Iacovides, A., & Kaprinis, G. (2008). Young people and binge drinking. *Annals of General Psychiatry, 7*(Suppl. 1), 1.

Pandey, A., Quick, J. C., Rossi, A. M., Nelson, D. L., & Martin, W. (2011). Stress and the workplace: 10 years of science, 1997–2007. In R. J. Contrada & A. Baum (Eds.), *The handbook of stress science: Biology, psychology, and health* (pp. 137–149). New York: Springer.

Pang, M., Chua, B., & Chu, C. (2008). Learning to stay ahead in an uncertain environment. *International Journal of Human Resource Management, 19*(7), 1383–1394.

Pansu, P., Lima, L., & Fointiat, V. (2014). When saying no leads to compliance: The door-in-the-face technique for changing attitudes and behaviors towards smoking at work. *European Review of Applied Psychology/Revue Européenne de Psychologie Appliquée, 64*(1), 19–27. doi:10.1016/j.erap.2013.11.001

Papaharitou, S., Nakopoulou, E., Kirana, P., Giaglis, G., Moraitou, M., & Hatzichristou, D. (2008). Factors associated with sexuality in later life: An exploratory study in a group of Greek married older adults. *Archives of Gerontology and Geriatrics, 46*, 191–201.

Papas, R. K., Belar, C. D., & Rozensky, R. H. (2004). The practice of clinical health psychology: Professional issues. In R. G. Frank, A. Baum, & J. L. Wallander (Eds.), *Handbook of clinical health psychology, Vol. 3* (pp. 293–319). Washington, DC: American Psychological Association.

Papernow, P. L. (1993). *Becoming a stepfamily: Patterns of development in remarried families.* San Francisco, CA: Jossey-Bass.

Pargament, K. I. (2011). Religion and coping: The current state of knowledge. In S. Folkman (Ed.), *The Oxford handbook of stress, health, and coping* (pp. 269–288). New York: Oxford University Press.

Park, C. L. (1998). Implications of posttraumatic growth for individuals. In R. G. Tedeschi, C. L. Park, & L. G. Calhoun (Eds.), *Posttraumatic growth: Positive changes in the aftermath of crisis* (pp. 153–178). Mahwah, NJ: Erlbaum.

Park, C. L., Bharadwaj, A. K., & Blank, T. O. (2011). Illness centrality, disclosure, and well-being in younger and middle-aged adult cancer survivors. *British Journal of Health Psychology, 16*(4), 880–889. doi:10.1111/j.2044-8287.2011.02024.x

Park, K. (2005). Choosing childlessness: Weber's typology of action and motives of the voluntarily childless. *Sociological Inquiry, 75*, 372–402.

Park, N., Peterson, C., & Seligman, M. E. P. (2004). Strengths of character and well-being. *Journal of Social and Clinical Psychology, 23*, 603–619.

Parker, K., & Patten, E. (2013). The Pew Research Center. The sandwich generation: Rising financial burdens for middle-aged Americans. Retrieved from www.pewsocialtrends.org/2013/01/30/the-sandwich-generation

Parker, R. (2000). Health literacy: A challenge for American patients and their health care providers. *Health Promotion International, 15*, 277–283.

Parrott, D. J., Peterson, J. L., Vincent, W., & Bakeman, R. (2008). Correlates of anger in response to gay men: Effects of male gender role beliefs, sexual prejudice, and masculine gender role stress. *Psychology of Men & Masculinity, 9*, 167–178.

Parrott, L. (2012). *You're stronger than you think: The power to do what you feel you can't.* Carol Stream, IL: Tyndale House.

Parwani, R., & Parwani, S. R. (2014). Does stress predispose to periodontal disease? *Dental Update, 41*, 260–264.

Pascoe, E. A., & Smart Richman, L. (2009). Perceived discrimination and health: A meta-analytic review. *Psychological Bulletin, 135*(4), 531–554. doi:10.1037/a0016059

Pashang, B., & Singh, M. (2008). Emotional intelligence and use of coping strategies. *Psychological Studies, 53*, 81–82.

Pasupathi, M. (2009). Arranged marriages. In H. T. Reis & S. Sprecher (Eds.), *Encyclopedia of human relationships, Vol. 2* (pp. 113–115). Los Angeles: Sage Reference.

Patterson, C. J. (2001). Family relationships of lesbians and gay men. In R. M. Milardo (Ed.), *Understanding families into the new millennium: A decade in review.* Minneapolis, MN: National Council on Family Relations.

Patterson, C. J. (2006). Children of lesbian and gay parents. *Current Directions in Psychological Science, 15*, 241–254.

Patterson, C. J. (2009). Lesbian and gay parents and their children: A social science perspective. In D. A. Hope (Ed.), *Contemporary perspectives on lesbian, gay, and bisexual identities* (pp. 141–182). New York: Springer Science and Business Media.

Patterson, C. J. (2013). Family lives of lesbian and gay adults. In G. W. Peterson & K. R. Bush (Eds.), *Handbook of marriage and the family* (3rd ed.; pp. 659–681). New York: Springer Science + Business Media. doi:10.1007/978-1-4614-3987-5_27

Patterson, M. L. (1988). Functions of nonverbal behavior in close relationships. In S. Duck (Ed.), *Handbook of personal relationships: Theory, research, and interventions.* New York: Wiley.

Paul, E. L., Wenzel, A., & Harvey J. (2008). Hookups: A facilitator or a barrier to relationship initiation and intimacy development? In S. Sprecher, A. Wenzel, & J. Harvey (Eds.), *Handbook of relationship initiation* (pp. 375–388). New York: Psychology Press.

Paul, K. I., & Moser, K. (2009). Unemployment impairs mental health: Meta-analyses. *Journal of Vocational Behavior, 74*(3), 264–282.

Paul, R. (2009). Parents ask: Am I risking autism if I vaccinate my children? *Journal of Autism and Developmental Disorders*, 39(6), 962–963.

Paulhus, D. L., Fridhandler, B., & Hayes, S. (1997). Psychological defense: Contemporary theory and research. In R. Hogan, J. Johnson, & S. Briggs (Eds), *Handbook of personality psychology.* San Diego, CA: Academic Press.

Paulsen, N., Callan, V. J., Grice, T. A., Rooney, D., Gallois, C., & Jones, E. (2005). Job uncertainty and personal control during downsizing: A comparison of survivors and victims. *Human Relations, 58*, 463–496.

Paunonen, S. V., & Hong, R. Y. (2015). On the properties of personality traits. In M. Mikulincer, P. R. Shaver, M. L. Cooper, & R. J. Larsen (Eds.), *APA handbook of personality and social psychology, Vol. 4: Personality processes and individual differences.* Washington, DC: American Psychological Association.

Paunonen, S. V., & LeBel, E. P. (2012). Socially desirable responding and its elusive effects on the validity of personality assessments. *Journal of Personality and Social Psychology, 103*(1), 158–175. doi:10.1037/a0028165

Pavelko, R. L., & Myrick, J. G. (2015). That's so OCD: The effects of disease trivialization via social media on user perceptions and impression formation. *Computers in Human Behavior, 49*, 251–258. doi:10.1016/j.chb.2015.02.061

Pavlov, I. P. (1906). The scientific investigation of psychical faculties or processes in the higher animals. *Science, 24*, 613–619.

Pavot, W., & Diener, E. (2013). Happiness experienced: The science of subjective well-being. In S. A. David, I. Boniwell, & A. Conley Ayers (Eds.), *The Oxford handbook of happiness.* New York: Oxford University Press.

Paxton, S. J., Norris, M., Wertheim, E. H., Durkin, S. J., & Anderson, J. (2005). Body dissatisfaction, dating, and importance of thinness to attractiveness in adolescent girls. *Sex Roles, 53*, 663–675.

Payne, B. K. (2006). Weapon bias: Split-second decisions and unintended sterotyping. *Current Directions in Psychological Science, 15*, 287–291.

Payne, S. C., Cook, A. L., & Diaz, I. (2012). Understanding childcare satisfaction and its effect on workplace outcomes: The convenience factor and the mediating role of work-family conflict. *Journal of Occupational and Organizational Psychology, 85*(2), 225–244. doi:10.1111/j.2044-8325.2011.02026.x

Pchelin, P., & Howell, R. T. (2014). The hidden cost of value-seeking: People do not accurately forecast the economic benefits of experiential purchases. *The Journal of Positive Psychology, 9*, 322–334. doi:10.1080/17439760.2014.898316

Pechnick, R. N., & Cunningham, K. A. (2011). Hallucinogens. In P. Ruiz & E. C. Strain (Eds.), *Lowinson and Ruiz's substance abuse: A comprehensive textbook* (5th ed.; pp. 267–276). Philadelphia: Lippincott Williams & Wilkins.

Pedersen, S., Vitaro, F., Barker, E. D., & Borge, A. I. H. (2007). The timing of middle-childhood peer rejection and friendship: Linking early behavior to early-adolescent adjustment. *Child Development, 78*, 1037–1051.

Pedregon, C. A., Farley, R. L., Davis, A., Wood, J. M., & Clark, R. D. (2012). Social desirability, personality questionnaires, and the 'better than average' effect. *Personality and Individual Differences, 52*(2), 213–217. doi:10.1016/j.paid.2011.10.022

Pelham, W. E., Jr., (2001). ADHD and behavioral modification. *Drug Benefit Trends, 13*, 11–14.

Pellowski, J. A., Kalichman, S. C., Matthews, K. A., & Adler, N. (2013). A pandemic of the poor: Social disadvantage and the U.S. HIV epidemic. *American Psychologist, 68*(4), 197–209. doi:10.1037/a0032694

Peng, Y., & Mao, C. (2015). The impact of person–job fit on job satisfaction: The mediator role of self efficacy. *Social Indicators Research, 121*(3), 805–813. doi:10.1007/s11205-014-0659-x

Pennebaker, J. W., Colder, M., & Sharp, L. K. (1990). Accelerating the coping process. *Journal of Personality and Social Psychology, 58*, 528–537.

Pennebaker, J. W., & Ferrell, J. D. (2013). Can expressive writing change emotions? An oblique answer to the wrong question. In D. Hermans, B. Rimé, B. Mesquita, D. (Eds.), *Changing Emotions* (pp. 183–186). New York: Psychology Press.

Penner, L. A., Dovidio, J. F., West, T. V., Gaertner, S. L., Albrecht, T. L., Dailey, R. K., & Markova, T. (2010). Aversive racism and medical interactions with black patients: A field study. *Journal of Experimental Social Psychology, 46*(2), 436–440. doi:10.1016/j.jesp.2009.11.004

Peper, J. S., & Dahl, R. E. (2013). The teenage brain: Surging hormones: Brain-behavior interactions during puberty. *Current Directions in Psychological Science, 22*(2), 134–139. doi:10.1177/0963721412473755

Peplau, L. A., & Fingerhut, A. W. (2007). The close relationships of lesbians and gay men. *Annual Review of Psychology, 58*, 405–424. doi:10.1146/annurev.psych.58.110405.085701

Peplau, L. A., Fingerhut, A., & Beals, K. P. (2004). Sexuality in the relationships of lesbians and gay men. In J. H. Harvey, A. Wenzel, & S. Sprecher (Eds.), *The handbook of sexuality in close relationships.* Mahwah, NJ: Lawrence Erlbaum.

Peplau, L. A., & Ghavami, N. (2009). Gay, lesbian, and bisexual relationships. In H. T. Reis & S. Sprecher (Eds.), *Encyclopedia of human relationships, Vol. 1* (pp. 746–751). Los Angeles: Sage Reference.

Peplau, L. A., Hill, C. T., & Rubin, Z. (1993). Sex role attitudes in dating and marriage: A 15-year follow-up of the Boston couples study. *Journal of Social Issues, 49*, 31–52.

Peplau, L. A., & Spalding, L. R. (2003). The close relationships of lesbians, gay men, and bisexuals. In L. D. Garnets & D. C. Kimmel (Eds.), *Psychological perspectives on lesbian, gay, and bisexual experiences.* New York: Columbia University Press.

Pereira, M. A., O'Reilly, E., Augustsson, K., Fraser, G. E., Goldbourt, U., Heitmann, B. L., . . . Ascherio, A. (2004). Dietary fiber and risk of coronary heart disease: A pooled analysis of cohort studies. *Archives of Internal Medicine, 164*, 370–376.

Perelman, M. A. (2014). The history of sexual medicine. In D. L. Tolman, L. M. Diamond, J. A. Bauermeister, W. H. George, J. G. Pfaus, & L. M. Ward (Eds.), *APA handbook of sexuality and psychology* (pp. 137–179). Washington, DC: American Psychological Association. doi:10.1037/14194-005

Perera, H. N., & DiGiacomo, M. (2015). The role of trait emotional intelligence in academic performance during the university transition: An integrative model of mediation via social support, coping, and adjustment. *Personality and Individual Differences, 83*, 208–213. doi:10.1016/j.paid.2015.04.001

Peretti, P. O., & Abplanalp, Jr., R. R. (2004). Chemistry in the college dating process: Structure and function. *Social Behavior and Personality, 32*(2), 147–154.

Perez, G. K., Cruess, D. G., & Kalichman, S. C. (2010). Effects of stress on health in HIV/AIDS. In R. Contrada & A. Baum (Eds.), *The handbook of stress science: Biology, psychology, and health* (pp. 447–460). New York: Springer.

Perilloux, C., Duntley, J. D., & Buss, D. M. (2012). The costs of rape. *Archives of Sexual Behavior, 41*(5), 1099–1106. doi:10.1007/s10508-011-9863-9

Perkins, A. B., Becker, J. V., Tehee, M., & Mackelprang, E. (2014). Sexting behaviors among college students: Cause for concern? *International Journal of Sexual Health, 26*(2), 79–92. doi:10.1080/19317611.2013.841792

Perkins, A. M., Inchley-Mort, S. L., Pickering, A. D., Corr, P. J., & Burgess, A. P. (2012). A facial expression for anxiety. *Journal of Personality and Social Psychology, 102*(5), 910–924. doi:10.1037/a0026825

Perkins, D. O., Miller-Anderson, L., & Lieberman, J. A. (2006). Natural history and predictors of clinical course. In J. A. Lieberman, T. S. Stroup, & D. O. Perkins (Eds.), *Textbook of schizophrenia* (pp. 289–302). Washington, DC: American Psychiatric Publishing.

Perkins, K. A., Parzynski, C., Mercincavage, M., Conklin, C. A., & Fonte, C. A. (2012). Is self-efficacy for smoking abstinence a cause of, or a reflection on, smoking behavior change? *Experimental and Clinical Psychopharmacology, 20*(1), 56–62. doi:10.1037/a0025482

Perlis, R. H., Perlis, C. S., Wu, Y., Hwang, C., Joseph, M., & Nierenberg, A. A. (2005). Industry sponsorship and financial conflict of interest in the reporting of clinical trials in psychiatry. *American Journal of Psychiatry, 162*, 1957–1960.

Perlman, D. (2007). The best of times, the worst of times: The place of close relationships in psychology and our daily lives. *Canadian Psychology/Psychologie Canadienne, 48*, 7–18.

Perlman, D., Stevens, N. L., & Carcedo, R. J. (2015). Friendship. In M. Mikulincer, P. R. Shaver, J. A. Simpson, & J. F. Dovidio (Eds.), *APA handbook of personality and social psychology, Vol. 3: Interpersonal relations* (pp. 463–493). Washington, DC: American Psychological Association. doi:10.1037/14344-017

Perloff, R. M. (1993). *The dynamics of persuasion.* Hillsdale, NJ: Erlbaum.

Perreault, S., & Bourhis, R. Y. (1999). Ethnocentrism, social identification, and discrimination. *Personality and Social Psychology Bulletin, 25*(1), 92–103.

Perrin, J. M., MacLean, W. E., Jr., Janco, R. L., & Gortmaker, S. L. (1996). Stress and incidence of bleeding in children and adolescents with hemophilia. *Journal of Pediatrics, 128*(1), 82–88.

Perry, J. C., & Bond, M. (2012). Change in defense mechanisms during long-term dynamic psychotherapy and five-year outcome. *The American Journal of Psychiatry, 169*, 916–925.

Perry-Jenkins, M., Repetti, R. L., & Crouter, A. C. (2001). Work and family in the 1990s. In R. M. Milardo (Ed.), *Understanding families into the new millennium: A decade in review.* Minneapolis, MN: National Council on Family Relations.

Pervin, L. A., & John, O. P. (2001). *Personality: Theory and research.* New York: Wiley.

Peters, M. N., Moscona, J. C., Katz, M. J., Deandrade, K. B., Quevedo, H. C., Tiwari, S., . . . Irimpen, A. M. (2014). Natural disasters and myocardial infarction: The six years after Hurricane Katrina. *Mayo Clinic Proceedings, 89*, 472–477. doi: 10.1016/j.mayocp.2013.12.013

Petersen, J. L., & Hyde, J. (2010a). Gender differences in sexuality. In J. C. Chrisler & D. R. McCreary (Eds.), *Handbook of gender research in psychology, Vol 1: Gender research in general and experimental psychology* (pp. 471–491). New York: Springer Science + Business Media.

Petersen, J. L., & Hyde, J. (2010b). A meta-analytic review of research on gender differences in sexuality, 1993–2007. *Psychological Bulletin, 136*(1), 21–38. doi:10.1037/a0017504

Petersen, J. L., & Hyde, J. (2011). Gender differences in sexual attitudes and behaviors: A review of meta-analytic results and large datasets. *Journal of Sex Research, 48*(2–3), 149–165. doi:10.1080/00224499.2011.551851

Peterson, C. (2006). *A primer in positive psychology.* New York: Oxford University Press.

Peterson, C., Maier, S. F., & Seligman, M. E. P. (1993). *Learned helplessness: A theory for the age of personal control.* New York: Oxford University Press.

Peterson, C., & Park, N. (2010). What happened to self-actualization? Commentary on Kenrick et al. (2010). *Perspectives on Psychological Science, 5*(3), 320–322. doi:10.1177/1745691610369471

Peterson, C., & Seligman, M. E. P. (2003). Positive organizational studies: Thirteen lessons from positive psychology. In K. S. Cameron, J. E. Dutton, & R. E. Quinn (Eds.), *Positive organizational scholarship: Foundations of a new discipline* (pp. 14–27). San Francisco: Berrett-Koehler.

Peterson, C., & Seligman, M. E. P. (2004). *Character strengths and virtues: A handbook and classification.* New York: Oxford University Press/Washington, DC: American Psychological Association.

Peterson, C., Seligman, M. E. P., Yurko, K. H., Martin, L. R., & Friedman, H. S. (1998). Castastrophizing and untimely death. *Psychological Science, 9*, 127–130.

Peterson, C., & Steen, T. A. (2009). Optimistic explanatory style. In S. J. Lopez & C. R. Snyder (Eds.), *Oxford handbook of positive psychology* (2nd ed., pp. 313–321). New York: Oxford University Press.

Peterson, C., & Vaidya, R. S. (2001). Explanatory style, expectations, and depressive symptoms. *Personality and Individual Differences, 31*, 1217–1223.

Peterson, G. W., & Bush, K. R. (2013). Introduction: Balancing connectedness and autonomy in diverse families. In G. W. Peterson & K. R. Bush (Eds.), *Handbook of marriage and the family* (3rd ed.; pp. 1–7). New York: Springer Science + Business Media. doi:10.1007/978-1-4614-3987-5_1

Peterson, S. H., Wingood, G. M., DiClemente, R. J., Davies, S., & Harrington, K. (2007). Images of sexual stereotypes in rap videos and the health of African American female adolescents. *Journal of Women's Health, 16*, 1157–1164.

Petrill, S. A. (2005). Behavioral genetics and intelligence. In O. Wilhelm & R. W. Engle (Eds.), *Handbook of understanding and measuring intelligence.* Thousand Oaks, CA: Sage.

Pettigrew, T. F. (2001). The ultimate attribution error: Extending Allport's cognitive analysis of prejudice. In M. A. Hogg & D. Abrams (Eds.), *Intergroup relations: Essential readings.* New York: Psychology Press.

Pettit, J. W., Lewinsohn, P. M., Seeley, J. R., Roberts, R. E., & Yaroslavsky, I. (2010). Developmental relations between depressive symptoms, minor hassles, and major events from adolescence through age 30 years. *Journal of Abnormal Psychology, 119*, 811–824. doi: 10.1037/a0020980

Petty, R. E., & Briñol, P. (2014). The elaboration likelihood and metacognitive models of attitudes: Implications for prejudice, the self, and beyond. In J. W. Sherman, B. Gawronski, & Y. Trope (Eds.), *Dual-process theories of the social mind* (pp. 172–187). New York: Guilford.

Petty, R. E., & Cacioppo, J. T. (1986). The elaboration likelihood model of persuasion. In L. Berkowitz (Ed.), *Advances in experimental social psychology, Vol. 19.* Orlando, FL: Academic Press.

Petty, R. E., & Cacioppo, J. T. (1990). Involvement and persuasion: Tradition versus integration. *Psychological Bulletin, 107*, 367–374.

Petty, R. E., Fleming, M. A., Priester, J. R., & Feinstein, A. H. (2001). Individual versus group interest violation: Surprise as a determinant of argument scrutiny and persuasion. *Social Cognition, 19*(4), 418–442.

Petty, R. E., Priester, J. R., & Wegener, D. T. (1994). Cognitive processes in attitude change. In R. S. Wyer & T. K. Srull (Eds.), *Handbook of social cognition, Vol. 2.* Hillsdale, NJ: Erlbaum.

Petty, R. E., & Wegener, D. T. (1998). Attitude change: Multiple roles for persuasion variables. In D. T. Gilbert, S. T. Fiske, & G. Lindzey (Eds.), *The handbook of social psychology, Vol. 1* (4th ed.). New York: McGraw-Hill.

Petty, R. E., Wegener, D. T., & Fabrigar, L. R. (1997). Attitudes and attitude change. *Annual Review of Psychology, 48*, 609–647.

Petty, S. C., Sachs-Ericsson, N., & Joiner, Jr., T. E. (2004). Interpersonal functioning deficits: Temporary or stable characteristics of depressed individuals. *Journal of Affective Disorders, 81*(2), 115–122.

Pew Research Center (2013). 10 findings about women in the workplace. Retrieved from www.pewsocialtrends.org/2013/12/11/10-findings-about-women-in-the-workplace

Pew Research Center (2015a, November). Raising kids and running a household: How working parents share the load. Retrieved from www.pewsocialtrends.org/files/2015/11/2015-11-04_working-parents_FINAL.pdf

Pew Research Center (2015b). Couples that live together beforehand are slightly less likely to survive the long haul. Retrieved from www.pewresearch.org/fact-tank/2015/12/04/education-and-marriage/ft_15-12-03-cohabitation-marriage

Pew Research Center (2015c). The American family today. Retrieved from www.pewsocialtrends.org/2015/12/17/1-the-american-family-today

Pfeiffer, B. E., Deval, H., Kardes, F. R., Hirt, E. R., Karpen, S. C., & Fennis, B. M. (2014). No product is perfect: The positive influence of acknowledging the negative. *Thinking & Reasoning, 20*(4), 500–512. doi:10.1080/13546783.2014.939225

Phelan, J. E., Moss-Racusin, C. A., & Rudman, L. A. (2008). Competent yet out in the cold: Shifting criteria for hiring reflect backlash toward agentic women. *Psychology of Women Quarterly, 32*(4), 406–413. doi:10.1111/j.1471-6402.2008.00454.x

Phillips, W. T., Kiernan, M., & King, A. C. (2001). The effects of physical activity on physical and psychological health. In A. Baum, T. A. Revenson, & J. E. Singer (Eds.), *Handbook of health psychology.* Mahwah, NJ: Erlbaum.

Phillips, A. G., & Silvia, P. J. (2010). Individual differences in self-discrepancies and emotional experience: Do distinct discrepancies predict distinct emotions? *Personality and Individual Differences, 49*, 148–151.

Pichenot, M., Deuffic-Burban, S., Cuzin, L., & Yazdanpanah, Y. (2012). Efficacy of new antiretroviral drugs in treatment-experienced HIV-infected patients: A systematic review and meta-analysis of recent randomized controlled trials. *HIV Medicine, 13*(3), 148–155. doi: 10.1111/j.1468-1293.2011.00953.x

Pierce, J. P., Distefan, J. M., Kaplan, R. M., & Gilpin, E. A. (2005). The role of curiosity in smoking initiation. *Addictive Behaviors, 30*, 685–696.

Pietromonaco, P. R., & Beck, L. A. (2015). Attachment processes in adult romantic relationships. In M. Mikulincer, P. R. Shaver, J. A. Simpson, & J. F. Dovidio (Eds.), *APA handbook of personality and social psychology, Vol. 3: Interpersonal relations* (pp. 33–64). Washington, DC: American Psychological Association. doi:10.1037/14344-002

Piff, P. K. (2014). Wealth and the inflated self: Class, entitlement, and narcissism. *Personality and Social Psychology Bulletin, 40*(1), 34–43. doi:10.1177/0146167213501699

Piff, P. K., Dietze, P., Feinberg, M., Stancato, D. M., & Keltner, D. (2015). Awe, the small self, and prosocial behavior. *Journal of Personality and Social Psychology, 108*, 883–889.

Piketty, T. (2014). *Capital in the twenty-first century.* A. Goldhammer (Trans.). Cambridge, MA: The Belknap Press of Harvard University Press.

Pilote, L., Dasgupta, K., Guru, V., Humphries, K. H., McGrath, J., Norris, C., . . . Tagalakis, V. (2007). A comprehensive review of sex-specific issues related to cardiovascular disease. *Canadian Medical Association Journal, 176*(6), S1–S44.

Pina, A., & Gannon, T. A. (2012). An overview of the literature on antecedents, perceptions and behavioural consequences of sexual harassment. *Journal of Sexual Aggression, 18*(2), 209–232. doi:10.1080/13552600.2010.501909

Pinel, J. P. J., Assanand, S., & Lehman, D. R. (2000). Hunger, eating, and ill health. *American Psychologist, 55*, 1105–1116.

Piper, W. E., & Hernandez, C. A. (2013). Group psychotherapies. In G. Stricker & T. A. Widiger (Eds.), *Handbook of psychology, Vol. 8: Clinical psychology* (2nd ed.). New York: Wiley.

Pitt, R. N., & Borland, E. (2008). Bachelorhood and men's attitudes about gender roles. *The Journal of Men's Studies, 16*, 140–158.

Planalp, S., Fitness, J., & Fehr, B. (2006). Emotion in theories of close relationships. In A. L. Vangelisti & D. Perlman (Eds.), *The Cambridge handbook of personal relationships.* New York: Cambridge University Press.

Planned Parenthood Federation of America (2014a). Morning-after pill (emergency contraception). Retrieved from https://www.plannedparenthood.org/learn/morning-after-pill-emergency-contraception

Planned Parenthood Federation of America (2014b). The abortion pill (medication abortion). Retrieved from https://www.plannedparenthood.org/learn/abortion/the-abortion-pill

Plante, T. G., Caputo, D., & Chizmar, L. (2000). Perceived fitness and responses to laboratory induced stress. *International Journal of Stress Management, 7*(1), 61–73.

Platje, E., Popma, A., Vermeiren, R., Doreleijers, T. A. H., Meeus, W. H. J., van Lier, P. A. C., . . . Jansen, L. M. C. (2015). Testosterone and cortisol in relation to aggression in a non-clinical sample of boys and girls. *Aggressive Behavior, 41*(5), 478–487. doi:10.1002/ab.21585

Platow, M. J., & Hunter, J. A. (2014). Necessarily collectivistic. *The Psychologist, 27*(11), 838–841.

Pleck, J. H. (1981). *The myth of masculinity.* Cambridge, MA: MIT Press.

Pleck, J. H. (1995). The gender role strain paradigm: An update. In R. F. Levant & W. S. Pollack (Eds.), *A new psychology of men.* New York: Basic Books.

Pleis, J. R., Lucas, J. W., & Ward, B. W. (2009). Summary health statistics for U.S. adults: National Health Interview Survey, 2008. National Center for Health Statistics. *Vital Health Statistics, 10*(242). Washington, DC: U.S. Government Printing Office.

Plötner, M., Over, H., Carpenter, M., & Tomasello, M. (2015). Young children show the bystander effect in helping situations. *Psychological Science, 26*(4), 499–506. doi:10.1177/0956797615569579

Podsiadlowski, A., Gröschke, D., Kogler, M., Springer, C., & van der Zee, K. (2013). Managing a culturally diverse workforce: Diversity perspectives in organizations. *International Journal of Intercultural Relations, 37*(2), 159–175. doi:10.1016/j.ijintrel.2012.09.001

Polivy, J., & Herman, C. P. (2002). Causes of eating disorder. *Annual Review of Psychology, 53,* 187–213.

Pollak, L. (2007). *Getting from college to career: 90 things to do before you join the real world.* New York: HarperCollins.

Pope, H. G., Gruber, A. J., & Yurgelun-Todd, D. (2001). Residual neuropsychologic effects of cannabis. *Current Psychiatry Report, 3,* 507–512.

Pope, J. (2012). Forgiveness is freedom, says holocaust survivor. *The Times-Picayune,* September 6.

Popkin, B. M. (2012). The changing face of global diet and nutrition. In K. D. Brownell & M. S. Gold (Eds.), *Food and addiction: A comprehensive handbook.* New York: Oxford University Press.

Pornpitakapan, C. (2004). The persuasiveness of source credibility: A critical review of five decades worth of evidence. *Journal of Applied Social Psychology, 34,* 243–281.

Post, R. M., & Altshuler, L. L. (2009). Mood disorders: Treatment of bipolar disorders. In B. J. Sadock, V. A. Sadock, & P. Ruiz (Eds.), *Kaplan & Sadock's comprehensive textbook of psychiatry* (pp. 1743–1812). Philadelphia: Lippincott Williams & Wilkins.

Powell, D. E., & Fine, M. A. (2009). Dissolution of relationships, causes. In H. T. Reis & S. Sprecher (Eds.), *Encyclopedia of human relationships, Vol. 1* (pp. 436–440). Los Angeles: Sage Reference.

Prati, G., & Pietrantoni, L. (2009). Optimism, social support, and coping strategies as factors contributing to posttraumatic growth: A meta-analysis. *Journal of Loss and Trauma, 1,* 364–388.

Pratkanis, A. R., & Aronson, E. (2000). *Age of propaganda: The everyday use and abuse of persuasion.* New York: Freeman.

Prat-Sala, M., & Redford, P. (2010). The interplay between motivation, self-efficacy, and approaches to studying. *British Journal of Educational Psychology, 80*(2), 283–305. doi:10.1348/000709909X480563

Prat-Sala, M., & Redford, P. (2012). Writing essays: Does self-efficacy matter? The relationship between self-efficacy in reading and in writing and undergraduate students' performance in essay writing. *Educational Psychology, 32*(1), 9–20. doi:10.1080/01443410.2011.621411

Pratto, F., & Walker, A. (2004). The bases of gendered power. In A. H. Eagly, A. E. Beall, & R. J. Sternberg (Eds.), *The psychology of gender.* New York: Guilford.

Pressman, S. (1993). *Outrageous betrayal: The real story of Werner Erhard, EST and the Forum.* New York: St. Martin's Press.

Pressman, S. D., & Cohen, S. (2012). Positive emotion word use and longevity in famous deceased psychologists. *Health Psychology, 31,* 297–305. doi: 10.1037/a0025339

Preuper, H. R. S., Boonstra, A. M., Wever, D., Heuts, P. H. T. G., Dekker, J. H. M., Smeets, R. J. E. M., Brouwer, S., Geertzen, J. H. B., & Reneman, M. F. (2011). Differences in the relationship between psychosocial distress and self-reported disability in patients with chronic low back pain in six pain rehabilitation centers in the Netherlands. *Spine, 36,* 969–976.

Prichard, I., Polivy, J., Provencher, V., Herman, C. P., Tiggemann, M., & Cloutier, K. (2015). Brides and young couples: Partners' weight, weight change, and perceptions of attractiveness. *Journal of Social and Personal Relationships, 32*(2), 263–278. doi:10.1177/0265407514529068

Priess, H. A., & Hyde, J. S. (2010). Gender and academic abilities and preferences. In J. C. Chrisler & D. R. McCreary (Eds.), *Handbook of gender research in psychology, Vol. 1* (pp. 297–316). New York: Springer.

Primack, B. A., Douglas, E. L., Fine, M. J., & Dalton, M. A. (2009). Exposure to sexual lyrics and sexual experience among urban adolescents. *American Journal of Preventive Medicine, 36*(4), 317–323. doi:10.1016/j.amepre.2008.11.011

Pritchard, C., & Hansen, L. (2015). Examining undetermined and accidental deaths as source of "under-reported-suicide" by age and sex in twenty Western countries. *Community Mental Health Journal, 51*(3), 365–376. doi:10.1007/s10597-014-9810-z

Prochnau, W., & Parker, L. (2010). *Miracle on the Hudson: The extraordinary real-life story behind flight 1549, by the survivors.* New York: Ballantine.

Pronin, E. (2008). How we see ourselves and how we see others. *Science, 320*(5880), 1177–1180. doi:10.1126/science.1154199

Pronin, E. (2013). When the mind races: Effects of thought speed on feeling and action. *Current Directions In Psychological Science, 22*(4), 283–288.

Pronin, E., Berger, J., & Moluki, S. (2007). Alone in a crowd of sheep: Asymmetric perceptions of conformity and their roots in an introspection illusion. *Journal of Personality and Social Psychology, 92,* 585–595.

Pronin, E., & Jacobs, E. (2008). Thought speed, mood, and the experience of mental motion. *Perspectives on Psychological Science, 3,* 461–485.

Pronin, E., Jacobs, E., & Wegner, D. M. (2008). Psychological effects of thought acceleration. *Emotion, 8,* 597–612.

Pronin, E., & Wegner, D. M. (2006). Independent effects of thought speed and thought content on mood. *Psychological Science, 17,* 807–813.

Prot, S., Gentile, D. A., Anderson, C. A., Suzuki, K., Swing, E., Lim, K. M., . . . Lam, B. C. P. (2014). Long-term relations among prosocial-media use, empathy, and prosocial behavior. *Psychological Science, 25*(2), 358–368.

Prudic, J. (2009). Electroconvulsive therapy. In B. J. Sadock, V. A. Sadock, & P. Ruiz (Eds.), *Kaplan & Sadock's comprehensive textbook of psychiatry* (pp. 3285–3300). Philadelphia: Lippincott Williams & Wilkins.

Pryor, F. L., & Schaffer, D. (1997, July). Wages and the university educated: A paradox resolved. *Monthly Labor Review,* 3–14.

Pseekos, A., Bullock-Yowell, E., & Dahlen, E. R. (2011). Examining Holland's person-environment fit, workplace aggression, interpersonal conflict, and job satisfaction. *Journal of Employment Counseling, 48*(2), 63–71. doi:10.1002/j.2161-1920.2011.tb00115.x

Puentes, J., Knox, D., & Zusman, M. E. (2008). Participants in "friends with benefits" relationships. *College Student Journal, 42,* 176–180.

Puurtinen, M., Heap, S., & Mappes, T. (2015). The joint emergence of group competition and within-group cooperation. *Evolution and Human Behavior, 36*(3), 211–217. doi:10.1016/j.evolhumbehav.2014.11.005

Pyc, M. A., Agarwal, P. K., & Roediger, H. I. (2014). Test-enhanced learning. In V. A. Benassi, C. E. Overson, & C. M. Hakala (Eds.), *Applying science of learning in education: Infusing psychological science into the curriculum.* Washington, DC: Society for the Teaching of Psychology.

Pyszczynski, T., Solomon, S., & Greenberg, J. (2003). *In the wake of 9/11: The psychology of terror.* Washington, DC: American Psychological Association.

Pyszczynski, T., Sullivan, D., & Greenberg, J. (2015). Experimental existential psychology: Living in the shadow of the facts of life. In M. Mikulincer, P. R. Shaver, E. Borgida, & J. A. Bargh (Eds.), *APA handbook of personality and social psychology, Vol. 1: Attitudes and social cognition.* Washington, DC: American Psychological Association.

Quick, B. L., Shen, L., & Dillard, J. P. (2013). Reactance theory and persuasion. In J. P. Dillard & L. Shen (Eds.), *The Sage handbook of persuasion: Developments in theory and practice* (2nd ed.; pp. 167–183). Thousand Oaks, CA: Sage.

Quoidbach, J., Mikolajczak, M., & Gross, J. J. (2015). Positive interventions: An emotion regulation perspective. *Psychological Bulletin, 141*(3), 655–693. doi:10.1037/a0038648

Rabelo, V. C., & Cortina, L. M. (2014). Two sides of the same coin: Gender harassment and heterosexist harassment in LGBQ work lives. *Law and Human Behavior, 38*(4), 378–391. doi:10.1037/lhb0000087

Rachman, S. J. (2009). Psychological treatment of anxiety: The evolution of behavior therapy and cognitive behavior therapy. *Annual Review of Clinical Psychology, 5,* 97–119.

Rae, K., & Sands, J. (2013). Using classroom layout to help reduce students' apprehension and increase communication. *Accounting Education, 22*(5), 489–491. doi:10.1080/09639284.2013.835534

Rahe, R. H., & Arthur, R. H. (1978). Life change and illness studies. *Journal of Human Stress, 4,* 3–15.

Rahim, M. A., & Magner, N. R. (1995). Confirmatory factor analysis of the styles of handling interpersonal conflict: First-order factor model and its invariance across groups. *Journal of Applied Psychology, 80,* 122–132.

Raikes, H. A., & Thompson R. A. (2008). Attachment security and parenting quality predict children's problem-solving, attributions, and loneliness with peers. *Attachment & Human Development, 10,* 319–344.

Rakel, D., Barrett, B., Zhang, Z., Hoeft, T., Chewning, B., Marchand, L., & Scheder, J. (2011). Perception of empathy in the therapeutic encounter: Effects on the common cold. *Patient Education & Counseling, 85*(3), 390–397. doi:10.1016/j.pec.2011.01.009

Ramaekers, J. G., Robbe, H. W. J., & O'Hanlon, J. F. (2000). Marijuana, alcohol and actual driving performance. *Human Psychopharmacology Clinical & Experimental, 15*(7), 551–558.

Ramanathan, S., & Williams, P. (2007). Immediate and delayed emotional consequences of indulgence: The moderating influence of personality type on mixed emotions. *Journal of Consumer Research, 34,* 212–223.

Ramirez, A., Sumner, E. M., Fleuriet, C., & Cole, M. (2015). When online dating partners meet offline: The effect of modality switching on relational communication between online daters. *Journal of Computer-Mediated Communication, 20*(1), 99–114. doi:10.1111/jcc4.12101

Rand, K. L., & Cheavens, J. S. (2009). Hope theory. In S. J. Lopez & C. R. Snyder (Eds.), *Oxford handbook of positive psychology* (2nd ed., pp. 323–333). New York: Oxford University Press.

Rapoport, J. L., Giedd, J. N., & Gogtay, N. (2012). Neurodevelopmental model of schizophrenia: Update 2012. *Molecular Psychiatry, 17,* 1228–1238. doi:10.1038/mp.2012.23

Raskin, N. J., Rogers, C. R., & Witty, M. C. (2011). Client-centered therapy. In R. J. Corsini & D. Wedding (Eds.), *Current psychotherapies* (9th ed.). Belmont, CA: Brooks/Cole.

Raskin, R., & Hall, C. S. (1979). A narcissistic personality inventory. *Psychological Reports, 40,* 590.

Raskin, R., & Hall, C. S. (1981). The Narcissistic Personality Inventory: Alternate form reliability and further evidence of construct validity. *Journal of Personality Assessment, 45,* 159–162.

Rassin, E. (2008). Individual differences in susceptibility to conformation bias. *Netherlands Journal of Psychology, 64*(2), 87–93.

Rathunde, K. (1988). Optimal experience and the family context. In M. Csikszentmihalyi & I. S. Csikszentmihalyi (Eds.), *Optimal experience* (pp. 342–363). Cambridge, UK: Cambridge University Press.

Raub, S., & Liao, H. (2012). Doing the right thing without being told: Joint effects of initiative climate and general self-efficacy on employee proactive customer service performance. *Journal of Applied Psychology, 97,* 651–667. doi:10.1037/a0026736

Ravindran, L. N., & Stein, M. B. (2009). Anxiety disorders: Somatic treatment. In B. J. Sadock, V. A. Sadock, & P. Ruiz (Eds.), *Kaplan & Sadock's comprehensive textbook of psychiatry* (pp. 1906–1914). Philadelphia: Lippincott Williams & Wilkins.

Ravizza, S. M., Hambrick, D. Z., & Fenn, K. M. (2014). Non-academic Internet use in the classroom is negatively related to classroom learning regardless of intellectual ability. *Computers & Education, 78,* 109–114. doi:10.1016/j.compedu.2014.05.007.

Ray, G. E., Cohen, R., Secrist, M. E., & Duncan, M. K. (1997). Relating aggressive and victimization behaviors to children's sociometric status and friendships. *Journal of Social and Personal Relationships, 14*(1), 95–108.

Read, J., Cartwright, C., & Gibson, K. (2014). Adverse emotional and interpersonal effects reported by 1829 New Zealanders while taking antidepressants. *Psychiatry Research, 21, 6*(1), 67–73. doi:10.1016/j.psychres.2014.01.042

Reardon, R. C., Lenz, J. G., Sampson, J. P., Jr., & Peterson, G. W. (2009). *Career development and planning: A comprehensive approach.* Belmont, CA: Cengage.

Reece, M., Herbenick, D., Sanders, S. A., Dodge, B. Ghassemi, A., & Fortenberry, J. D. (2009). Prevalence and characteristics of vibrator use by men in the United States. *Journal of Sexual Medicine, 6,* 1867–1874.

Reece, M., Herbenick, D., Schick, V., Sanders, S. A., Dodge, B., & Fortenberry, J. D. (2010). Sexual behaviors, relationships, and perceived health among adult men in the United States: Results from a national probability sample. *Journal of Sexual Medicine, 7*(5), 291–304.

Rees, C. J., & Metcalfe, B. (2003). The faking of personality questionnaire results: Who's kidding whom. *Journal of Managerial Psychology, 18,* 156–165.

Regan, P. C., & Berscheid, E. (1997). Gender differences in characteristics desired in potential sexual and marriage partners. *Journal of Psychology and Human Sexuality, 9*(1), 25–37.

Reger, G. M., Holloway, K. M., Candy, C., Rothbaum, B. O., Difede, J., Rizzo, A. A., & Gahm, G. A. (2011). Effectiveness of virtual reality exposure therapy for active duty soldiers in a military mental health clinic. *Journal of Traumatic Stress, 24*(1), 93–96. doi:10.1002/jts.20574

Regnerus, M. D. (2007). *Forbidden fruit: Sex and religion in the lives of American teenagers.* New York: Oxford Press.

Rehman, U. S., Rellini, A. H., & Fallis, E. (2011). The importance of sexual self-disclosure to sexual satisfaction and functioning in committed relationships. *Journal of Sexual Medicine, 8*(11), 3108–3115. doi:10.1111/j.1743-6109.2011.02439.x

Reicher, S., & Haslam, S. A. (2014). Camps, conflict and collectivism. *The Psychologist, 27*(11), 826–828.

Reid, M., Miller, W., & Kerr, B. (2004). Sex-based glass ceilings in U.S. state-level bureaucracies, 1987–1997. *Administration and Society, 36,* 377–405.

Reidy, D. E., Brookmeyer, K. A., Gentile, B., Berke, D. S., & Zeichner, A. (2015). Gender role discrepancy stress, high-risk sexual behavior, and sexually transmitted disease. *Archives of Sexual Behavior.* doi:10.1007/s10508-014-0413-0

Reilly, D., & Neumann, D. L. (2013). Gender-role differences in spatial ability: A meta-analytic review. *Sex Roles, 68*(9–10), 521–535. doi:10.1007/s11199-013-0269-0

Reis, H. T., & Carothers, B. J. (2014). Black and white or shades of gray: Are gender differences categorical or dimensional? *Current Directions in Psychological Science, 23*(1), 19–26. doi:10.1177/0963721413504105

Reis, H. T., & Holmes, J. G. (2012). Perspectives on the situation. In K. Deaux & M. Snyder (Eds.), *The Oxford handbook of personality and social psychology* (pp. 64–92). New York: Oxford University Press.

Reis, H. T., & Patrick. B. C. (1996). Attachment and intimacy: Component processes. In E. T. Higgins & A. Kruglanski (Eds.), *Social psychology: Handbook of basic principles.* New York: Guilford.

Reis, H. T., & Shaver, P. (1988). Intimacy as an interpersonal process. In S. W. Duck (Ed.), *Handbook of personal relationships.* New York: Wiley.

Reis, T. J., Gerrard, M., & Gibbons, F. X. (1993). Social comparison and the pill: Reactions to upward and downward comparison of contraceptive behavior. *Personality and Social Psychology Bulletin, 19,* 13–21.

Reissman, C., Aron, A., & Bergen, M. R. (1993). Shared activities and marital satisfaction: Causal direction and self-expansion versus boredom. *Journal of Social and Personal Relationships, 10,* 243–254.

Rennison, C. M., & Welchans, S. (2000). *Intimate partner violence.* Washington, DC: U.S. Department of Justice, Office of Justice Programs, Bureau of Justice Statistics.

Repetti, R. L., & Wang, S. (2009). Work-family spillover. In H. T. Reis & S. Sprecher (Eds.), *Encyclopedia of human relationships, Vol. 3* (pp. 1694–1697). Los Angeles: Sage Reference.

Reynolds, G. (2012, June 12). An argument for the slow-but-steady approach. *New York Times,* D5.

Reynolds, G. (2015, July 28). Piece of nature, peace of mind: A walk in the park can help city dwellers' mental health. *New York Times,* D6.

Rhoades, G. K., Stanley, S. M., Markman, H. J., & Ragan, E. P. (2012). Parents' marital status, conflict, and role modeling: Links with adult romantic relationship quality. *Journal of Divorce and Remarriage, 53*(5), 348–367. doi:10.1080/10502556.2012.675838

Riccardi, N. (2011, June 22). Self-help guru convicted in Arizona sweat lodge deaths. *Los Angeles Times.* Retrieved from http://articles.latimes.com/2011/jun/22/nation/la-na-sweat-lodge-trial-20110623

Rice, J. K., & Else-Quest, N. (2006). The mixed messages of motherhood. In J. Worrell & C. D. Goodheart (Eds.), *Handbook of girls' and women's psychological health.* New York: Oxford University Press.

Rice, K. G., Richardson, C. E., & Clark, D. (2012). Perfectionism, procrastination, and psychological distress. *Journal of Counseling Psychology, 59*(2), 288–302. doi:10.1037/a0026643

Rich, G. J. (2014). Positive institutions, communities, and nations: Methods and internationalizing positive psychology concepts. In H. Águeda Marujo, & L. M. Neto (Eds.), *Positive nations and communities: Collective, qualitative and cultural-sensitive processes in positive psychology* (pp. 17–32). New York: Springer Science + Business Media. doi:10.1007/978-94-007-6869-7_2

Richard, N. T., & Wright, S. C. (2010). Advantaged group members' reactions to tokenism. *Group Processes & Intergroup Relations, 13*(5), 559–569. doi:10.1177/1368430210362227

Richardson, C. R., Kriska, A. M., Lantz, P. M., & Hayword, R. A. (2004). Physical activity and mortality across cardiovascular disease risk groups. *Medicine and Science in Sports and Exercise, 36*(11), 1923–1929.

Richardson, D. S. (2014). Everyday aggression takes many forms. *Current Directions in Psychological Science, 23*(3), 220–224. doi:10.1177/0963721414530143

Richardson, F. C., & Guignon, C. B. (2008). Positive psychology and philosophy of social science. *Theory & Psychology, 18,* 605–627.

Richardson, H. B., Moyer, A. M., & Goldberg, A. E. (2012). "You try to be superman and you don't have to be": Gay adoptive fathers' challenges and tensions in balancing work and family. *Fathering: A Journal of Theory, Research, and Practice about Men as Fathers, 10*(3), 314–336. doi:10.3149/fth.1003.314

Richmond, V. P., & McCroskey, J. C. (1995). *Communication: Apprehension, avoidance, and effectiveness* (5th ed.). Boston: Allyn & Bacon.

Rick, S. I., Small, D. A., & Finkel, E. J. (2011). Fatal (fiscal) attraction: Spendthrifts and tightwads in marriage. *Journal of Marketing Research, 48*(2), 228–237. doi:10.1509/jmkr.48.2.228

Ridgeway, C. L., & Bourg, C. (2004). Gender as status: An expectation states theory approach. In A. H. Eagly, A. E. Beall, & R. J. Sternberg (Eds.), *The psychology of gender.* New York: Guilford.

Rieger, S., Göllner, R., Trautwein, U., & Roberts, B. W. (2015). low self-esteem prospectively predicts depression in the transition to young adulthood: A replication of Orth, Robins, and Roberts (2008). *Journal of Personality and Social Psychology.* doi:10.1037/pspp0000037

Riek, B. M., & Mania, E. W. (2012). The antecedents and consequences of interpersonal forgiveness: A meta-analytic review. *Personal Relationships, 19*(2), 304–325.

Righetti, F., Rusbult, C., & Finkenauer, C. (2010). Regulatory focus and the Michelangelo phenomenon: How close partners promote one another's ideal selves. *Journal of Experimental Social Psychology, 46*(6), 972–985. doi:10.1016/j.jesp.2010.06.001

Riis, J., Loewenstein, G., Baron, J., Jepson, C., Fagerlin, A., & Ubel, P. A. (2005). Ignorance of hedonic adaptation to hemodialysis: A study using ecological momentary assessment. *Journal of Experimental Psychology: General, 134,* 3–9.

Riley, B., & Kendler, K. S. (2011). Classical genetic studies of schizophrenia. In D. R. Weinberger & P. Harrison (Eds.), *Schizophrenia* (3rd ed.). Malden, MA: Wiley-Blackwell.

Riley, K., & Park, C. L. (2014). Problem-focused vs. meaning-focused coping as mediators of the appraisal-adjustment relationship in chronic stressors. *Journal of Social and Clinical Psychology, 33*(7), 587–611. doi:10.1521/jscp.2014.33.7.587

Ringström, G., Abrahamsson, H., Strid, H., & Simŕen, M. (2007). Why do subjects with irritable bowel syndrome seek health care for their symptoms? *Scandinavian Journal of Gastroenterology, 42,* 1194–1203.

Risch, N., Hoffmann, T. J., Anderson, M., Croen, L. A., Grether, J. K., & Windham, G. C. (2014). Familial recurrence of autism spectrum disorder: Evaluating genetic and environmental contributions. *The American Journal of Psychiatry, 171,* 1206–1213. doi:10.1176/appi.ajp.2014.13101359

Riskey, D. R., & Birnbaum, M. H. (1974). Compensatory effects in moral judgment: Two rights don't make up for a wrong. *Journal of Experimental Psychology, 103,* 171–173.

Ritchart, R., & Perkins, D. N. (2002). Life in the mindful classroom: Nurturing the disposition of mindfulness. *Journal of Social Issues, 56*(1), 27–47.

Roberson, L., Kulik, C. T., & Tan, R. Y. (2013). Effective diversity training. In Q. M. Roberson (Ed.), *The Oxford handbook of diversity and work* (pp. 341–365). New York: Oxford University Press.

Roberts, B. W., Caspi, A., & Moffitt, T. (2003). Work experiences and personality development in young adulthood. *Journal of Personality and Social Psychology, 84,* 582–593.

Roberts, B. W., Jackson, J. J., Fayard, J. V., Edmonds, G., & Meints, J. (2009). Conscientiousness. In M. R. Leary & R. H. Hoyle (Eds.), *Handbook of individual differences in social behavior* (pp. 369–381). New York: Guilford.

Roberts, B. W., Kuncel, N. R., Shiner, R., Caspi, A., & Goldberg, L. R. (2007). The power of personality: The comparative validity of personality traits, socioeconomic status, and cognitive ability for predicting important life outcomes. *Perspectives on Psychological Science, 2,* 313–345.

Roberts, C. J., Campbell, I. C., & Troop, N. (2014). Increases in weight during chronic stress are partially associated with a switch in food choice towards increased carbohydrate and saturated fat intake. *European Eating Disorders Review, 22*(1), 77–82. doi:10.1002/erv.2264

Roberts, M. E., Tchanturia, K., & Treasure, J. L. (2010). Exploring the neurocognitive signature of poor set-shifting in anorexia and bulimia nervosa. *Journal of Psychiatric Research, 44,* 964–970. doi:10.1016/j.jpsychires.2010.03.001

Robertson, B. R., Prestia, D., Twamley, E. W., Patterson, T. L., Bowie, C. R., & Harvey, P. D. (2014). Social competence versus negative symptoms as predictors of real world social functioning in schizophrenia. *Schizophrenia Research, 160*(1–3), 136–141. doi:10.1016/j.schres.2014.10.037

Robertson-Kraft, C., & Duckworth, A. (2014). True grit: Trait-level perseverance and passion for long-term goals predicts effectiveness and retention among novice teachers. *Teachers College Record, 116*(3), 1–27.

Robins, R. W., Mendelsohn, G. A., Connell, J. B., & Kwan, V. S. Y. (2004). Do people agree about the causes of behavior? A social relations analysis of behavior ratings and causal attribution. *Journal of Personality and Social Psychology, 86,* 334–344.

Robinson, B. E., Flowers, C., & Ng, K. (2006). The relationship between workaholism and marital disaffection: Husband's perspective. *Family Journal: Counseling and Therapy for Couples and Families, 14,* 213–220.

Robitaille, C., & Saint-Jacques, M. (2009). Social stigma and the situation of young people in lesbian and gay stepfamilies. *Journal of Homosexuality, 56*(4), 421–442. doi:10.1080/00918360902821429

Robles, T. F. (2014). Marital quality and health: Implications for marriage in the 21st century. *Current Directions in Psychological Science, 23*(6), 427–432. doi:10.1177/0963721414549043

Rodin, J., Schank, D., & Striegel-Moore, R. H. (1989). Psychological features of obesity. *Medical Clinics of North America, 73,* 47–66.

Roediger, H. L., III, Agarwal, P. K., Kang, S. K., & Marsh, E. J. (2010). Benefits of testing memory: Best practices and boundary conditions. In G. M. Davies & D. B. Wright (Eds.), *Current issues in applied memory research* (pp. 13–49). New York: Psychology Press.

Roediger, H. L., III, & Karpicke, J. D. (2006). Test-enhanced learning: Taking memory tests improves long-term retention. *Psychological Science, 17,* 249–255.

Roepke, A. M. (2015). Psychosocial interventions and posttraumatic growth: A meta-analysis. *Journal of Consulting and Clinical Psychology, 83*(1), 129–142. doi:10.1037/a0036872

Rogers, C. R. (1951). *Client-centered therapy: Its current practice, implications, and theory.* Boston: Houghton Mifflin.

Rogers, C. R. (1961). *On becoming a person: A therapist's view of psychotherapy.* Boston: Houghton Mifflin.

Rogers, C. R. (1986). Client-centered therapy. In I. L. Kutash & A. Wolf (Eds.), *Psychotherapist's casebook.* San Francisco: Jossey-Bass.

Rohde, P., Lewinsohn, P. M., Klein, D. N., Seeley, J. R., & Gau, J. M. (2013). Key characteristics of major depressive disorder occurring in childhood, adolescence, emerging adulthood, and adulthood. *Clinical Psychological Science, 1*(1), 41–53. doi:10.1177/2167702612457599

Rohner, J., & Rasmussen, A. (2012). Recognition bias and the physical attractiveness stereotype. *Scandinavian Journal of Psychology, 53*(3), 239–246. doi:10.1111/j.1467-9450.2012.00939.x

Rohner, R. P., & Veneziano, R. A. (2001). The importance of father love: History and contemporary evidence. *Review of General Psychology, 5*(4), 382–405.

Rohrer, D., Taylor, K., Pashler, H., Wixted, J. T., & Capeda, N. J. (2005). The effect of overlearning on long-term retention. *Applied Cognitive Psychology, 19,* 361–374.

Rollie, S. S., & Duck, S. (2006). Divorce and dissolution of romantic relationships. In M. A. Fine & J. H. Harvey (Eds.), *Handbook of divorce and relationship resolution.* Mahwah, NJ: Erlbaum.

Rook, K. S. (1998). Investigating the positive and negative sides of personal relationships: Through a lens darkly? In B. H. Spitzberg & W. R. Cupach (Eds.), *The dark side of close relationships.* Mahwah, NJ: Lawrence Erlbaum.

Rook, K. S. (2015). Social networks in later life: Weighing positive and negative effects on health and well-being. *Current Directions in Psychological Science, 24*(1), 45–51. doi:10.1177/0963721414551364

Rook, K. S., August, K. J., & Sorkin, D. H. (2011). Social network functions and health. In R. J. Contrada & A. Baum (Eds.), *The handbook of stress science: Biology, psychology, and health* (pp. 123–135). New York: Springer.

Rosario, M., & Schrimshaw, E. W. (2014). Theories and etiologies of sexual orientation. In D. L. Tolman, L. M. Diamond, J. A. Bauermeister, W. H. George, J. G. Pfaus, L. M. Ward (Eds.), *APA handbook of sexuality and psychology,* (pp. 555–596). Washington, DC: American Psychological Association. doi:10.1037/14193-018

Rose, D., Wykes, T., Leese, M., Bindman, J., & Fleischmann, P. (2003). Patient's perspectives on electroconvulsive therapy: Systematic review. *British Medical Journal, 326,* 1363–1365.

Rose, D. P. (1997). Dietary fatty acids and cancer. *American Journal of Clinical Nutrition, 66*(4), 998S–1003S.

Rose-Greenland, F., & Smock, P. J. (2013). Living together unmarried: What do we know about cohabiting families? In G. W. Peterson & K. R. Bush (Eds.), *Handbook of marriage and the family* (3rd ed.) (pp. 255–273). New York: Springer Science + Business Media. doi:10.1007/978-1-4614-3987-5_12

Rosen, G. M., Glasgow, R. E., Moore, T. E., & Barrera, M. J. (2015). Self-help therapy: Recent developments in the science and business of giving psychology away. In S. O. Lilienfeld, S. J. Lynn, & J. M. Lohr (Eds.), *Science and pseudoscience in clinical psychology* (2nd ed.; pp. 245–274). New York: Guilford.

Rosen, R. D. (1977). *Psychobabble.* New York: Atheneum.

Rosenbaum, J. E. (2009). Patient teenagers? A comparison of the sexual behavior of virginity pledgers and matched nonpledgers. *Pediatrics, 123,* 110–120.

Rosenman, R. H. (1993). Relationships of the Type A behavior pattern with coronary heart disease. In L. Goldberger & S. Breznitz (Eds.), *Handbook of stress: Theoretical and clinical aspects* (2nd ed.). New York: Free Press.

Rosenthal, H. (1988). *Not with my life I don't: Preventing suicide and that of others.* Muncie, IN: Accelerated Development.

Rosenthal, R. (2006). Applying psychological research on interpersonal expectations and covert communication in classrooms, clinics, corporations, and courtrooms. In S. I. Donaldson, D. E. Berger, & K. Pedzek (Eds.), *Applied psychology: New frontiers and rewarding careers.* Mahwah, NJ: Erlbaum.

Rospenda, K. M., Fujishiro, K., Shannon, C. A., & Richman, J. A. (2008). Workplace harassment, stress, and drinking behavior over time: Gender differences in a national sample. *Addictive Behaviors, 33*(7), 964–967.

Rospenda, K. M., Richman, J. A., Shannon, C. A. (2009). Prevalence and mental health correlates of harassment and discrimination in the workplace: Results from a national study. *Journal of Interpersonal Violence, 24*(5), 819–843.

Ross, C. A., & Ness, L. (2010). Symptom patterns in dissociative identity disorder patients and the general population. *Journal of Trauma & Dissociation, 11,* 458–468. doi:10.1080/15299732.2010.495939

Ross, L. D. (1977). The intuitive psychologist and his shortcomings: Distortions in the attribution process. In L. Berkowitz (Ed.), *Advances in experimental social psychology, Vol. 10.* New York: Academic Press.

Ross, M., & Wilson, A. E. (2002). It feels like yesterday: Self-esteem, valence of personal past experiences, and judgments of subjective distance. *Journal of Personality and Social Psychology, 82,* 792–803.

Roth, M. E., Gillis, J. M., & DiGennaro Reed, F. D. (2014). A meta-analysis of behavioral interventions for adolescents and adults with autism spectrum disorders. *Journal of Behavioral Education, 23*(2), 258–286. doi:10.1007/s10864-013-9189-x

Roth, P. L., BeVier, C. A., Switzer, F. S., & Schippmann, J. S. (1996). Meta-analyzing the relationship between grades and job performance. *Journal of Applied Psychology, 81*(5), 548–556.

Roth, P. L., & Clarke, R. L. (1998). Meta-analyzing the relationship between grades and salary. *Journal of Vocational Behavior, 53,* 386–400,

Rothberg, B., & Feinsten, R. E. (2014). Suicide. In J. L. Cutler (Ed.), *Psychiatry* (3rd ed.). New York: Oxford University Press.

Roughton, B. (2001, May 27). In Europe, workers' time off adds up. *The Atlanta Journal-Constitution,* pp. D1–D2.

Rounding, K., Lee, A., Jacobson, J. A., & Ji, L. (2012). Religion replenishes self-control. *Psychological Science, 23*(6), 635–642. doi:10.1177/0956797611431987

Rowa, K., & Antony, M. M. (2008). Generalized anxiety disorders. In W. E. Craighead, D. J. Miklowitz, & L. W. Craighead (Eds.), *Psychopathology: History, diagnosis, and empirical foundations.* New York: Wiley.

Rowatt, W. C., Shen, M. J., LaBouff, J. P., & Gonzalez, A. (2013). Religious fundamentalism, right-wing authoritarianism, and prejudice: Insights from meta-analyses, implicit social cognition, and social neuroscience. In R. F. Paloutzian & C. L. Park (Eds.), *Handbook of the psychology of religion and spirituality* (2nd ed.; pp. 457–475). New York: Guilford.

Rowny, S., & Lisanby, S. H. (2008). Brain stimulation in psychiatry. In A. Tasman, J. Kay, J. A. Lieberman, M. B. First, & M. Maj (Eds.), *Psychiatry* (3rd ed.). New York: Wiley-Blackwell.

Roy-Matton, N., Moutquin, J. M., Brown, C., Carrier, N., & Bell, L. (2011). The impact of perceived maternal stress and other psychosocial risk factors on pregnancy complications. *Journal of Obstetrics and Gynaecology Canada, 33*(4), 344–352.

Rubenstein, C. M., & Shaver, P. (1982). The experience of loneliness. In L. A. Peplau & D. Perlman (Eds.), *Loneliness: A sourcebook of current theory, research and therapy.* New York: Wiley.

Rubie-Davies, C. M., Peterson, E. R., Sibley, C. G., & Rosenthal, R. (2015). A teacher expectation intervention: Modeling the practices of high expectation teachers. *Contemporary Educational Psychology, 40,* 72–85. doi:10.1016/j.cedpsych.2014.03.003

Rubin, R. H. (2001). Alternative lifestyles revisited, or whatever happened to swingers, group marriages, and communes? *Journal of Family Issues, 22,* 711–726.

Rubin, Z., Peplau, L. A., & Hill, C. T. (1981). Loving and leaving: Sex differences in romantic attachments. *Sex Roles, 7,* 821–835.

Ruis, C., Postma, A., Bouvy, W., & van der Ham, I. (2015). Cognitive disorders after sporadic ecstasy use? A case report. *Neurocase, 21*(3), 351–357.

Ruiz, P., & Strain, E. C. (2011). *Lowinson and Ruiz's substance abuse: A comprehensive textbook* (5th ed.). Philadelphia: Wolters Kluwer Lippincott Williams & Wilkins.

Rupert, P. A., Miller, A. O., & Dorociak, K. E. (2015). Preventing burnout: What does the research tell us? *Professional Psychology: Research and Practice, 46*(3), 168–174. doi:10.1037/a0039297

Rupp, H. A., & Wallen, K. (2009). Sex-specific content preferences for visual sexual stimuli. *Archives of Sexual Behavior, 38,* 417–426.

Rüsch, N., Corrigan, P. W., Heekeren, K., Theodoridou, A., Dvorsky, D., Metzler, S., . . . Rössler, W. (2014). Well-being among persons at risk of psychosis: The role of self-labeling, shame, and stigma stress. *Psychiatric Services, 65,* 483–489. doi:10.1176/appi.ps.201300169

Rush, A. J. (1984). Cognitive therapy. In T. B. Karasu (Ed.), *The psychiatric therapies.* Washington, DC: American Psychiatric Association.

Russell, N. C. (2011). Milgram's obedience to authority experiments: Origins and early evolution. *British Journal of Social Psychology, 50*(1), 140–162. doi:10.1348/014466610X492205

Rutkowski, E. M., & Connelly, C. D. (2012). Self-efficacy and physical activity in adolescent and parent dyads. *Journal for Specialists in Pediatric Nursing, 17,* 51–60. doi:10.1111/j.1744-6155.2011.00314.x

Rutter, M. (2012). Gene–environment interdependence. *European Journal of Developmental Psychology, 9,* 391–412. doi:10.1080/17405629.2012.661174

Ruvio, A., Somer, E., & Rindfleisch, A. (2014). When bad gets worse: The amplifying effect of materialism on traumatic stress and maladaptive consumption. *Journal of the Academy of Marketing Science, 42,* 90–101. doi: 10.1007/s11747-013-0345-6

Ruz, M., & Tudela, P. (2011). Emotional conflict in interpersonal interactions. *Neuroimage, 54*(2), 1685–1691. doi:10.1016/j.neuroimage.2010.08.039

Ryan, K. M., King, E. B., Adis, C., Gulick, L. V., Peddie, C., & Hargraves, R. (2012). Exploring the asymmetrical effects of gender tokenism on supervisor–subordinate relationships. *Journal of Applied Social Psychology, 42*(Suppl. 1), E56–E102. doi:10.1111/j.1559-1816.2012.01025.x

Ryan, M. P. (2008). The antidepressant effects of physical activity: Mediating self-esteem and self-efficacy mechanisms. *Psychology and Health, 23,* 279–307.

Ryan, W. S., Legate, N., & Weinstein, N. (2015). Coming out as lesbian, gay, or bisexual: The lasting impact of initial disclosure experiences. *Self and Identity, 14*(5), 549–569. doi: 10.1080/15298868.2015.1029516

Rye, M. S., Folck, C. D., Heim, T. A., Olszewski, B. T., & Traina, E. (2004). Forgiveness of an ex-spouse: How does it relate to mental health following a divorce? *Journal of Divorce and Remarriage, 41,* 31–51.

Ryff, C. D., & Singer, B. (2003). Flourishing under fire: Resilience as a prototype of challenged thriving. In C. L. M. Keyes & J. Haidt (Eds.), *Flourishing: Positive psychology and the life well-lived* (pp. 15–36). Washington, DC: American Psychological Association.

Saad, L. (2007). Americans rate the morality of 16 social issues. Retrieved from www.galluppoll.com/content/?ci=27757&p=1

Saad, L. (2015). Fewer young people say I do—to any relationship. Retrieved from www.gallup.com/poll/183515/fewer-young-people-say-relationship.aspx

Sachdev, P. S. (2013). Is DSM-5 defensible? *Australian and New Zealand Journal of Psychiatry, 47*(1), 10–11. doi:10.1177/0004867412468164

Sackeim, H. A. (2014). Autobiographical memory and electroconvulsive therapy: Do not throw out the baby. *The Journal of ECT, 30*(3), 177–186. doi:10.1097/YCT.0000000000000117

Sackeim, H. A., Dillingham, E. M., Prudic, J., Cooper, T., McCall, W. V., Rosenquist, P., . . . Haskett, R. F. (2009). Effect of concomitant pharmacotherapy on electroconvulsive therapy outcomes: Short-term efficacy and adverse effects. *Archives of General Psychiatry, 66*(7), 729–737.

Saddleson, M. L., Kozlowski, L. T., Giovino, G. A., Hawk, L. W., Murphy, J. M., MacLean, M. G., . . . Mahoney, M. C. (2015). Risky behaviors, e-cigarette use and susceptibility of use among college students. *Drug and Alcohol Dependence, 149,* 25–30. doi:10.1016/j.drugalcdep.2015.01.001

Sadock, B. J., Sadock, V. A., & Ruiz, P. (2015). *Kaplan and Sadock's synopsis of psychiatry: Behavioral sciences/clinical psychiatry* (11th ed.). Philadelphia: Wolters Kluwer.

Salas-Wright, C. P., Robles, E. H., Vaughn, M. G., Córdova, D., & Pérez-Figueroa, R. E. (2015). Toward a typology of acculturative stress: Results among Hispanic immigrants in the United States.

Hispanic Journal of Behavioral Sciences, 37(2), 223–242. doi:10.1177/0739986315573967

Salerno, S. (2005). *Sham: How the self-help movement made America helpless.* New York: Crown Publishers.

Salovey, P., & Mayer, J. D. (1990). Emotional intelligence. *Imagination, Cognition, and Personality, 9,* 185–211.

Samberg, E., & Marcus, E. R. (2005). Process, resistance, and interpretation. In E. S. Person, A. M. Cooper, & G. O. Gabbard (Eds.), *Textbook of psychoanalysis.* Washington, DC: American Psychiatric Publishing.

Samios, C., Henson, D. F., & Simpson, H. J. (2014). Benefit finding and psychological adjustment following a non-marital relationship breakup. *Journal of Relationships Research, 5.* doi:10.1017/jrr.2014.6

Samovar, L. A., & Porter, R. E. (2004). *Communication between cultures.* Belmont, CA: Wadsworth.

Samovar, L. A., Porter, R. E., & McDaniel. E. R. (2007). *Communication between cultures.* Belmont, CA: Wadsworth.

Samson, A. C., & Gross, J. J. (2012). Humour as emotion regulation: The differential consequences of negative versus positive humour. *Cognition and Emotion, 26*(2), 375–384. doi:10.1080/02699931.2011.585069

Sana, F., Weston, T., & Cepeda, N. J. (2013). Laptop multitasking hinders classroom learning for both users and nearby peers. *Computers & Education, 62,* 24–31. doi:10.1016/j.compedu.2012.10.003.

Sanchez, D. T., Fetterolf, J. C., & Rudman, L. A. (2012). Eroticizing inequality in the United States: The consequences and determinants of traditional gender role adherence in intimate relationships. *Journal of Sex Research, 49*(2–3), 168–183.

Sandstrom, G. M., & Dunn, E. W. (2011). The virtue blind spot: Do affective forecasting errors undermine virtuous behavior? *Social and Personality Psychology Compass, 5*(10), 720–733. doi:10.1111/j.1751-9004.2011.00384.x

Sandstrom, G. M., & Dunn, E. W. (2014). Social interactions and well-being: The surprising power of weak ties. *Personality and Social Psychology Bulletin, 40,* 910–922. doi: 10.1177/0146167214529799

Sanger-Katz, M. (2015, July 28). Behind a drop in calories, a shift in cultural attitudes. *New York Times,* A3.

Sanjuán, P., Magallares, A., & Gordillo, R. (2011). Self-serving attributional bias and hedonic and eudaimonic aspects of well-being. In I. Brdar (Ed.), *The human pursuit of well-being: A cultural approach* (pp. 15–26). New York: Springer.

Sansone, R. A., & Sansone, L. A. (2010). Road rage: What's driving it? *Psychiatry, 7*(7), 14–18.

Saphire-Bernstein, S., & Taylor, S. E. (2013). Close relationships and happiness. In S. A. David, I. Boniwell, & A. Conley Ayers (Eds.), *The Oxford handbook of happiness.* New York: Oxford University Press.

Sapolsky, R. M. (2004). *Why zebras don't get ulcers: The acclaimed guide to stress, stress-related diseases, and coping.* New York: Holt.

Sarwer, D. B., Foster, G. D., & Wadden, T. A. (2004). Treatment of obesity I: Adult obesity. In J. K. Thompson (Ed.), *Handbook of eating disorders and obesity.* New York: Wiley.

Sassler, S., & Miller, A. J. (2011). Class differences in cohabitation processes. *Family Relations: An Interdisciplinary Journal of Applied Family Studies, 60*(2), 163–177. doi:10.1111/j.1741-3729.2010.00640.x

Saucier, G., & Srivastava S. (2015). What makes a good structural model of personality? Evaluating the big five and alternatives. In M. Mikulincer, P. R. Shaver, M. L. Cooper, & R. J. Larsen (Eds.), *APA handbook of personality and social psychology, Vol. 4: Personality processes and individual differences.* Washington, DC: American Psychological Association.

Saunders, J., Worth, R., & Fernandes, M. (2012). Repressive coping style and mnemic neglect. *Journal of Experimental Psychopathology, 3,* 346–367.

Savin-Williams, R. C., Pardo, S. T., Vrangalova, Z., Mitchell, R. S., & Cohen, K. M. (2010). Sexual and gender prejudice. In J. C. Chrisler & D. R. McCreary (Eds.), *Handbook of gender research in psychology, Vol 2: Gender research in social and applied psychology* (pp. 359–376). New York: Springer Science + Business Media. doi:10.1007/978-1-4419-1467-5_15

Sawdon, A. M., Cooper, M., & Seabrook, R. (2007). The relationship between self-discrepancies, eating disorder, and depressive symptoms in women. *European Eating Disorders Review, 15*(3), 207–212.

Sbarra, D. A., & Beck, C. A. (2013). Divorce and close relationships: Findings, themes, and future directions. In J. A. Simpson & L. Campbell (Eds.), *The Oxford handbook of close relationships* (pp. 795–822). New York: Oxford University Press.

Sbarra, D. A., Law, R. W., & Portley, R. M. (2011). Divorce and death: A meta-analysis and research agenda for clinical, social, and health psychology. *Perspectives on Psychological Science, 6*(5), 454–474. doi:10.1177/1745691611414724

Sbarra, D. A., Smith, H. L., & Mehl, M. R. (2012). When leaving your ex, love yourself: Observational ratings of self-compassion predict the course of emotional recovery following marital separation. *Psychological Science, 23*(3), 261–269. doi:10.1177/0956797611429466

Schachner, D. A., Shaver, P. R., & Mikulincer, M. (2005). Patterns of nonverbal behavior and sensitivity in the context of attachment relations. *Journal of Nonverbal Behavior, 29*(3), 141–169.

Schachter, R. (2011). Using the group in cognitive group therapy. *Group, 35*(2), 135–149.

Schachter, S. (1959). *The psychology of affiliation.* Stanford, CA: Stanford University Press.

Schaller, M., Kenrick, D. T., & Neuberg, S. L. (2012). Six degrees of Bob Cialdini and five principles of scientific influence. In D. T. Kenrick, N. J. Goldstein, & S. L. Braver (Eds.), *Six degrees of social influence: Science, application, and the psychology of Robert Cialdini* (pp. 3–13). New York: Oxford University Press.

Scharrer, E. L. (2013). Representations of gender in the media. In K. E. Dill (Ed.), *The Oxford handbook of media psychology* (pp. 267–284). New York: Oxford University Press.

Scheele, D., Striepens, N., Güntürkün, O., Deutschländer, S., Maier, W., Kendrick, K. M., & Hurlemann, R. (2012). Oxytocin modulates social distance between males and females. *The Journal of Neuroscience, 32*(46), 16074–16079. doi:10.1523/JNEUROSCI.2755-12.2012.

Scheiber, C., Reynolds, M. R., Hajovsky, D. B., & Kaufman, A. S. (2015). Gender differences in achievement in a large, nationally representative sample of children and adolescents. *Psychology in the Schools, 52*(4), 335–348. doi:10.1002/pits.21827

Scheier, M. F., & Carver, C. S. (1985). Optimism, coping, and health: Assessment and implications of generalized outcome expectancies. *Health Psychology, 4,* 219–247.

Schick, V., Calabrese, S. K., & Herbenick, D. (2014). Survey methods in sexuality research. In D. L. Tolman, L. M. Diamond, J. A. Bauermeister, W. H. George, J. G. Pfaus, L. M. Ward (Eds.), *APA handbook of sexuality and psychology,* (pp. 81–98). Washington, DC: American Psychological Association. doi:10.1037/14193-004

Schick, V., Herbenick, D., Reece, M., Sanders, S. A., Dodge, B., Middlestat, S. E., & Fortenberry, J. D. (2010). Sexual behaviors, condom use, and sexual health of Americans over 50: Implications for sexual health promotion for older adults. *Journal of Sexual Medicine, 7*(5), 315–329.

Schietroma, M., Piccione, F., Carlei, F., Clementi, M., Bianchi, Z., De Vita, F., & Amicucci, G. (2012). Peritonitis from perforated appendicitis: Stress response after laproscopic or open treatment. *The American Surgeon, 78,* 582–590.

Schilit, W. K. (1987). Thinking about managing your time. In A. D. Timpe (Ed.), *The management of time.* New York: Facts on File.

Schlapobersky, J., & Pines, M. (2009). Group methods in adult psychiatry. In M. C. Gelder, N. C. Andreasen, J. J. López-Ibor, Jr., & J. R. Geddes (Eds.), *New Oxford textbook of psychiatry, Vol. 1* (2nd ed.). New York: Oxford University Press.

Schlenger, W. E., Kulka, R. A., Fairbank, J. A., Hough, R. L., & Weiss, D. S. (1992). The prevalence of post-traumatic stress disorder in the Vietnam generation: A multimethod, multisource assessment of psychiatric disorder. *Journal of Traumatic Stress, 5,* 333–363.

Schlenker, B. R. (2003). Self-presentation. In M. R. Leary & J. P. Tangney (Eds.), *Handbook of self and identity.* New York: Guilford.

Schlösser, T., Dunning, D., Johnson, K. L., & Kruger, J. (2013). How unaware are the unskilled? Empirical tests of the "signal extraction" counterexplanation for the Dunning–Kruger effect in self-evaluation of performance. *Journal of Economic Psychology,* 3985–100. doi:10.1016/j.joep.2013.07.004

Schmaal, L., Veltman, D. J., van Erp, T. G., Sämann, P. G., Frodl, T., Jahanshad, N., . . . Hibar, D. P. (2015). Subcortical brain alterations in major depressive disorder: findings from the ENIGMA Major Depressive Disorder working group. *Molecular Psychiatry.* doi:10.1038/mp.2015.69

Schmader, T., Hall, W., & Croft, A. (2015). Stereotype threat in intergroup relations. In M. Mikulincer, P. R. Shaver, J. F. Dovidio, & J. A. Simpson (Eds.), *APA handbook of personality and social psychology, Vol. 2: Group processes* (pp. 447–471). Washington, DC: American Psychological Association. doi:10.1037/14342-017

Schmaling, K. B. (2012). Asthma. In A. M. Nezu, C. M. Nezu, P. A. Geller, & I. B. Weiner (Eds.), *Handbook of psychology, Vol. 9: Health psychology* (2nd ed.). New York: Wiley.

Schmitt, N. W., Highhouse, S., & Weiner, I. B. (Eds.). (2013). *Handbook of psychology, Vol. 12: Industrial and organizational psychology* (2nd ed.). Hoboken, NJ: Wiley.

Schmitz, J. M., & DeLaune, K. A. (2005). Nicotine. In J. H. Lowinson, P. Ruiz, R. B. Millman, & J. G. Langrod (Eds.), *Substance abuse: A comprehensive textbook.* Philadelphia: Lippincott/Williams & Wilkins.

Schneider, K. (2011). Toward a humanistic positive psychology: Why can't we just get along? *Existential Analysis, 22*(1), 32–38.

Schneier, F. R., Vidair, H. B., Vogel, L. R., & Muskin, P. R. (2014). Anxiety, obsessive-compulsive, and stress disorders. In J. L. Cutler (Ed.), *Psychiatry* (3rd ed.). New York: Oxford University Press.

Schnittker, J. (2008). An uncertain revolution: Why the rise of a genetic model of mental illness has not increased tolerance. *Social Science & Medicine, 67*(9), 1370–1381. doi:10.1016/j.socscimed.2008.07.007

Schoon, I., & Parsons, S. (2002). Teenage aspirations for future careers and occupational outcomes. *Journal of Vocational Behavior, 60*(2), 262–288.

Schor, J. (2011). *True wealth: How and why millions of Americans are creating a time rich, ecologically light, small-scale, high satisfaction economy.* New York: Penguin.

Schor, J. B. (1991). *The overworked American: The unexpected decline of leisure.* New York: Basic Books.

Schramm, D. G., Marshall, J. P., Harris, V. W., & Lee, T. R. (2005). After "I do": The newlywed transition. *Marriage & Family Review, 38,* 45–67.

Schramm, S. H., Moebus, S., Lehmann, N., Galli, U., Obermann, M., Bock, E., . . . Katsarava, Z. (2014). The association between stress and headache: A longitudinal population-based study. *Cephalalgia.* doi: 10.1177/0333102414563087

Schramm, W. (1955). *The process and effects of mass communication.* Urbana: University of Illinois Press.

Schraw, G., Wadkins, T., & Olafson, L. (2007). Doing the things we do: A grounded theory of academic procrastination. *Journal of Educational Psychology, 99*(1), 12–25.

Schuckit, M. A. (2000). Alcohol-related disorders. In B. J. Sadock & V. A. Sadock (Eds.), *Kaplan and Sadock's comprehensive textbook of psychiatry* (7th ed.). Philadelphia: Lippincott/Williams & Wilkins.

Schultz, D. S., & Brabender, V. M. (2013). More challenges since Wikipedia: The effects of exposure to Internet information about the Rorschach on selected comprehensive system variables. *Journal of Personality Assessment, 95*(2), 149–158. doi:10.1080/00223891.2012.725438

Schurtz, D. R., Blincoe, S., Smith, R. H., Powell, C. J., Combs, D. Y., & Kim, S. (2012). Exploring the social aspects of goose bumps and their role in awe and envy. *Motivation and Emotion, 36*(2), 205–217. doi:10.1007/s11031-011-9243-8

Schutte, N. S., & Malouff, J. M. (2014). A meta-analytic review of the effects of mindfulness meditation on telomerase activity. *Psychoneuroendocrinology, 42,* 45–48. doi:10.1016/j.psyneuen.2013.12.017

Schutte, N. S., Malouff, J. M., Thorsteinsson, E. B., Bhullar, N., & Rooke, S. E. (2007). A meta-analytic investigation of the relationship between emotional intelligence and health. *Personality and Individual Differences, 42,* 921–933.

Schwartz, B. (2004). *The paradox of choice: Why more is less.* New York: Ecco.

Schwartz, B., & Sommers, R. (2013). Affective forecasting and well-being. In D. Reisberg (Ed.), *The Oxford handbook of cognitive psychology,* 704–716. New York: Oxford University Press. doi:10.1093/oxfordhb/9780195376746.013.0044

Schwartz, N., Bless, H., & Bohner, G. (1991). Mood and persuasion: Affective states influence the processing of persuasive communications. In M. P. Zanna (Ed.), *Advances in experimental social psychology, Vol. 24* (pp. 161–199). New York: Academic Press.

Schwartz, P., & Young, L. (2009). Sexual satisfaction in committed relationships. *Sexuality Research & Social Policy: A Journal of the NSRC, 6*(1), 1–17.

Schwind, C., Buder, J., Cress, U., & Hesse, F. W. (2012). Preference-inconsistent recommendations: An effective approach for reducing confirmation bias and stimulating divergent thinking? *Computers & Education, 58*(2), 787–796. doi:10.1016/j.compedu.2011.10.003

Schwinger, M., Wirthwein, L., Lemmer, G., & Steinmayr, R. (2014). Academic self-handicapping and achievement: A meta-analysis. *Journal of Educational Psychology, 106*(3), 744–761. doi:10.1037/a0035832

Scully, J. A., Tosi, H., & Banning, K. (2000). Life event checklists: Revisiting the social readjustment rating scale after 30 years. *Educational & Psychological Measurement, 60*(6), 864–876.

Seay, T. A. (2016). Positive psychology: How to live the good life. In C. Tien-Lun Sun, C. Tien-Lun Sun (Eds.), *Psychology in Asia: An introduction* (pp. 491–510). Boston: Cengage.

Seccombe, K. (2001). Families in poverty in the 1990s: Trends, causes, consequences, and lessons learned. In R. M. Milardo (Ed.), *Understanding families into the new millennium: A decade in review.* Minneapolis, MN: National Council on Family Relations.

Sedikides, C., & Alicke, M. D. (2012). Self-enhancement and self-protection motives. In R. M. Ryan (Ed.), *The Oxford handbook of human motivation* (pp. 303–322). New York: Oxford University Press.

Seery, M. D. (2011). Resilience: A silver lining to experiencing adverse life events? *Current Directions in Psychological Science, 20*(6), 390–394. doi:10.1177/0963721411424740

Seery, M. D., Leo, R. J., Lupien, S. P., Kondrak, C. L., & Almonte, J. L. (2013). An upside to adversity? Moderate cumulative lifetime adversity is associated with resilient responses in the face of controlled stressors. *Psychological Science, 24,* 1181–1189. doi: 10.1177/0956797612469210

Segall, A. (1997). Sick role concepts and health behavior. In D. S. Gochman (Ed.), *Handbook of health behavior research I: Personal and social determinants.* New York: Plenum.

Segerstrom, S. C., & Miller, G. E. (2004). Psychological stress and the human immune system: A meta-analytic study of 30 years of inquiry. *Psychological Bulletin, 130,* 601–630.

Seiter, J. S. (2007). Ingratiation and gratuity: The effect of complimenting customers on tipping behavior in restaurants. *Journal of Applied Social Psychology, 37*(3), 478–485.

Sekerka, L. E., Vacharkulksemsuk, T., & Fredrickson, B. L. (2012). Positive emotions. In K. S. Cameron & G. M. Spreitzer (Eds.), *The Oxford handbook of positive organizational scholarship* (pp. 168–177). New York: Oxford University Press.

Selfhout, M., Denissen, J., Branje, S., & Meeus, W. (2009). In the eye of the beholder: Perceived, actual, and peer-rated similarity in personality, communication, and friendship intensity during the acquaintanceship process. *Journal of Personality and Social Psychology, 96,* 1152–1165.

Seligman, M. E. P. (1971). Phobias and preparedness. *Behavior Therapy, 2,* 307–321.

Seligman, M. E. P. (1974). Depression and learned helplessness. In R. J. Friedman & M. M. Katz (Eds.), *The psychology of depression: Contemporary theory and research.* New York: Wiley.

Seligman, M. E. P. (1990). *Learned optimism: How to change your mind and your life.* New York: Pocket Books.

Seligman, M. E. P. (1991). *Learned optimism.* New York: Alfred A. Knopf.

Seligman, M. E. P. (1992). *Helplessness: On depression, development, and death.* New York: Freeman.

Seligman, M. E. P. (1994). *What you can change and what you can't.* New York: Knopf.

Seligman, M. E. P. (1999). The president's address. *American Psychologist, 54,* 559–562.

Seligman, M. E. P. (2002). Positive psychology, prevention, and positive therapy. In C. R. Snyder & S. J. Lopez (Eds.), *Handbook of positive psychology* (pp. 3–13). New York: Oxford University Press.

Seligman, M. E. P. (2003). The past and future of positive psychology. In C. L. M. Keyes & J. Haidt (Eds.), *Flourishing: Positive psychology and the life well-lived.* Washington, DC: American Psychological Association.

Seligman, M. E. P. (2011). *Flourish: A visionary new understanding of happiness and well-being.* New York: Free Press.

Seligman, M. E. P., & Csikszentmihalyi, M. (2000). Positive psychology: An introduction. *American Psychologist, 55*(1), 5–14.

Seligman, M. E. P., Schulman, P., DeRubeis, R. J., & Hollon, S. D. (1999). The prevention of depression and anxiety. *Prevention and Treatment,* http://journals.apa.org/prevention/volume2/pre0020008a.html

Seligman, M. E. P., Schulman, P., & Tryon, A. M. (2007). Group prevention of depression and anxiety symptoms. *Behaviour Research and Therapy, 45,* 1111–1126.

Selye, H. (1936). A syndrome produced by diverse nocuous agents. *Nature, 138,* 32.

Selye, H. (1956). *The stress of life.* New York: McGraw-Hill.

Selye, H. (1982). History and present status of the stress concept. In L. Goldberger & S. Breznitz (Eds.), *Handbook of stress: Theoretical and clinical aspects.* New York: Free Press.

Semans, J. H. (1956). Premature ejaculation: A new approach. *Journal of Southern Medicine, 79,* 353–361.

Senders, A., Bourdette, D., Hanes, D., Yadav, V., & Shinto, L. (2014). Perceived stress in multiple sclerosis: The potential role of mindfulness in health and well-being. *Journal of Evidence-Based Complementary and Alternative Medicine, 19,* 104–111. doi: 10.1177/2156587214523291

Senecal, C., Lavoie, K., & Koestner, R. (1997). Trait and situational factors in procrastination: An interactional model. *Journal of Social Behavior and Personality, 12,* 889–903.

Settles, I. H., Cortina, L. M., Malley, J., & Stewart, A. J. (2006). The climate for women in academic science: The good, the bad, and the changeable. *Psychology of Women Quarterly, 30,* 47–58.

Shaffer, D. R. (1989). *Developmental psychology: Childhood and adolescence.* Pacific Grove, CA: Brooks/Cole.

Shah, J., & Higgins, E. T. (2001). Regulatory concerns and appraisal efficiency: The general impact of promotion and prevention. *Journal of Personality and Social Psychology, 80,* 693–705.

Shapiro, A. F., Gottman, J. M., & Carrère, S. (2000). The baby and marriage: Identifying factors that buffer against decline in marital satisfaction after the first baby arrives. *Journal of Family Psychology, 14*(1), 59–70.

Shapiro, D. L., & Burris, E. (2014). The role of voice in managing conflict. In O. B. Ayoko, N. M. Ashkanasy, & K. A. Jehn (Eds.), *Handbook of conflict management research* (pp. 173–192). Northampton, MA: Edward Elgar. doi:10.4337/9781781006948.00019

Shapiro, S. L., Schwartz, G. E. R., & Santerre, C. (2002). Meditation and positive psychology. In C. R. Snyder & S. J. Lopez (Eds.), *Handbook of positive psychology.* New York: Oxford University Press.

Shavelson, R. J., Hubner, J. J., & Stanton, G. C. (1976). Self-concept: Validation of construct interpretations. *Review of Educational Research, 46,* 407–411.

Shaver, P. R., & Hazan, C. (1993). Adult attachment: Theory and research. In W. Jones & D. Perlman (Eds.), *Advances in personal relationships, Vol. 4.* London: Jessica Kingsley.

Shaver, P. R., & Mikulincer, M. (2008). Augmenting the sense of security in romantic, leader-follower, therapeutic, and group relationships: A relational model of psychological change. In J. P. Forgas & J. Fitness (Eds.) *Social relationships: Cognitive, affective, and motivational processes* (pp. 55–74). New York: Psychology Press.

Shaw, L. H., & Gant, L. M. (2002). In defense of the internet: The relationship between internet communication and depression, loneliness, self-esteem, and perceived social support. *CyberPsychology, 5*(2), 157–171.

Shaw, R. (2011). Women's experiential journey toward voluntary childlessness: An interpretative phenomenological analysis. *Journal of Community and Applied Social Psychology, 21*(2), 151–163. doi:10.1002/casp.1072

Shedler, J. (2010). The efficacy of psychodynamic psychotherapy. *American Psychologist, 65*(2), 98–109. doi:10.1037/a0018378

Sheehan, S. (1982). *Is there no place on earth for me?* Boston: Houghton Mifflin.

Shelton, K. H., & Harold, G. T. (2007). Marital conflict and children's adjustment: The mediating and moderating role of children's coping strategies. *Social Development, 16,* 497–511.

Shen, B.-J., Stroud, L. R., Todaro, J. F., Spiro, A., Laurenceau, J.-P., Ward, K. D., . . . Niaura. (2008). Anxiety characteristics independently and prospectively predict myocardial infarction in men: The unique contribution of anxiety among psychologic factors. *Journal of the American College of Cardiology, 51,* 113–119.

Shepard, L. D. (2013). The impact of polygamy on women's mental health: A systematic review. *Epidemiology and Psychiatric Sciences, 22*(1), 47–62. doi:10.1017/S2045796012000121

Shepperd, J., Malone, W., & Sweeny, K. (2008). Exploring causes of the self-serving bias. *Social and Personality Psychology Compass, 2*(2), 895–908.

Shepperd, J. A., Klein, W. P., Waters, E. A., & Weinstein, N. D. (2013). Taking stock of unrealistic optimism. *Perspectives on Psychological Science, 8*(4), 395–411. doi:10.1177/1745691613485247

Shepperd, J. A., Waters, E. A., Weinstein, N. D., & Klein, W. P. (2015). A primer on unrealistic optimism. *Current Directions in Psychological Science, 24*(3), 232–237. doi:10.1177/0963721414568341

Sherif, M., Harvey, O., White, B., Hood, W., & Sherif, C. (1961). *Intergroup conflict and cooperation: The Robber's Cave experiment.* Norman, OK: University of Oklahoma, Institute of Group Behavior.

Sherman, A. M., & Zurbriggen, E. L. (2014). "Boys can be anything": Effect of Barbie play on girls' career cognitions. *Sex Roles, 70*(5–6), 195–208. doi:10.1007/s11199-014-0347-y

Shi, X., Brinthaupt, T. M., & McCree, M. (2015). The relationship of self-talk frequency to communication apprehension and public speaking anxiety. *Personality and Individual Differences, 75,* 125–129. doi:10.1016/j.paid.2014.11.023

Shiffman, S., Brockwell, S. E., Pillitteri, J. L., & Gitchell, J. G. (2008). Use of smoking-cessation treatments in the United States. *American Journal of Preventive Medicine, 34,* 102–111.

Shifron, R., & Reysen, R. R. (2011). Workaholism: Addiction to work. *The Journal of Individual Psychology, 67*(2), 136–146.

Shimazu, A., Kubota, K., & Bakker, A. B. (2015). How workaholism affects employees and their families. In I. Harpaz & R. Snir (Eds.), *Heavy work investment: Its nature, sources, outcomes, and future directions* (pp. 171–186). New York: Routledge/Taylor & Francis Group.

Shimazu, A., Schaufeli, W. B., Kamiyama, K., & Kawakami, N. (2015). Workaholism vs. work engagement: The two different predictors of future well-being and performance. *International Journal of Behavioral Medicine, 22*(1), 18–23. doi:10.1007/s12529-014-9410-x

Shin, N. (2006). Online learner's "flow" experience: An empirical study. *British Journal of Education Technology, 37*(5), 705–720.

Shiota, M. N. (2006). Silver linings and candles in the dark: Differences among positive coping strategies in predicting subjective well-being. *Emotion, 6,* 335–339.

Shirom, A. (2010). Employee burnout and health: Current knowledge and future research paths. In J. Houdmont & S. Leka (Eds.), *Contemporary occupational health psychology: Global perspectives on research and practice, Vol. 1* (pp. 59–76). Wiley-Blackwell. doi:10.1002/9780470661550.ch4

Shmotkin, D. (2005). Happiness in the face of adversity: Reformulating the dynamic and modular bases of subjective well-being. *Review of General Psychology, 9*(4), 291–325.

Shneidman, E. S., Farberow, N. L., & Litman, R. E. (1994). *The psychology of suicide: A clinician's guide to evaluation and treatment.* Northvale, NJ: Jason Aronson.

Shoda, Y., Mischel, W., & Peake, P. K. (1990). Predicting adolescent cognitive and self-regulatory competencies from preschool delay of gratification: Identifying diagnostic conditions. *Developmental Psychology, 26,* 978–986.

Showers. C. J., & Zeigler-Hill, V. (2012). Organization of self-knowledge: Features, functions, and flexibility. In M. R. Leary & J. P. Tangney (Eds.), *Handbook of self and identity* (2nd ed., pp. 105–123). New York: Guilford.

Shultz, K.S., Wang, M., & Olson, D.A. (2010). Role overload and underload in relation to occupational stress and health. *Stress and Health, 26,* 99–111.

Shupe, E. I., & Buchholz, K. A. (2013). The effects of not working: A psychological framework for understanding the experience of job loss. In A. G. Antoniou & C. L. Cooper (Eds.), *The psychology of the recession on the workplace* (pp. 209–229). Northampton, MA: Edward Elgar. doi:10.4337/9780857933843.00022

Sibley, C. G., & Duckitt, J. (2008). Personality and prejudice: A meta-analytic and theoretical review. *Personality and Social Psychology Review, 12*(3), 248–279.

Sidani, J. E., Shensa, A., Barnett, T. E., Cook, R. L., & Primack, B. A. (2014). Knowledge, attitudes, and normative beliefs as predictors of hookah smoking initiation: A longitudinal study of university students. *Nicotine & Tobacco Research*, 16(6), 647–654. doi:10.1093/ntr/ntt201

Siddiqui, R. N., & Pandey, J. (2003). Coping with environmental stressors by urban slum dwellers. *Enviroment and Behavior*, 35, 589–604.

Siegel, J. T., Thomson, A. L., & Navarro, M. A. (2014). Experimentally distinguishing elevation from gratitude: Oh, the morality. *The Journal of Positive Psychology*, 9(5), 414–427. doi:10.1080/17439760.2014.910825

Siegel, K., Schrimshaw, E. W., Lekas, H., & Parsons, J. T. (2008). Sexual behaviors of non-gay identified non-disclosing men who have sex with men and women. *Archives of Sexual Behavior*, 37(5), 720–735. doi:10.1007/s10508-008-9357-6

Sifferlin, A. (2015, July 7). Heroin use in the U.S. reaches epidemic levels. *Time*, retrieved from http://time.com/3946904/heroin-epidemic/.

Silton, N. R., Flannelly, K. J., & Lutjen, L. J. (2013). It pays to forgive! aging, forgiveness, hostility, and health. *Journal of Adult Development*, 20(4), 222–231. doi:10.1007/s10804-013-9173-7

Silver, R. C., Holman, E. A., Andersen, J. P., Poulin, M., McIntosh, D. N., & Gil-Rivas, V. (2013). Mental- and physical-health effects of acute exposure to media images of the September 11, 2001, attacks and the Iraq war. *Psychological Science*, 24(9), 1623–1634. doi

Silvia, P. J., & Duval, T. S. (2001). Objective self-awareness theory: Recent progress and enduring problems. *Personality and Social Psychology Review*, 5, 230–241.

Silvia, P. J., & Eddington, K. M. (2012). Self and emotion. In M. R. Leary & J. P. Tangney (Eds.), *Handbook of self and identity* (2nd ed., pp. 425–445). New York: Guilford.

Simeon, D., & Loewenstein, R. J. (2009). Dissociative disorders. In B. J. Sadock, V. A. Sadock, & P. Ruiz (Eds.), *Kaplan & Sadock's comprehensive textbook of psychiatry* (pp. 1965–2026). Philadelphia: Lippincott Williams & Wilkins.

Simpson, J. A., & Overall, N. C. (2014). Partner buffering of attachment insecurity. *Current Directions in Psychological Science*, 23(1), 54–59. doi:10.1177/0963721413510933

Simpson, J. A., Collins, W., & Salvatore, J. E. (2011). The impact of early interpersonal experience on adult romantic relationship functioning: Recent findings from the Minnesota longitudinal study of risk and adaptation. *Current Directions in Psychological Science*, 20(6), 355–359. doi:10.1177/0963721411418468

Simpson, J. R. (2008). Functional MRI lie detection: Too good to be true? *Journal of the American Academy of Psychiatry and the Law*, 36, 491–498.

Sinclair, R. C., Mark, M. M., & Clore, G. L. (1994). Mood-related persuasion depends on (mis)attributions. *Social Cognition*, 12, 309–326.

Sinke, C. A., Kret, M. E., & de Gelder, B. (2012). Body language: Embodied perception of emotion. In B. Berglund, G. B. Rossi, J. T. Townsend, & L. R. Pendrill (Eds.), *Measurement with persons: Theory, methods, and implementation areas* (pp. 335–352). New York: Psychology Press.

Sireci, S. G., & Sukin, T. (2013). Test validity. In K. F. Geisinger, B. A. Bracken, J. F. Carlson, J. C. Hansen, N. R. Kuncel, S. P. Reise, & M. C. Rodriguez (Eds.), *APA handbook of testing and assessment in psychology, Vol. 1: Test theory and testing and assessment in industrial and organizational psychology*. Washington, DC: American Psychological Association. doi:10.1037/14047-004

Sirois, F. M. (2014). Out of sight, out of time? A meta-analytic investigation of procrastination and time perspective. *European Journal of Personality*, 28(5), 511–520. doi:10.1002/per.1947

Sirois, F. M., & Kitner, R. (2015). Less adaptive or more maladaptive? A meta-analytic investigation of procrastination and coping. *European Journal of Personality*, 29, 433–444. doi:10.1002/per.1985

Skinner, B. F. (1953). *Science and human behavior*. New York: Macmillan.

Skinner, B. F. (1974). *About behaviorism*. New York: Knopf.

Skinner, B. F. (1990). Can psychology be a science of mind? *American Psychologist*, 45, 1206–1210.

Skinner, E. A., Edge, K., Altman, J., & Sherwood, H. (2003). Searching for the structure of coping: A review and critique of category systems for classifying ways of coping. *Psychological Bulletin*, 129, 216–269.

Skinner, P. H., & Shelton, R. L. (1985). *Speech, language, and hearing: Normal processes and disorders* (2nd ed.). New York: Wiley.

Skodol, A. E., Bender, D. S., Gunderson, J. G., & Oldham, J. M. (2014). Personality disorders. In R. E. Hales, S. C. Yudofsky, & L. W. Roberts (Eds.), *The American Psychiatric Publishing textbook of psychiatry* (6th ed.). Washington, DC: American Psychiatric Publishing.

Skodol, A. E., Bender, D. S., & Morey, L. C. (2014). Narcissistic personality disorder in DSM-5. *Personality Disorders: Theory, Research, and Treatment*, 5, 422–427. doi:10.1037/per0000023

Skogrand, L., Johnson, A. C., Horrocks, A. M., & DeFrain, J. (2011). Financial management practices of couples with great marriages. *Journal of Family and Economic Issues*, 32(1), 27–35. doi:10.1007/s10834-010-9195-2

Skowronski, J. J., & Carlston, D. E. (1992). Caught in the act: When impressions are based on highly diagnostic information behaviours are resistant to contradiction. *European Journal of Social Psychology*, 22, 435–452.

Slopen, N., Kontos, E. Z., Ryff, C. D., Ayanian, J. Z., Albert, M. A., & Williams, D. R. (2013). Psychosocial stress and cigarette smoking persistence, cessation, and relapse over 9–10 years: A prospective study of middle-aged adults in the United States. *Cancer Causes & Control*, 24, 1849–1863.

Slowinski, J. (2007). Sexual problems and dysfunctions in men. In A. F. Owens & M. S. Tepper (Eds.), *Sexual Health, Vol. 4: State-of-the-art treatments and research* (pp. 1–14). Westport, CT: Praeger/Greenwood.

Smedema, S. M., Chan, J. Y., & Phillips, B. N. (2014). Core self-evaluations and Snyder's hope theory in persons with spinal cord injuries. *Rehabilitation Psychology*, 59(4), 399–406. doi:10.1037/rep0000015

Smetana, J. G. (2009). Parent-adolescent communication. In H. T. Reis & S. Sprecher (Eds.), *Encyclopedia of human relationships, Vol. 3* (pp. 1189–1193). Los Angeles: Sage Reference.

Smith, A. K. (2000, November 6). Charting your own course. *U.S. News & World Report*, 56–60, 62, 64–65.

Smith, B. W., Epstein, E. M., Ortiz, J. A., Christopher, P. J., & Tooley, E. M. (2013). The foundations of resilience: What are the critical resources for bouncing back from stress? In S. Prince-Embury & D. H. Saklofske (Eds.), *Resilience in children, adolescents, and adults: Translating research into practice*. New York: Spring Science + Business Media.

Smith, G. C., James, L. E., Varnum, M. W., & Oyserman, D. (2014). Give up or get going? Productive uncertainty in uncertain times. *Self and Identity*, 13(6), 681–700. doi:10.1080/15298868.2014.919958

Smith, J. L., Hardy, T., & Arkin, R. (2009). When practice doesn't make perfect: Effort expenditure as an active behavioral self-handicapping strategy. *Journal of Research in Personality*, 43(1), 95–98.

Smith, M. L., & Glass, G. V. (1977). Meta-analysis of psychotherapy outcome studies. *American Psychologist*, 32, 752–760.

Smith, S. (2014). "Frazzled" on the job: More than 80 percent of American workers are stressed out. *EHS Today*. Retrieved from http://ehstoday.com/health/frazzled-job-more-80-percent-american-workers-are-stressed-out

Smith, S. W., & Wilson, S. R. (2010). *New directions in interpersonal communication research*. Thousand Oaks, CA: Sage.

Smith, T. W. (2006). Personality as risk and resilience in physical health. *Current Directions in Psychological Science*, 15, 227–231.

Smith, T. W., & Gallo, L. C. (1999). Hostility and cardiovascular reactivity during marital interaction. *Psychosomatic Medicine*, 61, 436–445.

Smith, T. W., & Gallo, L. C. (2001). Personality traits as risk factors for physical illness. In A. Baum, T. A. Revenson, & J. E. Singer (Eds.), *Handbook of health psychology*. Mahwah, NJ: Erlbaum.

Smith, T. W., Pope, M. K., Sanders, J. D., Allred, K. D., & O'Keefe, J. L. (1988). Cynical hostility at home and work: Psychosocial vulnerability across domains. *Journal of Research in Personality*, 22, 525–548.

Smith, T. W., Williams, P. G., & Segerstrom, S. C. (2015). Personality and physical health. In M. Mikulincer, P. R. Shaver, M. L. Cooper, & R. J. Larsen (Eds.), *APA handbook of personality and social psychology, Vol. 4: Personality processes*

and individual differences. Washington, DC: American Psychological Association.

Smith, W. P., Compton, W. C., & West, W. B. (1995). Meditation as an adjunct to a happiness enhancement program. *Journal of Clinical Psychology*, 51, 269–273.

Smock, P. J., Manning, W. D., & Gupta, S. (1999). The effect of marriage and divorce on women's economic well-being. *American Sociological Review*, 64, 794–812.

Smyth, J. M., & Pennebaker, J. W. (1999). Sharing one's story: Translating emotional experiences into words as a coping tool. In C. R. Snyder (Ed.), *Coping: The psychology of what works*. New York: Oxford University Press.

Smyth, J. M., & Pennebaker, J. W. (2001). What are the health effects of disclosure? In A. Baum, T. A. Revenson, & J. E. Singer (Eds.), *Handbook of health psychology*. Mahwah, NJ: Erlbaum.

Snell, J. C., & Marsh, M. (2008). Life cycle loneliness curve. *Psychology and Education: An Interdisciplinary Journal*, 45, 26–28.

Snowden, L. R. (2012). Health and mental health policies' role in better understanding and closing African American–White American disparities in treatment access and quality of care. *American Psychologist*, 67, 524–531. doi:10.1037/a0030054

Snyder, C. R. (1994/2000). *The psychology of hope: You can get there from here*. New York: Free Press.

Snyder, C. R. (2002). Hope theory: Rainbows of the mind. *Psychological Inquiry*, 13, 249–275.

Snyder, C. R., Harris, C., Anderson, J. R., Holeran, S. A., Irving, L. M., Sigmon, S. T., . . . Harney, P. (1991). The will and the ways: Development and validation of an individual-differences measure of hope. *Journal of Personality and Social Psychology*, 60, 570–585.

Snyder, C. R., Rand, K. L., & Sigmon, D. R. (2002). Hope theory: A member of the positive psychology family. In C. R. Snyder & S. J. Lopez (Eds.), *Handbook of positive psychology* (pp. 257–276). New York: Oxford University Press.

Snyder, C. R., Sympson, S. C., Ybasco, F. C., Borders, T. F., Babyak, M. A., & Higgins, R. L. (1996). Development and validation of the State Hope Scale. *Journal of Personality and Social Psychology*, 70, 321–335.

Snyder, H. R., Kaiser, R. H., Warren, S. L., & Heller, W. (2015). Obsessive-compulsive disorder is associated with broad impairments in executive function: A meta-analysis. *Clinical Psychological Science*, 3(2), 301–330. doi:10.1177/2167702614534210

Snyder, M. (1986). *Public appearances/Private realities: The psychology of self-monitoring*. New York: Freeman.

Society for Human Resource Management (SHRM). (2011). *2011 Employee benefits: Examining employee benefits amidst uncertainty*. Alexandria, VA: Society for Human Resource Management.

Solberg, L. M., Solberg, L. B., & Peterson, E. N. (2014). Measuring impact of stress in sandwich generation caring for demented parents. *Geropsych: The Journal of Gerontopsychology and Geriatric Psychiatry*, 27(4), 171–179. doi:10.1024/1662-9647/a000114

Solomon, S., Greenberg, J. L., & Pyszczynski, T. (1991). A terror management theory of social behavior: The psychological functions of self-esteem and cultural worldviews. In M. Zanna (Ed.), *Advances in experimental social psychology, Vol. 24*. Orlando, FL: Academic Press.

Solomon, S., Greenberg, J., & Pyszczynski, T. (2004a). The cultural animal: Twenty years of terror management. In J. Greenberg, S. L. Koole, & T. Pyszczynski (Eds.), *Handbook of experimental existential psychology*. New York: Guilford.

Solomon, S., Greenberg, J., & Pyszczynski, T. (2004b). Lethal consumption: Death-denying materialism. In T. Kasser & A. D. Kanner (Eds.), *Psychology and consumer culture: The struggle for a good life in a materialistic world*. Washington, DC: American Psychological Association.

Solomon, S. E., Rothblum, E. D., & Balsam, K. F. (2004). Pioneers in partnership: Lesbian and gay male couples in civil unions compared with those not in civil unions and married heterosexual siblings. *Journal of Family Psychology*, 18, 275–286.

Solowij, N., Stephens, R. S., Roffman, R. A., Babor, T., Kadden, R., Miller, M., Christiansen. K., McRee, B., & Vendetti, J. (2002). Cognitive functioning of long-term heavy cannabis users seeking treatment. *Journal of the American Medical Association*, 287, 1123–1131.

Sommer, K. L., & Baumeister, R. F. (2002). Self-evaluation, persistence, and performance following implicit rejection: The role of trait self-esteem. *Personality and Social Psychology Bulletin, 28*, 926–938.

Son Hing, L. S., Li, W., & Zanna, M. P. (2002). Inducing hypocrisy to reduce prejudicial responses among aversive racists. *Journal of Experimental Social Psychology, 38*, 71–78.

Sonfield A., Hasstedt K., & Gold R. B. (2014). *Moving forward: family planning in the era of health reform.* New York: Guttmacher Institute.

Sonnentag, S., & Frese, M. (2003). Stress in organizations. In W. C. Borman, D. R. Ilgen, & R. J. Klimoski (Eds.), *Handbook of psychology, Vol. 12: Industrial and organizational psychology.* New York: Wiley.

Sorokowski, P., Sorokowska, A., Oleszkiewicz, A., Frackowiak, T., Huk, A., & Pisanski, K. (2015). Selfie posting behaviors are associated with narcissism among men. *Personality and Individual Differences, 85*, 123–127. doi:10.1016/j.paid.2015.05.004

South, S. C., Reichborn-Kjennerud, T., Eaton, N. R., & Krueger, R. F. (2013). Genetics of personality. In H. Tennen, J. Suls, & I. B. Weiner (Eds.), *Handbook of psychology, Vol. 5: Personality and social psychology* (2nd ed.). New York: Wiley.

South, S. C., Reichborn-Kjennerud, T., Eaton, N. R., & Krueger, R. F. (2015). Genetics of personality. In M. Mikulincer, P. R. Shaver, M. L. Cooper, & R. J. Larsen (Eds.), *APA handbook of personality and social psychology, Vol. 4: Personality processes and individual differences.* Washington, DC: American Psychological Association.

South, S. J., Bose, S., & Trent, K. (2004). Anticipating divorce: Spousal agreement, predictive accuracy, and effects on labor supply and fertility. *Journal of Divorce and Remarriage, 40*(3–4), 1–22.

Souza, R., Bernatsky, S., Reyes, R., & de Jong, K. (2007). Mental health status of vulnerable tsunami-affected communities: A survey in Aceh Province, Indonesia. *Journal of Traumatic Stress, 20*, 263–269.

Sparks, E. A., & Baumeister, R. F. (2008). If bad is stronger than good, why focus on human strength? In S. J. Lopez (Ed.), *Positive psychology: Exploring the best in people, Vol. 1: Discovering human strengths* (pp. 55–79). Westport, CT: Praeger/Greenwood.

Sparks, J. A., Duncan, B. L., & Miller, S. D. (2008). Common factors in psychotherapy. In J. L. Lebow (Ed.), *Twenty-first century psychotherapies: Contemporary approaches to theory and practice.* New York: Wiley.

Spears, R. (2011). Group identities: The social identity perspective. In S. J. Schwartz, K. Luyckx, & V. L. Vignoles (Eds.), *Handbook of identity theory and research, Vols. 1 and 2* (pp. 201–224). New York: Springer.

Spears, R., & Stroebe, W. (2015). Two (or more?) cognitive approaches to stereotype formation: Biased or reality based? In S. J. Stroessner & J. W. Sherman (Eds.), *Social perception from individuals to groups* (pp. 141–158). New York: Psychology Press.

Special, W. P., & Li-Barber, K. T. (2012). Self-disclosure and student satisfaction with Facebook. *Computers in Human Behavior, 28*(2), 624–630. doi:10.1016/j.chb.2011.11.008

Spence, I., Yu, J. J., Feng, J., & Marshman, J. (2009). Women match men when learning a spatial skill. *Journal of Experimental Psychology, 35*, 1097–1103.

Spence, J. T. (1983). Comment on Lubinski, Tellegen, and Butcher's "Masculinity, femininity, and androgyny viewed and assessed as distinct concepts." *Journal of Personality and Social Psychology, 44*, 440–446.

Sperry, R. W. (1982). Some effects of disconnecting the cerebral hemispheres. *Science, 217*, 1223–1226, 1250.

Spiegler, M. D. (2016). *Contemporary behavior therapy* (6th ed.). Belmont, CA: Wadsworth.

Spielmans, G. I., & Kirsch, I. (2014). Drug approval and drug effectiveness. *Annual Review of Clinical Psychology, 10*, 741–766. doi:10.1146/annurev-clinpsy-050212-185533

Spitz, H. I. (2009). Group psychotherapy. In B. J. Sadock, V. A. Sadock, & P. Ruiz (Eds.), *Kaplan & Sadock's comprehensive textbook of psychiatry* (pp. 2832–2856). Philadelphia: Lippincott Williams & Wilkins.

Spitz, H. I., & Spitz, S. (2009). Family and couple therapy. In B. J. Sadock, V. A. Sadock, & P. Ruiz (Eds.), *Kaplan & Sadock's comprehensive textbook of psychiatry* (pp. 2845–2856). Philadelphia: Lippincott, Williams & Wilkins.

Spokane, A. R., & Cruza-Guet, M. C. (2005). Holland's theory of vocational personalities in work environments. In S. D. Brown & R. W. Lent (Eds.), *Career development and counseling: Putting theory and research to work.* Hoboken, NJ: Wiley.

Sprecher, S. (1994). Two sides to the breakup of dating relationships. *Personal Relationships, 1*, 199–222.

Sprecher, S. (2002). Sexual satisfaction in premarital relationships: Associations with satisfaction, love, commitment, and stability. *The Journal of Sex Research, 39*(3), 190–196.

Sprecher, S. (2014). Effects of actual (manipulated) and perceived similarity on liking in get-acquainted interactions: The role of communication. *Communication Monographs, 81*(1), 4–27. doi:10.1080/03637751.2013.839884

Sprecher, S., & Cate, R. M. (2004). Sexual satisfaction and sexual expression as predictors of relationship satisfaction and stability. In J. H. Harvey, A. Wenzel, & S. Sprecher (Eds.), *The handbook of sexuality and close relationships.* Mahwah, NJ: Lawrence Erlbaum.

Sprecher, S., & Treger, S. (2015). The benefits of turn-taking reciprocal self-disclosure in get-acquainted interactions. *Personal Relationships, 22*(3), 460–475. doi:10.1111/pere.12090

Sprecher, S., Brooks, J. E., & Avogo, W. (2013). Self-esteem among young adults: Differences and similarities based on gender, race, and cohort (1990–2012). *Sex Roles, 69*(5–6), 264–275. doi:10.1007/s11199-013-0295-y

Sprecher, S., Christopher, F. S., & Cate, R. (2006). Sexuality in close relationships. In A. L. Vangelisti & D. Perlman (Eds.), *The Cambridge handbook of personal relationships.* New York: Cambridge University Press.

Sprecher, S., Felmlee, D., Metts, S., & Cupach, W. (2015). Relationship initiation and development. In M. Mikulincer, P. R. Shaver, J. A. Simpson, & J. F. Dovidio (Eds.), *APA handbook of personality and social psychology, Vol. 3: Interpersonal relations* (pp. 211–245). Washington, DC: American Psychological Association. doi:10.1037/14344-008

Sprecher, S., Treger, S., & Wondra, J. D. (2013). Effects of self-disclosure role on liking, closeness, and other impressions in get-acquainted interactions. *Journal of Social and Personal Relationships, 30*(4), 497–514.

Sprecher, S., Treger, S., Wondra, J. D., Hilaire, N., & Wallpe, K. (2013). Taking turns: Reciprocal self-disclosure promotes liking in initial interactions. *Journal of Experimental Social Psychology, 49*(5), 860–866. doi:10.1016/j.jesp.2013.03.017

Springer, S. P., & Deutsch, G. (1998). *Left brain, right brain: Perspectives from cognitive neuroscience* (5th ed.). New York: Freeman.

Sproesser, G., Schupp, H. T., & Renner, B. (2014). The bright side of stress-induced eating: Eating more when stressed but less when pleased. *Psychological Science, 25*(1), 58–65. doi:10.1177/0956797613494849

Stafford, L., & Canary, D. J. (1991). Maintenance strategies and romantic relationship type, gender and relational characteristics. *Journal of Social and Personal Relationships, 8*, 217–242.

Staines, G. L. (2008). The relative efficacy of psychotherapy: Reassessing the methods-based paradigm. *Review of General Psychology, 12*(4), 330–343.

Stake, J. E., & Eisele, H. (2010). Gender and personality. In J. C. Chrisler & D. R. McCreary (Eds.), *Handbook of gender research in psychology, Vol. 2* (pp. 19–40). New York: Springer.

Stamler, J., Daviglus, M. L., Garside, D. B., Dyer, A. R., Greenland, P., & Neaton, J. D. (2000). Relationship of baseline serum cholesterol levels in 3 large cohorts of younger men to long-term coronary, cardiovascular, and all-cause mortality and to longevity. *Journal of the American Medical Association, 284*, 311–318.

Stangor, C., & Crandall, C. S. (2013). *Stereotyping and prejudice.* New York: Psychology Press.

Stanko, K. E., Cherry, K. E., Ryker, K. S., Mughal, F., Marks, L. D., Brown, J. S., . . . Jazwinski, S. M. (2015). Looking for the silver lining: Benefit finding after hurricanes Katrina and Rita in middle-aged, older, and oldest-old adults. *Current Psychology: A Journal for Diverse Perspectives on Diverse Psychological Issues.* doi:10.1007/s12144-015-9366-2

Stanley, M. A., & Beidel, D. C. (2009). Behavior therapy. In B. J. Sadock, V. A. Sadock, & P. Ruiz (Eds.), *Kaplan & Sadock's comprehensive textbook of psychiatry* (pp. 2781–2803). Philadelphia: Lippincott Williams & Wilkins.

Stanley, S. M., Rhoades, G. K., Amato, P. R., Markman, H. J., & Johnson, C. A. (2010). The timing of cohabitation and engagement: Impact on first and second marriages. *Journal of Marriage and Family, 72*(4), 906–918. doi:10.1111/j.1741-3737.2010.00738.x

Stanton, S. C. E., & Campbell, L. (2014). Psychological and physiological predictors of health in romantic relationships: An attachment perspective. *Journal of Personality, 82*(6), 528–538. doi:10.1111/jopy.12056

Starcevic, V. (2013). Is internet addiction a useful concept? *Australian and New Zealand Journal of Psychiatry, 47*, 16–19. doi: 10.1177/0004867412461693

Statista: The Statistics Portal (2015). Beliefs about online dating according to U.S. singles as of September 2013, by gender. Retrieved from www.statista.com/statistics/316481/us-beliefs-online-dating

Statistic Brain Research Institute (2015). Arranged/forced marriage statistics. Retrieved from www.statisticbrain.com/arranged-marriage-statistics

Stead, L. F., Perera, R., Bullen, C., Mant, D., & Lancaster, T. (2008). Nicotine replacement therapy for smoking cessation. *Cochrane Database of Systematic Reviews,* Cochrane AN: CD000146.

Steel, P. (2007). The nature of procrastination: A meta-analytic and theoretical review of quintessential self-regulatory failure. *Psychological Bulletin, 133*(1), 65–94.

Steele, C. M. (1997). A threat in the air: How stereotypes shape intellectual identity and performance. *American Psychologist, 52*, 613–629.

Steele, C. M. (2011). *Whistling Vivaldi: How stereotypes affect us and what we can do.* New York: Norton.

Steele, C. M., & Aronson, J. (1995). Stereotype threat and the intellectual test performance of African Americans. *Journal of Personality and Social Psychology, 69*, 797–811.

Steiger, H., Bruce, K. R., & Israël, M. (2003). Eating disorders. In G. Stricker & T. A. Widiger (Eds.), *Handbook of psychology, Vol. 8: Clinical psychology.* New York: Wiley.

Steiger, H., Bruce, K. R., & Israël, M. (2013). Eating disorders: Anorexia nervosa, bulimia nervosa, and binge eating disorder. In T. A. Widiger, G. Stricker, & I. B. Weiner (Eds.), *Handbook of psychology, Vol. 8: Clinical psychology* (2nd ed.). New York: Wiley.

Steil, J. M. (2009). Dual-earner couples. In H. T. Reis & S. Sprecher (Eds.), *Encyclopedia of human relationships, Vol. 2* (pp. 469–471). Los Angeles: Sage Reference.

Stephens, N. M., Markus, H. R., & Townsend, S. M. (2007). Choice as an act of meaning: The case of social class. *Journal of Personality and Social Psychology, 93*(5), 814–830. doi:10.1037/0022-3514.93.5.814

Steptoe, A., Shankar, A., Demakakos, P., & Wardle, J. (2013). Social isolation, loneliness, and all-cause mortality in older men and women. *PNAS Proceedings of the National Academy of Sciences of the United States of America, 110*, 5797–5801.

Stermer, P. S., & Burkley, M. (2012). Xbox or sexbox? an examination of sexualized content in video games. *Social and Personality Psychology Compass, 6*(7), 525–535. doi:10.1111/j.1751-9004.2012.00442.x

Stermer, P. S., & Burkley, M. (2015). SeX-box: Exposure to sexist video games predicts benevolent sexism. *Psychology of Popular Media Culture, 4*(1), 47–55. doi:10.1037/a0028397

Sternberg, R. J. (1986). A triangular theory of love. *Psychological Review, 93* 119–135.

Sternberg, R. J. (2012). Understanding love. *Psychologist, 25*(1), 27–28.

Sternberg, R. J. (2013). Searching for love. *Psychologist, 26*(2), 98–101.

Sterner, W. R. (2012). Integrating existentialism and super's life-span, life-space approach. *The Career Development Quarterly, 60*(2), 152–162. doi:10.1002/j.2161-0045.2012.00013.x

Stets, J. E., & Burke, P. J. (2003). A sociological approach to self and identity. In M. R. Leary & J. P. Tangney (Eds.), *Handbook of self and identity* (pp. 128–152). New York: Guilford.

Stevens, C. K., & Kristof, A. L. (1995). Making the right impression: A field study of applicant impression management during job interviews. *Journal of Applied Psychology, 80*(5), 587–606. http://dx.doi.org/10.1037/0021-9010.80.5.587

Stewart, G. L., Dustin, S. L., Barrick, M. R., & Darnold, T. C. (2008). Exploring the handshake in employment interviews. *Journal of Applied Psychology, 93*(5), 1139–1146. doi:10.1037/0021-9010.93.5.1139

Stewart, J. A., Russakoff, M., & Stewart, J. W. (2014). Pharmacotherapy, ECT, and TMS. In J. L. Cutler, (Ed.), *Psychiatry* (3rd ed). New York: Oxford University Press.

Stewart-Knox, B. J., Sittlington, J., Rugkasa, J., Harrisson, S., Treacy, M., & Abauza, P. S. (2005). Smoking and peer groups: Results from a longitudinal qualitative study of young people in Northern Ireland. *British Journal of Social Psychology, 44,* 397–414.

Stier, H., & Yaish, M. (2014). Occupational segregation and gender inequality in job quality: A multi-level approach. *Work, Employment and Society, 28*(2), 225–246. doi:10.1177/0950017013510758

Stiglitz, J. E. (2012). *The price of inequality: How today's divided society endangers our future.* New York: Norton.

Stith, S. M., Smith, D. B., Penn, C. E., Ward, D. B., & Tritt, D. (2004). Intimate partner physical abuse perpetration and victimization risk factors: A meta-analytic review. *Aggression and Violent Behavior, 10,* 65–98.

Stoet, G., & Geary, D. C. (2015). Sex differences in academic achievement are not related to political, economic, or social equality. *Intelligence, 48,* 137–151. doi:10.1016 /j.intell.2014.11.006

Stokstad, E. (2009, November 25). Americans' eating habits more wasteful than ever. *ScienceNOW.* Retrieved from http://news.sciencemag.org/sciencenow/2009/11/25-01 .html?ref=hp

Stoll, B. M., Arnaut, G. L., Fromme, D. K., & Felker-Thayer, J. A. (2005). Adolescents in stepfamilies: A qualitative analysis. *Journal of Divorce and Remarriage, 44,* 177–189.

Stone, A. A., Krueger, A. B., Steptoe, A., & Harter, J. K. (2010). The socioeconomic gradient in daily colds and influenza, headaches, and pain. *Archives of Internal Medicine, 170,* 570–572.

Stone, J., & McWhinnie, C. (2008). Evidence that blatant versus subtle stereotype threat cues impact performance through dual processes. *Journal of Experimental Social Psychology, 44*(2), 445–452.

Stone, P., & Lovejoy, M. (2004, November). Fast-track women and the "choice" to stay home. *Annals of the American Academy of Political and Social Science, 596,* 62–83.

Stone, W. N. (2008). Group psychotherapy. In A. Tasman, J. Kay, J. A. Lieberman, M. B. First, & M. Maj (Eds.), *Psychiatry* (3rd ed.). New York: Wiley-Blackwell.

Stoner, R., Chow, M. L., Boyle, M. P., Sunkin, S. M., Mouton, P. R., Roy, S., . . . Courchesne, E. (2014). Patches of disorganization in the neocortex of children with autism. *The New England Journal of Medicine, 370,* 1209–1219. doi:10.1056/NEJMoa1307491

Stoney, C. M. (2003). Gender and cardiovascular disease: A psychobiological and integrative approach. *Current Directions in Psychological Science, 12*(4), 129–133.

Stowell, J. R., Robles, T. F., & Kane, H. S. (2013). Psychoneuroimmunology: Mechanisms, individual differences, and interventions. In A. M. Nezu, C. M. Nezu, P. A. Geller, & I. B. Weiner (Eds.), *Handbook of psychology, Vol. 9: Health psychology* (2nd ed.). New York: Wiley.

Strahan, E. J., Lafrance, A., Wilson, A. E., Ethier, N., Spencer, S. J., & Zanna, M. P. (2008). Victoria's dirty secret: How sociocultural norms influence adolescent girls and women. *Personality and Social Psychology Bulletin, 34*(2), 288–301.

Strassberg, D. S., & Mackaronis, J. E. (2014). Sexuality and psychotherapy. In D. L. Tolman & L. M. Diamond (Eds.), *APA handbook of sexuality and psychology, Vol. 2* (pp. 105–136). Washington, D. C.: American Psychological Association.

Strassberg, D. S., Perelman, M. A., & Watter, D. N. (2014). Sexual dysfunction in males. In L. Grossman, S. Walfish, (Eds.), *Translating psychological research into practice* (pp. 435–442). New York: Springer.

Striegel-Moore, R. H., & Bulik, C. M. (2007). Risk factors for eating disorders. *American Psychologist, 62,* 181–198.

Stroebe, K., Barreto, M., & Ellemers, N. (2010). Experiencing discrimination: How members of disadvantaged groups can be helped to cope with discrimination. *Social Issues And Policy Review, 4*(1), 181–213. doi:10.1111/j.1751-2409.2010 .01021.x

Stroebe, K., Lodewijkx, H. F. M., & Spears, R. (2005). Do unto others as they do unto you: Reciprocity and social identification as determinants of ingroup favoritism. *Personality and Social Psychology Bulletin, 31,* 831–845.

Stroebe, M., Stroebe, W., van de Schoot, R., , Schut, H., Abakoumkin, G., & Li, J. (2014). Guilt in bereavement: The role of self-blame and regret in coping with loss. *PLoS One, 9*(5) .

Stroup, T. S., Lawrence, R. E., Abbas, A. I., Miller, B. R., Perkins, D. O., & Lieberman, J. A. (2014). Schizophrenia spectrum and other psychotic disorders. In R. E. Hales, S. C. Yudofsky & L. W. Roberts (Eds.), *The American Psychiatric Publishing textbook of psychiatry* (6th ed.). Washington, DC: American Psychiatric Publishing.

Stults-Kolehmainen, M. A., & Sinha, R. (2014). The effects of stress on physical activity and exercise. *Sports Medicine, 44*(1), 81–121. doi:10.1007/s40279-013-0090-5

Stunkard, A. J., Harris, J. R., Pederson, N. L., & McClearn, G. E. (1990). The body-mass index of twins who have been reared apart. *New England Journal of Medicine, 322,* 1483–1487.

Stunkard, A. J., Sorensen, T., Hanis, C., Teasdale, T. W., Chakraborty, R., Schull, W. J., & Schulsinger, F. (1986). An adoption study of human obesity. *New England Journal of Medicine, 314,* 193–198.

Stürmer, T., Hasselbach, P., & Amelang, M. (2006). Personality, lifestyle, and risk of cardiovascular disease and cancer: Follow-up of population based cohort. *British Medical Journal, 332,* 1359.

Substance Abuse and Mental Health Services Administration. (2011). Results from the 2010 National Survey on Drug Use and Health: Summary of National Findings, NSDUH Series H-41, HHS Publication No. (SMA) 11-4658. Rockville, MD: Substance Abuse and Mental Health Services Administration.

Sudak, H. S. (2005). Suicide. In B. J. Sadock & V. A. Sadock (Eds.), *Kaplan & Sadock's comprehensive textbook of psychiatry.* Philadelphia: Lippincott Williams & Wilkins.

Sue, S., Cheng, J. Y., Saad, C. S., & Chu, J. P. (2012). Asian American mental health: A call to action. *American Psychologist, 67,* 532–544. doi:10.1037/a0028900

Sue, S., Zane, N., & Young, K. (1994). Research on psychotherapy with culturally diverse populations. In A. E. Bergin & S. L. Garfield (Eds.), *Handbook of psychotherapy and behavior change* (4th ed.). New York: Wiley.

Suls, J., & Bunde, J. (2005). Anger, anxiety, and depression as risk factors for cardiovascular disease: The problems and implications of overlapping affective dispositions. *Psychological Bulletin, 131,* 260–300.

Suls, J., Davidson, K., & Kaplan, R. (Eds.). (2010). *Handbook of health psychology and behavioral medicine.* New York: Guilford.

Suls, J., & Wheeler, L. (2012). Social comparison theory. In P. M. Van Lange, A. W. Kruglanski, & E. T. Higgins (Eds.), *Handbook of theories of social psychology, Vol. 1* (pp. 460–482). Thousand Oaks, CA: Sage.

Sulsky, L., & Smith, C. (2005). *Work stress.* Belmont, CA: Wadsworth.

Summers, G., & Feldman, N. S. (1984). Blaming the perpetrator: An attributional analysis of spouse abuse. *Journal of Social and Clinical Psychology, 2,* 339–347.

Super, D. E. (1988). Vocational adjustment: Implementing a self-concept. *The Career Development Quarterly, 36,* 351–357.

Super, D. E. (1990). A life-span, life-space approach to career development. In D. Brown & L. Brooks (Eds.), *Career choice and development* (2nd ed., pp. 197–261). San Francisco, CA: Jossey-Bass.

Surra, C. A., & Boelter, J. M. (2013). Dating and mate selection. In G. W. Peterson & K. R. Bush (Eds.), *Handbook of marriage and the family* (3rd ed., pp. 211–232). New York: Springer Science + Business Media. doi:10.1007/978-1-4614-3987-5_10

Surtees, P. G., Wainwright, N. W., J., Luben, R., Day, N. E., & Khaw, K.-T. (2005). Prospective cohort study of hostility and the risk of cardiovascular disease mortality. *International Journal of Cardiology, 100,* 155–161.

Suschinsky, K. D., Lalumiere, M. L., & Chivers, M. L. (2009). Sex differences in patterns of genital sexual arousal: Measurement artifacts of true phenomena? *Archives of Sexual Behavior, 38,* 559–574.

Susser, E., Neugebauer, R., Hoek, H. W., Brown, A. S., Lin, S., Labovitz, D., & Gorman, J. M. (1996). Schizophrenia after prenatal famine: Further evidence. *Archives of General Psychiatry, 53,* 25–31.

Sussman, N. (2009). Selective serotonin reuptake inhibitors. In B. J. Sadock, V. A. Sadock, & P. Ruiz (Eds.), *Kaplan & Sadock's comprehensive textbook of psychiatry* (pp. 3190–3205). Philadelphia: Lippincott Williams & Wilkins.

Sutfin, E. L., McCoy, T. P., Morrell, H. R., Hoeppner, B. B., & Wolfson, M. (2013). Electronic cigarette use by college students. *Drug and Alcohol Dependence, 131*(3), 214–221. doi:10.1016/j.drugalcdep.2013.05.001

Sutin, A. R., Ferrucci, L., Zonderman, A. B., & Terracciano, A. (2011). Personality and obesity across the adult life span. *Journal of Personality and Social Psychology, 101*(3), 579–592.

Sutker, P. B., & Allain, A. J. (2001). Antisocial personality disorder. In P. B. Sutker & H. E. Adams (Eds.), *Comprehensive handbook of psychopathology* (3rd ed.). New York: Kluwer Academic/Plenum.

Swan, G. E., Hudmon, K. S., & Khroyan, T. V. (2003). Tobacco dependence. In A. M. Nezu, C. M. Nezu, & P. A. Geller (Eds.), *Handbook of psychology, Vol. 9: Health psychology.* New York: Wiley.

Swanson, J. L., & D'Achiardi, C. (2005). Beyond interests, needs/values, and abilities: Assessing other important career constructs over the life span. In S. D. Brown & R. W. Lent (Eds.), *Career development and counseling: Putting theory and research to work.* New York: Wiley.

Swanson, S. A., Crow, S. J., Le Grange, D., Swendsen, J., & Merikangas, K. R. (2011). Prevalence and correlates of eating disorders in adolescents: Results from the national comorbidity survey replication adolescent supplement. *Archives of General Psychiatry, 68,* 714–723. doi:10.1001 /archgenpsychiatry.2011.22

Swartz, J. R., Williamson, D. E., & Hariri, A. R. (2015). Developmental change in amygdala reactivity during adolescence: Effects of family history of depression and stressful life events. *The American Journal of Psychiatry, 172*(3), 276–283. doi:10.1176/appi.ajp.2014.14020195

Swencionis, J. K., & Fiske, S. T. (2014). How social neuroscience can inform theories of social comparison. *Neuropsychologia, 56,* 140–146. doi:10.1016/j.neuropsychologia.2014.01.009

Swendsen, J., Burstein, M., Case, B., Conway, K. P., Dierker, L., He, J., & Merikangas, K. R. (2012). Use and abuse of alcohol and illicit drugs in US adolescents: Results of the National Comorbidity Survey-Adolescent Supplement. *Archives of General Psychiatry, 69*(4), 390–398. doi:10.1001/archgenpsychiatry.2011.1503

Swithers, S. E., Martin, A. A., Clark, K. M., Laboy, A. F., & Davidson, T. L. (2010). Body weight gain in rats consuming sweetened liquids: Effects of caffeine and diet composition. *Appetite, 55*(3), 528–533.

Szasz, T. S. (1974). *The myth of mental illness.* New York: HarperCollins.

Szasz, T. S. (1993). *A lexicon of lunacy: Metaphoric malady, moral responsibility, and psychiatry.* New Brunswick, NJ: Transaction.

Szigethy, E. M., & Friedman, E. S. (2009). Combined psychotherapy and pharmacology. In B. J. Sadock, V. A. Sadock, & P. Ruiz (Eds.), *Kaplan & Sadock's comprehensive textbook of psychiatry* (pp. 2923–2931). Philadelphia: Lippincott Williams & Wilkins.

Tajfel, H. (1982). *Social identity and intergroup relations.* London: Cambridge University Press.

Tam, C. S., Garnett, S. P., Cowell, C. T., Campbell, K., Cabrera, G., & Baur, L. A. (2006). Soft drink consumption and excess weight gain in Australian school students: Results from the Nepean study. *International Journal of Obesity, 30,* 1091–1093.

Tamborski, M., & Brown, R. P. (2011). The measurement of trait narcissism in social-personality research. In W. K. Campbell & J. D. Miller (Eds.), *The handbook of narcissism and narcissistic personality disorder: Theoretical approaches, empirical findings, and treatments* (pp. 133–140). New York: Wiley.

Tang, C., Curran, M., & Arroyo, A. (2014). Cohabitors' reasons for living together, satisfaction with sacrifices, and relationship quality. *Marriage & Family Review, 50*(7), 598–620. doi:10.1080/01494929.2014.938289

Tang, J., Yu, Y., Du, Y., Ma, Y., Zhang, D., & Wang, J. (2014). Prevalence of internet addiction and its association with stressful life events and psychological symptoms among adolescent internet users. *Addictive Behaviors, 39,* 744–747. doi: 10.1016/j.addbeh.2013.12.010

Taormina, R. J., & Gao, J. H. (2013). Maslow and the motivation hierarchy: Measuring satisfaction of the needs. *The American Journal of Psychology, 126*(2), 155–177. doi:10.5406/amerjpsyc.126.2.0155

Tardy, C. H., & Dindia, K. (2006). Self-disclosure: Strategic revelation of information in personal and professional relationships. In O. Hargie (Ed.), *The handbook of communication skills* (3rd ed., pp. 229–266). New York: Routledge/Taylor & Francis Group.

Tavris, C. (1982). *Anger: The misunderstood emotion.* New York: Simon & Schuster.

Tavris, C. (1989). *Anger: The misunderstood emotion* (2nd ed.). New York: Simon & Schuster.

Taylor, D. A., & Altman, I. (1987). Communication in interpersonal relationships: Social penetration processes. In M. E. Roloff & G. R. Miller (Eds.), *Interpersonal processes: New directions in communication research.* Newbury Park, CA: Sage.

Taylor, M. C. (1995). White backlash to workplace affirmative action: Peril or myth? *Social Forces, 73,* 1385–1414.

Taylor, M. C. (2014). *Speed limits: Where time went and why we have so little left.* New Haven, CT: Yale University Press.

Taylor, S. E. (1981). The interface of cognitive and social psychology. In J. Harvey (Ed.), *Cognition, social behavior, and the environment* (pp. 189–211). Hillsdale, NJ: Lawrence Erlbaum.

Taylor, S. E. (2007). Social support. In H. S. Friedman & R. C. Silver (Eds.), *Foundations of health psychology.* New York: Oxford University Press.

Taylor, S. E. (2011a). Affiliation and stress. In S. Folkman (Ed.). *The Oxford handbook of stress, health, & coping* (pp. 86–100). New York: Oxford University Press.

Taylor, S. E. (2011b). Positive illusions: How ordinary people become extraordinary. In M. Gernsbacher, R. W. Pew, L. M. Hough, & J. R. Pomerantz (Eds.), *Psychology and the real world: Essays illustrating fundamental contributions to society* (pp. 224–228). New York: Worth.

Taylor, S. E., & Brown, J. D. (1988). Illusion and well-being: A social psychological perspective on mental health. *Psychological Bulletin, 103,* 193–210.

Taylor, S. E., & Brown, J. D. (1994). Positive illusions and well-being revisited: Separating fact from fiction. *Psychological Bulletin, 116,* 21–27.

Taylor, S. E., & Master, S. L. (2011). Social responses to stress: The tend-and-befriend model. In R. J. Contrada & A. Baum (Eds.), *The handbook of stress science: Biology, psychology, and health* (pp. 101–109). New York: Springer.

Taylor, S. E., Sherman, D. K., Kim, H. S., Jarcho, J., Takagi, K., & Dunagan, M. S. (2004). Culture and social support: Who seeks it and why? *Journal of Personality, 87,* 354–362.

Tazelaar, M. A., Van Lange, P. M., & Ouwerkerk, J. W. (2004). How to cope with 'noise' in social dilemmas: The benefits of communication. *Journal of Personality and Social Psychology, 87*(6), 845–859. doi:10.1037/0022-3514.87.6.845

Teachman, J. (2008). Complex life course patterns and the risk of divorce in second marriages. *Journal of Marriage and Family, 70,* 294–305.

Teachman, J., Tedrow, L., & Kim, G. (2013). The demography of families. In G. W. Peterson, K. R. Bush, G. W. Peterson, & K. R. Bush (Eds.), *Handbook of marriage and the family* (3rd ed., pp. 39–63). New York: Springer Science + Business Media. doi:10.1007/978-1-4614-3987-5_3

Tedeschi, R. G., & Calhoun, L. G. (1996). The traumatic growth inventory: Measuring the positive legacy of trauma. *Journal of Traumatic Stress, 9,* 455–471.

Tedeschi, R. G., & Calhoun, L. G. (2004). Posttraumatic growth: Conceptual foundations and empirical evidence. *Psychological Inquiry, 15*(1), 1–18.

Temoshok, L. R. (2004). Type C coping/behavior pattern. In A. J. Christensen, R. Martin, & J. Morrision Smyth (Eds.), *Encyclopedia of health psychology* (pp. 332–333). New York: Kluwer Academic/Plenum.

ten Brinke, L., MacDonald, S., Porter, S., & O'Connor, B. (2012). Crocodile tears: Facial, verbal and body language behaviours associated with genuine and fabricated remorse. *Law and Human Behavior, 36*(1), 51–59. doi:10.1037/h0093950

Teper, R., Segal, Z. V., & Inzlicht, M. (2013). Inside the mindful mind: How mindfulness enhances emotion regulation through improvements in executive control. *Current Directions in Psychological Science, 22*(6), 449–454. doi:10.1177/0963721413495869

Terracciano, A., Abdel-Khalak, A. M., Adám, N., Adamovová, L., Ahn, C. K., Ahn, H. N., . . . McCrae, R. R. (2005). National character does not reflect mean personality trait levels in 49 cultures. *Science, 310,* 96–100.

Tesser, A., Wood, J. V., & Stapel, D. A. (Eds.). (2005). *On building, defending, and regulating the self: A psychological perspective.* New York: Psychology Press.

Tetlock, P. E., & Fincher, K. (2015). Social functionalism. In B. Gawronski & G. V. Bodenhausen (Eds.), *Theory and explanation in social psychology* (pp. 266–282). New York: Guilford.

Thase, M. E. (2012). Social skills training for depression and comparative efficacy research: A 30-year retrospective. *Behavior Modification, 36,* 545–557. doi:10.1177/0145445512445610

Thase, M. E., Hahn, C., & Berton, O. (2014). Neurobiological aspects of depression. In I. H. Gotlib & C. L. Hammen (Eds.), *Handbook of depression* (3rd ed.). New York: Guilford.

Thomaes, S., & Bushman, B. J. (2011). Mirror, mirror, on the wall, who's the most aggressive of them all? Narcissism, self-esteem, and aggression. In P. R. Shaver & M. Mikulincer (Eds.), *Human aggression and violence: Causes, manifestations, and consequences* (pp. 203–219). Washington, DC: American Psychological Association. doi:10.1037/12346-011

Thompson, J. K., & Stice, E. (2001). Thin-ideal internalization: Mounting evidence for a new risk factor for body-image disturbance and eating pathology. *Current Directions in Psychological Science, 10*(5), 181–183.

Thompson, J. L., & Morris, S. B. (2013). What factors influence judges' rulings about the legality of affirmative action plans? *Journal of Business and Psychology, 28*(4), 411–424. doi:10.1007/s10869-013-9292-y

Thornton, L. M., Mazzeo, S. E., & Bulik, C. M. (2011). The heritability of eating disorders: Methods and current findings. In R. H. Adan & W. H. Kaye (Eds.), *Behavioral neurobiology of eating disorders* (pp. 141–156). New York: Springer-Verlag.

Thorogood, A., Mottillo, S., Shimony, A., Filion, K. B., Joseph, L., Genest, J., . . . Eisenberg, M. J. (2011). Isolated aerobic exercise and weight loss: A systematic review and meta-analysis of randomized controlled trials. *American Journal of Medicine, 124*(8), 747–755.

Thune, I., & Furberg, A. (2001). Physical activity and cancer risk: Dose-response and cancer, all sites and site specific. *Medicine and Science in Sports and Exercise, 33*(6), S530–S550.

Tice, D. M., & Baumeister, R. F. (1997). Longitudinal study of procrastination, performance, stress, and health: The cost and benefits of dawdling. *Psychological Science, 8,* 454–458.

Tice, D. M., Baumeister, R. F., Shmueli, D., & Muraven, M. (2007). Restoring the self: Positive affect helps improve self-regulation following ego depletion. *Journal of Experimental Social Psychology, 43*(3), 379–384.

Tidwell, N. D., Eastwick, P. W., & Finkel, E. J. (2013). Perceived, not actual, similarity predicts initial attraction in a live romantic context: Evidence from the speed-dating paradigm. *Personal Relationships, 20*(2), 199–215.

Tiggemann, M., Martins, Y., & Kirkbride, A. (2007). Oh to be lean and muscular: Body image ideals in gay and heterosexual men. *Psychology of Men & Masculinity, 8,* 15–24.

Tillotson, K., & Osborn, D. (2012). Effect of a résumé-writing workshop on résumé-writing skills. *Journal of Employment Counseling, 49*(3), 110–117. doi:10.1002/j.2161-1920.2012.00011.x

Timm, D. A., & Slavin, J. L. (2008). Dietary fiber and the relationship to chronic diseases. *American Journal of Lifestyle Medicine, 2,* 233–240.

Timonen, V., & Doyle, M. (2014). Life-long singlehood: Intersections of the past and the present. *Ageing & Society, 34*(10), 1749–1770. doi:10.1017/S0144686X13000500

Tims, M., Bakker, A. B., & Derks, D. (2014). Daily job crafting and the self-efficacy—Performance relationship. *Journal of Managerial Psychology, 29,* 490–507. doi:10.1108/JMP-05-2012-0148

To, M. L., Fisher, C. D., Ashkanasy, N. M., & Rowe, P. A. (2012). Within-person relationships between mood and creativity. *Journal of Applied Psychology, 97*(3), 599–612. doi:10.1037/a0026097

Toepfer, S. M., Cichy, K., & Peters, P. (2012). Letters of gratitude: Further evidence for author benefits. *Journal of Happiness Studies, 13*(1), 187–201. doi:10.1007/s10902-011-9257-7

Tolman, D. L., Bowman, C. P., & Fahs, B. (2014). Sexuality and embodiment. In D. L. Tolman, L. M. Diamond, J. A. Bauermeister, W. H. George, J. G. Pfaus, L. M. Ward (Eds.), *APA handbook of sexuality and psychology* (pp. 759–804). Washington, DC: American Psychological Association. doi:10.1037/14193-025

Tolstrup, J. S., Stephens, R., & Gronbaek, M. (2014). Does the severity of hangovers decline with age? Survey of the incidence of hangover in different age groups. *Alcoholism: Clinical and Experimental Research, 38*(2), 466–470. doi:10.1111/acer.12238.

Toma, C. L., & Hancock, J. T. (2010). Looks and lies: The role of physical attractiveness in online dating self-presentation and deception. *Communication Research, 37*(3), 335–351. doi:10.1177/0093650209356437

Tomko, R. L., Trull, T. J., Wood, P. K., & Sher, K. J. (2014). Characteristics of borderline personality disorder in a community sample: Comorbidity, treatment utilization, and general functioning. *Journal of Personality Disorders, 28,* 734–750. doi:10.1521/pedi_2012_26_093

Toossi, M. (2007, November). Labor force projections to 2016: More workers in their golden years. *Monthly Labor Review,* 33–52.

Torgersen, S. (2012). Epidemiology. In T. A. Widiger (Ed.), *The Oxford handbook of personality disorders.* New York: Oxford University Press.

Torres, A. R., Prince, M. J., Bebbington, P. E., Bhugra, D., Brugha, T. S., Farrell, M., Jenkins, R., Lewis, G., Meltzer, H., & Singleton, N. (2006). Obsessive-compulsive disorder: Prevalence, comorbidity, impact, and help-seeking in the British national psychiatric morbidity survey of 2000. *American Journal of Psychiatry, 163,* 1978–1985.

Tortolero, S. R., Johnson, K., Peskin, M., Cuccaro, P. M., Markham, C., Hernandez, B. F., Addy, R. C., Shegog, R., & Li, D. H. (2011). Dispelling the myth: What parents really think about sex education in schools. *Journal of Applied Research on Children: Informing Policy for Children at Risk, 2*(2).

Tosun, L. P. (2012). Motives for Facebook use and expressing "true self" on the internet. *Computers in Human Behavior, 28*(4), 1510–1517. doi:10.1016/j.chb.2012.03.018

Tov, W., & Diener, E. (2007). Culture and subjective well-being. In S. Kitayama & D. Cohen (Eds.), *Handbook of cultural psychology* (pp. 691–713). New York: Guilford.

Trace, S. E., Baker, J. H., Peñas-Lledó, E., & Bulik, C. M. (2013). The genetics of eating disorders. *Annual Review of Clinical Psychology, 9,* 589–620. doi:10.1146/annurev-clinpsy-050212-185546

Trachtenberg, J. D., & Sande, M. A. (2002). Emerging resistance to nonnucleoside reverse transcriptase inhibitors: A warning and a challenge. *Journal of the American Medical Association, 288*(2), 239–241.

Tracy, E. (2006). *The student's guide to exam success* (2nd ed.). New York: McGraw-Hill.

Tran, S., & Simpson, J. A. (2012). Attachment, commitment, and relationship maintenance: When partners really matter. In L. Campbell, J. G. La Guardia, J. M. Olson, & M. P. Zanna (Eds.), *The science of the couple* (pp. 95–117). New York: Psychology Press.

Traut-Mattausch, E., Jones, E., Frey, D., & Zanna, M. P. (2011). Are there "his" and "her" types of decisions? Exploring gender differences in the confirmation bias. *Sex Roles, 65,* 223–233. doi:10.1007/s11199-011-0009-2

Travers, K. M., Creed, P. A., & Morrissey, S. (2015). The development and initial validation of a new scale to measure explanatory style. *Personality and Individual Differences, 81,* 1–6. doi:10.1016/j.paid.2015.01.045

Travis, L. A., Bliwise, N. G., Binder, J. L., & Horne-Moyer, H. L. (2001). Changes in clients' attachment style over the course of time-limited dynamic psychotherapy. *Psychotherapy: Theory, Research, Practice, Training, 38*(2), 149–159.

Treadway, M. T., Waskom, M. L., Dillon, D. G., Holmes, A. J., Park, M. M., Chakravarty, M. M., . . . Pizzagalli, D. A. (2015). Illness progression, recent stress, and morphometry of hippocampal subfields and medial prefrontal cortex in major depression. *Biological Psychiatry, 77*(3), 285–294. doi:10.1016/j.biopsych.2014.06.018

Treger, S., & Sprecher, S. (2011). The influences of sociosexuality and attachment style on reactions to emotional versus sexual infidelity. *Journal of Sex Research, 48*(5), 413–422. doi:10.1080/00224499.2010.516845

Treger, S., Sprecher, S., & Erber, R. (2013). Laughing and liking: Exploring the interpersonal effects of humor use in initial social interactions. *European Journal of Social Psychology*, 43(6), 532–543.

Trevithick, P., & Wengraf, T. (2011). Special issue: Defences and defensiveness. *Journal of Social Work Practice*, 25(4), 383–387. doi:10.1080/02650533.2011.626641

Triandis, H. C. (1994). *Culture and social behavior*. New York: McGraw-Hill.

Triandis, H. C. (2001). Individualism-collectivism and personality. *Journal of Personality*, 69(6), 907–924.

Trogdon, J., Finkelstein, E., Feagan, C., & Cohen, J. (2012). State- and payer-specific estimates of annual medical expenditures attributable to obesity. *Obesity*, 20(1), 214–220. doi:10.1038.oby.2011.169

Troisi, J. D., & Gabriel, S. (2011). Chicken soup really is good for the soul: "Comfort food" fulfills the need to belong. *Psychological Science*, 22(6), 747–753. doi:10.1177/0956797611407931

Trope, Y., & Gaunt, R. (2003). Attribution and person perception. In M. A. Hogg & J. Cooper (Eds.), *The Sage handbook of social psychology*. Thousand Oaks, CA: Sage.

Tropp, L. R., & Page-Gould, E. (2015). Contact between groups. In M. Mikulincer, P. R. Shaver, J. F. Dovidio, & J. A. Simpson (Eds.), *APA handbook of personality and social psychology, Vol. 2: Group processes* (pp. 535–560). Washington, DC: American Psychological Association. doi:10.1037/14342-020

Trotter, P. B. (2009). Divorce, effects on adults. In H. T. Reis & S. Sprecher (Eds.), *Encyclopedia of human relationships, Vol. 2* (pp. 458–461). Los Angeles: Sage Reference.

Troy, A. B., Lewis-Smith, J., & Laurenceau, J. (2006). Interracial and intraracial romantic relationships: The search for differences in satisfaction, conflict, and attachment style. *Journal of Social and Personal Relationships*, 23, 65–80.

Trull, T. J., Carpenter, R. W., & Widiger, T. A. (2013). Personality disorders. In T. A. Widiger, G. Stricker, & I. B. Weiner (Eds.), *Handbook of psychology, Vol. 8: Clinical psychology* (2nd ed.). New York: Wiley.

Trull, T. J., Jahng, S., Tomko, R. L., Wood, P. K., & Sher, K. J. (2010). Revised NESARC personality disorder diagnoses: Gender, prevalence, and comorbidity with substance dependence disorders. *Journal of Personality Disorders*, 24, 412–426. doi:10.1521/pedi.2010.24.4.412

Trumbo, C. W., & Harper, R. (2013). Use and perception of electronic cigarettes among college students. *Journal of American College Health*, 61(3), 149–155. doi:10.1080/07448481.2013.776052

Tryon, M. S., DeCant, R., & Laugero, K. D. (2013). Having your cake and eating it too: A habit of comfort food may link chronic social stress exposure and acute stress-induced cortisol hyporesponsiveness. *Physiology & Behavior*, 114–115, 32–37. doi:10.1016/j.physbeh.2013.02.018

Trzesniewski, K. H., Donnellan, M. B., & Robins, R. W. (2003). Stability of self-esteem across the life span. *Journal of Personality and Social Psychology*, 84(1), 205–220.

Tsutsumi, A., Kayaba, K., & Ishikawa, S. (2011). Impact of occupational stress on stroke across occupational classes and genders. *Social Science & Medicine*, 72, 1652–1658.

Tucker, O. N., Szomstein, S., & Rosenthal, R. J. (2007). Nutritional consequences of weight loss surgery. *Medical Clinics of North America*, 91, 499–513.

Tugade, M. M., Devlin, H. C., & Fredrickson, B. L. (2014). Infusing positive emotions into life: The broaden-and-build theory and a dual-process model of resilience. In M. M. Tugade, M. N. Shiota & L. D. Kirby (Eds.), *Handbook of positive emotions* (pp. 28–43). New York: Guilford.

Tugade, M. M., Shiota, M. N., & Kirby, L. D. (Eds.). (2014). *Handbook of positive emotions*. New York: Guilford.

Turkle, S. (2011). *Alone together: Why we expect more from technology and less from each other*. New York: Basic Books.

Turner, J. C. (1987). *Rediscovering the social group: A self-categorization theory*. Oxford, UK: Basil Blackwell.

Turner-Frey, W. (2014). Homophobia is a global issue. *Social Work*, 59(3), 281–282. doi:10.1093/sw/swu017

Twenge, J. M. (2006). *Generation me: Why today's young Americans are more confident, assertive, entitled—and more miserable than ever before*. New York: Free Press.

Twenge, J. M. (2011). Generational differences in mental health: Are children and adolescents suffering more, or

less? *American Journal of Orthopsychiatry*, 81, 469–472. doi:10.1111/j.1939-0025.2011.01115.x

Twenge, J. M. (2014). Time period and birth cohort differences in depressive symptoms in the U.S., 1982–2013. *Social Indicators Research*, 121(2), 437–454. doi:10.1007/s11205-014-0647-1

Twenge, J. M., & Campbell W. K. (2003). Isn't it fun to get the respect that we're going to deserve? Narcissism, social rejection, and aggression. *Personality and Social Psychology*, 29(2), 261–272.

Twenge, J. M., & Campbell, W. K. (2009). *The narcissism epidemic: Living in the age of entitlement*. New York: Free Press.

Twenge, J. M., Campbell, W. K., & Foster, C. A. (2003). Parenthood and marital satisfaction: A meta-analytic review. *Journal of Marriage and Family*, 65, 574–83.

Twenge, J. M., Catanese, K. R., & Baumeister, R. F. (2002). Social exclusion causes self-defeating behavior. *Journal of Personality and Social Psychology*, 83(3), 606–615. doi:10.1037/0022-3514.83.3.606

Twenge, J. M., & Crocker, J. (2002). Race and self-esteem: Meta-analyses comparing whites, blacks, Hispanics, Asians, and American Indians and comment on Gray-Little and Hafdahl (2000). *Psychological Bulletin*, 128(3), 371–408.

Twenge, J. M., Gentile, B., & Campbell, W. K. (2015). Birth cohort differences in personality. In M. Mikulincer, P. R. Shaver, M. L. Cooper, & R. J. Larsen (Eds.), *APA handbook of personality and social psychology, Vol. 4: Personality processes and individual differences*. Washington, DC: American Psychological Association.

Twenge, J. M., & Kasser, T. (2013). Generational changes in materialism and work centrality, 1976–2007: Associations with temporal changes in societal insecurity and materialistic role modeling. *Personality and Social Psychology Bulletin*, 39(7), 883–897.

Twenge, J. M., Konrath, S., Foster, J. D., Campbell, W. K., & Bushman, B. J. (2008). Egos inflating over time: A cross-temporal meta-analysis of the Narcissistic Personality Inventory. *Journal of Personality*, 76, 903–917.

U.S. Bureau of Justice Statistics. (2011). Criminal victimization, 2010 (Washington, DC: U.S. Department of Justice, 2011), Table 1. Retrieved from http://bjs.ojp.usdoj.gov/content/pub/pdf/cv10.pdf

U.S. Bureau of Justice Statistics (2015). Prisoners in 2014. Retrieved from www.bjs.gov/content/pub/pdf/p14_Summary.pdf

U.S. Bureau of Labor Statistics. (2004). *Occupational outlook handbook: 2004–2005*. Washington, DC: U.S. Government Printing Office.

U.S. Bureau of Labor Statistics. (2006). *Occupational outlook handbook, 2006–2007*. Washington, D.C.: U.S. Government Printing Office.

U.S. Bureau of Labor Statistics. (2009). Vacations, holidays, and personal leave: Access, quantity, costs, and trends. Retrieved from www.bls.gov/opub/perspectives/issue2.pdf

U.S. Bureau of Labor Statistics. (2012a, Summer). High wages after high school without a bachelor's degree. *Occupational Outlook Quarterly*. Retrieved from www.bls.gov/opub/OOQ/2012/Summer/art03.pdf

U.S. Bureau of Labor Statistics. (2012b). Unemployed persons by duration of unemployment. Retrieved from www.bls.gov/news.release/empsit.t12.htm

U.S. Bureau of Labor Statistics. (2013a). U.S. Department of Labor, current population survey. Retrieved from www.bls.gov/cps/cpsaat03.htm

U.S. Bureau of Labor Statistics. (2013b). U.S. Department of Labor, current population survey. Retrieved from http://bls.gov/cps/cpsaat04.htm

U.S. Bureau of Labor Statistics. (2013c). U.S. Department of Labor, current population survey. Retrieved from www.bls.gov/opub/mlr/2013/article/labor-force-projections-to-2022-the-labor-force-participation-rate-continues-to-fall.htm

U.S. Bureau of Labor Statistics. (2014a). Employment characteristics of families summary. Retrieved from www.bls.gov/news.release/famee.nr0.htm

U.S. Bureau of Labor Statistics. (2014b). Labor force statistics from the current population survey: Absences from work of employed full time wage and salary workers by occupation and industry. Retrieved from www.bls.gov/cps/cpsaat47.htm

U.S. Bureau of Labor Statistics. (2015a). Databases, tables, and calculators by subject: Labor force statistics from the current population survey. Retrieved from http://data.bls.gov/timeseries/LNS14000000

U.S. Bureau of Labor Statistics. (2015b). Economic new release: Table A-12—Unemployed persons by duration of unemployment. Retrieved from www.bls.gov/news.release/empsit.t12.htm

U.S. Bureau of Labor Statistics. (2015c). Number of jobs held, labor market activity, and earnings growth among the youngest baby boomers: Results from a longitudinal survey. Retrieved from www.bls.gov/news.release/pdf/nlsoy.pdf

U.S. Bureau of the Census. (2006). *Statistical abstract of the United States: 2007*. Washington, DC: U.S. Government Printing Office.

U.S. Bureau of the Census. (2011). One-third of fathers with working wives regularly care for their children, Census Bureau reports. Retrieved from www.census.gov/newsroom/releases/archives/children/cb11-198.html

U.S. Bureau of the Census. (2012a). Labor force participation rates by marital status, sex, and age: 1970 to 2010. *Statistical Abstract of the United States: 2012*. Retrieved from www.census.gov/compendia/statab/2012/tables/12s0598.pdf

U.S. Bureau of the Census. (2012b). Labor force participation rates for wives, husband present, by age of own youngest child: 1990 to 2009. *Statistical Abstract of the United States: 2012*. Retrieved from www.census.gov/compendia/Statab/2012/tables/12s0599.pdf

U.S. Bureau of the Census. (2012c). 2010 Census shows interracial and interethnic married couples grew by 28 percent over decade. www.census.gov/newsroom/releases/archives/2010_census/cb12-68.html

U.S. Bureau of the Census (2015). Marital status. Retrieved from https://www.census.gov/hhes/families/data/marital.html

U.S. Bureau of the Census (2015). Population Projections. Retrieved from www.census.gov/population/projections/data/national/2014/summarytables.html

U.S. Department of Agriculture and U.S. Department of Health and Human Services (USDA & USDHHS). (2010). *Dietary guidelines for Americans, 2010* (7th ed.). Washington, DC: U.S. Government Printing Office.

U.S. Department of Health and Human Services. (1990). *The health benefits of smoking cessation: A report of the surgeon general*. Washington, DC: U.S. Government Printing Office.

U.S. Department of Health and Human Services. (2007). Impacts of four Title V, Section 510 abstinence education programs, final report. Retrieved from http://aspe.hhs.gov/hsp/abstinence07/index.htm

U.S. Department of Health and Human Services. (2010). Dietary guidelines for Americans. Retrieved from www.guideline.gov/content.aspx?id=34277&search=2005

U.S. Department of Health and Human Services. (2014). The Health Consequences of Smoking: 50 Years of Progress: A Report of the Surgeon General. Atlanta: U.S. Department of Health and Human Services, Centers for Disease Control and Prevention, National Center for Chronic Disease Prevention and Health Promotion, Office on Smoking and Health.

U.S. National Center for Health Statistics. (2010, December). National Vital Statistics Reports (NVSR), Deaths: Preliminary Data for 2008, 59(2). from https://www.census.gov/compendia/statab/cats/births_deaths_marriages_divorces/life_expectancy.html

Uleman, J. S., & Saribay, S. A. (2012). Initial impressions of others. In K. Deaux & M. Snyder (Eds.), *The Oxford handbook of personality and social psychology* (pp. 337–366). New York: Oxford University Press.

Uleman, J. S., Hon, A., Roman, R. J., & Moskowitz, G. B. (1996). Online evidence for spontaneous trait inferences at encoding. *Personality and Psychology Bulletin*, 22(4), 377–394.

Ullén, F., de Manzano, Ö., Almeida, R., Magnusson, P. E., Pedersen, N. L., Nakamura, J., . . . Madison, G. (2012). Proneness for psychological flow in everyday life: Associations with personality and intelligence. *Personality and Individual Differences*, 52(2), 167–172. doi:10.1016/j.paid.2011.10.003

Ullman, S. E., Filipas, H. H., Townsend, S. M., & Starzynski, L. L. (2007). Psychosocial correlates of PTSD symptom severity in sexual assault survivors. *Journal of Traumatic Stress*, 20, 821–831.

Ulrich, M., & Weatherall, A. (2000). Motherhood and infertility: Viewing motherhood through the lens of infertility. *Feminism & Psychology, 10*(3), 323–336. doi:10.1177/0959353500010003003

UNAIDS. (2007). *AIDS epidemic update, 2007.* Geneva, Switzerland: Joint United Nations Programme on HIV/AIDS.

UNAIDS. (2010). *Report on the global AIDS epidemic, 2010.* Geneva, Switzerland: Joint United Nations Programme on HIV/AIDS.

Unger-Saldaña, K., & Infante-Castañeda, C. B. (2011). Breast cancer delay: A grounded model of help-seeking behaviour. *Social Science & Medicine, 72*(7), 1096–1104. doi:10.1016/j.socscimed.2011.01.022

Ursano, A. M., Kartheiser, P. H., & Barnhill, L. J. (2008). Disorders usually first diagnosed in infancy, childhood, or adolescence. In R. E. Hales, S. C. Yudofsky, & G. O. Gabbard (Eds.), *The American Psychiatric Publishing textbook of psychiatry* (5th ed., pp. 861–920). Washington, DC: American Psychiatric Publishing.

Ursano, R. J., & Carr, R. B. (2014). Psychodynamic psychotherapy. In R. E. Hales, S. C. Yudofsky, & L. W. Roberts (Eds.), *The American Psychiatric Publishing textbook of psychiatry* (6th ed.). Washington, DC: American Psychiatric Publishing.

Utz, S. (2015). The function of self-disclosure on social network sites: Not only intimate, but also positive and entertaining self-disclosures increase the feeling of connection. *Computers in Human Behavior, 45,* 1–10. doi:10.1016/j.chb.2014.11.076

Uysal, A., & Knee, C. (2012). Low trait self-control predicts self-handicapping. *Journal of Personality, 80*(1), 59–79. doi:10.1111/j.1467-6494.2011.00715.x

Valentine, K. A., Li, N. P., Penke, L., & Perrett, D. I. (2014). Judging a man by the width of his face: The role of facial ratios and dominance in mate choice at speed-dating events. *Psychological Science, 25*(3), 806–811. doi:10.1177/0956797613511823

van Anders, S. M. (2012). Testosterone and sexual desire in healthy women and men. *Archives of Sexual Behavior, 41*(6), 1471–1484. doi:10.1007/s10508-012-9946-2

Van Blerkom, D. L. (2012). *College study skills: Becoming a strategic learner.* Belmont, CA: Wadsworth.

van Bommel, M., van Prooijen, J., Elffers, H., & Van Lange, P. M. (2012). Be aware to care: Public self-awareness leads to a reversal of the bystander effect. *Journal of Experimental Social Psychology.* doi:10.1016/j.jesp.2012.02.011

van Bommel, M., van Prooijen, J., Elffers, H., & Van Lange, P. M. (2014). Intervene to be seen: The power of a camera in attenuating the bystander effect. *Social Psychological and Personality Science, 5*(4), 459–466. doi:10.1177/1948550613507958

Van der Hart, O., & Nijenhuis, E. R. S. (2009). Dissociative disorders. In P. H. Blaney & T. Millon (Eds.), *Oxford textbook of psychopathology* (pp. 452–481). New York: Oxford University Press.

van der Meer, P. H. (2014). Gender, unemployment and subjective well-being: Why being unemployed is worse for men than for women. *Social Indicators Research, 115*(1), 23–44. doi:10.1007/s11205-012-0207-5

van der Pol, L. D., Groeneveld, M. G., van Berkel, S. R., Endendijk, J. J., Hallers-Haalboom, E. T., Bakermans-Kranenburg, M. J., & Mesman, J. (2015). Fathers' and mothers' emotion talk with their girls and boys from toddlerhood to preschool age. *Emotion, 15*(6), 854–864. doi:10.1037/emo0000085

van Eeden-Moorefield, B., & Pasley, B. K. (2013). Remarriage and stepfamily life. In G. W. Peterson, K. R. Bush, G. W. Peterson, & K. R. Bush (Eds.), *Handbook of marriage and the family* (3rd ed., pp. 517–546). New York: Springer Science + Business Media. doi:10.1007/978-1-4614-3987-5_22

van Erp, T. G. M., Hibar, D. P., Rasmussen, J. M., Glahn, D. C., Pearlson, G. D., Andreassen, O. A., . . . Turner, J. A. (2015). Subcortical brain volume abnormalities in 2028 individuals with schizophrenia and 2540 healthy controls via the ENIGMA consortium. *Molecular psychiatry.* doi:10.1038/mp.2015.63

van Gelderen, L., Bos, H. W., Gartrell, N., Hermanns, J., & Perrin, E. C. (2012). Quality of life of adolescents raised from birth by lesbian mothers: The US National Longitudinal Family Study. *Journal of Developmental and Behavioral Pediatrics, 33*(1), 17–23. doi:10.1097/DBP.0b013e31823b62af

van Kammen, D. P., Hurford, I., & Marder, S. R. (2009). First-generation antipsychotics. In B. J. Sadock, V. A. Sadock, & P. Ruiz (Eds.), *Kaplan & Sadock's comprehensive textbook of psychiatry* (pp. 3105–3126). Philadelphia: Lippincott Williams & Wilkins.

Van Kleef, G. A., De Dreu, C. W., & Manstead, A. R. (2006). Supplication and appeasement in conflict and negotiation: The interpersonal effects of disappointment, worry, guilt, and regret. *Journal of Personality and Social Psychology, 91*(1), 124–142. doi:10.1037/0022-3514.91.1.124

Van Lange, Paul A. M., & Balliet, D. (2015). Interdependence theory. In M. Mikulincer, P. R. Shaver, J. A. Simpson, & J. F. Dovidio (Eds.), *APA handbook of personality and social psychology, Vol. 3: Interpersonal relations* (pp. 65–92). Washington, DC: American Psychological Association. doi:10.1037/14344-003

van Winkel, R., & Kuepper, R. (2014). Epidemiological, neurobiological, and genetic clues to the mechanisms linking cannabis use to risk for nonaffective psychosis. *Annual Review of Clinical Psychology, 10,* 767–791. doi:10.1146/annurev-clinpsy-032813-153631

Vandenberg, S. G. (1987). Sex differences in mental retardation and their implications for sex differences in ability. In J. M. Reinisch, L. A. Rosenblum, & S. A. Sanders (Eds.), *Masculinity/Femininity: Basic perspectives.* New York: Oxford University Press.

Vandenbroucke, J. P., & Psaty, B. M. (2008). Benefits and risks of drug treatments: How to combine the best evidence on benefits with the best data about adverse effects. *Journal of the American Medical Association, 300*(20), 2417–2419.

Vangelisti, A. L. (2015). Communication in personal relationships. In M. Mikulincer, P. R. Shaver, J. A. Simpson, & J. F. Dovidio (Eds.), *APA handbook of personality and social psychology, Vol. 3: Interpersonal relations* (pp. 371–392). Washington, DC: American Psychological Association. doi:10.1037/14344-014

Varnum, M. W., Grossmann, I., Kitayama, S., & Nisbett, R. E. (2010). The origin of cultural differences in cognition: The social orientation hypothesis. *Current Directions in Psychological Science, 19*(1), 9–13. doi:10.1177/0963721409359301

Vartanian, L. R., Giant, C. L., & Passino, R. M. (2001). "Ally McBeal vs. Arnold Schwarzenegger": Comparing mass media, interpersonal feedback and gender as predictors of satisfaction with body thinness and masculinity. *Social Behavior and Personality, 29*(7), 711–723.

Veenhoven, R. (1993). *Happiness in nations.* Rotterdam, Netherlands: Risbo.

Ventura, M., Salanova, M., & Llorens, S. (2015). Professional self-efficacy as a predictor of burnout and engagement: The role of challenge and hindrance demands. *The Journal Of Psychology: Interdisciplinary And Applied, 149*(3), 277–302. doi:10.1080/00223980.2013.876380

Verderber, K. S., Verderber, R. F., & Berryman-Fink, C. (2007). *Inter-act: Interpersonal communication concepts, skills, and contexts.* New York: Oxford University Press.

Verderber, R. F., & Verderber, K. S. (2004). *Inter-Act: Interpersonal communication concepts, skills, and contexts.* New York: Oxford University Press.

Verderber, R. F., Verderber, K. S., & Berryman-Fink, C. (2008). *Communicate.* Belmont, CA: Wadsworth.

Verona, E., & Curtin, J. J. (2006). Gender differences in the negative affective priming of aggressive behavior. *Emotion, 6*(1), 115–124.

Verschuere, B., Suchotzki, K., & Debey, E. (2015). Detecting deception through reaction times. In P. A. Granhag, A. Vrij, B. Verschuere, P. A. Granhag, A. Vrij, & B. Verschuere (Eds.), *Detecting deception: Current challenges and cognitive approaches* (pp. 269–291). Wiley-Blackwell.

Vetter, M. L., Dumon, K. R., & Williams, N. N. (2011). Surgical treatments for obesity. *Psychiatric Clinics of North America, 34*(4), 881–893. doi:10.1016/j.psc.2011.08.012

Vida, M. D., & Maurer, D. (2012). The development of fine-grained sensitivity to eye contact after 6 years of age. *Journal of Experimental Child Psychology, 112*(2), 243–256. doi:10.1016/j.jecp.2012.02.002

Vidal, M. E., & Petrak, J. (2007). Shame and adult sexual assault: A study with a group of female survivors recruited from an east London population. *Sexual and Relationship Therapy, 22,* 159–171.

Vignoles, V. L., Manzi, C., Regalia, C., Jemmolo, S., & Scabini, E. (2008). Identity motives underlying desired and feared possible future selves. *Journal of Personality, 76,* 1165–1200.

Vita, R., Lapa, D., Trimarchi, F., & Benvenga, S. (2015). Stress triggers the onset and the recurrences of hyperthyroidism in patients with Graves' disease. *Endocrine, 48*(1), 254–263. doi: 10.1007/s12020-014-0289-8.

Vittengl, J. R., & Holt, C. S. (2000). Getting acquainted: The relationship of self-disclosure and social attraction to positive affect. *Journal of Social and Personal Relationships, 17*(1), 53–56.

Vivancos, R., Abubakar, I., Phillips-Howard, P., & Hunter, P. R. (2013). School-based sex education is associated with reduced risky sexual behaviour and sexually transmitted infections in young adults. *Public Health, 127*(1), 53–57. doi:10.1016/j.puhe.2012.09.016

Vohs, K. D., & Baumeister, R. F. (Eds.). (2011). *Handbook of self-regulation: Research, theory, and applications* (2nd ed.). New York: Guilford.

Vohs, K. D., Baumeister, R. F., & Ciarocco, N. J. (2005). Self-regulation and self-presentation: Regulatory resource depletion impairs impression management and effortful self-presentation depletes regulatory resources. *Journal of Personality and Social Psychology, 88,* 632–657.

Vohs, K., & Heatherton, T. F. (2001). Self-esteem and threats to self: Implications for self-construals and interpersonal perceptions. *Journal of Personality and Social Psychology, 81,* 1103–1118.

Volkmar, F. R., Klin, A., Schultz, R. T., & State, M. W. (2009). Pervasive developmental disorders. In B. J. Sadock, V. A. Sadock, & P. Ruiz (Eds.), *Kaplan & Sadock's comprehensive textbook of psychiatry* (9th ed., pp. 3540–3559). Philadelphia: Lippincott Williams & Wilkins.

Von Culin, K. R., Tsukayama, E., & Duckworth, A. L. (2014). Unpacking grit: Motivational correlates of perseverance and passion for long-term goals. *The Journal of Positive Psychology, 9*(4), 306–312.

Vonk, R. (1993). The negativity effect in trait rating and in open-ended descriptions of persons. *Personality and Social Psychology Bulletin, 19,* 269–278.

Vorauer, J. D., Cameron, J. J., Holmes, J. G., & Pearce, D. G. (2003). Invisible overtures: Fears of rejection and the signal amplification bias. *Journal of Personality and Social Psychology, 84*(4), 793–812.

Voyer, D., & Voyer, S. D. (2014). Gender differences in scholastic achievement: A meta-analysis. *Psychological Bulletin, 140*(4), 1174–1204. doi:10.1037/a0036620

Vrij, A. (2015). Deception detection. In B. L. Cutler, P. A. Zapf, B. L. Cutler, & P. A. Zapf (Eds.), *APA handbook of forensic psychology, Vol. 2: Criminal investigation, adjudication, and sentencing outcomes* (pp. 225–244). Washington, DC: American Psychological Association. doi:10.1037/14462-008

Vrij, A., Oliveira, J., Hammond, A., & Ehrlichman, H. (2015). Saccadic eye movement rate as a cue to deceit. *Journal of Applied Research in Memory and Cognition, 4*(1), 15–19. doi:10.1016/j.jarmac.2014.07.005

Vrugt, A., & Luyerink, M. (2000). The contribution of bodily posture to gender stereotypical impressions. *Social Behavior and Personality, 28*(1), 91–103.

Vukasović, T., & Bratko, D. (2015). Heritability of personality: A meta-analysis of behavior genetic studies. *Psychological Bulletin, 141*(4), 769–785. doi:10.1037/bul0000017

Wagner, B., Horn, A. B., & Maercker, A. (2014). Internet-based versus face-to-face cognitive-behavioral intervention for depression: A randomized controlled non-inferiority trial. *Journal of Affective Disorders, 152–154,* 113–121. doi:10.1016/j.jad.2013.06.032

Wagner, J., Lüdtke, O., & Trautwein, U. (2015). Self-esteem is mostly stable across young adulthood: Evidence from latent starts models. *Journal of Personality.* doi:10.1111/jopy.12178

Wai, J., Cacchio, M., Putallaz, M., & Makel, M. C. (2010). Sex differences in the right tail of cognitive abilities: A 30 year examination. *Intelligence, 38,* 412–423.

Waite, L. J. (2000). Trends in men's and women's well-being in marriage. In L. J. Waite (Ed.), *The ties that bind.* New York: Aldine de Gruyter.

Walker, L. S., Claar, R. L., & Garber, J. (2002). Social consequences of children's pain: When do they encourage symptoms of maintenance? *Journal of Pediatric Psychology, 27*(8), 689–698.

Wallace, H. M., Baumeister, R. F., & Vohs, K. D. (2005). Audience support and choking under pressure: A home disadvantage? *Journal of Sports Sciences, 23,* 429–438.

Wallace, L. S., Keenum, A. J., AbdurRaqeeb, O., Miser, W. F., & Wexler, R. K. (2013). Terminology matters: Patient understanding of "opioids" and "narcotics." *Pain Practice, 13*(2), 104–108.

Wallerstein, J. S. (2005). Growing up in the divorced family. *Clinical Social Work Journal, 33*, 401–418.

Wallerstein, J. S., & Blakeslee, S. (1989). *Second chances: Men, women, and children a decade after divorce.* Boston: Houghton Mifflin.

Wallerstein, J. S., & Lewis, J. M. (2004). The unexpected legacy of divorce: Report of a 25-year study. *Psychoanalytic Psychology, 21*, 353–370.

Wallerstein, J. S., & Lewis, J. M. (2007). Sibling outcomes and disparate parenting and stepparenting after divorce: Report from a 10-year longitudinal study. *Psychoanalytic Psychology, 24*, 445–458.

Wallerstein, J. S., Lewis, J. M., & Blakeslee, S. (2000). *The unexpected legacy of divorce: A 25-year landmark study.* New York: Hyperion.

Walsh, R. (2011). Lifestyle and mental health. *American Psychologist, 66*(7), 579–592. doi:10.1037/a0021769

Wampold, B. E. (2001). *The great psychotherapy debate.* Mahwah, NJ: Erlbaum.

Wampold, B. E. (2013). The good, the bad, and the ugly: A 50-year perspective on the outcome problem. *Psychotherapy, 50*(1), 16–24. doi:10.1037/a0030570

Wanberg, C. R. (2012). The individual experience of unemployment. *Annual Review of Psychology, 63*, 369–396. doi:10.1146/annurev-psych-120710-100500

Wang, H., & Amato, P. R. (2000). Predictors of divorce adjustment: Stressors, resources, and definitions. *Journal of Marriage and the Family, 62*, 655–668.

Wang, M., & Wong M. C. S. (2014). Happiness and leisure across countries: Evidence from international survey data. *Journal of Happiness Studies, 15*(1), 85–118. doi:10.1007/s10902-013-9417-z

Wang, Q., Fink, E. L., & Cai, D. A. (2012). The effect of conflict goals on avoidance strategies: What does not communicating communicate? *Human Communication Research, 38*(2), 222–252. doi:10.1111/j.1468-2958.2011.01421.x

Wang, W., Parker, K., & Taylor, P. (2013). Pew Research Center. Breadwinner Moms. Retrieved from www.pewsocialtrends.org/2013/05/29/breadwinner-moms

Wansink, B. (2012). Specific environmental drivers of eating. In K. D. Brownell, & M. S. Gold (Eds.), *Food and addiction: A comprehensive handbook.* New York: Oxford University Press.

Wansink, B., & van Ittersum, K. (2013). Portion size me: Plate-size induced consumption norms and win-win solutions for reducing food intake and waste. *Journal of Experimental Psychology: Applied, 19*(4), 320–332. doi:10.1037/a0035053

Warburton, D. E. R., Charlesworth, S., Ivey, A., Nettlefold, I., & Bredin, S. S. D. (2010). A systematic review of the evidence for Canada's physical activity guidelines for adults. *International Journal of Behavioral Nutrition and Physical Activity, 7*, 1–220.

Ward, A., & Brenner, L. (2006). Accentuate the negative: The positive effects of negative acknowledgement. *Psychological Science, 17*, 959–962.

Ward, L. M., Reed, L., Trinh, S. L., & Foust, M. (2014). Sexuality and entertainment media. In D. L. Tolman, L. M. Diamond, J. A. Bauermeister, W. H. George, J. G. Pfaus, & L. M. Ward, (Eds.), *APA handbook of sexuality and psychology* (pp. 373–423). Washington, DC: American Psychological Association. doi:10.1037/14194-012

Wardle, M. C., Kirkpatrick, M. G., & de Wit, H. (2015). "Ecstasy" as a social drug: MDMA preferentially affects responses to emotional stimuli with social content. *Social Cognitive and Affective Neuroscience, 9*(8), 1076–1081.

Ware, A., & Kowalski, G. S. (2012). Sex identification and love of sports: BIRGing and CORFing among sports fans. *Journal of Sport Behavior, 35*, 223–237.

Wareham, J., Boots, D. P., & Chavez, J. M. (2009). A test of social learning and intergenerational transmission among batterers. *Journal of Criminal Justice, 37*, 163–173.

Warner, E. (2014). Fact sheet: The women's leadership gap. Center for American Progress. Retrieved from https://www.americanprogress.org/issues/women/report/2014/03/07/85457/fact-sheet-the-womens-leadership-gap

Wäschle, K., Allgaier, A., Lachner, A., Fink, S., & Nückles, M. (2014). Procrastination and self-efficacy: Tracing vicious and virtuous circles in self-regulated learning. *Learning and Instruction, 29*, 103–114. doi:10.1016/j.learninstruc.2013.09.005

Waterman, A. S. (2013). The humanistic psychology–positive psychology divide: Contrasts in philosophical foundations. *American Psychologist, 68*(3), 124–133. doi:10.1037/a0032168

Waterman, A. S. (2014). Further reflections on the humanistic psychology–positive psychology divide. *American Psychologist, 69*(1), 92–94. doi:10.1037/a0034966

Waters, E. A., Klein, W. M. P., Moser, R. P., Yu, M., Waldron, W. R., McNeel, T. S., & Freedman, A. N. (2011). Correlates of unrealistic optimism in a nationally representative sample. *Journal of Behavioral Medicine, 34*(3), 225–235.

Waters, E., Merrick, S., Treboux, D., Crowell, J., & Albersheim, L. (2000). Attachment security in infancy and early adulthood: A twenty-year longitudinal study. *Child Development, 71*(3), 684–689.

Watkins, P. C. (2014). *Gratitude and the good life: Towards a psychology of appreciation.* New York: Springer.

Watson, D. (2002). Positive affectivity: The disposition to experience pleasurable emotional states. In C. R. Snyder & S. J. Lopez (Eds.), *Handbook of positive psychology* (pp. 106–119). New York: Oxford University Press.

Watson, D., & Clark, L. A. (1984). Negative affectivity: The disposition to experience aversive emotional states. *Psychological Bulletin, 96*, 465–490.

Watson, D., Klohnen, E. C., Casillas, A., Nus Simms, E., Haig, J., & Berry, D. S. (2004). Match makers and deal breakers: Analyses of assortative mating in newlywed couples. *Journal of Personality, 72*, 1029–1068.

Watson, D. L., & Tharp, R. G. (2007). *Self-directed behavior: Self-modification for personal adjustment.* Belmont, CA: Wadsworth.

Watson, D. L., & Tharp, R. G. (2013). *Self-directed behavior: Self-modification for personal adjustment* (10th ed.). Belmont, CA: Cengage.

Wayment, H. A., & O'Mara, E. M. (2008). The collective and compassionate consequences of downward social comparisons. In H. A. Wayment & J. J. Bauer (Eds.), *Transcending self-interest: Psychological explorations of the quiet ego* (pp. 159–169). Washington, DC: American Psychological Association.

Weaver, A. D., & Byers, E. S. (2006). The relationships among body image, body mass index, exercise, and sexual functioning in heterosexual women. *Psychology Of Women Quarterly, 30*(4), 333–339. doi:10.1111/j.1471-6402.2006.00308.x

Weber, S. R., & Pargament, K. I. (2014). The role of religion and spirituality in mental health. *Current Opinion in Psychiatry, 27*(5), 358–363. doi:10.1097/YCO.0000000000000080

Webster, D. M. (1993). Motivated augmentation and reduction of the overattribution bias. *Journal of Personality and Social Psychology, 65*, 261–271.

Webster, D. M., Richter, L., & Kruglanski, A. W. (1996). On leaping to conclusions when feeling tired: Mental fatigue effects on impressional primacy. *Journal of Experimental Social Psychology, 32*, 181–195.

Webster, G. D. (2009). Parental investment theory. In H. T. Reis & S. Sprecher (Eds.), *Encyclopedia of human relationships, Vol. 3* (pp. 1194–1197). Los Angeles: Sage Reference.

Wechsler, H., Lee, J. E., Kuo, M., Seibring, M., Nelson, T. F., & Lee, H. (2002). Trends in college binge drinking during a period of increased prevention efforts. *Journal of American College Health, 50*(5), 203–217.

Weems, C. F., Scott, B. G., Banks, D. M., & Graham, R. A. (2012). Is TV traumatic for all youths? The role of preexisting posttraumatic-stress symptoms in the link between disaster coverage and stress. *Psychological Science, 23*(11), 1293–1297. doi:10.1177/0956797612446952

Wegener, D. T., & Petty, R. E. (1994). Mood management across affective states: The hedonic contingency hypothesis. *Journal of Personality and Social Psychology, 66*, 1034–1048.

Weinberger, J. (1995). Common factors aren't so common: The common factors dilemma. *Clinical Psychology: Science and Practice, 2*(1), 45-69. doi:10.1111/j.1468-2850.1995.tb00024.x

Weiner, B. (Ed.). (1974). *Achievement motivation and attribution theory.* Morristown, NJ: General Learning Press.

Weiner, B. (1994). Integrating social and personal theories of achievement striving. *Review of Educational Research, 64*, 557–573.

Weiner, B. (2006). *Social motivation, justice, and the moral emotions: An attributional approach.* Mahwah, NJ: Erlbaum.

Weiner, B. (2012). An attribution theory of motivation. In P. M. Van Lange, A. W. Kruglanski, & E. Higgins (Eds.), *Handbook of theories of social psychology, Vol. 1* (pp. 135–155). Thousand Oaks, CA: Sage.

Weiner, I. B. (2013). Applying Rorschach assessment. In G. P. Koocher, J. C. Norcross, & B. A. Greene (Eds.), *Psychologists' desk reference* (3rd ed.). New York: Oxford University Press.

Weinstein, A. A., Lydick, S. E., & Biswabharati, S. (2014). Exercise and its relationship to psychological health and well-being. In R. Gomes, R. Resende, & A. Albuquerque, A. (Eds.). *Positive human functioning from a multidimensional perspective, Vol. 2* (pp. 147–166). Hauppauge, NY: Nova Science Publishers.

Weinstein, A., Curtiss, F., Rosenberg, K. P., & Dannon, P. (2014). Internet addiction disorder: Overview and controversies. In K. P. Rosenberg & L. Curtiss Feder (Eds.), *Behavioral addictions: Criteria, evidence, and treatment.* San Diego, CA: Elsevier Academic Press. doi: 10.1016/B978-0-12-407724-9.00005-7

Weinstein, A., Dorani, D., Elhadif, R., Bukovza, Y., Yarmulnik, A., & Dannon, P. (2015). Internet addiction is associated with social anxiety in young adults. *Annals of Clinical Psychiatry, 27*(1), 4–9.

Weinstein, N. D. (2003). Exploring the links between risk perceptions and preventive health behavior. In J. Suls & K. A. Wallston (Eds.), *Social psychological foundations of health and illness.* Malden, MA: Blackwell Publishing.

Weisbuch, M., & Ambady, N. (2008). Nonconscious routes to building culture: Nonverbal components of socialization. *Journal of Consciousness Studies, 15*, 159–183.

Weiss, R. S. (1973). *Loneliness: The experience of emotional and social isolation.* Cambridge, MA: MIT Press.

Weiss, R. S. (1975). *Marital separation.* New York: Basic Books.

Wells, J. C. K. (2011). An evolutionary perspective on the trans-generational basis of obesity. *Annals of Human Biology, 38*(4), 400–409.

Wentland, D. (2015). *Is your organization a great place to work?* Charlotte, NC: IAP Information Age Publishing.

Wentzel, K. R., & Looney, L. (2007). Socialization in School Settings. In J. E. Grusec, P. D. Hastings, J. E. Grusec, & P. D. Hastings (Eds.), *Handbook of socialization: Theory and research* (pp. 382–403). New York: Guilford.

West, D. S., Harvey-Berino, J., & Raczynski, J. M. (2004). Behavioral aspects of obesity, dietary intake, and chronic disease. In J. M. Raczynski & L. C. Leviton (Eds.), *Handbook of clinical health psychology, Vol. 2: Disorders of behavior and health.* Washington, DC: American Psychological Association.

West, K., Holmes, E., & Hewstone, M. (2011). Enhancing imagined contact to reduce prejudice against people with schizophrenia. *Group Processes & Intergroup Relations, 14*(3), 407–428. doi:10.1177/1368430210387805

Westefeld, J. S., Maples, M. R., Buford, B., & Taylor, S. (2001). Gay, lesbian, and bisexual college students: The relationship between sexual orientation and depression, loneliness and suicide. *Journal of College Student Psychotherapy, 15*(3), 71–82.

Westen, D., Gabbard, G. O., & Ortigo, K. M. (2008). Psychoanalytic approaches to personality. In O. P. John, R. W. Robins, & L. A. Pervin (Eds.), *Handbook of personality: Theory and research* (pp. 61–113). New York: Guilford.

Westman, M. (2010). Flexible-working time arrangements and their impact on work-family interface and mental wellbeing at work. In C. L. Cooper, J. Field, U. Goswami, R. Jenkins, B. J. Sahakian, C. L. Cooper, et al. (Eds.), *Mental capital and wellbeing* (pp. 663–672). Wiley-Blackwell.

Wetherby, A. M., & Prizant, B. M. (2005). Enhancing language and communication development in autism spectrum disorders: Assessment and intervention guidelines. In D. Zager (Ed.), *Autism spectrum disorders: Identification, education, and treatment* (3rd ed., pp. 327–365). Hillside, NJ: Lawrence Erlbaum.

Whang, W., Kubzansky, L. D., Kawachi, I., Rexrode, K. M., Kroenke, C. H., Glynn, R. J., . . . Albert, C. M. (2009). Depression and risk of sudden cardiac death and coronary heart disease in women: Results from the Nurses' Health Study. *Journal of the American College of Cardiology, 53,* 950–958.

Wheeler, L., Koestner, R., & Driver, R. (1982). Related attributes in the choice of comparison others: It's there, but it isn't all there is. *Journal of Experimental Social Psychology, 18,* 489–500.

Wheeler, L., & Suls, J. (2005). Social comparison and self-evaluations of competence. In A. J. Elliot & C. S. Dweck (Eds.), *Handbook of competence and motivation.* New York: Guilford.

Whelan, C. B. (2009, October 25). For these "spiritual warriors," the casualties were real. *The Washington Post.*

Whelan, C. W., Wagstaff, G., & Wheatcroft, J. M. (2015). High stakes lies: Police and non-police accuracy in detecting deception. *Psychology, Crime & Law, 21*(2), 127–138. doi:10.1080/1068316X.2014.935777

Whitaker, R. (2009). Deinstitutionalization and neuroleptics: The myth and reality. In Y. O. Alanen, M. González de Chávez, A. S. Silver, & B. Martindale (Eds.), *Psychotherapeutic approaches to schizophrenic psychoses: Past, present and future.* New York: Routledge /Taylor & Francis Group.

White, C. M., & Hoffrage, U. (2009). Testing the tyranny of too much choice against the allure of more choice. *Psychology & Marketing, 26*(3), 280–298. doi:10.1002/mar.20273

White, L. K., & Rogers, S. J. (2001). Economic circumstances and family outcomes: A review of the 1990s. In R. M. Milardo (Ed.), *Understanding families into the new millennium: A decade in review.* Minneapolis, MN: National Council on Family Relations.

White, M. A., & Murray, A. S. (2015). Building a positive institution. In M. A. White, A. S. Murray, M. A. White, & A. S. Murray (Eds.), *Evidence-based approaches in positive education: Implementing a strategic framework for well-being in schools* (pp. 1–26). New York: Springer Science + Business Media. doi:10.1007/978-94-017-9667-5_1

White, M. P., Alcock, I., Wheeler, B. W., & Depledge, M. H. (2013). Would you be happier living in a greener urban area? A fixed-effects analysis of panel data. *Psychological Science, 24*(6), 920–928. doi:10.1177/0956797612464659

Whitehouse, W. G., Orne, E. C., & Orne, M. T. (2007). Relaxation techniques. In G. Fink (Ed.), *Encyclopedia of stress: Vols. 1–4* (2nd ed., pp. 345–350). San Diego, CA: Elsevier Academic Press.

Whiteman, S. D., McHale, S. M., & Crouter, A. C. (2003). What parents learn from experience: The first child as a first draft? *Journal of Marriage and Family, 65,* 608–621.

Whitley, B. E., & Kite, M. E. (2006). *The psychology of prejudice and discrimination.* Belmont, CA: Wadsworth.

Whitton, S. W., Waldinger, R. J., Schulz, M. S., Allen, J. P., Crowell, J. A., & Hauser, S. T. (2008). Prospective associations from family-of-origin interactions to adult marital interactions and relationship adjustment. *Journal of Family Psychology, 22,* 274–286.

Whitty, M. T. (2013). Online romantic relationships. In Y. Amichai-Hamburger (Ed.), *The social net: Understanding our online behavior* (2nd ed., pp. 62–78). New York: Oxford University Press. doi:10.1093/acprof:oso /9780199639540.003.0004

Whybrow, P. C. (2005). *American mania: When more is not enough.* New York: Norton.

Wickrama, K. A. S., Lorenz, F. O., Conger, R. D., & Elder, G. H. (1997). Marital quality and physical illness: A latent growth curve analysis. *Journal of Marriage and Family, 59,* 143–155.

Widiger, T. A. (2009). Neuroticism. In M. R. Leary & R. H. Hoyle (Eds.), *Handbook of individual differences in social behavior* (pp. 129–146). New York: Guilford.

Widiger, T. A., & Crego, C. (2013). Diagnosis and classification. In T. A. Widiger, G. Stricker, I. B. Weiner, G. Stricker, T. A. Widiger, & I. B. Weiner (Eds.), *Handbook of psychology, Vol. 8: Clinical psychology* (2nd ed.). New York: Wiley.

Widom, C. S., Czaja, S. J., & Paris, J. (2009). A prospective investigation of borderline personality disorder in abused and neglected children followed up into adulthood. *Journal of Personality Disorders, 23*(5), 433–446. doi:10.1521/pedi .2009.23.5.433

Wilfong, J. D. (2006). Computer anxiety and anger: The impact of computer use, computer experience, and self-efficacy beliefs. *Computers in Human Behavior, 22,* 1001–1011.

Wilkins, K. G., & Tracey, T. G. (2014). Person environment fit and vocational outcomes. In M. Coetzee, & M. Coetzee (Eds.), *Psycho-social career meta-capacities: Dynamics of contemporary career development* (pp. 123–138). Cham, Switzerland: Springer International. doi:10.1007/978-3-319-00645-1_7

Willett, W. C., & Stampfer, W. J. (2003). Rebuilding the food pyramid. *Scientific American, 288*(1), 64–71.

Williams, C. G., Gagne, M., Ryan, R. M., & Deci, E. L. (2002). Facilitating autonomous motivation for smoking cessation. *Health Psychology, 21,* 40–50.

Williams, E. F., Gilovich, T., & Dunning, D. (2012). Being all you can be: How potential performances influence assessment of self and others. *Personality and Social Psychology Bulletin, 38,* 143–154.

Williams, J. E., Paton, C. C., Siegler, I. C., Eigenbrodt, M. L., Neito, F. J., & Tyroler, H. A. (2000). Anger proneness predicts coronary heart disease risk. *Circulation, 101,* 2034–2039.

Williams, J. E., Satterwhite, R. C., & Best, D. L. (1999). Pancultural gender stereotypes revisited: The five-factor model. *Sex Roles, 40,* 513–526.

Williams, K. B., Radefeld, P. S., Binning, J. F., & Sudak, J. R. (1993). When job candidates are "hard-" versus "easy-to-get": Effects of candidate availability on employment decisions. *Journal of Applied Social Psychology, 23*(3), 169–198.

Williams, L. A., & Bartlett, M. Y. (2015). Warm thanks: Gratitude expression facilitates social affiliation in new relationships via perceived warmth. *Emotion, 15*(1), 1–5. doi:10.1037/emo0000017

Williams, P. (2005). What is psychoanalysis? What is a psychoanalyst? In E. S. Person, A. M. Cooper, & G. O. Gabbard (Eds.), *Textbook of psychoanalysis.* Washington, DC: American Psychiatric Publishing.

Williams, S. L. (1995). Self-efficacy, anxiety, and phobic disorders. In J. E. Maddux (Ed.), *Self-efficacy, adaptation, and adjustment: Theory, research, and application.* New York: Plenum.

Williamson, I., & Gonzales, M. H. (2007). The subjective experience of forgiveness: Positive construals of the forgiveness experience. *Journal of Social and Clinical Psychology, 26,* 407–446.

Willness, C. R., Steel, P., & Lee, K. (2007). A meta-analysis of antecedents and consequences of workplace sexual harassment. *Personnel Psychology, 60*(1), 127–162. doi:10.1111 /j.1744-6570.2007.00067.x

Willoughby, B. J., Carroll, J. S., & Busby, D. M. (2014). Differing relationship outcomes when sex happens before, on, or after first dates. *Journal of Sex Research, 51*(1), 52–61. doi:10.1080/00224499.2012.714012

Willoughby, B. J., Hall, S. S., & Goff, S. (2015). Marriage matters but how much? Marital centrality among young adults. *The Journal of Psychology: Interdisciplinary and Applied, 149*(8), 796-817. doi:10.1080/00223980.2014 .979128

Wilson, T. D. (2011). *Redirect: The surprising new science of psychological change.* New York: Litte, Brown.

Wilson, T. D., & Gilbert, D. T. (2003). Affective forecasting. In M. P. Zanna (Ed.), *Advances in experimental social psychology* (pp. 345–411). San Diego, CA: Elsevier Academic Press. doi:10.1016/S0065-2601(03)01006-2

Wilson, T. D., & Gilbert, D. T. (2005). Affective forecasting: Knowing what to want. *Current Directions in Psychological Science, 14*(3), 131–134.

Wilson, T. D., Wheatley, T. P., Meyers, J. M., Gilbert, D. T., & Axsom, D. (2000). Focalism: A source of durability bias in affective forecasting. *Journal of Personality and Social Psychology, 78,* 821–836.

Wilt, J., & Revelle, W. (2009). Extraversion. In M. R. Leary & R. H. Hoyle (Eds.), *Handbook of individual differences in social behavior* (pp. 27–45). New York: Guilford.

Wing, J. F., Schutte, N. S., & Byrne, B. (2006). The effect of positive writing on emotional intelligence and life satisfaction. *Journal of Clinical Psychology, 62,* 1291–1302.

Wing, L., & Potter, D. (2009). The epidemiology of autism spectrum disorders: Is the prevalence rising? In S. Goldstein, J. A. Naglieri, & S. Ozonoff (Eds.), *Assessment of autism spectrum disorders* (pp. 18–54). New York: Guilford.

Wing, R. R., & Phelan, S. (2012). Obesity. In A. Baum, T. A. Revenson, & J. Singer (Eds.), *Handbook of health psychology* (pp. 333–352). New York: Guilford.

Winton-Brown, T. T., Fusar-Poli, P., Ungless, M. A., & Howes, O. D. (2014). Dopaminergic basis of salience dysregulation in psychosis. *Trends in Neurosciences, 37*(2), 85–94. doi:10.1016/j.tins.2013.11.003

Wipfli, B. M., Rethorst, C. D., & Landers, D. M. (2008). The anxiolytic effect of exercise: A meta-analysis of randomized trials and dose-response analysis. *Journal of Sport and Exercise Psychology, 30,* 392–410.

Wise, D., & Rosqvist, J. (2006). Explanatory style and well-being. In J. C. Thomas, D. L. Segal, & M. Hersen (Eds.), *Comprehensive handbook of personality and psychopathology: Personality and everyday functioning.* Hoboken, NJ: Wiley.

Wise, T. (2015). *Under the affluence: Shaming the poor, praising the rich and sacrificing the future of America.* San Francisco, CA: City Lights Open Media.

Wissink, I. B., Dekovic, M., & Meijer, A. M. (2006). Parenting behavior, quality of the parent-adolescent functioning in four ethnic groups. *Journal of Early Adolescence, 26,* 133–159.

Wlodarski, R., & Dunbar, R. I. M. (2013). Examining the possible functions of kissing in romantic relationships. *Archives of Sexual Behavior, 42*(8), 1415-1423. doi:10.1007 /s10508-013-0190-1

Wlodarski, R., & Dunbar, R. I. M. (2014). What's in a kiss? The effect of romantic kissing on mating desirability. *Evolutionary Psychology, 12*(1), 178-199.

Wohl, M. J. A., & McLaughlin, K. J. (2014). Self-forgiveness: The good, the bad, and the ugly. *Social and Personality Psychology Compass, 8*(8), 422–435. doi:10.1111/spc3.12119

Wolitzky, D. L. (2006). Psychodynamic theories. In J. C. Thomas & D. L. Segal (Eds.), *Comprehensive handbook of personality and psychopathology.* New York: Wiley.

Wollman, S. C., Alhasson, O. M., Stern, M. J., Hall, M. G., Rompogren, J., Kimmel, C. L., & Perez-Figueroa, A. M. (2015). White matter abnormalities in long-term heroin users: A preliminary neuroimaging meta-analysis. *The American Journal of Drug and Alcohol Abuse, 41*(2), 133–138.

Woloshin, S., Schwartz L.M., & Welch H. G. (2002). Risk charts: Putting cancer in context. *Journal of the National Cancer Institute, 94,* 803.

Wolpe, J. (1958). *Psychotherapy by reciprocal inhibition.* Stanford, CA: Stanford University Press.

Wolpe, J. (1987). The promotion of scientific therapy: A long voyage. In J. K. Zeig (Ed.), *The evolution of psychotherapy.* New York: Brunner/Mazel.

Wonderlich, S. A. (2002). Personality and eating disorders. In C. G. Fairburn & K. D. Brownell (Eds.), *Eating disorders and obesity: A comprehensive handbook.* New York: Guilford.

Wong, L. (2015). *Essential study skills* (8th ed.). Boston: Cengage.

Wood, A. M., Froh, J. J., & Geraghty, A. A. (2010). Gratitude and well-being: A review and theoretical integration. *Clinical Psychology Review, 30*(7), 890–905. doi:10.1016 /j.cpr.2010.03.005

Wood, E., Desmarais, S., & Gugula, S. (2002). The impact of parenting experience on gender stereotyped toy play of children. *Sex Roles, 47*(1–2), 39–49.

Wood, J. M., Garb, H. N., Nezworski, M. T., Lilienfeld, S. O., & Duke, M. C. (2015). A second look at the validity of widely used Rorschach indices: Comment on Mihura, Meyer, Dumitrascu, and Bombel (2013). *Psychological Bulletin, 141*(1), 236–249. doi:10.1037/a0036005

Wood, J. M., Lilienfeld, S. O., Nezworski, M. T., Garb, H. N., Allen, K. H., & Wildermuth, J. L. (2010). Validity of Rorschach Inkblot scores for discriminating psychopaths from nonpsychopaths in forensic populations: A meta-analysis. *Psychological Assessment, 22,* 336–349. doi:10.1037/a0018998

Wood, J. T. (2010). *Interpersonal communication: Everyday encounters* (6th ed.). Belmont, CA: Wadsworth.

Wood, J. T. (2015). *Communication in our lives* (7th ed.). Belmont, CA: Cengage.

Wood, J. V. (1989). Theory and research concerning social comparisons of personal attributes. *Psychological Bulletin, 106,* 231–248.

Wood, J. V., & Wilson, A. E. (2003). How important is social comparison? In M. R. Leary & J. P. Tangney (Eds.), *Handbook of self and identity.* New York: Guilford.

Wood, N., & Cowan, N. (1995). The cocktail party phenomenon revisited: How frequent are attention shifts to one's name in an irrelevant auditory channel? *Journal of Experimental Psychology: Learning, Memory, and Cognition, 21,* 255–260.

Wood, W., & Quinn, J. M. (2003). Forewarned and fore-armed? Two meta-analytic syntheses of forewarnings of influence appeals. *Psychological Bulletin, 129*(1), 119–138.

Wood, W., Conway, M., Pushkar, D., & Dugas, M. J. (2005). People's perceptions of women's and men's worry about life issues: Worrying about love, accomplishment, or money? *Sex Roles, 53*, 545–551.

Woodcock, E. A., Lundahl, L. H., Stoltman, J. K., & Greenwald, M. K. (2015). Progression to regular heroin use: Examination of patterns, predictors, and cnsequences. *Addictive Behaviors, 45*, 287–293.

Woodzicka, J. A., & LaFrance, M. (2005). The effects of subtle sexual harassment on women's performance in a job interview. *Sex Roles, 53*, 67–77.

Woolfolk, R. L. (2002). The power of negative thinking: Truth, melancholia, and the tragic sense of life. *Journal of Theoretical and Philosophical Psychology, 22*(1), 19–27. doi:10.1037/h0091192

Worthington, R. L., Flores, L. Y., & Navarro, R. L. (2005). Career development in context: Research with people of color. In S. D. Brown & R. W. Lent (Eds.), *Career development and counseling: Putting theory and research to work.* New York: Wiley.

Worthington, R. L., Soth-McNett, A. M., & Moreno, M. V. (2007). Multicultural counseling competencies research: A 20-year content analysis. *Journal of Counseling Psychology, 54*, 351–361.

Wright, C. E., O'Donnell, K., Brydon, L., Wardle, J., & Steptoe, A. (2007). Family history of cardiovascular disease is associated with cardiovascular responses to stress in healthy young men and women. *International Journal of Psychophysiology, 63*, 275–282.

Wright, J. H., Thase, M. E., & Beck, A. T. (2014). Cognitive-behavior therapy. In R. E. Hales, S. C. Yudofsky, & L. W. Roberts (Eds.), *The American Psychiatric Publishing textbook of psychiatry* (6th ed.). Washington, DC: American Psychiatric Publishing.

Wright, Jr., M. J. (2015). Legalizing marijuana for medicinal purposes will increase the risk of long-term, deleterious consequences for adolescents. *Drug and Alcohol Dependence, 149*, 298–303.

Wright, P. H. (2006). Toward an expanded orientation to the comparative study of women's and men's same-sex friendships. In K. Dindia & D. J. Canary (Eds.), *Sex differences and similarities in communication.* Mahwah, NJ: Erlbaum.

Wright, S. C., & Taylor, D. M. (2003). The social psychology of cultural diversity: Social stereotyping, prejudice, and discrimination. In M. A. Hogg & J. Cooper (Eds.), *The Sage handbook of social psychology.* Thousand Oaks, CA: Sage.

Wrosch, C., Scheier, M. F., & Miller, G. E. (2013). Goal adjustment capacities, subjective well-being, and physical health. *Social and Personality Psychology Compass, 7*(12), 847–860.

Wrosch, C., Scheier, M. F., Miller, G. E., & Carver, C. S. (2012). When meaning is threatened: The importance of goal adjustment for psychological and physical health. In P. T. P. Wong (Ed.), Human quest for meaning: Theories, research, and applications (2nd ed.). New York: Routledge /Taylor & Francis Group.

Wrzesniewski, A. (2012). Callings in work. In K. S. Cameron & G. M. Spreitzer (Eds.), *The Oxford handbook of positive organizational scholarship* (pp. 45–55). New York: Oxford University Press.

Wrzesniewski, A., McCauley, C., Rozin, P., & Schwartz, B. (1997). Jobs, careers, and callings: People's relations to their work. *Journal of Research in Personality, 31*, 21–33.

Wrzus, C., Luong, G., Wagner, G. G., & Riediger, M. (2015). Can't get it out of my head: Age differences in affective responsiveness vary with preoccupation and elapsed time after daily hassles. *Emotion, 15*(2), 257–269. doi:10.1037/emo0000019

Wurm, S., Warner, L. M., Ziegelmann, J. P., Wolff, J. K., & Schüz, B. (2013). How do negative self-perceptions of aging become a self-fulfilling prophecy? *Psychology And Aging, 28*(4), 1088–1097. doi:10.1037/a0032845

Wynder, E. L., Cohen, L. A., Muscat, J. E., Winters, B., Dwyer, J. T., & Blackburn, G. (1997). Breast cancer: Weighing the evidence for a promoting role of dietary fat. *Journal of the National Cancer Institute, 89*(11), 766–775.

Xie, J. (2011). Relationship between emotional intelligence, job burnout and job satisfaction. *Chinese Journal of Clinical Psychology, 19*(3), 372–373.

Yang, A. C., Tsai, S-J., & Huang, N. E. (2011). Decomposing the association of completed suicide with air pollution, weather, and unemployment data at different time scales. *Journal of Affective Disorders, 129*(1–3), 275–281. doi:10.1016/j.jad.2010.08.010

Yang, K., Friedman-Wheeler, D. G., & Pronin, E. (2014). Thought acceleration boosts positive mood among individuals with minimal to moderate depressive symptoms. *Cognitive Therapy and Research, 38*(3), 261–269. doi:10.1007/s10608-014-9597-9

Yao, M. Z., & Zhong, Z. (2014). Loneliness, social contacts and internet addiction: A cross-lagged panel study. *Computers in Human Behavior, 30*, 164–170. doi:10.1016/j.chb.2013.08.007

Yao, M. Z., Mahood, C., & Linz, D. (2010). Sexual priming, gender stereotyping, and likelihood to sexually harass: Examining the cognitive effects of playing a sexually-explicit video game. *Sex Roles, 62*(1–2), 77–88. doi:10.1007/s11199-009-9695-4

Yate, M. (2006). *Knock 'em dead: The ultimate job search guide.* Avon, MA: Adams Media.

Yehuda, R., & Wong, C. M. (2007). Acute stress disorder and posttraumatic stress disorder. In G. Fink (Ed.), *Encyclopedia of stress: Vols. 1–4* (2nd ed., pp. 2–6). San Diego, CA: Elsevier Academic Press.

Yi, H, Chen CM, Williams GD. (2006). Trends in alcohol-related fatal traffic crashes, United States, 1982–2004 (Surveillance Report No. 76), Bethesda, MD: National Institute on Alcohol Abuse and Alcoholism, Division of Epidemiology and Prevention Research.

Yoder, J. D., & Kahn, A. S. (2003). Making gender comparisons more meaningful: A call for more attention to social context. *Psychology of Women Quarterly, 27*, 281–290.

Young, J. E. (1982). Loneliness, depression and cognitive therapy: Theory and application. In L. A. Peplau & D. Perlman (Eds.), *Loneliness: A sourcebook of current theory, research and therapy.* New York: Wiley.

Young, K. (2015). The evolution of internet addiction disorder (pp. 3–17). New York: Springer Science + Business Media.

Young, K. S. (2009). Assessment and treatment of Internet addiction. In A. Browne-Miller (Ed.), *The Praeger international collection on addictions, Vol 4: Behavioral addictions from concept to compulsion* (pp. 217–234). Santa Barbara, CA: Praeger/ABC-CLIO.

Young, L. (2012, April 30). What's the value of a college degree? Retrieved from www.reuters.com/article/2012/04/30/us-personalfinance-grad-qa-idUSBRE83T0WK20120430

Young, L. R., & Nestle, M. (2002). The contribution of expanding portion sizes to the US obesity epidemic. *American Journal of Public Health, 92*, 246–249.

Young, R., & Sweeting, H. (2004). Adolescent bullying, relationships, psychological well-being, and gender-atypical behavior: A gender diagnosticity approach. *Sex Roles, 50*, 525–537.

Young, S. G., Hugenberg, K., Bernstein, M. J., & Sacco, D. F. (2012). Perception and motivation in face recognition: A critical review of theories of the cross-race effect. *Personality and Social Psychology Review, 16*, 116–142.

Yousaf, O., Popat, A., & Hunter, M. S. (2015). An investigation of masculinity attitudes, gender, and attitudes toward psychological help-seeking. *Psychology of Men & Masculinity, 16*(2), 234–237. doi:10.1037/a0036241

Yu, X., Bao, Z., Zou, J., & Dong, J. (2011). Coffee consumption and risk of cancers: A meta-analysis of cohort studies. *BMC Cancer, 11*, 96.

Yzerbyt, V., & Demoulin, S. (2010). Intergroup relations. In S. T. Fiske, D. T. Gilbert, & G. Lindzey (Eds.), *The handbook of social psychology* (5th ed., pp. 1024–1083). New York: McGraw-Hill.

Zahorodny, W., Shenouda, J., Howell, S., Rosato, N. S., Peng, B., & Mehta, U. (2014). Increasing autism prevalence in metropolitan New Jersey. *Autism, 18*(2), 117–126. doi:10.1177/1362361312463977

Zajonc, R. B. (1968). Attitudinal effects of mere exposure. *Journal of Personality and Social Psychology, 9*, 1–27.

Zane, N., Hall, G. C. N., Sue, S., Young, K., & Nunez, J. (2004). Research on psychotherapy with culturally diverse populations. In M. J. Lambert (Ed.), *Bergin and Garfield's handbook of psychotherapy and behavior change.* New York: Wiley.

Zárate, M. A., Quezada, S. A., Shenberger, J. M., & Lupo, A. K. (2014). Reducing racism and prejudice. In F. L. Leong, L. Comas-Díaz, G. C. Nagayama Hall, V. C. McLoyd, & J. E. Trimble (Eds.), *APA handbook of multicultural psychology, Vol. 2: Applications and training* (pp. 593–606). Washington, DC: American Psychological Association. doi:10.1037/14187-033

Zell, E., & Alicke, M. D. (2009). Self-evaluative effects of temporal and social comparison. *Journal of Experimental Social Psychology, 45*, 223–227.

Zell, E., Krizan, Z., & Teeter, S. R. (2015). Evaluating gender similarities and differences using metasynthesis. *American Psychologist, 70*(1), 10–20. doi:10.1037/a0038208

Zentner, M., & Mitura, K. (2012). Stepping out of the caveman's shadow: Nations' gender gap predicts degree of sex differentiation in mate preferences. *Psychological Science, 23*(10), 1176–1185. doi:10.1177/0956797612441004

Zhang, J. W., & Howell, R. T. (2011). Do time perspectives predict unique variance in life satisfaction beyond personality traits? *Personality and Individual Differences, 50*, 1261–1266. doi:10.1016/j.paid.2011.02.021

Zhang, J. W., Howell, R. T., & Howell, C. J. (2014). Living in wealthy neighborhoods increases material desires and maladaptive consumption. *Journal of Consumer Culture, 0*, 1–20. doi:10.1177/1469540514521085

Zhu, S., Tse, S., Cheung, S., & Oyserman, D. (2014). Will I get there? Effects of parental support on children's possible selves. *British Journal of Educational Psychology, 84*(3), 435–453. doi:10.1111/bjep.12044

Ziersch, A. M., Baum, F., Woodman, R. J., Newman, L., & Jolley, G. (2014). A longitudinal study of the mental health impacts of job loss: The role of socioeconomic, sociodemographic, and social capital factors. *Journal Of Occupational And Environmental Medicine, 56*(7), 714–720. doi:10.1097/JOM.0000000000000193

Zimbardo, P. G. (1977). *Shyness: What it is, what to do about it.* Reading, MA: Addison-Wesley.

Zimbardo, P. G. (1990). *Shyness.* Reading, MA: Addison-Wesley.

Zimmerman, M., & Strouse, D. (2002). *Choosing a psychotherapist: A guide to navigating the mental health maze.* Lincoln, NE: Writers Club Press.

Zinbarg, R. E., & Griffith, J. W. (2008). Behavior therapy. In J. L. Lebow (Ed.), *Twenty-first century psychotherapies: Contemporary approaches to theory and practice.* New York: Wiley.

Zivin, K., Ratliff, S., Heisler, M. M., Langa, K. M., & Piette, J. D. (2010). Factors influencing cost-related nonadherence to medication in older adults: A conceptually based approach. *Value in Health, 13*(4), 338–345. doi:10.1111/j.1524-4733.2009.00679.x

Zohar, J., Fostick, L., & Juven-Wetzler, E. (2009). Obsessive-compulsive disorder. In M. C. Gelder, N. C. Andreasen, J. J. López-Ibor, Jr., & J. R. Geddes (Eds.), *New Oxford textbook of psychiatry, Vol. 1* (2nd ed.). New York: Oxford University Press.

Zolnierek, K. B., & DiMatteo, R. M. (2009). Physician communication and patient adherence: A meta-analysis. *Medical Care, 47*, 826–834.

Zuckerman, M. (2013). Biological bases of personality. In H. Tennen, J. Suls, & I. B. Weiner (Eds.), *Handbook of psychology, Vol. 5: Personality and social psychology* (2nd ed.). New York: Wiley.

Zwan, J. E., Vente, W., Huizink, A. C., Bögels, S. M., & Bruin, E. I. (2015). Physical activity, mindfulness meditation, or heart rate variability biofeedback for stress reduction: A randomized controlled trial. *Applied Psychophysiology and Biofeedback.* doi:10.1007/s10484-015-9293-x

Zweig, J. S. (2015). Are woman happier than men? Evidence from the Gallup World Poll. *Journal of Happiness Studies, 16*(2), 515–541. doi:10.1007/s10902-014-9521-8

Zytowski, D. G. (2001). Kuder career search with person match: Career assessment for the 21st century. *Journal of Career Assessment, 9*(3), 229–242. doi:10.1177/106907270100900302

Name Index

Kraft, S., 4
Kramer, P. D., 38
Krause, K., 117
Kreider, R. M., 280, 295, 297
Krendl, A. C., 204
Kret, M. E., 231
Krimsky, S., 446
Kring, A. M., 312
Kristof, A. L., 183
Krizan, Z., 52, 309
Kroenke, K., 443
Krosnick, J. A., 14
Krueger, A. B., 147
Krueger, J. I., 169, 194
Krueger, R. F., 17
Krueger, W. C. F., 23
Kruger, J., 138, 182
Kruger, M. L., 72, 73
Kruglanski, A. W., 198
Krumrei, E., 296
Krusemark, E. A., 177
Kteily, N., 201
Kubota, K., 388
Kuepper, R., 417
Kuhl, E. A., 401
Kuipers, E., 419
Kukla, I., 174
Kulick, A. R., 415
Kulik, C. T., 381
Kulik, L., 386
Kuncel, N. R., 21
Kung, H. C., 123
Kunkel, D., 339
Kuper, L., 342
Kupfer, D. J., 401
Kurdek, L. A., 260, 298, 327, 388
Kuroki, T., 129
Kushlev, K., 287, 288
Kuyper, H., 165
Kwan, V. S., 53
Kwon, P., 472
Kypri, K., 134

L

Ladd, G. W., 477
la Fleur, S. E., 99
LaFrance, M., 385
La Greca, A. M., 81
Lakein, A., 115, 117
Lakey, B., 18
Lalumiere, M. L., 345
Lamb, M. E., 295
Lambert, A. J., 197
Lambert, M. J., 438, 439, 451, 453
Lamers, L. M., 147
Lamkin, J., 52
Lammers, J., 353
Lamont, R. A., 204
Lampert, R, 126
Lancaster, L. C., 190
Landau, M. J., 52, 159
Landers, D. M., 143
Landfield, K., 192
Landrum, R. E., 369
Lane, S. D., 154
Langelle, C., 473
Langer, E. J., 173, 204, 468, 469, 482
Langlois, J. H., 195, 253
Lansford, J. E., 296, 297
LaPiere, R. T., 198
Lapierre, V., 347
Lapp, L. K., 406
LaRose, R., 226
Larsen, R. J., 475

Larson, K. A., 260
Laska, K. M., 439, 453
Laskoff, M. B., 387
Lassiter, G. D., 234, 235
Lau, J. Y., 411
Lau, S., 179
Lauer, J., 267
Lauer, R., 267
Laugero, K. D., 99
Laughlin, H., 403
Laurenceau, J., 237, 238, 283
Laursen, B., 320
Lautsch, B. A., 376
Lavallee, L. F., 167
Lavee, Y., 285
Lavie, C. J., 128
LaViolette, A. D., 302
Lavoie, K., 116
Lavrakas, P. J., 14
Lawrence, E., 288
Lawrie, S. M., 418
Lawson, T. J., 173
Lay, C. H., 117
Layton, J. B., 83
Lazarus, A. A., 448, 453
Lazarus, R. S., 64, 65, 71, 92, 478
Le, B., 266
Leal, S., 234
Leaper, C., 312, 318, 321
Leary, M. R., 170
LeBel, E. P., 58
Le Blanc, P. M., 43
Le Boeuf, M., 116
Lebow, J. L., 432, 437
Lechner, S. C., 107, 474
Ledbetter, A. M., 256
Lederman, S. J., 232
Ledermann, T., 285
Ledgerwood, A., 165
LeDoux, J. E., 413
Lee, A., 114
Lee, D., 107
Lee, I.-M., 142, 143
Lee, J. D., 152
Lee, K., 331, 385
Lee, M. J., 322, 339
Lee, S., 160
Lee, S. Y., 51
Leeds, E. M., 241
Lefcourt, H. M., 106
LeFevre, J., 468
Lefringhausen, L., 51
Legate, N., 343
Lehman, K., 180
Leibel, R. L., 138
Leitenberg, H., 347, 348
Leiter, M. P., 79, 80, 384
LeMay, E. J., 195
Lengua, L. J., 65
Lenhart, A., 269, 270
Lenmon, G., 330
Lenton, R. L., 270
Leonard, N. H., 116
Leondari, A., 160
Leonhardt, D., 370
Leslie, L. A., 283
Letiecq, B. L., 283
Lett, H. S., 128
Leutner, F., 30
Levant, R. F., 322, 323
Levenson, J. L., 443, 445
Levenson, R. W., 290, 293
Leventhal, E. A., 123, 147
Leventhal, H., 123, 147
Levin, A. R., 384

Levin, T., 128
Levin, Z., 421
Levine, J. M., 209
Levine, M. P., 425
Levine, T. R., 234
Levinthal, C. F., 151
Levy, D., 139
Levy, I., 197
Levy, P. E., 382
Levy, S. R., 201
Lewin, K., 68, 214
Lewis, J. M., 296, 297
Lewis, K., 226
Lewis-Fernández, R., 449
Lewis-Smith, J., 283
Li, M., 311
Li, N. P., 255, 261
Li, S., 228
Li, T., 265
Li, W., 200
Li, Y., 446
Li, Yee-lam, 100
Li, Y-M, 228
Liao, H., 44
Liao, Y., 95
Li-Barber, K. T., 238
Libby, L. K., 475
Lichiello, S., 473
Lick, D. J., 66, 344
Lieberman, J. A., 416
Lieberman, M. D., 196
Liewer, L., 125
Lilienfeld, S. O., 5, 7, 59, 192, 407, 438, 451
Lilienthal, R., 389
Lim, B. T., 472
Lima, L., 217
Lin, C. A., 224
Lin, H., 406
Lin, Y., 238
Lindberg, L. D., 354
Lindberg, S. M., 309, 310
Linden, W., 128
Lindgren, H. C., 23
Lindholm, T., 321
Links, P. S., 423
Linley, P. A., 459, 460
Linn, M. C., 310
Linz, D., 339
Lippa, R. A., 253, 283, 314, 315, 321, 322
Lippman, J. R., 322
Lips, H. M., 378
Liptak, A., 279
Lisanby, S. H., 447
Litman, R. E., 411
Little, A. C., 252
Littlefield, M. B., 318
Liu, H., 273
Livingston, B. A., 30
Livingston, G., 280, 281, 287, 290, 297
Livingston, R. W., 183
Llera, S. J., 403
Llorca, P., 149
Llorens, S., 180
Lloyd, M., 369, 370
Lloyd, S. A., 284, 301
Lobel, A., 98
Lock, R. D., 377, 387, 393, 394
Lockwood, P., 164
Lodewijkx, H. F. M., 203
Loewenstein, G., 17, 20, 133
Loewenstein, R. J., 407
Loflin, M., 153
Lofquist, D., 300

Lohmer, M., 384
Long, J., 370
Longmore, M. A., 288
Looney, L., 320
Lopes, P. N., 110
Lopez, S. J., 86, 459, 464, 469
Lopez, S. R., 448
Loth, K., 80
Lourenco, P. M., 139
Love, S., 210, 211
Lovejoy, M., 389
Loving, T. J., 83, 267
Lozano, B. E., 180
Lu, F. G., 445, 448
Lu, S., 82
Luborsky, E. B., 432
Luborsky, L., 452
Lucas, A. R., 425
Lucas, L. E., 16, 19
Lucas, R. E., 20, 65, 459
Lucas, S., 343
Lucassen, P. J., 76
Lüdtke, O., 168
Lueders, A., 236
Luhtanen, R., 203
Lukow, H. I., 473
Lulofs, R. S., 242, 243
Lundberg-Love, P. K., 302
Luthans, F., 476
Lutjen, L. J., 112
Lutz, C. J., 181
Luyerink, M., 232
Lyddy, C., 65
Lydick, S. E., 112
Lydon, J. E., 267
Lyness, K. S., 329
Lynn, D. J., 38
Lynn, S. J., 407
Lyons, H., 337
Lyons-Ruth, K., 75
Lytton, H., 318
Lyubomirsky, S., 19, 287, 288, 413, 460

M

Maass, A., 322, 330, 331
Maccoby, M. M., 318, 320
MacGeorge, E. L., 207
MacGregor, J. D., 238
Mack, A. H., 136
Mackaronis, J. E., 449
Mackenzie, R. A., 115, 117
Mackie, D. M., 193, 206
MacLeod, A. K., 411
Macritchie, K., 411
Madathil, J., 282
Madden, M., 269, 270
Maddi, S. R., 86
Maddox, W., 79
Maddux, J. E., 180, 458
Madey, S. F., 262, 267
Madon, S., 193
Madsen, O. J., 6
Maercker, A., 450, 451
Magallares, A., 177
Magnavita, J. J., 129, 434
Magner, N. R., 242, 243
Mahar, I., 413
Maher, B. A., 415
Maher, I., 77
Mahoney, A., 338
Mahoney, M. J., 107
Mahood, C., 339
Maier, S. F., 175
Maier, W., 353

Subject Index

conformity
   compliance vs., 211
   defined, 209
   dynamics of, 210–211
   group size and, 211
   resisting, 212
   self-actualizers and, 47
   social expectations and, 189, 210
   whys of, 69, 211–212
congruence, 45, 46
conscientiousness
   characteristics of, 30
   evolutionary psychology and, 49
   NEO Inventory measure of, 57
   nonverbal decoding and, 236
conscious, Freud's view of, 32
consistency principle
   foot-in-the-door technique, 215
   lowball technique, 215–216
constructive coping
   appraisal-focused, 103, 104–107
   defined, 104–105
   emotion-focused, 103, 109–114
   problem-focused, 103, 107–109
contagious diseases, 123
content, of communication, 222
contraception
   abstinence-only programs, 338
   condoms, 147, 338, 349, 355–359
   effective, constraints on, 354
   emergency, 357
   failure rates, 354
   information sources, 337, 340
   method selection, 354–357
control groups, 10–11
controlled processing, 172–173,
   204, 208
conventional personality orientation, 373
conversational rerouting, 242
coping, 95–119
   adaptive value of, 96, 110, 114
   appraisal-focused, 103, 104–107
   defensive, 101–102
   defined, 78
   emotion-focused, 103, 109–114
   flexibility in, 95–96
   general adaption syndrome and, 76
   limited-value, 96–102
   problem-focused, 103, 107–109
   repressive style, 35
   with self-discrepancies, 163
   self-esteem and, 170
   strategies, 96
   with stress, 9, 29, 49, 63, 65, 72
   See also constructive coping
coronary heart disease. *See* heart disease
correlation, defined, 12
correlational coefficient, 12
correlational research
   advantages, disadvantages, 14–15
   case studies, 14
   causal relations in, 15
   measuring correlation, 12
   naturalistic observation, 12–13
   survey methods, 14
   See also experimental research
corticosteroids, 76–77
cortisol, 77
cosmetic surgery, 254
counseling psychologists, 430–431
counselors, 431–432
counter-arguing, 208
counterproductive behavior, 181

couples (marital) therapy, 437–438
courtships
   cohabitation phase, 299
   vs. marriage, 290
   mate selection and, 282, 284, 285
   whirlwind, 266
*Crazy: A Father's Search Through America's Mental
   Health Madness* (Earley), 442
creativity
   career choices and, 368
   in effective therapy, 453
   flow and, 468
   positive mood and, 461–462
credibility, of source, 206
cross-gender-typing, 327
cultural differences
   in abnormal behavior, 400
   in attitudes toward homosexuality, 357
   in attitudes towards love, marriage, 280–283
   in display of emotions, 230
   in expressing anger, 230
   in eye contact, 231
   in facial expressions, 229–230
   in gender-role socialization, 318
   in marital satisfaction, 282
   in mate selection, 281–282
   in nonverbal communication, 227–230
   in personality traits, 54
   in personal space, 228–229
   in person perception, 198
   in prejudice, 53, 202
   in relationships, 166
   in seeking help, 109
   in self-concept, 159–160, 163, 165–166, 171
   in self-enhancement, 54
   in self-esteem, 52
   in sexual values, 335–336
   in social communication, 223
   in subjective well-being, 18
   in textbooks, 166
   in touch, 232
   in trait scores, 53
culture
   communication and, 223
   consideration in therapy, 448–449
   drinking and, 135
   emotional expressions and, 230
   gender-role socialization, 318
   happiness and, 18
   influence on thought, 166
   interaction with biology, 307
   marriage and, 281–282
   nonverbal messages and, 190, 227
   of organizations, 373
   personality and, 53–54
   personal space and, 228
   self-actualization and, 47
   self-concept and, 165–166
   social trends, 272
   stress and, 66, 71
cunnilingus, 347, 348, 349
cutting off reflected failure (CORFing), 177
cynicism
   anger, hostility, and, 127
   burnout and, 79, 80, 384
   heart disease and, 127

D

date rape, 302–303
dating
   ability-achievement gap and, 325
   boredom in, 268

challenges for homosexuals, 261
matching hypothesis of, 255
online vs. face-to-face, 269–270
resource exchange in, 255–256
role of physical attractiveness, 252
role of similarity in, 256–257, 283
satisfaction factors, 262
sexual behavior in, 351
as step in mate selection, 282
death rates, for diseases, 123, 124
deception
   detecting, 227–228, 234–236
   nonverbal cues, 226, 227
   self-deception, 33, 34, 102–103
   on self-report inventories, 58–59
decline stage, in career choice, 374,
   375–376
decoding, 222
deep processing, 25
defense mechanisms
   conflict and, 32–35
   defined/nature of, 101–102
   psychodynamic theory and, 38
   types of, 102
   value of, 102
defensive attributions, 202
defensive coping, 101–102
defensiveness
   in communication, 223, 232, 241, 293–294
   Rogers' view of, 45–46
delusions of grandeur, 415
denial
   as defense mechanism, 101, 102
   emotional intelligence and, 110
   of gays, 341
   health-impairing habits and, 130
   of illness, 147
   of sexual harassment, 385
   stress and, 86
   unrealistic optimism and, 130
dependent variables, 10
depression
   Beck's cognitive theory of, 441
   choice overload and, 2
   coming out, by gay men and, 344
   drug use and, 150, 152, 154–155
   exercise and, 143
   from financial difficulties, 293
   forgiveness and, 112, 296
   gender differences in, 309, 313
   happiness and, 2
   humor and, 106
   immune function and, 125, 129–130
   increased prevalence of, 6
   in later life, 161
   learned helplessness model of, 413
   loneliness and, 273
   marriage and, 282
   parenthood and, 288
   from partner abuse, 301
   postpartum, 287
   premature ejaculation and, 362
   problem solving and, 107
   rape and, 303
   rumination and, 409–410, 413
   self-blame and, 101
   self-concept and, 102, 161
   self-discrepancies and, 162
   self-esteem and, 167–168
   sexual harassment and, 385
   slow speed of thought in, 463
   social anxiety and, 100
   from unemployment, 386

friends with benefits (FWB), 350
frustration
  advertising and, 3
  communication and, 226
  compulsive shopping and, 17
  defined, 67
  fixation and, 35
  from job dissatisfaction, 292
  from life changes, 68
  from overexercising, 143
  as source of stress, 67, 71, 97
frustration-aggression hypothesis, 97
fundamental attribution error, 201
future-oriented people, 109

G

galvanic skin response (GSR), 235
gambling, 99
gamma hydroxybutyrate (GHB), 303
Gardisil vaccine, 359
gastric bypass surgery, 139
gays. See homosexuals
gaze. See eye contact (mutual gaze)
gender, defined, 307
gender-appropriate behavior, 317
gender bias, 320, 328, 371
gender differences
  in aggression, 311, 322
  in alcohol abuse, 312–313
  biological origins of, 314–316
  in body image, 313
  in brain organization, 315–316
  in cardiovascular disease, 125
  in close relationships, 312
  in cognitive abilities, 309–310
  in communication, 312
  in crimes, 311
  in depressive disorders, 309, 313, 410
  in eating disorders, 313
  in emotional expression, 312
  environmental origins of, 317–322
  evolutionary perspective on, 314–315, 340
  in expressing anger, 354
  in eye contact, 231
  in feeling negative emotions, 312, 340
  in happiness, 17
  in infants' response to threats, 75
  in mate selection, 283
  in mathematical abilities, 309–310
  in mating strategies, 255–256, 283
  in mood disorders, 313
  in motivations for sexual infidelity, 352–353
  in nonverbal communication, 312
  in panic disorder, 404
  in patterns of orgasm, 346
  in personality traits, social behavior, 311–312
  in psychological disorders, 312–313
  in role expectations, 322–326
  in self-esteem, 172, 311
  sexism, sexual harassment and, 331
  in sexual arousal, 344
  in sexual attitudes, behavior, 312
  in sexual desire, 303
  in sexual fantasies, 347
  in sexual socialization, 340
  in sharing pain, 322
  in socialization, 310, 314
  social role theory on, 314, 317
  in spatial abilities, 310, 314
  stereotype threat, 203–204
  in touch, 232–233
  in verbal abilities, 309

in violent crime, 311
in the workplace, 309, 325, 329–331
gender-neutral characters, in picture books, 319
gender-role expectations
  for females, 324–326
  for males, 322–324
  See also role expectations
gender-role identity, 326–327
gender roles
  alternatives to, 326–328
  defined, 307, 317
  domestic violence and, 302
  in other-gender relationships, 238–239
  reasons for changes in, 3, 326
  in same-sex relationships, 291
  transitions, in marriage, 280
  transitions in, 280, 290–291
gender-role socialization
  male "macho" sexual image and, 324
  mating patterns and, 256
  processes in, 317–318
  sexual problems and, 324, 325–326
  sources of, 318–322
gender-role transcendence, 327–328
gender schemas, 307, 318, 319, 320
gender similarities hypothesis, 309
gender stereotypes
  defined, 307
  development/persistence of, 314, 340
  gender-neutral books and, 319, 320
  gender roles relation to, 317
  masculine, feminine, 308
  in television commercials, 321–322
  in video games, 322
  in the workplace, 329–331
gender-typing, 327
gender variance, 328
general adaptation syndrome, 75–76
generalized anxiety disorder, 403, 450
genetic predisposition
  to anxiety-related disorders, 405
  to depressive/bipolar disorders, 411–412
  to eating disorders, 425
  to happiness, 19
  to loneliness, 272
  to obesity, 137
  to schizophrenic disorders, 417
  to sexual orientation, 342
  See also heredity
genital herpes virus (HSV-2), 358
genital stage, 35, 36–37
Gen-X, 390
geriatrics, therapists for, 431–432
giving up
  as coping response, 78, 96–97
  interdependence theory and, 259
  learned helplessness and, 413
  Oedipal complex and, 36
  by pessimists, 86
glass ceiling, 329–330, 381
gonads (sex glands), 336
gonorrhea, 358
good moods. See positive moods
GPA. See grade point average
grade point average (GPA)
  career success and, 370
  grit and, 474–475
  high school-college correlation, 12
  time management and, 117
grandiose narcissism, 51–52
gratification
  ego and, 31–32
  fixation and, 35

pleasure principle and, 31, 33
  reality principle and, 31
gratitude, 72, 463, 469, 475, 479–480
gratitude letter, 479–480
grief, 71
grit, 474–475
grooming, attractiveness and, 253–254
group competition, 202
group therapy, 436–437
  in blended therapy, 448
  choosing, 451
  over the telephone, 450
growth needs, 46
growth stage, in career choice, 374, 375

H

Haldol (haloperidol), 443
hallucinations, 136, 151, 414–416, 440, 443
hallucinogens, 150, 151, 153, 154
Hamm, Jon, 408
hand gestures, 232
handwashing, 404
happiness, 16–20
  age and, 17
  attractiveness and, 17
  culture and, 18
  facial expression of, 230
  genetics and, 19
  health and, 17–18
  intelligence and, 17
  leisure activity and, 18
  marital status and, 18
  money and, 16–17
  parenthood and, 17
  personality and, 19
  relationship satisfaction and, 18–19
  religious belief and, 18
  self-boosting of, 479–481
  social relations and, 18
  subjective well-being and, 3, 16–20, 84
  work and, 19
hardiness, 83, 86
hard to get, playing, 217
hashish, 151, 153
Hathaway, Anne, 408
headaches, migraine, 129
health
  biopsychosocial model, 123, 124
  happiness and, 17–18
  mindfulness and, 469
  nutrition and, 139–142
  See also mental health
health-impairing habits, 130
health psychology, 123–124
heart attack, 64, 107, 112, 125–127, 132, 404
heart disease, 123, 124
  anger and, 126, 127–128
  depression and, 128
  emotional reactions and, 127–128
  exercise and, 125
  hostility and, 125–127
  nutrition and, 140
  obesity and, 125–126, 136
  risk factors, 125
  rumination and, 128
hedonic adaptation, 20
help, seeking, in problem solving, 108–109
Hemingway, Ernest, 408
hemophilia, 129
heredity
  obesity and, 137
  personality and, 48, 49, 50, 423

Personal Explorations Workbook

PERSONAL EXPLORATIONS WORKBOOK CONTENTS

INTRODUCTION

In your textbook, *Psychology Applied to Modern Life,* the value of developing an accurate self-concept is emphasized repeatedly. A little self-deception may occasionally be adaptive (see Chapter 4), but most theories of psychological health endorse the importance of forming a realistic picture of one's personal qualities and capabilities. This *Personal Explorations Workbook* contains two types of exercises intended to help you achieve this goal. They are (1) a series of *Self-Assessments,* or self-scoring psychological scales, intended to help you gain insight into your attitudes and personality traits, and (2) a series of *Self-Reflections* intended to help you systematically analyze various aspects of your life in relation to adjustment issues.

How you use these personal exploration exercises will depend, in large part, on your instructor. Some instructors will formally assign some of these exercises and then collect them for individual scrutiny or class discussion. That is why the pages of this workbook are perforated—to make it convenient for those instructors who like to assign the exercises as homework. Other instructors may simply encourage students to complete the exercises that they find intriguing. We believe that, even if the exercises are not assigned, you will find many of them very interesting and we encourage you to complete them on your own. Let's briefly take a closer look at these exercises.

Self-Assessments

The Self-Assessments are a collection of attitude scales and personality tests that psychologists have used in their research. One Self-Assessment questionnaire has been selected for each chapter in your text. Instructions are provided so that you can administer these scales to yourself and then compute your score. Each Self-Assessment also includes an explanation of what the scale measures followed by a brief review of the research on the scale. These reviews discuss the evidence on the reliability, validity, and behavioral correlates of each scale. The final section of each Self-Assessment provides information which allows you to interpret the meaning of your score. Test norms are supplied to indicate what represents a high, intermediate, or low score on the scale. We hope you may gain some useful insights about yourself by responding to these scales.

However, you should be careful about attributing too much significance to your scores. As explained in Chapter 2 in your text, the results of psychological tests can be misleading, and caution is always in order when interpreting test scores. It is probably best to view your scores as interesting "food for thought" rather than as definitive statements about your personal traits or abilities.

Most of the scales included in this book are self-report inventories. Your scores on such tests are only as accurate as the information that you provide in your responses. Hence, we hasten to emphasize that the Self-Assessments will only be as valuable as you make them by striving to respond honestly. Usually, people taking a scale do not know what the scale measures. The conventional approach is to put some sort of vague or misleading title, such as "Biographical Inventory," at the top of the scale. We have not adhered to this practice because you could easily find out what any scale measures simply by reading ahead a little. Thus, you will be taking each scale with some idea (based on the title) of what the scale measures. Bear in mind, however, that these scales are intended to satisfy your curiosity. There is no reason to try to impress or mislead anyone—including yourself. Your test scores will be accurate and meaningful only if you try very hard to respond in a candid manner.

Self-Reflections

The Self-Reflections consist of sets of questions designed to make you think about yourself and your personal experiences in relation to specific issues and topics raised in your text. They involve systematic inquiries into how you behave in certain situations, how your behavior has been shaped by past events, how you feel about certain issues, how you might improve yourself in some areas, how you anticipate behaving under certain circumstances in the future, and so forth. There is one Self-Reflection for each of the sixteen chapters in your textbook. The aspects of life probed by these inquiries are, of course, tied to the content of the chapters in your text. You will probably derive the most benefit from them if you read the corresponding text chapter before completing the Self-Reflections.

Wayne Weiten
Dana S. Dunn
Elizabeth Yost Hammer

REFERENCES

Ames, D. R., Rose, P., & Anderson, C. P. (2006). The NPI-16 as a short measure of narcissism. *Journal of Research in Personality, 40*, 440–450.

Ames, S. C., Jones, G. N., Howe, J. T., & Brantley, P. J. (2001). A prospective study of the impact of stress on quality of life: An investigation of low-income individuals with hypertension. *Annals of Behavioral Medicine, 23*(2), 112–119.

Anderson, N. H. (1968). Likableness ratings of 555 personality trait words. *Journal of Personality and Social Psychology, 9*, 272–279.

Arnaut, G. L. Y. (2006). Sensation seeking, risk taking, and fearlessness. In J. C. Thomas & D. L. Segal (Eds.), *Comprehensive handbook of personality and psychopathology, Vol 1: Personality and everyday functioning* (pp. 322–344). New York: Wiley.

Barnes, G. E., & Vulcano, B. A. (1982). Measuring rationality independent of social desirability. *Personality and Individual Differences, 3*, 303–309.

Baumeister, R. F., & Vohs, K. D. (2001). Narcissism as addiction to esteem. *Psychological Inquiry, 12*, 206–210.

Becker, H. A. (1980). The Assertive Job-Hunting Survey. *Measurement and Evaluation in Guidance, 13*, 43–48.

Compton, W. C. (2005). *An introduction to positive psychology.* Belmont, CA: Thompson/Wadsworth.

Denisoff, E., & Endler, N. S. (2000). Life experiences, coping, and weight preoccupation in young adult women. *Canadian Journal of Behavioural Science, 32*(2), 97–103.

Egan, G. (1977). *You and me: The skills of communicating and relating to others.* Pacific Grove, CA: Brooks/Cole.

Ellis, A. (1962). *Reason and emotion in psychotherapy.* Secaucus, NJ: Lyle Stuart.

Ellis, A. (1973). *Humanistic psychotherapy: The rational-emotive approach.* New York: Julian Press.

Fischer, E. H., & Turner, J. L. (1970). Orientations to seeking professional help: Development and research utility of an attitude scale. *Journal of Consulting and Clinical Psychology, 35*, 82–83.

Hatfield, E., & Sprecher, S. (1986). Measuring passionate love in intimate relationships. *Journal of Adolescence, 9*, 383–410.

Hodgson, R. J. (1977). Obsessional-compulsive complaints. *Behavior Research & Therapy, 15*, 389–395.

Ickes, W., & Barnes, R. D. (1977). The role of sex and self-monitoring in unstructured dyadic interactions. *Journal of Personality and Social Psychology, 35*, 315–330.

Infante, D. A., & Rancer, A. S. (1982). A conceptualization and measure of argumentativeness. *Journal of Personality Assessment, 46*, 72–80.

Malefo, V. (2000). Psycho-social factors and academic performance among African women students at a predominantly white university in South Africa. *South African Journal of Psychology, 30*(4), 40–45.

Miller, L. C., Berg, J. H., & Archer, R. L. (1983). Openers: Individuals who elicit intimate self-disclosure. *Journal of Personality and Social Psychology, 44*, 1234–1244.

Peterson, C. (2006). *A primer in positive psychology.* New York: Oxford University Press.

Peterson, C., Park, N., & Seligman, M. E. P. (2005). Orientations to happiness and life satisfaction: The full life versus the empty life. *Journal of Happiness Studies, 6*, 25–41.

Raskin, R., & Terry, H. (1988). A principal-components analysis of the Narcissistic Personality Inventory and further evidence of its construct validity. *Journal of Personality and Social Psychology, 54*, 890–902.

Rhodewalt, F., & Morf, C. C. (2005). Reflections in troubled waters: Narcissism and the vicissitudes of an interpersonality contextualized self. In A. Tesser, J. V. Wood, & D. A. Staper (Eds.), *On Building, defending, and regulating the self* (pp. 127–152). New York: Psychology Press.

Rhodewalt, F. & Peterson, B. (2009). Narcissism. In M. R. Leary & R. H. Hoyle (Eds.), *Handbook of individual differences in social behavior* (pp. 547–560). New York: Guilford.

Rosenbaum, M. (1980). A schedule for assessing self-control behaviors: Preliminary findings. *Behavior Therapy, 11*, 109–121.

Rotter, J. B. (1966). Generalized expectancies for internal versus external control of reinforcement. *Psychological Monographs, 80* (Whole No. 609).

Sarason, I. G., Johnson, J. H., & Siegel, J. M. (1978). Assessing the impact of life changes: Development of the Life Experiences Survey. *Journal of Consulting and Clinical Psychology, 46*, 932–946.

Snell, W. E., Jr., & Papini, D. R. (1989). The sexuality scale: An instrument to measure sexual-esteem, sexual-depression, and sexual-preoccupation. *Journal of Sex Research, 26*, 256–263.

Snyder, M. (1974). Self-monitoring of expressive behavior. *Journal of Personality and Social Psychology, 30*, 526–537.

Spence, J. T., & Helmreich, R. L. (1978). *Masculinity and femininity: Their psychological dimensions, correlates, and antecedents.* Austin: University of Texas Press.

Sternberger, L. G., & Burns, G. L. (1990). Compulsive activity checklist and the Maudsley Obsessional-Compulsive Inventory: Psychometric properties of two measures of obsessive-compulsive disorder. *Behavior Therapy, 21*, 117–127.

Suinn, R. M. (1968). Removal of social desirability and response set items from the Manifest Anxiety Scale. *Educational and Psychological Measurement, 28*, 1189–1192.

Taylor, J. A. (1953). A personality scale of manifest anxiety. *Journal of Abnormal and Social Psychology, 48*, 285–290.

Twenge, J. M., & Campbell, W. K. (2009). *The narcissism epidemic: Living in the age of entitlement.* New York: Free Press.

Twenge, J. M., Konrath, S., Foster, J. D., Campbell, W. K., & Bushman, B. J. (2008). Egos inflating over time: A cross-temporal meta-analysis of the Narcissistic Personality Inventory. *Journal of Personality, 76*(4), 903–917.

U.S. Department of Health and Human Services. (1981). *Health style: A self-test.* Washington, DC: Department of Health and Human Services, Public Health Service, PHS 81–50155.

Wallston, K. A. (2005). The validity of the Multidimensional Health Locus of Control Scales. *Journal of Health Psychology, 10*, 623–631.

Wallston, K. A., Wallston, B. S., & DeVellis, R. (1978). Development of the Multidimensional Health Locus of Control (MHLC) Scales. *Health Education Monographs, 6*, 160–170.

Watson, D. L., & Friend, R. (1969). Measurement of social-evaluative anxiety. *Journal of Consulting and Clinical Psychology, 33*, 448–457.

Weiten, W. (1988). Pressure as a form of stress and its relationship to psychological symptomatology. *Journal of Social and Clinical Personality, 13*, 51–68.

Weiten, W. (1998). Pressure, major life events, and psychological symptoms. *Journal of Social Behavior and Personality, 13*, 51–68.

Zuckerman, M. (1979). *Sensation seeking: Beyond the optimal level of arousal.* Hillsdale, NJ: Erlbaum.

Zuckerman, M. (1994). *Behavioral expressions and biosocial bases of sensation seeking.* New York: Cambridge University Press.

Zuckerman, M. (2007). *Sensation seeking and risky behavior.* Washington, DC: American Psychological Association.

CHAPTER 1 Adjusting to Modern Life

EXERCISE 1.1 *Self-Assessment:* Narcissistic Personality Inventory

INSTRUCTIONS

Read each pair of statements below and place an "X" by the one that comes closest to describing your feelings and beliefs about yourself. You may feel that neither statement describes you well, but pick the one that comes closest. **Please complete all pairs.**

The Scale

____ 1. A. When people compliment me I sometimes get embarrassed.
   B. I know that I am good because everybody keeps telling me so.

____ 2. A. I prefer to blend in with the crowd.
   B. I like to be the center of attention.

____ 3. A. I am no better or worse than most people.
   B. I think I am a special person.

____ 4. A. I like to have authority over other people.
   B. I don't mind following orders.

____ 5. A. I find it easy to manipulate people.
   B. I don't like it when I find myself manipulating people.

____ 6. A. I insist upon getting the respect that is due me.
   B. I usually get the respect that I deserve.

____ 7. A. I try not to be a show off.
   B. I will usually show off if I get the chance.

____ 8. A. I always know what I am doing.
   B. Sometimes I am not sure of what I am doing.

____ 9. A. Sometimes I tell good stories.
   B. Everybody likes to hear my stories.

____ 10. A. I expect a great deal from other people.
   B. I like to do things for other people.

____ 11. A. I really like to be the center of attention.
   B. It makes me uncomfortable to be the center of attention.

____ 12. A. Being an authority doesn't mean that much to me.
   B. People always seem to recognize my authority.

____ 13. A. I am going to be a great person.
   B. I hope I am going to be successful.

____ 14. A. People sometimes believe what I tell them.
   B. I can make anybody believe anything I want them to.

____ 15. A. I am more capable than other people.
   B. There is a lot that I can learn from other people.

____ 16. A. I am much like everybody else.
   B. I am an extraordinary person.

Scoring the Scale

The scoring key is reproduced below. You should circle your response of A or B each time it corresponds to the keyed response below. Add up the number of responses you circled. This total is your score on the Narcissistic Personality Inventory. Record your score below.

1. B	5. A	9. B	13. A
2. B	6. A	10. A	14. B
3. B	7. B	11. A	15. A
4. A	8. A	12. B	16. B

My score _____

What the Scale Measures

As noted briefly in Chapter 1, *narcissism* is a personality trait marked by an inflated sense of importance, a need for attention and admiration, a sense of entitlement, and a tendency to exploit others. Those who score high in narcissism tend to exhibit feelings of superiority, although their feelings of self-esteem are actually quite fragile and constantly require validation (Rhodewalt & Morf, 2005). This insecurity creates an insatiable need for expressions of admiration from others that leads to grandiose self-presentations (Rhodewalt & Peterson, 2009). Baumeister and Vohs (2001) compare narcissists' craving for approval and admiration to an addiction. Twenge and Campbell (2009) emphasize narcissists' sense of entitlement—the expectation that everything should revolve around them and that they should receive special favors and treatment.

The Narcissistic Personality Inventory (NPI) was developed by Robert Raskin and colleagues (Raskin & Hall, 1979, 1981; Raskin & Terry, 1988) to assess normal levels of narcissism on a continuum. The original 54-item measure was reduced to a 40-item scale in 1988. The assessment you took here is a 16-item version devised and validated by Ames, Rose, and Anderson (2006). There is extensive evidence that the various versions of the NPI accurately measure what they set out to measure.

Interpreting Your Score

Our norms are based on data from five studies reported by Ames, Rose, and Anderson (2006). Our high and low scores are basically ¾ of a standard deviation above and below the mean, with a little rounding (the standard deviation is an index of how much variability there tends to be on a measure). Roughly speaking, that means high scorers fall in the upper 25% on this trait, medium scorers in the middle 50%, and low scorers in the bottom 25%. There are some small gender differences on the NPI-16, so norms are reported separately for males and females.

Norms

	Males	Females
High score:	9–16	7–16
Medium score:	4–8	3–6
Low score:	0–3	0–2

Source: From Ames, D. R., Rose, P., & Anderson, C. P. (2006). The NPI-16 as a short measure of narcissism. *Journal of Research in Personality, 40*(4), 440–450. Appendix A. Reprinted with permission from Elsevier.

EXERCISE 1.2 *Self-Reflection:* What Are Your Study Habits Like?

Do you usually complete your class assignments on time?   YES   NO

Do you usually find time to prepare adequately for your exams?   YES   NO

Do you frequently delay schoolwork until the last minute?   YES   NO

When do you usually study (mornings, evenings, weekends, etc.)?

Do you write out and follow a study schedule?   YES   NO

Are your study times planned for when you're likely to be alert?   YES   NO

Do you allow time for brief study breaks?   YES   NO

Where do you usually study (library, kitchen, bedroom, etc.)?

Do you have a special place set up for studying and nothing else?   YES   NO

What types of auditory, visual, and social distractions are present in your study areas?

Can you suggest any changes to reduce distractions in your study areas?

CHAPTER 2 Theories of Personality

EXERCISE 2.1 *Self-Assessment:* Sensation-Seeking Scale

INSTRUCTIONS

Each of the items below contains two choices, A and B. Please indicate in the spaces provided on the left which of the choices most describes your likes or the way you feel. It is important that you respond to all items with only one choice, A or B. In some cases you may find that both choices describe your likes or the way you feel. Please choose the one that better describes your likes or feelings. In some cases you may not like either choice. In these cases mark the choice you dislike least. We are interested only in your likes or feelings, not in how others feel about these things or how one is supposed to feel. There are no right or wrong answers. Be frank and give your honest appraisal of yourself.

The Scale

_____ 1. A. I would like a job that would require a lot of traveling.

   B. I would prefer a job in one location.

_____ 2. A. I am invigorated by a brisk, cold day.

   B. I can't wait to get indoors on a cold day.

_____ 3. A. I find a certain pleasure in routine kinds of work.

   B. Although it is sometimes necessary, I usually dislike routine kinds of work.

_____ 4. A. I often wish I could be a mountain climber.

   B. I can't understand people who risk their necks climbing mountains.

_____ 5. A. I dislike all body odors.

   B. I like some of the earthy body smells.

_____ 6. A. I get bored seeing the same old faces.

   B. I like the comfortable familiarity of everyday friends.

_____ 7. A. I like to explore a strange city or section of town by myself, even if it means getting lost.

   B. I prefer a guide when I am in a place I don't know well.

_____ 8. A. I find the quickest and easiest route to a place and stick to it.

   B. I sometimes take different routes to a place I often go, just for variety's sake.

_____ 9. A. I would not like to try any drug that might produce strange and dangerous effects on me.

   B. I would like to try some of the new drugs that produce hallucinations.

_____ 10. A. I would prefer living in an ideal society where everyone is safe, secure, and happy.

   B. I would have preferred living in the unsettled days of our history.

_____ 11. A. I sometimes like to do things that are a little frightening.

   B. A sensible person avoids activities that are dangerous.

_____ 12. A. I order dishes with which I am familiar, so as to avoid disappointment and unpleasantness.

   B. I like to try new foods that I have never tasted before.

_____ 13. A. I can't stand riding with a person who likes to speed.

   B. I sometimes like to drive very fast because I find it exciting.

_____ 14. A. If I were a salesperson, I would prefer a straight salary rather than the risk of making little or nothing on a commission basis.

   B. If I were a salesperson, I would prefer working on a commission if I had a chance to make more money than I could on a salary.

_____ 15. A. I would like to take up the sport of water skiing.

   B. I would not like to take up the sport of water skiing.

_____ 16. A. I don't like to argue with people whose beliefs are sharply divergent from mine, since such arguments are never resolved.

   B. I find people who disagree with my beliefs more stimulating than people who agree with me.

_____ 17. A. When I go on a trip, I like to plan my route and timetable fairly carefully.

   B. I would like to take off on a trip with no pre-planned or definite routes or timetables.

_____ 18. A. I enjoy the thrills of watching car races.

   B. I find car races unpleasant.

_____ 19. A. Most people spend entirely too much money on life insurance.

   B. Life insurance is something that no one can afford to be without.

_____ 20. A. I would like to learn to fly an airplane.

   B. I would not like to learn to fly an airplane.

_____ 21. A. I would not like to be hypnotized.

   B. I would like to have the experience of being hypnotized.

_____ 22. A. The most important goal of life is to live it to the fullest and experience as much of it as you can.

   B. The most important goal of life is to find peace and happiness.

_____ 23. A. I would like to try parachute jumping.

   B. I would never want to try jumping out of a plane, with or without a parachute.

_____ 24. A. I enter cold water gradually, giving myself time to get used to it.

   B. I like to dive or jump right into the ocean or a cold pool.

_____ 25. A. I do not like the irregularity and discord of most modern music.

   B. I like to listen to new and unusual kinds of music.

_____ 26. A. I prefer friends who are excitingly unpredictable.

   B. I prefer friends who are reliable and predictable.

_____ 27. A. When I go on a vacation, I prefer the comfort of a good room and bed.

   B. When I go on a vacation, I prefer the change of camping out.

_____ 28. A. The essence of good art is in its clarity, symmetry of form, and harmony of colors.

   B. I often find beauty in the "clashing" colors and irregular forms of modern paintings.

_____ 29. A. The worst social sin is to be rude.

B. The worst social sin is to be a bore.

_____ 30. A. I look forward to a good night of rest after a long day.

B. I wish I didn't have to waste so much of a day sleeping.

_____ 31. A. I prefer people who are emotionally expressive even if they are a bit unstable.

B. I prefer people who are calm and even-tempered.

_____ 32. A. A good painting should shock or jolt the senses.

B. A good painting should give one a feeling of peace and security.

_____ 33. A. When I feel discouraged, I recover by relaxing and having some soothing diversion.

B. When I feel discouraged, I recover by going out and doing something new and exciting.

_____ 34. A. People who ride motorcycles must have some kind of an unconscious need to hurt themselves.

B. I would like to drive or ride on a motorcycle.

Scoring the Scale

The scoring key is reproduced below. You should circle your response of A or B each time it corresponds to the keyed response below. Add up the number of responses you circled. This total is your score on the Sensation-Seeking Scale. Record your score below.

1. A	8. B	15. A	22. A	29. B
2. A	9. B	16. B	23. A	30. B
3. B	10. B	17. B	24. B	31. A
4. A	11. A	18. A	25. B	32. A
5. B	12. B	19. A	26. A	33. B
6. A	13. B	20. A	27. B	34. B
7. A	14. B	21. B	28. B	

My score _____

What the Scale Measures

As its name implies, the Sensation-Seeking Scale (SSS) measures one's need for a high level of stimulation. Sensation seeking involves the active pursuit of experiences that many people would find very stressful. As discussed in the chapter, Marvin Zuckerman (1994, 2007) believes that this thirst for sensation is a highly heritable personality trait that leads people to seek thrills, adventures, and new experiences.

The scale you have just responded to is the second version of the SSS (Zuckerman, 1979), but it shares a great deal of overlap with the current version (Arnaut, 2006). Sensation seeking is distributed along a continuum, and many people fall in the middle. Factor analyses indicate that the personality trait of sensation seeking consists of four related components. When compared to low sensation seekers, those high in sensation seeking display the following four sets of characteristics (Arnaut, 2006; Zuckerman, 1994):

- *Thrill and adventure seeking.* They're more willing to engage in activities that may involve a physical risk. Thus, they're more likely to go mountain climbing, skydiving, surfing, and scuba diving.
- *Experience seeking.* They're more willing to volunteer for unusual experiments or activities that they may know little about. They tend to relish extensive travel, provocative art, wild parties, and unusual friends.
- *Disinhibition.* They are relatively uninhibited. Hence, they are prone to engage in heavy drinking, recreational drug use, gambling, and sexual experimentation.
- *Susceptibility to boredom.* Their chief foe is monotony. They have a low tolerance for routine and repetition, and they quickly and easily become bored.

Test-retest reliabilities are quite respectable and there is ample evidence to support the scale's predictive validity. For example, studies show that high sensation seekers appraise hypothetical situations as less risky than low sensation seekers do and are more willing to volunteer for an experiment in which they will be hypnotized. The scale also shows robust positive correlations with measures of change seeking, novelty seeking, and impulsiveness. Interestingly, SSS scores tend to decline with age.

Interpreting Your Score

Our norms are based on percentiles reported by Zuckerman and colleagues for a sample of 62 undergraduates. Although males generally tend to score a bit higher than females on the SSS, the differences are small enough to report one set of (averaged) norms. Remember, sensation-seeking scores tend to decline with age. So, if you're not in the modal college student age range (17–23), these norms may be a bit high.

Norms

High score:	21–34
Intermediate score:	11–20
Low score:	0–10

Source: From Zuckerman, M. (1979). *Sensation seeking: Beyond the optimal level of arousal* (pp. 385–387). Hillsdale, NJ: Lawrence Erlbaum Associates. Reprinted with permission of Taylor & Francis Group LLC.

EXERCISE 2.2 *Self-Reflection:* Who Are You?

Below you will find 75 personality trait words taken from an influential list assembled by Anderson (1968). Try to select the 20 traits (20 only!) that describe you best. Check them.

sincere	forgetful	truthful	imaginative	outgoing
pessimistic	crafty	mature	impolite	dependable
open-minded	methodical	skeptical	diligent	persistent
suspicious	sly	efficient	prideful	orderly
patient	headstrong	resourceful	optimistic	energetic
tense	naive	perceptive	considerate	modest
cooperative	sloppy	punctual	courteous	smart
neat	grouchy	prejudiced	candid	kind
logical	ethical	friendly	idealistic	good-humored
vain	persuasive	gracious	warm	unselfish
sociable	nervous	shy	versatile	cordial
scornful	clumsy	short-tempered	courageous	wholesome
cheerful	rebellious	compulsive	tactful	generous
honest	studious	sarcastic	loyal	boastful
reasonable	understanding	respectful	reliable	daring

Review the 20 traits that you chose. Overall, is it a favorable or unfavorable picture that you have sketched?

Considering Carl Rogers's point that we often distort reality and construct an overly favorable self-concept, do you feel that you were objective?

What characteristics make you unique?

What are your greatest strengths?

What are your greatest weaknesses?

CHAPTER 3 Stress and Its Effects

EXERCISE 3.1 *Self-Assessment:* Pressure Inventory

INSTRUCTIONS

Pressure involves expectations and demands that we behave in a certain manner. Basically, there are two kinds of pressure: (1) the pressure to perform various tasks and responsibilities efficiently, successfully, and quickly, and (2) the pressure to conform to others' expectations about how we ought to act, think, and spend our time. On this questionnaire you will find a number of examples of the kinds of pressure that many people experience. They are divided into six common sources of pressure: (1) family relations, (2) work relations, (3) intimate relations, (4) school relations, (5) peer relations, and (6) self-imposed pressures. Although some of these sources of pressure may not seem relevant to you (for example: work relations if you are not employed), please read all of the items in the inventory.

For each item, circle a number on the right to indicate whether you have experienced that pressure **during the last 3 months**, and to indicate how severe the pressure was. If you have not experienced the pressure described in the item during the last 3 months, simply circle 0. This inventory does not list all of the pressures that people experience. Thus, in each category, there is a blank item where you can list an additional example of pressure that you have experienced in the last 3 months. If you list any additional examples of pressure in these blank spaces, please indicate the severity of the pressure by circling one of the numbers between 1 and 5 on the right.

The Scale

	None	Mild		Moderate		Severe
FAMILY RELATIONS—I have been under pressure:						
1. To spend more time with my parents or children	0	1	2	3	4	5
2. To conform to my parents' values and expectations	0	1	2	3	4	5
3. To take on a larger share of responsibilities or chores around the house	0	1	2	3	4	5
4. To become more independent from my parents or family	0	1	2	3	4	5
5. To hide something from my parents or family (for example: money problems)	0	1	2	3	4	5
6. To get along better with members of my family	0	1	2	3	4	5
7. To achieve success expected by my parents or family	0	1	2	3	4	5
8. Other: (describe) _____	0	1	2	3	4	5
WORK RELATIONS—I have been under pressure:						
9. To get a job, or find a better job	0	1	2	3	4	5
10. To conform to my co-workers' values or expectations	0	1	2	3	4	5
11. To improve the quality of my work to satisfy co-workers or supervisors	0	1	2	3	4	5
12. To get more done at work in less time and to meet numerous deadlines	0	1	2	3	4	5
13. To get along better with co-workers or supervisors	0	1	2	3	4	5
14. To learn new job skills or to take on new work responsibilities	0	1	2	3	4	5
15. To be more assertive with my co-workers	0	1	2	3	4	5
16. Other: (describe) _____	0	1	2	3	4	5
INTIMATE RELATIONS—I have been under pressure:						
17. To find or develop a new intimate relationship	0	1	2	3	4	5
18. To conform to the values or expectations of my spouse, boyfriend, or girlfriend	0	1	2	3	4	5
19. To spend more time with my spouse, girlfriend, or boyfriend	0	1	2	3	4	5
20. To impress my spouse, boyfriend, or girlfriend with my competence or success	0	1	2	3	4	5
21. To engage in sexual encounters more or less frequently with my partner	0	1	2	3	4	5
22. To improve the quality of my relationship with my spouse, girlfriend, or boyfriend	0	1	2	3	4	5
23. To make a decision about divorce or breaking up with my boyfriend or girlfriend	0	1	2	3	4	5
24. Other: (describe) _____	0	1	2	3	4	5
SCHOOL RELATIONS—I have been under pressure:						
25. To get excellent grades or to improve my grades	0	1	2	3	4	5
26. To make a good impression on my instructors	0	1	2	3	4	5
27. To impress my classmates	0	1	2	3	4	5
28. To complete lots of school work in little time	0	1	2	3	4	5
29. To conform to the expectations and values of my classmates or instructors	0	1	2	3	4	5
30. To make important decisions about my educational future	0	1	2	3	4	5
31. To earn a scholarship or to earn admission to another school	0	1	2	3	4	5
32. Other: (describe) _____	0	1	2	3	4	5

	None		Mild		Moderate		Severe
PEER RELATIONS—I have been under pressure:							
33. To develop or find more or better friends	0	1	2	3	4	5	
34. To provide help or emotional support to friends or neighbors	0	1	2	3	4	5	
35. To conform to the values and expectations of my friends or neighbors (other than those from work or school)	0	1	2	3	4	5	
36. To spend more time with certain friends	0	1	2	3	4	5	
37. To maintain "appearances" for friends or neighbors (by having an attractive home, car, clothes, etc.)	0	1	2	3	4	5	
38. To achieve greater success in the eyes of my friends	0	1	2	3	4	5	
39. To be clever or witty to impress others	0	1	2	3	4	5	
40. Other: (describe) _____	0	1	2	3	4	5	
SELF-IMPOSED PRESSURES—I have been under pressure:							
41. To make more money or improve my social status	0	1	2	3	4	5	
42. To do something to make myself more attractive (such as losing weight, changing hair, etc.)	0	1	2	3	4	5	
43. To change or improve my personality	0	1	2	3	4	5	
44. To improve my self-control over everyday bad habits (such as smoking, drinking, overspending etc.)	0	1	2	3	4	5	
45. To inhibit or hide emotions that I don't want others to see	0	1	2	3	4	5	
46. To find more private time for myself	0	1	2	3	4	5	
47. To be more efficient in my use of my personal time	0	1	2	3	4	5	
48. Other: (describe) _____	0	1	2	3	4	5	

Scoring the Scale

Arriving at your score on the Pressure Inventory is very simple. Just add up all the numbers that you circled for the forty-eight items. The total is your score on the Pressure Inventory. Record your score below.

My score _____

What the Scale Measures

As its name clearly indicates, the Pressure Inventory developed by Weiten (1988, 1998) measures pressure as a form of stress. It assesses the degree to which you have subjectively felt like you were under pressure over the last 3 months. Research with the scale suggests that pressure may have ramifications for one's mental health. For example, Weiten (1998) found that scores on the Pressure Inventory were predictive of subjects' levels of anxiety, depression, alienation, and psychological discomfort. Indeed, the measure of pressure was found to correlate more strongly with each of these variables than a measure of life change (the Life Experiences Survey). The same study also analyzed stress diaries compiled by subjects and determined that pressure is a common source of everyday stress. The test-retest reliability of the scale (.72 over 2 weeks) appears to be satisfactory (Weiten, 1988).

Interpreting Your Score

The norms for the Pressure Inventory are based on two diverse samples of undergraduates, totaling 150 subjects. The high score shown below corresponds roughly to scoring in the upper 20% on the scale, whereas the low score corresponds roughly to scoring in the lowest 20% on the scale.

Norms

High score:	80 and above
Medium score:	31–79
Low score:	0–30

Although there is merit in getting an estimate of how much stress you have experienced lately, scores on the Pressure Inventory should be interpreted with caution. You need not panic if you find that your score falls in the "high" category. For one thing, the strength of the association between stress and adaptational problems is modest. Second, stress interacts with many other factors, such as lifestyle, coping skills, social support, hardiness, and genetic inheritance, in influencing one's mental and physical health.

Source: Weiten, W. (1998). Pressure, major life events, and psychological symptoms. *Journal of Social Behavior and Personality, 13,* 51–68.

EXERCISE 3.2 *Self-Reflection:* Stress—How Do You Control It?

1. Do modern lifestyles create more stress than in the past? How so?

2. How do *you* create stress in your own life?

3. How could you change the nature of our society to make it less stressful?

4. It could be said that some stress comes from leading "out-of-balance" lives. What can people do to "keep it simple"? Furthermore, in what ways can individuals control the stressors they will encounter beforehand?

5. How could you change the way in which you interact with your school demands or your work demands to change the amount of stress that you feel?

CHAPTER 4 Coping Processes

EXERCISE 4.1 *Self-Assessment:* Barnes-Vulcano Rationality Test

INSTRUCTIONS

For each of the following statements, please indicate the degree to which you tend to either agree or disagree with the statement according to the following five-point scale:

1	2	3	4	5
Agree Strongly	Agree	Neither Agree nor Disagree	Disagree	Disagree Strongly

The Scale

_____ 1. I do not need to feel that everyone I meet likes me.

_____ 2. I frequently worry about things over which I have no control.

_____ 3. I find it easy to overcome irrational fears.

_____ 4. I can usually shut off thoughts that are causing me to feel anxious.

_____ 5. Life is a ceaseless battle against irrational worries.

_____ 6. I frequently worry about death.

_____ 7. Crowds make me nervous.

_____ 8. I frequently worry about the state of my health.

_____ 9. I tend to worry about things before they actually happen.

_____ 10. If I were told that someone had a criminal record I would not hire him or her to work for me.

_____ 11. When I make a mistake I feel worthless and inadequate.

_____ 12. When someone is wrong I sure let them know.

_____ 13. When I am frustrated the first thing I do is ask myself whether there is anything I can do to change it now.

_____ 14. Whenever something goes wrong I ask myself, "Why did this have to happen to me?"

_____ 15. Whenever things go wrong I say to myself, "I don't like this, I can't stand it."

_____ 16. I usually find a cure for my own depression when it occurs.

_____ 17. Once I am depressed it takes me a long while to recover.

_____ 18. I feel that when I become depressed or unhappy it is caused by other people or the events that happen.

_____ 19. People have little or no ability to control their sorrows or rid themselves of their negative feelings.

_____ 20. When I become angry I usually control my anger.

_____ 21. I can usually control my appetite for food and alcohol.

_____ 22. The value of a human being is directly proportionate to her/his accomplishments; if s/he is not thoroughly competent and adequate in achieving, s/he might as well curl up and die.

_____ 23. The important part of playing the game is that you succeed.

_____ 24. I feel bad when my achievement level is lower than others'.

_____ 25. I feel that I must succeed at everything I undertake.

_____ 26. When I feel doubts about potential success, I avoid participating and risking the chance of failure.

_____ 27. When I set out to accomplish a task I stick with it to the end.

_____ 28. If I find difficulties in life, I discipline myself to face them.

_____ 29. If I try to do something and encounter problems, I give up easily.

_____ 30. I find it difficult to work at tasks that have a long-range payoff.

_____ 31. I usually like to face my problems head on.

_____ 32. A person never learns from his/her mistakes.

_____ 33. Life is what you make of it.

_____ 34. Unhappy childhoods inevitably lead to problems in adult life.

_____ 35. I try not to brood over past mistakes.

_____ 36. People who are selfish make me mad because they really should not be that way.

_____ 37. If I had to nag someone to get what I wanted I would not think it was worth the trouble.

_____ 38. I frequently find that life is boring.

_____ 39. I often wish that something new and exciting would happen.

_____ 40. I experience life as just the same old thing from day to day.

_____ 41. I often wish life were more stimulating.

_____ 42. I often feel that everything is tiresome and dull.

_____ 43. I wish I could change places with someone who lives an exciting life.

_____ 44. I often wish life were different than it is.

Scoring the Scale

To score this scale, you must reverse the numbers you entered for 12 of the items. The responses to be reversed are those for items 1, 3, 4, 13, 16, 20, 21, 27, 28, 31, 33, and 35. For each of these items, make the following conversions: If you chose 1, change it to 5. If you chose 2, change it to 4. If you chose 3, leave it unchanged. If you chose 4, change it to 2. If you chose 5, change it to 1.

Now add up the numbers for all 44 items, using the new numbers for the reversed items. This sum, which should fall somewhere between 44 and 220, is your score on the Barnes-Vulcano Rationality Test. Enter it below.

My score _____

What the Scale Measures

Devised by Gordon Barnes and Brent Vulcano (1982), the Barnes-Vulcano Rationality Test (BVRT) measures the degree to which people do or do not subscribe to the irrational assumptions described by Albert Ellis (1973). As Chapter 4 in your text explains, Ellis believes that troublesome emotions and overreactions to stress are caused by negative self-talk or catastrophic thinking. Such thinking is thought to be derived from irrational assumptions that people hold. The items on the BVRT are based on 10 of the irrational assumptions described by Ellis, such as the idea that one must receive love and affection from certain people, or the idea that one must be thoroughly competent in all endeavors.

The scale is set up so that high scores indicate that one tends to think relatively rationally, whereas low scores indicate that one is prone to the irrational thinking described by Ellis. The BVRT has excellent reliability, and the authors took steps to minimize contamination from social desirability bias. Evidence regarding the test's validity can be gleaned from various correlational analyses. For example, high scores on the BVRT have been found to correlate negatively with measures of neuroticism (−.50), depression (−.55), and fear (−.31), indicating that respondents who score high on the test tend to be less neurotic, depressed, or fearful than those who score lower.

Interpreting Your Score

Our norms, which are shown below, are based on combined data from two sets of adults studied by Barnes and Vulcano (1982). The first sample consisted of 172 subjects (with a mean age of 22), and the second included 177 subjects (with a mean age of 27).

Norms
High score: 166–220
Medium score: 136–165
Low score: 44–135

Source: From Barnes, G. E., & Vulcano, B. A. (1982). Measuring rationality independent of social desirability. *Personality and Individual Differences, 3,* 303–309. Reprinted with permission from Elsevier and Brent Vulcano.

EXERCISE 4.2 *Self-Reflection:* Analyzing Coping Strategies

1. You just generally feel "lousy" but are unsure as to what might be causing it. How would you go about figuring out what is wrong? What questions would you ask yourself to ensure that you come to an accurate conclusion?

2. What are some of the phrases that a person might use who is operating in the mode of "learned helplessness"? How could you help individuals tell the difference between something they have control over and something they do not?

3. Rationalization is a mechanism fraught with consequences. List some negative consequences of rationalization in the following areas: school, work, home, and relationships.

4. Discuss the issue of deadlines as they apply to any area of your life. How do you react to deadline pressures? What are some positive and negative coping strategies you have used in dealing with deadlines?

5. How do you explain negative events that occur in your life? What is your explanatory style?

Source: © Cengage Learning

CHAPTER 5 Psychology and Physical Health

EXERCISE 5.1 *Self-Assessment:* Multidimensional Health Locus of Control Scales

INSTRUCTIONS

Each item below is a belief statement with which you may agree or disagree. Beside each statement is a scale that ranges from strongly disagree (1) to strongly agree (6). For each item we would like you to circle the number that represents the extent to which you agree or disagree with that statement. The more you agree with a statement, the higher will be the number you circle. The more you disagree with a statement, the lower will be the number you circle. Please make sure that you answer *every item* and that you circle *only one* number per item. This is a measure of your personal beliefs; obviously, there are no right or wrong answers. The scale for responding is shown below.

1	2	3	4	5	6
Strongly disagree	Moderately disagree	Slightly disagree	Slightly agree	Moderately agree	Strongly agree

The Scale

1. If I become sick, I have the power to make myself well again.
   1   2   3   4   5   6

2. Often I feel that no matter what I do, if I am going to get sick, I will get sick.
   1   2   3   4   5   6

3. If I see an excellent doctor regularly, I am less likely to have health problems.
   1   2   3   4   5   6

4. It seems that my health is greatly influenced by accidental happenings.
   1   2   3   4   5   6

5. I can only maintain my health by consulting health professionals.
   1   2   3   4   5   6

6. I am directly responsible for my health.
   1   2   3   4   5   6

7. Other people play a big part in whether I stay healthy or become sick.
   1   2   3   4   5   6

8. Whatever goes wrong with my health is my own fault.
   1   2   3   4   5   6

9. When I am sick, I just have to let nature run its course.
   1   2   3   4   5   6

10. Health professionals keep me healthy.
    1   2   3   4   5   6

11. When I stay healthy, I'm just plain lucky.
    1   2   3   4   5   6

12. My physical well-being depends on how well I take care of myself.
    1   2   3   4   5   6

13. When I feel ill, I know it is because I have not been taking care of myself properly.
    1   2   3   4   5   6

14. The type of care I receive from other people is what is responsible for how well I recover from an illness.
    1   2   3   4   5   6

15. Even when I take care of myself, it's easy to get sick.
    1   2   3   4   5   6

16. When I become ill, it's a matter of fate.
    1   2   3   4   5   6

17. I can pretty much stay healthy by taking good care of myself.
    1   2   3   4   5   6

18. Following doctor's orders to the letter is the best way for me to stay healthy.
    1   2   3   4   5   6

Scoring the Scale

This assessment instrument actually consists of three subscales that measure health-related attitudes and beliefs. In the blanks below record the numbers you circled for the indicated items. Then add up the numbers in each column to calculate your score on each subscale. Record your score for each scale in the Total space at the bottom of each column.

IHLC Scale	PHLC Scale	CHLC Scale
1. _____	3. _____	2. _____
6. _____	5. _____	4. _____
8. _____	7. _____	9. _____
12. _____	10. _____	11. _____
13. _____	14. _____	15. _____
17. _____	18. _____	16. _____
Total _____	Total _____	Total _____

What the Scale Measures

These scales all relate to a personality dimension called *locus of control* originally described by Julian Rotter (1966). Locus of control is a generalized expectancy about the degree to which individuals control their outcomes. Individuals with an *external locus of control* believe that their successes and failures are governed by external factors such as fate, luck, and chance. They feel that their outcomes are largely beyond their control—that they're pawns of fate. In contrast, individuals with an *internal locus of control* believe that their successes and failures are determined by their actions and abilities (internal, or personal, factors). They consequently feel that they have more influence over their outcomes than people with an external locus of control. Of course, locus of control is not an either-or proposition. Like any other dimension of personality, it should be thought of as occurring on a continuum. Some people are very external, some are very internal, but most people fall somewhere in between.

Developed by Wallston, Wallston, and DeVellis (1978), the *Multidimensional Health Locus of Control Scales* assess individuals' locus of control in relation to health concerns. The *Internal Health Locus of Control Scale* (IHLC) measures internality in the realm of health. The other two scales measure different aspects of externality. The *Powerful Others Health Locus of Control Scale* (PHLC) measures a form of externality marked by the belief that one's health rests in the hands of medical personnel. The *Chance Health Locus of Control Scale* (CHLC) assesses a form of externality marked by the belief that one's health is a matter of chance and luck. The assumption underlying these scales is that people's scores should predict health-related behaviors, such as seeking information related to health issues, engaging in preventive measures to maintain good health, and adherence to medical advice. Some studies have provided support for this assumption, although the findings have been a mixed bag and the observed correlations have generally been rather modest (Wallston, 2005).

Interpreting Your Score

Our norms are based on data from Wallston, Wallston, and DeVellis (1978). Our cutoffs for high and low scores are based on being one standard deviation above or below the mean.

Norms

	IHLC	PHLC	CHLC
High score:	30–36	27–36	21–36
Intermediate score:	21–29	15–26	10–20
Low score:	0–20	0–15	0–9

Source: Scale reproduced with permission of Kenneth A. Wallston, Ph.D.

EXERCISE 5.2 *Self-Reflection:* How Do Your Health Habits Rate?

	Almost Always	Sometimes	Almost Never
Eating Habits			
1. I eat a variety of foods each day, such as fruits and vegetables, whole-grain breads and cereals, lean meats, dairy products, dry peas and beans, and nuts and seeds.	4	1	0
2. I limit the amount of fat, saturated fat, and cholesterol I eat (including fat on meats, eggs, butter, cream, shortenings, and organ meats such as liver).	2	1	0
3. I limit the amount of salt I eat by cooking with only small amounts, not adding salt at the table, and avoiding salty snacks.	2	1	0
4. I avoid eating too much sugar (especially frequent snacks of sticky candy or soft drinks).	2	1	0

Eating Habits Score: _____

	Almost Always	Sometimes	Almost Never
Exercise/Fitness			
1. I maintain a desired weight, avoiding overweight and underweight.	3	1	0
2. I do vigorous exercises for 15 to 30 minutes at least three times a week (examples include running, swimming, and brisk walking).	3	1	0
3. I do exercises that enhance my muscle tone for 15 to 30 minutes at least three times a week (examples include yoga and calisthenics).	2	1	0
4. I use part of my leisure time participating in individual, family, or team activities that increase my level of fitness (such as gardening, bowling, golf, and baseball).	2	1	0

Exercise/Fitness Score: _____

	Almost Always	Sometimes	Almost Never
Alcohol and Drugs			
1. I avoid drinking alcoholic beverages or I drink no more than one or two drinks a day.	4	1	0
2. I avoid using alcohol or other drugs (especially illegal drugs) as a way of handling stressful situations or the problems in my life.	2	1	0
3. I am careful not to drink alcohol when taking certain medicines (for example, medicine for sleeping, pain, colds, and allergies).	2	1	0
4. I read and follow the label directions when using prescribed and over-the-counter drugs.	2	1	0

Alcohol and Drugs Score: _____

What Your Scores Mean:

9–10	**Excellent**
6–8	**Good**
3–5	**Mediocre**
0–2	**Poor**

Do any of your scores surprise you? Why?

Source: © Cengage Learning

CHAPTER 6 The Self

EXERCISE 6.1 *Self-Assessment:* Self-Control Schedule

INSTRUCTIONS

Indicate how characteristic or descriptive each of the following statements is of you by using the numeral given below.

+3   Very characteristic of me, extremely descriptive
+2   Rather characteristic of me, quite descriptive
+1   Somewhat characteristic of me, slightly descriptive
−1   Somewhat uncharacteristic of me, slightly undescriptive
−2   Rather uncharacteristic of me, quite undescriptive
−3   Very uncharacteristic of me, extremely undescriptive

Record your responses in the spaces provided on the left.

The Scale

_____ 1. When I do a boring job, I think about the less boring parts of the job and the reward that I will receive once I am finished.

_____ 2. When I have to do something that is anxiety-arousing for me, I try to visualize how I will overcome my anxieties while doing it.

_____ 3. Often by changing my way of thinking I am able to change my feelings about almost everything.

_____ 4. I often find it difficult to overcome my feelings of nervousness and tension without any outside help.

_____ 5. When I am feeling depressed, I try to think about pleasant events.

_____ 6. I cannot avoid thinking about mistakes I have made in the past.

_____ 7. When I am faced with a difficult problem, I try to approach its solution in a systematic way.

_____ 8. I usually do my duties quicker when somebody is pressuring me.

_____ 9. When I am faced with a difficult decision, I prefer to postpone making a decision even if all the facts are at my disposal.

_____ 10. When I find that I have difficulties in concentrating on my reading, I look for ways to increase my concentration.

_____ 11. After I plan to work, I remove all the things that are not relevant to my work.

_____ 12. When I try to get rid of a bad habit, I first try to find out all the factors that maintain this habit.

_____ 13. When an unpleasant thought is bothering me, I try to think about something pleasant.

_____ 14. If I smoked two packages of cigarettes a day, I probably would need outside help to stop smoking.

_____ 15. When I am in a low mood, I try to act cheerful so my mood will change.

_____ 16. If I had the pills with me, I would take a tranquilizer whenever I felt tense and nervous.

_____ 17. When I am depressed, I try to keep myself busy with things that I like.

_____ 18. I tend to postpone unpleasant duties even if I could perform them immediately.

_____ 19. I need outside help to get rid of some of my bad habits.

_____ 20. When I find it difficult to settle down and do a certain job, I look for ways to help me settle down.

_____ 21. Although it makes me feel bad, I cannot avoid thinking about all kinds of possible catastrophes in the future.

_____ 22. First of all I prefer to finish a job that I have to do and then start doing the things I really like.

_____ 23. When I feel pain in a certain part of my body, I try not to think about it.

_____ 24. My self-esteem increases once I am able to overcome a bad habit.

_____ 25. In order to overcome bad feelings that accompany failure, I often tell myself that it is not so catastrophic and that I can do something about it.

_____ 26. When I feel that I am too impulsive, I tell myself, "Stop and think before you do anything."

_____ 27. Even when I am terribly angry at somebody, I consider my actions very carefully.

_____ 28. Facing the need to make a decision, I usually find out all the possible alternatives instead of deciding quickly and spontaneously.

_____ 29. Usually, I do first the things I really like to do even if there are more urgent things to do.

_____ 30. When I realize that I cannot help but be late for an important meeting, I tell myself to keep calm.

_____ 31. When I feel pain in my body, I try to divert my thoughts from it.

_____ 32. I usually plan my work when faced with a number of things to do.

_____ 33. When I am short of money, I decide to record all my expenses in order to plan carefully for the future.

_____ 34. If I find it difficult to concentrate on a certain job, I divide the job into smaller segments.

_____ 35. Quite often I cannot overcome unpleasant thoughts that bother me.

_____ 36. Once I am hungry and unable to eat, I try to divert my thoughts away from my stomach or try to imagine that I am satisfied.

Scoring the Scale

The items listed below are reverse-scored items. Thus, for each of them you should go back and simply change the + or − sign in front of the number you recorded.

4	9	18	29
6	14	19	35
8	16	21	

After making your reversals, all you need to do is add up the numbers you recorded for each of the thirty-six items. Of course, it is important to pay close attention to the algebraic sign in front of each number. The easiest way to calculate your score is to add up all the positive numbers first and jot that down. Then add up all the negative numbers and subtract that total from the positive total. The result you arrive at is your score on the Self-Control Schedule (SCS). Record your score below.

My score _____

What the Scale Measures

Developed by Michael Rosenbaum (1980), the Self-Control Schedule assesses your ability to employ self-management methods to solve common behavioral problems. Specifically, it measures your tendency to (1) use rational self-talk to modify emotional responses, (2) use systematic problem-solving strategies, and (3) delay immediate gratification when necessary. It also measures your perceptions regarding your self-control skills.

Rosenbaum (1980) administered the SCS to a diversified batch of six samples including both student and nonstudent populations. Test-retest reliability (.86 for 4 weeks) was excellent. Support for the validity of the scale was derived from evidence that it correlates negatively with established measures of irrational thinking. Additional supportive evidence was garnered in an experimental study wherein high scorers on the SCS showed better self-control on a laboratory task than did low scorers.

Interpreting Your Score

Our norms are based on an American sample of 111 undergraduate students studied by Rosenbaum (1980). Although females tend to score a little higher on the scale than do males, the difference is not large enough to merit separate norms (so their means have been averaged).

Norms

High score:	Above 48
Medium score:	6–47
Low score:	Below 6

Source: Rosenbaum, M. (1980). A schedule for assessing self-control behaviors: Preliminary findings. *Behavior Therapy, 11,* 109–121.

Below you will find a list of 15 traits, each portrayed on a 9-point continuum. Mark with an X where you think you fall on each trait. Try to be candid and accurate; these marks will collectively describe a portion of your self-concept. When you are finished, go back and circle where you *wish* you could be on each dimension. These marks describe your self-ideal. Finally, in the spaces on the right, indicate the size of the discrepancy between self-concept and self-ideal for each trait (subtract one score from the other).

1. Decisive   Indecisive _____
   9   8   7   6   5   4   3   2   1

2. Anxious   Relaxed _____
   9   8   7   6   5   4   3   2   1

3. Easily influenced   Independent thinker _____
   9   8   7   6   5   4   3   2   1

4. Very intelligent   Less intelligent _____
   9   8   7   6   5   4   3   2   1

5. In good physical shape   In poor physical shape _____
   9   8   7   6   5   4   3   2   1

6. Undependable   Dependable _____
   9   8   7   6   5   4   3   2   1

7. Deceitful   Honest _____
   9   8   7   6   5   4   3   2   1

8. A leader   A follower _____
   9   8   7   6   5   4   3   2   1

9. Unambitious   Ambitious _____
   9   8   7   6   5   4   3   2   1

10. Self-confident   Insecure _____
   9   8   7   6   5   4   3   2   1

11. Conservative   Adventurous _____
   9   8   7   6   5   4   3   2   1

12. Extraverted   Introverted _____
   9   8   7   6   5   4   3   2   1

13. Physically attractive   Physically unattractive _____
   9   8   7   6   5   4   3   2   1

14. Lazy   Hardworking _____
   9   8   7   6   5   4   3   2   1

15. Funny   Little sense of humor _____
   9   8   7   6   5   4   3   2   1

Overall, how would you describe the discrepancy between your self-concept and your self-ideal (large, moderate, small, large on a few dimensions)?

How do sizable gaps on any of the traits affect your self-esteem?

Do you feel that any of the gaps exist because you have had others' ideals imposed on you or because you have thoughtlessly accepted others' ideals?

CHAPTER 7 Social Thinking and Social Influence

EXERCISE 7.1 *Self-Assessment:* Argumentativeness Scale

INSTRUCTIONS

This questionnaire contains statements about arguing controversial issues. Indicate how often each statement is true for you personally by placing the appropriate number in the blank to the left of the statement:

1	2	3	4	5
Almost Never True	Rarely True	Occasionally True	Often True	Almost Always True

The Scale

_____ 1. While in an argument, I worry that the person I am arguing with will form a negative impression of me.

_____ 2. Arguing over controversial issues improves my intelligence.

_____ 3. I enjoy avoiding arguments.

_____ 4. I am energetic and enthusiastic when I argue.

_____ 5. Once I finish an argument I promise myself that I will not get into another.

_____ 6. Arguing with a person creates more problems for me than it solves.

_____ 7. I have a pleasant, good feeling when I win a point in an argument.

_____ 8. When I finish arguing with someone I feel nervous and upset.

_____ 9. I enjoy a good argument over a controversial issue.

_____ 10. I get an unpleasant feeling when I realize I am about to get into an argument.

_____ 11. I enjoy defending my point of view on an issue.

_____ 12. I am happy when I keep an argument from happening.

_____ 13. I do not like to miss the opportunity to argue a controversial issue.

_____ 14. I prefer being with people who rarely disagree with me.

_____ 15. I consider an argument an exciting intellectual challenge.

_____ 16. I find myself unable to think of effective points during an argument.

_____ 17. I feel refreshed and satisfied after an argument on a controversial issue.

_____ 18. I have the ability to do well in an argument.

_____ 19. I try to avoid getting into arguments.

_____ 20. I feel excitement when I expect that a conversation I am in is leading to an argument.

Scoring the Scale

Add up the numbers that you have recorded for items 2, 4, 7, 9, 11, 13, 15, 17, 18, and 20. This total reflects your tendency to approach argumentative situations. Next, add up the numbers that you have recorded for items 1, 3, 5, 6, 8, 10, 12, 14, 16, and 19. This total reflects your tendency to avoid getting into arguments. Record these subtotals in the spaces below. Subtract your avoidance score from your approach score to arrive at your overall score.

_____	−	_____	=	_____
Approach score		**Avoidance score**		**Total score**

What the Scale Measures

This questionnaire measures an aspect of your social influence behavior. Specifically, it assesses your tendency to argue with others in persuasive efforts. Persons who score high on this scale are not bashful about tackling controversial issues, are willing to attack others verbally to make their points, and are less compliant than the average person. Developed by Infante and Rancer (1982), this scale has high test-retest reliability (.91 for a period of one week). Examinations of the scale's validity show that it correlates well with other measures of communication tendencies and with friends' ratings of subjects' argumentativeness.

Interpreting Your Score

Our norms are based on the responses of over 800 undergraduate subjects studied by Infante and Rancer (1982).

Norms

High score:	16 and above
Intermediate score:	6 to 15
Low score:	5 and below

Source: From Infante, D. A., & Rancer, A. S. (1982). A Conceptualization and measure of argumentativeness. *Journal of Personality Assessment, 46,* 72–80. Copyright © Lawrence Erlbaum Associates, Inc. Reprinted by permission of Taylor & Francis, and Dominic Infante.

EXERCISE 7.2 *Self-Reflection:* Can You Identify Your Prejudicial Stereotypes?

1. List and briefly describe examples of three prejudicial stereotypes that you hold or have held at one time.

   Example 1:

   Example 2:

   Example 3:

2. Try to identify the sources (family, friends, media, etc.) of each of these stereotypes.

   Example 1:

   Example 2:

   Example 3:

3. For each stereotype, how much actual interaction have you had with the stereotyped group, and has this interaction affected your views?

   Example 1:

   Example 2:

   Example 3:

4. Can you think of any ways in which the fundamental attribution error or defensive attribution has contributed to these stereotypes?

   Fundamental attribution error:

   Defensive attribution:

CHAPTER 8 Interpersonal Communication

EXERCISE 8.1 *Self-Assessment:* Opener Scale

INSTRUCTIONS

For each statement, indicate your degree of agreement or disagreement, using the scale shown below. Record your responses in the spaces on the left.

4 = I strongly agree
3 = I slightly agree
2 = I am uncertain
1 = I slightly disagree
0 = I strongly disagree

The Scale

_____ 1. People frequently tell me about themselves.

_____ 2. I've been told that I'm a good listener.

_____ 3. I'm very accepting of others.

_____ 4. People trust me with their secrets.

_____ 5. I easily get people to "open up."

_____ 6. People feel relaxed around me.

_____ 7. I enjoy listening to people.

_____ 8. I'm sympathetic to people's problems.

_____ 9. I encourage people to tell me how they are feeling.

_____10. I can keep people talking about themselves.

Scoring the Scale

This scale is easy to score! Simply add up the numbers that you have recorded in the spaces on the left. This total is your score on the Opener Scale.

My Score _____

What the Scale Measures

Devised by Lynn Miller, John Berg, and Richard Archer (1983), the Opener Scale is intended to measure your perception of your ability to get others to "open up" around you. In other words, the scale assesses your tendency to elicit intimate self-disclosure from people. The items assess your perceptions of (a) others' reactions to you ("People feel relaxed around me"), (b) your interest in listening ("I enjoy listening to people"), and (c) your interpersonal skills ("I can keep people talking about themselves").

In spite of its brevity, the scale has reasonable test-retest reliability (.69 over a period of six weeks). Correlations with other personality measures were modest, but in the expected directions. For instance, scores on the Opener Scale correlate positively with a measure of empathy and negatively with a measure of shyness. Further evidence for the validity of the scale was obtained in a laboratory study of interactions between same-sex strangers. Subjects who scored high on the scale compared to those who scored low elicited more self-disclosure from people who weren't prone to engage in much disclosure.

Interpreting Your Score

Our norms are based on the original sample of 740 undergraduates studied by Miller, Berg, and Archer (1983). They found a small but statistically significant difference between males and females.

Norms

	Females	Males
High score:	35–40	33–40
Intermediate score:	26–34	23–32
Low score:	0–25	0–22

Source: From Miler, L. C., Berg, J. H., & Archer, R. L. (1983). Openers: individuals who elicit intimate self-disclosure. *Journal of Personality and Social Psychology, 44,* 1234–1244. Table 1, p. 1235 (adapted). Copyright © 1983 by the American Psychological Association. Adapted with permission of the publisher and R. L. Archer. No further reproduction or distribution is permitted without written permission from the American Psychological Association.

EXERCISE 8.2 *Self-Reflection:* How Do You Feel About Self-Disclosure?

This exercise is intended to make you think about your self-disclosure behavior. Begin by finishing the incomplete sentences below (adapted from Egan, 1977). Go through the sentences fairly quickly; do not ponder your responses too long. There are no right or wrong answers.

1. I dislike people who . . .

2. Those who really know me . . .

3. When I let someone know something I don't like about myself . . .

4. When I'm in a group of strangers . . .

5. I envy . . .

6. I get hurt when . . .

7. I daydream about . . .

8. Few people know that I . . .

9. One thing I really dislike about myself is . . .

10. When I share my values with someone . . .

Based on your responses to the incomplete sentences, do you feel you engage in the right amount of self-disclosure? Too little? Too much?

In general, what prevents you from engaging in self-disclosure?

Are there particular topics on which you find it difficult to be self-disclosing?

Are you the recipient of much self-disclosure from others, or do people have difficulty opening up to you?

CHAPTER 9 Friendship and Love

EXERCISE 9.1 *Self-Assessment:* Social Avoidance and Distress Scale

INSTRUCTIONS

The statements below inquire about your personal reactions to a variety of situations. Consider each statement carefully. Then indicate whether the statement is true or false in regard to your typical behavior. Record your responses (T or F) in the space provided on the left.

The Scale

_____ 1. I feel relaxed even in unfamiliar social situations.

_____ 2. I try to avoid situations that force me to be very sociable.

_____ 3. It is easy for me to relax when I am with strangers.

_____ 4. I have no particular desire to avoid people.

_____ 5. I often find social occasions upsetting.

_____ 6. I usually feel calm and comfortable at social occasions.

_____ 7. I am usually at ease when talking to someone of the opposite sex.

_____ 8. I try to avoid talking to people unless I know them well.

_____ 9. If the chance comes to meet new people, I often take it.

_____ 10. I often feel nervous or tense in casual get-togethers in which both sexes are present.

_____ 11. I am usually nervous with people unless I know them well.

_____ 12. I usually feel relaxed when I am with a group of people.

_____ 13. I often want to get away from people.

_____ 14. I usually feel uncomfortable when I am in a group of people I don't know.

_____ 15. I usually feel relaxed when I meet someone for the first time.

_____ 16. Being introduced to people makes me tense and nervous.

_____ 17. Even though a room is full of strangers, I may enter it anyway.

_____ 18. I would avoid walking up and joining a large group of people.

_____ 19. When my superiors want to talk with me, I talk willingly.

_____ 20. I often feel on edge when I am with a group of people.

_____ 21. I tend to withdraw from people.

_____ 22. I don't mind talking to people at parties or social gatherings.

_____ 23. I am seldom at ease in a large group of people.

_____ 24. I often think up excuses in order to avoid social engagements.

_____ 25. I sometimes take the responsibility for introducing people to each other.

_____ 26. I try to avoid formal social occasions.

_____ 27. I usually go to whatever social engagements I have.

_____ 28. I find it easy to relax with other people.

Scoring the Scale

The scoring key is reproduced below. Circle your true or false response each time it corresponds to the keyed response below. Add up the number of responses you circle, and this total is your score on the Social Avoidance and Distress (SAD) Scale. Record your score below.

1. False	8. True	15. False	22. False
2. True	9. False	16. True	23. True
3. False	10. True	17. False	24. True
4. False	11. True	18. True	25. False
5. True	12. False	19. False	26. True
6. False	13. True	20. True	27. False
7. False	14. True	21. True	28. False

My Score _____

What the Scale Measures

As its name implies, this scale measures avoidance and distress in social interactions. David Watson and Ronald Friend (1969) developed the scale to assess the extent to which individuals experience discomfort, fear, and anxiety in social situations and the extent to which they therefore try to evade many kinds of social encounters. To check the validity of the scale, they used it to predict subjects' social behavior in experimentally contrived situations. As projected, they found that people who scored high on the SAD Scale were less willing than low scorers to participate in a group discussion. The high scorers also reported anticipating more anxiety about their participation in the discussion than the low scorers. Additionally, Watson and Friend found a strong negative correlation (−.76) between the SAD and a measure of affiliation drive (the need to seek the company of others).

Interpreting Your Score

Our norms are based on data collected by Watson and Friend (1969) on over 200 university students.

Norms

High score:	16–28
Intermediate score:	6–15
Low score:	0–5

Source: From Watson, D. L., & Friend, R. (1969). Measure of social-evaluative anxiety. *Journal of Consulting and Clinical Psychology, 33,* 448–457. Table 1, p. 450 (adapted). Copyright © 1969 by the American Psychological Association. Adapted with permission of the publisher and David Watson. No further reproduction or distribution is permitted without written permission from the American Psychological Association.

EXERCISE 9.2 *Self-Reflection:* How Do You Relate to Friends?

The following questions (adapted from Egan, 1977) are designed to help you think about how you deal with friendships.

1. Do you have many friends or very few?

2. Whether many or few, do you usually spend a lot of time with your friends?

3. What do you like in other people—that is, what makes you choose them as friends?

4. Are the people you hang out with like you or different from you? Or are they in some ways like you and in other ways different? How?

5. Do you like to control others, to get them to do things your way? Do you let others control you? Do you give in to others much of the time?

6. Are there ways in which your friendships are one-sided?

7. What would make your friendships more satisfying?

CHAPTER 10 Marriage and Intimate Relationships

EXERCISE 10.1 *Self-Assessment:* Passionate Love Scale

INSTRUCTIONS

We would like to know how you feel (or once felt) about the person you love, or have loved, most passionately. Some common terms for passionate love are romantic love, infatuation, love sickness, or obsessive love. Please think of the person whom you love most passionately right now. If you are not in love, please think of the last person you loved. If you have never been in love, think of the person you came closest to caring for in that way.

Try to describe the way you felt when your feelings were most intense.

Whom are you thinking of?

_____ Someone I love right now.
_____ Someone I once loved.
_____ I have never been in love.

Your answers should range from (1) Not at all true to (9) Definitely true. Enter your responses in the blank spaces before each item.

1	2	3	4	5	6	7	8	9
Not at all true								Definitely true

The Scale

_____ 1. I would feel deep despair if _____ left me.

_____ 2. Sometimes I feel I can't control my thoughts; they are obsessively on _____.

_____ 3. I feel happy when I am doing something to make _____ happy.

_____ 4. I would rather be with _____ than anyone else.

_____ 5. I'd get jealous if I thought _____ was falling in love with someone else.

_____ 6. I yearn to know all about _____.

_____ 7. I want _____ physically, emotionally, and mentally.

_____ 8. I have an endless appetite for affection from _____.

_____ 9. For me, _____ is the perfect romantic partner.

_____ 10. I sense my body responding when _____ touches me.

_____ 11. _____ always seems to be on my mind.

_____ 12. I want _____ to know me—my thoughts, my fears, and my hopes.

_____ 13. I eagerly look for signs indicating _____'s desire for me.

_____ 14. I possess a powerful attraction for _____.

_____ 15. I get extremely depressed when things don't go right in my relationship with _____.

Scoring the Scale

Scoring this scale is extremely simple. Just add up the numbers entered in the 15 blanks above. The total is your score on the Passionate Love Scale.

My Score _____

What the Scale Measures

Developed by Elaine Hatfield and Susan Sprecher (1986), this scale measures feelings of *passionate love,* which they define as a state of intense longing for union with another. *Cognitive features* of passionate love include preoccupation with the partner, idealization of the relationship, and desire to know the other person. *Emotional features* of passionate love include sexual attraction, physiological arousal, and longing for reciprocity. *Behavioral features* include maintaining physical closeness, trying to determine how the other person feels about you, and demonstrating your love to your partner. Evidence for validity of the scale mostly consists of data showing that the scale correlates with other measures in the way that one would expect. For example, robust positive correlations have been found between the scores on the scale and measures of relationship commitment, relationship trust, relationship satisfaction, and sexual satisfaction.

Interpreting Your Score

Our norms are based on data available at Elaine Hatfield's website.

Extremely passionate: 106–135 points
Wildly, even recklessly in love

Passionate: 86–105 points
Passionate, but less intense

Average: 66–85 points
Occasional bursts of passion

Cool: 45–65 points
Tepid or infrequent passion

Extremely cool: 15–44 points
No thrill, never was

Source: Reprinted from Hatfield, E., & Sprecher, S. (1986). Measuring passionate love in intimate relationships. *Journal of Adolescence 4*(9), p. 391, Figure 1. © 1986 with permission from Elsevier and Elaine Hatfield.

EXERCISE 10.2 *Self-Reflection:* Thinking Through Your Attitudes About Marriage and Cohabitation

1. Regardless of your current marital status, what are your ideal criteria for selecting a mate?

2. How do you know if you are really ready for marriage?

3. What areas of self-awareness or knowledge of self do you feel you need to explore before you make a long-term commitment to a relationship?

4. In what ways is cohabitation a realistic preparation for marriage, and in what ways is it not?

CHAPTER 11 Gender and Behavior

EXERCISE 11.1 *Self-Assessment:* Personal Attributes Questionnaire (PAQ)

INSTRUCTIONS

The items below inquire about what kind of a person you think you are. Each item consists of a pair of characteristics, with the letters A–E in between. For example:

Not at all artistic   A   B   C   D   E   Very artistic

Each pair describes contradictory characteristics—that is, you cannot be both at the same time, such as very artistic and not at all artistic.

The letters form a scale between the two extremes. You are to enter a letter that describes where you fall on the scale. For example, if you think you have no artistic ability, you would enter A. If you think you are pretty good, you might enter D. If you are only medium, you might enter C, and so forth.

The Scale

_____ 1. Not at all aggressive	A	B	C	D	E	Very aggressive
_____ 2. Not at all independent	A	B	C	D	E	Very independent
_____ 3. Not at all emotional	A	B	C	D	E	Very emotional
_____ 4. Very submissive	A	B	C	D	E	Very dominant
_____ 5. Not at all excitable in a major crisis	A	B	C	D	E	Very excitable in a major crisis
_____ 6. Very passive	A	B	C	D	E	Very active
_____ 7. Not at all able to devote self completely to others	A	B	C	D	E	Able to devote self completely to others
_____ 8. Very rough	A	B	C	D	E	Very gentle
_____ 9. Not at all helpful to others	A	B	C	D	E	Very helpful to others
_____10. Not at all competitive	A	B	C	D	E	Very competitive
_____11. Very home oriented	A	B	C	D	E	Very worldly
_____12. Not at all kind	A	B	C	D	E	Very kind
_____13. Indifferent to others' approval	A	B	C	D	E	Highly needful of others' approval
_____14. Feelings not easily hurt	A	B	C	D	E	Feelings easily hurt
_____15. Not at all aware of feelings of others	A	B	C	D	E	Very aware of feelings of others
_____16. Can make decisions easily	A	B	C	D	E	Have difficulty making decisions
_____17. Give up very easily	A	B	C	D	E	Never give up easily
_____18. Never cry	A	B	C	D	E	Cry very easily
_____19. Not at all self-confident	A	B	C	D	E	Very self-confident
_____20. Feel very inferior	A	B	C	D	E	Feel very superior
_____21. Not at all understanding of others	A	B	C	D	E	Very understanding of others
_____22. Very cold in relations with others	A	B	C	D	E	Very warm in relations with others
_____23. Very little need for security	A	B	C	D	E	Very strong need for security
_____24. Go to pieces under pressure	A	B	C	D	E	Stand up well under pressure

Scoring the Scale

The Personal Attributes Questionnaire (PAQ) is made up of three 8-item subscales, but we are only going to compute scores for two of these subscales, so the first step is to eliminate the 8 items from the unused subscale. Put an X in the spaces to the left of the items for the following items: 1, 4, 5, 11, 13, 14, 18, and 23. These items belong to the subscale that we won't be using, and they can be ignored. Of the remaining items, one (item 16) is reverse-scored as follows: If you circled A, enter 4 in the space to the left of the item if you circled B, enter 3; if you circled C, enter 2; if you circled D, enter 1; and if you circled E, enter 0. All the rest of the items are scored in the following manner: A = 0, B = 1, C = 2, D = 3, and E = 4. Based on the responses you circled, enter the appropriate numbers for the remaining items in the spaces to the left of the items.

The next step is to compute your scores on the femininity and masculinity subscales of the PAQ. To compute your score on the *femininity* subscale, add up the numbers next to items 3, 7, 8, 9, 12, 15, 21, and 22, and enter your score in the space below. To compute your score on the *masculinity* subscale, add up the numbers next to items 2, 6, 10, 16, 17, 19, 20, and 24, and enter your score in the space below.

My score on the femininity subscale _____

My score on the masculinity subscale _____

What the Scale Measures

Devised by Janet Spence and Robert Helmreich (1978), the PAQ assesses masculinity and femininity in terms of respondents' self-perceived possession of various personality traits that are stereotypically believed to differentiate the sexes. The authors emphasize that the PAQ taps only limited aspects of sex roles: certain self-assertive/instrumental traits traditionally associated with masculinity and certain interpersonal/expressive traits traditionally associated with femininity. Although the PAQ should not be viewed as a global measure of masculinity and femininity, it has been widely used in research to provide a rough classification of subjects in terms of their gender-role identity. As explained in your text, people who score high in both masculinity and femininity are said to be androgynous. People who score high in femininity and low in masculinity are said to be feminine sex-typed. Those who score high in masculinity and low in femininity are characterized as masculine sex-typed, and those who score low on both dimensions are said to be sex-role undifferentiated.

Interpreting Your Score

You can use the chart here to classify yourself in terms of gender-role identity. Our norms are based on a sample of 715 college students studied by Spence and Helmreich (1978). The cutoffs for "high" scores on the masculinity and femininity subscales are the medians for each scale.

Obviously, these are arbitrary cutoffs, and results may be misleading for people who score very close to the median on either scale, as a difference of a point or two could change their classification. Hence, if either of your scores is within a couple of points of the median, you should view your gender-role classification as tentative. Also, keep in mind that the perception of some of these traits has changed over time. As mentioned in your text, some of the traditional masculine traits aren't viewed as strictly masculine today.

My classification _____

What percentage of subjects falls into each of the four gender-role categories? The exact breakdown will vary depending on the nature of the sample, but Spence and Helmreich (1978) reported the following distribution for their sample of 715 college students.

Category	Males	Females
Androgynous	25%	35%
Feminine	8%	32%
Masculine	44%	14%
Undifferentiated	23%	18%

Source: Adapted from Spence, J. T., & Helmreich, R. L. (1978). *Masculinity and femininity: Their psychological dimensions, correlates, and antecedents.* Austin: University of Texas Press. Copyright © 1978. By permission of the University of Texas Press.

EXERCISE 11.2 *Self-Reflection:* How Do You Feel About Gender Roles?

1. Can you recall any experiences that were particularly influential in shaping your attitudes about gender roles? If yes, give a couple of examples.

2. Have you ever engaged in cross-sex-typed behavior? Can you think of a couple of examples? How did people react?

3. Do you ever feel restricted by gender roles? If so, in what ways?

4. Have you ever been a victim of sex discrimination (sexism)? If so, describe the circumstances.

5. How do you think the transition in gender roles has affected you personally?

CHAPTER 12 Development and Expression of Sexuality

EXERCISE 12.1 *Self-Assessment:* Sexuality Scale

INSTRUCTIONS

For the 30 items that follow, indicate the extent of your agreement or disagreement with each statement, using the key shown below. Record your responses in the spaces to the left of the items.

+2	+1	0	−1	−2
Agree	Slightly Agree	Neither Agree nor Disagree	Slightly Disagree	Disagree

The Scale

_____ 1. I am a good sexual partner.

_____ 2. I am depressed about the sexual aspects of my life.

_____ 3. I think about sex all the time.

_____ 4. I would rate my sexual skill quite highly.

_____ 5. I feel good about my sexuality.

_____ 6. I think about sex more than anything else.

_____ 7. I am better at sex than most other people.

_____ 8. I am disappointed about the quality of my sex life.

_____ 9. I don't daydream about sexual situations.

_____ 10. I sometimes have doubts about my sexual competence.

_____ 11. Thinking about sex makes me happy.

_____ 12. I tend to be preoccupied with sex.

_____ 13. I am not very confident in sexual encounters.

_____ 14. I derive pleasure and enjoyment from sex.

_____ 15. I'm constantly thinking about having sex.

_____ 16. I think of myself as a very good sexual partner.

_____ 17. I feel down about my sex life.

_____ 18. I think about sex a great deal of the time.

_____ 19. I would rate myself low as a sexual partner.

_____ 20. I feel unhappy about my sexual relationships.

_____ 21. I seldom think about sex.

_____ 22. I am confident about myself as a sexual partner.

_____ 23. I feel pleased with my sex life.

_____ 24. I hardly ever fantasize about having sex.

_____ 25. I am not very confident about myself as a sexual partner.

_____ 26. I feel sad when I think about my sexual experiences.

_____ 27. I probably think about sex less often than most people.

_____ 28. I sometimes doubt my sexual competence.

_____ 29. I am not discouraged about sex.

_____ 30. I don't think about sex very often.

Scoring the Scale

To arrive at your scores on the three subscales of this questionnaire, transfer your responses into the spaces provided below. If an item number has an R next to it, this item is reverse-scored, so you should change the + or − sign in front of the number you recorded. After recording your responses, add up the numbers in each column, taking into account the algebraic sign in front of each number. The totals for each column are your scores on the three subscales of the Sexuality Scale. Record your scores at the bottom of each column.

Sexual Esteem	Sexual Depression	Sexual Preoccupation
1. _____	2. _____	3. _____
4. _____	5. R _____	6. _____
7. _____	8. _____	9. R _____
10. R _____	11. R _____	12. _____
13. R _____	14. R _____	15. _____
16. _____	17. _____	18. _____
19. R _____	20. _____	21. R _____
22. _____	23. R _____	24. _____
25. R _____	26. _____	27. R _____
28. R _____	29. R _____	30. R _____
_____	_____	_____
	My Scores	

What the Scale Measures

Developed by William Snell and Dennis Papini (1989), the Sexuality Scale measures three aspects of your sexual identity. The Sexual Esteem subscale measures your tendency to evaluate yourself in a positive way in terms of your capacity to relate sexually to others. The Sexual Depression subscale measures your tendency to feel saddened and discouraged by your ability to relate sexually to others. The Sexual Preoccupation subscale measures your tendency to become absorbed in thoughts about sex on a persistent basis.

Internal reliability is excellent. Thus far, the scale's validity has been examined through factor analysis, which can be used to evaluate the extent of overlap among the subscales. The factor analysis showed that the three subscales do measure independent aspects of one's sexuality.

Interpreting Your Score

Our norms are based on Snell and Papini's (1989) sample of 296 college students drawn from a small university in the Midwest. Significant gender differences were found only on the Sexual Preoccupation subscale, so we report separate norms for males and females only for this subscale.

Source: From Snell, W. E., & Papini, D. R. (1989). The sexuality scale: An instrument to measure sexual-esteem, sexual-depression, and sexual-preoccupation. *Journal of Sex Research, 26*(2), 256–263. Copyright © 1989 Society for Scientific Study of Sex. Reprinted with permission from Taylor & Francis and W. E. Snell.

Norms

	Sexual Esteem Both sexes	Sexual Depression Both sexes	Sexual Preoccupation Males	Sexual Preoccupation Females
High score:	+14 to +20	+1 to +20	+8 to +20	−1 to +20
Intermediate score:	0 to +13	−12 to 0	−2 to +7	−10 to −2
Low score:	−20 to −1	−20 to −13	−20 to −3	−20 to −11

EXERCISE 12.2 *Self-Reflection:* How Did You Acquire Your Attitudes About Sex?

1. Who do you feel was most important in shaping your attitudes regarding sexual behavior (parents, teachers, peers, early girlfriend or boyfriend, and so forth)?

2. What was the nature of their influence?

3. If the answer to the first question was not your parents, what kind of information did you get at home? Were your parents comfortable talking about sex?

4. In childhood, were you ever made to feel shameful, guilty, or fearful about sex? How?

5. Were your parents open or secretive about their own sex lives?

6. Do you feel comfortable with your sexuality today?

CHAPTER 13 Careers and Work

EXERCISE 13.1 *Self-Assessment:* Assertive Job-Hunting Survey

INSTRUCTIONS

This inventory is designed to provide information about the way in which you look for a job. Picture yourself in each of these job-hunting situations and indicate how likely it is that you would respond in the described manner. If you have never job-hunted before, answer according to how you would try to find a job. Please record your responses in the spaces to the left of the items. Use the following key for your responses:

1	2	3	4	5	6
Very Unlikely	Somewhat Unlikely	Slightly Unlikely	Slightly Likely	Somewhat Likely	Very Likely

The Scale

_____ 1. When asked to indicate my experience for a position, I would mention only my paid work experience.

_____ 2. If I heard someone talking about an interesting job opening, I'd be reluctant to ask for more information unless I knew the person.

_____ 3. I would ask an employer who did not have an opening if he knew of other employers who might have job openings.

_____ 4. I downplay my qualifications so that an employer won't think I'm more qualified than I really am.

_____ 5. I would rather use an employment agency to find a job than apply to employers directly.

_____ 6. Before an interview, I would contact an employee of the organization to learn more about that organization.

_____ 7. I hesitate to ask questions when I'm being interviewed for a job.

_____ 8. I avoid contacting potential employers by phone or in person because I feel they are too busy to talk with me.

_____ 9. If an interviewer were very late for my interview, I would leave or arrange for another appointment.

_____ 10. I believe an experienced employment counselor would have a better idea of what jobs I should apply for than I would have.

_____ 11. If a secretary told me that a potential employer was too busy to see me, I would stop trying to contact that employer.

_____ 12. Getting the job I want is largely a matter of luck.

_____ 13. I'd directly contact the person for whom I would be working, rather than the personnel department of an organization.

_____ 14. I am reluctant to ask professors or supervisors to write letters of recommendation for me.

_____ 15. I would not apply for a job unless I had all the qualifications listed on the published job description.

_____ 16. I would ask an employer for a second interview if I felt the first one went poorly.

_____ 17. I am reluctant to contact an organization about employment unless I know there is a job opening.

_____ 18. If I didn't get a job, I would call the employer and ask how I could improve my chances for a similar position.

_____ 19. I feel uncomfortable asking friends for job leads.

_____ 20. With the job market as tight as it is, I had better take whatever job I can get.

_____ 21. If the personnel office refused to refer me for an interview, I would directly contact the person I wanted to work for, if I felt qualified for the position.

_____ 22. I would rather interview with recruiters who come to the college campus than contact employers directly.

_____ 23. If an interviewer says "I'll contact you if there are any openings," I figure there's nothing else I can do.

_____ 24. I'd check out available job openings before deciding what kind of job I'd like to have.

_____ 25. I am reluctant to contact someone I don't know for information about career fields in which I am interested.

Scoring the Scale

To score this scale, you have to begin by reversing your responses on 18 of the items. On these items, convert the response you entered as follows: 1 = 6, 2 = 5, 3 = 4, 4 = 3, 5 = 2, and 6 = 1. The items to be reversed are 1, 2, 4, 5, 7, 8, 10, 11, 12, 14, 15, 17, 19, 20, 22, 23, 24, and 25. After making your reversals, add up the numbers that you have recorded for the 25 items on the scale. This total is your score on the Assertive Job-Hunting Survey.

My Score _____

What the Scale Measures

Developed by Heather Becker, Susan Brown, Pat LaFitte, Mary Jo Magruder, Bob Murff, and Bill Phillips, this scale measures your job-seeking style (Becker, 1980). Some people conduct a job search in a relatively passive way—waiting for jobs to come to them. Others tend to seek jobs in a more vigorous, assertive manner. They act on their environment to procure needed information, obtain helpful contacts, and get their foot in the door at attractive companies. This scale measures your tendency to pursue jobs assertively.

Test-retest reliability for this scale is reasonable (.77 for an interval of two weeks). The scale's validity has been supported by demonstrations that subjects' scores increase as a result of training programs designed to enhance their job-hunting assertiveness. Also, those who have job-hunted before tend to score higher than those who have never job-hunted.

Interpreting Your Score

Our norms are based on a sample of college students who had applied to a university counseling center for career-planning assistance

Norms	
High score:	117–150
Intermediate score:	95–116
Low score:	0–94

Source: Adapted from Becker, H. (1980). Assertive job-hunting survey. *Measurement and Evaluation in Guidance, (13)*1, 43–48.

EXERCISE 13.2 *Self-Reflection:* What Do You Know About the Career That Interests You?

Important vocational decisions require information. Your assignment in this exercise is to pick a vocation and research it. You should begin by reading some occupational literature. Then you should interview someone in the field. Use the outline below to summarize your findings.

1. *The nature of the work.* What are the duties and responsibilities on a day-to-day basis?

2. *Working conditions.* Is the working environment pleasant or unpleasant, low-key or high-pressure?

3. *Job entry requirements.* What kind of education and training are required to break into this occupational area?

4. *Potential earnings.* What are entry-level salaries, and how much can you hope to earn if you're exceptionally successful?

5. *Opportunities for advancement.* How do you move up in this field? Are there adequate opportunities for promotion and advancement?

6. *Intrinsic job satisfaction.* What can you derive in the way of personal satisfaction from this job?

7. *Future outlook.* How is supply and demand projected to shape up in the future for this occupational area?

Source: © Cengage Learning

CHAPTER 14 Psychological Disorders

EXERCISE 14.1 *Self-Assessment:* Maudsley Obsessional-Compulsive Inventory

INSTRUCTIONS

Please answer each question by putting a circle around T for "true" or F for "false" in response to each question. There are no right or wrong answers, and no trick questions. Work quickly and do not think too long about the exact meaning of the question.

The Scale

T   F   **1.** I avoid using public telephones because of possible contamination.

T   F   **2.** I frequently get nasty thoughts and have difficulty in getting rid of them.

T   F   **3.** I am more concerned than most people about honesty.

T   F   **4.** I am often late because I can't seem to get through everything on time.

T   F   **5.** I don't worry unduly about contamination if I touch an animal.

T   F   **6.** I frequently have to check things (e.g., gas or water taps, doors, etc.) several times.

T   F   **7.** I have a very strict conscience.

T   F   **8.** I find that almost every day I am upset by unpleasant thoughts that come into my mind against my will.

T   F   **9.** I do not worry unduly if I accidently bump into somebody.

T   F   **10.** I usually have serious doubts about the simple everyday things I do.

T   F   **11.** Neither of my parents was very strict during my childhood.

T   F   **12.** I tend to get behind in my work because I repeat things over and over again.

T   F   **13.** I use only an average amount of soap.

T   F   **14.** Some numbers are extremely unlucky.

T   F   **15.** I do not check letters over and over again before mailing them.

T   F   **16.** I do not take a long time to dress in the morning.

T   F   **17.** I am not excessively concerned about cleanliness.

T   F   **18.** One of my major problems is that I pay too much attention to detail.

T   F   **19.** I can use well-kept public toilets without any hesitation.

T   F   **20.** My major problem is repeated checking.

T   F   **21.** I am not unduly concerned about germs and diseases.

T   F   **22.** I do not tend to check things more than once.

T   F   **23.** I do not stick to a very strict routine when doing ordinary things.

T   F   **24.** My hands do not feel dirty after touching money.

T   F   **25.** I do not usually count when doing a routine task.

T   F   **26.** I take rather a long time to complete my washing in the morning.

T   F   **27.** I do not use a great deal of antiseptics.

T   F   **28.** I spend a lot of time every day checking things over and over again.

T   F   **29.** Hanging and folding my clothes at night does not take up a lot of time.

T   F   **30.** Even when I do something very carefully, I often feel that it is not quite right.

Scoring the Scale

The scoring key is shown below. You should circle your response of true (T) or false (F) each time it corresponds to the keyed response below. Add up the number of responses you circle. This total is your score on the scale. Record your response below.

1. True	7. True	13. False	19. False	25. False
2. True	8. True	14. True	20. True	26. True
3. True	9. False	15. False	21. False	27. False
4. True	10. True	16. False	22. False	28. True
5. False	11. False	17. False	23. False	29. False
6. True	12. True	18. True	24. False	30. True

My Score _____

What the Scale Measures

This scale was never intended to serve as an aid in diagnosing obsessive-compulsive disorder (OCD). Rather it was developed to provide an objective measure of symptom severity that could be used in research to check whether patients improved from various types of therapeutic interventions. As such, it should be viewed as a *rough index of obsessive-compulsive tendencies.* To gather supportive evidence for the validity of the scale, the original investigators compared the scores of individuals with a known diagnosis of obsessive-compulsive disorder against those of a control group. As one would predict, if the scale effectively measures obsessive-compulsive tendencies, those with OCD scored significantly higher than the controls. The reliability of the scale over a period of 1 month was found to be .80, which is very good for a measure of personality.

Interpreting Your Score

Our norms are based on a sample of 579 university students (Sternberger & Burns, 1990). Remember that these norms provide only a rough estimate of obsessive-compulsive tendencies. Even a high score does not indicate that one has an obsessive-compulsive disorder.

Norms

High score:	**17 and above**
Medium score:	**9–16**
Low score:	**0–8**

Source: Hodgson, R. J. (1977). Obsessional-compulsive complaints. *Behavior Research & Therapy,* 15, 389-395.

EXERCISE 14.2 *Self-Reflection:* What Are Your Attitudes on Mental Illness?

1. List seven adjectives that you associate with people who are diagnosed as mentally ill.

2. If you meet someone who was once diagnosed as mentally ill, what are your immediate reactions?

3. List some comments about people with psychological disorders that you heard when you were a child.

4. Have you had any actual interactions with "mentally ill" people that have supported or contradicted your expectations?

5. Do you agree with the idea that psychological disorders should be viewed as an illness or disease? Defend your position.

Source: © Cengage Learning

CHAPTER 15 Psychotherapy

EXERCISE 15.1 *Self-Assessment:* Attitudes Toward Seeking Professional Psychological Help

INSTRUCTIONS

Read each statement carefully and indicate your agreement or disagreement, using the scale below. Please express your frank opinion in responding to each statement, answering as you honestly feel or believe.

0 = Disagreement
1 = Probable disagreement
2 = Probable agreement
3 = Agreement

The Scale

_____ 1. Although there are clinics for people with mental troubles, I would not have much faith in them.

_____ 2. If a good friend asked my advice about a mental health problem, I might recommend that he see a psychiatrist.

_____ 3. I would feel uneasy going to a psychiatrist because of what some people would think.

_____ 4. A person with a strong character can get over mental conflicts by himself, and would have little need of a psychiatrist.

_____ 5. There are times when I have felt completely lost and would have welcomed professional advice for a personal or emotional problem.

_____ 6. Considering the time and expense involved in psychotherapy, it would have doubtful value for a person like me.

_____ 7. I would willingly confide intimate matters to an appropriate person if I thought it might help me or a member of my family.

_____ 8. I would rather live with certain mental conflicts than go through the ordeal of getting psychiatric treatment.

_____ 9. Emotional difficulties, like many things, tend to work out by themselves.

_____ 10. There are certain problems that should not be discussed outside of one's immediate family.

_____ 11. A person with a serious emotional disturbance would probably feel most secure in a good mental hospital.

_____ 12. If I believed I was having a mental breakdown, my first inclination would be to get professional attention.

_____ 13. Keeping one's mind on a job is a good solution for avoiding personal worries and concerns.

_____ 14. Having been a psychiatric patient is a blot on a person's life.

_____ 15. I would rather be advised by a close friend than by a psychologist, even for an emotional problem.

_____ 16. A person with an emotional problem is not likely to solve it alone; he or she is likely to solve it with professional help.

_____ 17. I resent a person—professionally trained or not—who wants to know about my personal difficulties.

_____ 18. I would want to get psychiatric attention if I was worried or upset for a long period of time.

_____ 19. The idea of talking about problems with a psychologist strikes me as a poor way to get rid of emotional conflicts.

_____ 20. Having been mentally ill carries with it a burden of shame.

_____ 21. There are experiences in my life I would not discuss with anyone.

_____ 22. It is probably best not to know everything about oneself.

_____ 23. If I were experiencing a serious emotional crisis at this point in my life, I would be confident that I could find relief in psychotherapy.

_____ 24. There is something admirable in the attitude of a person who is willing to cope with his conflicts and fears without resorting to professional help.

_____ 25. At some future time I might want to have psychological counseling.

_____ 26. A person should work out his own problems; getting psychological counseling would be a last resort.

_____ 27. Had I received treatment in a mental hospital, I would not feel that it had to be "covered up."

_____ 28. If I thought I needed psychiatric help, I would get it no matter who knew about it.

_____ 29. It is difficult to talk about personal affairs with highly educated people such as doctors, teachers, and clergymen.

Scoring the Scale

Begin by reversing your response (0 = 3, 1 = 2, 2 = 1, 3 = 0) for items 1, 3, 4, 6, 8, 9, 10, 13, 14, 15, 17, 19, 20, 21, 22, 24, 26, and 29. Then add up the numbers for all 29 items on the scale. This total is your score. Record your score below.

My Score _____

What the Scale Measures

The scale assesses the degree to which you have favorable attitudes toward professional psychotherapy (Fischer & Turner, 1970). As discussed in your text, there are many negative stereotypes about therapy, and many people are reluctant to pursue therapy. This situation is unfortunate, because negative attitudes often prevent people from seeking therapy that could be beneficial to them.

Interpreting Your Score

Our norms are shown below. The higher your score, the more positive your attitudes about therapy.

Norms
High score:	64–87
Medium score:	50–63
Low score:	0–49

Source: From Fischer, E. H., & Turner, J. L. (1970). Orientation to seeking professional help: development and research utility of an attitude scale. *Journal of Consulting and Clinical Psychology, 35*, 82–83. Table 1 (adapted). Copyright © 1970 by the American Psychological Association. Adapted with permission of the publisher and Edward Fischer. No further reproduction or distribution is permitted without written permission from the American Psychological Association. For educational use only.

EXERCISE 15.2 *Self-Reflection:* What Are Your Feelings About Therapy?

1. What type of therapeutic approach do you think you would respond to best if you were seeking a therapist? In thinking about this question, consider not only theoretical approaches and professions, but whether you would prefer a male versus a female, individual therapy versus group therapy, and so on.

2. What personal traits would you look for in a therapist?

3. Do you have a sense of what your family beliefs are about psychotherapy and its use? If you had to articulate these beliefs in a few sentences, what would you say?

4. Before you read Chapter 15, what did you picture in your mind as happening in a therapy session? How accurate was that picture? What were some of your inaccurate perceptions about therapy?

5. Statistics show that more women seek psychotherapy than men. Why do you think this is so?

CHAPTER 16 Positive Psychology

EXERCISE 16.1 *Self-Assessment:* What Is Your Happiness Profile?

INSTRUCTIONS

All of the questions below reflect statements that many people would find desirable, but answer only in terms of whether the statement describes how you actually live your life. Please be honest and accurate. Use the following scale to answer the questions:

5 = Very much like me
4 = Mostly like me
3 = Somewhat like me
2 = A little like me
1 = Not like me at all

The Scale

_____ 1. My life serves a higher purpose.

_____ 2. Life is too short to postpone the pleasures it can provide.

_____ 3. I seek out situations that challenge my skills and abilities.

_____ 4. I keep score at life.

_____ 5. Whether at work or play, I am usually "in a zone" and not conscious of myself.

_____ 6. I am always very absorbed in what I do.

_____ 7. I am rarely distracted by what is going on around me.

_____ 8. I have a responsibility to make the world a better place.

_____ 9. My life has a lasting meaning.

_____10. No matter what I am doing, it is important for me to win.

_____11. In choosing what to do, I always take into account whether it will be pleasurable.

_____12. What I do matters to society.

_____13. I want to accomplish more than other people.

_____14. I agree with this statement: "Life is short—eat dessert first."

_____15. I love to do things that excite my senses.

_____16. I love to compete.

Scoring the Scale

Your Orientation to Pleasure score is the sum of points for questions 2, 11, 14, and 15; your Orientation to Engagement score is the sum of points for questions 3, 5, 6, and 7; your Orientation to Meaning score is the sum of points for questions 1, 8, 9, and 12; your Orientation to Victory score is the sum of points for questions 4, 10, 13, and 16.

My Orientation to Pleasure Score _____

My Orientation to Engagement Score _____

My Orientation to Meaning Score _____

My Orientation to Victory Score _____

Interpreting Your Scores

The questionnaire measures four possible routes to happiness: through pleasure, engagement, meaning, and victory. What is your highest score of the four? This is your dominant orientation. And what is the configuration of your scores? That is, are you "high" (> 15) on all four orientations? If so, you are oriented toward a full life and are likely to be highly satisfied. Or are you "low" (< 9) on all four orientations? If so, you may have a more empty life and are likely to be dissatisfied. You might consider doing something different—anything!—in your life. And if you are high on one or two orientations, chances are that you are satisfied with life, although you might seek further opportunities for pursuing your signature way of being happy.

Source: Based on Peterson, C. (2006). *A primer in positive psychology.* New York: Oxford University Press; and Peterson, C., Park, N., & Seligman, M. E. P. (2005). Orientations to happiness and life satisfaction: The full life versus the empty life. *Journal of Happiness Studies, 6,* 25–41.

EXERCISE 16.2 *Self-Reflection:* Thinking About How You Construe Happiness

Imagine that medicine has developed a new "happiness" pill. If you take this pill everyday it will make you feel positive emotions more frequently. There are also no negative side effects, and it is inexpensive to buy. Would you take it? Why or why not?

Imagine that you have found the famous "Aladdin's Lamp" and the genie has granted you three wishes. What would you wish for? Sorry, you can't wish for more wishes.

1.

2.

3.

What do your answers tell you about your idea of happiness or the good life?

Are your answers based on any specific assumptions about human nature or the relationships between people and the societies they live in? What are those assumptions?

Source: Based on Compton, W. C. (2005). *An introduction to positive psychology.* Belmont, CA: Thompson/Wadsworth.